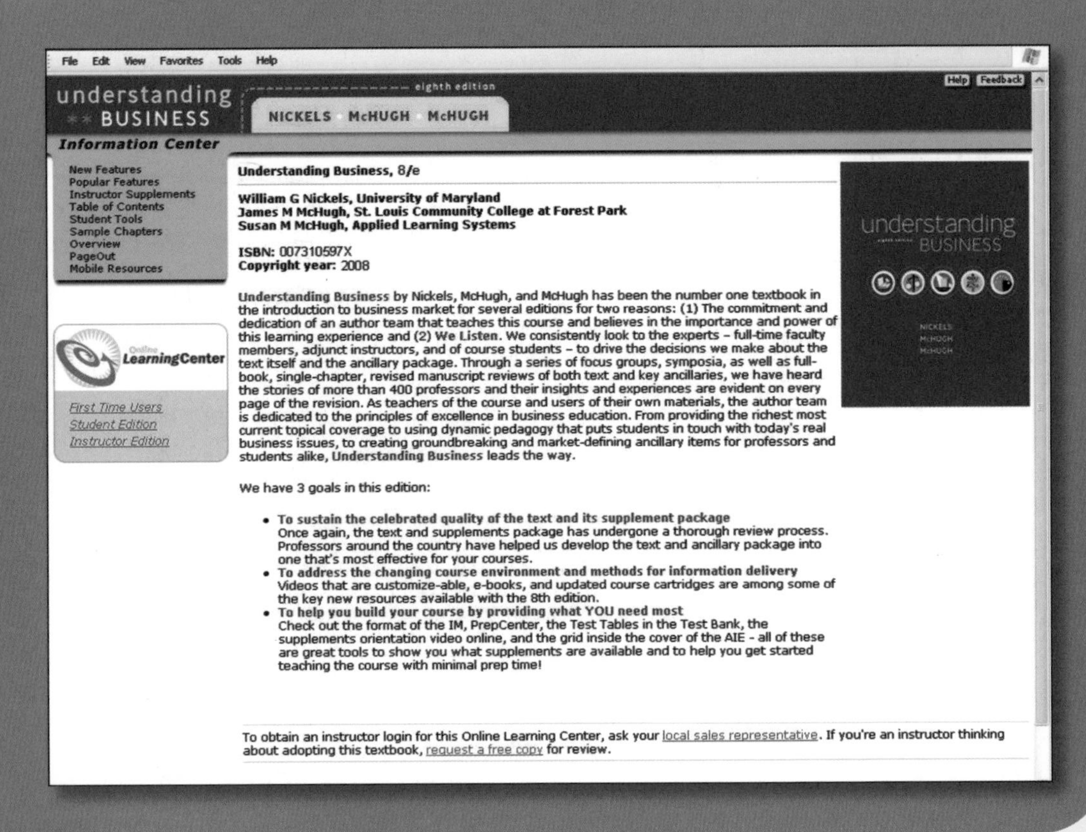


# www.mhhe.com/ub8e

The Online Learning Center is your access to resources that will help you review and study in this course.

Log in to use course-related materials such as interactive exercises, video clips, career resources, and the McGraw-Hill Investments Trader (stock-market game). Chapter-level materials, such as chapter summaries, flashcards, chapter quizzes, Casing the Web cases referenced in the text, Internet assignments, and student study PowerPoints, are also provided to help you review the chapter content more carefully.

Simply go to the site and click on "Student Edition" to get started.

# understanding BUSINESS

eighth edition


**William G. Nickels**
University of Maryland

**James M. McHugh**
St. Louis Community College at Forest Park

**Susan M. McHugh**
Applied Learning Systems

Boston Burr Ridge, IL Dubuque, IA Madison, WI New York San Francisco St. Louis
Bangkok Bogotá Caracas Kuala Lumpur Lisbon London Madrid Mexico City
Milan Montreal New Delhi Santiago Seoul Singapore Sydney Taipei Toronto

UNDERSTANDING BUSINESS

Published by McGraw-Hill/Irwin, a business unit of The McGraw-Hill Companies, Inc., 1221 Avenue of the Americas, New York, NY, 10020. 

This book is printed on acid-free paper.

2 3 4 5 6 7 8 9 0 DOW/DOW 0 9 8 7

ISBN 978-0-07-310597-0 (student edition)
MHID 0-07-310597-X (student edition)
ISBN 978-0-07-310609-0 (annotated instructor's edition)
MHID 0-07-310609-7 (annotated instructor's edition)

Editorial director: *John E. Biernat*
Executive editor: *John Weimeister*
Developmental editors: *Natalie J. Ruffatto and Laura Griffin*
Marketing manager: *Sarah Reed*
Producer, Media technology: *Janna Martin*
Lead project manager: *Mary Conzachi*
Manager, New book production: *Heather D. Burbridge*
Senior designer: *Kami Carter*
Senior photo research coordinator: *Jeremy Cheshareck*
Photo researcher: *Jennifer Blankenship*
Supplement producer: *Ira C. Roberts*
Senior media project manager: *Susan Lombardi*
Cover and interior design: *Pam Verros, pv design*
Typeface: *10/12 New Aster*
Compositor: *Techbooks*
Printer: *R. R. Donnelley*

**Library of Congress Cataloging-in-Publication Data**

Nickels, William G.
Understanding business / William G. Nickels, James M. McHugh, Susan M. McHugh.—8th ed.
p. cm.
Includes index.
ISBN-13: 978-0-07-310597-0 (student edition : alk. paper)
ISBN-10: 0-07-310597-X (student edition : alk. paper)
ISBN-13: 978-0-07-310609-0 (annotated instructor's edition : alk. paper)
ISBN-10: 0-07-310609-7 (annotated instructor's edition : alk. paper)
1. Industrial management. 2. Business. 3. Business—Vocational guidance.
I. McHugh, James M. II. McHugh, Susan M. III. Title.
HD31.N4897 2008
650—dc22

2006025567

www.mhhe.com

# dedication

**To our families: their energy inspires us, their love warms us, and their tuition bills keep us working.**

and

**To all the business educators who have worked with us over the years to improve this text and who have become friends as well as colleagues.**

# brief CONTENTS


**Preface xix**

**Prologue: Getting Ready for Prime Time P-1**

part 1

**Business Trends: Cultivating a Business in Diverse, Global Environments**

1 Managing within the Dynamic Business Environment: Taking Risks and Making Profits 2
2 How Economics Affects Business: The Creation and Distribution of Wealth 28
3 Competing in Global Markets 58
4 Demonstrating Ethical Behavior and Social Responsibility 88

part 2

**Business Ownership: Starting a Small Business**

5 Choosing a Form of Business Ownership 116
6 Entrepreneurship and Starting a Small Business 148

part 3

**Business Management: Empowering Employees to Satisfy Customers**

7 Management, Leadership, and Employee Empowerment 180
8 Adapting Organizations to Today's Markets 204
9 Producing World-Class Goods and Services 232

part 4

**Management of Human Resources: Motivating Employees to Produce Quality Goods and Services**

10 Motivating Employees and Building Self-Managed Teams 258
11 Human Resource Management: Finding and Keeping the Best Employees 286
12 Dealing with Employee–Management Issues and Relationships 320

part 5

**Marketing: Developing and Implementing Customer-Oriented Marketing Plans**

13 Marketing: Building Customer Relationships 348
14 Developing and Pricing Products and Services 374
15 Distributing Products Quickly and Efficiently 402
16 Using Effective Promotional Techniques 430

part 6

**Managing Financial Resources**

17 Understanding Financial Information and Accounting 454
18 Financial Management 482
19 Securities Markets: Financing and Investing Opportunities 510
20 Understanding Money, Financial Institutions, and the Federal Reserve 544

**Bonus Chapters**

A Working within the Legal Environment of Business 572
B Using Technology to Manage Information 594
C Managing Risk 618
D Managing Your Personal Finances 632

**Endnotes EN-1**

**Glossary G-1**

**Credits PC-1**

**Name Index I-1**

**Organization Index I-8**

**Subject Index I-13**

**Preface xix**

**Prologue: Getting Ready for Prime Time P-1**

part 1

**Business Trends: Cultivating a Business in Diverse, Global Environments**

Chapter One

2 Managing within the Dynamic Business Environment: Taking Risks and Making Profits

**Profile: Getting to Know Michele Hoskins of Michele Foods 2**

**Business and Entrepreneurship: Revenues, Profits, and Losses 4**

Matching Risk with Profit 4

Businesses Add to the Standard of Living and Quality of Life 5


# contents


Responding to the Various Business Stakeholders 5

*Spotlight on Small Business: Social Entrepreneurship* 7

Using Business Principles in Nonprofit Organizations 7

**Entrepreneurship versus Working for Others 8**

Opportunities for Entrepreneurs 8

The Importance of Entrepreneurs to the Creation of Wealth 9

*Reaching Beyond Our Borders: Freedom Equals Prosperity* 10

**The Business Environment 10**

The Economic and Legal Environment 11

The Technological Environment 12

*Making Ethical Decisions: Ethics Begin with You* 13

*Dealing with Change: Amazon.com Must Change with the Times* 14

The Competitive Environment 15

The Social Environment 16

The Global Environment 18

**The Evolution of American Business 20**

Progress in the Agricultural and Manufacturing Industries 20

Progress in Service Industries 21

Your Future in Business 21

**Video Case: No Clowning Around—Cirque du Soleil 27**

Chapter Two

28 How Economics Affects Business: The Creation and Distribution of Wealth

**Profile: Getting to Know Hernando de Soto, Economist for the Poor 28**

**How Economic Conditions Affect Businesses 30**

What Is Economics? 31

Why Economics Was Known as the "Dismal Science" 31

Growth Economics and Adam Smith 32

How Businesses Benefit the Community 32

*Making Ethical Decisions: Helping Disaster Victims* 34

**Understanding Free-Market Capitalism 34**

The Foundations of Capitalism 35

How Free Markets Work 36

How Prices Are Determined 37

The Economic Concept of Supply 37

The Economic Concept of Demand 37

The Equilibrium Point, or Market Price 37

*Dealing with Change: Adapting to Swings in Demand* 39

Competition within Free Markets 39

Benefits and Limitations of Free Markets 40

**Understanding Socialism 41**

The Benefits of Socialism 41

The Negative Consequences of Socialism 41

**Understanding Communism 42**

*Spotlight on Small Business: China's Entrepreneurs Create Wealth* 43

**The Trend toward Mixed Economies 43**

*Reaching Beyond Our Borders: Finding New Markets Overseas* 44

**Understanding the Economic System of the United States 46**

Key Economic Indicators 46

Productivity in the United States 48

Productivity in the Service Sector 49

The Business Cycle 49

Stabilizing the Economy through Fiscal Policy 50

Using Monetary Policy to Keep the Economy Growing 50

**Video Case: Katrina's Aftermath 57**

## Chapter Three

58 Competing in Global Markets

**Profile: Getting to Know Li Yifei, President of MTV Networks China 58**

**The Dynamic Global Market 60**

*Dealing with Change: Asia's 800-Pound Gorilla* 61

**Why Trade with Other Nations? 61**

The Theories of Comparative and Absolute Advantage 61

**Getting Involved in Global Trade 62**

Importing Goods and Services 63

Exporting Goods and Services 63

*Spotlight on Small Business: Going Global: It's "Bearly" Possible* 64

Measuring Global Trade 64

**Strategies for Reaching Global Markets 66**

Licensing 66

Exporting 67

Franchising 67

*Reaching Beyond Our Borders: The Winner and Still World's Champion* 68

Contract Manufacturing 69

International Joint Ventures and Strategic Alliances 69

Foreign Direct Investment 70

**Forces Affecting Trading in Global Markets 71**

Sociocultural Forces 71

Economic and Financial Forces 72

Legal and Regulatory Forces 74

Physical and Environmental Forces 74

**Trade Protectionism 75**

The World Trade Organization (WTO) 76

Common Markets 77

The North American and Central American Free Trade Agreements 78

**The Future of Global Trade 79**

The Challenge of Offshore Outsourcing 81

*Making Ethical Decisions: You Can Call Me Ray or You Can Call Me Sanjay* 82

Globalization and Your Future 82

**Video Case: The Mouse that Doesn't Come with a Computer 87**

## Chapter Four

88 Demonstrating Ethical Behavior and Social Responsibility

**Profile: Getting to Know Howard Schultz of Starbucks 88**

**Ethics Is More Than Legality 90**

Ethical Standards Are Fundamental 90

*Legal Briefcase: Accused Corporate Executives Have Their Day in Court* 91

Ethics Begins with Each of Us 91

*Making Ethical Decisions: Not All Pirates Wield Swords—Some Sport MP3 Players* 93

**Managing Businesses Ethically and Responsibly 94**

Setting Corporate Ethical Standards 96

*Legal Briefcase: SOX It to 'Em: Whistleblowers Move from Snitches to Corporate Heroes* 98

**Corporate Social Responsibility 99**

*Spotlight on Small Business: Myths about Small-Business Philanthropy* 101

Responsibility to Customers 101

Responsibility to Investors 102

*Dealing with Change: Martha Stewart Living, Again* 103

Responsibility to Employees 104

Responsibility to Society and the Environment 105

Social Auditing 106

**International Ethics and Social Responsibility 108**

*Reaching Beyond Our Borders: Ethical Culture Clash* 110

**Video Case: If It Isn't Ethical, It Isn't Right 113**

# * part 2

## Business Ownership: Starting a Small Business

## Chapter Five

116 Choosing a Form of Business Ownership

**Profile: Getting to Know Donald and Susan Sutherland of Cold Stone Creamery 116**

**Basic Forms of Business Ownership 118**

**Sole Proprietorships 119**

Advantages of Sole Proprietorships 119

Disadvantages of Sole Proprietorships 119

**Partnerships 121**

Advantages of Partnerships 122

Disadvantages of Partnerships 122

*Making Ethical Decisions: Outsourcing or Outsmarting?* 123

**Corporations 124**

*Spotlight on Small Business: Choose Your Partner* 125

Advantages of Corporations 125

Disadvantages of Corporations 127

Individuals Can Incorporate 128

S Corporations 129

Limited Liability Companies 130

**Corporate Expansion: Mergers and Acquisitions 132**

*Dealing with Change: The Urge to Merge Rises Again* 134

**Special Forms of Business Ownership 134**
**Franchises 134**
Advantages of Franchises 135
Disadvantages of Franchises 136
*Legal Briefcase: Scam Artists Don't Paint Pretty Pictures* 137
Diversity in Franchising 138
Home-Based Franchises 139
E-Commerce in Franchising 140
Using Technology in Franchising 140
Franchising in International Markets 140
**Cooperatives 141**
**Which Form of Ownership Is for You? 142**
**Video Case: Sonic Is Booming 146**

Chapter Six

148 Entrepreneurship and Starting a Small Business

**Profile: Getting to Know Nina Vaca, Founder and CEO of Pinnacle Technical Resources Inc. 148**
**The Age of the Entrepreneur 150**
**The Job-Creating Power of Entrepreneurs in the United States 150**
**Why People Take the Entrepreneurial Challenge 151**
What Does It Take to Be an Entrepreneur? 151
Entrepreneurial Teams 154
Micropreneurs and Home-Based Businesses 154
Web-Based Businesses 156
Entrepreneurship within Firms 158
Encouraging Entrepreneurship—What Government Can Do 159
**Getting Started in Small Business 159**
Small versus Big Business 160
*Spotlight on Small Business: Inner-City Opportunities* 161
Importance of Small Business 161
Small-Business Success and Failure 162
**Learning about Small-Business Operations 163**
Learn from Others 163
Get Some Experience 163
*Making Ethical Decisions: Going Down with the Ship* 164
Take Over a Successful Firm 164
**Managing a Small Business 165**
Begin with Planning 165
Writing a Business Plan 166
Getting Money to Fund a Small Business 166
The Small Business Administration (SBA) 168
Knowing Your Customers 170
Managing Employees 170
Keeping Records 171
Looking for Help 171
**Going International: Small-Business Prospects 173**
*Reaching Beyond Our Borders: Steve & Barry's Tariff Engineering* 174
**Video Case: Are You Still Going Around with that Old Bag? 178**

* part 3

**Business Management: Empowering Employees to Satisfy Customers**

Chapter Seven

180 Management, Leadership, and Employee Empowerment

**Profile: Getting to Know Oprah Winfrey, Businesswoman and TV Personality 180**
**Managers' Roles Are Evolving 182**
**Functions of Management 182**
*Reaching Beyond Our Borders: Mickey Mouse Brings the Magic to China* 183
**Planning: Creating a Vision Based on Values 184**
*Dealing with Change: Hitting the Retail Bull's-Eye* 186
*Spotlight on Small Business: On-the-Fly Decision Making after Hurricane Katrina* 188
Decision Making: Finding the Best Alternative 189
**Organizing: Creating a Unified System 190**
Tasks and Skills at Different Levels of Management 191
The Stakeholder-Oriented Organization 192
Staffing: Getting and Keeping the Right People 193
**Leading: Providing Continuous Vision and Values 193**
*Making Ethical Decisions: To Share or Not to Share* 194
Leadership Styles 194
Empowering Workers 196
Managing Knowledge 196
**Controlling: Making Sure It Works 197**
A New Criterion for Measurement: Customer Satisfaction 198
**Video Case: Bread Lines Are Back at Panera! 203**

Chapter Eight

204 Adapting Organizations to Today's Markets

**Profile: Getting to Know Anne Mulcahy of Xerox 204**
**Everyone Is Doing It 206**
Building an Organization from the Bottom Up 206
*Making Ethical Decisions: Safety versus Profit* 207
The Changing Organization 207
The Development of Organization Design 208
Turning Principles into Organization Design 210
**Issues Involved in Structuring Organizations 211**
Centralization versus Decentralization of Authority 211

Choosing the Appropriate Span of Control 212
Tall versus Flat Organization Structures 213
Advantages and Disadvantages of Departmentalization 214
**Organization Models 216**
Line Organizations 217
Line-and-Staff Organizations 217
Matrix-Style Organizations 217
Cross-Functional Self-Managed Teams 219
**Managing the Interactions among Firms 220**
Benchmarking and Core Competencies 221
**Adapting to Change 223**
Restructuring for Empowerment 223
*Dealing with Change: Riding Hurd at HP* 224
Focusing on the Customer 225
Creating a Change-Oriented Organizational Culture 225
*Spotlight on Small Business: All This and Ice Cream Too* 226
The Informal Organization 226
**Video Case: One Smooth Stone 231**

## Chapter Nine

232 Producing World-Class Goods and Services
**Profile: Getting to Know Richard Dauch of American Axle & Manufacturing 232**
**U.S. Manufacturing in Perspective 234**
*Making Ethical Decisions: Stay or Leave?* 235
What Manufacturers Have Done to Become More Competitive 235
**From Production to Operations Management 236**
Operations Management in the Service Sector 237
**Production Processes 238**
The Need to Improve Production Techniques and Cut Costs 239
Computer-Aided Design and Manufacturing 240
Flexible Manufacturing 240
Lean Manufacturing 241
Mass Customization 241
**Operations Management Planning 242**
Facility Location 242
*Dealing with Change: Responding to a Major Disaster* 244
Facility Layout 245
*Reaching Beyond Our Borders: Lockheed Martin Goes Global* 245
Materials Requirement Planning 246
Purchasing 247
Just-in-Time Inventory Control 247
Quality Control 248
*Spotlight on Small Business: Meeting the Six Sigma Standard* 249
**Control Procedures: PERT and Gantt Charts 250**
**Preparing for the Future 252**
**Video Case: Reality On Request—Digital Domain 256**

# part 4

## Management of Human Resources: Motivating Employees to Produce Quality Goods and Services

## Chapter Ten

258 Motivating Employees and Building Self-Managed Teams
**Profile: Getting to Know Elizabeth McLaughlin, CEO of Hot Topic 258**
**The Importance of Motivation 260**
Frederick Taylor: The Father of Scientific Management 260
*Legal Briefcase: UPS and Scientific Management* 261
Elton Mayo and the Hawthorne Studies 262
**Motivation and Maslow's Hierarchy of Needs 263**
Applying Maslow's Theory 264
**Herzberg's Motivating Factors 265**
Applying Herzberg's Theories 266
**Job Enrichment 267**
*Spotlight on Small Business: Small Businesses Can Motivate without Big Costs* 269
**McGregor's Theory X and Theory Y 269**
Theory X 270
Theory Y 270
**Ouchi's Theory Z 271**
**Goal-Setting Theory and Management by Objectives 273**
**Meeting Employee Expectations: Expectancy Theory 274**
**Reinforcing Employee Performance: Reinforcement Theory 274**
**Treating Employees Fairly: Equity Theory 275**
**Building Teamwork through Open Communication 276**
Applying Open Communication in Self-Managed Teams 277
*Making Ethical Decisions: Motivating Temporary Employees* 278
**Motivation in the Future 278**
*Reaching Beyond Our Borders: Global Teamwork* 279
**Video Case: Motivation Is a Hot Topic 284**

## Chapter Eleven

286 Human Resource Management: Finding and Keeping the Best Employees
**Profile: Getting to Know Wegmans Food Markets 286**
**Working with People Is Just the Beginning 288**
Developing the Ultimate Resource 288
The Human Resource Challenge 289
*Dealing with Change: Replacing the Old Guard* 290
**Determining Your Human Resource Needs 290**

**Recruiting Employees from a Diverse Population 292**
*Spotlight on Small Business: Attracting Qualified Employees* 293
**Selecting Employees Who Will Be Productive 294**
Hiring Contingent Workers 295
**Training and Developing Employees for Optimum Performance 297**
Management Development 299
Networking 299
Diversity in Management Development 300
**Appraising Employee Performance to Get Optimum Results 300**
**Compensating Employees: Attracting and Keeping the Best 302**
Pay Systems 302
Compensating Teams 303
Fringe Benefits 304
*Reaching Beyond Our Borders: Working Worldwide* 306
**Scheduling Employees to Meet Organizational and Employee Needs 306**
Flextime Plans 306
Home-Based and Other Mobile Work 307
Job-Sharing Plans 308
**Moving Employees Up, Over, and Out 309**
Promoting and Reassigning Employees 309
Terminating Employees 309
Retiring Employees 310
Losing Employees 310
**Laws Affecting Human Resource Management 311**
*Legal Briefcase: Government Legislation* 312
Law Protecting the Disabled and Older Employees 313
Effects of Legislation 313
**Video Case: Surf's Up at Patagonia! 318**

## Chapter Twelve

**320** Dealing with Employee-Management Issues and Relationships
**Profile: Getting to Know James P. Hoffa, President of the International Brotherhood o Teamsters 320**
**Employee-Management Issues 322**
**Labor Unions from Different Perspectives 323**
The Early History of Organized Labor 323
**Labor Legislation and Collective Bargaining 324**
Objectives of Organized Labor 326
*Dealing with Change: The Unions versus Wal-Mart* 327
Resolving Labor-Management Disagreements 329
*Reaching Beyond Our Borders: Are the Good Times Really Over for Good?* 330
Mediation and Arbitration 330
**Tactics Used in Labor-Management Conflicts 331**
Union Tactics 331
Management Tactics 333
The Future of Unions and Labor-Management Relations 333
*Making Ethical Decisions: Let Your Conscience Be Your Guide* 334
*Spotlight on Small Business: Nursing the Unions Back to Health* 335
**Controversial Employee-Management Issues 336**
Executive Compensation 336
*Legal Briefcase: Saying Goodbye the Gold-Lined Way* 337
Pay Equity 338
Sexual Harassment 339
Child Care 340
Elder Care 341
Drug Testing 342
Violence in the Workplace 342
**Video Case: United We Stand 347**

## * part 5

## Marketing: Developing and Implementing Customer-Oriented Marketing Plans

## Chapter Thirteen

**348** Marketing: Building Customer Relationships
**Profile: Getting to Know Lance Fried, Entrepreneur 348**
**What Is Marketing? 350**
The Evolution of the Field of Marketing 350
Nonprofit Organizations and Marketing 351
**The Marketing Mix 352**
Applying the Marketing Process 352
*Dealing with Change: Four Ps Drive Marketing* 353
Designing a Product to Meet Needs 354
Setting an Appropriate Price 355
Getting the Product to the Right Place 355
Developing an Effective Promotional Strategy 355
**Providing Marketers with Information 356**
The Marketing Research Process 356
The Marketing Environment 358
*Making Ethical Decisions: No Kidding* 359
*Reaching Beyond Our Borders: Responding to the Needs of People in Other Countries* 360
Two Different Markets: Consumer and Business-to-Business (B2B) 361
**The Consumer Market 362**
Segmenting the Consumer Market 363
Reaching Smaller Market Segments 364
Moving toward Relationship Marketing 364
*Spotlight on Small Business: Marketing Helps Small Firms Compete* 365
The Consumer Decision-Making Process 366
**The Business-to-Business Market 367**
**Your Prospects in Marketing 369**
**Video Case: MTV Goes Everywhere 372**

## Chapter Fourteen


374 Developing and Pricing Products and Services

**Profile: Getting to Know Bill and Vieve Gore of W. L. Gore & Associates 374**

**Product Development and the Total Product Offer 376**

*Dealing with Change: Making Bread* 377

*Spotlight on Small Business: When You Don't Have Time to Cook at Home* 378

Developing a Total Product Offer 378

*Dealing with Change: Using the Web to Differentiate a Product* 379

Product Lines and the Product Mix 379

**Product Differentiation 380**

Marketing Different Classes of Consumer Goods and Services 380

*Reaching Beyond Our Borders: Designing Products for the Poor* 381

Marketing Industrial Goods and Services 382

**Packaging Changes the Product 383**

The Growing Importance of Packaging 384

**Branding and Brand Equity 385**

Brand Categories 385

Generating Brand Equity and Loyalty 386

*Making Ethical Decisions: Are We Too Star Struck?* 387

Creating Brand Associations 387

Brand Management 387

**The New-Product Development Process 388**

Generating New-Product Ideas 388

Product Screening 388

Product Analysis 388

Product Development and Testing 389

Commercialization 389

**The Product Life Cycle 389**

Example of the Product Life Cycle 390

The Importance of the Product Life Cycle 390

**Competitive Pricing 392**

Pricing Objectives 392

Cost-Based Pricing 393

Demand-Based Pricing 393

Competition-Based Pricing 393

Break-Even Analysis 393

Other Pricing Strategies 394

How Market Forces Affect Pricing 395

**Nonprice Competition 395**

**Video Case: SolutionPeople Have the Idea 400**


## Chapter Fifteen


402 Distributing Products Quickly and Efficiently

**Profile: Getting to Know A. Jayson Adair of Copart Inc. 402**

**The Emergence of Marketing Intermediaries 404**

Why Marketing Needs Intermediaries 404

How Intermediaries Create Exchange Efficiency 405

The Value versus the Cost of Intermediaries 406

**The Utilities Created by Intermediaries 407**

Form Utility 407

Time Utility 408

Place Utility 408

Possession Utility 408

Information Utility 408

*Making Ethical Decisions: Look One Place, Buy Another* 409

Service Utility 409

**Wholesale Intermediaries 410**

Merchant Wholesalers 410

Agents and Brokers 410

**Retail Intermediaries 411**

Retail Distribution Strategy 412

Nonstore Retailing 412

Electronic Retailing 413

*Reaching Beyond Our Borders: What You Want, When You Want It* 414

Telemarketing 414

Vending Machines, Kiosks, and Carts 414

Direct Selling 415

Multilevel Marketing 415

Direct Marketing 415

**Building Cooperation in Channel Systems 416**

Corporate Distribution Systems 416

Contractual Distribution Systems 416

Administered Distribution Systems 417

Supply Chains 417

**The Emergence of Logistics 418**

**Getting Goods from Producers to Consumers Efficiently 419**

**Dealing with Change: Responding to National Emergencies 420**

Choosing the Right Distribution Mode 420

The Storage Function 422

Tracking Goods 423

**What All This Means to You 423**

**Video Case: Feeding the Poor of Chicago 428**


## Chapter Sixteen


430 Using Effective Promotional Techniques

**Profile: Getting to Know Dietrich Mateschitz of Red Bull 430**

**Promotion and the Promotion Mix 432**

**Advertising: Fighting to Keep Consumer Interest 433**

The Growing Use of Infomercials 435

*Dealing with Change: You Can't TiVo Your Way Away from Product Placement* 436

Advertisers Are Moving to the Internet 436

Global Advertising 437

*Reaching Beyond Our Borders: Let's Stop at Starbucks for Some Coffee* 438
**Personal Selling: Providing Personal Attention 438**
Steps in the Selling Process 439
The Business-to-Consumer (B2C) Sales Process 441
**Public Relations: Building Relationships 442**
Publicity: The Talking Arm of PR 443
**Sales Promotion: Getting a Good Deal 443**
Sampling 445
Word of Mouth 445
*Making Ethical Decisions: A Tobacco Industry Smoke Screen?* 446
How New Technologies Are Affecting Promotion 447
*Spotlight on Small Business: Help, I'm Getting Married* 448
**Managing the Promotion Mix: Putting It All Together 448**
Promotional Strategies 448
**Video Case: Promotion Gets a Big Push 453**

# * part 6

## Managing Financial Resources

### Chapter Seventeen

**454** Understanding Financial Information and Accounting
**Profile: Getting to Know Roxanne Coady of R. J. Julia Booksellers 454**
**The Importance of Accounting Information 456**
**What Is Accounting? 456**
**Areas of Accounting 457**
Managerial Accounting 457
Financial Accounting 457
*Dealing with Change: Accountants Reading Between the Lines* 459
Auditing 459
Tax Accounting 460
Government and Not-for-Profit Accounting 460
**The Accounting Cycle 461**
Using Computers in Accounting 462
**Understanding Key Financial Statements 463**
The Fundamental Accounting Equation 463
The Balance Sheet 464
Classifying Assets 464
Liabilities and Owners' Equity Accounts 466
*Spotlight on Small Business: You Incorporated* 467
The Income Statement 467
*Legal Briefcase: The Last Shall Be First* 469
Revenue 469
Cost of Goods Sold (Cost of Goods Manufactured) 469
Operating Expenses 470
Net Profit or Loss 470
The Statement of Cash Flows 471
The Importance of Cash Flow Analysis 472
*Making Ethical Decisions: On the Accounting Hot Seat* 473
**Analyzing Financial Statements: Ratio Analysis 473**
Liquidity Ratios 473
Leverage (Debt) Ratios 474
Profitability (Performance Ratios) 474
Activity Ratios 475
**Video Case: When the Goal Line Meets the Bottom Line 481**

### Chapter Eighteen

**482** Financial Management
**Profile: Getting to Know Jonathan Mariner, CFO of Major League Baseball 482**
**The Role of Finance and Financial Managers 484**
*Dealing with Change: Bringing Financial Goodwill to Goodwill Industries* 485
The Importance of Understanding Finance 486
**What Is Financial Management? 486**
**Financial Planning 487**
Forecasting Financial Needs 488
Working with the Budgeting Process 488
Establishing Financial Controls 489
*Spotlight on Small Business: You Incorporated Monthly Budget* 490
*Making Ethical Decisions: Playing It Safe or Stupid* 491
**The Need for Operating Funds 491**
Managing Day-by-Day Needs of the Business 491
Controlling Credit Operations 492
Acquiring Needed Inventory 492
Making Capital Expenditures 493
Alternative Sources of Funds 493
**Obtaining Short-Term Financing 494**
Trade Credit 494
Family and Friends 495
Commercial Banks 495
Different Forms of Short-Term Loans 496
Factoring Accounts Receivable 497
*Reaching Beyond Our Borders: Guaranteeing That the Deal Gets Done* 498
Commercial Paper 498
Credit Cards 499
**Obtaining Long-Term Financing 500**
Debt Financing 500
Equity Financing 502
Making Decisions on Using Financial Leverage 504
**Video Case: It's My Money 509**

### Chapter Nineteen

**510** Securities Markets: Financing and Investing Opportunities
**Profile: Getting to Know Jim Cramer, the Mad Man of Wall Street 510**

**The Function of Securities Markets 512**
The Role of Investment Bankers 513
**Debt Financing by Selling Bonds 513**
Learning the Language of Bonds 513
Advantages and Disadvantages of Issuing Bonds 514
Different Classes of Bonds 515
Special Bond Features 515
**Equity Financing by Selling Stock 516**
Learning the Language of Stock 516
Advantages and Disadvantages of Issuing Stock 517
Issuing Shares of Preferred Stock 517
Special Features of Preferred Stock 518
Issuing Shares of Common Stock 518
*Dealing with Change: A Change at the Exchange* 519
**Stock Exchanges 519**
U.S. Exchanges 519
Securities Regulations and the Securities and Exchange Commission 520
Global Stock Exchanges 521
*Legal Briefcase: Ins and Outs of Insider Trading* 522
**How to Invest in Securities 522**
*Making Ethical Decisions: What Will It Be: Your Bark or Your Bite?* 523
Investing Online 523
*Reaching Beyond Our Borders: It Really Is a Small World* 524
Choosing the Right Investments Strategy 524
**Investing in Bonds 525**
**Investing in Stocks 526**
Stock Splits 527
**Investing in Mutual Funds and Exchange-Traded Funds 527**
*Dealing with Change: Diamonds and Spiders and Vipers, Oh My!* 529
Diversifying Investments 530
**Investing in High-Risk Investments 530**
Investing in High-Risk (Junk) Bonds 530
Buying Stock on Margin 530
Investing in Commodities 531
**Understanding Information from Securities Markets 532**
Understanding Bond Quotations 532
Understanding Stock Quotations 532
Understanding Mutual Fund Quotations 534
Stock Market Indicators 535
The Market's Roller-Coaster Ride 536
Investing Challenges in the 21st-Century Market 537
**Video Case: A Fool and His Money: Motley Fool 542**

## Chapter Twenty

544 Understanding Money, Financial Institutions, and the Federal Reserve
**Profile: Getting to Know Ben S. Bernanke of the Federal Reserve 544**
**Why Money Is Important 546**
What Is Money? 546
What Is the Money Supply? 547
Why Does the Money Supply Need to Be Controlled? 548
The Global Exchange of Money 548
**Control of the Money Supply 548**
Basics about the Federal Reserve 549
The Reserve Requirement 550
Open-Market Operations 550
The Discount Rate 551
The Federal Reserve's Check-Clearing Role 551
**The History of Banking and the Need for the Fed 551**
Banking and the Great Depression 553
**The American Banking System 554**
Commercial Banks 554
*Making Ethical Decisions: To Tell the Teller or Not* 555
*Spotlight on Small Business: You Won't Loan Me Money? Isn't That What Banks Are For?* 556
Savings and Loan Associations (S&Ls) 557
Credit Unions 557
Other Financial Institutions (Nonbanks) 557
**How the Government Protects Your Funds 559**
The Federal Deposit Insurance Corporation (FDIC) 559
The Savings Association Insurance Fund (SAIF) 559
The National Credit Union Administration (NCUA) 559
*Legal Briefcase: What Are Your Rights?* 560
**The Future of Banking 560**
Electronic Banking on the Internet 560
Using Technology to Make Banking More Efficient 561
**International Banking and Banking Services 563**
Leaders in International Banking 563
The World Bank and the International Monetary Fund (IMF) 564
*Reaching Beyond Our Borders: What Can Be Done to Help the World's Poor?* 565
**Video Case: Would You Like Banking with that Insurance? 570**

## Bonus Chapter A

572 Working within the Legal Environment of Business
**Profile: Getting to Know David Boies, Corporate Attorney 572**

The Need for Laws 574
Statutory and Common Law 574
Administrative Agencies 575
Tort Law 576
Product Liability 576
Law Protecting Ideas Patents, Copyrights, and Trademarks 577
Sales Law: The Uniform Commercial Code 579
Warranties 579
Negotiable Instruments 580
Contract Law 580
Breach of Contract 581
Laws to Promote Fair and Competitive Practices 582
The History of Antitrust Legislation 582
Laws to Protect Consumers 584
Tax Laws 584
Bankruptcy Laws 585
Deregulation 588

Bonus Chapter B
594 Using Technology to Manage Information
Profile: Getting to Know Eva Chen, Cofounder and CEO of Trend Micro 594
The Role of Information Technology 596
How Information Technology Changes Business 596
Moving from Information toward Knowledge and Business Intelligence 597
Types of Information 599
Managing Information 600
Storing and Mining Data 601
The Road to Knowledge: The Internet, Intranets, Extranets, and Virtual Private Networks 601
The Front Door: Enterprise Portals 603
Broadband Technology 603
The Enabling Technology: Hardware 604
Cutting the Cord: Wireless Information Appliances 605
Computer Networks 605
Software 606
Effects of Information Technology on Management 608
Human Resource Issues 608
Security Issues 609
Privacy Issues 611
Stability Issues 612
Technology and You 613

Bonus Chapter C
618 Managing Risk
Profile: Getting to Know A. G. Gaston, Insurance Entrepreneur and Risk Taker 618
Understanding Business Risks 620
How Rapid Change Affects Risk Management 621
Managing Risk 621
Reducing Risk 621
Avoiding Risk 622
Self-Insuring 622
Buying Insurance to Cover Risk 623
Understanding Insurance Policies 624
Rule of Indemnity 624
Types of Insurance Companies 625
Insurance Coverage for Various Kinds of Risk 625
Health Insurance 625
Disability Insurance 626
Workers' Compensation 626
Liability Insurance 626
Other Business Insurance 627
Life Insurance for Businesses 627
Insurance Coverage for Home-Based Businesses 627
The Risk of Damaging the Environment 627

Bonus Chapter D
632 Managing Personal Finances
Profile: Getting to Know Millionaires You Can Follow to Financial Success 632
The Need for Personal Financial Planning 634
Financial Planning Begins with Making Money 634
Six Steps in Learning to Control Your Assets 634
Building Your Financial Base 637
Real Estate: Historically, a Relatively Secure Investment 638
Where to Put Your Savings 639
Learning to Manage Credit 640
Protecting Your Financial Base: Buying Insurance 641
Health Insurance 643
Homeowner's or Renter's Insurance 643
Other Insurance 644
Planning Your Retirement 644
Social Security 644
Individual Retirement Accounts (IRAs) 644
401(k) Plans 646
Keogh Plans 647
Financial Planners 647
Estate Planning 648

Endnotes EN-1
Glossary G-1
Credits PC-1
Name Index I-1
Organization Index I-8
Subject Index I-13

# ABOUT THE authors

The *Understanding Business* author team possesses a unique blend of university, community college, industry, public service, small business, and curriculum development experience that helps them breathe life into the dynamic business concepts presented in the text. As instructors who use the text and supplements in their own classrooms, Bill Nickels and Jim McHugh have a personal stake in the quality of the entire project. As a curriculum specialist, Susan McHugh is committed to making certain that Bill and Jim (and all of the other *Understanding Business* users) have the best materials possible for creating interesting and useful classes that make learning business an exciting experience.

**Bill Nickels** is emeritus professor of business at the University of Maryland, College Park. He has over 30 years' experience teaching graduate and undergraduate business courses including introduction to business, marketing, and promotion. He has won the Outstanding Teacher on Campus award four times and was nominated for the award dozens of other times. He received his M.B.A. degree from Western Reserve University and his Ph.D. from The Ohio State University. He has written a marketing communications text and two marketing principles texts in addition to many articles in business publications. He has taught many seminars to businesspeople on subjects like power communications, marketing, non-business marketing, and stress and life management. His son, Joel, will be getting his Ph.D. from The University of California (Cal) soon and will be the third Ph.D. in the family. He, too, will be a professor.

**Jim McHugh** is an associate professor of business at St. Louis Community College/Forest Park. He holds an M.B.A. degree from Lindenwood University and has had broad experience in education, business, and government. In addition to teaching several sections of introduction to business each semester for over 25 years, Jim teaches in the marketing and management areas at both the undergraduate and graduate levels. Jim enjoys conducting business seminars and consulting with small and large businesses. Jim is actively involved in the public service sector. When he is not in the classroom or boardroom, Jim enjoys figuring out who Donald Trump's next apprentice is going to be.

**Susan McHugh** is a learning specialist with extensive training and experience in adult learning and curriculum development. She holds a M.Ed. degree from the University of Missouri and completed her course work for a Ph.D. in education administration with a specialty in adult learning theory. As a professional curriculum developer, she has directed numerous curriculum projects and educator training programs. She has worked in the public and private sector as a consultant in training and employee development. While Jim and Susan treasure their participation in the *Understanding Business* project, their greatest accomplishment is their collaboration on their three children, Casey, Molly, and Michael, who have all grown up regarding the text as a fourth sibling. Casey was a fervent user of the 4th edition, Molly eagerly used the 6th edition, and Michael had his chance to understand business with the 7th edition. Newborn grandson, Colin, will have to wait for the 15th edition.

As authors, it is thrilling to see the results of the work we love be embraced by colleagues in hundreds of colleges and universities throughout the United States and around the world. Not only is *Understanding Business* the most widely used text in introduction to business courses across the country, but it is also the text we use day-in and day-out in our own intro classes. When you use the materials yourself, you have a strong vested interest in making the text and supplements the very best possible.

While we did play a significant role in the development of this text, the greatest joy we find in performing this task comes from working with the many people who deserve credit for the evolution of this remarkable project. Over 250 faculty who teach the course and hundreds of students who have used the book and its supplements were formally involved in various stages of our research and writing of this edition. We continue to hear informally from students and faculty throughout the country who call and e-mail us with comments and suggestions. We encourage you to do the same. We enjoy the interaction.

Prior to writing this edition, we held several close-to-the-customer focus groups in cities around the country. Discussions with instructors and students in these sessions helped us define, clarify, and test the needs of the diverse group who teach and take this course. Additionally, more than 20 instructors provided us with in-depth evaluations of the seventh edition, providing insights for the improvements that you will encounter on every page of this edition. Once the first draft was written, another group of instructors critiqued our initial effort, which led to many more important refinements.

Many consider this process the most extensive product development process ever implemented for a text of this type. While that's probably true, we consider this talking and sharing of ideas with our colleagues and students across the country as one of the greatest perks of our jobs.

## KEEPING UP WITH WHAT'S NEW

Users of *Understanding Business* have always appreciated the currency of the material and the large number of examples from companies of *all* sizes and industries (e.g., service, manufacturing, profit and nonprofit) in the United States and around the world. A glance at the Chapter Notes will show you that most of them are from 2005 or 2006. Accordingly, this edition features the latest business practices and other developments affecting business, including:

- Effects of Hurricane Katrina and other natural disasters.
- Identity theft.
- Bernanke at the Federal Reserve.
- Blogging and podcasting.
- Off-shore outsourcing—and insourcing.
- A new, unifying case study of a vegetarian restaurant.
- Social security developments.
- Central American Free Trade Agreement.
- Corporate social initiatives.
- SEC's fair disclosure rule.
- Homeland security developments.
- Privacy and security issues with information technology.
- Corporate and other scandals.
- Fall of companies such as Enron and WorldCom.
- The Sarbanes-Oxley Act.
- E-commerce's impact on the role of intermediaries.
- The latest population trends.

- Viral marketing.
- Internet2.
- XM radio.
- Online banking and smart cards.
- Storing and mining data.
- Radio-Frequency Identification Tags (RFID).
- The latest issues regarding the World Bank and IMF.
- Latest quality standards.
- and much, much more.

We firmly believe that no course in college is more important than the introduction to business course. That's why we enjoy teaching it so much and why we are willing to spend so much time helping others make this the best course on campus. We are proud of the text and the integrated teaching and testing system that you have helped us develop over the years. We thank the many text and supplements users who have supported us through the years and welcome new instructors to the team. We look forward to a continuing relationship with all of you and to sharing what we consider the most exciting classroom experience possible: teaching introduction to business.

**Bill Nickels** **Jim McHugh** **Susan McHugh**

# acknowledgments

Our remarkable team of talented people at Irwin/McGraw-Hill was artfully led by our executive editor John Weimeister. We appreciate his dedication and thank him for enlisting and guiding such a talented team of professionals.

Natalie Ruffatto took the helm as the developmental editor of this edition. Natalie's excellent production experience proved invaluable as we targeted ever-shortening deadlines. It was Natalie's job to make certain that all of the pieces of this complex project came together at the right moment.

Copyeditor Janet Renard continues to amaze us with her ability to improve the text. Michael Hannon provided much appreciated research assistance in addition to his many other text development responsibilities. Kami Carter created the new fresh, open interior design and extraordinary cover. Jennifer Blankenship carried out the extensive research for photos that was necessary to effectively reflect the concepts presented in the text. Mary Conzachi did a splendid job of keeping the production of the text on schedule. Manufacturing was kept on time under the watchful eye of Heather Burbridge. Chris Cole, Jennifer Cole, and Dan Mack used their remarkable creative talents to produce the fabulous new videos. Susan Lombardi and Janna Martin expertly supervised the print supplements and media assets. Joanne Butler graciously arranged the focus groups and managed the text reviews that have proven so helpful in revising the text and the supplements.

Many dedicated educators made extraordinary contributions to the quality and utility of this text and package. Barbara Barrett of St. Louis Community College at Meramec once again prepared an exemplary student assessment and learning guide that truly guides students on the path to mastering the course concepts. Carol Johnson of Denver University did an exceptional job in revising the Test Bank and creating the quizzes for the Online Learning Center. Gayle Ross of Ross Publishing continued to achieve miracles for us with her contributions to and management of the various resources that eventually came together to form the Instructor's Manual and AIE. Amit Shah of Frostburg State University did a superb job of creating the PowerPoint slides and transparency acetates. He also enhanced the teaching value of the transparency acetates by preparing insightful lecture notes that accompany the acetates. Stephanie Bibb prepared a handy media resource guide that adds instructional value to the video package. Many students would not be happy without the audio CD-ROMs prepared by Soph-Ware. McGraw-Hill's Charles Pelto was responsible for quality assurance. And many more people than we can ever acknowledge worked behind the scenes to translate our manuscript into the text you see; we thank them all.

Some suggested that taking over the market-leading text and guiding it again to record-breaking sales would be an impossible task. However, our outstanding marketing manager, Sarah Reed, was up to the challenge. With the assistance of the market's finest sales professionals, she again led the text to record sales. We appreciate her commitment and the renowned product knowledge, service, and dedication of the McGraw-Hill/Irwin sales reps.

We want to thank the many instructors who contributed to the development of *Understanding Business*. An exceptional group of reviewers dedicated many long hours to critiquing the previous edition and subsequent drafts of this edition, and attending our focus groups. Their recommendations and contributions were invaluable in making this edition a stronger instructional tool. Our sincere thanks to the following reviewers:

## REVIEWERS OF THE EIGHTH EDITION

We would like to thank the following instructors and students who generously provided the input and advice on which the refinements and enhancements to the Eighth Edition of the text and supplements are based.

## 8E REVIEWERS AND FOCUS GROUP AND SYMPOSIA

Dave Aiken, *Hocking College*
M.T. Alabbassi, *University of North Florida*
Sylvia Allen, *Los Angeles Valley College*
Kenneth Anderson, *CUNY-Boro of Manhattan Community College*
Marilyn Anderson, *Phoenix College*
Chi Anyansi-Archibong, *North Carolina A&T State University*
Vondra O. Armstrong, *Pulaski Technical College*
Robert Ash, *Santiago Canyon College*
Lee Ash, *Skagit Valley College*
Harold Babson, *Columbus State Community College*
Mike Baran, *South Puget Sound Community College*
Robert Barker, *Daytona Beach Community College*
Cora Barnhart, *Palm Beach Atlantic College*
William Barrett, *University of Wisconsin-Milwaukee*
Charles Beavin, *Miami Dade/ North Campus*
Lori Bennett, *Moorpark College*
Robert Bennett, *Delaware County Community College*
Michael Bento, *Owens Community College*
Bill Bettencourt, *Edmonds Community College*
Iris Berdrow, *Bentley College*
Carol Bibly, *Triton College*
Chris Bjornson, *Indiana University Southeast*
Margaret Black, *San Jacinto College, North Campus*
Mary Jo Boehms, *Jackson State Community College*
Steven Bradley, *Austin Community College*
David Braun, *Pierce College*
Harvey Bronstein, *Oakland Community College*
Deborah M. Brown, *North Carolina State University*
Joe Brum, *Fayetteville Tech Community College*
Judy Bulin, *Monroe Community College*
Cathleen Burns, *University of Missouri–Columbia*
John Burns, *Tomball College*
Harrison Burris, *DeVry University*
Paul Callahan, *Cincinnati State Tech Community College*
Nate Calloway, *University of Maryland–Metro University College*
Jim Carey, *Onandaga Community College*
Marilyn Carlson, *Clark State Community College*
Ron Cereola, *James Madison University*
Kevin Chandler, *DeVry Institute of Technology–Orlando*
Glen Chapuis, *St. Charles Community College*
Bonnie Chavez, *Santa Barbara City College*
Michael Cicero, *Highline Community College*
Antoinette Clegg, *Delta College*
Cindy Cloud, *Phoenix College*
Paul Coakley, *Community College of Baltimore County–Catonsville*
Barbara Connelly, *DeVry Institute–Phoenix*
Elijah Cooks, *Prince Georges Community College*
Ron Cooley, *South Suburban College*
Yolanda Cooper, *Collin County Community College*
Bobbie Corbett, *North Virginia Community College–Annandale*
Amy Daniel, *Saddleback College*
Dean Danielson, *San Joaquin Delta College*
Helen M. Davis, *Jefferson Community College*
Cory Dobbs, *Rio Salado College*
Ron Dolch, *Wor-Wi Community College*
Richard Drury, *North Virginia Community College–Annandale*
Beverly Dunlop-Loach, *Central Piedmont Community College*
Steven M. Dunphy, *Indiana University Northwest*
Timothy R. Durfield, *Citrus College*
Linda Durkin, *Delaware County Community College*
James Eason, *Coastal Carolina University*
Joe Eble, *Burlington Community College*
Nancy Evans, *Heartland Community College*

Joyce Fairchild, *North Virginia Community College–Alexandria*

Nancy J. Feather, *Pittsburgh Technical Institute*

Janice M. Feldbauer, *Austin Community College*

Ivan Figueroa, *Miami Dade College–Kendall*

Ronald E. Foshee, *North Harris College*

Dennis Foster, *Northern Arizona University*

John Foster, *Montgomery College–Rockville*

Barry Freeman, *Bergen Community College*

Steven L. Fuller, *Waubonsee Community College*

Ellen S. Kaye Gehrke, *Alliant International University*

Richard Ghirdella, *Citrus College*

Vic Giardini, *University of Delaware*

Sofia Gill, *Palm Beach Community College*

Alfredo Gomez, *Broward Community College*

Mary Gorman, *University of Cincinnati*

Mark Goudreau, *Johnson and Wales University*

Chris W. Grevesen, *DeVry College of New Jersey*

Karen Halpern, *South Puget Sound Community College*

Carnella Hardin, *Glendale Community College*

Carnella Hardin, *Glendale Community College*

Jeri Harper, *Western Illinois University*

Rowland Harvey, *DeVry Institute–Houston*

Carolyn Hatton, *Cincinnati State University*

Karen H. Hawkins, *Miami Dade College*

Linda Heffin, *Elgin Community College*

Dennis Heiner, *College of Southern Idaho*

Jack Heinsius, *Modesto Junior College*

Charlane Held, *Onondaga Community College*

Dave Hickman, *Frederick Community College*

Nate Himelstein, *Essex Community College*

Merrily Hoffman, *San Jacinto College–Central*

Alice J. Holt, *Benedict College*

Julie Huang, *Rio Hondo College*

Richard Hunting, *Montgomery College–Houston*

Donald Inman, *Grand Valley State University*

Bill Jackson, *Green River Community College*

Charlotte Jacobsen, *Montgomery College–Rockville*

Andrew Johnson, *Bellevue Community College*

Jack Johnson, *Consumnes River College*

Marie Johnson, *Skagit Valley College*

Edgar Joya, *St. Augustine College*

Jehan Kavoosi, *Clarion University*

Donald Kelley, *Francis Marion University*

Ann Kelly, *Georgia Southern University*

Marce Kelly, *Santa Monica College*

Mary Beth Klinger, *College of Southern Maryland*

Tom Knoll, *DeVry Institute of Technology–Houston*

Steve Kober, *Pierce College*

Barbara Kriechbaum, *Hagerstown Business College*

Gary Langdale, *Saddleback College*

Michael LaSala, *Westchester Business Institute*

Dane Leonard, *Chabot College*

Harry Lepinske, *Purdue/ Calumet–Hammond*

Rich Lewis, *Lansing Community College*

Ellen Ligons, *Pasadena City College*

Bryon Lilly, *DeAnza College*

Vasant Limaye, *SouthWest Collegiate Institute for the Deaf (SWCID) of Howard College*

Robert Livingston, *Cerritos College*

Beverly Loach, *Central Piedmont Community College*

Terry Lovell, *Yavapai College*

B. Tim Lowder, *Francis Marion University*

Yvonne I. Lucas, *Southwestern College*

Elaine Luther, *Point Park College*

Richard Lyons, *Indian River Community College*

Ashford Marahaja, *Berkeley College–White Plains*

Suzanne K. Markow, *Des Moines Area Community College*

Larry Martin, *Community College of Southern Nevada*

Randy Martin, *Germanna Community College*

Robert Matthews, *Oakton Community College*

Susan Smith McClaren, *Mt. Hood Community College*

Tim McHeffey, *Suffolk County Community College*

Andrea G. McKeon, *Florida Community College at Jacksonville*

Noel E. McKeon, *Florida Community College at Jacksonville*

Pat McMahon, *Palm Beach Community College*

Lasche McRorey, *Southwest Texas Junior College*

Michelle Meyer, *Joliet Junior College*

Herbert L. Meyer, *Scott Community College*

Bob Meyers, *Palm Beach Atlantic Community College*

Jacqueline Middleton, *Montgomery College–Germantown*

Rebecca Miles, *Delaware Tech Community College*

Willie Minor, *Rio Salado College*

Ed Mitchell, *Hillsborough Community College*

Alison Mukweyi, *Midland College*

Liz Murata, *Edmonds Community College*

Jerry Myers, *Stark State College*

Tom Nagle, *Northland Pioneer College*

Andrew Nelson, *Montgomery College–Germantown*

Linda Newell, *Saddleback College*

Linda Newell, *Saddleback College*

Ken Newgren, *Illinois State University*

Janet Nichols, *Northeastern University*

Cynthia Nicola, *Carlow University*

Ed O'Brien, *Scottsdale Community College*

John O'Brien, *Valencia Community College*

Tibor Osztreicher, *Baltimore County Community College–Baltimore Campus*

Karen Overton, *Houston Community College Northwest*

Norman Pacula, *College of Marin*

Roger Pae, *Cuyahoga Community College*

Esther S. Page-Wood, *Western Michigan University*

Richard Paradiso, *Thomas Nelson Community College*

Ron Pardee, *Riverside Community College*

Rex A. Parker, *Rock Valley College*

Jack Partlow, *North Virginia Community College–Annandale*

Lou Pearsall, *DeVry University*

Jeffrey D. Penley, *Catawba Community College*

Steven Peters, *Walla Walla Community College*

Jim Pfister, *St. Petersburg Junior College*

John Phillips, *North Virginia Community College–Manassas*

Anita Pinkston, *Vincennes University*

Alison Adderley-Pittman, *University of Central Florida*

Michael Potter, *DeVry Institute–Phoenix*

Lana Powell, *Valencia Community College–West*

Mark Preising, *Florida Metro University*

Ian Priestman, *Linn Benton Community College*

Kathy Pullins, *Columbus State Community College*

Charles C. Quinn, *Austin Community College*

Michael Quinn, *James Madison University*

Gregg Rapp, *Portland Community College–Sylvania*

Robert Reck, *Western Michigan University*

Phil Reffitt, *Florida Metro University*

Robert Reichl, *Morton College*

Jeffrey R. Ricciardi, *North Harris Montgomery College*

Levi Richard, *Citrus College*

Karen Richardson, *Tarrant County Community College–Northeast*

Dan Ricica, *Sinclair Community College*

Denver Riffe, *National College of Business & Technology*

Pollis Robertson, *Kellogg Community College*

Harriett Rojas, *Indiana Wesleyan*

Eric Rothenburg, *Kingsborough Community College*

Carol Rowey, *Community College of Rhode Island*

Joan Ryan, *Clackamas Community College*

James Sagner, *Berkeley College-Westchester*

Timothy E. Samolis, Pittsburgh Technical Institute

Marcy Satterwhite, Lake Land Community College

Pookie Truly Sautter, *New Mexico State University*

Gerry Scheffelmaier, *Middle Tennessee State University*

Ron Schloemer, *Miami University*

Lewis Schlossinger, *Community College of Aurora*

Marcianna Schusler, *Prairie State College*

Tom Secrest, *Coastal Carolina University*

Patty Serrano, *Clark College*

Pat Setlik, *William Rainey Harper College*

Martin Shapiro, *Berkeley College–White Plains*

Dick Sharman, *Montgomery College*

Richard Sherer, *Los Angeles Trade–Tech College*

Charlie Shi, *Diablo Valley College*

Lynette Shishido, *Santa Monica College*

Gerald Silver, *Purdue/Calumet–Hammond*

Cynthia Singer, *Union City College*

Leon Singleton, *Santa Monica College*

Rajendra Sinhaa, *Des Moines Area Community College*

Steven Skaggs, *Waubonsee Community College*

Noel Smith, *Palm Beach Community College–South*

Stephen Snyder, University of West Florida

Ray Sparks, *Pima Community College–East Campus*

Rieann Spence-Gale, *North Virginia Community College–Alexandria*

Sandra Spencer, *DeAnza College*

Camille Stallings, *Pima Community College*

Camille Stallings, *Pima Community College–Downtown*

Vernon Stauble, *San Bernardino Valley College*

Jeffery Stauffer, *Ventura College*

*William A.* Steiden, *Jefferson Community College Southwest Campus*

Leo Stevenson, *Western Michigan University*

Edith Strickland, *Tallahassee Community College*

David Stringer, *De Anza College*

Lynn Suksdorf, *Salt Lake Community College*

Dottie Sutherland, *Pima Community College–East Campus*

Verna Swanljung, *North Seattle Community College*

Susan Thompson, *Palm Beach Community College–Lake Worth*

Tom Thompson, *University of Maryland–University College*

Frank Titlow, *St. Petersburg College*

Shafi Ullah, *Broward Community College (South campus)*

Vern Urlacher, *Colorado Technical University*

Margie Vance, *Albuquerque Vo-Tech Institute*

Michael Vijuk, *William Rainey Harper College*

Nancy Waldron, *Lasell College*

Tom Walker, *Seminole Community College*

Carl Wall, *Broward Community College–North*

Roger Waller, *San Joaquin Delta College*

Joyce Walsh-Portillo, *Broward Community College–Central*

Leatha Ware, *Waubonsee Community College*

Richard C. Warner, *Lehigh Carbon Community College*

Dorothy S. Warren, *Middle Tennessee State University*

Louis Watanabe, *Bellevue Community College*

Warren Wee, *Hawaii Pacific University*

William Weisgerber, *Saddleback College*

Gregor Weiss, *Prince Georges Community College*

Dick Westfall, *Cabrillo College*

Jay Whitelock, *Community College of Baltimore County–Catonsville*

Jean Wicks, *Bowie State University*

Timothy Wiedman, *Thomas Nelson Community College*

Paul Wilcox, *DeVry Institute of Technology–Orlando*

Lynn Wilson, *Saint Leo University*

Greg Winter, *Barry University*

Colette Wolfson, *Ivy Tech Community College*

Steve Wong, *Rock Valley College*

Nathaniel Woods, *Columbus State Community College*

Daniel Wubbena, *Western Iowa Tech Community College*

Ron Young, *Kalamazoo Valley Community College*

Nancy Zimmerman, *Community College of Baltimore County—Cantonsville*

Gail A. Zwart, *Riverside Community College District, Norco Campus*

The eighth edition continues to be the market's gold standard due to involvement of these committed instructors and students. We thank them all for their help, support, and friendship.

**Bill Nickels** **Jim McHugh** **Susan McHugh**

## REVIEWERS AND OTHER PARTICIPANTS IN THE DEVELOPMENT OF PREVIOUS EDITIONS

Larry Aaronson, *Catonsville Community College;* Milton Alderfer, *Miami-Dade Community College;* Dennis G. Allen, *Grand Rapids Community College;* Dan Anderson, *Sullivan Jr. College;* Kenneth Anderson, *Charles S. Mott Community College;* Kenneth F. Anderson, *CUNY–Borough of Manhattan Community College;* Lydia E. Anderson, *Fresno City College;* John Anstey, *University of Nebraska–Omaha;* Maria Zak Aria, *Camden County College;* Glenann Arnold, *Pueblo Community College;* Ed Aronson, *Golden West College;* Larry Arp, *University of Southern Indiana;* Doug Ashby, *Lewis & Clark;* Hal Babson, *Columbus State Community College;* Harold Babson, *Columbus State Community College;* Chani Badrian, *CUNY–Baruch College;* Herm Baine, *Broward Community College;* Morris Baird, *The Community College of Baltimore County;* Russell Baker, *Florida Metropolitan University;* Xenia Balabkins, *Middlesex County College;* Michael Baldigo, *Sonoma State University;* Lee R. Baldwin, *Mt. San Antonio College;* John Balek, *Morton College;* Fran Ballard, *Florida Community College;* Barbara Barrett, *St. Louis Community College;* Richard Bartlett, *Muskigan Area Technical College;* Lorraine Bassette, *Prince George's Community College;* Robert Bennett, *Delaware County Community College;* Ellen Benowitz, *Mercer County Community College;* Alec Beudoin, *Triton College;* Jade Beavers, *Jefferson State Community College;* Charles Beavin, *Miami-Dade–North;* John Beem, *College of DuPage;* Michael Bejtlich, *Cape Cod Community College;* Larry Benke, *Sacramento City College;* Marcel Berard, *Community College of Rhode Island;* Janet L. Bernard, *Tampa College;* Patricia Bernson, *County College of Morris;* John Berry, *Antelope Valley College;* Carol Bibly, *Triton College;* Dean Bittick, *East Central College;* John Blackburn, *Ohio State University;* Jane Bloom, *Palm Beach Community College;* James H. Boeger, *Rock Valley College;* Mary Jo Boehms, *Jackson State Community College;* Jessee Bolton, *Charles County Community College;* Robert Bouck, *Lansing Community College;* John Bowdidge, *Southwest Missouri State University;* Barbara Ann Boyington, *Brookdale Community College;* Steven E. Bradley, *Austin Community College–Riverside;* Stephen Branz, *Triton College;* Robert Brechner, *Miami-Dade Community College;* Sonya Brett, *Macomb Community College;* Harvey Bronstein, *Oakland Community College;* Richard Brooke, *Florida Community College at Jacksonville;* Deborah M. Brown, *Santa Fe Community College;* Joseph Brum, *Fayetteville Technical Community College;* Thomas Buchl, *Northern Michigan University;* Howard Budner, *CUNY–Borough of Manhattan Community College;* Albert Bundons, *Johnson County Community College;* Nichole Burnes, *FMU–Tampa College;* Barrett R. Burns, *Houston Community College;* William F. Burtis, *DeAnza College;* Dennis Butler, *Orange Coast Community College;* Ron Bytnar, *South Suburban College;* Willie Caldwell, *Houston Community College;* J. Callahan, *Florida Institute of Technology;* Nathaniel Calloway, *University of Maryland–University College;* Nathaniel R. Calloway, *University of Maryland–University College;* B. J. Campsey, *San Jose State University;* Michele Lynn Carver, *The Community College of Baltimore County;* Lesley Casula, *Lord Fairfax Community College;* Mary Margaret Cavera, *Davenport College;* Sandra Cece, *Triton College;* Sam Chapman, *Diablo Valley College;* Bruce Charnov, *Hofstra University;* Bonnie Chavez, *Santa Barbara City College;* Barbara Ching, *Los Angeles City College;* William Chittenden, *Texas Tech University;* Larry Chonko, *Baylor University;* Jill Chown, *Mankato State University;* Nancy Christenson, *Brevard Community College;* Peter D. Churchill, *Diablo Valley College;* Gary Ciampa, *Wayne County Community College;* Michael Cicero, *Highline Community College;* J. Cicheberger, *Hillsborough Community College;* Monico Cisneros, *Austin Community College;* Robert Clobes, *St. Charles County Community College;* Paul

Coakley, *The Community College of Baltimore County;* James Cocke, *Pima County Community College;* Jerry Cohen, *Raritan Valley Community College;* Jeffrey Conte, *Westchester Community College;* Ron Cooley, *South Suburban College;* Allen Coon, *Robert Morris College;* Doug Copeland, *Johnson County Community College;* John Coppage, *Saginaw Valley State University;* Bobbie Corbett, *Northern Virginia Community College–Annandale;* John Courtney, *University of Maryland, University College;* James Cox, *Jefferson Community College;* William Crandall, *College of San Mateo;* Susan Cremins, *Westchester Community College;* Bruce Cudney, *Middlesex Community College;* C. Culbreth, *Brevard Community College;* Rex Cutshall, *Vincennes University;* Lawrence Danks, *Camden County College;* Clifford Davis, *SUNY–Cobleskill;* R.K. Davis, *University of Akron;* Burton V. Dean, *San Jose State University;* Cindy Del Medico, *Oakton Community College;* Evelyn Delaney, *Daytona Beach Community College;* Peter DelPiano, *Florida Metropolitan University;* Vincent Deni, *Oakland Community College;* Kathleen Denisco, *SUNY–Buffalo;* S. Desai, *Cedar Valley College;* Jack Dilbeck, *Ivy Tech State College;* Katherine Dillon, *Ocean County College;* Samuel DiRoberto, *Penn State University–Ogontz;* Steve Dolvin, *Pensacola Christian College;* Frank Dumas, *Baker College–Flint;* Dana Dye, *Gulf Coast Community College;* Shannon M. Ebersol, *Hagerstown Community College;* Ronald Eggers, *Barton College;* Pat Ellsberg, *Lower Columbia College;* Frank Emory, *Northern Virginia Community College–Woodbridge;* Warren Enos, *Ohlone College;* David Erickson, *College of Lake County;* Ted Erickson, *Normandale Community College;* Alton Evans, *Tarrant County Community College;* John Evans, *New Hampshire College;* C. S. Everett, *Des Moines Area Community College;* Shad Ewart, *Anne Arundel Community College;* Al Fabian, *IVY Tech;* Karen Fager, *Umpqua Community College;* Frank Falcetta, *Middlesex Community College;* S. Fante, *Central Florida Community College;* Bob Farris, *Mt. San Antonio College;* James Fatina, *College of Lake County–Harper College;* Edward Fay, *Canton College of Technology;* Janice Feldbauer, *Austin Community College;* Kevin Feldt, *University of Akron;* David Felt, *Northern Virginia Community College–Manassas;* Bob Ferrentino, *Lansing Community College;* Ivan Figueroa, *Miami-Dade Community College;* Robert Fineran, *East-West University;* Robert Fishco, *Middlesex County Community College;* Charles FitzPatrick, *Central Michigan University;* Joseph L. Flack, *Washtenaw Community College;* Jane Flagello, *DeVry Institute of Technology–Lombard;* H. Steven Floyd, *Manatee Community College;* Ronald E. Foshee, *North Harris College;* John Foster, *Montgomery College;* Robin Frazee, *Anne Arundel Community College;* Barry Freeman, *Bergen Community College;* Leatrice Freer, *Pitt Community College;* Roger Fremier, *Monterey Peninsula College;* Edward Friese, *Okaloosa Walton Community College;* John Frith, *Central Texas College;* Michael Fritz, *Portland Community College;* Thomas Frizzel, *Massasoit Community College;* J. Pat Fuller, *Brevard Community College;* Arlen Gastineau, *Valencia Community College;* Alan Gbur, *Richard J. Daley College;* Michael Geary, *Pensacola Christian College;* Lucille S. Genduso, *Nova Southeastern University;* James George, Jr., *Seminole Community College;* Tom Gilbertson, *Baker College;* Julie Giles, *DeVry Institute of Technology DuPage Campus;* Peter Giuliani, *Franklin University;* Eileen Baker Glassman, *Montgomery College;* Bernette Glover, *Olive Harvey College;* Don Gordon, *Illinois Central College;* Ron Gordon, *Florida Metropolitan University;* Donald Gordon, *Illinois Central College;* Mary E. Gorman, *Bellevue Community College;* Kay Gough, *Bellevue Community College;* Patricia Graber, *Middlesex Country College;* Mike Graves, *Portland Community College;* Joe Gray, *Nassau Community College;* Gary Greene, *Manatee Community College;* Roberta Greene, *Central Piedmont Community College;* Stephen Griffin, *Tarrant County Junior College;* John Gubbay, *Moraine Valley Community College;* Jonathan Gueverra, *Newbury College;* Paula Gulbicki, *Middlesex Community College;* Bill Hafer, *South Suburban College;* James Hagel, *Davenport College;* Jim Hagen, *Cornell University;* Dan Hall, *East Central College;*

Daniel Hallock, *St. Edward's University;* Clark Hallpike, *Elgin Community College;* Ron Halsac, *Community College Allegheny North;* Maurice Hamington, *Lane Community College;* E. Hamm, *Tidewater Community College;* Crystal Hance, *Charles County Community College;* Dennis L. Hansen, *Des Moines Area Community College;* Paula W. Hansen, *Des Moines Area Community College;* Jean Harlan, *Glendale College;* Bob Harmel, *Midwestern State University;* Karen Harris, *Montgomery College;* Gene Hastings, *Portland Community College;* Frederic Hawkins, *Westchester Business Institute;* Lewis Jerome Healy, *Chesapeake College;* Joseph Hecht, *Montclair State College;* Douglas Heeter, *Ferris State University;* Linda Hefferin, *Elgin Community College;* Michael Heim, *Lakewood Community College;* Sanford B. Helman, *Middlesex County College;* Tim Helton, *Juliet Junior College;* Edward Henn, *Broward Community College;* Charles P. Hiatt, *Central Florida Community College;* Dave Hickman, *Frederick Community College;* David Hickman, *Frederick Community College;* Leslie Hickman, *Frederick Community College;* George Hicks, *Muskigan Area Technical College;* George M. Hihn, III, *University of Akron;* Nathan Himelstein, *Essex County College;* Kevin Hofert, *Elgin Community College;* Stacey Hofert, *Elgin Community College;* Merrily Hoffman, *San Jacinto College–Central;* William Leigh Holt, *Mercer County Community College;* Cheryl Lynn Holliday, *Calvert County Community College;* Trinh Hong Hoang, *Mt. San Antonio College;* B. Hoover, *Brevard Community College;* Vince Howe, *University of North Carolina–Wilmington;* Joseph Hrebenak, *Community College Allegheny County;* Tom Humphrey, *Palomar College;* Howard Hunnius, *John Tyler Community College;* Curtis W. Hwang, *Mt. San Antonio College;* Robert Ironside, *North Lake College;* Jim Isherwood, *Community College of Rhode Island;* Gary Izumo, *Moorpark College;* Gloria Jackson, *San Antonio College;* Henry Jackson, *Delaware County Community College;* Ralph Jagodka, *Mt. San Antonio College;* Paloma Jalife, *SUNY–Oswego;* Bill Jedlicka, *Harper College;* William Jedlicka, *William Rainey Harper College;* Paul Jenner, *Southwest Missouri State University;* Velma Jesser, *Lane Community College;* Lauren Jeweler, *Frederick Community College;* Constance Johnson, *Tampa College;* Gene Johnson, *Clarke College;* Herbert J. Johnson, *Blinn College;* M. E. "Micki" Johnson, *Nova Southeastern University;* M. Gwen Johnson, *Black Hawk College;* Mike Johnson, *Delaware County Community College;* Michael Johnson, *Delaware County Community College;* Wallace Johnston, *Virginia Commonwealth University;* Valerie Jones, *Kalamazoo Valley Community College;* John Kalaras, *DeVry Institute of Technology;* Alan Kardoff, *Northern Illinois University;* Norman Karl, *Johnson County Community College;* Janice Karlen, *LaGuardia Community College;* Allen Kartchner, *Utah State University;* Bob Kegel, *Cypress College;* Warren Keller, *Grossmont College;* Roland Kelley, *Tarrant County Junior College–NE Campus;* Jim Kennedy, *Angelina College;* Daniel Kent, *Northern Kentucky University;* Robert Kersten, *St. Louis Community College–Florissant Valley;* Scott Key, *Pensacola Junior College;* Emogene King, *Tyler Junior College;* James H. King, *McLennan Community College;* Jerry Kinskey, *Sinclair Community College;* Betty Ann Kirk, *Tallahassee Community College;* Gregory Kishel, *Fullerton College;* Patricia Kishel, *Cypress College;* Charles C. Kitzmiller, *Indian River Community College;* Karl Kleiner, *Ocean County College;* John A.Knarr, *University of Maryland–European Division;* Anna Kostorizos, *Middlesex Community College;* Pat Laidler, *Massasoit Community College;* Barbara G. Kreichbaum, *Hagerstown Business College;* Patrick C. Kumpf, *University of Cincinnati;* Kenneth Lacho, *University of New Orleans;* Micheale LaFalce, *Tampa College;* Fay Lamphear, *San Antonio College;* Keith Lane, *Fresno City College;* Jennifer Landig, *Saddleback Valley Community College;* Roger Lattanza, *University of New Mexico;* Amy J. Lee, *Parkland College;* Donna Lees, *Butte College;* Jay LeGregs, *Tyler Junior College;* Jim Lentz, *Moraine Valley Community College;* George Leonard, *St. Petersburg Junior College;* Bruce Leppien, *Delta College;* Dawn Lerman, *CUNY–Bernard*

*Baruch College;* Thomas Lerra, *Quinsigamond Community College;* Murray Levy, *Glendale Community College;* Richard Lewis, *Lansing Community College;* Joseph Liebreich, *Reading Area Community College;* Tom Lifvendahl, *Cardinal Stritch College;* Ellen Reynolds Ligons, *Pasadena City College;* Yet Mee Lim, *Alabama State University;* Stephen Lindsey, *Citrus College;* Telissa K. Lindsey, *Peirce College;* Donald Linner, *Essex County College;* Corinne B. Linton, *Valencia Community College;* John Lloyd, *Monroe Community College;* Thomas Lloyd, *Westmoreland County Community College;* Paul Londrigan, *Charles S. Mott Community College;* Hanh Long, *DeAnza College;* Patricia Long, *Tarrant Junior College;* Anthony Lucas, *Allegheny Community College;* Barbara Luck, *Jackson Community College;* Joyce Luckman, *Jackson Community College;* Carmelo Luna, *DeVry–DuPage;* Judith Lyles, *Illinois State University;* Jerry Lunch, *Purdue University;* Richard Lyons, *Indian River Community College;* Rippy Madan, *Frostburg State University;* James W. Marco, *Wake Technical Community College;* Richard Maringer, *University of Akron–Wayne College;* Leon E. Markowicz, *Lebanon Valley College;* Alan Marks, *DeVry Institute of Technology;* Larry Martin, *Community College of Southern Nevada;* Travaul Martin, *East-West University;* Randolph L. Martin, *Germanna Community College;* Thomas Mason, *Brookdale Community College;* Bob Mathews, *Oakton Community College;* Jane Mattes, *Community College of Baltimore College–Dundalk Campus;* Stacy McAfee, *College of Southern Maryland;* Christine McCallum, *University of Akron–Wayne College;* Diana McCann, *Kentucky College of Business;* Mark M. McCarthy, *Davenport College;* Paul McClure, *Mt. San Antonio College;* Tom McFarland, *Mt. San Antonio College;* Jimmy McKenzie, *Tarrant County Junior College;* Noel McKeon, *Florida Community College;* Pat McMahon, *Palm Beach Community College–Glades;* Michael McNutt, *Orlando College South/FL Metropolitan Univ.;* Carl Meskimen, *Sinclair Community College;* Athena Miklos, *The College of Southern Maryland;* Duane Miller, *SUNY–Cobleskill;* Herbert Miller, *Indiana University–Kokomo;* Terrance Mitchell, *South Suburban College;* Kimberly Montney, *Kellogg Community College;* Joyce Mooneyhan, *Pasadena City College;* Willy Morris, *Northwestern Business College;* Richard Morrison, *Northeastern University;* William Morrison, *San Jose State University;* Ed Mosher, *Laramie County Community College;* William Motz, *Lansing Community College;* Carolyn Mueller, *Ball State University;* Micah Mukabi, *Essex County College;* Gary R. Murray, *Rose State College;* Winford C. Naylor, *Santa Barbara City College;* Herschel Nelson, *Polk Community College;* Linda Newell, *Saddleback College;* Joe Newton, *Bakersfield College;* Janet Nichols, *Northeastern University;* Sharon J. Nickels, *St. Petersburg Junior College;* Carolyn Nickeson, *Del Mar College;* Elaine Novak, *San Jacinto College;* Phil Nufrio, *Essex County College;* Edward O'Brien, *Scotsdale Community College;* Eugene O'Connor, *California Polytechnical University–San Luis Obispo;* Marie D. O'Dell, *Anne Arundel Community College;* Cletus O'Drobinak, *South Suburban College;* Ron O'Neal, *Pierce College;* Susan Ockert, *Charles County Community College;* Susan Oleson, *Central Piedmont Community College;* David Oliver, *Edison Community College;* Katherine Olson, *Northern Virginia Community College;* Kenneth A. Olson, *County College of Morris;* J. Ashton Oravetz, *Tyler Junior College;* George Otto, *Truman College;* Nikki Paahana, *DeVry Institute of Technology;* Robert A. Pacheco, *Massasoit Community College;* Richard Packard, *City College–Richard J. Daley;* Mike Padbury, *Arapahoe Community College;* Teresa Palmer, *Illinois State University;* Dennis Pappas, *Columbus State Community College;* Dennis Pappas, *Columbus Technical Institute;* Knowles Parker, *Wake Technical Community College;* Patricia Parker, *Maryville University;* Jack Partlow, *Northern Virginia Comm. College;* Janis Pasquali, *University of California–Riverside;* Charlotte A. Patterson, *Tampa College;* Don Paxton, *Pasadena City College;* Darlene Raney Perry, *Columbus State;* Stephen Peters, *Walla Walla Community College;* Melinda Philabaum, *Indiana University–Kelley School of Business;* John P. Phillips, *Northern*

*Virginia Community College–Manassas;* Marie Pietak, *Bucks County Community College;* Warren Pitcher, *Des Moines Area Community College;* Alison Adderley-Pittman, *Brevard Community College–Melbourn;* Joseph Platts, *Miami-Dade Community College;* Wayne Podgorski, *University of Memphis;* Raymond Pokhon, *MATC;* Robert Pollero, *Anne Arundel Community College;* Geraldine Powers, *Northern Essex Community College;* Roderick Powers, *Iowa State University;* Fred Pragasam, *University of North Florida;* Renee Prim, *Central Piedmont Community College;* Marva Pryor, *Valencia Community College;* Brokke Quigg, *Pierce College;* Charles C. Quinn, *Austin Community College–Northridge;* Donald Radtke, *Richard J. Daley College;* Anne Ranczuch, *Monroe Community College;* Richard Randall, *Nassau Community College;* Richard J. Randolph, *Johnson County Community College;* Mary E. Ray, *Indiana Business College;* Robert A. Redick, *Lincoln Land Community College;* Scott Reedy, *Brookes College;* Robert O. Reichl, *Morton College;* James Reinemann, *College of Lake County;* Dominic Rella, *Polk Community College;* Carla Rich, *Pensacola Junior College;* John Rich, *Illinois State University;* Doug Richardson, *Eastfield College;* Karen Richardson, *Tarrant County Junior College;* Al Rieger, *Burlington County College;* Kathryn Roberts, *Chipola Junior College;* Pollis Robertson, *Kellogg Community College;* Paul Rompala, *Triton College;* Ali Roodsari, *Baltimore City Community College;* Barbara Rosenthal, *Miami-Dade Community College;* Bob Roswell, *Jackson Community College;* Linda Roy, *Evergreen Valley College;* Jeri Rubin, *University of Alaska;* Bonnie S. Rucks, *DeVry Institute–DuPage;* Jill Russell, *Camden County College;* Karl Rutkowski, *Pierce Jr. College;* Tom Rutkowski, *SUNY–Cobleskill;* Maurice M. Sampson, *Community College of Philadelphia;* Roy Sanchez, *San Jacinto College;* Cathy Sanders, *San Antonio College;* Joseph C. Santora, *Essex County College;* Nicholas Sarantakes, *Austin Community College;* Billie Sargent, *National College;* Quinn Sasaki, *Mt. San Antonio College;* Jim (Wallace) Satchell, *St. Philips College;* Gordon Saul, *National Business College;* Larry Saville, *Des Moines Area Community College;* Robert R. Schaller, *Charles County Community College;* Kurt Schindler, *Wilbur Wright College;* Lance Schmeidler, *Northern Virginia Community College;* Linda Schmitigal, *Lake Superior State University;* Dennis Schmitt, *Emporia State University;* Marilyn Schwartz, *College of Marin;* Jim Seeck, *Harper College;* Daniel C. Segebath, *South Suburban College;* Justin Selden, *The University of Akron;* Patricia A. Serraro, *Clark College;* Greg Service, *Broward Community College–North;* Guy Sessions, *Spokane Falls Community College;* Phyllis T. Shafer, *Brookdale Community College;* Dennis Shannon, *Belleville Area College;* Richard Shapiro, *Cuyahoga Community College;* Charles Shatzer, *Solano Community College;* Mark Sheehan, *Bunker Hill Community College;* Nora Jo Sherman, *Houston Community College;* Donald Shifter, *Fontbonne College;* Lynette Shishido, *Santa Monica College;* Leon Singleton, *Santa Monica College;* Jerry Sitek, *Southern Illinois University;* Michelle Slagle, *The George Washington University;* James A. Smalley, *DeVry–DuPage;* Noel Smith, *Palm Beach Community College;* Bill Snider, *Cuesta College;* Paul Solomon, *San Jose State University;* Sol A. Solomon, *Community College of Rhode Island;* Carl Sonntag, *Pikes Peak Community College;* Melinda Soto, *Mt. San Antonio Community College;* Russell W. Southall, *Laney College;* Rieann Spence-Gale, *Northern Virginia Community College;* Sandra Spencer, *DeAnza College;* Richard Stanish, *Tulsa Junior College;* Elizabeth Stanley, *Northern Virginia Community College;* Lynda St. Clair, *Bryant College;* Emanual Stein, *Queensborough Community College;* Scott Steinkamp, *Northwestern Business College;* Kenneth Steinkruger, *DeVry Institute of Technology–Chicago;* Carl Stem, *Texas Tech University;* Richard Stewart, *Gulf Coast Community College;* Robert Stivender, *Wake Technical Community College;* David Stringer, *DeAnza College;* Charles I. Stubbart, *Southern Illinois University;* Jacinto Suarez, *Bronx Community College;* Paul Sunko, *Olive Harvey College;* George Sutcliffe, *Central Piedmont Community College;* Lorraine Suzuki, *University of Maryland–Asian Division;* Carl

Swartz, *Three Rivers Community College;* William Syvertsen, *Fresno City College;* James Taggart, *University of Akron;* Robert Tansky, *St. Clair County Community College;* Daryl Taylor, *Pasadena City College;* Merle E. Taylor, *Santa Barbara City College;* Verna Teasdale, *Prince George's Community College;* Ray Tewell, *American River College;* Gary W. Thomas, *Anne Arundel Community College;* Bill Thompson, *Foothill Community College;* Darrell Thompson, *Mountain View College;* Linda Thompson, *Massasoit Community College;* Susan Thompson, *Palm Beach Community College;* Tom Thompson, *University of Maryland University College;* Linda Tibbetts, *Sinclair Community College;* Darlene Tickle, *Southern Arkansas University–Magnolia;* Vern Timmer, *SUNY–Alfred;* Patricia Torpey, *National American University;* Amy Toth, *Northampton County Area Community College;* Jane A. Treptow, *Broward Community College;* Bonnie Luck-Yan Tsang, *DeAnza College;* Stephen Tsih, *San Jose City College;* Chuck Tychsen, *Northern Virginia Community College;* J. Robert Ulbrich, *Parkland College;* Pablo Ulloa, *El Paso Community College;* Robert Vandellen, *Baker College–Cadillac;* Richard Van Ness, *Schenectady County Community College;* Sal Veas, *Santa Monica College;* Heidi Vernon-Wortzel, *Northeastern University;* Julie C.Verrati, *Montgomery College;* Janna P. Vice, *Eastern Kentucky University;* Michael Vijuk, *William Rainey Harper College;* Martha Villarreal, *San Joaquin Delta College;* William Vincent, *Santa Barbara City College;* Douglas S. Viska, *William Rainey Harper College;* Cortez Walker, *Baltimore City Community College;* Steve Walker, *Midwestern State University;* Christopher Walsh, *Hagerstown Community College;* W. J. Waters, *Central Piedmont Community College;* Philip Weatherford, *Embry-Riddle Aeronautical University;* Connie Wedemeyer, *McLennan Community College;* Ron Weidenfeller, *Grand Rapids Community College;* Pete Weiksner, *Lehigh County Community College;* Henry Weiman, *Bronx Community College;* Bernard Weinrich, *St. Louis Community College–Forest Park;* Bill Weisgerber, *Saddleback College;* Martin Welc, *Saddleback College;* William A. Weller, *Modesto Junior College;* James H. Wells, *Daytona Beach Community College;* Sally Wells, *Columbia College;* Michael David Wentz, *Hagerstown Community College;* Richard Westfall, *Cabrillo College;* Aimee Wheaton, *Regis University;* Cammie White, *Santa Monica College;* Donald White, *Prince Georges Community College;* Frederick D. White, *Indian River Community College;* John Whitlock, *Community College of Baltimore County–Cantonsville;* Jean Wicks, *Bowie State University;* Walter Wilfong, *Florida Technical College;* Dick Williams, *Laramie County Community College;* Mary E. Williams, *University of Central Oklahoma;* Paul Williams, *Mott Community College;* Stanley Williams, *Pensacola Christian College;* Gayla Jo Wilson, *Mesa State College;* Wallace Wirth, *South Suburban Community College;* Amy Wojciechowski, *West Shore Community College;* Judy Eng Woo, *Bellevue Community College;* Joyce Wood, *Northern Virginia Community College;* Bennie Woods, *Burlington County College;* Greg Worosz, *Schoolcraft College;* William Wright, *Mt. Hood Community College;* Merv Yeagle, *Hagerstown Junior College;* C. Yin, *DeVry Institute of Technology;* Ned Young, *Sinclair Community College;* Ron Young, *Kalamazoo Valley Community College;* Charles D. Zarubba, *Florida Metropolitan University–Tampa College;* C. Zarycki, *Hillsborough Community College;* John Ziegler, *Hagerstown Community College;* Richard Zollinger, *Central Piedmont College*.

## to our fellow Introduction to Business Instructors

**How quickly things are changing!** The ways instructors teach, the ways students learn, and the ways information is delivered are all changing rapidly. This evolution is affecting college courses across the country. As authors, we must consider all of these changes both in the types of resources we offer and in the way we provide them to you.

### WE HAVE 3 GOALS IN THIS EDITION:

- To sustain the celebrated quality of the text and its supplement package
- To address the changing course environment and methods for information delivery
- To help you build your course by providing what YOU need most

We remain dedicated to listening vigilantly to what you tell us you need in this course. We have made changes and enhancements in this revision that are all based on what we heard from you. As you look through the next few pages, you'll find what you need to navigate your way most effectively through this book and its supplements.

We firmly believe that no course in college is more important than the introduction to business course. We thank all the dedicated instructors who have shared their work with us in previous editions and look forward to welcoming new instructors to the *Understanding Business* team.

Bill Nickels Jim McHugh Susan McHugh

# text changes

CURRENCY * THEMES

* You may notice this edition has gone through a bit of a makeover—organizationally and visually. The new design helps us highlight the important information in the text, and the revised table of contents focuses on the material you have told us is most important...but everything you know and love about ***Understanding Business*** is still here.

## BONUS CHAPTERS

*Using Technology to Manage Information* and *Managing Personal Finances to Achieve Financial Security* have been changed to bonus chapters that are at the end of the text. Along with previous appendixes: *Working within the Legal Environment of Business*, and *Managing Risk*, **these 4 new bonus chapters** cover material that you told us are not always covered in your courses. It is important to note that **all the accompanying supplemental materials (PowerPoints, test questions, etc.) are included for these bonus chapters**. Our bonus chapters are easy to include in your lectures *and* easy to skip if you don't cover this material in your course.

## THE DYNAMIC NATURE OF BUSINESS

Key topics and issues are still incorporated as themes throughout the text, with particular emphasis given to change, small business, global business, legal issues, and ethics through boxes in each chapter:

- Cultural diversity issues and examples
- **Dealing with change**
- **Small business and entrepreneurship**
- **Global business**
- Technology and change
- Pleasing customers
- **Ethics and social responsibility**
- Teams
- Quality
- E-commerce
- **Legal briefcase**

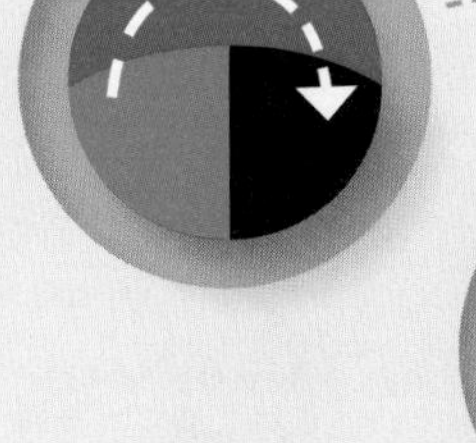

# students

## * understanding

**SCANS** The Secretary's Commission on Achieving Necessary Skills identifies the skills people need to succeed in the workplace. The purpose of SCANS is to encourage a high-performance economy characterized by high-skill, high-wage employment. To help your students connect to what they learn in class to the world outside, it is important they understand five workplace competencies: l. resource skills, 2. interpersonal skills, 3. information ability, 4. systems understanding, and 5. technology ability. Throughout the 8th edition, several pedagogical devices are used to help students develop their skills.

**LEARNING GOALS** Everything in the text and supplements package ties back to the chapter learning goals. The learning goals help students preview what they should know after reading the chapter, and then the chapter summaries test students' knowledge by asking questions related to the learning goals. The Test Bank, Instructor's Manual, and Student Assessment and Learning Guide are all organized according to the learning goals as well.

**DEVELOPING WORKPLACE SKILLS** This section has activities designed to increase student involvement in the learning process. Some of these miniprojects require Internet searches, while others can be used as team activities either in or out of the classroom.

**GETTING READY FOR PRIME TIME** This section, found at the front of the text, introduces students to the skills they need to succeed in this course, in future courses, and in their careers. It includes material on business etiquette, study skills and time management, and career management advice.

**GETTING TO KNOW BUSINESS PROFESSIONALS** Every chapter and bonus chapter opens with the profile of a business professional whose career relates closely to the material in the chapter. These business professionals work for a variety of businesses from small businesses and nonprofit organizations to large corporations. These career profiles are an engaging way to open the chapter and to introduce students to a variety of business career paths.

**CRITICAL THINKING QUESTIONS** In each chapter (now at the end of the chapter) these questions ask students to pause and think about how the material they're reading applies to their own lives.

competing in global markets

learning goals

CHAPTER 3

Getting to Know Li Yifei, President of MTV Networks China

www.mtv.com

Learning tools are included to help students understand and review necessary business concepts and to give them an introduction to the functional areas of business.

**STUDENT ASSESSMENT AND LEARNING GUIDE** The Student Assessment and Learning Guide contains various forms of open-ended questions, key term review, practice tests and answers, and Internet exercises to help them be successful in the introduction to business course.

**PROGRESS ASSESSMENTS** To help students understand and retain the material in the chapters, progress assessments will stop them at important points in the chapters to assess what they should have learned before proceeding. This is also a great tool for reviewing the material for quizzes/tests.

**KEY TERMS** The key terms from each chapter are highlighted in the text and defined in the margin. They're again listed at the end of each chapter and in the glossary at the end of the text. Matching exercises in the Student Assessment and Learning Guide help to reinforce the key business terms they need to know and understand. Multilingual glossaries are also provided on the Online Learning Center (Mandarin Chinese, Spanish, and Russian) to help ESL students understand basic terminology. The text glossary also includes definitions of frequently used slang terms to help ESL students understand typical jargon.

**TAKING IT TO THE NET** Each chapter contains optional Taking It to the Net exercises that allow students to research topics and issues on the Web and make decisions based on their research. These are updated on the Online Learning Center (**www.mhhe.com/ub8e**) as necessary.

**CASING THE WEB** Short cases are provided on the text Web site (**www.mhhe.com/ub8e**) that allow students to practice managerial decision making. They are meant to be discussion starters rather than comprehensive cases that require a large percentage of class time. These cases are provided for every chapter and are referenced in the text (but housed on the text Web site.)

**SUMMARIES** The end-of-chapter summaries are directly tied with the learning objectives from the beginning of the chapters and are written in a unique question-and-answer format to help students review the chapter material more effectively.

**iPOD CONTENT** Quizzes and narrated slides are available to students to help them review the chapters. This content is only available if the Enhanced Cartridge is packaged with the book.

* We know how much material instructors must cover in this course, and there is a wealth of resources available to you with this text. One of our main goals with *Understanding Business* is to help you piece together which supplements can be most useful to **YOU** in your course. All of the supplements in this package are fully integrated with the text, easy to use, author-reviewed, and responsive to instructors' requests.

## prep**

**INSTRUCTOR'S MANUAL** This 2-volume print instructor's manual uses the ground-breaking format that others in many other disciplines now copy. Detailed lecture outlines are included and contain marginal notes recommending where to use other supplementary material from the text such as PowerPoint slides, supplementary cases, lecture links, and critical thinking exercises. Each chapter begins with a list of every resource available to teach that chapter. Many instructors, especially part-time faculty, tell us that the IM is a valuable time-saver and a very easy way to start using the text quickly.

**ANNOTATED INSTRUCTOR'S EDITION** The AIE is the same as the student edition with the addition of marginal notes that suggest where to use various instructional tools such as PowerPoints, supplementary cases, lecture links, and critical thinking exercises. It also identifies the activities that facilitate the SCANS competencies.

**SUPPLEMENTS ORIENTATION VIDEO ONLINE** **(www.mhhe.com/ub8e)** Let author Jim McHugh walk you through the supplements package. New and part-time professors can easily see what supplements are available, and full-time professors who are interested in seeing how to revitalize their courses with fresh instructor support will enjoy a video walkthrough. A perfect introduction for adjunct instructors!

NICKELS
McHUGH
McHUGH
understanding
eighth edition
BUSINESS
INSTRUCTOR:
ANNOTATED INSTRUCTOR EDITION
INSTRUCTOR MANUAL
TEST BANK
COMPUTERIZED TEST BANK
TELETEST
POWERPOINT/ACETATES
IRCD
VIDEOS
MEDIA RESOURCE GUIDE
TELECOURSE INSTRUCTOR MANUAL
PREP CENTER
STUDENT:
STUDENT ASSESSMENT AND
LEARNING GUIDE
AUDIO CDS
TELECOURSE STUDY GUIDE
WSJ EDITION
TECHNOLOGY:
ONLINE LEARNING CENTER
ENHANCED CARTRIDGE
BUSINESS PLAN SOFTWARE
INVESTMENTS TRADER
PRIMIS/CUSTOM


**INSTRUCTOR'S RESOURCE CD** The IRCD includes electronic versions of the Instructor's Resource Manual, PowerPoint slides, videos, and Test Bank, as well as the complete library of figures and photos from the text.

**PREPCENTER** One thing we hear often from instructors using UB, is "There's so much here, it's difficult to know what's available!" PrepCenter is a perfect tool to help you prepare for and organize your course. It puts the power in your hands to organize the teaching assets that are available to you with this book. Browse either by chapter or by concept or by media type (video, images, audio files, PowerPoints, and teaching notes); preview the resource and then drag and drop it into your file for future lectures. It's fast and easy and it's a great way for a course coordinator to standardize the lecture materials.

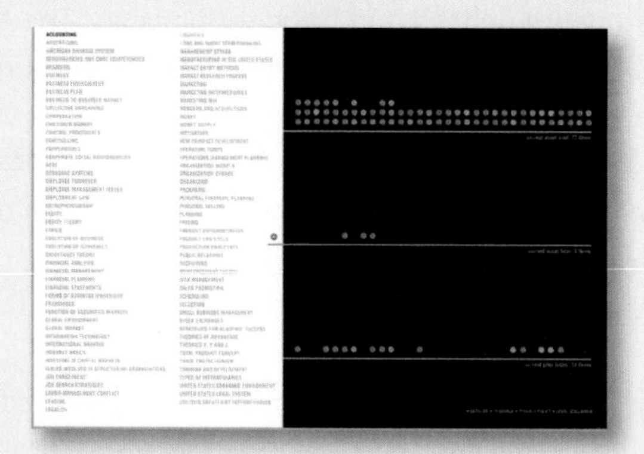

**REFERENCE TABLE** The reference table, on the inside front cover of the Annotated Instructor's Edition, also gives you—at a glance—an idea of the topics/concepts/resources available with this book and where they're provided to you and your students.

# instructor

## testing **

**TEST BANK** The Nickels/McHugh/McHugh test bank has set the standard. It is designed to test three levels of learning:

1) Knowledge of key terms
2) Understanding of concepts and principles
3) Application of principles

Rationales for the correct answer and the page references are included for each of the 6000+ questions that have all been reviewed for accuracy. The Test Bank also asks questions about the boxed material and end-of-chapter material. Last but not least, each chapter and bonus chapter in the test bank includes a **Test Table** that organizes the questions by learning objective and level of learning, as well as identifies what type of question each is (multiple-choice, true-false, essay, question on boxed material, etc). A quick quiz is also provided in each chapter as an easy handout.

**E-Z TEST** The Test Bank also comes in a computerized version that allows you to add and edit questions, save and reload multiple test versions, and select questions based on type, difficulty, or key word.

**TELETEST** If you prefer not to use the computerized test-generator, McGraw-Hill/Irwin provides a Teletest Service. A master copy of the exam, with answer key, is sent first-class mail the same day it is requested. Please call 1-800-338-3987 (prompt #3) and then follow the rest of the prompts.

## * presentation

**VIDEOS** ***Understanding Business*** is known for high-quality videos and this edition is no exception. We have provided 13 new videos for this edition in an exciting new format. They are broken out into modules that are much shorter clips and allow you to place them in the order you'd prefer. So, you can customize your own video depending on the length of video you want to use or depending on what you'd like to emphasize from each video. Video cases are also included in every chapter discussing the key concepts of each video.

**POWERPOINT™** Over **500** slides are available that include material from the text as well as slides that support and expand the text discussion. The PowerPoints have detailed teaching notes as well as page references and correlation to the learning objectives. The slides can be modified and are available on the OLC as well as on the Instructor's CD. A PowerPoint presentation of basic concepts is available to students on the OLC to help them review the chapter material.

**TRANSPARENCY ACETATES WITH NOTES** Over **250** acetates enhance the concepts in the chapters and each also includes a very detailed teaching note to help you craft your lectures.

**MEDIA RESOURCE GUIDE** This print guide includes teaching notes for all of the media material available with the book. Detailed teaching notes to accompany the chapter videos are available, as well as teaching notes on the business planning software, the Online Learning Center, and the Investments Trader.

**TELECOURSE GUIDE** The Telecourse Instructor's Manual to accompany the "It's Strictly Business" Dallas Telecourse organizes lesson overviews and questions from the Test Bank to the 26 telecourse videos. There is also a student study guide available that organizes student study material (like quizzes and key term reviews) according to the telecourse lessons.

# online components

* We know the number of hybrid and online courses is increasing every day. For those of you who have some sort of online component to your course, we offer a number of options depending on how much material you need—from a basic text Web site to a fully loaded course cartridge enabling your course to run entirely online.

## ONLINE LEARNING CENTER

**www.mhhe.com/ub8e**

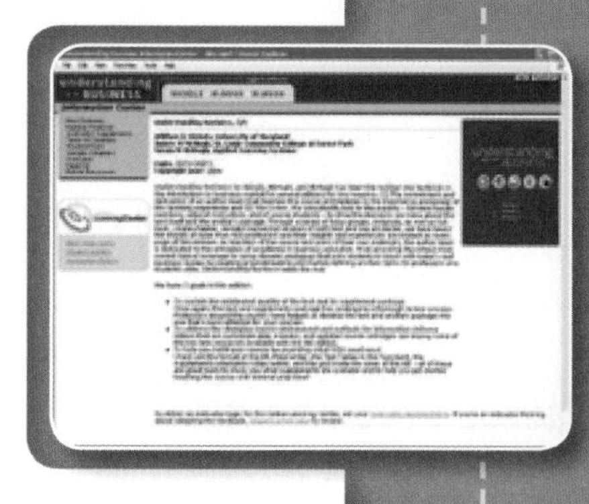

The Online Learning Center contains material for both instructors and students. **None of the student material here requires a password**. Instructor supplements are available here to view or download, and students can find resources such as the Taking It to the Net exercises from the book, Casing the Web cases referenced in the text, small business, global, and technology resources, the McGraw-Hill Investments Trader, news links, chapter quizzes, and multi-lingual glossaries.

If you are using a course management system in your course, all of this material is available as a cartridge.

## MCGRAW-HILL ENHANCED CARTRIDGE

We've heard you tell us about the importance of course management systems. In response to your suggestions, McGraw-Hill is pleased to offer a new, ENHANCED COURSE CARTRIDGE that populates your CMS (such as Blackboard or WebCT, or whatever CMS you use) with instructor and student supplements, directly from ***Understanding Business***. There is no need to upload content unless you want to! But you still have the capability to add any of your own material or hide the material that we provide. Our content includes all the material on the OLC plus a wealth of study material for students such as self-assessments, pre- and post-tests, discussion topics, key term review, progress assessments, iPod content, videos, and video quizzes. Contact your McGraw-Hill/Irwin sales representative for more information.

**PAGEOUT** PageOut is the easiest way to create a Web site for your Introduction to Business course. There's no need for HTML coding, graphic design, or a thick how-to book. Just fill in a series of boxes and click on one of our professional designs. In no time, your course is online! To learn more, please visit www.pageout.net.

# options

* Consider the options for you and your students—there are different methods of delivering the textbook as well as packaging options available to you for your course.

**ZINIO** Offer your students the choice to buy an e-book. Students can save approximately 50% off the bookstore price of the text if they'd rather access an electronic copy of the book. They can download the text to their computer, and have printing capabilities so they can study/review. **http://textbookszinio.com**

**PRIMIS** Primis Online allows you to build your own custom textbook if you don't use the entire text. Select the content and chapters that you are interested in from this book, arrange them in the order that's most effective for your class, personalize them with the information from your course, and request a complimentary print copy for your review and approval. Visit **www.primisonline.com** or talk to your McGraw-Hill/Irwin sales representative for more details.

**AUDIO CDS** The entire book is available for purchase on audio CDs. This set is perfect for instructors to listen to as they travel to class, for students who are visually impaired, or for non-native English-speaking students to help reinforce chapter content.

**BUSINESS PLANNING SOFTWARE** You have two options if you incorporate a business planning project into your course. The New Business Mentor 2007 and the Business Plan Writer are both available as packaging options with the text. Both software packages provide sample business plans and resources, along with financial worksheets and help along the way.

BusinessWeek

**BUSINESSWEEK**
Expand your students' current business knowledge by offering a *BusinessWeek* subscription with the text. For $8.25 your students can receive the magazine for 15 weeks—substantially less than the lowest subscription rate. *BusinessWeek* is available in print or digital format.

**THE WALL STREET JOURNAL** Students can receive a subscription to the *Wall Street Journal* for 15 weeks for $20. They'll also receive a "How to Use the WSJ" handbook and access to wsj.com in the package.

**CLASSROOM PERFORMANCE SYSTEM (CPS) BY eINSTRUCTION**
CPS is a great tool to help encourage class participation. CPS enables you to record responses from students to questions posed in a PowerPoint slide, record attendance, and offers a variety of reporting features. For your students, it's as easy as using a remote control. Questions can be designed by you, or you can choose from the set of questions included with the *Understanding Business* PowerPoint. CPS now integrates with Blackboard version 6.0 (and higher) and WebCT Vista and Campus Edition 6.0—meaning grades can be recorded in your CMS. The newest generation of response pads also include self-paced testing on the pads (eliminating the need for a projector), and will show the answer as correct or incorrect on the pad. Talk to your McGraw-Hill/Irwin sales representative if you're interested in packaging CPS with *Understanding Business*.

PROLOGUE

# getting ready for prime time

## Top 10 Reasons to Read This Introduction

**(Even If It Isn't Assigned)**

**10** You don't want the only time you get a raise to be when the government increases the minimum wage.

**9** What the heck—you already bought the book, so you might as well get your money's worth.

**8** You can learn what professional behavior is all about so that you don't suddenly find yourself all alone in your own section of the classroom.

**7** You need to know that a time management course is not a class on clock repair.

**6** Most employers reject résumés written in crayon on looseleaf paper.

**5** Not many job-producing interviews start with "Like, you know, this is, like, what I want to, like, do, you know."

**4** Getting off to a good start in the course can improve your chances of getting a higher grade, and your Uncle Ernie will send you a quarter for every A you get.

**3** It must be important because the authors spent so much time writing it.

**2** You want to run with the big dogs someday.

**And the number one reason for reading this introductory section is . . .**

**1** It could be on a test.

# LEARNING THE SKILLS NEEDED TO SUCCEED TODAY AND TOMORROW

Your life is full. You're starting a new semester, probably even beginning your college career, and you're feeling pulled in many directions. Why take time to read this introductory section? We lightheartedly offer our top 10 reasons to read it on page P-1, but the real importance of this section to your success is no joking matter. The purpose of this introduction and of the entire text is to help you learn principles, strategies, and skills for success that will help you not only in this course but also in your career and entire life. Whether or not you learn these skills is up to you. Learning them won't guarantee success, but not learning them—well, you get the picture.

We hope you invest the time to read the entire Getting Ready for Prime Time section. However, we realize that some parts of the material may be more relevant to your individual needs at a particular time than others. To help you focus on the most important information for your needs, we've divided the material into two major categories:

1. **Succeeding in This Course**. An overview of the skills you'll need to succeed in this course and throughout college as well as the skills needed to succeed in your career after you earn your diploma. READ THIS SECTION BEFORE YOUR FIRST CLASS and make a great first impression!
2. **Getting the Job You Want**. Guidelines to finding and getting the job you want with an emphasis on job search, résumé writing, and interviewing skills.

This is an exciting and challenging time. Never before have there been more opportunities to become successful. And never before have there been more challenges. Success in any venture comes from understanding basic principles and having the skills to apply those principles effectively. What you learn now could help you be a success—for the rest of your life. Begin applying these skills now to gain an edge on the competition. Good luck. We wish you the best.

**Bill Nickels** **Jim McHugh** **Susan McHugh**

## SUCCEEDING IN THIS COURSE

Since you've signed up for this course, we're guessing you already know the value of a college education. But just to give you some numerical backup, you should know that the gap between the earnings of high school graduates and college graduates, which is growing every year, now ranges to more than 80 percent. According to the U.S. Census Bureau, the holders of bachelor's degrees will make an average of $51,206 per year as opposed to just $27,915 for high school graduates. That's a whopping additional $23,291 a year (nearly double that of a high school graduate).[1] Thus, what you invest in a college education is likely to pay you back many times.[2] See Figure P.1 to get an idea of how much salary difference a college degree makes by the end of a 30-year career. That doesn't mean there aren't good careers available to non–college graduates. It just means that those with an education are more likely to have higher earnings over their lifetime.

The value of a college education is more than just a larger paycheck. Other benefits include increasing your ability to think critically and communicate your ideas to others, improving your ability to use technology, and preparing yourself to live in a diverse world. Knowing you've met your goals and earned a college degree also gives you the self-confidence to continue to strive to meet your future goals.[3]

Experts say it is likely that today's college graduates will hold seven or eight different jobs (often in several different careers) in their lifetime. There are many returning students in college today who are changing their careers and their plans for life. In fact, 32 percent of the people enrolled in college today are 25 or older. More than 1.4 million students are over 40.[4] Talk to them and learn from their successes and mistakes. You too may want to change careers someday. Often that is the path to long-term happiness and success. That means you will have to be flexible and adjust your strengths and talents to new opportunities. Many of the best jobs of the future don't even exist today. Learning has become a lifelong job. You will have to constantly update your skills if you want to achieve and remain competitive.

If you're typical of many college students, you may not have any idea what career you'd like to pursue. That isn't necessarily a big disadvantage in today's fast-changing job market. There are no perfect or certain ways to

figure P.1

**SALARY COMPARISON OF HIGH SCHOOL VERSUS COLLEGE GRADUATES**

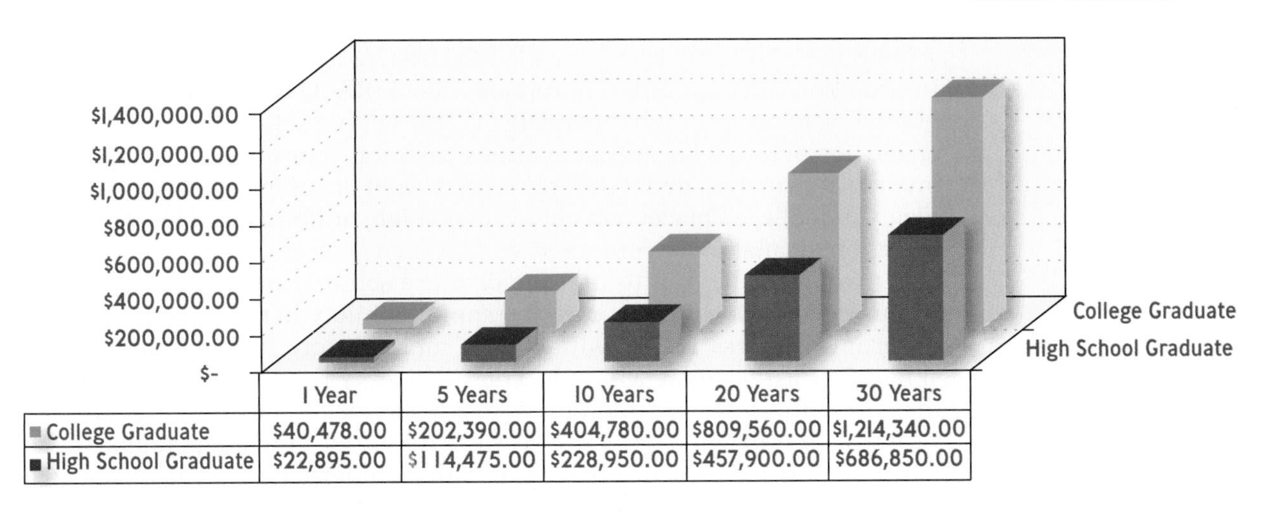


| | 1 Year | 5 Years | 10 Years | 20 Years | 30 Years |
|---|---|---|---|---|---|
| College Graduate | $40,478.00 | $202,390.00 | $404,780.00 | $809,560.00 | $1,214,340.00 |
| High School Graduate | $22,895.00 | $114,475.00 | $228,950.00 | $457,900.00 | $686,850.00 |

College graduation is a reason to smile not only for students, but also for businesses. For students the rewards of college are well worth the effort. College graduates can expect to earn 60 percent to 80 percent more than high school graduates. For businesses the growing needs of a global workplace require knowledgeable workers to fill the jobs of the future. What additional benefits do you see from earning a college degree?

prepare for the most interesting and challenging jobs of tomorrow. Rather, you should continue your college education, develop strong computer skills, improve your verbal and written communication skills, and remain flexible while you explore the job market.[5]

## USING THIS COURSE TO PREPARE FOR YOUR CAREER

One of the objectives of this class is to help you choose an area in which you might enjoy working and in which you might succeed. This book and this course together may be one of your most important learning experiences ever. They're meant to help you understand business so that you can use business principles throughout your life. You'll learn about economics, global business, entrepreneurship, management, marketing, accounting, finance, and more. At the end of the course, you should have a much better idea about what careers would be best for you and what careers you would not enjoy.

But you don't have to be in business to use business principles. You can use marketing principles to get a job and to sell your ideas to others. You can use your knowledge of investments to make money in the stock market. Similarly, you'll be able to use management skills and general business knowledge wherever you go and in whatever career you pursue—including government agencies, charities, and social causes.

## ASSESSING YOUR SKILLS AND PERSONALITY

The earlier you can do a personal assessment of your interests, skills, and values, the better it will be for you in finding some career direction. In recognition of this need, many colleges offer self-assessment programs. Hundreds of schools use a software exercise called the System for Interactive Guidance and Information (SIGI). A different version, called DISCOVER, is used at hundreds of other schools. Both SIGI and DISCOVER feature self-assessment exercises, create personalized lists of occupations based on your interests and skills, and provide information about different careers and the preparation each requires. Visit your college's placement center, career lab, or library and learn what programs are available for you.

It would be helpful to use one or more self-assessment programs early in this course so that you can determine, while you're learning about the different business fields, which ones most closely fit your interests and skills. Self-assessment will help you determine the kind of work environment you'd prefer (e.g., technical, social service, or business); what values you seek to fulfill in a career (e.g., security, variety, or independence); what abilities you have (e.g., creative/artistic, numerical, or sales); and what important job characteristics you stress most (e.g., income, travel, or amount of job pressure).

Even if you're one of the college students over 30 years old, an assessment of your skills will help you choose the right courses and career path to follow next. Many returning students have taken such tests because they are not satisfied with what they're doing and are seeking a more rewarding occupation. Armed with the results of your self-assessment, you are more likely to make a career choice that will be personally fulfilling.

## LEARNING PROFESSIONAL BUSINESS STRATEGIES

Business professionals have learned the importance of networking and of keeping files on subjects that are important to them. These are two secrets to success that students should begin practicing now: retention of knowledge and keeping contacts. One thing that links students in all colleges is the need to retain what they learn. You need a strategy to help you meet this need. It's also extremely important to keep the names of contact people at various organizations. In addition, you may want to keep facts and figures of all kinds about the economy and business-related subjects. These are all reasons why you should develop resource files.

An effective way to become an expert on almost any business subject is to set up your own information system. Eventually you may want to store data on computer disks for retrieval on your personal computer and to access professional databases as businesspeople do. Meanwhile, it's effective to establish a comprehensive filing system on paper.

If you start now, you'll soon have at your fingertips information that will prove invaluable for use in term papers and throughout your career. Few college students do this filing; those who don't lose much of the information they read in college or thereafter. Developing this habit is one of the most effective ways of educating yourself and having the information available when you need it. The only space you'll need to start is a 12-inch-square corner of your room to hold a portable file box. The box should hold hanging folders in which you can place a number of tabbed file folders. To start filling these files, you might put your course notes in them with the names of your professors and the books you used. You may need this information later for employment references. Also, be sure to keep all the notes you make when talking with people about careers, including salary information, courses needed, and contacts.

Each time you read a story about a firm that interests you, either cut it out of the publication or photocopy it and then place it in an appropriate file. You might begin with files labeled Careers, Small Business, Economics, Management, and Resource People. You might summarize the article on a Post-it note and stick this summary on the front for later reference. Today, it is possible to find the latest data on almost any subject on the Internet. Good students know, or quickly learn, how to find such information efficiently. The best students know the importance of keeping such information in files so that it is readily accessible. Those files may be in their computers or on their desktops, ready for easy access.

You definitely want to have a personal data file titled Credentials for My Résumé or something similar. In that file, you'll place all reference letters and other information about jobs you may have held. Soon you'll have a tremendous amount of information available to you. You can add to these initial files until you have your own comprehensive information system.

Businesspeople are constantly seeking ways to increase their knowledge of the business world and to increase their investment returns. One way they do so is by watching television shows such as *Nightly Business Report* and Jim Cramer's *Mad Money.* Watching such programs is like getting a free graduate education in business. Try viewing some of these shows or listening to similar shows on the radio, and see which ones you like best. Take notes and put them in your files. Another way, one of the best, to increase your business knowledge is to read your local newspaper. Keep up with the business news in your local area so that you know what jobs are available and where. You may also want to join local business groups to begin networking with people and learning the secrets of the local business scene. Many business groups and professional societies accept student members.

## LEARNING TO BEHAVE LIKE A PROFESSIONAL

Good manners are back, and for a good reason. As the world becomes increasingly competitive, the gold goes to the individuals and the teams that have an extra bit of polish. The person who makes a good impression will be the one who gets the job, wins the promotion, or clinches the deal. Manners and professionalism must become second nature to anyone who wants to achieve and maintain a competitive edge.[6]

Many businesses have adopted business casual as the proper work attire, but others still require traditional attire. How does your appearance impact both you and the company?

Often, students focus on becoming experts in their particular field and neglect other concerns, including proper attire and etiquette. Their résumés look great, and they may get through the interview process, but then they get in the workplace and may not succeed. Their behavior, including their verbal behavior, is so unacceptable that they are rejected by their peers.[7]

The lesson is this: You can have good credentials, but a good presentation is everything. You can't neglect etiquette, or somewhere in your career you will be at a competitive disadvantage because of your inability to use good manners or to maintain your composure in tense situations. You must constantly practice the basics until they become second nature to you. Such basics include saying "Please" and "Thank you" when you ask for something. They also include opening doors for others, standing when an older person enters the room, and using a polite tone of voice. You may want to take a class in etiquette to learn the proper way to eat in a nice restaurant and handle the various utensils, the proper way to act at a formal party, and so on. Of course, it is critical that you are honest, reliable, dependable, and ethical at all times.

You can probably think of sports stars who have earned a bad reputation by not acting professionally (e.g., spitting, swearing, and criticizing teammates in front of others). People in professional sports are fined if they are late to meetings or refuse to follow the rules established by the team and coach. Business professionals also must follow set rules. Many of these rules are not formally written anywhere, but every successful businessperson learns them through experience.

You can begin the habits now while you are in college so that you will have the skills needed for success when you start your career. Those habits include the following:

1. **Making a good first impression**. An old saying goes, "You never get a second chance to make a good first impression." You have just a few seconds to make an impression. Therefore, how you dress and how you look are important. Take a clue as to what is appropriate at any specific company by studying the people there who are most successful. What do they wear? How do they act?
2. **Focusing on good grooming**. Be aware of your appearance and its impact on those around you. Consistency is essential—you can't project a good image by dressing well a few times a week and then showing up looking like you're getting ready to mow a lawn. Wear appropriate, clean clothing and accessories. For example, revealing shirts, nose rings, and such may not be appropriate in a work setting. It is not appropriate for men to wear hats inside buildings. It is also not appropriate, usually, to wear wrinkled clothing or to have shirttails hanging out of your pants. Many businesses have adopted "business casual" policies, but others still require traditional attire, so it may be helpful to ask what the organization's policies are and choose your wardrobe accordingly.

   What is business casual to some may not be acceptable to others, but there are a few guidelines most organizations accept. First, casual doesn't mean sloppy or shabby. For women, business casual attire includes simple skirts and slacks (no jeans), cotton shirts, sweaters (not too tight), blazers, low-heeled shoes or boots (always with socks or stockings). For men, acceptable business casual attire includes khaki trousers, sport shirts with collars, sweaters or sport jackets, casual loafers or lace-up shoes (no athletic shoes).
3. **Being on time**. When you don't come to class or to work on time, you're sending a message to your teacher or boss. You're saying, "My time is more important than your time. I have more important things to do than be here." In addition to the lack of respect tardiness shows to your teacher or boss, it rudely disrupts the work of your colleagues. Promptness may not be a priority in some circles, but in the workplace promptness is essential. But being punctual doesn't always mean just being on time. You have to pay attention to the corporate culture. Sometimes you have to come earlier than others and leave later to get that promotion you desire. To develop good work habits and get good grades, it is important to get to class on time and not leave early.
4. **Practicing considerate behavior**. Considerate behavior includes listening when others are talking—for example, not reading the newspaper or eating in class. Don't interrupt others when they are speaking. Wait for your turn to present your views in classroom or workplace discussions. Of course, eliminate all words of profanity from your vocabulary. Use appropriate body language by sitting up attentively and not slouching. Sitting up has the added bonus of helping you stay awake! Professors and managers get a favorable impression from those who look and act alert. That may help your grades in school and your advancement at work.
5. **Practicing good "netiquette."** Computer technology, particularly e-mail, can be a great productivity tool. The basic courtesy rules of face-to-face communication also apply to e-mail exchanges. As in writing a

letter, you should introduce yourself at the beginning of your first e-mail message. Next, you should let your recipients know how you got their names and e-mail addresses. Then you can proceed with your clear but succinct message, and finally close the e-mail with a signature. Do not send an attachment (a text or graphics file) with your e-mail unless your correspondent has indicated that he or she will accept it. Ask first! You can find much more information about proper Internet etiquette (netiquette) on the Internet. For example, Onlinenetiquette.com offers netiquette advice.

6. **Practicing good cell phone manners**. Cellular phones are a vital part of today's world, but it is important to be polite when using the phone. Turn off the phone during class or in a business meeting unless you are expecting a critical call. Your Introduction to Business class is not the place to be arranging a date for tonight. If you are expecting a critical call, turn off the audible phone ring and use the vibrating ring if your phone has that feature. If you do have to have your cellular phone turned on, sit by the aisle and near the door. If your phone does ring, leave the room before answering it. Apologize to the professor after class and explain the nature of the emergency. Most professors will be sympathetic when you explain why you left the room abruptly.
7. **Being prepared**. A businessperson would never show up for a meeting without reading the materials assigned for that meeting and being prepared to discuss the topics of the day. To become a professional, you must practice acting like a professional. For students, that means reading assigned materials before class, asking questions and responding to questions in class, and discussing the material with fellow students.

In many cultures bowing is a form of greeting to show respect. It's important that people learn the business etiquette appropriate for the countries in which they do business. Behavior that's taken for granted in the United States might be insulting in other cultures. It's best to do your homework in learning about other cultures.

From the minute you enter your first job interview until the day you retire, people will notice whether you follow the proper business etiquette. Just as traffic laws enable people to drive more safely, business etiquette allows people to conduct business with the appropriate amount of dignity. How you talk, how you eat, and how you dress all create an impression on others. We encourage you to add a course or seminar on etiquette to your college curriculum. Many businesses today require their employees to complete such a course. Taking the initiative to do so on your own will help sharpen your competitive edge.

Business etiquette may encompass different rules in different countries. It is important, therefore, to learn the proper business etiquette for each country you visit. Areas that require proper etiquette include greeting people (shaking hands is not always appropriate); eating (Europeans, for example, often hold their knives and forks the whole time they are eating); giving gifts; presenting and receiving business cards; and conducting business in general. Honesty, high ethical standards, and good character (e.g., reliability and trustworthiness) are important ingredients to success in any country.

Having a reputation for integrity will enable you to be proud of who you are and will contribute a great deal to your business success. Unethical behavior can ruin your reputation, so think carefully before you act. When in doubt, don't! Ethics is so important to success that we include ethics discussions throughout the text.

## DOING YOUR BEST IN SCHOOL

The skills you need to succeed in college are the same skills you need to succeed in life after college. Career, family, and hobbies all involve the same organizational and time management skills. Applying these skills during your college years will ensure that you will have the life skills you need for a successful career. We will try to help you hone your skills by offering hints for improving your study habits, taking tests, and managing your time.

### Study Hints

Studying is your business now. When you fill out a form you write "Student" in the occupation box, right? So until you get out of school and into a full-time job, studying is your business. Like any good businessperson, you aim for success. Let us suggest some strategies for success:

1. **Go to class**. It is often tempting to cut a class on a nice day or when there are other things to do. But nothing is more important to doing well in school than going to class every time. If possible, sit in the front near the instructor. This will help you focus more on what is being said and less on distractions in the room.
2. **Listen well**. It's not enough to show up for class if you use the time for a siesta. Make eye contact with the instructor. In your mind, form a picture of what is discussed. Try to include past experiences in your picture. This ties new knowledge to what you already know.
3. **Take careful notes**. Make two columns in your notebook and use one side to write down the important concepts and the other side to write examples or more detailed explanations. Use abbreviations and symbols whenever possible. Use wide spacing to make the notes easier to read. Rewrite the notes after class because hastily written notes are often difficult to decipher much later. Rereading and rewriting notes also helps store the information in your long-term memory. You learn the concepts in the course the same way you learn the words to your favorite song: through repetition and review.
4. **Find a good place to study**. Find a place with good lighting and a quiet atmosphere. Some students do well with classical music or other music without lyrics playing in the background. Keep your study place equipped with extra supplies such as pens, pencils, calculator, folders, and paper so that you don't have to interrupt study time to hunt for what you need.
5. **Read the text using a strategy such as "survey, question, read, recite, review" (SQ3R)**.

   a. *Survey* or scan the chapter first to see what it is all about. This means looking over the table of contents, learning goals, headings, photo essays, and charts so you get a broad idea of the content. Scanning will provide an introduction and help get your mind in a learning mode.

By following the study system of "survey, question, read, recite, and review (SQ3R)," you can stay up with the class and be ready to shine in class every day. Work today pays off tomorrow. Go for it!

b. Write *questions*, first by changing the headings into questions. For example, you could change the heading of this section to "What hints can I use to study better?" Read the questions that appear throughout each chapter in the Progress Assessment sections. The Progress Assessment questions give you a chance to recall what you've read.
c. *Read* the chapter to find the answers to your questions. Be sure to read the boxes throughout the text as well. They offer extended examples or discussions of the concepts in the text. You've probably asked, "Will the stuff in the boxes be on the tests?" Even if your instructor chooses not to test over them directly, they are often the most interesting parts and will help you retain the concepts.
d. *Recite* your answers to yourself or to others in a study group. Make sure you say the answers in your own words so that you clearly understand the concepts. Research has shown that saying things is a more effective way to learn them than seeing, hearing, or reading about them. Used in study groups, recitation is also good practice for working in teams in the work world.
e. *Review* by rereading and recapping the information. The chapter summaries are written in a question-and-answer form, much like a classroom dialogue. Cover the written answers and see if you can answer the questions yourself first. The summaries are directly tied to the learning goals so you can see whether you've accomplished the chapter's objectives.

6. **Use the study guide**. The Student Assessment Learning Guide gives you the chance to practice thinking through answers and writing them down. It also includes practice multiple-choice tests.
7. **Use flash cards**. Much of the material in this course consists of terminology. To review the key terms in the book (see page P-15), write any terms you don't know on index cards and go through your cards between classes and when you have other free time.
8. **Use this text's Online Learning Center**. Using the Online Learning Center (OLC) on this text's Web site (www.mhhe.com/ub8e) is a great way to practice your test-taking skills. The OLC contains sample test questions. It will analyze your achievement and tell you not only if you were correct or incorrect but also why. Then it will provide page references to concepts you have trouble understanding and even pop up a picture of the appropriate text page so that you don't have to fumble through your text while you are at the computer.
9. **Go over old exams, if possible**. Sometimes a professor will make old exams available so that you can see the style of the exam. If such exams are not available, ask your professor exactly how the exam will be given. That is, ask how many multiple-choice questions and how many true–false and essay questions there will be. It is not unethical to ask

your professor's former students what kind of questions are given and what material is usually emphasized. It is unethical, though, to go over illegally obtained exams.

10. **Use as many of your senses in learning as possible**. If you're an auditory learner—that is, if you learn best by hearing—record yourself reading your notes and answering the questions you've written. Listen to the tape while you're dressing in the morning. You can also benefit from reading or studying aloud. Use the text on tape (a set of audio CDs) that is available with this book. If you're a visual learner, you should use pictures, charts, colors, and graphs. Your professor has a set of videotapes that illustrate the concepts in this text. If you're a kinesthetic learner, you remember best by doing, touching, and experiencing. You can benefit from doing some of the Developing Workplace Skills and Taking It to the Net exercises at the end of each chapter.

## Test-Taking Hints

Often students will say, "I know this stuff, but I'm just no good at taking multiple-choice (or essay) tests." Other students find test-taking relatively easy. A survey of such students reveals the following test-taking hints:

1. **Get plenty of sleep and a good meal**. It is better to be alert and awake during an exam than to study all night and be groggy. If you keep up with your reading and your reviews, there is no need to pull an all-nighter just before the exam. Proper nutrition plays an important part in your brain's ability to function.
2. **Bring all you need for the exam**. Sometimes you will need number 2 pencils, erasers, and a calculator. Ask beforehand what you'll need.
3. **Relax**. Begin at home before the test. Take deep, slow breaths. Picture yourself in the testing session, relaxed and confident. Get to class early to settle down. If you start to get nervous during the test, stop and take deep breaths. Turn the test over and write down information you remember. Sometimes this helps you connect the information you know to the questions on the test.
4. **Read the directions on the exam carefully**. You don't want to miss anything or do something you are not supposed to do.
5. **Read all the answers in multiple-choice questions**. Often there is more than one correct-sounding answer to a multiple-choice question, but one is clearly better. Be sure to read them all to be sure that the one you pick is best. A technique that may help you is to cover up the choices while reading the question. If the answer you think of is one of the choices, it is probably the correct answer. If you are still unsure of the answer, start eliminating options you know are wrong. Narrowing the choices to two or three improves your odds.
6. **Answer all the questions**. Unless your instructor takes off more for an incorrect answer than no answer at all, you have nothing to lose by guessing. Also, skipping a question can lead to inadvertently misaligning your answers on a scan sheet. You could end up with all of your subsequent answers scored wrong!
7. **Read true–false questions carefully**. All parts of the statement must be true or the entire statement is false. Watch out for absolutes such as *never*, *always*, and *none*. These most likely make a statement false.

8. **Organize your thoughts before answering essay questions**. Think of the sequence you intend to use to present what you want to say. Use complete sentences with correct grammar and punctuation. Explain or defend your answers.
9. **Go over the test at the end**. Make sure you have answered all the questions and that you have put your name on the exam and followed all the other directions.

## Time Management Hints

Throughout your life, the most important management skill you will learn is to manage your time. Now is as good a time to learn as any. Here are some hints that other students have learned—often the hard way:

1. **Write weekly goals for yourself**. Make certain your goals are realistic and attainable. Write the steps you will use to achieve each goal. Reward yourself when you reach a goal.
2. **Keep a "to do" list**. It is easy to forget things unless you have them written down. Jot tasks down the first time you think of them so that you don't rediscover chores when you think of them again. Writing them down gives you one less thing to do: remembering what you have to do.
3. **Prepare a daily schedule**. Use a commercial daily planner or create your own. Write the days of the week across the top of the page. Write the hours of the day from the time you get up until the time you go to bed down the left side. Draw lines to form columns and rows and fill in all the activities you have planned in each hour. Hopefully, you will be surprised to see how many slots of time you have available for studying.
4. **Prepare for the next day the night before**. Having everything ready to go will help you make a quick, unfrenzied start in the morning.
5. **Prepare weekly and monthly schedules**. Use a calendar to fill in activities and upcoming assignments. Include both academic and social activities so you can balance your work and fun.
6. **Space out your work**. Don't wait until the last week of the course to write all your papers and study for your exams. If you do a few pages a day, you can do a 20-page paper in a couple of weeks with little effort. It is really difficult to push out 20 pages in a day or two.
7. **Defend your study time**. Fraternities and sororities often set aside time for everyone to study. It is important to study some every day. Use the time between classes to go over your flash cards and read the next day's assignments. Make it a habit to defend your study time so you don't slip.
8. **Take time for fun**. If you have some fun every day, life will be full. But if you don't have fun, life can be a real drag. Schedule your fun times along with your study schedule so that you have balance.

"Time is money" the saying goes. Some, however, would argue that time is more valuable than money. If your bank account balance falls, you might be able to build it back up by finding a better paying job, taking on a second job, or even selling something you own. But you only have a limited amount of time and there is no way to make more. Don't steal someone else's valuable time by being late for class or appointments. If you do, what message are you sending?

## MAKING THE MOST OF THE RESOURCES FOR THIS COURSE

College courses are best at teaching you concepts and ways of thinking about business. However, to learn firsthand about real-world applications, you will need to explore and interact with actual businesses. Textbooks are like comprehensive tour guides in that they tell you what to look for and where to look, but they can never replace experience.

This text, then, isn't meant to be the only resource for this class. In fact, it's not even the primary resource. Your professor will be much better than the text at responding to your specific questions and needs. This book is just one of the resources he or she can use with you to satisfy your desire to understand what the business world is all about. There are seven basic resources for the class in addition to the text and study guide:

Your professor is not a person put on earth just to make your life difficult. Your professor is one of the most valuable resources and contacts you will encounter in college as you chart and develop your career path. Get to know your professor soon!

1. **The professor**. One of the most valuable facets of college is the chance to study with experienced professors. Your instructor is more than a teacher of facts and concepts. He or she is a resource who's there to answer questions and guide you to the answers for others. It's important for you to develop a friendly relationship with all of your professors. One reason for doing so is that many professors get job leads they can pass on to you. Professors are also excellent references for future jobs. By following the rules of dress and etiquette outlined earlier, you can create a good impression, which will be valuable should you ask a professor to write a good letter of recommendation for you. Finally, your professor is one more experienced person who can help you find and access resource materials, both at your college and in the business world.

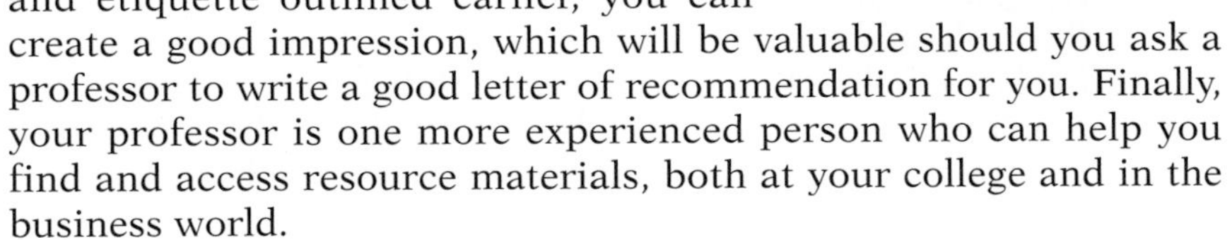

2. **The supplements that come with this text: the Online Learning Center, the Student Assessment Learning Guide, and the audio CDs**. The OLC and study guide will help you review and interpret key material and give you practice answering test questions. Even if your professor does not assign the study guide and OLC, you may want to use them anyhow. Doing so will improve your test scores and help you compete successfully with the other students. If you are an auditory learner (you learn best by listening) or if you have a long commute to class, you'll find the audio version of this text to be a great resource.
3. **Outside readings**. We recommend that you review the following magazines and newspapers as well as other resources during the course and throughout your career: *The Wall Street Journal*, *Forbes*, *BusinessWeek*, *Fortune*, *Money*, *Hispanic Business*, *Smart Money*, *Harvard Business Review*, *Black Enterprise*, and *Entrepreneur*. You may also want to read your local newspaper's business section and national news magazines such as *Time* and *Newsweek* to keep up with current issues. If you're not familiar with these sources, it's time to get to know them. You don't necessarily have to become a regular subscriber, but you should learn what information is available in these sources over time. All of these

sources are probably available free of charge in your school's learning resource center or the local public library. One secret to success in business is staying current, and these magazines will help you do so.

4. **Your own experience and that of your classmates**. Many college students have had experience working in business or nonprofit organizations. Talking together about those experiences exposes you to many real-life examples that are invaluable for understanding business. Don't rely totally on the professor for answers to the cases and other exercises in this book. Often there is no single "right" answer, and your classmates may open up new ways of looking at things for you.

   Part of being a successful businessperson is knowing how to work with others. College classrooms are excellent places to practice this skill. Some professors provide opportunities for their students to work together in small groups. Such exercises build teamwork as well as presentation and analytical skills. If you have students from other countries in your class, working with them can help you learn about different cultures and different approaches to handling business problems. There is strength in diversity, so seek out people different from yourself to work with on teams.
5. **Outside contacts**. One of the best ways to learn about different businesses is to visit them in person. Who can tell you more about what it's like to start a career in accounting than someone who's doing it now? The same is true of other jobs. The world can be your classroom if you let it. When you go shopping, for example, think about whether you would enjoy working in and managing a store. Talk with the clerks and the manager to see how they feel about the job. Think about the possibilities of owning or managing a restaurant, an auto body shop, a health club, a print shop, or any other establishment you visit. If something looks interesting, talk to the employees and learn more about their jobs and the industry. Soon you may discover fascinating careers in places such as the zoo or a health club or in industries such as travel or computer sales. In short, be constantly on the alert to find career possibilities, and don't hesitate to talk with people about their careers. Typically, they'll be pleased to give you their time.
6. **The Internet**. Never before have students had access to information as easily as they do today. What makes information gathering so easy now is the Internet. In fact, you will find more material than you could use in a lifetime. On the Internet you can search through library catalogs all over the world, find articles from leading business journals, view paintings from leading museums, and more—much more. Throughout this text we will present information and exercises that require you to use the Internet. This resource will become even more important in the future. Information changes rapidly, and it is up to you to stay current.
7. **The library or learning resource center**. The library is a great complement to the Internet as a valuable resource. Work with your librarian to learn how to best access the information you need.

## Getting the Most from This Text

Many learning aids appear throughout this text to help you understand the concepts:

1. **List of Learning Goals at the beginning of each chapter**. Reading through these goals will help you set the framework and focus for the

chapter material. Since every student at one time or other has found it difficult to get into studying, the Learning Goals are there to provide an introduction and to get your mind into a learning mode.

2. **Self-test questions**. Periodically, within each chapter, you'll encounter set-off lists of questions called Progress Assessment. These questions give you a chance to pause, think carefully about, and recall what you've just read.
3. **Key terms**. Developing a strong business vocabulary is one of the most important and useful aspects of this course. To assist you, all key terms in the book are highlighted in boldface type. Key terms are also defined in the margins, and page references to these terms are given at the end of each chapter. A full glossary is located in the back of the book. You should rely heavily on these learning aids in adding these terms to your vocabulary.
4. **Boxes**. Each chapter contains a number of boxes that offer extended examples or discussions of concepts in the text. This material is designed to highlight key concepts and to make the book more interesting to read. The boxes cover major themes of the book: (*a*) ethics (Making Ethical Decisions); (*b*) small business (Spotlight on Small Business); (*c*) legal environment of business (Legal Briefcase); (*d*) global business (Reaching Beyond Our Borders); and (*e*) constant change (Dealing with Change).
5. **End-of-chapter summaries**. The chapter summaries are directly tied to the chapter Learning Goals so that you can see whether you've accomplished the chapter's objectives.
6. **Critical Thinking Questions**. The end-of-chapter questions will help you relate the material to your own experiences.
7. **Developing Workplace Skills exercises**. Regardless of how hard we try to make learning easier, the truth is that students tend to forget most of what they read and hear. To really remember something, it's best to do it. That's why there are Developing Workplace Skills sections at the end of each chapter. The purpose of Developing Workplace Skills questions is to suggest small projects that reinforce what you've read and help you develop the skills you need to succeed in the workplace. These activities will help you develop skills in using resources, interpersonal skills, skills in managing information, skills in understanding systems, and computer skills.
8. **Taking It to the Net exercises**. These exercises not only give you practice surfing the Internet but, more important, direct you to dynamic outside resources that reinforce the concepts introduced in the text.
9. **Video cases**. These cases feature companies, processes, practices, and managers that highlight the key concepts in the chapter and bring them to life.
10. **Casing the Web cases**. These cases give you another chance to think about the material and apply it in real-life situations. These cases are referenced at the end of each chapter and can be found on the text's Web site (www.mhhe.com/ub8e).

If you use the suggestions we've presented here, you will not simply "take a course in business." Instead, you will actively participate in a learning experience that will help you greatly in your chosen career. The most important secret to success may be to enjoy what you are doing and to do your best in everything. You can't do your best without taking advantage of all the learning aids that are available to you.

## GETTING THE JOB YOU WANT

One of the more important objectives of this text is to help you get the job you want. First, you have to decide what you want to do. We'll help you explore this decision by explaining what people do in the various business functions: human resource management, marketing, accounting, finance, and so on. There are many good books about finding the job you want, so we can only introduce the subject here to get you thinking about careers as you read the various chapters.

"I got the job!" is what students look forward to saying after years of college study. Job fairs are among the many resources students can use to help find the right match. Do you think it's ever too early to start thinking about your career?

If you are a returning student, you have both blessings and handicaps that younger students do not have. First, you may have had a full-time job already. Second, you are more likely to know what kind of job you don't want. That is a real advantage. By exploring the various business careers in depth, you should be able to choose a career path that will meet your objectives. If you have a full-time job right now, you've already discovered that working while going to school is exhausting. Many older students must juggle family responsibilities in addition to the responsibilities of school and work. But take heart. You have also acquired many skills from these experiences. Even if they were acquired in unrelated fields, these skills will be invaluable as you enter your new career. You should have no trouble competing with younger students because you have more focus and experience. We enjoy having both kinds of students in class because of the different perspectives they have.

So, whether you're beginning your first career or your latest career, it's time to develop a strategy for finding and obtaining a personally satisfying job.

## JOB SEARCH STRATEGY

It is never too early to begin thinking about a future career or careers. The following strategies will give you some guidance in that pursuit:

1. **Begin with self-analysis**. You might begin your career quest by completing a self-analysis inventory. You can refer to Figure P.2 for a sample of a simple assessment.
2. **Search for jobs you would enjoy**. Begin at your college's career planning office or placement office, if your school has one. Keep interviewing people in various careers, even after you've found a job. Career progress demands continuous research.
3. **Begin the networking process**. According to a Seattle-based job placement firm, networking remains the number one way for new job seekers to get their foot in the door, even beating using the Internet.[8] In fact, a leading magazine states that as many as 85 percent of jobs are secured through networking.[9] You can start with your fellow students, family, relatives, neighbors, friends, professors, and local businesspeople. Be sure to keep a file with the names, addresses, and phone numbers of contacts—where they work, the person who recommended them to you, and the relationship between the source person and the contact. A great way to make contacts and a good impression on

**Interests**

1. How do I like to spend my time?
2. Do I enjoy being with people?
3. Do I like working with mechanical things?
4. Do I enjoy working with numbers?
5. Am I a member of many organizations?
6. Do I enjoy physical activities?
7. Do I like to read?

**Abilities**

1. Am I adept at working with numbers?
2. Am I adept at working with mechanical things?
3. Do I have good verbal and written communication skills?
4. What special talents do I have?
5. In which abilities do I wish I were more adept?

**Education**

1. Have I taken certain courses that have prepared me for a particular job?
2. In which subjects did I perform the best? The worst?
3. Which subjects did I enjoy the most? The least?
4. How have my extracurricular activities prepared me for a particular job?
5. Is my GPA an accurate picture of my academic ability? Why?
6. Do I want a graduate degree? Do I want to earn it before beginning my job?
7. Why did I choose my major?

**Experience**

1. What previous jobs have I held? What were my responsibilities in each?
2. Were any of my jobs applicable to positions I may be seeking? How?
3. What did I like the most about my previous jobs? Like the least?
4. Why did I work in the jobs I did?
5. If I had to do it over again, would I work in these jobs? Why?

**Personality**

1. What are my good and bad traits?
2. Am I competitive?
3. Do I work well with others?
4. Am I outspoken?
5. Am I a leader or a follower?
6. Do I work well under pressure?
7. Do I work quickly, or am I methodical?
8. Do I get along well with others?
9. Am I ambitious?
10. Do I work well independently of others?

**Desired job environment**

1. Am I willing to relocate? Why?
2. Do I have a geographic preference? Why?
3. Would I mind traveling in my job?
4. Do I have to work for a large, nationally known firm to be satisfied?
5. Must I have a job that initially offers a high salary?
6. Must the job I assume offer rapid promotion opportunities?
7. In what kind of job environment would I feel most comfortable?
8. If I could design my own job, what characteristics would it have?

**Personal goals**

1. What are my short- and long-term goals? Why?
2. Am I career-oriented, or do I have broader interests?
3. What are my career goals?
4. What jobs are likely to help me achieve my goals?
5. What do I hope to be doing in 5 years? In 10 years?
6. What do I want out of life?

figure P.2
**A PERSONAL ASSESSMENT**

employers is to do part-time work and summer internships at those firms you find interesting. Many young professionals use online social-networking sites, such as Tribe or Friendster, to expand their networks. If you choose to post to one of these Web sites, be careful to include only information you would want a potential hiring agent to see and not something that might hurt your chances for landing a job. For example, a recruiter at HireAbility.com, a recruiting-services company, turned to Tribe to find information on a sales candidate for one of his clients. The recruiter saw that the applicant posted photos of himself shirtless and exposing body art. Since the hiring company was concerned about the presentation of candidates (that is, how they dress and present themselves), the recruiter quickly ruled out the tattooed-and-pierced candidate.[10]

4. **Go to the Internet for help**. You will find details about finding jobs on a variety of Web sites. Many of these sites can help you write your résumé as well as help you search for jobs that meet your interests and skills.[11] Later we'll list a number of these sites.
5. **Prepare a good cover letter and résumé**. Once you know what you want to do and where you would like to work, you need to develop a good résumé and cover letter. Your résumé lists your education, work experience, and activities. We'll talk about these key job search tools in more detail.
6. **Develop interviewing skills**. Interviewers will be checking your appearance (clothes, haircut, fingernails, shoes); your attitude (friendliness is desired); your verbal ability (speak loud enough to be heard clearly); and your motivation (be enthusiastic). Note also that interviewers want you to have been active in clubs and activities and to have set goals. Have someone evaluate you on these scales now to see if you have any weak points. You can then work on those points before you have any actual job interviews. We'll give you some clues on how to do this later.
7. **Follow up**. Write a thank-you note after interviews, even if you think they didn't go well. You have a chance to make a lasting impression with a follow-up note. Keep in touch with companies in which you have an interest. Show your interest by calling periodically or sending e-mail and letting the company know you are still interested. Indicate your willingness to travel to various parts of the country or the world to be interviewed. Get to know people in the company and learn from them whom to contact and what qualifications to emphasize.

## MORE HINTS ON THE JOB SEARCH

The placement bureau at your school is a good place to begin reading about potential employers. On-campus interviewing is often a great source of jobs (see Figure P.3). Another good source of jobs involves writing to companies and sending a good cover letter and résumé. You can identify companies to contact in your library or on the Internet. Check such sources as the *Million Dollar Directory* or the *Standard Directory of Advertisers*. Your library and the Internet may also have annual reports that will give you even more information about your selected companies.

Other good sources of jobs include the want ads, job fairs, summer and other internship programs, placement bureaus, and sometimes walking into firms that appeal to you and asking for an interview. The *Occupational Outlook Quarterly*, produced by the U.S. Department of Labor, says this about job hunting:

> *The skills that make a person employable are not so much the ones needed on the job as the ones needed to get the job, skills like the ability to find a job opening, complete an application, prepare the résumé, and survive an interview.*

Here are a few printed sources you can use for finding out about jobs and other career choices:

*Occupational Outlook Handbook* (Washington, DC: U.S. Department of Labor, 2006–2007 edition).

figure P.3

**WHERE COLLEGE STUDENTS FIND JOBS**

| SOURCE OF JOB | PERCENTAGE OF NEW EMPLOYEES |
|---|---|
| On-campus interviewing | 49.3% |
| Write-ins | 9.8 |
| Current employee referrals | 7.2 |
| Job listings with placement office | 6.5 |
| Responses from want ads | 5.6 |
| Walk-ins | 5.5 |
| Cooperative education programs | 4.8 |
| Summer employment | 4.7 |
| College faculty/staff referrals | 4.5 |
| Internship programs | 4.5 |
| High-demand major programs | 4.4 |
| Minority career programs | 2.9 |
| Part-time employment | 2.4 |
| Unsolicited referrals from placement | 2.1 |
| Women's career programs | 2.1 |
| Job listings with employment agencies | 1.9 |
| Referrals from campus organizations | 1.8 |

*The Big Book of Jobs* (New York: VGM Career Books, McGraw-Hill, 2005–2006 edition).

Michael Farr, *100 Fastest Growing Careers: Your Complete Guidebook to Major Jobs with the Most Growth and Openings* (Indianapolis, IN: JIST, 2006).

Michael Farr, *Best Jobs of the Twenty-First Century*, 4th ed. (Indianapolis, IN: JIST, 2006).

Richard Nelson Bolles (with Mark Emery Bolles, ed.), *What Color Is Your Parachute?* (Berkeley, CA: Ten Speed Press, 2006 edition).

Martin Yate, *Knock 'Em Dead 2006* (Holbrook, MA: Adams Media Corporation, 2005).

Caryl Krannich and Ron Krannich, *Interview for Success*, 8th ed. (Manassas Park, VA: Impact, 2003).

*The Directory of Executive Recruiters 2005–2006* (Peterborough, NH: Kennedy Information, 2004).

Richard Wallace, *The National Job Bank 2006: The Complete Employment Guide to Over 20,000 Companies* (Avon, MA: Adams Media Corporation, 2006).

You can also use the Internet to search for job information. To find information about careers or internships, try these sites (though keep in mind that addresses on the Internet are subject to sudden and frequent change):[12]

CareerBuilder: www.careerbuilder.com

Hoover's: www.hoovers.com

Monster: www.monster.com

America's Job Bank: www.ajb.dni.us

Yahoo! Classifieds: www.classifieds.yahoo.com

It's never too early in your career to begin designing a résumé and thinking of cover letters. Preparing such documents reveals your strengths and weaknesses more clearly than most other techniques. By preparing a résumé now, you may discover that you haven't been involved in enough outside activities to impress an employer. That information may prompt you to join some student groups, to become a volunteer, or to otherwise enhance your social skills.[13]

You may also discover that you're weak on experience, and seek an internship or part-time job to fill in that gap.[14] In any event, it's not too soon to prepare a résumé. It will certainly help you decide what you'd like to see in the area marked Education and, if you haven't already done so, help you choose a major and other coursework. Given that background, let's discuss how to prepare these materials.

## WRITING YOUR RÉSUMÉ

A résumé is a document that lists information an employer would need to evaluate you and your background. It explains your immediate goals and career objectives. This information is followed by an explanation of your educational background, experience, interests, and other relevant data. Be sure to use industry buzzwords in your résumé (see Figure P.4) because companies use keywords to scan such résumés.[15] Having experience working in teams, for example, is important to many companies. For online résumé help, go to www1.umn.edu/ohr/ecep/resume.

If you have exceptional abilities but your résumé doesn't communicate them to the employer, those abilities aren't part of the person he or she will evaluate. You must be comprehensive and clear in your résumé if you are to communicate all your attributes.

Your résumé is an advertisement for yourself. If your ad is better than the other person's ad, you're more likely to get the interview. In this case, *better* means that your ad highlights your attributes attractively. In discussing your education, for example, be sure to highlight your extracurricular activities such as part-time jobs, sports, and clubs. If you did well in school, include your grades. The idea is to make yourself look as good on paper as you are in reality.

The same is true for your job experience. Be sure to describe what you did, any special projects in which you participated, and any responsibilities you had. For the interests section, if you include one, don't just list your interests, but describe how deeply you were involved. If you organized the club, volunteered your time, or participated more often than usual in an organization, make sure to say so in the résumé. See Figure P.5 for a sample résumé. Most companies prefer that you keep your résumé to one page unless you have many years of experience.

figure P.4

**SAMPLE ACTION WORDS**

| | | | |
|---|---|---|---|
| Managed | Wrote | Budgeted | Improved |
| Planned | Produced | Designed | Increased |
| Organized | Scheduled | Directed | Investigated |
| Coordinated | Operated | Developed | Teamed |
| Supervised | Conducted | Established | Served |
| Trained | Administered | Implemented | Handled |

figure P.5

SAMPLE RÉSUMÉ

**Yann Ng**
345 Big Bend Boulevard
Kirkwood, Missouri, 63122
314-555-5385
YNG@AOL.COM

**Job objective:** Sales representative in business-to-business marketing

**Education:**

**St. Louis Community College at Meramec**
A.A. in Business (3.6 grade point average)
Served on Student Representative Board

**University of Missouri, St. Louis**
B.S. in Business: Marketing major (3.2 grade point average, 3.5 in major)
Earned 100 percent of college expenses working 35 hours a week.
Member of Student American Marketing Association
Vice President of Student Government Association
Dean's List for two semesters

**Work experience:**
Schnuck's Supermarket: Worked checkout evenings and weekends for four years while in school. Learned to respond to customer requests quickly, and communicate with customers in a friendly and helpful manner.

Mary Tuttle's Flowers: For two summers, made flower arrangements, managed sales transactions, and acted as assistant to the manager. Also trained and supervised three employees. Often handled customer inquiries and complaints.

**Special skills:**
Fluent in Vietnamese, French, and English. Proficient at using WordPerfect and Word. Developed my own website (www.yan@stilnet.com) and use the Internet often to do research for papers and for personal interests.

**Other interests:**
Cooking: often prepare meals for my family and friends. Reading, especially the classics. Piano playing and aerobics. Traveling: Asia, Europe, and America. Doing research on the Internet.

## PUTTING YOUR RÉSUMÉ ON THE INTERNET

You might want to post your résumé on the Internet because many larger firms seek candidates on the Net. While Internet résumés allow you to cast a wide net by allowing you to reach the greatest number of potential employers with the least amount of effort, the Internet is not always the most effective job search tool. It may have been more effective a couple of years ago, but today thousands of other eager job hunters send résumés online and the volume can overwhelm recruiters. That doesn't mean you shouldn't post your résumé online; it does mean, though, that you can't just send a few hundred résumés into cyberspace and then sit back and wait for the phone to ring. Include online résumés as a tool in your job search process, but continue to use the more traditional tools such as networking.

Afraid your résumé might make a monkey out of you? Following proper procedures in résumé writing will help your chance of having your résumé considered. Remember, the key is getting the reader's attention.

An Internet résumé is different from a standard one because the elimination process is done by computer. Thus, you must understand what the computer is programmed to look for. It wants nouns, not verbs. Whereas the traditional résumé is built on verbs like *managed* and *supervised*, résumés on the Internet are built around nouns like *program management* and *teams*. They also emphasize software programs you have mastered, like Microsoft Word. Listing jobs chronologically is no longer the best thing to do. Instead, emphasize knowledge, skills, and abilities. At the beginning of your résumé or after the Experience section, you may write a new section called Key Skills or Functional Expertise and list all the nouns that fit your experience.

For example, a salesperson might put terms that apply to selling such as *prospect*, *approach*, *presentations*, *close sale*, *follow up*, *focus groups*, and *service*.

Here are some hints on preparing your résumé for the Internet:

- Keep it simple. Use text only. Put a summary of your skills and your objective at the top so that the reader can capture as much as possible in the first 30 seconds.
- If you e-mail your résumé, send it in the text of the message; don't put it as an attachment. It takes too long for the receiver to open an attachment.
- Customize each mailing to that specific company. You may use a standard résumé, but add data to customize it and to introduce it.
- Put your cover letter and résumé in one file.
- Use any advertised job title as the subject of your e-mail message, citing any relevant job numbers. (Note that some companies don't want you to e-mail them your résumé and cover letter, preferring letters or faxes instead.)

Posting résumés to Internet job sites can cause privacy nightmares for job seekers, resulting in everything from identity theft to losing their current job when their employers, who use the same job search services, find out that they are looking for new jobs. Sometimes posted résumés are sold to other sites or individuals willing to pay for them. Scam artists posing as recruiters, meanwhile, also can download all the résumés they want and do virtually whatever they want with them. At worst, online résumés can give identity thieves a starting point to steal personal information. Here are tips to protect your résumé and your identity:

- *Never* include highly private information, such as Social Security numbers and birthdays.
- Check job boards' privacy policies to see how information is used and resold.
- Post résumés directly to employers if possible.
- Date résumés and remove them promptly after finding a job.
- If possible, withhold confidential information such as telephone numbers and your name and use temporary e-mail addresses for contacts.

You can find more details about applying for jobs on the Internet in Margaret Riley Dikel and Frances E. Roehm's 2006–2007 edition of *Guide to Internet Job Searching*. See Figure P.6 for a sample Internet résumé.

figure P.6

**SAMPLE INTERNET RÉSUMÉ**

Yann Ng
345 Big Bend Boulevard
Kirkwood, Missouri, 63122
314-555-5385
YNG@AOL.COM

Job objective: Sales representative in business-to-business marketing

Education:
St. Louis Community College at Meramec
A.A. in Business (3.6 grade point average)
Service on Student Representative Board
Courses included introduction to business, accounting, and marketing.

University of Missouri, St. Louis
B.S. in Business: Marketing major
(3.2. grade point average, 3.5 in major)
Earned 100 percent of college expenses working 35 hours a week.
Member of Student American Marketing Association
Vice President of Student Government Association
Dean's List for two semesters

Work experience:
Schnuck's Supermarket: Worked checkout evenings and weekends for four years while in school. Learned to respond to customer requests quickly, and communicate with customers in a friendly and helpful manner.

Mary Tuttle's Flowers: For two summers, made flower arrangements, managed sales transactions, and acted as assistant to the manager. Also trained and supervised three employees. Often handled customer inquiries and complaints.

Special skills: Fluent in Vietnamese, French, and English. Proficient at using MS Word 2000, MS Excel 2000, and MS PowerPoint 2000. Developed my own website (www.yan@stilnet.com) and use the Internet often to do research for papers and for personal interests. Sales skills include conducting focus groups, prospecting, making presentations, and customer service.

Other interests: Cooking: often prepare meals for my family and friends. Reading, especially the classics. Piano playing and aerobics. Traveling: Asia, Europe, and America. Doing research on the Internet.

## WRITING A COVER LETTER

A cover letter is used to announce your availability and to introduce the résumé. The cover letter is probably one of the most important advertisements anyone will write in a lifetime—so it should be done right.

First, the cover letter should indicate that you've researched the organization in question and are interested in a job there. Let the organization know what sources you used and what you know about it in the first paragraph to get the attention of the reader and show your interest.

You may have heard people say, "What counts is not what you know, but whom you know." This is only partly true—because both knowledge and personal contacts are necessary but it's important nonetheless. If you don't know someone, you can get to know someone. You do this by calling the organization (or better yet, visiting its offices) and talking to people who already have the kind of job you're hoping to get. Ask about training, salary, and other relevant issues. Then, in your cover letter, mention that you've talked with some of the firm's employees and that this discussion increased your interest. You thereby show the letter reader that you "know someone," if only casually, and that you're interested enough to actively pursue the organization. This is all part of networking.

Second, in the description of yourself, be sure to say how your attributes will benefit the organization. For example, don't just say, "I will be graduating with a degree in marketing." Say, "You will find that my college training in marketing and marketing research has prepared me to learn your marketing system quickly and begin making a contribution right away." The sample cover letter in Figure P.7 will give you a better feel for how this looks.

Third, be sure to "ask for the order." That is, say in your final paragraph that you're available for an interview at a time and place convenient for the interviewer. Again, see the sample cover letter in Figure P.7 for guidance. Notice in this letter how the writer subtly shows that she reads business publications and draws attention to her résumé.

Principles to follow in writing a cover letter and preparing your résumé include the following:

- Be confident. List all your good qualities and attributes.
- Don't be apologetic or negative. Write as one professional to another, not as a humble student begging for a job.
- Describe how your experience and education can add value to the organization.
- Research every prospective employer thoroughly before writing anything. Use a rifle approach rather than a shotgun approach. That is, write effective marketing-oriented letters to a few select companies rather than to a general list.
- Have your materials prepared by an experienced keyboarder if you are not highly skilled yourself. If you have access to a word processing system with a letter-quality laser printer, you can produce individualized letters efficiently.
- Have someone edit your materials for spelling, grammar, and style. Don't be like the student who sent out a second résumé to correct "some mixtakes." Or another who said, "I am acurite with numbers."
- Don't send the names of references until asked.

figure P.7

SAMPLE COVER LETTER

345 Big Bend Blvd.
Kirkwood, MO 63122
October 10, 2007

Mr. Carl Karlinski
Premier Designs
45 Apple Court
Chicago, Illinois 60536

Dear Mr. Karlinski: [Note that it's best to know whom to write by name.]

Recent articles in *Inc.* and *Success* have praised your company for its innovative products and strong customer orientation. I'm familiar with your creative display materials. In fact, we've used them at Mary Tuttle's Flower Shop—my employer for the last two summers. Christie Bouchard, your local sales representative, told me all about your products and your training program at Premier Designs.

Christie mentioned the kind of salespeople you are seeking. Here's what she said and my qualifications.

Requirement: Men and women with proven sales ability.

Qualifications: Success making and selling flower arrangements at Mary Tuttle's and practicing customer relations at Schnuck's Supermarket. As you know, Schnuck's has one of the best customer-oriented training programs in the food industry.

Requirement: Self-motivated people with leadership ability.

Qualifications: Paid my way through college working nights and summers. Selected to be on the Student Representative Board at St. Louis Community College at Meramec and active in student government at the University of Missouri. Paid my own way to Asia, Europe, and the Americas.

Could you use such a successful salesperson at Premier Designs? I will be in the Chicago area the week of January 4–9. What time and date would be most convenient for us to discuss career opportunities at Premier? I'll phone your secretary to set up an appointment.

Sincerely,

Yann Ng

## PREPARING FOR JOB INTERVIEWS

Companies usually don't conduct job interviews unless they're somewhat certain that the candidate has the requirements for the job. The interview, therefore, is pretty much a make-or-break situation. If it goes well, you have a greater chance of being hired. That's why you must be prepared for your interviews. There are five stages of interview preparation:

1. **Do research about the prospective employers**. Learn what industry the firm is in, its competitors, the products or services it produces and their acceptance in the market, and the title of your desired position. You can find such information in the firm's annual reports, in

- How would you describe yourself?
- What are your greatest strengths and weaknesses?
- How did you choose this company?
- What do you know about the company?
- What are your long-range career goals?
- What courses did you like best? Least?
- What are your hobbies?
- Do you prefer a specific geographic location?
- Are you willing to travel (or move)?
- Which accomplishments have given you the most satisfaction?
- What things are most important to you in a job?
- Why should I hire you?
- What experience have you had in this type of work?
- How much do you expect to earn?

figure P.8

**FREQUENTLY ASKED QUESTIONS**

Standard & Poor's, Hoover's, Moody's manuals, and various business publications such as *Fortune*, *BusinessWeek*, and *Forbes*. Ask your librarian for help or search the Internet. You can look in the *Reader's Guide to Business Literature* to locate the company name and to look for articles about it. This important first step shows you have initiative and interest in the firm.

2. **Practice the interview**. Figure P.8 lists some of the more frequently asked questions in an interview. Practice answering these questions and more at the placement office and with your roommate, parents, or friends.[16] Don't memorize your answers, but do be prepared—know what you're going to say. Interviewers will be impressed if you thought enough to prepare questions for them about the products, job, company culture, and so on.[17] Figure P.9 shows sample questions you might ask. Be sure you know whom to contact, and write down the names of everyone you meet. Review the action words in Figure P.4 and try to fit them into your answers.
3. **Be professional during the interview**. You should look and sound professional throughout the interview. Do your homework and find out how managers dress at the firm. Make sure you wear an appropriate outfit. When you meet the interviewers, greet them by name, smile, and maintain good eye contact. Sit up straight in your chair and be alert and enthusiastic. If you have practiced, you should be able to relax and be confident. Other than that, be yourself, answer questions, and be friendly and responsive. (You will learn more about what types of questions job interviewers are legally allowed to ask you in Chapter 11.) Remember, the interview is not one-way communication; don't forget to ask the questions you've prepared before the interview. Do *not* ask about salary,

figure P.9

**SAMPLE QUESTIONS TO ASK THE INTERVIEWER**

- Who are your major competitors, and how would you rate their products and marketing relative to yours?
- How long does the training program last, and what is included?
- How soon after school would I be expected to start?
- What are the advantages of working for this firm?
- How much travel is normally expected?
- What managerial style should I expect in my area?
- How would you describe the working environment in my area?
- How would I be evaluated?
- What is the company's promotion policy?
- What is the corporate culture?
- What is the next step in the selection procedures?
- How soon should I expect to hear from you?
- What other information would you like about my background, experience, or education?
- What is your highest priority in the next six months and how could someone like me help?

figure P.10

TRAITS RECRUITERS SEEK IN JOB PROSPECTS

1. **Ability to communicate**. Do you have the ability to organize your thoughts and ideas effectively? Can you express them clearly when speaking or writing? Can you present your ideas to others in a persuasive way?
2. **Intelligence**. Do you have the ability to understand the job assignment? Learn the details of operation? Contribute original ideas to your work?
3. **Self-confidence**. Do you demonstrate a sense of maturity that enables you to deal positively and effectively with situations and people?
4. **Willingness to accept responsibility**. Are you someone who recognizes what needs to be done and is willing to do it?
5. **Initiative**. Do you have the ability to identify the purpose for work and to take action?
6. **Leadership**. Can you guide and direct others to obtain the recognized objectives?
7. **Energy level**. Do you demonstrate a forcefulness and capacity to make things move ahead? Can you maintain your work effort at an above-average rate?
8. **Imagination**. Can you confront and deal with problems that may not have standard solutions?
9. **Flexibility**. Are you capable of changing and being receptive to new situations and ideas?
10. **Interpersonal skills**. Can you bring out the best efforts of individuals so they become effective, enthusiastic members of a team?
11. **Self-knowledge**. Can you realistically assess your own capabilities? See yourself as others see you? Clearly recognize your strengths and weaknesses?
12. **Ability to handle conflict**. Can you successfully contend with stress situations and antagonism?
13. **Competitiveness**. Do you have the capacity to compete with others and the willingness to be measured by your performance in relation to that of others?
14. **Goal achievement**. Do you have the ability to identify and work toward specific goals? Do such goals challenge your abilities?
15. **Vocational skills**. Do you possess the positive combination of education and skills required for the position you are seeking?
16. **Direction**. Have you defined your basic personal needs? Have you determined what type of position will satisfy your knowledge, skills, and goals?

Source: "So You're Looking for a Job?" The College Placement Council.

however, until you've been offered a job. When you leave, thank the interviewers and, if you're still interested in the job, tell them so. If they don't tell you, ask them what the next step is. Maintain a positive attitude. Figures P.10 and P.11 on page P-28 outline what the interviewers will be evaluating.

4. **Follow up on the interview**. First, write down what you can remember from the interview: names of the interviewers and their titles, dates for training, and so on. Put the information in your career file. You can send a follow-up letter thanking each interviewer for his or her time. You can also send a letter of recommendation or some other piece of added information to keep their interest. "The squeaky wheel gets the grease" is the operating slogan. Your enthusiasm for working for the company could be a major factor in hiring you.
5. **Be prepared to act**. Know what you want to say if you do get a job offer. You may not want the job once you know all the information. Don't expect to receive a job offer from everyone you meet, but do expect to learn something from every interview. With some practice and persistence, you should find a rewarding and challenging job.

figure P.II

**INTERVIEW RATING SHEET**

Candidate: "For each characteristic listed below there is a rating scale of 1 through 7, where '1' is generally the most unfavorable rating of the characteristic and '7' the most favorable. Rate each characteristic by *circling* just one number to represent the impression you gave in the interview that you have just completed."

**Name of Candidate** ______________

**1. Appearance**

| | | | | | | | | |
|---|---|---|---|---|---|---|---|---|
| Sloppy | 1 | 2 | 3 | 4 | 5 | 6 | 7 | Neat |

**2. Attitude**

| | | | | | | | | |
|---|---|---|---|---|---|---|---|---|
| Unfriendly | 1 | 2 | 3 | 4 | 5 | 6 | 7 | Friendly |

**3. Assertiveness/Verbal Ability**

a. Responded completely to questions asked

| | | | | | | | | |
|---|---|---|---|---|---|---|---|---|
| Poor | 1 | 2 | 3 | 4 | 5 | 6 | 7 | Excellent |

b. Clarified personal background and related it to job opening and description

| | | | | | | | | |
|---|---|---|---|---|---|---|---|---|
| Poor | 1 | 2 | 3 | 4 | 5 | 6 | 7 | Excellent |

c. Able to explain and sell job abilities

| | | | | | | | | |
|---|---|---|---|---|---|---|---|---|
| Poor | 1 | 2 | 3 | 4 | 5 | 6 | 7 | Excellent |

d. Initiated questions regarding position and firm

| | | | | | | | | |
|---|---|---|---|---|---|---|---|---|
| Poor | 1 | 2 | 3 | 4 | 5 | 6 | 7 | Excellent |

e. Expressed thorough knowledge of personal goals and abilities

| | | | | | | | | |
|---|---|---|---|---|---|---|---|---|
| Poor | 1 | 2 | 3 | 4 | 5 | 6 | 7 | Excellent |

**4. Motivation**

| | | | | | | | | |
|---|---|---|---|---|---|---|---|---|
| Poor | 1 | 2 | 3 | 4 | 5 | 6 | 7 | High |

**5. Subject/Academic Knowledge**

| | | | | | | | | |
|---|---|---|---|---|---|---|---|---|
| Poor | 1 | 2 | 3 | 4 | 5 | 6 | 7 | Good |

**6. Stability**

| | | | | | | | | |
|---|---|---|---|---|---|---|---|---|
| Poor | 1 | 2 | 3 | 4 | 5 | 6 | 7 | Good |

**7. Composure**

| | | | | | | | | |
|---|---|---|---|---|---|---|---|---|
| Ill at ease | 1 | 2 | 3 | 4 | 5 | 6 | 7 | Relaxed |

**8. Personal Involvement/Activities, Clubs, Etc.**

| | | | | | | | | |
|---|---|---|---|---|---|---|---|---|
| Low | 1 | 2 | 3 | 4 | 5 | 6 | 7 | Very high |

**9. Mental Impression**

| | | | | | | | | |
|---|---|---|---|---|---|---|---|---|
| Dull | 1 | 2 | 3 | 4 | 5 | 6 | 7 | Alert |

**10. Adaptability**

| | | | | | | | | |
|---|---|---|---|---|---|---|---|---|
| Poor | 1 | 2 | 3 | 4 | 5 | 6 | 7 | Good |

**11. Speech Pronunciation**

| | | | | | | | | |
|---|---|---|---|---|---|---|---|---|
| Poor | 1 | 2 | 3 | 4 | 5 | 6 | 7 | Good |

**12. Overall Impression**

| | | | | | | | | |
|---|---|---|---|---|---|---|---|---|
| Unsatisfactory | 1 | 2 | 3 | 4 | 5 | 6 | 7 | Highly satisfactory |

**13. Would you hire this individual if you were permitted to make a decision right now?**

Yes No

## BE PREPARED TO CHANGE CAREERS

If you're like most people, you'll find that you'll follow several different career paths over your lifetime. This is a good thing in that it enables you to try different jobs and stay fresh and enthusiastic. The key to moving forward in your career is a willingness to change jobs, always searching for the career that will bring the most personal satisfaction and growth. This means that you'll have to write many cover letters and résumés and go through many interviews. Each time you change jobs, go through the steps in this section of the Prologue to be sure you're fully prepared. Good luck!

# understanding BUSINESS

eighth edition

# MANAGING WITHIN THE dynamic business environment

## Taking Risks and Making Profits

profile

**Getting to Know**

**X** Michele Hoskins

**of Michele Foods**

Not all businesspeople make the headlines. But their stories are interesting nonetheless. For example, Michele Hoskins says she comes from "a family of cooking women." Her mother was a great cook who made sure that Hoskins learned everything about cooking. One of the recipes Hoskins's mother taught her had been passed down from her great-great-grandmother, America Washington. Mrs. Washington, who was born a slave in the 1860s, served a family who did not like molasses on their pancakes. She developed a syrup for them made out of churned butter, cream, and honey. Today it is known as Honey Creme Syrup.

Hoskins's parents told her, "Anything that the mind can conceive can be achieved." When Hoskins was going through a divorce and was working at one part-time job after another, she read an article about women entrepreneurs and how they were succeeding. She decided then and there to become an entrepreneur herself because she wanted to be independent and to control her own destiny. So, she thought, why not form a company to sell her great-great-grandmother's syrup? She began to visualize the bottles and all the stores that would be selling the syrup. She sold her home, her car, and her jewelry to get the money she needed to start her business. Then she began making the syrup in her basement and taking it around to the local stores to sell. She would often go back and buy some herself to get the flow of sales going.

It took a lot of persistence for Hoskins to finally succeed. Eventually she got a $3 million contract from Denny's—after calling on the company *every week* for three years. So, how is she doing now? Honey Creme Syrup is being sold in 10,000 grocery stores, including Stop & Shop, Super Wal-Mart, and Albertson's. Sales are over $8 million. In addition to the syrup, Hoskins's company also sells condiments; for example, it sells condiments for Church's Chicken. Now Hoskins is so successful that she is eager to pass down her success to her own three children.

Hoskins has written a book about her experiences called *Sweet Expectations*. She writes about the obstacles she has faced, including a brain tumor that temporarily blinded her. Of course, she also writes about her many successes. For example, she was named the 2002 Entrepreneur of the Year by the Woman's Foodservices Forum. She has been on many TV shows, including *Oprah*. She believes that anything can be

LEARNING **goals**

After you have read and studied this chapter, you should be able to

1. Describe the relationship of businesses' profit to risk assumption and discuss how businesses and nonprofit organizations add to the standard of living and quality of life for all.
2. Explain the importance of entrepreneurship to the wealth of an economy.
3. Examine how the economic environment and taxes affect businesses.
4. Illustrate how the technological environment has affected businesses.
5. Identify various ways in which businesses can meet and beat competition.
6. Demonstrate how the social environment has changed and tell what the reaction of the business community has been.
7. Analyze what businesses must do to meet the global challenge, which includes war and terrorism.
8. Review how trends from the past are being repeated in the present and what such trends will mean for tomorrow's college graduate.

CHAPTER

**www.michelefoods.com**

achieved by "faith, hard work, and perseverance." Her enthusiasm makes her a great speaker. Because she believes in contributing to her community, Hoskins also mentors individuals who have an interest in the food business. (You can hear Hoskins tell the story of how and why she started her own business by visiting the company Web site at www.michelefoods.com and clicking on the video.)

The purpose of this text is to introduce you to the exciting and challenging world of business. Each chapter will begin with a story like this one. You will meet more successful entrepreneurs like Michele Hoskins who have started businesses of all kinds. You will also learn about people who work for others and have succeeded far beyond their original expectations. You will learn about all aspects of business: management, human resource management, marketing, accounting, finance, and more. You will also learn about businesses of all sizes, from hot-dog vendors in a local street market to huge global concerns like IBM. We begin by looking at some key terms and exploring the rapidly changing business environment so that you can start preparing to meet tomorrow's challenges today.

Sources: "Sweet Expectations: A Recipe for Success," *Black Enterprise,* December 2004, pp. 116–19, and www.michelefoods.com/, April 28, 2006.

**business**
Any activity that seeks to provide goods and services to others while operating at a profit.

**profit**
The amount of money a business earns above and beyond what it spends for salaries and other expenses.

**entrepreneur**
A person who risks time and money to start and manage a business.

**revenue**
The total amount of money a business takes in during a given period by selling goods and services.

**loss**
When a business's expenses are more than its revenues.

# BUSINESS AND ENTREPRENEURSHIP: REVENUES, PROFITS, AND LOSSES

Michele Hoskins is just one of thousands of people who have learned that one of the best ways to become a success in the United States, or almost anywhere else in the world, is to start a business. A **business** is any activity that seeks to provide goods and services to others while operating at a profit. **Profit** is the amount of money a business earns above and beyond what it spends for salaries and other expenses. Since not all businesses make a profit, starting a business can be risky. An **entrepreneur** is a person who risks time and money to start and manage a business.

Businesses provide people with the opportunity to become wealthy. Sam Walton of Wal-Mart began by opening one store in Arkansas and, over time, became the richest person in America; his heirs now have many billions of dollars. Bill Gates started Microsoft and is now the richest person in the world. *Forbes* magazine reports that there are at least 793 billionaires in over 40 different countries.[1] Maybe you will be one of them someday if you start your own business.

Businesses don't just make money for entrepreneurs. Businesses provide all of us with necessities such as food, clothing, housing, medical care, and transportation, as well as other goods and services that make our lives easier and better.

## Matching Risk with Profit

Profit, remember, is the amount of money a business earns *above and beyond* what it pays out for salaries and other expenses. For example, if you were to start a business selling hot dogs in the summer, you would have to pay for the cart rental, for the hot dogs and other materials, and for someone to run the cart while you were away. After you paid your employee and yourself, paid for the food and materials you used, paid the rent on the cart, and paid your taxes, any money left over would be profit. Keep in mind that profit is over and above the money you pay yourself in salary. You could use any profit you make to rent or buy a second cart and hire other employees. After a few summers, you might have a dozen carts employing dozens of workers.

**Revenue** is the total amount of money a business takes in during a given period by selling goods and services. A **loss** occurs when a business's expenses are more than its revenues. If a business loses money over time, it will likely have to close, putting its employees out of work. In fact, approximately 80,000 businesses in the United States close each year. Some owners close down one business to start another one or retire. Even though such closings are not failures, they are often reported as such in the statistics.

Hot dog vendors have expenses to pay, just like any other business. They have to subtract those expenses from revenues to determine what profit they make. What kind of expenses might street vendors avoid relative to those entrepreneurs who establish restaurants?

Starting a business involves risk. **Risk** is the chance an entrepreneur takes of losing time and money on a business that may not prove profitable. Even among companies that do make a profit, not all make the same amount. Those companies that take the most risk may make the most profit. There is a lot of risk involved, for example, in making a new kind of automobile. Similarly, it may involve additional risk to open a business in the inner city because insurance and land costs there are usually higher than in suburban areas, but the chance of making substantial profits in the inner city is also good because there's often less competition there than in other areas.[2]

**risk**
The chance an entrepreneur takes of losing time and money on a business that may not prove profitable.

## Businesses Add to the Standard of Living and Quality of Life

**standard of living**
The amount of goods and services people can buy with the money they have.

**quality of life**
The general well-being of a society in terms of political freedom, a clean natural environment, education, health care, safety, free time, and everything else that leads to satisfaction and joy.

**stakeholders**
All the people who stand to gain or lose by the policies and activities of a business.

Entrepreneurs such as Sam Walton (Wal-Mart) and Bill Gates (Microsoft) not only became wealthy themselves by starting successful businesses; they also provided employment for other people. Wal-Mart is currently the nation's largest private employer. Employees pay taxes that the federal government and local communities use to build hospitals, schools, playgrounds, and other facilities. Taxes are also used to help keep the environment clean and to support people in need. Businesses pay taxes to the federal government and local communities. That money can be used for schools, libraries, hospitals, and other such facilities. Thus, the wealth businesses generate and the taxes they pay may help everyone in their communities. A nation's businesses are part of an economic system that contributes to the standard of living and quality of life for everyone in the country.

The term **standard of living** refers to the amount of goods and services people can buy with the money they have. For example, the United States has one of the highest standards of living in the world, even though a few workers in some other countries, such as Germany and Japan, may make more money per hour. How can that be? Prices for goods and services in Germany and Japan are higher than in the United States, so what a person can buy in those countries is less than what a person in the United States can buy with the same amount of money. For example, a bottle of beer that in Japan may cost $7 may in the United States cost less than $1. A pound of rice may be five times more expensive in Japan than in the United States. Often, the reasons goods cost more in one country versus another include higher taxes and stricter government regulations. Finding the right level of taxes and regulation is an important step toward making a country (or a city) prosperous. We'll explore that issue more deeply in Chapter 2. At this point, it is enough to understand that the United States has such a high standard of living largely because of the wealth created by its businesses.

The term **quality of life** refers to the general well-being of a society in terms of political freedom, a clean natural environment, education, health care, safety, free time, and everything else that leads to satisfaction and joy. It is the joy life brings beyond the possession of goods. Maintaining a high quality of life requires the combined efforts of businesses, nonprofit organizations, and government agencies. The more money businesses create, the more is potentially available to improve the quality of life for everyone.

**You know that people have a high standard of living in areas where you see stores selling expensive merchandise. That includes major cities in relatively poor countries. A high standard of living doesn't necessarily translate into a high quality of life. Is it more important to have what you want or to want what you have?**

## Responding to the Various Business Stakeholders

**Stakeholders** are all the people who stand to gain or lose by the policies and activities of a business. Stakeholders include customers, employees, stockholders, suppliers, dealers, bankers, people in the surrounding community (e.g., community interest groups), environmentalists, and elected government leaders (see Figure 1.1 on page 6). All of these groups are figure I.I

**A BUSINESS AND ITS STAKEHOLDERS**

Often the needs of a firm's various stakeholders will conflict. For example, paying employees more may cut into stockholders' profits. Balancing such demands is a major role of business managers.

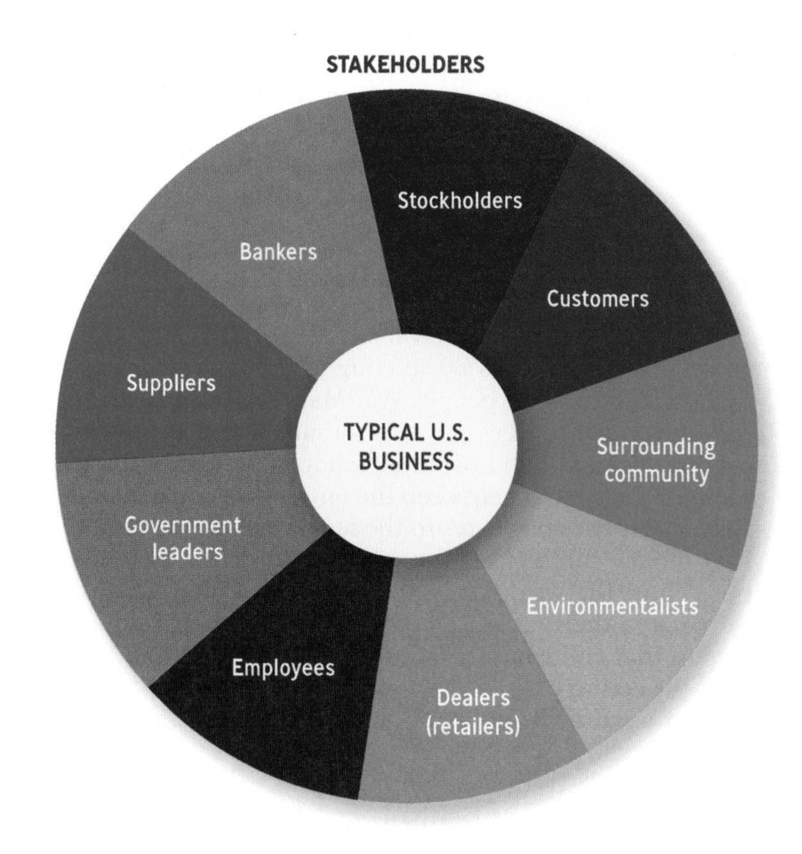


affected by the products, policies, and practices of businesses, and their concerns need to be addressed.

The challenge of the 21st century will be for organizations to balance, as much as possible, the needs of all stakeholders.[3] For example, the need for the business to make profits may be balanced against the needs of employees for sufficient income. The need to stay competitive may call for outsourcing jobs to other countries, but that might do great harm to the community because many jobs would be lost.[4] **Outsourcing** means contracting with other companies (often in other countries) to do some or all of the functions of a firm (e.g., production or accounting).[5] Outsourcing has had serious consequences in states where many jobs have been lost to overseas competitors. Companies have gone from outsourcing production jobs to outsourcing research and development and design functions. Such outsourcing may prove disastrous to those firms, in that overseas companies may use the information to produce their own, competitive products.[6]

**outsourcing**
Assigning various functions, such as accounting, production, security, maintenance, and legal work, to outside organizations.

The other side of the coin is *insourcing*. Many companies are setting up design and production facilities here in the United States.[7] For example, Hyundai is doing design and engineering work in Detroit and producing cars in Montgomery, Alabama. Honda and Toyota have been producing cars in the United States for years. Such insourcing creates many new jobs, and helps offset the number of jobs being outsourced.[8] It may be legal to outsource, but is that best for all the stakeholders, including workers? Business leaders must make a decision based on all factors, including the need to make a profit. As you can see, pleasing all stakeholders is not easy and calls for trade-offs that are not always pleasing to one or another stakeholder.

SPOTLIGHT ON small business www.ashoka.org

### Social Entrepreneurship

Bill Drayton has the kind of credentials that would make any businessperson proud. He was graduated from Harvard and went on to study at Oxford and Yale Law. He then worked for McKinsey, a consulting firm, and the Environmental Protection Agency. He is now the founder and chief executive of a group called Ashoka (it was named for a peace-minded, third-century-BC Indian emperor). Ashoka seeks out social entrepreneurs (it now supports some 1,500) and creates a network among them so that they can learn from one another.

For example, poor farmers in Bolivia were using the sharp edges of cans to shear alpaca. An entrepreneur created incentives for farmers to use shears instead of the cans, and to wash the fiber. He also came up with a simple but efficient distribution system that includes grading the wool. This results in more income for the farmers. Ashoka linked this entrepreneur with others around the world so they could learn from one another. In this case, a social entrepreneur in Nepal's Tibetan plateau learned about the new methods in Bolivia and was able to implement them quickly.

As Ashoka raises more money, it will be able to support projects such as this throughout the world. However, it needs more people who have creative ideas that they can apply to social problems, such as the need for clean water. The ideas have to be general enough to be used in multiple countries or areas, and the social entrepreneurs must have the highest ethical values so that they can become trusted change agents in the areas they serve. Can you see yourself as such a person? You could become a small-business owner in the United States, but you could also use the business skills you learn in this course to be a social entrepreneur in other countries. Can you see the possibilities?

Sources: Keith H. Hammonds, "A Lever Long Enough to Move the World," *Fast Company*, January 2005, pp. 61–63; www.ashoka.org, 2006; and Cheryl Dahle, "Next: A Nonprofit IPO?," *Fast Company*, April 2006, p. 36.

## Using Business Principles in Nonprofit Organizations

Despite their efforts to satisfy all their stakeholders, businesses cannot do everything that is needed to make a community all it can be. Nonprofit organizations—such as public schools, civic associations, charities, and groups devoted to social causes—also make major contributions to the welfare of society. A **nonprofit organization** is an organization whose goals do not include making a personal profit for its owners or organizers.[9] Nonprofit organizations often do strive for financial gains, but such gains are used to meet the stated social or educational goals of the organization rather than personal profit.[10] *Social entrepreneurs* are people who use business principles to start and manage organizations that are not for profit and help countries with their social issues.[11] One such entrepreneur is featured in the Spotlight on Small Business box.

**nonprofit organization**
An organization whose goals do not include making a personal profit for its owners or organizers.

Your interests may lead you to work for a nonprofit organization. That doesn't mean, however, that you shouldn't study business. If you want to start or work in a nonprofit organization, you'll need to learn business skills such as information management, leadership, marketing, and financial management. Therefore, the knowledge and skills you acquire in this and other business courses will be useful for careers in any organization, including nonprofits.

Businesses, nonprofit organizations, and volunteer groups often strive to accomplish the same objectives.[12] All such groups can help feed people, provide them with clothing and housing, clean up the environment and keep it clean, and improve the standard of living and quality of life for all.

Starting any business, profit or nonprofit, can be risky. Once an entrepreneur has started a business, there is usually a need for good managers and other workers to keep the business going. Not all entrepreneurs are skilled at being managers. We shall explore entrepreneurship in more detail right after the Progress Assessment.

Entrepreneurship is available to everyone in the United States. Statistics show that the number of new ventures being started by Hispanic entrepreneurs is many times greater than the average. But other ethnic groups are also eager to start their own businesses and improve the standard of living and quality of life for them and the people they hire. Who are the new entrepreneurs in your town?

**progress assessment**

- What is the difference between *revenue* and *profit*?
- What is the difference between *standard of living* and *quality of life*?
- What is risk, and how is it related to profit?
- What do the terms *stakeholders* and *outsourcing* mean?

## ENTREPRENEURSHIP VERSUS WORKING FOR OTHERS

There are two ways to succeed in business. One way is to rise up through the ranks of large companies like IBM or General Electric. The advantage of working for others is that somebody else assumes the entrepreneurial risk and provides you with benefits such as paid vacation time and health insurance. Most people choose that option. It is a very good option and can lead to a happy and prosperous life.

The other, riskier path is to start your own business (become an entrepreneur). The national anthem, "The Star Spangled Banner," says that the United States is the "land of the free and the home of the brave." Part of being free is being able to own your own business and to reap the profits from that business. But freedom to succeed also means freedom to fail, and many small businesses fail each year. Thus, it takes a brave person, like Michele Hoskins (see this chapter's Opening Profile), to start a small business. Furthermore, as an entrepreneur you don't receive any benefits such as paid vacation time, day care, a company car, or health insurance. You have to provide them for yourself! Before you take on the challenge of entrepreneurship, you should study those who have succeeded to learn the process. You can do that by talking to them personally or by reading about them in Chapter 6 of this text and in other books and magazines.

### Opportunities for Entrepreneurs

The United States provides opportunities for all. Often the most attractive opportunity is that of owning and managing your own business. Millions of people from all over the world have taken the entrepreneurial challenge and succeeded. For example, the number of Hispanic-owned businesses in the United States is growing three times the national average.[13] There is also rapid growth in businesses owned by Asians, Pacific Islanders, Native Americans, and Alaskan Natives. Some 30 percent of Koreans who immigrated to the United States now own their own businesses.

Top African American business leaders include Kase Lawal of CAMAC International, Gregory Jackson of Prestige Automotive, Bill Easter III of Duke Energy, Ann M. Fudge of Young & Rubicam Brands, and John W. Thompson of Symantec.[14] Tremendous opportunities exist for all men and women willing to take the risk of starting a business. Notice that we said *men and women*. The number of women business owners has dramatically increased in the last 20 years. In 1980, there were about 3 million women business owners; by 2005, there were over 10.6 million firms that were 50 percent or more women-owned. Women now own over a third of all businesses. Names you may be familiar with include Oprah Winfrey, Donna Karan, and Lillian Vernon.[15]

## The Importance of Entrepreneurs to the Creation of Wealth

Have you ever wondered why some countries are relatively wealthy and others poor? Economists have been studying the issue of wealth creation for many years. They began the process by studying potential sources of wealth to determine which are the most important. Over time, they came up with five factors that seemed to contribute to wealth. They called them **factors of production**. Figure 1.2 shows those five factors. They are:

**factors of production**
The resources used to create wealth: land, labor, capital, entrepreneurship, and knowledge.

1. Land (or natural resources).
2. Labor (workers).
3. Capital. (This includes machines, tools, buildings, or whatever else is used in the production of goods. It does *not* include money; money is used to buy factors of production—it is not a factor itself.)
4. Entrepreneurship.
5. Knowledge.

Traditionally, business and economics textbooks emphasized only four factors of production: land, labor, capital, and entrepreneurship. But the late management expert and business consultant Peter Drucker said that the most important factor of production in our economy is and always will be knowledge. Workers in the high-tech industries in the Silicon Valley area of California are sometimes called *knowledge workers*. Many have become millionaires while still in their 20s.

If you were to analyze rich countries versus poor countries to see what causes the differences in the levels of wealth, you'd have to look at the factors of production in each country. Such analyses have revealed that some relatively poor countries often have plenty of land and natural resources. Russia, for example, has vast areas of land with many resources, but is not a rich country. In contrast, Japan is a relatively rich country but is poor in land and other natural resources. Therefore, land isn't the critical element for wealth creation.

figure 1.2
THE FIVE FACTORS OF PRODUCTION

| | |
|---|---|
| Land: | Land and other natural resources are used to make homes, cars, and other products. |
| Labor: | People have always been an important resource in producing goods and services, but many people are now being replaced by technology. |
| Capital: | Capital includes machines, tools, buildings, and other means of manufacturing. |
| Entrepreneurship: | All the resources in the world have little value unless entrepreneurs are willing to take the risk of starting businesses to use those resources. |
| Knowledge: | Information technology has revolutionized business, making it possible to quickly determine wants and needs and to respond with desired goods and services. |

www.heritage.org

### Freedom Equals Prosperity

Recent studies have found that the freer a country is, the wealthier its citizens are. Freedom includes freedom from excess taxation, government regulations, and restrictions on trade. The average per capita gross domestic product (GDP)—the total value of all final goods and services produced in a country divided by the number of people in the country—for the freest countries greatly exceeds that in less-free countries. For example, Hong Kong is considered one of the freest economies in the world and has a per capita GDP of $25,576. The same is true of Singapore, with a per capita GDP of $27,321. At the other end of the scale, you will find Libya, with a per capita GDP of $4,579. Some countries make even less per capita: Haiti, for example, has a GDP of $338, and Burundi's is just $143.

For the United States, there is good news and bad news in these figures. The bad news is that the United States has slipped from number 4 on the list of most-free countries to 12th—tied with Switzerland. The good news is the reason the United States has fallen is that other countries—such as Luxembourg, Ireland, Estonia, the United Kingdom, and Denmark—have become more free. That is good news because freedom means freedom of trade as well as other freedoms, such as lower taxes and fewer regulations. Nonetheless, the United States is a relatively free country and its per capita GDP is a high $32,517. As more countries become free, the standard of living around the world increases. And that is a good thing.

Sources: Donald Lambro, "Economic Freedom Slippage," *Washington Times,* January 13, 2005, p. A17; William Peterson, "Global Competiton," *Washington Times,* February 15, 2005, p. A19; and Mary Anastasia O'Grady, "Wish They All Could Be Like Estonia," *The Wall Street Journal,* January 4, 2006, p. A10.

Most poor countries have many laborers, so it's not labor that's the primary source of wealth today. Laborers need to find work to make a contribution; that is, they need entrepreneurs to provide jobs for them. Furthermore, capital—machinery and tools—is now becoming available in world markets, so capital isn't the missing ingredient. Capital is not productive without entrepreneurs to put it to use.

What makes rich countries rich today is a combination of entrepreneurship and the effective use of knowledge. Together, lack of entrepreneurship and the absence of knowledge among workers, along with the lack of freedom, contribute to keeping poor countries poor. The box called Reaching Beyond Our Borders discusses the importance of freedom to economic development.

Entrepreneurship also makes some states and cities in the United States rich while others remain relatively poor. The business environment either encourages or discourages entrepreneurship. In the following section, we'll explore what makes up the business environment and how to build an environment that encourages growth and job creation.

### progress assessment

- What are some of the advantages of working for others?
- What benefits do you lose by being an entrepreneur and what do you gain?
- What are the five factors of production? Which factors are the key to wealth?

**business environment**
The surrounding factors that either help or hinder the development of businesses.

## THE BUSINESS ENVIRONMENT

The **business environment** consists of the surrounding factors that either help or hinder the development of businesses. Figure 1.3 shows the five elements in the business environment:

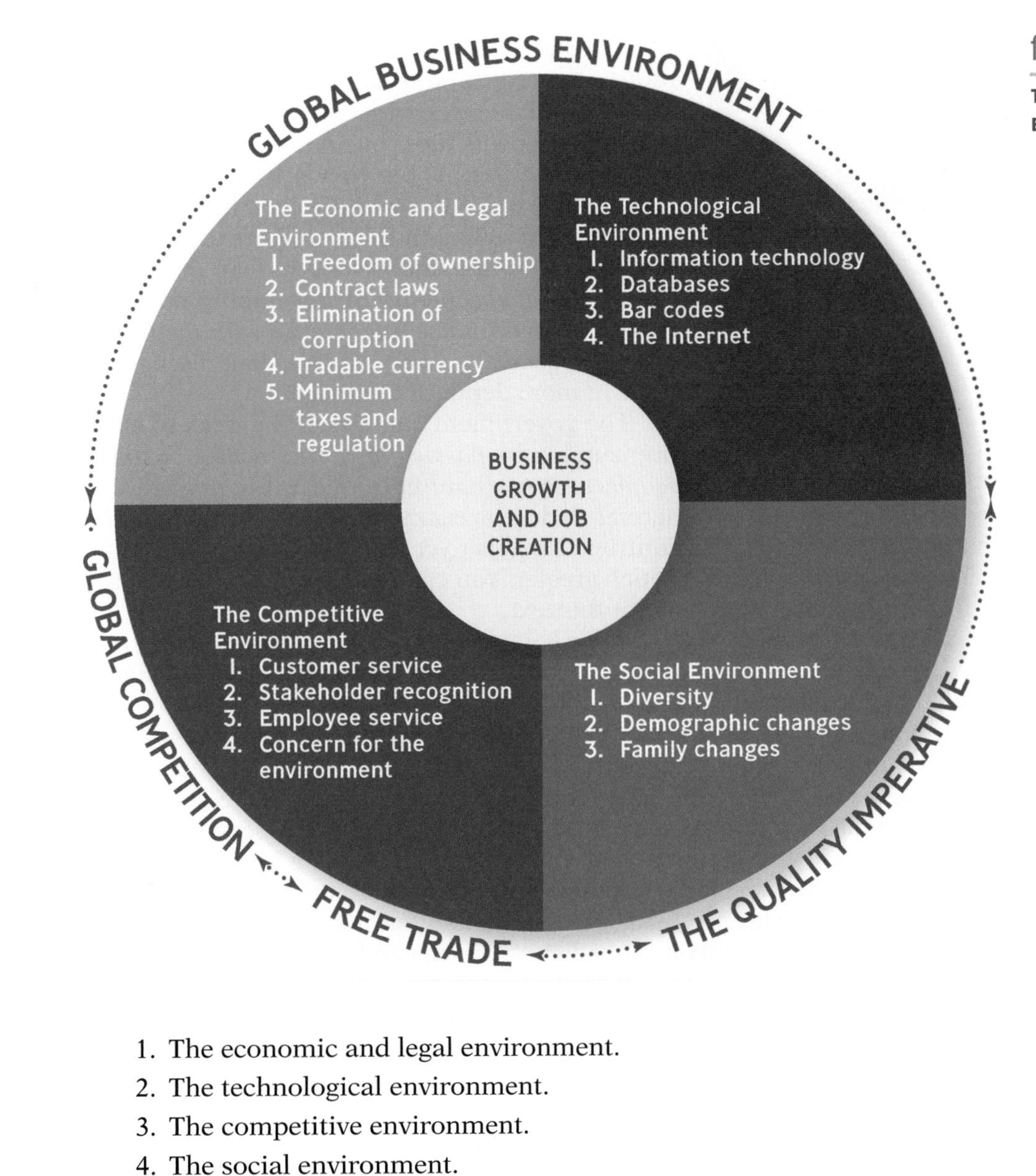


figure 1.3
**TODAY'S DYNAMIC BUSINESS ENVIRONMENT**

1. The economic and legal environment.
2. The technological environment.
3. The competitive environment.
4. The social environment.
5. The global business environment.

Businesses grow and prosper in a healthy environment. The results are job growth and the wealth that makes it possible to have both a high standard of living and a high quality of life. The wrong environmental conditions, in contrast, lead to business failure, loss of jobs, and a low standard of living and quality of life. In short, creating the right business environment is the foundation for social progress of all kinds, including good schools, clean air and water, good health care, and low rates of crime.

## The Economic and Legal Environment

People are willing to start new businesses if they believe that the risk of losing their money isn't too great. Part of that risk involves the economic system and how government works with or against businesses. Government can do a lot to lessen the risk of starting businesses and thus increase entrepreneurship and wealth. For example, a government can *keep taxes and regulations to a minimum.*

Starting a business in some countries is much harder than in others. In India, for example, a person has to go through an extraordinary and time-consuming bureaucratic process to get permission to start a business—and with no certainty of success. Nonetheless, those businesses that do get started can become a major source of wealth and employment. This jewelry business is one small example. Can you imagine the opportunities and wealth that might be created with just a little more freedom in this country of over a billion people?

Another way for government to actively promote entrepreneurship is to *allow private ownership of businesses.* In some countries, the government owns most businesses, and there's little incentive for people to work hard or create profit. All around the world today, however, governments are selling those businesses to private individuals to create more wealth. One of the best things the governments of developing countries can do is to *minimize interference with the free exchange of goods and services.* We shall discuss that issue in more depth in Chapter 2.

The government can lessen the risks of entrepreneurship by *passing laws that enable businesspeople to write contracts that are enforceable in court.* The Universal Commercial Code, for example, covers things like contracts and warranties. In countries that don't yet have such laws, the risks of starting a business are that much greater. You can read more about such laws in Bonus Chapter A at the end of this text.

The government can also *establish a currency that's tradable in world markets.* That is, you can buy and sell goods and services anywhere in the world using that currency.

Finally, the government can help *minimize corruption* in business and in its own ranks. It's hard to do business in many poor countries because the governments are so corrupt. It's very difficult in such countries to get permission to build a factory or open a store without a government permit, which is obtained largely through bribery of public officials. Among businesses themselves, leaders can threaten competitors and minimize competition.

There are many laws in the United States to minimize corruption, and businesses can flourish as a result. Nonetheless, corrupt and illegal activities at some companies do negatively affect the business community and the economy as a whole.[16] The news media widely report scandals involving people like Martha Stewart and companies such as Enron. You also hear about sports scandals (e.g., the taking of performance enhancers), church scandals, and government scandals. Such scandals go across borders and across organizations. Ethics is so important to the success of businesses and the economy as a whole that we feature ethics boxes in each chapter and devote Chapter 4 to the subject.

The capitalist system relies heavily on honesty, integrity, and high ethical standards. Failure of those fundamentals can weaken the whole system; the faltering economy of the early 2000s was due in part to such failure. It is easy to see the damage caused by the poor moral and ethical behavior of some businesspeople. What is not so obvious is the damage caused by the moral and ethical lapses of the everyday consumer—that is, you and me. The Making Ethical Decisions box on page 13 discusses that issue in more depth.

## The Technological Environment

Since prehistoric times, humans have felt the need to create tools that make their jobs easier. Various tools and machines developed throughout history have changed the business environment tremendously, but few technological changes have had a more comprehensive and lasting impact on businesses than the emergence of information technology (IT): computers, modems, cellular phones, and so on. Chief among these developments is the Internet. Although many Internet firms have failed in recent years, the Internet is a major force in business

*** MAKING

## ethical decisions

### Ethics Begins with You

Despite the fact that the vast majority of businesspeople are ethical, television, movies, and the print media all paint a dismal picture of ethics among businesspeople, government officials, students, and citizens in general. It is easy to criticize the ethics of people whose names appear in the headlines. It is more difficult to see the moral and ethical misbehavior of your own social group. Do you find some of the behaviors of your friends morally or ethically questionable? A recent study found that 26 percent of business majors admitted to cheating.

A recent survey found that among the number of employees calling in sick, which has reached a five-year high, three-fifths were not sick at all. Other employees have been caught doing personal business at work, such as doing their taxes. And others play video games on their work computers. We're sure you can add many more examples of employees choosing to do unethical things at work. One of the major trends in business today is that many companies are creating ethics codes to guide their employees' behavior. We believe that this trend toward improving ethical behavior is so important that we've made it a major theme of this book. Throughout the text you'll see boxes, like this one, called Making Ethical Decisions. The boxes contain short descriptions of situations that pose ethical dilemmas and ask what you would do to resolve them. The idea is for you to think about the moral and ethical dimensions of every decision you make.

Here is your first ethical dilemma: You are doing a project outside of your work. The project will need paper, pens, and other materials available at work. You have noticed other employees taking home such materials. You are thinking about doing the same. What is the problem in this situation? What are your alternatives? What are the consequences of each alternative? Which alternative will you choose? Is your choice ethical?

Source: Sue Shellenbarger, "How and Why We Lie at the Office: From Pilfered Pens to Padded Accounts," *The Wall Street Journal,* March 24, 2005, p. DI, and Helena Oh, "Biz Majors Get an F for Honesty," *BusinessWeek,* February 6, 2006, p. 14.

today.[17] We discuss the Internet's impact on businesses throughout the text. In addition, we provide Internet exercises at the end of each chapter to give you some hands-on experience with various Internet uses.

**How Technology Benefits Workers and You** One of the advantages of working for others is that the company often provides the tools and technology to make your job more productive. **Technology** means everything from phones and copiers to computers, medical imaging devices, personal digital assistants, and the various software programs that make business processes more effective, efficient, and productive. *Effectiveness* means producing the desired result. *Efficiency* means producing goods and services using the least amount of resources. **Productivity** is the amount of output you generate given the amount of input (e.g., hours worked). The more you can produce in any given period of time, the more money you are worth to companies.

**technology**
Everything from phones and copiers to computers, medical imaging devices, personal digital assistants, and the various software programs that make business processes more efficient and productive.

**productivity**
The amount of output you generate given the amount of input.

Technology affects people in all industries. For example, Don Glenn, a farmer in Decatur, Alabama, uses his personal computer to compare data from last year's harvest with infrared satellite photos of his farm that show which crops are flourishing. He has a desktop terminal called a DTN that allows him to check the latest grain prices, and he uses AgTalk, a Web-based bulletin board, to converse with other farmers from all over the world. He also bids for

## DEALING WITH change

### Amazon.com Must Change with the Times

Jeff Bezos started Amazon.com back in 1995. His first task was to raise a million dollars through private financing. Eventually, 22 different investors put up the money, but the venture was considered very risky. By the year 2000, people were predicting that the company would be unable to service its debt and would soon go bankrupt. Bezos had to dodge and weave to keep the company going and to assure investors that it was viable. As companies like Amazon.com grew more successful, traditional retailers started their own online services to compete. Bezos had to counter these new competitors by expanding the company's offerings. For example, he began to offer free shipping for orders of $99 or more. Then he made it $49 or more. Eventually, he ended up with free shipping for orders over $25.

Constant adjustments to the market have made Amazon.com one of the fastest-growing companies in the United States. Over time, the company added new products to its offerings. Now it sells everything from automobiles and baby items to video games and watches.

Dealing with change is such an important subject in businesses today that we will have boxes like this in almost every chapter. The idea is to keep you informed of the changes that are occurring and the ways that companies are adapting. You have seen, for example, how automobile companies are trying to adapt to higher gas prices. Some are producing hybrid vehicles and diesel cars that use less gas. Small companies are learning to compete with larger companies by going on the Internet.

Sources: Bob Walker, "Because Optimism Is Essential," *Inc.*, April 2004, pp. 149–50; Robert Buderi, "E-Commerce Gets Smarter," *Technology Review*, April 2005, pp. 54–59, and www.amazon.com, 2006.

www.amazon.com

bulk fertilizer on XSAg.com, an online agricultural exchange. High-tech equipment tells Glenn how and where to spread fertilizer and seed, tracks yields yard by yard, and allows him to maintain high profit margins.

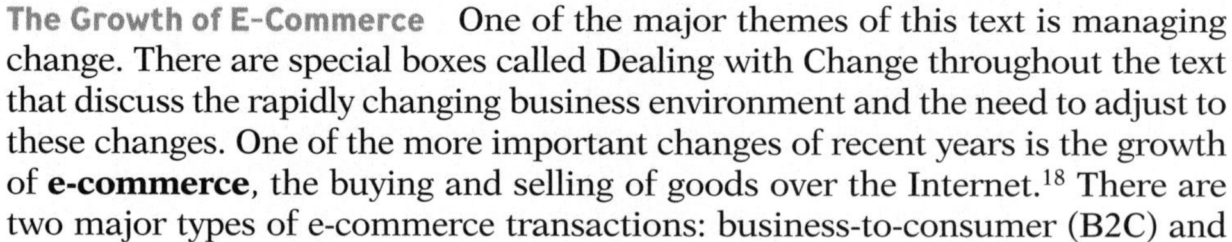

**The Growth of E-Commerce** One of the major themes of this text is managing change. There are special boxes called Dealing with Change throughout the text that discuss the rapidly changing business environment and the need to adjust to these changes. One of the more important changes of recent years is the growth of **e-commerce**, the buying and selling of goods over the Internet.[18] There are two major types of e-commerce transactions: business-to-consumer (B2C) and business-to-business (B2B). As important as the Internet has been in the consumer market, it has become even more important in the B2B market, which consists of selling goods and services from one business to another, such as IBM selling consulting services to a local bank.[19]

EBay is one of the big winners in the fight for Internet attention. What Internet sites are your favorites? Do you think that buying items over the Internet is going to greatly affect the shopping malls in your area?

The rise of Internet marketing came so fast and furious that it drew hundreds of competitors into the fray. Many of the new Internet companies failed. Companies such as Pets.com, CDnow, Internet Capital Group, Peapod, eToys, and Drkoop.com have failed entirely or seen their stock prices drop dramatically. Many B2B stocks experienced similar failures. There is no question that some Internet businesses will grow and prosper, but along the way there will continue to be lots of failures, just as there have been in traditional businesses. Traditional businesses will have to learn how to deal with the new competition from B2B and B2C firms, and vice versa. The Dealing with Change box discusses how Amazon.com is adapting to rapid change.

**e-commerce**
The buying and selling of goods and services over the Internet.

**Using Technology to Be Responsive to Customers** Another of the major themes of this text is that businesses succeed or fail largely because of how they treat their customers.[20] The businesses that are most responsive to customer wants and needs will succeed, and those that do not respond to customers will not be as successful.[21] One way traditional retailers can respond to the Internet revolution is to use technology to become much more responsive to customers. For example, businesses mark goods with Universal Product Codes (bar codes)—those series of lines and numbers that you see on most consumer packaged goods. Bar codes can be used to tell retailers what product you bought, in what size and color, and at what price. A scanner at the checkout counter can read that information and put it into a database.

**database**
An electronic storage file where information is kept; one use of databases is to store vast amounts of information about consumers.

**identity theft**
The obtaining of private information about a person, such as Social Security number and/or credit card number, and using that information for illegal purposes, such as buying things with it.

A **database** is an electronic storage file where information is kept. One use of databases is to store vast amounts of information about consumers. For example, a retailer may ask for your name, address, and telephone number so that it can put you on its mailing list. The information you give the retailer is added to the database. Because companies routinely trade database information, many retailers know what you buy and from whom you buy it. Using that information, companies can send you catalogs and other direct mail advertising that offers the kind of products you might want, as indicated by your past purchases. The use of databases enables stores to carry only the merchandise that the local population wants.

Unfortunately, the gathering of personal information about people has also led to identity theft. **Identity theft** is the obtaining of private information about a person, such as Social Security number and/or credit card number, and using that information for illegal purposes, such as buying things with it. ChoicePoint, the leading provider of identification and verification services for businesses, for example, sold private data on 145,000 people to criminals. Some 180,000 people who used MasterCard credit cards at Polo Ralph Lauren may have had their private information stolen.[22] The Federal Trade Commission estimates that about 10 million Americans are victims of identity theft each year. What you should learn from these examples is to be very careful to limit those to whom you give your private information such as credit card numbers and Social Security number.[23]

Once an identity thief has obtained your social security number, credit card number, address, and such he or she can charge goods and services to your account. Do you know the limit you are liable for?

## The Competitive Environment

Competition among businesses has never been greater than it is today. Some companies have found a competitive edge by focusing on quality. The goal for many companies is zero defects—no mistakes in making products.[24] However, simply making a high-quality product isn't enough to allow a company to stay competitive in world markets. Companies now have to offer both high-quality products and outstanding service at competitive prices (value). Figure 1.4 on page 16 shows how competition has changed businesses from the traditional model to a new, world-class model.

figure 1.4

**HOW COMPETITION HAS CHANGED BUSINESS**

| TRADITIONAL BUSINESSES | WORLD-CLASS BUSINESSES |
|---|---|
| Customer satisfaction | Delighting the customer[1] |
| Customer orientation | Customer and stakeholder orientation[2] |
| Profit orientation | Profit and social orientation[3] |
| Reactive ethics | Proactive ethics[4] |
| Product orientation | Quality and service orientation |
| Managerial focus | Customer focus |

[1] *Delight* is a term from total quality management. *Bewitch* and *fascinate* are alternative terms.

[2] Stakeholders include employees, stockholders, suppliers, dealers (retailers), and the community; the goal is to please *all* stakeholders.

[3] A social orientation goes beyond profit to do what is right and good for others.

[4] *Proactive* means doing the right thing before anyone tells you to do it. *Reactive* means responding to criticism after it happens.

**Competing by Exceeding Customer Expectations** Manufacturers and service organizations throughout the world have learned that today's customers are very demanding. Not only do they want good quality at low prices, but they want great service as well. Every manufacturing and service organization in the world should have a sign over its door telling its workers that the customer is king. Business is becoming customer-driven, not management-driven as in the past. This means that customers' wants and needs must come first.[25]

Customer-driven organizations include Nordstrom department stores (which have a very generous return policy) and Disney amusement parks (which are kept clean and appeal to all ages). Successful organizations must now listen more closely to customers to determine their wants and needs, then adjust the firm's products, policies, and practices to meet those demands. We will explore these concepts in more depth in Chapter 13.

**Competing by Restructuring and Empowerment** To meet the needs of customers, firms must give their frontline workers (office clerks, front-desk people at hotels, salespeople, etc.) the responsibility, authority, freedom, training, and equipment they need to respond quickly to customer requests and to make other decisions essential to producing quality goods and providing good service. This is called **empowerment**, and we'll be talking about that process throughout this book. To implement a policy of empowerment, managers must train frontline people to make decisions without the need to consult managers.

**empowerment**
Giving frontline workers the responsibility, authority, and freedom to respond quickly to customer requests.

Empowering employees leads to developing entirely new organization structures to meet the changing needs of customers and employees. As many companies have discovered, it sometimes takes years to restructure an organization so that managers are willing to give up some of their authority and employees are willing to assume more responsibility. We'll discuss such organizational changes and models in Chapter 8.

## The Social Environment

**demography**
The statistical study of the human population with regard to its size, density, and other characteristics such as age, race, gender, and income.

**Demography** is the statistical study of the human population with regard to its size, density, and other characteristics such as age, race, gender, and income. In this book, we're particularly interested in the demographic trends that most affect businesses and career choices. The U.S. population is going through major changes that are dramatically affecting how people live, where they live, what they buy, and how they spend their time. Furthermore, tremendous population shifts are leading to new opportunities for some firms and to declining opportunities for others.

**Managing Diversity** Diversity has come to mean much more than recruiting and keeping minorities and women. Many more groups are now included in diversity efforts. For example, the list of 26 diversity groups identified by Federated Department Stores includes seniors, the disabled, homosexuals, atheists, extroverts, introverts, married people, singles, and the devout.

Companies have responded to a diverse customer base by hiring a more diverse workforce to serve them. AT&T, for example, is one of the largest data communications companies in the world. The company's workforce is 51 percent female and 34 percent people of color; people of color also represent 26 percent of SBC's management team. More than 75 percent of Fortune 1,000 companies have some sort of diversity initiative. Some, like Kodak, have a chief diversity officer (CDO) in the executive suite. In short, companies are taking diversity management seriously.[26]

When you do business in more than 60 countries, you learn the value of diversity.
Each day Cargill does business in food, nutrition, agriculture and supply chain management. With more than 100,000 employees in 60 countries around the world, our work in such diverse communities has made us very aware of the importance of diversity. We've learned that no one has a monopoly on good ideas and that they can come from anyone, anywhere. We're committed to employee and supplier diversity because we know it adds value to what we do for our customers ... as well as promoting prosperity in communities everywhere. For more information, visit Cargill.com
Cargill
Nourishing Ideas. Nourishing People.
www.cargill.com
©2005 Cargill, Incorporated


Many large companies are emphasizing their diversity initiatives. Diversity means more than ethnicity or race. It makes sense for companies to search for a diverse workforce because the customer base is likely to be just as diverse and often needs special attention. Do you see lots of diversity among college students? What are the benefits and drawbacks?

The number of legal and illegal immigrants has had a dramatic effect on many cities. The schools and hospitals have been especially affected. Governments are adapting to the inflows by changing signs, brochures, and forms to other languages. They are also changing voting ballots and making every effort possible to adapt. Is your city one of those that has experienced such changes? What are some of the impacts you've noticed?

**The Increase in the Number of Older Americans** People ages 45 to 54 are currently the richest group in U.S. society. They spend more than others on everything except health care and thus represent a lucrative market for restaurants, transportation, entertainment, education, and so on. By 2010 the number of citizens over 60 will be about 56 million, and by 2020 they will be more than 23 percent of the population. What do such demographics mean for you and for businesses in the future? Think of the products and services the middle-aged and elderly will need—travel, medicine, nursing homes, assisted-living facilities, adult day care, home health care, recreation, and the like—and you'll see opportunities for successful businesses of the 21st century. Businesses that cater to older consumers will have the opportunity for exceptional growth in the near future. For example, there are lots of computer games for young people, but senior citizens may enjoy playing games and doing other things on the computer as well. The market is huge.

On the other hand, retired people will be draining the economy of wealth. The Social Security issue has become one of the major issues today. The pay-as-you-go system (this means that today's workers pay for today's retirees) worked just fine in 1940, when 42 workers supported each retiree. But by 1960 there were only five workers per retiree, and today that number is barely three and dropping.[27] When the baby-boom generation (those people born between 1946 and 1964) retires, it will be closer to two.

Here is the situation: Since 1985, Social Security tax revenues have exceeded benefit payments. But the government has been spending that money instead of leaving it in a Social Security account. In 2018, less money will be coming into Social Security than will be going out.[28] The government will have to do something to make up for the shortfall. There are several options, none of them particularly good for you: raise taxes, cut Social Security benefits (e.g., raise the retirement age), reduce spending elsewhere (e.g., cut social programs), or borrow on the world market.[29]

In short, paying Social Security to senior citizens in the future will draw huge amounts of money from the economy.[30] That is why there is so much discussion about what to do with Social Security in the media today. One option involves setting up personal savings accounts to allow young people to invest part of their Social Security money.[31] This is just one of many options available to the government today. You may want to research other options that are being discussed. After all, your welfare at retirement age depends on the decisions made now.

**Two-Income Families** Several factors have led to a dramatic growth in two-income families in the United States. The high costs of housing and of maintaining a comfortable lifestyle, the high level of taxes, and the cultural emphasis on "having it all" have made it difficult if not impossible for many households to live on just one income. Furthermore, many women today simply want a career outside the home.

One result of this trend is a host of programs that companies have implemented in response to the demands of busy two-income families. IBM and Procter & Gamble, for example, each offer employees pregnancy benefits, parental leave, flexible work schedules, and elder care programs. Some companies offer referral services that provide counseling to parents in search of child care or elder care. Such trends are creating many new opportunities for graduates in human resource management.

Workplace changes due to the rise of two-income families create many job opportunities in day care, counseling, and other related fields. You'll learn more about what's happening in human resource management in Chapter 11.

**Single Parents** The rapid growth of single-parent households has had a major effect on businesses as well. It is a tremendous task to work full-time and raise a family. Welfare rules force single parents to work after a certain period. Single parents have encouraged businesses to implement programs such as family leave (where workers can take time off to attend to a sick child) and flextime (where workers can come in or leave at selected times). Again, you will be able to read about such programs in more detail in Chapter 11.

## The Global Environment

The global environment of business is so important that we show it as surrounding all other environmental influences (see again Figure 1.3). Two important environmental changes in recent years have been the growth of international competition and the increase of free trade among nations. Two things that have led to more trade are the improvements in transportation and communication. These changes include more efficient distribution systems (we'll talk about these in Chapter 15) and communication advances such as the Internet. World trade (sometimes called globalization) has greatly improved living standards around the world. For example, the number of East Asian people living on less than a dollar a day has declined from 56 percent to less than 16 percent.[32] China and India have become major U.S. competitors. Lenovo, a Chinese firm, recently bought IBM's PC unit.[33] Shop at Wal-Mart or most other American retail stores and you can't help but be impressed by the

The agreement between Lenovo and IBM is just one of many that you can expect now that the world has become so interdependent. Companies from the United States are building many of their products overseas, but many foreign companies, such as auto firms, are building their products in the United States. Do you see the globalization of companies as basically a good thing or not?

number of "Made in China" stickers you see. Call for computer help and you are as likely to be talking with someone in India as someone in the United States.

World trade has its benefits and costs. You'll read much more about the importance of global business in Chapter 3 and in the Reaching Beyond Our Borders boxes throughout the text.

**War and Terrorism** The war in Iraq that began in 2003 has drawn billions of dollars from the American economy. Some companies, including those that make bullets and tanks and uniforms, have benefited greatly. Most companies, however, have lost workers to the armed forces and have grown more slowly as money has been diverted to the war effort. The threat of other wars makes it necessary to spend even more money on the military. Such expenditures are a major focus of the government and are subject to much debate.

The threat of terrorism also adds greatly to organizational costs, including the cost of security personnel, security equipment, and insurance (firms are finding it difficult to get insurance against terrorist attacks). Airlines, for example, have had to install stronger cockpit doors, buy more security equipment, and hire new security personnel. The U.S. government has also experienced huge cost increases because of domestic security issues.

There seems to be a movement toward democracy in many parts of the world, and that could mean greater prosperity and peace.[34] Businesspeople, like all citizens, benefit from a peaceful and prosperous world. One way to lessen tensions around the world is to foster global economic growth using both profit-making organizations and nonprofit organizations, as discussed earlier.

**How Global Changes Affect You** As businesses expand to serve global markets, new jobs will be created in both manufacturing and service industries. U.S. exports are expected to continue to increase under new trade agreements that will lead to expansion of the job market both in the United States and globally. Global trade also means global competition. The students who will prosper are those who are prepared for the markets of tomorrow. That means that you must prepare yourself now to compete in a rapidly changing worldwide environment. Rapid changes create a need for continuous learning. In other words, be prepared to continue your education throughout your career. Colleges will offer updated courses in computer technology, telecommunications, language skills, and other subjects you'll need to stay competitive. Students have every reason to be optimistic about job opportunities in the future if they prepare themselves well.

**progress assessment**

- What are four ways the government can foster entrepreneurship?
- What's the definition of productivity?
- What is *empowerment*?
- What are some of the major issues having to do with Social Security today?

**goods**
Tangible products such as computers, food, clothing, cars, and appliances.

## THE EVOLUTION OF AMERICAN BUSINESS

Many managers and workers are losing their jobs in major manufacturing firms. Businesses in the United States have become so productive that, compared to the past, fewer workers are needed in industries that produce goods. **Goods** are tangible products such as computers, food, clothing, cars, and appliances. Due to the increasing impact of technology and global competition, shouldn't we be concerned about the prospect of high unemployment rates and low incomes? Where will the jobs be when you graduate? These important questions force us all to look briefly at the U.S. economy and its future.

### Progress in the Agricultural and Manufacturing Industries

The United States has seen strong economic development since the 1800s. The agricultural industry led the way, providing food for the United States and much of the world. Cyrus McCormick's invention of the harvester in 1834 and other inventions, such as the cotton gin, and modern improvements on such equipment did much to make farming successful. The modern farming industry has become so efficient through the use of technology that the number of farmers has dropped from about 33 percent of the population to less than 2 percent today. The number of farms in the United States declined from some 5.7 million at the beginning of the 20th century to under 2 million today. However, average farm size is now about 455 acres versus 160 acres in the past. In other words, agriculture is still a major industry in the United States. What has changed is that the millions of small farms that existed previously have been replaced by some huge farms, some merely large farms, and some small but highly specialized farms. The loss of farmwork-

Agriculture is one of the largest and most important industries in the United States. Use of technology has led to increased productivity and made farmers more efficient, resulting in larger farms. This trend has meant less expensive food for us, but a continual reduction in the number of small, family-run farms. Does the new technology also help smaller farms compete?

ers over the past century is not a negative sign; it is instead an indication that U.S. agricultural workers are the most productive in the world.

Most farmers who lost their jobs went to work in factories. The manufacturing industry, much like agriculture, used technology to become more productive. As you read earlier in this chapter, that productivity was due to tools and machines. The consequence, as in farming, was the elimination of many jobs. Again, the loss to society is minimal if the wealth created by increased productivity and efficiency creates new jobs elsewhere—and that's exactly what has happened over the past 50 years. Many workers in the industrial sector found jobs in the service sector. Most of those who can't find work today are people who need retraining and education to become qualified for jobs that now exist. We'll discuss the manufacturing sector and production in more detail in Chapter 9.

## Progress in Service Industries

As noted above, many workers who could no longer find employment in manufacturing were able to find jobs in the service industry. **Services** are intangible products (i.e., products that can't be held in your hand) such as education, health care, insurance, recreation, and travel and tourism. In the past, the dominant industries in the United States produced goods (steel, railroads, machine tools, etc.). Today, the leading firms are in services (legal, health, telecommunications, entertainment, financial, etc.). Together, services make up more than half of the American economy. Since the mid-1980s, the service industry has generated almost all of the U.S. economy's increases in employment. Although service-sector growth has slowed, it remains the largest area of growth. Chances are very high that you'll work in a service job at some point in your career. Figure 1.5 on page 22 lists many service-sector jobs; look it over to see where the careers of the future are likely to be. Retailers like Gap are part of the service sector. Each new retail store creates many managerial jobs for college graduates.

**services**
Intangible products (i.e., products that can't be held in your hand) such as education, health care, insurance, recreation, and travel and tourism.

Another bit of good news is that there are more high-paying jobs in the service sector than in the goods-producing sector. High-paying service-sector jobs can be found in health care, accounting, finance, entertainment, telecommunications, architecture, law, and software engineering. Projections are that some areas of the service sector will grow rapidly, while others may have much slower growth. The strategy for college graduates is to remain flexible, to find out where the jobs are being created, and to move when appropriate.

## Your Future in Business

Despite growth in the service sector, the service era now seems to be coming to a close as a new era is beginning. We're now in the midst of an information-based global revolution that will alter all sectors of the economy: agricultural, industrial, and service. It's exciting to think about the role you'll play in that revolution. You may be a leader; that is, you may be one of the people who will implement the changes and accept the challenges of world competition based on world quality standards. This book will introduce you to some of the concepts that will make such leadership possible.

Remember that most of the concepts and principles that make businesses more effective and efficient are applicable in government agencies and nonprofit organizations as well. This is an introductory business text, so we'll tend to focus on business. Nonetheless, we'll remind you periodically that you can apply these concepts in other areas. Business can't prosper in the future without the cooperation of government and social leaders throughout the world.

There's much talk about the service sector, but few discussions actually list what it includes. Here's a representative list of services as classified by the government:

**LODGING SERVICES**

Hotels, rooming houses, and other lodging places
Sporting and recreation camps
Trailer parks and camp sites for transients

**PERSONAL SERVICES**

| | |
|---|---|
| Laundries | Child care |
| Linen supply | Shoe repair |
| Diaper service | Funeral homes |
| Carpet cleaning | Tax preparation |
| Photographic studios | Beauty shops |
| Health clubs | |

**BUSINESS SERVICES**

| | |
|---|---|
| Accounting | Exterminating |
| Ad agencies | Employment agencies |
| Collection agencies | Computer programming |
| Commercial photography | Research and development labs |
| Commercial art | Management services |
| Stenographic services | Public relations |
| Window cleaning | Detective agencies |
| Consulting | Interior design |
| Equipment rental | Web design |

**AUTOMOTIVE REPAIR SERVICES AND GARAGES**

| | |
|---|---|
| Auto rental | Tire retreading |
| Truck rental | Exhaust system shops |
| Parking lots | Car washes |
| Paint shops | Transmission repair |

**MISCELLANEOUS REPAIR SERVICES**

| | |
|---|---|
| Radio and television | Welding |
| Watch | Sharpening |
| Reupholstery | Septic tank cleaning |

**MOTION PICTURE INDUSTRY**

| | |
|---|---|
| Production | Theaters |
| Distribution | Drive-ins |

**AMUSEMENT AND RECREATION SERVICES**

| | |
|---|---|
| Dance halls | Racetracks |
| Symphony orchestras | Golf courses |
| Pool halls | Amusement parks |
| Bowling alleys | Carnivals |
| Fairs | Ice skating rinks |
| Botanical gardens | Circuses |
| Video rentals | Infotainment |

**HEALTH SERVICES**

| | |
|---|---|
| Physicians | Nursery care |
| Dentists | Medical labs |
| Chiropractors | Dental labs |

**LEGAL SERVICES**

**EDUCATIONAL SERVICES**

| | |
|---|---|
| Libraries | Computer schools |
| Schools | |

**SOCIAL SERVICES**

| | |
|---|---|
| Child care | Family services |
| Job training | |

**NONCOMMERCIAL MUSEUMS, ART GALLERIES, AND BOTANICAL AND ZOOLOGICAL GARDENS**

**SELECTED MEMBERSHIP ORGANIZATIONS**

| | |
|---|---|
| Business associations | Civic associations |

**FINANCIAL SERVICES**

| | |
|---|---|
| Banking | Real estate agencies |
| Insurance | Investment firms (brokers) |

**MISCELLANEOUS SERVICES**

| | |
|---|---|
| Architectural | Surveying |
| Engineering | Utilities |
| Telecommunications | |

figure I.5

**WHAT IS THE SERVICE SECTOR?**

**progress assessment**

- What is the major factor that caused people to move from farming to manufacturing and from manufacturing to the service sector?
- What does the future look like for tomorrow's college graduates?

## summary

1. A business is any activity that seeks to provide goods and services to others while operating at a profit.

   - **What are the relationships between risk, profit, and loss?**

   *Profit* is money a business earns above and beyond the money that it spends for salaries and other expenses. Businesspeople make profits by taking risks. *Risk* is the chance an entrepreneur takes of losing time and money on a business that may not prove profitable. A loss occurs when a business's costs and expenses are more than its revenues.

   - **How do businesses add to the standard of living and quality of life of a community?**

   Businesses and their employees create the wealth that people use to buy goods and services. Businesses, through taxes, also are the source of funds for government agencies and nonprofit organizations that help improve the quality of life of society. *Quality of life* refers to the general well-being of a country's people in terms of political freedom, a clean natural environment, safety, education, health care, free time, and other things that lead to satisfaction and joy (other than goods). Thus, businesses may add to both the quality of life and standard of living of society by creating the wealth needed to fund progress in those areas.

   - **What groups are considered stakeholders, and which stakeholders are most important to a business?**

   Stakeholders include customers, employees, stockholders, suppliers, dealers, bankers, people in the local community, environmentalists, and elected government leaders. The goal of business leaders is to try to balance the needs of all these stakeholders and still make a profit. That is a challenge when the opportunity for outsourcing comes up. Businesspeople often must choose between cheaper labor and more profits by sending jobs overseas or keeping their employees at home and trying to make them more productive.

**1.** Describe the relationship of businesses' profit to risk assumption and discuss how businesses and nonprofit organizations add to the standard of living and quality of life for all.

2. Entrepreneurs are people who risk time and money to start and manage a business.

   - **What importance does entrepreneurship hold in the list of the five factors of production?**

   Businesses use five factors of production: land (natural resources), labor (workers), capital (buildings and machinery), entrepreneurship, and knowledge. Of these, the most important are entrepreneurship and knowledge (managed information) because without them land, labor, and capital are not of much use.

**2.** Explain the importance of entrepreneurship to the wealth of an economy.

3. Economic factors affect business by increasing or decreasing the risks of starting a business.

   - **What are some things that the government in developing countries can do to lessen the risk of starting businesses?**

   The government may allow private ownership of businesses, pass laws that enable businesspeople to write contracts that are enforceable in court, establish a currency that's tradable in world markets, help to lessen corruption in business and government, and keep taxes and regulations to a minimum. From a business perspective, lower taxes mean lower risks, more growth, and thus more money for workers and the government.

**3.** Examine how the economic environment and taxes affect businesses.

**4.** Illustrate how the technological environment has affected businesses.

4. Adapting to technological change is one of the most important tasks of management.
   - **How has technology benefited workers, businesses, and consumers?**

   Technology enables workers to be more effective, efficient and productive. *Effectiveness* means doing the right thing in the right way. *Efficiency* means producing items using the least amount of resources. *Productivity* is the amount of output you generate given the amount of input (e.g., hours worked). The more workers can produce in any given period of time, the more money they are worth to companies, and the more they earn.

**5.** Identify various ways in which businesses can meet and beat competition.

5. Competition among business firms has never been greater.
   - **What are some ways in which businesses meet and beat competition?**

   Some companies have found a competitive edge by focusing on making high-quality products, all the way to zero defects. Companies also aim to exceed customer expectations. Often that means *empowering* frontline workers by giving them more training and more responsibility and authority.

**6.** Demonstrate how the social environment has changed and tell what the reaction of the business community has been.

6. The United States is going through a social revolution that's having a dramatic impact on how people live, where they live, what they buy, and how they spend their time.
   - **How have such social changes affected businesses?**

   A diverse population challenges businesses to manage a diverse workforce. As more women have entered the labor force, companies have implemented a variety of programs to assist two-income and single-parent families. Many employers provide child care benefits of some type to keep their valued employees. The biggest threat to business may be the loss of trust caused by scandals. That is why this text puts so much emphasis on business ethics.

**7.** Analyze what businesses must do to meet the global challenge, which includes war and terrorism.

7. Global competition has never been greater.
   - **Which countries are creating the greatest challenge?**

   China has taken over much of the production process from U.S. manufacturers. Chinese companies will continue to be a competitive threat for many years to come. India is also a major competitor, especially in providing some information services.
   - **What will be the impact of future wars and terrorism?**

   Some businesses, such as those in the defense industry, may prosper. Others, such as tourism, may suffer. One way to minimize world tensions is to help less developed countries to become more prosperous.

**8.** Review how trends from the past are being repeated in the present and what such trends will mean for tomorrow's college graduate.

8. The United States has matured from an economy based on industry to one based on services and from one dominated by domestic issues to one dominated by global issues.
   - **What do these trends mean for tomorrow's graduates?**

   Check over Figure 1.5, which outlines the service sector. That is where you are most likely to find the fast-growing firms of the future.
   - **What is the history of our economic development in the United States, and what does it tell us about the future?**

   What has sustained the United States as the world's economic leader is the development and use of technology to improve productivity. The agricultural sector, for example, has been able to produce more food with fewer workers. Displaced agricultural workers eventually went to work in factories, producing more industrial goods. Improved productivity resulting from technology and increased competition from foreign firms combined to reduce the need for factory workers and contributed to the development of a service economy in the United States. The service era is now giving way to an information-based global revolution that will affect all sectors of the economy. The secret to long-term success in such an economy is flexibility and continuing education to be prepared for the opportunities that are sure to arise.

## key terms

**business** 4
**business environment** 10
**database** 15
**demography** 16
**e-commerce** 15
**empowerment** 16
**entrepreneur** 4
**factors of production** 9
**goods** 20
**identity theft** 16
**loss** 4
**nonprofit organization** 7
**outsourcing** 6
**productivity** 13
**profit** 4
**quality of life** 5
**revenue** 4
**risk** 5
**services** 21
**stakeholders** 5
**standard of living** 5
**technology** 13

## critical thinking questions

Imagine that you are thinking of starting a restaurant in your community and answer the following questions.

1. Who would be the various stakeholders of your restaurant?
2. What are some of the things you could do to benefit your community other than providing jobs and tax revenue?
3. How could you establish good relationships with your suppliers? With your employees?
4. Do you see any conflict between your desire to be as profitable as possible and your desire to pay employees a living wage?
5. Which of the environmental factors outlined in this chapter might have the biggest impact on your restaurant? How?

## developing workplace skills

1. Imagine that you are a local businessperson who has to deal with the various issues involved with outsourcing. You want to begin with the facts. How many jobs have been lost to outsourcing in your area, if any? Are there any foreign firms in your area that are creating jobs (insourcing)? You may want to use the Internet to find the data you need.
2. What are some of the signs that you and other people in the United States have a high standard of living? What are some signs that such a high standard of living may be negatively affecting their quality of life?

3. As a consumer and worker, it is hard to ignore the growth trend in the numbers of businesses in the service sector. Look through your local phone book to find and list five businesses that provide services in your area. For each of the five, describe how social trends might affect it. Include both negative effects and positive effects. Be prepared to explain your answers.

4. Prepare to defend or attack the idea of using personal savings accounts for helping solve the Social Security problem. Would a person your age benefit or not from such accounts? What are the advantages and disadvantages? What other potential solutions do you see for the Social Security problem?

5. Form teams of four or five students and discuss the technological and e-commerce revolutions. How many students now shop for goods and services online? What have been their experiences? What other high-tech equipment do they use (e.g., cell phones, pagers, laptop computers, desktop computers, personal digital assistants, portable music players)?

## taking it to the net

### Purpose

To gather data regarding trends in population and the social environment and to analyze how these changes affect American businesses.

### Exercise

1. Select the link to the U.S. Population Clock from the Census Bureau's home page at www.census.gov. Record the time and the population for the United States.
2. The U.S. Commerce Department conducts an economic census every five years (in years ending with 2 and 7). How do businesses use the information gathered in this census? To help answer this question, go to the Census Bureau's home page, click on Economic Census, then click on Guide to the Economic Census. There you'll find information on the scope and use of the economic census. What are the three major ways businesses use the economic census data?
3. Return to the U.S. Census Bureau's home page. Check the population of the nation again. Has the population changed since you started this exercise? If so, how? What does this tell you about the U.S. population? How could businesses use this information?

## casing the web

To access the case *"Moving Up the Corporate Ladder,"* visit **www.mhhe.com/ub8e**

video case

## No Clowning Around—Cirque du Soleil

Several themes were introduced in this first chapter, including the importance of entrepreneurship to the success of the overall economy, the need for entrepreneurs to take risks (and the greater the risk, the higher the profit may be), and the dynamic business environment and the challenges it presents. Few organizations in today's society are more indicative of the new challenges than Cirque du Soleil (sounds like Serk due Solay).

In the first place, Guy Laliberte took a great risk by challenging the established circus tradition. The elaborate shows are expensive to start, and the talent must be the best in the world. But the risk paid off big time with sales of almost one billion dollars per year. Cirque du Soleil creates thousands of new jobs and contributes greatly to the communities it serves. It does this not only through the taxes it pays, but through community outreach programs as well. Because of the entertainment value, Cirque contributes to both the standard of living (through the taxes it pays) and the quality of life (the fun it provides for citizens of all ages).

Like all organizations, Cirque du Soleil has many stakeholders. They include the owners, employees, and local community. The organization is especially focused on the stakeholder group called customers. It wants to put on the best show possible, and that means providing the best talent in the best locations. To reach as many people as possible, many of the shows go on the road. You can even watch some of the performances on TV.

The business environment presents many challenges to Cirque du Soleil, as it does for all businesses. The economic and legal environment of the United States greatly supports entrepreneurs like Laliberte.

The technological environment in the United States is also supportive of new business ventures. No circus in the past came close to the elaborate technological devices used by Cirque du Soleil. The stage of the Cirque productions in Las Vegas, for example, is a huge pool that delights the audience with its ability to change from a place where the actors can seem to walk on water to one where they can dive from many feet above the pool.

The social environment is also conducive to new businesses. The diversity of the U.S. population has contributed greatly to the ability of the circus to find diverse acts and to recruit such acts from all over the world. The ability of the organization to adapt to many cultures is shown by its success in various cities throughout the world.

Of course, success is likely to breed much competition, and Cirque has its share. Even traditional circuses are tending to offer more exciting programs that reflect what Cirque has been doing for years. Competition is good for business. It prompts all businesses to offer the best products possible.

One of the best things about this video is that is allows you to see part of Cirque du Soleil in action. If you have never seen the show, search it out—even if only on TV. It is exciting and fun, and it shows that entrepreneurship is alive and well and providing wonderful new services. The result is profits for the owners and a better quality of life for us.

### Thinking It Over

1. What lessons can you take from Guy Laliberte about how to be a successful entrepreneur?
2. What are some of the challenges and opportunities you see for Cirque du Soleil in today's dynamic business environment?
3. How would you compare the excitement and fun of working for a new entrepreneurial venture like Cirque du Soleil with working for a large, traditional business? What are the risks? The rewards? The challenges?

# HOW economics affects business

## The Creation and Distribution of Wealth

profile

### Getting to Know

### X Hernando de Soto,

### Economist for the Poor

Crowded together, eager fans push to get a glimpse of a celebrity visiting a poor community in Peru. Who is this person who has the town so excited? A rock singer, a famous athlete, a movie star? No. Would you believe an economist? Hernando de Soto, a noted economist, wrote one of Peru's best-selling books, and the crowds were eager to hear his ideas about improving the country's economy—and thus their own lives.

Hernando de Soto was born in Peru. He went on to study in Canada, the United States, and Switzerland. Eventually he got a graduate degree in international economics and law at the University of Geneva. He was successful enough to become managing director of Universal Engineering Corporation, a Swiss consulting firm. He made enough money to retire but decided instead to devote his time to studying what makes some countries rich and others poor. He returned to Peru and studied the entrepreneurs there to see what held them back. What he learned was that the business owners were locked out of the formal, legal economy because there were no laws that provided property titles. That is, people could have houses, but no titles to them; farms, but no deeds to them; and businesses, but no certificates of incorporation. The lack of formal titling prevented owners from using their property as collateral, and thus prevented the capital embedded in these assets to be used for other purposes. In other words, entrepreneurs could not sell their property and use the money to invest. They also could not borrow money from banks to expand or improve their businesses. De Soto's book, *The Other Path,* outlines his arguments.

De Soto found that another barrier to wealth in Peru and other less developed countries is government bureaucracy. It took de Soto and others six and a half years and 207 administrative steps in 52 government offices to obtain legal authorization to build a house on state-owned land. It took 289 six-hour days

**LEARNING goals**

After you have read and studied this chapter, you should be able to

1. Compare and contrast the economics of despair with the economics of growth.
2. Explain what capitalism is and how free markets work.
3. Discuss the major differences between socialism and communism.
4. Explain the trend toward mixed economies.
5. Discuss the economic system of the United States, including the significance of key economic indicators (especially GDP), productivity, and the business cycle.
6. Define *fiscal policy* and *monetary policy*, and explain how each affects the economy.

CHAPTER 2

**www.policylibrary.com/desoto**

and $1,231 in fees (that's about 31 times the monthly minimum wage in Peru) to legally open a garment workshop. In short, it is often very difficult and very expensive to become an entrepreneur in less developed countries. And entrepreneurship is the major source of wealth.

De Soto estimates that the value of real estate held, but not owned, by the poor in less developed countries is worth at least $9.3 trillion. That's a lot of money that could be used to start or expand businesses, hire more people, and create wealth. De Soto's second book, *The Mystery of Capital*, goes into more detail about how property ownership leads to the creation of wealth.

De Soto is now the president of the Institute for Liberty and Democracy, a Lima-based think tank. He says that two-thirds of humanity is not in a state to participate in a modern market economy, and that is his biggest challenge. De Soto finds this to be true around the world—from Peru to Egypt, Russia, Africa, and the Philippines. He found, for example, that it takes 25 years of red tape to legally gain the kind of home in Manila that people now get through squatting. He cites Switzerland and Japan as two countries that went from relative poverty to wealth by modifying their property laws. As you can imagine, de Soto has his share of people who don't agree with him. Articles have been written challenging his thinking, and his life has been threatened. But such challenges only help him bring the issue of poverty to the forefront and urge countries to change their laws to make prosperity a reality.

Many people don't realize the importance of the economic environment to the success of business. That is what this chapter is all about. You will learn to compare different economic systems to see the benefits and drawbacks of each. You will learn how the free-market system of the United States works. And you will learn more about what makes some countries rich and other countries poor. By the end of the chapter, you should understand the direct effect that economic systems have on the wealth and the happiness of communities throughout the world.

Sources: Hernando de Soto, *The Mystery of Capital: Why Capitalism Triumphs in the West and Fails Everywhere Else* (New York: Basic Books, 2000); Hernando de Soto, *The Other Path: The Invisible Revolution in the Third World* (New York: Harper & Row, 1989); Hernando de Soto's biography, www.Cato.org/special/friedman/desoto/ (accessed March 7, 2006; Jeremy Main, "How to Make Poor Countries Rich," *Fortune*, January 16, 1989; N. Stephan Kinsella, ed., book review, *Journal of Libertarian Studies*, Winter 2002; and www.nytimes.com/books/00/12/24/reviews/00124.24skidelt.html, 2002 (accessed in 2006).

## HOW ECONOMIC CONDITIONS AFFECT BUSINESSES

Unlike Peru and other developing countries, the United States is a relatively wealthy country. Its entrepreneurs can get funding for risky projects like starting a business.[1] South America, on the other hand, is relatively poor, and there is less money available for entrepreneurial ventures. Why is that? Why is South Korea comparatively wealthy and North Korea suffering economically, with many of its people starving?[2] Why is China's annual income per person ($944) much less than Taiwan's ($13,010)? Such questions are part of the subject of economics. In this chapter, we explore the various economic systems of the world and how they either promote or hinder business growth, the creation of wealth, and a higher quality of life for all.

A major part of America's business success is due to an economic and social climate that allows businesses to operate freely. People are free to start a business anywhere and are just as free to fail. The freedom to fail and start again motivates people to try until they succeed because the rewards are often so great. Any change in the U.S. economic or political system has a major influence on the success of the business system. *Global* economics and politics also have a major influence on businesses in the United States. Therefore, to understand business, you must also understand basic economics and politics.

Sam Walton, founder of Wal-Mart, is just one of millions of men and women who have created wealth for their families and their countries when given the chance. That chance comes when a free market (one not controlled by government) is introduced and people can find a little money to get started.[3]

The economic contrast is remarkable. Business is booming in Seoul, South Korea (pictured on left). But North Korea, a communist country, is not doing well, as the picture on the right of thousands of workers using old fashioned tools in a work-for-food program shows. South Korea has 110 telephones per 100 residents while North Korea has just 5. The annual income per person in the North is 8 percent of that in the South. What do you think accounts for the dramatic differences in the economies of these two neighboring countries?

## What Is Economics?

**Economics** is the study of how society chooses to employ resources to produce goods and services and distribute them for consumption among various competing groups and individuals. Remember from Chapter 1 that these resources (land, labor, capital, entrepreneurship, and knowledge) are called *factors of production*.

There are two major branches of economics: **macroeconomics** looks at the operation of a nation's economy as a whole and **microeconomics** looks at the behavior of people and organizations in particular markets. For example, while macroeconomics looks at how many jobs exist in the whole economy, microeconomics examines how many people will be hired in a particular industry or a particular region of the country. Topics discussed in this chapter that are part of macroeconomics include gross domestic product (GDP), the unemployment rate, and price indexes. Chapter topics that deal with microeconomic issues include pricing and supply and demand.

Some economists define economics as the allocation of "scarce" resources. They believe that resources are scarce and need to be carefully divided among people, usually by the government. There's no way to maintain peace and prosperity in the world by merely dividing the resources we have today among the existing nations. There aren't enough known resources available to do that. **Resource development** is the study of how to increase resources and to create the conditions that will make better use of those resources (e.g., recycling and oil conservation).[4] Outside of government, businesses may contribute to an economic system by inventing products that greatly increase available resources. For example, businesses may discover new energy sources (e.g., hydrogen), new ways of growing food, and new ways of creating needed goods and services.[5] For example, people are starting to raise more fish in pens out in the ocean in a process known as *mariculture*.[6] Such processes could lead to more food for everyone and more employment.

**economics**
The study of how society chooses to employ resources to produce goods and services and distribute them for consumption among various competing groups and individuals.

**macroeconomics**
The part of economics that looks at the operation of a nation's economy as a whole.

**microeconomics**
The part of economics that looks at the behavior of people and organizations in particular markets.

**resource development**
The study of how to increase resources and to create the conditions that will make better use of those resources.

## Why Economics Was Known as the "Dismal Science"

Imagine the world when kings and other rich landowners had most of the wealth and the majority of the people were peasants. The peasants had many children, and it may have seemed a natural conclusion that there would soon be too many people and not enough food and other resources. Thomas Malthus made this argument in the late 1700s and early 1800s. In response to such views, Thomas Carlyle called economics the "dismal science." Followers of Malthus today (who are called neo-Malthusians) still believe that there are too many people in the world and that the solution to poverty is birth control, which includes such measures as forced abortions and forced sterilization. The latest statistics, however, show that the world population is growing more slowly than was expected, and in some industrial countries (e.g., Japan, Germany, Italy, Russia) growth may be so slow so that there will be too many old people and too few young people to care for them.[7] The problem with Social Security in the United States is largely due to too few young people to support retired people.

In the developing world, however, population will continue to climb relatively quickly. Some figures may help you understand these trends: In 1950, the 25 countries of North Africa and West Asia had a combined population less than half that of Europe—163 million compared to 350 million. By 2050, the combined population of North Africa and West Asia will be more than three times larger than that of Europe—1.3 billion to 401 million.[8] Such population increases may lead to greater poverty and more unrest. Studies about

the effects of population growth on the economy are part of *macroeconomics*.

Some macroeconomists believe that a large population can be a valuable resource, especially if the people are educated. They believe that one of the keys to economic growth throughout the world is to better educate people. You've probably heard or read the saying "Give a man a fish and you feed him for a day, but teach a man to fish and you feed him for a lifetime." You can add to that: "Teach a person to start a fish farm, and he or she will be able to feed a village for a lifetime." *The secret to economic development is contained in this last statement.* Business owners provide jobs and economic growth for their employees and communities as well as for themselves.

No sentence in this whole text may be more important than the one that says, "Teach a person to start a fish farm, and he or she will be able to feed a village for a lifetime." That is a much more important concept than the traditional saying: "Teach a man to fish and you feed him for a lifetime." The answer to ending poverty in the world is to teach people how to form their own businesses so that they can provide food, clothing, and other needed goods and services to others. What skills are likely to be needed first?

The challenge for macroeconomists is to determine what makes some countries relatively wealthy and other countries relatively poor, and then to implement policies and programs that lead to increased prosperity for everyone in all countries.[9] One way to begin understanding this challenge is to consider the theories of Adam Smith.

## Growth Economics and Adam Smith

Adam Smith was one of the first people to imagine a system for creating wealth and improving the lives of everyone. Rather than believing that fixed resources had to be divided among competing groups and individuals, Smith envisioned creating more resources so that everyone could become wealthier. The year was 1776. Adam Smith's book *An Inquiry into the Nature and Causes of the Wealth of Nations* often is called simply *The Wealth of Nations*.

Adam Smith believed that *freedom* was vital to the survival of any economy, especially the freedom to own land or property and the freedom to keep the profits from working the land or running a business. He believed that people will work hard if they have incentives for doing so—that is, if they know they will be rewarded.

He made the desire for improving one's condition in life the basis of his theory. According to Smith, as long as farmers, laborers, and businesspeople (entrepreneurs) could see economic reward for their efforts (i.e., receive enough money in the form of profits to support their families), they would work long hours and work hard. As a result of those efforts, the economy would prosper—with plenty of food and all kinds of products available to everyone. Smith's ideas were later challenged by Malthus and others who believed that economic conditions would only get worse, but it is Smith, not Malthus, who is considered by some to be the *father of modern economics*.

## How Businesses Benefit the Community

**invisible hand**
A phrase coined by Adam Smith to describe the process that turns self-directed gain into social and economic benefits for all.

Under Adam Smith's theory, businesspeople don't necessarily deliberately set out to help others. They work primarily for their own prosperity and growth. Yet as people try to improve their own situation in life, Smith said, their efforts serve as an "invisible hand" that helps the economy grow and prosper through the production of needed goods, services, and ideas. Thus, the **invisible hand** turns self-directed gain into social and economic benefits for all.

Entrepreneurs like Bill Gates are often quite generous with their money. He and his wife have given billions of dollars to other countries. Other businesspeople are equally generous, but don't always receive the same amount of attention because the dollar amounts are much smaller. Nonetheless, the compassion is still there. Why do you suppose you don't read or hear more about the generosity of businesspeople in the news media?

How is it that people working in their own self-interest produce goods, services, and wealth for others? The only way farmers in a given area can become wealthy is to sell some of their crops to others. To become even wealthier, farmers would have to hire workers to produce more food. As a consequence, people in that area would have plenty of food available and some would have jobs on the farms. So the farmers' self-centered efforts to become wealthy lead to jobs for some and food for almost all. Stop and envision that process for a minute, because it is critical to your understanding of economic growth in the United States and other free countries. The same principles apply to other products as well—everything from clothing to houses to iPods.

Smith assumed that as people became wealthier, they would naturally reach out to help the less fortunate in the community.[10] That has not always happened. Today, however, many U.S. businesspeople are becoming more concerned about social issues and their obligation to return to society some of what they've earned. For example, Bill Gates (the cofounder of Microsoft) and his wife, Melinda, have set up the largest charitable foundation in history, worth some $29 billion.[11] The foundation has helped save at least 700,000 lives in poor countries through its investments in vaccinations.[12] The Bill and Melinda Gates Foundation works to improve schools; wire libraries to the Internet; and improve world health by providing vaccines, training people in health matters, and more.[13] Ninety percent of U.S. business owners contribute money to charities, compared with 70 percent of U.S. households. Businesses donated millions of dollars to help the victims of Hurricane Katrina, and many businesspeople were on the scene as volunteers. As we mentioned in Chapter 1, it is important for businesses to be ethical as well as generous. Unethical practices undermine the whole economic system; therefore, there needs to be more emphasis on ethics at all stages in business education. You can explore your own ethical position regarding responses to people in need by looking at the Making Ethical Decisions box on page 34.

MAKING **ethical decisions**

### Helping Disaster Victims

Hurricane Katrina, which struck the U.S. Gulf Coast in late August 2005, has been called "the greatest natural disaster in the history of the United States." Thousands of people in Louisiana, Mississippi, and Alabama lost their homes and were sent to other areas of the country with no money, no job, and no permanent place to live. Some were put up in motels. Others found refuge in football arenas or people's homes. Many of the people left without any identification, bank statements, or insurance papers. Chances are that some of the people who were made homeless and jobless will remain so for many months, if not years.

There has been a lot of attention given to the failures of various organizations after Hurricane Katrina. But there were and are many successes as well. The problem is simply too large for most organizations to handle. The Red Cross is just one of many organizations doing their best to help people get through the crisis.

Imagine you live in an area where the homes are medium priced. You have plenty of food to eat and spare rooms in the house. You know that the need is great and the ethical thing is for everyone to do his or her part. "We are all Americans," the news media are saying, and you understand what such a message means. You can send money to the Red Cross, the Salvation Army, or other charities; you can go down to the endangered areas and try to help; or you can offer your home for protection and aid until things get better. What are the potential consequences of each action? What action are you most likely to take, if any? And why? What can ethical businesspeople do to help?

Sources: Anna Mulrine, "To the Rescue," *U.S. News and World Report*, September 12, 2005, pp. 20–26; "The Lost City," *Newsweek*, September 12, 2005, pp. 40–52; and various news reports on TV and radio, 2005–2006.

**progress assessment**

- What is the difference between macroeconomics and microeconomics?
- Why was economics known as the "dismal science"?
- What is better for an economy than teaching a person to fish?
- What does Adam Smith's term *invisible hand* mean? How does the invisible hand create wealth for a country?

## UNDERSTANDING FREE-MARKET CAPITALISM

Basing their ideas on free-market principles, such as those of Adam Smith, businesspeople in the United States, Europe, Japan, Canada, and other countries began to create more wealth than had ever been created before. They hired others to work on their farms and in their factories, and their nations began to prosper as a result. Businesspeople soon became the wealthiest people in society.

**capitalism**
An economic system in which all or most of the factors of production and distribution are privately owned and operated for profit.

Great disparities in wealth remained or even increased. Many businesspeople owned large homes and fancy carriages, while most workers lived in

**Frank and Ernest**

THE BIRTH OF FREE MARKET ECONOMICS
I WISH I HAD A ROCK.
I WISH I HAD A STICK.
THAVES

humble surroundings. Nonetheless, there was always the promise of better times. One way to be really wealthy was to start a successful business of your own.[14] Of course, it wasn't that easy—it never has been. Then and now, you have to accumulate some money to buy or start a business, and you have to work long hours to make it grow. But the opportunities are there.[15]

The economic system that has led to wealth creation in much of the world is known as capitalism. **Capitalism** is an economic system in which all or most of the factors of production and distribution (e.g., land, factories, railroads, and stores) are privately owned (not owned by the government) and are operated for profit. In capitalist countries, businesspeople decide what to produce; how much to pay workers; how much to charge for goods and services; whether to produce certain goods in their own countries, import those goods, or have them made in other countries; and so on. No country is purely capitalist, however. Often the government gets involved in issues such as determining minimum wages and setting farm prices, as it does in the United States. But the *foundation* of the U.S. economic system is capitalism. Similarly, capitalism is the foundation for the economies of England, Australia, Canada, and most other developed nations.

## The Foundations of Capitalism

Some people don't understand how the free-market system (capitalism) works or what rights it confers. As a result, they can't determine what the best economic system is. You should learn how the U.S. economy works and what mechanisms exist to promote economic growth. People under free-market capitalism have four basic rights:

1. *The right to private property.* This is the most fundamental of all rights under capitalism. It means that individuals can buy, sell, and use land, buildings, machinery, inventions, and other forms of property. They can also pass property on to their children. Would farmers work as hard as they do if they didn't own the land and

ZAPRASZAMY

The people of Poland have learned that moving from a communist to a capitalist system is not easy. However, some entrepreneurs flourished. Wala Lukaszuk, for example, enjoyed early success with her own salad bar, but she is now experiencing competition from larger businesses. Capitalism does not guarantee success; it only affords the opportunity to try. Have you talked with someone familiar with socialism or communism to compare the advantages and disadvantages with capitalism?

couldn't keep the profits from what they earned? It is the right to private property that Hernando de Soto is fighting for (see this chapter's Opening Profile).

2. *The right to own a business and to keep all of that business's profits.* Recall from Chapter 1 that profits equal revenues minus expenses (salaries, materials, taxes). Profits act as important incentives for business owners.
3. *The right to freedom of competition.* Within certain guidelines established by the government, individuals are free to compete with other individuals or businesses by offering new products and promotions. To survive and grow, businesses need laws and regulations, such as the laws of contracts, which ensure that people will do what they say they'll do.
4. *The right to freedom of choice.* People are free to choose where they want to work and what career they want to follow. Other freedoms of choice include where to live and what to buy or sell.

One benefit of such rights and freedoms is that people are willing to take more risks than they would otherwise. President Franklin D. Roosevelt believed that four additional freedoms were essential to economic success. They were the freedom of speech and expression, the freedom of every person to worship God in his or her own way, freedom from want, and freedom from fear. Do you see the benefits of these additional freedoms? Now that you understand these rights and freedoms, let's explore how the free market works. What role do consumers play in the process? How do businesses learn what consumers need and want? These questions and more are answered next.

## How Free Markets Work

A free market is one in which decisions about what to produce and in what quantities are made by the market—that is, by buyers and sellers negotiating prices for goods and services. You and I and other consumers in the United States and in other free-market countries send signals to tell producers what to make, how many, in what color, and so on. We do that by choosing to buy (or not to buy) certain products and services.

For example, if all of us decided we wanted T-shirts supporting our favorite baseball team, the clothing industry would respond in certain ways. (Imagine, for example, what happened when the Chicago White Sox won the World Series in 2005.)[16] Manufacturers and retailers would increase the price of T-shirts, because they know people are willing to pay more than before. People in the clothing industry would also realize they could make more money by making more White Sox T-shirts. Thus, they would have incentive to pay workers to start work earlier and end later. Furthermore, the number of clothing companies making White Sox T-shirts would increase. How many T-shirts they make depends on how many we request or buy in the stores. The prices and quantities would continue to change as the amount of T-shirts we buy changed.

People in Chicago are eager to buy White Sox T-shirts when the team is winning. That is especially true when they win the World Series. What happened to the price of White Sox T-shirts when the team won the World Series?

The same process occurs with most other products. The price tells producers how much to produce. As a consequence, there's rarely a long-term shortage of goods in the United States. If something is wanted but isn't available, the price tends to go up until someone begins making more of that product, sells the ones already on hand, or makes a substitute.

## How Prices Are Determined

How free markets work is an important part of economics. The main point is that, in a free market, prices are not determined by sellers; they are determined by buyers and sellers negotiating in the marketplace. A seller may want to receive $50 for a White Sox T-shirt, but the quantity demanded at that price may be quite low. If the seller lowers the price, the quantity demanded is likely to increase. How is a price determined that is acceptable to both buyers and sellers? The answer is found in the microeconomic concepts of supply and demand. We shall explore both next.

## The Economic Concept of Supply

**supply**
The quantity of products that manufacturers or owners are willing to sell at different prices at a specific time.

**Supply** refers to the quantity of products that manufacturers or owners are willing to sell at different prices at a specific time. Generally speaking, the amount supplied will increase as the price increases because sellers can make more money with a higher price.

Economists show this relationship between quantity supplied and price on a graph. Figure 2.1 on page 38 shows a simple supply curve for T-shirts. The price of the shirts in dollars is shown vertically on the left of the graph. The quantity of shirts sellers are willing to supply is shown horizontally at the bottom of the graph. The various points on the curve indicate how many T-shirts sellers would provide at different prices. For example, at a price of $5 a shirt, a T-shirt vendor would provide only 5 T-shirts, but at $50 a shirt the vendor would supply 50 shirts. The supply curve indicates the relationship between the price and the quantity supplied. All things being equal, the higher the price, the more the vendor will be willing to supply.

## The Economic Concept of Demand

**demand**
The quantity of products that people are willing to buy at different prices at a specific time.

**Demand** refers to the quantity of products that people are willing to buy at different prices at a specific time. Generally speaking, the quantity demanded will increase as the price decreases. Again, the relationship between price and quantity demanded can be shown in a graph. Figure 2.2 on page 38 shows a simple demand curve for T-shirts. The various points on the graph indicate the quantity demanded at various prices. For example, at a price of $45, the quantity demanded is just 5 shirts; but if the price were $5, the quantity demanded would increase to 35 shirts. The line connecting the dots is called a demand curve. It shows the relationship between quantity demanded and price.

## The Equilibrium Point, or Market Price

It should be clear to you after reviewing Figures 2.1 and 2.2 that the key factor in determining the quantity supplied and the quantity demanded is *price*. Sellers prefer a high price, and buyers prefer a low price. If you were to lay one of the two graphs on top of the other, the supply curve and the demand curve would cross. At that crossing point, the quantity demanded and the quantity supplied would be equal. Figure 2.3 illustrates that point. At a price of $15, the quantity of T-shirts demanded and the quantity supplied are equal (25 shirts).

## figure 2.1

**THE SUPPLY CURVE AT VARIOUS PRICES**

The supply curve rises from left to right. Think it through. The higher the price of T-shirts goes (the vertical axis), the more sellers will be willing to supply.

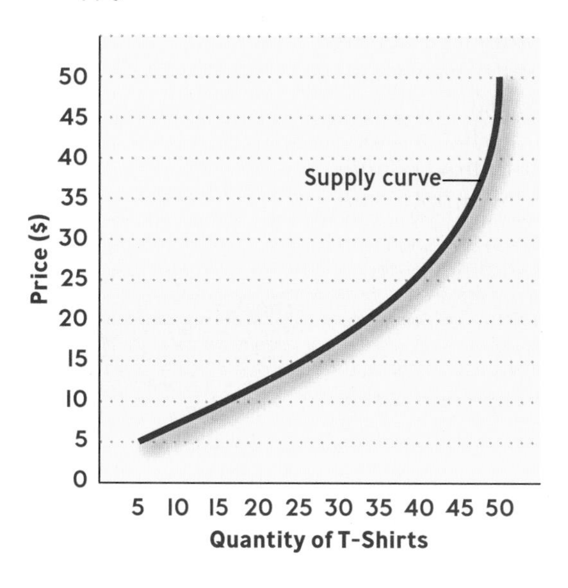


## figure 2.2

**THE DEMAND CURVE AT VARIOUS PRICES**

This is a simple demand curve showing the quantity of T-shirts demanded at different prices. The demand curve falls from left to right. It is easy to understand why. The lower the price of T-shirts, the higher the quantity demanded.

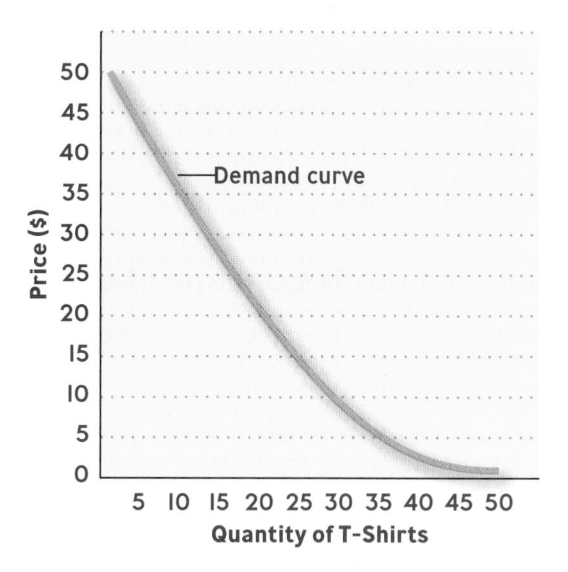


## figure 2.3

**THE EQUILIBRIUM POINT**

The place where quantity demanded and supplied meet is called the equilibrium point. When we put both the supply and demand curves on the same graph, we find that they intersect at a price where the quantity supplied and the quantity demanded are equal. In the long run, the market price will tend toward the equilibrium point.

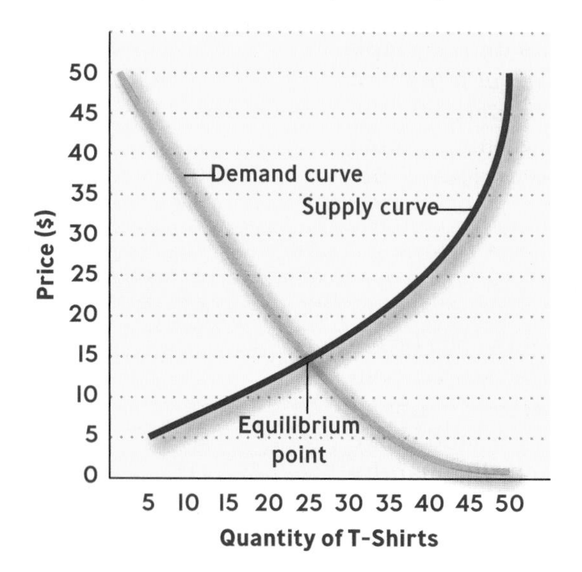


That crossing point is known as the *equilibrium point* or the equilibrium price. In the long run, that price would become the market price. **Market price**, then, is determined by supply and demand.

Proponents of a free market would argue that, because supply and demand interactions determine prices, there is no need for government involvement or government planning. If surpluses develop (i.e., if quantity supplied exceeds quantity demanded), a signal is sent to sellers to lower the price. If shortages develop (i.e., if quantity supplied is less than quantity demanded), a signal is sent to sellers to increase the price. Eventually, supply will again equal demand if nothing interferes with market forces. You saw such price swings when the oil supply was cut in 2005 because of Hurricane Katrina. When supplies were low because of the hurricane, the price of gasoline went up (dramatically). When supplies were again plentiful, the price of gas fell, and went up again dramatically when overseas demand increased. The Dealing with Change box shows you what happens when changes occur faster than a company is able to adapt.

In countries without a free market, there is no such mechanism to reveal to businesses (via price) what to produce and in what amounts, so there are often shortages (not enough products) or surpluses (too many products). In such countries, the government decides what to produce and in what quantity, but the government has no way of knowing what the proper quantities are. Furthermore, when the government interferes in otherwise free markets, such as when it subsidizes farm goods, surpluses and shortages may also develop.

## DEALING WITH change

### Adapting to Swings in Demand

Imagine that your local professional baseball team has not been winning many games in the last few years. I'm sure many of you can identify with that. Ticket prices are set, and the season begins. Because of a few new people on the team, the team begins winning game after game and the demand for tickets goes up. The owners cannot raise the prices without creating great tumult among the fans, so the price remains stable. But an informal market (among fans) grows for tickets, often on the Internet. Prices go up. Revenue also goes up for the owners because they sell a lot more hot dogs and beverages.

But what happens if the team starts losing again? Demand for tickets falls. The owners begin losing money at the concession stand. What can the owners do to adjust? You can see how adapting to changes in demand are often difficult to make.

The same is true with auto sales. When gas prices went up dramatically in 2005 and 2006, auto dealers found themselves with too many SUVs in their inventories. Also, there weren't enough hybrid cars (combination gas/electric vehicles with high gas mileage). Auto manufacturers simply could not respond quickly to the rapid changes in demand. What other examples could you cite that show the lag between changes in supply and/or demand and the reaction by businesspeople?

Sources: Larry Armstrong, "Are You Ready for a Hybrid?," *BusinessWeek*, April 25, 2005, pp. 118–26, and Victoria Murphy, "Seattle's Best-Kept Secret," *Forbes*, April 25, 2005, pp. 86–88.

## Competition within Free Markets

**market price**
The price determined by supply and demand.

Economists generally agree that there are four different degrees of competition: (1) perfect competition, (2) monopolistic competition, (3) oligopoly, and (4) monopoly.

**perfect competition**
The market situation in which there are many sellers in a market and no seller is large enough to dictate the price of a product.

**Perfect competition** exists when there are many sellers in a market and no seller is large enough to dictate the price of a product. Under perfect competition, sellers produce products that appear to be identical. Agricultural products (e.g., apples, corn, potatoes) are often considered to be the closest examples of such products. You should know, however, that there are no true examples of perfect competition. Today, government price supports and drastic reductions in the number of farms make it hard to argue that even farming is an example of perfect competition.

**monopolistic competition**
The market situation in which a large number of sellers produce products that are very similar but that are perceived by buyers as different.

**Monopolistic competition** exists when a large number of sellers produce products that are very similar but are perceived by buyers as different (e.g., hot dogs, candy, personal computers, T-shirts). Under monopolistic competition, product differentiation (the attempt to make buyers think similar products are different in some way) is a key to success. Think about what that means for just a moment. Through tactics such as advertising, branding, and packaging, sellers try to convince buyers that their products are different from those of competitors. Actually, the competing products may be similar or even interchangeable. The fast-food industry, in which there are often pricing battles between hamburger places, offers a good example of monopolistic competition.

**oligopoly**
A form of competition in which just a few sellers dominate the market.

An **oligopoly** is a form of competition in which just a few sellers dominate a market. Oligopolies exist in industries that produce products such as breakfast cereals, tobacco, automobiles, soft drinks, aluminum, and aircraft. One reason some industries remain in the hands of a few sellers is that the initial investment required to enter the business is tremendous.

In an oligopoly, prices for products from different companies tend to be close to the same. The reason for this is simple: Intense price competition would lower profits for all the competitors, since a price cut on the part of one producer would most likely be matched by the others. As in monopolistic competition, product differentiation, rather than price, is usually the major factor in market success in a situation of oligopoly. Note, for example, that most cereals are priced about the same, as are soft drinks. Thus, advertising is a major factor in which of the few available brands consumers buy because often it is advertising that creates the perceived differences.

**monopoly**
A market in which there is only one seller for a product or service.

A **monopoly** occurs when there is only one seller for a product or service. That is, one seller controls the total supply of a product and the price. In the United States, laws prohibit the creation of monopolies. The U.S. legal system has permitted monopolies in the markets for public utilities that sell natural gas, water, and electric power. These utility companies' prices and profits usually have been monitored and controlled by public service commissions that are supposed to protect the interest of buyers. For example, the Florida Public Service Commission is the administering agency over the Florida Power and Light utility company. New legislation has ended the monopoly status of utilities in some areas, and consumers in those areas are able to choose among utility providers. The intention of this *deregulation* is to increase competition among utility companies and, ultimately, lower prices for consumers.

## Benefits and Limitations of Free Markets

One benefit of the free market is that it allows open competition among companies. Businesses must provide customers with quality products at fair prices with good service; otherwise, they will lose customers to those businesses that do provide good products, good prices, and good service.

The free market—with its competition and incentives—was a major factor in creating the wealth that industrialized countries now enjoy. Some people even talk of the free market as an economic miracle. Free-market capitalism, more than any other economic system, provides opportunities for poor people to work their way out of poverty.[17] Capitalism also encourages businesses to be more efficient so they can successfully compete on price and quality.

Yet even as free-market capitalism has brought prosperity to the United States and to much of the rest of the world, it has brought inequality as well. Business owners and managers make more money and have more wealth than lower-level workers.[18] Similarly, people who are old, disabled, or sick may not be able to start and manage a business. Others may not have the talent or the drive to start and manage a business or farm. What should society do about such inequality? Not everyone in the United States is as generous as Bill Gates. In fact, the desire to produce as much as possible and to create as much wealth as possible has led some businesspeople (throughout history and even in some places still today) to use such practices as slavery and child labor.

One of the dangers of free markets is that businesspeople and others may let greed dictate how they act. Recent charges made against some big businesses—oil companies, accounting firms, telecommunications firms, insurance companies, drug companies, and others—indicate the scope of this danger. Some businesspeople have deceived the public about their products, and others have deceived their stockholders about the value of their stock.[19] All this was done in order to increase the executives' personal assets.

Clearly, some government laws, rules, and regulations are necessary to make sure that all of businesses' stakeholders are protected and that people who are unable to work get the basic care they need. To overcome the limitations of capitalism, some countries have adopted an economic system called socialism. It, too, has its good and bad points. We explore the advantages and disadvantages of socialism after the Progress Assessment questions.

**progress assessment**

- What are the four basic rights that people have under free-market capitalism?
- How do businesspeople know what to produce and in what quantity?
- How are prices determined?
- What are some of the limitations of free markets?

**socialism**
An economic system based on the premise that some, if not most, basic businesses should be owned by the government so that profits can be evenly distributed among the people.

## UNDERSTANDING SOCIALISM

**Socialism** is an economic system based on the premise that some, if not most, basic businesses—such as steel mills, coal mines, and utilities—should be owned by the government so that profits can be more evenly distributed among the people.[20] Entrepreneurs often own and run the smaller businesses, but private businesses and individuals are taxed relatively steeply to pay for social programs. The top federal personal income tax rate in the United States, for example, is 35 percent, but in some socialist countries the top rate is as much as 60 percent. While people in the United States pay state sales taxes of about 5 percent, more or less (more in California, less—in fact, nothing—in Delaware), socialist countries charge a value-added tax (which is something like a sales tax) of 15 to 20 percent or more. Socialists acknowledge the major benefit of capitalism—wealth creation—but believe that wealth should be more evenly distributed than occurs in free-market capitalism. They believe that the government should be the agency that carries out the distribution.

Socialism has been a lot more successful in some countries than others. This photo shows Denmark's modern and clean public transportation system. On the other hand, France experienced street riots from young people who resisted legislation that would have allowed businesses to fire younger workers. That legislation was then withdrawn. What other factors may lead to slow growth in socialist countries?

### The Benefits of Socialism

The major benefit of socialism is supposed to be social equality. There is supposed to be more equality of outcome in socialism than in capitalism because income is taken from the wealthier people, in the form of taxes, and redistributed to the poorer members of the population through various government programs. Free education (even through the college level), free health care, and free child care are some of the benefits socialist governments distribute to their people (using the money from taxes). Workers in socialist countries usually get longer vacations than workers in capitalist countries. They also tend to work fewer hours per week and have more employee benefits, such as generous sick leave.

### The Negative Consequences of Socialism

Socialism may create more equality than capitalism, but it takes away some of businesspeople's incentives to start work early and leave work late. For example, tax rates in some nations once reached 85 percent. Today, doctors, lawyers, business owners, and others who earn a lot of money have very high tax rates. As a consequence, many of them leave socialist countries for capitalistic countries with lower taxes, such as the United States. This loss of the best and brightest people to other countries is called a **brain drain**.

**brain drain**
The loss of the best and brightest people to other countries.

Imagine an experiment in socialism in your own class: Say that after the first exam, those students with grades of 90 and above have to give some of their points to those who make 70 and below so that everyone ends up with grades in the 80s. What would happen to the incentive of those who got an A on the first exam? Would they study as hard for the second exam, knowing that they would have to give away any points above 80? What about those who got 70s? Would they work less hard if they knew that they would get extra points if they didn't do well? Can you see why workers may not work as hard or as well if they all get the same benefits regardless of how hard they work?

Socialism also results in fewer inventions and less innovation because those who come up with new ideas usually don't receive as much reward as they would in a capitalist system. Over the past decade or so, most socialist countries have simply not kept up with the United States in new inventions, job creation, or wealth creation.[21] Communism may be considered as a version of socialism. We shall explore that system next.

**communism**
An economic and political system in which the state (the government) makes almost all economic decisions and owns almost all the major factors of production.

## UNDERSTANDING COMMUNISM

**Communism** is an economic and political system in which the state (the government) makes *almost all* economic decisions and owns almost all the major factors of production. It intrudes further into the lives of people than socialism does. For example, some communist countries have not allowed their citizens to practice certain religions, change jobs, or move to the town of their choice.

When you live in a relatively rich country with free markets, scarcity of goods or services is a rarity indeed. But that is not true worldwide. This photo, for example, shows what happens when there is a scarcity of water. People must scramble to find enough water to drink and bathe. What other goods and services are often unavailable in countries without free markets?

One problem with communism is that the government has no way of knowing what to produce because prices don't reflect supply and demand as they do in free markets. The government must guess what the economic needs of the people are. As a result, shortages of many items may develop, including shortages of food and basic clothing. Another problem with communism is that it doesn't inspire businesspeople to work hard because the government takes most of their earnings. Therefore, although communists once held power in many nations around the world, communism is slowly disappearing as an economic form.

Most communist countries today are now suffering severe economic depression, and some people (for example, in North Korea) are starving. The people in Cuba are suffering from the lack of goods and services readily available in most other countries, and some people fear the government.[22] There seems to be a movement toward communist principles in Venezuela, following the Cuban model.[23] Other countries in the region may follow. Some parts of the former Soviet Union remain under communist concepts, but the movement there, until recently, has been toward free markets. In fact, Russia now has a flat tax of 13 percent, much lower than the tax rate in the United States. When Russia introduced that flat rate, tax revenues jumped by nearly 30 percent, in part because people no longer did whatever they could to avoid paying their taxes. The trend away from communism toward free markets is now appearing in Vietnam[24] and parts of China.[25] The regions in China that are most free have prospered greatly while the rest of the country has grown relatively slowly. The Spotlight on Small Business box has some interesting stories about entrepreneurship and growth in China.

SPOTLIGHT ON small business

## China's Entrepreneurs Create Wealth

Economically, there are two Chinas. One China is the farming interior, where the people are very poor and the prospects for the future are rather dim. The other China consists of fast-growing urban areas, where incomes are much higher and the prospects for growth are very good. As a consequence, the share of China's population living in towns and cities has risen to 40 percent today from only 18 percent in 1978. The entrepreneurial stories of those who have left the farm are the stories of the future of China.

Yu Chengyu was a farmer who tried to support his family of five on a small farm. It is difficult to save money to move away from a farm in China because the government still owns the land and people cannot sell the land to get funds to start a business. Nonetheless, several years ago Yu moved to a city to sell homemade furniture. Now he has the biggest shop on his block, selling motor scooters, TV sets, and washing machines. He employs six other people in his business, creating more wealth for the community.

Han Dexun has a similar story to tell. He moved to Beijing from a village a decade ago to work for an uncle who had started a small furniture factory. Eventually he left to start his own business doing interior renovations. He has brought many relatives, friends, and neighbors into Beijing to find jobs, and he employs several of them on his own crews.

You don't have to look far to see the results of the rapid growth of Chinese businesses. There are "Made in China" stickers on clothes, furniture, and other products in stores throughout the United States. The more freedoms the people in China experience, the faster the overall economy is sure to grow. The same is true in India and other developing countries. One way you can help poor people in such countries to prosper and grow is to contribute to microlending firms like Grameen or the Foundation for International Community Assistance (FINCA). Such firms provide small loans to small businesses to get them started or to help them grow. More prosperity throughout the world could lead to less international tensions and greater peace.

Sources: Jason Dean, "Living the Chinese Dream," *The Wall Street Journal*, April 26, 2005, p. A12; Jeffrey Gangemi, "Microcredit Missionary," *BusinessWeek*, December 26, 2005, p. 20; and Dexter Roberts, "How Rising Wages Are Changing the Game in China," *BusinessWeek*, March 27, 2006, pp. 32–35.

## THE TREND TOWARD MIXED ECONOMIES

The nations of the world have largely been divided between those that followed the concepts of capitalism and those that adopted the concepts of communism or socialism. Thus, to sum up the preceding discussion, the two major economic systems vying for dominance in the world today can be defined as follows:

1. **Free-market economies** exist when the market largely determines what goods and services get produced, who gets them, and how the economy grows. *Capitalism* is the popular term used to describe this economic system.
2. **Command economies** exist when the government largely decides (commands) what goods and services will be produced, who will get them, and how the economy will grow. *Socialism* and *communism* are the popular terms used to describe variations of this economic system.

**free-market economies**
Economic systems in which the market largely determines what goods and services get produced, who gets them, and how the economy grows.

**command economies**
Economic systems in which the government largely decides what goods and services will be produced, who will get them, and how the economy will grow.

The experience of the world has been that neither free-market nor command economies have resulted in optimum economic conditions. Free-market mechanisms haven't been responsive enough to the needs of the poor, the old, or the disabled. Some people also believe that businesses in free-market economies have not done enough to protect the environment. Over time, voters in free-market countries, such as the United States, have therefore elected officials who have adopted many social and environmental programs such as Social Security, welfare, unemployment compensation, and various clean air and water acts.

REACHING BEYOND

our borders

## Finding New Markets Overseas

Growth in many U.S. companies has slowed in recent years. This includes companies in the once fast-growing service sector. One solution to the problem is to explore markets in other countries. That is just what Citigroup is doing. Citigroup is one of the largest financial services companies in the world. It has about 120 million customers in more than 100 countries. Citibank is its banking arm. Despite its worldwide success, Citigroup is not standing still. It is reaching out to such fast-growing countries as Brazil, Mexico, Russia, India, and China—54 more countries in all.

It is not as easy as you might imagine to open banks in other countries. You have to work with government officials and regulators to allow you to create the legal mechanisms to open a bank, provide loans, and distribute credit cards. But that is only the beginning. You then have to convince people who have never used a bank or have lost money in banks to trust the bank to keep their money. You have to teach people how to use credit cards. You also have to adapt to the many rules and regulations that apply to banking or help the country to create new rules. That is what Citigroup had to do in Russia, where there was no system for deposit insurance, for example. Charging interest for credit card use was also new to the country.

Many other companies are going through similar struggles in their attempts to develop markets overseas. Each country has its own economic system, legal system, banking system, and regulations regarding the sale of goods and services. That is an opportunity for you. If you are willing to learn other languages; move to another country; learn that country's laws, customs, and culture; and adapt to its needs, you can become quite successful. Often the markets are wide open and the possibilities almost endless. Sound interesting?

Sources: Bernard Condon, Michael Freedman, and Naazneen Karmali, "Globetrotter," *Fortune,* April 18, 2005, pp. 66–86; www.citigroup.com (accessed March 7, 2006); and Kate Linebaugh, "How Foreign Banks Scaled the Chinese Wall," *The Wall Street Journal,* February 23, 2006, pp. C1 and C5.

Socialism and communism, for their part, haven't always created enough jobs or wealth to keep economies growing fast enough. As a consequence, communist governments are disappearing and socialist governments have been cutting back on social programs and lowering taxes on businesses and workers. The idea is to generate more business growth and thus generate more revenue.[26] The Reaching Beyond Our Borders box discusses the problems companies may face when expanding markets overseas.

The trend, then, has been for so-called capitalist countries (e.g., England) to move toward more socialism and for so-called socialist countries (e.g., France) to move toward more capitalism. We say "so-called" because no country in the world is purely capitalist or purely socialist. All countries have some mix of the two systems. Thus, the long-term global trend is toward a blend of capitalism and socialism. This trend likely will increase with the opening of global markets caused by the Internet.[27] The net effect of capitalist systems moving toward socialism and socialist systems moving toward capitalism is the emergence throughout the world of mixed economies.

**mixed economies**
Economic systems in which some allocation of resources is made by the market and some by the government.

**Mixed economies** exist where some allocation of resources is made by the market and some by the government. Most countries don't have a name for such a system. If the dominant way of allocating resources is by free-market mechanisms, then the leaders of such countries still call their system capitalism. If the dominant way of allocating resources is by the government, then the leaders call their system socialism. Figure 2.4 compares the various economic systems.

Like most other nations of the world, the United States has a mixed economy. The degree of government involvement in the economy today is a matter of some debate, as it has been at various times in the past. The government has now become the largest employer in the United States, which means that the number of workers in the public sector is more than the number in the entire manufacturing sector.

| | CAPITALISM | SOCIALISM | COMMUNISM | MIXED ECONOMY |
|---|---|---|---|---|
| **Social and economic goals** | Private ownership of land and business. Liberty and the pursuit of happiness. Free trade. Emphasis on freedom and the profit motive for economic growth. | Public ownership of major businesses. Some private ownership of smaller businesses and shops. Government control of education, health care, utilities, mining, transportation, and media. Very high taxation. Emphasis on equality. | Public ownership of all businesses. Government-run education and health care. Emphasis on equality. Many limitations on freedom, including freedom to own businesses, change jobs, buy and sell homes, and to assemble to protest government actions. | Private ownership of land and business with government regulation. Government control of some institutions (e.g., mail). High taxation for defense and the common welfare. Emphasis on a balance between freedom and equality. |
| **Motivation of workers** | Much incentive to work efficiently and hard because profits are retained by owners. Workers are rewarded for high productivity. | Capitalist incentives exist in private businesses. Government control of wages in public institutions limits incentives. | Very little incentive to work hard or to produce quality goods or services. | Incentives are similar to capitalism except in government-owned enterprises, which may have fewer incentives. |
| **Control over markets** | Complete freedom of trade within and among nations. No government control of markets. | Some markets are controlled by the government and some are free. Trade restrictions among nations vary and include some free-trade agreements. | Total government control over markets except for illegal transactions. | Some government control of trade within and among nations (trade protectionism). |
| **Choices in the market** | A wide variety of goods and services is available. Almost no scarcity or oversupply exists for long because supply and demand control the market. | Variety in the marketplace varies considerably from country to country. Choice is directly related to government involvement in markets. | Very little choice among competing goods. | Similar to capitalism, but scarcity and over-supply may be caused by government involvement in the market (e.g., subsidies for farms). |
| **Social freedoms** | Freedom of speech, press, assembly, religion, job choice, movement, and elections. | Similar to mixed economy. Governments may restrict job choice, movement among countries, and who may attend upper-level schools (i.e., college). | Very limited freedom to protest the government, practice religion, or change houses or jobs. | Some restrictions on freedoms of assembly and speech. Separation of church and state may limit religious practices in schools. |

figure 2.4

**COMPARISONS OF KEY ECONOMIC SYSTEMS**

**progress assessment**

- What led to the emergence of socialism?
- What are the benefits and drawbacks of socialism?
- What countries still practice communism?
- What are the characteristics of a mixed economy?

## UNDERSTANDING THE ECONOMIC SYSTEM OF THE UNITED STATES

**gross domestic product (GDP)**
The total value of final goods and services produced in a country in a given year.

The following sections will introduce the terms and concepts you'll need to understand the issues facing government and business leaders today in the United States. As an informed citizen, you can then become a leader in helping to create a world economy that is best for all.

### Key Economic Indicators

**unemployment rate**
The number of civilians at least 16 years old who are unemployed and tried to find a job within the prior four weeks.

Three major indicators of economic conditions are (1) the gross domestic product (GDP), (2) the unemployment rate, and (3) the price indexes. Another important statistic is the increase or decrease in productivity. When you read business literature, you'll see these terms used again and again. It will greatly increase your understanding if you learn the terms now.

**Gross Domestic Product** **Gross domestic product (GDP)** is the total value of final goods and services produced in a country in a given year. Either a domestic company or a foreign-owned company may produce the goods and services included in the GDP as long as the companies are located within the country's boundaries. For example, production values from Japanese automaker Honda's factory in Ohio would be included in the U.S. GDP. Likewise, revenue generated by the Ford car factory in Mexico would be included in Mexico's GDP, even though Ford is a U.S. company.

If GDP growth slows or declines, there are often many negative effects on businesses. A major influence on the growth of GDP is how productive the workforce is, that is, how much output workers create with a given amount of input. In 2004, world GDP was growing at its fastest rate in 30 years. It was expected to continue that pace into 2005.[28]

The overall unemployment rate in the United States is less than 5 percent. That doesn't mean, however, that certain areas of the country or certain cities are not experiencing much higher unemployment rates. Unemployment insurance only goes so far to relieve such unemployment. How high is the unemployment rate in your area?

Almost every discussion about a nation's economy is based on GDP. The total U.S. GDP in the early 2000s was over $11 trillion. The level of U.S. economic activity is actually larger than the GDP figures show because the figures don't take into account illegal activities (e.g., sales of illegal drugs). The high GDP in the United States is what enables Americans to enjoy such a high standard of living.[29]

**The Unemployment Rate** The **unemployment rate** refers to the number of civilians at least 16 years old who are unemployed and tried to find a job within the prior four weeks. In 2000, the U.S. unemployment rate reached its lowest point in over 30 years, falling as low as 3.9 percent, but the rate rose rapidly to over 6 percent as a result of the

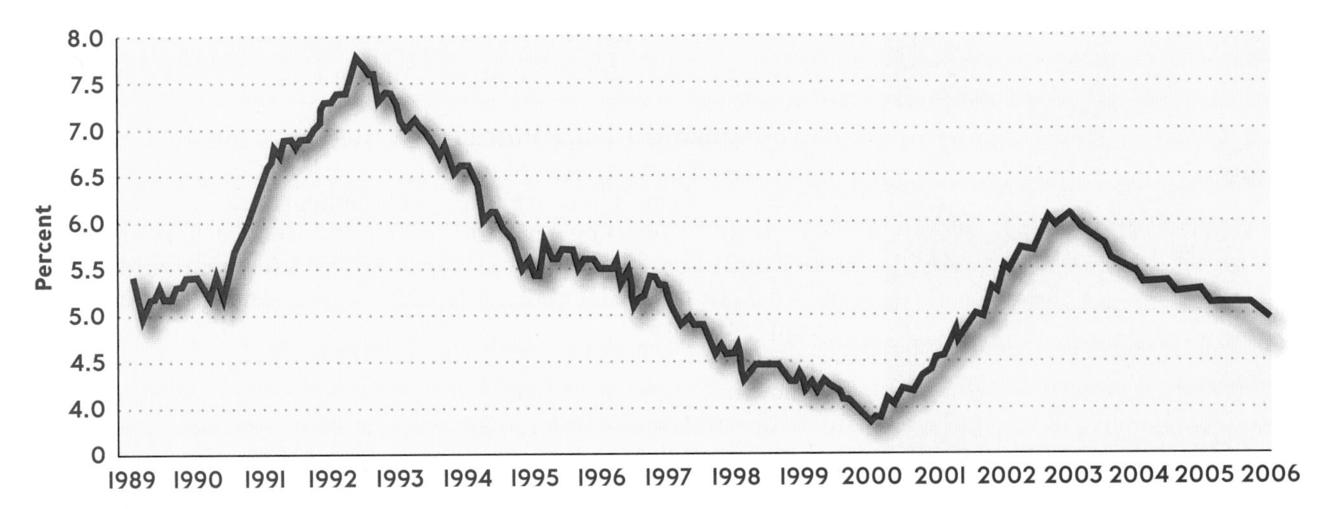


figure 2.5

**U.S. UNEMPLOYMENT RATE, 1989–2006**

economic slowdown of 2002–2003. It fell to less than 5 percent in 2006 (see Figure 2.5).[30] Figure 2.6 describes the four types of unemployment: frictional, structural, cyclical, and seasonal. The United States tries to protect those who are unemployed because of recessions, industry shifts, and other cyclical factors. Nonetheless, for a variety of reasons, many of these individuals do not receive unemployment benefits.

**inflation**
A general rise in the prices of goods and services over time.

**The Price Indexes** The price indexes help to measure the health of the economy by measuring the levels of inflation, disinflation, deflation, and stagflation. **Inflation** refers to a general rise in the prices of goods and services over time.[31] Rapid inflation is scary.[32] If the cost of goods and services goes up by just 7 percent a year, everything would double in cost in just 10 years or so. You can read more about such numbers in the Practicing Management Decisions Case at www.mhhe.com/ub8e.

**disinflation**
A situation in which price increases are slowing (the inflation rate is declining).

**Disinflation** describes a situation in which price increases are slowing (the inflation rate is declining). That was the situation in the United States throughout the 1990s. **Deflation** means that prices are actually declining.[33] It occurs when countries produce so many goods that people cannot afford to

**deflation**
A situation in which prices are declining.

figure 2.6

**TYPES OF UNEMPLOYMENT**

**There are several kinds of unemployment:**

- *Frictional unemployment* refers to those people who have quit work because they didn't like the job, the boss, or the working conditions and who haven't yet found a new job. It also refers to those people who are entering the labor force for the first time (e.g., new graduates) or are returning to the labor force after significant time away (e.g., parents who reared children). There will always be some frictional unemployment because it takes some time to find a first job or a new job.
- *Structural unemployment* refers to unemployment caused by the restructuring of firms or by a mismatch between the skills (or location) of job seekers and the requirements (or location) of available jobs (e.g., coal miners in an area where mines have been closed).
- *Cyclical unemployment* occurs because of a recession or a similar downturn in the business cycle (the ups and downs of business growth and decline over time). This type of unemployment is the most serious.
- *Seasonal unemployment* occurs where demand for labor varies over the year, as with the harvesting of crops.

It's hard to imagine the damage caused by runaway inflation. In Germany, runaway inflation meant that you had to have a wheelbarrow full of money just to shop for groceries. These children are stacking up money for just such a shopping trip. One job of the Federal Reserve is to keep inflation in check. Can you see the effects of higher gasoline prices on other items in the store, or are the changes too small to notice?

buy them all (too few dollars are chasing too many goods). *Stagflation* occurs when the economy is slowing but prices are going up anyhow.[34]

The **consumer price index (CPI)** consists of monthly statistics that measure the pace of inflation or deflation. Costs of goods and services—including food, apparel, and medical care—are computed to see if they are going up or down (see Figure 2.7). The CPI is an important figure because some wages and salaries, rents and leases, tax brackets, government benefits, and interest rates are based on it. Recently the government created a new index called the chained consumer price index (C-CPI). The CPI failed to take into account the fact that consumers would shift their purchases as prices went up or down. For example, if the price of beef went up, consumers may switch to less-expensive chicken. The C-CPI takes such decisions into account; thus, the C-CPI is usually a lower figure than the CPI.[35]

The **producer price index (PPI)** measures prices at the wholesale level. Other indicators of the economy's condition include housing starts, retail sales, and changes in personal income. You can learn more about such indicators by reading business periodicals, listening to business broadcasts on radio and television, and exploring the Internet.

**consumer price index (CPI)**
Monthly statistics that measure the pace of inflation or deflation.

## Productivity in the United States

An increase in productivity means that a worker can produce more goods and services in the same period of time than before, usually through the use of machinery or other equipment. Productivity in the United States has gone up in recent years because computers and other technology have made the process of production faster and easier for many workers.[36] The higher productivity is, the lower costs are in producing goods and services, and the lower prices can be. Therefore, businesspeople are eager to increase productivity.

Starbucks is one firm that is very concerned about productivity. The faster an employee can make a venti-sized cold beverage, the more profits the store can make and the more productive the employee becomes. The more productive an employee becomes, the more he or she can be paid. Therefore, when someone discovered that it took two scoops of ice to make a venti-sized drink, a double-size scoop was invented that cut the production time by 14 seconds. A tall black drip coffee can be made in under 20 seconds, while a Venti Double Chocolate Chip Frappuccino Blended Crème takes closer to 90 seconds. Which drink would be more profitable for the store?[37]

figure 2.7

**HOW THE CONSUMER PRICE INDEX IS PUT TOGETHER**

1. 400 data collectors visit stores and gather 80,000 retail price quotes and 5,000 housing rent quotes, transmitting data daily to Washington.
2. 40 commodity analysts at the Bureau of Labor Statistics review about a quarter of this avalanche of price data.
3. About nine days before the release of the CPI, the office is locked down—with bright red "restricted area" signs posted on all the doors.
4. 90 people—a mix of commodity analysts and other economists who specialize in assembling the CPI—compute basic indexes for 211 item categories, which are divided into 38 index areas.
5. Final results are released at 8:30 a.m., Eastern time, about two weeks after the end of the month in question.

Now that the U.S. economy is a service economy, productivity is an issue, because service firms are so labor-intensive. Spurred by foreign competition, productivity in the manufacturing sector is rising rapidly. In the service sector, productivity is growing more slowly because there are fewer new technologies available to assist service workers (e.g., teachers, clerks, lawyers, and personal service providers like barbers) than there are for factory workers.

**producer price index (PPI)**
An index that measures prices at the wholesale level.

## Productivity in the Service Sector

In the service sector, other technological innovations are beginning to make workers more productive. The United States is ahead of much of the world in service productivity. However, one problem with the service industry is that an influx of machinery may add to the *quality* of the service provided but not to the *output per worker* (productivity).

For example, you've probably noticed how many computers have been installed on college campuses. They add to the quality of education, but they don't necessarily boost professors' productivity. The same is true of some new equipment in hospitals, such as CAT scanners and PET scanners (more modern versions of the X-ray machine). They improve patient care but don't necessarily increase the number of patients that can be seen. In other words, today's productivity measures fail to capture the increase in quality caused by new technology.

Clearly, the United States and other countries need to develop new measures of productivity for the service economy, measures that include quality as well as quantity of output. Despite productivity improvement, the economy is likely to go through a series of ups and downs, much as it has over the past few years. We'll explore that process next.

## The Business Cycle

**business cycles**
The periodic rises and falls that occur in all economies over time.

**Business cycles** are the periodic rises and falls that occur in economies over time.[38] Economists look at a number of types of cycles, from seasonal cycles that occur within a year to cycles that occur every 48 to 60 years.

Economist Joseph Schumpeter identified the four phases of long-term business cycles as boom–recession–depression–recovery:

1. An economic boom is just what it sounds like—business is booming.
2. A **recession** is two or more consecutive quarters of decline in the GDP. In a recession prices fall, people purchase fewer products, and businesses fail. A recession has many negative consequences for an economy: high unemployment, increased business failures, and an overall drop in living standards.
3. A **depression** is a severe recession usually accompanied by deflation. Business cycles rarely go through a depression phase. In fact, while there were many business cycles during the 20th century, there was only one severe depression (1929–1933).
4. A recovery occurs when the economy stabilizes and starts to grow. This eventually leads to an economic boom, starting the cycle all over again.

**recession**
Two or more consecutive quarters of decline in the GDP.

**depression**
A severe recession.

One goal of economists is to predict ups and downs in the economy. That is very difficult to do. Business cycles are based on facts, but what those facts describe can be explained only by using theories.[39] Therefore, one cannot say with certainty what will happen next. One can only theorize. But one thing is for sure: The economy and the stock market *will* rise and fall.[40]

Business cycles show that over time the stock market is likely to rise *or* fall by significant amounts. Such cycles have shown to be rather consistent; that is, long periods of growth are typically followed by periods of decline. Investing, therefore, always involves a certain degree of risk, but usually the greater the risk the higher the payoff. Can you see why investors may be wise to study past trends before putting their money into stocks?

Since dramatic swings up and down in the economy cause all kinds of disruptions to businesses, the government tries to minimize such changes. The government uses fiscal policy and monetary policy to try to keep the economy from slowing too much or growing too rapidly.

## Stabilizing the Economy through Fiscal Policy

**Fiscal policy** refers to the federal government's efforts to keep the economy stable by increasing or decreasing taxes or government spending. The first half of fiscal policy involves taxation. Theoretically, high tax rates tend to slow the economy because they draw money away from the private sector and put it into the government. High tax rates may discourage small-business ownership because they decrease the profits businesses can make and make the effort less rewarding. It follows, then, that (theoretically) low tax rates would tend to give the economy a boost.

In the United States, the percentage of GDP taken by the government through taxes at all levels (federal, state, and local) was about 20.7 percent in 1995. That rate had fallen to 18.4 percent by 2001, but it has been going up since then and is about 20.3 percent today.[41] When you count all fees, sales taxes, and more, taxes on the highest-earning citizens could exceed 50 percent. In your opinion, is that figure too high or not high enough? Why?

The second half of fiscal policy involves government spending. The government spends money on highways, social programs, education, defense, and so on. The *national deficit* is the amount of money that the federal government spends over and above the amount it gathers in taxes for a specific period (namely a fiscal year). Over time, such deficits increase the national debt. The **national debt** is the sum of government deficits over time. Recently, the national debt was over 8 trillion (see Figure 2.8). That's over $28,000 for every man, woman, and child in the United States, or over $112,000 for a family of four. (You can see what your current share of the national debt is by checking out the National Debt Clock at www.brillig.com/debt_clock.) At times, there is a *national surplus,* where tax revenues exceed expenditures, but that is a relatively rare event.

**fiscal policy**
The federal government's efforts to keep the economy stable by increasing or decreasing taxes or government spending.

**national debt**
The sum of government deficits over time.

One way to lessen the annual deficits is to cut government spending. Many presidents have promised to make the government "smaller," that is, to lower government spending—but that doesn't happen very often. There seems to be a need for more social programs or more defense spending each year, and thus the deficits continue and add to the national debt. Some people believe that spending by the government helps the economy to grow. Others believe that the money the government spends comes out of the pockets of consumers and businesspeople and thus slows growth. What do you think?

## Using Monetary Policy to Keep the Economy Growing

Have you ever wondered what organization adds or subtracts money from the economy? The answer is the Federal Reserve Bank (the Fed). The Fed is a semiprivate organization that is not under the direct control of the government but does have members who are appointed by the president of the United

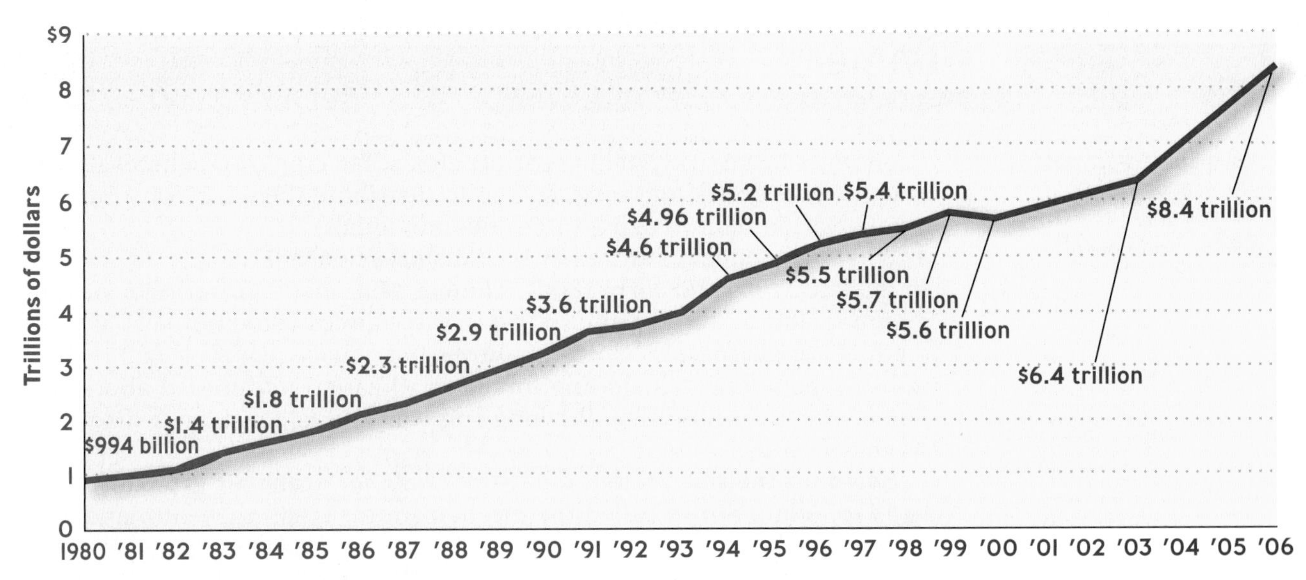


figure 2.8

**THE NATIONAL DEBT**

Source: Government data.

States. We will discuss the Fed in detail later in the book when we look at the subject of banking in Chapter 20. Our goal in this chapter is to simply introduce you to the concept of monetary policy and the role of the Fed in controlling the economy.

**monetary policy**
The management of the money supply and interest rates.

**Monetary policy** is the management of the money supply and interest rates. That policy is controlled by the Federal Reserve System. The most obvious role of the Federal Reserve is the raising and lowering of interest rates. When the economy is booming, the Fed tends to raise interest rates. This makes money more expensive to borrow. Businesses thus borrow less, and the economy slows as businesspeople spend less money on everything they need to grow, including labor and machinery. The opposite is true when the Fed lowers interest rates. Businesses tend to borrow more, and the economy takes off. Raising and lowering interest rates should therefore help control the rapid ups and downs of the economy.

The Federal Reserve also controls the money supply. A simple explanation is that the more money that the Fed makes available to businesspeople and others, the faster the economy grows. To slow the economy, the Fed lowers the money supply. If you are eager to learn more about the Fed and the money supply, you can turn to Chapter 20 now. You don't need to know all the details, however, to understand that there are two major efforts being made to control the economy of the United States: fiscal policy (taxes and spending) and monetary policy (control over interest rates and the money supply).[42] The economic goal is to keep the economy growing so that more people can rise up the economic ladder and enjoy a satisfying quality of life.[43]

## progress assessment

- Name the three economic indicators and describe how well the United States is doing according to each indicator.
- What's the difference between a recession and a depression?
- How does the government manage the economy using fiscal policy?
- What does the term *monetary policy* mean? What organization is responsible for monetary policy?

## summary

**1.** Compare and contrast the economics of despair with the economics of growth.

1. Economics is the study of how society chooses to employ resources to produce various goods and services and to distribute them for consumption among various competing groups and individuals.

- **Why was economics known as the "dismal science"?**

In the late 1700s and early 1800s, Thomas Malthus theorized that the human population would grow so fast that resources could not keep up. On the basis of his theories, some countries today have placed severe restrictions on population, including forced sterilization and forced abortions. The economic outlook for the long run was and is considered dismal in some countries.

- **How does the government create a climate for economic growth?**

In 1776, Adam Smith called the mechanism for creating wealth and jobs an invisible hand. Under his system (capitalism), businesspeople don't deliberately set out to help others. In fact, they work mostly for their own prosperity and growth. Yet people's efforts to improve their own situation in life act like an invisible hand to help the economy grow and prosper through the production of needed goods, services, and ideas.

**2.** Explain what capitalism is and how free markets work.

2. Capitalism is an economic system in which all or most of the means of production and distribution (e.g., land, factories, railroads, and stores) are privately owned and operated for profit.

- **Who decides what to produce under capitalism?**

In capitalist countries, businesspeople decide what to produce; how much to pay workers; how much to charge for goods and services; whether to produce certain goods in their own countries, import those goods, or have them made in other countries; and so on.

- **What are the basic rights people have under capitalism?**

The four basic rights under capitalism are (1) the right to private property, (2) the right to own a business and to keep all of that business's profits after taxes, (3) the right to freedom of competition, and (4) the right to freedom of choice. President Franklin D. Roosevelt felt that other economic freedoms were also important: the freedom of speech and expression, the freedom of every person to worship God in his or her own way, freedom from want, and freedom from fear.

- **How does the free market work?**

The free market is one in which decisions about what to produce and in what quantities are made by the market—that is, by buyers and sellers negotiating prices for goods and services. Buyers' decisions in the marketplace tell sellers what to produce and in what quantity. When buyers demand more goods, the price goes up, signaling suppliers to produce more. The higher the price, the more goods and services suppliers are willing to produce. Price, then, is the mechanism that allows free markets to work.

**3.** Discuss the major differences between socialism and communism.

3. Socialism is an economic system based on the premise that some businesses should be owned by the government.

- **What are the advantages and disadvantages of socialism?**

Socialism creates more social equity. Compared to workers in capitalist countries, workers in socialist countries not only receive more free education and health care benefits but also work fewer hours, have longer vacations, and receive more free benefits in general, such as child care. The major disadvantage of socialism is that it lowers the profits of owners and managers, thus cutting the incentive to start a business or to work hard. Socialist economies tend to have a higher unemployment rate and a slower growth rate than capitalist economies.

- **How does socialism differ from communism?**

Under communism, the government owns almost all major production facilities and dictates what gets produced and by whom. Communism is also more restrictive when it comes to personal freedoms, such as religious freedom. While there are many countries practicing socialism, there are only a small number (e.g., North Korea, Cuba, Vietnam) still practicing communism.

**4.** Explain the trend toward mixed economies.

4. A mixed economy is one that is part capitalist and part socialist. That is, some businesses are privately owned, but taxes tend to be high to distribute income more evenly among the population.

- **What countries have mixed economies?**

The United States has a mixed economy, as do most other countries of the world.

- **What are the benefits of mixed economies?**

A mixed economy has most of the benefits of wealth creation that free markets bring plus the benefits of greater social equality and concern for the environment that socialism offers.

**5.** Discuss the economic system of the United States, including the significance of key economic indicators (especially GDP, productivity, and the business cycle.)

5. Three major indicators of economic conditions are (1) the gross domestic product (GDP), (2) the unemployment rate, and (3) the price indexes.

- **What are the key terms used to describe the U.S. economic system?**

Gross domestic product (GDP) is the total value of final goods and services produced in a country in a given year. The unemployment rate refers to the number of civilians at least 16 years old who are unemployed and who tried to find a job within the most recent four weeks. The consumer price index (CPI) measures changes in the prices of about 400 goods and services that consumers buy. It contains monthly statistics that measure the pace of inflation (consumer prices going up) or deflation (consumer prices going down). Recently, the government created a new index called the chained consumer price index (C-CPI) because the CPI failed to take into account the fact that consumers would shift their purchases as prices went up or down. Productivity is the total volume of goods and services one worker can produce in a given period. Productivity in the United States has increased due to the use of machinery and other technology.

- **What are the four phases of business cycles?**

In an economic boom, businesses do well. A recession occurs when two or more quarters show declines in the GDP, prices fall, people purchase fewer products, and businesses fail. A depression is a severe recession. Recovery occurs when the economy stabilizes and starts to grow.

**6.** Define *fiscal policy* and *monetary policy*, and explain how each affects the economy.

6. Fiscal policy consists of government efforts to keep the economy stable by increasing or decreasing taxes or government spending. The search is for a good balance between taxes and spending so that the economy can grow and the government can fund its various programs.

- **What is the importance of monetary policy to the economy?**

Monetary policy is the management of the money supply and interest rates. When unemployment gets too high, the Federal Reserve Bank (the Fed) may put more money into the economy and lower interest rates. That provides a boost to the economy as businesses borrow and spend more money and hire more people.

## key terms

**brain drain** 41
**business cycles** 49
**capitalism** 34
**command economies** 43
**communism** 42
**consumer price index (CPI)** 48
**deflation** 47
**demand** 37
**depression** 49
**disinflation** 47
**economics** 31
**fiscal policy** 50
**free-market economies** 43
**gross domestic product (GDP)** 46
**inflation** 47
**invisible hand** 32
**macroeconomics** 31
**market price** 38
**microeconomics** 31
**mixed economies** 44
**monetary policy** 51
**monopolistic competition** 39
**monopoly** 40
**national debt** 50
**oligopoly** 39
**perfect competition** 39
**producer price index (PPI)** 49
**recession** 49
**resource development** 31
**socialism** 41
**supply** 37
**unemployment rate** 46

## critical thinking questions

1. Recently, the U.S. Supreme Court ruled that cities could have voucher programs that give money directly to parents, and the parents can then choose between competing schools: public and private. The idea for promoting such a ruling was to create competition among schools. As with businesses, schools were expected to improve their products (how effectively they teach) to win students from competitors. Supposedly, that would mean an improvement in all schools, private and public, and would benefit many students.

    a. Do you believe that such economic principles apply in both private and public organizations? Be prepared to defend your answer.

    b. Are there other public functions that might benefit from more competition, including competition from private firms?

2. Many people say that businesspeople do not do enough for society. Some students choose to go into the public sector instead of business because they "want to help others." However, businesspeople say that they do more to help others than nonprofit groups do because they provide jobs for people rather than giving them charity, which often precludes them from searching for work. Furthermore, they believe that businesses create all the wealth that nonprofit groups distribute.

    a. Can you find some middle ground in this debate that would show that both businesspeople and those who work for nonprofit organizations contribute to society and need to work together more closely to help people?

    b. Could you use the concepts of Adam Smith to help illustrate your position?

## developing workplace skills

1. In teams, develop a list of the advantages of living in a capitalist society. Then develop lists headed "What are the disadvantages?" and "How could such disadvantages be minimized?" Describe why a poor person in a socialist country might reject capitalism and prefer a socialist state.
2. Show your understanding of the principles of supply and demand by looking at the employment market today. Explain, for example, the high salaries that computer scientists are getting at Microsoft. Also explain why some people with graduate degrees aren't getting better pay than computer scientists who only have undergraduate degrees. Why do some librarians make less than some garbage collectors, even though the librarians may have a better education?
3. This exercise is intended to help you understand socialism from different perspectives. Form three groups. Each group should adopt a different role in a socialist economy: One group will be the business owners, another group will be workers, and another will be government leaders. Within your group discuss and list the advantages and disadvantages to you of lowering taxes on businesses. Then have each group choose a representative to go to the front of the class and debate the tax issue with the representatives from the other groups.
4. Draw a line and mark one end "free-market capitalism" and the other end "central planning." Mark where on the line the United States is now. Explain why you marked the spot you chose. Students from other countries may want to do this exercise for their own countries and explain the differences to the class.
5. Break into small groups. In your group discuss how the following changes have affected people's purchasing behavior and attitudes toward the United States and its economy: the war in Iraq; the creation of the Department of Homeland Security; the growth of the Internet; and the numerous charges against big businesses behaving illegally, unethically, and immorally. Have a group member prepare a short summary for the class.

## taking it to the net * 1

### Purpose

To compare the value of the dollar based on variances in the consumer price index.

### Exercise

Do your parents ever tire of telling you how much things cost back in their day? Sure, things were cheaper then, but the value of a dollar was different too. Think about something you bought today (shoes, soda, candy bar, haircut—whatever). How much did the good or service you bought today cost your parents when they were your age? Find out by using the handy tool on the Federal Reserve Bank of Minneapolis's Woodrow Web site (http://woodrow.mpls.frb.fed.us/research/data/us/calc). The calculator uses the consumer price index to compare the value of the dollar in different years. Enter the cost of the item you bought today, the year you would like to compare it with, and—presto—you'll find out how Mom and Pop could get along on such a small paycheck. (For an even bigger shock, compare the current dollar to the dollar in your grandparents' day!)

1. How much would a $50 pair of jeans bought today have cost the year you were born?
2. How much would a job paying $6 an hour today have paid in 1970?
3. How much would a new car costing $18,000 today have cost the year your mother first got her driver's license?

## taking it to the net * 2

### Purpose

To familiarize you with the sources of economic information that are important to business decision makers.

### Exercise

Imagine your boss asked you to help her in preparing the company's sales forecast for the next two years. In the past she felt that trends in the nation's GDP, U.S. manufacturing, and manufacturing in Illinois were especially helpful in forecasting sales. She would like you to do the following:

1. Go to the Bureau of Economic Analysis's Web site (www.bea.doc.gov) and locate the gross domestic product data. Compute an annual figure for the last four years by averaging the quarterly data. Plot this on graph paper or a spreadsheet. Leave enough space for six years so that you can draw a projection line for the next two years.
2. On the Bureau of Labor Statistics' Web site (www.bls.gov), under Industries, click on Industries at a Glance to find information about the manufacturing industry. What is the employment trend in manufacturing over the last four years?
3. Return to the Bureau of Labor Statistics' home page and use the Search feature to find the manufacturing employment for the state of Illinois. Using the data from July, plot the trend in manufacturing employment in Illinois over the last four years.
4. If sales in your company tend to increase as the GDP increases and as employment in manufacturing in the United States and Illinois remains stable or increases, what do you think is going to happen to your company's sales?

## casing the web

To access the case "The Rule of 72," visit **www.mhhe.com/ub8e**

## Katrina's Aftermath

Free market capitalism has been credited with the marvelous growth and prosperity enjoyed by the United States and other developed countries. But no country really has a totally free market system. Always, the government acts to help assure those who are poor, elderly, or disabled that they will receive some minimum amount of assistance. Usually that assistance includes education or some kind of welfare assistance (e.g., food, housing, or tax relief). The resulting system is called a mixed economic system because it is a mixture of free market capitalism and government social programs. If the government programs are extensive, the system might be called socialism.

Despite numerous efforts by businesses, government agencies, and nonprofit organizations to end poverty in the United States, poverty still persists. That point was illustrated vividly when hurricane Katrina hit the Gulf Coast region of the United States.

Who is to blame for persistent poverty? And why did the people in New Orleans suffer for so many days before assistance arrived? Is the government indifferent to the needs of some? Is the city government responsible, or the state government, or the federal government? Almost always, citizens try to help, but the task is simply too great. At times, even the state and federal government are overwhelmed by the need.

In the case of New Orleans, businesses like Wal-Mart responded rather quickly, but they couldn't get food and materials to people without help. Nonprofit groups of all kinds drove down to help, but government bureaucracy made it difficult, if not impossible, to get a coordinated effort going. Communications between and among various government, private, and nonprofit organizations was almost nonexistent. Much of the infrastructure (roads, rivers, water system, electricity, and so forth) were not operating.

Capitalism is a great system for creating wealth in a macroeconomic environment where supply and demand dictate through prices what gets produced and in what quantity and quality. In the short run, however, shortages can exist for a while without the appropriate response. In the long run, the free market system will do its work. The demand for supplies will result in flows of goods. Homes will be rebuilt. Businesses will reopen. Jobs will be created.

Wars and natural disasters create a real challenge for any economic system. The fastest response usually comes when people are free to create their own businesses, free to own their own land, free to set their own prices, and free to keep the profits from what they earn. Acadian Ambulance is an example of what free markets can do. In the midst of the Katrina disaster, the company had a satellite communication system up and running. Acadian was thus able to coordinate hospitals, law enforcement, and rescue workers.

Ultimately, you and I, as taxpayers, will have to pay for the damages in the Gulf region. The government uses fiscal policy, taxes and spending, to keep the economy growing and to respond to people in need. The government also uses monetary policy to keep the economy growing at the right pace. That means that the Federal Reserve will raise or lower interest rates and control the money supply so that businesses can prosper and grow—creating jobs and minimizing poverty.

There have always been ups and downs in the economy. People have always helped their neighbors and those throughout the world who have less. More countries are adopting the concepts of free markets and free trade. The results are obvious in places like China, India, and South Korea. A good understanding of economics is the basis for all such growth—and the reason for discussing economics early in this text.

### Thinking It Over

1. No economic system has been able to respond quickly to the devastation caused by war or major natural disasters. Why is the free market system more likely to respond faster? What advantages might a socialist system have in responding to the needs of the poor?
2. What could the government do to better coordinate the efforts of churches, other nonprofit organizations, government agencies, businesses, and individual citizens when emergencies strike? What factors have hindered such coordination in the past?
3. When disasters hit an area, the cost of everything seems to go up immediately: food, water, housing, gas, and so forth. Explain why this phenomenon may be a good thing, using the laws of supply and demand to explain your answer. What would happen if prices did not go up?

# competing in global markets

*

profile

**Getting to Know**

**X** Li Yifei,

**President of MTV Networks China**

MTV has had tremendous influence on the music, style, innovation, and attitude of the teenage and 20-plus population. Imagine bringing MTV's marketing power to China, the most populous nation on earth, and a country with not only emerging economic potential but also increasing demand among its young people. Viacom, the owner of MTV, envisions such a future and has entrusted Li Yifei, president of MTV Networks China, to make it happen.

Viacom's chief executive chose Li Yifei for the job because of what he called the three Cs—character, competence, and commitment. Li added one more C—Chinese. Li brings an interesting background and credentials to the job. A native of Beijing (China's capital city), Li was a national champion in tai chi (a form of martial arts) at 13 and a supporting actor in China's first action movie. She earned the opportunity to attend the most elite foreign-language university in Beijing. At age 21, she left China to come to the United States after receiving a scholarship to attend Baylor University in Waco, Texas. Li earned a master's degree in political science at Baylor and also observed firsthand the differences between the U.S. and Chinese cultures.

After graduation, she was one of 40 students selected for a prestigious internship at the United Nations. There she had the opportunity to produce the television program *U.N. Calling Asia*. After deciding that diplomacy was not her career calling, Li became manager of the Beijing office of Burson-Marsteller, a large public relations company. She assisted the firm's clients in business dealings with the Chinese bureaucracy, helped handle complicated paperwork the government required, and assisted with cultural details involved with trade contacts of all kinds. Her work caught the eye of Viacom, and she was hired as the general manager of MTV Networks China in 1999.

To call her job a challenge would be an understatement. With a population of 1.3 billion and an emerging middle class, China is projected to be the second-largest advertising market in the world in the next 10 years. However, China is not really just one market. It's fragmented into many local and cable stations

After you have read and studied this chapter, you should be able to

1. Discuss the growing importance of the global market and the roles of comparative advantage and absolute advantage in global trade.
2. Explain the importance of importing and exporting, and understand key terms used in global business.
3. Illustrate the strategies used in reaching global markets and explain the role of multinational corporations in global markets.
4. Evaluate the forces that affect trading in global markets.
5. Debate the advantages and disadvantages of trade protectionism.
6. Discuss the changing landscape of the global market and the issue of offshore outsourcing.

CHAPTER 3

www.mtv.com

and has a state-owned TV network, making the Chinese system very complex. Li is in charge of bringing everything together.

To add to this challenge, Li must adapt her management style to fit the Chinese culture. Traditional media regulators in China are very conservative and not typically concerned with program ratings (as regulators are in the United States). They are not receptive to broadcasting attractive, sometimes scantily clad vee-jays who work for a foreign network. When dealing with her mostly male Chinese business associates, Li reins in her usual straightforward, confident business style, since Chinese culture expects a woman to be soft and humble when conducting business. Li also knows it's easier to gain access to markets in China if you have the support of a Chinese partner.

Due to this understanding of Chinese culture, Li has created a win-win situation for Viacom and China. For example, she has persuaded over 300 Chinese cities to carry MTV programming and convinced CCTV, China's state-owned national TV network, to co-produce the Chinese version of the MTV awards. She has also been instrumental in helping Viacom lay plans for a 24-hour MTV China channel through a partnership with Beijing Television.

Li Yifei is a strong example of an emerging global businessperson, that is, a person who speaks different languages, understands cultural and economic differences, and visualizes the vast potential and challenges of global markets. *Fortune* magazine has named her one of its "25 Rising Stars of the Next Generation of Global Leaders." Li places great value on her time spent in the United States and strongly believes that people from different cultures can have an effective dialogue. Her dream, and the mission of Viacom, she says, is to narrow the cultural divide: "I strongly believe that different cultures can have effective dialogue as long as we have tolerance. It's a matter of attitude."

The future of U.S. economic growth and the continued economic expansion of developing nations such as China are both tied to open markets and global trade. This chapter will explain the opportunities that exist in global markets and the challenges businesspeople such as Li Yifei must face to succeed globally.

Sources: Michael Paoletta, "Music Makes the World Go 'Round: MTV Networks Gets Back to Its Roots," *Billboard*, April 30, 2005; "Li Yifei: A Chinese Businesswoman and MTV in China," www.womenofchina.com, March 24, 2005; Normandy Madden, "Reaching China's Youth a Balancing Act," *Advertising Age*, June 6, 2005; and Anna Quinlan, "The Sign of the Times," *Newsweek*, May 1, 2006.

## THE DYNAMIC GLOBAL MARKET

Have you ever dreamed of traveling to exotic cities like Paris, Tokyo, Rio de Janeiro, or Cairo? In times past, the closest most Americans ever got to working in such cities was in their dreams. Today, the situation has changed. It's hard to find a major U.S. company that does not cite global expansion as a link to its future growth. A recent study noted that 91 percent of the companies doing business globally believe it's important to send employees on assignments in other countries.[1]

If a career in global business has never crossed your mind, maybe a few facts will make the possibility of such a career more interesting: The United States is a market of about 290 million people, but there are over 6 billion potential customers in the 193 countries that make up the global market. (See Figure 3.1 for a map of the world and important statistics about world population.) Perhaps more interesting is that approximately 75 percent of the world's population lives in developing areas where technology, education, and per capita income still lag considerably behind those of developed (or industrialized) nations such as the United States.

Today Americans buy billions of dollars' worth of goods from China.[2] United Parcel Service (UPS) saw 45 percent market growth in India last year and an even higher rate in China.[3] Major league baseball teams, the National Basketball Association (NBA), and the National Football League (NFL) play games in Mexico, Italy, Japan, and elsewhere. Born in China, Yao Ming of the NBA's Houston Rockets is one of the most recognized athletes in the world.[4] Johnny Depp, Will Smith, and Julia Roberts continuously draw crowds to movie theaters around the globe as American movies take center stage in the global entertainment market.[5]

**importing**
Buying products from another country.

**exporting**
Selling products to another country.

The United States is the largest importing nation in the world. **Importing** is buying products from another country. The United States is also the largest exporting nation as well. **Exporting** is selling products to another country. Competition in exporting is very intense.[6] U.S. companies face aggressive competition from exporters such as Germany, China, and Japan.[7] Read the Dealing with Change box to see how this competition promises to intensify in the future.

The purpose of this chapter is to familiarize you with the potential of global business, including its many challenges. The demand for students with

figure 3.1
**WORLD POPULATION BY CONTINENT**

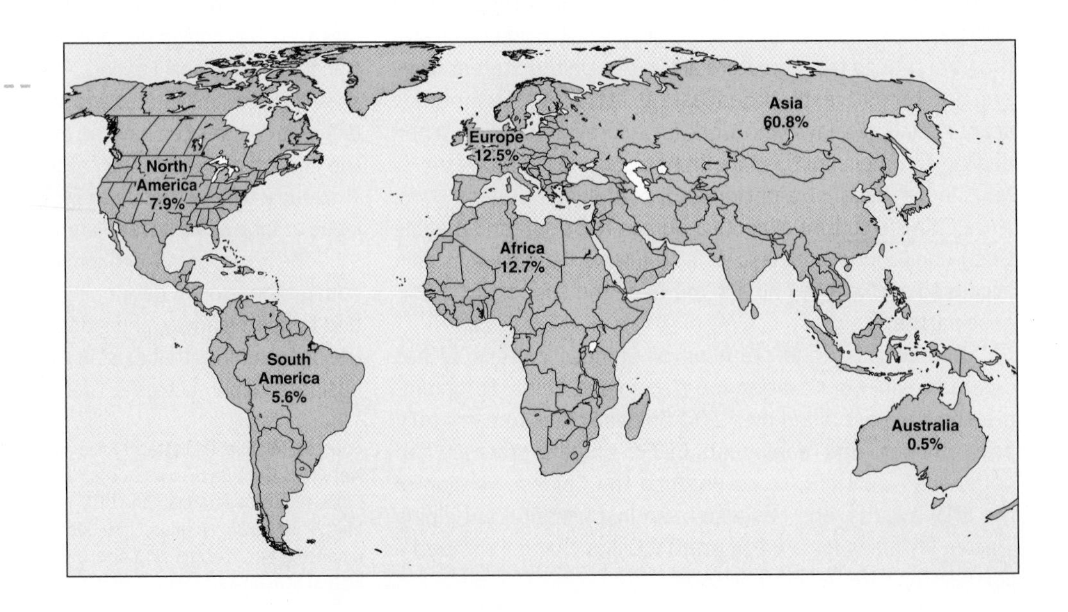

DEALING WITH change

## Asia's 800-Pound Gorilla

It's a statistic that may be a bit mind-boggling: two out of every six people on Earth live in either China or India. This fact forces competitive nations to face the reality that these two emerging powers could reshape the world's economic order. That's why the announcement by the two Asian giants that they are forming a strategic partnership, forging closer economic ties, and establishing a task force to consider a free trade pact has quickened the pulse of businesspeople around the globe. Some economists even suggest the two powers will be vying with the United States and the European Union for global economic superiority by 2020.

By virtue of its exporting prowess and huge market, China transformed the economic map of Asia in the early 2000s. India's economy has the potential to match China. One key business area that would clearly benefit from a strengthened China/India alliance is information technology (IT). Chinese premier Wen Jiabao has even suggested that he envisions a "two pagodas" alliance in which China concentrates on producing computer hardware and India focuses on software and services. A successful Indo-Chinese strategy could create real issues for the United States in setting IT standards. Additionally, U.S. firms such as Dell and Hewlett-Packard could also face a powerful personal computer (PC) vendor like China's Lenovo Group Ltd., which acquired IBM's PC and laptop business.

Still some doubt that trade temptations can ease decades of political and territory battles between the two nations and old wounds will resurface. China and India have a long-standing border dispute involving 16,000 square miles of territory in the Kashmir region that China holds yet India claims. China is also a main trading partner of Pakistan and a major backer of its military; India has fought three wars with Pakistan. Time will tell if the two rivals can cooperate and put commerce before conflict.

Sources: Peter Mandelson, "India's New Leadership Role: An Economic Giant," *International Herald Tribune*, January 15, 2005; John Diamond, "Prediction: India, China Will Be Economic Giants," *USA Today*, January 14, 2005, p. 8A; Jo Johnson, "China and India Pledge to Boost Trade and End Border Dispute," *Financial Times*, April 12, 2005, p. 5; John Larkin, "China and India Declare Era of Cooperation," *The Wall Street Journal*, April 12, 2005, pp. A19–A21; Paul McDougall, "Tech Powerhouse," *Information Week*, April 18, 2005, pp. 20–22.

www.globalpolicy.org

training in global business is almost certain to grow as the number of businesses competing in global markets increases.[8] You might decide that a career in global business is your long-term goal. If you make that choice, prepare yourself to work hard and always be ready for new challenges.[9]

## WHY TRADE WITH OTHER NATIONS?

There are several reasons why countries trade with other countries. First, no nation, not even a technologically advanced one, can produce all of the products that its people want and need. Second, even if a country did become self-sufficient, other nations would seek to trade with that country in order to meet the needs of their own people. Third, some nations (e.g., China, Russia) have an abundance of natural resources but limited technological know-how, while other countries (e.g., Japan, Switzerland) have sophisticated technology but few natural resources. Global trade enables a nation to produce what it is most capable of producing and to buy what it needs from others in a mutually beneficial exchange relationship. This happens through a process called free trade.[10] **Free trade** is the movement of goods and services among nations without political or economic barriers. It is often a hotly debated concept.[11] Figure 3.2 on page 62 offers some of the pros and cons of free trade.

**free trade**
The movement of goods and services among nations without political or economic barriers.

### The Theories of Comparative and Absolute Advantage

Global trade involves the exchange of goods and services across national borders. Exchanges between and among countries involve more than goods and services, however. Countries also exchange art, sports, cultural events, medical

| PROS | CONS |
| --- | --- |
| • The global market contains over 6 billion potential customers for goods and services.<br>• Productivity grows when countries produce goods and services in which they have a comparative advantage.<br>• Global competition and less-costly imports keep prices down, so inflation does not curtail economic growth.<br>• Free trade inspires innovation for new products and keeps firms competitively challenged.<br>• Uninterrupted flow of capital gives countries access to foreign investments, which help keep interest rates low. | • Domestic workers (particularly in manufacturing-based jobs) can lose their jobs due to increased imports or productions shifts to low-wage global markets.<br>• Workers may be forced to accept pay cuts from employers, who can threaten to move their jobs to lower-cost global markets.<br>• Moving operations overseas because of intense competitive pressure often means the loss of service jobs and growing numbers of white-collar jobs.<br>• Domestic companies can lose their comparative advantage when competitors build advanced production operations in low-wage countries. |

figure 3.2

**THE PROS AND CONS OF FREE TRADE**

**comparative advantage theory**
Theory that states that a country should sell to other countries those products that it produces most effectively and efficiently, and buy from other countries those products that it cannot produce as effectively or efficiently.

**absolute advantage**
The advantage that exists when a country has a monopoly on producing a specific product or is able to produce it more efficiently than all other countries.

advances, space exploration, and labor. Comparative advantage theory, suggested in the early 19th century by English economist David Ricardo, was the guiding principle that supported this idea of free economic exchange.[12] **Comparative advantage theory** states that a country should sell to other countries those products that it produces most effectively and efficiently, and buy from other countries those products it cannot produce as effectively or efficiently.

The United States has a comparative advantage in producing goods and services, such as software and engineering services. In contrast, the United States lacks a comparative advantage in growing coffee or making shoes; thus, it imports most of these products. Through specialization and trade, the United States and its trading partners can realize mutually beneficial exchanges.[13]

A country has an **absolute advantage** if it has a monopoly on producing a specific product or is able to produce it more efficiently than all other countries. For instance, South Africa once had an absolute advantage in diamond production. Today there are very few instances of absolute advantage in global markets.

## GETTING INVOLVED IN GLOBAL TRADE

People interested in finding a job in global business often think of firms like Boeing, Ford, or IBM, which have large multinational accounts. The real job potential, however, may be with small businesses. Today in the United States, small businesses account for almost half of the private-sector commerce but only about 30 percent of exports.[14] With the help and encouragement of the U.S. Department of Commerce, many small businesses are becoming more involved in global markets.[15]

Getting started globally is often a matter of observation, determination, and risk. For example, years ago an American traveler in an African country noticed there was no ice available for drinks, for keeping foods fresh, and so on. Further research showed there was no ice factory for hundreds of miles, yet the market seemed huge. The man returned to the United States, found some investors, and returned to Africa to build an ice-making plant. The job was tough. Much negotiation was necessary with local authorities (negotiation often best done by local citizens and businesspeople who know the system), and the plant was built. This forward-thinking entrepreneur gained a considerable return on his idea, and the people in that country gained a needed product.

## Importing Goods and Services

Foreign students attending U.S. colleges and universities often notice that some products widely available in their countries are not available in the United States, or are more expensive here. By working with producers in their native country, finding some start-up financing, and putting in long hours of hard work, many students have become major importers while still in school.

Howard Schultz, chairman of Starbucks, found his opportunity while traveling in Italy. Schultz became enthralled with the neighborhood coffee and espresso bars he frequented there. He loved the ambience, the aroma, and especially the sense of community he saw and wondered why we lacked such great gathering places in the United States. In 1987, Schultz bought the original Starbucks coffee shop in Seattle and transformed it according to his vision.[16] Because the Italian coffee bars caught Schultz's attention, people across America now know what a "grande latte" is.[17]

Things may not have started off "pretty" for Ugly Dolls but the two-person company has grown into a global business selling its product in over 1,000 stores around the world. The dolls are particular favorites in Japan. Does a career in exporting or importing sound appealing to you?

## Exporting Goods and Services

You may be surprised at what you can sell in other countries. Who would think that U.S. firms could sell beer in Germany, the home of so many good beers? Well, around the corner from a famous beer hall in Munich you can buy Samuel Adams Boston Lager. America's largest brewer, Anheuser-Busch, also saw such opportunities. It owns 27 percent of Tsingtao Brewing, the largest brewing company in central China.[18] Only the Chinese government, with 31 percent ownership, has a larger financial investment in the company.[19] If these global moves surprise you, imagine selling sand in the Middle East. Meridan Group exports a special kind of sand used in swimming pool filters that sells well.

The fact is, you can sell just about any good or service used in the United States to other countries—and sometimes the competition is not nearly as intense in global markets as it is at home. You can, for example, sell snowplows to the Saudi Arabians, who use them to plow sand off their driveways. Tropical Blossom Honey Company in Edgewater, Florida, found that Saudis are significant consumers of honey because the Koran (the Muslim holy book) suggests it has healing properties. GlobalSight Corporation, a global consulting and software company in San Jose, California, has expanded opportunities for clients like Herbalife by developing Web sites to the cultural and linguistic needs of a particular country or region.[20] The possibilities for global trade seem almost limitless. Read the Spotlight on Small Business box on page 64 about a company that can't bear to avoid the global market.

It's important for businesses to be aware of these great opportunities. It's also important to note that exporting is a terrific boost to the U.S. economy. C. Fred Bergsten, director of the Institute for International Economics, estimates that every $1 billion in U.S. exports generates 25,000 jobs at home. But don't be misled: Selling in global markets is by no means easy. Adapting products to specific global markets is potentially profitable but can be very difficult. We shall discuss a number of forces that affect global trading later in this chapter.

If you are interested in exporting, write for "The Basic Guide to Exporting," a brochure available from the U.S. Government Printing Office; Superintendent

SPOTLIGHT ON small business

www.buildabear.com

## Going Global: It's "Bearly" Possible

Maxine Clark had a distinguished career in the retailing industry when she decided she could bear it no longer. She opened her first Build-A-Bear Workshop in St. Louis, Missouri, in 1997. Build-A-Bear is a teddy-bear-themed experience retail store that allows kids ages 3 to 103 to create their own huggable best friends. From this single store in a St. Louis mall, the company expanded to stores in 42 states. However, the "chief executive bear" (Clark) does not intend to stop. Build-A-Bear Workshop Inc. is intent on establishing a global brand with stores across Europe, the Middle East, and Asia.

Apart from its U.S. stores, the company currently operates stores in Australia, Denmark, England, Japan, and South Korea, with stores expected to open in France and Taiwan soon. Eventually Build-A-Bear hopes to operate 350 to 400 stores globally. Will the global market be willing to bear such expansion? Clark notes that the teddy bear is a universally loved symbol around the globe. She's also quick to point out that Build-A-Bear is not just selling a product; it's selling the experience of making your own stuffed animal.

However, like all companies that venture into the global market, Build-A-Bear must overcome certain challenges. One key problem is the differences that exist in shopping in a particular country. For example, in some countries malls are very prevalent while in others they are just starting to grow. Retail space also tends to be expensive in Europe, Asia, and Canada since there is less retail space per person than in the United States. Add to that the problems of finding the right international personnel to operate the stores, managing currency fluctuations, and calculating differences in consumer income—and the challenges can seem unbearable. Maxine Clark, however, is not discouraged and plans to push forward. She's even thinking about putting her stores on cruise ships, a "beary" interesting idea.

Sources: Mary Jo Feldstein, "Build-A-Bear Builds a Presence," *St. Louis Post-Dispatch*, May 13, 2005, p. B1, and Arlene Weintraub, "The 100 Best Small Companies," *BusinessWeek*, June 6, 2005, pp. 63–92.

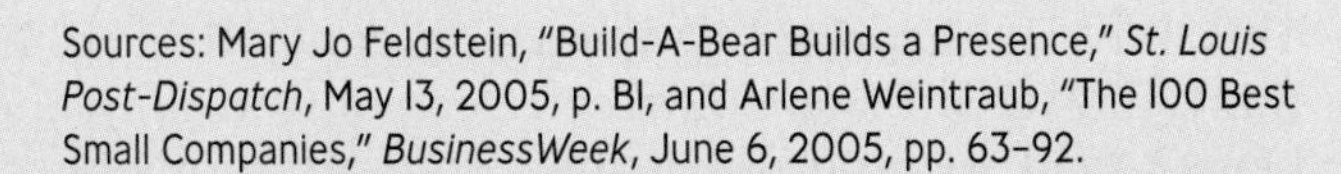

of Documents; Washington, D.C. 20402. More advice can be found at Web sites such as those of the U.S Department of Commerce (www.doc.gov), the Bureau of Export Administration (www.bea.gov), the Small Business Administration (www.sba.gov), and the Small Business Exporters Association (www.sbea.org).

**balance of trade**
The total value of a nation's exports compared to its imports measured over a particular period.

**trade deficit**
An unfavorable balance of trade; occurs when the value of a country's imports exceeds that of its exports.

**balance of payments**
The difference between money coming into a country (from exports) and money leaving the country (for imports) plus money flows from other factors such as tourism, foreign aid, military expenditures, and foreign investment.

## Measuring Global Trade

In measuring global trade, nations follow two key indicators: balance of trade and balance of payments. The **balance of trade** is the total value of a nation's exports compared to its imports measured over a particular period. A *favorable* balance of trade, or trade surplus, occurs when the value of the country's exports exceeds that of its imports. An *unfavorable* balance of trade, or **trade deficit**, occurs when the value of the country's imports exceeds that of its exports. It's easy to understand why countries prefer to export more than they import. If I sell you $200 worth of goods and buy only $100 worth, I have an extra $100 available to buy other things. However, I'm in an unfavorable position if I buy $200 worth of goods from you and sell you only $100.

The **balance of payments** is the difference between money coming into a country (from exports) and money leaving the country (for imports) plus money flows coming into or leaving a country from other factors such as tourism, foreign aid, military expenditures, and foreign investment. The goal is always to have more money flowing into the country than flowing out of the country; in other words a *favorable* balance of payments. Conversely, an *unfavorable* balance of payments exists when more money is flowing out of a country than coming in.

For many years, the United States exported more goods and services to other countries than it imported. However, since 1975 the United States has bought more goods from other nations than it has sold to other nations (a trade deficit, or unfavorable balance of trade).[21] Recently, the United States ran its highest trade deficits with China.[22] How, then, is the United States one of the world's largest exporting nations? Good question; let's look at the answer.

Even though the United States exports a vast amount of goods globally, it exports a much lower *percentage* of its products than other countries do. (Figure 3.3 lists the major trading countries in the world.) In fact, in the early 1980s, no more than 10 percent of American businesses exported products. Today, most large businesses are involved in global trade and growing numbers of small- and medium-sized businesses are going global as well. The Internet helped make such expansion much easier.

In supporting free trade, the United States, like other nations, wants to make certain that global trade is conducted fairly. To ensure this level playing field, the United States and other countries enforce laws to prohibit unfair practices such as dumping.[23] **Dumping** is the practice of selling products in a foreign country at lower prices than those charged in the producing country. This tactic is sometimes used to reduce surplus products in foreign markets or to gain a foothold in a new market by offering products for lower prices than domestic competitors do. There's also evidence that some governments offer financial incentives to certain industries to sell goods in global markets for less than they sell them at home. Japan, Brazil, and Russia, for example, have been penalized for dumping steel in the United States; Canada for dumping softwood lumber.[24] U.S. laws against dumping are specific and require foreign firms to price their products to include 10 percent overhead costs plus an 8 percent profit margin.

Now that you understand some of the basic terms used in global business, we can begin to discuss this topic more deeply. We'll begin by looking at different strategies a business can use to enter global markets. Before doing so, let's assess your progress so far.

## figure 3.3

**THE LARGEST TRADING NATIONS IN THE WORLD**

- United States
- Germany
- China (includes Hong Kong)
- Japan
- France
- Great Britain
- Canada
- Italy
- Netherlands

**dumping**
Selling products in a foreign country at lower prices than those charged in the producing country.

DANZIGER
CartoonArts International / NYTimes Syndicate

China accounts for the highest U.S. trade deficit with any nation. It's no wonder then that "Made in China" is a phrase very familiar to most Americans. How many products can you think of that we import from China?

### progress assessment

- How do world population and market statistics support the expansion of U.S. businesses into global markets?
- What is comparative advantage, and what are some examples of this concept in actual global markets?
- How are a nation's balance of trade and balance of payments determined?
- What is dumping?

## STRATEGIES FOR REACHING GLOBAL MARKETS

**licensing**
A global strategy in which a firm (the licensor) allows a foreign company (the licensee) to produce its product in exchange for a fee (a royalty).

Businesses may use different strategies to compete in global markets. The key strategies include licensing, exporting, franchising, contract manufacturing, creating international joint ventures and strategic alliances, creating foreign subsidiaries, and engaging in foreign direct investment. Each strategy provides opportunities for becoming involved in global markets, along with specific commitments and risks. Figure 3.4 places the strategies on a continuum showing the amount of commitment, control, risk, and profit potential associated with each one. Take a few minutes to look over Figure 3.4 before you continue reading.

The sun never sets on Mickey and the gang, which is making the Disney Company very happy. The firm has had great success licensing the famous mouse and his cast of characters in Europe and Asia. Here Mickey welcomes visitors to Tokyo Disneyland. What challenges does a company like Disney face in global markets?

### Licensing

A firm (the licensor) may decide to compete in a global market by **licensing** the right to manufacture its product or use its trademark to a foreign company (the licensee) for a fee (a royalty). A company with an interest in licensing generally sends company representatives to the foreign producer to help set up operations. The licensor may also assist or work with a licensee in such areas as distribution, promotion, and consulting.

A licensing agreement can be beneficial to a firm in several different ways. Through licensing, an organization can gain additional revenues it normally would not have generated in its home market. In addition, foreign licensees often must purchase start-up supplies, component materials, and consulting services from the licensing firm. Such agreements have been very profitable for companies like Disney, Coca-Cola, and Altria. These firms often enter foreign markets through licensing agreements that typically extend into long-term service contracts. For example, Oriental Land Company owns and operates Tokyo Disneyland and Tokyo Disney Sea Park under a licensing agreement; Disney also collects management and consulting fees.[25] Altria, the parent company of Philip Morris, has an agreement pending with the Chinese government to permit Marlboro to be manufactured and sold in China, the world's largest cigarette market.[26]

A final advantage of licensing is that licensors spend little or no money to produce and market their products. These costs come from the licensee's

figure 3.4
**STRATEGIES FOR REACHING GLOBAL MARKETS**

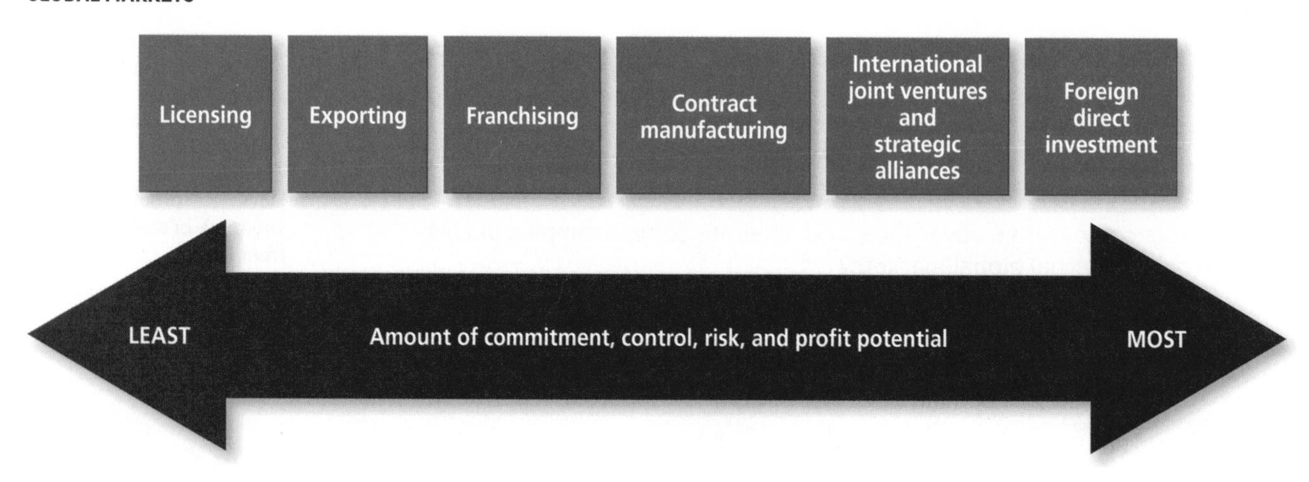

pocket. Therefore, licensees generally work very hard to see that the product they license succeeds in their market. However, licensors may also experience problems. One major problem is that often a firm must grant licensing rights to its product for an extended period, maybe 20 years or longer. If a product experiences remarkable growth and success in the foreign market, the bulk of the revenues earned belong to the licensee. Perhaps even more threatening is that a licensing firm is actually selling its expertise in a product area. If a foreign licensee learns the company's technology or product secrets, it may break the agreement and begin to produce a similar product on its own. If legal remedies are not available, the licensing firm may lose its trade secrets, not to mention the agreed-on royalties.

## Exporting

As global competition intensified, the U.S. Department of Commerce created Export Assistance Centers (EACs). EACs provide hands-on exporting assistance and trade-finance support for small and medium-sized businesses that wish to directly export goods and services. An EAC network exists in more than 100 U.S. cities and 80 countries, with further expansion planned.[27] This activity is critical because it is estimated that small and midsize firms represented 98 percent of the growth in the exporter population in the United States from 1994 to 2004.[28]

Still, even with the help of EACs available, many U.S. firms are reluctant to go through the trouble of establishing foreign trading relationships. In such cases specialists called export trading companies (or export-management companies) are available to assist in negotiating and establishing the trading relationships desired. An export-trading company not only matches buyers and sellers from different countries but also provides needed services (such as dealing with foreign customs offices, documentation, even weights and measures) to ease the process of entering global markets. Export-trading companies also help exporters with a key and risky element of doing business globally: getting paid. Companies that work with export-trading companies are involved in indirect exporting. If you are considering a career in global business, export-trading companies often provide internships or part-time opportunities for students.

## Franchising

Franchising is an arrangement whereby someone with a good idea for a business sells the rights to use the business name and sell a product or service to others in a given territory in a specified manner. Franchising is popular both domestically and internationally, and will be discussed in depth in Chapter 5. U.S. franchisors such as McDonald's, Holiday Inn, and Dunkin' Donuts have many global units operated by foreign franchisees. However, global franchising is not limited to the large franchisors. For example, Rocky Mountain Chocolate Factory, a Colorado-based producer of premium chocolate candies with 286 retail stores worldwide, has franchising agreements with the Muhairy

Getting tired from reading and need a quick snack? How about a piping hot Domino's pizza with squid and sweet mayonnaise or a duck gizzard with bean sprouts to satisfy your craving? Domino's serves pizzas around the globe that appeal to different tastes. Franchises like Domino's and McDonald's know the world is a big place with wide differences in foods and tastes. How can franchises ensure their products are appropriate for global markets?

REACHING BEYOND

www.mcdonalds.com

our borders

## The Winner and Still World's Champion

Franchising is an arrangement whereby someone with a good idea for a business sells the rights to use the business name and to sell a product or service to others in a given territory. The United States led the way in the expansion of franchising and changed the global market's landscape. Today small, midsize, and large franchises cover the globe, offering business opportunities in areas from chicken to pizza to exercise. For example, Yum! Brands has more than 1,000 KFCs and 120 Pizza Huts in China, Domino's Pizza has more than 7,500 stores in more than 50 countries, and Jazzercise and Curves have countries like Japan and Greece dancing to their music.

Still, when the word *franchise* comes to mind, one name dominates all others: McDonald's. Whether in New Zealand, South Africa, Mexico, Germany, Brazil, or Indonesia, no other company adapts better and blends the franchise values into the local culture better than McDonald's. Some even use the term *McDonaldization* to symbolize the spread of franchising and the weaving of American pop culture into the world fabric. Today, McDonald's is the largest food-service company in the world and operates more than 30,000 local restaurants in 119 countries.

In Hong Kong, Israel, India, and all other markets in which McDonald's operates, the company continuously listens to customers and adapts to their culture and preferences. For example, having set up its first franchises in Hong Kong in 1975, McDonald's altered the breakfast menu after realizing that customers there liked burgers for breakfast, then preferred chicken or fish for the rest of the day. The company also offers unique products such as curry potato pie and red bean sundaes for its Hong Kong customers. In Israel, all meat served in McDonald's restaurants is 100 percent kosher beef. The company also closes its restaurants on the Sabbath and on religious holidays. However, the company also operates nonkosher restaurants for Israelis who don't keep a strict kosher diet and desire to visit McDonald's on the Sabbath and religious holidays. In India, to meet the unique challenge of respecting the religious sentiments of the population, McDonald's did not introduce beef or pork into its menu.

As a global enterprise, the company must respond to different problems and challenges that emerge at its global restaurants—challenges such as the outbreak of mad cow disease in Europe and Asia or lawsuits claiming that McDonald's food caused it customers to be overweight. McDonald's helped fund research that would let it test for the presence of *E. coli* or mad cow disease in its beef. The company also introduced an adult Happy Meal with salad, bottled water, a pedometer, and a booklet of walking tips to ensure good health. Other causes of global grief for McDonald's are weak currencies in many countries and government regulations.

Yet, even with its problems and challenges, McDonald's is the leading restaurant in the world, serving almost 50 million customers worldwide per day. By adapting to cultural, social, economic, and environmental needs, the company has reaped a large payoff. Today, McDonald's derives more than half of its sales from abroad.

Sources: Julia Boorstein, "Delivering at Domino's Pizza," *Fortune*, February 7, 2005, p. 28, and Lauren Foster, "McDonald's Sales Show Weakness in Europe," *Financial Times*, March 9, 2005, p. 19.

Group of the United Arab Emirates. It operates stores in Saudi Arabia, Oman, Kuwait, Bahrain, and Qatar, where chocolate is considered a gourmet luxury much like caviar is in the United States.[29]

Franchisors, however, have to be careful to adapt their product or service to the countries they serve. KFC's first 11 Hong Kong outlets failed within two years. Apparently the chicken was too greasy, and eating with fingers was too messy for the fastidious people of Hong Kong. Pizza Hut and Domino's learned that preferences in pizza toppings also differ globally. Japanese customers, for example, enjoy squid and sweet mayonnaise pizza. Read the Reaching Beyond our Borders box that highlights McDonald's, the undisputed champion of franchisors.

## Contract Manufacturing

**contract manufacturing**
A foreign country's production of private-label goods to which a domestic company then attaches its brand name or trademark.

**Contract manufacturing** involves a foreign company producing private-label goods to which a domestic company then attaches its own brand name or trademark. The practice falls under the broad category of *outsourcing,* which we discussed in Chapter 1 and will discuss in more depth later.[30] For example, Dell contracts with Quanta Computer of Taiwan to make notebook PCs on which it puts the Dell brand name. Flextronics of Singapore manufactures cell phones, printers, and telecom equipment for many U.S. firms. Nike has more than 700 contract factories around the world that manufacture its footwear and apparel.[31]

Contract manufacturing enables a company to experiment in a new market without incurring heavy start-up costs such as a manufacturing plant. If the brand name becomes a success, the company has penetrated a new market with relatively low risk. A firm can also use contract manufacturing temporarily to meet an unexpected increase in orders and, of course, labor costs are often very low.

## International Joint Ventures and Strategic Alliances

**joint venture**
A partnership in which two or more companies (often from different countries) join to undertake a major project.

A **joint venture** is basically a partnership in which two or more companies (often from different countries) join to undertake a major project. Joint ventures are often mandated by governments such as China as a condition of doing business in their country. For example, General Motors and Volkswagen since 1995 have had a joint venture with Shanghai Automotive Industrial Corporation, China's largest domestic car company, to build cars in China.[32] Joint ventures with foreign firms produce 27 percent of China's industrial output.

Joint ventures are developed for other business reasons as well. In the early 2000s, Campbell Soup formed a joint venture with Japan's Nakano Vinegar, called Campbell Nakano Inc., to expand its rather low share of the soup market in Japan. Nestlé and L'Oréal formed a joint venture to develop a line of inner-beauty products to improve the quality of a person's skin, hair, and nails.[33] Some joint ventures are truly unique, such as the University of Pittsburgh and the Italian government's joint venture to bring a new medical transplant center to Sicily.

The benefits of international joint ventures are clear:

1. Shared technology and risk.
2. Shared marketing and management expertise.
3. Entry into markets where foreign companies are often not allowed unless goods are produced locally.

The drawbacks are not so obvious but are important. One partner can learn the other's technology and practices, and go off and use what it learned to its own advantage only. Also, a shared technology may become obsolete or the joint venture may become too large to be as flexible as needed.

**strategic alliance**
A long-term partnership between two or more companies established to help each company build competitive market advantages.

The global market is also fueling the growth of strategic alliances. A **strategic alliance** is a long-term partnership between two or more companies established to help each company build competitive market advantages. Unlike joint ventures, however, strategic alliances do not typically involve sharing costs, risks, management, or even profits. Such alliances provide access to markets, capital, and technical expertise, causing executives and global consultants to predict that few companies in the future will succeed globally by going it alone.[34] Plus, because of their flexibility, they can effectively link firms from different countries and firms of vastly different sizes. Hewlett-Packard has strategic alliances with Hitachi and Samsung; Chevron has alliances with the Western Australia Energy Research Alliance and Nantucket Nectars (a small maker of juice-based beverages from New England).[35]

## Foreign Direct Investment

**foreign direct investment** The buying of permanent property and businesses in foreign nations.

**foreign subsidiary** A company owned in a foreign country by another company (called the *parent company*).

**Foreign direct investment** is the buying of permanent property and businesses in foreign nations. The most common form of foreign direct investment is a foreign subsidiary. A **foreign subsidiary** is a company that is owned in a foreign country by another company (called the *parent company*). Such a subsidiary operates like a domestic firm, with production, distribution, promotion, pricing, and other business functions under the control of the foreign subsidiary's management. The legal requirements of both the country where the parent firm is located (called the *home country*) and the foreign country where the subsidiary is located (called the *host country*) have to be observed. The primary advantage of a subsidiary is that the company maintains complete control over any technology or expertise it may possess. The major shortcoming of a subsidiary is that the parent company commits a large amount of funds and technology within foreign boundaries. Should relations with a host country falter, the firm's assets could be taken over by the foreign government. Such a takeover is called an *expropriation*.

**multinational corporation** An organization that manufactures and markets products in many different countries and has multinational stock ownership and multinational management.

Swiss-based Nestlé is an example of a major firm with many foreign subsidiaries. The consumer-products giant spent billions of dollars acquiring foreign subsidiaries such as Ralston Purina, Chef America (maker of Hot Pockets), and Dreyer's Ice Cream in the United States as well as Perrier in France. All told, Nestlé has over 500 factories in 80 countries and employs 250,000 people globally.[36] Nestlé is also an example of a multinational corporation. A **multinational corporation** is an organization that manufactures and markets products in many different countries and has multinational stock ownership and multinational management. Multinational corporations are typically extremely large corporations like Nestlé, but not all large firms involved in global business are multinationals. For example, a business could literally be exporting everything it produces, deriving 100 percent of its sales and profits globally, and still not be considered a multinational corporation. Only firms that have *manufacturing capacity* or some other physical presence in different nations can truly be called multinational. Figure 3.5 lists the 10 largest multinational corporations in the world.

Getting involved in global business requires selecting an entry strategy that best fits the goals of the business. The different strategies discussed reflect different levels of ownership, financial commitment, and risk that a company can assume. However, this is just the beginning. It's important to be aware of key market forces that affect a business's ability to trade in global markets. After the Progress Assessment, we'll discuss these forces.

figure 3.5

**THE LARGEST MULTINATIONAL CORPORATIONS IN THE WORLD**

| COMPANY | COUNTRY | SALES (BILLION) |
|---|---|---|
| Wal-Mart | United States | $217 |
| Exxon Mobil | United States | 213 |
| General Motors | United States | 175 |
| BP | United Kingdom | 174 |
| Ford Motor | United States | 162 |
| DaimlerChrysler | Germany | 136 |
| Royal Dutch/Shell | United Kingdom/Netherlands | 135 |
| General Electric | United States | 125 |
| Toyota Motor | Japan | 121 |
| Mitsubishi | Japan | 112 |

Sources: *BusinessWeek;* Morgan Stanley Capital International; and S&P Compustat.

**progress assessment**

- What are the advantages to a firm of using licensing as a method of entry in global markets? What are the disadvantages?
- What services are usually provided by an export-trading company?
- What is the key difference between a joint venture and a strategic alliance? What is a multinational corporation? Can you name at least three multinational corporations?

## FORCES AFFECTING TRADING IN GLOBAL MARKETS

Succeeding in any business takes effort. Unfortunately, the hurdles are higher and more complex in global markets. This is particularly true when dealing with differences in sociocultural forces, economic and financial forces, legal and regulatory forces, and physical and environmental forces. Let's look at each of these global market forces to see how they challenge even the most established and experienced global businesses.

### Sociocultural Forces

The United States is a multicultural nation, yet understanding cultural diversity in America is one of the business challenges of the 21st century. The word *culture* refers to the set of values, beliefs, rules, and institutions held by a specific group of people.[37] Culture can include social structures, religion, manners and customs, values and attitudes, language, and personal communication. If you hope to get involved in global trade, it's critical to be aware of the cultural differences among nations. Unfortunately American businesspeople are notoriously bad at adapting to those differences. In fact, American businesspeople have consistently been accused of *ethnocentricity,* which is an attitude that one's own culture is superior to all others. In contrast, foreign businesspeople are very good at adapting to U.S. culture. Think how effectively German and Japanese carmakers have adapted to Americans' wants and needs in the auto industry. Japanese manufacturer Toyota now sells more vehicles in the United

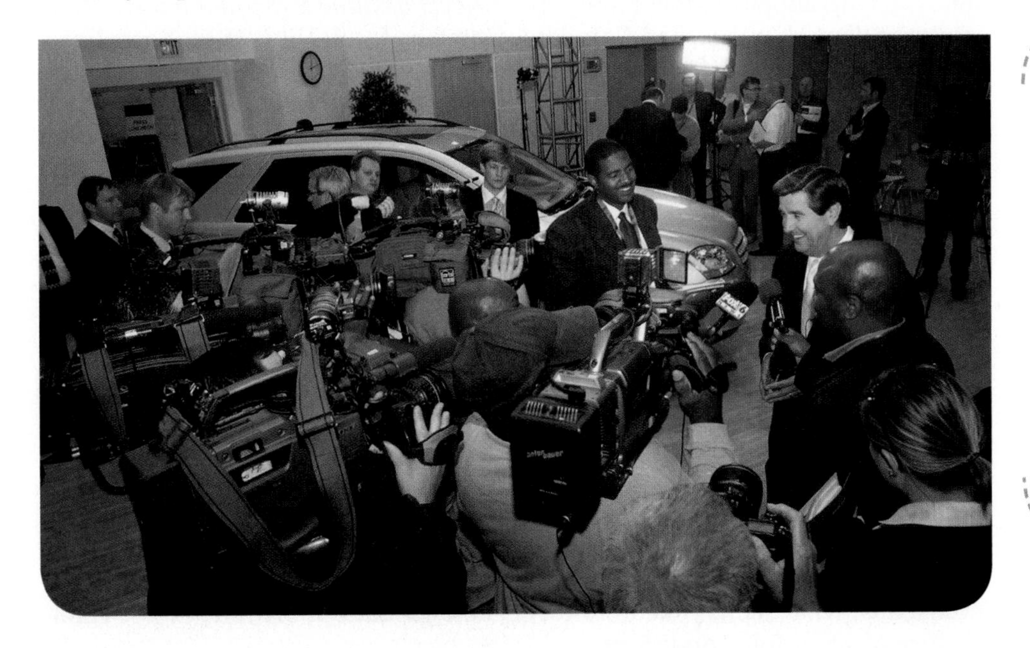

The United States has been and remains a popular global spot for foreign direct investment. Global automobile manufacturers like Toyota, Honda, and Mercedes have spent millions of dollars building facilities in the United States like the Mercedes plant pictured here in Tuscaloosa, Alabama. Do you consider a Mercedes produced in Tuscaloosa an American car or a German car?

States than in Japan.[38] Its Camry model has been the best-selling car in the United States in seven of the last eight years (in 2001 Honda Accord was the winner).[39] In contrast, for many years U.S. auto producers didn't adapt automobiles to drive on the left side of the road, as is done in many countries, and printed owner's manuals only in English. Also, the United States is one of only five nations in the world that still has not conformed to the metric system. Let's look at other experiences American businesses have faced in adapting to important sociocultural (societal and cultural) differences in global markets.

Religion is an important part of any society's culture and can have a significant impact on business operations. Consider the violent clashes between religious communities in India, Pakistan, Northern Ireland, and the Middle East—clashes that have wounded these areas' economies. Companies sometimes ignore religious implications in business decisions. Both McDonald's and Coca-Cola offended Muslims in Saudi Arabia by putting the Saudi Arabian flag on their packaging. The flag's design contains a passage from the Koran (Islam's sacred scripture), and Muslims feel their holy writ should never be wadded up and thrown away. In a classic story, an American manager in Islamic Pakistan toured a new plant under his control. While the plant was in full operation, he went to his office to make some preliminary forecasts of production. Suddenly all the machinery in the plant stopped. He rushed out, suspecting a power failure, but found his production workers on their prayer rugs. Upon learning that Muslims are required to pray five times a day, he returned to his office and lowered his production estimates.

Understanding sociocultural differences can also be important in managing employees. In Latin American countries, workers believe managers are in positions of authority to make decisions and be responsible for the well-being of the workers under their control. Consider what happened to one American manager in Peru who was unaware of this cultural characteristic and believed workers should participate in managerial functions. This manager was convinced he could motivate his workers to higher levels of productivity by instituting a more democratic decision-making style. Soon workers began quitting their jobs in droves. When asked why, the workers said the new manager did not know his job and was asking the workers what to do. All stated they wanted to find new jobs, since this company was doomed due to incompetent management.

The truth is that many U.S. companies still fail to think globally. A sound philosophy to adopt in global markets is: *Never assume that what works in one country will work in another*. Companies such as Intel, Nike, IBM, Sony, Ford, Dell, and Toyota have developed brand names with widespread global appeal and recognition. However, even these successful global businesses often face difficulties. For example, translating an advertising theme into a different language can be disastrous. To get an idea of the problems companies have faced with translations, take a look at Figure 3.6. "Think global, act local" is a valuable motto to follow.

## Economic and Financial Forces

Economic differences can also muddy the water in global markets. Surely it's hard for us to imagine buying chewing gum by the stick instead of by the package. Yet this buying behavior is commonplace in economically depressed nations like Haiti, where customers can buy only small quantities. You might suspect with over 1 billion people, India would be a dream market for companies like Hershey's, Skippy, and Coca-Cola.[40] However, Indians annually consume an average of only three soft drinks per person and the vast majority cannot afford chocolate or peanut butter due to India's low per capita income level. Thus, what seems like an unbelievable global opportunity is not viable because of economic conditions.

- PepsiCo attempted a Chinese translation of "Come Alive, You're in the Pepsi Generation" that read to Chinese customers as "Pepsi Brings Your Ancestors Back from the Dead."
- Coors Brewing Company put its slogan "Turn It Loose" into Spanish and found it translated as "Suffer from Diarrhea."
- Perdue Chicken used the slogan "It Takes a Strong Man to Make a Chicken Tender," which was interpreted in Spanish as "It Takes an Aroused Man to Make a Chicken Affectionate."
- KFC's patented slogan "finger-lickin' good" was understood in Japanese as "Bite Your Fingers Off."
- On the other side of the translation glitch, Electrolux, a Scandinavian vacuum manufacturer, tried to sell its products in the U.S. market with the slogan "Nothing Sucks Like an Electrolux."

figure 3.6

**OOPS, DID WE SAY THAT?**

A global marketing strategy can be very difficult to implement. Look at the problems these well-known companies encountered in global markets.

Global financial markets do not have a worldwide currency. Mexicans shop with pesos, South Koreans with won, Japanese with yen, and Americans with dollars. Globally, the U.S. dollar is considered the world's dominant and most stable currency. However, this doesn't mean that the dollar always retains the same market value. In an international transaction today, one dollar may be exchanged for eight pesos; tomorrow you may only get seven pesos for the same dollar. The **exchange rate** is the value of one nation's currency relative to the currencies of other countries.

**exchange rate** The value of one nation's currency relative to the currencies of other countries.

Changes in a nation's exchange rates can have important implications in global markets.[41] A *high value of the dollar* means that a dollar would be traded for more foreign currency than previously. Therefore, products of foreign producers would be cheaper because it takes fewer dollars to buy them. However, the cost of U.S.-produced goods would become more expensive because of the dollar's high value. Conversely, a *low value of the dollar* means that a dollar is traded for less foreign currency—foreign goods become more expensive because it takes more dollars to buy them, but American goods become cheaper to foreign buyers because it takes less foreign currency to buy them.[42]

The euro officially became the common currency of most of the members of the EU on January 1, 2002, replacing the mark, franc, lira, peseta, and other former currencies. Do you think the euro will replace the American dollar for leadership among the world's currencies?

Global financial markets operate under a system called *floating exchange rates,* in which currencies "float" according to the supply and demand in the global market for the currency. This supply and demand is created by global currency traders, who develop a market for a nation's currency based on the perceived trade and investment potential of the country. Changes in currency values cause many problems globally. Consider multinational corporations like Nestlé or General Electric. Labor costs at their many operations can vary considerably as currency values shift, causing them to juggle production from one country to another.[43] Medium-sized companies like H. B. Fuller of St. Paul, Minnesota, and smaller businesses like Superior Products of Cleveland are also impacted by currency fluctuations. Fuller has operations in 34 countries, and Superior operates in 6 countries. Both have learned to use currency fluctuations to their advantage in dealing with their global markets.[44]

Currency valuation problems can be especially harsh on developing economies. At certain times a nation's government will intervene and adjust the value of its currency, often to increase the export potential of its products. **Devaluation** is lowering the value of a nation's currency relative to other currencies. In other instances, due to a nation's weak currency, the only possibility of trade is through one of its oldest forms: *bartering,* which is the exchange of merchandise for

**devaluation** Lowering the value of a nation's currency relative to other currencies.

**countertrading**
A complex form of bartering in which several countries may be involved, each trading goods for goods or services for services.

merchandise or service for service with no money involved.[45] **Countertrading** is a complex form of bartering in which several countries may be involved, each trading goods for goods or services for services. Estimates are that countertrading accounts for over 20 percent of all global exchanges, especially deals involving developing countries. For example, let's say a developing country such as Jamaica wants to buy vehicles from Ford Motor Company in exchange for Jamaican bauxite. Ford, however, does not have a need for Jamaican bauxite, but does have a need for computer monitors. In a countertrade agreement, Ford may trade vehicles to Jamaica, which then trades bauxite to another country, say India, which then exchanges computer monitors with Ford. This countertrade is thus beneficial to all three parties. Trading products for products helps businesses avoid some of the financial problems and currency constraints that exist in global markets. Understanding economic conditions, currency fluctuations, and countertrade opportunities is vital to a company's success in the global market.

## Legal and Regulatory Forces

In any economy, the conduct and direction of business are firmly tied to the legal and regulatory environment. In the United States federal, state, and local laws, as well as other government regulations, heavily impact business practices. In global markets, no central system of law exists, so different systems of laws and regulations may apply. This makes the task of conducting global business extremely difficult as businesspeople navigate a sea of laws and regulations in global markets that are often inconsistent. Important legal questions related to antitrust rules, labor relations, patents, copyrights, trade practices, taxes, product liability, child labor, prison labor, and other issues are written and interpreted differently country by country.[46]

American businesses are required to follow U.S. laws and regulations in conducting business globally. U.S. legislation, such as the Foreign Corrupt Practices Act of 1978, can create competitive disadvantages for American businesspeople when competing with foreign competitors.[47] This law specifically prohibits "questionable" or "dubious" payments to foreign officials to secure business contracts. The problem is that this law runs contrary to beliefs and practices in many countries, where corporate or government bribery is not only acceptable but perhaps the only way to secure a lucrative contract.[48] Members of the Organization for Economic Cooperation and Development (OECD) have been urged to lead a global effort to fight corruption and bribery in foreign markets, but little has been accomplished. For a partial list of countries where bribery or other unethical business practices are most common, see Figure 3.7.

figure 3.7

**COUNTRIES RATED HIGHEST ON CORRUPT BUSINESS PRACTICES**

1. Haiti
2. Bangladesh
3. Nigeria
4. Myanmar
5. Chad
6. Paraguay
7. Azerbaijan
8. Turkmenistan
9. Tajikistan
10. Indonesia

Source: Transparency International.

It's important to remember that to be successful in global markets it's often useful to contact local businesspeople in the host countries and gain their cooperation and sponsorship. Such local contacts can help a company penetrate the market and deal with what can be imposing bureaucratic barriers. Local businesspeople are also familiar with laws and regulations that could have an important impact on a foreign firm's business in their country.

## Physical and Environmental Forces

Certain physical and environmental forces can also impact a company's ability to conduct business in global markets. In fact, technological constraints may make it difficult or perhaps impossible to build a large global market. For example, some developing countries have such primitive transportation and storage systems that international distribution is ineffective, if not impossible. This is especially true with regard to food, which is often spoiled by the time it reaches the market in certain countries. Compound this fact with unclean water and the lack of effective sewer systems, and you can sense the intensity of the problem.

American exporters must also be aware that certain technological differences affect the nature of exportable products. For example, houses in most developing countries do not have electrical systems that match those of U.S. homes, in kind or capacity. How would the differences in electricity available (110 versus 220 volts) affect an American appliance manufacturer wishing to export? Also, computer and Internet usage in many developing countries is thin or nonexistent. You can see how this would make for a tough business environment in general and would make e-commerce difficult, if not nearly impossible. After the progress assessment, we will explore how trade protectionism affects global business.

**trade protectionism**
The use of government regulations to limit the import of goods and services.

**tariff**
A tax imposed on imports.

progress assessment

- What are the major hurdles to successful global trade?
- What does *ethnocentricity* mean?
- Which cultural and societal differences are most likely to affect global trade efforts? (Name at least two.)

## TRADE PROTECTIONISM

As we discussed in the previous section, sociocultural, economic and financial, legal and regulatory, and physical and environmental forces are all challenges to trading globally. What is often a much greater barrier to global trade, however, is trade protectionism. **Trade protectionism** is the use of government regulations to limit the import of goods and services. Advocates of trade protectionism believe it allows domestic producers to survive and grow, producing more jobs. Countries often use protectionist measures to guard against such practices as dumping (discussed earlier); others are wary of foreign competition in general. To understand how protectionism affects global business, let's briefly review some global economic history.

Business, economics, and politics have always been closely linked. What we now call economics was once referred to as *political economy,* indicating the close ties between politics (government) and economics. In the 17th and 18th centuries, businesspeople and government leaders endorsed an economic belief called *mercantilism*. The idea of mercantilism was for a nation to sell more goods to other nations than it bought from them, that is, to have a favorable balance of trade.[49] According to mercantilists, this resulted in a flow of money to the country that sold the most globally. This philosophy led governments to implement **tariffs,** which are basically taxes on imports, thus making imported goods more expensive to buy.

Generally, there are two different kinds of tariffs: protective and revenue. *Protective tariffs* (import taxes) are designed to raise the retail price of imported products so that domestic goods are more

The United Steelworkers Union claims it lost 70 percent of its members over the past 20 years because of the growth of imported steel. Should governments protect such industries by placing tariffs on imported products? Why or why not?

competitively priced. These tariffs are meant to save jobs for domestic workers and to keep industries (especially *infant industries,* new companies in the early stages of growth) from closing down because of foreign competition. *Revenue tariffs* are designed to raise money for the government. They are commonly used by developing countries to help infant industries compete in global markets. An **import quota** limits the number of products in certain categories that a nation can import. The United States has import quotas on a number of products, including sugar; there are also U.S. tariffs on products such as shrimp.[50] The goal is to protect U.S. companies in order to preserve jobs. An **embargo** is a complete ban on the import or export of a certain product or the stopping of all trade with a particular country. Political disagreements have caused many countries to establish embargoes such as the U.S. embargo against Cuba, in effect since 1962.[51] Nations also prohibit the export of specific products globally.[52] Antiterrorism laws and the U.S. Export Administration Act of 1979 prohibit the exporting of goods (e.g., high-tech weapons) that could endanger national security.

**import quota**
A limit on the number of products in certain categories that a nation can import.

**embargo**
A complete ban on the import or export of a certain product or stopping all trade with a particular country.

*Nontariff barriers* are not as specific or formal as tariffs, import quotas, and embargoes but can be as detrimental to free trade.[53] It's common for nations to set restrictive standards that detail exactly how a product must be sold in a country. For example, Denmark requires companies to sell butter in cubes, not tubs. For many years Japan argued it had some of the lowest tariffs in the world and welcomed foreign exports, yet American businesses found it difficult to establish trade relationships with the Japanese. A Japanese tradition called *keiretsu* (pronounced "care-yet-sue") built "corporate families" (like Mitsui and Mitsubishi) that forged semipermanent ties with suppliers, customers, and distributors with full support of the government.[54] The Japanese believed these corporate alliances would provide economic payoffs by nurturing long-term strategic thinking and mutually beneficial cooperation. Today, U.S. businesses are finding Japan a much friendlier place for imports.[55]

Would-be exporters might easily view the trade barriers discussed above as good reasons to avoid global trade. Still, wherever you stand on the tariff issue, it's obvious that overcoming trade constraints creates business opportunities. Next, we'll look at organizations and agreements that attempt to eliminate barriers to trade among nations.

## The World Trade Organization (WTO)

In 1948, government leaders from 23 nations throughout the world formed the **General Agreement on Tariffs and Trade (GATT)**, an international forum for negotiating mutual reductions in trade restrictions. These countries agreed to negotiate trade agreements to facilitate the exchange of goods, services, ideas, and cultural programs. In 1986, the Uruguay Round of the GATT was convened to specifically deal with the renegotiation of trade agreements. After eight years of meetings, 124 nations at the Uruguay Round voted to modify the GATT. The U.S. Congress approved the agreement in 1994. Under the agreement, tariffs were lowered an average of 38 percent worldwide, and new trade rules were expanded to areas such as agriculture, services, and the protection of patents.

**General Agreement on Tariffs and Trade (GATT)**
A 1948 agreement that established an international forum for negotiating mutual reductions in trade restrictions.

The Uruguay Round also established the **World Trade Organization (WTO)** to assume the task of mediating trade disputes among nations. The WTO, headquartered in Geneva, Switzerland, is an independent entity now comprised of 148 member nations whose purpose is to oversee cross-border trade issues and global business practices.[56] It's the world's first attempt at establishing a global mediation center. Trade issues are expected to be resolved by the WTO within 12 to 15 months instead of languishing for years, as was the case in the past. The WTO celebrated its 10th anniversary in 2005.

**World Trade Organization (WTO)**
The international organization that replaced the General Agreement on Tariffs and Trade, and was assigned the duty to mediate trade disputes among nations.

Not everyone sees the WTO as an independent entity attempting to improve global business practices. Protests in cities like Seattle, Prague, and Genoa involved demonstrators expressing their distrust of globalization and the WTO in particular. The demonstrators believe that multinational corporations and international financial institutions have worked to their own benefit rather than addressing the needs of developing nations. What do you think should be the role of the WTO in dealing with global trade issues?

It would be a mistake to assume the WTO has solved all the problems in global trade. Legal and regulatory problems (discussed previously) often impede trade expansion. Also, a wide divide exists between developing nations (which comprise 80 percent of the WTO membership) and industrialized nations such as the United States.[57] The 2001 WTO meetings in Doha, Qatar (located in the Middle East), addressed topics including dismantling protection of manufactured goods, eliminating subsidies on agricultural products, and overturning temporary protectionist measures that impede global trade. China became a member of the WTO in 2001; Russia is hoping to be admitted to the WTO possibly in 2006. WTO challenges will likely persist throughout the current decade.

## Common Markets

An issue not resolved by the GATT or the WTO is whether common markets create regional alliances at the expense of global expansion. A **common market** (also called a *trading bloc*) is a regional group of countries that have a common external tariff, no internal tariffs, and the coordination of laws to facilitate exchange among member countries. Two examples are the European Union (EU) and the South American Common Market called the Mercosur. Let's look briefly at both.

**common market**
A regional group of countries that have a common external tariff, no internal tariffs, and a coordination of laws to facilitate exchange; also called a *trading bloc.* An example is the European Union.

The EU began in the late 1950s as an alliance of six trading partners (then known as the Common Market and later the European Economic Community). Today the EU is a group of 25 nations with a population of 455 million (see Figure 3.8 on page 78). EU nations united to make Europe the world's second-largest economy and an even stronger competitor in global commerce.[58] The EU sees economic integration as the major way to compete for global business, particularly with the United States, China, and Japan.[59]

The path to European unification was not easy, but the EU took a significant step in 1999, when it officially launched its currency, the euro. The formal transition to the euro occurred three years later, when 12 of the then 15 EU member nations agreed to a single monetary unit. (Great Britain, Sweden, and Denmark elected not to convert to the euro.) EU businesses saved billions each year with the entry of the euro, whose adoption eliminated currency conversions. Globally, the euro is certainly a worthy challenger to the U.S. dollar's dominance in global markets due to the economic strength and size of the EU.

figure 3.8

**MEMBERS OF THE EUROPEAN UNION**

Current EU members are highlighted in dark blue. Countries that have applied for membership are in light blue.

Mercosur is an organization that groups Brazil, Argentina, Paraguay, Uruguay, and associate members Chile and Bolivia. Like the EU, Mercosur had economic goals that included a single currency. There was even talk of an agreement combining Mercosur and the Andean Pact (which includes Venezuela, Colombia, Peru, and Ecuador) to pave the way for an economic free-trade zone spanning South America. However, more than a decade after its formation, the Mercosur trade bloc has not advanced its goals.

## The North American and Central American Free Trade Agreements

**North American Free Trade Agreement (NAFTA)** Agreement that created a free-trade area among the United States, Canada, and Mexico.

A widely debated issue of the early 1990s was the ratification of the **North American Free Trade Agreement (NAFTA)**, which created a free-trade area among the United States, Canada, and Mexico. NAFTA was signed into law in 1994. The objectives of NAFTA were to (1) eliminate trade barriers and facilitate cross-border movement of goods and services among the three countries; (2) promote conditions of fair competition in this free-trade area; (3) increase investment opportunities in the territories of the three nations; (4) provide effective protection and enforcement of intellectual property rights (patents, copyrights, etc.) in each nation's territory; (5) establish a framework for further regional trade cooperation; and (6) improve working conditions in North America.

Opponents of NAFTA warned that it would have serious economic consequences such as the loss of U.S. jobs and loss of capital leaving the United States. In contrast, supporters predicted that NAFTA would open a vast new market for U.S. exports and would create jobs and market opportunities in the long term. Today, the three NAFTA countries have a combined population of 426 million people and a gross domestic product (GDP) of more than $12 trillion.[60] The agreement permits the United States, Canada, and Mexico to reduce trade barriers with one another while maintaining independent trade agreements with other countries.

NAFTA remains hotly debated. On the positive side, the value of U.S. exports to NAFTA partners has increased from approximately $135 billion to $250 billion since the agreement was signed. Trade volume among the three partners has expanded from $289 billion in 1994 to $623 billion today. On the downside, the U.S. Department of Labor estimates that the United States has lost 500,000 jobs since enacting NAFTA; others put the number at close to 1 million.[61] Also, annual per capita income in Mexico (about $9,000) still lags considerably behind that of the United States (about $36,000), causing illegal immigration to remain a major problem. Many argue that work conditions have become even more unsafe, especially southern Mexico.[62]

NAFTA controversies have not changed the U.S. commitment to free-trade agreements. In 2005, Congress passed the Central American Free Trade Agreement (CAFTA), which created a free-trade zone with Central American nations Costa Rica, the Dominican Republic, El Salvador, Guatemala, Honduras, and Nicaragua.[63] Supporters claim that CAFTA will open new markets, lower tariffs, and ease regulations between the member nations.[64] Critics again insist the measure will cost American jobs, especially in the sugar and textile industries. CAFTA is expected to become fully operational soon after the six Central American partners make specific technical changes required in the agreement. Some hope the passage of CAFTA is a stepping-stone to the creation of a Free Trade Area of the Americas (FTAA), which would create a free-trade area of 800 million people and range in scope from Patagonia to Alaska. This agreement, however, remains stalled due to the U.S. political environment and trade differences among potential partners.[65]

The issues surrounding common markets and free-trade areas will extend far into the 21st century. Some economists resoundingly praise such unions, while others express concern that the world is dividing itself into major trading blocs (EU, NAFTA, etc.). Many fear that poor and developing countries that don't fit into the plans of the trading blocs will suffer. After the Progress Assessment, we'll look at the future of global trade and the controversial issue of outsourcing.

**progress assessment**

- What are the advantages and disadvantages of trade protectionism and of tariffs?
- What is the primary purpose of the World Trade Organization (WTO)?
- What is the primary objective of a common market like the EU?
- Which three nations comprise NAFTA? Which nations comprise CAFTA?

## The Future of Global Trade

Global trade opportunities grow more interesting yet more challenging each day. New and expanding markets present great potential for trade and development. Changes in technology, especially through the Internet, have changed the landscape of global trade. Increases in Internet usage and advances in e-commerce enable companies worldwide to bypass normally required distribution channels to reach a large market that is only a mouse click away. Take New England Pottery Company, for example. Using the Internet, the company was able to speed up the flow of information between buyers and its manufacturing partners in Europe, South America, and Asia. The company became the world's largest vendor in the garden pottery industry. However, issues like terrorism have cast a bit of a dark shadow on global markets. Let's conclude this chapter by looking at issues certain to influence global markets and perhaps your business career in the 21st century.

The lure of over 6 billion customers is hard to pass up, especially since the Internet makes global markets instantly accessible. With more than two-thirds of U.S. adults and more than 600 million people worldwide now plugged into the Net, the global market is where the opportunities exist.[66] However, nowhere on this planet is the lure to global markets keener than in the world's most populous country, China. With more than 1.3 billion people, China has shifted its economy into high gear since changing its economic philosophy from central planning to free markets. In 2005, China surpassed Japan and became the world's third-largest exporter behind the United States and Germany.[67]

Not long ago, foreign direct investment in China was considered risky and not worth the effort. Today, U.S. foreign direct investment surpasses exports as the primary means by which U.S. companies deliver goods to China. In fact, since 2003, China has attracted more global foreign direct investment than the United States. Multinational companies such as General Motors have invested heavily in China's future. Why? According to *The Economist*, if automobile ownership in China rose to current American levels of ownership, there would be 650 million cars on China's roads—more than all the cars in the world today. China has already become the largest global consumer of commodities such as steel, copper, coal, and cement and is second only to the United States in the consumption of oil. Wal-Mart has 42 stores in China but plans to open hundreds more with its Hong Kong partner CITIC Pacific.[68] The New York Stock Exchange has even applied to open offices in China.[69] Manufacturers now use the term *China price* to mean the lowest price possible.[70]

Many view China as the fulfillment of a free trader's dream, where global investment and entrepreneurship are leading a nation to wealth and economic interdependence with the rest of the world. However, concerns remain about China's one-party political system, human rights policies, and growing trade imbalance.[71] Product piracy and counterfeiting are also significant problems. China's underground economy is still actively counterfeiting everything from Callaway golf clubs to Kiwi shoe polish to Louis Vuitton bags.[72] However, since its admission to the World Trade Organization (WTO) in 2001, China has been more receptive to dealing with piracy and counterfeiting. Still, few expect the problems to disappear anytime soon. Economists have warned that profits will take a long time to materialize for most companies doing business in China. Nonetheless, in a relatively short time, China has become an economic phenomenon. With its openness to trade and investment, educated workforce, and stable infrastructure, China could join the United States as a key driver of the world economy.

Planning on improving your golf game with a brand new set of Callaway clubs? Well, maybe you better look closely. In many nations active counterfeiting runs rampant and what buyers may think is the buy of a lifetime is nothing but trademark piracy.

While China clearly attracts most of the attention in Asia, it's important not to forget the rest of the continent. For example, both India's population of 1.1 billion (600 million of whom are under 25 years old) and Russia's 150 million potential customers represent opportunities too good to pass up. India and Russia are emerging markets that present enormous business opportunities. India has seen huge growth in information technology, pharmaceuticals, and biotechnology.[73] Still, it remains a nation with extreme poverty and difficult trade laws. Russia is an industrialized nation with large reserves of oil, gas, and gold.[74] Chevron and Exxon Mobil are hard at work to develop vast oil reserves; Bristol-Myers Squibb and Procter & Gamble have Russian manufacturing facilities. Unfortunately, political, currency, and social problems still persist in Russia. The developing nations of Asia, including Indonesia, Thailand, Singapore, the Philippines, Korea, Malaysia, and Vietnam, also offer great potential for U.S. businesses—and possibly for you.

Ever wonder where those Nikes you are wearing were made? Hard to say, but it's a safe bet they were not made in Nike's home city of Beaverton, Oregon. Nike is one of many companies that have outsourced the manufacturing of its products to plants in other countries. Today, there is a "second wave" of outsourcing as many companies move service-sector jobs offshore. Is there anything U.S. workers can do to make sure their jobs are not shifted offshore?

## The Challenge of Offshore Outsourcing

As you learned in Chapter 1, *outsourcing* is the purchase of goods and services from sources outside a firm rather than providing them within the company. In the United States, companies have outsourced payroll functions, accounting, and some manufacturing operations for many years. However, the shift in outsourcing manufacturing and services from domestic businesses to primarily low-wage markets has become a major issue in the United States. This shift is referred to as *offshore outsourcing*. The Making Ethical Decisions box on page 82 offers an example.

The truth is that American companies like Levi-Strauss and Nike have outsourced manufacturing offshore for decades. Fundamentally, as lower-level manufacturing became more simplified, U.S. companies shifted focus from assembling products to design and architecture. Today, economists argue, we are moving into the "second wave" of offshore outsourcing that involves sizable numbers of skilled, well-educated, middle-income workers in service-sector jobs such as accounting, law, financial and risk management, health care, and information technology that were thought to be safe from foreign market competition. This shift is potentially more disruptive to the U.S. job market than was the first—which primarily involved manufacturing jobs. Forrester Research estimates that more than 3 million U.S. jobs could be moved to global markets in the next 10 years. To take a look at the pros and cons of offshore outsourcing, see Figure 3.9.

China and India are at the center of the offshore outsourcing controversy. Currently, China is primarily involved with manufacturing at the low end of the technology scale whereas India focuses on call centers, telemarketing, data

figure 3.9

**THE PROS AND CONS OF OFFSHORE OUTSOURCING**

**PROS**

1. Less-strategic tasks can be outsourced globally so that companies can focus on areas in which they can excel and grow.
2. Outsourced work allows companies to create efficiencies that in fact let them hire more workers.
3. Consumers benefit from lower prices generated by effective use of global resources and developing nations grow, thus fueling global economic growth.

**CONS**

1. Jobs are lost permanently and wages fall due to low-cost competition offshore.
2. Offshore outsourcing reduces product quality and can therefore cause permanent damage to a company's reputation.
3. Communication among company members, with suppliers, and with customers becomes much more difficult.

www.spu.edu/depts/sbe/ethics

MAKING ethical decisions

### You Can Call Me Ray or You Can Call Me Sanjay

Imagine that you're having a problem with your computer. Not able to fix the problem yourself, you take out the operator's manual and dial customer service. Your call is answered by a service technician who identifies himself as Jeff. You explain to Jeff the problem you are having and wait for his reply. Unfortunately, Jeff cannot solve your problem and transfers your call to his colleague Jennifer. Jennifer analyzes the situation and promptly provides a suggestion that fixes your computer. Impressed, you ask Jennifer for her direct line so that you can call her number if you have additional questions. She says that company policy prevents her from giving you her direct number.

Upset, you call customer relations and ask why a service technician cannot give her direct number to a customer. The company representative says, in a rather disgusted tone, "Because the service center is in India. You were talking to people trained to speak like Americans and told to identify themselves as Jeff and Jennifer."

Should a company let customers know that its service facilities are being outsourced? Should service people be required to give their real names when dealing with customers? What are the consequences of each alternative? What would you do?

entry, billing, and low-end software development. However, China is intent on developing advanced manufacturing technology and India has a deep pool of scientists, software engineers, chemists, accountants, lawyers, and physicians.[75] For example, radiologists from Wipro Health Science in India now read CAT scans and MRIs for Massachusetts General and other U.S. hospitals.[76] The technology talent in these nations also keeps growing: China graduates 250,000 engineers each year, and India about 150,000.

Is it time to push the panic button in the United States? Not necessarily, but America must stay aware of the global challenge and maintain its strength in innovation and entrepreneurship. It's increasingly important for U.S. workers to get the proper education and training to preserve the "skill premium" they possess today to stay ahead in the future.[77] The key things to remember as you progress through this text are that globalization is for real and that competition promises to intensify.

## Globalization and Your Future

Whether you aspire to be an entrepreneur, manager, or other type of business leader, it's increasingly important to think globally in planning your career. As this chapter points out, global markets offer many opportunities yet are laced with significant challenges and complexities. By studying foreign languages, learning about foreign cultures, and taking business courses (including a global business course), you can develop a global perspective on your future.[78] But remember, the potential of global markets does not belong only to large, multinational corporations. Small and medium-sized businesses are often better prepared to leap into global markets and react quickly to opportunities than are large firms saddled with bureaucracies. Also don't forget the global potential of franchising, which we will examine in more detail in Chapter 5.

### progress assessment

- What are the economic risks of doing business in countries like China?
- What might be some important factors that will have an impact on global trading?
- What is meant by offshore outsourcing?

## summary

1. The world market for trade is huge. Major U.S. companies routinely cite expansion to global markets as a route to future growth.
   - **Why should nations trade with other nations?**

   (1) No country is self-sufficient, (2) other countries need products that prosperous countries produce, and (3) natural resources and technological skills are not distributed evenly around the world.
   - **What is the theory of comparative advantage?**

   The theory of comparative advantage contends that a country should make and then sell those products it produces most efficiently but buy those it cannot produce as efficiently.
   - **What is absolute advantage?**

   Absolute advantage means that a country has a monopoly on a certain product or can produce the product more efficiently than any other country can. There are few examples of absolute advantage.

**1.** Discuss the growing importance of the global market and the roles of comparative advantage and absolute advantage in global trade.

2. Anyone, students included, can get involved in world trade through importing and exporting. Businesspeople do not have to work for big multinational corporations.
   - **What kinds of products can be imported and exported?**

   Just about any kind of product can be imported and exported. Companies can sometimes find surprising ways to succeed in either activity. Selling in global markets is not necessarily easy, though.
   - **What terms are important in understanding world trade?**

   *Exporting* is selling products to other countries. *Importing* is buying products from other countries. The *balance of trade* is the relationship of exports to imports. The *balance of payments* is the balance of trade plus other money flows such as tourism and foreign aid. *Dumping* is selling products for less in a foreign country than in your own country. See the Key Terms list at the end of this chapter to be sure you know the other important terms.

**2.** Explain the importance of importing and exporting, and understand key terms used in global business.

3. A company can participate in world trade in a number of ways.
   - **What are some ways in which a company can get involved in global business?**

   Ways of entering world trade include licensing, exporting, franchising, contract manufacturing, joint ventures and strategic alliances, and direct foreign investment.
   - **How do multinational corporations differ from other companies that participate in global business?**

   Unlike other companies that are involved in exporting or importing, multinational corporations also have manufacturing facilities or some other type of physical presence in different nations.

**3.** Illustrate the strategies used in reaching global markets and explain the role of multinational corporations in global markets.

4. There are many restrictions on foreign trade.
   - **What are some of the forces that can discourage participation in global business?**

   Potential stumbling blocks to world trade include sociocultural forces, economic and financial forces, legal and regulatory forces, and physical and environmental forces.

**4.** Evaluate the forces that affect trading in global markets.

5. Political differences are often the most difficult hurdles to global trade.
   - **What is trade protectionism?**

   Trade protectionism is the use of government regulations to limit the import of goods and services; advocates believe that it allows domestic

**5.** Debate the advantages and disadvantages of trade protectionism.

producers to survive and grow, producing more jobs. The key tools of protectionism are tariffs, import quotas, and embargoes.

- **What are tariffs?**

Tariffs are taxes on foreign products. There are two kinds of tariffs: (1) protective tariffs, which are used to raise the price of foreign products, and (2) revenue tariffs, which are used to raise money for the government.

- **What is an embargo?**

An embargo prohibits the importing or exporting of certain products.

- **Is trade protectionism good for domestic producers?**

That is debatable. Trade protectionism offers pluses and minuses.

- **Why do governments continue such practices?**

The theory of mercantilism started the practice of trade protectionism and it has persisted, though in a lesser form, ever since.

**6.** Discuss the changing landscape of the global market and the issue of offshore outsourcing.

6. Technology is changing the way businesses communicate around the globe. The Internet has made distant global markets instantly accessible. E-commerce enables companies to bypass normal distribution channels to reach large global markets quickly.

- **What is offshore outsourcing? Why is it a major concern for the future?**

Outsourcing is the purchase of goods and services from outside a firm rather than providing them inside the company. It has been a large part of business for many years. Today, more businesses are outsourcing manufacturing and services offshore (globally.) Many fear growing numbers of jobs in the United States will be lost due to offshore outsourcing.

## key terms

**absolute advantage** 62
**balance of payments** 64
**balance of trade** 64
**common market** 77
**comparative advantage theory** 62
**contract manufacturing** 69
**countertrading** 74
**devaluation** 73
**dumping** 65
**embargo** 76
**exchange rate** 73
**exporting** 60
**foreign direct investment** 70
**foreign subsidiary** 70
**free trade** 61
**General Agreement on Tariffs and Trade (GATT)** 76
**importing** 60
**import quota** 76
**joint venture** 69
**licensing** 66
**multinational corporation** 70
**North American Free Trade Agreement (NAFTA)** 78
**strategic alliance** 69
**tariff** 75
**trade deficit** 64
**trade protectionism** 75
**World Trade Organization (WTO)** 76

## critical thinking questions

1. About 95 percent of the world's population lives outside the United States, but many U.S. companies, especially small businesses, still do not engage in global trade. Why is that? Do you think more small business will participate in global trade in the future? Why or why not?

2. Countries like the United States that have a high standard of living are referred to as *industrialized nations*; countries with a low standard of living

and quality of life are called *developing countries* (other terms include *underdeveloped* or *less developed countries*). What prevents developing nations from fully industrializing?

3. The forces affecting trade in global markets include sociocultural forces, economic and financial forces, legal and regulatory forces, and physical and environmental forces. What can businesses do to prevent unexpected problems in dealing with these forces in global markets?

4. Two different types of tariffs, revenue and protective, are used by governments to protect a nation's trade. How would you justify the use of either a revenue or protective tariff in today's global market?

## developing workplace skills

1. Find out firsthand the global impact on your life. With a group of your classmates check the labels on your clothes. How many different countries' names appear on the product labels? How many languages are spoken by your fellow class members? List the ethnic restaurants that are in your community. Are they family-owned or corporate chains?
2. Call, e-mail, or visit a local business involved with importing foreign goods (perhaps a wine or specialty foods importer). Check with the owner or manager about the problems and joys of global trade, and compile a list of advantages and disadvantages. Compare notes with your classmates about what they found in their search.
3. Visit four or five public locations in your community such as schools, hospitals, city/county buildings, or airports. See how many signs are posted in different languages (by the way, don't forget to check the restrooms). Also check for other information, such as brochures or handouts, in other languages. Do any of the locations fly flags from different nations recognizing the diversity of employees or students? What does your search tell you about your community?
4. Suppose that Representative I. M. Wright just delivered a passionate speech at your college on the topic of tariffs. He argues tariffs are needed to
   a. Provide revenues to protect our young industries.
   b. Encourage Americans to buy U.S.-made products because doing so is patriotic.
   c. Protect Americans jobs and wages.
   d. Help us to attain a favorable balance of trade and balance of payments.

   Do you agree with Representative Wright? Evaluate each of his major points and decide whether you consider it valid or invalid. Be sure to justify your position.
5. Form a joint venture with three classmates and select a product, service, or idea the group would like to market to a specific country. Have each team member select a key global market force (sociocultural, economic and financial, legal and regulatory, or physical and environmental) to research concerning the selected market. Have each member report his or her findings, and then have the group prepare a short explanation of whether the market is worth pursuing.

## taking it to the net * 1

### Purpose

To compare the shifting exchange rates of various countries and to predict the effects of such exchange shifts on global trade.

### Exercise

One of the difficulties of engaging in global trade is the constant shift in exchange rates. How much do exchange rates change over a 30-day period? Research this by choosing five currencies (e.g., the euro, the British pound, the Japanese yen, the Mexican peso, the Saudi Arabian riyal) and recording their exchange rates relative to the U.S. dollar for 30 days. The rates are available on the Internet at http://finance.yahoo.com/currency.

At the end of the tracking period, choose a company and describe what effects the currency shifts you noted might have on this company's trade with each of the countries or areas whose currency you chose.

## taking it to the net * 2

### Purpose

To identify those nations with high export potential and those with low export potential (except for basic goods, such as food).

### Exercise

Imagine your company is ready to expand its products to foreign countries. Which countries are most likely to buy your products? The potential to export to a specific country is based on a number of factors, including the size of its population and the strength of its GDP.

1. From the population data given on the United Nations Population Information Network's Web site (www.un.org/popin), prepare a list of the 20 countries with the largest population.
2. Go to the InfoNation section of the UN's Cyber School Bus Web site (www.un.org/Pubs/CyberSchoolBus) and find the GDP per person for each of the nations on your population list. Rate each of the nations in your population list for its export potential. Using the GDP per capita and the population size, place each of those nations into the following categories:
   a. High export potential (those nations whose population is one of the 10 largest and whose GDP per capita is greater than $20,000).
   b. Medium-high export potential (those nations whose population is ranked 11 to 21 and whose GDP per capita is greater than $20,000).
   c. Medium export potential (those nations whose population is one of the 10 largest and whose GDP per capita is between $3,000 and $20,000).
   d. Low export potential (those nations whose population is ranked 11 to 21 and whose GDP per capita is less than $3,000).

## casing the web

To access the case "Cooling off the Sweatshops," visit **www.mhhe.com/ub8e**

video case

## The Mouse that Doesn't Come with a Computer

What could be more American than Mickey Mouse? Em I C kay ee y. Em O you es ee. How would you say that in Chinese or Japanese or French? Would it have the same meaning, the same appeal? Those are the questions Disney faced when planning to take the Disneyland experience overseas. Would the "Happiest Place on Earth" be equally happy for people who hadn't been exposed since birth to Mickey Mouse and Donald Duck and the other Disney characters?

Walt Disney Imagineering is the creative arm of the Walt Disney Company. It is the function of the people in Imagineering to come up with the solutions to the questions posed above. The problem may be easier to solve than you imagine because people all over the world have similar likes, fears, and imaginations. Just because they come from a different culture and speak a different language doesn't mean that they won't be equally enchanted by Cinderella, Snow White, and Mickey. On the other hand, there may be huge differences in the way people react. So, what can you do to minimize the potential for disharmony? One answer is to hire local people to help in every phase of the project. They know the culture. They know the language. And they know what people like and dislike—in the specific country or town or village.

Taking Disney to China would have many positive benefits for both countries. It would create jobs in China and bring new entertainment. For the United States, a Chinese Disneyland would create a more favorable balance of trade and possibly lead the way toward more trade with China. Chinese labor is less expensive than U.S. labor, so a Disney park could perhaps be built for less—if local architects, engineers, and set designers were used. Then everything would have to be planned with a Chinese audience in mind.

The same would be true in other countries. For example, in Japan people like to shop for gifts, so the gift shop might be bigger and have more clerks. In France, the people may prefer to drink wine instead of Coke. Local laws must be considered and local tastes. In short, taking a business overseas is a real challenge. It involves more than copying what you have done in the United States. It means listening to what locals have to say and then adapting your offerings accordingly.

Ethically, would it be fair to pay U.S. employees a different wage than locals? After all, locals may pay much less for rent, autos, etc. What if the locals found out you were paying them less? What ethical issues do you see with spreading the American culture to other countries? Are you OK with spreading American dress styles, movies, food, and music to the rest of the world? Are you open to having other cultures have an equal effect in you?

Speaking of food, is it a good idea to open fast-food restaurants in Disney parks selling the same kind of food sold in the U.S. parks? Would people in other countries be willing to spend the same amount of money to enter the parks? Are there alternative ways to charge for the experience? Which of the Disney characters would appeal the most to people from China? How would you find out?

### Thinking It Over

1. Working in another country can be a fun and challenging experience. If you had to choose one country to live in other than the United States, where would it be? What American companies are located there?
2. What products have you bought lately that were made in a different country? What countries produced them? Did you have any difficulty accepting the fact that the product came from there? Did you have any difficulty with the directions or the follow-up service? What does that tell you about global marketing and global business?
3. Imagine yourself trying to sell someone from France on the idea of visiting the Disney park. What issues might you expect to encounter? What issues may you encounter when trying to get someone visiting from France to go to the Disneyland park in the United States?

# DEMONSTRATING ethical behavior and social responsibility

*

profile

**Getting to Know**

**X** Howard Schultz

**of Starbucks**

A cup of coffee may be able to perk up your spirits, but can it brew a better world? Probably not, but Howard Schultz, founder and chairman of Starbucks, believes that Starbucks can certainly help make the world a nicer place—one latte at a time. "Contributing positively to our communities and environment is at the heart of Starbucks," said Schultz. "Starbucks is committed to constantly improving our environmental footprint in every level of our supply chain, from coffee farmer to customer."

This commitment isn't just a sound bite or a paragraph in the company's annual report. Starbucks' efforts toward meeting the company's goal of improving the environment have been so successful that the World Environment Center awarded the company the 2005 Gold Medal for International Corporate Achievement in Sustainable Development. Starbucks' success can be attributed to a set of coffee-buying guidelines it calls Coffee and Farmer Equity (C.A.F.E.) Practices. These environmentally, socially, and economically responsible guidelines are designed to contribute to the livelihoods of coffee farmers while emphasizing environmental conservation. The C.A.F.E. guidelines provide incentives for suppliers who meet high quality, environmental, and labor standards. These incentives include low-cost loans, long-term contracts, and guaranteed prices. Starbucks has pledged to purchase more than 60 percent of its coffee from suppliers who grow coffee under C.A.F.E. guidelines by 2007. Gold Medal Jury chairman Dr. Joel Abrams said, "This creative new way of doing business has the potential to improve the lives of people and the global environment."

Coffee production affects the lives of over 25 million farmers in more than 70 countries around the world, many in developing regions. Deforestation and the chemicals used in traditional coffee production can often harm the surrounding environment. Although Starbucks buys only 2 percent of the world's coffee, it has demonstrated how innovation in combining corporate social responsibility and business policies can lead to long-term economic and environmental improvements.

Starbucks doesn't confine its social responsibility efforts to its relationships with coffee growers. The company strives to balance fiscal responsibility with the goals of enhancing the lives of all of its stakeholders, including its employees, customers, coffee farmers, shareholders, community members, and suppliers. For example, when Starbucks acquired Ethos Water, a privately held bottled water company based in Santa Monica, California, in 2005, it promised to meet Ethos Water's goal to help children around the world get clean water. The goal

LEARNING **goals**

**After you have read and studied this chapter, you should be able to**

1. Explain why legality is only the first step in behaving ethically.
2. Ask the three questions one should answer when faced with a potentially unethical action.
3. Describe management's role in setting ethical standards.
4. Distinguish between compliance-based and integrity-based ethics codes, and list the six steps in setting up a corporate ethics code.
5. Define *corporate social responsibility* and examine corporate responsibility to various stakeholders.
6. Analyze the role of American businesses in influencing ethical behavior and social responsibility in global markets.

CHAPTER 4

**www.starbucks.com**

involved donating $250,000 by the end of fiscal 2005 and $1 million by the end of fiscal 2006 to water projects in developing countries around the world. Starbucks strives to improve each of the communities it serves. Given that there are almost 30,000 Starbucks stores in more than 35 countries, that's a considerable portion of the world.

One of the reasons Starbucks was included on *Fortune* magazine's Most Admired Companies and 100 Best Companies to Work For lists is how it treats its partners (employees). The company was among the first to offer health care and stock options to part-time partners. It encourages and rewards volunteerism and participation in organizations that are important to its partners, including local schools, literacy programs, walk-a-thons, and Earth Day activities. It encourages and supports partners to make a difference in their local communities. For example, through a program called Make Your Mark, Starbucks matches partner and customer volunteer hours with cash contributions to nonprofit organizations. Partners are also able to contribute to the Caring Unites Partners (CUP) Fund, a financial assistance program to help other partners in need. These are just a few examples of Starbucks' many social responsibility efforts. For more information about its programs, visit the company's Web site (www.starbucks.com).

"Success is not an entitlement, and each day we strive to earn the trust and confidence of the millions of customers who come to Starbucks each week," said Schultz. "The phenomenal success Starbucks has achieved confirms my belief that a company can do good and do well at the same time." Since Starbucks' stock price is up 5,000 percent since the company went public in 1992, it is certainly doing well.

With the media saturated by stories of high-profile business scandals, why do we open this chapter on ethics with a story about a company doing good? Because we want you to know that few businesspeople let greed guide their actions, and that there are many honest, ethical people in the business world. In this chapter, we explore the responsibility of businesses to all of their stakeholders: customers, investors, employees, and society. We look at the responsibilities of individuals as well. After all, responsible business behavior depends on responsible behavior of each individual in the business.

Sources: "Starbucks Demonstrates Commitment to Stakeholder Engagement in Fiscal 2004 Corporate Social Responsibility Annual Report," Business Wire, March 25, 2005; "100 Best Corporate Citizens for 2005," *Business Ethics,* Spring 2005; Chris O'Brien, "Starbucks CEO Hopes to Brew Up Social Responsibility," *San Jose (California) Mercury News,* January 16, 2005; and Mangu-Ward, Katherine, "The Age of Corporate Environmentalism," *Reason*, February 1, 2006.

# ETHICS IS MORE THAN LEGALITY

In the early 2000s, the American public was shocked when it learned that Enron, the giant energy trading company, created off-the-books partnerships to hide debts and losses. The Enron disgrace soon was followed by more scandals at major companies like WorldCom, Tyco International, ImClone, HealthSouth, and Boeing.[1] (See the Legal Briefcase box for a brief summary of a few of these cases.) Such scandals aren't limited to major companies. Small companies have faltered as well. For example, Lacrad International, a small multimedia publisher, admitted that it lied to lenders when it claimed to have revenue in the millions in order to get loans to buy such things as a $2.5 million corporate jet. In reality, the company's revenues never exceeded $100,000. What did Lacrad sell? Religious sermons and CDs of gospel music.[2]

The giant accounting firm Arthur Andersen became famous for shredding Enron-related documents. While the Andersen employees shown here thought it was funny to give document shredding lessons at an Arthur Andersen Night before an Oregon baseball game in 2002, no one is laughing now. Andersen's 28,000 employees lost their jobs when the company was found guilty of obstructing the government's investigation of Enron. The verdict was later overturned. Although the document shredding was eventually deemed to be legal, do you believe it was ethical?

Given the ethical lapses that are so prevalent today, what can be done to restore trust in the free-market system and leaders in general? First, those who have broken the law need to be punished accordingly. Arresting business leaders, putting them in handcuffs, and carting them off to jail may seem harsh, but it is a first step toward showing the public that it is time to get serious about legal and ethical behavior in business. No one should be above the law: not religious people, not government people, and not businesspeople. New laws making accounting records more transparent (easy to read and understand) and making businesspeople and others more accountable may help. But laws don't make people honest, reliable, or truthful. If laws alone were a big deterrent, there would be much less crime than exists today.

The danger in writing new laws to correct behavior is that people may begin to think that any behavior that is within the law is also acceptable. The measure of behavior, then, becomes "Is it legal?" A society gets in trouble when it considers ethics and legality to be the same. Ethics and legality are two very different things. Although following the law is an important first step, ethical behavior requires more than that. Ethics reflects people's proper relations with one another: How should people treat others? What responsibility should they feel for others? Legality is more narrow. It refers to laws we have written to protect ourselves from fraud, theft, and violence. Many immoral and unethical acts fall well within our laws.[3]

## Ethical Standards Are Fundamental

**ethics**
Standards of moral behavior, that is, behavior that is accepted by society as right versus wrong.

We define **ethics** as the standards of moral behavior, that is, behavior that is accepted by society as right versus wrong. Many Americans today have few moral absolutes. Many decide situationally whether it's OK to steal, lie, or drink and drive. They seem to think that what is right is whatever works best for the individual, that each person has to work out for himself or herself the difference between right and wrong. That is the kind of thinking that has led to the recent scandals in government and business.

This isn't the way it always was. When Thomas Jefferson wrote that all men have the right to life, liberty, and the pursuit of happiness, he declared it to be a self-evident truth. Going back even further in time, the Ten Commandments were not called the "The Ten Highly Tentative Suggestions."

In a country like the United States, with so many diverse cultures, you might think it is impossible to identify common standards of ethical behavior. However,

* * *

LEGAL briefcase

### Accused Corporate Executives Have Their Day in Court

The following is a brief summary of some of the recent high-profile corporate scandals:

- Enron: Former Enron chairman and chief executive officer (CEO) Kenneth Lay, former CEO Jeffrey Skilling, and chief accounting officer Richard Causey were convicted in 2006 of committing accounting fraud by setting up partnerships that the company used to improperly enhance profits while moving billions of dollars of debt off its balance sheet. That made its financial picture look better than it was and artificially inflated the company's stock and bond prices. The executives sold millions of dollars' worth of stock just before the fraud became public while the company's pension regulations prohibited regular employees from selling their stock. The result was that the executives who bankrupted the company made millions while the employees and other small investors lost millions.
- Arthur Andersen: In 2002, Arthur Andersen, one of the largest accounting firms at the time, was convicted of tampering with witnesses when it told its employees to shred two tons of Enron documents. The government claimed that Andersen conducted the massive document destruction to obstruct what the company knew was a coming Securities and Exchange Commission investigation. At the trial, Andersen said it was merely reminding employees to follow the company's established document retention and destruction policy and that it did so at a time when it had not yet been notified of any investigation or asked for any documents. In 2005, the U.S. Supreme Court agreed with Andersen and overturned the conviction. However, there was no one left at Andersen to celebrate—the company's 28,000 employees had already lost their jobs when the earlier conviction forced the company out of business.
- Tyco International: In a 2005 retrial, former Tyco CEO Dennis Kozlowski and former chief financial officer Mark Swartz were convicted of stealing $600 million from the company. They were both sentenced to $8\frac{1}{3}$ to 25 years in New York state prison. A state judge declared the 2004 trial a mistrial because, he said, there had been undue pressure on one juror.
- Adelphia Communications: In 2004, Aldelphia founder John Rigas and his son Timothy were convicted of conspiracy, bank fraud, and securities fraud. John was sentenced to 15 years in prison and Timothy to 20 years. Another Rigas son, Michael, pleaded guilty in 2005 to making a false entry in a financial record, eliminating a need for a retrial after his first trial ended in a mistrial. A fourth executive, Michael Mulcahey, was found not guilty of conspiracy and securities fraud.
- WorldCom: In June 2002, WorldCom admitted that intentional accounting irregularities made the company look almost $4 billion more profitable than it was. This led to more scrutiny of the company's books. It was discovered that WorldCom's practice of counting revenue twice dated back as far as 1999, that additional debt continued to be undisclosed, and that revenue that was not received was entered in the books—pushing the irregularities to more than $11 billion. In 2005, former CEO Bernie Ebbers was convicted of fraud, conspiracy, and making false regulatory filings. He was sentenced to 25 years in federal prison. The company has emerged from bankruptcy and now operates under the name of MCI Inc.

Sources: Erin McClam, "Scandal-Tainted CEOs Have Year of Reckoning," AP Online, December 14, 2005; "Status of High-profile U.S. Corporate Scandals," AP Worldstream, December 12, 2005; and Carrie Johnson, "Taking Enron to Task; Government's Prosecutors Are Ambitious, Driven and Accustomed to Winning," *Washington Post*, January 18, 2006.

among sources from many different times and places—such as the Bible, Aristotle's *Ethics,* William Shakespeare's *King Lear,* the Koran, and the *Analects* of Confucius—you'll find the following statements of basic moral values: Integrity, respect for human life, self-control, honesty, courage, and self-sacrifice are right; cheating, cowardice, and cruelty are wrong. Furthermore, all of the world's major religions support a version of the Golden Rule, even if it is stated only in the negative form: Do not do unto others as you would not have them do unto you.[4]

## Ethics Begins with Each of Us

It is easy to criticize business and political leaders for their moral and ethical shortcomings, but we must be careful in our criticism to note that Americans in general are not always as honest or honorable as they should be. One study revealed that two-thirds of the American population reported never giving any time to the community in which they live. Nearly one-third said they never contributed to a charity. Both managers and workers cited low managerial ethics as a major cause of American business's competitive woes. Employees reported that they often violate safety standards and goof off as much as seven hours a week.

Young people learn from such behavior. In a study on one college campus, 80 percent of the students surveyed admitted to cheating. At the University of Maryland recently, a group of instructors conducted a "techno sting." They posted false answers to an accounting exam on a Web site. Twelve students used the false answers, including a few who admitted getting the answers from the site during the exam itself by using their cell phones. Plagiarizing material from the Internet is the most common form of cheating today. One school reported that half of its plagiarism cases involved students cutting and pasting information from a Web site without crediting the source. To fight this problem, many instructors now use services like TurnItIn.com, which scans students' papers against 6 billion pages of documents and provides evidence of copying in seconds.[5]

Two recent studies found that there is a strong relationship between academic dishonesty among undergraduate students and dishonesty later, when these same students were in the working world.[6] In response, many schools are adopting stricter honor policies that provide heavy consequences for cheating. Do you think such policies make a difference to student behavior?

It is always healthy when discussing moral and ethical issues to remember that ethical behavior begins with you and me. We cannot expect society to become more moral and ethical unless we as individuals commit to becoming more moral and ethical ourselves.

The purpose of the Making Ethical Decisions boxes you see throughout the text—like the accompanying one on music piracy—is to demonstrate to you that it is important to keep ethics in mind whenever you are making a business decision. The choices are not always easy. Sometimes the obvious solution from an ethical point of view has drawbacks from a personal or professional point of view. For example, imagine that your supervisor at work has asked you to do something you feel is unethical. You have just taken out a mortgage on a new house to make room for your first baby, due in two months. Not carrying out your supervisor's request may get you fired. What would you do? Sometimes there is no desirable alternative. Such situations are called ethical dilemmas because you must choose between equally unsatisfactory alternatives. It can be very difficult to maintain a balance between ethics and other goals such as pleasing stakeholders or advancing in your career. It is helpful to ask yourself the following questions when facing an ethical dilemma.[7]

1. *Is it legal?* Am I violating any law or company policy? Whether you are thinking about having a drink and then driving home, gathering marketing intelligence, designing a product, hiring or firing employees, planning on how to get rid of waste, or using a questionable nickname for an employee, it is necessary to think about the legal implications of what you do. This question is the most basic one in behaving ethically in business, but it is only the first.
2. *Is it balanced?* Am I acting fairly? Would I want to be treated this way? Will I win everything at the expense of another party? Win–lose situations often end up as lose–lose situations. There is nothing like a major loss to generate retaliation from the loser. You can see that in

* * * MAKING

# ethical decisions

www.riaa.com/issues/piracy

## Not All Pirates Wield Swords—Some Sport MP3 Players

Would you walk into a music store and slip a few compact discs (CDs) into your pocket and walk out without paying for them? Have you ever downloaded free music from the Internet rather than buying the CD? If so, you should know that the Recording Industry Association of America (RIAA), as well as the U.S. court system, considers both of these methods of getting music as piracy—and it may have a bounty on your head. In early 2005, the RIAA, which represents the major record labels, announced that it planned to sue college students across the country for copyright infringement. The lawsuits target "the most egregious users," those sharing more than 2,300 songs (the equivalent of more than 175 CDs). Combined, the first round of 405 students who were sued had illegally distributed more than 930,000 songs. To date, more than 9,000 users have been sued. Many have settled their lawsuits by paying penalties of $2,500 to $10,000.

When 19-year-old Shawn Fanning began writing a new software program, his goal was to create a tool for helping people search for music files on the Internet and to talk to each other about the types of music they liked. When he finished the project and got Napster up on the Web in 1999, it attracted thousands of college kids looking for an easy way to find tunes. The number of users doubled every five to six weeks. Soon Fanning had the attention of most college students—and just about all of the record companies.

The court ordered Napster to close down in 2001. Even though German media giant Bertelsmann had invested $85 million in the file-sharing company, Napster filed Chapter 7 bankruptcy. Interestingly, a few years later, CD-burning-software maker Roxio paid $5 million for the Napster name and technology. Roxio combined Napster with an online music service by Vivendi Universal and Sony, two of the record labels that forced Napster out of business. Napster resurfaced as a publicly held company, once again providing listeners with unlimited music downloads—this time for a fee.

Through all of this Napster claimed that it never did anything illegal. Much of the music industry felt otherwise. People were reproducing CDs and other products for free. To record companies, that's like walking into music stores and stealing CDs. But Napster argued that since no one was selling the music, it wasn't illegal. (Don't get the idea that Napster didn't bring in money simply because it didn't actually sell music. Bertelsmann didn't invest $85 million in Napster just so cash-poor students could get free music.) In 2005, the Supreme Court ruled that file-sharing services can be sued if they promote the use of their technology for the illegal downloading of copyrighted music and movies.

Some Napster supporters said that file sharing was a way of sampling music risk-free and that when people found an artist's work they liked, they actually bought more CDs than they would have bought otherwise. But Linda Zirkelbach, a lawyer for the RIAA, said illegal downloading has cost the music industry more than 5,000 jobs. "Unauthorized use has decimated the music industry," she said. "We have seen a 22 percent decline in CD sales since 1999." According to the RIAA Web site, "Each year, the industry loses about $4.2 billion to piracy worldwide. We estimate we lose millions of dollars a day to all forms of piracy." This drives up the cost of the legitimate product for everyone else.

The debate about file-sharing sites like Napster is really a concern about intellectual property ownership. With Napster, we're talking about music. But the issue includes almost anything in the creative realm: movies, books, art, and so on. Should musicians work without getting paid? Movie producers? Authors? Engineers? If people don't get paid adequately, will they continue to work to produce high-quality music, software, or books? Would you work if you didn't get paid fairly?

Technology changes so rapidly that as soon as sites similar to the old Napster are forced out of business, others take their place. It's more difficult now, but it is still possible to find free music online. Remember that just because something is possible doesn't mean it is ethical. How will you respond to these ethical challenges? Are you willing to pass up the opportunity to get free music if you think that free file sharing is unethical?

Sources: Scott Mervis, "CMU, Pitt Students Targeted in Action Against Illegal Online Music Swapping," *Pittsburgh Post-Gazette*, April 13, 2005; Dawn C. Chmielewski, "Court Decision Could Spur Interest in Legal File-Sharing Services," *San Jose Mercury News*, June 28, 2005; and Ethan Smith, "Digital-Music Officials Criticize Subscription Prices," *The Wall Street Journal*, January 12, 2006, p. B2.

the stock market today. Many companies that were merely suspected of wrongdoing have seen their stock drop dramatically. Not every situation can be completely balanced, but it is important to the health of our relationships that we avoid major imbalances over time. An ethical businessperson has a win–win attitude. In other words, such a person tries to make decisions that benefit all parties involved.

The Birmingham Change Fund (BCF) is a giving circle for African American professionals hosted by the Community Foundation of Greater Birmingham. Giving circles are charitable foundations designed to save individual donors the cost of setting up their own private foundations. Members commit to making annual contributions to the fund to address some common purpose. You can learn about giving circles in your area through givingforum .org/giving circles.

3. *How will it make me feel about myself?* Would I feel proud if my family learned of my decision? My friends? Would I be able to discuss the proposed situation or action with my immediate supervisor? The company's clients? How would I feel if my decision were announced on the evening news? Will I have to hide my actions or keep them secret? Has someone warned me not to disclose my actions? Am I feeling unusually nervous? Decisions that go against our sense of right and wrong make us feel bad—they corrode our self-esteem. That is why an ethical businessperson does what is proper as well as what is profitable.

There are no easy solutions to ethical dilemmas. Individuals and companies that develop a strong ethics code and use the three ethics-check questions just presented have a better chance than most of behaving ethically. If you would like to know which style of recognizing and resolving ethical dilemmas you favor, fill out the ethical orientation questionnaire in Figure 4.1.

**progress assessment**

- What are ethics?
- How does ethics differ from legality?
- When faced with ethical dilemmas, what questions can you ask yourself that might help you make ethical decisions?

## MANAGING BUSINESSES ETHICALLY AND RESPONSIBLY

Organizational ethics begin at the top. Ethics is caught more than it is taught. That is, people learn their standards and values from observing what others do, not from hearing what they say. This is as true in business as it is at home. The leadership and example of strong top managers can help instill corporate values in employees. The majority of CEOs surveyed recently attributed unethical employee conduct to the failure of the organization's leadership in establishing ethical standards and culture.[8]

Any trust and cooperation between workers and managers must be based on fairness, honesty, openness, and moral integrity. The same can be said about relationships among businesses and among nations. A business should be managed ethically for many reasons: to maintain a good reputation; to keep existing customers; to attract new customers; to avoid lawsuits; to reduce employee turnover; to avoid government intervention (the passage of new laws and regulations controlling business activities); to please customers, employees, and society; and simply to do the right thing.

Some managers think that ethics is a personal matter—that either individuals have ethical principles or they don't. These managers feel that they are not responsible for an individual's misdeeds and that ethics has nothing to do with management. But a growing number of people think that ethics has everything to do with management. Individuals do not usually act alone; they

Please answer the following questions.

1. Which is worse?
   A. Hurting someone's feelings by telling the truth.
   B. Telling a lie and protecting someone's feelings.
2. Which is the worse mistake?
   A. To make exceptions too freely.
   B. To apply rules too rigidly.
3. Which is it worse to be?
   A. Unmerciful.
   B. Unfair.
4. Which is worse?
   A. Stealing something valuable from someone for no good reason.
   B. Breaking a promise to a friend for no good reason.
5. Which is it better to be?
   A. Just and fair.
   B. Sympathetic and feeling.
6. Which is worse?
   A. Not helping someone in trouble.
   B. Being unfair to someone by playing favorites.
7. In making a decision you rely more on
   A. Hard facts.
   B. Personal feelings and intuition.
8. Your boss orders you to do something that will hurt someone. If you carry out the order, have you actually done anything wrong?
   A. Yes.
   B. No.
9. Which is more important in determining whether an action is right or wrong?
   A. Whether anyone actually gets hurt.
   B. Whether a rule, law, commandment, or moral principle is broken.

To score: The answers fall in one of two categories, J or C. Count your number of J and C answers using this key: 1. A = C; B = J; 2. A = J; B = C; 3. A = C; B = J; 4. A = J; B = C; 5. A = J; B = C; 6. A = C; B = J; 7. A = J; B = C; 8. A = C; B = J; 9. A = C; B = J

What your score means: The higher your J score, the more you rely on an ethic of *justice*. The higher your C score, the more you prefer an ethic of *care*. Neither style is better than the other, but they are different. Because they appear so different they may seem opposed to one another, but they're actually complementary. In fact, your score probably shows you rely on each style to a greater or lesser degree. (Few people end up with a score of 9 to 0.) The more you can appreciate both approaches, the better you'll be able to resolve ethical dilemmas and to understand and communicate with people who prefer the other style.

An ethic of justice is based on principles like justice, fairness, equality, or authority. People who prefer this style see ethical dilemmas as conflicts of rights that can be solved by the impartial application of some general principle. The advantage of this approach is that it looks at a problem logically and impartially. People with this style try to be objective and fair, hoping to make a decision according to some standard that's higher than any specific individual's interests. The disadvantage of this approach is that people who rely on it might lose sight of the immediate interests of particular individuals. They may unintentionally ride roughshod over the people around them in favor of some abstract ideal or policy. This style is more common for men than women.

An ethic of care is based on a sense of responsibility to reduce actual harm or suffering. People who prefer this style see moral dilemmas as conflicts of duties or responsibilities. They believe that solutions must be tailored to the special details of individual circumstances. They tend to feel constrained by policies that are supposed to be enforced without exception. The advantage of this approach is that it is responsive to immediate suffering and harm. The disadvantage is that, when carried to an extreme, this style can produce decisions that seem not simply subjective, but arbitrary. This style is more common for women than men.

To learn more about these styles and how they might relate to gender, go to www.ethicsandbusiness.org/kgl.htm.

Source: Thomas I. White, *Discovering Philosophy—Brief Edition*, 1e, © Copyright 1996. Adapted by permission of Pearson Education, Inc., Upper Saddle River, NJ.

figure 4.1

**ETHICAL ORIENTATION QUESTIONNAIRE**

need the implied, if not the direct, cooperation of others to behave unethically in a corporation.

For example, when Sears, Roebuck & Company was besieged with complaints about its automotive services, Sears management introduced new goals and incentives for its auto center employees. The increased pressure on the Sears employees to meet service quotas caused them to become careless and to exaggerate to customers the need for repairs. Did the managers say directly,

figure 4.2

**OVERVIEW OF JOHNSON & JOHNSON'S CODE OF ETHICS**

This is an overview of Johnson & Johnson's code of ethics, what it calls its Credo. To see the company's complete Credo, go to its Web site at www.jnj.com/careers/ourcredo.html.

Written in 1943 by long-time Chairman General Robert Wood Johnson, the Johnson & Johnson Credo serves as a conscious plan that represents and encourages a unique set of values. Our Credo sums up the responsibilities we have to the four important groups we serve:

- Our customers—We have a responsibility to provide high-quality products they can trust, offered at a fair price.
- Our employees—We have a responsibility to treat them with respect and dignity, pay them fairly and help them develop and thrive personally and professionally.
- Our communities—We have a responsibility to be good corporate citizens, support good works, encourage better health and protect the environment.
- Our stockholders—We have a responsibility to provide a fair return on their investment.

The deliberate ordering of these groups—customers first, stockholders last—proclaims a bold business philosophy: If we meet our first three responsibilities, the fourth will take care of itself . . . To ensure our adherence to Credo values, we periodically ask every employee to evaluate the company's performance in living up to them. We believe that by monitoring our actions against the ethical framework of Our Credo, we will best ensure that we make responsible decisions as a company.

"Deceive the customers"? No, but the message was clear anyway. The goals and incentives created an environment in which mistakes did occur and managers did not make efforts to correct the mistakes. Sears settled pending lawsuits by offering coupons to customers who had paid for unnecessary repairs. The estimated cost to Sears was $60 million. Such misbehavior does not reflect a management philosophy that intends to deceive. It does, however, show an insensitivity or indifference to ethical considerations.[9] In an effort to remedy this insensitivity, Sears replaced 23,000 pages of policies and procedures with a simple booklet called "Freedoms & Obligations," which discusses the company's code of business conduct from a commonsense approach.

## Setting Corporate Ethical Standards

Formal corporate ethics codes are popular these days. Eighty-nine percent of the organizations surveyed recently have written codes of ethics.[10] Figure 4.2 offers a sample from one company's code of ethics.

Although ethics codes vary greatly, they can be classified into two major categories: compliance-based and integrity-based. **Compliance-based ethics codes** emphasize preventing unlawful behavior by increasing control and by penalizing wrongdoers. Whereas compliance-based ethics codes are based on avoiding legal punishment, **integrity-based ethics codes** define the organization's guiding values, create an environment that supports ethically sound behavior, and stress a shared accountability among employees. See Figure 4.3 for a comparison of compliance-based and integrity-based ethics codes.

**compliance-based ethics codes**
Ethical standards that emphasize preventing unlawful behavior by increasing control and by penalizing wrongdoers.

**integrity-based ethics codes**
Ethical standards that define the organization's guiding values, create an environment that supports ethically sound behavior, and stress a shared accountability among employees.

The following six-step process can help improve America's business ethics:

1. Top management must adopt and unconditionally support an explicit corporate code of conduct.
2. Employees must understand that expectations for ethical behavior begin at the top and that senior management expects all employees to act accordingly.

| FEATURES OF COMPLIANCE-BASED ETHICS CODES | | FEATURES OF INTEGRITY-BASED ETHICS CODES | |
|---|---|---|---|
| Ideal: | Conform to outside standards (laws and regulations) | Ideal: | Conform to outside standards (laws and regulations) and chosen internal standards |
| Objective: | Avoid criminal misconduct | Objective: | Enable responsible employee conduct |
| Leaders: | Lawyers | Leaders: | Managers with aid of lawyers and others |
| Methods: | Education, reduced employee discretion, controls, penalties | Methods: | Education, leadership, accountability, decision processes, controls, and penalties |

figure 4.3

**STRATEGIES FOR ETHICS MANAGEMENT**

Integrity-based ethics codes move beyond legal compliance to create a "do-it-right" climate that emphasizes core values such as honesty, fair play, good service to customers, a commitment to diversity, and involvement in the community. These values are ethically desirable, but not necessarily legally mandatory.

3. Managers and others must be trained to consider the ethical implications of all business decisions.
4. An ethics office must be set up. Phone lines to the office should be established so that employees who don't necessarily want to be seen with an ethics officer can inquire about ethical matters anonymously. **Whistleblowers** (people who report illegal or unethical behavior) must feel protected from retaliation. In 2002, President George W. Bush signed the Corporate and Criminal Fraud Accountability (Sarbanes-Oxley) Act. The act contains historic protections for corporate whistleblowers. See the Legal Briefcase box on page 98 for more information about this important legislation. (Sarbanes-Oxley is covered in more detail in Chapter 17.)
5. Outsiders such as suppliers, subcontractors, distributors, and customers must be told about the ethics program. Pressure to put aside ethical considerations often comes from the outside, and it helps employees resist such pressure when everyone knows what the ethical standards are.
6. The ethics code must be enforced. It is important to back any ethics program with timely action if any rules are broken. That is the best way to communicate to all employees that the code is serious.[11]

**whistleblowers**
People who report illegal or unethical behavior.

This last step is perhaps the most critical. No matter how well intended a company's ethics code is, it is worthless if it is not enforced. Enron had a written code of ethics. However, by ignoring this code both Enron's board and management sent employees the message that rules could be shelved when inconvenient.[12]

An important factor to the success of enforcing an ethics code is the selection of the ethics officer. The most effective ethics officers set a positive tone, communicate effectively, and relate well with employees at every level of the company. They are equally comfortable serving as counselors or as investigators. While many ethics officers have a background in law, it is more important that they have strong communication skills than a background in specific rules, regulations, and risks. Effective ethics officers are people who can be trusted to maintain confidentiality, conduct objective investigations, and ensure the process is fair, and they can demonstrate to stakeholders that ethics are important in everything that the company does. While there are no statistics about the number of companies that have ethics officers, membership of the Ethics and Compliance Officer Association has increased over 60 percent since the managerial misconduct at Enron became known.[13]

www.healthsouth.com

LEGAL briefcase

## SOX It to 'Em: Whistleblowers Move from Snitches to Corporate Heroes

As vice president for corporate development at Enron, Sherron Watkins sensed that something was rotten with the financial reporting at the company. She blew the whistle on her bosses who hid billions of dollars of debt and operating losses from investors and employees. She said she would have come forward sooner, but she was afraid of losing her job. The Sarbanes-Oxley Act (SOX), passed in 2002, now protects whistleblowers like Watkins from any company retaliation. SOX provides for reinstatement and back pay to people who were punished by their employers for passing information about frauds on to authorities.

SOX requires all public corporations to provide a system that allows employees to submit concerns regarding accounting and auditing issues confidentially and anonymously. Obviously, the purpose is to motivate employees to report any wrongdoing. It seems to be working—40 percent of business frauds detected in 2004 came to authorities' attention through tips from whistleblowers. Not all whistleblowers are employees. For example, James DeVage was a HealthSouth customer. He reported questionable charges that his insurance company paid to HealthSouth for his physical therapy. DeVage's complaints resulted in a Justice Department investigation. The department claimed that HealthSouth made false claims to Medicare and sought reimbursement for unallowable costs, including "lavish entertainment and certain travel costs for HealthSouth's annual administrators' meeting at Disney World."

HealthSouth agreed to settle the claim by paying $325 million to the government. Under the False Claims Act, whistleblower DeVage was eligible to receive a percentage of the amount recovered by the government—he received $8.1 million. The eighty-three-year-old DeVage doesn't regard the money as his true reward: "The reward for me is that I did something that some other people should have been doing. . . . Someone had to pick up the ball and go forward with it."

Would you "blow the whistle" on your supervisors at work if you saw wrongdoing on their part? What penalties or punishment do you think should be imposed on corporate executives who knowingly cheat investors or employees?

DECEMBER 30, 2002 / JANUARY 6, 2003
SPECIAL DOUBLE ISSUE
PERSONS OF THE YEAR
TIME
The Whistleblowers
CYNTHIA COOPER OF WORLDCOM
COLEEN ROWLEY OF THE FBI
SHERRON WATKINS OF ENRON
www.time.com AOL Keyword: TIME


Sources: Curtis Verschoor, "Is This the Age of Whistleblowers?" *Strategic Finance*, February 1, 2005; Guillermo Contreras, "San Antonio Whistleblower Doubly Rewarded in Exposing HealthSouth Fraud," *San Antonio Express News*, January 14, 2005; and Paul K. Mcmasters, "Inside the First Amendment: Blowing the Whistle Can Also Blow a Career," Gannett News Service, January 16, 2006.

**progress assessment**

- What are compliance-based and integrity-based ethics codes?
- What are the six steps to follow in establishing an effective ethics program in a business?

## CORPORATE SOCIAL RESPONSIBILITY

Just as you and I need to be good citizens, contributing what we can to society, corporations need to be good citizens as well. **Corporate social responsibility (CSR)** is the concern businesses have for the welfare of society. It is based on a company's concern for the welfare of all its stakeholders, not just the owners. CSR goes well beyond merely being ethical. It is based on a commitment to such basic principles as integrity, fairness, and respect.[14]

**corporate social responsibility**
A business's concern for the welfare of society.

You may be surprised to know that not everyone thinks that CSR is a good thing. Some critics of CSR believe that a manager's sole role is to compete and win in the marketplace. American economist Milton Friedman made a classic statement when he said that the only social responsibility of business is to make money for stockholders. He thought that doing anything else was moving dangerously toward socialism. CSR critics believe that managers who pursue CSR are doing so with other people's money—money they invested to make more money, not to improve society. They view spending money on CSR activities as stealing from their investors.

CSR defenders, in contrast, believe that businesses owe their existence to the societies they serve. Businesses cannot succeed in societies that fail. They are given access to society's labor pool and its natural resources, things that every member of the society has a stake in. Even Adam Smith, the father of capitalism, believed that self-interested pursuit of profit was wrong. He argued that benevolence was the highest virtue. CSR defenders acknowledge that businesses have deep obligations to investors and that they should not attempt government-type social responsibility projects. However, they also argue that CSR makes more money for investors in the long run. They base their arguments on studies that have shown that companies with good ethical reputations attract and retain better employees, draw more customers, and enjoy greater employee loyalty. A Harvard and University of Michigan analysis of 95 studies on CSR showed that most of them revealed a positive correlation between corporate social performance and corporate financial performance.[15]

The social performance of a company has several dimensions:

- **Corporate philanthropy** includes charitable donations to nonprofit groups of all kinds. Eighty percent of the business leaders surveyed in

**corporate philanthropy**
Dimension of social responsibility that includes charitable donations.

Timberland is a company with a long-standing commitment to community service. The company's "Path of Service" program offers employees 40 hours of paid time off to serve in their communities. Here at a sales meeting in Jacksonville, Florida, employees gather together for a day of community service. Do companies have responsibilities to the environment beyond obeying environmental laws?

a recent study say that their companies participate in philanthropic activities.[16] Strategic philanthropy involves companies making long-term commitments to one cause, such as McDonald's founding and support of Ronald McDonald Houses, which house families whose critically ill children require treatment away from home. The Bill & Melinda Gates Foundation is by far the nation's largest philanthropic foundation, with assets of nearly $29 billion.[17] Philanthropy isn't limited to large corporations like McDonald's and Microsoft. The Spotlight on Small Business box describes how small businesses can become involved in such generous giving.

**corporate social initiatives**
Enhanced forms of corporate philanthropy that are more directly related to the company's competencies.

- **Corporate social initiatives** include enhanced forms of corporate philanthropy. Corporate social initiatives differ from traditional philanthropy in that they are more directly related to the company's competencies. For example, as part of the 2004 Asian tsunami disaster relief, UPS and FedEx shipped emergency relief supplies for free from all around the world; Johnson & Johnson sent medical supplies; and other pharmaceutical companies sent antibiotics, nutritional supplements, and baby formula.[18]

**corporate responsibility**
Dimension of social responsibility that includes everything from hiring minority workers to making safe products.

- **Corporate responsibility** includes everything from hiring minority workers to making safe products, minimizing pollution, using energy wisely, and providing a safe work environment—essentially everything that has to do with acting responsibly within society.

**corporate policy**
Dimension of social responsibility that refers to the position a firm takes on social and political issues.

- **Corporate policy** refers to the position a firm takes on social and political issues.

So much news coverage has been devoted to the problems caused by corporations that people tend to get a negative view of the impact that companies have on society. If the news were more balanced, much more could be said about the positive contributions that businesses make. Few people know, for example, that Xerox has a program called Social Service Leave, which allows employees to leave for up to a year and work for a nonprofit organization. While on Social Leave, the Xerox employee gets full salary and benefits, including job security.[19] IBM and Wells-Fargo Bank have similar programs. In fact, many companies are jumping on the volunteerism bandwagon by allowing employees to give part-time help to social agencies of all kinds.[20] In 2002, President George W. Bush signed an executive order establishing the USA Freedom Corps to oversee Citizen Corps, a program designed to strengthen homeland security efforts through the help of volunteers. Volunteers handle administrative work at local police departments and spread antiterrorism information as part of expanded Neighborhood Watch programs. Some donate their professional health care skills to support emergency medical efforts, and some train others in disaster response and emergency preparedness.[21] VolunteerConnections.org, NetworkforGood.org, and VolunteerMatch.org are Web-based services that link volunteers with nonprofit and public sector organizations around the country. Volunteers enter a zip code or indicate the geographic area in which they'd like to work, and the programs list organizations that could use their help.

Two-thirds of the MBA students surveyed by a group called Students for Responsible Business said they would take a lower salary to work for a socially responsible company. But when the same students were asked to define *socially responsible*, things got complicated. It appears that even those who support the idea of social responsibility can't agree on what it involves. Maybe it would be easier to understand social responsibility if we looked at the concept through the eyes of the stakeholders to whom businesses are responsible: customers, investors, employees, and society in general.

SPOTLIGHT ON small business

www.giftsinkind.org

### Myths about Small-Business Philanthropy

Many entrepreneurs have a hard time determining how to start a charitable-giving program in their businesses. Often this is because of misconceptions.

*Myth 1:* Charities need cash, so struggling small businesses can't help them without jeopardizing their own cash flow.

*Reality:* Sure, charities need money. But they also need equipment (such as used computers), food, clothing, and volunteers. Pat Heffron, a franchisee of Chem-Dry (which specializes in carpet and upholstery cleaning), found a way to train his employees and help the community at the same time. New Chem-Dry employees learn how to do their jobs by cleaning discarded furniture, which Heffron then donates to local shelters for battered women and the homeless. Another way a small business can contribute to charities without taking a penny out of the cash register is to shop for business supplies through Internet charity sites such as GreaterGood.com. Companies listed on such sites donate between 2 and 20 percent of their revenues to the buyer's charity of choice. One extra click—no extra money.

*Myth 2:* If your business is small, you can't make a significant difference.

*Reality:* If you target your involvement to small programs within your community, you'll be able to have a notable impact. For instance, one Chicago manufacturer invested just $1,500 in a new local early-childhood literacy program that rewarded inner-city parents with grocery money when they read to their children.

*Myth 3:* Charity organizers will pay attention only to large contributors with well-known names.

*Reality:* Nonprofits look for ways to form partnerships with both large and small companies. For example, Dine Across America, a fund-raising effort for a national antihunger organization, received funding for administrative expenses from American Express. But more important, it was small businesses—restaurants and food wholesalers—that donated the food and labor.

Business owners who don't know how to locate nonprofit organizations that need donations can call Gifts in Kind International (703-836-2121), which serves as an intermediary by collecting clothing, office equipment, and other useful materials and distributing them to more than 50,000 nonprofit organizations and schools across the nation.

## Responsibility to Customers

One responsibility of business is to satisfy customers by offering them goods and services of real value. A recurring theme of this book is the importance of pleasing customers. This responsibility is not as easy to meet as it seems. Keep in mind that three out of five new businesses fail—perhaps because their owners failed to please their customers. One of the surest ways of failing to please customers is to be less than totally honest with them. For example, a consumer magazine reported that the Suzuki Samurai was likely to roll over if a driver swerved violently in an emergency. When Suzuki executives denied there was a problem, sales plummeted.

In contrast, Daimler-Benz suffered a similar problem during a test simulating a swerve around a wayward elk, when its A-class Baby Benz rolled over. The company quickly admitted a problem, came up with a solution, and committed the money necessary to put that solution into action. In addition, company representatives continued to answer questions in spite of aggressive press coverage. Daimler took out full-page ads that read: "We should like to thank our customers most warmly for their loyalty. You have given us the chance to remedy a mistake." After the test flip, only 2 percent of the orders for the vehicle were canceled. The solution cost the company $59 million the first year and $118 million the next; analysts say those costs probably eliminated any profit on the vehicle. However, the quick resolution of the problem protected the company's reputation, thus allowing its other models to become such hits that Daimler's net earnings remained the same.[22]

The payoff for socially conscious behavior could result in new business as customers switch from rival companies simply because they admire the company's social efforts—a powerful competitive edge. Consumer behavior studies show that, all else being equal, a socially conscious company is likely to be viewed more favorably than less socially responsible companies. The important point to remember is that customers prefer to do business with companies they trust and, even more important, do not want to do business with companies they don't trust.

Bernie Ebbers, former CEO of WorldCom, was once revered in his home-state of Mississippi. However, after it was disclosed that WorldCom hid billions of dollars in expenses and was forced into bankruptcy due to accounting irregularities, Ebber tumbled from hero to corporate hooligan. Here Ebber leaves the federal courthouse after being sentenced to 25 years in prison for his role in the $11 billion accounting fraud. Do you think this is an appropriate punishment for a convicted corporate executive?

## Responsibility to Investors

As we stated earlier, ethical behavior is good for shareholder wealth. It doesn't subtract from the bottom line; it adds to it. In contrast, unethical behavior does cause financial damage. Those cheated by corporate wrongdoing are the shareholders themselves. Unethical behavior may seem to work for the short term, but it guarantees eventual failure.[23] For example, in just 11 business days in June 2002, 44 CEOs left American corporations amid accusations of wrongdoing, and stock prices plummeted.

Some people believe that before you can do good you must do well (i.e., make a lot of money); others believe that by doing good, you can also do well.[24] For example, Bagel Works, a New England–based chain of bagel stores, has a dual-bottom-line approach that focuses on the well-being of the planet in addition to profits. Bagel Works has received national recognition for social responsibility. Its mission involves commitments to the environment and to community service. Each store not only employs environmentally protective practices such as in-store recycling, composting, using organically grown ingredients, and using nontoxic cleaners, but also includes donations for community causes in its budget. The company donates 10 percent of its pretax profits to charities each year.

Many people believe that it makes financial as well as moral sense to invest in companies that are planning ahead to create a better environment. By choosing to put their money into companies whose goods and services benefit the community and the environment, investors can improve their own financial health while improving society's health.

A few investors, known as inside traders, have chosen unethical means to improve their own financial health. **Insider trading** involves insiders using private company information to further their own fortunes or those of their family and friends. A high-profile case related to insider trading involved home style diva Martha Stewart. While Stewart was never charged with insider trading, she was found guilty of lying to authorities who were investigating the possibility of such trading. See the Dealing with Change box for a summary of Stewart's story.

**insider trading**
An unethical activity in which insiders use private company information to further their own fortunes or those of their family and friends.

Insider trading isn't limited to company executives and their friends. For example, before it was publicly known that IBM was going to take over Lotus Development, an IBM secretary told her husband, who told two co-workers, who told friends, relatives, business associates, and even a pizza delivery man. A total of 25 people received the information and traded illegally on the insider tip within a six-hour period. When the deal was announced publicly, the stock soared 89 percent. One of the inside traders, a stockbroker who passed the

## DEALING WITH change

### Martha Stewart Living, Again

Often when a felon leaves prison with over a billion dollars in assets waiting on the outside, that person obtained those riches illegally. Martha Stewart, however, the leading guru of hearth and home, earned her treasures by demonstrating that she is capable and, more important, willing to change with the times. Following her stint in jail, Stewart has become a humble woman—a woman who has suffered, a *real* woman in her public's eyes—and the price of her stock has soared because of it.

How did Stewart end up in prison in the first place? When Stewart sold her ImClone stock one day before bad news caused the stock price to dip, she was investigated for using insider information for her own gain. Stewart was convicted of lying to investigators about the stock deal. Stewart's conviction sent the stock price in her company, Martha Stewart Omnimedia, into a tailspin and led to a string of losses and sales declines.

Instead of delaying her sentence by remaining free while appealing the conviction, Stewart chose to do her time. By going to prison voluntarily, she gained the sympathy of some. "There's an element of martyrdom that rattles around Martha Stewart now," says Jeffrey Sonnenfeld, associate dean of the Yale School of Management. Due to a massive public relations campaign, Martha salvaged the reputation that the scandal nearly destroyed. Rather than sulk quietly in the shadows and hope that the public forgets about the five months of prison time, Martha jumped back into the spotlight as a changed woman. No longer the godlike sage of all things home related, she has become personable and modest; most of all, homemakers everywhere can at last relate to her. She is seen as someone who has been trampled underfoot by society, one who has suffered through the worst and is now bouncing back into the world with as much tenacity and vigor as ever.

Stewart has a number of different things to keep her busy as she rebuilds her empire. For starters, she is starring in a new television series. In the daily morning show, she displays her domestic prowess to a live studio audience. (A spin-off of NBC's hit reality show *The Apprentice*, with Martha Stewart as head honcho rather than Donald Trump, was canceled after one season.) Besides her television ventures, Stewart gave her once-central moneymaker, *Martha Stewart Living*, a much needed boost by reinstating the beloved "Ask Martha" column. She also hopes to win back key advertisers by making herself the star once again in this postimprisonment Martha Stewart world. Finally, the upcoming merger between Sears and Kmart is expected to provide Stewart's line of furniture, clothing, and various housewares with even more shelf space. Not bad for an ex-con.

Americans adore cutting down the very people they worship, but what they enjoy even more than watching the mighty fall is seeing how they get back up again. By shedding her unapproachable brand of domesticity and donning a new, more relatable image to her public, Martha Stewart is poised to take the world's kitchens and gardens by storm and reestablish her rule over the home. Martyrdom seems to have been good for Marthadom.

Sources: Keith Naughton, "Martha Breaks Out," *Newsweek*, March 7, 2005, pp. 36–44; Philip Sherwell, "Martha Stewart Watches Her Fortunes Soar from a Jail Cell," *Sunday Telegraph*, February 20, 2005; "Federal Appeals Court Upholds Martha Stewart's Conviction," *The Wall Street Journal*, January 7, 2006, p. B3; and "Martha Stewart Plans to Test a New Magazine for Women," Associated Press, January 12, 2006.

www.marthastewart.com

information to a few of his customers, made $468,000 in profits. The U.S. Securities and Exchange Commission (SEC) filed charges against the secretary, her husband, and 23 others. Four of the defendants settled out of court by paying penalties that equaled twice their profit. Prosecutors are placing increased emphasis on the prosecution of insider trading cases in order to ensure that the public is able to conduct business in a securities market that is fair and equally accessible to all.

After the deluge of insider trader cases made public in the early 2000s, the SEC adopted a new rule called Regulation FD for "fair disclosure." The rule doesn't specify what information can and cannot be disclosed. It simply requires companies that release any information to share it with everybody, not just a few select people. In other words, if companies tell anyone, they must tell everyone—at the same time.[25]

Some companies have misused information for their own benefit at investors' expense. In the case of WorldCom, when the company admitted that accounting irregularities made the company look billions of dollars more profitable than it was, the stock plummeted and the company filed for bankruptcy a month later. Investors who purchased stock on the basis of the company's false financial reports saw share prices free-fall from the mid-teens in January 2002 to less than a dime by the following July. The pain was even greater for long-term investors who bought the stock at around $60 in 1999.

## Responsibility to Employees

Businesses have several responsibilities to employees. First, they have a responsibility to create jobs if they want to grow. It's been said that the best social program in the world is a job. Once a company creates jobs, it has an obligation to see to it that hard work and talent are fairly rewarded. Employees need realistic hope of a better future, which comes only through a chance for upward mobility. People need to see that integrity, hard work, goodwill, ingenuity, and talent pay off. Studies have shown that the factor that most influences a company's effectiveness and financial performance is human resource management. We will discuss human resource management in Chapter 11.

If a company treats employees with respect, they usually will respect the company as well. That respect can make a huge difference in a company's bottom line. In their book *Contented Cows Give Better Milk*, Bill Catlette and Richard Hadden compared "contented cow" companies with "common cow" companies. The companies with the contented employees outgrew their counterparts by four to one for more than 10 years. The "contented cow" companies outearned the "common cow" companies by nearly $40 billion and generated 800,000 more jobs. Catlette and Hadden attribute this difference in performance to the commitment and caring the companies demonstrated for their employees.[26]

One way a company can demonstrate commitment and caring is to give employees salaries and benefits that help them reach their personal goals. For example, the wage and benefit packages offered by Costco are among the best in hourly retail. Even part-time workers are covered by Costco's health plan, and the workers pay less for their coverage than at other retailers such as Wal-Mart. The increased benefits reduce employee turnover. Employee turnover at Costco is less than a third of the industry average. Given that the U.S. Department of Labor estimates that replacing employees costs between 150 and 250 percent of their annual salaries, retaining workers is good for business as well as for morale.[27]

When employees feel they've been treated unfairly, they often strike back. Getting even is one of the most powerful incentives for good people to do bad things. Not many disgruntled workers are desperate enough to resort to violence in the workplace, but a great number do relieve their frustrations in more subtle ways, such as blaming mistakes on others, not accepting responsibility for decision making, manipulating budgets and expenses, making commitments they intend to ignore, hoarding resources, doing the minimum needed to get by, and making results look better than they are. The loss of employee commitment, confidence, and trust in the company and its management can be very costly indeed. Employee theft costs U.S. businesses approximately $660 billion annually, according to a report from the Association of Certified Fraud Examiners.[28] You will read more about issues that affect employee management relations in Chapter 12.

## Responsibility to Society and the Environment

One of business's major responsibilities to society is to create new wealth. If businesses don't do it, who will? More than a third of working Americans receive their salaries from nonprofit organizations that in turn receive their funding from others, who in turn receive their money from business. Foundations, universities, and other nonprofit organizations own billions of shares in publicly held companies. As those stock prices increase, more funds are available to benefit society.

Businesses are also partially responsible for promoting social justice. Business is perhaps the most crucial institution of civil society. For its own well-being, business depends on its employees being active in politics, law, churches and temples, arts, charities, and so on. Many companies believe that business has a role in building a community that goes well beyond giving back. To them, charity is not enough. Their social contributions include cleaning up the environment, building community toilets, providing computer lessons, caring for the elderly, and supporting children from low-income families.[29] Samsung, a Korean electronics conglomerate, emphasizes volunteer involvement. For example, a busload of Samsung employees and managers are transported each month to a city park, where they spread out to pick up garbage, pull weeds, and plant saplings. Managers even volunteer to help spruce up employee homes. Local employees feel such loyalty to the company that in the height of an unrest that destroyed many businesses in Indonesia, local employees and their neighbors pulled together to protect Samsung's refrigerator factory there and shielded foreign managers from violence. With the help of relatives in the countryside, the local employees

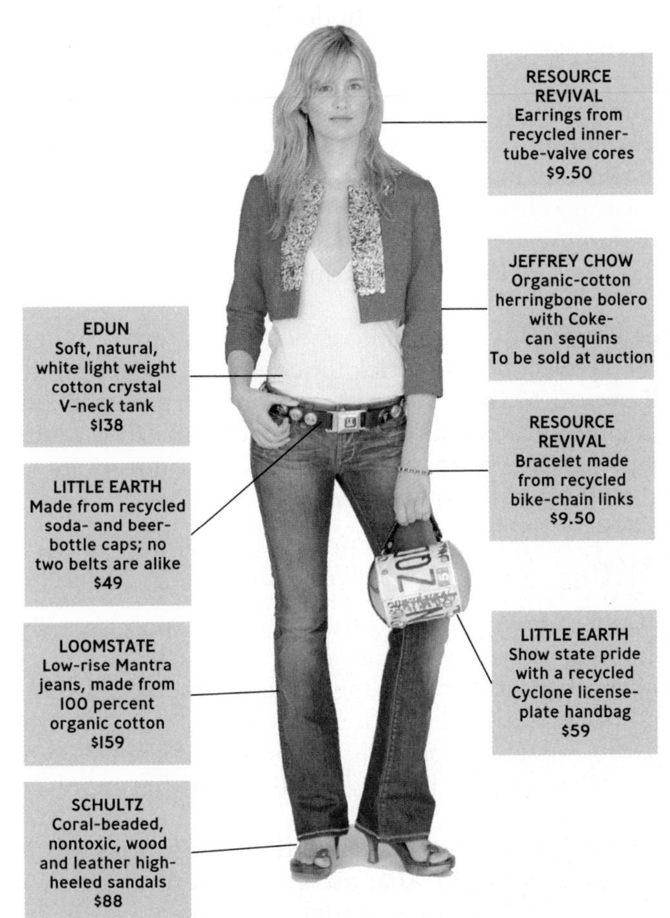


Goodbye fabric spun by silkworms; hello fabric spun from corn and recycled Coke cans. Ecofashion could very well change the closet of the future. New technologies are leading to more versatile earth-friendly fabrics that appeal to customers who refuse to sacrifice style in order to save the planet. Designers feel confident that consumers may be ready to buy clothes that match their healthier lifestyles. Are you ready to join the conscious commerce movement?

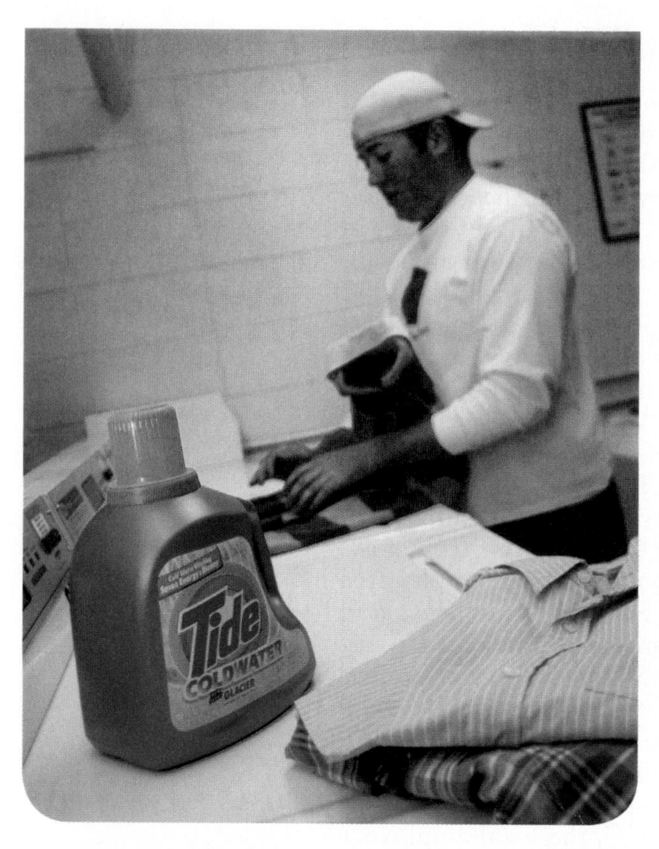


Consumer products giant Procter & Gamble is doing its part to help the environment. The company formulated a laundry detergent called Coldwater Tide to help consumers reduce their utility bills while delivering deep cleaning in cold water. Would you be willing to pay a bit extra for products that offered a clear benefit to the environment?

set up a food supply network that helped protect their colleagues from skyrocketing prices for food staples such as rice and palm oil.

Businesses are clearly taking responsibility for helping to make their own environment a better place. Environmental efforts may increase the company's costs, but they also may allow the company to charge higher prices, to increase market share, or both. For example, Ciba Specialty Chemicals, a Swiss textile-dye manufacturer, developed dyes that require less salt than traditional dyes. Since used dye solutions must be treated before they are released into rivers or streams, having less salt and unfixed dye in the solution means having lower water-treatment costs. Patents protect Ciba's low-salt dyes, so the company can charge more for its dyes than other companies can charge for theirs. Ciba's experience illustrates that, just as a new machine enhances labor productivity, lowering environmental costs can add value to a business.

Not all environmental strategies prove to be as financially beneficial to the company as Ciba's, however. For instance, in the early 1990s StarKist responded to consumer concerns about dolphins dying in the process of tuna fishing because the nets meant to capture tuna also caught dolphins swimming over the yellowfin tuna schools in the eastern Pacific. The company announced that it would sell only tuna from the western Pacific, where the skipjack tuna do not swim underneath dolphins. Unfortunately, the company found that customers were unwilling to pay a premium for the dolphin-safe tuna and that they considered the taste of the skipjack inferior to that of yellowfin tuna. In addition, it turned out that there was no clear environmental gain: In exchange for every dolphin saved by not fishing in the eastern Pacific, thousands of immature tuna and dozens of sharks, turtles, and other marine animals died in the western Pacific fishing process.

Environmental quality is a public good; that is, everyone gets to enjoy it regardless of who pays for it. The trick for companies is to find the right public good that will appeal to their customers. Many corporations are publishing reports that document their net social contribution. To do that, a company must measure its positive social contributions and subtract its negative social impacts. We shall discuss that process next.

## Social Auditing

It is nice to talk about having organizations become more socially responsible. It is also encouraging to see some efforts made toward creating safer products, cleaning up the environment, designing more honest advertising, and treating women and minorities fairly. But is there any way to measure whether organizations are making social responsibility an integral part of top management's decision making? The answer is yes, and the term that represents that measurement is *social auditing*.

**social audit**
A systematic evaluation of an organization's progress toward implementing programs that are socially responsible and responsive.

A **social audit** is a systematic evaluation of an organization's progress toward implementing programs that are socially responsible and responsive. One of the major problems of conducting a social audit is establishing

- Community-related activities such as participating in local fund-raising campaigns, donating executive time to various nonprofit organizations (including local government), and participating in urban planning and development.
- Employee-related activities such as establishing equal opportunity programs, offering flextime and other benefits, promoting job enrichment, ensuring job safety, and conducting employee development programs. (You'll learn more about these activities in Chapters 11 and 12.)
- Political activities such as taking a position on nuclear safety, gun control, pollution control, consumer protection, and other social issues; and working more closely with local, state, and federal government officials.
- Support for higher education, the arts, and other nonprofit social agencies.
- Consumer activities such as ensuring product safety, creating truthful advertising, handling complaints promptly, setting fair prices, and conducting extensive consumer education programs.

figure 4.4

**SOCIALLY RESPONSIBLE BUSINESS ACTIVITIES**

procedures for measuring a firm's activities and their effects on society. What should be measured? Many social audits consider such things as workplace issues, the environment, product safety, community relations, military weapons contracting, international operations and human rights, and respecting the rights of local people.[30] See Figure 4.4 for an outline of business activities that could be considered socially responsible.

There is some question as to whether positive actions should be added (e.g., charitable donations, pollution control efforts) and then negative effects subtracted (e.g., layoffs, overall pollution levels) to get a net social contribution. Or should just positive actions be recorded? In general, social responsibility is becoming one of the aspects of corporate success that business evaluates, measures, and develops.

In addition to the social audits conducted by the companies themselves, there are four types of groups that serve as watchdogs regarding how well companies enforce their ethical and social responsibility policies:

1. *Socially conscious investors* who insist that a company extend its own high standards to all its suppliers. Social responsibility investing (SRI) is on the rise, with approximately $2 trillion invested in SRI funds in the United States already.[31]
2. *Environmentalists* who apply pressure by naming names of companies that don't abide by the environmentalists' standards. For example, after months of protests coordinated by the San Francisco–based Rainforest Action Network (RAN), J. P. Morgan Chase & Co. adopted sweeping guidelines that restrict its lending and underwriting practices for industrial projects that are likely to have a negative impact on the environment. RAN activists first go after an industry leader, as it did with J. P. Morgan, and then smaller companies. "We call it, 'Rank 'em and spank 'em,'" says RAN's executive director.[32]
3. *Union officials* who hunt down violations and force companies to comply to avoid negative publicity.
4. *Customers* who take their business elsewhere if a company demonstrates what they consider unethical or socially irresponsible practices. For example, a group in Largo, Florida, called Children of God for Life called for a boycott of General Electric products when the company planned to conduct embryonic stem-cell research.[33]

What these groups look for constantly changes as the worldview changes. For example, until September 11, 2001, no group formally screened publicly traded companies to determine potential links to terrorism or the spread of weapons of mass destruction. Now some groups have targeted companies that may be even peripherally linked as the United States focuses on terrorism. One important thing to remember is that it isn't enough for a company to be right when it comes to ethics and social responsibility—it also has to convince its customers and society that it's right.

**progress assessment**

- What is corporate social responsibility, and how does it relate to each of a business's major stakeholders?
- What is a social audit, and what kinds of activities does it monitor?

## INTERNATIONAL ETHICS AND SOCIAL RESPONSIBILITY

Ethical problems and issues of social responsibility are not unique to the United States. Top business and government leaders in Japan were caught in a major influence-peddling (i.e., bribery) scheme in Japan. Similar charges have been brought against top officials in South Korea, the People's Republic of China, Italy, Brazil, Pakistan, and Zaire. What is new about the moral and ethical standards by which government leaders are being judged? They are much stricter than in previous years. Top leaders are now being held to higher standards.

Ethical responsibility does not stop at America's borders. Many colleges have adopted standards that prohibit their school's name or logo from being displayed on apparel made in foreign sweatshops. Sweatshops are factories with very low pay and poor health and safety standards. Would you be willing to buy products from a manufacturer that produces its goods in substandard facilities in foreign nations?

Government leaders are not the only ones being held to higher standards. Many American businesses are demanding socially responsible behavior from their international suppliers by making sure their suppliers do not violate U.S. human rights and environmental standards. For example, Sears will not import products made by Chinese prison labor. The clothing manufacturer Phillips–Van Heusen said it would cancel orders from suppliers that violate its ethical, environmental, and human rights code. Dow Chemical expects its suppliers to conform to tough American pollution and safety laws rather than just to local laws of their respective countries. McDonald's denied rumors that one of its suppliers grazes cattle on cleared rain-forest land but wrote a ban on the practice anyway.

In contrast to companies that demand that their suppliers demonstrate socially responsible behavior are those that have been criticized for exploiting workers in less developed countries. Nike, the world's largest athletic shoe company, has been accused by human rights and labor groups of treating its workers poorly while lavishing millions of dollars on star athletes to endorse its products. Cartoonist Garry Trudeau featured an anti-Nike campaign in his popular syndicated series *Doonesbury*. An Ernst & Young report on Nike's operations in Asia indicated that thousands of young women labored over 10 hours a day, six days a week, in excessive heat, noise, and foul air, for slightly more than $10 a week.

Nike is working to improve its reputation in part by joining forces with Patagonia, Gap, and five other companies and six leading antisweatshop groups to create a single set of labor standards with a common factory-inspection system. The goal of the Joint Initiative on Corporate Accountability and Workers' Rights, as the project is called, is to replace the current multitude of approaches with something that is easier and cheaper to use, in the hope that more companies will then adopt the standards as well.[34] If the 30-month experiment works, one of the outcomes is that the common guidelines will keep companies from undercutting one another on labor standards. One of the toughest issues for the group is the local living-wage proposal. It is a sticking point because the living wage must be subjectively determined and will likely exceed the local legal minimum wage. Success of the Joint Initiative should benefit all of the companies' stakeholders (i.e., employees, investors, community, customers). While customers still seem to favor brand, price, and quality over their perception of a company's humane treatment and social responsibility, surveys show that the vast majority of respondents would pay an extra few dollars for a garment that had been made in a worker-friendly environment.

The justness of requiring international suppliers to adhere to American ethical standards is not as clear-cut as you might think. For example, what could be considered a gift in one culture is a bribe in another.[35] Is it always ethical for companies to demand compliance with the standards of their own countries? What about countries where child labor is an accepted part of the society and families depend on the children's salaries for survival? What about foreign companies doing business in the United States? Should they expect American companies to comply with their ethical standards? What about multinational corporations? Since they span different societies, do they not have to conform to any one society's standards? Why is Sears applauded for not importing goods made in Chinese prisons when there are many prison-based enterprises in the United States? None of these questions are easy to answer, but they give you some idea of the complexity of social responsibility issues in international markets. (See the Reaching Beyond Our Borders box on page 110 for an example of an ethical culture clash.)

In an effort to identify some form of common global ethic and to fight corruption in global markets, the partners in the Organization of American States signed the Inter-American Convention Against Corruption.[36] The United Nations adopted a formal condemnation of corporate bribery, as did the European Union and the Organization for Economic Cooperation and Development.[37] The International Organization for Standardization (ISO) developed a new standard on social responsibility which includes guidelines on product manufacturing, fair pay rates, appropriate employee treatment and hiring practices. These standards are advisory only and will not be used for certification purposes.[38] The formation of a single set of international rules governing multinational corporations is unlikely in the near future. In many places "Fight corruption" remains just a slogan, but even a slogan is a start.

### progress assessment

- How are American businesses demanding socially responsible behavior from their international suppliers?
- Why is it unlikely that there will be a single set of international rules governing multinational companies soon?

## REACHING BEYOND our borders

www.motorola.com

### Ethical Culture Clash

Communications and electronics giant Motorola describes itself as dedicated to "uncompromising integrity." Robert W. Galvin, Motorola's former board chairman, says that the company's ethical values and standards are an "indispensable foundation" for the company's work, relationships, and business success. Almost half of Motorola's employees live outside the United States, and more than half of its revenues come from non-U.S. markets. Is it difficult for Motorola employees to adhere to the company's ethical values while at the same time respecting the values of the host countries in which Motorola manufactures and markets its products?

Here's an example of how corporate ethics can clash with cultural ethics. Joe, the oldest son of a poor South American cloth peddler, managed to move to the United States, earn an engineering degree, and get a job with Motorola. After five years, Joe seemed to have bought into the Motorola culture and was happy to have been granted a transfer back to his home country. Joe was told that the company expected him to live there in a safe and presentable home of his choice. To help him afford such a residence, Motorola agreed to reimburse him a maximum of $2,000 a month for the cost of his rent and servants. Each month Joe submitted rental receipts for exactly $2,000. The company later found out that Joe was living in what was, by Western standards, a shack in a dangerous slum area of town. Such a humble home could not have cost more than $200 a month. The company was concerned for Joe's safety as well as for the effect the employee's unseemly residence would have on Motorola's image. The human resource manager was ultimately concerned about Joe's lack of integrity, given that he had submitted false receipts for reimbursement.

Joe was upset with what he considered the company's invasion of his privacy. He argued that he should receive the full $2,000 monthly reimbursement that all of the other Motorola employees received. He explained his choice of housing by saying that he was making sacrifices so he could send the extra money to his family and put his younger siblings through school. This was especially important since his father had died and his family had no one else to depend on but Joe. "Look, my family is poor," Joe said, "so poor that most Westerners wouldn't believe our poverty even if they saw it. This money means the difference between hope and despair for all of us. For me to do anything less for my family would be to defile the honor of my late father. Can't you understand?"

Often it is difficult to understand what others perceive as being ethical. Different situations often turn the clear waters of "rightness" downright muddy. Clearly, Joe was trying to do the honorable thing for his family. Yet Motorola's wish to have its higher-level people live in safe housing is not unreasonable, given the dangerous conditions of the city in which Joe lived. The policy of housing reimbursement supports Motorola's intent to make its employees' stay in the country reasonably comfortable and safe, not to increase their salaries. If Joe worked in the United States, where he would not receive a housing supplement, it would be unethical for him to falsify expense reports in order to receive more money to send to his family. In South America, though, the issue is not so clear.

Sources: R. S. Moorthy, Robert C. Solomon, William J. Ellos, and Richard T. De George, "Friendship or Bribery?" *Across the Board,* January 1999, pp. 43–47, and Steven K. Paulson, "An Integrated Social Science Perspective on Global Business Ethics," *International Journal of Commerce and Management,* September 11, 2005.

## summary

**1.** Explain why legality is only the first step in behaving ethically.

1. Ethics goes beyond obeying laws. It also involves abiding by the moral standards accepted by society.
   - **How is legality different from ethics?**

   Ethics reflects people's proper relations with one another. Legality is more limiting; it refers only to laws written to protect people from fraud, theft, and violence.

**2.** Ask the three questions one should answer when faced with a potentially unethical action.

2. It is often difficult to know when a decision is ethical.
   - **How can we tell if our business decisions are ethical?**

   Our business decisions can be put through an ethics check by asking three questions: (1) Is it legal? (2) Is it balanced? and (3) How will it make me feel?

3. Some managers think ethics is an individual issue that has nothing to do with management, while others believe ethics has everything to do with management.
   - **What is management's role in setting ethical standards?**

   Managers often set formal ethical standards, but more important are the messages they send through their actions. Management's tolerance or intolerance of ethical misconduct influences employees more than any written ethics codes do.

**3.** Describe management's role in setting ethical standards.

4. Ethics codes can be classified as compliance-based or integrity-based.
   - **What's the difference between compliance-based and integrity-based ethics codes?**

   Whereas compliance-based ethics codes are concerned with avoiding legal punishment, integrity-based ethics codes define the organization's guiding values, create an environment that supports ethically sound behavior, and stress a shared accountability among employees.

**4.** Distinguish between compliance-based and integrity-based ethics codes, and list the six steps in setting up a corporate ethics code.

5. Corporate social responsibility is the concern businesses have for society.
   - **How do businesses demonstrate corporate responsibility toward stakeholders?**

   Business is responsible to four types of stakeholders: (1) business's responsibility to customers is to satisfy them with goods and services of real value; (2) business is responsible for making money for its investors; (3) business has several responsibilities to employees: to create jobs, to maintain job security, and to see that hard work and talent are fairly rewarded; and (4) business has several responsibilities to society: to create new wealth, to promote social justice, and to contribute to making its own environment a better place.
   - **How are a company's social responsibility efforts measured?**

   A corporate social audit measures an organization's progress toward social responsibility. Some people believe that the audit should add together the organization's positive actions and then subtract the negative effects of business to get a net social benefit.

**5.** Define *corporate social responsibility* and examine corporate responsibility to various stakeholders.

6. Many customers are demanding that companies deal only with other companies that share a commitment to environmental and human rights issues.
   - **How can American companies influence ethical behavior and social responsibility in global markets?**

   Companies like Sears, Phillips–Van Heusen, and Dow Chemical will not import products from companies that do not meet their ethical and social responsibility standards.

**6.** Analyze the role of American businesses in influencing ethical behavior and social responsibility in global markets.

## key terms

**compliance-based ethics codes** 96
**corporate philanthropy** 99
**corporate policy** 100
**corporate responsibility** 100
**corporate social initiatives** 100
**corporate social responsibility** 99
**ethics** 90
**insider trading** 102
**integrity-based ethics codes** 96
**social audit** 106
**whistleblowers** 97

## critical thinking questions

Think of a situation you have been involved in that tested your ethical behavior. For example, maybe your best friend forgot about a term paper due the next day and asked you if he could copy and hand in a paper you wrote for another instructor last semester.

1. What are your alternatives, and what are the consequences of each one?
2. Would it have been easier to resolve the dilemma if you had asked yourself the three questions listed in the chapter? Try answering them now and see if you would have made a different choice.

## developing workplace skills

1. What sources have helped shape your personal code of ethics and morality? What influences, if any, have ever pressured you to compromise those standards? Think of an experience you had at work or school that tested your ethical standards. What did you decide to do to resolve your dilemma? Now that time has passed, are you comfortable with the decision you made? If not, what would you do differently?
2. Newspapers and magazines are full of stories about individuals and businesses that are not socially responsible. What about those individuals and organizations that do take social responsibility seriously? We don't normally read or hear about them. Do a little investigative reporting of your own. Identify a public interest group in your community and identify its officers, objectives, sources and amount of financial support, and size and characteristics of membership. List some examples of its recent actions and/or accomplishments. You should be able to choose from environmental groups, animal protection groups, political action committees, and so on. Call the local chamber of commerce, the Better Business Bureau, or local government agencies for help. Try using one of the Internet search engines to help you find more information.
3. You are manager of a coffeehouse called the Morning Cup. One of your best employees desires to be promoted to a managerial position; however, the owner is grooming his slow-thinking son for the promotion your employee seeks. The owner's act of nepotism may hurt a valuable employee's chances for advancement, but complaining may hurt your own chances for promotion. What do you do?
4. Contact a local corporation and ask for a copy of its written ethics code. Would you classify its code as compliance-based or integrity-based? Explain.
5. What effects have the new laws protecting whistleblowers had on the business environment? Use the Internet or the library to research individuals who reported their employers' illegal and/or unethical behavior. Did the companies change their policies? If so, what effect have these policies had on the companies' stakeholders? What effect did reporting the problems have on the whistleblowers themselves?

## taking it to the net

**Purpose**

To demonstrate the level of commitment one business has to social responsibility.

**Exercise**

Richard Foos of Rhino Records built a multimillion-dollar entertainment experience out of a pile of dusty old records, and did it by sticking to his ideals. Foos fosters ethical practices in Rhino's day-to-day business, supporting numerous charitable groups and promoting community service by Rhino employees. See for yourself how Foos responds to social and environmental issues by going to Rhino's Web site at www.rhino.com. Then answer the following questions:

1. What is the social mission of Rhino Records?
2. What does the Social and Environmental Responsibility Team (SERT) do to implement this mission?
3. How does Rhino Records encourage its employees to get involved in community service?
4. How do Rhino employees communicate the company's social mission to their customers?

## casing the web

To access the case *"Got a Deadline? Click Here,"* visit **www.mhhe.com/ub8e**

## video case

### If It Isn't Ethical, It Isn't Right

Cancer affects the lives of millions of people each year. While there has been significant progress made toward fighting the disease, finding a cure is considered by many to be the "holy grail" of medicine. For most of the 20th century, cancer-fighting drugs were like World War II bombers. They'd drop thousands of bombs hoping that a few would get lucky and hit the target. Since the drugs couldn't tell the difference between a cancer cell and a healthy cell, they killed them both. But new generations of drugs are more precise and target individual disease cells and leave healthy cells unharmed.

Unfortunately developing effective new treatments for cancer is a lengthy and costly process. Every step in the process of developing a new drug calls for ethical decision making. The temptation may be to rush the process and cut corners to minimize costs and maximize profits. Does the drug violate a patent that already exists? How far should we go in testing the effectiveness and the side effects of the new product? Should we test it on animals? Should we test it on humans? How much should we charge for the drug? What should we say in our promotions?

Jennie Mather founded a company called Raven Biotechnologies to develop solutions to the most serious cancer illnesses. She understood from the beginning that ethical decisions were based on ethical management. She used the latest monoclonal technology because it enabled the company to target and attack a single disease cell like a cancer. This is a much safer and ethical way of solving the problem because it dramatically reduces the serious side effects caused by "shotgun" type treatments. Because of these precautions, such drugs tend to go through the government screening process faster and easier.

Mather hires employees who have the same ethical approach to business and the same kind of scientific approach that she has. She knows that management sets the ethical parameters, but that employees must keep those standards. Businesspeople today are conscious of the fact that the public is very sensitive to ethical practices because of companies, like Enron, that violated ethical principles. The public is particularly sensitive to issues surrounding pharmaceutical companies. One popular movie focused on the ethics of product testing. Should drugs be tested on humans? If so, how should people taking the test drugs be treated? Is it right to give some people the medicine and others a placebo (a fake medicine)?

Another fundamental issue is price. It costs a lot of money to develop a new drug and companies cannot come up with new solutions to illnesses without making up those huge costs. On the other hand, people without health insurance and people in developing countries simply cannot afford high prices for drugs. Who should bear the cost of providing life-saving drugs to these people?

It's comforting to know that people like Mather are willing to take the entrepreneurial risks demanded of a pioneering company like Raven. It is even more comforting to know that Mather and her employees take an ethical approach to everything they do. Everyone looks forward to the day when there are drugs to take for pancreatic cancer, colorectal cancer, and other serious illnesses. We look to science to solve those problems, and we look to ethical managers to apply the science in the right way.

### Thinking It Over

1. What ethical issues concern you most about the development and sale of pharmaceutical drugs? Does Raven address all of your issues?
2. One of the major issues involving pharmaceutical drugs is their high cost. Do you understand why drug companies have to charge such high prices? Should they charge lower prices in countries where the people don't have the money to buy expensive drugs?
3. Is the need for high ethical standards more or less important in the pharmaceutical industry? Why? What could be done to assure the public that the highest standards are being used?

# choosing A FORM OF business ownership

profile

**Getting to Know**

**X** Donald and Susan Sutherland

**of Cold Stone Creamery**

Cold Stone Creamery isn't just any ice cream shop. After waiting in what are typically long lines, customers order custom-made concoctions of their own design. First they choose the flavor ice cream they want, then any of the dozens of available mix-ins such as sponge cake, graham-cracker piecrust, apple pie filling, cookie dough, brownies, candies, nuts, fruit, and coconut. (During a *Survivor*-inspired promotion, the company even offered what turned out to be a surprisingly popular mix-in: chocolate-dipped crickets!) The ice cream is mixed together by employees brandishing metal spades on a granite surface that is refrigerated from underneath—the "cold stone." Employees break out into song on a whim, especially when they receive tips.

Cold Stone Creamery was listed as the 12th fastest-growing franchise in 2005 by *Entrepreneur* magazine. Success in such a business is a long way from what founders Donald and Susan Sutherland originally envisioned for themselves. After owning a picture-framing shop in Texas, the Sutherlands moved to Arizona with the hope of getting into telecommunications. A real estate slump at the time promptly dashed that dream.

In their funk, the Sutherlands missed the comforting handmade ice cream they used to get from the store near their old Texas shop. The couple searched everywhere in their new hometown for ice cream that was smooth and creamy—ice cream that was neither hard-packed nor soft-serve like traditional varieties. When they couldn't find what they were looking for, they decided to open their own ice cream shop.

When the Sutherlands opened the first Cold Stone Creamery in 1988 next to a popular pizza place, they soon learned that the passing crowds were more interested in beer than in ice cream. "Six dollars was a good day, $10 was a great day," Sutherland said, cringing at the thought. With few customers to interrupt them, the Sutherlands spent their time perfecting ice cream recipes. Sales grew slowly, but Cold Stone eventually won a couple of Best of Phoenix awards.

The Sutherlands opened their second store in 1992. A friend opened a third store and soon wanted to open two more. The first franchise store opened in 1995, and the small company soon began getting inquiries from people all around the United States who wanted to open stores in their areas. "I got to the point where I realized I was a great mom-and-pop operator, and I either had to slow down or get professional help," Donald admitted. He decided he would rather own part of a big company than all of a small one.

The Sutherlands brought on Ken Burk, a veteran in the food-service industry, as a partner and CEO to establish the foundation of the fast-growing company in 1994. The following year, Doug Ducey joined Cold Stone Creamery as a partner

**LEARNING goals**

After you have read and studied this chapter, you should be able to

1. Compare the advantages and disadvantages of sole proprietorships.
2. Describe the differences between general and limited partners, and compare the advantages and disadvantages of partnerships.
3. Compare the advantages and disadvantages of corporations, and summarize the differences between C corporations, S corporations, and limited liability companies.
4. Define and give examples of three types of corporate mergers, and explain the role of leveraged buyouts and taking a firm private.
5. Outline the advantages and disadvantages of franchises, and discuss the opportunities for diversity in franchising and the challenges of global franchising.
6. Explain the role of cooperatives.

# CHAPTER 5

www.coldstonecreamery.com

and took on the role of president. His role was to handle business development and strategic direction. Ducey had previously worked for Procter & Gamble and had struggled to market Folgers coffee when Starbucks was turning the drink into an experience. His goal now is to turn Cold Stone Creamery into the Starbucks of ice cream shops. Under Ducey's leadership, the franchise has grown to 1,000 stores, with another 1,000 in the planning stages. Business is indeed hot for the $285 million ice cream chain.

Franchisees range from an ex-waitress to a former business-school dean. What they have in common, Ducey says, is prior success, energy, and a good attitude toward a business where most of the work comes at night and on weekends. The Sutherlands say that what sets Cold Stone apart from other ice cream chains is that it makes its ice cream, brownies, and waffle cones daily in its stores. Franchisees are taught to make the product rather than having it shipped in from across town or across the country. "The product is first and foremost," Donald Sutherland said. "It is the one thing that can't be changed. You have to have the best."

Just like the Sutherlands, all business owners must decide for themselves which form of business is best for them. Whether you dream of starting a business for yourself, going into business with a partner, or someday being a leading franchisor, it's important to know that each form of ownership has its advantages and disadvantages. You will learn about them in this chapter.

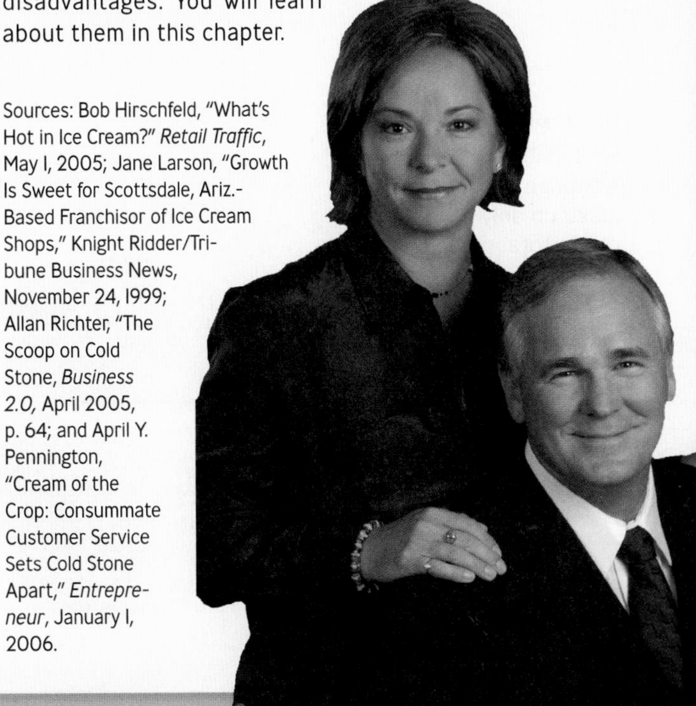

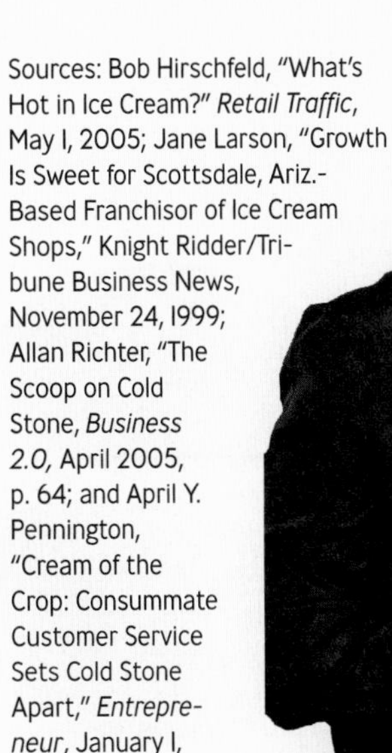

Sources: Bob Hirschfeld, "What's Hot in Ice Cream?" *Retail Traffic*, May 1, 2005; Jane Larson, "Growth Is Sweet for Scottsdale, Ariz.-Based Franchisor of Ice Cream Shops," Knight Ridder/Tribune Business News, November 24, 1999; Allan Richter, "The Scoop on Cold Stone, *Business 2.0*, April 2005, p. 64; and April Y. Pennington, "Cream of the Crop: Consummate Customer Service Sets Cold Stone Apart," *Entrepreneur*, January 1, 2006.

# BASIC FORMS OF BUSINESS OWNERSHIP

Like Donald and Susan Sutherland, hundreds of thousands of people have started new businesses in the United States. In fact, more than 500,000 new U.S. businesses are started each year.[1] Chances are, you have thought of owning your own business or know someone who has. One key to success in starting a new business is understanding how to get the resources you need. You may have to take on partners or find other ways of obtaining money. To stay in business, you may need help from someone with more expertise than you have in certain areas, or you may need to raise more money to expand. How you form your business can make a tremendous difference in your long-term success. You can form a business in one of several ways. The three major forms of business ownership are (1) sole proprietorships, (2) partnerships, and (3) corporations.

It can be easy to get started in your own business. You can begin a word processing service out of your home, open a car repair center, start a restaurant, develop a Web site, or go about meeting other wants and needs of your community. A business that is owned, and usually managed, by one person is called a **sole proprietorship**. That is the most common form of business ownership.

**sole proprietorship**
A business that is owned, and usually managed, by one person.

Many people do not have the money, time, or desire to run a business on their own. They prefer to have someone else or some group of people get together to form the business. When two or more people legally agree to become co-owners of a business, the organization is called a **partnership**.

**partnership**
A legal form of business with two or more owners.

There are advantages to creating a business that is separate and distinct from the owners. A legal entity with authority to act and have liability separate from its owners is called a **corporation**. The almost 5 million corporations in the United States comprise only 20 percent of all businesses, but they earn 81 percent of the total receipts (see Figure 5.1).[2]

**corporation**
A legal entity with authority to act and have liability separate from its owners.

As you will learn in this chapter, each form of business ownership has its advantages—and disadvantages. It is important to understand these advantages and disadvantages before attempting to start a business. Keep in mind that just because a business starts in one form of ownership, it doesn't have to stay in that form. Many companies start out in one form, then add (or drop) a partner or two, and eventually become corporations, limited liability companies, or franchisors. Let's begin our discussion by looking at the most basic form of ownership—the sole proprietorship.

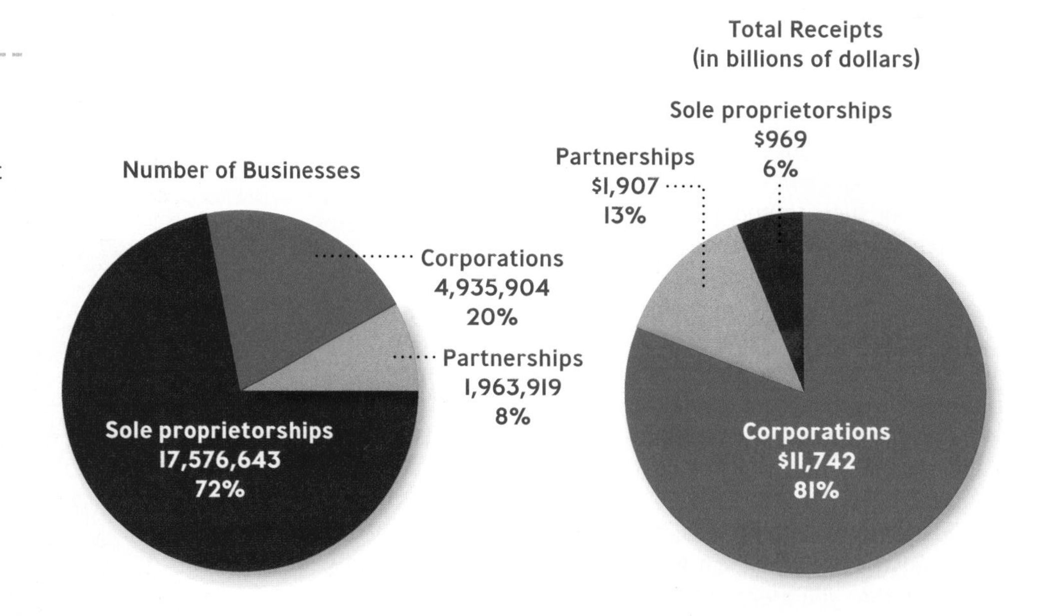


figure 5.1

**FORMS OF BUSINESS OWNERSHIP**

Although corporations make up only 20 percent of the total number of businesses, they make 81 percent of the total receipts. Sole proprietorships are the most common form (72 percent), but they only earn 6 percent of the receipts.

Source: U.S. Internal Revenue Service.

# SOLE PROPRIETORSHIPS

## Advantages of Sole Proprietorships

Sole proprietorships are the easiest kind of businesses for you to explore in your quest for an interesting career. Every town has sole proprietors you can visit. Talk with some of these businesspeople about the joys and frustrations of being on their own. Most will mention the benefits of being their own boss and setting their own hours. Other advantages they mention may include the following:

1. *Ease of starting and ending the business.* All you have to do to start a sole proprietorship is buy or lease the needed equipment (e.g., a saw, a word processor, a tractor, a lawn mower) and put up some announcements saying you are in business. It is just as easy to get out of business; you simply stop. There is no one to consult or to disagree with about such decisions. You may have to get a permit or license from the local government, but often that is no problem.
2. *Being your own boss.* Working for others simply does not have the same excitement as working for yourself—at least, that's the way sole proprietors feel. You may make mistakes, but they are your mistakes—and so are the many small victories each day.
3. *Pride of ownership.* People who own and manage their own businesses are rightfully proud of their work. They deserve all the credit for taking the risks and providing needed goods or services.
4. *Leaving a legacy.* Business owners have something to leave behind for future generations.
5. *Retention of company profit.* Other than the joy of being your own boss, there is nothing like the pleasure of knowing that you can earn as much as possible and not have to share that money with anyone else (except the government, in taxes).
6. *No special taxes.* All the profits of a sole proprietorship are taxed as the personal income of the owner, and the owner pays the normal income tax on that money. (However, owners do have to estimate their taxes and make quarterly payments to the government or suffer penalties for nonpayment.)

**unlimited liability**
The responsibility of business owners for all of the debts of the business.

Warren Brown's career is finally "rising." Brown left a promising law career to create Cakelove, a bustling bakery that specializes in making pastries from scratch using all natural ingredients. Cakes, however, are his passion and the company's signature dish. Brown has appeared on the Oprah Winfrey show and is regularly seen on the Food Network. Do you have a passion you would like to pursue as a business?

## Disadvantages of Sole Proprietorships

Not everyone is equipped to own and manage a business. Often it is difficult to save enough money to start a business and keep it going. The costs of inventory, supplies, insurance, advertising, rent, computers, utilities, and so on may be too much to cover alone. There are other disadvantages of owning your own business:

1. *Unlimited liability—the risk of personal losses.* When you work for others, it is their problem if the business is not profitable. When you own your own business, you and the business are considered one. You have **unlimited liability**; that is, any debts or

damages incurred by the business are your debts and you must pay them, even if it means selling your home, your car, or whatever else you own. This is a serious risk, and one that requires not only thought but also discussion with a lawyer, an insurance agent, an accountant, and others.

2. *Limited financial resources.* Funds available to the business are limited to the funds that the one (sole) owner can gather. Since there are serious limits to how much money one person can raise, partnerships and corporations have a greater probability of obtaining the needed financial backing to start a business and keep it going.
3. *Management difficulties.* All businesses need management; that is, someone must keep inventory records, accounting records, tax records, and so forth. Many people who are skilled at selling things or providing a service are not so skilled in keeping records. Sole proprietors often find it difficult to attract good, qualified employees to help run the business because they cannot compete with the salary and fringe benefits offered by larger companies.
4. *Overwhelming time commitment.* Though sole proprietors may say they set their own hours, it's hard to own a business, manage it, train people, and have time for anything else in life. This is true of any business, but a sole proprietor has no one with whom to share the burden. The owner often must spend long hours working. The owner of a store, for example, may put in 12 hours a day, at least six days a week—almost twice the hours worked by a nonsupervisory employee in a large company. Imagine how this time commitment affects the sole proprietor's family life. Tim DeMello, founder of the successful company Wall Street Games Inc., echoes countless other sole proprietors when he says, "It's not a job, it's not a career, it's a way of life."
5. *Few fringe benefits.* If you are your own boss, you lose the fringe benefits that often come from working for others. You have no paid health insurance, no paid disability insurance, no sick leave, and no vacation pay. These and other benefits may add up to approximately 30 percent of a worker's income.[3]
6. *Limited growth.* Expansion is often slow since a sole proprietorship relies on its owner for most of its creativity, business know-how, and funding.
7. *Limited life span.* If the sole proprietor dies, is incapacitated, or retires, the business no longer exists (unless it is sold or taken over by the sole proprietor's heirs).

Don't forget to talk with a few local sole proprietors about the problems they have faced in being on their own. They are likely to have many interesting stories to tell about problems getting loans from the bank, problems with theft, problems simply keeping up with the business, and so on. These problems are also reasons why many sole proprietors choose to find partners to share the load.

**progress assessment**

- Most people who start businesses in the United States are sole proprietors. What are the advantages and disadvantages of sole proprietorships?
- Why would unlimited liability be considered a major drawback to sole proprietorships?

## PARTNERSHIPS

A partnership is a legal form of business with two or more owners. There are several types of partnerships: (1) general partnerships, (2) limited partnerships, and (3) master limited partnerships. A **general partnership** is a partnership in which all owners share in operating the business and in assuming liability for the business's debts. A **limited partnership** is a partnership with one or more general partners and one or more limited partners. A **general partner** is an owner (partner) who has unlimited liability and is active in managing the firm. Every partnership must have at least one general partner. A **limited partner** is an owner who invests money in the business but does not have any management responsibility or liability for losses beyond the investment. **Limited liability** means that limited partners are not responsible for the debts of the business beyond the amount of their investment—their liability is *limited* to the amount they put into the company; their personal assets are not at risk.

A newer form of partnership, the **master limited partnership (MLP)**, looks much like a corporation (which we discuss next) in that it acts like a corporation and is traded on the stock exchanges like a corporation, but it is taxed like a partnership and thus avoids the corporate income tax. For example, Sunoco Inc. formed MLP Sunoco Logistics (SXL) to acquire, own, and operate a group of crude oil and refined-product pipelines and storage facilities. SXL began trading on the New York Stock Exchange in 2002. Income received by SXL is not taxed before it is passed on to investors in the form of dividends as it would have been if SXL were a corporation.

Another newer type of partnership was created to limit the disadvantage of unlimited liability. All states are now allowing partners to form what is called a

**general partnership**
A partnership in which all owners share in operating the business and in assuming liability for the business's debts.

**limited partnership**
A partnership with one or more general partners and one or more limited partners.

**general partner**
An owner (partner) who has unlimited liability and is active in managing the firm.

**limited partner**
An owner who invests money in the business but does not have any management responsibility or liability for losses beyond the investment.

Kate and Andy Spade (David's brother) started a business selling a $155 black nylon handbag in 1993. Their business has grown into a $175 million global brand with 25 shops worldwide. More than 600 other stores also carry the brand. What makes the pair of Spades such great business partners? It's their differences: Kate is the creative soul who designs the products and Andy is the risk taker who shapes the brand. What problems might partners who share both business and home encounter that other partners might not?

**limited liability**
The responsibility of a business's owners for losses only up to the amount they invest; limited partners and shareholders have limited liability.

**master limited partnership (MLP)**
A partnership that looks much like a corporation (in that it acts like a corporation and is traded on a stock exchange) but is taxed like a partnership and thus avoids the corporate income tax.

**limited liability partnership (LLP)**
A partnership that limits partners' risk of losing their personal assets to only their own acts and omissions and to the acts and omissions of people under their supervision.

**limited liability partnership (LLP)**. LLPs limit partners' risk of losing their personal assets to only their own acts and omissions and to the acts and omissions of people under their supervision. This means that the LLP allows you to operate without the fear that one of your partners might commit an act of malpractice that would result in a judgment that takes away your house, car, retirement plan, and collection of vintage Star Wars action figures, as would be the case in a general partnership. However, in many states this personal protection does not extend to contract liabilities such as bank loans, lease obligations, and trade creditors; loss of personal assets is still a risk in these situations. In the states that do have additional contract liability protections for LLPs, the LLP is in many ways similar to an LLC (discussed later in the chapter).

All states except Louisiana have adopted the Uniform Partnership Act (UPA) to replace laws relating to partnerships. The UPA defines the three key elements of any general partnership as (1) common ownership, (2) shared profits and losses, and (3) the right to participate in managing the operations of the business.

## Advantages of Partnerships

There are many advantages to having one or more partners in a business. Often, it is much easier to own and manage a business with one or more partners. Your partner can cover for you when you are sick or go on vacation. Your partner may be skilled at inventory control and accounting, while you do the selling or servicing. A partner can also provide additional money, support, and expertise. Partnerships usually have the following advantages:

1. *More financial resources.* When two or more people pool their money and credit, it is easier to pay the rent, utilities, and other bills incurred by a business. A limited partnership is specially designed to help raise money. As mentioned earlier, a limited partner invests money in the business but cannot legally have any management responsibility and has limited liability.
2. *Shared management and pooled/complementary skills and knowledge.* It is simply much easier to manage the day-to-day activities of a business with carefully chosen partners. Partners give each other free time from the business and provide different skills and perspectives. Some people find that the best partner is a spouse. That is why you see so many husband-and-wife teams managing restaurants, service shops, and other businesses.[4]
3. *Longer survival.* One study that examined 2,000 businesses started since 1960 reported that partnerships were four times as likely to succeed as sole proprietorships. Being watched by a partner can help a businessperson become more disciplined.
4. *No special taxes.* As with sole proprietorships, all profits of partnerships are taxed as the personal income of the owners, and the owners pay the normal income tax on that money. Similarly, partners must estimate their taxes and make quarterly payments or suffer penalties for nonpayment.

## Disadvantages of Partnerships

Anytime two people must agree, there is the possibility of conflict and tension. Partnerships have caused splits among families, friends, and marriages. Let's explore the disadvantages of partnerships:

1. *Unlimited liability.* Each *general* partner is liable for the debts of the firm, no matter who was responsible for causing those debts. You are

## * * * MAKING ethical decisions

### Outsourcing or Outsmarting?

Imagine that you and your partner own a construction company. You receive a bid from a subcontractor that you know is 20 percent too low. Such a loss to the subcontractor could put him out of business. Accepting the bid will certainly improve your chances of winning the contract for a big shopping center project. Your partner wants to take the bid and let the subcontractor suffer the consequences of his bad estimate. What do you think you should do? What will be the consequences of your decision?

liable for your partners' mistakes as well as your own. Like sole proprietors, general partners can lose their homes, cars, and everything else they own if the business loses a lawsuit or goes bankrupt.

2. *Division of profits.* Sharing risk means sharing profits, and that can cause conflicts. There is no set system for dividing profits in a partnership, so profits are not always divided evenly. For example, two people form a partnership in which one puts in more money and the other puts in more hours working the business. Each may feel justified in asking for a bigger share of the profits. Imagine the resulting conflicts.
3. *Disagreements among partners.* Disagreements over money are just one example of potential conflict in a partnership. Who has final authority over employees? Who hires and fires employees? Who works what hours? What if one partner wants to buy expensive equipment for the firm and the other partner disagrees? Potential conflicts are many. (See the Making Ethical Decisions box for an example.) Because of such problems, all terms of partnership should be spelled out in writing to protect all parties and to minimize misunderstandings.[5]
4. *Difficulty of termination.* Once you have committed yourself to a partnership, it is not easy to get out of it (other than by death, which immediately terminates the partnership). Sure, you can end a partnership just by quitting. However, questions about who gets what and what happens next are often very difficult to solve when the partnership ends. Surprisingly, law firms often have faulty partnership agreements and find that breaking up is hard to do. How do you get rid of a partner you don't like? It is best to decide such questions up front in the partnership agreement. Figure 5.2 on page 124 gives you more ideas about what should be included in partnership agreements.

The best way to learn about the advantages and disadvantages of partnerships is to interview several people who have experience with such agreements. They will give you insights and hints on how to avoid problems. The Spotlight on Small Business box on page 125 offers a few tips about choosing a partner.

One common fear of owning your own business or having a partner is the fear of losing everything you own if the business loses a lot of money or someone sues the business. Many businesspeople try to avoid this and the other disadvantages of sole proprietorships and partnerships by forming corporations. We discuss this basic form of business ownership in the following section.

Once a giant in the accounting industry; now just a name from the past. The lowering of the Andersen name from its lofty spot atop the Center City building in Philadelphia reminds us that even the mighty can fall. It also reminds us of the importance of choosing your partners wisely. What do you feel is the greatest risk of being a general partner in a partnership.

figure 5.2

HOW TO FORM A PARTNERSHIP

It's not hard to form a partnership, but it's wise for each prospective partner to get the counsel of a lawyer experienced with such agreements. Lawyers' services are usually expensive, so would-be partners should read all about partnerships and reach some basic agreements before calling a lawyer.

For your protection, be sure to put your partnership agreement in writing. The Model Business Corporation Act recommends including the following in a written partnership agreement:

1. The name of the business. Many states require the firm's name to be registered with state and/or county officials if the firm's name is different from the name of any of the partners.
2. The names and addresses of all partners.
3. The purpose and nature of the business, the location of the principal offices, and any other locations where business will be conducted.
4. The date the partnership will start and how long it will last. Will it exist for a specific length of time, or will it stop when one of the partners dies or when the partners agree to discontinue?
5. The contributions made by each partner. Will some partners contribute money, while others provide real estate, personal property, expertise, or labor? When are the contributions due?
6. The management responsibilities. Will all partners have equal voices in management, or will there be senior and junior partners?
7. The duties of each partner.
8. The salaries and drawing accounts of each partner.
9. Provision for sharing of profits or losses.
10. Provision for accounting procedures. Who'll keep the accounts? What bookkeeping and accounting methods will be used? Where will the books be kept?
11. The requirements for taking in new partners.
12. Any special restrictions, rights, or duties of any partner.
13. Provision for a retiring partner.
14. Provision for the purchase of a deceased or retiring partner's share of the business.
15. Provision for how grievances will be handled.
16. Provision for how to dissolve the partnership and distribute the assets to the partners.

progress assessment

- What is the difference between a limited partner and a general partner?
- What are some of the advantages and disadvantages of partnerships?

## CORPORATIONS

Although the word *corporation* makes people think of big businesses like General Motors, IBM, Ford, Exxon, General Electric, Microsoft, and Wal-Mart, it is not necessary to be big in order to incorporate. Obviously, many corporations are big and contribute substantially to the U.S. economy. However, incorporating may be beneficial for small businesses as well.

**conventional (C) corporation**
A state-chartered legal entity with authority to act and have liability separate from its owners.

A **conventional (C) corporation** is a state-chartered legal entity with authority to act and have liability separate from its owners (the corporation's

SPOTLIGHT ON small business www.entrepreneur.com

## Choose Your Partner

Suppose you need money and want help running your business, and you decide to take on a partner. You know that partnerships are like marriages and that you won't really know the other person until after you live together. How do you choose the right partner? Before you plunge into a partnership, do three things:

1. Talk to people who have been in successful—and unsuccessful—partnerships. Find out what worked and what didn't. Ask them how conflicts were resolved and how decisions were made.
2. Interview your prospective partner very carefully. Do you share the same goals? What skills does the person have? Are they the same as yours, or do they complement your skills? What contacts, resources, or special attributes will the person bring to the business? Do you both feel the same about family members working for the business? Do you share the same vision for the company's future?
3. Evaluate your prospective partner as a decision maker. Ask yourself, "Is this someone with whom I could happily share authority for all major business decisions?"

As in a good marriage, the best way to avoid major conflicts is to begin with an honest communication of what each partner expects to give and get from the partnership.

stockholders are its owners). What this means for the owners is that they are not liable for the debts or any other problems of the corporation beyond the money they invest. Owners no longer have to worry about losing personal belongings such as their house, car, or other property because of some business problem—a significant benefit. A corporation not only limits the liability of owners but often enables many people to share in the ownership (and profits) of a business without working there or having other commitments to it. Corporations can choose whether to offer such ownership to outside investors or whether to remain privately held. (We will discuss stock ownership in Chapter 19.) Figure 5.3 on page 126 describes various types of corporations.

## Advantages of Corporations

Most people are not willing to risk everything to go into business. Yet for a business to grow and prosper and create economic opportunity, many people would have to be willing to invest their money in it. One way to solve this problem is to create an artificial being, an entity that exists only in the eyes of the law—a corporation. Let's explore some of the advantages of corporations:

1. *Limited liability.* A major advantage of corporations is the limited liability of owners. Corporations in England and Canada have the letters *Ltd.* after their name, as in British Motors Ltd. The *Ltd.* stands for "limited liability," probably the most significant advantage of corporations. Remember, limited liability means that the owners of a business are responsible for losses only up to the amount they invest.
2. *More money for investment.* To raise money, a corporation can sell ownership (stock) to anyone who is interested. This means that millions of people can own part of major companies like IBM, Xerox, and General Motors and smaller companies as well. If a company sold 10 million shares for $50 each, it would have $500 million available to build plants, buy materials, hire people, manufacture products, and so on. Such a large amount of money would be difficult to raise any other way.

   Corporations can also borrow money from individual investors through issuing bonds. Corporations may also find it easier to obtain loans from financial institutions, since lenders find it easier to place a

figure 5.3

**CORPORATE TYPES**

Corporations can fit in more than one category.

You may find some confusing types of corporations when reading about them. Here are a few of the more widely used terms:

An *alien corporation* does business in the United States but is chartered (incorporated) in another country.

A *domestic corporation* does business in the state in which it's chartered (incorporated).

A *foreign corporation* does business in one state but is chartered in another. About one-third of all corporations are chartered in Delaware because of its relatively attractive rules for incorporation. A foreign corporation must register in states where it operates.

A *closed (private) corporation* is one whose stock is held by a few people and isn't available to the general public.

An *open (public) corporation* sells stock to the general public. General Motors and Exxon Mobil are examples of public corporations.

A *quasi-public corporation* is a corporation chartered by the government as an approved monopoly to perform services to the general public. Public utilities are examples of quasi-public corporations.

A *professional corporation* is one whose owners offer professional services (doctors, lawyers, etc.). Shares in professional corporations aren't publicly traded.

A *nonprofit corporation* is one that doesn't seek personal profit for its owners.

A *multinational corporation* is a firm that operates in several countries.

value on the company when they can review how the stock is trading. Many small or individually owned corporations that do not trade actively may not have such opportunities, however. You can read about how corporations raise funds through the sale of stocks and bonds in Chapter 19.

3. *Size.* That one word summarizes many of the advantages of some corporations. Because they have the ability to raise large amounts of money to work with, corporations can build modern factories or software development facilities with the latest equipment. They can also hire experts or specialists in all areas of operation. Furthermore, they can buy other corporations in other fields to diversify their risk. (What this means is that a corporation can be involved in many businesses at once so that if one fails, the effect on the total corporation is lessened.) In short, a large corporation with numerous resources can take advantage of opportunities anywhere in the world.

   Remember, however, that corporations do not have to be large to enjoy the benefits of incorporating. Many doctors, lawyers, and individuals, as well as partners in a variety of businesses, have incorporated. The vast majority of corporations in the United States are small businesses.
4. *Perpetual life.* Because corporations are separate from those who own them, the death of one or more owners does not terminate the corporation.
5. *Ease of ownership change.* It is easy to change the owners of a corporation. All that is necessary is to sell the stock to someone else.
6. *Ease of drawing talented employees.* Corporations can attract skilled employees by offering such benefits as stock options (the right to purchase shares of the corporation for a fixed price).

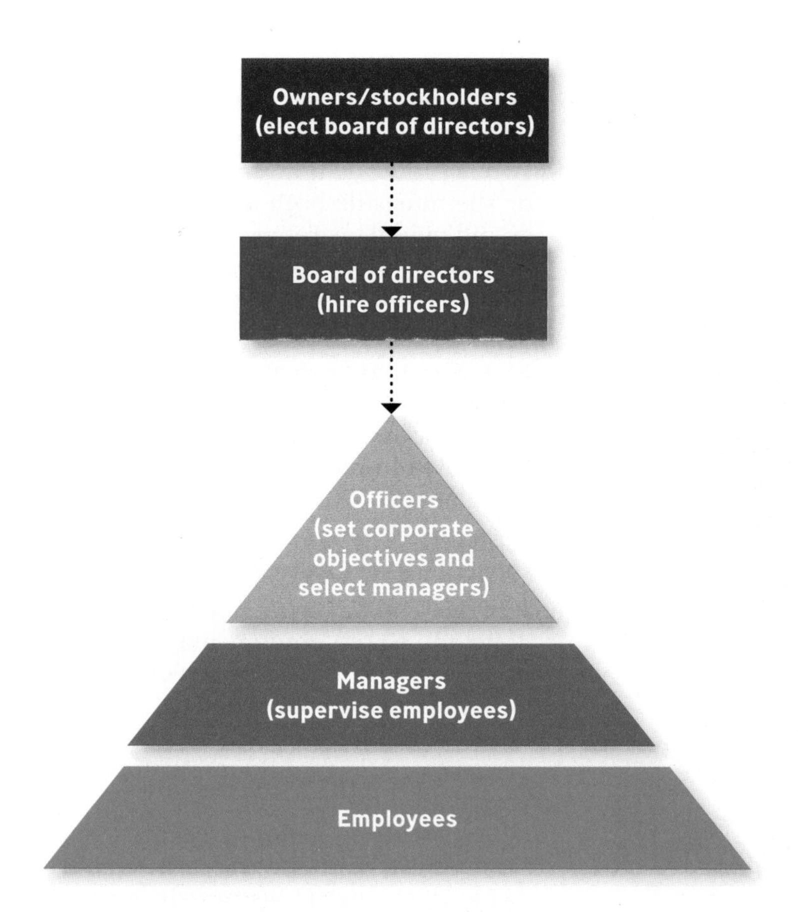


figure 5.4

**HOW OWNERS AFFECT MANAGEMENT**

Owners have an influence on how business is managed by electing a board of directors. The board hires the top managers (or fires them). It also sets the pay for top managers. Top managers then select other managers and employees with the help of the human resources department.

7. *Separation of ownership from management.* Corporations are able to raise money from many different investors without getting them involved in management. A corporate hierarchy is shown in Figure 5.4.

The pyramid in Figure 5.4 shows that the owners/stockholders are separate from the managers and employees. The owners/stockholders elect a board of directors. The directors hire the officers of the corporation and oversee major policy issues. The owners/stockholders thus have some say in who runs the corporation, but they have no control over the daily operations.

## Disadvantages of Corporations

There are so many sole proprietorships and partnerships in the United States that clearly there must be some disadvantages to incorporating. Otherwise, more people would incorporate their businesses. The following are a few of the disadvantages:

1. *Extensive paperwork.* The paperwork filed to start a corporation is just the beginning. Tax laws demand that a corporation prove that all its expenses and deductions are legitimate. Corporations must therefore process many forms. A sole proprietor or a partnership may keep rather broad accounting records; a corporation, in contrast, must keep detailed financial records, the minutes of meetings, and more.
2. *Double taxation.* Corporate income is taxed twice. First the corporation pays tax on income before it can distribute any to stockholders. Then the stockholders pay tax on the income (dividends) they receive from the corporation. States often tax corporations more harshly than

When Mark Beckloff and Dan Dye's neighbors sniffed the all-natural treats Mark and Dan baked for their own dogs, they came begging for biscuits. It didn't take the two friends long to decide to form a partnership and open a bakery just for dogs. Today, their business is incorporated with more than 30 bakeries in the United States as well as stores in Canada, Japan, and South Korea. Can you think of innovative products that might fit into a specialized market?

they tax other enterprises. Sometimes they levy special taxes that apply to corporations but not to other forms of business.

3. *Two tax returns.* If an individual incorporates, he or she must file both a corporate tax return and an individual tax return. Depending on the size of the corporation, a corporate return can be quite complex and require the assistance of a certified public accountant (CPA).
4. *Size.* Size may be one advantage of corporations, but it can be a disadvantage as well. Large corporations sometimes become too inflexible and too tied down in red tape to respond quickly to market changes.
5. *Difficulty of termination.* Once a corporation is started, it's relatively hard to end.
6. *Possible conflict with stockholders and board of directors.* Some conflict may brew if the stockholders elect a board of directors that disagrees with the present management. Since the board of directors chooses the company's officers, entrepreneurs could find themselves forced out of the very company they founded. This is what happened to Rod Canion, one of the founders of Compaq Computer, and Steve Jobs, a founder of Apple Computer (Jobs has since returned to the company).
7. *Initial cost.* Incorporation may cost thousands of dollars and involve expensive lawyers and accountants. There are less expensive ways of incorporating in certain states (see the next subsection in this chapter), but many people do not have the time or confidence to go through this procedure without the help of a lawyer.

Many people are discouraged by the costs, paperwork, and special taxes corporations must pay. However, many other businesspeople believe the hassles of incorporation outweigh the advantages.

## Individuals Can Incorporate

Not all corporations are large organizations with hundreds of employees or thousands of stockholders. Individuals (e.g., truckers, doctors, lawyers, plumbers, athletes, and movie stars) can also incorporate. Normally, individuals who incorporate do not issue stock to outsiders; therefore, they do not share all of the same advantages and disadvantages of large corporations (such as more money for investment and size). Their major advantage is limited liability and possible tax benefits. As noted in Figure 5.3, many firms incorporate in Delaware because the state's laws make the process easier than it is in other states.[6] Although you are not required to file for incorporation through a lawyer, it is usually wise to consult one. In addition to lawyers' fees, the secretary of state's office charges a fee for incorporating a business. Such fees vary widely by state, from a low of $50 in six states to a high of $300 in Texas.[7] Like the fee, the length of time it will take to actually have your business incorporated will vary widely by state. The average time is approximately 30 days from the date of application. Figure 5.5 outlines how to incorporate.

figure 5.5

**HOW TO INCORPORATE**

The process of forming a corporation varies somewhat from state to state. The articles of incorporation are usually filed with the secretary of state's office in the state in which the company incorporates. The articles contain:

- The corporation's name.
- The names of the people who incorporated it.
- Its purposes.
- Its duration (usually perpetual).
- The number of shares that can be issued, their voting rights, and any other rights the shareholders have.
- The corporation's minimum capital.
- The address of the corporation's office.
- The name and address of the person responsible for the corporation's legal service.
- The names and addresses of the first directors.
- Any other public information the incorporators wish to include.

Before a business can so much as open a bank account or hire employees, it needs a federal tax identification number. To apply for one, get an SS-4 form from the IRS.

In addition to the articles of incorporation listed, a corporation has bylaws. These describe how the firm is to be operated from both legal and managerial points of view. The bylaws include

- How, when, and where shareholders' and directors' meetings are held, and how long directors are to serve.
- Directors' authority.
- Duties and responsibilities of officers, and the length of their service.
- How stock is issued.
- Other matters, including employment contracts.

## S Corporations

**S corporation**
A unique government creation that looks like a corporation but is taxed like sole proprietorships and partnerships.

One issue that has received much attention in recent years is the formation of S corporations. An **S corporation** is a unique government creation that looks like a corporation but is taxed like sole proprietorships and partnerships. The paperwork and details of S corporations are similar to those of conventional (C) corporations. S corporations have shareholders, directors, and employees, and have the benefit of limited liability, but their profits are taxed as the personal income of the shareholders—thus avoiding the double taxation of C corporations.

Avoiding double taxation is reason enough for approximately 3 million U.S. companies to operate as S corporations.[8] Yet not all businesses can become S corporations. In order to qualify, a company must:

1. Have no more than 100 shareholders. (As of 2004, all members of a family can be counted as one shareholder.)[9]
2. Have shareholders that are individuals or estates and are citizens or permanent residents of the United States.
3. Have only one class of outstanding stock. (You can read more about the various classes of stock in Chapter 19.)
4. Not have more than 25 percent of income derived from passive sources (rents, royalties, interest, etc.).

An S corporation that loses its status as such may not reelect S corporation status for a minimum of five years. The tax structure of S corporations isn't attractive to all businesses. It's important to note that the benefits of S corporations change every time the tax rules change.[10] The best way to learn all the benefits or shortcomings for a specific business is to go over the tax advantages and liability differences with a lawyer, an accountant, or both.

## Limited Liability Companies

**limited liability company (LLC)**
A company similar to an S corporation but without the special eligibility requirements.

Many businesses are being attracted to the newest form of business ownership: the limited liability company (LLC). Billed as the "business entity of the future," a **limited liability company (LLC)** is similar to an S corporation but without the special eligibility requirements. LLCs were introduced in Wyoming in 1977 and were recognized by the Internal Revenue Service as a partnership for federal income tax purposes in 1988. In 1995 the National Conference of Commissioners on Uniform State Laws approved the final version of the Uniform Limited Liability Company Act. By 1996, all 50 states and the District of Columbia recognized LLCs. The number of LLCs has risen dramatically since 1988, when there were fewer than 100 filings. Today more than half of new business registrations in some states are LLCs.[11]

Why the drive toward forming LLCs? LLCs offer businesses the best of all corporate worlds. Advantages include:[12]

1. *Limited liability.* Personal assets are protected. Limited liability was previously available only to limited partners and shareholders of C corporations.
2. *Choice of taxation.* LLCs can choose to be taxed as partnerships or as corporations. Partnership-level taxation was previously a benefit normally reserved for partners or S corporation owners.
3. *Flexible ownership rules.* LLCs do not have to comply with ownership restrictions as S corporations do. Owners can be a person, partnership, or corporation.
4. *Flexible distribution of profit and losses.* Profit and losses don't have to be distributed in proportion to the money each person invests. LLC members agree on the percentage to be distributed to each member. Regular and S corporations must distribute profits and losses in proportion to shares held.
5. *Operating flexibility.* LLCs do have to submit articles of organization, which are similar to articles of incorporation, but they are not required to keep minutes, file written resolutions, or hold annual meetings. An LLC also submits a written operating agreement, similar to a partnership agreement, describing how the company is to be operated.

Of course, LLCs have their disadvantages as well. These include:

1. *No stock.* LLC ownership is nontransferable. LLC members need the approval of the other members in order to sell their interests. In contrast, regular and S corporation stockholders can sell their shares as they wish.
2. *Limited life span.* LLCs are required to identify dissolution dates in the articles of organization (no more than 30 years in some states). The death of a member can cause LLCs to dissolve automatically. Members may choose to reconstitute the LLC after it dissolves.
3. *Fewer incentives.* Unlike corporations, LLCs can't deduct the cost of fringe benefits. Since there's no stock, you can't use stock options as incentives to employees.
4. *Taxes.* LLC members must pay self-employment taxes—the Medicare/Social Security taxes paid by sole proprietors and partnerships—on profits. In contrast, S corporations pay self-employment tax on salary but not on the entire profits.
5. *Paperwork.* While the paperwork required of LLCs is not as great as that required of corporations, it is more than what is required of sole proprietors.

| | | Partnerships | | Corporations | | |
|---|---|---|---|---|---|---|
| | **SOLE PROPRIETORSHIP** | **GENERAL PARTNERSHIP** | **LIMITED PARTNERSHIP** | **CONVENTIONAL CORPORATION** | **S CORPORATION** | **LIMITED LIABILITY COMPANY** |
| **Documents Needed to Start Business** | None; may need permit or license | Partnership agreement (oral or written) | Written agreement; must file certificate of limited partnership | Articles of incorporation, bylaws | Articles of incorporation, bylaws, must meet criteria | Articles of organization and operating agreement; no eligibility requirements |
| **Ease of Termination** | Easy to terminate: just pay debts and quit | May be hard to terminate, depending on the partnership agreement | Same as general partnership | Hard and expensive to terminate | Same as conventional corporation | May be difficult, depending upon operating agreement |
| **Length of Life** | Terminates on the death of owner | Terminates on the death or withdrawal of partner | Same as general partnership | Perpetual life | Same as conventional corporation | Varies according to dissolution dates in articles of organization |
| **Transfer of Ownership** | Business can be sold to qualified buyer | Must have other partner(s)' agreement | Same as general partnership | Easy to change owners; just sell stock | Can sell stock, but with restrictions | Can't sell stock |
| **Financial Resources** | Limited to owner's capital and loans | Limited to partners' capital and loans | Same as general partnership | More money to start and operate; may sell stocks and bonds | Same as conventional corporation | Same as partnership |
| **Risk of Losses** | Unlimited liability | Unlimited liability | Limited liability | Limited liability | Limited liability | Limited liability |
| **Taxes** | Taxed as personal income | Taxed as personal income | Same as general partnership | Corporate, double taxation | Taxed as personal income | Varies |
| **Management Responsibilities** | Owner manages *all* areas of the business | Partners share management | Can't participate in management | Separate management from ownership | Same as conventional corporation | Varies |
| **Employee Benefits** | Usually fewer benefits and lower wages | Often fewer benefits and lower wages; promising employee could become a partner | Same as general partnership | Usually better benefits and wages, advancement opportunities | Same as conventional corporation | Varies, but are not tax deductible |

figure 5.6

**COMPARISON OF FORMS OF BUSINESS OWNERSHIP**

The start-up cost for an LLC is approximately $2,500, with annual charges of $1,500 for tax-return preparation and legal fees. Information about LLCs is available on the Small Business Administration's Web site at www.onlinewbc.gov/docs/growing/llcs.html. Figure 5.6 lists the advantages and disadvantages of the major forms of business ownership.

**merger** The result of two firms forming one company.

**acquisition** One company's purchase of the property and obligations of another company.

**vertical merger** The joining of two companies involved in different stages of related businesses.

**horizontal merger** The joining of two firms in the same industry.

**conglomerate merger** The joining of firms in completely unrelated industries.

**leveraged buyout (LBO)** An attempt by employees, management, or a group of investors to purchase an organization primarily through borrowing.

### progress assessment

- What are the major advantages and disadvantages of incorporating a business?
- What is the role of owners (stockholders) in the corporate hierarchy?
- If you buy stock in a corporation and someone gets injured by one of the corporation's products, can you be sued? Why or why not?
- Why are so many new businesses choosing a limited liability company (LLC) form of ownership?

## CORPORATE EXPANSION: MERGERS AND ACQUISITIONS

The merger mania of the late 1990s reached its peak in 2000, when the total spent on mergers and acquisitions hit a stunning $3.4 trillion and a new deal was being struck every 17 minutes. It seemed as though each deal made was intended to top the one before. Most of the new deals involved companies trying to expand within their own fields to save costs, enter new markets, position for international competition, or adapt to changing technologies or regulations. Those proved to be unattainable goals for many of the merged giants (see the Dealing with Change box on page 134).

What's the difference between mergers and acquisitions? A **merger** is the result of two firms forming one company. It is similar to a marriage joining two individuals as one. An **acquisition** is one company's purchase of the prop-

figure 5.7

TYPES OF MERGERS

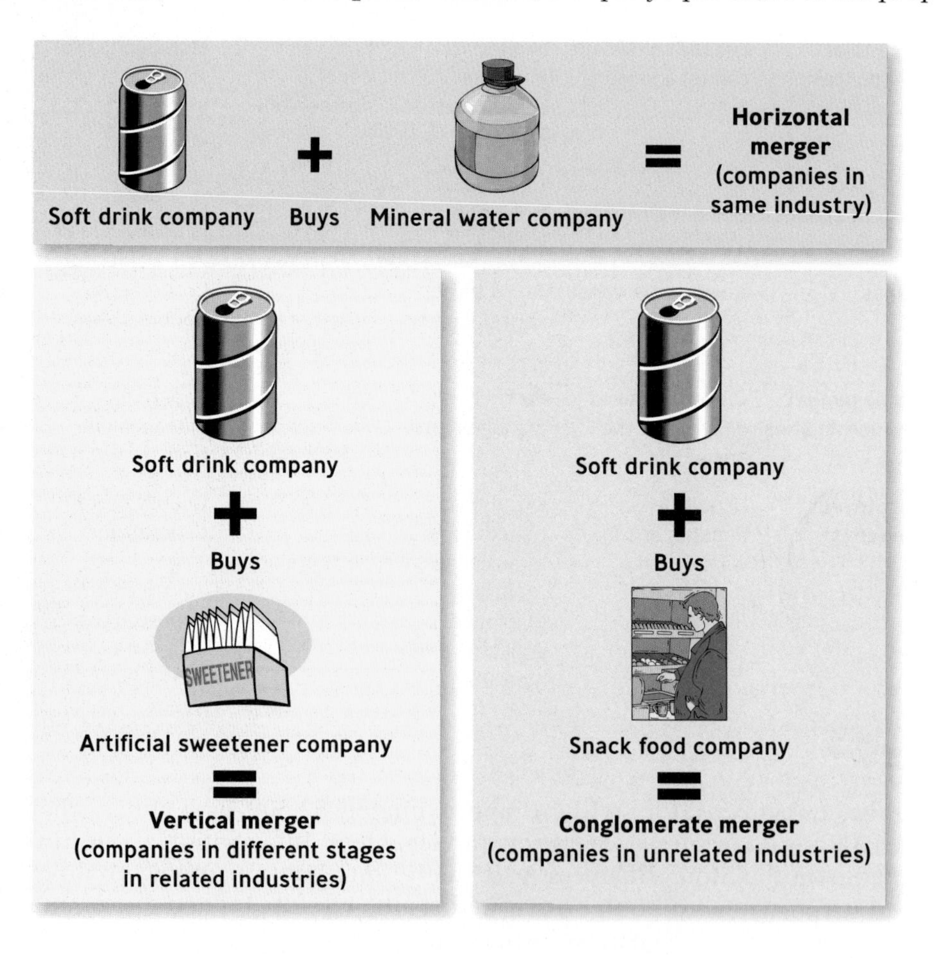

erty and obligations of another company. It is more like buying a house than entering a marriage.

There are three major types of corporate mergers: vertical, horizontal, and conglomerate. A **vertical merger** is the joining of two firms involved in different stages of related businesses. Think of a merger between a soft drink company and a company that produces artificial sweetener. Such a merger would ensure a constant supply of sweetener needed by the soft drink manufacturer. It could also help ensure quality control of the soft drink company's products. A **horizontal merger** joins two firms in the same industry and allows them to diversify or expand their products. An example of a horizontal merger is the merger of a soft drink company and a mineral water company. The business can now supply a variety of drinking products. A **conglomerate merger** unites firms in completely unrelated industries. The primary purpose of a conglomerate merger is to diversify business operations and investments. The merger of a soft drink company and a snack food company would be an example of a conglomerate merger. Figure 5.7 illustrates the differences in the three types of mergers.

Rather than merge or sell to another company, some corporations decide to maintain control, or in some cases regain control, of a firm internally. For example, Steve Stavro, the majority owner and head of a group that invested in the Maple Leaf Gardens Ltd. (owners of the Toronto Maple Leafs hockey team), decided to take the firm private. *Taking a firm private* involves the efforts of a group of stockholders or management to obtain all the firm's stock for themselves.[13] In the Maple Leaf Gardens situation, Stavro's investors group successfully gained total control of the company by buying all of the company's stock. For the first time in 65 years, investors in the open market could no longer purchase stock in the Maple Leafs.

Suppose the employees in an organization feel there is a good possibility they may lose their jobs. Or what if the managers believe that corporate performance could be enhanced if they owned the company? Do either of these groups have an opportunity of taking ownership of the company? Yes—they might attempt a leveraged buyout. A **leveraged buyout (LBO)** is an attempt by employees, management, or a group of investors to purchase an organization primarily through borrowing. The funds borrowed are used to buy out the stockholders in the company. The employees, managers, or investors now become the owners of the firm. LBOs have ranged in size from $50 million to $31 billion and have involved everything from small family businesses to giant corporations like R. J. R. Nabisco, Toys "R" Us, and Northwest Airlines.[14]

Today, merger mania isn't restricted to American companies. Foreign companies are gobbling up U.S. companies. The $41 billion merger of Stuttgart, Germany–based Daimler-Benz and U.S. automaker Chrysler in 1998 created a global automotive giant, DaimlerChrysler. Foreign companies have found that often the quickest way to grow is to buy an established operation and bring the brands and technology back to their home countries. However, such deals are not always welcomed. In 2005, U.S. lawmakers were concerned that the proposed purchase of U.S. oil company Unocal by a Chinese oil company

Tony Lee took a job cleaning bathrooms in a factory until a job opened up for him on the production line. He worked so hard he eventually became supervisor. When the owners announced plans to close the factory, Lee knew he had to do something. With the help of a local law professor and an economic development group, Tony prepared a business plan. After attracting five investors, selling his motorcycle and taking a second mortgage on his home, Lee completed a leveraged buyout. Now he and the other investors own the $3 million company.

DEALING WITH change

## The Urge to Merge Rises Again

Two-thirds of the merged giants of the late 1990s failed to meet their goals. The greatest merger mania in history unraveled before our eyes. These failing corporate giants lost trillions of dollars in market value. The once high-flying WorldCom filed for bankruptcy. The AOL/Time Warner marriage was so rocky that, even though the company overcame the threat of divorce, its stock lost two-thirds its value in 2001 and has not recovered since.

Why did CEOs have the urge to merge if so many land mines lay in the way? The booming markets in the mid-1990s convinced many CEOs that they needed to beef up in order to compete and to achieve the double-digit growth Wall Street expected. Deregulation in telecommunications and banking primed the merger pump, and the flow of mergers quickly spread to other industries. The remarkable upward spiral of the stock market gave dot-com entrepreneurs rising stock prices. They used that high-priced stock to buy other companies, which increased their earnings, which raised their stock prices higher, which allowed them to buy more and bigger businesses. Of course, if the CEOs got a big bonus for merger deals no matter what happened to the share price, they were even more eager to merge. Joseph Nacchio, CEO of Qwest Communications, received a $26 million "growth payment" when Qwest bought US West, and Solomon Trujillo of US West got $15 million for selling. (The deal was not so profitable for the company's shareholders. Qwest's value fell $20–$30 billion in late 2000 when the merger was completed and continued the free fall for the next two years. If you had bought 100 shares of the stock at its height in mid-2000, you'd have paid $8,500. If you still held the stock in 2005, the shares would have been worth a mere $400—that's a 95 percent loss.)

Some economists see merger waves in terms of games CEOs play. When one company merges with another, its competitors ask themselves what their next move should be in order to get not the best outcome, but the least bad outcome. Since they fear being left behind, the first deal inspires others. For example, after Daimler bought Chrylser, Ford and General Motors each bought other carmakers. But which carmakers have remained the most profitable? BMW, Porsche, and Toyota—all of which stayed out of the mania.

Change is constant, of course, so every merger wave is followed by a counterwave. More than a third of the companies formed in the largest international mergers of the preceding decade are now being "demerged." For example, luxury goods giant LVMH sold bits of the empire it accumulated in the 1990s. However, after avoiding big deals for more than three years, a new wave of mergers surged in early 2005 as corporations announced 48 deals of $1 billion or more, totaling $357 billion in just three months. Procter & Gamble (P&G) paid $57 billion for Gillette. Will P&G's shares collapse, as have many of the megamergers of the past? According to analysts, P&G must increase profits from Gillette's razor, batteries, and other businesses by 12 percent each year for the next five years to cover the costs of the merger. Gillette's profits have risen at only one-third that rate in the past five years, so meeting that goal may be a close shave.

Sources: Harry Berkowitz. "Time Warner Pays $2.4B to Settle Class-Action Suit," *Newsday*, August 4, 2005; Shawn Tully, "The Urge to Merge," *Fortune*, February 21, 2005; Robert Barker, "P&G's $57 Billion Bargain," *BusinessWeek*, July 25, 2005; and Gregory Zuckerman and Ian McDonald, "Time to Slice the Mergers," *The Wall Street Journal*, January 10, 2006, p. C1.

www.pg.com

might threaten American economic and national security interests. CNOOC, the Chinese company, eventually withdrew its bid.[15]

# SPECIAL FORMS OF OWNERSHIP

In addition to the three basic forms of business ownership, we shall discuss two special forms of ownership: franchises and cooperatives. Let's look at franchises first.

# FRANCHISES

**franchise agreement**
An arrangement whereby someone with a good idea for a business sells the rights to use the business name and sell a product or service to others in a given territory.

**franchisor**
A company that develops a product concept and sells others the rights to make and sell the products.

Basically, a **franchise agreement** is an arrangement whereby someone with a good idea for a business (the **franchisor**) sells the rights to use the business name and to sell a product or service (the **franchise**) to others (the **franchisee**) in a given territory.

Some people are uncomfortable with the idea of starting their own business from scratch. They would rather join a business with a proven track record through a franchise agreement. A franchise can be formed as a sole proprietorship, partnership, or corporation. Some of the best-known franchises are McDonald's, Jiffy Lube, 7-Eleven, Weight Watchers, and Holiday Inn.[16]

**franchise**
The right to use a specific business's name and sell its products or services in a given territory.

Approximately 10 million people in the United States work in a franchise. Franchised businesses now account for approximately $1.5 trillion, or 10 percent, of America's gross domestic product (GDP)—that's more than China's total GDP.[17] The most popular businesses for franchising are restaurants (more than 80 percent of all franchises), retail stores, hotels and motels, and automotive parts and service centers. McDonald's is the largest restaurant chain in the United States and is considered the gold standard of franchising.[18]

**franchisee**
A person who buys a franchise.

## Advantages of Franchises

Franchising has penetrated every aspect of American and global business life by offering products and services that are reliable, convenient, and competitively priced. The worldwide growth of franchising could not have been accomplished by accident. Franchising clearly has some advantages:

1. *Management and marketing assistance.* Compared with someone who starts a business from scratch, a franchisee (the person who buys a franchise) usually has a much greater chance of succeeding because he or she has an established product (e.g., Wendy's hamburgers, Domino's pizza); help with choosing a location and promotion; and assistance in all phases of operation. It is like having your own store with full-time consultants available when you need them. Franchisors provide intensive training. For example, McDonald's sends all new franchisees and managers to Hamburger University in Oak Brook, Illinois.

   Some franchisors are helping their franchisees succeed by helping with local marketing efforts rather than having them depend solely on national advertising. Furthermore, franchisees have a whole network of fellow franchisees who are facing similar problems and can share their experiences. For example, The UPS Store provides its 5,300 franchisees with a software program that helps them build data banks of customer names and addresses. The company also provides one-on-one phone support and quick e-mail access through its help desk. The help desk focuses on personalizing contact with the company's franchisees by immediately addressing their questions and concerns.
2. *Personal ownership.* A franchise operation is still your store, and you enjoy much of the incentives and profit of any sole proprietor. You are still your own boss, although you must follow more rules, regulations, and procedures than you would with your own privately owned store.
3. *Nationally recognized name.* It is one thing to open a gift shop or ice cream store. It is quite another to open a new Hallmark store or a Baskin-Robbins. With an established franchise, you get instant recognition and support from a product group with established customers from around the world.
4. *Financial advice and assistance.* A major problem with small businesses is arranging financing and learning to keep good records. Franchisees get valuable assistance and periodic advice from people with expertise in these areas. In fact, some franchisors will even provide financing to potential franchisees they feel will be valuable parts of the franchise system. For example, SRA International Inc., an executive-recruiting franchise, eases entry for selected new franchisees by allowing $20,000 of the $35,000 initiation fee to be paid from revenue over a period of two years or more.

Holiday Inn's InterContinential Amstel hotel in Amsterdam has been celebrated as the Netherland's most beautiful and luxurious hotel. Holiday Inn franchises try to complement the environment of the area they serve. This hotel is on the crossroads of Amsterdam's financial and exclusive shopping districts. What do you think would have been the reaction if Holiday Inn built the typical American-style hotel in this area?

5. *Lower failure rate.* Historically, the failure rate for franchises has been lower than that of other business ventures. Some experts say that independent businesses fail eight times more often than franchised businesses.[19] However, franchising has grown so rapidly that many weak franchises have entered the field, so you need to be careful and invest wisely.

## Disadvantages of Franchises

It almost sounds like franchising is too good to be true. There are, however, some potential pitfalls. You must be sure to check out any such arrangement with present franchisees and possibly discuss the idea with an attorney and an accountant. Disadvantages of franchises include the following:

1. *Large start-up costs.* Most franchises will demand a fee just for the rights to the franchise. Fees for franchises can vary considerably. Start-up costs for a Jazzercise franchise, for example, range from $2,000 to $3,000; but if it's Krispy Kreme you're after, you'd better have a lot more dough. An average Krispy Kreme store will cost you approximately $2 million.[20]
2. *Shared profit.* The franchisor often demands either a large share of the profits in addition to the start-up fees or a percentage commission based on sales, not profit.[21] This share demanded by the franchisor is generally referred to as a *royalty.* For example, if a franchisor demands a 10 percent royalty on a franchise's net sales, 10 cents of every dollar collected at the franchise (before taxes and other expenses) must be paid to the franchisor.
3. *Management regulation.* Management "assistance" has a way of becoming managerial orders, directives, and limitations. Franchisees feeling burdened by the company's rules and regulations may lose the spirit and incentive of being their own boss with their own business. One of the biggest changes in franchising in recent years has been the banding together of franchisees to resolve their grievances with franchisors rather than each fighting their battles alone. For example, franchisees joined forces to sue franchisor Meineke Discount Muffler Shops Inc. for fraudulently pocketing money they gave the company for advertising. The

www.ftc.gov/bcp/conline/pubs/invest/homewrk.htm

LEGAL briefcase

### Scam Artists Don't Paint Pretty Pictures

Did you know you can bid on a business on eBay? For example, one entrepreneur offered to franchise his used golf ball business—he said you could sort balls while watching movies on TV and make big bucks.

It's a story we've all heard before. Uncle Dick, Aunt Jane, or some enterprising person down the street dips into his or her life savings, retirement accounts, or other personal funds to invest in a new franchise opportunity. The next thing we hear is that the franchisee is basking on a beach on the French Riviera. Sounds like we better get to the bank pronto and then make a quick stop to pick up some suntan lotion.

Actually, you'd better not move too fast. It's true that a franchise is often a quick and efficient way for people who lack experience or detailed business training to grow a business. The lure of some franchises can almost be seductive. It's important to remember, though, that not all franchises have fairy-tale endings. In fact, investors lose hundreds of millions of dollars a year to ill-conceived franchises and, worse, franchise scams.

Many fraudulent franchise schemes are advertised at business opportunity and franchise shows, in newspaper ads, and by e-mail. For example, one e-mail ad for a business distributing music albums promised, "We will show you step by step how to earn $150,000 per year just working a few hours per week. Imagine that!" Bob Keith, 54, of Philadelphia, said he lost $13,000 after signing up and being promised a supply of current popular music to sell. "I got recordings from artists that have been dead for 30 years," he said. Other customers said they were sent CDs of whale songs.

Sleazy salespersons peddle franchise opportunities to wide-eyed would-be millionaires, yet the businesses are clearly destined to flop. Fatty Arburgers might sound like the next McDonald's, and Kelly's Coffee & Fudge Factory the next Starbucks, but be sure the franchise has stores up and operating before putting your money on the table. The important thing to remember is this: Beware of business opportunities that sound too good to be true—they probably are. To protect yourself against franchise fraud, do your homework and don't be afraid to ask questions.

Sources: "The Federal Trade Commission's Consumer Guide to Buying a Franchise," *Franchising World*, April 1, 2005; David Ho, "Charges Filed vs. Work-at-Home Scams," AP Online, June 20, 2002; "Before You Ink That Contract," *BusinessWeek*, April 14, 2005; and Karen Richardson, "Reports Help Uncover Red Flags," *The Wall Street Journal*, January 18, 2006, p. C5.

franchisees won an initial judgment of $390 million against the company, but the award was overturned on appeal.

4. *Coattail effects.* What happens to your franchise if fellow franchisees fail? Quite possibly you could be forced out of business even if your particular franchise has been profitable. This is often referred to as a *coattail effect.* The actions of other franchisees clearly have an impact on your future growth and level of profitability. Franchisees must also look out for competition from fellow franchisees. For example, TCBY franchisees' love for frozen yogurt melted as the market became flooded with new TCBY stores. McDonald's franchisees complain that due to the McDonald's Corporation's relentless growth formula, some of the new stores have cannibalized (taken away) business at existing locations, squeezing franchisees' profits per outlet.
5. *Restrictions on selling.* Unlike owners of private businesses, who can sell their companies to whomever they choose on their own terms, many franchisees face restrictions in the reselling of their franchises. In order to control the quality of their franchisees, franchisors often insist on approving the new owner, who must meet their standards.
6. *Fraudulent franchisors.* Contrary to common belief, most franchisors are not large systems like McDonald's and Subway. Many are small, rather obscure companies that prospective franchisees may know little about. Most franchisors are honest, but there has been an increase in complaints to the Federal Trade Commission about franchisors that delivered little or nothing of what they promised. Before you buy a franchise, make certain you check out the facts fully.[22] The saying "You get what you pay for" may be old, but it's not old-fashioned. See the Legal Briefcase box for advice about avoiding fraudulent practices.

Since buying a franchise is a major investment, be sure to check out a company's financial strength before you get involved. Watch out for scams, too. Scams called *bust-outs* usually involve people coming to town, renting nice offices, taking out ads, and persuading people to invest. Then they disappear with the investors' money. For example, in San Francisco a company called T.B.S. Inc. sold distributorships for in-home AIDS tests. It promised an enormous market and potential profits of $3,000 for an investment of less than $200. The test turned out to be nothing more than a mail-order questionnaire about lifestyle.

A good source of information about evaluating a franchise deal is the handbook *Investigate before Investing,* available from International Franchise Association Publications.

**CHECKLIST FOR EVALUATING A FRANCHISE**

**The Franchise**

Did your lawyer approve the franchise contract you're considering after he or she studied it paragraph by paragraph?

Does the franchise give you an exclusive territory for the length of the franchise?

Under what circumstances can you terminate the franchise contract and at what cost to you?

If you sell your franchise, will you be compensated for your goodwill (the value of your business's reputation and other intangibles)?

If the franchisor sells the company, will your investment be protected?

**The Franchisor**

How many years has the firm offering you a franchise been in operation?

Does it have a reputation for honesty and fair dealing among the local firms holding its franchise?

Has the franchisor shown you any certified figures indicating exact net profits of one or more going firms that you personally checked yourself with the franchisee? Ask for the company's disclosure statement.

Will the firm assist you with
- A management training program?
- An employee training program?
- A public relations program?
- Capital?
- Credit?
- Merchandising ideas?

Will the firm help you find a good location for your new business?

Has the franchisor investigated you carefully enough to assure itself that you can successfully operate one of its franchises at a profit both to itself and to you?

**You, the Franchisee**

How much equity capital will you need to purchase the franchise and operate it until your income equals your expenses?

Does the franchisor offer financing for a portion of the franchising fees? On what terms?

Are you prepared to give up some independence of action to secure the advantages offered by the franchise? Do you have your family's support?

Does the industry appeal to you? Are you ready to spend much or all of the remainder of your business life with this franchisor, offering its product or service to the public?

**Your Market**

Have you made any study to determine whether the product or service that you propose to sell under the franchise has a market in your territory at the prices you'll have to charge?

Will the population in the territory given to you increase, remain static, or decrease over the next five years?

Will demand for the product or service you're considering be greater, about the same, or less five years from now than it is today?

What competition already exists in your territory for the product or service you contemplate selling?

Sources: U.S. Department of Commerce, *Franchise Opportunities Handbook,* and Rhonda Adams, "Franchising Is No Simple Endeavor," Gannett News Services, March 14, 2002.

figure 5.8

**BUYING A FRANCHISE**

Figure 5.8 also gives you some tips on becoming a franchisee.

## Diversity in Franchising

The private consulting firm Women in Franchising (WIF) found that female franchise ownership decreases as franchise cost increases. "There's not so much of a glass ceiling keeping women from purchasing a franchise as there is a green ceiling—money," says Samuel Crawford, a WIF senior franchise consultant and author of the study. While women own about half of all U.S. companies, they receive less than 4 percent of venture capital.[23] And although access to capital is increasing, the amount of credit granted to women still trails that granted to men. Many experts believe that more needs to be done to educate women business owners about the appropriate forms of financing for each stage of business growth.[24]

A growing number of women are getting the message. In fact, women aren't just franchisees anymore either; they are becoming franchisors as well. When women have difficulty obtaining financing for expanding their businesses, they often turn to finding franchisees to sidestep expansion costs. For example, the top-rated franchise companies Auntie Anne's, Decorating Den, and Jazzercise are owned by women. Entrepreneur Mry Ellen Sheets moved into the male-dominated trucking industry when she started Two Men and a Truck as a way to help her college-age sons earn money part-time. Sheets bought an old pickup truck for $350 and managed her sons' moving-job schedules. When the boys went back to school, Sheets kept the business going by hiring two men to do the heavy lifting. Business grew, and Sheets decided to expand through franchising. Today, Two Men and a Truck has 152 locations in 27 states and generates $150 million in revenue. (Sheets's sons have returned—one as a franchise owner and the other as director of franchise licensing. Her daughter is president and chief operating officer.)

Cleaning offices may not be glamorous, but it's a stable job that technology won't make obsolete. Mark Melton's Coverall Cleaning Franchises are accessible to franchisees at a fraction of the cost of most franchises. For $11,750 the company provides an initial client base that guarantees an income while the franchise builds. Melton now has 250 franchisees, many of them Hmong and Hispanic immigrants. Can you think of any other low-cost franchise opportunities?

Minority-owned businesses are growing at more than six times the national rate. According to the U.S. secretary of commerce, minorities own 15 percent of the nation's businesses, employ 4.5 million people, and generate $591.3 billion in revenue.[25] As a result, franchisors are becoming more focused on recruiting minority franchisees. For example, Marriott held an "education summit" for aspiring minority hotel owners. This was one of many initiatives the company implemented in order to meet its goal of doubling its 270 franchisees in five years.[26] *Black Enterprise* magazine publisher Earl Graves encourages African Americans to look for opportunities in franchising in his book *How to Succeed in Business without Being White.* Franchising opportunities seem perfectly attuned to the needs of aspiring minority businesspeople. The U.S. Commerce Department's Federal Minority Business Development Agency provides minorities with training in how to run franchises.

## Home-Based Franchises

Home-based businesses offer many obvious advantages, including relief from the stress of commuting, extra time for family activities, and low overhead expenses. But one of the disadvantages of owning a business based at home is the feeling of isolation. Compared to home-based entrepreneurs, home-based franchisees feel less isolated. Experienced franchisors share their knowledge of building a profitable enterprise with franchisees. For example, when Henry and Paula Feldman decided to quit sales jobs that kept them on the road for weeks, they wanted to find a business to run at home together.

The Feldmans started their home-based franchise, Money Mailer Inc. (a direct mail advertiser), with nothing more than a table and a telephone. Five years later, they owned 15 territories, which they ran from an office full of state-of-the-art equipment. They grossed more than $600,000 during their fifth year. Henry says that the real value of being in a franchise is that the systems are in place: "You don't have to develop them yourself. Just be willing to work hard, listen, and learn. There's no greater magic than that." See the Taking It to the Net exercise at the end of this chapter for a Web site that can help you explore home-based franchise opportunities.

## E-Commerce in Franchising

We've already talked about how e-commerce revolutionized the way we do business. Many franchisees with existing brick-and-mortar stores are expanding their businesses online. Franchisees that started with a limited territory are now branching out globally. For example, Carole Shutts owns a Rocky Mountain Chocolate Factory franchise in Galena, Illinois. Her Web site generates 15 percent of her sales. Other Rocky Mountain franchisees have competing Web sites. Right now, Shutts isn't concerned about the competition from her colleagues because she thinks multiple sites will build brand awareness.

Many franchisors prohibit franchisee-sponsored Web sites. Conflicts between franchisors and franchisees can erupt if the franchisor then creates its own Web site. The franchisees may be concerned that the site will pull sales from their brick-and-mortar locations. Sometimes the franchisors send "reverse royalties" to outlet owners who feel their sales were hurt by the franchisor's Internet sales, but that doesn't always bring about peace. Before buying a franchise, you would be wise to read the small print regarding online sales.

## Using Technology in Franchising

Franchisors often use technology to meet the needs of both their customers and their franchisees. For example, U.S. Web Corporation set up its Web site to streamline processes of effective communication for its employees, customers, and vendors. It built a computer network to allow communication among its 50 franchisees, almost eliminating paperwork. Using the Web site, every franchisee has immediate access to every subject that involves the franchise operation, even the forms to fill out. There is a chat room where franchisees can discuss issues with each other. All franchisees are kept up-to-date on company news via e-mail. The company has found that the Internet is a great way of disseminating information and is revolutionizing franchisor support and franchisee communications.

## Franchising in International Markets

The attraction of global markets has carried over into franchising. Today, American franchisors are counting their profits in pesos, won, euros, krona, baht, yen, and many other currencies. More than 450 of America's 3,000 franchisors have outlets overseas. For example, McDonald's has more than 30,000 restaurants in 119 countries serving 50 million customers.[27]

Because of proximity and language, Canada is by far the most popular target for U.S.-based franchises. Many other franchisors are finding it surprisingly easy to move into South Africa and the Philippines. Even though franchisors find the costs of franchising high in these markets, the costs are counterbalanced by less competition and a rapidly expanding consumer base.

Newer, smaller franchises are going international as well. Smaller franchises such as SpeeDee Oil Change & Tune-Up, Rug Doctor Pro, and Merry Maids have all ventured into the international market. Long Island–based Nathan's Famous Inc. sells hot dogs in the Caribbean and the Middle East. Auntie Anne sells hand-rolled pretzels in Indonesia, Malaysia, the Philippines, Singapore, Japan, Venezuela, and Thailand.

What makes franchising successful in international markets is what makes it successful in the United States: convenience and a predictable level of service and quality. Franchisors, though, must be careful to adapt to the region. In France, people thought a furniture-stripping place called Dip 'N' Strip was a bar that featured strippers. In general, however, U.S. franchises are doing well all over the world and are adapting to the local customs and desires of consumers.

International franchising travels both ways. Just as McDonald's and Starbucks have exported the golden arches and the long-haired mermaid symbols worldwide, foreign franchises are changing tastes here. For example, Maria's Bakery customers in the United States enjoy sweet pastries made from the recipes perfected by franchisor Maria Lee, who is considered the Martha Stewart of Hong Kong. Asian franchisors have added stores throughout the entire United States, whereas businesses from Latin America more often focus on California, Texas, and Florida. Just as U.S. franchisors must adapt to their foreign markets, foreign franchisors must tinker with menus and store layouts to better fit the U.S. market. For example, Maria's Bakery franchises in the United States carry milk tea drinks and ice cream, products the Hong Kong stores never sold because there was so much competition from other food vendors there.

KFC is as finger-licking good in Japan as it is in the United States. Why have franchisors like KFC been so successful in international markets?

## COOPERATIVES

Some people dislike the notion of having owners, managers, workers, and buyers as separate individuals with separate goals. These people have formed a different kind of organization to meet their needs for things such as electricity, child care, housing, health care, food, and financial services. Such an organization, called a **cooperative**, is owned and controlled by the people who use it—producers, consumers, or workers with similar needs who pool their resources for mutual gain. In many rural parts of the country, for example, electrical power is sold through cooperatives. The government sells wholesale power to electric cooperatives at rates that are, on average, from 40 to 50 percent below the rates nonfederal utilities charge. Electric cooperatives serve 37 million people in 47 states and 80 percent of the country's counties.[28]

**cooperative**
A business owned and controlled by the people who use it—producers, consumers, or workers with similar needs who pool their resources for mutual gain.

There are 47,000 cooperatives in the United States today. Some co-ops ask members/customers to work at the cooperative for a number of hours a month as part of their duties. Members democratically control these businesses by electing a board of directors that hires professional management. You may have one of the country's 4,000 food cooperatives near you. If so, stop by and chat with the people there to learn more about this growing aspect of the U.S. economy. If you are interested in knowing more about cooperatives, contact the National Cooperative Business Association at 202-638-6222 or visit its Web site at www.ncba.org.

There is another kind of cooperative in the United States, set up for different reasons. These cooperatives are formed to give members more economic power as a group than they would have as individuals. The best example of such cooperatives is a farm cooperative. The idea at first was for farmers to join together to get better prices for their food products. Eventually, however, the organization expanded so that farm cooperatives now buy and sell fertilizer, farm equipment, seed, and other products needed on the farm. This has become a multibillion-dollar industry. The cooperatives now own many manufacturing facilities. Farm cooperatives do not pay the same kind of taxes that corporations do and thus have an advantage in the marketplace.

In spite of debt and mergers, cooperatives are still a major force in agriculture today. Some top co-ops have familiar names such as Land O Lakes, Sunkist, Ocean Spray, Blue Diamond, Associated Press, Ace Hardware, True Value Hardware, Riceland Foods, and Welch's.

## WHICH FORM OF OWNERSHIP IS FOR YOU?

As you can see, you may participate in the business world in a variety of ways. You can start your own sole proprietorship, partnership, corporation, or cooperative—or you can buy a franchise and be part of a larger corporation. There are advantages and disadvantages to each. However, there are risks no matter which form you choose. Before you decide which form is for you, you need to evaluate all the alternatives carefully.

The miracle of free enterprise is that the freedom and incentives of capitalism make risks acceptable to many people, who go on to create the great corporations of America. You know many of their names: J. C. Penney, Malcolm Forbes, Richard Warren Sears and Alvah C. Roebuck, Levi Strauss, Henry Ford, Thomas Edison, and so on. They started small, accumulated capital, grew, and became industrial leaders. Could you do the same?

### progress assessment

- What are some of the factors to consider before buying a franchise?
- What opportunities are available for starting a global franchise?
- What is a cooperative?

## summary

**1.** Compare the advantages and disadvantages of sole proprietorships.

1. The major forms of business ownership are sole proprietorships, partnerships, and corporations.

- **What are the advantages and disadvantages of sole proprietorships?**

The advantages of sole proprietorships include ease of starting and ending, being your own boss, pride of ownership, retention of profit, and no special taxes. The disadvantages include unlimited liability, limited financial resources, difficulty in management, overwhelming time commitment, few fringe benefits, limited growth, and limited life span.

**2.** Describe the differences between general and limited partners, and compare the advantages and disadvantages of partnerships.

2. The three key elements of a general partnership are common ownership, shared profits and losses, and the right to participate in managing the operations of the business.

- **What are the main differences between general and limited partners?**

General partners are owners (partners) who have unlimited liability and are active in managing the company. Limited partners are owners (partners) who have limited liability and are not active in the company.

- **What does unlimited liability mean?**

Unlimited liability means that sole proprietors and general partners must pay all debts and damages caused by their business. They may have to sell their houses, cars, or other personal possessions to pay business debts.

- **What does limited liability mean?**

Limited liability means that corporate owners (stockholders) and limited partners are responsible for losses only up to the amount they invest. Their other personal property is not at risk.

- **What is a master limited partnership?**

A master limited partnership is a partnership that acts like a corporation but is taxed like a partnership.

- **What are the advantages and disadvantages of partnerships?**

The advantages include more financial resources, shared management and pooled knowledge, and longer survival. The disadvantages include unlimited liability, division of profits, disagreements among partners, and difficulty of termination.

**3.** Compare the advantages and disadvantages of corporations, and summarize the differences between C corporations, S corporations, and limited liability companies.

3. A corporation is a state-chartered legal entity with authority to act and have liability separate from its owners.

- **What are the advantages and disadvantages of corporations?**

The advantages include more money for investment, limited liability, size, perpetual life, ease of ownership change, ease of drawing talented employees, and separation of ownership from management. The disadvantages include initial cost, paperwork, size, difficulty of termination, double taxation, and possible conflict with a board of directors.

- **Why do people incorporate?**

Two important reasons for incorporating are special tax advantages and limited liability.

- **What are the advantages of S corporations?**

S corporations have the advantages of limited liability (like a corporation) and simpler taxes (like a partnership). In order to qualify for S corporation status, a company must have fewer than 100 stockholders (members of a family count as one shareholder); its stockholders must be individuals or estates and U.S. citizens or permanent residents; and the company cannot have more than 25 percent of its income derived from passive sources.

- **What are the advantages of limited liability companies?**

Limited liability companies have the advantage of limited liability without the hassles of forming a corporation or the limitations imposed by S corporations. LLCs may choose whether to be taxed as partnerships or corporations.

**4.** Define and give examples of three types of corporate mergers, and explain the role of leveraged buyouts and taking a firm private.

4. The number of mergers reached a peak at the start of the new millennium.

- **What is a merger?**

A merger is the result of two firms forming one company. The three major types of mergers are vertical mergers, horizontal mergers, and conglomerate mergers.

- **What are leveraged buyouts, and what does it mean to take a company private?**

Leveraged buyouts are attempts by managers and employees to borrow money and purchase the company. Individuals who, together or alone, buy all of the stock for themselves are said to take the company private.

**5.** Outline the advantages and disadvantages of franchises, and discuss the opportunities for diversity in franchising and the challenges of global franchising.

5. A person can participate in the entrepreneurial age by buying the rights to market a new product innovation in his or her area.

- **What is this arrangement called?**

An arrangement to buy the rights to use the business name and sell its products or services in a given territory is called a franchise.

- **What is a franchisee?**

A franchisee is a person who buys a franchise.

- **What are the benefits and drawbacks of being a franchisee?**

The benefits include a nationally recognized name and reputation, a proven management system, promotional assistance, and pride of ownership. Drawbacks include high franchise fees, managerial regulation, shared profits, and transfer of adverse effects if other franchisees fail.

- **What is the major challenge to global franchises?**

It is often difficult to transfer an idea or product that worked well in the United States to another culture. It is essential to adapt to the region.

**6.** Explain the role of cooperatives.

6. People who dislike organizations in which owners, managers, workers, and buyers have separate goals often form cooperatives.

- **What is the role of a cooperative?**

Cooperatives are organizations that are owned by members/customers. Some people form cooperatives to give members more economic power than they would have as individuals. Small businesses often form cooperatives to give them more purchasing, marketing, or product development strength.

## key terms

**acquisition** 132
**conglomerate merger** 132
**conventional (C) corporation** 124
**cooperative** 141
**corporation** 118
**franchise** 135
**franchise agreement** 134
**franchisee** 135
**franchisor** 134
**general partner** 122
**general partnership** 121
**horizontal merger** 132
**leveraged buyout (LBO)** 132
**limited liability** 122
**limited liability company (LLC)** 130
**limited liability partnership (LLP)** 122
**limited partner** 122
**limited partnership** 121
**master limited partnership (MLP)** 122
**merger** 132
**partnership** 118
**S corporation** 129
**sole proprietorship** 118
**unlimited liability** 119
**vertical merger** 132

## critical thinking questions

Imagine that you are considering starting your own business.

1. What kind of products or services would you offer?
2. What talents or skills do you have that you could use to run the business?
3. Do you have all of the skills and resources you would need to start the business or would you need to find one or more partners? If so, what skills would your partners need to have?
4. What form of business ownership would you choose—sole proprietorship, partnership, corporation, S corporation, or LLC? Why?

## developing workplace skills

1. Research businesses in your area and identify companies that use each of the following forms of ownership: sole proprietorship, partnership, corporation, and franchise. Arrange interviews with managers from each form of ownership and get their impressions, hints, and warnings. (If you are able to work with a team of fellow students, divide the interviews among team members.) How much does it cost to start? How many hours do they work? What are the specific benefits? Share the results with your class.

2. Have you thought about starting your own business? What opportunities seem attractive? Think of a friend or friends whom you might want for a partner or partners in the business. List all the financial resources and personal skills you will need to launch the business. Then make separate lists of the personal skills and the financial resources that you and your friend(s) might bring to your new venture. How much capital and what personal skills do you need but neither of you have? Develop an action plan to obtain them.

3. Let's assume you want to open one of the following new businesses. What form of business ownership would you choose for each business? Why?
   *a.* Video game rental store.
   *b.* Wedding planning service.
   *c.* Software development firm.
   *d.* Computer hardware manufacturing company.
   *e.* Online bookstore.

4. Successful businesses continually change. Methods of change discussed in this chapter include mergers, acquisitions, taking a firm private, and leveraged buyouts. Find an article in the library or on the Internet that illustrates how one of these methods changed an organization. What led to the change? How will this change affect the company's stakeholders? What benefits does the change provide? What new challenges does it create?

5. Go on the Internet and find information about a business cooperative. Find out how it was formed, who can belong to it, and how it operates.

## taking it to the net

### Purpose

To explore current franchising opportunities and to evaluate the strengths and weaknesses of a selected franchise.

### Exercise

Go to Be the Boss: The Virtual Franchise Expo (www.betheboss.com).

1. Take the self-test to see if franchising is a good personal choice for you. (Find the test by clicking on Resources, then on Introduction to Franchising. Then, under Franchising Basics, click on Franchising—An Interactive Self-Test.)

2. Go back to the home page and use the search tool to find a franchise that has the potential of fulfilling your entrepreneurial dreams. Navigate to the profile of the franchise you selected. Explore the franchise's Web site if such a link is available. Refer to the questions listed in Figure 5.8 on page 138 in this chapter and assess the strengths and weaknesses of your selected franchise. (Hint: The Web site also contains tips for evaluating a franchise listing.)
3. Did your search give you enough information to answer most of the questions in Figure 5.8? If not, what other information do you need, and where can you obtain it?

## casing the web

To access the case *"Keeping the Air in Blimpie,"* visit **www.mhhe.com/ub8e**

## video case

### Sonic Is Booming

Entrepreneurship is the path to success throughout the world. More millionaires come from the ranks of entrepreneurs than any other place. Because the work is so hard, however, fewer people than you would imagine are willing to take the plunge.

One of the major decisions an entrepreneur must make is what form of business to use: sole proprietorship, partnership, corporation, franchise, or what? Sonic is a large chain of fast-food restaurants with over 3,000 drive-ins located from coast to coast. It began as a sole proprietorship, evolved into a partnership, later added many franchises, and eventually became a publicly traded corporation. This is not an unusual progression for a business, but Sonic did it relatively quickly and effectively.

Troy Smith started the first Sonic in 1954. It was a sole proprietorship that took the form of a drive-in restaurant, much like other drive-ins of that era. Smith brought in a partner in 1956, and the business began to grow. The partner shared profits and liability with Smith. When the partner died, Smith found many other people who were interested in becoming franchisees. The company grew even faster then. In fact, Cody Barnett's father owned seven Sonic franchises. Cody eventually took over those franchises and added 15 more. There is much to learn about buying and running a number of franchises, and Cody schooled himself in the managerial techniques and strategies that he would need. Like most franchisors, Sonic was a big help in that regard.

Clearly, understanding the various forms of business is key to both getting started in business and then growing the business later. If you plan to franchise the business, it is critical to find franchisees like the Barnetts who understand that the business is their own and also understand the value of having the foundation of a well-known brand name and a ready customer base.

One thing franchisees learn from the very beginning is that running your own business takes a lot of work. At first, you have to be there whenever the business is open. That means long, long hours at work—and away from the family. That is true of many businesses and the search for balanced living is one of the most important skills a business owner must learn.

You don't have to go very far in most towns to see the results of franchising. On every corner, there is a fast-food restaurant of some other franchise that is serving the area and travelers who come to that area. Many are obviously very successful. Sonic is one of them. But, as you can see in this video, the success does not come easily. It takes lots of time and hard work.

### Thinking It Over

1. Sonic started as a sole proprietorship and gradually evolved to a partnership, then to a corporation, and finally to franchisor. Do you think that Sonic would have grown as large as it is today if it had remained a sole proprietorship? Why or why not?
2. What were the advantages and disadvantages to Sonic of each form of business ownership?
3. There have been lots of drive-in and fast-food restaurants over time. In your opinion, what makes Sonic and other major franchises more successful than the others?

# entrepreneurship AND STARTING A small business

profile

**Getting to Know**

**X** Nina Vaca-Humrichouse,

**Founder and CEO of Pinnacle Technical Resources Inc.**

"Being an entrepreneur is in my blood," says Nina Vaca-Humrichouse, founder, chairman, and CEO of Pinnacle Technical Resources, Inc. Indeed, her grandfather was a highly successful entrepreneur in Quito, the capital of Ecuador. Her parents immigrated to the United States in the mid-1960s. By the time Vaca-Humrichouse was born in 1971, her father owned and operated three travel agencies and her mother owned retail stores in the Los Angeles area.

When Vaca-Humrichouse was 17, her father was tragically killed in a robbery at his place of business, leaving behind his wife and five children. Along with their mother, Nina and her sister Jessica took over the operations of the travel business. It was then that she learned many of the challenges of being an entrepreneur. The family later sold the business in order to put Nina through college.

Vaca-Humrichouse graduated from Texas State University where she majored in communications and business. Upon graduation, she accepted a job with a New York-based information technology recruiting firm, where she gained valuable experiences and skills that would be helpful later in her career.

In 1996, when Vaca-Humrichouse was 25, she was ready to start out on her own. She says, "I was single and bought a computer, sat down and went to work." It was two and a half months before she had her first client. Pinnacle initially focused on systems integration but later evolved its business model to include custom application development, data warehousing, and IT-enabled business process outsourcing solutions. She surrounded herself with talented business and technical people. Most importantly, her sister Jessica, her two brothers, Freddy and Chris, and her husband Jim all joined the firm at various stages, creating a core of management and talent that she expects will drive the success of Pinnacle for decades to come.

Vaca-Humrichouse also sought out experienced businesspeople as mentors to help her establish and guide her firm. These executives provided critical advice regarding the firm's strategy and operations through periods of rapid growth

LEARNING **goals**

**After you have read and studied this chapter, you should be able to**

1. Explain why people are willing to take the risks of entrepreneurship, list the attributes of successful entrepreneurs, describe the benefits of entrepreneurial teams and intrapreneurs, and explain the growth of home-based and Web-based businesses.
2. Discuss the importance of small business to the American economy and summarize the major causes of small-business failure.
3. Summarize ways to learn about how small businesses operate.
4. Analyze what it takes to start and run a small business.
5. Outline the advantages and disadvantages small businesses have in entering global markets.

CHAPTER 6

**www.pinnacle.com**

and expansion. Still, she considers her parents to be her most important mentors. She learned perseverance and the value of hard work from them—and the importance of getting good people to do the job well.

Vaca-Humrichouse also believes her company's success can be attributed to good old-fashioned bootstrapping. *Bootstrapping* refers to the practice of growing a small firm without the aid of bank loans or other forms of money. As a young entrepreneur, Vaca-Humrichouse encountered many barriers to financing her growth. Some banks were reluctant to invest in a company without three years of growth and profits; others wanted to see a broader client base. However, after several years of demonstrating the commitment to re-invest her own funds back into the firm, rather than take them out on a yearly basis as so many do, the banks were persuaded. Seven years and three banks later, Pinnacle's performance enabled it to raise its borrowings from an initial level of $100,000 to the present level of $4 million and growing.

Pinnacle now has revenues of $42 million and is on track for another record year. Its customers include Fortune 500 companies such as AT&T, EDS, and Citigroup. The company has grown from only 25 employees in mid-2002 to over 600 by 2006; and it expects to continue to add people rapidly. The Dallas-based firm currently serves clients in 32 states, and has offices in Washington, D.C., New York, Los Angeles, Houston, and Orlando.

And Nina Vaca-Humrichouse? She earned many honors including being named National Hispanic Businesswoman of the Year (2003 and 2004) by the U.S. Hispanic Chamber of Commerce, a Marshall Memorial Fellow (2003), one of the top 25 Women Business Builders by *Fast Company* magazine, Entrepreneur of the Year (2004 and 2005) by *Hispanic Business Magazine*, and Entrepreneur of the Year (2005) by Ernst & Young. In 2005, Pinnacle ranked #78 on the Inc. 500 and garnered accolades from numerous organizations across the United States. Quite a set of accomplishments for a woman and a company that hasn't even hit their 10-year anniversary!

Stories about people who take risks, like Nina Vaca-Humrichouse, are commonplace in this age of the entrepreneur. As you read about such risks takers in this chapter, maybe you'll be inspired to take the risk to become an entrepreneur yourself.

Sources: Margaret Allen, "Intelligent Growth," *Dallas Business Journal*, January 7, 2005; Robert Miller, "The Dallas Morning News Robert Miller Column," *Dallas Morning News*, March 7, 2005; Allison Overholt, "25 Top Women Business Builders," *Fast Company*, May 2005; and Barry Shlachter, Jim Fuquay, and Doug Tsuruoka, "Making Her Entrepreneurial Mark," *Investor's Business Daily*, July 5, 2005.

## THE AGE OF THE ENTREPRENEUR

Of the 14 million people in the United States who are self-employed, about 20 percent are 16 to 34 years old.[1] "The perception is out there among young people that a job with IBM for 30 years is not likely to happen," said Bruce Phillips, a senior fellow in regulatory studies at the National Federation of Independent Business Research Foundation. "Thus, working in or starting a small business has increased appeal . . . where there is a feeling that you control more of your own destiny."[2] Colleges around the country are responding to this trend by offering more courses on the subject of entrepreneurship. **Entrepreneurship** is accepting the risk of starting and running a business. Explore this chapter and think about the possibility of entrepreneurship in your future.

**entrepreneurship** Accepting the risk of starting and running a business.

## THE JOB-CREATING POWER OF ENTREPRENEURS IN THE UNITED STATES

One of the major issues in the United States today is the need to create more jobs. You can get some idea about the job-creating power of entrepreneurs when you look at some of the great American entrepreneurs from the past and the present. The history of the United States is the history of its entrepreneurs. Consider just a few of the many entrepreneurs who have helped shape the American economy:[3]

- Du Pont, which manufactures thousands of products under such brand names as Teflon and Lycra, was started in 1802 by French immigrant Éleuthère Irénée du Pont de Nemours. Some 18 shareholders provided $36,000 in start-up money.
- Avon started in 1886 on $500 David McConnell borrowed from a friend.
- George Eastman launched Kodak in 1880 with a $3,000 investment.
- Procter & Gamble was formed in 1837 by William Procter and James Gamble with a total of $7,000 in capital.
- Ford Motor Company began with an investment of $28,000 by Henry Ford and 11 associates.
- Amazon.com began with investments by founder Jeff Bezos's family and friends. Bezos's parents invested $300,000, a huge portion of their retirement account. Today they are billionaires.

The stories are all about the same. One entrepreneur or a couple of entrepreneurs had a good idea, borrowed some money from friends and family, and started a business. That business now employs thousands of people and helps the country prosper.

The United States still has plenty of entrepreneurial talent. Names such as Steve Jobs (Apple Computer), Ross Perot (Electronic Data Systems), Michael Dell (Dell Inc.), Bill Gates (Microsoft), Howard Schultz (Starbucks), Scott Cook (Intuit), and Ted Turner (Cable News Network) have become as familiar as those of the great entrepreneurs of the past.

Wacky grocer Jim Bonaminio may put on his wizard suit and roller skate through his Jungle Jim's International Market, but he's serious when it comes to his business. Instead of competing on price against mega-giants like Wal-Mart, Jungle Jim's competes on product variety. A case holding 1,200 kinds of hot sauce rests beneath an antique fire engine. Why do you think customers might remain loyal to Jungle Jim's?

## WHY PEOPLE TAKE THE ENTREPRENEURIAL CHALLENGE

Taking the risks of starting a business can be scary and thrilling at the same time. One entrepreneur described it as almost like bungee jumping. You might be scared, but if you watch six other people do it and they survive, you're then able to do it yourself. The following are some of the many reasons people are willing to take the risks of starting a business:[4]

- *Opportunity.* The opportunity to share in the American dream is a tremendous lure. Many people, including those new to this country, may not have the necessary skills for working in today's complex organizations. However, they may have the initiative and drive to work the long hours demanded by entrepreneurship. The same is true of many corporate managers who left the security of the corporate life (either by choice or as a result of corporate downsizing) to run businesses of their own. Other people, including an increasing number of people with disabilities, find that starting their own businesses offers them more opportunities than working for others.
- *Profit.* Profit is another important reason to become an entrepreneur. At one time the richest person in America was Sam Walton, the entrepreneur who started Wal-Mart. Now the richest person in America is Bill Gates, the entrepreneur who founded Microsoft Corporation.
- *Independence.* Many entrepreneurs simply do not enjoy working for someone else. Many lawyers, for example, do not like the stress and demands of big law firms. Some have found enjoyment and self-satisfaction in starting their own businesses.
- *Challenge.* Some people believe that entrepreneurs are excitement junkies who flourish on taking risks. Nancy Flexman and Thomas Scanlan, however, in their book *Running Your Own Business*, contend that entrepreneurs take moderate, calculated risks; they are not just gambling. In general, though, entrepreneurs seek achievement more than power.

### What Does It Take to Be an Entrepreneur?

Would you succeed as an entrepreneur? You can learn about the managerial and leadership skills needed to run a firm. However, you may not have the personality to assume the risks, take the initiative, create the vision, and rally others to follow your lead. Those traits are harder to learn or acquire. A list of entrepreneurial attributes you would look for in yourself includes the following:[5]

- *Self-directed.* You should be thoroughly comfortable and thoroughly self-disciplined even though you are your own boss. You will be responsible for your success or failure.
- *Self-nurturing.* You must believe in your idea even when no one else does, and be able to replenish your own enthusiasm. When Walt Disney suggested the possibility of a full-length animated feature film, *Snow White,* the industry laughed. His personal commitment and enthusiasm caused the Bank of America to back his venture. The rest is history.
- *Action-oriented.* Great business ideas are not enough. The most important thing is a burning desire to realize, actualize, and build your dream into reality.
- *Highly energetic.* It's your business, and you must be emotionally, mentally, and physically able to work long and hard. For example, Tabitha

Mageto and Remi Pageon, co-owners of Artisan Bakery in Virginia, often spend 18 hours a day in their shop. During the Christmas season, each pulls a 48-hour shift. "But that is better than working 18-hour days for someone else," says Mageto.[6]

- *Tolerant of uncertainty.* Successful entrepreneurs take only calculated risks (if they can help it). Still, they must be able to take some risks. Remember, entrepreneurship is not for anyone who is squeamish or bent on security.

It is important to know that most entrepreneurs don't get the ideas for their products and services from some flash of inspiration. Rather than a flash, the source of innovation is more like a flash*light.* Imagine a search party, walking around in the dark, shining lights, looking around, asking questions, and looking some more. The late Sam Walton used such a flashlight approach. He visited his stores and those of competitors and took notes. He'd see a good idea on Monday, and by Tuesday every Wal-Mart manager in the country would know about it. He expected his managers to use flashlighting too. Every time they traveled on business, they were expected to come back with at least one idea worth more than the cost of their trip. "That's how most creativity happens," says business author Dale Dauten. "Calling around, asking questions, saying 'What if?' till you get blisters on your tongue."

Keep in mind that necessity isn't always the mother of invention. Entrepreneurs don't always look for what customers need—they look for what they *don't* need as well. Aaron Lapin thought we didn't need the hassles of the touchy process of whipping heavy cream to top our pies. He made millions selling his invention: Reddi Wip. Although we'd rather reach for a can in the refrigerator than whip our own cream, Reddi Wip isn't a necessity. If you think you may have the entrepreneurial spirit in your blood, complete the Entrepreneurial Readiness Questionnaire below. There is also some advice for would-be entrepreneurs in Figure 6.1 on page 154.

### ENTREPRENEUR READINESS QUESTIONNAIRE

Not everyone is cut out to be an entrepreneur. The fact is, though, that all kinds of people with all kinds of personalities have succeeded in starting small and large businesses. There are certain traits, however, that seem to separate those who'll be successful as entrepreneurs from those who may not be. The following questionnaire will help you determine in which category you fit. Take a couple of minutes to answer the questions and then score yourself at the end. Making a low score doesn't mean you won't succeed as an entrepreneur. It does indicate, however, that you may be happier working for someone else.

Each of the following items describes something that you may or may not feel represents your personality or other characteristics about you. Read each item and then circle the response (1, 2, 3, 4, or 5) that most nearly reflects the extent to which you agree or disagree that the item seems to fit you.

Scoring:

Give yourself one point for each 1 or 2 response you circled for questions 1, 2, 6, 8, 10, 11, 16, 17, 21, 22, 23.

Give yourself one point for each 4 or 5 response you circled for questions 3, 4, 5, 7, 9, 12, 13, 14, 15, 18, 19, 20, 24, 25.

Add your points and see how you rate in the following categories:

| | |
|---|---|
| 21–25 | Your entrepreneurial potential looks great if you have a suitable opportunity to use it. What are you waiting for? |
| 16–20 | This is close to the high entrepreneurial range. You could be quite successful if your other talents and resources are right. |
| 11–15 | Your score is in the transitional range. With some serious work you can probably develop the outlook you need for running your own business. |
| 6–10 | Things look pretty doubtful for you as an entrepreneur. It would take considerable rearranging of your life philosophy and behavior to make it. |
| 0–5 | Let's face it. Entrepreneurship isn't really for you. Still, learning what it's all about won't hurt anything. |

| Looking at My Overall Philosophy of Life and Typical Behavior, I Would Say That . . . | Response | | | | |
|---|---|---|---|---|---|
| | AGREE COMPLETELY (1) | MOSTLY AGREE (2) | PARTIALLY AGREE (3) | MOSTLY DISAGREE (4) | DISAGREE COMPLETELY (5) |
| 1. I am generally optimistic. | 1 | 2 | 3 | 4 | 5 |
| 2. I enjoy competing and doing things better than someone else. | 1 | 2 | 3 | 4 | 5 |
| 3. When solving a problem, I try to arrive at the best solution first without worrying about other possibilities. | 1 | 2 | 3 | 4 | 5 |
| 4. I enjoy associating with co-workers after working hours. | 1 | 2 | 3 | 4 | 5 |
| 5. If betting on a horse race I would prefer to take a chance on a high-payoff "long shot." | 1 | 2 | 3 | 4 | 5 |
| 6. I like setting my own goals and working hard to achieve them. | 1 | 2 | 3 | 4 | 5 |
| 7. I am generally casual and easy-going with others. | 1 | 2 | 3 | 4 | 5 |
| 8. I like to know what is going on and take action to find out. | 1 | 2 | 3 | 4 | 5 |
| 9. I work best when someone else is guiding me along the way. | 1 | 2 | 3 | 4 | 5 |
| 10. When I am right I can convince others. | | | | | |
| 11. I find that other people frequently waste my valuable time. | 1 | 2 | 3 | 4 | 5 |
| 12. I enjoy watching football, baseball, and similar sports events. | 1 | 2 | 3 | 4 | 5 |
| 13. I tend to communicate about myself very openly with other people. | 1 | 2 | 3 | 4 | 5 |
| 14. I don't mind following orders from superiors who have legitimate authority. | 1 | 2 | 3 | 4 | 5 |
| 15. I enjoy planning things more than actually carrying out the plans. | 1 | 2 | 3 | 4 | 5 |
| 16. I don't think it's much fun to bet on a "sure thing." | 1 | 2 | 3 | 4 | 5 |
| 17. If faced with failure, I would shift quickly to something else rather than sticking to my guns. | 1 | 2 | 3 | 4 | 5 |
| 18. Part of being successful in business is reserving adequate time for family. | 1 | 2 | 3 | 4 | 5 |
| 19. Once I have earned something, I feel that keeping it secure is important. | 1 | 2 | 3 | 4 | 5 |
| 20. Making a lot of money is largely a matter of getting the right breaks. | 1 | 2 | 3 | 4 | 5 |
| 21. Problem solving is usually more effective when a number of alternatives are considered. | 1 | 2 | 3 | 4 | 5 |
| 22. I enjoy impressing others with the things I can do. | 1 | 2 | 3 | 4 | 5 |
| 23. I enjoy playing games like tennis and handball with someone who is slightly better than I am. | 1 | 2 | 3 | 4 | 5 |
| 24. Sometimes moral ethics must be bent a little in business dealings. | 1 | 2 | 3 | 4 | 5 |
| 25. I think that good friends would make the best subordinates in an organization. | 1 | 2 | 3 | 4 | 5 |

Source: Kenneth R. Van Voorhis, *Entrepreneurship and Small Business Management* (New York: Allyn & Bacon, 1980).

figure 6.1

**ADVICE FOR POTENTIAL ENTREPRENEURS**

- Work for other people first and learn on their money.
- Research your market, but don't take too long to act.
- Start your business when you have a customer. Maybe try your venture as a sideline at first.
- Set specific objectives, but don't set your goals too high. Remember, there's no easy money.
- Plan your objectives within specific time frames.
- Surround yourself with people who are smarter than you—including an accountant and an outside board of directors who are interested in your well-being and who'll give you straight answers.
- Don't be afraid to fail. Former football coach Vince Lombardi summarized the entrepreneurial philosophy when he said, "We didn't lose any games this season, we just ran out of time twice." New entrepreneurs must be ready to run out of time a few times before they succeed.

Sources: Kathleen Lynn, "Entrepreneurs Get Tips on Weathering Recession," *Bergen County (New Jersey) Record,* March 5, 2002, p. 15, and "Get Your Business on the Fast Track," *Entrepreneur*, January 1, 2006.

**entrepreneurial team**
A group of experienced people from different areas of business who join together to form a managerial team with the skills needed to develop, make, and market a new product.

## Entrepreneurial Teams

An **entrepreneurial team** is a group of experienced people from different areas of business who join together to form a managerial team with the skills needed to develop, make, and market a new product.[7] A team may be better than an individual entrepreneur because team members can combine creative skills with production and marketing skills right from the start. Having a team also can ensure more cooperation and coordination among functions.

When you think of the start of Apple Computers, the name of Steven Jobs may spring to mind. However, while Jobs was the charismatic folk hero and visionary, it was Steve Wozniack who invented the first personal computer model and Mike Markkula who offered the business expertise and access to venture capital.[8] The key to Apple's early success was that the company was built around this "smart team" of entrepreneurs. The team wanted to combine the discipline of a big company with an environment in which people could feel they were participating in a successful venture. The trio of entrepreneurs recruited seasoned managers with similar desires. All the managers worked as a team. Everyone worked together to conceive, develop, and market products.

**micropreneurs**
Entrepreneurs willing to accept the risk of starting and managing the type of business that remains small, lets them do the kind of work they want to do, and offers them a balanced lifestyle.

## Micropreneurs and Home-Based Businesses

Not every person who starts a business has the goal of growing it into a mammoth corporation. Some are interested in simply enjoying a balanced lifestyle while doing the kind of work they want to do. Business writer Michael LeBoeuf calls such business owners **micropreneurs**. While other entrepreneurs are committed to the quest for growth, micropreneurs know they can be happy even if their companies never appear on a list of top-ranked businesses.

Many micropreneurs are home-based business owners. More than 20 million small businesses in the United States are run out of the owner's home. Nearly half of those home-based businesses are in service industries. Micropreneurs include writers, consultants, video producers, architects, bookkeepers, and such. In fact, the development of this textbook involved many home-based business owners. The authors, the developmental editors, the copy editor, and even the text designer operate home-based businesses.

Many home-based businesses are owned by people who are trying to combine career and family.[9] Don't misunderstand and picture home-based workers as women with young children; nearly 50 percent are men. In addition to helping business owners balance work and family, other reasons for the growth of home-based businesses include the following:[10]

- Computer technology has leveled the competitive playing field, allowing home-based businesses to look and act as big as their corporate competitors. Broadband Internet connections, personal digital assistants (PDAs), and other technologies are so affordable that setting up a business takes a much smaller initial investment than it used to.
- Corporate downsizing has made workers aware that there is no such thing as job security, leading many to venture out on their own. Meanwhile, the work of the downsized employees still needs to be done and corporations are outsourcing much of the work to smaller companies; that is, they are contracting with small companies to temporarily fill their needs. (We'll talk more about outsourcing in Chapter 8.)
- Social attitudes have changed. Whereas home-based entrepreneurs used to be asked when they were going to get a "real" job, they are now likely to be asked instead for how-to-do-it advice.
- New tax laws have loosened the restrictions regarding deductions for home offices.

Working at home has its challenges, of course. In setting up a home-based business, you could expect the following major challenges:[11]

- *Getting new customers.* Getting the word out can be difficult because you don't have signs or a storefront.
- *Managing time.* Of course, you save time by not commuting, but it takes self-discipline to use that time wisely.
- *Keeping work and family tasks separate.* Often it is difficult to separate work and family tasks. It's great to be able to throw a load of laundry

Not all home-based business owners sit in front of computer screens. Chocolatier Jeanne Marie Miller has a degree in clinical psychology as well as training as a professional chef. When she was working in a mental health clinic, she began testing her confections on co-workers and friends. Encouraged by their rave reviews, Miller decided to start her own business, Coco's Chocolate Dreams, based in her New Hudson, Michigan home. She enjoys sweet success!

figure 6.2

**POTENTIAL HOME-BASED BUSINESSES**

Many businesses can be started at home. Listed below are 10 businesses that have low start-up costs, don't require an abundance of administrative tasks, and are in relatively high demand and easy to sell:

1. Cleaning service.
2. Gift-basket business.
3. Web merchant.
4. Mailing list service.
5. Microfarming (small plots of land for such high-value crops as mushrooms, edible flowers, or sprouts).
6. Tutoring.
7. Résumé service.
8. Web design.
9. Medical claims assistance.
10. Personal coaching.

Look for a business that meets these important criteria: (1) The job is something you truly enjoy doing; (2) you know enough to do the job well or you are willing to spend time learning it while you have another job; and (3) you can identify a market for your product or service.

Source: www.entrepreneur.com, May 15, 2006.

in the washer in the middle of the workday if you need to, but you have to keep such distractions to a minimum. It is also difficult to leave your work at the office if the office is at home. Again, it takes self-discipline to keep work from trickling out of the home office and into the family room.

- *Abiding by city ordinances.* Government ordinances restrict such things as the types of businesses that are allowed in certain parts of the community and how much traffic a home-based business can attract to the neighborhood.
- *Managing risk.* Home-based entrepreneurs should review their homeowner's insurance policy, since not all policies cover business-related claims. Some even void the coverage if there is a business in the home.

Those who wish to get out of an office building and into a home office should focus on finding opportunity instead of accepting security, getting results instead of following routines, earning a profit instead of earning a paycheck, trying new ideas instead of avoiding mistakes, and creating a long-term vision instead of seeking a short-term payoff. Figure 6.2 lists 10 ideas for potentially successful home-based businesses, and Figure 6.3 highlights clues for avoiding home-based business scams. You can find a wealth of online information about starting a home-based business at www.entrepreneur.com.

## Web-Based Businesses

The Internet has sprouted a world of small Web-based businesses that sell everything from staplers to refrigerator magnets to wedding dresses. In 2005, online sales in the United States reached $165 billion, or approximately 8 percent of all retail sales. By 2010, the online channel is expected to account for $331 billion, or 13 percent of retail sales.[12]

Atlanta's KEH Camera Brokers began as a hobby, grew into a mail-order business, and is now a flourishing Web-based business (www.keh.com). More than 57 percent of the store's sales are made online. Customers have found that the Web site is an efficient pipeline for buying and selling cameras. The far reach of the Web was a natural fit for the company. "The Web is a so much better vehicle for our customers [compared with a mail-order catalog]," store

You've probably read many newspaper and magazine ads selling home-based businesses. You may have even received unsolicited e-mail messages touting the glory of particular work-at-home opportunities. Beware of work-at-home scams! Here are a few clues that tell you a home business opportunity is a scam:

1. The ad promises that you can earn hundreds or even thousands of dollars a week working at home.
2. No experience is needed.
3. You only need to work a few hours a week.
4. There are loads of CAPITAL LETTERS and exclamation points!!!!!
5. You need to call a 900 number for more information.
6. You're asked to send in some money to receive a list of home-based business opportunities.
7. You're pressured to make a decision NOW!!!!

Do your homework before investing in a business opportunity. Call and ask for references. Contact the Better Business Bureau (www.bbb.org), county and state departments of consumer affairs, and the state attorney general's office. Conduct an Internet search and ask people in chat rooms, Usenet discussion groups, or bulletin boards if they've dealt with the company. Visit Web sites such as www.friendsinbusiness.com to find advice on specific online scams. Most important, don't pay a great deal of money for a business opportunity until you've talked to an attorney.

figure 6.3

**WATCH OUT FOR SCAMS**

manager Pat Mulherin said. "They want to be able to see our inventory." When KEH's first Web page went active, it was an immediate success. "Within two months it was accounting for 35 percent of our business, then quickly went up." Prior to establishing itself on the Web, the small store produced mail-order catalogs listing used cameras for sale. Creating and mailing the catalogs was a slow process; by the time a customer saw a product and tried to order it, another customer could have already purchased it. The KEH Web site's listing of available cameras is updated every four hours. A used camera is listed for sale on the Web site a few hours after it enters KEH's inventory.

Web-based businesses have to do more than simply offer the same merchandise customers can easily buy at their local stores—they must offer unique products or services.[13] Even though the fuse to the dot-com bomb had already been lit by the time Karen Booth Adams began PoshTots in November 2000, the online baby decor retailer not only survived the blast but also grew to 22 employees and a projected $10 million in sales for 2005. PoshTots had no particular technological edge over its competitors in online retailing. It prospered for the simple reason that no one, online or off, offered what Adams did—a single, convenient place to go for high-end children's decor and furnishings. "We picked a niche, stuck to it and did it the best," Adams says.[14]

**Netflix CEO Reed Hastings sits in a mail delivery case of thousands of DVDs at their distribution plant in San Jose, California. The online DVD rental company is one of the Internet's rising stars. Hastings launched the subscription service in 1999. It grew to one million subscribers in less than four years. By 2005 Netflix had more than 4 million subscribers and hopes to reach 20 million by 2010. What advantages does doing business online offer businesses like Netflix?**

The Internet community has numerous sites that lend entrepreneurs a helping hand in setting up their online stores:

- DistributorMatch.com plays matchmaker between manufacturers and distributors. If you're looking for ideas about what you might like to sell online, this site may get you started.
- Hypermart.com offers full e-commerce capability that allows small businesses to build their own security or electronic shopping carts.
- Sitecritique.net offers constructive criticism of your Web site by other users, a resource directory, a Web design and usability magazine, and Web design products and services.

**intrapreneurs**
Creative people who work as entrepreneurs within corporations.

**enterprise zones**
Specific geographic areas to which governments try to attract private business investment by offering lower taxes and other government support.

Don't get the idea that a Web-based business is always a fast road to success. It can sometimes be a shortcut to failure. Hundreds of high-flying dot-coms crashed after promising to revolutionize the way we shop.[15] That's the bad news. The good news is that you can learn from someone else's failure and spare yourself some pain. To help future Web-based entrepreneurs understand online-business fundamentals and how to avoid the failed dot-coms' mistakes, the University of Maryland maintains a database of dot-com business plans and marketing documents. Check out the school's Business Plan Archive at www.businessplanarchive.org for more information.

## Entrepreneurship within Firms

Entrepreneurship in a large organization is often reflected in the efforts and achievements of intrapreneurs. **Intrapreneurs** are creative people who work as entrepreneurs within corporations. The idea is to use a company's existing resources—human, financial, and physical—to launch new products and generate new profits.[16] At 3M, which produces a wide array of products from adhesives (Scotch tape) to nonwoven materials for industrial use, managers are expected to devote 15 percent of their time to thinking up new products or services.[17] You know those bright-colored Post-it Notes people use to write messages on just about everything? That product was developed by Art Fry, a 3M employee. He needed to mark the pages of a hymnal in a way that wouldn't damage the book or fall out. He came up with the idea of the self-stick, repositionable paper. The 3M labs soon produced a sample, but distributors thought the product wasn't important and market surveys were inconclusive. Nonetheless, 3M kept sending samples to secretaries of top executives. Eventually, after launching a major sales and marketing program, the orders began pouring in, and Post-it Notes became a big winner. The company continues to update the product; making the notes from recycled paper is just one of the many innovations. Post-it Notes have gone international as well—the notepads sent to Japan are long and narrow to accommodate vertical writing. You can even use Post-it Notes electronically—the Post-it Software Notes program allows you to type messages onto brightly colored notes and store them on memo boards, embed them in documents, or send them through e-mail.

When you come up with a winning idea, stick with it. That's certainly been the motto of the 3M company, the maker of Post-its. 3M encourages intrapreneurship among its employees by requiring them to devote at least 15 percent of their time to thinking about new products. How has this commitment to innovation paid off for the company and its employees?

The classic intrapreneurial venture is the Skunkworks of Lockheed Martin Corporation. The Skunkworks is a top-secret research and development center that turned out such monumental products as America's first fighter jet in 1943 and the Stealth fighter in 1991.

## Encouraging Entrepreneurship—What Government Can Do

Part of the Immigration Act passed by Congress in 1990 was intended to encourage more entrepreneurs to come to the United States. The act created a category of "investor visas" that allows 10,000 people to come to the United States each year if they invest $1 million in an enterprise that creates or preserves 10 jobs.[18] Some people are promoting the idea of increasing the number of such immigrants. They believe the more entrepreneurs that can be lured to the United States, the more jobs will be created and the more the economy will grow.

One way to encourage entrepreneurship is through enterprise zones. **Enterprise zones** are specific geographic areas to which governments try to attract private business investment by offering lower taxes and other government support. The government could have a significant effect on entrepreneurship by offering investment tax credits that would give tax breaks to businesses that make the kind of investments that would create jobs. To learn more about the benefits of enterprise zones and to see a map of their locations throughout the United States, go to www.ezec.gov.

States are becoming stronger supporters of entrepreneurs as they create programs that invest directly in new businesses. Often, state commerce departments serve as clearinghouses for such investment programs. States are also creating incubators and technology centers to reduce start-up capital needs. **Incubators** are centers that offer new businesses low-cost offices with basic business services such as accounting, legal advice, and secretarial help. Incubators help companies survive because they provide assistance in the critical stage of early development.[19] One incubator graduate, Visual Networks, grew so rapidly that it displaced the incubator that housed it, forcing the Maryland Technology Development Center to move elsewhere. According to a recent study conducted by the National Business Incubator Association (NBIA), 80 percent of incubator graduates remain in business.[20] To learn more about what incubators offer and to find links to incubators in your area, visit the NBIA's Web site at www.nbia.org.

Sixteen-year-old Natasha Spedalle sells her jewelry to students at New York's Laboratory Institute of Merchandising. Spedalle started her business with $200 in capital. In 2005, the Initiative for Competitive Inner City added Spedalle to its list of most successful inner-city businesses. The ICIC says that local governments can lure more small businesses to the inner city by providing tax incentives, grants, and other perks. What advantages can you see to running a business in an inner city?

**progress assessment**

- Why are people willing to take the risks of entrepreneurship?
- What are the advantages of entrepreneurial teams?
- How do micropreneurs differ from other entrepreneurs?
- What are some of the opportunities and risks of Web-based businesses?

## GETTING STARTED IN SMALL BUSINESS

Let's suppose you have a great idea for a new business, you have the attributes of an entrepreneur, and you are ready to take the leap into business for yourself. How do you start a business? How much paperwork is involved?

**incubators**
Centers that offer new businesses low-cost offices with basic business services.

Faust Capobianco loved baseball and knew making the major leagues was a long shot. He finally made it when his company, Majestic Athletic, beat out Adidas, Nike, and Reebok to become the executive licensee for Major League Baseball. Majestic simply outplayed its larger rivals by focusing all its efforts on one sport. Can you think of other companies that have earned success by focusing on a single market?

That is what the rest of this chapter is about. We will explore small businesses, their role in the economy, and small-business management. It may be easier to identify with a small neighborhood business than with a giant global firm, yet the principles of management are similar. The management of charities, government agencies, churches, schools, and unions is much the same as the management of small and large businesses. So, as you learn about small-business management, you will make a giant step toward understanding management in general. All organizations demand capital, good ideas, planning, information management, budgets (and financial management in general), accounting, marketing, good employee relations, and good overall managerial know-how. We shall explore these areas as they relate to small businesses and then, later in the book, apply the concepts to large firms, even global organizations.

## Small versus Big Business

**small business**
A business that is independently owned and operated, is not dominant in its field of operation, and meets certain standards of size (set by the Small Business Administration) in terms of employees or annual receipts.

The Small Business Administration (SBA) defines a **small business** as one that is independently owned and operated, is not dominant in its field of operation, and meets certain standards of size in terms of employees or annual receipts (e.g., less than $2 million a year for service businesses). A small business is considered "small" only in relation to other businesses in its industry. A wholesaler may sell up to $22 million and still be considered a small business by the SBA. In manufacturing, a plant can have 1,500 employees and still be considered small.[21] Let's look at some interesting statistics about small businesses:[22]

- There are over 20 million full- and part-time home-based businesses in the United States.
- Nearly 750,000 tax-paying, employee-hiring businesses are started every year.
- Small businesses create 75 percent of the new jobs in the United States.
- Of all nonfarm businesses in the United States, almost 97 percent are considered small by SBA standards.
- Small businesses account for more than 50 percent of the gross domestic product (GDP).
- The total number of U.S. employees who work in small business is greater than the populations of Australia and Canada combined.
- About 80 percent of Americans find their first jobs in small businesses.
- The number of women owning small businesses has increased rapidly. Women now own nearly 6 million small businesses.
- Minority-owned businesses are one of the fastest-growing segments of the U.S. economy. In the past decade, the number of small businesses owned by Asians has grown 463 percent, Hispanics 417 percent, and African Americans 108 percent.

SPOTLIGHT ON small business

www.icic.org

## Inner-City Opportunities

When most people think of the inner city they don't think of entrepreneurial success. But that is what the Initiative for a Competitive Inner City (ICIC) cites as a trend in today's inner cities. The ICIC is a nonprofit that promotes small businesses in what were formerly depressed areas of U.S. cities. Many of the new inner-city entrepreneurs are young people; their average age is 33, and some are under 20, with a few as young as 13.

Jason Lutz is 31 years old and runs Sneaker Villa, a store targeting young urban youth that started out in Reading and now has branches in three other Pennsylvania cities. Lutz's store was listed in the ICIC's Inner City 100 for 2005 as one of the country's most successful inner-city businesses. He says that costs in the urban areas are low, customers live close by, and he finds his workers "awfully loyal."

The ICIC agrees. Dorothy Terrell, ICIC president and CEO, points out that in addition to low costs, necessities like phone lines, utilities, and other technology are readily available because of the metropolitan location. Also, the inner-city boasts a loyal diverse workforce with low turnover. An ICIC study showed that the turnover rate for inner-city business employees was 15 percent, compared to a national average of 25 percent. "It's about location, location, location," Terrell said. "The inner-city is a strategic location because there's an underserved market and an underutilized workforce there." The demographic of inner-city entrepreneurs is changing as well. Latinos make up 19 percent of the inner-city entrepreneurs, African-Americans 16 percent, Asians 4 percent, and American Indians 1 percent.

Some inner-city businesses find their success in areas—niches—that larger companies have abandoned. In recent years the music industry has suffered a 10 percent drop in CD sales. As a result, some big labels have dropped jazz as being too marginal. The Manchester Craftsman Guild in Pittsburgh found itself ready to fill the void. For years its members had been producing music concerts as part of their mission "to preserve, present, and promote" jazz. Looking for a steadier source of income, the guild's music director, Marty Ashby, arranged financing to produce a release of a performance of the Count Basie Orchestra at the guild's hall. The CD was so well done that it won a Grammy for large jazz ensemble in 1996. Since then the label has produced 12 CDs, won another Grammy, and had one CD reach the *Billboard* Top Five for jazz.

As these examples show, when one company leaves an opening, sometimes an enterprising young entrepreneur can fill the void with new products or services.

Sources: Doug Tsuruoka, "Younger Entrepreneurs Transforming Inner Cities," *Investor's Business Daily*, July 11, 2005; Joe Williams, "These Bizkids Know How to Make Bread," *New York Daily News*, April 27, 2005; Paulette Thomas, "Small Competitors Can Conquer Tough Markets," *The Wall Street Journal Online*, April 2005; and John Schmid, "Corporate Catalyst for Stricken Cities," *Milwaukee Journal Sentinel*, January 8, 2006.

As you can see, small business is really a big part of the U.S. economy. How big a part? We'll explore that question next.

## Importance of Small Businesses

Since 75 percent of the nation's new jobs are in small businesses, there is a very good chance that you will either work in a small business someday or start one. A quarter of the small businesses list "lack of qualified workers" as one of their biggest obstacles to growth.

In addition to providing employment opportunities, small firms believe they offer other advantages that larger companies do not. Owners of small companies report that their greatest advantages over big companies are their more personal customer service and their ability to respond quickly to opportunities.[23]

Bigger is not always better. Picture a hole in the ground. If you fill it with big boulders, there are many empty spaces between them. However, if you fill it with sand, there is no space between the grains. That's how it is in business. Big businesses don't serve all the needs of the market. There is plenty of room for small companies to make a profit filling those niches. See the Spotlight on Small Business box for examples of how small businesses can fill the void left by big businesses.

## Small-Business Success and Failure

You can't be naive about business practices, or you'll go broke. There is some debate about how many new small businesses fail each year. Conventional wisdom says that a third of all small businesses fail in their first four years, and the SBA reports a 60 percent death rate within six years.[24] Yet a study by economist Bruce Kirchhoff shows that the failure rate is only 18 percent over the first eight years. Kirchhoff contends that the other failure rates are the result of misinterpretations of Dun & Bradstreet statistics. When small-business owners closed down one business to start new and different businesses, they were included in the "business failure" category even though obviously that was not the case. Similarly, when a business changed its form of ownership from partnership to corporation, it was counted as a failure. Retirements of sole owners were also included as business failures. All in all, the good news for entrepreneurs is that business failures are much lower than has traditionally been reported.

Although the chances of business survival may be greater than some used to think, keep in mind that even the most optimistic interpretation of the statistics shows that nearly one out of five businesses that cease operations is left owing money to creditors. Figure 6.4 lists reasons for small-business failures, among which are managerial incompetence and inadequate financial planning.

Choosing the right type of business is critical. Many of the businesses with the lowest failure rates require advanced training to start—veterinary services, dental practices, medical practices, and so on. While training and degrees may buy security, they do not tend to produce much growth. If you want to be both independent and rich, you need to go after growth. Often high-growth businesses, such as technology firms, are not easy to start and are even more difficult to keep going.

In general it seems that the easiest businesses to start are the ones that tend to have the least growth and the greatest failure rate (e.g., restaurants). The easiest businesses to keep alive are difficult ones to get started (e.g., manufacturing). And the ones that can make you rich are the ones that are both hard to

figure 6.4

**CAUSES OF SMALL-BUSINESS FAILURE**

The following are some of the causes of small-business failure:

- Plunging in without first testing the waters on a small scale.
- Underpricing or overpricing goods or services.
- Underestimating how much time it will take to build a market.
- Starting with too little capital.
- Starting with too much capital and being careless in its use.
- Going into business with little or no experience and without first learning something about the industry or market.
- Borrowing money without planning just how and when to pay it back.
- Attempting to do too much business with too little capital.
- Not allowing for setbacks and unexpected expenses.
- Buying too much on credit.
- Extending credit too freely.
- Expanding credit too rapidly.
- Failing to keep complete, accurate records, so that the owners drift into trouble without realizing it.
- Carrying habits of personal extravagance into the business.
- Not understanding business cycles.
- Forgetting about taxes, insurance, and other costs of doing business.
- Mistaking the freedom of being in business for oneself for the liberty to work or not, according to whim.

figure 6.5

**SITUATIONS FOR SMALL-BUSINESS SUCCESS**

The following factors increase the chances of small-business success:

- The customer requires a lot of personal attention, as in a beauty parlor.
- The product is not easily made by mass-production techniques (e.g., custom-tailored clothes or custom auto-body work).
- Sales are not large enough to appeal to a large firm (e.g., a novelty shop).
- The neighborhood is not attractive because of crime or poverty. This provides a unique opportunity for small grocery stores and laundries.
- A large business sells a franchise operation to local buyers. (Don't forget franchising as an excellent way to enter the world of small business.)
- The owner pays attention to new competitors.
- The business is in a growth industry (e.g., computer services or Web design).

start and hard to keep going (e.g., automobile assembly). See Figure 6.5 to get an idea of the business situations that are most likely to lead to success.

When you decide to start your own business, you must think carefully about what kind of business you want. You are not likely to find everything you want in one business—easy entry, security, and reward. Choose those characteristics that matter the most to you; accept the absence of the others; plan, plan, plan; and then go for it!

## LEARNING ABOUT SMALL-BUSINESS OPERATIONS

Hundreds of would-be entrepreneurs of all ages have asked the same question: "How can I learn to run my own business?" Many of these people had no idea what kind of business they wanted to start; they simply wanted to be in business for themselves. That seems to be a major trend among students today. Therefore, here are some hints for learning about small business.

### Learn from Others

Your search for small-business knowledge might begin by investigating your local community college for classes on the subject. There are thousands of entrepreneurship programs in postsecondary schools throughout the United States.[25] One of the best things about such courses is that they bring together entrepreneurs from diverse backgrounds. An excellent way to learn how to run a small business is to talk to others who have already done it. They will tell you that location is critical. They will caution you not to be undercapitalized, that is, not to start without enough money. They will warn you about the problems of finding and retaining good workers. And, most of all, they will tell you to keep good records and hire a good accountant and lawyer before you start. Free advice like this is invaluable.

### Get Some Experience

There is no better way to learn small-business management than by becoming an apprentice or working for a successful entrepreneur. Many small-business owners got the idea for their businesses from their prior jobs. The rule of thumb is: Have three years' experience in a comparable business.

## MAKING ethical decisions

### Going Down with the Ship

Suppose you've worked for two years in a company and you see signs that the business is beginning to falter. You and a co-worker have ideas about how to make a company like your boss's succeed. Rather than share your ideas with your boss, you and your friend are considering quitting your jobs and starting your own company together. Should you approach other co-workers about working for your new venture? Will you try to lure your old boss's customers to your own business? What are your alternatives? What are the consequences of each alternative? What's the most ethical choice?

Many new entrepreneurs come from corporate management. They are tired of the big-business life or are being laid off because of corporate downsizing. Such managers bring their managerial expertise and enthusiasm with them.

Getting experience before you start your own business isn't a new concept. In fact, way back in 1818, Cornelius Vanderbilt sold his own sailing vessels and went to work for a steamboat company so he could learn the rules of the new game of steam. After learning what he needed to know, he quit, started his own steamship company, and became the first American to accumulate $100 million.

By running a small business part-time, during your off hours or on weekends, you can experience the rewards of working for yourself while still enjoying a regular paycheck. Learning a business while working for someone else may also save you money because you are less likely to make "rookie mistakes" when you start your own business. The Making Ethical Decisions box presents ethical questions about starting your own business.

Katrina Markoff believes that chocolate can save the world. As founder of Vosges Haut-Chocolat, Markoff introduces her customers to different cultures by mixing her chocolate with exotic flavors from around the globe. It's easy to think of Japan when trying a wasabi truffle or of Italy when sampling a chocolate laced with taleggio cheese. After receiving a SBA loan, Markoff opened her first store in Chicago and then others in New York City and Las Vegas and soon Japan.

## Take Over a Successful Firm

Small-business management takes time, dedication, and determination. Owners work long hours and rarely take vacations. After many years, they may feel stuck in their business. They may think they can't get out because they have too much time and effort invested. Consequently, there are millions of small-business owners out there eager to get away, at least for a long vacation.

This is where you come in. Find a successful businessperson who owns a small business. Tell him or her that you are eager to learn the business and would like to serve an apprenticeship, that is, a training period. Say that at the end of the training period (one year or so), you would like to help the owner or manager by becoming assistant manager. As assistant manager, you would free the owner to take off weekends and holidays, and to take a long vacation—a good deal for him or her. For another year or so, work very hard to learn all about the business—suppliers, inventory, bookkeeping, customers, promotion, and so on. At the end of two years, make the owner this offer: He or she can retire or work only part-time, and you will take over the business. You can establish a profit-sharing plan for yourself plus a salary. Be generous with yourself; you will earn it if you manage the business. You can even ask for 40 percent or more of the profits.

The owner benefits by keeping ownership in the business and making 60 percent of what he or she earned before—without having to work. You benefit by making 40 percent of the profits of a successful firm. This is an excellent deal for an owner about to retire—he or she is able to keep the firm and a healthy profit flow. It is also a clever and successful way to share in the profits of a successful small business without any personal money investment.

If profit sharing doesn't appeal to the owner, you may want to buy the business outright. How do you determine a fair price for a business? Value is based on (1) what the business owns, (2) what it earns, and (3) what makes it unique. Naturally, your accountant will need to help you determine the business's value.

If your efforts to take over the business through either profit sharing or buying fail, you can quit and start your own business fully trained.

**business plan**
A detailed written statement that describes the nature of the business, the target market, the advantages the business will have in relation to competition, and the resources and qualifications of the owner(s).

## MANAGING A SMALL BUSINESS

The Small Business Administration has reported that 90 percent of all small-business failures are a result of poor management. Keep in mind, though, that the term *poor management* covers a number of faults. It could mean poor planning, poor record keeping, poor inventory control, poor promotion, or poor employee relations. Most likely it would include poor capitalization.[26] To help you succeed as a business owner, in the following sections we explore the functions of business in a small-business setting:

- Planning your business.
- Financing your business.
- Knowing your customers (marketing).
- Managing your employees (human resource development).
- Keeping records (accounting).

Although all of the functions are important in both the start-up and management phases of the business, the first two functions—planning and financing—are the primary concerns when you start your business. The remaining functions are the heart of the actual operations once the business is started.

### Begin with Planning

It is amazing how many people are eager to start a small business but have only a vague notion of what they want to do. Eventually, they come up with an idea for a business and begin discussing the idea with professors, friends, and other businesspeople. It is at this stage that the entrepreneur needs a business plan. A **business plan** is a detailed written statement that describes the nature of the business, the target market, the advantages the business will have in relation to competition, and the resources and qualifications of the owner(s). A business plan forces potential owners of small businesses to be quite specific about the products or services they intend to offer. They must

Some people may think that aging baby boomers are getting ready to retire to their rocking chairs to watch *I Love Lucy* reruns. No way, according to Franny Martin and 5.6 million other Americans age 50 and older who run their own businesses. Franny started her business, Cookies on Call, when she was nearly 56. She sells 47 kinds of chocolate-chunk cookies through her Web site for $16 to $17 a dozen and has no plans to slow down. Do you think it's ever too late to start a business?

analyze the competition, calculate how much money they need to start, and cover other details of operation. A business plan is also mandatory for talking with bankers or other investors.

Michael Celello, president of the People's Commercial Bank, says that fewer than 10 percent of prospective borrowers come to a bank adequately prepared. He offers several tips to small-business owners, including picking a bank that serves businesses the size of yours, having a good accountant prepare a complete set of financial statements and a personal balance sheet, making an appointment before going to the bank, going to the bank with an accountant and all the necessary financial information, and demonstrating to the banker that you're a person of good character: civic minded and respected in business and community circles. Finally, he says to ask for all the money you need, be specific, and be prepared to personally guarantee the loan.

## Writing a Business Plan

A good business plan takes a long time to write, but you've got to convince your readers in five minutes not to throw the plan away. While there is no such thing as a perfect business plan, prospective entrepreneurs do think out the smallest details. Jerrold Carrington of Inroads Capital Partners advises that one of the most important parts of the business plan is the executive summary. The summary has to catch the reader's interest. Bankers receive many business plans every day. "You better grab me up front," says Carrington. The box on pages 167–168 gives you an outline of a comprehensive business plan.

Sometimes one of the most difficult tasks in undertaking complex projects, such as writing a business plan, is knowing where to start. There are many computer software programs on the market now to help you get organized. One highly rated business-plan program is Business Plan Pro by Palo Alto Software. You can find online help with the MiniPlan (www.miniplan.com), a free interactive Web tool that guides you through the business-plan writing process.

Employees at Concurrent Pharmaceuticals hope the infusion of $16 million in venture capital will help the firm follow in the footsteps of market giants like Intel and Cisco that used venture capital financing to grow their businesses. Venture capitalists can be a source of start-up funds for a small business, but they generally require an ownership stake in the firm.

Getting the completed business plan into the right hands is almost as important as getting the right information in the plan. Finding funding requires research. Next we will discuss some of the many sources of money available to new business ventures. All of them call for a comprehensive business plan. The time and effort you invest before starting a business will pay off many times later. With small businesses, the big payoff is survival.

## Getting Money to Fund a Small Business

An entrepreneur has several potential sources of capital: personal savings, relatives, former employers, banks, finance companies, venture capitalists, and government agencies such as the Small Business Administration (SBA), the Farmers Home Administration, the Economic Development Authority, and the Minority Business Development Agency. An estimated 90 percent of all start-ups receive money from friends and family.[27] You may even want to consider borrowing from a

## OUTLINE OF A COMPREHENSIVE BUSINESS PLAN

A good business plan is between 25 and 50 pages long and takes at least six months to write.

**Cover letter**

Only one thing is certain when you go hunting for money to start a business: You won't be the only hunter out there. You need to make potential funders want to read *your* business plan instead of the hundreds of others on their desks. Your cover letter should summarize the most attractive points of your project in as few words as possible. Be sure to address the letter to the potential investor by name. "To whom it may concern" or "Dear Sir" is not the best way to win an investor's support.

**Section 1—Executive Summary**

Begin with a two-page or three-page management summary of the proposed venture. Include a short description of the business, and discuss major goals and objectives.

**Section 2—Company Background**

Describe company operations to date (if any), potential legal considerations, and areas of risk and opportunity. Summarize the firm's financial condition, and include past and current balance sheets, income and cash flow statements, and other relevant financial records (you will read about these financial statements in Chapter 17). It is also wise to include a description of insurance coverage. Investors want to be assured that death or other mishaps do not pose major threats to the company.

**Section 3—Management Team**

Include an organization chart, job descriptions of listed positions, and detailed résumés of the current and proposed executives. A mediocre idea with a proven management team is funded more often than a great idea with an inexperienced team. Managers should have expertise in all disciplines necessary to start and run a business. If not, mention outside consultants who will serve in these roles and describe their qualifications.

**Section 4—Financial Plan**

Provide five-year projections for income, expenses, and funding sources. Don't assume the business will grow in a straight line. Adjust your planning to allow for funding at various stages of the company's growth. Explain the rationale and assumptions used to determine the estimates. Assumptions should be reasonable and based on industry/historical trends. Make sure all totals add up and are consistent throughout the plan. If necessary, hire a professional accountant or financial analyst to prepare these statements.

Stay clear of excessively ambitious sales projections; rather, offer best-case, expected, and worst-case scenarios. These not only reveal how sensitive the bottom line is to sales fluctuations but also serve as good management guides.

**Section 5—Capital Required**

Indicate the amount of capital needed to commence or continue operations, and describe how these funds are to be used. Make sure the totals are the same as the ones on the cash-flow statement. This area will receive a great deal of review from potential investors, so it must be clear and concise.

**Section 6—Marketing Plan**

Don't underestimate the competition. Review industry size, trends, and the target market segment. Sources like *American Demographics* magazine and the *Rand McNally Commercial Atlas and Marketing Guide* can help you put a plan together. Discuss strengths and weaknesses of the product or service. The most important things investors want to know are what makes the product more desirable than what's already available and whether the product can be patented. Compare pricing to the competition's. Forecast sales in dollars and units. Outline sales, advertising, promotion, and public relations programs. Make sure the costs agree with those projected in the financial statements.

**Section 7—Location Analysis**

In retailing and certain other industries, the location of the business is one of the most important factors. Provide a comprehensive demographic analysis of consumers in the area of the proposed business as well as a traffic-pattern analysis and vehicular and pedestrian counts.

(*continued*)

**Section 8—Manufacturing Plan**

Describe minimum plant size, machinery required, production capacity, inventory and inventory-control methods, quality control, plant personnel requirements, and so on. Estimates of product costs should be based on primary research.

**Section 9—Appendix**

Include all marketing research on the product or service (off-the-shelf reports, article reprints, etc.) and other information about the product concept or market size. Provide a bibliography of all the reference materials you consulted. This section should demonstrate that the proposed company won't be entering a declining industry or market segment.

If you would like to see sample business plans that successfully secured funding, go to the sample business plan resource center at www.bplans.com/samples. You can also learn more about writing business plans on the Small Business Administration Web site at www.sba.gov/starting.

potential supplier to your future business. Helping you get started may be in the supplier's interest if there is a chance you will be a big customer later. It's usually not a good idea to ask such an investor for money at the outset. Begin by asking for advice; if the supplier likes your plan, he or she may be willing to help you with funding.

Other than personal savings, individual investors are the primary source of capital for most entrepreneurs. *Angel investors* are private individuals who invest their own money in potentially hot new companies before they go public.[28] Web sites are now available that link entrepreneurs with potential investors; examples are www.financehub.com and www.garage.com.

**venture capitalists**
Individuals or companies that invest in new businesses in exchange for partial ownership of those businesses.

Investors known as **venture capitalists** may finance your project—for a price. Venture capitalists may ask for a hefty stake (as much as 60 percent) in your company in exchange for the cash to start your business. If the venture capitalist demands too large a stake, you could lose control of the business. Since the burst of the dot-com bubble, venture capitalists have tightened the purse strings on how much they are willing to invest in a business and have multiplied the return they expect on their investment if the new company is sold.[29] Therefore, if you're a very small company, you don't have a good chance getting venture capital. You'd have a better chance finding an angel investor.

If your proposed venture does require millions of dollars to start, experts recommend that you talk with at least five investment firms and their clients in order to find the right venture capitalist. You can get a list of venture capitalists from the Small Business Administration. Ask for the brochure called "Directory of Operating Small Business Investment Companies." Or visit the National Venture Capital Association's Web site at www.nvca.org. You can also follow the ups and downs of venture capital availability in *Inc.* magazine.

**Small Business Administration (SBA)**
A U.S. government agency that advises and assists small businesses by providing management training and financial advice and loans.

## The Small Business Administration (SBA)

The **Small Business Administration (SBA)** is a U.S. government agency that advises and assists small businesses by providing management training and financial advice and loans (see Figure 6.6). The SBA started a microloan demonstration program in 1991. The program provides very small loans (up to $35,000) and technical assistance to "prebankable" small-business owners. The program is administered through a nationwide network of 170 nonprofit organizations chosen by the SBA. Rather than base the awarding of loans on

The SBA may provide the following types of financial assistance:

- *Guaranteed loans*—loans made by a financial institution that the government will repay if the borrower stops making payments. The maximum individual loan guarantee is capped at $1 million.
- *Microloans*—amounts ranging from $100 to $35,000 (average $10,500) to people such as single mothers and public housing tenants.
- *Export Express*—loans made to small businesses wishing to export. The maximum guaranteed loan amount is $250,000.
- *Community Adjustment and Investment Program (CAIP)*—loans to businesses to create new, sustainable jobs or to preserve existing jobs in eligible communities that have lost jobs due to changing trade patterns with Mexico and Canada following the adoption of NAFTA.
- *Pollution control loans*—loans to eligible small businesses for the financing of the planning, design, or installation of a pollution control facility. This facility must prevent, reduce, abate, or control any form of pollution, including recycling. The maximum guaranteed loan amount is $1 million.
- *504 certified development company (CDC) loans*—loans for purchasing major fixed assets, such as land and buildings for businesses in eligible communities, typically rural communities or urban areas needing revitalization. The program's goal is to expand business ownership by minorities, women, and veterans. The maximum guaranteed loan amount is $1.3 million.

figure 6.6

**TYPES OF SBA FINANCIAL ASSISTANCE**

collateral, credit history, or previous business success, these programs decide worthiness on the basis of belief in the borrowers' integrity and the soundness of their business ideas.[30]

The SBA microloan program helps people like Karla Brown start their own businesses. Newly divorced and facing a mountain of debt, Brown needed to find a way to support her daughter. She bought two buckets of flowers and headed to the subway to sell them. Continuing the process, she made enough money to keep a steady inventory, but she needed help from her friends to pay her bills. She thought she could make a living if she could take her flowers out of the subway and into a store. She obtained a $19,000 SBA microloan and rented a store in the heart of Boston; soon after, Brown's flower shop brought in $100,000 in sales.[31]

You may also want to consider requesting funds from the **Small Business Investment Company (SBIC) Program**. SBICs are private investment companies licensed by the Small Business Administration to lend money to small businesses. An SBIC must have a minimum of $5 million in capital and can borrow up to $2 from the SBA for each $1 of capital it has. It lends to or invests in small businesses that meet its criteria. Often SBICs are able to keep defaults to a minimum by identifying a business's trouble spots early, giving entrepreneurs advice, and in some cases rescheduling payments.[32]

**Small Business Investment Company (SBIC) Program**
A program through which private investment companies licensed by the Small Business Administration lend money to small businesses.

Perhaps the best place for young entrepreneurs to start shopping for an SBA loan is a Small Business Development Center (SBDC). SBDCs are funded jointly by the federal government and individual states, and are usually associated with state universities. SBDCs can help you evaluate the feasibility of your idea, develop your business plan, and complete your funding application—all for free. The SBA recently reduced the size of its application from 150 pages to 1 page for loans under $50,000.[33]

You may want to go to the SBA's Web site (www.sba.gov) for the latest information about SBA programs. The SBA site gives detailed information on the agency and other business services.

Not all small businesses stay small; some become business superstars. Take Staples, for example. The office supply chain with almost 1,800 stores worldwide, started with the help of an SBA loaned in 1986. It is now a $16.1 billion retailer. The government, acting through the Small Business Administration, is a great supporter of entrepreneurship. Have you contacted the SBA for information about starting a small business?

Obtaining money from banks, venture capitalists, and government sources is very difficult for most small businesses. (You will learn more about financing in Chapter 18.) Those who do survive the planning and financing of their new ventures are eager to get their businesses up and running. Your success in running a business depends on many factors. Three important factors for success are knowing your customers, managing your employees, and keeping efficient records.

## Knowing Your Customers

One of the most important elements of small-business success is knowing the market. In business, a **market** consists of people with unsatisfied wants and needs who have both the resources and the willingness to buy. For example, we can confidently state that most of our students have the willingness to own a brand-new Maserati sports car. However, few of them have the resources necessary to satisfy this want. Would they be considered a good market for a luxury car dealer to pursue?

Once you have identified your market and its needs, you must set out to fill those needs. The way to meet your customers' needs is to offer top quality at a fair price with great service. Remember, it isn't enough to get customers—you have to keep them. As Victoria Jackson, founder of the $50 million Victoria Jackson Cosmetics Company, says of the stars who push her products on television infomercials, "All the glamorous faces in the world wouldn't mean a thing if my customers weren't happy with the product and didn't come back for more." Everything must be geared to bring customers the satisfaction they deserve.

One of the greatest advantages that small businesses have over larger ones is the ability to know their customers better and to adapt quickly to their ever-changing needs. You will gain more insights about markets in Chapters 13–16. Now let's consider the importance of effectively managing the employees who help you serve your market.

**market**
People with unsatisfied wants and needs who have both the resources and the willingness to buy.

## Managing Employees

As a business grows, it becomes impossible for an entrepreneur to oversee every detail, even if he or she is putting in 60 hours per week. This means that hiring, training, and motivating employees is critical.

It is not easy to find good, qualified help when you offer less money, skimpier benefits, and less room for advancement than larger firms do. That is one reason employee relations is such an important part of small-business management. Employees of small companies are often more satisfied with their jobs than are their counterparts in big business. Why? Quite often they find their jobs more challenging, their ideas more accepted, and their bosses more respectful.

Often entrepreneurs reluctantly face the reality that to keep growing, they must delegate authority to others. Nagging questions such as "Who should be delegated authority?" and "How much control should they have?" create perplexing problems.

This can be a particularly touchy issue in small businesses with long-term employees, and in family businesses. As you might expect, entrepreneurs who have built their companies from scratch often feel compelled to promote employees who have been with them from the start—even when those employees aren't qualified to serve as managers. Common sense probably tells you this could be detrimental to the business.

The same can be true of family-run businesses that are expanding. Attitudes such as "You can't fire family" or you must promote certain workers because "they're family" can hinder growth. Entrepreneurs can best serve themselves and the business if they gradually recruit and groom employees for management positions. By doing this, entrepreneurs can enhance trust and support of the manager among other employees and themselves.[34]

When Heida Thurlow of Chantal Cookware suffered an extended illness, she let her employees handle the work she once had insisted on doing herself. The experience transformed her company from an entrepreneurial company into a managerial one. She says, "Over the long run that makes us stronger than we were." You'll learn more about managing employees in Chapters 7–12.

## Keeping Records

Small-business owners often say that the most important assistance they received in starting and managing their business involved accounting. A businessperson who sets up an effective accounting system early will save much grief later. Computers simplify record keeping and enable a small-business owner to follow the daily progress of the business (sales, expenses, profits). An inexpensive computer system can also help owners with other record-keeping chores, such as inventory control, customer records, and payroll.

A good accountant is invaluable in setting up such systems and showing you how to keep the system operating smoothly. Many business failures are caused by poor accounting practices. A good accountant can help you decide whether to buy or lease equipment and whether to own or rent a building. He or she may also help you with tax planning, financial forecasting, choosing sources of financing, and writing up requests for funds.[35]

Other small-business owners may tell you where to find an accountant experienced in small business. It pays to shop around for advice. You'll learn more about accounting in Chapter 17.

## Looking for Help

Small-business owners have learned, sometimes the hard way, that they need outside consulting advice early in the process. This is especially true of legal, tax, and accounting advice but may also be true of marketing, finance, and other areas. Most small and medium-sized firms cannot afford to hire such experts as employees, so they must turn to outside assistance.

A necessary and invaluable aide is a competent, experienced lawyer—one who knows and understands small businesses. Partners have a way of forgetting agreements unless the contract is written by a lawyer and signed. Lawyers can help with a variety of matters, including leases, contracts, and protection against liabilities. Lawyers don't have to be expensive. In fact, there are several prepaid legal plans that offer services (such as drafting legal documents) for an annual rate of $150 to $350.[36] Of course, you can find plenty of legal services online. For example, the SBA's BusinessLaw.com offers plain-English guides and minitutorials that will help you gain a basic understanding of the laws that affect each phase of the life of a small business. Findforms.com offers a search tool that helps you find free legal forms from all over the Web as well as advice, links, books, and more. Remember, "free" isn't a bargain if the information isn't correct, so check the sources carefully and double-check any legal actions with an attorney.

Marketing decisions should be made long before a product is produced or a store opened. An inexpensive marketing research study may help you determine where to locate, whom to select as your target market, and what would be an effective strategy for reaching those people. Thus, a marketing consultant with small-business experience can be of great help to you.

Given the marketing power of the Internet, your business will benefit from a presence on the Internet even if you do not sell products or services directly from the Web. For example, Brandt's Cafe, a small restaurant in St. Louis, has a Web site (www.brandtscafe.com) that features the day's menu and specials, highlights the credentials of the head chef, and displays photos of the restaurant. It also includes an interactive calendar that lists the scheduled live entertainment. Click on the names of the entertainers to learn what kind of music they play. Some entertainers even include audio samples of their work for you to preview. Web sites such as Workz.com give you access to tools to build your own site, including sources for Web graphic design and search engine submission tactics.

**Service Corps of Retired Executives (SCORE)** An SBA office with volunteers from industry, trade associations, and education who counsel small businesses at no cost (except for expenses).

Two other invaluable experts are a commercial loan officer and an insurance agent. The commercial loan officer can help you design an acceptable business plan and give you valuable financial advice as well as lend you money when you need it. An insurance agent will explain all the risks associated with a small business and how to cover them most efficiently with insurance and other means (e.g., safety devices and sprinkler systems).

An important source of information for small businesses is the **Service Corps of Retired Executives (SCORE)**. This SBA office has volunteers from industry, trade associations, and education who counsel small businesses at no cost (except for expenses).[37] You can find a SCORE counselor by calling (800) 634-0245 or logging on to www.score.org. The SBA also offers a free, comprehensive online entrepreneurship course for aspiring entrepreneurs.

Often local colleges have business professors who will advise small-business owners for a small fee or for free. Some universities have clubs or programs that provide consulting services by master of business administration (MBA) candidates for a nominal fee. For example, the University of Maryland and Virginia Tech have internship programs that pair MBA students with budding companies in local incubator programs. The incubator companies pay half of the intern's salary, which is around $20 an hour.

It also is wise to seek the counsel of other small-business owners. The Web site YoungEntrepreneur.com offers experienced entrepreneurs and young start-ups an open forum to exchange advice and ideas. Visitors also have access to articles on topics such as marketing, business planning, incorporation and financial management.

Other sources of counsel include local chambers of commerce, the Better Business Bureau, national and local trade associations, the business reference section of your library, and many small-business-related sites on the Internet. There are Web sites that can help you find the help you need by matching your consulting needs with the proper consultant. Such sites include National Consultant Referrals Inc. at www.4consulting-services.com.

When Sharon Lee and her brother Darryl wanted to start up a new seafood restaurant they turned to Ben Pelton for advice. Lee met Pelton, a retired sales and marketing executive, through the Service Corps of Retired Executives (SCORE). Pelton helped Lee complete her business plan and later sort through the stack of investment proposals from prospective backers that read about her business planning in a local newspaper article. How did Lee's business planning affect her chances of success?

progress assessment

- A business plan is probably the most important document a small-business owner will ever create. There are nine sections in the business plan outline on pages 167–168. Can you describe at least five of those sections now?
- What are three of the reasons given by the SBA for why small businesses fail financially?

## GOING INTERNATIONAL: SMALL-BUSINESS PROSPECTS

As we noted in Chapter 3, there are only about 290 million people in the United States but more than 6 billion people in the world. Obviously, the world market is potentially a much larger, much more lucrative market for small businesses than the United States alone. In spite of that potential, most small businesses still do not think internationally. According to the U.S. Department of Commerce, only a small percentage of small businesses export even though the number of small exporters has tripled in the last decade. In fact, in the past five years, the value of small-business exports has increased by 300 percent.[38] Despite this surge in export activity, many small businesses continue to have difficulty getting started in global business.

Why are so many companies missing the boat to the huge global markets? Primarily because the voyage involves a few major hurdles: (1) Financing is often difficult to find, (2) many would-be exporters don't know how to get started, (3) potential global businesspeople do not understand the cultural differences of prospective markets, and (4) the bureaucratic paperwork can threaten to bury a small business. See the Reaching Beyond Our Borders box for a story about how one company turned some of these hurdles into advantages.

Besides the fact that most of the world's market lies outside the United States, there are other good reasons for going international. For instance, exporting products can absorb excess inventory, soften downturns in the domestic market, and extend product lives. It can also spice up dull routines.

Small businesses have several advantages over large businesses in international trade:

- Overseas buyers enjoy dealing with individuals rather than with large corporate bureaucracies.
- Small companies can usually begin shipping much faster.
- Small companies provide a wide variety of suppliers.
- Small companies can give more personal service and more undivided attention, because each overseas account is a major source of business to them.

The growth potential of small businesses overseas is phenomenal. For example, John Stollenwerk found customers for his Wisconsin-made shoes in Italy, and Ohio's Andrew Bohnengel opened his tape company to the rest of the world by adopting the metric standard. Web-based business applications are helping small businesses cross boundaries like never before. CPI Process Systems Inc., a six-employee import/export oil-field equipment company in Houston, Texas, won a contract away from Swiss giant ABB to build a power station

REACHING BEYOND our borders

www.steveandbarrys.com

## Steve & Barry's Tariff Engineering

Have you ever thought something was so complicated that it was useless for anything but causing headaches? A lot of people feel that way about international tariff laws. Barry Prevor, one of the founders of Steve & Barry's University Sportswear, though, considers himself a "tariff engineer."

Steve Shore and Barry Prevor started out selling T-shirts for $1 each in flea markets during summers in college. After graduating, they opened sportswear stores on or near college campuses. Their chain numbered 100 stores by 2005 and is projected to increase to 200 by the end of 2006. They hope to top 5,000 stores someday. Sales are now nearly $1 billion a year. *Forbes* magazine and the International Council of Shopping Centers named Steve & Barry's one of their 50 Hottest Retailers for 2005.

Shore and Prevor got to that position because they "look at every single detail," selling at high volume, buying off-season production, filling trucks to capacity to save on freight, and other cost-saving measures. Highest among these is the tariff engineer's mastery of the tariff laws that cover the U.S. apparel trade.

For instance, goods that come from certain industrial parks that were designed to promote good relations between Jordan and Israel are duty free—if a certain part of their value comes from work done in the protected zone. Thus, material such as fabric, buttons, and zippers can be sent to Jordan and Israel, where shorts can be cut, sewn and assembled for $5.00 a pair. If those shorts had been made in China, they would have cost $6.40 a pair. In 2004, Steve & Barry's sold 500,000 pairs of Jordanian shorts. You do the math.

Nylon jackets from China typically carry a duty of 28 percent. But the tariff engineer orders a design that uses fabric with a water-resistant coating; this means that the garment can be reclassified as rainwear, for which the duty is as little as 4 percent. The reclassification results in a savings of millions of dollars. Similarly, women's cotton khakis have a duty of 17 percent; synthetic khakis have a duty of 29 percent. Steve & Barry's has their khakis made from more than 50 percent ramie (a strong, stain-resistant natural fiber), for which the duty drops to 3 percent. For 5 million pairs of pants, that means a savings of $3.5 million.

The success Steve & Barry's is enjoying shows that attention to detail and the "headache" of mastering complicated laws can sometimes pay off very well.

Sources: Peter Lattman, "Cheapskates," *Forbes*, July 4, 2005; John Hayes, "Rave Reviews," *Marion Star*, March 24, 2005; Greta Guest, "Steve & Barry's Retail Revolution: The Price Is Right," *Detroit Free Press*, July 26, 2005; "Steve & Barry's University Sportswear Tags GERS Solutions to Improve Retail Operations," Business Wire, January 13, 2006; and Ben Dobbin, "Steve & Barry's Grows with Low-Cost Formula," *Wisconsin State Journal*, January 10, 2006.

in China. CPI won the deal thanks to a strong relationship with small overseas suppliers—a relationship facilitated by frequent e-mail. Dave Hammond, inventor and founder of Wizard Vending, began to push his gum-ball machines into the international market via a Web site. In the site's first year, Hammond sold machines in Austria, Belgium, and Germany, and Internet sales accounted for 10 percent of the company's revenues.

There is an abundance of information about exporting on the Internet. A good place to start is with the Department of Commerce's Bureau of Industry and Security (www.bxa.doc.gov). Other sources of information include the SBA's list of international business resources (www.sba.gov/hotlist/internat.html). The SBA's Export Express loan program provides export financing opportunities for small businesses. The program is designed to finance a variety of needs of small-business exporters, including participation in foreign trade shows, catalog translations for use in foreign markets, lines of credit for export purposes, and real estate and equipment for the production of goods or services to be exported.

### progress assessment

- Why do many small businesses avoid doing business overseas?
- What are some of the advantages small businesses have over large businesses in selling in global markets?

## summary

1. There are many reasons people are willing to take the risks of entrepreneurship.
   - **What are a few of the reasons people start their own businesses?**

   Reasons include profit, independence, opportunity, and challenge.
   - **What are the attributes of successful entrepreneurs?**

   Successful entrepreneurs are self-directed, self-nurturing, action-oriented, highly energetic, and tolerant of uncertainty.
   - **What have modern entrepreneurs done to ensure longer terms of management?**

   They have formed entrepreneurial teams that have expertise in the many different skills needed to start and manage a business.
   - **What is a micropreneur?**

   Micropreneurs are people willing to accept the risk of starting and managing the type of business that remains small, lets them do the kind of work they want to do, and offers them a balanced lifestyle.
   - **What is intrapreneuring?**

   Intrapreneuring is the establishment of entrepreneurial centers within a larger firm where people can innovate and develop new product ideas internally.
   - **Why has there been such an increase in the number of home-based and Web-based businesses in the last few years?**

   The increase in power and decrease in price of computer technology has leveled the field and made it possible for small businesses to compete against larger companies—regardless of location.

1. Explain why people are willing to take the risks of entrepreneurship, list the attributes of successful entrepreneurs, describe the benefits of entrepreneurial teams and intrapreneurs, and explain the growth of home-based and Web-based businesses.

2. Of all the nonfarm businesses in the United States, almost 97 percent are considered small by the Small Business Administration.
   - **Why are *small* businesses important to the U.S. economy?**

   Small business accounts for almost 50 percent of gross domestic product (GDP). Perhaps more important to tomorrow's graduates, 80 percent of American workers' first jobs are in small businesses.
   - **What does the small in small business mean?**

   The Small Business Administration defines a small business as one that is independently owned and operated, not dominant in its field of operation, and meets certain standards of size in terms of employees or sales (depending on the size of others in the industry).
   - **Why do many small businesses fail?**

   Many small businesses fail because of managerial incompetence and inadequate financial planning. See Figure 6.4 (page 162) for a list of causes of business failure.

2. Discuss the importance of small business to the American economy and summarize the major causes of small-business failure.

3. Most people have no idea how to go about starting a small business.
   - **What hints would you give someone who wants to learn about starting a small business?**

   First, learn from others. Take courses and talk with some small-business owners. Second, get some experience working for others. Third, take over a successful firm. Finally, study the latest in small-business management techniques, including the use of computers for things like payroll, inventory control, and mailing lists.

3. Summarize ways to learn about how small businesses operate.

4. Writing a business plan is the first step in organizing a business.
   - **What goes into a business plan?**

   See the box on pages 167–168.

4. Analyze what it takes to start and run a small business.

- **What sources of funds should someone wanting to start a new business consider investigating?**

A new entrepreneur has several sources of capital: personal savings, relatives, former employers, banks, finance companies, venture capital organizations, government agencies, and more.

- **What are some of the special problems that small-business owners have in dealing with employees?**

Small-business owners often have difficulty finding competent employees and grooming employees for management responsibilities.

- **Where can budding entrepreneurs find help in starting their businesses?**

Help can be found from many sources: accountants, lawyers, marketing researchers, loan officers, insurance agents, the SBA, SBDCs, SBICs, and even college professors.

**5.** Outline the advantages and disadvantages small businesses have in entering global markets.

5. The future growth of some small businesses is in foreign markets.

- **What are some advantages small businesses have over large businesses in global markets?**

Foreign buyers enjoy dealing with individuals rather than large corporations because (1) small companies provide a wider variety of suppliers and can ship products more quickly and (2) small companies give more personal service.

- **Why don't more small businesses start trading internationally?**

There are several reasons: (1) Financing is often difficult to find, (2) many people don't know how to get started, (3) many do not understand the cultural differences in foreign markets, and (4) the bureaucratic red tape is often overwhelming.

## key terms

**business plan** 165
**enterprise zones** 158
**entrepreneurial team** 154
**entrepreneurship** 150
**incubators** 159
**intrapreneurs** 158
**market** 170
**micropreneurs** 154
**Service Corps of Retired Executives (SCORE)** 172
**small business** 160
**Small Business Administration (SBA)** 168
**Small Business Investment Company (SBIC) Program** 169
**venture capitalists** 168

## critical thinking questions

1. Do you have the entrepreneurial spirit? What makes you say that?

2. Are there any similarities between the characteristics demanded of an entrepreneur and those of a professional athlete? Would an athlete be a good prospect for entrepreneurship? Why or why not? Could teamwork be important in an entrepreneurial effort?

3. Imagine yourself starting a small business. What kind of business would it be? How much competition is there? What could you do to make your business more attractive than those of competitors? Would you be willing to work 60 to 70 hours a week to make the business successful?

## developing workplace skills

1. Find issues of *Entrepreneur*, *Success*, and *Inc.* magazines in the library or on the Internet. Read about the entrepreneurs who are heading today's dynamic new businesses. Write a profile about one entrepreneur.
2. Select a small business that looks attractive as a career possibility for you. Talk to at least one person who manages such a business. Ask how he or she started the business. Ask about financing; personnel problems (hiring, firing, training, scheduling); accounting problems; and other managerial matters. Prepare a summary of your findings, including whether the job was rewarding, interesting, and challenging—and why or why not.
3. Contact the Small Business Administration by visiting a local office or by going to the organization's website at www.sba.gov. Write a brief summary of the services the SBA offers.
4. Select a small business in your area that has failed. List the factors you think led to its failure. Compile a list of actions the business owners might have taken to keep the company in business.
5. Choose a partner from among your classmates and put together a list of factors that might mean the difference between success and failure of a new company entering the business software industry. Can small start-ups realistically hope to compete with companies such as Microsoft and Intel? Discuss the list and your conclusions in class.

## taking it to the net

### Purpose

To assess your potential to succeed as an entrepreneur and to evaluate a sample business plan.

### Exercise

1. Go to www.bizmove.com/other/quiz.htm and take the interactive entrepreneurial quiz to find out if you have the qualities to be a successful entrepreneur.

2. If you have entrepreneurial traits and decide you would like to start your own business, you will need to develop a business plan. Go to www.quicken.com/small business/cch/tools/retailer.rtf and review the business plan for Joe's Redhots. Although Joe's plan does not follow the same format as the business plan outline on pages 167–168, does it contain all of the necessary information listed in the outline? If not, what is missing?

## casing the web

To access the case *"BMOC; Starting a Small Business at School,"* visit **www.mhhe.com/ub8e**

## video case

### Are You Still Going Around with that Old Bag?

Entrepreneurs provide 80 percent of entry-level jobs and contribute almost half to the Gross Domestic Product. However, many people are reluctant to start their own businesses because there is too much risk and uncertainty. One person who did assume the risk is Jennifer Velarde. Like all entrepreneurs, Velarde saw a marketing opportunity—in her case, accessories for women. Velarde thinks that one of the most important accessories is the handbag a woman carries. It can make a statement, show her taste. Velarde made sketches of unusual bags while she was still employed elsewhere, but didn't feel that she had full freedom of expression where she worked. Eventually she decided to go out on her own and make customized handbags.

Velarde made 20 finished bags and took them to a street fair in Chicago. It occurred to her that if she sold the bags quickly she would have no inventory left to sell to others. Therefore, she began taking orders and produced the bags later. That became the model for the company: Learn what people want first, and make the bags later.

Imagine this. You want a handbag that says YOU. You want it to be original, different, exciting, new, and eye catching. You have some idea in mind of what it should look like, but can't find anything that meets your needs. And then you step into Velarde's store called 1154 LILL. (Why that name? Because that was the address of Velarde's first home of her own in Chicago where she sewed her first customized handbags.) Anyhow, you see about 20 handbag designs to choose from, and a few look interesting, but you would just love to make some personal changes to have the handbag meet your exact specifications. You're in luck because that's exactly what you can do at 1154 LILL. You can choose the lining color, the external fabric, and the handle you want. In short, you can have a handbag that is just the way you want it.

You don't have to go to a 1154 LILL store to design your own bag. Velarde learned the value of handbag home parties early on. A LILL associate will come to your home or office armed with fabrics and bag samples. Velarde believes her customized handbags are not her only product. Her product offer is the full "LILL Experience" that is created when you visit one of her stores, attend a handbag party, or order online. The LILL experience is now available in 25 cities across the country.

Getting started in business is one thing. Learning how to grow is quite another. One place to turn for help is the Small Business Administration. For example, the SBA led Velarde to an accountant to do payroll taxes. Naturally, you will need employees to help grow the business. Velarde started with a childhood friend. But the two of them couldn't make the bags fast enough, so they had to outsource that task to others. Eventually, Velarde had to hire more artists and salespeople to help market the bags. In some ways, such employees are mini-entrepreneurs because they too have to take the risk of working for a small firm. However, they too enjoy the freedom and opportunity that goes along with such work.

One soon learns, when starting a small business, that there is technology out there that can make the job a lot easier; things like computers, the Internet, and Web pages. There are also people with marketing skills who can take such products to unexpected places—like in the home—and make the business grow. "Bag parties," like many home-based selling ideas, have become a big success.

What can you learn from Velarde? First, you need a business plan that outlines the money you will need, the personnel you will need, and so forth. Second, you need to establish upfront how much time you will spend with the business. It could be 24/7 if you let it. You must build in time for family, friends, travel, and self. There are many reasons to start a small business; that is, to become an entrepreneur. They include the freedom to do your own thing and see it to completion, to follow your passion, to do what's fun for you, and, of course, you can make a lot of money.

### Thinking It Over

1. Velarde has not done much business with overseas companies, either buying or selling. Do you see her doing so in the future? Why or why not?
2. Does the story of 1154 Lill encourage you to be an entrepreneur yourself some day? Where might you begin? Whom might you seek for help?
3. What other accessories might women want to help design themselves? Do you see the opportunity for another such business? Could it be an extension of this business? Where might you look for ideas?
4. What do you see as the advantages and disadvantages of working for others rather than starting your own business?

# management, leadership, AND employee empowerment

*

profile

**Getting to Know**

**X** Oprah Winfrey,

**Businesswoman and TV Personality**

Oprah Winfrey is one of the most famous women in the world. She was born in Kosciusko, Mississippi. When she was young, she lived in a home with no electricity or running water. Her name was supposed to be Orpah, after the daughter-in-law of Naomi in the Bible. It turned out that her name was spelled wrong on her birth certificate, so it became Oprah. Now Oprah is much more famous than Orpah.

Oprah went to Tennessee State University and majored in speech communications. After some earlier work, she went to a TV station in Baltimore, Maryland. The station bosses wanted her to change her hair, nose, and just about everything else. Not surprisingly, she wanted to leave Baltimore and host the morning Chicago show. She applied for the job, and not only did they hire her, but they let Oprah be Oprah. The name of the show was changed from *A.M. Chicago* to *The Oprah Winfrey Show.* Oprah went on from there to become the nation's first female African American billionaire.

Oprah's biggest source of wealth is Harpo Inc. (*Harpo* is *Oprah* spelled backward.) *The Oprah Winfrey Show* reaches millions of viewers and is the number one daytime television talk show in the United States. *O*, the Oprah magazine, was the most successful magazine launch ever. It is now in its fifth year.

So, what is Oprah's management style? How does she stay so successful? If you were to ask Oprah what her management style is, she would hesitate to say because she just tries to be herself and trusts others to manage her affairs. In many ways, Oprah displays the characteristics of today's progressive managers. She is more a leader than a manager. She sets the tone and direction of her enterprises. She is flexible and sees opportunities as they arise. For example, she was able to get Pontiac to donate 276 cars to give away at the beginning of her 19th season. Pontiac wanted to promote its new sports sedan, so Oprah struck a deal. Both Oprah and Pontiac got lots and lots of publicity because of this giveaway.

She doesn't believe much in long-range planning but is quick to seize an opportunity when it comes. Her message is "You are responsible for your own life." Few people model that belief system better than Oprah herself. Although Oprah tends to use a manage-by-instinct style herself, she works closely with others—like Jeff Jacobs, the president of

## LEARNING goals

After you have read and studied this chapter, you should be able to

1. Explain how the changes that are occurring in the business environment are affecting the management function.
2. Describe the four functions of management.
3. Relate the planning process and decision making to the accomplishment of company goals.
4. Describe the organizing function of management.
5. Explain the differences between leaders and managers, and describe the various leadership styles.
6. Summarize the five steps of the control function of management.

CHAPTER 7

Harpo—who have a more traditional managerial style. While Oprah enables others to make operational decisions, she is very involved in the content of her shows and her magazine. She reads every word in the magazine before it comes out and looks closely at every photo. That's why she was so harsh on James Frey whose book she had promoted. She forced Frey to tell the truth about *"A Million Little Pieces"* to restore integrity and honesty to her show.

Oprah has donated 10 percent of her annual income to charity most of her adult life. Most of her giving is done anonymously. She focuses on three causes: women, children, and education. In everything she does, Oprah's goal is to do better. Her rise to success has been so rapid that she hasn't had much time to sit down and create a vision for her future, but she has had an internal vision that has suited her well so far.

In this chapter, you will read about management and the changes occurring in that area. Like Oprah, most managers today are flexible and open to new ideas. They see opportunity and act much faster than they did in the past. They tend to give their workers more responsibility and authority and act more like leaders (visionaries) than hands-on managers who tell people what to do and how to do it.

Sources: Patricia Sellers, "The Business of Being Oprah," *Fortune*, April 1, 2001, pp. 50 ff.; Tara Burghart, "Oprah's Car Giveaway Hailed as Marketing Coup," *Enquirer*, September 15, 2004; "Oprah Winfrey," www.achievement.org/autodoc/page/winOpro-1, February 5, 2005; "Winfrey," *Television Week*, January 17, 2005; and Jonathan Darman, "The Wrath of Oprah," *Newsweek*, February 6, 2006, pp. 42–43.

## MANAGERS' ROLES ARE EVOLVING

Managers must practice the art of getting things done through organizational resources (e.g., workers, financial resources, information, and equipment). At one time, managers were called bosses, and their job consisted of telling people what to do and watching over them to be sure they did it. Bosses tended to reprimand those who didn't do things correctly and generally acted stern. Many managers still behave that way. Perhaps you've witnessed such behavior.[1]

Today, management is more progressive. Oprah Winfrey is just one example. Such managers are educated to guide, train, support, motivate, and coach employees rather than to tell them what to do.[2] There is much more emphasis on working in teams and team building. Managers of high-tech firms realize that workers often know much more about technology than they do. Thus, most modern managers emphasize teamwork and cooperation rather than discipline and order giving.[3] Managers in some high-tech firms and in progressive firms of all kinds tend to be friendly, and generally treat employees as partners rather than unruly workers.

**management**
The process used to accomplish organizational goals through planning, organizing, leading, and controlling people and other organizational resources.

In the past, a worker would expect to work for the same company for many years, maybe even a lifetime. Similarly, companies would hire people and keep them for a long time. Today, many companies don't hesitate to lay off employees, and employees don't hesitate to leave if their needs are not being met. Today's top leaders of Fortune 100 companies are younger, more of them are female, and fewer of them were educated at elite universities. They tend to move from one company to another as their careers unfold.[4] Traditional long-term contracts between management and employees—and the accompanying trust—are often no longer there. This increases the difficulty of the management task because managers must earn the trust of their employees, which includes listening to them, rewarding them, and finding ways to encourage them to stay in the firm.

In general, management is experiencing a revolution. Managers in the future are likely to be working in teams and to be assuming completely new roles in the firm. Furthermore, they will be doing more expansion overseas (see the Reaching Beyond Our Borders box). We'll discuss these roles and the differences between managers and leaders in detail later in the chapter.

What this means for you and other graduates of tomorrow is that management will demand a new kind of person: a skilled communicator and team player as well as a planner, coordinator, organizer, and supervisor. These trends will be addressed in the next few chapters to help you decide whether management is the kind of career you would like.

Today's employees tend to be younger and more aware of job alternatives. Companies such as Yahoo! have adapted by making the workplace more open and comfortable for multitaskers. What kind of perks would appeal to you the most?

## FUNCTIONS OF MANAGEMENT

Managers give direction to their organizations, provide leadership, and decide how to use organizational resources to accomplish goals.[5] Such descriptions give you some idea of what managers do. In addition to those tasks, managers today must deal with conflict resolution, create trust in an atmosphere where trust has been badly shaken, and help create balance between work lives and family lives.[6] Managers look at the big picture, and their decisions make a major difference in organizations.[7] The following definition provides the outline of this chapter: **Management** is the process used to accomplish organizational goals through planning,

www.disney.com

## REACHING BEYOND our borders

### Mickey Mouse Brings the Magic to China

Sometimes opportunities overseas seem very promising when compared with domestic growth. Take the Walt Disney Company, for example. There are 290 million people under the age of 14 in China—more potential Mousketeers than the entire U.S. population. You can see, then, why Disney president Robert Iger went to China to promote Winnie-the-Pooh books and Disney products in general. Part of the attraction was to take basketball star Yao Ming and other NBA stars with him. It is not easy doing business in China, however. American managers must deal with cultural, regulatory, and other barriers to succeed.

Despite the managerial obstacles, Disney opened its Hong Kong theme park in 2005 and hopes to open another one in Shanghai, China. Some 70 percent of overseas sales now come from slow-growing Europe, and Iger wants to expand into fast-growing regions like China and India. But the challenges are sometimes daunting. For example, the Mickey Mouse Club must be called the Dragon Club and there are many other restrictions on the use of Chinese TV for American firms. To break into the culture, Disney has teamed up with the 70-million-member Communist Youth League to build reading skills and creativity. Disney performers tell stories and encourage children to draw pictures of Mickey Mouse and other Disney characters. Disney's *The Lion King* was the first foreign film released in China. Since then, the company has introduced many other films, including *Toy Story* and *Finding Nemo.* What other problems do you think Disney management might face when trying to introduce Disney theme parks and products in other countries?

Source: Clay Chandler, "Mickey Mao," *Fortune*, April 18, 2005, pp. 170–178; G. Pascal Zachary, "Making It in China," *Business 2.0*, August 2005, pp. 59–66; and Bay Fang, "Spending Spree," *U.S. News & World Report*, May 1, 2006, pp. 43–50.

organizing, leading, and controlling people and other organizational resources (see Figure 7.1).

**Planning** includes anticipating trends and determining the best strategies and tactics to achieve organizational goals and objectives. One of those

**Planning**
- Setting organizational goals.
- Developing strategies to reach those goals.
- Determining resources needed.
- Setting precise standards.

**Organizing**
- Allocating resources, assigning tasks, and establishing procedures for accomplishing goals.
- Preparing a structure (organization chart) showing lines of authority and responsibility.
- Recruiting, selecting, training, and developing employees.
- Placing employees where they'll be most effective.

**Leading**
- Guiding and motivating employees to work effectively to accomplish organizational goals and objectives.
- Giving assignments.
- Explaining routines.
- Clarifying policies.
- Providing feedback on performance.

**Controlling**
- Measuring results against corporate objectives.
- Monitoring performance relative to standards.
- Rewarding outstanding performance.
- Taking corrective action when necessary.

figure 7.1

**WHAT MANAGERS DO**

Some modern managers perform all of these tasks with the full cooperation and participation of workers. Empowering employees means allowing them to participate more fully in decision making.

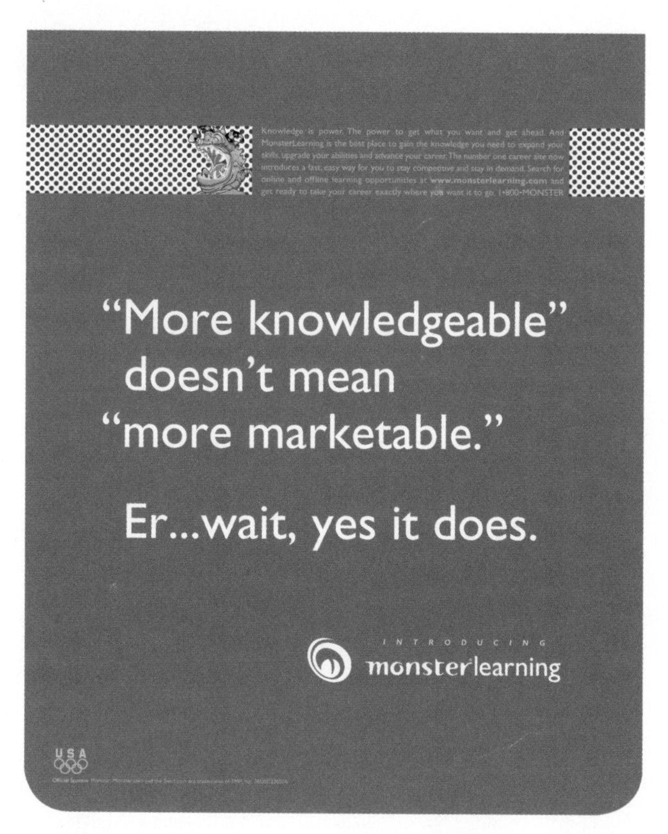


Many of today's workers are called "knowledge workers" because they have the education and skill to compete with companies anywhere in the world. Much of that learning comes from community colleges, universities, and online learning centers of all kinds. What skills will make you more competitive in tomorrow's job market?

**planning**
A management function that includes anticipating trends and determining the best strategies and tactics to achieve organizational goals and objectives.

**organizing**
A management function that includes designing the structure of the organization and creating conditions and systems in which everyone and everything work together to achieve the organization's goals and objectives.

objectives is to please customers.[8] The trend today is to have *planning teams* to help monitor the environment, find business opportunities, and watch for challenges. Planning is a key management function because the other functions depend heavily on having a good plan.

**Organizing** includes designing the structure of the organization and creating conditions and systems in which everyone and everything work together to achieve the organization's goals and objectives.[9] Many of today's organizations are being designed around the customer. The idea is to design the firm so that everyone is working to please the customer at a profit. Thus, organizations must remain flexible and adaptable because customer needs change, and organizations must either change along with them or risk losing their business. General Motors, for example, has lost much of its customer base to manufacturers of more fuel-efficient cars.[10] It hopes to win back market share by offering hydrogen-powered vehicles that could save consumers much money for fuel.[11]

**Leading** means creating a vision for the organization and communicating, guiding, training, coaching, and motivating others to work effectively to achieve the organization's goals and objectives. The trend is to empower employees, giving them as much freedom as possible to become self-directed and self-motivated. This function was once known as *directing*; that is, telling employees exactly what to do. In many smaller firms, that is still the role of managers. In most large modern firms, however, managers no longer tell people exactly what to do because knowledge workers and others often know how to do their jobs better than the manager does. Nonetheless, leadership is necessary to keep employees focused on the right tasks at the right time along with training, coaching, motivating, and the other leadership tasks.[12]

**Controlling** involves establishing clear standards to determine whether an organization is progressing toward its goals and objectives, rewarding people for doing a good job, and taking corrective action if they are not. Basically, it means measuring whether what actually occurs meets the organization's goals.

The four functions just addressed—planning, organizing, leading, and controlling—are the heart of management, so let's explore them in more detail. The process begins with planning; we'll look at that right after the Progress Assessment.

### progress assessment

- What are some of the changes happening in management today?
- What's the definition of *management* used in this chapter?
- What are the four functions of management?

## PLANNING: CREATING A VISION BASED ON VALUES

Planning, the first managerial function, involves setting the organizational vision, goals, and objectives. Executives rate planning as the most valuable tool in their workbench. Part of the planning process involves the creation of a vision for the organization. A **vision** is more than a goal; it's an encompassing explanation of why the organization exists and where it's trying to go. A vision gives the organization a sense of purpose and a set of values that, together, unite workers in a common destiny. Managing an organization without first establishing a vision can be counterproductive. It's like motivating everyone in a rowboat to get excited about going somewhere, but not telling them exactly where. As a result, the boat will just keep changing directions rather than speeding toward an agreed-on goal.

Usually employees work with managers to design a **mission statement**, which is an outline of the organization's fundamental purposes.[13] A meaningful mission statement should address:

- The organization's self-concept.
- Company philosophy and goals.
- Long-term survival.
- Customer needs.
- Social responsibility.
- The nature of the company's product or service.

Figure 7.2 contains Starbucks' mission statement. How well does Starbucks address all of the issues listed above?

The mission statement becomes the foundation for setting specific goals and selecting and motivating employees. **Goals** are the broad, long-term accomplishments an organization wishes to attain. Goals need to be mutually agreed on by workers and management. Thus, goal setting is often a team process.

**Objectives** are specific, short-term statements detailing how to achieve the organization's goals. One of your goals for reading this chapter, for example, may be to learn basic concepts of management. An objective you could use to achieve this goal is to answer correctly the chapter's Progress Assessment questions. Objectives must be measurable. For example, you can measure your progress in answering questions by determining what percentage you answer correctly over time.

Planning is a continuous process. It's unlikely that a plan that worked yesterday would be successful in today's market. Most planning follows a pattern. The procedure you would follow in planning your life and career is basically the same as that used by businesses for their plans. Planning answers several fundamental questions for businesses:

1. What is the situation now? What is the state of the economy and other environments? What opportunities exist for meeting people's needs? What products and customers are most profitable? Why do people buy

**leading**
Creating a vision for the organization and guiding, training, coaching, and motivating others to work effectively to achieve the organization's goals and objectives.

**controlling**
A management function that involves establishing clear standards to determine whether or not an organization is progressing toward its goals and objectives, rewarding people for doing a good job, and taking corrective action if they are not.

**vision**
An encompassing explanation of why the organization exists and where it's trying to head.

**mission statement**
An outline of the fundamental purposes of an organization.

**goals**
The broad, long-term accomplishments an organization wishes to attain.

**objectives**
Specific, short-term statements detailing how to achieve the organization's goals.

figure 7.2

**STARBUCKS' MISSION STATEMENT**

To establish Starbucks as the premier purveyor of the finest coffee in the world while maintaining our uncompromising principles as we grow. The following six guiding principles will help us measure the appropriateness of our decisions:

- Provide a great work environment and treat each other with dignity and respect.
- Embrace diversity as an essential component in the way we do business.
- Apply the highest of standards in excellence to the purchasing, roasting, and fresh delivery of our coffee.
- Develop enthusiastically satisfied customers all of the time.
- Contribute positively to our community and our environment.
- Recognize that profitability is essential to our future success.

DEALING WITH change

www.target.com

## Hitting the Retail Bull's-Eye

Target is certainly one of the success stories of the recent past. It has the reputation that Sears, Kmart, and other large retailers once had. As the competition slows, Target management seems to be finding the right path to success. For one thing, Target managers have found a market niche for its online sales. Stores are good for buying items for yourself, but Web sites are often better for finding gifts for someone else. Therefore, management decided to go to the Web. Target.com aims at people who need to buy gifts. One fall, for example, Target.com sold thousands of Student Survival Kits to parents and other relatives of returning students. Some 22 percent of the site's sales come from bridal and baby registries. By responding quickly to such market opportunities, Target managers can keep the company in the vanguard. Soon management will add Target's sister store, Mervyn's, to its Web site. Target is also allied with Amazon.com. In short, Target seems to be on target when it comes to adapting to the Internet challenge. In this area, Target's success seems comparable to that of Wal-Mart.

What about the challenge of Wal-Mart in the area of superstores? Here Target management has been less successful. Target's superstores are less productive than its regular stores. Was it a mistake to go after Wal-Mart's supercenters? Wal-Mart has its own grocery warehouses, giving it a cost advantage. Target could create its own distribution centers to become more competitive, but that is dangerous ground. Such centers are costly. Adapting to change is never easy, but adapting to Wal-Mart is truly daunting.

Target has its own image and its own customer base. Sometimes change is good and sometimes it's not. By listening to its customer base and responding appropriately, Target's managers should be able to expand and increase profits. That may mean sticking to what Target knows best and not venturing out into Wal-Mart's strengths. It may not. That's the future challenge for Target's managers.

Sources: Jim Collins, "Bigger, Better, Faster," *Fast Company,* June 2003, pp. 74–78; www.Target.com, 2006; and Michael Barbaro, "Pinch Me—Is That a Wal-Mart?," *Washington Post*, August 7, 2005, pp. Fl and F6.

**SWOT analysis**
A planning tool used to analyze an organization's strengths, weaknesses, opportunities, and threats.

(or not buy) our products? Who are our major competitors? What threats are they to our business? These questions are part of what is called **SWOT analysis**, which is an analysis of the organization's **s**trengths, **w**eaknesses, **o**pportunities, and **t**hreats. The company begins such a process with an analysis of the business environment in general. Then it identifies strengths and weaknesses. Finally, as a result of the environmental analysis, it identifies opportunities and threats. These are often external to the firm and cannot always be anticipated. The Dealing with Change box discusses one company's strengths and weaknesses, and Figure 7.3 lists some of the potential issues companies consider when conducting a SWOT analysis: Where do we want to go? How much growth do we want? What is our profit goal? What are our social objectives? What are our personal development objectives?

2. How can we get there from here? This is the most important part of planning. It takes four forms: strategic, tactical, operational, and contingency (see Figure 7.4).

**strategic planning**
The process of determining the major goals of the organization and the policies and strategies for obtaining and using resources to achieve those goals.

**Strategic planning** determines the major goals of the organization. It provides the foundation for the policies, procedures, and strategies for obtaining and using resources to achieve those goals. In this definition, policies are broad guides to action, and strategies determine the best way to use resources. At the strategic planning stage, the company decides which customers to serve,

| Potential Internal STRENGTHS | Potential Internal WEAKNESSES |
| --- | --- |
| • Core competencies in key areas<br>• An acknowledged market leader<br>• Well-conceived functional area strategies<br>• Proven management<br>• Cost advantages<br>• Better advertising campaigns | • No clear strategic direction<br>• Obsolete facilities<br>• Subpar profitability<br>• Lack of managerial depth and talent<br>• Weak market image<br>• Too narrow a product line |
| **Potential External OPPORTUNITIES** | **Potential External THREATS** |
| • Ability to serve additional customer groups<br>• Expand product lines<br>• Ability to transfer skills/technology to new products<br>• Falling trade barriers in attractive foreign markets<br>• Complacency among rival firms<br>• Ability to grow due to increases in market demand | • Entry of lower-cost foreign competitors<br>• Rising sales of substitute products<br>• Slower market growth<br>• Costly regulatory requirements<br>• Vulnerability to recession and business cycles<br>• Changing buyer needs and tastes |

figure 7.3

**SWOT MATRIX**

This matrix identifies potential strengths, weaknesses, opportunities, and threats organizations may consider in a SWOT analysis.

what products or services to sell, and the geographic areas in which the firm will compete.[14] For example, GM is going through the painful process of deciding which products to keep and which to cut.[15] Its poor decision making in the past has had disastrous consequences.

In today's rapidly changing environment, strategic planning is becoming more difficult because changes are occurring so fast that plans—even those set for just months into the future—may soon be obsolete.[16] Therefore, some companies are making shorter-term plans that allow for quick responses to customer needs and requests.[17] The goal is to be flexible and responsive to the market.

**Tactical planning** is the process of developing detailed, short-term statements about what is to be done, who is to do it, and how it is to be done. Tactical planning is normally done by managers or teams of managers at *lower* levels of the organization, whereas strategic planning is done by the *top* managers of the firm (e.g., the president and vice presidents of the organization). Tactical planning, for example, involves setting annual budgets and deciding on other details and activities necessary to meet the strategic objectives. If the strategic plan of a truck manufacturer, for example, is to sell more trucks in

**tactical planning**
The process of developing detailed, short-term statements about what is to be done, who is to do it, and how it is to be done.

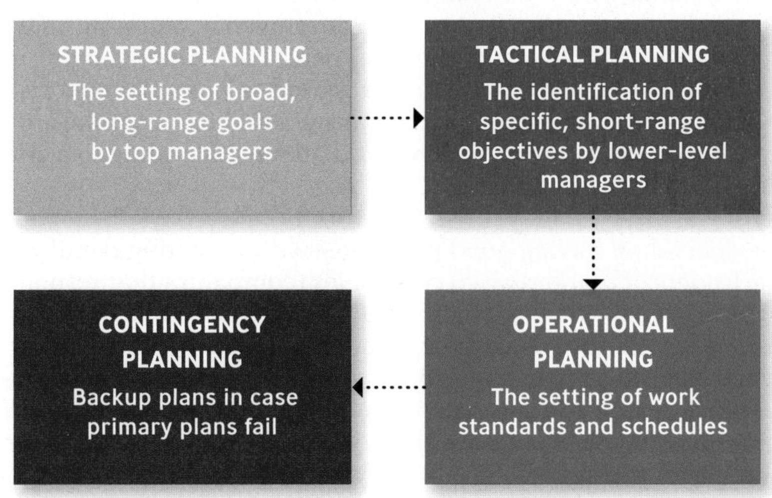


figure 7.4

**PLANNING FUNCTIONS**

Very few firms bother to make contingency plans. If something changes the market, such companies may be slow to respond. Most organizations do strategic, tactical, and operational planning.

SPOTLIGHT ON small business

## On-the-Fly Decision Making after Hurricane Katrina

Julie Rodriguez bought her father's oil-field service business in Harvey, Louisiana, in 1991. The company, Epic Divers & Marine, repairs offshore pipelines and platforms, the kind that were destroyed by Hurricane Katrina. The company suffered severe damage from the storm, and many of the employees were left homeless. Working below water is always dangerous, but now the workers were stressed by their situations at home as well as at work.

Whether they worked or not the two weeks following Katrina, Rodriguez kept everyone on the payroll. Long-range planning was no longer an option for her. She faced many short-term issues: Would the office be torn down? When would employees be allowed to come back to Jefferson Parish? Where would she be working next week? Rodriguez needed a contingency plan to move to another building if her building could not be repaired in a reasonable amount of time.

Management is often like that. You think you have the situation under control, and suddenly the whole world has changed. Rodriguez found that participative leadership was best under such circumstances. She had learned over time that managing a firm is more a matter of listening and responding to workers than telling them what to do. Change brings opportunities: Many companies were calling for Rodriguez's help. But change also brings tremendous challenges, especially for a small business. Rodriguez had to make employment decisions, building decisions, and other managerial decisions on the fly. She hopes that the tragedy will lead to more collaboration and camaraderie. She has long empowered employees to do what they feel best, and that is helping the company through this crisis. Such situations make managing a small business a challenging endeavor.

Source: Lucas Conley, "25 Top Women Business Leaders, #11: Julie Rodriguez," *Fast Company*, May 2005, p. 72; Chuck Salter, "It's Never Been This Hard," *Fast Company*, November 2005, pp. 72–79; and Jon Birger, "Man on a Mission," *Fortune*, April 3, 2006, pp. 86–92.

**operational planning**
The process of setting work standards and schedules necessary to implement the company's tactical objectives.

**contingency planning**
The process of preparing alternative courses of action that may be used if the primary plans don't achieve the organization's objectives.

the South, the tactical plan might be to fund more research of southern truck drivers' wants and needs, and to plan advertising to reach those people.

**Operational planning** is the process of setting work standards and schedules necessary to implement the company's tactical objectives. Whereas strategic planning looks at the organization as a whole, operational planning focuses on specific supervisors, department managers, and individual employees. The operational plan is the department manager's tool for daily and weekly operations. An operational plan may include, say, the specific dates for certain truck parts to be completed and the quality specifications those parts must meet.

**Contingency planning** is the process of preparing alternative courses of action that may be used if the primary plans don't achieve the organization's objectives. The economic and competitive environments change so rapidly that it's wise to have alternative plans of action ready in anticipation of such changes. For example, if an organization doesn't meet its sales goals by a certain date, the contingency plan may call for more advertising or a cut in prices at that time. Crisis planning is a part of contingency planning that involves reacting to sudden changes in the environment. For example, many cities and businesses are now developing plans to respond to potential terrorist attacks. You can imagine how important such plans would be to hospitals, the police, and other such organizations. You can read about responding to a crisis in the Spotlight on Small Business box.

Planning is a key management function because the other management functions depend on having good plans. Instead of creating detailed strategic plans, the leaders of market-based companies (companies that respond quickly to changes in competition or to other environmental changes) set direction. The idea is to stay flexible, listen to customers, and seize opportunities when they come, whether or not those opportunities were expected.[18] The opportunities, however, must fit into the company's overall goals and objectives or the company could lose its focus. Clearly, then, much of management and planning involves decision making.

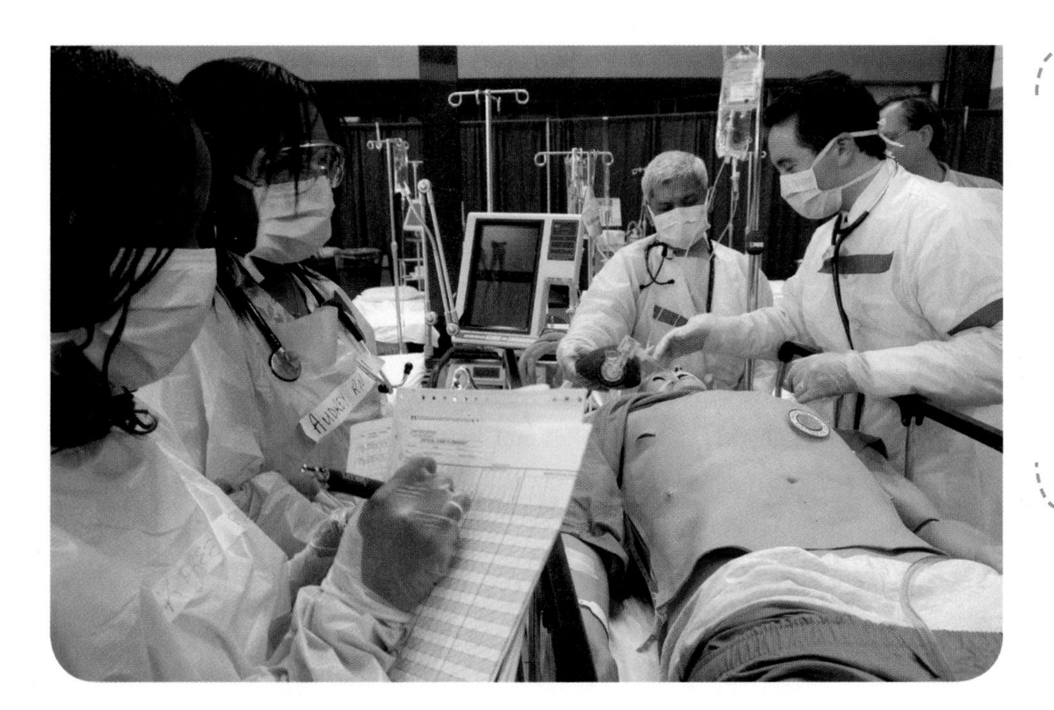

All organizations need to have contingency plans for unexpected events. Note the chaos in New Orleans when hospitals and other organizations were not prepared for a major hurricane. This photo shows a hospital preparing for a terrorist attack. What responsibilities do you have, as a citizen, to prepare for a terrorist attack or some other major emergency?

## Decision Making: Finding the Best Alternative

All management functions involve some kind of decision making.[19] **Decision making** is choosing among two or more alternatives. It sounds easier here than it is in practice. In fact, decision making is the heart of all the management functions. The rational decision-making model is a series of steps managers often follow to make logical, intelligent, and well-founded decisions.[20] These steps can be thought of as the seven Ds of decision making:

**decision making**
Choosing among two or more alternatives.

1. Define the situation.
2. Describe and collect needed information.
3. Develop alternatives.
4. Develop agreement among those involved.
5. Decide which alternative is best.
6. Do what is indicated (begin implementation).
7. Determine whether the decision was a good one and follow up.

Managers don't always go through this seven-step process. Sometimes decisions have to be made *on the spot—with little information available*. Managers must make good decisions in all such circumstances. **Problem solving** is the process of solving the everyday problems that occur. It is less formal than the decision-making process and usually calls for quicker action. Problem-solving teams are made up of two or more workers who are given an assignment to solve a specific problem (e.g., Why are customers not using our service policies?). Problem-solving techniques that companies use include **brainstorming** (i.e., coming up with as many solutions as possible in a short period of time with no censoring of ideas) and **PMI** (i.e., listing all the **p**luses for a solution in one column, all the **m**inuses in another, and the **i**mplications in a third column). You can practice using the PMI system on almost all of your decisions to get some practice. For example, should you stay home and study tonight? You would list all the benefits of your choice (pluses) in one column: better grades, more self-esteem, more responsible, and so on. In the other column, you would

**problem solving**
The process of solving the everyday problems that occur. Problem solving is less formal than decision making and usually calls for quicker action.

**brainstorming**
Coming up with as many solutions to a problem as possible in a short period of time with no censoring of ideas.

**PMI**
Listing all the pluses for a solution in one column, all the minuses in another, and the implications in a third column.

put the negatives (minuses): boredom, less fun, and so on. We hope that the pluses outweigh the minuses most of the time and that you study often. But sometimes it is best to go out and have some fun. In that case the implications would be that having fun would not hurt your grades or job prospects.

**progress assessment**

- What's the difference between goals and objectives?
- What does a company analyze when it does a SWOT analysis?
- What's the difference between strategic, tactical, and operational planning?
- What are the seven Ds in decision making?

**organization chart**
A visual device that shows relationships among people and divides the organization's work; it shows who is accountable for the completion of specific work and who reports to whom.

**top management**
Highest level of management, consisting of the president and other key company executives who develop strategic plans.

## ORGANIZING: CREATING A UNIFIED SYSTEM

After managers have planned a course of action, they must organize the firm to accomplish their goals. Operationally, organizing means allocating resources (such as funds for various departments), assigning tasks, and establishing procedures for accomplishing the organizational objectives. An **organization chart** is a visual device that shows relationships among people and divides the organization's work; it shows who is accountable for the completion of specific work and who reports to whom (see Figure 7.5).

**Top management** (the highest level of management) consists of the president and other key company executives who develop strategic plans. Terms you're likely to see often are chief executive officer (CEO), chief operating officer (COO), chief financial officer (CFO), and chief information officer (CIO) or (in some companies) chief knowledge officer (CKO). The CEO is often the president of the firm and is responsible for all top-level decisions in the firm.

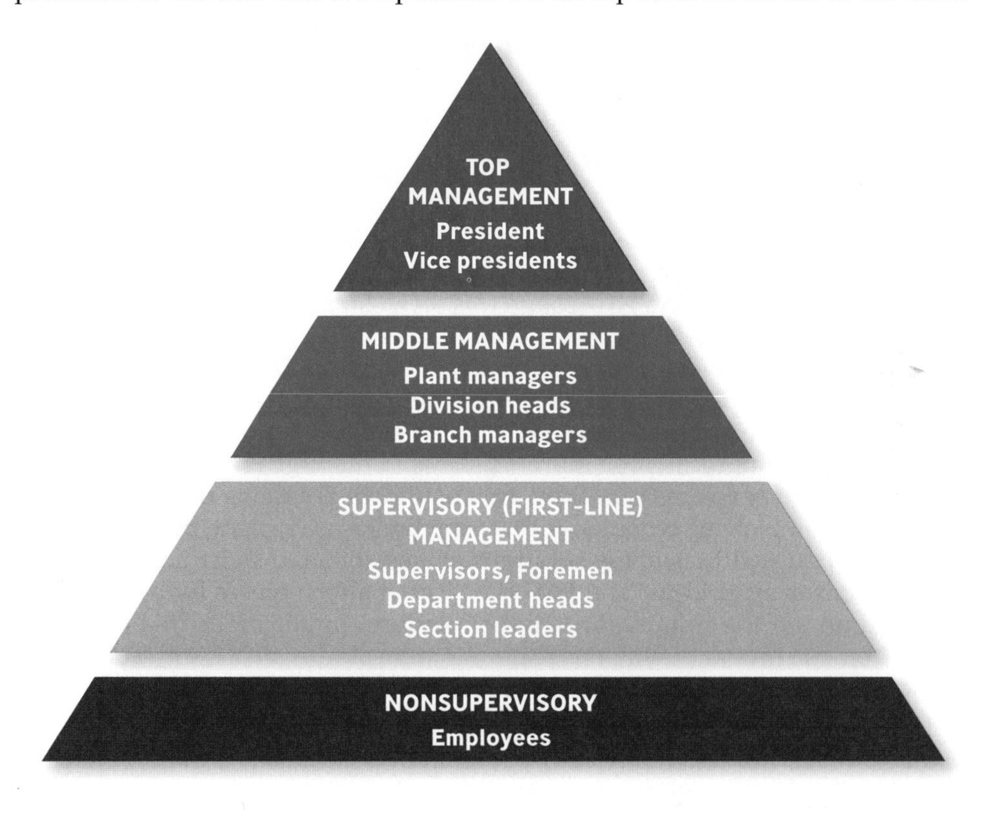


figure 7.5

**LEVELS OF MANAGEMENT**

This figure shows the three levels of management. In many firms, there are several levels of middle management. Recently, however, firms have been eliminating middle-level managers because fewer are needed to oversee self-managed teams of employees.

CEOs are responsible for introducing change into an organization. The COO is responsible for putting those changes into effect. His or her tasks include structuring work, controlling operations, and rewarding people to ensure that everyone strives to carry out the leader's vision. Many companies today are eliminating the COO function as a cost-cutting measure and are assigning that role to the CEO.[21] Often, the CFO participates in the decision to cut the COO position. The CFO is responsible for obtaining funds, planning budgets, collecting funds, and so on. The CIO or CKO is responsible for getting the right information to other managers so they can make correct decisions.

**Middle management** includes general managers, division managers, and branch and plant managers (in colleges, deans and department heads) who are responsible for tactical planning and controlling. Many firms have eliminated some middle managers through downsizing, and have given the remaining managers more employees to supervise.

**middle management**
The level of management that includes general managers, division managers, and branch and plant managers who are responsible for tactical planning and controlling.

**Supervisory management** includes those who are directly responsible for supervising workers and evaluating their daily performance; they're often known as first-line managers (or supervisors) because they're the first level above workers.[22]

**supervisory management**
Managers who are directly responsible for supervising workers and evaluating their daily performance.

## Tasks and Skills at Different Levels of Management

Few people are trained to be good managers. Usually a person learns how to be a skilled accountant or sales representative or production-line worker, and then—because of his or her skill—is selected to be a manager. The tendency is for such managers to become deeply involved in showing others how to do things, helping them, supervising them, and generally being very active in the operating task.

The further up the managerial ladder a person moves, the less important his or her original job skills become. At the top of the ladder, the need is for people who are visionaries, planners, organizers, coordinators, communicators,

"... GO AHEAD,... ASK ME ANYTHING..."

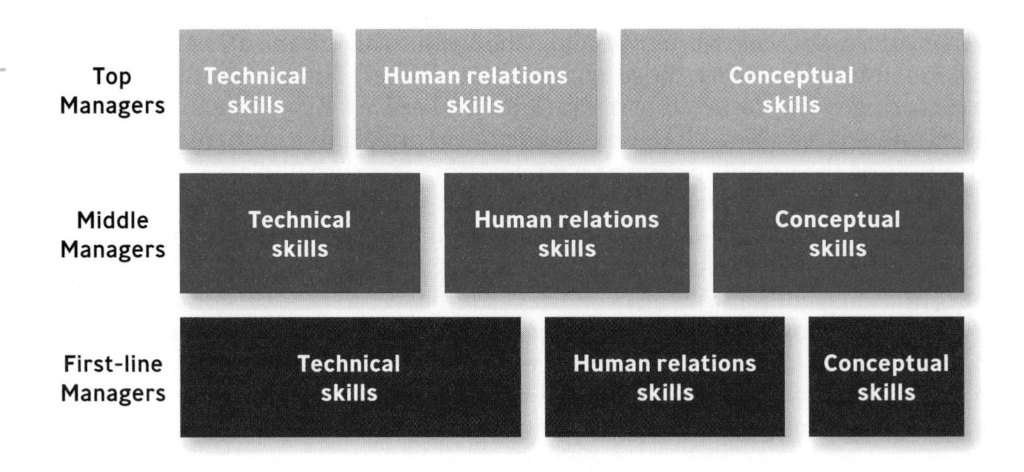


figure 7.6

**SKILLS NEEDED AT VARIOUS LEVELS OF MANAGEMENT**

All managers need human relations skills. At the top, managers need strong conceptual skills and rely less on technical skills. First-line managers need strong technical skills and rely less on conceptual skills. Middle managers need to have a balance between technical and conceptual skills.

morale builders, and motivators. Figure 7.6 shows that a manager must have three categories of skills:

**technical skills**
Skills that involve the ability to perform tasks in a specific discipline or department.

**human relations skills**
Skills that involve communication and motivation; they enable managers to work through and with people.

**conceptual skills**
Skills that involve the ability to picture the organization as a whole and the relationship among its various parts.

1. **Technical skills** involve the ability to perform tasks in a specific discipline (such as selling a product or developing software) or department (such as marketing or information systems).
2. **Human relations skills** involve communication and motivation; they enable managers to work through and with people. Such skills also include those associated with leadership, coaching, morale building, delegating, training and development, and help and supportiveness.
3. **Conceptual skills** involve the ability to picture the organization as a whole and the relationships among its various parts. Conceptual skills are needed in planning, organizing, controlling, systems development, problem analysis, decision making, coordinating, and delegating.

Looking at Figure 7.6, you'll notice that first-line managers need to be skilled in all three areas. However, most of their time is spent on technical and human relations tasks (assisting operating personnel, giving directions, etc.). First-line managers spend little time on conceptual tasks. Top managers, in contrast, need to use few technical skills. Instead, almost all of their time is devoted to human relations and conceptual tasks. A person who is competent at a low level of management may not be competent at higher levels, and vice versa. The skills needed are different at different levels.

## The Stakeholder-Oriented Organization

A dominating question of the past 20 years or so has been how to best organize a firm to respond to the needs of customers and other stakeholders. Remember, stakeholders include anyone who's affected by the organization and its policies and products. That includes employees, customers, suppliers, dealers, environmental groups, and the surrounding communities. The consensus seems to be that smaller organizations are more responsive than larger organizations. Therefore, many large firms are being restructured into smaller, more customer-focused units.

The point is that companies are no longer organizing to make it easy for managers to have control. Instead, they're organizing so that customers have the greatest influence. The change to a customer orientation is being aided by technology. For example, establishing a dialogue with customers on the Internet enables some firms to work closely with customers and respond quickly to their wants and needs.

There's no way an organization can provide high-quality goods and services to customers unless suppliers provide world-class parts and materials with which to work. Thus, managers have to establish close relationships with suppliers, including close Internet ties.[23] To make the entire system work, similar relationships have to be established with those organizations that sell directly to consumers—retailers.

In the past, the goal of the organization function in the firm was to clearly specify who does what *within* the firm. Today, the organizational task is much more complex because firms are forming partnerships, joint ventures, and other arrangements that make it necessary to organize the *whole system*, that is, several firms working together, often across national boundaries.[24] One organization working alone is often not as effective as many organizations working together. Creating a unified system out of multiple organizations will be one of the greatest management challenges of the 21st century.

To get the right kind of people to staff an organization, the firm has to offer the right kind of incentives. Google's gourmet chefs cook up free lunch, dinner, and snacks for employees. Would such an incentive appeal to you? How important to you is pay relative to other incentives?

## Staffing: Getting and Keeping the Right People

**Staffing** involves recruiting, hiring, motivating, and retaining the best people available to accomplish the company's objectives. Recruiting good employees has always been an important part of organizational success. Today, however, it is critical, especially in the Internet and high-tech areas. At most high-tech companies, like IBM, Sony, and Microsoft, the primary capital equipment is brainpower. One day the company may be selling books (Amazon.com) and suddenly an employee comes up with the idea of selling music or having auctions online or whatever. Any of these opportunities may prove profitable in the long run. The opportunities seem almost limitless. Thus, the firms with the most innovative and creative workers can go from start-up to major competitor with leading companies in just a few years.

**staffing** A management function that includes hiring, motivating, and retaining the best people available to accomplish the company's objectives.

Once they are hired, good people must be retained. Many people are not willing to work at companies unless they are treated well and get fair pay. Employees may leave to find companies that offer them a better balance between work and home. Staffing is becoming a greater part of each manager's assignment, and all managers need to cooperate with human resource management to win and keep good workers.

Staffing is such an important subject that we cannot cover it fully in this chapter. It is enough for now to understand that staffing is becoming more and more important as companies search for skilled and talented workers. All of Chapter 11 is devoted to human resource issues, including staffing.

# LEADING: PROVIDING CONTINUOUS VISION AND VALUES

In business literature there's a trend toward separating the notion of management from that of leadership.[25] One person might be a good manager but not a good leader.[26] Another might be a good leader without being a good manager. One difference between managers and leaders is that managers strive to produce order and stability whereas leaders embrace and manage change. Leadership is creating a vision for others to follow, establishing corporate values and ethics, and transforming the way the organization does business in order to improve its effectiveness and efficiency.[27] Good leaders motivate workers and create the environment for workers to motivate themselves. *Management*

## MAKING ethical decisions

### To Share or Not to Share

First-line managers assist in the decisions made by their department heads. The department heads retain full responsibility for the decisions—if a plan succeeds, it's their success; if a plan fails, it's their failure. Now picture this: As a first-line manager, you have new information that your department head hasn't seen yet. The findings in this report indicate that your manager's recent plans are sure to fail. If the plans do fail, the manager will probably be demoted and you're the most likely candidate to fill the vacancy. Will you give your department head the report? What is the ethical thing to do? What might be the consequences of your decision?

*is the carrying out of the leadership's vision.* Can you see how Oprah Winfrey (the subject of this chapter's Opening Profile) might be considered more of a leader than a manager?

Now and in the future, all organizations will need leaders who can supply the vision as well as the moral and ethical foundation for growth. You don't have to be a manager to be a leader. All employees can lead. That is, any employee can contribute to producing order and stability and can motivate others to work well. All employees can also add to a company's ethical environment and report ethical lapses when they occur.

Phil Jackson has been successful as an autocratic leader. That makes sense, since you don't want basketball players deciding whether or not to play as a team. On the other hand, can you see why it is not so good using autocratic leadership with doctors? What kind of leadership would you expect in a nonprofit agency full of volunteers?

Organizations will need workers and managers who share a vision and know how to get things done cooperatively. The workplace is changing from an environment in which a few dictate the rules to others to an environment in which all employees work together to accomplish common goals. Furthermore, managers must lead by doing, not just by saying.

In summary, leaders must:

- *Communicate a vision and rally others around that vision.* In doing so, the leader should be openly sensitive to the concerns of followers, give them responsibility, and win their trust.[28]
- *Establish corporate values.* These values include a concern for employees, for customers, for the environment, and for the quality of the company's products. When companies set their business goals today, they're defining the values of the company as well.
- *Promote corporate ethics.* Ethics include an unfailing demand for honesty and an insistence that everyone in the company gets treated fairly. That's why we stress ethical decision making throughout this text. Many businesspeople are now making the news by giving away huge amounts to charity, thus setting a model of social concern for their employees and others (see the Making Ethical Decisions box).
- *Embrace change.* A leader's most important job may be to transform the way the company does business so that it's more effective (does things better) and efficient (uses fewer resources to accomplish the same objectives).

## Leadership Styles

Nothing has challenged researchers in the area of management more than the search for the "best" leadership traits, behaviors, or styles. Thousands of studies have been made just to find leadership traits, that is, characteristics that make leaders different from other people.[29] Intuitively, you would conclude about the same thing that researchers have found: Leadership

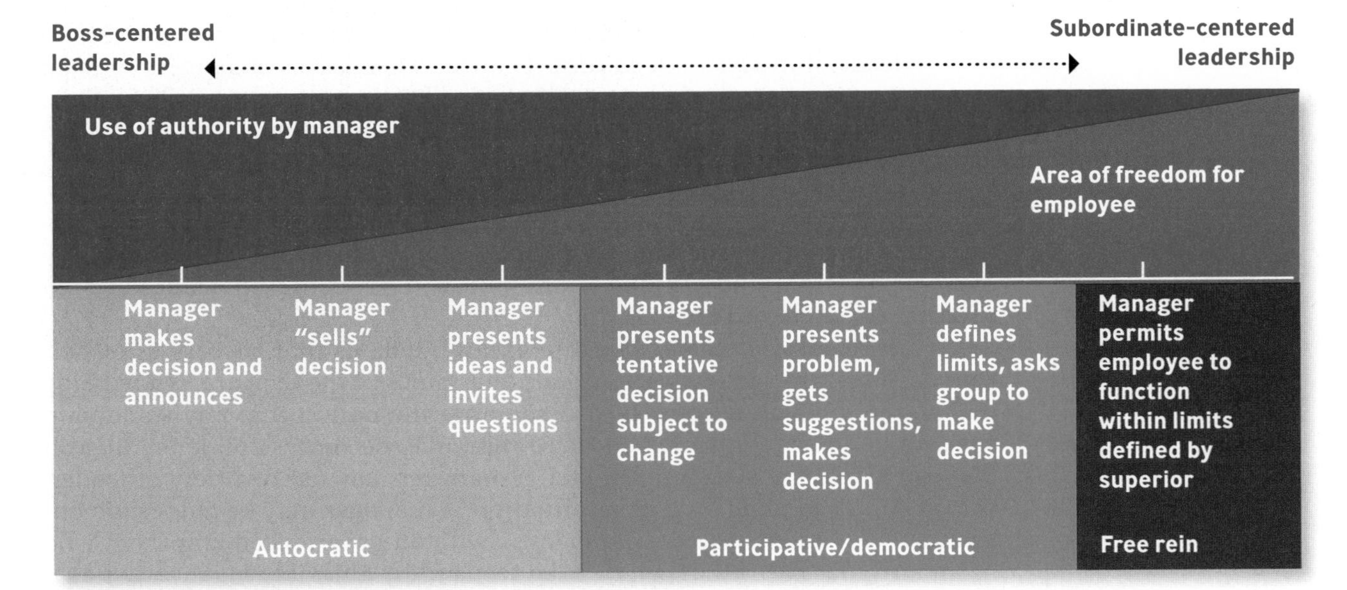


figure 7.7

**VARIOUS LEADERSHIP STYLES**

Source: Reprinted by permission of the *Harvard Business Review.* An exhibit from "How to Choose a Leadership Pattern" by Robert Tannenbaum and Warren Schmidt (May/June 1973). Copyright © 1973 by the Harvard Business School Publishing Corporation, all rights reserved.

traits are hard to pin down. In fact, results of most studies on leadership have been neither statistically significant nor reliable. Some leaders are well groomed and tactful, while others are unkempt and abrasive—yet the latter may be just as effective as the former.

Just as there's no one set of traits that can describe a leader, there's also no one style of leadership that works best in all situations.[30] Even so, we can look at a few of the most commonly recognized leadership styles and see how they may be effective (see Figure 7.7):

1. **Autocratic leadership** involves making managerial decisions without consulting others.[31] Such a style is effective in emergencies and when absolute followership is needed—for example, when fighting fires. Autocratic leadership is also effective sometimes with new, relatively unskilled workers who need clear direction and guidance. Coach Phil Jackson used an autocratic leadership style to take the Los Angeles Lakers to three consecutive National Basketball Association championships. By following his leadership, a group of highly skilled individuals became a winning team. How is the team doing now?
2. **Participative (democratic) leadership** consists of managers and employees working together to make decisions. Research has found that employee participation in decisions may not always increase effectiveness, but it usually increases job satisfaction. Many progressive organizations are highly successful at using a democratic style of leadership that values traits such as flexibility, good listening skills, and empathy.

   Organizations that have successfully used this style include Wal-Mart, FedEx, IBM, Cisco, AT&T, and most smaller firms. At meetings in such firms, employees discuss management issues and resolve those issues together in a democratic manner. That is, everyone has some opportunity to contribute to decisions. Many firms have placed meeting rooms throughout the company and allow all employees the right to request a meeting.
3. **Free-rein leadership** involves managers setting objectives and employees being relatively free to do whatever it takes to accomplish those objectives. In certain organizations, where managers deal with

**autocratic leadership** Leadership style that involves making managerial decisions without consulting others.

**participative (democratic) leadership** Leadership style that consists of managers and employees working together to make decisions.

**free-rein leadership** Leadership style that involves managers setting objectives and employees being relatively free to do whatever it takes to accomplish those objectives.

doctors, engineers, or other professionals, often the most successful leadership style is free rein. The traits needed by managers in such organizations include warmth, friendliness, and understanding. More and more firms are adopting this style of leadership with at least some of their employees.

Individual leaders rarely fit neatly into just one of these categories. Researchers illustrate leadership as a continuum with varying amounts of employee participation, ranging from purely boss-centered leadership to subordinate-centered leadership.

Which leadership style is best? Research tells us that successful leadership depends largely on what the goals and values of the firm are, who's being led, and in what situations. It also supports the notion that any leadership style, ranging from autocratic to free-rein, may be successful depending on the people and the situation. In fact, a manager may use a variety of leadership styles, depending on a given situation. A manager may be autocratic but friendly with a new trainee; democratic with an experienced employee who has many good ideas that can only be fostered by a flexible manager who's a good listener; and free-rein with a trusted, long-term supervisor who probably knows more about operations than the manager does.

There's no such thing as a leadership trait that is effective in all situations, or a leadership style that always works best. A truly successful leader has the ability to use the leadership style most appropriate to the situation and the employees involved.

## Empowering Workers

Historically, many leaders gave explicit instructions to workers, telling them what to do to meet the goals and objectives of the organization. The term for such a process is *directing*. In traditional organizations, directing involves giving assignments, explaining routines, clarifying policies, and providing feedback on performance.[32] Many organizations still follow this model, especially in firms like fast-food restaurants and small retail establishments where the employees don't have the skill and experience needed to work on their own, at least at first.

Progressive leaders, such as those in many high-tech firms and Internet companies, are less likely than traditional leaders to give specific instructions to employees. Rather, they're more likely to empower employees to make decisions on their own. Empowerment means giving employees the authority (the right to make a decision without consulting the manager) and responsibility (the requirement to accept the consequences of one's actions) to respond quickly to customer requests. Managers are often reluctant to give up the power they have to make such decisions; thus, empowerment is often resisted. In those firms that are able to implement the concept, the manager's role is becoming less that of a boss and director and more that of a coach, assistant, counselor, or team member. **Enabling** is the term used to describe giving workers the education and tools they need to make decisions. Clearly, enabling is the key to the success of empowerment. Without the right education, training, coaching, and tools, workers cannot assume the responsibilities and decision-making roles that make empowerment work.

**enabling**
Giving workers the education and tools they need to make decisions.

## Managing Knowledge

There's an old saying that still holds true today: "Knowledge is power." Empowering employees means giving them knowledge—that is, getting them the information they need to do the best job they can. Finding the right information, keeping the information in a readily accessible place, and making the information known to everyone in the firm together constitute **knowledge management**.[33]

**knowledge management** Finding the right information, keeping the information in a readily accessible place, and making the information known to everyone in the firm.

The first step to developing a knowledge management system is determining what knowledge is most important. Do you want to know more about your customers? Do you want to know more about competitors? What kind of information would make the company more effective or more efficient or more responsive to the marketplace? Once you have decided what you need to know, you set out to find answers to those questions.

Knowledge management tries to keep people from reinventing the wheel—that is, duplicating the work of gathering information—every time a decision needs to be made. A company really progresses when each person in the firm asks continually, "What do I still not know?" and "Whom should I be asking?" It's as important to know what's not working as what is working. Employees and managers now have e-mail, fax machines, intranets, and other means of keeping in touch with each other, with customers, and with other stakeholders. The key to success is learning how to process that information effectively and turn it into knowledge that everyone can use to improve processes and procedures. That is one way to enable workers to be more effective.

## CONTROLLING: MAKING SURE IT WORKS

The control function involves measuring performance relative to the planned objectives and standards, rewarding people for work well done, and then taking corrective action when necessary. Thus, the control process (see Figure 7.8) is one key to a successful management system because it provides the feedback that enables managers and workers to adjust to any deviations from plans and to changes in the environment that have affected performance. Controlling consists of five steps:

1. Establishing clear performance standards. This ties the planning function to the control function. Without clear standards, control is impossible.
2. Monitoring and recording actual performance (results).
3. Comparing results against plans and standards.
4. Communicating results and deviations to the employees involved.
5. Taking corrective action when needed and providing positive feedback for work well done.

figure 7.8

**THE CONTROL PROCESS**

The whole control process is based on clear standards. Without such standards, the other steps are difficult, if not impossible. With clear standards, performance measurement is relatively easy and the proper action can be taken.

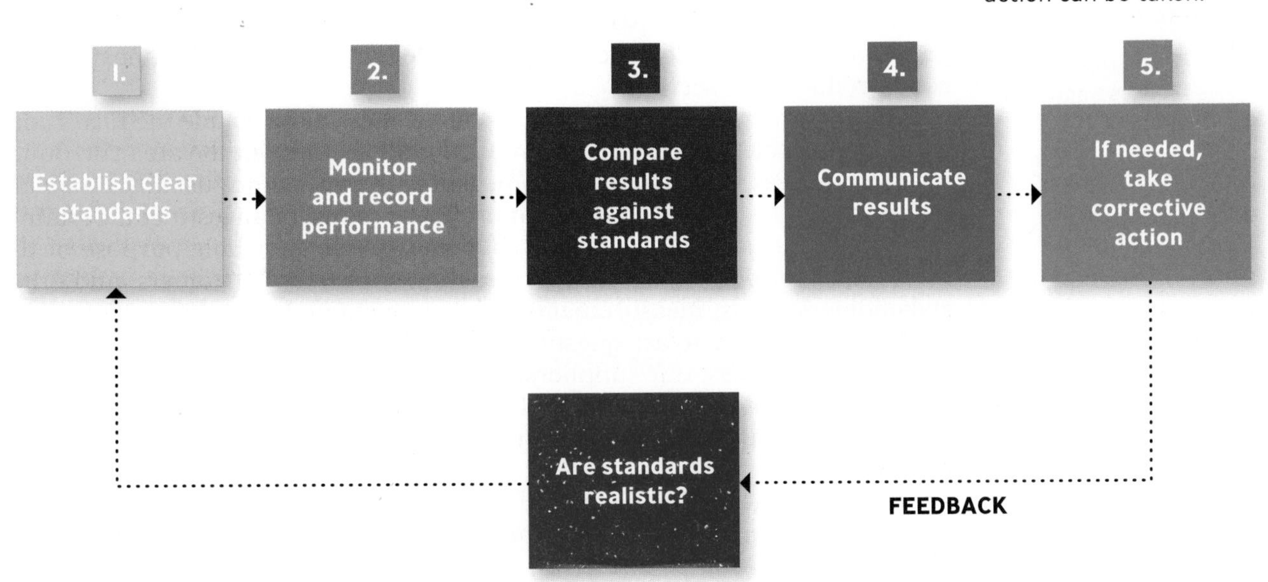
1.
Establish clear standards
2.
Monitor and record performance
3.
Compare results against standards
4.
Communicate results
5.
If needed, take corrective action
Are standards realistic?
FEEDBACK

As indicated, the control system's weakest link tends to be the setting of standards. To measure results against standards, the standards must be specific, attainable, and measurable. Setting such clear standards is part of the planning function. Vague goals and standards such as "better quality," "more efficiency," and "improved performance" aren't sufficient because they don't describe in enough detail what you're trying to achieve. For example, let's say you're a runner and you have made the following statement: "My goal is to improve my distance." When you started your improvement plan last year, you ran 2 miles a day; now you run 2.1 miles a day. Did you meet your goal? Well, you did increase your distance, but certainly not by very much. A more appropriate statement would be "My goal is to increase my running distance from two miles a day to four miles a day by January 1." It's important to establish a time period for reaching goals. The following examples of goals and standards meet these criteria:

- Cutting the number of finished product rejects from 10 per 1,000 to 5 per 1,000 by March 31.
- Increasing the number of times managers praise employees from 3 per week to 12 per week by the end of the quarter.
- Increasing sales of product X from 10,000 per month to 12,000 per month by July.

One way to make control systems work is to establish clear procedures for monitoring performance. Accounting and finance are often the foundations for control systems because they provide the numbers management needs to evaluate progress. We shall explore both accounting and finance in detail later in the text.

## A New Criterion for Measurement: Customer Satisfaction

**external customers**
Dealers, who buy products to sell to others, and ultimate customers (or end users), who buy products for their own personal use.

**internal customers**
Individuals and units within the firm that receive services from other individuals or units.

The criterion for measuring success in a customer-oriented firm is customer satisfaction. This includes satisfaction of both external and internal customers. **External customers** include dealers, who buy products to sell to others, and ultimate customers (also known as end users) such as you and me, who buy products for their own personal use. **Internal customers** are individuals and units within the firm that receive services from other individuals or units. For example, the field salespeople are the internal customers of the marketing research people who prepare research reports for them. One goal today is to go beyond simply satisfying customers to "delighting" them with unexpectedly good products and services.

Other criteria of organizational effectiveness may include the firm's contribution to society and its environmental responsibility in the area surrounding the business.[34] The traditional measures of success are usually financial; that is, success is defined in terms of profits or return on investment. Certainly these measures are still important, but they're not the whole purpose of the firm. Other purposes may include pleasing employees, customers, and other stakeholders. Thus, measurements of success may take all these groups into account. Firms have to ask questions such as these: Do we have good relations with our employees, our suppliers, our dealers, our community leaders, the local media, our stockholders, and our bankers? What more could we do to please these groups? Are the corporate needs (such as making a profit) being met as well?

Management will be discussed in more detail in the next few chapters. Let's pause now, review, and do some exercises. Management is doing, not just reading.

### progress assessment

- How does enabling help empowerment?
- What are the five steps in the control process?
- What's the difference between internal and external customers?

## summary

1. Explain how the changes that are occurring in the business environment are affecting the management function.

1. Many managers are changing their approach to corporate management.
   - **What reasons can you give to account for these changes in management?**

   Businesspeople are being challenged to be more ethical and to make their accounting practices more visible to investors and the general public. Change is now happening faster than ever, and global competition is just a click away. Managing change is an important element of success, particularly in light of today's emphasis on speed in the global marketplace. National borders mean much less now than ever before, and cooperation and integration among companies have greatly increased. Within companies, knowledge workers are demanding managerial styles that allow for freedom, and the workforce is becoming increasingly diverse, educated, and self-directed.
   - **How are managers' roles changing?**

   Managers are being educated to guide, train, support, and teach employees rather than tell them what to do. Before employees can be empowered, they must receive extensive training and development.

2. Describe the four functions of management.

2. Managers perform a variety of functions.
   - **What are the four primary functions of management?**

   The four primary functions are (1) planning, (2) organizing, (3) leading, and (4) controlling.

3. Relate the planning process and decision making to the accomplishment of company goals.

3. The planning function involves the process of setting objectives to meet the organizational goals.
   - **What's the difference between goals and objectives?**

   Goals are broad, long-term achievements that organizations aim to accomplish, whereas objectives are specific, short-term plans made to help reach the goals.
   - **What is a SWOT analysis?**

   Managers look at the Strengths, Weaknesses, Opportunities, and Threats facing the firm.
   - **What are the four types of planning, and how are they related to the organization's goals and objectives?**

   Strategic planning is broad, long-range planning that outlines the goals of the organization. Tactical planning is specific, short-term planning that lists organizational objectives. Operational planning is part of tactical planning and involves setting specific timetables and standards. Contingency planning involves developing an alternative set of plans in case the first set doesn't work out.
   - **What are the steps involved in decision making?**

   The seven Ds of decision making are (1) define the situation, (2) describe and collect needed information, (3) develop alternatives, (4) develop agreement among those involved, (5) decide which alternative is best, (6) do what is indicated (begin implementation), and (7) determine whether the decision was a good one and follow up.

**4.** Describe the organizing function of management.

4. Organizing means allocating resources (such as funds for various departments), assigning tasks, and establishing procedures for accomplishing the organizational objectives.

- **What are the three levels of management in the corporate hierarchy?**

The three levels of management are (1) top management (highest level consisting of the president and other key company executives who develop strategic plans); (2) middle management (general managers, division managers, and plant managers who are responsible for tactical planning and controlling); and (3) supervisory management (first-line managers/supervisors who evaluate workers' daily performance).

- **What skills do managers need?**

Managers must have three categories of skills: (1) technical skills (ability to perform specific tasks such as selling products or developing software), (2) human relations skills (ability to communicate and motivate), and (3) conceptual skills (ability to see organizations as a whole and how all the parts fit together).

- **Are these skills equally important at all management levels?**

Managers at different levels need different skills. Top managers rely heavily on human relations and conceptual skills and rarely use technical skills, while first-line supervisors need strong technical and human relations skills but use conceptual skills less often. Middle managers need to have a balance of all three skills (see Figure 7.6).

- **What are some of the latest trends in organizational management?**

One trend is toward stakeholder-oriented management. In those cases, management tries to satisfy the needs of all stakeholders, including employees, customers, suppliers, dealers, environmental groups, and the surrounding communities.

- **What changes in the marketplace have made staffing more important?**

E-commerce CEOs must spend a lot of time recruiting because their companies grow so fast and run on the knowledge of mostly young workers. Keeping people is also critical because there are lots of companies seeking new talent and people feel free today to go where the action is fastest.

**5.** Explain the differences between leaders and managers, and describe the various leadership styles.

5. Executives today must be more than just managers; they must be leaders as well.

- **What's the difference between a manager and a leader?**

A manager plans, organizes, and controls functions within an organization. A leader has vision and inspires others to grasp that vision, establishes corporate values, emphasizes corporate ethics, and doesn't fear change.

- **Describe the various leadership styles.**

Figure 7.7 shows a continuum of leadership styles ranging from boss-centered to subordinate-centered leadership.

- **Which leadership style is best?**

The best (most effective) leadership style depends on the people being led and the situation. The challenge of the future will be to empower self-managed teams to manage themselves. This is a move away from autocratic leadership.

- **What does empowerment mean?**

Empowerment means giving employees the authority and responsibility to respond quickly to customer requests. Enabling is the term used to describe giving workers the education and tools they need to assume their new decision-making powers. Knowledge management involves finding the right information, keeping the information in a readily accessible place, and making the information known to everyone in the firm.

6. The control function of management involves measuring employee performance against objectives and standards, rewarding people for a job well done, and taking corrective action if necessary.
   - **What are the five steps of the control function?**

   Controlling incorporates (1) setting clear standards, (2) monitoring and recording performance, (3) comparing performance with plans and standards, (4) communicating results and deviations to employees, and (5) providing positive feedback for a job well done and taking corrective action if necessary.
   - **What qualities must standards possess to be used to measure performance results?**

   Standards must be specific, attainable, and measurable.

**6.** Summarize the five steps of the control function of management.

## key terms

**autocratic leadership** 195
**brainstorming** 189
**conceptual skills** 192
**contingency planning** 188
**controlling** 185
**decision making** 189
**enabling** 196
**external customers** 198
**free-rein leadership** 195
**goals** 185
**human relations skills** 192
**internal customers** 198
**knowledge management** 197
**leading** 185
**management** 182
**middle management** 191
**mission statement** 185
**objectives** 185
**operational planning** 188
**organization chart** 190
**organizing** 184
**participative (democratic) leadership** 195
**planning** 184
**PMI** 189
**problem solving** 189
**staffing** 193
**strategic planning** 186
**supervisory management** 191
**SWOT analysis** 186
**tactical planning** 187
**technical skills** 192
**top management** 190
**vision** 185

## critical thinking questions

Many students say they would like to be a manager someday. Here are some questions to get you started thinking like a manager:

1. Would you like to work for a large firm or a small business? Private or public? In an office or out in the field?

2. What kind of leader would you be? Do you have evidence to show that?

3. Do you see any problems with a participative (democratic) leadership style? Can you see a manager getting frustrated when he or she can't control others?

4. Can someone who's trained to give orders (e.g., a military sergeant) be retrained to be a participative leader? What problems may emerge?

## developing workplace skills

1. Allocate some time to do some career planning by doing a SWOT analysis of your present situation. What does the marketplace for your chosen career(s) look like today? What skills do you have that will make you a winner in that type of career? What weaknesses might you target to improve? What are the threats to that career choice? What are the opportunities? Prepare a two-minute presentation to the class.
2. Bring several decks of cards to class and have the class break up into teams of four or so members. Each team should then elect a leader. Each leader should be assigned a leadership style: autocratic, participative (democratic), or free rein. Have each team try to build a house of cards by stacking them on top of each other. The team with the highest house wins. Each team member should then report his or her experience under that style of leadership.
3. In class, discuss the advantages and disadvantages of becoming a manager. Does the size of the business make a difference? What are the advantages of a career in a profit-seeking business versus a career in a nonprofit organization?
4. Review Figure 7.7 and discuss managers you have known, worked for, or read about who have practiced each style. Students from other countries may have interesting experiences to add. Which managerial style did you like best? Why? Which were most effective? Why?
5. Because of the illegal and unethical behavior of a few managers, managers in general are under suspicion for being greedy and dishonest. Discuss the fairness of such charges, given the thousands of honest and ethical managers, and what could be done to improve the opinion of managers among the students in your class.

## taking it to the net

**Purpose**

To perform a simple SWOT analysis.

**Exercise**

Go to www.marketingteacher.com, click on SWOT, and review the SWOT analysis for Toys "R" Us.

1. What are the store's strengths, weaknesses, opportunities, and threats?
2. Analyze the store's weaknesses. How do you think the company's strengths might be used to overcome some of its weaknesses?
3. Analyze the store's opportunities and threats. What additional opportunities can you suggest? What additional threats can you identify?

## casing the web

To access the case *"Leading in a Leaderless Company,"* visit **www.mhhe.com/ub8e**

video case

## Bread Lines Are Back at Panera!

During the Great Depression, people sadly stood in long lines waiting to get bread. Today, people are eager to wait in lines (which are much shorter and faster) to get at the bread, soup, and sandwiches, at Panera Bread. The company started in 1981 and was known as Au Bon Pain. In 1991, the company went public (sold stock to people) and bought the St. Louis Bread Company. In 1994, Ron Shaich, the president of the organization, prepared a vision he called "Concept Essence" that described how the company should compete in the marketplace. Since then the company has been working diligently to apply the concepts from that original vision.

Based on the vision, Shaich developed long-term goals for the firm. Broad strategic plans led to tactical plans that would direct the company to the goals Shaich identified. Every step along the way called for decision making: Defining the situation, collecting information, developing alternatives, choosing the best alternative, and so forth. That process led to the company's decision to focus solely on Panera Bread and to sell all other business units, including the original Au Bon Pain stores. The idea was to focus on the mission and keep that focus. That meant, among other things, placing the stores in the right locations, keeping the stores relatively small, maintaining the atmosphere of friendliness, and building a team of employees who enjoy the work and serve customers well. Of course, the whole enterprise was built upon offering quality products.

Periodically, the company has to examine its strengths, weaknesses, opportunities and threats. It's always tempting to grow rapidly, but that might lead to poorer quality. Similarly, one may be tempted to look overseas for growth, but choosing to do so should not be at the expense of maintaining control over quality and personnel.

So, how do the managers at Panera Bread test how well they are doing? They listen to customers and then they listen again and again. They also listen to employees and anyone else who has interesting ideas and suggestions. The key question today for most firms is: "Would you recommend us to others?" In Panera's case, the answer is a resounding YES. What do they love? It depends. Some love the soups. Others the bagels. Others the coffee. And, clearly, some like it all.

First-line managers (supervisors) at Panera must have strong technical skills needed to keep the place running smoothly. They must also have great human relations skills to work successfully with employees. It takes a wise manager to step back and let the employees do the work and not step in and do it for them. The word to describe that process is empowerment. It is one of the more difficult managerial tasks to learn. But when people are given the freedom to make decisions on their own and they can respond to customer wants and needs without delay, the whole company benefits. Proof is in the rapid growth of the company.

The kind of leadership that works best for Panera is participative (democratic). While employees need goals, direction, and guidance, they also need to be able to give input on how to reach those goals. Employees are the front-line people who hear what customers have to say day after day. They know what's working and what's not. Working with management as a team, the store's personnel enjoy the surroundings and create a great atmosphere for customers.

### Thinking It Over

1. Who are the major competitors to Panera Bread in your area? What managerial differences, if any, do you see? Given the description of Panera Bread in this case, for which company would you rather work? Why?
2. Thus far Panera Bread has not gone international, nor does it open stores as fast as some franchises do. What do you see as the benefits and drawbacks of such a policy?
3. Ron Shaich has applied almost everything you learned in this chapter to the management of Panera Bread. Would these management skills be equally useful to him if he were to go to a different organization to work? What about a nonprofit organization?

# adapting ORGANIZATIONS TO today's markets

profile

## Getting to Know X Anne Mulcahy of Xerox

Anne Mulcahy didn't anticipate being the chief executive officer of Xerox when she was majoring in English and journalism at Marymount College in New York. She knew about Xerox because she had grown up in Connecticut, the company's home state. Furthermore, both her husband and brother worked for Xerox.

She began her Xerox career as a field sales representative and moved up through the organization rather quickly. She became the vice president for human resources and served from 1992 to 1995. She became chief staff officer in 1997 and corporate senior vice president in 1998. She also gained some experience overseas as vice president and staff officer for customer operations in places like Europe, Asia, and Africa. Clearly, Mulcahy was not afraid of change or of taking on new challenges. But the challenge of being CEO was the biggest challenge of all.

When Mulcahy was chosen to be CEO, Xerox was in bad shape. It was called before the U.S. Securities and Exchange Commission to explain questionable accounting practices. In addition, the company was $14 billion in debt! Bankruptcy was on the horizon, but Mulcahy began the work of restructuring the organization. She cut the debt down to $9.6 billion and built up the cash reserve to $3.5 billion. She cut 38,000 workers, brought in a new financial officer, and began meeting with customers to see what could be done to restore the image of the firm. "Turnaround or

LEARNING **goals**

**After you have read and studied this chapter, you should be able to**

1. Explain the organizational theories of Fayol and Weber.
2. Explain the various issues involved in structuring organizations.
3. Describe and differentiate the various organizational models.
4. Discuss the concepts involved in interfirm cooperation and coordination.
5. Explain how restructuring, organizational culture, and informal organizations can help businesses adapt to change.

CHAPTER 08

**www.xerox.com**

growth, it's getting your people focused on the goal that is still the job of leadership," she said.

She took Xerox back to the foundations of its corporate culture—innovation and customer care. "You need to change and adapt," she said. And changing and adapting is what she did. Her focus is now on winning the printing, copying, and services businesses of leading companies. That puts her in direct competition with companies like Dell and Kodak. *Fortune* magazine called Mulcahy "the hottest turnaround act since Lou Gerstner [of IBM]." She was one of the top five Alpha Females of business that year.

Here are some of the things Mulcahy has to say about reorganizing a business: "First, change is the most difficult thing." For example, she outsourced most of the manufacturing operations. She also invested in research and development and global services when her company was deep in debt. Difficult stuff. But, she says, "in a crisis, you have the opportunity to move quickly and change a lot." Then again, "Change doesn't happen if you don't work at it."

Xerox is only partway through a technological shift from analog to digital copying and from black-and-white to color. It is trying to be more like a document consulting company and less like a copier maker. The bottom line is that Xerox stock rose from $5 to $15 a share. Mulcahy must be doing something right.

This chapter is about adapting organizations to today's markets. Nobody is better suited for this Opening Profile than Anne Mulcahy. She has carried Xerox from the brink of disaster to a viable competitor among some of the biggest firms in the world. She is one of few women running a top public company. What does she say about being a successful manager? Work hard. Measure the results. Tell the truth. Because of her philosophy and success, Mulcahy also serves on the boards of leading companies such as Citigroup and Target.

Sources: Keith H. Hammonds, "What I Know Now," *Fast Company*, March 2005, p. 96; "The Best and Worst Managers of 2004—The Best Managers," *BusinessWeek*, January 10, 2005; www.xerox.com, April 2005; "Anne Mulcahy," *Forbes*, August 15, 2005, p. 46; Betsy Morris, "The Accidental CEO," *Fortune*, June 23, 2005, pp. 58–67; and Reshma Kapadia, "A Study in Contrast," *Smartmoney,* March, 2006, p. 30.

# EVERYONE IS DOING IT

You don't have to look far to find examples of companies going through the process of reorganizing. Xerox is just one of many—and sometimes the process is quite painful. When the headlines say "Ford to Axe 25,000 Jobs and Close Seven Plants," what are we to think?[1] As this book was going to press, the country was still reeling from the announcement that General Motors (GM) was cutting some 30,000 workers.[2] Then the headlines said "Toyota Gears Up for Michigan" and the article talked about how the Japanese company was about to become the world's biggest car manufacturer, taking over from GM. Ford and GM are likely to make a comeback; nonetheless, there is an obvious need for U.S. auto manufacturers to reorganize to become better competitors.[3]

The airline industry also needs to reorganize. Many airlines have gone bankrupt, and there is much talk about merging with foreign airlines. Kodak is in the middle of a major reorganization; it is moving away from film toward digital cameras, and the process has been difficult and slow. Kraft Foods announced it was cutting 8,000 jobs and shutting down 20 plants.[4] IBM sold its personal computer (PC) business to a Chinese company in its effort to become more competitive.

If you didn't know that the unemployment rate in the United States was below 5 percent, you might get very worried. You may be thinking, "What is happening to U.S. producers?" But the fact is that adjusting to changing markets is a normal function in a capitalist economy. In Germany, the electronics company Siemens is going through a similar process.[5] There will be big winners, like Google, and big losers as well.[6] The key to success is to remain flexible and to adapt to the changing times. Often that means going back to basic principles and building the organization on a sound foundation. This chapter will discuss such basic principles; the goal is to prepare you for the future by helping you understand the past.

## Building an Organization from the Bottom Up

No matter the size of the business, the principles of organization are much the same. Let's say, for example, that you and two of your friends plan to start a lawn-mowing business. One of the first steps is to organize your business. Organizing, or structuring, begins with determining what work needs to be done (mowing, edging, trimming, etc.) and then dividing up the tasks among the three of you; this is called a *division of labor.* One of you, for example, might have a special talent for trimming bushes, while another is better at mowing. Dividing tasks into smaller jobs is called *job specialization.* The success of a firm often depends on management's ability to identify each worker's strengths and assign the right tasks to the right person. Many jobs can be done quickly and well when each person specializes.

If your business is successful, you will probably hire more workers to help. You might then organize them into teams or departments to do the various tasks. One team, for example, might mow the lawns while another team uses blowers to clean up the leaves and grass. If you are really successful over time, you might hire an accountant to keep records for you, various people to do your marketing (e.g., advertising), and repair people to keep the equipment in good shape. You can see how your business might evolve into a company with several departments: production (mowing the lawns and everything related to that), marketing, accounting, and repair. The process of setting up individual departments to do specialized tasks is called *departmentalization.* Finally, you would need to assign authority and responsibility to people so that you could control the whole process. If something went wrong in the accounting department, for example, you would know who was responsible.

* * * **MAKING**

# ethical decisions

## Safety versus Profit

Imagine that you have begun a successful lawn-mowing service in your neighborhood. You observe other lawn-mowing services in the area. Several seem to hire untrained workers, many of them from other countries. The companies pay the workers minimum wage or slightly more. Most obviously, however, the owners often provide no safety equipment. Workers don't have ear protection against the loud mowers and blowers. Most don't wear goggles when operating the shredder. Very few workers wear masks when spraying potentially harmful fertilizers.

You are aware that there are many hazards connected with yardwork. You also know that safety gear can be expensive and that workers often prefer to work without such protection. You are interested in making as much money as possible, but you also are concerned about the safety and welfare of your workers. Furthermore, you are aware of the noise pollution caused by blowers and other equipment and would like to keep noise levels down, but quiet equipment is expensive.

Clearly, most other lawn services don't seem too concerned about safety and the environment. On the one hand, you know that the corporate culture you create as you begin your service will last for a long time. If you emphasize safety and environmental concern from the start, your workers will adopt your values. On the other hand, you can see the potential for making faster profits by ignoring safety rules and by paying little attention to the environment. What are the consequences of each choice? Which would you choose?

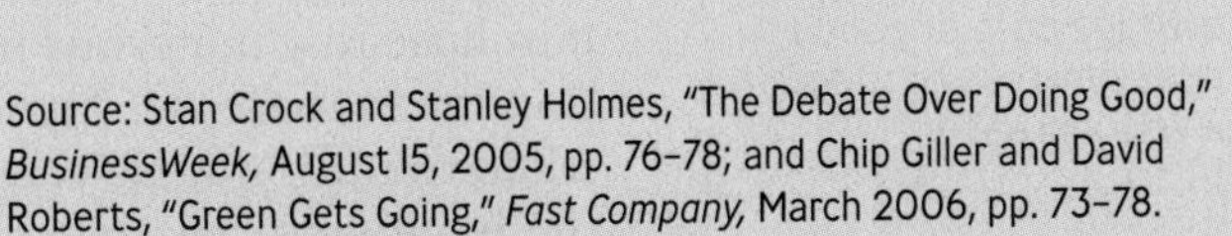

Source: Stan Crock and Stanley Holmes, "The Debate Over Doing Good," *BusinessWeek,* August 15, 2005, pp. 76–78; and Chip Giller and David Roberts, "Green Gets Going," *Fast Company,* March 2006, pp. 73–78.

Structuring an organization, then, consists of devising a division of labor (sometimes resulting in specialization); setting up teams or departments to do specific tasks (e.g., production and accounting); and assigning responsibility and authority to people. Part of the process would include allocating resources (such as funds for various departments), assigning specific tasks, and establishing procedures for accomplishing the organizational objectives. Right from the start, you have to make some ethical decisions about how you will treat your workers (see the Making Ethical Decisions box). You may develop an organization chart that shows relationships among people: It shows who is accountable for the completion of specific work and who reports to whom. Finally, you have to monitor the environment to see what competitors are doing and what customers are demanding. Then you must adjust to the new realities. For example, a major lawn care company may begin promoting in your area. You might have to make some organizational changes to offer even better service at competitive prices. What would be the first thing you would do if you began to lose business to competitors?

## THE CHANGING ORGANIZATION

Never before in the history of business has so much change been introduced so quickly; sometimes too quickly.[7] As you learned in earlier chapters, much of that change is due to the changing business environment, including more global competition and faster technological change.[8] Equally important to many businesses is the change in customer expectations. Consumers today expect high-quality products and fast, friendly service—at a reasonable cost.[9] *Managing change*, then, has become a critical managerial function. That sometimes includes changing the whole organization structure. Many organizations in the past were designed more to facilitate management than to please the customer. Companies designed many rules and regulations to give managers control over employees. As you will learn later in this chapter, that is called *bureaucracy.* You saw the results when Hurricane Katrina hit New Orleans in August 2005. The country seemed to be paralyzed and didn't know how to respond. Blame was placed on federal bureaucracy, state bureaucracy, and local bureaucracy. Meanwhile, less bureaucratic businesses in the area adjusted to

the new conditions, reopened, and waited for the government to catch up. Where did bureaucracy come from? What are the alternatives? To understand where we are, it helps to know where we've been.

## The Development of Organization Design

**economies of scale** The situation in which companies can reduce their production costs if they can purchase raw materials in bulk; the average cost of goods goes down as production levels increase.

Until the 20th century, most businesses were rather small, the processes for producing goods were relatively simple, and organizing workers was fairly easy. Organizing workers is still not too hard in most small firms, such as a lawn-mowing service or a small shop that produces custom-made boats. Not until the 1900s and the introduction of *mass production* (efficiently producing large quantities of goods) did business production processes and organization become complex. Usually, the bigger the plant, the more efficient production became.

Business growth led to what was called **economies of scale**. This term refers to the fact that companies can reduce their production costs if they can purchase raw materials in bulk; the average cost of goods goes down as production levels increase. The cost of building a car, for example, got much cheaper when the automobile companies went to mass production. It was in this era that the huge factories that produce GM and Ford cars were introduced. You may have noticed the same benefits of mass production with houses and computers.

During the era of mass production, organization theorists emerged. In France, economic theoritician Henri Fayol published his book *Administration industrielle et générale* in 1919. It was popularized in the United States in 1949 under the title *General and Industrial Management*.

**Fayol's Principles of Organization** Fayol introduced such principles as the following:

- *Unity of command.* Each worker is to report to one, and only one, boss. The benefits of this principle are obvious. What happens if two different bosses give you two different assignments? Which one should you follow? To prevent such confusion, each person is to report to only one manager.
- *Hierarchy of authority.* All workers should know to whom they should report. Managers should have the right to give orders and expect others to follow. As you learned in Chapter 7, this concept has gone through major changes and empowerment is often more important now.
- *Division of labor.* Functions are to be divided into areas of specialization such as production, marketing, and finance. This principle, as you will read later, is now being questioned or modified, and cross-functional teamwork is being given more emphasis.
- *Subordination of individual interests to the general interest.* Workers are to think of themselves as a coordinated team. The goals of the team are more important than the goals of individual workers. This concept is still very much in use.
- *Authority.* Managers have the right to give orders and the power to enforce obedience. Authority and responsibility are related: Whenever authority is exercised, responsibility arises. This principle is also being modified as managers are beginning to empower employees.
- *Degree of centralization.* The amount of decision-making power vested in top management should vary by circumstances. In a small organization, it's possible to centralize all decision-making power in the top manager. In a larger organization, however, some decision-making power should be delegated to lower-level managers and employees on both major and minor issues.

- *Clear communication channels.* All workers should be able to reach others in the firm quickly and easily.
- *Order.* Materials and people should be placed and maintained in the proper location.
- *Equity.* A manager should treat employees and peers with respect and justice.
- *Esprit de corps.* A spirit of pride and loyalty should be created among people in the firm.

Management courses in colleges throughout the world taught these principles for years, and they became synonymous with the concept of management. Organizations were designed so that no person had more than one boss, lines of authority were clear, and everyone knew to whom they were to report. Naturally, these principles tended to be written down as rules, policies, and regulations as organizations grew larger. That process of rule making often led to rather rigid organizations that didn't always respond quickly to consumer requests. For example, in various cities in the past, the Department of Motor Vehicles (DMV) and auto repair facilities were often cited as relatively slow to adapt to the needs of their customers. Recently, it was the Department of Homeland Security and the Federal Emergency Management Agency (FEMA) that were slow to respond to threats. So where did the idea of bureaucracy come from? We talk about that next.

**Max Weber and Organizational Theory** Max Weber's book *The Theory of Social and Economic Organizations*, like Fayol's, also appeared in the United States in the late 1940s. It was Weber, a German sociologist and economist, who promoted the pyramid-shaped organization structure that became so popular in large firms. Weber put great trust in managers and felt that the firm would do well if employees simply *did what they were told*. The less decision making employees had to do, the better. Clearly, this is a reasonable way to operate if you're dealing with relatively uneducated and untrained workers. *Where are you likely to find such workers today?* Often, such workers were the only ones available at the time Weber was writing; most employees did not have the kind of educational background and technical skills that today's workers generally have.

Max Weber promoted an organizational structure composed of middle managers who implement the orders of top managers. He believed that less educated workers were best managed by having them follow strict rules and regulations monitored by managers or supervisors. What industries or businesses today would benefit by using such controls?

Weber's principles of organization were similar to Fayol's. In addition, Weber emphasized

- Job descriptions.
- Written rules, decision guidelines, and detailed records.
- Consistent procedures, regulations, and policies.
- Staffing and promotion based on qualifications.

Weber believed that large organizations demanded clearly established rules and guidelines that were to be followed precisely. In other words, he was in favor of bureaucracy. Although his principles made a great deal of sense at the time, the practice of establishing rules and procedures sometimes became so rigid in some companies that they became counterproductive. Some organizations today still thrive on Weber's theories. United Parcel Service (UPS), for example, still has written rules and decision guidelines that enable the firm to deliver packages quickly because employees don't have to pause to make decisions—the procedures to follow are clearly spelled out for them. Other organizatio[illegible]s are not as effective because they don't allow employees to respond qui[illegible] to new challenges. That is clearly the case with disaster relief in many areas. Later, we shall explore what can be done to make organizations more responsive. First, let's look again at some basic terms and concepts.

## Turning Principles into Organization Design

**hierarchy**
A system in which one person is at the top of the organization and there is a ranked or sequential ordering from the top down of managers who are responsible to that person.

**chain of command**
The line of authority that moves from the top of a hierarchy to the lowest level.

**bureaucracy**
An organization with many layers of managers who set rules and regulations and oversee all decisions.

Following the concepts of theorists like Fayol and Weber, managers in the latter part of the 1900s began designing organizations so that managers could *control* workers. Many companies are still organized that way, with everything set up in a hierarchy. A **hierarchy** is a system in which one person is at the top of the organization and there is a ranked or sequential ordering from the top down of managers and others who are responsible to that person. Since one person can't keep track of thousands of workers, the top manager needs many lower-level managers to help. The **chain of command** is the line of authority that moves from the top of the hierarchy to the lowest level. Figure 8.1 shows a typical hierarchical organization structure.

Some organizations have a dozen or more layers of management between the chief executive officer (CEO) and the lowest-level employees. If employees want to introduce work changes, they ask a supervisor (the first level of management), who asks his or her manager, who asks a manager at the next level up, and so on. Eventually a decision is made and passed down from manager to manager until it reaches the employees. Such decisions can take weeks or months to be made. Max Weber used the word *bureaucrat* to describe a middle manager whose function was to implement top management's orders. Thus, **bureaucracy** came to be the term used for an organization with many layers of managers who set rules and regulations and oversee all decisions. Recently, IBM went through a major reorganization that included firing more than 10,000 people. The company said it wanted to "reduce bureaucracy and move more of our people and resources out to the field (closer to the customer)."[10]

When employees have to ask their managers for permission to make a change, the process may take so long that customers become annoyed. Such consumer discontent may happen either in a small organization, such as a flower shop, or in a major organization such as an automobile dealership or a large construction firm. The employee has to find the manager, get permission to make the requested change, come back to the customer, explain what the management decision was, and so on. Has this happened to you in a department store or some other organization? Since many customers want efficient service—and they want it *now*—slow service is simply not acceptable in today's competitive firms.

figure 8.1

**TYPICAL ORGANIZATION CHART**

This is a rather standard chart with managers for major functions and supervisors reporting to the managers. Each supervisor manages three employees.

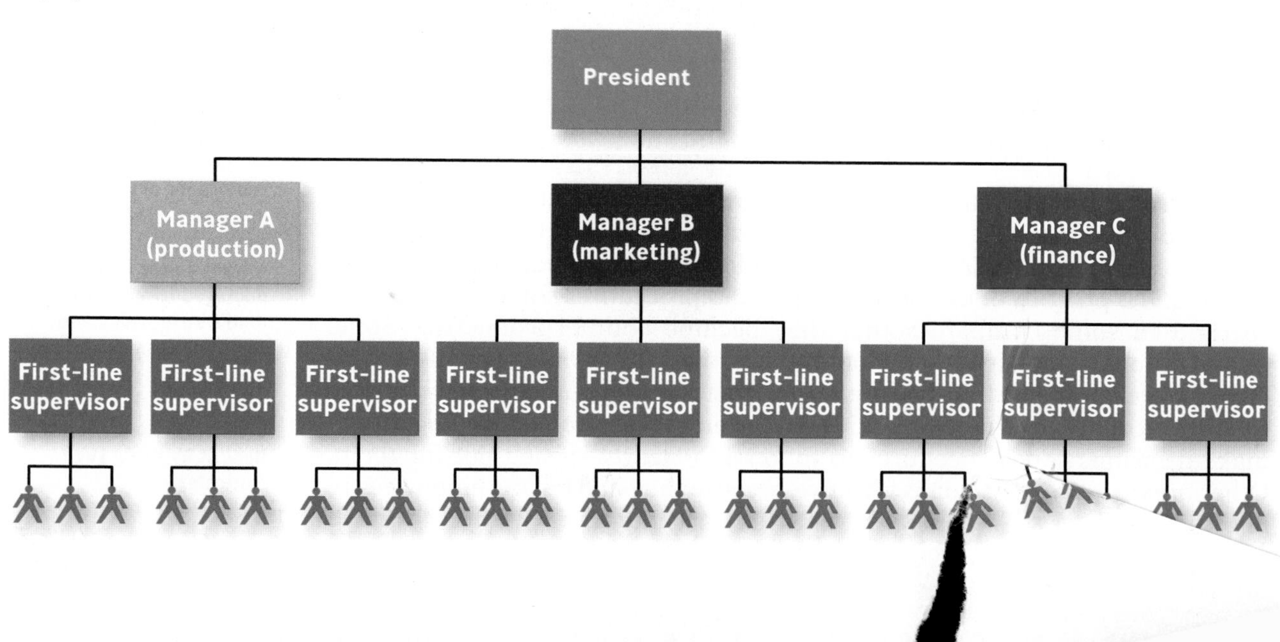

To make customers happier, some companies are reorganizing to give employees power to make more decisions on their own. Rather than always having to follow strict rules and regulations, they are encouraged to please the customer no matter what. Home Depot is trying such an approach to win more customers from competitors.[11] Similarly, at Nordstrom, a chain of upscale department stores, an employee can accept a return from a customer without seeking managerial approval, even if the garment was not originally sold at that store. As you read earlier, giving employees such authority and responsibility to make decisions and please customers is called *empowerment*. Remember that empowerment works only when employees are given the proper training and resources to respond. Can you see how such training would help first responders in crisis conditions?

**progress assessment**

- What do the terms *division of labor* and *specialization* mean?
- What are the principles of management outlined by Fayol?
- What did Weber add to the principles of Fayol?

## ISSUES INVOLVED IN STRUCTURING ORGANIZATIONS

When designing responsive organizations, firms have had to deal with several organizational issues: (1) centralization versus decentralization, (2) span of control, (3) tall versus flat organization structures, and (4) departmentalization.

### Centralization versus Decentralization of Authority

Sara Lee is a company that sells everything from air fresheners and Kiwi shoe polish to Sara Lee desserts and Earth Grain breads. You might expect a company with such diverse products to have decentralized authority. That is, managers of highly diverse products would be given the power to make decisions about what they are selling. When Brenda Barnes took over the company, however, she instituted a centralized plan.[12] For example, she immediately sold to other companies products that accounted for $18.3 billion in revenue. Industry experts said that a major restructuring was in order, and that's what they got.[13]

When a company needs radical changes, centralized decision making is often necessary, at least for a while. On the other hand, computer and printer maker Hewlett-Packard (HP) may be moving in the opposite direction. Its former CEO, Carly Fiorina, changed what was once a decentralized organization structure into a more centralized form. HP's new CEO, Mark Hurd, is likely to go back to a more decentralized form of management to get more ideas from his various divisions.[14]

**centralized authority** An organization structure in which decision-making authority is maintained at the top level of management at the company's headquarters.

**Centralized authority** occurs when decision-making authority is maintained at the top level of management at the company's headquarters.[15] **Decentralized authority** occurs when decision-making authority is delegated to lower-level managers and employees who are more familiar with local conditions than headquarter's management could be. Figure 8.2 on page 212 lists some advantages and disadvantages of centralized versus decentralized authority.

**decentralized authority** An organization structure in which decision-making authority is delegated to lower-level managers more familiar with local conditions than headquarters management could be.

JCPenney customers in California, for example, are likely to demand clothing styles different from those demanded in Minnesota or Maine. It makes

figure 8.2

**ADVANTAGES AND DISADVANTAGES OF CENTRALIZED VERSUS DECENTRALIZED MANAGEMENT**

| ADVANTAGES | DISADVANTAGES |
|---|---|
| **Centralized** | |
| • Greater top-management control | • Less responsiveness to customers |
| • More efficiency | • Less empowerment |
| • Simpler distribution system | • Interorganizational conflict |
| • Stronger brand/corporate image | • Lower morale away from headquarters |
| **Decentralized** | |
| • Better adaptation to customer wants | • Less efficiency |
| • More empowerment of workers | • Complex distribution system |
| • Faster decision making | • Less top-management control |
| • Higher morale | • Weakened corporate image |

**span of control**
The optimum number of subordinates a manager supervises or should supervise.

sense, therefore, to give store managers in various cities the authority to buy, price, and promote merchandise appropriate for each area. Such a delegation of authority is an example of decentralized management.

In contrast, McDonald's feels that purchasing, promotion, and other such decisions are best handled centrally. There's usually little need for each McDonald's restaurant to carry different food products. McDonald's would therefore lean toward centralized authority. However, today's rapidly changing markets, added to global differences in consumer tastes, tend to favor more decentralization and thus more delegation of authority, even at McDonald's. Its restaurants in England offer tea, those in France offer a Croque McDo (a hot ham-and-cheese sandwich), those in Japan offer rice, those in China offer taro and red bean desserts, and so on.[16] Rosenbluth International is a service organization in the travel industry. It too has decentralized so that its separate units can offer the kinds of services demanded in each region while still getting needed resources from corporate headquarters. What other service organizations might benefit from having more freedom at the local level?

There was a time when every McDonald's restaurant looked much the same and carried the same kind of food. Centralized management decisions were appropriate in such circumstances. Today, however, McDonald's restaurants are all over the world and decentralized decision making has become more appropriate as managers adapt to the local tastes of each country. Which country would you expect to serve beer? Tea?

## Choosing the Appropriate Span of Control

**Span of control** refers to the optimum number of subordinates a manager supervises or should supervise. There are many factors to consider when determining span of control.[17] At lower levels, where work is standardized, it's possible to implement a broad span of control (15 to 40 workers). For example, one supervisor can be responsible for 20 or more workers who are assembling computers or cleaning up movie theaters. However, the number gradually narrows at higher levels of the organization because work is less standardized and there's more need for face-to face communication.

In businesses today, the span of control varies widely. The number of people reporting to a company president may range from 1 to 80 or more. The trend is to expand the span of control as organizations reduce the number of middle managers and hire more educated and talented lower-level employees. That is all included in the idea of *empowerment*. It's possible to increase the span of control as employees become more professional, as information technology

*"Shaded blue box on our org chart, meet dotted red arrow."*

Cross-functional work teams often call for new organizational charts to show the relationships among employees. A person may work in the design department, but be assigned with people in engineering and marketing to come up with a new product design. Would you enjoy working with different people on new assignments over time?

makes it possible for managers to handle more information, and as employees take on more responsibility for self-management. At Rowe Furniture in Salem, Virginia, for example, the manufacturing chief dismantled the assembly line and gave the people who had previously performed limited functions (sewing, gluing, stapling) the freedom to make sofas as they saw fit. That is, the chief empowered the company's workers. Productivity and quality soared. The company's delivery time was six weeks in the 1980s; this had been cut to just 10 days by early 2006.[18] More companies could expand their span of control if they trained their employees better and were willing to trust them more.

## Tall versus Flat Organization Structures

In the early 20th century, organizations grew bigger and bigger, adding layer after layer of management until they came to have what are called tall organization structures. A **tall organization structure** is one in which the pyramidal organization chart would be quite tall because of the various levels of management. Some organizations had as many as 14 levels, and the span of control was small (that is, there were few people reporting to each manager). You can imagine how a message might be distorted as it moved up the organization from manager to manager and then back down. When viewing such a tall organization, you saw a huge complex of managers, management assistants, secretaries, assistant secretaries, supervisors, trainers, and so on. The cost of keeping all these managers and support people was quite high. The paperwork they generated was enormous, and the inefficiencies in communication and decision making often became intolerable.

**tall organization structure**
An organizational structure in which the pyramidal organization chart would be quite tall because of the various levels of management.

The result was the movement toward flatter organizations. A **flat organization structure** is one that has fewer layers of management (see Figure 8.3) and a broad span of control (that is, there are many people reporting to each manager). Such structures can be highly responsive to customer demands because authority and responsibility for making decisions may be given to

**flat organization structure**
An organization structure that has few layers of management and a broad span of control.

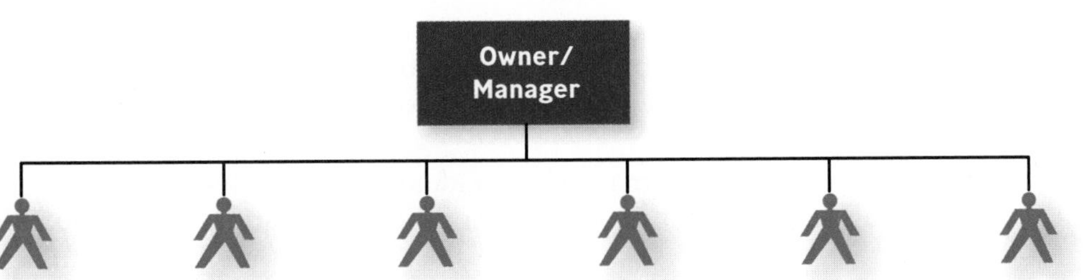


figure 8.3

**A FLAT ORGANIZATION STRUCTURE**

figure 8.4

**ADVANTAGES AND DISADVANTAGES OF A NARROW VERSUS A BROAD SPAN OF CONTROL**

The flatter the organization, the broader the span of control.

| ADVANTAGES | DISADVANTAGES |
| --- | --- |
| **Narrow** | |
| • More control by top management | • Less empowerment |
| • More chances for advancement | • Higher costs |
| • Greater specialization | • Delayed decision making |
| • Closer supervision | • Less responsiveness to customers |
| **Broad** | |
| • Reduced costs | • Fewer chances for advancement |
| • More responsiveness to customers | • Overworked managers |
| • Faster decision making | • Loss of control |
| • More empowerment | • Less management expertise |

lower-level employees, and managers can be spared from certain day-to-day tasks. DaimlerChrysler is dumping 6,000 white-collar jobs in the next few years for just that reason.[19]

In a bookstore that has a flat organization structure, employees may have the authority to arrange shelves by category, process special orders for customers, and so on. In many ways, large organizations are trying to match the friendliness of small firms, whose workers often know the customers by name. The flatter organizations become, the broader the span of control becomes for most managers, and many managers lose their jobs. Figure 8.4 lists some advantages and disadvantages of a narrow versus a broad span of control.

## Advantages and Disadvantages of Departmentalization

**departmentalization** The dividing of organizational functions into separate units.

**Departmentalization** is the dividing of organizational functions (design, production, marketing, accounting, etc.) into separate units. The traditional way to departmentalize organizations is by function. Functional structure is the grouping of workers into departments based on similar skills, expertise, or resource use. A company might have, for example, a production department, a transportation department, and a finance department. Departmentalization by function enables employees to specialize and work together efficiently. It may also save costs. Other advantages include the following:

1. Employees can develop skills in depth and can progress within a department as they master those skills.
2. The company can achieve economies of scale in that it can centralize all the resources it needs and locate various experts in that area.
3. There's good coordination within the function, and top management can easily direct and control various departments' activities.

As for disadvantages of departmentalization by function,

1. There may be a lack of communication among the different departments. For example, production may be so isolated from marketing that the people making the product do not get the proper feedback from customers.[20]
2. Individual employees may begin to identify with their department and its goals rather than with the goals of the organization as a whole. For

example, the purchasing department may find a good value somewhere and buy a huge volume of goods that have to be stored at a high cost to the firm. Such a deal may make the purchasing department look good, but it hurts the overall profitability of the firm.

3. The company's response to external changes may be slow.
4. People may not be trained to take different managerial responsibilities; rather, they tend to become narrow specialists.
5. People in the same department tend to engage in groupthink (think alike) and may need input from outside the department to become more creative.

**Alternative Ways to Departmentalize** Functional separation isn't always the most responsive form of organization. So what are the alternatives? Figure 8.5 on page 216 shows five ways a firm can departmentalize. One form of departmentalization is by product. A book publisher might have a trade book department (books sold to the general public), a textbook department, and a technical book department. Customers for each type of book are different, so separate development and marketing processes may be created for each product. Such product-focused departmentalization usually results in good customer relations.

It makes more sense in some organizations to departmentalize by customer group. A pharmaceutical company, for example, might have one department that focuses on the consumer market, another that calls on hospitals (the institutional market), and another that targets doctors. You can see how the customer groups might benefit from having specialists satisfying their needs.

Some firms group their units by geographic location because customers vary so greatly by region. Japan, Europe, and Korea may involve separate departments. Again, the benefits are rather obvious.

The decision about which way to departmentalize depends greatly on the nature of the product and the customers served. A few firms find that it's most efficient to separate activities by process. For example, a firm that makes leather coats may have one department cut the leather, another dye it, and a third sew the coat together. Such specialization enables employees to do a better job because they can focus on a few, critical skills.

Some firms use a combination of departmentalization techniques; they would be called *hybrid forms*. For example, a company could departmentalize by function, geographic location, *and* customer groups.

The development of the Internet has created whole new opportunities for reaching customers. Not only can companies sell to customers directly over the Internet, but they can also interact with customers, ask them questions, and provide them with any information they may want. Companies must now learn to coordinate the efforts made by their traditional departments and their Internet people to create a friendly, easy-to-use process for accessing information and buying goods and services.[21] The firms that have implemented such coordinated systems for meeting customer needs are winning market share.

**progress assessment**

- Why are organizations becoming flatter?
- What are some reasons for having a narrow span of control in an organization?
- What are the advantages and disadvantages of departmentalization?
- What are the various ways a firm can departmentalize?

figure 8.5

**WAYS TO DEPARTMENTALIZE**

A computer company may want to departmentalize by geographic location (countries), a manufacturer by function, a pharmaceutical company by customer group, a leather manufacturer by process, and a publisher by product. In each case the structure must fit the firm's goals.

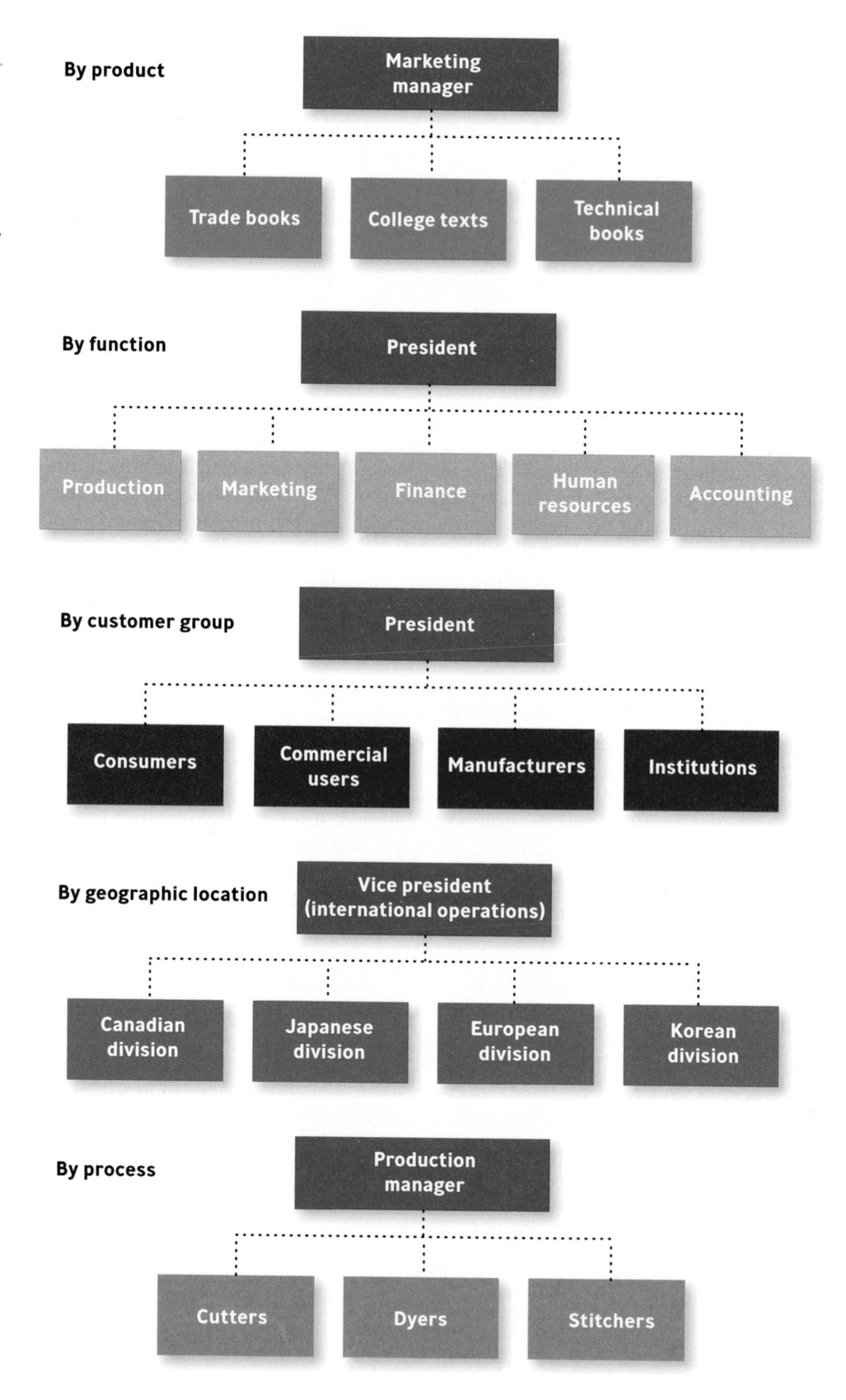


## ORGANIZATION MODELS

Now that we've explored the basic issues of organization design, we can explore in depth the various ways to structure an organization. We'll look at four models: (1) line organizations, (2) line-and-staff organizations, (3) matrix-style organizations, and (4) cross-functional self-managed teams. You'll see that some of these models violate traditional management principles. The business community is in a period of transition, with some traditional organizational models giving way to new structures. Such transitions can be not only painful but also fraught with problems and errors. It will be easier for you to understand the issues involved after you have learned the basics of organizational modeling.

**line organization**
An organization that has direct two-way lines of responsibility, authority, and communication running from the top to the bottom of the organization, with all people reporting to only one supervisor.

## Line Organizations

A **line organization** has direct two-way lines of responsibility, authority, and communication running from the top to the bottom of the organization, with all people reporting to only one supervisor. The military and many small businesses are organized this way. For example, Mario's Pizza Parlor has a general manager and a shift manager. All the general employees report to the shift manager, and he or she reports to the general manager or owner. A line organization does not have any specialists who provide managerial support. For example, there would be no legal department, no accounting department, no personnel department, and no information technology (IT) department. Such organizations follow all of Fayol's traditional management rules. Line managers can issue orders, enforce discipline, and adjust the organization as conditions change.

In large businesses, a line organization may have the disadvantages of being too inflexible, of having few specialists or experts to advise people along the line, of having lines of communication that are too long, and of being unable to handle the complex decisions involved in an organization with thousands of sometimes unrelated products and literally tons of paperwork. Such organizations usually turn to a line-and-staff form of organization.

## Line-and-Staff Organizations

**line personnel**
Employees who are part of the chain of command that is responsible for achieving organizational goals.

**staff personnel**
Employees who advise and assist line personnel in meeting their goals.

To minimize the disadvantages of simple line organizations, many organizations today have both line and staff personnel. A couple of definitions will help. **Line personnel** are part of the chain of command that is responsible for directly achieving organizational goals. Included are production workers, distribution people, and marketing personnel. **Staff personnel** *advise and assist* line personnel in meeting their goals (e.g., marketing research, legal advising, information technology, and human resource management). See Figure 8.6 for a diagram of a line-and-staff organization. One important difference between line and staff personnel is authority. Line personnel have formal authority to make policy decisions. Staff personnel have the authority to *advise* the line personnel and make suggestions that might influence those decisions, but they can't make policy changes themselves. The line manager may choose to seek or to ignore the advice from staff personnel.

Many organizations have benefited from the expert advice of staff assistants in areas such as safety, legal issues, quality control, database management, motivation, and investing. Staff positions strengthen the line positions and are not inferior or lower-paid. Having people in staff positions is like having well-paid consultants on the organization's payroll.

## Matrix-Style Organizations

Both line and line-and-staff organization structures may suffer from inflexibility. Both allow for established lines of authority and communication, and both work well in organizations with a relatively unchanging environment and slow product development, such as firms selling consumer products like toasters and refrigerators. In such firms, clear lines of authority and relatively fixed organization structures are assets that ensure efficient operations.

figure 8.6

A SAMPLE LINE-AND-STAFF ORGANIZATION

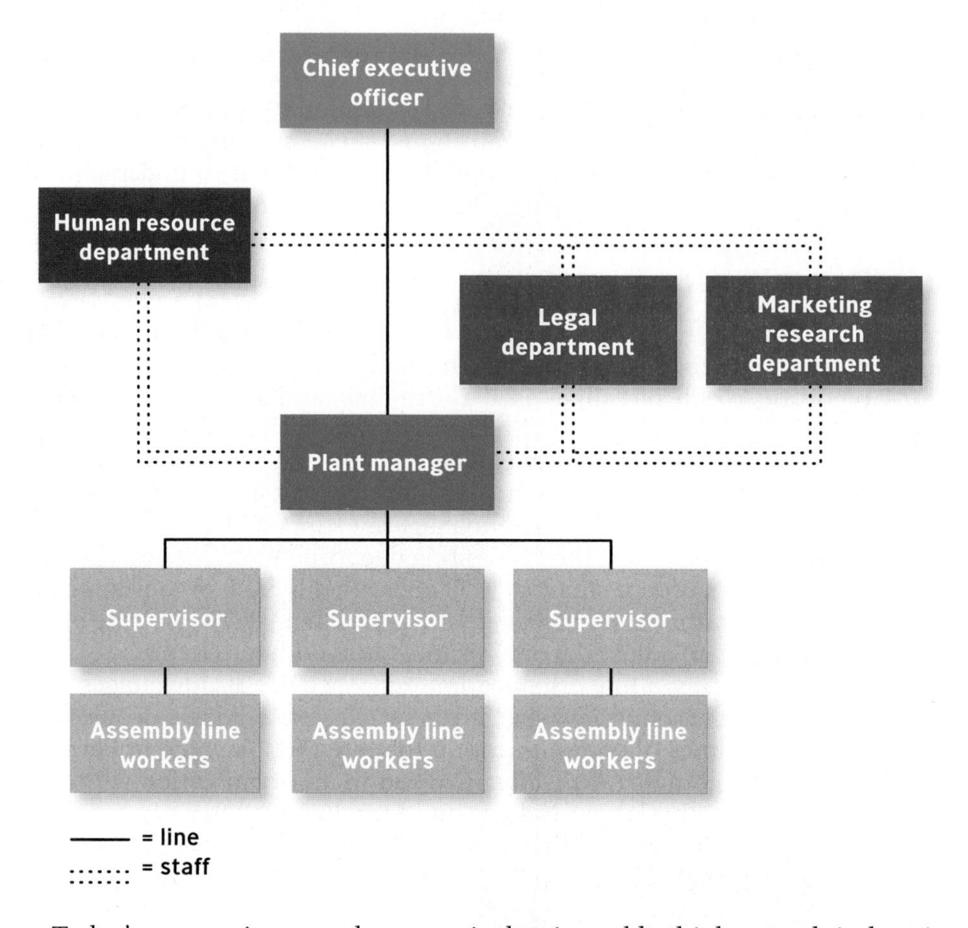


Today's economic scene, however, is dominated by high-growth industries (e.g., telecommunications, nanotechnology, robotics, biotechnology, and aerospace) unlike anything seen in the past. In such industries, competition is stiff and the life cycle of new ideas is short. Emphasis is on product development, creativity, special projects, rapid communication, and interdepartmental teamwork.[22] The economic, technological, and competitive environments are rapidly changing.

**matrix organization**
An organization in which specialists from different parts of the organization are brought together to work on specific projects but still remain part of a line-and-staff structure.

From those changes grew the popularity of the matrix organization. In a **matrix organization**, specialists from different parts of the organization are brought together to work on specific projects but still remain part of a line-and-staff structure. (See Figure 8.7 for a diagram of a matrix organization.) In other words, a project manager can borrow people from different departments to help design and market new product ideas.

Matrix organization structures were first developed in the aerospace industry at firms such as Boeing and Lockheed Martin. The structure is now used in banking, management consulting firms, accounting firms, ad agencies, and school systems. Advantages of a matrix organization structure include the following:

- It gives flexibility to managers in assigning people to projects.
- It encourages interorganizational cooperation and teamwork.
- It can result in creative solutions to problems such as those associated with product development.
- It provides for efficient use of organizational resources.

Although it works well in some organizations, the matrix style doesn't work well in others. As for disadvantages,

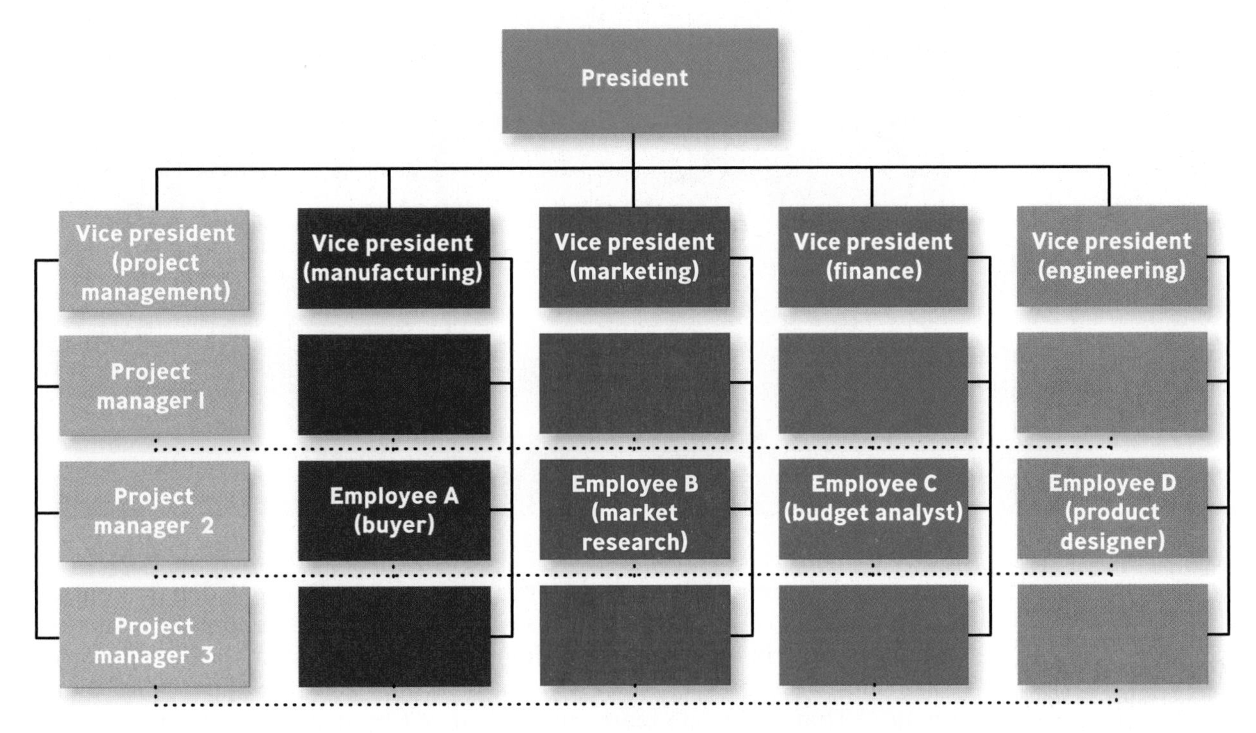


figure 8.7

**A MATRIX ORGANIZATION**

In a matrix organization, project managers are in charge of teams made up of members of several departments. In this case, project manager 2 supervises employees A, B, C, and D. These employees are accountable not only to project manager 2 but also to the head of their individual departments. For example, employee B, a market researcher, reports to project manager 2 *and* to the vice president of marketing.

- It's costly and complex.
- It can cause confusion among employees as to where their loyalty belongs—to the project manager or to their functional unit.
- It requires good interpersonal skills and cooperative employees and managers; communication problems can emerge.
- It may be only a temporary solution to a long-term problem.

If it seems to you that matrix organizations violate some traditional managerial principles, you're right. Normally a person can't work effectively for two bosses. Who has the real authority? Which directive has the first priority: the one from the project manager or the one from the employee's immediate supervisor? In reality, however, the system functions more effectively than you might imagine. To develop a new product, a project manager may be given temporary authority to "borrow" line personnel from production, marketing, and other line functions. Together, the employees work to complete the project and then return to their regular positions. Thus, no one really reports to more than one manager at a time. The effectiveness of matrix organizations in high-tech firms has led to the adoption of similar concepts in many firms, including such traditional firms as Rubbermaid. During the past decade, Rubbermaid turned out an average of one new product every day using the team concept from matrix management.

A potential problem with matrix management, however, is that the project teams are not permanent. They are formed to solve a problem or develop a new product, and then they break up. There is little chance for cross-functional learning because experts from each function are together for so little time.

## Cross-Functional Self-Managed Teams

An answer to the disadvantage of the *temporary* teams created by matrix management is to establish *long-lived* teams and to empower them to work closely with suppliers, customers, and others to quickly and efficiently bring out new, high-quality products while giving great service.[23] **Cross-functional self-**

**cross-functional self-managed teams**
Groups of employees from different departments who work together on a long-term basis.

Teams at Rubbermaid have turned out new products at a pace of one per day. Does this elaborate storage system look as attractive to you as it does to me?

**managed teams** are groups of employees from different departments who work together on a long-term basis (as opposed to the temporary teams established in matrix style organizations).[24] Usually the teams are empowered to make decisions on their own without having to seek the approval of management.[25] That's why the teams are called *self-managed*. The barriers between design, engineering, marketing, distribution, and other functions fall when interdepartmental teams are created. Sometimes the teams are interfirm. Toyota, for example, works closely with teams at other firms to produce its cars.

**Going Beyond Organizational Boundaries** Cross-functional teams work best when the voice of the customer is brought into organizations.[26] Customer input is especially valuable to product development teams. Suppliers and distributors should be included on the team as well. A cross-functional team that includes customers, suppliers, and distributors goes beyond organizational boundaries.

Some firms' suppliers and distributors are in other countries. Thus, cross-functional teams may share market information across national boundaries. The government may encourage the networking of teams, and government coordinators may assist such projects. In that case, cross-functional teams break the barriers between government and business. The use of cross functional teams is only one way in which businesses have changed to interact with other companies. In the next section of this chapter we look at other ways that organizations manage their various interactions.

**progress assessment**

- What is the difference between line and staff personnel?
- What management principle does a matrix-style organization challenge?
- What is the main difference between a matrix-style organization's structure and the use of cross-functional teams?

**networking**
Using communications technology and other means to link organizations and allow them to work together on common objectives.

## MANAGING THE INTERACTIONS AMONG FIRMS

Whether it involves customers, suppliers and distributors, or the government, **networking** is using communications technology and other means to link organizations and allow them to work together on common objectives.[27]

Operating in real time can be a real advantage, but it can be intrusive as well. Have you seen people on vacation using cell phones and laptop computers to stay in touch?

Organizations are so closely linked by the Internet that each can find out what the others are doing in real time. **Real time** simply means the present moment or the actual time in which something takes place. Internet data are available in real time because they are sent instantly to various organizational partners as they are developed or collected. The net effect is a rather new concept called transparency. **Transparency** occurs when a company is so open to other companies working with it that the once-solid barriers between them become see-through and electronic information is shared as if the companies were one. Because of this integration, two companies can now work as closely together as two departments once did in traditional firms.

**real time**
The present moment or the actual time in which something takes place.

**transparency**
A concept that describes a company being so open to other companies working with it that the once-solid barriers between them become see-through and electronic information is shared as if the companies were one.

Can you see the implications for organizational design? Most organizations are no longer self-sufficient or self-contained. Rather, many modern organizations are part of a vast network of global businesses that work closely together. An organization chart showing what people do within any one organization is simply not complete because the organization is part of a much larger system of firms. A modern organization chart would show people in different organizations and indicate how they are networked. This is a relatively new concept, however, so few such charts are yet available.

The organization structures tend to be flexible and changing. That is, one company may work with a design expert from a different company in Italy for a year and then not need that person anymore. Another expert from another company in another country may be hired next time for another project. Such a temporary networked organization, made up of replaceable firms that join and leave as needed, is called a **virtual corporation** (see Figure 8.8 on page 222). This may sound confusing because it is so different from traditional organization structure; in fact, traditional managers do often have trouble adapting to the speed of change and the impermanence of relationships that have come about in the age of networking. We discuss adaptation to change in the final section of this chapter; first, though, we describe how organizations are using benchmarking and outsourcing to manage their interactions with other firms.

**virtual corporation**
A temporary networked organization made up of replaceable firms that join and leave as needed.

## Benchmarking and Core Competencies

Traditionally, organizations have tried to do all functions themselves. That is, each organization had a separate department for accounting, finance, marketing, production, and so on. Today's organizations are looking to other organizations to help them in areas where they are not able to generate world-class quality. **Benchmarking** involves comparing an organization's practices,

**benchmarking**
Comparing an organization's practices, processes, and products against the world's best.

figure 8.8

**A VIRTUAL CORPORATION**

A virtual corporation has no permanent ties to the firms that do its production, distribution, legal, and other work. Such firms are very flexible and can adapt to changes in the market quickly.

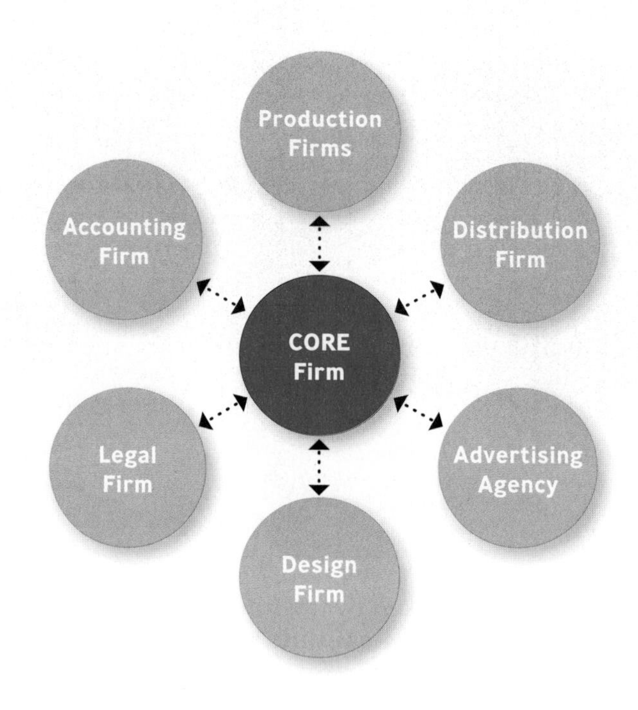


processes, and products against the world's best.[28] For example, K2 is a company that makes skis, snowboards, in-line skates, and related products. It studied the compact-disc industry and learned to use ultraviolet inks to print graphics on skis. It went to the aerospace industry to get Piezo technology to reduce vibration in its snowboards (the aerospace industry uses the technology for wings on planes). It learned from the cable-TV industry how to braid layers of fiberglass and carbon, and adapted that knowledge to make skis. Wyeth, a pharmaceutical company, benchmarked the aerospace industry for project management, the shipping industry for standardization of processes, and computer makers to learn the most efficient way to make products.[29]

Knowledge is increasing and technology is developing so fast that companies can only maintain a leading edge by benchmarking everything they do against the best in all industries. That's how K-2 was able to find the best materials and processes for making its skis. Whom might you study to learn the best way to prepare for classes and exams?

Benchmarking is also used in a more directly competitive way. For example, Target may compare itself to Wal-Mart to see what, if anything, Wal-Mart does better. Target would then try to improve its practices or processes to become even better than Wal-Mart. Sam Walton used to do competitive benchmarking regularly. He would visit the stores of competitors and see what, if anything, the competitor was doing better. When he found something better—say, a pricing program—he would come back to Wal-Mart and make the appropriate changes.

If an organization can't do as well as the best in any particular area, such as shipping, it often will try to outsource the function to an organization that *is* the best (e.g., UPS or FedEx). Outsourcing, remember, means assigning various functions, such as accounting, production, security, maintenance, and legal work, to outside organizations. We have already discussed some problems associated with outsourcing, especially when companies outsource functions to other countries. Jobs are lost in the United States, leaving some states severely hurt. Some functions, such as information management and marketing, may be too important to assign to outside firms. In that case, the organization should benchmark on the best firms and restructure its departments to try to be equally good.

When a firm has completed its outsourcing process, the remaining functions are the firm's core competencies. **Core competencies** are those functions that the organization can do as well as or better than any other organization in the world. For example, Nike is great at designing and marketing athletic shoes. Those are its core competencies. It outsources manufacturing, however, to other companies that can assemble shoes better and less expensively than Nike itself can. Similarly, Dell is best at marketing computers and outsources most other functions, including manufacturing and distribution, to others. IBM has also outsourced most of its manufacturing functions.

**core competencies**
Those functions that the organization can do as well as or better than any other organization in the world.

## ADAPTING TO CHANGE

Once you have structured an organization, you must be prepared to adapt that structure to changes in the market. As you read in the case of Xerox (see the chapter's Opening Profile), that is not always easy to do. Over a number of years, it is easy for an organization to become stuck in its ways. Employees have a tendency to say, "That's the way we've always done things. If it isn't broken, don't fix it." Managers also get stuck in their ways. Managers may say that they have 20 years' experience when the truth is that they've had one year's experience 20 times. Introducing change into an organization is thus one of the hardest challenges facing any manager. Nonetheless, that is what is happening at GM, Ford, Kodak, and the other companies cited earlier in this chapter. Traditional companies are used to operating in traditional ways. Such ways are often no longer appropriate. But change is hard. If you have old facilities that are no longer efficient, you have to get rid of them. That's exactly what Ford and other companies are doing. You may have to cut your labor force to lower costs. Again, that is what companies are doing. They hope to rehire those people in the future when the reorganization results in a faster-growing firm.

**restructuring**
Redesigning an organization so that it can more effectively and efficiently serve its customers.

Several companies have been cited in the business literature as having difficulty reinventing themselves in response to changes in the competitive environment. They include Kmart and Polaroid. Digital cameras and new kinds of film brought about the downfall of Polaroid, which filed for bankruptcy and was later sold. Kmart was unable to manage the competition from Wal-Mart, Sears, and Target, and filed for bankruptcy. Edward Lampert joined Sears Holding with Kmart Holding and is trying to make the Kmart stores more competitive with wider aisles and Sears products, including appliances.[30] Can Lampert create a new image for Kmart—and more profits? Only time will tell.

Kmart is not the only company going through changes. The Dealing with Change box on page 224 discusses the new management at Hewlett-Packard, and the challenges facing Mark Hurd, its CEO. Hurd is dealing with issues of decentralization, empowerment, and corporate culture—all subjects of this chapter.

Often it's the little things that can make a big difference in consumer perceptions. The piano player in this Nordstrom store adds a lot to the atmosphere. However, an even more important Nordstrom difference is the power it gives its employees to make decisions about customer returns, etc. How does this empowerment help the store build relationships with its customers?

### Restructuring for Empowerment

To implement the empowerment of employees, firms often must reorganize dramatically. Sometimes that may mean restructuring the firm to make frontline workers the most important people in the organization. **Restructuring** is redesigning an organization so that it can more effectively and efficiently serve its customers.[31] Until recently, front-desk people in hotels, clerks in department

## DEALING WITH change

www.hp.com

### Riding Hurd at HP

Few managers have received more attention in the last few years than Carleton (Carly) Fiorina. She led the fight to unite her company, Hewlett-Packard (HP), with Compaq Computer. The news media and the stock market experts all expected the attempt to fail, but the integration took place and Fiorina had the task of reorganizing the two companies into one.

Fiorina had to get rid of duplicate products and eliminate some employees to realize the cost savings that the integration made available. She hoped to cut costs by $3 billion annually. The 2002 stock market downturn occurred right in the middle of her reorganization attempt and made the whole process more difficult. Eventually, Fiorina was ousted from the firm and Mark Hurd took over. Hurd came from NCR, a much smaller firm, where he was known as a cost cutter and strong operations manager. In other words, he was more involved in the day-to-day operations of the firm than Fiorina had been at HP.

Experts suggested that Hurd should adopt a decentralized form of management at first, especially with consumer products, with which he had no experience at NCR. They also suggested that he restructure the sales force and focus more on innovation, especially in the printer business. Finally, Hurd was advised to restore the old corporate culture, which emphasized simple objectives, enlightened business practices, and trust in employees to make the right decisions (empowerment). It will be interesting to follow the success or failure of Hurd as he struggles with organizational issues at HP. Making organizational changes is never easy, but it is especially difficult in a large firm that is struggling to stay viable in a highly competitive market.

Sources: Peter Burrows and Ben Elgin, "Memo to: Mark Hurd," *BusinessWeek*, April 11, 2005, pp. 38–39; Michael S. Malone, "What's the Hurd Instinct?," *The Wall Street Journal*, May 19, 2005, p. A14; and Pui-Wing Tam, "H-P Net Rises on Gains Across Units," *Wall Street Journal*, February 16, 2006, p. A3.

**inverted organization**
An organization that has contact people at the top and the chief executive officer at the bottom of the organization chart.

stores, and tellers in banks hadn't been considered the key personnel. Instead, managers were considered the key people, and they were responsible for directing the work of the front-line people. The organization chart in a typical firm looked something like the organization pyramid shown in Figure 8.1.

A few service-oriented organizations have turned the traditional organization structure upside down. An **inverted organization** has contact people at the top and the chief executive officer at the bottom. There are few layers of management, and the manager's job is to assist and support frontline people, not boss them around. Figure 8.9 illustrates the difference between an inverted and a traditional organizational structure.

Companies based on this organization structure support frontline personnel with internal and external databases, advanced communication systems,

figure 8.9

**COMPARISON OF AN INVERTED ORGANIZATION STRUCTURE AND A TRADITIONAL ORGANIZATION STRUCTURE**

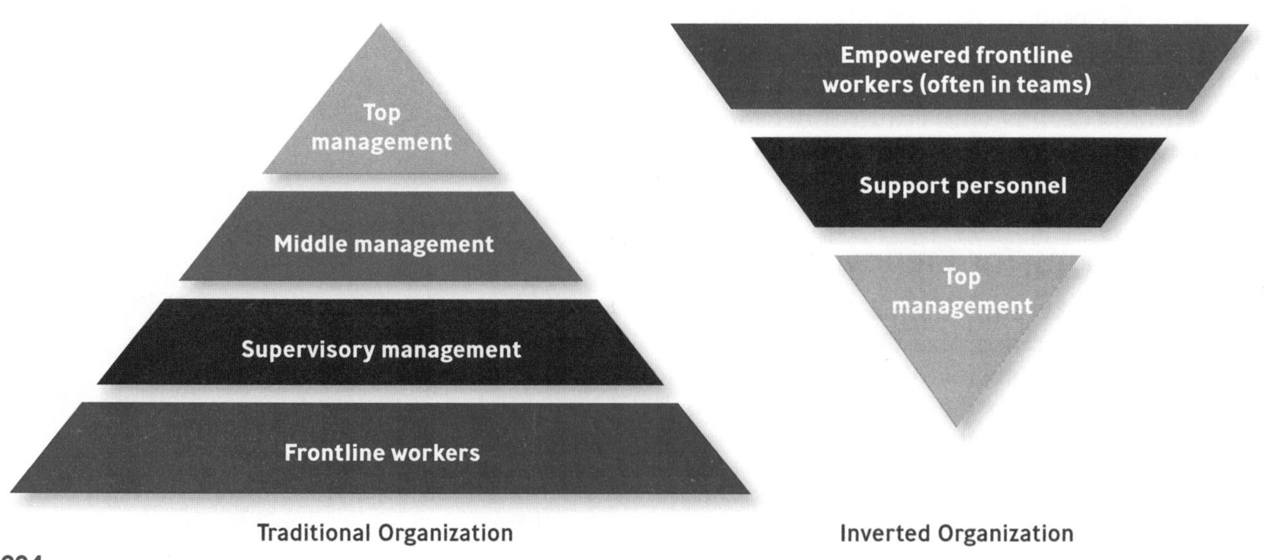

and professional assistance. Naturally, this means that frontline people have to be better educated, better trained, and better paid than in the past. It takes a lot of trust for top managers to implement such a system—but when they do, the payoff in customer satisfaction and in profits is often well worth the effort. In the past, managers controlled information—and that gave them power. In more progressive organizations, everyone shares information, often through an elaborate database system. Today, that information sharing is among firms as well as within firms. Organizations have formed close alliances with other firms—for example, one firm may design the product and the other firm produce it. The communication among such firms is often just as close and personal as within a single firm.[32]

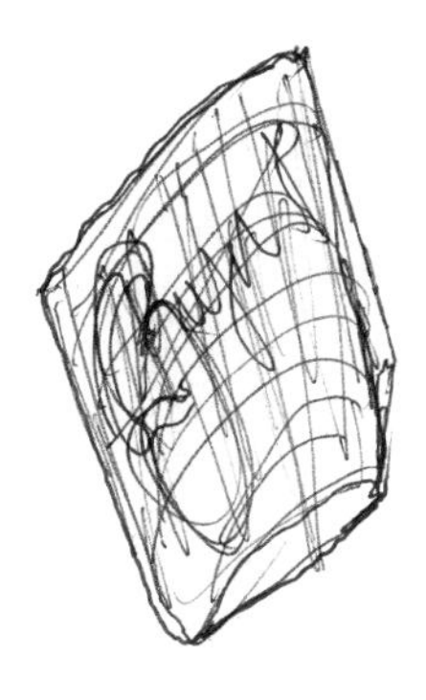

## Focusing on the Customer

No matter what organizational model you choose or how much you empower your employees, the secret to successful organization change is to focus on customers and give them what they want. That's what Ford is now doing. CEO Bill Ford has introduced a new program called "The Way Forward." "True customer focus means that our business decisions originate from our knowledge of what the customer wants," Ford says. He confessed that product plans in the past were "defined by our capacity" and vehicles were designed to utilize plant capacity "sometimes at the expense of creativity."[33]

One thing Ford, GM, and Chrysler have learned is that customers today want fuel-efficient (usually small) cars or hybrids.[34] Sometimes it is hard for such large companies to adapt to market changes, like higher gas prices, but eventually they *do* change, or they go out of business.

## Creating a Change-Oriented Organizational Culture

**organizational (or corporate) culture**
Widely shared values within an organization that provide unity and cooperation to achieve common goals.

Any organizational change is bound to cause some stress and resistance among members of the firm. Firms adapt best when they have a change-oriented culture. **Organizational (or corporate) culture** may be defined as widely shared values within an organization that provide unity and cooperation to achieve common goals. Usually the culture of an organization is reflected in stories, traditions, and myths. It's obvious from visiting any McDonald's restaurant that effort has been made to maintain a culture that emphasizes quality, service, cleanliness, and value. Each restaurant has the same feel, the same look, the same atmosphere. In short, each has a similar organizational culture.

An organizational culture can also be negative. Have you ever been in an organization where you feel that no one cares about service or quality? The clerks may seem uniformly glum, indifferent, and testy. The mood seems to pervade the atmosphere so that patrons become unhappy or upset. It may be hard to believe that an organization, especially a profit-making one, can be run so badly and still survive. When searching for a job, therefore, it is important to study the organizational culture to see if you will thrive in the present culture.[35]

The very best organizations have cultures that emphasize service to others, especially customers.[36] The atmosphere is one of friendly, concerned, caring people who enjoy working together to provide a good product at a reasonable price. Those companies that have such cultures have less need for close supervision of employees, not to mention policy manuals; organization charts; and formal rules, procedures, and controls. The key to a productive culture is mutual trust. You get such trust by giving it. The very best companies stress high moral and ethical values such as honesty, reliability, fairness, environmental protection, and social involvement. The Spotlight on Small Business box on page 226 looks at how one small organization successfully implemented a customer-oriented culture.

SPOTLIGHT ON small business www.amysicecreams.com

## All This and Ice Cream Too

Amy's Ice Creams parlors in Austin and Houston, Texas, attract a lot of customers because of their offbeat corporate culture. On any given night, you might see the servers juggling with their serving spades, tossing scoops of ice cream to each other, or break-dancing on the freezer top. If there is a long line, they pass out samples or give a free cone to any customer who will sing, dance, recite a poem, or otherwise entertain those in line. Employees might be wearing pajamas (Sleepover Night) or masks (Star Wars Night). Lighting may be provided by candles (Romance Night) or strobe lights (Disco Night). You get the idea. It's fun at Amy's—for the customers and for the employees. Amy's is careful to choose employees who will fit in with the organizational culture. For example, in job interviews candidates are asked to decorate a plain bag to show how creative they are. Organizational culture can go a long way toward making a small company a success or a failure.

Thus far, we've been talking as if organizational matters were mostly controllable by management. The fact is that the formal organization structure is just one element of the total organizational system. In the creation of organizational culture, the informal organization is of equal or even greater importance. Let's explore this notion next.

## The Informal Organization

All organizations have two organizational systems. One is the **formal organization**, which is the structure that details lines of responsibility, authority, and position. It's the structure shown on organization charts. The other is the **informal organization**, which is the system of relationships that develop spontaneously as employees meet and form power centers. It consists of the various cliques, relationships, and lines of authority that develop outside the formal organization. It's the human side of the organization that doesn't show on any organization chart.[37]

No organization can operate effectively without both types of organization. The formal system is often too slow and bureaucratic to enable the organization to adapt quickly. However, the formal organization does provide helpful guides and lines of authority to follow in routine situations.

The informal organization is often too unstructured and emotional to allow careful, reasoned decision making on critical matters. It's extremely effective, however, in generating creative solutions to short-term problems and providing a feeling of camaraderie and teamwork among employees.

In any organization, it's wise to learn quickly who the important people are in the informal organization. Typically, there are formal rules and procedures to follow for getting certain supplies or equipment, but those procedures may take days. Who in the organization knows how to obtain supplies immediately without following the normal procedures? Which administrative assistants should you see if you want your work given first priority? These are the questions to answer to work effectively in many organizations.

The informal organization's nerve center is the *grapevine* (the system through which

Richard Tait (left) calls himself the grand poo-bah for Cranium, producer of the highly successful board game of that name. Whit Alexander, who does product development and manufacturing, is called the chief noodler. Their criteria for decision making are clever, high quality, innovative, friendly, and fun (CHIFF). What kind of leadership style and company culture might you expect in a company that is so casual?

unofficial information flows between and among managers and employees). The key people in the grapevine usually have considerable influence in the organization.

In the old "us-versus-them" system of organizations, where managers and employees were often at odds, the informal system often hindered effective management. In the new, more open organizations, where managers and employees work together to set objectives and design procedures, the informal organization can be an invaluable managerial asset that often promotes harmony among workers and establishes the corporate culture. That's a major advantage, for example, of self-managed teams.

As effective as the informal organization may be in creating group cooperation, it can still be equally powerful in resisting management directives. Employees may form unions, go on strike together, and generally disrupt operations. Learning to create the right corporate culture and to work within the informal organization is a key to managerial success.

**formal organization**
The structure that details lines of responsibility, authority, and position; that is, the structure shown on organization charts.

**informal organization**
The system of relationships and lines of authority that develops spontaneously as employees meet and form power centers; that is, the human side of the organization that does not appear on any organization chart.

## progress assessment

- What is an inverted organization?
- Why do organizations outsource functions?
- What is organizational culture?

## summary

1. Companies like Ford, GM, and Kodak are going through the painful process of reorganization. They are closing plants, firing workers, and restructuring their operations to be more competitive. They are basing such changes on basic organizational principles that apply to all organizations.
   - **What concepts did Fayol and Weber contribute?**

   Fayol introduced principles such as unity of command, hierarchy of authority, division of labor, subordination of individual interests to the general interest, authority, clear communication channels, order, and equity. Weber added principles of bureaucracy such as job descriptions, written rules and decision guidelines, consistent procedures, and staffing and promotions based on qualifications. Today, bureaucratic organizations are simply too slow moving to handle the rapidly changing conditions facing most corporations and government agencies.

**1.** Explain the organizational theories of Fayol and Weber.

2. Issues involved in structuring and restructuring organizations include (1) centralization versus decentralization, (2) span of control, (3) tall versus flat organization structures, and (4) departmentalization.
   - **What are the basics of each?**

   Departments are often being replaced or supplemented by matrix organizations and cross-functional teams. Use of cross-functional teams results in decentralization of authority. The span of control becomes larger as employees become self-directed. The problem with tall organizations is that they slow communications. The trend is to eliminate managers and flatten organizations.

**2.** Explain the various issues involved in structuring organizations.

3. Organizational design is the coordinating of workers so that they can best accomplish the firm's goals. New forms of organization are emerging that enable firms to be more responsive to customers.

**3.** Describe and differentiate the various organizational models.

- **What are the traditional forms of organization and their advantages?**

The two traditional forms of organization explored in the text are (1) line organizations and (2) line-and-staff organizations. A line organization has the advantages of having clearly defined responsibility and authority, being easy to understand, and providing one supervisor for each person. Most organizations have benefited from the expert advice of staff assistants in areas such as safety, quality control, computer technology, human resource management, and investing.

- **What are the alternative forms of organization?**

Matrix organizations and cross-functional self-managed teams.

- **How do they differ?**

Matrix organizations involve *temporary* assignments (projects) that give flexibility to managers in assigning people to projects and encourage interorganizational cooperation and teamwork. Cross-functional self-managed teams are *long term* and have all the benefits of the matrix style.

**4.** Discuss the concepts involved in interfirm cooperation and coordination.

4. Networking is using communications technology and other means to link organizations and allow them to work together on common objectives.

- **What is a virtual corporation?**

A virtual corporation is a networked organization made up of replaceable firms that join the network and leave it as needed.

- **Why do firms outsource some of their functions?**

Some firms are very good at one function: for example, marketing. Competitive benchmarking tells them that they are not as good as some companies at production or distribution. The company may then outsource those functions to companies that can perform those functions more effectively and efficiently. The functions left are called the firm's core competencies.

**5.** Explain how restructuring, organizational culture, and informal organizations can help businesses adapt to change.

5. Organizational culture may be defined as widely shared values within an organization that provide coherence and cooperation to achieve common goals.

- **How do inverted organizations fit into these concepts?**

An inverted organization usually results from a major restructuring effort because the changes are dramatic in that employees are placed at the top of the hierarchy and are given much training and support while managers are at the bottom and are there to train and assist employees.

- **How can organizational culture and the informal organization hinder or assist organizational change?**

The very best organizations have cultures that emphasize service to others, especially customers. The atmosphere is one of friendly, concerned, caring people who enjoy working together to provide a good product at a reasonable price. Companies with such cultures have less need than other companies for close supervision of employees; policy manuals; organization charts; and formal rules, procedures, and controls. This opens the way for self-managed teams.

## key terms

**benchmarking** 221
**bureaucracy** 210
**centralized authority** 211
**chain of command** 210
**core competencies** 223
**cross-functional self-managed teams** 219
**decentralized authority** 211
**departmentalization** 214
**economies of scale** 208
**flat organization structure** 213
**formal organization** 227
**hierarchy** 210
**informal organization** 227
**inverted organization** 224
**line organization** 217
**line personnel** 217

**matrix organization** 218
**networking** 220
**organizational (or corporate) culture** 225
**real time** 221
**restructuring** 223
**span of control** 212
**staff personnel** 217
**tall organization structure** 213
**transparency** 221
**virtual corporation** 221

## critical thinking questions

Now that you have learned some of the basic principles of organization, pause and think of where you have already applied such concepts yourself or when you have been involved with an organization that did.

1. Did you find that a division of labor was necessary and helpful?
2. Were you assigned specific tasks or were you left on your own to decide what to do?
3. Were promotions based strictly on qualifications, as Weber suggested? What other factors may have been considered?
4. What problems seem to emerge when an organization gets larger?
5. What organizational changes might you recommend to the auto companies? The airline companies?

## developing workplace skills

1. There is no way to better understand the effects of having many layers of management on communication accuracy than to play the game of Message Relay. Choose seven or more members of the class and have them leave the classroom. Then choose one person to read the following paragraph and another student to listen. Call in one of the students from outside and have the "listener" tell him or her what information was in the paragraph. Then bring in another student and have the new listener repeat the information to him or her. Continue the process with all those who left the room. Do not allow anyone in the class to offer corrections as each listener becomes the storyteller in turn. In this way, all the students can hear how the facts become distorted over time. The distortions and mistakes are often quite humorous, but they are not so funny in organizations such as Ford, which once had 22 layers of management.

   Here's the paragraph:

   *Dealers in the midwest region have received over 130 complaints about steering on the new Commander and Roadhandler models of our minivans. Apparently, the front suspension system is weak and the ball joints are wearing too fast. This causes slippage in the linkage and results in oversteering. Mr. Berenstein has been notified, but so far only 213 out of 4,300 dealers have received repair kits.*

2. Describe some informal groups within an organization with which you are familiar (at school, at work, etc.). What have you noticed about how those groups help or hinder progress in the organization?

3. Imagine you are working for Kitchen Magic, an appliance manufacturer that produces, among other things, dishwashers for the home. Imagine further that a competitor introduces a new dishwasher that uses sound waves to clean dishes. The result is a dishwasher that cleans even the worst burned-on food and sterilizes the dishes and silverware as well. You need to develop a similar offering fast, or your company will lose the market. Write an e-mail to management outlining the problem and explaining your rationale for recommending use of a cross-functional team to respond quickly.
4. Divide the class into teams of five. Imagine that your firm has been asked to join a virtual network. You are a producer of athletic shoes. What might you do to minimize the potential problems of being involved with a virtual corporation? Begin by defining a virtual corporation and listing the potential problems. Also, list the benefits of being part of such a system.
5. As discussed in this chapter, many of the work groups of the future, including management, will be cross-functional and self-managed. To practice working in such an organization, break your class up into groups of five or so students. (Try to find students with different backgrounds and interests.) Each group must work together to prepare a report on the advantages and disadvantages of working in teams. Many of the problems and advantages should emerge in your group as you try to complete this assignment.

## taking it to the net

### Purpose

To describe Ford Motor Company's formal and informal organizational structures.

### Exercise

When you think of how Ford Motor Company is organized, you may think of it in terms of its brands (Mazda, Mercury, Lincoln, Aston Martin, Jaguar, Land Rover, Volvo) or its businesses (Automotive Operations, Ford Financial, Hertz). However, the company serves all of its brands and businesses through what it calls hiring organizations. Learn more about it by going to **www.mycareer.ford.com/OurCompany.asp**.

1. How are Ford's hiring organizations organized?
2. Click on the link of one of the hiring organizations. What types of positions does this function provide? What are the preferred qualifications of the candidates Ford would like to find to fill these positions?
3. Describe Ford's unique hiring process. If you've applied for jobs before, how does Ford's hiring process differ from what you've experienced? What could this process tell you about Ford's organizational culture? How does the process help Ford find employees who will fit in its culture?

## casing the web

To access the case *"IBM Is Both an Outsourcer and a Major Outsource for Others,"* visit **www.mhhe.com/ub8e**

video case

## One Smooth Stone

David slew Goliath with one smooth stone, and thus was born the name of the company One Smooth Stone (OSS). It's an unusual name for an unusually interesting company. The company is in the business of providing materials for big corporate events: sales meetings, client meetings, and product presentations. Most people in the industry have attended many such meetings, so to keep them entertained is a major challenge. And that's where OSS comes in: It uses project teams to come up with original and captivating presentations for its customers.

You read about the history of organizational design in this chapter. You learned, for example, about Fayol and his principles of organization. The first principle is unity of command (every worker is to report to one, and only one, boss). Other principles include order, equity, and esprit de corps. This video shows that OSS is one company that understands the importance of esprit de corps. It is a fun and interesting place to work, and turnover is very low. The company does not follow many of Weber's principles dealing with written rules and consistent procedures. Quite the contrary: OSS is structured to be flexible and responsive to its clients. There are no set rules, and the company is certainly not consistent with its projects. Everything is custom made to the needs of each client.

OSS uses a flat organization structure. There are a few project managers, who have workers under them, but they don't look over the employees' shoulders telling them what to do or how to do it. That means there is decentralized authority. Whereas many companies are structured by department—design, engineering, marketing, finance, accounting, and so forth—OSS is structured using project teams. Each team is structured to meet the needs of an individual client. For example, the company will go out and hire people with specific skills as they are needed. The term for this is *outsourcing,* and OSS outsources many of its tasks to freelance professionals. Together, they work as self-managed teams. The focus of the team is on client needs. There are some staff workers to help with personnel, legal, and other such services.

The company is not keen on making strategic plans because its environment changes so rapidly that such plans are obsolete as soon as they are made. So the company does what is calls "strategic improvising." Although OSS sounds less structured and more informal than most companies, it still focuses on total quality and it practices continuous improvement.

In addition, the company is particularly concerned about its corporate culture. It has three values: smart, fast, and kind. It works smart, responds quickly, and is always kind to others, including its own workers. Because of its culture and responsiveness, the company has been able to capture big accounts like Motorola, Sun Microsystems, and International Truck and Engine.

The long-run success of the firm, however, is based on its project management teams. They carefully listen to what clients are trying to accomplish and then come up with solutions to their problems. You can see the creativity in this video. Clearly, OSS has been able to impress the Goliaths of big business with its presentations.

### Thinking It Over

1. What have you learned from this video about the use of teams as an organizational tool versus the traditional line or line-and-staff forms of organization?
2. Does working at OSS look like more or less fun than working for a company with a more traditional approach to organizational structure and operations? Why?
3. From what you saw in the video, what do you think the core competencies of the company might be?

PRODUCING

# world-class goods AND services

profile

## Getting to Know

X Richard Dauch

## of American Axle & Manufacturing

Richard Dauch (pronounced *Dauck*) was reared on a dairy farm in Norwalk, Ohio—the youngest of seven children. He could drive a pickup truck by the age of 6 and was repairing farm machinery by the age of 16. You can see, then, why he decided to take technical and engineering courses at Purdue University. After college, he got an engineer-in-training job in Chevrolet's auto and truck plant in Flint, Michigan. He decided to learn from the bottom up, so he began working on the truck assembly line. What he learned surprised him. He found, for example, that workers were not always treated very well. He also noted some inattention to quality. Furthermore, union contracts were often so restrictive that they hindered productivity. Dauch would use those insights later in his career, when he was a manager.

At the age of 30, Dauch became Chevrolet's youngest plant manager. He went from one plant with 3,000 employees to an axle plant in Detroit with 7,000 employees. He was so successful that he was recruited by Volkswagen to be vice president for manufacturing in North America. He took an old Chrysler plant in Pennsylvania, a former American Motors plant in West Virginia, and a U.S. government plant in Michigan and began turning out 1,000 Volkswagen Rabbits a day.

His successes caught the attention

LEARNING **goals**

**After you have read and studied this chapter, you should be able to**

1. Describe the evolution of production in the United States.
2. Define operations management.
3. Distinguish between the various production processes and describe several of the production techniques that have improved the productivity of U.S. companies, including computer-aided design and manufacturing, flexible manufacturing, lean manufacturing, and mass customization.
4. Describe the operations management planning issues involved in both the manufacturing and service sectors, including facility location, facility layout, materials requirement planning, purchasing, just-in-time inventory control, and quality control.
5. Explain the use of PERT and Gantt charts to control manufacturing processes.

CHAPTER 9

**www.aam.com**

of Chrysler's Lee Iacocca, who made him executive vice president for diversified operations, which included manufacturing. Dauch was successful in improving both productivity and quality. He introduced flexible manufacturing (which you'll learn about in this chapter).

When General Motors (GM) was restructuring, it had to sell five old axle and drivetrain plants in Detroit. Dauch found the funding and bought them all. The plants were in really bad shape, but Dauch was determined to make them a success. He named his company American Axle & Manufacturing (AAM). GM promised to buy parts (crankshafts, transmission parts, and the like) from AAM if quality was improved. AAM spent more than $2 billion modernizing and rebuilding. It doubled productivity and boosted the number of gear sets it made daily from 5,000 to 13,000. Dauch is proud of the fact that he can produce quality products to compete with products from China and other low-cost countries.

To meet its customers' requirements around the world, AAM now has sales and business offices in Japan and Germany. According to Dauch, "Status quo is never acceptable at American Axle & Manufacturing or any of our subsidiaries. We know that competition on a global scale requires the best we have to offer. That's why we continually improve not only the skills of our associates, but also our technology, equipment, systems, and facilities. Our products, systems, and processes are designed to help us precisely meet customers' needs, and we consistently offer products that deliver power for affordable prices and the highest value."

There is a lot of talk about outsourcing manufacturing to other countries. But people like Richard Dauch are showing the world that U.S. workers and U.S. productivity are as good as any in the world. This chapter will discuss the developments that have made America's manufacturing base strong enough to compete globally. There is a great need in the United States for people who are interested in innovation and production. Perhaps this chapter will motivate you to consider such a career.

Sources: Gene Bylinsky, "Heroes of Manufacturing," *Fortune*, March 8, 2004, pp. 190D–190H; Peter Coy, "Asian Competition: Is the Cup Half Empty—or Half Full?," *BusinessWeek*, August 22/29, 2005, pp. 134–35; and www.aam.com, 2006.

## U.S. MANUFACTURING IN PERSPECTIVE

Fifty years or so ago, the head of GM said, "What's good for the country is good for General Motors, and vice versa."[1] He was right in many ways. That may cause you some concern if you've read recent business journal headlines such as: "GM Hits the Skids" or "GM Plants to Cut 25,000 Jobs by '08 in Restructuring."[2] GM pays its assembly line workers some $8.7 billion a year. In one way or another, GM supports some 900,000 jobs (including auto workers, advertising writers, car salespeople, office-supply vendors, and the like).[3] There is no doubt that GM's troubles affect the economy of the United States. So when things are not going well for GM, the country *does* feel the impact.

Meanwhile, a recent headline about Toyota read, "The Smartest Company of the Year," and another observed, "Hyundai: Crowding into the Fast Lane."[4] When gasoline prices skyrocketed toward the end of 2005, it looked as if the U.S. auto industry was dead in its tracks.[5] Would Toyota take the market with its hybrid Prius and Lexus RX 400h? Would the United States lose most of its manufacturing jobs to countries like India and China? To many in the United States, such questions bring on a feeling of déjà vu. U.S. citizens had heard in the 1980s how Japanese firms would dominate manufacturing. Of course, that was before Japan's economy collapsed and bumped along for years.[6]

Certainly, the 60 percent share of the U.S. auto market American companies hold today is considerably less than the 95 percent share they held in the 1950s.[7] However, today's picture of U.S. auto manufacturing isn't all gloomy. In fact, Harbour Consulting says that GM has three of the five most productive auto assembly plants in North America, and Ford has one of the others.[8] The United States is still a good place to make cars. That's one reason Honda, Toyota, BMW, Mercedes, Nissan, and Hyundai have all built plants in the United States. In short, the United States is still one of the premier manufacturing centers of the world. But clearly the world is trying hard to win away much of that work. Many U.S. companies *are* outsourcing manufacturing jobs to other countries. Of course, many others are outsourcing manufacturing *to* the

Hyundai is just one of many auto manufacturers that have insourced jobs to the United States. Why do you suppose so many articles emphasize outsourcing when thousands of jobs are created by insourcing?

* * * MAKING

## ethical decisions

www.ethics.ubc.ca/resources/business

### Stay or Leave?

Suppose that the hypothetical company ChildrenWear Industries has long been the economic foundation for its hometown. Most of the area's small businesses and schools support ChildrenWear, either by supplying the materials needed for production or by training its employees. ChildrenWear has learned that if it were to move its production facilities to Asia, it could increase its profits by 25 percent. Closing operations in the company's hometown would cause many of the town's other businesses to fail and schools to close, leaving a great percentage of the town unemployed, with no options for reemployment there. As a top manager at ChildrenWear, you must help decide whether the plant should be moved and, if so, when to tell the employees about the move. The law says that you must tell them at least 60 days before closing. What alternatives do you have? What are the consequences of each? Which will you choose?

United States as well. The battle is fierce and real.[9] The Making Ethical Decisions box looks at the kind of decisions companies must make when it comes to outsourcing.

The production picture in the United States is probably better than you may think. North American auto plants built 15.8 million vehicles in 2005, the same as in 2004. Overall production is expected to rise to 16.8 million by 2009. Of course, some 5.8 million of those vehicles will have foreign brand names. "The domestic auto industry is as healthy as it has ever been," says Eric Noble, president of Car Lab, an industry consulting firm in Santa Ana, California. "The names on the plates are just changing."[10] We know this is not much consolation to those who have lost their jobs in the North (the traditional region for auto manufacturing), but it is good news to those finding new jobs in the South (the region in which many new auto plants have been built).

## What Manufacturers Have Done to Become More Competitive

Obviously manufacturing involves more than just building cars. Overall U.S. manufacturing output rose by 3.7 percent a year from 1990 to 1995. That figure increased to 5.7 percent a year from 1995 to 2001.[11] Manufacturers were expected to be a source of strength to the economy in 2006.[12] More than 60 percent of U.S. manufacturers planned on hiring new workers in 2006.[13] What have American manufacturers done to regain a competitive edge? They've emphasized the following:[14]

- Focusing on customers.[15]
- Maintaining close relationships with suppliers and other companies to satisfy customer needs.
- Practicing continuous improvement.
- Focusing on quality.
- Saving on costs through site selection.
- Relying on the Internet to unite companies.
- Adopting new production techniques such as enterprise resource planning, computer integrated manufacturing, flexible manufacturing, and lean manufacturing.

What will the United States have to do to continue to strengthen its manufacturing base? Here's what David Audretsch, the director of the Institute for Development Strategies at Indiana University, says: "You're not going to be able to compete on price. You're going to have to live off having a new idea that other companies around the globe don't have."[16] A *Wall Street Journal* writer agrees: "Research, particularly in the physical sciences and engineering, is the foundation of our innovative economy. It has spawned the transistor, fiber optics, integrated circuits, wireless communication, liquid crystal displays, lasers, the Web, the GPS, hybrid automobiles and medical technologies too numerous to list. . . . When an innovation is found, the U.S. entrepreneurial spirit is quick to develop, produce and market it, creating new jobs and revenue."[17]

**production** The creation of finished goods and services using the factors of production: land, labor, capital, entrepreneurship, and knowledge.

**production management** The term used to describe all the activities managers do to help their firms create goods.

**operations management** A specialized area in management that converts or transforms resources (including human resources) into goods and services.

There is much room for optimism in the United States when it comes to innovation. Think of the spin-offs from the iPod revolution. Think of all the innovations that have gone into Motorola's phones.[18] The U.S. workforce is creative and dynamic. Nonetheless, it cannot stand still. Some universities are including new-product design into their curricula.[19] Businesses must keep up with the latest production techniques and processes.

The service sector of the economy will also continue to get attention as it becomes a larger and larger part of the overall economy. Service productivity is a real issue, as is the blending of service and manufacturing through the Internet. This chapter will devote attention to operations management in both the service and the manufacturing sectors. Since the majority of tomorrow's graduates will likely find jobs in the service sector, it is important to understand the latest operations management concepts for this sector.

## FROM PRODUCTION TO OPERATIONS MANAGEMENT

**Production** is the creation of goods and services using the factors of production: land, labor, capital, entrepreneurship, and knowledge. Production has historically been associated with manufacturing, but the nature of business has changed significantly in the last 20 years or so. The service sector, including Internet services, has grown dramatically. The United States now has what is called a service economy—that is, one dominated by the service sector. This can be a benefit to future college graduates because many of the top-paying jobs are in legal services; medical services; entertainment; broadcasting; and business services such as accounting, finance, and management consulting.

**Production management** has been the term used to describe all the activities managers do to help their firms create goods. To reflect the change in importance from manufacturing to services, the term *production* often has been replaced by *operations* to reflect both goods and services production. **Operations management**, then, is a specialized area in management that converts or transforms resources (including human resources) into goods and services. It includes inventory management, quality control, production scheduling, follow-up services, and more. In an automobile plant, operations management transforms raw materials, human resources, parts, supplies, paints, tools, and other resources into automobiles. It does this through the processes of fabrication and assembly. In a college, operations management takes inputs such as information, professors, supplies, buildings, offices, and computer systems—and creates services that

Each year companies discover new ways of automating that eliminate the need for human labor. This photo shows an automated apparatus known as a Flipper. Are McDonald's or any other restaurants in your area already using equipment like this?

transform students into educated people. It does this through a process called education.

Some organizations—such as factories, farms, and mines—produce mostly goods. Others—such as hospitals, schools, and government agencies—produce mostly services. Still others produce a combination of goods and services. For example, an automobile manufacturer not only makes cars but also provides services such as repairs, financing, and insurance. And at Wendy's you get goods such as hamburgers and fries, but you also get services such as order taking, order filling, and cleanup.

## Operations Management in the Service Sector

Most of us have been conditioned to think of operations management in the manufacturing sector. Let's look at the life of an operations manager in the service sector to see what it entails. After many years of hotel management experience, Horst Schulze became the president and CEO of the Ritz-Carlton Hotel Company. He is now the president and CEO of the West Paces Hotel Group. Schulze's commitment to quality is apparent in the many innovations and changes that he initiated over the years. These innovations include installation of a sophisticated computerized guest recognition program and a quality management program designed to ensure that all employees are "certified" in their positions.

Operations management in the service industry is all about creating a good experience for those who use the service. In a Ritz-Carlton hotel, operations management includes restaurants that offer the finest in service, elevators that run smoothly, and a front desk that processes people quickly. It may include placing fresh-cut flowers in the lobbies and dishes of fruit in every room. More important, it may mean spending thousands of dollars to provide training in quality management for every new employee.

Operations management in luxury hotels is changing with today's new executives. As customers in hotels, executives are likely to want in-room Internet access and a help center with toll-free telephone service. Also, when an executive has to give a speech or presentation, he or she needs video equipment and a whole host of computer hardware and other aids. Foreign visitors would like

Operations management in hotels is customer based. The idea is to offer services that exceed the customer's expectations. The key to success is training and more training. What operations in hotels have most disappointed and most pleased you in the past?

multilingual customer-support services. Hotel shops need to carry more than souvenirs, newspapers, and some drugstore and food items to serve today's high-tech travelers. The shops may also carry laptop computer supplies, electrical adapters, and the like. Operations management is responsible for locating and providing such amenities to make customers happy. In his speeches today, Horst Schulze talks about the need for having an internal measurement system to assess the performance results of your service delivery system.

In short, delighting customers by anticipating their needs has become the quality standard for luxury hotels, as it has for most other service businesses. But knowing customer needs and satisfying them are two different things. That's why operations management is so important: It is the implementation phase of management.

**form utility**
The value added by the creation of finished goods and services, such as the value added by taking silicon and making computer chips or putting services together to create a vacation package.

**progress assessment**

- What have U.S. manufacturers done to regain a competitive edge?
- What must U.S. companies do to continue to strengthen the country's manufacturing base?
- What led to the focus on operations management rather than production?

The United States can maintain a leadership position in production by designing new and better products. This *BusinessWeek* edition showed many examples. What new products are you now using?

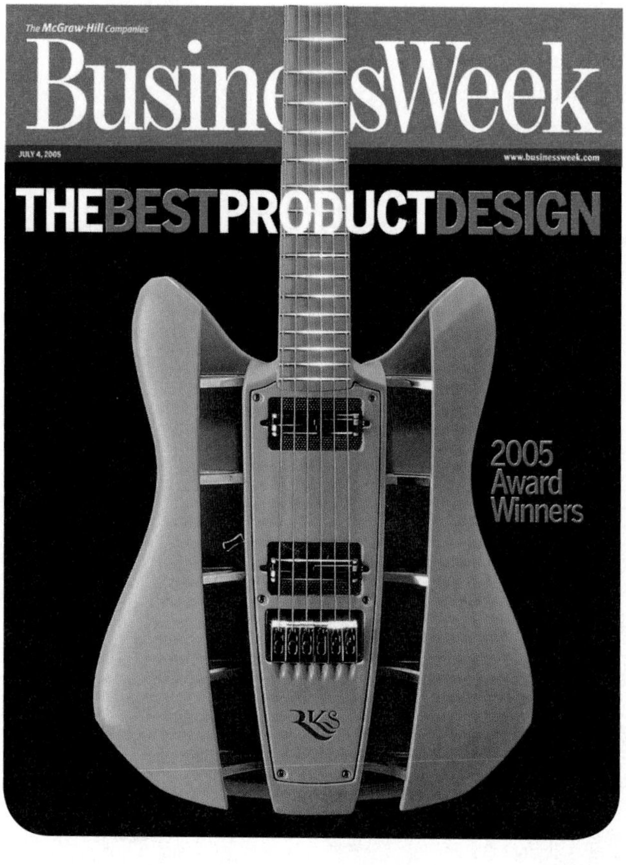

## PRODUCTION PROCESSES

Common sense and some experience have already taught you much of what you need to know about production processes. You know what it takes to write a term paper or prepare a dinner. You need money to buy the materials, you need a place to work, and you need to be organized to get the task done. The same is true of the production process in industry. It uses basic inputs to produce outputs (see Figure 9.1). Production adds value, or utility, to materials or processes. **Form utility** is the value added by the creation of finished goods and services, such as the value added by taking silicon and making computer chips or putting services together to create a vacation package. Form utility can exist at the retail level as well. For example, a butcher can produce a specific cut of beef from a whole cow, or a baker can make a specific type of cake out of basic ingredients. We'll be discussing utility in more detail in Chapter 15.

There are several different processes manufacturers use to produce goods. Andrew S. Grove, chairman of computer chip manufacturer Intel, uses a great analogy to explain production:

> *To understand the principles of production, imagine that you're a chef . . . and that your task is to serve a breakfast consisting of a three-minute soft-boiled egg, buttered toast, and coffee. Your job is to prepare and deliver the three items simultaneously, each of them fresh and hot.*

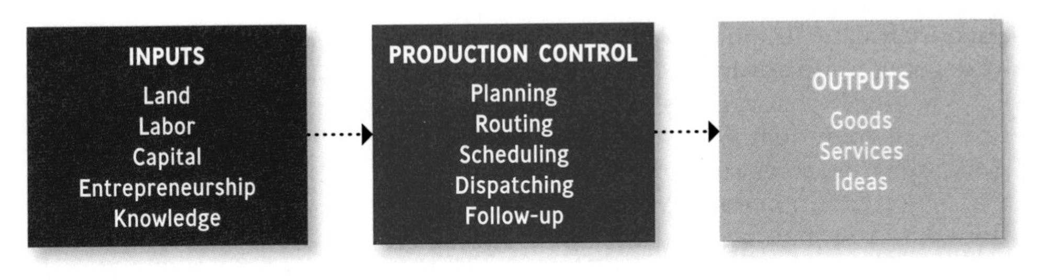


figure 9.1

**THE PRODUCTION PROCESS**

The production process consists of taking the factors of production (land, etc.) and using those inputs to produce goods, services, and ideas. Planning, routing, scheduling, and the other activities are the means to accomplish the objective—output.

Grove goes on to say that the task here encompasses the three basic requirements of production: (1) to build and deliver products in response to the demands of the customer at a scheduled delivery time, (2) to provide an acceptable quality level, and (3) to provide everything at the lowest possible cost.

Using the breakfast example, it's easy to understand two production terms: process and assembly. **Process manufacturing** physically or chemically changes materials. For example, boiling physically changes the egg. (Similarly, process manufacturing turns sand into glass or computer chips.) The **assembly process** puts together components (eggs, toast, and coffee) to make a product (breakfast). (Cars are made through an assembly process that puts together the frame, engine, and other parts.)

In addition, production processes are either continuous or intermittent. A **continuous process** is one in which long production runs turn out finished goods over time. As the chef in our diner, you could have a conveyor belt that lowers eggs into boiling water for three minutes and then lifts them out on a continuous basis. A three-minute egg would be available whenever you wanted one. (A chemical plant, for example, is run on a continuous process.)

It usually makes more sense when responding to specific customer orders to use an **intermittent process**. This is an operation where the production run is short (one or two eggs) and the machines are changed frequently to make different products (like the oven in a bakery or the toaster in the diner). (Manufacturers of custom-designed furniture would use an intermittent process.)

Today many new manufacturers use intermittent processes. Computers, robots, and flexible manufacturing processes allow firms to turn out custom-made goods almost as fast as mass-produced goods were once turned out.[20] We'll discuss how they do that in more detail in the next few sections as we explore advanced production techniques and the latest technology being used to cut costs.

**process manufacturing**
That part of the production process that physically or chemically changes materials.

**assembly process**
That part of the production process that puts together components.

**continuous process**
A production process in which long production runs turn out finished goods over time.

**intermittent process**
A production process in which the production run is short and the machines are changed frequently to make different products.

## The Need to Improve Production Techniques and Cut Costs

The ultimate goal of manufacturing and operations management is to provide high-quality goods and services instantaneously in response to customer demand. As we stress throughout this book, traditional organizations were simply not designed to be so responsive to the customer. Rather, they were designed to make goods efficiently (inexpensively). The whole idea of mass production was to make a large number of a limited variety of products at very low cost.

Over the years, low cost often came at the expense of quality and flexibility. Furthermore, suppliers didn't always deliver when they said they would, so manufacturers had to carry large inventories of raw materials and components.

Such inefficiencies made U.S. companies subject to foreign competitors who were using more advanced production techniques.

As a result of new global competition, companies have had to make a wide variety of high-quality custom-designed products at very low cost. Clearly, something had to change on the production floor to make that possible. Several major developments have radically changed the production process in the United States, making U.S. companies more competitive: (1) computer-aided design and manufacturing, (2) flexible manufacturing, (3) lean manufacturing, and (4) mass customization.

**computer-aided design (CAD)**
The use of computers in the design of products.

**computer-aided manufacturing (CAM)**
The use of computers in the manufacturing of products.

**computer-integrated manufacturing (CIM)**
The uniting of computer-aided design with computer-aided manufacturing.

**flexible manufacturing**
Designing machines to do multiple tasks so that they can produce a variety of products.

## Computer-Aided Design and Manufacturing

The one development in the recent past that appears to have changed production techniques and strategies more than any other has been the integration of computers into the design and manufacturing of products. The first thing computers did was help in the design of products; this is called **computer-aided design (CAD)**. The latest CAD systems allow designers to work in three dimensions. The next step was to involve computers directly in the production process; this is called **computer-aided manufacturing (CAM)**.

CAD/CAM (the use of both computer-aided design and computer-aided manufacturing) makes it possible to custom-design products to meet the needs of small markets with very little increase in cost. A manufacturer programs the computer to make a simple design change, and that change can be incorporated directly into the production line. For example, CAD and CAM is used in the clothing industry. A computer program establishes a pattern and cuts the cloth automatically. Today, a person's dimensions can be programmed into the machines to create custom-cut clothing at little additional cost.[21] In food service, CAM is used to make cookies in fresh-baked cookie shops. On-site, small-scale, semiautomated, sensor-controlled baking makes consistent quality easy to achieve.

CAD has doubled productivity in many firms. But it is one thing to design a product and quite another to set the specifications to make a machine do the work. The problem in the past was that CAD machines couldn't talk to CAM machines directly. Today, however, software programs unite CAD with CAM: the result is **computer-integrated manufacturing (CIM)**. The software is expensive, but it cuts as much as 80 percent of the time needed to program machines to make parts. The printing company JohnsByrne uses CIM in its Niles, Illinois, plant. It noticed a decreased cost in overhead, reduced outlay of resources, and fewer errors. IBM also uses CIM in a semiconductor facility. You can consult the *International Journal of Computer-Integrated Manufacturing* for other examples.

This photo shows computer-aided design (CAD) in operation. When linked with computer-aided manufacturing (CAM), these software systems can greatly improve the design and production process. What advantages might this technology offer to smaller manufacturing companies?

## Flexible Manufacturing

**Flexible manufacturing** involves designing machines to do multiple tasks so that they can produce a variety of products. Allen-Bradley (part of Rockwell Automation), a maker of industrial automation controls, uses flexible manufacturing to build motor starters. Orders come in daily, and within 24 hours the company's 26 machines and robots manufacture, test, and package the starters—which are untouched by human hands. Allen-Bradley's machines are so flexible that a special order, even a single item, can be included in the assembly without slowing down the process. Did you notice that these products were made without any labor? One way to compete with cheap labor is to have as few workers as possible.

## Lean Manufacturing

**Lean manufacturing** is the production of goods using less of everything compared to mass production: less human effort, less manufacturing space, less investment in tools, and less engineering time to develop a new product. A company becomes lean by continuously increasing its capacity to produce high-quality goods while decreasing its need for resources.[22] That's called "increasing productivity." You can see how technological improvements are largely responsible for the increase in productivity and efficiency of U.S. plants. That makes labor more productive and makes it possible to pay higher wages.

**lean manufacturing**
The production of goods using less of everything compared to mass production.

**mass customization**
Tailoring products to meet the needs of individual customers.

## Mass Customization

To *customize* means to make a unique product or provide a specific service to specific individuals. Although it once may have seemed impossible, **mass customization**, which means tailoring products to meet the needs of a large number of individual customers, is now practiced widely. The National Bicycle Industrial Company in Japan, for example, makes 18 bicycle models in more than 2 million combinations, with each combination designed to fit the needs of a specific customer. The customer chooses the model, size, color, and design. The retailer takes various measurements from the buyer and faxes the data to the factory, where robots handle the bulk of the assembly.

More and more manufacturers are learning to customize their products.[23] For example, some General Nutrition Center (GNC) stores feature machines that enable shoppers to custom-design their own vitamins, shampoo, and lotions. Other companies produce custom-made books with a child's name inserted in key places, and custom-made greeting cards have appeared on the market. The Custom Foot stores use infrared scanners to precisely measure each foot so that shoes can be crafted to fit perfectly. Adidas can make each shoe fit perfectly for each customer.[24] InterActive Custom Clothes offers a wide variety of options in custom-made jeans, including four different rivet colors. You can even buy custom-made M&M's.[25]

Mass customization can be used in the *service sector* as well. Capital Protective Insurance (CPI), for example, sells customized risk-management plans to companies. The latest in computer software and hardware makes it possible for CPI to develop such policies. Health clubs now offer unique fitness programs for individuals, travel agencies provide vacation packages that vary according to individual choices, and some colleges allow students to design their own majors. Actually, it is much easier to custom-design service programs than it is to custom-make goods, because there is no fixed tangible good that has to be adapted. Each customer can specify what he or she wants, within the limits of the service organization—limits that seem to be ever widening.

The Igus manufacturing plant in Cologne, Germany, can shrink or expand in a flash. Its flexible design keeps it competitive in a fast-changing market. Because the layout of the plant changes so often, some employees use scooters in order to more efficiently provide needed skills, supplies, and services to multiple workstations. A fast-changing plant needs a fast-moving employee base to achieve maximum productivity.

**progress assessment**

- What is form utility?
- Define and differentiate the following: process manufacturing, assembly process, continuous process, and intermittent process.
- What do you call the integration of CAD and CAM?
- What is mass customization?

# OPERATIONS MANAGEMENT PLANNING

*Operations management planning* involves many of the same issues in both the service and manufacturing sectors. These issues include facility location, facility layout, materials requirement planning, purchasing, inventory control, and quality control. The resources used may be different, but the management issues are similar.

## Facility Location

**facility location**
The process of selecting a geographic location for a company's operations.

**Facility location** is the process of selecting a geographic location for a company's operations. In keeping with the need to focus on customers, one strategy in facility location is to find a site that makes it easy for consumers to access the company's services and to maintain a dialogue about their needs. Thus, flower shops and banks are putting facilities in supermarkets so that their products and services are more accessible than they are in freestanding facilities. You can find a McDonald's inside some Wal-Mart stores. There are even McDonald's outlets in some gas stations. Customers can order and pay for their meals at the pumps and by the time they are finished filling their tanks, they go to the window to pick up their food orders.

Of course, the ultimate in convenience is never having to leave home at all to get services. That's why there is so much interest in Internet banking, Internet car shopping, Internet education, and so on. For brick-and-mortar businesses (e.g., retail stores) to beat such competition, they have to choose good locations

Briggs & Stratton moved many of its operations from a huge factory outside Milwaukee to a series of new factories in America's rural South. The new facilities are all nonunion. Unionized workers in the plant outside of Milwaukee would not concede to pay and benefit concessions, and the company felt it needed to cut costs to remain competitive. Besides cheaper labor, what other factors may influence companies like Briggs & Stratton to relocate?

and offer outstanding service to those who do come. Study the location of service-sector businesses—such as hotels, banks, athletic clubs, and supermarkets—and you will see that the most successful are conveniently located.

**Facility Location for Manufacturers** A major issue of the recent past has been the shift of manufacturing organizations from one city or state to another in the United States or to foreign sites. VW, for example, has a factory in Bratislava, Slovakia, that turns out 250,000 cars a year. It recently won the bid to produce Audi's Q7 SUV from Western European plants.[26] Such shifts sometimes result in pockets of unemployment in some geographic areas and lead to tremendous economic growth in others.

Why would companies spend millions of dollars to move their facilities from one location to another? Issues that influence site selection include labor costs; availability of resources, such as labor; access to transportation that can reduce time to market; proximity to suppliers; proximity to customers; low crime rates; quality of life for employees; cost of living; and the ability to train or retrain the local workforce.

One of the most common reasons for a business move is the availability of inexpensive labor or the right kind of skilled labor. Even though labor cost is becoming a smaller percentage of total cost in some highly automated industries, the low cost of labor remains a key reason many producers move their plants. For example, low-cost labor is one reason why some firms are moving to Malaysia, China, India, Mexico, and other countries with low wage rates. In general, manufacturing firms from the United States tend to pay more and offer more benefits than local firms throughout the world. However, some U.S. firms have been charged with providing substandard working conditions and/or exploiting children in the countries where they have set up factories. Others, such as Grupo Moraira (Grupo M), a real estate construction and sales company in the Dominican Republic, are being used as role models for global manufacturing. Grupo M provides its employees with higher pay relative to local businesses, transportation to and from work, day care centers, discounted food, and health clinics. Its operations are so efficient that it can compete in world markets and provide world-class services to its employees.

Inexpensive resources are another major reason for moving production facilities. Companies usually need water, electricity, wood, coal, and other basic resources. By moving to areas where natural resources are inexpensive and plentiful, firms can significantly lower not only the cost of buying such resources but also the cost of shipping finished products. Often the most important resource is people, so companies tend to cluster where smart and talented people are. Witness Silicon Valley in California and similar areas in Colorado, Massachusetts, Virginia, Texas, Maryland, and other states.

Reducing time-to-market is another decision-making factor. As manufacturers attempt to compete globally, they need sites that allow products to move through the system quickly, at the lowest costs, so that they can be delivered rapidly to customers.[27] Access to various modes of transportation (i.e., highways, rail lines, airports, and the like) is thus critical. Information technology (IT) is also important to quicken response time, so many firms are seeking countries with the most advanced information systems.

Another way to work closely with suppliers to satisfy customers' needs is to locate production facilities near supplier facilities. That cuts the cost of distribution and makes communication easier.[28]

Many businesses are building factories in foreign countries to get closer to their international customers. That's a major reason why the Japanese automaker Honda builds cars in Ohio and the German company Mercedes builds them in Alabama. When U.S. firms select foreign sites, they consider whether they are near airports, waterways, and highways so that raw materials and finished goods can be moved quickly and easily.

DEALING WITH change

## Responding to a Major Disaster

Hurricane Katrina, which hit the U.S. Gulf Coast in August 2005, has been called "the largest natural disaster in American history." What do you do if you have your corporate headquarters in New Orleans, where almost the whole city was flooded, and your only factory is in Long Beach, Mississippi, where the devastation was enormous? If you are Thomas Oreck, you plan to resume manufacturing in just two weeks. Here was the situation: The Oreck vacuum cleaner factory in Long Beach had no phone service, no electricity, and no water. Roads in and out of town were blocked. Hundreds of employees had lost their homes and hundreds more were missing. The list of things needed to restart production was long: diesel fuel, generators, food, water, and housing. One team of workers went looking for generators while another team searched for mobile homes.

Arrangements were made with United Parcel Service to distribute the vacuum cleaners and bring in food and water. The grounds around the manufacturing facility became a campus of sorts with housing, health clinics, and offices. Web sites were established so that workers could contact each other and family members. The company was operating again as soon as it possibly could.

Other businesses responded to the disaster in many ways. Getting old factories started again was a major contribution because it renewed old jobs and created some hope. Although Katrina closed down 126 Wal-Mart facilities, all but 14 were operating within a couple of weeks. Hundreds of businesses did what they could to help, and they responded quickly. Springs Industries of Fort Mill, South Carolina, sent sheets, blankets, and comforters. Anheuser-Busch sent 2.5 million cans of drinking water *a week*! Bristol-Myers Squibb sent many cartons of baby formula. Eli Lilly sent 40,000 vials of insulin. Kellogg sent seven truckloads of crackers and cookies. Pfizer sent $2 million and lots of medicines, and other pharmaceutical companies were equally or more generous—Amgen, for example, sent $2.5 million and offered to match any contributions from employees. The list goes on and on.

Change management means more than adjusting to day-to-day challenges. It also means adjusting to catastrophic disasters, and reacting quickly. That is true for both manufacturing firms like Oreck and service firms like Wal-Mart.

Sources: Jeffrey H. Birnbaum, "Stepping Up," *Washington Post*, September 4, 2005, pp. F1 and F4; Jonathan Eig, "Manufacturer Finds More Than Vacuums at Stake in Recovery," *The Wall Street Journal*, September 9, 2005, pp. B1 and B5; Susan Morse, "A Tide of Giving," *Washington Post*, September 13, 2005, p. F3; and Anne Hull, "After Katrina," *Washington Post*, January 26, 2006, pp. A1 and A8.

www.oreck.com

Businesses also study the quality of life for workers and managers. Quality-of-life questions include these: Are there good schools nearby? Is the weather nice? Is the crime rate low? Does the local community welcome new businesses? Do the chief executive and other key managers want to live there? Sometimes a region with a high quality of life is also an expensive one, which complicates the decision. In short, facility location has become a critical issue in operations management. The Dealing with Change box looks at how a major natural disaster can affect manufacturing and service organizations within the region and beyond. Nothing challenges firms more.

**Taking Operations Management to the Internet** Many of today's rapidly growing companies do very little production themselves. Instead, they outsource engineering, design, manufacturing, and other tasks to other companies—such as Solectron, Flextronics, and SCI Systems—that specialize in those functions. Furthermore, companies are creating whole new relationships with suppliers over the Internet so that operations management is becoming an interfirm process in which companies work together to design, produce, and ship products to customers. Coordination among companies today can be as close as coordination among departments in a single firm was in the past.

Many of the major manufacturing companies (e.g., Microsoft) are developing new Internet-focused strategies that will enable them and others to compete more effectively in the future.[29] These changes are having a dramatic effect on operations managers as they adjust from a one-firm system to an interfirm environment and from a relatively stable environment to one that is constantly changing and evolving.

www.lockheedmartin.com

REACHING BEYOND our borders

**Lockheed Martin Goes Global**

Can you imagine how hard it would be to manage the construction of a combat jet airplane? Now try to imagine how hard it would be if the plane was being built by 80 different suppliers in 187 different locations. Furthermore, while the plane is being constructed, the U.S. Air Force, Navy, and Marines; the British Defense Ministry; and eight other U.S. allies will be watching the progress, making comments, and changing the plans if necessary. What kind of person could pull all of that together?

The man responsible for this huge project is Dain Hancock of Lockheed Martin. One of his successes at Lockheed was to consolidate three operating units into a single company. Now he has the responsibility, with the help of others, of uniting some 80 companies into a single production unit. To do that, Lockheed and its partner companies will be using a system of 90 Web software tools to share designs, track the exchange of documents, and keep an eye on progress. The Internet enables people from different companies with incompatible computer systems to meet on Web sites and speak a common language. They will be able to talk via their computers while looking at shared documents. They can also use electronic white boards on which two or more people can draw pictures or charts, in real time, as others watch and comment.

Hancock and other managers are taking operations management beyond the control of one plant to the control of multiple plants in multiple locations, often in multiple countries. The Internet has changed business in many ways, but no other may be as dramatic as this.

**Facility Location in the Future** Developments in information technology (computers, modems, e-mail, voice mail, teleconferencing, etc.) are giving firms and employees more flexibility than ever before in choosing locations while staying in the competitive mainstream. Telecommuting (working from home via computer and modem) is a major trend in business.[30] Companies that no longer need to locate near sources of labor will be able to move to areas where land is less expensive and the quality of life may be nicer.[31]

One big incentive to locate or relocate in a particular city or state is the tax situation and the degree of government support. Some states and local governments have higher taxes than others, yet many engage in fierce competition by giving tax reductions and other support, such as zoning changes and financial aid, so that businesses will locate there. The Reaching Beyond Our Borders box explores how one company has handled the complex role of handling production facilities all over the world.

## Facility Layout

**facility layout**
The physical arrangement of resources (including people) in the production process.

**Facility layout** is the physical arrangement of resources (including people) in the production process. The idea is to have offices, machines, storage areas, and other items in the best possible position to enable workers to produce goods and provide services for customers. Facility layout depends greatly on the processes that are to be performed. For services, the layout is usually designed to help the consumer find and buy things. More and more, that means helping consumers find and buy things on the Internet. Some stores have added kiosks that enable customers to search for goods on the Internet and then place orders in the store. The store also handles returns and other customer-contact functions. In short, service organizations are becoming more and more customer oriented in how they design their facilities and their Internet services.[32] Some service-oriented organizations, such as hospitals, use layouts that improve the efficiency of the operations process, just as manufacturers do. For manufacturing plants, facilities layout has become critical because the possible cost savings are enormous.

Many companies are moving from an *assembly line layout,* in which workers do only a few tasks at a time, to a *modular layout,* in which teams of workers combine to produce more complex units of the final product.[33] For

**PRODUCT LAYOUT (also called Assembly Line Layout)**
Used to produce large quantities of a few types of products.

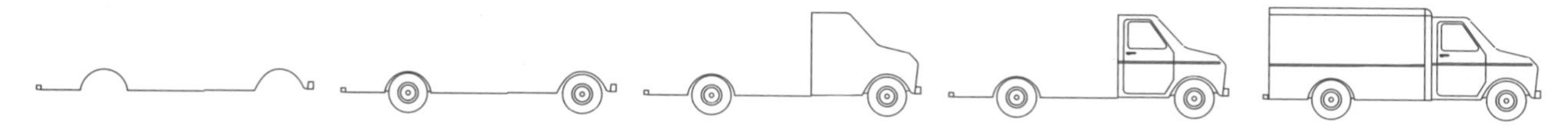

**PROCESS LAYOUT**
Frequently used in operations that serve different customers' different needs.

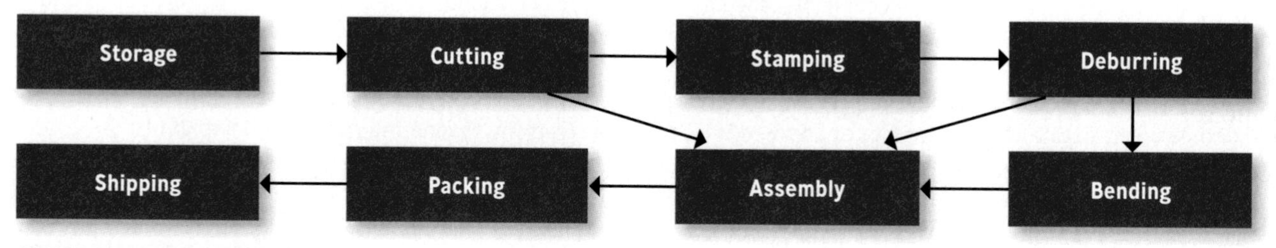


**CELLULAR or MODULE LAYOUT**
Can accommodate changes in design or customer demand.

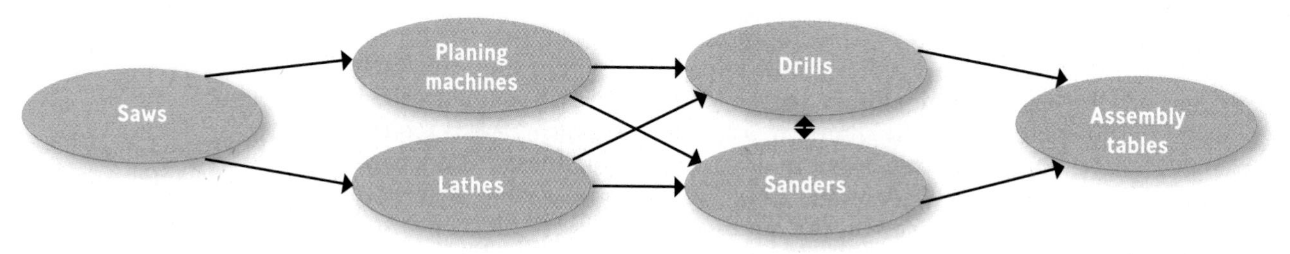


**FIXED-POSITION LAYOUT**
A major feature of planning is scheduling work operations.

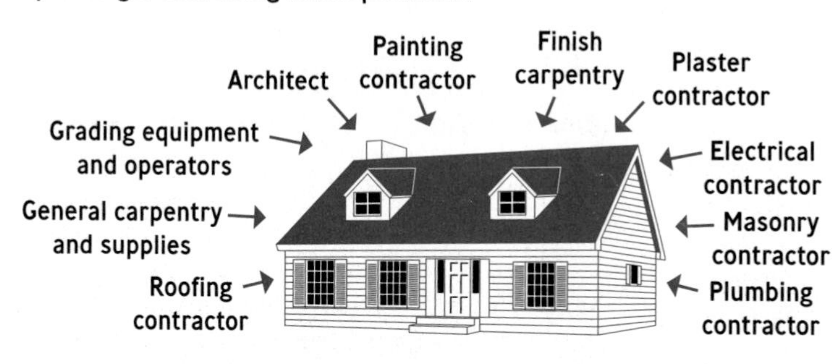


figure 9.2
**TYPICAL LAYOUT DESIGNS**

example, there may have been a dozen or more workstations on an assembly line to complete an automobile engine in the past, but all of that work may be done in one module today. A *process layout* is one in which similar equipment and functions are grouped together. The order in which the product visits a function depends on the design of the item. This allows for flexibility. When working on a major project, such as a bridge or an airplane, companies use a *fixed-position layout* that allows workers to congregate around the product to be completed. Figure 9.2 illustrates typical layout designs.

## Materials Requirement Planning

**materials requirement planning (MRP)**
A computer-based production management system that uses sales forecasts to make sure that needed parts and materials are available at the right time and place.

**Materials requirement planning (MRP)** is a computer-based operations management system that uses sales forecasts to make sure that needed parts and materials are available at the right time and place *in a specific company*. The newest variation of MRP is **enterprise resource planning (ERP)**. ERP is a computer application that enables *multiple* firms to manage all of their operations

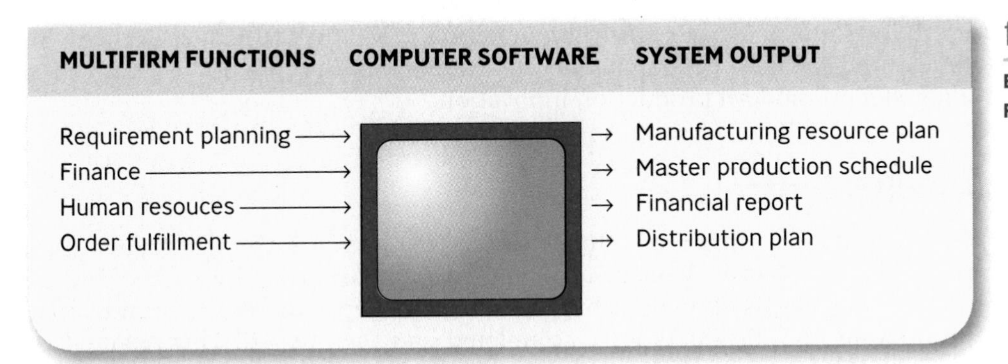


figure 9.3

**ENTERPRISE RESOURCE PLANNING**

(finance, requirements planning, human resources, and order fulfillment) on the basis of a single, integrated set of corporate data (see Figure 9.3). The result is shorter time between orders and payment, less staff to do ordering and order processing, reduced inventories, and better customer service for all the firms involved. By entering customer and sales information in an ERP system, a manufacturer can generate the next period's demand forecast, which in turn generates orders for raw materials, production scheduling, and financial projections.[34]

**enterprise resource planning (ERP)**
A computer application that enables multiple firms to manage all of their operations (finance, requirements planning, human resources, and order fulfillment) on the basis of a single, integrated set of corporate data.

## Purchasing

**Purchasing** is the function in a firm that searches for quality material resources, finds the best suppliers, and negotiates the best price for quality goods and services. In the past, manufacturers tended to deal with many different suppliers with the idea that, if one supplier or another couldn't deliver, materials would be available from someone else. Today, however, manufacturers are relying more heavily on one or two suppliers because the firms share so much information that they don't want to have too many suppliers knowing their business. The relationship between suppliers and manufacturers is thus much closer than ever before.[35]

**purchasing**
The function in a firm that searches for quality material resources, finds the best suppliers, and negotiates the best price for goods and services.

The Internet has transformed the purchasing function in recent years. For example, a business looking for supplies can contact an Internet-based purchasing service and find the best supplies at the best price. Similarly, a company wishing to sell supplies can use the Internet to find all the companies looking for such supplies. The cost of purchasing items has thus been reduced tremendously.[36]

## Just-in-Time Inventory Control

One major cost of production is holding parts, motors, and other items in storage for later use. Storage not only subjects items to obsolescence, pilferage, and damage but also requires construction and maintenance of costly warehouses. To cut such costs, many companies have implemented a concept called **just-in-time (JIT) inventory control**. JIT systems keep a minimum of inventory on the premises—and parts, supplies, and other needs are delivered just in time to go on the assembly line.[37] To work effectively, however, the process requires excellent coordination with carefully selected suppliers. Sometimes the suppliers build new facilities close to the main producer to minimize distribution time. JIT runs into problems when suppliers are farther away. Weather may delay shipments, for example.

**just-in-time (JIT) inventory control**
A production process in which a minimum of inventory is kept on the premises and parts, supplies, and other needs are delivered just in time to go on the assembly line.

Here's how it works: A manufacturer sets a production schedule (using ERP) to determine what parts and supplies will be needed. Suppliers are connected electronically, so they know immediately what will be needed and when. The suppliers must then deliver the goods just in time to go on the assembly line. Naturally, this calls for more effort (and more costs) on the suppliers' part. The manufacturer maintains efficiency by linking electronically to the suppliers so that the suppliers become more like departments in the firm than separate businesses.

JIT systems make sure the right materials are at the right place at the right time at the cheapest cost to meet both customer and production needs. That's a key step in modern production innovation.

**quality**
Consistently producing what the customer wants while reducing errors before and after delivery to the customer.

## Quality Control

**Quality** is consistently producing what the customer wants while reducing errors before and after delivery to the customer. Earlier in the United States, quality control was often done by quality control departments at the end of the production line. Products were completed and then tested. This resulted in several problems:

1. There was a need to inspect other people's work. This took extra people and resources.
2. If an error was found, someone would have to correct the mistake or scrap the product. This, of course, was costly.
3. If the customer found the mistake, he or she might be dissatisfied and might even buy from someone else thereafter.

Such problems led to the realization that quality is not an outcome; it is a never-ending process of continually improving what a company produces. Therefore, quality control should be part of the operations management planning process rather than simply an end-of-the-line inspection.

**six sigma quality**
A quality measure that allows only 3.4 defects per million opportunities.

Companies have turned to the use of modern quality control standards, such as six sigma. **Six sigma quality** (just 3.4 defects per million opportunities) detects potential problems to prevent their occurrence. That's important to a company like Bank of America, which makes 4 million transactions a day.[38] The Spotlight on Small Business box explores how small businesses can apply six sigma to their operations.

**statistical quality control (SQC)**
The process some managers use to continually monitor all phases of the production process to assure that quality is being built into the product from the beginning.

**statistical process control (SPC)**
The process of taking statistical samples of product components at each stage of the production process and plotting those results on a graph. Any variances from quality standards are recognized and can be corrected if beyond the set standards.

**Statistical quality control (SQC)** is the process some managers use to continually monitor all phases of the production process to assure that quality is being built into the product from the beginning. **Statistical process control (SPC)** is the process of taking statistical samples of product components at each stage of the production process and plotting those results on a graph. Any variances from quality standards are recognized and can be corrected if beyond the set standards. Making sure that products meet standards all along the production process eliminates or minimizes the need for having a quality control inspection at the end. Any mistakes would have been caught much earlier in the process. SQC and SPC thus save companies much time and many dollars. Some companies call such an approach to quality control the Deming cycle (after the late W. Edwards Deming, the father of the movement toward quality).[39] It consists of Plan, Do, Check, Act (PDCA). Again, the idea is to find potential errors *before* they happen.

The customer is ultimately the one who determines what the standard for quality should be. American businesses are getting serious about providing top customer service, and many are already doing it. Service organizations are finding it difficult to provide outstanding service every time because the process is so labor intensive. Physical goods (e.g., a gold ring) can be designed and manufactured to near perfection. However, it is hard to reach such perfection when designing and providing a service experience such as a dance on a cruise ship or a cab drive through New York City.

**Quality Standards: The Baldrige Awards** In the United States in 1987, a standard was set for overall company quality with the introduction of the Malcolm Baldrige National Quality Awards, named in honor of the late U.S. secretary of

## Meeting the Six Sigma Standard

Six sigma is a quality measure that allows only 3.4 defects per million opportunities. It is one thing for Motorola or General Electric to reach for such standards, but what about a small company like Dolan Industries? Dolan is a 41-person manufacturer of fasteners. It spent a few years trying to meet ISO 9000 standards, which are comparable to six sigma.

Once the company was able to achieve six sigma quality itself, it turned to its suppliers and demanded six sigma quality from them as well. It had to do that because its customers were demanding that level of quality. Companies such as General Electric, Honeywell, and Motorola are all seeking six sigma quality. The benefits include increases in product performance and, more important, happy customers—and profit growth.

Here is how six sigma works: If you can make it to the level of one sigma, two out of three products will meet specifications. If you can reach the two sigma level, then more than 95 percent of products will qualify. But when you meet six sigma quality, as we've said, you have only 3.4 defects in a million opportunities (which means that 99.99966 percent of your products will qualify). The bottom line is that small businesses are being held to a higher standard, one that reaches near perfection. Service organizations are also adopting six sigma standards.

So how can a small business learn about such processes quickly? The answer is to use TRIZ. TRIZ is a Russian acronym for the theory of inventive problem solving. The ideas are these:

1. Somebody, somewhere, has already solved your problem or one similar to it. Creativity means finding that solution and adapting it to the current problem.
2. Don't accept compromises. Eliminate them.

For example, farmers learned how to process manure to remove the water from it by studying the orange juice industry (i.e., the making of concentrated orange juice). The pharmaceutical industry learned to manage foam in the production process by studying the beer industry. You get the idea. Today, searching for answers on the Internet is critical to a company's success. You might look at publications like *Quality Digest* for examples.

Sources: Ellen Domb, "Enhance Six Sigma Creativity with TRIZ," *Quality Digest*, February 2004; Ellen Domb, "Think TRIZ for Creative Problem Solving," *Quality Digest*, August 2005; pp. 35–40; and www.TRIZ-journal.com, 2006.

commerce. Companies can apply for these awards in each of the following areas: manufacturing, services, small businesses, education, and health care. To qualify, an organization has to show quality in seven key areas: leadership, strategic planning, customer and market focus, information and analysis, human resources focus, process management, and business results. Major criteria for earning the award include whether customer wants and needs are being met and whether customer satisfaction ratings are better than those of competitors. As you can see, the focus is shifting away from just making quality goods and services to providing top-quality customer service in all respects.

One Baldrige Award winner was Sunny Fresh Foods, a small company that makes about 200 different egg products. Sunny Fresh was the first food company to win the award, and one of only a few small companies. It won again in 2006.[40] The company used the Baldrige criteria to drive business systems development and business systems redesign. The Bama Company of Tulsa, Oklahoma, makes pies, biscuits, and pizza crusts. Using Baldrige criteria, the company increased overall customer satisfaction from 75 percent in 2001 to almost 100 percent.[41] Richland College, in Dallas, Texas, was the first community college to receive a Baldrige Award. With over 20,000 students, Richland dropped its operational costs while improving services, and implemented stakeholder listening services to measure satisfaction.[42]

**ISO 9000 and ISO 14000 Standards** The International Organization for Standardization (ISO) is a worldwide federation of national standards bodies from more than 140 countries that set the global measures for the quality of individual products. ISO is a nongovernmental organization established in 1947 to promote the development of world standards to facilitate the international exchange of goods and services. (ISO is not an acronym. It comes from the Greek word *isos*, meaning "oneness.") **ISO 9000** is the common name given to quality management and assurance standards. The latest standards are called ISO 9000: 2004.[43] The standards require that a company must determine what customer needs are, including regulatory and legal requirements. The company must also make communication arrangements to handle issues such as complaints. Other standards involve process control, product testing, storage, and delivery. Improving quality is an investment that can pay off in better customer relations and higher sales.[44]

**ISO 9000**
The common name given to quality management and assurance standards.

What makes ISO 9000 so important is that the European Union (EU) is demanding that companies that want to do business with the EU be certified by ISO standards. Some major U.S. companies are also demanding that suppliers meet such standards. There are several accreditation agencies in Europe and in the United States whose function is to certify that a company meets the standards for all phases of its operations, from product development through production and testing to installation.

**ISO 14000** is a collection of the best practices for managing an organization's impact on the environment. It does not prescribe a performance level. ISO 14000 is an environmental management system (EMS). The requirements for certification include having an environmental policy, having specific improvement targets, conducting audits of environmental programs, and maintaining top management review of the processes. Certification in both ISO 9000 and ISO 14000 would show that a firm has a world-class management system in both quality and environmental standards. In the past, firms assigned employees separately to meet both standards. Today, ISO 9000 and 14000 standards have been blended so that an organization can work on both at once. ISO is now working on social responsibility guidelines to go with the other standards.

**ISO 14000**
A collection of the best practices for managing an organization's impact on the environment.

**progress assessment**

- What are the major criteria for facility location?
- What is the difference between MRP and ERP?
- What is just-in-time inventory control?
- What are six sigma quality, the Baldrige Award, ISO 9000, and ISO 14000?

## CONTROL PROCEDURES: PERT AND GANTT CHARTS

An important function of an operations manager is to be sure that products are manufactured and delivered on time, on budget, and to specifications. The question is: How can one be sure that all of the assembly processes will go smoothly and end up completed by the required time? One popular technique for maintaining some feel for the progress of production was developed in the 1950s for constructing nuclear submarines: the **program evaluation and**

**program evaluation and review technique (PERT)**
A method for analyzing the tasks involved in completing a given project, estimating the time needed to complete each task, and identifying the minimum time needed to complete the total project.

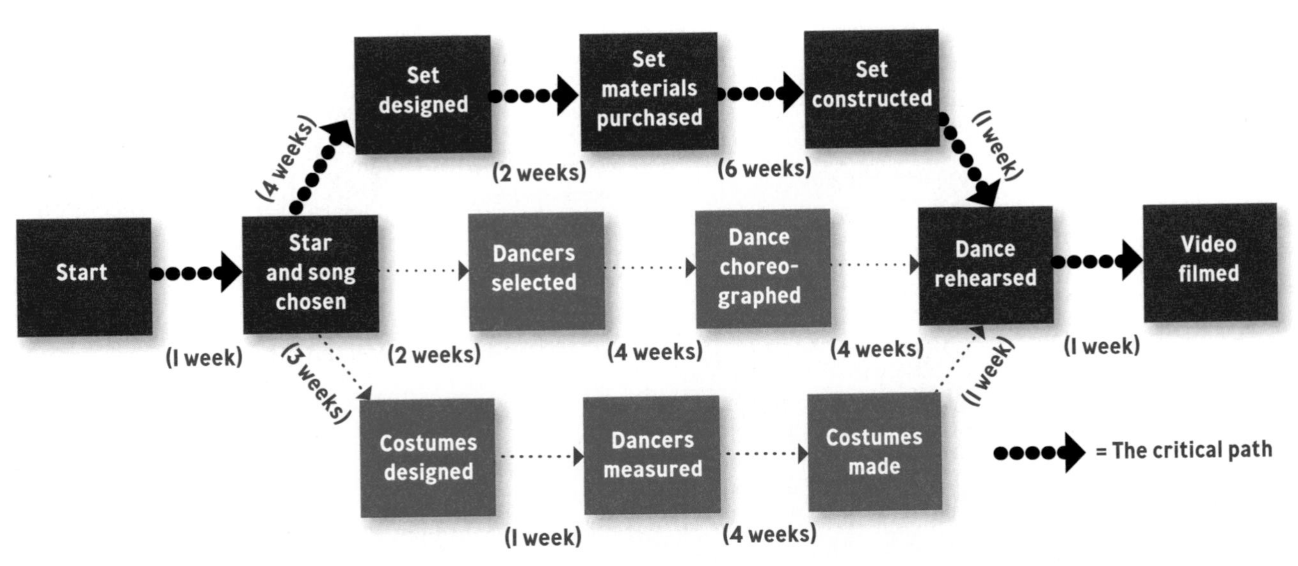


figure 9.4

**PERT CHART FOR A VIDEO**

The minimum amount of time it will take to produce this video is 15 weeks. To get that number, you add the week it takes to pick a star and a song to the four weeks to design a set, the two weeks to purchase set materials, the six weeks to construct the set, the week before rehearsals, and the final week when the video is made. That's the critical path. Any delay in that process will delay the final video.

**review technique (PERT)**. PERT users analyze the tasks involved in completing a given project, estimate the time needed to complete each task, and identify the minimum time needed to complete the total project.

Formally, the steps involved in using PERT are (1) analyzing and sequencing tasks that need to be done, (2) estimating the time needed to complete each task, (3) drawing a PERT network illustrating the information from steps 1 and 2, and (4) identifying the critical path. The **critical path** is the sequence of tasks that takes the longest time to complete. The word *critical* is used in this term because a delay in the time needed to complete this path would cause the project or production run to be late.

Figure 9.4 illustrates a PERT chart for producing a music video. Note that the squares on the chart indicate completed tasks and the arrows leading to the squares indicate the time needed to complete each task. The path from one completed task to another illustrates the relationships among tasks. For example, the arrow from "set designed" to "set materials purchased" shows that designing the set must be completed before the materials can be purchased. The critical path (indicated by the bold black arrows) reflects that producing the set takes more time than auditioning dancers and choreographing dances as well as designing and making costumes. The project manager now knows that it's critical that set construction remain on schedule if the project is to be completed on time, but short delays in dance and costume preparation shouldn't affect completing the total project on time.

A PERT network can be made up of thousands of events over many months. Today, this complex procedure is done by computer. Another, more basic strategy used by manufacturers for measuring production progress is a Gantt chart. A **Gantt chart** (named for its developer, Henry L. Gantt) is a bar graph that clearly shows what projects are being worked on and how much has been completed at any given time. Figure 9.5 on page 252 shows a Gantt chart for a doll manufacturer. The chart shows that the dolls' heads and bodies should be completed before the clothing is sewn. It also shows that at the end of week 3, the dolls' bodies are ready, but the heads are about half a week behind. All of this calculation was once done by hand. Now computers have taken over. Using a Gantt-like computer program, a manager can trace the production process minute by minute to determine which tasks are on time and which are behind so that adjustments can be made to allow the company to stay on schedule.

**critical path**
In a PERT network, the sequence of tasks that takes the longest time to complete.

**Gantt chart**
Bar graph showing production managers what projects are being worked on and what stage they are in at any given time.

figure 9.5

**GANTT CHART FOR A DOLL MANUFACTURER**

A Gantt chart enables a production manager to see at a glance when projects are scheduled to be completed and what the status is now. For example, the dolls' heads and bodies should be completed before the clothing is sewn, but they could be a little late as long as everything is ready for assembly in week 6. This chart shows that at the end of week 3, the dolls' bodies are ready, but the heads are about half a week behind.

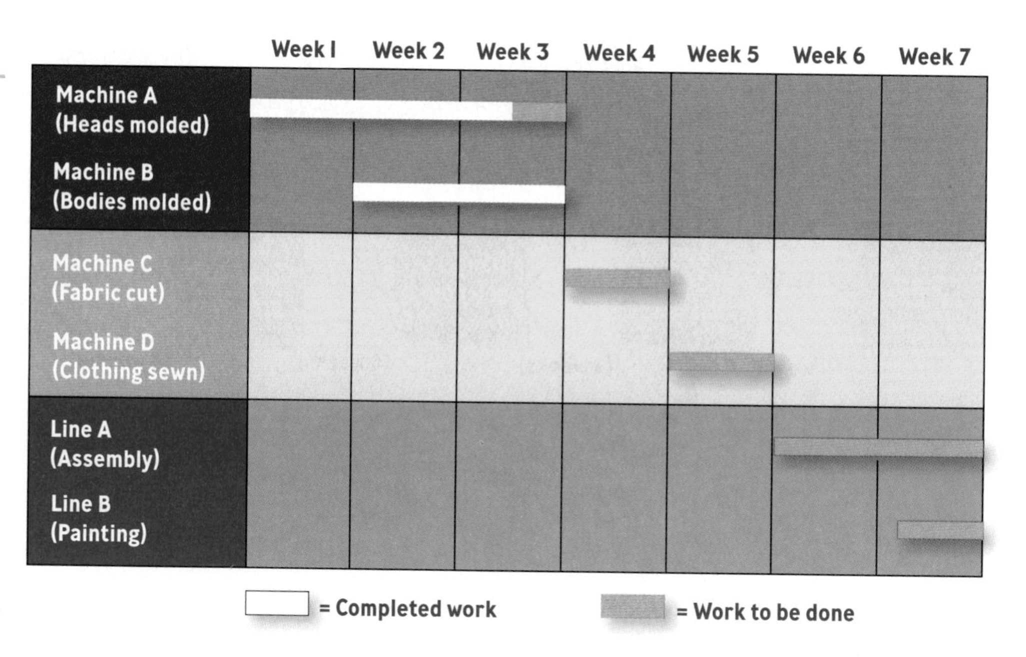


## PREPARING FOR THE FUTURE

The United States remains a major industrial country, but competition is growing stronger each year. This means that there are tremendous opportunities for careers in operations management, as companies fight to stay competitive. Today relatively few college students major in product design, production and operations management, inventory management, and other areas involving manufacturing and operations management in the service sector.[45] That means more opportunities for those students who can see the future trends and have the skills to own or work in tomorrow's highly automated, efficient factories, mines, service facilities, and other production locations.

### progress assessment

- Draw a PERT chart for making a breakfast of three-minute eggs, buttered toast, and coffee. Define the critical path.
- How could you use a Gantt chart to keep track of production?

## summary

**1.** Describe the evolution of production in the United States.

1. U.S. manufacturing output rose by 3.7 percent a year from 1990 to 1995. That figure increased to 5.7 percent a year from 1995 to 2001. 2006 was expected to be a good year for manufacturing.
   - **What have American manufacturers done in order to achieve this increased output?**

   U.S. manufactures have increased output by emphasizing close relationships with suppliers and other companies to satisfy customer needs; continuous improvement; quality; site selection; the Internet to unite companies; and production techniques such as enterprise resource planning, computer integrated manufacturing, flexible manufacturing, and lean manufacturing.

- **What can the United States do to keep more jobs in the country?**

One solution is to come up with new products to create more new jobs.

2. Operations management is a specialized area in management that converts or transforms resources (including human resources) into goods and services.

**2.** Define operations management.

- **What kind of firms use operations managers?**

Firms in both the manufacturing and service sectors use operations managers.

3. There are several different processes manufacturers use to produce goods.

**3.** Distinguish between the various production processes and describe several of the production techniques that have improved the productivity of U.S. companies, including computer-aided design and manufacturing, flexible manufacturing, lean manufacturing, and mass customization.

- **What is process manufacturing, and how does it differ from assembly processes?**

Process manufacturing physically or chemically changes materials. Assembly processes put together components.

- **How do CAD/CAM systems work?**

Design changes made in computer-aided design (CAD) are instantly incorporated into the computer-aided manufacturing (CAM) process. The linking of the two systems—CAD and CAM—is called computer-integrated manufacturing (CIM).

- **What is flexible manufacturing?**

Flexible manufacturing involves designing machines to produce a variety of products.

- **What is lean manufacturing?**

Lean manufacturing is the production of goods using less of everything compared to mass production: less human effort, less manufacturing space, less investment in tools, and less engineering time to develop a new product.

- **What is mass customization?**

Mass customization means making custom-designed goods and services for a large number of individual customers. Flexible manufacturing makes mass customization possible. Given the exact needs of a customer, flexible machines can produce a customized good as fast as mass-produced goods were once made. Mass customization is also important in service industries.

4. Operations management planning involves facility location, facility layout, materials requirement planning, purchasing, inventory control, and quality control.

**4.** Describe the operations management planning issues involved in both the manufacturing and service sectors, including facility location, facility layout, materials requirement planning, purchasing, just-in-time inventory control, and quality control.

- **What is facility location and how does it differ from facility layout?**

Facility location is the process of selecting a geographic location for a company's operations. Facility layout is the physical arrangement of resources (including people) to produce goods and services effectively and efficiently.

- **What criteria are used to evaluate different sites?**

Labor costs and land costs are two major criteria for selecting the right sites. Other criteria include whether resources are plentiful and inexpensive, skilled workers are available or are trainable, taxes are low and the local government offers support, energy and water are available, transportation costs are low, and the quality of life and quality of education are high.

- **What relationship does materials requirement planning (MRP) and Enterprise resource planning (ERP) have with the production process?**

MRP is a computer application that uses sales forecasts to make sure the needed parts and materials are available at the right time and place in a *specific company*. ERP, an advanced form of MRP, enables *multiple firms* to manage all of their operations (finance, requirements planning, human resources, and order fulfillment) on the basis of a single, integrated set of corporate data. The result is shorter time between orders and payment, less staff to do ordering and order processing, reduced inventories, and better customer service.

- **How have purchasing agreements changed?**

Purchasing agreements now involve fewer suppliers who supply quality goods and services at better prices in return for getting the business. Many new Internet companies have emerged to help both buyers and sellers complete the exchange process more efficiently.

- **What is just-in-time (JIT) inventory control?**

JIT involves having suppliers deliver parts and materials just in time to go on the assembly line so they don't have to be stored in warehouses.

- **What is six sigma quality?**

Six sigma quality (just 3.4 defects per million opportunities) detects potential problems before they occur. Statistical quality control (SQC) is the process some managers use to continually monitor all processes in the production process to assure that quality is being built into the product from the beginning. Statistical process control (SPC) is the process of taking statistical samples of product components at each stage of the production process and plotting those results on a graph. Any variances from quality standards are recognized and can be corrected.

- **What quality standards do firms use in the United States?**

Many firms try for the Malcolm Baldrige National Quality Awards. To qualify for one of these awards, a company has to show quality in seven key areas: leadership, strategic planning, customer and market focus, information and analysis, human resources focus, process management, and business results. International standards U.S. firms strive to meet include ISO 9001:2004 (ISO 9000) and ISO 14000. The first is a European standard for quality and the second is a collection of the best practices for managing an organization's impact on the environment.

**5.** Explain the use of PERT and Gantt charts to control manufacturing processes.

5. The program evaluation and review technique (PERT) is a method for analyzing the tasks involved in completing a given project, estimating the time needed to complete each task, and identifying the minimum time needed to complete the total project. A Gantt chart is a bar graph that clearly shows what projects are being worked on and how much has been completed at any given time.

- **Is there any relationship between a PERT chart and a Gantt chart?**

Figure 9.4 shows a PERT chart. Figure 9.5 shows a Gantt chart. Whereas PERT is a tool used for planning, a Gantt chart is a tool used to measure progress.

## key terms

**assembly process** 239
**computer-aided design (CAD)** 240
**computer-aided manufacturing (CAM)** 240
**computer-integrated manufacturing (CIM)** 240
**continuous process** 239
**critical path** 251
**enterprise resource planning (ERP)** 247
**facility layout** 245
**facility location** 242
**flexible manufacturing** 240
**form utility** 238
**Gantt chart** 251
**intermittent process** 239
**ISO 14000** 250
**ISO 9000** 250
**just-in-time (JIT) inventory control** 247
**lean manufacturing** 241
**mass customization** 241
**materials requirement planning (MRP)** 246
**operations management** 236
**process manufacturing** 239
**production** 236
**production management** 236
**program evaluation and review technique (PERT)** 250
**purchasing** 247
**quality** 248
**six sigma quality** 248
**statistical process control (SPC)** 248
**statistical quality control (SQC)** 248

## critical thinking questions

1. People on the manufacturing floor are being replaced by robots and other machines. On the one hand, that is one way companies compete with cheap labor from other countries. No labor at all is less expensive than cheap labor. On the other hand, automation eliminates many jobs. Are you concerned that automation may increase unemployment or underemployment in the United States and around the world? Why?
2. Computer-integrated manufacturing (CIM) has revolutionized the production process. Now everything from cookies to cars can be designed and manufactured much more cheaply than before. Furthermore, customized changes can be made with very little increase in cost. What will such changes mean for the clothing industry, the shoe industry, and other fashion-related industries? What will they mean for other consumer and industrial goods industries? How will you benefit as a consumer?
3. One solution to the creation of new jobs in the United States is to have more innovation. Much innovation comes from new graduates from engineering and the sciences. What could the United States do to motivate more students to major in those areas?

## developing workplace skills

1. Choosing the right location for a manufacturing plant or a service organization is often critical to its success. Form small groups and have each group member pick one manufacturing plant or one service organization in town and list at least three reasons why its location helps or hinders its success. If its location is not ideal, where would be a better one?
2. In teams of four or five, discuss the need for better operations management at airports and with the airlines in general. Have the team develop a report listing (*a*) problems team members have encountered in traveling by air and (*b*) suggestions for improving operations so such problems won't occur in the future.
3. Discuss some of the advantages and disadvantages of producing goods overseas using inexpensive labor. Summarize the moral and ethical issues of this practice.
4. Think of any production facility (e.g., sandwich shop or woodworking facility) or service center (e.g., library, copy room) at your school and redesign the layout (make a pencil drawing placing people and materials) so that the facility could more effectively serve its customers and so that the workers would be more effective and efficient.
5. Think about some of the experiences you have had with service organizations recently (e.g., the admissions office at your school), and select one incident in which you had to wait for an unreasonable length of time to get what you wanted. Tell what happens when customers are inconvenienced, and explain how management could make the operation more efficient and customer-oriented.

## taking it to the net * 1

### Purpose

To illustrate production processes.

### Exercise

Take a virtual tour of the Hershey Foods Corporation's chocolate factory by going to www.hersheys.com/tour/index.shtml. If you have a high-speed Internet connection, you can choose the video tour. If not, the picture tour is a faster choice.

1. Does Hershey use process manufacturing or the assembly process? Is the production of Hershey's chocolate an example of an intermittent or continuous production process? Justify your answers.
2. What location factors might go into the selection of a manufacturing site for Hershey's chocolate?

## taking it to the net * 2

### Purpose

To learn more about the Baldrige Award.

### Exercise

Go to the Baldrige Web page at www.quality.NIST.gov, and then click on Why Apply?

1. What are four ways in which companies might benefit by applying for the Baldrige Award?
2. What companies are cited as examples?
3. Discuss what you learned about companies that have applied for the award.

## casing the web

To access the case *"Griffin Hospital,"* visit **www.mhhe.com/ub8e**

## video case

### Reality On Request—Digital Domain

As Chairman and CEO of Digital Domain in Venice, California, Scott Ross runs one of the largest digital production studios in the world. His studio won an Academy Award for doing the simulation of the sinking of the *Titanic* in the movie with the same name. It also created the digital waves that wiped out the horsemen in *Lord of the Rings.*

Operations management is unique at Digital Domain because no two projects are ever the same. One day they may be making a digital cow (*O Brother, Where Art Thou*), on another a digital spaceship (*Apollo 13*), and on still another digital waves (*Titanic*). Digital is both a production and service provider. How so? In addition to producing digital scenes for movies, the company advises movie producers as to what is possible to do digitally. Still, certain activities, such as facility location and facility layout, are common to both service organizations and production firms.

Since many movies are made in Los Angeles, it's important for Digital Domain to be close to the city. Actors are often chosen from that area, as are workers and specialists at Digital. The company's most important resource, however, is its workers. Thus, facilities layout is designed to make the job of workers easier, yet efficient. For example, there's a combination conference room and cafeteria. Given the company's passion for *quality,* everything is designed to be clean and logical. Facility layout assists workers in developing the highest-quality product possible given time and money constraints.

Materials requirement planning (MRP) is a computer-based operations management system that uses sales forecasts to make needed parts and materials available at the right time and place. Since Digital's primary resource is people, the company lists 54 key disciplines in its database, so it's easy to find the right person for the right job. For example, a project may come up on Wednesday that demands having resources available the next Monday. People have to be contacted and hired just in time to keep the project on time and within budget.

The company does much of its purchasing on the Internet. It also uses *flexible manufacturing.* To keep costs down, Digital also used *lean manufacturing,* the production of goods using less of everything: less human effort, less manufacturing space, less investment in tools, and less engineering time for a given project. To keep costs down the company does a lot of pre-visualizing—simulating projects to determine the best way to proceed.

Of course, *mass customization* is basically what Digital Domain is all about: creating new and different scenes that can't be duplicated. However, once the company learns to create artificial waves or some other image, it is easier to duplicate a similar image next time. Since film is very expensive, many ideas are created using pen and pencil first. From such "primitive" tools, the company goes on to use *computer-aided design.*

Making movies is expensive. Everything needs to be done as planned. Scott Ross knows it's show *business,* and the accent is on business, and making a profit. For this reason, Digital uses PERT charts to follow projects and to determine what series of steps is critical to getting things out in time. It also uses computerized GANTT charts to follow goods in process. Getting things done right and on time is the hallmark at Digital Domain.

### Thinking It Over

1. Do you have an appreciation for operations management now that you've seen how exciting such a job can be at a company like Digital Domain?
2. Mass customization is critical in the production of movies and special effects. As a consumer, what benefits do you see in being able to buy custom-made shoes, clothes, automobiles, and more?
3. What lessons did you learn from this video that you could apply at any job you might get?
4. This video points out that certain workers are very focused on quality and that there comes a time when you have to stop improving things because time has a cost. Have you had to make a trade-off between perfection and "good enough"? What were the consequences?

# motivating employees AND building self-managed teams

profile

**Getting to Know**

X Elizabeth McLaughlin,

**CEO of Hot Topic**

Hot Topic is a clothing store that rocks because of its high volume of sales, rapid product flow, and great customer service. Its music-influenced clothing and other trendy products are displayed amid hip decor while music blasts everywhere. Televisions in the store are always tuned to MTV, MTV2, FUSE or VH-1. Young customers are drawn to the stores by T-shirts, CDs, cool clothes, and accessories, and, most important, a friendly staff.

Hot Topic employees focus on customer service, whether it is helping a teenager look for a T-shirt or answering questions from a bewildered parent. This emphasis on customer service begins at the top, with CEO Elizabeth "Betsy" McLaughlin. McLaughlin is a charismatic leader who personally makes six to eight phone calls a day to customers to find out what they are seeking. She also asks employees what they like and what they think would be cool. "Upper management really sets the tone to work well within their organization and to put the right face out there when customers walk through the door," explains Aaron Miller, a principal with Tompkins Associates, of Raleigh, North Carolina, who helped set up Hot Topic's warehouse management system in Nashville, Tennessee.

Betsy McLaughlin started her career in fashion retailing when she was in college. She worked her way through school by clerking in The Broadway, a department store in Los Angeles. After she earned her degree in economics from the University of California–Irvine, she continued to work for the store—moving to the planning and budgeting department. Later she joined Millers Outpost, a specialty retailer, as the director of planning, and eventually became the director of stores. In 1993, she moved to Hot Topic as the vice president of operations and helped to expand the company nationally. She became CEO in 2000.

Hot Topic is a trend-oriented business. How does McLaughlin know what teens will want before it's so 15 minutes ago? One strategy is to pay her employees to go to concerts and clubs so that they can write about the latest trends they spot. In fact, McLaughlin entrusts many of the buying decisions to store employees, who are tuned in to their customers. "It's an enlightened way of management to put that much trust in employees," said Elizabeth Pierce, an analyst with Wedbush Morgan Securities. "In return, they get tremendous loyalty at the employee base." Hot Topic was chosen as one of *Fortune*'s Best Companies to Work For three years in a row. (*Fortune* chooses the companies on its list primarily through employee surveys.) Hot Topic employees like working for the company because they enjoy what they do.

There are no offices with doors at the Hot Topic headquarters. Everybody, including McLaughlin, works in one big, colorful office with televisions and monitors scattered

LEARNING goals

**After you have read and studied this chapter, you should be able to**

1. Explain Taylor's scientific management.
2. Describe the Hawthorne studies, and relate their significance to management.
3. Identify the levels of Maslow's hierarchy of needs, and relate their importance to employee motivation.
4. Distinguish between the motivators and hygiene factors identified by Herzberg.
5. Explain how job enrichment affects employee motivation and performance.
6. Differentiate among Theory X, Theory Y, and Theory Z.
7. Explain goal-setting theory and how management by objectives (MBO) exemplifies the theory.
8. Describe the key principles of expectancy, reinforcement, and equity theories.
9. Explain how open communication builds teamwork, and describe how managers are likely to motivate teams in the future.

# CHAPTER 10

**www.hottopic.com**

throughout the space. There is a lot of comfortable furniture that looks more like what would be found at home than in an office. Of course, music is always playing. McLaughlin and her employees believe that the open environment helps them get work done. Miller agrees. During one of Miller's visits, the chief information officer (CIO) overheard his conversation with a Hot Topic employee. "If he were tucked away in an office, we would not have gotten his input, which we used," Miller said.

There are many reasons Hot Topic created such an open and friendly work environment. "People spend more time in the workplace than they do anywhere else in their life, so you want people to feel comfortable, to feel like it is a special place, and be proud of it, and to treat it well," explains Sue McPherson, Hot Topic's vice president of distribution.

"We work hard to develop people," McPherson says, "and hold people accountable for development of their employees. We look for people who have talent and passion for what they do, as opposed to experience. We believe that talented people can be trained on the functional aspects of any job. We encourage managers to take the time to sit down with their employees and ask them what they are passionate about. What do they really want to do? What is exciting to them? What gets their blood pumping? We have people moving cross-departmentally from stores to headquarters, from headquarters to stores, from human resources to the DC [distribution center], from DC to purchasing. It really depends on what their passions and talents are."

In this chapter, you will learn about the theories and practices managers like Betsy McLaughlin use to motivate their employees to focus on goals common to both the employees and the organization.

Sources: Lisa M. Kempfer, "Music, Put-to-Light Keeps Hot Topic in Sync," *Material Handling Engineering*, July 1, 2005; Lynn Fosse, "Betsy Mclaughlin, President and Chief Executive Officer, Hot Topic, Inc.—Interview," *Wall Street Corporate Reporter*, November 1, 2000; and Geoff Colvin, "The 100 Best Companies to Work For, 2006," *Fortune*, January 23, 2006.

# THE IMPORTANCE OF MOTIVATION

"If work is such fun, how come the rich don't do it?" quipped comedian Groucho Marx. Well, the rich do work—Bill Gates didn't make his billions playing computer games. And workers can have fun—if managers make the effort to motivate them. The importance of satisfaction among the workforce cannot be overstated. Happy workers lead to happy customers, and happy customers lead to successful businesses.[1] On the opposite side, unhappy workers are likely to leave the company, and when this happens, the company usually loses out. Losing a valuable, highly skilled employee could cost more than $100,000 for such things as exit interviews, severance pay, the process of hiring a replacement worker, and lost productivity while the new employee is learning the job.[2] The "soft" costs are even greater: loss of intellectual capital, decreased morale, increased employee stress, and a negative reputation. As Hot Topic CEO Betsy McLaughlin emphasized in this chapter's Opening Profile, motivating the right people to join and remain with the organization is a key function of managers.

**intrinsic reward**
The personal satisfaction you feel when you perform well and complete goals.

**extrinsic reward**
Something given to you by someone else as recognition for good work; extrinsic rewards include pay increases, praise, and promotions.

People are willing to work, and work hard, if they feel that their work makes a difference and is appreciated. People are motivated by a variety of things, such as recognition, accomplishment, and status.[3] An **intrinsic reward** is the personal satisfaction you feel when you perform well and complete goals. The belief that your work makes a significant contribution to the organization or society is a form of intrinsic reward. An **extrinsic reward** is something given to you by someone else as recognition for good work. Such things as pay increases, praise, and promotions are examples of extrinsic rewards. Although ultimately motivation—the drive to satisfy a need—comes from within an individual, there are ways to stimulate people that bring out their natural drive to do a good job.

The purpose of this chapter is to help you understand the concepts, theories, and practice of motivation. The most important person to motivate, of course, is yourself. One way to do that is to find the right job in the right organization—one that enables you to reach your goals in life. The whole purpose of this book is to help you in that search and to teach you how to succeed once you get there. One secret of success is to recognize that everyone else is on a similar search. Naturally, some are more committed than others. The job of a manager is to find that commitment, encourage it, and focus it on some common goal.

This chapter begins with a look at some of the traditional theories of motivation. You will learn about the Hawthorne studies because they created a new interest in worker satisfaction and motivation. Then you'll look at some assumptions about employees that come from the traditional theorists. You will see the names of these theorists over and over in business literature and courses: Taylor, Mayo, Maslow, Herzberg, and McGregor. Finally, you will learn the modern applications of motivation theories and the managerial procedures for implementing them.

## Frederick Taylor: The Father of Scientific Management

Several books in the 19th century presented management principles, but not until the early 20th century did there appear any significant works with lasting implications. One of the most well known, *The Principles of Scientific Management*, was written by American efficiency engineer Frederick Taylor and published in 1911. This book earned Taylor the title "father of scientific management." Taylor's goal was to increase worker productivity in order to benefit both the firm and the worker. The way to improve productivity, Taylor thought, was to scientifically study the most efficient ways to do things, determine the one "best way" to perform each task, and then teach people those methods.[4]

www.ups.com

LEGAL briefcase

## UPS and Scientific Management

With over $36 billion in revenues and 384,000 employees in 200 countries and territories, United Parcel Service (UPS) is the world's largest package distribution company. *Fortune* magazine rates UPS as one of the most admired companies in the country. The company grew from a small bicycle messenger service in 1907 to today's mammoth delivery service in part by dictating every task for its employees. Drivers are required to step out of their trucks with their right foot, fold their money faceup, and carry packages under their left arm. If a driver is considered slow, a supervisor rides along, prodding the driver with stopwatches and clipboards. To improve productivity to meet increased competition from other delivery services, UPS added 20 new services that required more skill. Drivers had to learn an assortment of new codes and billing systems and deliver an increasing number of time-sensitive packages that have special-handling requirements.

Drivers have long accepted such work requirements, taking comfort in good wages, generous benefits, and an attractive profit-sharing plan. All of this pressure, however, has taken its toll. Many UPS drivers have suffered from anxiety, phobias, or back strain, and at one point UPS had twice the injury rate of other delivery companies. In 1994, UPS settled a $3 million complaint from the Occupational Safety and Health Administration that it did not provide adequate safety for workers who handle hazardous wastes. UPS has spent nearly $1.5 billion since 1995 on improving health and safety programs. The total of days lost to disability has been on the decline.

In August 1997, the Teamsters Union, which represents 210,000 of UPS's employees, called a nationwide strike against the company because workers and managers couldn't reach agreement on a new contract. The Teamsters said they wanted better wages and pensions, and a safer workplace. They also wanted the company to limit its use of part-time workers, who receive limited benefits, and provide more full-time jobs. The 15-day strike ended when the union and UPS managers agreed on a five-year deal that created 10,000 new full-time jobs from existing part-time positions, increased full-time pay by $3.10 an hour, and retained the pension plan. Workers threatened to strike again in 2002 but were successful in negotiating a 25 percent increase over the next six years before the contract deadline.

UPS believes it is using new technologies and better planning to achieve greater productivity without overloading employees. Competition from companies such as FedEx (where workers earn 30 to 50 percent less than UPS workers) also requires greater efficiency. The variety of new UPS services requires drivers to remember more things. Because the jobs require more thinking, the company has begun hiring a new breed of skilled, college-educated workers. Do you think the new breed of UPS workers will be more or less tolerant of the company's rules and demands? Why?

Sources: "America's Most Admired Companies," *Fortune*, March 7, 2005; "Package Flow Technologies: Innovation at Work," www.ups.com; and Harry R. Weber, "UPS Will Purchase Overnite Corp.," *St. Louis Post-Dispatch*, May 17, 2005.

This became known as **scientific management**. Three elements were basic to Taylor's approach: time, methods, and rules of work. His most important tools were observation and the stopwatch. It's Taylor's thinking that is behind today's measures of how many burgers McDonald's expects its flippers to flip and how many callers the phone companies expect operators to assist.

**scientific management** Studying workers to find the most efficient ways of doing things and then teaching people those techniques.

A classic Taylor story involves his study of men shoveling rice, coal, and iron ore with the same type of shovel. Taylor felt that different materials called for different shovels. He proceeded to invent a wide variety of sizes and shapes of shovels and, with stopwatch in hand, measured output over time in what were called **time-motion studies**—studies of the tasks performed to complete a job and the time needed to do each task. Sure enough, an average person could shovel more (in fact, from 25 to 35 tons more per day) using the most efficient motions and the proper shovel. This finding led to time-motion

**time-motion studies** Studies, begun by Frederick Taylor, of which tasks must be performed to complete a job and the time needed to do each task.

studies of virtually every factory job. As researchers determined the most efficient ways of doing things, efficiency became the standard for setting goals.[5]

Taylor's scientific management became the dominant strategy for improving productivity in the early 1900s. Hundreds of time-motion specialists developed standards in plants throughout the country. One follower of Taylor was Henry L. Gantt, who developed charts by which managers plotted the work of employees a day in advance down to the smallest detail. (See Chapter 9 for a discussion of Gantt charts.) American engineers Frank and Lillian Gilbreth used Taylor's ideas in a three-year study of bricklaying. They developed the **principle of motion economy**, which showed that every job could be broken down into a series of elementary motions called a *therblig* (Gilbreth spelled backward with the *t* and *h* transposed). They then analyzed each motion to make it more efficient.

**principle of motion economy**
Theory developed by Frank and Lillian Gilbreth that every job can be broken down into a series of elementary motions.

Scientific management viewed people largely as machines that needed to be properly programmed.[6] There was little concern for the psychological or human aspects of work. Taylor felt simply that workers would perform at a high level of effectiveness (that is, be motivated) if they received high enough pay.

Some of Taylor's ideas are still being implemented. Some companies continue to place more emphasis on conformity to work rules than on creativity, flexibility, and responsiveness.[7] For example, United Parcel Service (UPS) tells drivers how fast to walk (three feet per second), how many packages to pick up and deliver a day (an average of 400), and how to hold their keys (teeth up, third finger). Drivers even wear "ring scanners," electronic devices on their index fingers wired to a small computer on their wrists that shoot a pattern of photons at a bar code on a package to let a customer tracking his or her package via the Internet know exactly where it is at any given moment. See the Legal Briefcase box for more about scientific management at UPS.

The benefits of relying on workers to come up with solutions to productivity problems have long been recognized, as we shall discover next.

## Elton Mayo and the Hawthorne Studies

One of the studies that grew out of Frederick Taylor's research was conducted at the Western Electric Company's Hawthorne plant in Cicero, Illinois. The study began in 1927 and ended six years later. Let's see why it was one of the major studies in management literature.

Little did Elton Mayo and his research team from Harvard University know that they would forever change the fixed beliefs of managers about employee motivation. Their research at the Hawthorne plant of Western Electric in Cicero, Illinois (pictured here), gave birth to the concept of human-based motivation. Before the Hawthorne studies, workers were often programmed to behave like human robots.

Elton Mayo and his colleagues from Harvard University came to the Hawthorne plant to test the degree of lighting associated with optimum productivity. In this respect, theirs was a traditional scientific management study; the idea was to keep records of the workers' productivity under different levels of illumination. But the initial experiments revealed what seemed to be a problem: The productivity of the experimental group compared to that of other workers doing the same job went up regardless of whether the lighting was bright or dim. This was true even when the lighting was reduced to about the level of moonlight. These results confused and frustrated the researchers, who had expected productivity to fall as the lighting was dimmed.

A second series of experiments was conducted. In these, a separate test room was set up where temperature, humidity, and other environmental factors could be manipulated. In the series of 13 experimental periods, productivity went up each time; in fact, it increased by 50 percent overall. When the experimenters repeated the original condition (expecting productivity to fall to original levels), productivity increased yet again. The experiments were considered a total failure at this point. No matter what the experimenters did, productivity went up. What was causing the increase?

In the end, Mayo guessed that some human or psychological factor was involved. He and his colleagues then interviewed the workers, asking them about their feelings and attitudes toward the experiment. The researchers' findings began a profound change in management thinking that has had repercussions up to the present. Here is what they concluded:

- The workers in the test room thought of themselves as a social group. The atmosphere was informal, they could talk freely, and they interacted regularly with their supervisors and the experimenters. They felt special and worked hard to stay in the group. This motivated them.
- The workers were involved in the planning of the experiments. For example, they rejected one kind of pay schedule and recommended another, which was used. The workers felt that their ideas were respected and that they were involved in managerial decision making. This, too, motivated them.
- No matter what the physical conditions were, the workers enjoyed the atmosphere of their special room and the additional pay they got for more productivity. Job satisfaction increased dramatically.

**Hawthorne effect**
The tendency for people to behave differently when they know they are being studied.

Researchers now use the term **Hawthorne effect** to refer to the tendency for people to behave differently when they know they're being studied.[8] The Hawthorne study's results encouraged researchers to study human motivation and the managerial styles that lead to more productivity. The emphasis of research shifted away from Taylor's scientific management and toward Mayo's new human-based management.

Mayo's findings led to completely new assumptions about employees. One of those assumptions, of course, was that pay was not the only motivator. In fact, money was found to be a relatively ineffective motivator. That change in assumptions led to many theories about the human side of motivation. One of the best-known motivation theorists was Abraham Maslow, whose work we discuss next.

## MOTIVATION AND MASLOW'S HIERARCHY OF NEEDS

Psychologist Abraham Maslow believed that to understand motivation at work, one must understand human motivation in general. It seemed to him that motivation arises from need. That is, people are motivated to satisfy unmet needs; needs that have been satisfied no longer provide motivation. He thought that needs could be placed on a hierarchy of importance.

**Maslow's hierarchy of needs**
Theory of motivation based on unmet human needs from basic physiological needs to safety, social, and esteem needs to self-actualization needs.

Figure 10.1 on page 264 shows **Maslow's hierarchy of needs**, whose levels are as follows:

*Physiological needs:* basic survival needs, such as the need for food, water, and shelter.

*Safety needs:* the need to feel secure at work and at home.

*Social needs:* the need to feel loved, accepted, and part of the group.

*Esteem needs:* the need for recognition and acknowledgment from others, as well as self-respect and a sense of status or importance.

*Self-actualization needs:* the need to develop to one's fullest potential.

figure 10.1

**MASLOW'S HIERARCHY OF NEEDS**

Maslow's hierarchy of needs is based on the idea that motivation comes from need. If a need is met, it's no longer a motivator, so a higher-level need becomes the motivator. Higher-level needs demand the support of lower-level needs. This chart shows the various levels of need. Do you know where you are on the chart right now?

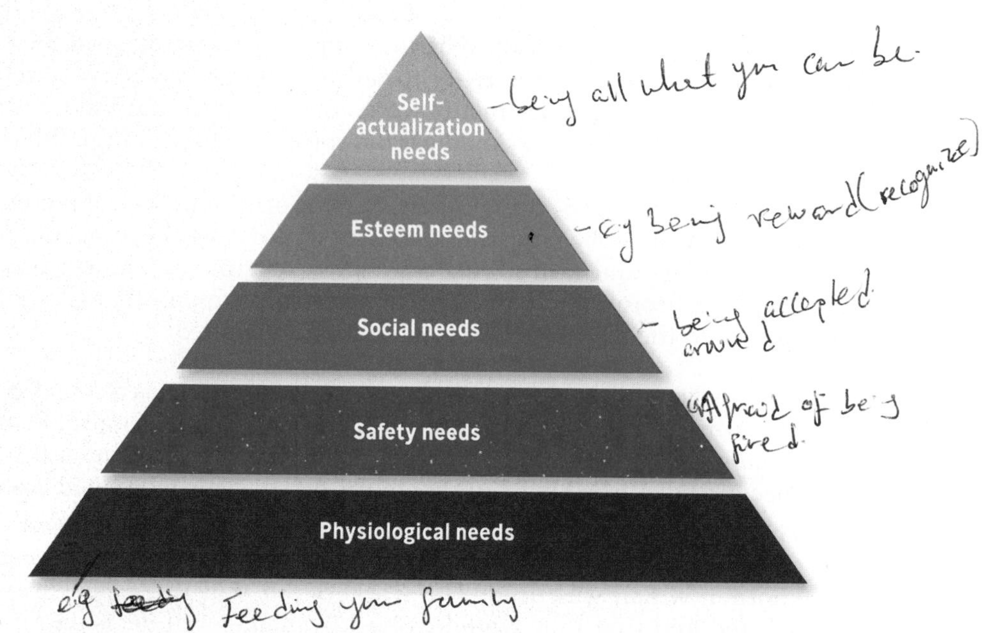


When one need is satisfied, another, higher-level need emerges and motivates the person to do something to satisfy it. The satisfied need is no longer a motivator. For example, if you just ate a full-course dinner, hunger would not (at least for several hours) be a motivator, and your attention may turn to your surroundings (safety needs) or family (social needs). Of course, lower-level needs (e.g., thirst) may emerge at any time they are not met and take your attention away from higher-level needs such as the need for recognition or status.

Most of the world's workers struggle all day simply to meet the basic physiological and safety needs. In developed countries, such needs no longer dominate, and workers seek to satisfy growth needs (social, esteem, and self-actualization needs).

To compete successfully, U.S. firms must create a work environment that motivates the best and the brightest workers. That means establishing a work environment that includes goals such as social contribution, honesty, reliability, service, quality, dependability, and unity.

Andrew Grove, former CEO of Intel, remains one of the most respected business minds in the United States. His best-selling books (*Swimming Across, Only the Paranoid Survive*) are considered must reads for aspiring businesspersons. Grove believes that managers can use Maslow's concepts to improve workers' job performance. How do you think managers can make use of Maslow's theory in the workplace?

## Applying Maslow's Theory

Andrew Grove, former CEO and current chairman of Intel, observed Maslow's concepts in action in his firm.[9] One woman, for example, took a low-paying job that did little for her family's standard of living. Why? Because she needed the companionship her work offered (social/affiliation need). One of Grove's friends had a midlife crisis when he was made a vice president. This position had been a lifelong goal, and when the man reached it he felt unsettled because he had to find another way to motivate himself (self-actualization need). People at a research and development lab were motivated by the desire to know more about their field of interest, but they had little desire to produce marketable results and thus little was achieved. Grove had to find new people who wanted to learn not just for the sake of learning but to achieve results as well.

Once managers understand the need level of employees, it is easier to design programs that will trigger self-motivation.[10] Grove believes that all motivation comes from within. He believes that self-actualized persons are achievers.

Personally, Grove was motivated to earn a doctorate from the University of California at Berkeley after surviving a childhood in communist Hungary. He also wrote several best-selling books, including his memoir *Swimming Across,* and designed a managerial program at Intel that emphasized achievement. Now Intel's managers are highly motivated to achieve their objectives because they feel rewarded for doing so.[11]

## HERZBERG'S MOTIVATING FACTORS

Another direction in managerial theory is to explore what managers can do with the job itself to motivate employees (a modern-day look at Taylor's research). In other words, some theorists ask: Of all the factors controllable by managers, which are most effective in generating an enthusiastic work effort?

The most discussed study in this area was conducted in the mid-1960s by psychologist Frederick Herzberg. He asked workers to rank various job-related factors in order of importance relative to motivation. The question was: What creates enthusiasm for workers and makes them work to full potential? The results showed that the most important motivating factors were the following:

1. Sense of achievement.
2. Earned recognition.
3. Interest in the work itself.
4. Opportunity for growth.
5. Opportunity for advancement.
6. Importance of responsibility.
7. Peer and group relationships.
8. Pay.
9. Supervisor's fairness.
10. Company policies and rules.
11. Status.
12. Job security.
13. Supervisor's friendliness.
14. Working conditions.

Herzberg noted that the factors receiving the most votes were all clustered around job content. Workers like to feel that they contribute to the company (sense of achievement was number 1). They want to earn recognition (number 2) and feel their jobs are important (number 6). They want responsibility (which is why learning is so important) and want recognition for that responsibility by having a chance for growth and advancement. Of course, workers also want the job to be interesting.

Herzberg noted further that factors having to do with the job environment were not considered motivators by workers. It was interesting to find that one of those factors was pay. Workers felt that the absence of good pay, job security, friendly supervisors, and the like could cause dissatisfaction, but the presence of those factors did not motivate them to work harder; they just provided satisfaction and contentment in the work situation.

The conclusions of Herzberg's study were that certain factors, called **motivators**, did cause employees to be productive and gave them a great deal of satisfaction. These factors mostly had to do with job content. Herzberg called other elements of the job **hygiene factors** (or maintenance factors). These had

**motivators**
In Herzberg's theory of motivating factors, job factors that cause employees to be productive and that give them satisfaction.

**hygiene factors**
In Herzberg's theory of motivating factors, job factors that can cause dissatisfaction if missing but that do not necessarily motivate employees if increased.

figure 10.2

**HERZBERG'S MOTIVATORS AND HYGIENE FACTORS**

There's some controversy over Herzberg's results. For example, sales managers often use money as a motivator. Recent studies have shown that money can be a motivator if used as part of a recognition program.

| MOTIVATORS | HYGIENE (MAINTENANCE) FACTORS |
|---|---|
| (These factors can be used to motivate workers.) | (These factors can cause dissatisfaction, but changing them will have little motivational effect.) |
| Work itself | Company policy and administration |
| Achievement | Supervision |
| Recognition | Working conditions |
| Responsibility | Interpersonal relations (co-workers) |
| Growth and advancement | Salary, status, and job security |

to do mostly with the job environment and could cause dissatisfaction if missing but would not necessarily motivate employees if increased. See Figure 10.2 for a list of both motivators and hygiene factors.

Considering Herzberg's motivating factors, we come up with the following conclusion: The best way to motivate employees is to make their jobs interesting, help them achieve their objectives, and recognize their achievement through advancement and added responsibility.

## Applying Herzberg's Theories

Twenty-two companies have appeared on *Fortune*'s list of 100 best companies to work for every year since the list started in 1998. Why do employees say they want to work for these companies? Here are just a few examples:[12]

- Nordstrom, the retailer known for its great customer service, gives its employees the tools they need to do their job and then gets out of the way.
- Synovus, a Georgia-based bank and payment processor, credits its success to what it calls its pat-on-the-back culture.
- Timberland, a footwear and apparel maker, offers a six-month, fully paid sabbatical to employees who want "to pursue a personal dream that benefits the community in a meaningful way."
- W. L. Gore, maker of Gore-Tex fabric, keeps its employees engaged by letting them choose what they work on.

Improved working conditions (such as better wages or increased security) are taken for granted after workers get used to them. This is what Herzberg meant by hygiene (or maintenance) factors: Their absence causes dissatisfaction, but their presence (maintenance) does not motivate. The best motivator for some employees is a simple and sincere "Thanks, I really appreciate what you're doing."

Many surveys conducted to test Herzberg's theories have supported his finding that the number one motivator is not money but a sense of achievement and recognition for a job well done.[13] If you're skeptical about this, think about the limitations of money as a motivating force. Most organizations review an employee's performance only once a year and allocate raises at that time. To inspire and motivate employees to perform at their highest level of capability, managers must recognize their achievements and progress more than once a year. In the National Survey of the Changing Workforce conducted by the Families and Work Institute in New York, salary ranked 16th in a list of items considered very important in rating jobs. A study prepared by Robert Half International, a

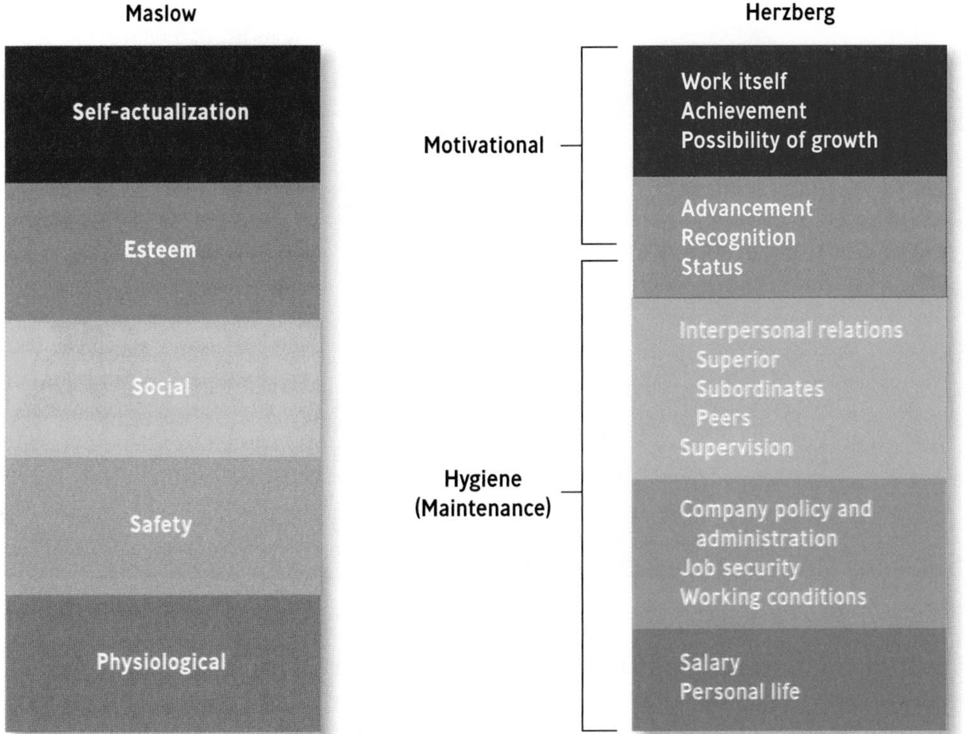


figure 10.3

COMPARISON OF MASLOW'S HIERARCHY OF NEEDS AND HERZBERG'S THEORY OF FACTORS

staffing and recruitment firm in Menlo Park, California, identified lack of enough praise and recognition as the primary reason employees leave their job.

Look back at Herzberg's list of motivating factors and identify the ones that tend to motivate you. Rank them in order of importance to you. Keep these factors in mind as you consider jobs and careers. What motivators do your job opportunities offer to you? Are they the ones you consider important? Evaluating your job offers in terms of what's really important to you will help you make a wise career choice.

A review of Figure 10.3 shows that there is a good deal of similarity in Maslow's hierarchy of needs and Herzberg's theory of factors.

### progress assessment

- What are the similarities and differences between Taylor's time-motion studies and Mayo's Hawthorne studies?
- How did Mayo's findings influence scientific management?
- Draw a diagram of Maslow's hierarchy of needs. Label and describe the parts.
- Explain the distinction between what Herzberg called motivators and hygiene factors.

## JOB ENRICHMENT

Both Maslow's and Herzberg's theories have been extended by job enrichment theory. **Job enrichment** is a motivational strategy that emphasizes motivating the worker through the job itself. Work is assigned to individuals so that they

**job enrichment**
A motivational strategy that emphasizes motivating the worker through the job itself.

Nobody said Gary Kelly, CEO of Southwest Airlines, had an easy job succeeding company co-founder Herb Kelleher and his Elvis imitations. Kelly, however, shocked his co-workers at the company Halloween party when he showed up dressed as Gene Simmons, front man for the rock group Kiss. Kelly remains fiercely committed to his predecessor's goal of developing employees who are happy, productive, and loyal. It seems likely that Kelly will keep rocking the airline industry.

have the opportunity to complete an identifiable task from beginning to end. They are held responsible for successful completion of the task. The motivational effect of job enrichment can come from the opportunities for personal achievement, challenge, and recognition. Go back and review Maslow's and Herzberg's work to see how job enrichment grew out of those theories.

Those who advocate job enrichment believe five characteristics of work to be important in affecting individual motivation and performance:

1. *Skill variety*. The extent to which a job demands different skills.
2. *Task identity*. The degree to which the job requires doing a task with a visible outcome from beginning to end.
3. *Task significance*. The degree to which the job has a substantial impact on the lives or work of others in the company.
4. *Autonomy*. The degree of freedom, independence, and discretion in scheduling work and determining procedures.
5. *Feedback*. The amount of direct and clear information that is received about job performance.

Variety, identity, and significance contribute to the meaningfulness of the job. Autonomy gives people a feeling of responsibility, and feedback contributes to a feeling of achievement and recognition.

Job enrichment is what makes work fun. The word *fun* can be misleading. We're not talking about having parties all the time. For example, Roger Sant, founder and chairman of the global electricity company AES Corporation, says that what makes working at AES fun is that people are fully engaged: "They have total responsibility for decisions. They are accountable for results. What they do every day matters to the company, and it matters to the communities we operate in. We do celebrate a lot—because lots of great things are happening. We just did a billion-dollar deal, for instance, and that called for a party. But it's what happens before the celebrations that's really fun."[14]

As mentioned above, job enrichment is based on Herzberg's higher motivators such as responsibility, achievement, and recognition. It stands in contrast to *job simplification*, which produces task efficiency by breaking down a job into simple steps and assigning people to each of those steps.

## SPOTLIGHT ON small business

### Small Businesses Can Motivate without Big Costs

Often small businesses cannot offer their employees the financial incentives that larger business can. So how can they motivate their workers to perform their best? Celine Rattray of Plum Pictures, a small independent movie production company, says that you must offer them something that money can't buy. "On a small-budget film, you offer typecasted actors different roles. You offer crew members a position above what they're used to doing—the makeup assistant might be the lead make-up artist. And we compensate writers by including them more in the production. We paid nothing for one script; a studio might have paid $10,000. The writer is helping choose a director and a cast. It's an exchange."

According to Rhonda Abrams, author of *Wear Clean Underwear: Business Wisdom from Mom*, the surest way to get the best value from your employees is to treat them with respect: "When you allow your employees to think about how to solve problems, not just carry out specific tasks, you can unleash an amazing amount of creativity and energy. To do so, however, they'll need information, patience, and a sense they won't be 'punished' if they make an honest mistake."

To help your employees be more productive, Abrams recommends that you:

- *Train your employees to do a wide variety of tasks.* In a small business, employees have to pitch in on many jobs, so instead of teaching them specific tasks, you need to teach them about the whole business and encourage problem solving.
- *Communicate frequently.* You could hold frequent, brief motivation sessions in which employees compliment each other for recent behaviors, both minor and major. Then each person could share something they've done well. These meetings raise individual self-esteem and set the tone for the rest of the day. According to Abrams, "Giving people positive feedback isn't just about building their self-esteem or empty flattery, it's about creating a strong, productive, atmosphere."
- *Empower your employees to make decisions.* Let them use their brains, not just their backs.
- *Acknowledge your employees' contributions.* The least productive thing you can say is "I don't need to thank employees; I pay them." We all need to be thanked and recognized.

It's important for small-business owners to make every employee feel valued, included, and respected. As your employees grow, your business is more likely to grow.

Sources: Rhonda Abrams, "Say It with Compliments," Gannett News Service, February 11, 2005; Lucas Conley and Danielle Sacks, "A Plum Partnership," *Fast Company*, March 2005, p. 39; and Rhonda Abrams, "Twenty Years Reaps Many Entrepreneurial Lessons," Gannett News Service, January 26, 2006.

Another type of job enrichment used for motivation is **job enlargement**, which combines a series of tasks into one challenging and interesting assignment. For example, Maytag, the home appliance manufacturer, redesigned the production process of its washing machines so that employees could assemble an entire water pump instead of just one part. **Job rotation** also makes work more interesting and motivating by moving employees from one job to another. One problem with job rotation, of course, is having to train employees to do several different operations. However, the resulting increase in employee motivation and the value of having flexible, cross-trained employees offsets the additional costs.[15]

**job enlargement**
A job enrichment strategy that involves combining a series of tasks into one challenging and interesting assignment.

**job rotation**
A job enrichment strategy that involves moving employees from one job to another.

Job enrichment is one way to ensure that workers enjoy responsibility and a sense of accomplishment. The Spotlight on Small Business box offers advice on using job enrichment strategies in small businesses.

## MCGREGOR'S THEORY X AND THEORY Y

The way managers go about motivating people at work depends greatly on their attitudes toward workers. Management theorist Douglas McGregor observed that managers' attitudes generally fall into one of two entirely different sets of managerial assumptions, which he called Theory X and Theory Y.

## Theory X

The assumptions of Theory X management are as follows:

- The average person dislikes work and will avoid it if possible.
- Because of this dislike, workers must be forced, controlled, directed, or threatened with punishment to make them put forth the effort to achieve the organization's goals.
- The average worker prefers to be directed, wishes to avoid responsibility, has relatively little ambition, and wants security.
- Primary motivators are fear and money.

Theory X managers do not come in one-size-fits-all packages. Take Salina Lo of Alteon Websystems, for example. She doesn't match the typical theory X stereotype, but on the job this University of California at Berkeley graduate is a tough and exacting Theory X manager. Her in-your-face style has earned her a reputation as one of the industry's toughest managers. Would you prefer to work for a Theory X or a Theory Y manager?

The natural consequence of such attitudes, beliefs, and assumptions is a manager who is very "busy" and who watches people closely, telling them what to do and how to do it. Motivation is more likely to take the form of punishment for bad work rather than reward for good work. Theory X managers give workers little responsibility, authority, or flexibility. With his scientific management, Taylor and other theorists who preceded him would have agreed with Theory X. That is why management literature focused on time-motion studies that calculated the one best way to perform a task and the optimum time to be devoted to a task. It was assumed that workers needed to be trained and carefully watched to see that they conformed to the standards.

Theory X management still dominates some organizations. Many managers and entrepreneurs still suspect that employees cannot be fully trusted and need to be closely supervised. No doubt you have seen such managers in action. How did this make you feel? Were these managers' assumptions accurate regarding the workers' attitudes?

## Theory Y

Theory Y makes entirely different assumptions about people:

- Most people like work; it is as natural as play or rest.
- Most people naturally work toward goals to which they are committed.
- The depth of a person's commitment to goals depends on the perceived rewards for achieving them.
- Under certain conditions, most people not only accept but also seek responsibility.
- People are capable of using a relatively high degree of imagination, creativity, and cleverness to solve problems.
- In industry, the average person's intellectual potential is only partially realized.
- People are motivated by a variety of rewards. Each worker is stimulated by a reward unique to that worker (time off, money, recognition, etc.).

Rather than emphasize authority, direction, and close supervision, Theory Y emphasizes a relaxed managerial atmosphere in which workers are free to set objectives, be creative, be flexible, and go beyond the goals set by management. A key technique in meeting these objectives is empowerment. Empowerment gives employees the authority to make decisions and the tools to implement the decisions they make. For empowerment to be a real motivator, management should follow these three steps:

1. Find out what people think the problems in the organization are.
2. Let them design the solutions.
3. Get out of the way and let them put those solutions into action.

Keeping on schedule and making sure the job is done according to customer expectations is the key to survival in the growing home cleaning industry. At Mini Maids, the emphasis is on teamwork and employee empowerment to deal with on-the-job problems that arise. The company values the principles of Theory Y management where employees are looked on as partners. What businesses do you feel are most appropriate to use the principles of theory Y management?

Often employees complain that although they're asked to become involved in company decision making, their managers fail to actually empower them to make decisions. Have you ever worked in such an atmosphere? How did that make you feel?

The trend in many U.S. businesses is toward Theory Y management. One reason for this trend is that many service industries are finding Theory Y helpful in dealing with on-the-spot problems. Dan Kaplan of Hertz Rental Corporation would attest to this. He empowers his employees in the field to think and work as entrepreneurs. Leona Ackerly of Mini Maid Inc. agrees: "If our employees look at our managers as partners, a real team effort is built."

## OUCHI'S THEORY Z

In addition to the reasons given above for the trend toward Theory Y management, another reason for companies to adopt a more flexible managerial style is to meet competition from foreign firms such as those in Japan, China, and the European Union. Back in the 1980s, Japanese companies seemed to be outperforming American businesses. William Ouchi, a management professor at the University of California–Los Angeles, wondered if the secret to Japanese success was the way Japanese companies managed their workers. The Japanese management approach (what Ouchi called Type J) involved lifetime employment, consensual decision making, collective responsibility for the outcomes of decisions, slow evaluation and promotion, implied control mechanisms, nonspecialized career paths, and holistic concern for employees. In contrast, the American management approach (what Ouchi called Type A) involved short-term employment, individual decision making, individual responsibility for the outcomes of decisions, rapid evaluation and promotion, explicit control mechanisms, specialized career paths, and segmented concern for employees.

Type J firms are based on the culture of Japan, which includes a focus on trust and intimacy within the group and family. Conversely, Type A firms are based on the culture of America, which includes a focus on individual rights and achievements. Ouchi wanted to help American firms adopt the successful Japanese strategies, but he realized that it wouldn't be practical to expect

figure 10.4

**THEORY Z: A BLEND OF AMERICAN AND JAPANESE MANAGEMENT APPOACHES**

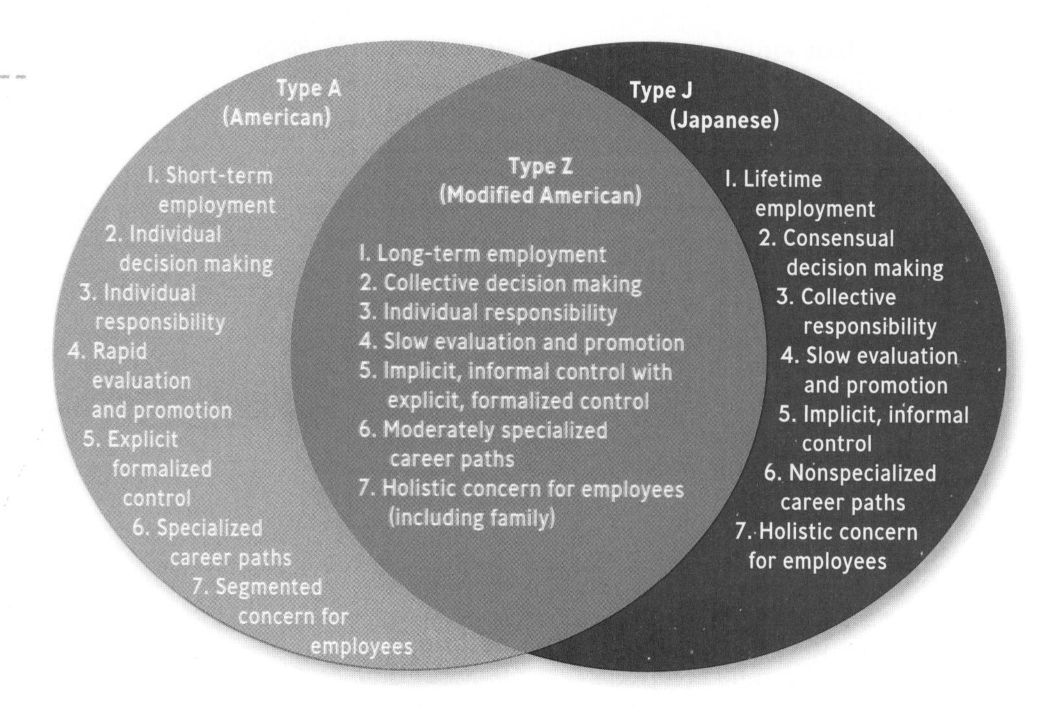


American managers to accept an approach based on the culture of another country. Judge for yourself. A job for life in a firm may sound good until you think of the implications: no chance to change jobs and no opportunity to move up quickly through the ranks. Therefore, Ouchi recommended a hybrid of the two approaches in what he called Theory Z (see Figure 10.4). Theory Z blends the characteristics of Type J and Type A into an approach that involves long-term employment, collective decision making, individual responsibility for the outcomes of decisions, slow evaluation and promotion, moderately specialized career paths, and holistic concern for employees (including family). The theory views the organization as a family that fosters cooperation and organizational values.

Today, economic decline, demographic and social changes, and fierce global competition have forced Japanese managers to reevaluate the way they conduct business. Whereas the Japanese system of the 1980s was admired for its focus on building long-term business relationships, today there is a realization that Japanese firms need to become both more dynamic and more efficient in order to compete effectively in the rapidly changing global economy.[16] Feeling the pain of the worst recession in their country's history, some Japanese managers are changing the way they do business.[17] For example, electronics giant Hitachi was the first major Japanese company to announce it had quit requiring corporate calisthenics—exercises done in groups not only for health but also to foster cohesion among employees. Having everyone start the day with group exercises symbolized doing the same thing the same way and reinforced the cultural belief that employees should not take risks or think for themselves. Many managers think that such conformity is what has hurt Japanese business. Will Japanese managers move toward the hybrid Theory Z in the future? We'll have to wait and see. The appropriate managerial style is one that matches the culture, the situation, and the specific needs of the organization and its employees. (See Figure 10.5 for a summary of Theories X, Y, and Z.)

| THEORY X | THEORY Y | THEORY Z |
|---|---|---|
| 1. Employees dislike work and will try to avoid it. | 1. Employees view work as a natural part of life. | 1. Employee involvement is the key to increased productivity. |
| 2. Employees prefer to be controlled and directed. | 2. Employees prefer limited control and direction. | 2. Employee control is implied and informal. |
| 3. Employees seek security, not responsibility. | 3. Employees will seek responsibility under proper work conditions. | 3. Employees prefer to share responsibility and decision making. |
| 4. Employees must be intimidated by managers to perform. | 4. Employees perform better in work environments that are nonintimidating. | 4. Employees perform better in environments that foster trust and cooperation. |
| 5. Employees are motivated by financial rewards. | 5. Employees are motivated by many different needs. | 5. Employees need guaranteed employment and will accept slow evaluations and promotions. |

figure 10.5

**A COMPARISON OF THEORIES X, Y, AND Z**

## GOAL-SETTING THEORY AND MANAGEMENT BY OBJECTIVES

**Goal-setting theory** is based on the idea that setting ambitious but attainable goals can motivate workers and improve performance if the goals are accepted, accompanied by feedback, and facilitated by organizational conditions. All members of an organization should have some basic agreement about the overall goals of the organization and the specific objectives to be met by each department and individual. It follows, then, that there should be a system to involve everyone in the organization in goal setting and implementation.

Peter Drucker developed such a system in the 1960s. Drucker asserted, "Managers cannot motivate people; they can only thwart people's motivation because people motivate themselves." Managers, he believed, can only create the proper environment for the seed to grow. Thus, he designed his system to help employees motivate themselves. Called **management by objectives (MBO)**, it is a system of goal setting and implementation that involves a cycle of discussion, review, and evaluation of objectives among top and middle-level managers, supervisors, and employees. Large corporations such as the Ford Motor Company have used MBO, as has the U.S. Department of Defense. MBO also spread to other companies and government agencies. MBO calls on managers to formulate goals in cooperation with everyone in the organization, to commit employees to those goals, and then to monitor results and reward accomplishment.[18]

MBO is most effective in relatively stable situations in which long-range plans can be made and implemented with little need for major changes. It is also important to MBO that managers understand the difference between helping and coaching subordinates. Helping means working with the subordinate and doing part of the work if necessary. Coaching means acting as a resource—teaching, guiding, and recommending—but not helping (that is, not participating actively or doing the task). The central idea of MBO is that employees need to motivate themselves.

Problems can arise when management uses MBO as a strategy for forcing managers and workers to commit to goals that are not really agreed on mutually but are instead set by top management. Employee involvement and expectations are important.[19]

Victor Vroom identified the importance of employee expectations and developed a process called expectancy theory. Let's examine this concept next.

**goal-setting theory**
The idea that setting ambitious but attainable goals can motivate workers and improve performance if the goals are accepted, accompanied by feedback, and facilitated by organizational conditions.

**management by objectives (MBO)**
A system of goal setting and implementation that involves a cycle of discussion, review, and evaluation of objectives among top and middle-level managers, supervisors, and employees.

figure 10.6

**EXPECTANCY THEORY**

The amount of effort employees exert on a task depends on their expectations of the outcome.

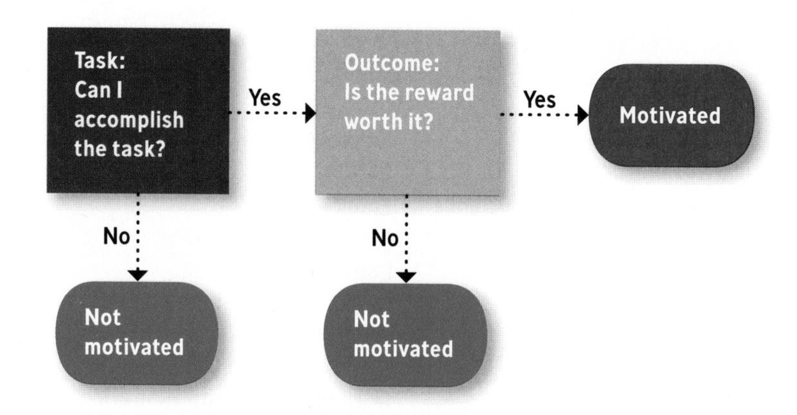


**expectancy theory** Victor Vroom's theory that the amount of effort employees exert on a specific task depends on their expectations of the outcome.

## MEETING EMPLOYEE EXPECTATIONS: EXPECTANCY THEORY

According to Victor Vroom's **expectancy theory**, employee expectations can affect an individual's motivation. Therefore, the amount of effort employees exert on a specific task depends on their expectations of the outcome.[20] Vroom contends that employees ask three questions before committing maximum effort to a task: (1) Can I accomplish the task? (2) If I do accomplish it, what's my reward? (3) Is the reward worth the effort? (See Figure 10.6.)

Think of the effort you might exert in your class under the following conditions: Suppose that your instructor says that to earn an A in the course you must achieve an average of 90 percent on coursework plus jump eight feet high. Would you exert maximum effort toward earning an A if you knew you could not possibly jump eight feet high? Or suppose that your instructor said any student can earn an A in the course, but you know that this instructor has not awarded an A in 25 years of teaching. If the reward of an A seems unattainable, would you exert significant effort in the course? Better yet, let's say that you read in the newspaper that businesses actually prefer hiring C-minus students to hiring A-plus students. Does the reward of an A seem worth it? Now think of the same types of situations that may occur on the job.

Expectancy theory does note that expectation varies from individual to individual. Employees therefore establish their own views in terms of task difficulty and the value of the reward. Researchers David Nadler and Edward Lawler modified Vroom's theory and suggested that managers follow five steps to improve employee performance:

1. Determine what rewards are valued by employees.
2. Determine each employee's desired performance standard.
3. Ensure that performance standards are attainable.
4. Guarantee rewards tied to performance.
5. Be certain that rewards are considered adequate.[21]

**reinforcement theory** Theory that positive and negative reinforcers motivate a person to behave in certain ways.

## REINFORCING EMPLOYEE PERFORMANCE: REINFORCEMENT THEORY

**Reinforcement theory** is based on the idea that positive and negative reinforcers motivate a person to behave in certain ways. In other words, motivation is the result of the carrot-and-stick approach (reward and punishment).

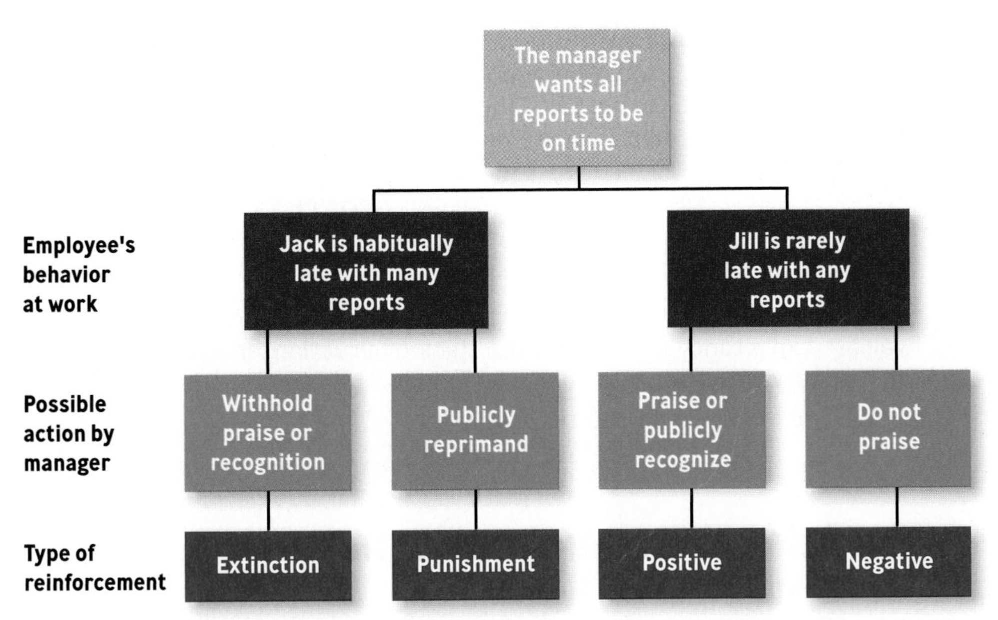


figure 10.7

**REINFORCEMENT THEORY**

A manager can use both positive and negative reinforcement to motivate employee behavior.

Individuals act to receive rewards and avoid punishment. Positive reinforcements are rewards such as praise, recognition, or a pay raise. Negative reinforcement includes reprimands, reduced pay, and layoff or firing. A manager might also try to stop undesirable behavior by not responding to it. This is called *extinction* because the hope is that the unwanted behavior will eventually become extinct. Figure 10.7 illustrates how a manager can use reinforcement theory to motivate workers.

## TREATING EMPLOYEES FAIRLY: EQUITY THEORY

**equity theory** The idea that employees try to maintain equity between inputs and outputs compared to others in similar positions.

**Equity theory** deals with the questions "If I do a good job, will it be worth it?" and "What's fair?" It has to do with perceptions of fairness and how those perceptions affect employees' willingness to perform. The basic principle is that employees try to maintain equity between inputs and outputs compared to others in similar positions. Equity comparisons are made from the information that is available through personal relationships, professional organizations, and so on.[22]

When workers do perceive inequity, they will try to reestablish equitable exchanges in a number of ways. For example, suppose you compare the grade you earned on a term paper with your classmates' grades. If you think you received a lower grade compared to the students who put out the same effort as you, you will probably react in one of two ways: (1) by reducing your effort on future class projects or (2) by rationalizing. The latter may include saying, "Grades are overvalued anyway!" If you think your paper received a higher grade than comparable papers, you will probably (1) increase your effort to justify the higher reward in the future or (2) rationalize by saying, "I'm worth it!" In the workplace, inequity may lead to lower productivity, reduced quality, increased absenteeism, and voluntary resignation.

Remember that equity judgments are based on perceptions and are therefore subject to errors in perception. When workers overestimate their own contributions—as happens often they are going to feel that any rewards given out for performance are inequitable. Sometimes organizations try to deal with this by keeping employee salaries secret, but secrecy may make things worse; employees are likely to overestimate the salaries of others in addition to overestimating their own contribution.[23] In general, the best remedy is clear and frequent communication. Managers must communicate as clearly as possible both the results they expect and the outcomes that will occur when those results are achieved or when they are not.

**progress assessment**

- Briefly describe the managerial attitudes behind Theories X, Y, and Z.
- Explain goal-setting theory.
- Evaluate expectancy theory. Can you think of situations in which expectancy theory could apply to your efforts or lack of effort?
- Explain the principles of equity theory.

## BUILDING TEAMWORK THROUGH OPEN COMMUNICATION

Companies with highly motivated workforces usually have several things in common. Among the most important factors are open communication systems and self-managed teams.[24] Open communication helps both top managers and team members understand the objectives and work together to achieve them. Communication must flow freely throughout the organization when teams are empowered to make decisions—they can't make these decisions in a vacuum. It is crucial for people to be able to access the knowledge they need when they need it.

Having teams creates an environment in which learning can happen because most learning happens at the peer level—peers who have an interest in helping each other along. Empowerment works when people volunteer to share their knowledge with their colleagues. For example, when Flora Zhou, a business development manager at global power company AES, was putting together a bid to the government of Vietnam, she sent a detailed e-mail about what she was planning to bid and why to about 300 people within AES. She asked for and received lots of advice and comments. Most people thought her proposal was fine, but Sarah Slusser, a group manager in Central America, sent Zhou a three-page response that contained a wealth of information about a similar situation she had encountered with a plant in the Yucatan. Slusser told Zhou what technology issues she needed to pay attention to. A few days later, Zhou made the bid. It was the lowest bid by two-tenths of a percent. Did Slusser tell Zhou the exact dollar to bid? No, but she and many others, including plant leaders and board members, gave her the best information and judgments they had to help her make her decision. They shared everything they knew with her.

Teamwork does not happen by itself. The whole organization must be structured to make it easy for managers and employees to talk to one another. Procedures for encouraging open communication include the following:[25]

- *Create an organizational culture that rewards listening.* Top managers must create places to talk, and they must show employees that talking with superiors counts—by providing feedback, adopting employee suggestions, and rewarding upward communication—even if the discussion is negative. Employees must feel free to say anything they deem appropriate. Jerry Stead, chairman of technology provider Ingram Micro, has his own 24-hour toll-free phone line to take calls from employees. Yes, he really answers it. He says: "If we are doing something right, I love to hear about it. If there's something we should be doing differently, I want to know that too." Stead has also given his home number to all 13,000 Ingram Micro employees.

- *Train supervisors and managers to listen.* Most people receive no training in how to listen, either in school or anywhere else, so organizations must do such training themselves or hire someone to do it.
- *Remove barriers to open communication.* Having separate offices, parking areas, bathrooms, and dining rooms for managers and workers only sets up barriers in an organization. Other barriers are different dress codes and different ways of addressing one another (e.g., calling workers by their first names and managers by their last). Removing such barriers may require imagination and willingness on the part of managers to give up their special privileges.
- *Actively undertake efforts to facilitate communication.* Large lunch tables at which all organization members eat, conference rooms, organizational picnics, organizational athletic teams, and other such efforts all allow managers to mix with each other and with workers.

Let's see how one organization addresses the challenge of open communication in teams.

## Applying Open Communication in Self-Managed Teams

Kenneth Kohrs, vice president of car product development at Ford Motor Company, says that an inside group known as Team Mustang sets the guidelines for how production teams should be formed. Given the challenge to create a car that would make people dust off their old "Mustang Sally" records and dance into the showrooms, the 400-member team was also given the freedom to make decisions without waiting for approval from headquarters or other departments. The team moved everyone from various departments into cramped offices under one roof of an old warehouse. Drafting experts sat next to accountants, engineers next to stylists. Budgetary walls that divided departments were knocked down as department managers were persuaded to surrender some control over their subordinates.

When the resulting Mustang convertible displayed shaking problems, suppliers were called in, and the team worked around the clock to solve the problem. The engineers were so motivated to complete the program on schedule and under budget that they worked late into the night and slept on the floors of the warehouse when necessary. The senior Ford executives were tempted to overrule the program, but they stuck with their promise not to meddle. The team solved the shaking problem and still came in under budget and a couple of months early. The new car was a big hit in the marketplace, and sales soared.[26] In fact, the 2005 Mustang was the hottest-selling car in the industry; nearly one out of two sports cars sold in the United States is a Mustang.[27]

In the car business nothing works like the "WOW" factor. At Ford Motor Company, the 400-member "Team Mustang" group was empowered to create such a response for the company's sleek Mustang convertible. The work team, suppliers, company managers, and even customers worked together to make the Mustang a winner in the very competitive automobile market.

To implement such teams, managers at most companies must reinvent work. This means respecting workers, providing interesting work, rewarding good work, developing workers' skills, allowing autonomy, and decentralizing authority. In the process of reinventing work, it is essential that managers behave ethically toward all employees. The Making Ethical Decisions box on page 278 illustrates a problem managers may face when filling temporary positions.

www.manpower.com

## MAKING ethical decisions

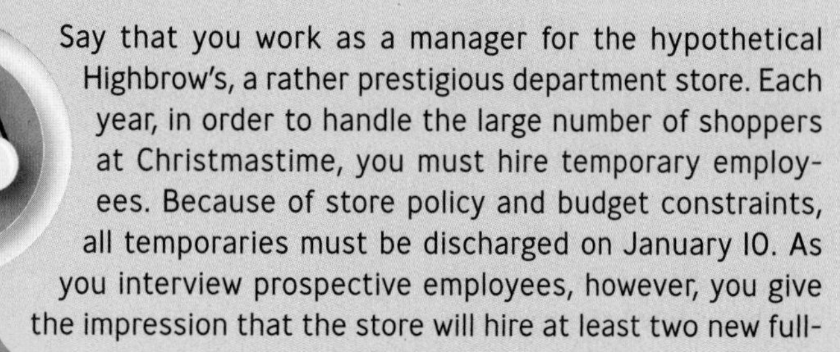

### Motivating Temporary Employees

Say that you work as a manager for the hypothetical Highbrow's, a rather prestigious department store. Each year, in order to handle the large number of shoppers at Christmastime, you must hire temporary employees. Because of store policy and budget constraints, all temporaries must be discharged on January 10. As you interview prospective employees, however, you give the impression that the store will hire at least two new full-time retail salespeople for the coming year. You hope that this will serve to motivate the temporary workers and even foster some competition among them. You also instruct your permanent salespeople to reinforce the falsehood that good work during the Christmas season is the path to full-time employment. Is this an ethical way to try to motivate your employees? What are the dangers of using a tactic such as this?

## MOTIVATION IN THE FUTURE

Today's customers expect high-quality, customized goods and services. This means that employees must provide extensive personal service and pay close attention to details. Employees will have to work smart as well as hard. No amount of supervision can force an employee to smile or to go the extra mile to help a customer. Managers need to know how to motivate their employees to meet customer needs.

Tomorrow's managers will not be able to use any one motivational formula for all employees. Rather, they will have to get to know each worker personally and tailor the motivational effort to the individual. As you have learned in this chapter, different employees respond to different managerial and motivational styles. This is further complicated by the increase in global business and the fact that managers now work with employees from a variety of cultural backgrounds. Different cultures experience motivational approaches differently; therefore, the manager of the future will have to study and understand these cultural factors in designing a reward system. The Reaching Beyond Our Borders box describes how Digital Equipment Corporation dealt with these cultural issues within global teams.

Generation X employees believe there is more to life than work; they also believe that stress at the job stalls company productivity. That's why at Excite.com, workers can take out their frustrations by putting on the over-sized boxing gloves and going a few rounds during the workday. What is important to your satisfaction on the job?

Cultural differences are not restricted to groups of people from various countries. Such differences also exist between generations raised in the same country. Members of generations such as the baby boomers (born between 1946 and 1964); Generation X (born between 1965 and 1980); and Generation Y or echo boomers (born after 1980) are linked through shared life experiences in their formative years—usually the first 10 years of life. The beliefs you gather as a child affect how you view risk, challenge, authority, technology, relationships, and economics. If you are in a management position, they can even affect whom you hire, fire, or promote. Boomers were raised in families that experienced unprecedented economic prosperity, secure jobs, and optimism about the future.[28] "Gen Xers" were raised in dual-career families with parents who focused on work. As children, they attended day care or became latchkey kids. Their parents' successive layoffs added to their insecurity about a lifelong job.

www.hp.com

## REACHING BEYOND our borders

### Global Teamwork

The global economy has altered the world landscape by bringing products and services to every corner of the earth and helping many people in less developed countries improve their quality of life. Business globalization has also resulted in the creation of global work teams, a rather formidable task.

Even though the concept of teamwork is nothing new, building a harmonious global work team is a new task and can be complicated. Global companies must recognize differing attitudes and competencies in the team's cultural mix and the technological capabilities among team members. For example, a global work team needs to determine whether the culture of its members is high-context or low-context. In a high-context team culture, members build personal relationships and develop group trust before focusing on tasks. In a low-context culture, members often view relationship building as a waste of time that diverts attention from the task. Koreans, Thais, and Saudis (high-context cultures), for example, often view American team members as insincere due to their need for data and quick decision making.

When Digital Equipment Corporation (now a part of Hewlett-Packard) decided to consolidate its operations at six manufacturing sites, the company recognized the need to form multicultural work teams. Realizing the challenge it faced, Digital hired an internal organization development specialist to train the team in relationship building, foreign languages, and valuing differences. All team members from outside the United States were assigned American partners and invited to spend time with their families. Digital also flew the flags of each employee's native country at all its manufacturing sites. As communication within the teams increased, the company reduced the time of new-product handoffs from three years to just six months.

Understanding the motivational forces in global organizations and building effective global teams is still new territory for most companies. Developing group leaders who are culturally astute, flexible, and able to deal with ambiguity is a challenge businesses must face in the 21st century.

Sources: Patricia Sellers, "Blowing in the Wind: To Build a Better Wind Turbine, General Electric Built a Global Team of Researchers in Germany, China, India, and the U.S.," *Fortune*, July 25, 2005, and Katherine Sima, "Global Design Focuses on Regional Needs," *Plastics News*, January 2, 2006.

How do these generational differences affect motivation in the workplace? For the boomer managers, it means that they will need to be flexible with their Gen X employees or they will lose them. For Gen X employees, it means that they will need to use their enthusiasm for change and streamlining to their advantage. Although many Gen Xers are unwilling to pay the same price for success that their parents and grandparents did, concern about undue stress and long work hours does not mean they lack ambition. Gen Xers' desire for security typically equals that of older workers, but there is a big difference in their approach to achieving it. Rather than focusing on job security, Gen Xers tend to focus on career security. As they look for opportunities to expand their skills and grow professionally, they are willing to change jobs to do it.

Many Gen Xers are now or soon will be managers themselves and responsible for motivating other employees. What type of management will this generation provide? In general, Gen X managers will be well equipped to motivate people. They understand that there is more to life than work, and they think a big part of motivating people is letting them know you recognize that fact. As a result, Gen X managers may tend to focus more on results than on hours in the workplace. They will tend to be flexible and good at collaboration and consensus building. They may tend to think in broader terms than their predecessors because, through the media, they have been exposed to a lot of problems around the world. They may also have a great impact on their team members because they will likely give the people working for them the goals and the parameters of the project and then leave them alone to do their work.[29]

Perhaps their best asset might be their ability to give their employees feedback, especially positive feedback. One reason they may be better at providing feedback is that they expect more of it themselves. One new employee remarked that he was frustrated because he hadn't received feedback from his boss since he was hired—two weeks earlier. In short, managers will need to realize that young workers demand performance reviews and other forms of feedback more than once or twice a year.

In every generational shift, the old generation says the same thing about the new generation: They break the rules. The generation that lived through the Great Depression and World War II said it of the baby boomers. Now boomers look at Gen Xers and say, "Why are they breaking the rules?" And you can be sure the Gen Xers are looking at the Gen Yers and saying, "What's wrong with these kids?" In fact, Gen Yers are entering the professional workforce now at 70 million strong; creating a workplace four generations deep.[30] As a group, Generation Yers tend to share a number of common characteristics: They are considered impatient, skeptical, blunt and expressive, image driven, and inexperienced. Like any generation, what may make Generation Y difficult to deal with on the job is also what could make it uniquely skilled. For example, a number of talents and tendencies dominate the Gen Yers: They are adaptable, tech savvy, able to grasp new concepts, practiced at multitasking, efficient, and tolerant. Perhaps the most surprising attribute many Gen Yers share is a sense of commitment.[31] What do you think are the most effective strategies managers can use to motivate Gen Y workers?

One thing in business is likely to remain constant, though: Motivation will come from the job itself rather than from external punishments or rewards. Managers will need to give workers what they need to do a good job: the right tools, the right information, and the right amount of cooperation.

Motivation doesn't have to be difficult. It begins with acknowledging a job well done. You can simply tell those who do such a job that you appreciate them—especially if you make this statement in front of others. After all, as we said earlier in this chapter, the best motivator is frequently a sincere "Thanks, I really appreciate what you're doing."[32]

### progress assessment

- What are several steps firms can take to increase internal communications and thus motivation?
- What problems may emerge when trying to implement participative management?
- Why is it important today to adjust motivational styles to individual employees? Are there any general principles of motivation that today's managers should follow?

## summary

**1.** Explain Taylor's scientific management.

1. Human efficiency engineer Frederick Taylor was one of the first people to study management.
   - **What is Frederick Taylor known for?**

   Frederick Taylor has been called the father of scientific management. He did time-motion studies to learn the most efficient way of doing a job and then trained workers in those procedures. He published his book *The Principles of Scientific Management* in 1911. Henry L. Gantt and Frank and Lillian Gilbreth were followers of Taylor.

2. Management theory moved away from Taylor's scientific management and toward theories that stress human factors of motivation.
   - **What led to the more human managerial styles?**

   The greatest impact on motivation theory was generated by the Hawthorne studies in the late 1920s and early 1930s. In these studies, Elton Mayo found that human factors such as feelings of involvement and participation led to greater productivity gains than did physical changes in the workplace.

**2.** Describe the Hawthorne studies, and relate their significance to management.

3. Abraham Maslow studied basic human motivation and found that motivation was based on needs; he said that a person with an unfilled need would be motivated to satisfy it and that a satisfied need no longer served as motivation.
   - **What were the various levels of need identified by Maslow?**

   Starting at the bottom of Maslow's hierarchy of needs and going to the top, the levels of need are physiological, safety, social, esteem, and self-actualization.
   - **Can managers use Maslow's theory?**

   Yes, they can recognize what unmet needs a person has and design work so that it satisfies those needs.

**3.** Identify the levels of Maslow's hierarchy of needs, and relate their importance to employee motivation.

4. Frederick Herzberg found that some factors are motivators and others are hygiene (or maintenance) factors; hygiene factors cause job dissatisfaction if missing but are not motivators if present.
   - **What are the factors called motivators?**

   The work itself, achievement, recognition, responsibility, growth, and advancement.
   - **What are hygiene (maintenance) factors?**

   Factors that do not motivate but must be present for employee satisfaction, such as company policies, supervision, working conditions, interpersonal relations, and salary.

**4.** Distinguish between the motivators and hygiene factors identified by Herzberg.

5. Job enrichment describes efforts to make jobs more interesting.
   - **What characteristics of work affect motivation and performance?**

   The job characteristics that influence motivation are skill variety, task identity, task significance, autonomy, and feedback.
   - **Name two forms of job enrichment that increase motivation.**

   Job enrichment strategies include job enlargement and job rotation.

**5.** Explain how job enrichment affects employee motivation and performance.

6. Douglas McGregor held that managers will have one of two opposing attitudes toward employees. They are called Theory X and Theory Y. William Ouchi introduced Theory Z.
   - **What is Theory X?**

   Theory X assumes that the average person dislikes work and will avoid it if possible. Therefore, people must be forced, controlled, and threatened with punishment to accomplish organizational goals.
   - **What is Theory Y?**

   Theory Y assumes that people like working and will accept responsibility for achieving goals if rewarded for doing so.
   - **What is Theory Z?**

   Theory Z comes out of Japanese management and stresses long-term employment; collective decision making; individual responsibility; slow evaluation and promotion; implicit, informal control with explicit, formalized control; moderately specialized career paths; and a holistic concern for employees (including family).

**6.** Differentiate among Theory X, Theory Y, and Theory Z.

7. Goal-setting theory is based on the notion that setting ambitious but attainable goals will lead to high levels of motivation and performance if the goals are accepted, accompanied by feedback, and facilitated by organizational conditions.

**7.** Explain goal-setting theory and how management by objectives (MBO) exemplifies the theory.

- **What is management by objectives (MBO)?**

MBO is a system of goal setting and implementation that involves a cycle of discussion, review, and evaluation of objectives among top and middle-level managers, supervisors, and employees.

**8.** Describe the key principles of expectancy, reinforcement, and equity theories.

8. According to Victor Vroom's expectancy theory, employee expectations can affect an individual's motivation.

- **What are the key elements involved in expectancy theory?**

Expectancy theory centers on three questions employees often ask about performance on the job: (1) Can I accomplish the task? (2) If I do accomplish it, what's my reward? and (3) Is the reward worth the effort?

- **What are the variables in reinforcement theory?**

Positive reinforcers are rewards like praise, recognition, or raises that a worker might strive to receive after performing well. Negative reinforcers are punishments such as reprimands, pay cuts, or firing that a worker might be expected to try to avoid.

- **According to equity theory, employees try to maintain equity between inputs and outputs compared to other employees in similar positions. What happens when employees perceive that their rewards are not equitable?**

If employees perceive that they are underrewarded, they will either reduce their effort or rationalize that it isn't important. If they perceive that they are overrewarded, they will either increase their effort to justify the higher reward in the future or rationalize by saying, "I'm worth it!" Inequity leads to lower productivity, reduced quality, increased absenteeism, and voluntary resignation.

**9.** Explain how open communication builds teamwork, and describe how managers are likely to motivate teams in the future.

9. Companies with highly motivated workforces often have open communication systems and self-managed teams.

- **Why is open communication so important in building effective self-managed teams?**

Open communication helps both top managers and team members understand the objectives and work together to achieve them. Teams establish an environment in which learning can happen because most learning happens at the peer level.

- **How are Generation X managers likely to be different from their baby boomer predecessors?**

Baby boomers are willing to work long hours to build their careers and often expect their subordinates to do likewise. Gen Xers strive for a more balanced lifestyle and are likely to focus on results rather than on how many hours their teams work. Gen Xers are better than previous generations at working in teams and providing frequent feedback. They are not bound by traditions that may constrain those who have been with an organization for a long time and are willing to try new approaches to solving problems.

## key terms

**equity theory** 275
**expectancy theory** 274
**extrinsic reward** 260
**goal-setting theory** 273
**Hawthorne effect** 263
**hygiene factors** 265
**intrinsic reward** 260
**job enlargement** 269
**job enrichment** 267
**job rotation** 269
**management by objectives (MBO)** 273
**Maslow's hierarchy of needs** 263
**motivators** 265
**principle of motion economy** 262
**reinforcement theory** 274
**scientific management** 261
**time-motion studies** 261

## critical thinking questions

Your job right now is to finish reading this chapter. How strongly would you be motivated to do that if you were sweating in a 105-degree Fahrenheit room? Imagine now that your roommate has turned on the air-conditioning. Once you are more comfortable, are you more likely to read? Look at Maslow's hierarchy of needs to see what need would be motivating you at both times. Can you see how helpful Maslow's theory is in understanding motivation by applying it to your own life?

## developing workplace skills

1. Talk with several of your friends about the subject of motivation. What motivates them to work hard or not work hard in school and on the job? How important is self-motivation to them?

2. Look over Maslow's hierarchy of needs and try to determine where you are right now on the hierarchy. What needs of yours are not being met? How could a company go about meeting those needs and thus motivate you to work better and harder?

3. One recent managerial idea is to let employees work in self-managed teams. There is no reason why such teams could not be formed in colleges as well as businesses. Discuss the benefits and drawbacks of dividing your class into self-managed teams for the purpose of studying, doing cases, and so forth.

4. Think of all the groups with which you have been associated over the years—sports groups, friendship groups, and so on—and try to recall how the leaders of those groups motivated the group to action. Did the leaders assume a Theory X or a Theory Y attitude? How often was money used as a motivator? What other motivational tools were used and to what effect?

5. Herzberg concluded that pay was not a motivator. If you were paid to get better grades, would you be motivated to study harder? In your employment experiences, have you ever worked harder to obtain a raise or as a result of receiving a large raise? Do you agree with Herzberg?

## taking it to the net * 1

**Purpose**

To assess your personality type using the Keirsey Character Sorter and to evaluate how well the description of your personality type fits you.

**Exercise**

Sometimes understanding differences in employees' personalities helps managers understand how to motivate them. Find out about your personality by going to the Keirsey Temperament Sorter Web site (www.keirsey.com) and answer the 36-item Keirsey Character Sorter questionnaire or the 70-item Keirsey Temperament Sorter questionnaire. Each test identifies four temperament types:

Guardian, Artisan, Idealist, and Rational. (Disclaimer: The Keirsey tests, like all other personality tests, are only preliminary and rough indicators of personality.)

1. After you identify your personality, read the corresponding personality portrait. How well or how poorly does the identified personality type fit?
2. Sometimes a personality test does not accurately identify your personality, but it may give you a place to start looking for a portrait that fits. After you have read the portraits on the Keirsey Web site, ask a good friend or relative which one best describes you.

## taking it to the net * 2

**Purpose**

To analyze why employees of the Container Store agree with *Fortune* magazine that their employer is an excellent company to work for.

**Exercise**

Employees at the Container Store sell boxes and garbage cans for a living. Find out why *Fortune* magazine has rated the Container Store at or near the top of its "100 Best Companies to Work For" list for many years. Go to the company's Web site (www.containerstore.com) and click on About Us.

1. What are the Container Store's foundation principles?
2. Give an example of how the Container Store employees are empowered to please their customers.
3. The national average annual turnover rate for salespeople is 73.6 percent. The Container Store's annual turnover rate is a mere 28 percent. Many of its employees took pay cuts to join the company. Identify at least five ways the company motivates its employees and explain why it has one of the most motivated workforces in America.

## casing the web

To access the case *"Making Teams Work in a Changing Market,"* visit **www.mhhe.com/ub8e**

## video case

### Motivation Is a Hot Topic

We all have witnessed retail employees who seem indifferent at best to customer satisfaction. They are as likely to be talking to one another as to customers—sometimes on the phone. It doesn't take a retailing expert to know that such employees do not contribute to the success of the firm. So, how do you get retail employees to be passionate about their work? To find that answer, we went to a company that has won the Best Small Companies and Best Small Companies to Work for lists often. That company is Hot Topic.

Hot Topic stores sell clothing and accessories that appeal to the alternative culture. Emphasis is on the latest music trends and the fashions that go with them. Employees, therefore, need to be familiar with the newest bands and the latest music. That means going to concerts and observing what the people wear and becoming very familiar with the cultural trends within those groups.

Torrid is another store run by the same company. It caters to an entirely different audience: more mature women who are looking for fashionable plus sizes. Hot Topic Incorporated runs both stores. The CEO of the company is Betsy McLaughlin. She has learned how to motivate the employees at both stores using well established managerial techniques that are outlined in this chapter.

There is much emphasis in this text on employee empowerment. At Hot Topic, that means that employees are paid to attend music concerts where they not only have a good time, but learn more about the culture of the people they will be serving. Since promotions come from within, that culture carries over into headquarters. There are not the usual offices that designate hierarchy. Instead, all employees are encouraged to make decisions on their own, within reason, and to be responsive to customer needs. As you read in this chapter, Herzberg says that employees have certain needs which are not motivating, but result in dissatisfaction (and possible poor performance) if not present. They include salary and other benefits. Thus the salary and benefits at both stores have to be competitive.

Employees feel good about their work when they are empowered to do what it takes to please customers. Empowerment often demands some in-house training to teach employees the skills they need to be responsive to customer demands. All of this falls under the concepts of Theory Y that says that people are willing to work hard if given the freedom and opportunity to do so. Such freedom is what Hot Topic Incorporated is all about.

One way to see these principles in action is to visit a Hot Topic or Torrid store for yourself and watch the employees in action. What is the atmosphere like? The store may not reflect your values or your culture, but does it seem to reflect the values and culture of the people being served? Are the clothes at Torrid attractive for plus-sized women? Is every effort being made to help women find what they want?

### Thinking It Over

1. What motivators identified by Herzberg are used at Hot Topic?
2. How do you think Hot Topic employees would react if the company gave them each a small raise, but stopped paying them to attend music concerts? Would they be more or less motivated to please customers? Why?
3. How well would a Theory X manager perform at Hot Topic? Why?

# human resource management

## Finding and Keeping the Best Employees

profile

**Getting to Know**

X Wegmans Food Markets

An employee of Wegmans Food Markets once described the company as "a $3 billion dollar company run by 16-year-old cashiers." Obviously, this is an exaggeration. The worker was referring to Wegmans' employee-centered organizational culture that contributed to it being listed in *Fortune*'s "100 Best Companies to Work For" eight years in a row. And in 2005, Wegmans made it all the way to the top of the list as the number one company to work for in the United States.

Wegmans is a grocery chain that was founded by two brothers, John and Walter Wegman, in Rochester, New York, in 1930. The showcase store was 20,000 square feet—large for the time—and featured a cafeteria with seating for 300. Through the years, Wegmans steadily expanded to its present 69 supermarkets in New York, Pennsylvania, New Jersey, Maryland, and Virginia. It plans to have 72 stores soon. The newer stores are 130,000 square feet—three times larger than typical supermarkets—and offer fancy organic and gourmet foods as well as the usual brands, all at competitive prices. Their vast selection, various on-site services, and massive prepared-foods departments make them desirable to customers. In 2004, the company received over 3,000 letters from consumers pleading with Wegmans to come to their towns.

One of the things that the customers like about Wegmans is the friendly, helpful, knowledgeable employees in the stores. The company works hard to achieve those qualities in its workers. First, the wages and

**LEARNING** goals

**After you have read and studied this chapter, you should be able to**

1. Explain the importance of human resource management, and describe current issues in managing human resources.
2. Summarize the five steps in human resource planning.
3. Describe methods that companies use to recruit new employees, and explain some of the issues that make recruitment challenging.
4. Outline the six steps in selecting employees.
5. Illustrate the use of various types of employee training and development methods.
6. Trace the six steps in appraising employee performance.
7. Summarize the objectives of employee compensation programs, and describe various pay systems and fringe benefits.
8. Explain scheduling plans managers use to adjust to workers' needs.
9. Describe the ways employees can move through a company: promotion, reassignment, termination, and retirement.
10. Illustrate the effects of legislation on human resource management.

CHAPTER

**www.wegmans.com**

salaries it pays are at the high end of the industry scale. In 1953, John Wegman's son, Robert, as the new president, added new employee benefits such as profit sharing and fully funded medical coverage. (With the increasing costs of health insurance, Wegmans had to ask employees to contribute to those costs in 2005.) Another benefit is a college scholarship program that since 1984 has given $54 million in scholarships to more than 17,500 full- and part-time employees. It is not unusual for employees to be sent on tours to learn about cheesemaking in Europe or on a trek through the Napa Valley in California to visit wineries.

Perhaps the most attractive thing about working at Wegmans is its employee empowerment. This is where the 16-year-old cashiers come in. Employees are encouraged to do whatever they think is necessary to make a customer happy. They do not have to check with a supervisor or clear it with the boss first. Sometimes that has meant going to a customer's home to straighten out a food order or cooking the Thanksgiving turkey at the store when it proves too big for a buyer's oven. When some larger ideas do need approval, there is no stifling hierarchy. When a bakery employee in the Pittsford, New York, store thought it would be a good idea to sell "chocolate meatball cookies" made from her ancestors' family recipe, she talked directly to then-president Danny Wegman. A part-time meat department employee commented, "They let me do whatever comes into my head, which is kind of scary sometimes." Now CEO, Danny Wegman says, "We have tried to create an environment where our people's ideas are listened to and where they can feel empowered to make decisions that impact their work."

Of course, Wegmans benefits by keeping its employees happy. Its labor costs may be high (estimated to be 16 percent of sales, compared with 12 percent for most supermarkets), but its annual full-time employee turnover rate is just 6 percent, a fraction of the 19 percent rate for comparable grocery chains. This is important because the cost of a supermarket chain's employee turnover can exceed its profits by 40 percent, according to the Coca-Cola Retailing Research Council. You can understand then what Danny Wegman's, father, Robert, meant when he said, "No matter how much we invest in our people, we get much more in return."

Sources: Matthew Boyle, "The Wegman Way," *Fortune*, January 10, 2005; Michael Garry, "Danny Wegman: CEO Wegman Food Market," *Supermarket News*, July 2005; Jeffrey Woldt, "The Employees Always Come First at Wegmans," *Mass Market Retailers*, January 24, 2005; and www.wegmans.com 2006.

# WORKING WITH PEOPLE IS JUST THE BEGINNING

**human resource management**
The process of determining human resource needs and then recruiting, selecting, developing, motivating, evaluating, compensating, and scheduling employees to achieve organizational goals.

Students have been known to say they want to go into human resource management because they want to "work with people." It is true that human resource managers work with people, but they are also deeply involved in planning, record keeping, and other administrative duties. To begin a career in human resource management, you need to develop a better reason than "I want to work with people." This chapter will discuss various aspects of human resource management. **Human resource management** is the process of determining human resource needs and then recruiting, selecting, developing, motivating, evaluating, compensating, and scheduling employees to achieve organizational goals (see Figure 11.1). Let's explore some of the trends in human resource management.

## Developing the Ultimate Resource

One reason human resource management is receiving increased attention now is that the U.S. economy has experienced a major shift from traditional manufacturing industries to service and high-tech manufacturing industries that require highly technical job skills. This shift means that many workers must be retrained for new, more challenging jobs.

Some people have called employees the "ultimate resource," and when you think about it, nothing could be truer. People develop the ideas that eventually become the products that satisfy consumers' wants and needs. Take away their

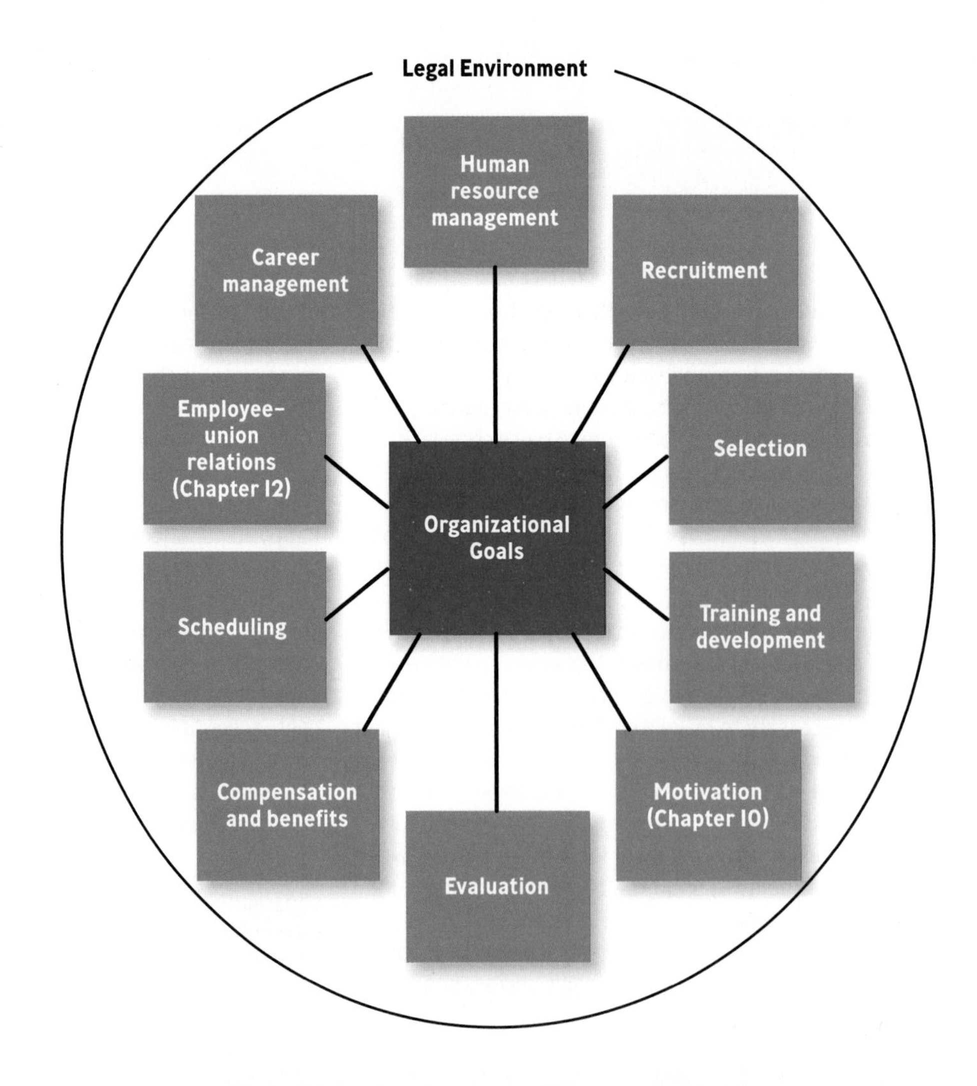


figure 11.1
**HUMAN RESOURCE MANAGEMENT**
As this figure shows, human resource management is more than hiring and firing personnel. All activities are designed to achieve organizational goals within the laws that affect human resource management. (Note that human resource management includes motivation, as discussed in Chapter 10, and employee–union relations, as discussed in Chapter 12.)

creative minds, and leading firms such as Google, General Electric, Hewlett-Packard, and Microsoft would be nothing. The problem is that in the past human resources were relatively plentiful, so there was little need to nurture and develop them. If you needed qualified people, you simply went out and hired them. If they didn't work out, you fired them and found others. But *qualified* employees are scarcer today, and that makes recruiting more difficult.

Historically, most firms assigned the job of recruiting, selecting, training, evaluating, compensating, motivating, and, yes, firing people to the various functional departments. For years, the personnel department was more or less responsible for clerical functions such as screening applications, keeping records, processing the payroll, and finding people when necessary.

Today the job of human resource management has taken on an entirely new role in the firm.[1] In the future it may become *the* most critical function, in that it will be responsible for dealing with all aspects of a business's most critical resource—people. In fact, the human resource function has become so important that it is no longer the function of just one department; it is a function of all managers. Most human resource functions are shared between the professional human resource manager and the other managers. What are some of the challenges in the human resource area that managers face? We'll outline a few of those challenges next.

## The Human Resource Challenge

The changes in the American business system that have had the most dramatic impact on the workings of the free enterprise system are the changes in the labor force. The ability of the U.S. business system to compete in global markets depends on new ideas, new products, and new levels of productivity—in other words, on people with good ideas. The following are some of the challenges and opportunities being encountered in the human resource area:

- Shortages in people trained to work in the growth areas of the future, such as computers, biotechnology, robotics, and the sciences.[2]
- A huge population of skilled and unskilled workers from declining industries, such as steel, automobiles, and garment making, who are unemployed or underemployed and who need retraining. Underemployed workers are those who have more skills or knowledge than their current jobs require.[3]
- A growing percentage of new workers who are undereducated and unprepared for jobs in the contemporary business environment.[4]
- A shift in the age composition of the workforce, including aging baby boomers, many of whom are deferring retirement.[5] The Dealing with Change box on page 290 discusses the new human resource challenges faced by an aging workforce.
- A complex set of laws and regulations involving hiring, safety, unionization, and equal pay that require organizations to go beyond a profit orientation and be more fair and socially conscious.[6]
- An increasing number of both single-parent and two-income families, resulting in a demand for day care, job sharing, maternity leave, and special career advancement programs for women.[7]
- A shift in employee attitudes toward work. Leisure time has become a much higher priority, as have concepts such as flextime and a shorter workweek.[8]
- Continued downsizing that is taking a toll on employee morale as well as increasing the demand for temporary workers.[9]

DEALING WITH change

### Replacing the Old Guard

Wine connoisseurs believe that most great wines get better with age. Unfortunately, the decision makers of most industrialized countries don't see it that way when evaluating people. By 2050, the average age of the world's population is expected to rise from 26 to 36. Millions of American baby boomers will reach retirement age in the next 5 to 10 years. This aging of the population presents huge economic implications. Who will do the work in geriatric societies? Who will support the increasing number of pensioners? What will happen to economic growth with a declining labor force?

For the past two decades the United States has been importing workers to increase the labor force. These workers supply important technical and scientific talent, start new companies, and help hold down prices by filling low-wage jobs. Even with this influx of foreign workers, the United States could experience labor shortages by 2010.

As critical as the impending labor shortage is, most companies are more concerned about the brain drain caused by experienced knowledgeable workers taking their irreplaceable knowledge with them as they retire. For instance, Raytheon Vision Systems, a national defense contractor in Goleta, California, realized that more than 35 percent of its workforce would be eligible to retire by 2009. "In many situations, the person [set to retire] was the only one in the whole nation who knew how to do something. They invented it," says Marilyn Weixel, a senior human resource manager. Raytheon needed a powerful solution. Weixel created a training program called Leave-A-Legacy, which pairs employees who have vital knowledge with high-potential younger employees. Not only has the mentoring program successfully encouraged near-retirees to share knowledge on a daily basis, but it has also given them a sense of purpose. As one retiring employee said, "This program is the first time I believed I was really valued—after nearly 20 years [at Raytheon]." At the same time, the program locks in the commitment of high-potential employees by giving them higher-level work.

Mentoring is not the only way companies are working to transfer knowledge. Hewlett-Packard (HP) uses online communities of different professional groups, such as sales and software engineering. "They're online knowledge repositories for people who do the same kind of work. They post how they do things, solutions and experience," explains James R. Malanson, an HP human resource executive. The federal government uses similar online learning portals as a way to transfer knowledge in preparation for a mass departure, as half of its employees will be eligible to retire in the next five years.

Many industries and businesses are trying to keep potential retirees as long as possible by offering consultant positions, flexible work schedules, job sharing, and gradual retirement. The challenge is to keep mature workers on the job—at least until they've shared their knowledge with their younger colleagues.

Sources: Marguerite Smith, "Aging Workers: Overlooked No More?" *Public Management*, January 1, 2005; Anne Fisher, "How to Battle the Coming Brain Drain," *Fortune*, March 21, 2005; Kathryn Tyler, "Training Revs Up," *HRMagazine*, April 1, 2005; and Susannah Patton, "Beating the Boomer Brain Drain Blues," *CIO*, January 15, 2006.



- A challenge from overseas labor pools whose members are available for lower wages and subject to many fewer laws and regulations. This results in many jobs being outsourced overseas.[10]
- An increased demand for benefits tailored to the individual.[11]
- A growing concern over such issues as health care, elder care, child care (discussed in Chapter 12), equal opportunities for people with disabilities, and special attention given to affirmative action programs.[12]
- A decreased sense of employee loyalty, resulting in increased employee turnover and increased costs of replacing lost workers.[13]

Given all of these issues, and others that are sure to develop, you can see why human resource management has taken a more central position in management thinking than ever before.

## DETERMINING YOUR HUMAN RESOURCE NEEDS

All management, including human resource management, begins with planning. Five steps are involved in the human resource planning process:

1. *Preparing a human resource inventory of the organization's employees.* This inventory should include ages, names, education, capabilities,

training, specialized skills, and other information pertinent to the specific organization (e.g., languages spoken). Such information reveals whether or not the labor force is technically up-to-date, thoroughly trained, and so forth.

2. *Preparing a job analysis.* A **job analysis** is a study of what is done by employees who hold various job titles. Such analyses are necessary in order to recruit and train employees with the necessary skills to do the job. The results of job analysis are two written statements: job descriptions and job specifications. A **job description** specifies the objectives of the job, the type of work to be done, the responsibilities and duties, the working conditions, and the relationship of the job to other functions. **Job specifications** are a written summary of the minimum qualifications (education, skills, etc.) required of workers to do a particular job. In short, job descriptions are statements about the job, whereas job specifications are statements about the person who does the job. See Figure 11.2 for hypothetical examples of a job description and job specifications.
3. *Assessing future human resource demand.* Because technology changes rapidly, training programs must be started long before the need is apparent. Human resource managers who are proactive—that is, who anticipate the organization's requirements identified in the forecast process—make sure that trained people are available when needed.
4. *Assessing future supply.* The labor force is constantly shifting: getting older, becoming more technically oriented, attracting more women, and so forth. There are likely to be increased shortages of some workers in the future (e.g., computer and robotic repair workers) and oversupplies of others (e.g., assembly line workers).

**job analysis**
A study of what is done by employees who hold various job titles.

**job description**
A summary of the objectives of a job, the type of work to be done, the responsibilities and duties, the working conditions, and the relationship of the job to other functions.

**job specifications**
A written summary of the minimum qualifications required of workers to do a particular job.

**JOB ANALYSIS**

Observe current sales representatives doing the job.
Discuss job with sales managers.
Have current sales reps keep a diary of their activities.

| JOB DESCRIPTION | JOB SPECIFICATIONS |
| --- | --- |
| Primary objective is to sell company's products to stores in Territory Z. Duties include servicing accounts and maintaining positive relationships with clients. Responsibilities include<br>• Introducing the new products to store managers in the area.<br>• Helping the store managers estimate the volume to order.<br>• Negotiating prime shelf space.<br>• Explaining sales promotion activities to store managers.<br>• Stocking and maintaining shelves in stores that wish such service. | Characteristics of the person qualifying for this job include<br>• Two years' sales experience.<br>• Positive attitude.<br>• Well-groomed appearance.<br>• Good communication skills.<br>• High school diploma and two years of college credit. |

figure 11.2
**JOB ANALYSIS**
A job analysis yields two important statements: job descriptions and job specifications. Here you have a job description and job specifications for a sales representative.

5. *Establishing a strategic plan.* The plan must address recruiting, selecting, training and developing, appraising, compensating, and scheduling the labor force. Because the previous four steps lead up to this one, this chapter will focus on these elements of the strategic human resource plan.

Some companies use advanced technology in order to perform this human resource planning process more efficiently. For example, IBM manages its global workforce of about 100,000 as well as its 100,000 subcontractors by using software and a database that catalogs employee skills, experiences, schedules, and references. IBM uses the system to match employee skills with the jobs needed. For example, if a client in Nova Scotia has a month-long project that needs a consultant who can speak English and French, has an advanced degree in engineering, and has experience with Linux programming, the IBM system can search the database to find the best-suited consultant available and arrange for the employee to contact the client.[14]

**recruitment**
The set of activities used to obtain a sufficient number of the right people at the right time.

## RECRUITING EMPLOYEES FROM A DIVERSE POPULATION

**Recruitment** is the set of activities used to obtain a sufficient number of the right people at the right time; its purpose is to select those who best meet the needs of the organization. One would think that, with a continuous flow of new people into the workforce, recruiting would be easy. On the contrary, recruiting has become very difficult, for several reasons:

- Some organizations have policies that demand promotions from within, operate under union regulations, or offer low wages, which

figure II.3

**EMPLOYEE SOURCES**

Internal sources are often given first consideration. So it's useful to get a recommendation from a current employee of the firm for which you want to work. College placement offices are also an important source. Be sure to learn about such facilities early so that you can plan a strategy throughout your college career.

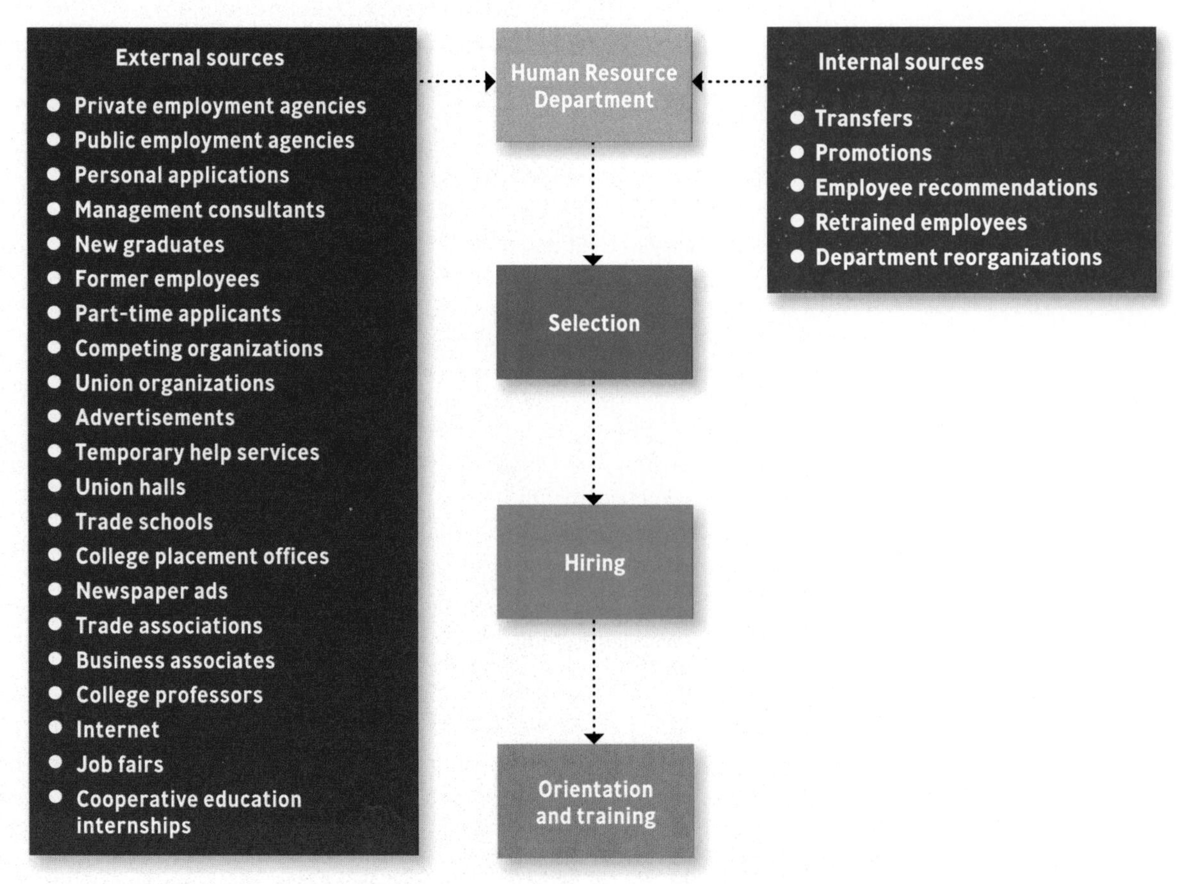

SPOTLIGHT ON small business www.careerbuilder.com

## Attracting Qualified Employees

It is difficult for small-business owners to find qualified employees. Small businesses want top talent but often can't afford corporate-level benefits or expensive recruiters to hunt down the best people. Despite the hurdles, small-business management consultants say there are many ways to lure desirable workers:

- *Transform ads into promotional tools*. For example, Ecoprint, a small print shop in Maryland, brags in its advertisements about the benefits of working for this collegial company.
- *Post job openings on the Internet*. Running a 20-line ad on an online service like CareerBuilder or Monster.com costs about $400 for 30 days. A comparable ad in the *New York Times* can cost $2,210 for only one week.
- *Let your staff help select hires*. The more staff people involved in the interview process, the better chance you have to find out who has the personality and skills to fit in.
- *Create a dynamic workplace to attract local, energetic applicants*. Sometimes word of mouth is the most effective recruiting tool.
- *Test-drive an employee*. Hiring temporary workers can allow you to test candidates for a few months before deciding whether to make an offer or not.
- *Hire your customer*. Loyal customers sometimes make the smartest employees.
- *Check community groups and local government agencies*. Don't forget to check out state-run employment agencies. The welfare-to-work programs may turn up excellent candidates you can train.
- *Lure candidates with a policy of promotions and raises*. Most employees want to know that they can move up in the company. Give employees an incentive for learning the business.
- *Outsource fringe benefit management to a professional employer organization (PEO)*. PEOs may be able to offer lower insurance rates for benefit programs because of greater economies of scale. While this may not bring a small business's benefits program all the way up to the level of those offered by most large companies, it may help close the gap and therefore help attract qualified workers.

Sources: J. Holly Dolloff, "Companies Compete for Shrinking Work Force Pool," *Nashville Business Journal*, July 22, 2005; Heather Gooch, "Aspire to Hire: Little Things Go a Long Way in Attracting and Retaining Loyal Employees," *Pest Control*, January 1, 2005; Anne Field, "Hire Right," *Registered Rep*, February 1, 2006; and Debra Morrill, "How to Tackle the Looming Labor Shortage," *Wisconsin State Journal*, February 1, 2006.

makes recruiting and keeping employees difficult or subject to outside influence and restrictions.

- The emphasis on corporate culture, teamwork, and participative management makes it important to hire people who not only are skilled but also fit in with the culture and leadership style of the organization.[15]
- Sometimes people with the necessary skills are not available; in this case, workers must be hired and then trained internally.[16]

Because recruiting is a difficult chore that involves finding, hiring, and training people who are an appropriate technical and social fit, human resource managers turn to many sources for assistance (see Figure 11.3). These sources are classified as either internal or external. Internal sources include employees who are already within the firm (and may be transferred or promoted) and employees who can recommend others to hire. Using internal sources is less expensive than recruiting outside the company. The greatest advantage of hiring from within is that it helps maintain employee morale. It isn't always possible to find qualified workers within the company, however, so human resource managers must use external recruitment sources such as advertisements, public and private employment agencies, college placement bureaus, management consultants, professional organizations, referrals, and walk-in applications.

Recruiting qualified workers may be particularly difficult for small businesses that don't have enough staff members to serve as internal sources and may not be able to offer the sort of competitive compensation that attracts external sources. The Spotlight on Small Business box outlines some ways that small businesses can address their recruiting needs. Newer tools for recruiting employees include Internet services such as CareerBuilder.com and Monster.com (see the first Taking It to the Net exercise at the end of this chapter).

**selection**
The process of gathering information and deciding who should be hired, under legal guidelines, for the best interests of the individual and the organization.

## SELECTING EMPLOYEES WHO WILL BE PRODUCTIVE

**Selection** is the process of gathering information and deciding who should be hired, under legal guidelines, for the best interests of the individual and the organization. Selecting and training employees have become extremely expensive processes in some firms. Think of what's involved: interview time, medical exams, training costs, unproductive time spent learning the job, moving expenses, and so on. It's easy to see how selection expenses can amount to over $130,000 for a top-level manager. It can even cost one and a half times the employee's annual salary to recruit, process, and train an entry-level worker.[17] Thus, the selection process is an important element of any human resource program. A typical selection process would involve six steps:

1. *Obtaining complete application forms.* Once this was a simple procedure with few complications. Today, however, legal guidelines limit the kinds of questions that may appear on an application form. Nonetheless, such forms help the employer discover the applicant's educational background, past work experience, career objectives, and other qualifications directly related to the requirements of the job. Large employers like Target, Blockbuster, and sporting goods chain G.I. Joe's make the application process more effective and efficient by using an artificial intelligence program called Smart Assessment, developed by application-service provider Unicru. An applicant sits down at a computer and spends a half hour answering questions about job experience, time available to work, and personality. Ten minutes later, a report is e-mailed to a hiring manager. The reports tell the manager whether to interview the applicant or not. If an interview is recommended, the report even suggests questions the manager can ask to find the best-fitting position for the applicant. G.I. Joe's says the smart-hiring program reduced turnover among hourly employees by more than half. It also cut almost two weeks off the time it takes to replace employees, from 30 days to 17. Ed Ariniello, G.I. Joe's vice president of operations, says, "Our managers hire better because of the tools they have." Because the employees are better suited for their new jobs, workers are more productive. The company's average sale per transaction rose by 3.5 percent a year for the past three years, and customer satisfaction jumped to 90 percent from the mid-80 percent range.[18]
2. *Conducting initial and follow-up interviews.* A staff member from the human resource department often screens applicants in a first interview. If the interviewer considers the applicant a potential employee, the manager who will supervise the new employee interviews the applicant as well. It's important that managers prepare adequately for the interview to avoid selection decisions they may regret.[19] Certain mistakes, such as asking an interviewee about his or her family, no matter how innocent the intention, could later be used as evidence if that applicant files discrimination charges.[20]
3. *Giving employment tests.* Organizations use tests to measure basic competencies in specific job skills (e.g., welding, word processing) and to help evaluate applicants' personalities and interests.[21] In using employment tests, it's important that they be directly related to the job. Employment tests have been severely criticized as potential sources of illegal discrimination. For example, several Bell South employees sued the company for

discrimination because they were not promoted when they failed math/logic tests. The employees said the tests did not assess the interpersonal skills needed for the job.[22] Many companies test potential employees in assessment centers where applicants perform actual tasks of the real job. Such testing is likely to make the selection process more efficient and will generally satisfy legal requirements.

4. *Conducting background investigations.* Most organizations now investigate a candidate's work record, school record, credit history, and references more carefully than they have in the past.[23] It is simply too costly to hire, train, and motivate people only to lose them and have to start the process over. Background checks help an employer identify which candidates are most likely to succeed in a given position. Web sites such as PeopleWise allow prospective employers not only to conduct speedy background checks of criminal records, driving records, and credit histories but also to verify work experience and professional and educational credentials.
5. *Obtaining results from physical exams.* There are obvious benefits to hiring physically and mentally healthy people. However, medical tests cannot be given just to screen out individuals. (See the discussion of the Americans with Disabilities Act on page 313.) In some states, physical exams can be given only after an offer of employment has been accepted. In states that allow preemployment physical exams, the exams must be given to everyone applying for the same position. There has been some controversy about preemployment testing to detect drug or alcohol abuse, as well as screening to detect carriers of the virus that causes AIDS. Over 70 percent of U.S. companies now test both current and potential employees for drug use.[24]
6. *Establishing trial (probationary) periods.* Often an organization will hire an employee conditionally. This enables the person to prove his or her worth on the job. After a specified probationary period (perhaps six months or a year), the firm may either permanently hire or discharge that employee on the basis of evaluations from supervisors. Although such systems make it easier to fire inefficient or problem employees, they do not eliminate the high cost of turnover.[25]

Choosing qualified employees is a difficult task. Psychologist Turhan Canli believes he can tell what makes some people better suited to a job than others by using human physiology mechanisms. Canli uses brain scans to see how people react to certain word-image combinations and believes you can read personalities from them. What do you think are key criteria to check in evaluating job candidates?

The selection process is often long and difficult, but it is worth the effort to select new employees carefully because of the high costs of replacing workers. The process helps ensure that new employees meet the requirements in all relevant areas, including communication skills, education, technical skills, experience, personality, and health.

## Hiring Contingent Workers

When more workers are needed in a company, human resource managers may want to consider finding creative staffing alternatives rather than simply hiring new full-time employees. A company with varying needs for employees—from hour to hour, day to day, week to week, and season to season—may find it cost-effective to hire contingent workers. **Contingent workers** are defined as workers who do not have the expectation of regular, full-time employment. Such workers include part-time workers (anyone who works 1 to 34 hours per

**contingent workers**
Workers who do not have the expectation of regular, full-time employment.

week), temporary workers (workers paid by temporary employment agencies), seasonal workers, independent contractors, interns, and co-op students.

A varying need for employees is the most common reason for hiring contingent workers. Companies may also look to hire contingent workers when full-time employees are on some type of leave (such as maternity leave), when there is a peak demand for labor, or when quick service to customers is a priority. Companies in areas where qualified contingent workers are available, and in which the jobs require minimum training, are most likely to consider alternative staffing options.

Contingent workers receive few benefits; they are rarely offered health insurance, vacation time, or private pensions. They also tend to earn less than permanent workers do. On the positive side, many of those on temporary assignments are eventually offered full-time positions. Managers see using temporary workers as a way of weeding out poor workers and finding good hires. Because temporary workers are often told that they may, at some point, be hired as permanent workers, they are often more productive than those on the permanent payroll. "We're seeing . . . temporary workers with the motivation to become full timers," said Joe Jotkowitz, senior consultant with Communication Development Associates, a human resources consulting firm in Woodland Hills, California. "They go out of their way because they're trying to impress."[26]

Although exact numbers are difficult to gather, experts say temps are increasingly being used to fill openings in a broad range of jobs, from unskilled manufacturing and distribution positions to middle managers. In fact, the San Fernando Valley Economic Research Center at Cal State Northridge estimates that about half of the business and professional workers added in the region in 2005 were temporary workers. An increasing number of contingent workers are educated professionals such as accountants, attorneys, and engineers.

Many people find that temporary work offers them a lot more flexibility than permanent employment. For example, student Daniel Butrym found that the transition from student to temp worker was not difficult. Butrym says, "You come back in town. You don't have to interview. You don't have to run across town and do a drug test. You don't have to waste a lot of time looking for a job. The first time you walk into [the temporary staffing] office, they meet you, sit you down and they find out your skills. Once you're in their computer, they have all your stats, they know what you can do and you're done. [Later] I can call from school, say 'I'm going to be home for spring break, I need some money.' " As soon as Butrym calls, he's put into the system for work assignments.

Butrym is not alone. Andy Williams of Randstad North America, the staffing services giant, welcomes college students. "A lot of the college students are computer literate, and they are familiar with many of the popular software programs that companies use. And, they are quick to get up to speed on [any] proprietary software an employer might use . . . Every customer is different. Some assignments come for one day. Some assignments are for weeks or for the whole summer," Williams says.[27]

In an era of downsizing and rapid change, some contingent workers have even found that temping can be more secure than full-time employment.

**progress assessment**

- What is human resource management?
- What are the five steps in human resource planning?
- What factors make it difficult to recruit qualified employees?
- What are the six steps in the selection process?
- What are contingent workers? Why do companies hire such workers?

## TRAINING AND DEVELOPING EMPLOYEES FOR OPTIMUM PERFORMANCE

Because employees need to learn how to work with equipment—such as computers and robots—companies are finding that they must offer training programs that often are quite sophisticated. Employers find that spending money on training is usually money well spent. A quality training program could lead to higher retention rates, increased productivity, and greater job satisfaction among employees.[28] It can also boost the company's stock performance. A recent study of 575 companies that invested approximately twice the industry norm in employee development outperformed the S&P 500 index by as much as 35 percent.[29]

**Training and development** include all attempts to improve productivity by increasing an employee's ability to perform. Training focuses on short-term skills, whereas development focuses on long-term abilities. But both training and development programs include three steps: (1) assessing the needs of the organization and the skills of the employees to determine training needs; (2) designing training activities to meet the identified needs; and (3) evaluating the effectiveness of the training. Some common training and development activities are employee orientation, on-the-job training, apprenticeships, off-the-job training, vestibule training, job simulation, and management training.

**training and development** All attempts to improve productivity by increasing an employee's ability to perform. Training focuses on short-term skills, whereas development focuses on long-term abilities.

**employee orientation** The activity that introduces new employees to the organization; to fellow employees; to their immediate supervisors; and to the policies, practices, and objectives of the firm.

**on-the-job training** Training in which the employee immediately begins his or her tasks and learns by doing, or watches others for a while and then imitates them, all right at the workplace.

- **Employee orientation** is the activity that initiates new employees to the organization; to fellow employees; to their immediate supervisors; and to the policies, practices, and objectives of the firm. Orientation programs include everything from informal talks to formal activities that last a day or more. They may involve such activities as scheduled visits to various departments and required reading of handbooks.[30] For example, at British Airways new employees participate in meetings that provide an education in the company's values and in its brand integrity. Part history lesson, part rules-of-the-road orientation, the training covers everything from principles of customer service to the choice of colors on the aircraft.
- **On-the-job training** is the most fundamental type of training. The employee being trained on the job immediately begins his or her tasks and learns by doing, or watches others for a while and then imitates them, right at the workplace. Salespeople, for example, are often trained by watching experienced salespeople perform (often called *shadowing*). Naturally, this can be either quite effective or disastrous, depending on the skills and habits of the person being watched. On-the-job training is obviously the easiest kind of training to implement when the job is relatively simple (such as clerking in a store) or repetitive (such as collecting refuse, cleaning carpets, or mowing lawns). More demanding or intricate jobs require a more intense training effort. Intranets and other new forms of technology are leading to cost-effective on-the-job training programs available 24 hours a day, all year long. Computer systems can monitor workers' input and give them instructions if they become confused about what

At FedEx time is money. That's why they spend six times more than the average company on employee training. Does the added cost pay off? You bet, FedEx enjoys a remarkably low 4 percent employee turnover rate. Should other companies follow the FedEx commitment to training? Why?

to do next. Such an intranet system helped Big Boy Restaurants realize training cost savings at an average of 2–4 percent per year.[31] The Web allows greater flexibility, but most companies believe its greatest advantage is the ability to make changes and updates in real time.[32]

**apprentice programs** Training programs involving a period during which a learner works alongside an experienced employee to master the skills and procedures of a craft.

**off-the-job training** Training that occurs away from the workplace and consists of internal or external programs to develop any of a variety of skills or to foster personal development.

**online training** Training programs in which employees "attend" classes via the Internet.

- **Apprentice programs** involve a period during which a learner works alongside an experienced employee to master the skills and procedures of a craft. Some apprenticeship programs also involve classroom training. Many skilled crafts, such as bricklaying and plumbing, require a new worker to serve as an apprentice for several years. Trade unions often require new workers to serve apprenticeships to ensure excellence among their members as well as to limit entry to the union. Workers who successfully complete an apprenticeship earn the classification of *journeyman.* In the future, there are likely to be more but shorter apprenticeship programs to prepare people for skilled jobs in changing industries. For example, auto repair will require more intense training as new automobile models include advanced computers and other electronic devices.[33]
- **Off-the-job training** occurs away from the workplace and consists of internal or external programs to develop any of a variety of skills or to foster personal development. Training is becoming more sophisticated as jobs become more sophisticated. Furthermore, training is expanding to include education (through the Ph.D.) and personal development—subjects may include time management, stress management, health and wellness, physical education, nutrition, and even art and languages.
- **Online training** offers an example of how technology is improving the efficiency of many off the-job training programs. In such training, employees "attend" classes via the Internet. Many colleges and universities now offer a wide variety of Internet courses. Such programs are sometimes called *distance learning* because the students are separated by distance from the instructor or content source. Pep Boys, an automotive retail chain, saved $2.6 million through reduced employee turnover after implementing an online training system. Workers use onsite computers to access a Web site that delivers more than 70 animated courses on topics like tires, spark plugs, automotive suspensions, the corporate dress code, management skills, sales skills, and customer service.[34] Online training gives employers the ability to provide consistent content that is tailored to specific employee training needs at convenient times to a large number of employees.
- **Vestibule training** (near-the-job training) is done in classrooms where employees are taught on equipment similar to that used on the job. Such classrooms enable employees to learn proper methods and safety procedures before assuming a specific job assignment in an organization. Computer and robotics training is often completed in a vestibule classroom.

It takes years of training on Earth before astronauts can safely travel in space. How do they learn how to work in space before they go there? One way is to participate in flight training in an aircraft that flies a series of parabola patterns over the Gulf of Mexico to simulate weightlessness in space. What other jobs would benefit from simulation training?

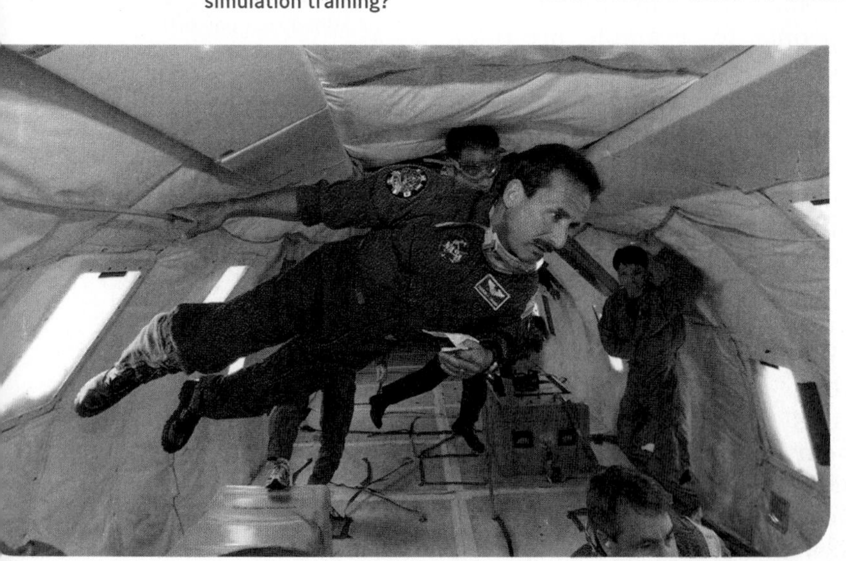

- **Job simulation** is the use of equipment that duplicates job conditions and tasks so that trainees can learn skills before attempting them on the job. Job simulation differs from vestibule training in that the simulation attempts to duplicate the *exact* combination of conditions that occur on the job. This is the kind of training given to astronauts, airline pilots, army tank operators, ship captains, and others who must learn difficult procedures off the job.

**vestibule training**
Training done in schools where employees are taught on equipment similar to that used on the job.

**job simulation**
The use of equipment that duplicates job conditions and tasks so that trainees can learn skills before attempting them on the job.

## Management Development

Managers need special training. To be good communicators, they especially need to learn listening skills and empathy. They also need time management, planning, and human relations skills.

**Management development**, then, is the process of training and educating employees to become good managers, and then monitoring the progress of their managerial skills over time. Management development programs have sprung up everywhere, especially at colleges, universities, and private management development firms. Managers participate in role-playing exercises, solve various management cases, and attend films and lectures.

**management development**
The process of training and educating employees to become good managers, and then monitoring the progress of their managerial skills over time.

Management development is increasingly being used as a tool to accomplish business objectives. For example, Ford Motor Company is teaching executives how to be more responsive to customers. General Electric's and Motorola's effective management teams were built with significant investment in management development.[35] Most management training programs include several of the following:

- *On-the-job coaching*. This means that a senior manager will assist a lower-level manager by teaching him or her needed skills and generally providing direction, advice, and helpful feedback.
- *Understudy positions*. Job titles such as *undersecretary* and *assistant* are part of a relatively successful way of developing managers. Selected employees work as assistants to higher-level managers and participate in planning and other managerial functions until they are ready to assume such positions themselves.
- *Job rotation*. So that they can learn about different functions of the organization, managers are often given assignments in a variety of departments. Through job rotation, top managers gain the broad picture of the organization necessary to their success.
- *Off-the-job courses and training*. Managers periodically go to schools or seminars for a week or more to hone their technical and human relations skills. Companies such as McDonald's Corporation have their own "colleges" for managers. At McDonald's Hamburger University, managers and potential franchise owners attend six days of classes, a course of study equivalent to 36 hours of college business-school credit.

**networking**
The process of establishing and maintaining contacts with key managers in one's own organization and other organizations and using those contacts to weave strong relationships that serve as informal development systems.

## Networking

**Networking** is the process of establishing and maintaining contacts with key managers in one's own organization and in other organizations, and using those contacts to weave strong relationships that serve as informal development systems. Of equal or greater importance to potential managers is a **mentor**, a corporate manager who supervises, coaches, and guides selected lower-level employees by introducing them to the right people and generally acts as their organizational sponsor. In reality, an informal type of mentoring goes on in most

**mentor**
An experienced employee who supervises, coaches, and guides lower-level employees by introducing them to the right people and generally being their organizational sponsor.

organizations on a regular basis as older employees assist younger workers. However, many organizations, such as Intel, use a formal system of assigning mentors to employees considered to have strong potential.[36]

It's also important to remember that networking and mentoring can go beyond the business environment.[37] For example, college is a perfect place to begin networking. Associations you nurture with professors, with local businesspeople through internships, and especially with your classmates might provide you with a valuable network you can turn to for the rest of your career.

## Diversity in Management Development

Angela Morris knew that diversity recruiting was the career she wanted to pursue; and how networking might help her advance that career. She asked a former colleague to pass her résumé to the human resource manager at her new company. Nothing happened immediately but Angela persisted and kept a dialogue going with the company. Her patience resulted in her being named the firm's diversity recruiter.

As women moved into management, they also learned the importance of networking and of having mentors. But since most older managers are male, women often have more difficulty than men do in finding mentors and entering the network. Women managers won a major victory when the U.S. Supreme Court ruled that it was illegal to bar women from certain clubs, long open to men only, where business activity flows and contacts are made. More and more, women are now entering established networking systems or, in some instances, creating their own.[38]

Similarly, African American managers are learning the value of networking. Working together, African Americans are forming pools of capital and new opportunities that are helping many individuals overcome traditional barriers to success.[39] *Black Enterprise* magazine sponsors several networking forums each year for African American professionals.

Other ethnic groups are networking as well. For example, Mark Shir, a financial and computer specialist from Taiwan, felt that he would never get ahead in the U.S. companies he had worked in for 10 years. When he joined Monte Jade, an association that helps Taiwanese and Chinese assimilate in American business, he met people who helped him start his own successful hardware-packaging company.[40]

Companies that take the initiative to develop female and minority managers understand three crucial principles: (1) Grooming women and minorities for management positions isn't about legality, morality, or even morale; it is about bringing more talent in the door—the key to long-term profitability; (2) the best women and minorities will become harder to attract and retain, so the companies that start now will have an edge later; and (3) having more women and minorities at all levels means that businesses can serve their increasingly female and minority customers better. If you don't have a diversity of people working in the back room, how are you going to satisfy the diversity of people coming in the front door?

**performance appraisal** An evaluation in which the performance level of employees is measured against established standards to make decisions about promotions, compensation, additional training, or firing.

# APPRAISING EMPLOYEE PERFORMANCE TO GET OPTIMUM RESULTS

Managers must be able to determine whether or not their workers are doing an effective and efficient job, with a minimum of errors and disruptions. They do so by using performance appraisals. A **performance appraisal** is an evaluation in which the performance level of employees is measured against established standards to make decisions about promotions, compensation, additional training, or firing. Performance appraisals consist of these six steps:

1. *Establishing performance standards.* This is a crucial step. Standards must be understandable, subject to measurement, and reasonable. They must be accepted by both the manager and subordinates.
2. *Communicating those standards.* Often managers assume that employees know what is expected of them, but such assumptions are dangerous at best. Employees must be told clearly and precisely what the standards and expectations are and how they are to be met.
3. *Evaluating performance.* If the first two steps are done correctly, performance evaluation is relatively easy. It is a matter of evaluating the employee's behavior to see if it matches standards.
4. *Discussing results with employees.* Most people will make mistakes and fail to meet expectations at first. It takes time to learn a new job and do it well. Discussing an employee's successes and areas that need improvement can provide managers with an opportunity to be understanding and helpful and to guide the employee to better performance. Additionally, the performance appraisal can be a good source of employee suggestions on how a particular task could be better performed.
5. *Taking corrective action.* As an appropriate part of the performance appraisal, a manager can take corrective action or provide corrective feedback to help the employee perform his or her job better. Remember, the key word is *performance.* The primary purpose of conducting this type of appraisal is to improve employee performance if possible.
6. *Using the results to make decisions.* Decisions about promotions, compensation, additional training, or firing are all based on performance evaluations. An effective performance appraisal system is also a way of satisfying certain legal conditions concerning such decisions.

Effective management means getting results through top performance by employees. That is what performance appraisals are for—at all levels of the organization. Even top-level managers benefit from performance reviews made by their subordinates.

One of the latest forms of performance appraisal, the 360-degree review, calls for feedback from all directions in the organization. Instead of basing an appraisal solely on the employee's and the supervisor's perceptions, management gathers opinions from those under, above, and on the same level as the worker. The goal is to get an accurate, comprehensive idea of the worker's abilities. Figure 11.4 illustrates how managers can make performance appraisals more meaningful.

figure 11.4

**CONDUCTING EFFECTIVE APPRAISALS AND REVIEWS**

1. **DON'T** attack the employee personally. Critically evaluate his or her work.
2. **DO** allow sufficient time, without distractions, for appraisal. (Take the phone off the hook or close the office door.)
3. **DON'T** make the employee feel uncomfortable or uneasy. *Never* conduct an appraisal where other employees are present (such as on the shop floor).
4. **DO** include the employee in the process as much as possible. (Let the employee prepare a self-improvement program.)
5. **DON'T** wait until the appraisal to address problems with the employee's work that have been developing for some time.
6. **DO** end the appraisal with positive suggestions for employee improvement.

progress assessment

- Can you name and describe four training techniques?
- What is the primary purpose of a performance appraisal?
- What are the six steps in a performance appraisal?

# COMPENSATING EMPLOYEES: ATTRACTING AND KEEPING THE BEST

Companies don't just compete for customers; they also compete for employees. Compensation is one of the main marketing tools companies use to attract qualified employees, and it is one of the largest operating costs for many organizations. The long-term success of a firm—perhaps even its survival—may depend on how well it can control employee costs and optimize employee efficiency. For example, service organizations such as hospitals, airlines, and banks have recently struggled with managing high employee costs. This is not unusual since these firms are considered labor intensive. That is, their primary cost of operations is the cost of labor. Manufacturing firms in the auto, airline, and steel industries have asked employees to take reductions in wages to make the firms more competitive. Many employees have agreed, even union employees who have traditionally resisted such cuts. They know that not to do so is to risk going out of business and losing their jobs forever. In other words, the competitive environment is such that compensation and benefit packages are being given special attention. In fact, some experts believe that determining how best to pay people has replaced downsizing as today's greatest human resources challenge.

A carefully managed compensation and benefit program can accomplish several objectives:

- Attracting the kinds of people needed by the organization, and in sufficient numbers.
- Providing employees with the incentive to work efficiently and productively.
- Keeping valued employees from leaving and going to competitors, or starting competing firms.
- Maintaining a competitive position in the marketplace by keeping costs low through high productivity from a satisfied workforce.
- Providing employees with some sense of financial security through insurance and retirement benefits.

## Pay Systems

How an organization chooses to pay its employees can have a dramatic effect on efficiency and productivity. Managers want to find a system that compensates employees fairly. Figure 11.5 outlines some of the most common pay systems.

Many companies still use the pay system devised by Edward Hay for General Foods. Known as the Hay system, this compensation plan is based on job tiers, each of which has a strict pay range. In some firms, employees are guaranteed a raise after 13 weeks if they're still breathing. Conflict can arise when an employee who is performing well earns less than an employee who is not performing well simply because the latter has worked for the company longer.

John Whitney, author of *The Trust Factor*, believes that companies should begin with some base pay and give all employees the same percentage merit raise.

figure II.5

PAY SYSTEMS

Some of the different pay systems are as follows:

- **Salary:** fixed compensation computed on weekly, biweekly, or monthly pay periods (e.g., $1,600 per month or $400 per week). Salaried employees do not receive additional pay for any extra hours worked.
- **Hourly wage or daywork:** wage based on number of hours or days worked, used for most blue-collar and clerical workers. Often employees must punch a time clock when they arrive at work and when they leave. Hourly wages vary greatly. The federal minimum wage is $5.15, and top wages go as high as $30 to $40 per hour for skilled craftspeople. This does not include benefits such as retirement systems, which may add 30 percent or more to the total package.
- **Piecework system:** wage based on the number of items produced rather than by the hour or day. This type of system creates powerful incentives to work efficiently and productively.
- **Commission plans:** pay based on some percentage of sales. Often used to compensate salespeople, commission plans resemble piecework systems.
- **Bonus plans:** extra pay for accomplishing or surpassing certain objectives. There are two types of bonuses: monetary and cashless. Money is always a welcome bonus. Cashless rewards include written thank-you notes, appreciation notes sent to the employee's family, movie tickets, flowers, time off, gift certificates, shopping sprees, and other types of recognition.
- **Profit-sharing plans:** annual bonuses paid to employees based on the company's profits. The amount paid to each employee is based on a predetermined percentage. Profit-sharing is one of the most common forms of performance-based pay.
- **Gain-sharing plans:** annual bonuses paid to employees based on achieving specific goals such as quality measures, customer satisfaction measures, and production targets.
- **Stock options:** right to purchase stock in the company at a specific price over a specific period of time. Often this gives employees the right to buy stock cheaply despite huge increases in the price of the stock. For example, if over the course of his employment a worker received options to buy 10,000 shares of the company stock at $10 each and the price of the stock eventually grows to $100, he can use those options to buy the 10,000 shares (now worth $1 million) for $100,000.

Doing so, he says, sends the message that everyone in the company is important. Fairness remains the issue. What do you think is the fairest pay system?

## Compensating Teams

Thus far we've talked about compensating individuals. What about teams? Since you want your teams to be more than simply a group of individuals, would you compensate them as you would individuals? If you can't answer that question immediately, you are not alone. While most managers believe in using teams, fewer are sure about how to pay them. This suggests that team-based pay programs are not as effective or as fully developed as managers would hope. Measuring and rewarding individual performance on teams, while at the same time rewarding team performance, can be tricky. Nonetheless, it can be done. Football players are rewarded as a team when they go to the playoffs and to the Super Bowl, but they are paid individually as well. Companies are now experimenting with and developing similar incentive systems.

Jay Schuster, coauthor of an ongoing study of team pay, found that when pay is based strictly on individual performance, it erodes team cohesiveness and makes it less likely that the team will meet its goals as a collaborative effort. Schuster recommends basing pay on team performance. In fact, a recent study indicates that over 50 percent of team compensation plans are based on team goals.[41] Skill-based pay and profit sharing are the two most common compensation methods for teams.

*Skill-based pay* is related to the growth of both the individual and the team. Base pay is raised when team members learn and apply new skills. For example, Baldrige Award winner Eastman Chemical Company rewards its teams for proficiency in technical, social, and business knowledge skills. A cross-functional compensation policy team defines the skills. The drawbacks of the skill-based pay system are twofold: the system is complex, and it is difficult to correlate skill acquisition and profit gains.

In most gain-sharing systems, bonuses are based on improvements over a previous performance baseline. For example, Behlen Manufacturing, a diversified maker of agricultural and industrial products, calculates its bonuses by dividing quality pounds of product by worker hours. *Quality* means no defects; any defects are subtracted from the total. Workers can receive a monthly gain-sharing bonus of up to $1 an hour when their teams meet productivity goals.

It is important to reward individual team players also. Outstanding team players—those who go beyond what is required and make an outstanding individual contribution to the firm—should be separately recognized for their additional contribution.[42] Recognition can include cashless as well as cash rewards. A good way to avoid alienating recipients who believe that team participation was uneven is to let the team decide which members get what type of individual award. After all, if you really support the team process, you need to give teams freedom to reward themselves.

**fringe benefits**
Benefits such as sick-leave pay, vacation pay, pension plans, and health plans that represent additional compensation to employees beyond base wages.

## Fringe Benefits

**Fringe benefits** include sick-leave pay, vacation pay, pension plans, and health plans that provide additional compensation to employees beyond base wages. Fringe benefits in recent years grew faster than wages. In fact, employee benefits can't really be considered "fringe" anymore. While such benefits accounted for less than 2 percent of payrolls in 1929, they account for approximately 30 percent of payrolls today.[43] Many employees request more fringe benefits, instead of more salary, to avoid higher taxes. This has resulted in much debate and much government investigation.

Beyond vacation pay and health plans, fringe benefits can include recreation facilities, company cars, country club memberships, discounted massages, special home-mortgage rates, paid and unpaid sabbaticals, day care services, and executive dining rooms.[44] Employees want packages to include dental care, mental health care, elder care, legal counseling, eye care, and short workweeks. As the cost of health care continues to spiral higher, however, many employers are now asking their employees to pay a larger share of their health insurance bill.[45]

Understanding that it takes many attractions to retain the best employees, dozens of companies on *Fortune* magazine's list of the "100 Best Companies to Work For" offer so-called soft benefits. *Soft benefits* help workers maintain the balance between work and family life that is as important to hardworking employees as the nature of the job itself. These perks include things such as on-site haircuts and shoe repair, concierge services, and free breakfasts.[46] Freeing employees from spending time on errands and chores gives them more time for family—and work.

**cafeteria-style fringe benefits**
Fringe benefits plan that allows employees to choose the benefits they want up to a certain dollar amount.

To counter employees' growing demands, over half of all large firms offer **cafeteria-style fringe benefits** plans, in which employees can choose the benefits they want, up to a certain dollar amount. Choice is the key to these flexible plans. At one time, most employees' needs were similar. Today, employee

## Less Rest Assured

***Is your downtime too far down?***

**TRAVEL—Americans rank lowest in the world for the average number of vacation days allotted by employers. But not too many of us are complaining. In fact, most Americans don't even use all of their vacation time. Here is how we rank, according to the World Trade Organization, when compared with other countries.**

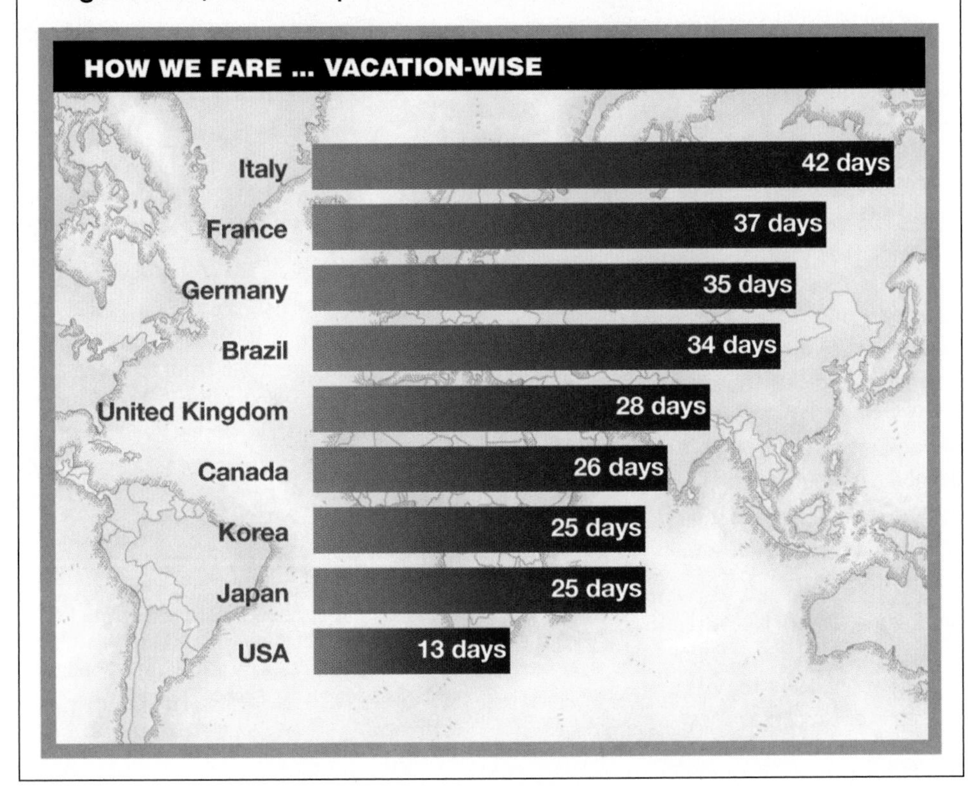


Does vacation time for trips to sunny beaches or ski trips to the mountains top your list of benefits you look for in a job? If so, you better check the want ads in Naples or Palermo, Italy. As this illustration shows, Italians take an average of 42 days of vacation per year compared to the average American worker who receives about 13 days. In fact, many American workers take no vacation at all. Why do you think Americans take so little time off their jobs?

demands are more varied. Some employees may need child care benefits, whereas others may need relatively large pension benefits. Rather than giving all employees identical benefits, managers can equitably and cost-effectively meet employees' individual needs by allowing employees some choice.[47]

Managing the benefits package will continue to be a major human resource issue in the future. The cost of administering benefits programs has become so great that a number of companies outsource this function—that is, they are hiring outside companies to run their employee benefits plans.[48] IBM, for example, decided to spin off its human resources and benefits operation into a separate company, Workforce Solutions, which provides customized services to each of IBM's independent units. The new company saves IBM $45 million each year. Workforce Solutions also handles benefits for other organizations such as the National Geographic Society.

Managing benefits can be especially complicated when employees are located in other countries. The Reaching Beyond Our Borders box on page 306 discusses the new human resource challenges faced by global businesses. To put it simply, benefits are as important to wage negotiations and recruitment now as salary. In the future, benefits may become even more important than salary.

REACHING BEYOND **our borders**

www.shrm.org

### Working Worldwide

Human resource people who manage a global workforce begin by understanding the customs, laws, and local business needs of every country in which the organization operates.

Varying cultural and legal standards can affect a variety of human resource functions:

- *Compensation.* Salaries must be converted to and from foreign currencies. Often employees with international assignments receive special allowances for relocation, children's education, housing, travel, or other business-related expenses.
- *Health and pension standards.* Human resource managers must consider the different social contexts for benefits in other countries. For example, in the Netherlands the government provides retirement income and health care.
- *Paid time off.* Cultural differences can be quite apparent when it comes to paid time off. Employees in other countries enjoy more vacation time than those in the United States. For example, four weeks of paid vacation is the standard of many European employers. But other countries do not have the short-term and long-term absence policies we have in the United States. They do not have sick leave, personal leave, or family and medical leave. Global companies need a standard definition of what time off is.
- *Taxation.* Different countries have varying taxation rules, and the payroll department is an important player in managing immigration information.
- *Communication.* When employees leave to work in another country they often feel disconnected from their home country. Wise companies use their intranet and the Internet to help these faraway employees keep in direct contact.

Human resource policies will be influenced more and more by conditions and practices in other countries and cultures. Human resource managers will need to move away from the assumed dominance and/or superiority of American business practices and sensitize themselves and their organizations to the cultural and business practices of other nations.

Sources: Anthony Kshanika, "Managing Globally: Managing a Diverse, Global Environment Is Critical Today—How You Do It Depends on Where You Are," *HRMagazine*, August 1, 2005; "How to Prepare Your Expatriate Employees for Cross-Cultural Work Environments," *Managing and Training Development*, February 1, 2005; and "Proposed Hong Kong Law Gives Business Shudders," Agence France Presse, English, January 19, 2006.

## SCHEDULING EMPLOYEES TO MEET ORGANIZATIONAL AND EMPLOYEE NEEDS

**flextime plan**
Work schedule that gives employees some freedom to choose when to work, as long as they work the required number of hours.

**core time**
In a flextime plan, the period when all employees are expected to be at their job stations.

By now, you are familiar with the trends occurring in the workforce that result in demands for more flexibility and responsiveness from companies. From these demands have emerged several new or renewed ideas such as flextime, in-home employment, and job sharing.

### Flextime Plans

A **flextime plan** gives employees some freedom to choose what hours to work, as long as they work the required number of hours. The most popular plans allow employees to come to work between 7:00 and 9:00 a.m. and leave between 4:00 and 6:00 p.m. Usually, flextime plans will incorporate what is called core time. **Core time** refers to the period when all employees are expected to

Flexible hours

Core time | Lunch period | Core time

6:30 7:00 7:30 8:00 8:30 9:00 9:30 10:00 10:30 11:00 11:30 12:00 12:30 1:00 1:30 2:00 2:30 3:00 3:30 4:00 4:30 5:00 5:30 6:00 6:30

Sarah's starting time

Sarah's lunch period

Sarah's quitting time

figure 11.6

**A FLEXTIME CHART**

At this company, employees can start work anytime between 6:30 and 9:30 a.m. They take a half hour for lunch anytime between 11:00 a.m. and 1:30 p.m. and can leave between 3:00 and 6:30 p.m. Everyone works an eight-hour day. The blue arrows show a typical employee's flextime day.

be at their job stations. For example, an organization may designate core time as between 9:30 and 11:00 a.m. and between 2:00 and 3:00 p.m. During these hours all employees are required to be at work (see Figure 11.6). Flextime plans, like job-sharing plans, are designed to allow employees to adjust to the demands of the times; two-income families find them especially helpful. Companies such as Sun Microsystems find that flextime boosts employee productivity and morale.[49]

There are some real disadvantages to flextime as well. Flextime is certainly not for all organizations. For example, it cannot be offered in assembly line processes where everyone must be at work at the same time. It also is not effective for shift work.

Another disadvantage to flextime is that managers often have to work longer days in order to assist and supervise employees. Some organizations operate from 6:00 a.m. to 6:00 p.m. under flextime—a long day for supervisors. Flextime also makes communication more difficult; certain employees may not be there when others need to talk to them. Furthermore, if not carefully supervised, some employees could abuse the system, and that could cause resentment among others. You can imagine how you'd feel if half the workforce left at 3:00 p.m. on Friday and you had to work until 6:00 p.m.

**compressed workweek**
Work schedule that allows an employee to work a full number of hours per week but in fewer days.

Another popular option used in approximately 24 percent of companies is a **compressed workweek**. That means that an employee works a full number of hours in less than the standard number of days. For example, an employee may work four 10-hour days and then enjoy a long weekend instead of working five 8-hour days with a traditional weekend. There are the obvious advantages of working only four days and having three days off, but some employees get tired working such long hours, and productivity could decline. Many employees find such a system of great benefit, however, and are quite enthusiastic about it.

Although many companies offer flexible schedules, few employees take advantage of them. Most workers report that they resist using the programs because they fear it will hurt their careers. Managers signal (directly or indirectly) that employees who change their hours are not serious about their careers.

## Home-Based and Other Mobile Work

As we noted in Chapter 1, telecommuting has grown tremendously in recent years. Nearly 10 million U.S. workers now work at least several days per month at home. Home-based workers can choose their own hours, interrupt

All of Jet Blue's reservation agents work from home through the company's virtual reservations center. What do you think would be the biggest problem working from home?

| | BENEFITS | CHALLENGES |
|---|---|---|
| **To organization** | • Increases productivity due to fewer sick days, fewer absences, higher job satisfaction, and higher work performance ratings<br>• Broadens available talent pool<br>• Reduces costs of providing on-site office space | • Makes it more difficult to appraise job performance<br>• Can negatively affect the social network of the workplace and can make it difficult to promote team cohesiveness<br>• Complicates distribution of tasks (Should office files, contact lists, and such be allowed to leave the office?) |
| **To individual** | • Makes more time available for work and family by reducing or eliminating commute time<br>• Reduces expenses of buying and maintaining office clothes<br>• Avoids office politics<br>• Helps balance work and family<br>• Expands employment opportunities for disabled individuals | • Can cause feeling of isolation from social network<br>• Can raise concerns regarding promotions and other rewards due to being "out of sight, out of mind"<br>• May diminish individual's influence within company due to limited opportunity to learn the corporate culture |
| **To society** | • Decreases traffic congestion<br>• Discourages community crime that might otherwise occur in bedroom communities<br>• Increases time available to build community ties | • Increases need to resolve zoning regulations forbidding business deliveries in residential neighborhoods<br>• May reduce ability to interact with other people in a personal, intimate manner |

figure 11.7

**BENEFITS AND CHALLENGES OF HOME-BASED WORK**

Home-based work (also known as telecommuting) offers many benefits and challenges to organizations, individuals, and to society as a whole.

work for child care and other tasks, and take time out for various personal reasons. Working at home isn't for everyone, however. To be successful, a home-based worker must have the discipline to stay focused on the work and not be easily distracted.

Telecommuting can be a cost saver for employers. For example, IBM used to have a surplus of office space, maintaining more offices than there were employees. Now the company has cut back on the number of offices, with employees telecommuting, "hoteling" (being assigned to a desk through a reservations system), and "hot-desking" (sharing a desk with other employees at different times). Many companies are hiring U.S. home-based call agents rather than using more expensive in-house operators or less-qualified offshore call centers. Office Depot says it saves 30 or 40 percent on the cost of each call because it's not providing work space or benefits for its home-based call-center workers. JetBlue's entire reservation system is handled by 900 home-based workers in Salt Lake City. The company claims it results in high worker retention and more satisfied customers, not to mention weather-proof operations.[50] Figure 11.7 outlines the benefits and challenges of home-based work to organizations, individuals, and society.

## Job-Sharing Plans

**job sharing**
An arrangement whereby two part-time employees share one full-time job.

**Job sharing** is an arrangement whereby two part-time employees share one full-time job. The concept has received great attention as more and more women with small children have entered the labor force. Job sharing enables parents to work only during the hours their children are in school. It has also proved beneficial to others with special needs, such as students and older people who want to work part-time before fully retiring. The benefits include

- Employment opportunities for those who cannot or prefer not to work full-time.
- A high level of enthusiasm and productivity.
- Reduced absenteeism and tardiness.
- Ability to schedule people into peak demand periods (e.g., banks on payday) when part-time people are available.
- Retention of experienced employees who might have left otherwise.

Disadvantages include having to hire, train, motivate, and supervise twice as many people and to prorate some fringe benefits. Nonetheless, most firms that were at first reluctant to try job sharing are finding that the benefits outweigh the disadvantages.

## MOVING EMPLOYEES UP, OVER, AND OUT

Employees don't always stay in the position they were initially hired to fill. They may excel and move up the corporate ladder or fail and move out the front door. In addition to being moved through promotion and termination, employees can be moved by reassignment and retirement. Of course, employees often choose to move themselves by quitting and going to another company.

### Promoting and Reassigning Employees

Many companies find that promotion from within the company improves employee morale. Promotions are also cost-effective in that the promoted employees are already familiar with the corporate culture and procedures, and do not need to spend valuable time on basic orientation.

Due to the prevalence of flatter corporate structures, there are fewer levels for employees to reach now than there were in the past. Therefore, it is more common today for workers to move *over* to a new position than to move *up* to one. Such transfers allow employees to develop and display new skills and to learn more about the company overall. This is one way of motivating experienced employees to remain in a company with few advancement opportunities.

### Terminating Employees

As we discussed in previous chapters, downsizing and restructuring, increasing customer demands for greater value, the relentless pressure of global competition, and shifts in technology have human resource managers struggling to manage layoffs and firings. Even companies that regain financial strength, however, are hesitant to rehire new full-time employees. Why? One reason is that the cost of terminating employees is prohibitively high. The cost of firing comes from lost training costs as well as damages and legal fees paid in wrongful discharge suits. To save money, many companies are either using temporary employees or outsourcing certain functions.

If you think sex discrimination and sexual harassment lawsuits are only an American phenomenon, think again. Stephanie Villalba, who managed the private client business for Merrill Lynch in London sued for sexual harassment, unequal pay, and unfair dismissal from the company. Even though she lost the multimillion pounds lawsuit against the company, the issues in the case promise not to go away soon.

figure 11.8

**HOW TO AVOID WRONGFUL-DISCHARGE LAWSUITS**

Sources: "In Economics Old and New, Treatment of Workers Is Paramount," *Washington Post*, February 11, 2001, p. L1, and www.uslaw.com.

Consultants offer this advice to minimize the chance of a lawsuit for wrongful discharge:

- Prepare before hiring by requiring recruits to sign a statement that retains management's freedom to terminate at will.
- Don't make unintentional promises by using such terms as *permanent employment*.
- Document reasons before firing and make sure you have an unquestionable business reason for the firing.
- Fire the worst first and be consistent in discipline.
- Buy out bad risk by offering severance pay in exchange for a signed release from any claims.
- Be sure to give employees the true reasons they are being fired. If you do not, you cannot reveal it to a recruiter asking for a reference without risking a defamation lawsuit.
- Disclose the reasons for an employee's dismissal to that person's potential new employers. For example, if you fired an employee for dangerous behavior and you withhold that information from your references, you can be sued if the employee commits a violent act at his or her next job.

At one time the prevailing employment doctrine in the United States was "employment at will." This meant that managers had as much freedom to fire workers as workers had to leave voluntarily. Most states now have written employment laws that limit the at-will doctrine to protect employees from wrongful firing. For example, an employer can no longer fire an employee simply because that person exposed the company's illegal actions, refused to violate a law, or was a member of a minority or other protected group. This well-intended legislation restricted management's ability to terminate employees as it increased workers' rights to their jobs. In some cases, workers fired for using illegal drugs have sued on the ground that they have an illness (addiction) and are therefore protected by laws barring discrimination against the handicapped. See Figure 11.8 for advice about how to minimize the chance of wrongful discharge lawsuits.

## Retiring Employees

In addition to layoffs, another tool used to downsize companies is to offer early retirement benefits to entice older (and more expensive) workers to retire. Such benefits usually involve financial incentives such as one-time cash payments, known in some companies as *golden handshakes*. The advantage of offering early retirement benefits over firing employees is that early retirement offers increase the morale of the surviving employees. Retiring senior workers earlier also increases promotion opportunities for younger employees.

## Losing Employees

In spite of a company's efforts to retain talented workers by offering flexible schedules, competitive salaries, and attractive fringe benefits, some employees will choose to pursue opportunities elsewhere. Learning about their reasons for leaving can be invaluable in preventing the loss of other good people in the future. One way to learn the real reasons employees leave is to have a third party (not the employee's direct manager) conduct an exit interview. Many companies contract with outside vendors to conduct exit interviews. Outsiders can provide confidentiality and anonymity features that can result in honest feedback that employees may feel uncomfortable giving in face-to-face interviews with their bosses. Today there are Web-based exit interview management systems that capture, track, and statistically analyze employee exit interview data and generate reports that identify retention trouble areas. Such programs can also coordinate exit interview data with employee satisfaction surveys to predict which departments should expect turnover to occur.[51]

**progress assessment**

- Can you name and describe five alternative compensation techniques?
- What advantages do compensation plans such as profit sharing offer an organization?
- What are the benefits and challenges of flextime? Telecommuting? Job sharing?

## LAWS AFFECTING HUMAN RESOURCE MANAGEMENT

Legislation has made hiring, promoting, firing, and managing employee relations in general very complex and subject to many legal complications and challenges. Let's see how changes in the law have expanded the role and the challenge of human resource management.

The U.S. government had little to do with human resource decisions until the 1930s. Since then, though, legislation and legal decisions have greatly affected all areas of human resource management, from hiring to training and working conditions (see the Legal Briefcase box). These laws were passed because many businesses would not exercise fair labor practices voluntarily.

One of the more important pieces of social legislation passed by Congress was the Civil Rights Act of 1964. This act generated much debate and was actually amended 97 times before final passage. Title VII of that act brought the government directly into the operations of human resource management. Title VII prohibits discrimination in hiring, firing, compensation, apprenticeships, training, terms, conditions, or privileges of employment based on race, religion, creed, sex, or national origin. Age was later added to the conditions of the act. The Civil Rights Act of 1964 was expected to stamp out discrimination in the workplace. However, specific language in the act often made its enforcement quite difficult.[52] With this in mind, Congress took on the task of amending the law.

In 1972, the Equal Employment Opportunity Act (EEOA) was added as an amendment to Title VII. It strengthened the Equal Employment Opportunity Commission (EEOC), which was created by the Civil Rights Act of 1964. Congress gave rather broad powers to the EEOC. For example, it permitted the commission to issue guidelines for acceptable employer conduct in administering equal employment opportunity. The EEOC also set forth specific recordkeeping procedures as mandatory. In addition, Congress vested the commission with the power of enforcement to ensure that these mandates were carried out. The EEOC became a formidable regulatory force in the administration of human resource management.

Probably the most controversial program enforced by the EEOC concerns **affirmative action**; that is, activities designed to "right past wrongs" by increasing opportunities for minorities and women. Interpretation of the affirmative-action law eventually led employers to actively recruit and give preference to qualified women and minority group members. Interpretation of the law has

**affirmative action**
Employment activities designed to "right past wrongs" by increasing opportunities for minorities and women.

www.eeoc.gov/welcome.html

LEGAL briefcase

## Government Legislation

*National Labor Relations Act of 1935.* Established collective bargaining in labor–management relations and limited management interference in the right of employees to have a collective bargaining agent.

*Fair Labor Standards Act of 1938.* Established a minimum wage and overtime pay for employees working more than 40 hours a week. The act has been amended in subsequent decades with changes expanding the classes of workers covered, raising the minimum wage, redefining regular-time work, raising overtime payments, and equalizing pay scales for men and women.

*Manpower Development and Training Act of 1962.* Provided for the training and retraining of unemployed workers.

*Equal Pay Act of 1963.* Specified that men and women doing equal jobs must be paid the same wage.

*Civil Rights Act of 1964.* Outlawed discrimination in employment based on sex, race, color, religion, or national origin. Applies to employers with 15 or more employees.

*Age Discrimination in Employment Act of 1967.* Outlawed personnel practices that discriminate against people ages 40 and above. An amendment outlaws company policies that require employees to retire by a specific age.

*Occupational Safety and Health Act of 1970.* Regulated the degree to which employees can be exposed to hazardous substances and specified the safety equipment to be provided by the employer.

*Equal Employment Opportunity Act of 1972.* Strengthened the Equal Employment Opportunity Commission (EEOC) and authorized the EEOC to set guidelines for human resource management.

*Comprehensive Employment and Training Act of 1973.* Provided funds for training unemployed workers. (Was known as the *CETA program.*)

*Employee Retirement Income Security Act of 1974.* Regulated company retirement programs and provided a federal insurance program for bankrupt retirement plans. (Known as *ERISA.*)

*Immigration Reform and Control Act of 1986.* Required employers to verify the eligibility for employment of *all* their new hires (including U.S. citizens).

*Supreme Court ruling against set-aside programs (affirmative action), 1989.* Declared that setting aside 30 percent of contracting jobs for minority businesses was reverse discrimination and therefore unconstitutional.

*Older Workers Benefit Protection Act, 1990.* Protects older people from signing away their rights to things like pensions or to fight against illegal age discrimination.

*Civil Rights Act of 1991.* Applies to firms with over 15 employees. It extends the right to a jury trial and punitive damages to victims of intentional job discrimination.

*Americans with Disabilities Act of 1990 (1992 implementation).* Prohibits employers from discriminating against qualified individuals with disabilities in hiring, advancement, or compensation, and requires them to adapt the workplace if necessary.

*Family and Medical Leave Act of 1993.* Businesses with 50 or more employees must provide up to 12 weeks of unpaid leave per year upon birth or adoption of an employee's child or upon serious illness of a parent, spouse, or child.

**reverse discrimination**
Discrimination against whites or males in hiring or promoting.

often been controversial, and enforcement difficult. Questions have persisted about the legality of affirmative action and the effect the program could have in creating a sort of reverse discrimination in the workplace. **Reverse discrimination** has been defined as discrimination against whites or males. Charges of reverse discrimination have occurred when companies have been perceived as unfairly giving preference to women or minority group members in hiring and promoting. The term has generated much heated debate. A 2003 lawsuit challenged the University of Michigan's law school admissions policy that assigned a certain number of points to minorities when they applied to the university. The U.S. Supreme Court ruled that the points system was equivalent to a quota and was unconstitutional. However, it also ruled that considering race was acceptable to achieve an academically diverse environment.[53]

The Civil Rights Act of 1991 expanded the remedies available to victims of discrimination by amending Title VII of the Civil Rights Act of 1964. Now victims of discrimination have the right to a jury trial and punitive damages. Human resource managers continue to follow court cases closely to see how the law is enforced. This issue is likely to persist for years to come.

## Laws Protecting the Disabled and Older Employees

The courts have continued their activity in issues involving human resource management. As you read earlier in the chapter, the courts look carefully into any improprieties concerning possible discrimination in hiring, firing, training, and so forth specifically related to race or sex. The Vocational Rehabilitation Act of 1973 extended the same protection to people with disabilities. Today, businesses cannot discriminate against people on the basis of any physical or mental disability.

The Americans with Disabilities Act of 1990 (ADA) requires employers to give disabled applicants the same consideration for employment as people without disabilities. It also requires that businesses make "reasonable accommodations" for people with disabilities. This means doing such things as modifying equipment or widening doorways. Making reasonable accommodations is not always expensive. For example, a company can provide an inexpensive headset that allows someone with cerebral palsy to talk on the phone. The ADA also protects disabled individuals from discrimination in public accommodations, transportation, and telecommunications.

The Americans with Disabilities Act guarantees that all Americans have equal opportunity in employment. This legislation requires businesses to make "reasonable accommodations" for people with disabilities on the job. What do you think would be "reasonable accommodations" a business should be required to provide?

Equal opportunity for people with disabilities promises to be a continuing issue into the next decade. Most companies are not having trouble making structural changes to be accommodating; what they are finding difficult are the cultural changes. Employers used to think being fair meant treating everyone the same. Now a key concept is *accommodation*, which means treating people according to their specific needs. In 1997, the EEOC issued new ADA guidelines that tell employers how they are supposed to treat workers and applicants with mental disabilities. The accommodations include putting up barriers to isolate people readily distracted by noise, reassigning workers to new tasks, and making changes in supervisors' management styles.

Older employees are also guaranteed protection against discrimination in the workplace. Courts have ruled against firms in unlawful-discharge suits where age appeared to be the major factor in the dismissal. The Age Discrimination in Employment Act of 1967 (ADEA) protects individuals who are 40 years of age or older from employment discrimination based on age. The ADEA's protections apply to both employees and job applicants. Under the ADEA, it is unlawful to discriminate against a person because of age with respect to hiring, firing, promotion, layoff, compensation, benefits, job assignments, and training.[54] The ADEA applies to employers with 20 or more employees. Additionally, the ADEA outlawed mandatory retirement in most organizations. It does allow age limits for certain professions if evidence shows the ability to perform a particular job significantly diminishes with age, or imposes a danger to society. This includes professions such as airline pilot and bus driver because research shows ability to perform these occupations may decrease with age.

## Effects of Legislation

Clearly, legislation affects all areas of human resource management. Such legislation ranges from the Social Security Act of 1935, to the Occupational Safety and Health Act of 1970, to the Employment Retirement Income Security Act of 1974. Human resource managers must read *The Wall Street Journal*, *BusinessWeek*, and other current publications to keep up with all human resource legislation and rulings.

We have devoted so much space to civil rights and related legislation because such decisions have greatly affected human resource programs and will continue to do so. It's apparent that a career in human resource management offers a challenge to anyone willing to put forth the effort. In summary:

- Employers must know and act in accordance with the legal rights of their employees or risk costly court cases.
- Legislation affects all areas of human resource management, from hiring and training to compensating employees.
- Court cases have made it clear that it is sometimes legal to go beyond providing equal rights for minorities and women to provide special employment (affirmative action) and training to correct discrimination in the past.
- New court cases and legislation change human resource management almost daily; the only way to keep current is to read the business literature and become familiar with the issues.

### progress assessment

Can you explain what was covered by the following laws?

- The Civil Rights Act of 1964.
- The Civil Rights Act of 1991.
- The Equal Employment Opportunity Act of 1972.
- The Americans with Disabilities Act of 1990.

## summary

1. Explain the importance of human resource management, and describe current issues in managing human resources.

1. Human resource management is the process of evaluating human resource needs, finding people to fill those needs, and getting the best work from each employee by providing the right incentives and job environment, all with the goal of meeting organizational objectives.
   - **What are some of the current challenges and opportunities in the human resource area?**

   Many of the current challenges and opportunities revolve around the changing demographics of workers: more women, minorities, immigrants, and older workers. Other challenges concern a shortage of trained workers and an abundance of unskilled workers, skilled workers in declining industries requiring retraining, changing employee work attitudes, and complex laws and regulations.

2. Summarize the five steps in human resource planning.

2. Like all other types of management, human resource management begins with planning.
   - **What are the steps in human resource planning?**

   The five steps are (1) preparing a human resource inventory of the organization's employees; (2) preparing a job analysis; (3) assessing future demand; (4) assessing future supply; and (5) establishing a plan for recruiting, hiring, educating, appraising, compensating, and scheduling employees.

3. Recruitment is the set of activities used to obtain a sufficient number of the right people at the right time to select those who best meet the needs of the organization.
   - **What methods do human resource managers use to recruit new employees?**

   Recruiting sources are classified as either internal or external. Internal sources include hiring from within the firm (transfers, promotions, etc.) and employees who recommend others to hire. External recruitment sources include advertisements, public and private employment agencies, college placement bureaus, management consultants, professional organizations, referrals, walk-in applications, and the Internet.
   - **Why has recruitment become more difficult?**

   Legal restrictions complicate hiring and firing practices. Finding suitable employees can also be made more difficult if companies are considered unattractive workplaces.

**3.** Describe methods that companies use to recruit new employees, and explain some of the issues that make recruitment challenging.

4. Selection is the process of gathering and interpreting information to decide which applicants should be hired.
   - **What are the six steps in the selection process?**

   The steps are (1) obtaining complete application forms, (2) conducting initial and follow-up interviews, (3) giving employment tests, (4) conducting background investigations, (5) obtaining results from physical exams, and (6) establishing a trial period of employment.

**4.** Outline the six steps in selecting employees.

5. Employee training and development include all attempts to improve employee performance by increasing an employee's ability to perform through learning.
   - **What are some of the activities used for training?**

   After assessing the needs of the organization and the skills of the employees, training programs are designed that may include the following activities: employee orientation, on- and off-the-job training, apprentice programs, online training, vestibule training, and job simulation. The effectiveness of the training is evaluated at the conclusion of the activities.
   - **What methods are used to develop managerial skills?**

   Management development methods include on-the job-coaching, understudy positions, job rotation, and off-the-job courses and training.
   - **How does networking fit in this process?**

   Networking is the process of establishing contacts with key managers within and outside the organization to get additional development assistance.

**5.** Illustrate the use of various types of employee training and development methods.

6. A performance appraisal is an evaluation of the performance level of employees against established standards to make decisions about promotions, compensation, additional training, or firing.
   - **How is performance evaluated?**

   The steps are (1) establish performance standards; (2) communicate those standards; (3) evaluate performance; (4) discuss results; (5) take corrective action when needed; and (6) use the results for decisions about promotions, compensation, additional training, or firing.

**6.** Trace the six steps in appraising employee performance.

7. Employee compensation is one of the largest operating costs for many organizations.
   - **What kind of compensation systems are used?**

   They include salary systems, hourly wages, piecework, commission plans, bonus plans, profit-sharing plans, and stock options.

**7.** Summarize the objectives of employee compensation programs, and describe various pay systems and fringe benefits.

- **What types of compensation systems are appropriate for teams?**

The most common are gains-sharing and skill-based compensation programs. It is also important to reward outstanding individual performance within teams.

- **What are fringe benefits?**

Fringe benefits include such items as sick leave, vacation pay, pension plans, and health plans that provide additional compensation to employees beyond base wages. Many firms offer cafeteria-style fringe benefits plans, in which employees can choose the benefits they want, up to a certain dollar amount.

**8.** Explain scheduling plans managers use to adjust to workers' needs.

8. Workers' increasing need for flexibility has generated new innovations in scheduling.

- **What scheduling plans can be used to adjust to employees' need for flexibility?**

Such plans include job sharing, flextime, compressed workweeks, and working at home.

**9.** Describe the ways employees can move through a company: promotion, reassignment, termination, and retirement.

9. Employees often move from their original positions in a company.

- **How can employees move within a company?**

Employees can be moved up (promotion), over (reassignment), or out (termination or retirement) of a company. Employees can also choose to leave a company to pursue opportunities elsewhere.

**10.** Illustrate the effects of legislation on human resource management.

10. There are many laws that affect human resource planning.

- **What are those laws?**

See the Legal Briefcase box on page 312 and review the text section on laws. This is an important subject for future managers to study.

## key terms

**affirmative action** 311
**apprentice programs** 298
**cafeteria-style fringe benefits** 304
**compressed workweek** 307
**contingent workers** 295
**core time** 306
**employee orientation** 297
**flextime plan** 306
**fringe benefits** 304
**human resource management** 288
**job analysis** 291
**job description** 291
**job sharing** 308
**job simulation** 299
**job specifications** 291
**management development** 299
**mentor** 299
**networking** 299
**off-the-job training** 298
**online training** 298
**on-the-job training** 297
**performance appraisal** 300
**recruitment** 292
**reverse discrimination** 312
**selection** 294
**training and development** 297
**vestibule training** 298

## critical thinking questions

1. Given the complex situations you'd be addressing, does human resource management seem like a career area that interests you? What have been your experiences in dealing with people who work in human resource management?

2. What effects have dual-career families had on the human resource function?
3. What problems can arise when family members work together in the same firm?
4. If you were a human resource manager, how would you address the "brain drain" as knowledgeable workers retire?
5. Imagine that you must fire an employee. What effect might the employee's dismissal have on your other workers? Explain how you would tell the employee and your remaining subordinates.

## developing workplace skills

1. Look in the classified ads in your local newspaper or on the Internet and find at least two positions that you might like to have when you graduate. List the qualifications specified in each of the ads. Identify methods the companies might use to determine how well applicants meet each of those qualifications.
2. Read several current business periodicals to find information on the latest court rulings involving fringe benefits, affirmative action, and other human resource issues. Compose a summary of your findings. What seems to be the trend? What will this mean for tomorrow's college graduates?
3. Recall the various training programs you have experienced. Think of both on-the-job and off-the-job training sessions. What is your evaluation of such programs? Write a brief critique of each. How would you improve them? Share your ideas with the class.
4. Consider the following occupations: doctor, computer salesperson, computer software developer, teacher, and assembly worker. Identify the method of compensation you think is appropriate for determining the wages for each of these workers. Explain your answer.
5. Choose one of these positions: a human resource manager notifying employees of mandatory drug testing or an employee representative protesting such testing. Write a memorandum supporting your position.

## taking it to the net * 1

### Purpose

To use job-search Web sites to identify employment options and to compare the services offered by several recruiting-related sites.

### Exercise

There are many recruiting-related sites on the Internet. You can find links to such sites at Careers.org. Select three job-search Web sites. Use the search feature in each site to try to identify a position for which you might qualify after graduation. Find the Web site for the companies offering the jobs.

1. Do some job-search sites offer services that the others don't? Compare the strengths and weaknesses of each site from the perspective of both job seekers and employers. Include such criteria as variety of occupations in

the database, volume of jobs, number of employers, geographical locations, ease of use, supplemental job hunting advice, and unique features.

2. What types of information did the individual companies' Web sites offer to attract potential employees?

## taking it to the net * 2

### Purpose

The purpose of this exercise is twofold. From a manager's perspective, the purpose is to illustrate the types of questions managers typically ask during interviews. From an applicant's perspective, the purpose is to practice answering such questions in a safe environment.

### Exercise

Go to www.monstertrak.monster.com. After registering (it's free), click on "Resource," then answer the sample interview questions in the Virtual Interview section. This interactive section gives you the opportunity to test your answers so that when you do go on an actual interview you are less likely to fumble for an answer.

## casing the web

To access the case *"Dual-Career Planning,"* visit **www.mhhe.com/ub8e**

## video case

### Surf's Up at Patagonia!

Human resource management (HRM) can be one of the most exciting and fun parts of a firm depending upon management commitment to the workers' needs. No company reflects this commitment better than Patagonia. Patagonia's HRM doesn't have to worry about where it's going to get its next worker. Workers are lined up to get a job there. Why? Because this is a firm with passion—passion for making the best products possible, passion for making its employees happy, and passion about the environment.

Patagonia believes that a great business begins with great products. Who could argue with that? Great products meet the needs of customers. In this case, that means that they will be long-lasting and are backed by a full guarantee. But great products do more than satisfy consumers. They also have a minimal impact on the environment.

Workers at Patagonia are pleased that the company's commitment to the environment is not just a slogan. Ten percent of pretax profit goes to environmental groups of all kinds. Employees are encouraged to get to know these groups and to participate in selecting the groups that receive the company's donations. If an environmental group is not familiar with best business practices, such as writing a business plan, Patagonia will give them that training.

Given that thousands of people are willing to work for Patagonia, how does the HRM department choose which ones to hire? They are looking for people who are as passionate as they are. What kind of passion? Any kind: a passion for cooking, for cleaning, for life. When your employees have passion, they will stick with you. That's why the turnover rate at Patagonia is a low 4 percent a year. Some businesses have a turnover rate approaching 100 percent a year. Such businesses have to constantly train and retrain their employees. Patagonia can put all that effort into satisfying the needs of employees who want to stay.

What does the company do for its employees that make it stand out from other companies? For one thing, Patagonia knows that parents often feel uncomfortable leaving their children with child-care centers. Not at Patagonia. The company provides onsite day care—and they did so long before other companies even dreamed about offering such a benefit. Children thus become part of the company's atmosphere. There are children everywhere, and the parents feel comfortable having them near.

All employees have those days when the sun is shining and nature is calling. You simply can't get your work done because you are dreaming about fishing or golfing or mountain climbing or whatever. How would you like it if your manager said, "Go ahead, take off. Have fun!" How can a company do that? One way is to have a flexible work schedule. With such a schedule, workers can take off early or come in late when the "surf's up." That is, when recreation calls. The top managers of Patagonia have a passion for sports and sports equipment—the kind that Patagonia sells. Since they expect their employees to have the same kind of passion that means letting them go when they need to go. What is the result? That employee passion comes across to customers, and they buy more. It's a win, win deal for the company. Employees are happy with the freedom they have and the company is happy with the productivity that such freedom creates.

What other company offers surfing lessons for its employees? Perhaps there are few companies that let their employees leave when the surf's up, but there are many other companies that offer employees flexible work schedules and other incentives that allow them to balance their work and personal lives. These companies also have workers who are passionate about the company and their work. Who organizes all these activities for workers? HRM.

### Thinking It Over

1. Patagonia stresses the importance of hiring employees with passion—a passion for anything, not just sports. Why do they place such importance upon passion? Why would they think that someone with a passion for something unrelated to sports (i.e. cooking) might be an excellent employee for their company?
2. What effect do Patagonia's practices of providing child-care and donating to environmental groups have upon employee productivity and retention? Why?
3. Can you see possible abuses of a flextime program? What could a company do to prevent such abuses before they occur?

# dealing with EMPLOYEE-MANAGEMENT issues AND relationships

profile

**Getting to Know**

**X James P. Hoffa,**

**President, International Brotherhood of Teamsters**

The Teamsters Union is the most fabled labor union in the United States. Jimmy Hoffa, who was elected president of the Teamsters in 1957, was one of the best-known labor leaders of his time. It didn't take Hoffa long to earn the loyalty of his members by negotiating labor contracts that significantly improved the average Teamster's standard of living. Under Hoffa's leadership, the Teamsters achieved their first national trucking contract. Not all his efforts were good for the union—in 1967, Hoffa was sentenced to prison for jury tampering and fraud. After receiving a presidential pardon in 1971, he set out to regain the Teamsters' leadership. However, the end of the story is a mystery; Hoffa disappeared on June 30, 1975, and was never heard from again. The search for him continues.

Jimmy Hoffa's son, James P. Hoffa, ascended to the leadership of the Teamsters Union in 1998, 41 years after his father did. The younger Hoffa learned early in his life about hard work and competition. In high school in Detroit, Michigan, he was an honor student and an all-state football player. After receiving dozens of scholarship offers, he chose Michigan State University, where he played football until an injury during his sophomore year ended his football career. At the urging of his father, young Hoffa studied harder than ever. After earning a degree in economics from Michigan State, he was accepted at the University of Michigan's law school, where he earned his law degree.

After law school, James P. Hoffa worked as a labor lawyer in Detroit. He practiced law for 25 years and became a successful and respected attorney. But James P. Hoffa never forgot spending his growing-up years on picket lines and in union meetings. He often recalled his childhood days when he tagged along with his father and watched him mix with his fellow Teamsters and conduct union business. He also remembered spending days with striking workers and hearing his father encourage strikers not to give up because better wages mean better lives. James P. Hoffa, attorney-at-law, also never lost his allegiance to the Teamsters. In 1993, he left his law practice and went to work full-time as an executive assistant to the president of Teamsters Joint Council 43 in Detroit. In 1996, he ran for president of the Teamsters Union but was defeated by Ron Carey by 16,000 votes. When Carey was forced to resign his office due to a financial scandal, Hoffa was elected president in 1998. Upon taking office, Hoffa pledged to gain industry-leading contracts through collective bargaining. He also promised a corruption-free union.

LEARNING **goals**

**After you have read and studied this chapter, you should be able to**

1. Trace the history of organized labor in the United States.
2. Discuss the major legislation affecting labor unions.
3. Outline the objectives of labor unions.
4. Describe the tactics used by labor and management during conflicts, and discuss the role of unions in the future.
5. Explain some of today's controversial employee–management issues, such as executive compensation, pay equity, child care and elder care, drug testing, and violence in the workplace.

# CHAPTER 12

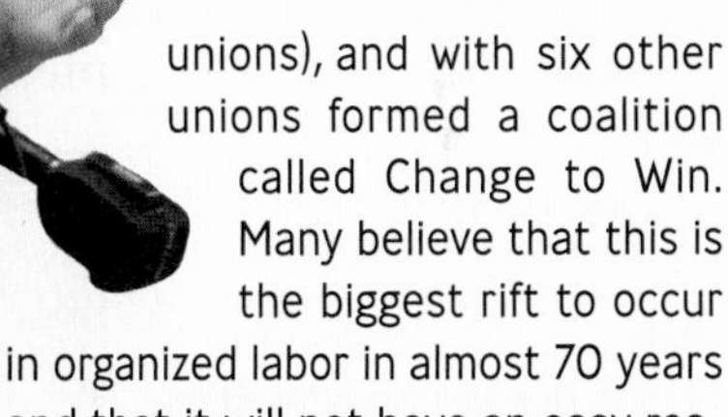

Today, James P. Hoffa, like other labor leaders, is facing a challenging future. Globalization, technology, automation, and the transition from an industrial-based economy to a service economy have created serious challenges for labor unions. Hoffa is an ardent opponent of free-trade agreements and offshore outsourcing, which he believes have cost Americans countless jobs. He also laments the decline in the number of workers who now belong to labor unions. In the 1980s, the Teamsters Union boasted that its membership was over 2 million; today, its membership is down to approximately 1.3 million. Research indicates that less than 8 percent of American workers in the private sector belong to labor unions, compared to 33 percent in 1955.

Hoffa has become the center of attention in the labor movement. In 2005, the Teamsters renounced their membership in the AFL-CIO (the nation's largest federation of unions), and with six other unions formed a coalition called Change to Win. Many believe that this is the biggest rift to occur in organized labor in almost 70 years and that it will not have an easy resolution. Some even believe that the survival of the labor movement may be at stake. The actions of labor leaders like James P. Hoffa and similar labor–management activities promise to dominate headlines and the business environment in the coming years. This chapter discusses such union issues and other employee–management controversies, including executive pay, pay equity, child care, elder care, drug testing, and violence in the workplace.

Sources: Ron Fournier, "Teamsters, Service Union Split from AFL-CIO," *USA Today*, July 25, 2005, p. 1; Aaron Bernstein, "Struggle for the Soul of the AFL-CIO," *BusinessWeek*, July 25, 2005; Todd G. Buchholz, "What Color Is Your Collar?," *The Wall Street Journal*, September 30, 2005, p. W11; and Lynne Duke, "Love, Labor, Loss," *Washington Post*, January 3, 2006.

## EMPLOYEE–MANAGEMENT ISSUES

The relationship between managers and employees has never been very smooth. Management has the responsibility of producing a profit through maximum productivity. Thus, managers have to make hard decisions that often do not let them win popularity contests. Labor (the collective term for nonmanagement workers) is interested in fair and competent management, human dignity, and a reasonable share in the wealth its work generates. Many issues affect the relationship between managers and labor: union activity, executive compensation, pay equity, child care and elder care, drug testing, and violence in the workplace.

**union**
An employee organization that has the main goal of representing members in employee–management bargaining over job-related issues.

Like other managerial challenges, employee–management issues must be worked out through open discussion, goodwill, and compromise. It is important to know both sides of an issue in order to make reasoned decisions. A good starting point in discussing employee–management relations in the United States is with a discussion of labor unions. A **union** is an employee organization that has the main goal of representing its members in employee–management negotiation concerning job-related issues. Workers originally formed unions to protect themselves from intolerable work conditions and unfair treatment. They also united to secure some say in the operations of their jobs. As the number of union members grew, workers gained more negotiating power with managers and more political power as well.

Labor unions were largely responsible for the establishment of minimum-wage laws, overtime rules, workers' compensation, severance pay, child-labor laws, job safety regulations, and more. Recently, however, union strength has waned.[1] Throughout the 1990s and into the 2000s, unions failed to regain the economic and political power they once had, and membership continued to decline. Business observers suggest that global competition, shifts from manufacturing to service and high-tech industries, growth in part-time work, and changes in management philosophies are some of the reasons for labor's decline. Others contend that the membership decline is related to labor's success in seeing the issues it championed become law.[2]

Some labor analysts forecast that unions will regain strength as companies become more involved with practices such as outsourcing; others insist

When the United States rolled into the Industrial Revolution in the late 19th century workers faced great demands in terms of productivity. Workers toiled 60 to 80 hours per week, wages were low, job conditions unsafe, and the use of child labor rampant. From this environment labor unions emerged. Today, as this union member illustrates, fair wages remains a goal of organized labor. What do you consider to be a "fair" wage? What should be the United States minimum wage?

that unions have seen their brightest days. Few doubt that the role and influence of unions—particularly in selected regions—will continue to arouse emotions and opinions that contrast considerably. Let's briefly look at labor unions and then analyze other key issues affecting employee–management relations.

## LABOR UNIONS FROM DIFFERENT PERSPECTIVES

Are labor unions essential in the American economy today? An electrician carrying a picket sign in New York City would say yes, and he or she might elaborate on the dangers to a free society if employers continue to try to bust, or break apart, authorized unions. A small manufacturer would likely embrace a different perspective and complain about having to operate under union wage and benefit obligations in an increasingly competitive global economy.

Historians generally agree that today's unions are an outgrowth of the economic transition caused by the Industrial Revolution of the 19th and early 20th centuries. Workers who once toiled in the fields, dependent on the mercies of nature for survival, suddenly became dependent on the continuous roll of the factory presses and assembly lines for their living.[3] Making the transition from an agricultural economy to an industrial economy was quite difficult. Over time, workers learned that strength through unity (unions) could lead to improved job conditions, better wages, and job security.

Today, critics of organized labor maintain that few of the inhuman conditions that once dominated U.S. industry still exist in the workplace. They charge that organized labor has in fact become a large industrial entity in itself and that the real issue of protecting workers has become secondary. They also maintain that the current legal system and changing management philosophies minimize the chances that the sweatshops (workplaces with unsatisfactory and often unsafe or oppressive labor conditions) of the late 19th and early 20th centuries will reappear in the United States.[4] A short discussion of the history of labor unions will help cast some light on the issues involved.

### The Early History of Organized Labor

The presence of formal labor organizations in the United States dates back close to the time of the American Revolution. As early as 1792, cordwainers (shoemakers) in Philadelphia met to discuss fundamental work issues of pay, hours, conditions, and job security—pretty much the same issues that dominate labor negotiations today. The cordwainers were a **craft union**, which is an organization of skilled specialists in a particular craft or trade. They were typical of the labor organizations formed before the Civil War in that they were local or regional in membership. Also, most were established to achieve some short-range goal such as curtailing the use of convict labor as an alternative to available free labor (an issue still present in some states). Often, after attaining a specific objective, the labor group disbanded. This situation changed dramatically in the late 19th century with the expansion of the Industrial Revolution, which changed the economic structure of the United States. Enormous productivity increases gained through mass production and job specialization made the United States a world economic power. This growth, however, brought problems for workers in terms of productivity expectations, hours of work, wages, and unemployment.

**craft union**
An organization of skilled specialists in a particular craft or trade.

Workers were faced with the reality that productivity was vital. Anyone who failed to produce lost his or her job. People had to go to work even if they were ill or had family problems. Over time, the increased emphasis on production led firms to expand the hours of work. The length of the average workweek in 1900 was 60 hours, but an 80-hour week was not uncommon for some industries. Wages were low, and the use of child labor was widespread. Minimum-wage laws and unemployment benefits were nonexistent, which meant that periods of unemployment were hard on families who earned subsistence wages. As you can sense, these were not short-term issues that would easily go away. The workplace was ripe for the emergence of national labor organizations.[5]

**Knights of Labor**
The first national labor union; formed in 1869.

The first truly national labor organization was the **Knights of Labor**, formed by Uriah Smith Stephens in 1869. By 1886, the Knights claimed a membership of 700,000. The organization offered membership to all working people, including employers, and promoted social causes as well as labor and economic issues.[6] The intention of the Knights was to gain significant *political* power and eventually restructure the entire U.S. economy. The organization fell from prominence after being blamed for a bomb that killed eight policemen during a labor rally at Haymarket Square in Chicago in 1886.[7]

**American Federation of Labor (AFL)**
An organization of craft unions that championed fundamental labor issues; founded in 1886.

A rival group, the **American Federation of Labor (AFL)**, was formed that same year. By 1890, the AFL, under the dynamic leadership of Samuel Gompers, stood at the forefront of the labor movement. The AFL was an organization of craft unions that championed fundamental labor issues. It intentionally limited membership to skilled workers (craftspeople), assuming they would have better bargaining power than unskilled workers in attaining concessions from employers. Note that the AFL was never one big union.[8] Rather, it functioned as a federation of many individual unions that could become members yet keep their separate union status. Over time, an unauthorized AFL group, called the Committee of Industrial Organizations, began to organize workers in **industrial unions**, which consisted of unskilled and semiskilled workers in mass-production industries such as automobile manufacturing and mining. John L. Lewis, president of the United Mine Workers, led this committee.

**industrial unions**
Labor organizations of unskilled and semiskilled workers in mass-production industries such as automobiles and mining.

Lewis's objective was to organize both craftspeople and unskilled workers.[9] When the AFL rejected his proposal in 1935, Lewis broke away to form the **Congress of Industrial Organizations (CIO)**.[10] The CIO soon rivaled the AFL in membership, partly because of the passage of the National Labor Relations Act (also called the Wagner Act) that same year (see the next section). For 20 years, the two organizations struggled for power in the labor movement. It wasn't until passage of the Taft-Hartley Act in 1947 (discussed on page 328) that the two organizations saw the benefits of a merger. In 1955, under the leadership of George Meany, 16 million labor members united to form the AFL-CIO. Recently, as you read in this chapter's Opening Profile, the AFL-CIO has begun to weaken. Seven unions, including the Service Employees International Union (SEIU), left the AFL-CIO in 2005 and formed a coalition called Change to Win. The SEIU was the AFL-CIO's largest union, with 1.8 million members.[11] Today, the AFL-CIO maintains affiliations with 53 national and international labor unions and has about 9 million members.[12]

**Congress of Industrial Organizations (CIO)**
Union organization of unskilled workers; broke away from the American Federation of Labor (AFL) in 1935 and rejoined it in 1955.

## LABOR LEGISLATION AND COLLECTIVE BARGAINING

The growth and influence of organized labor in the United States has depended primarily on two major factors: the law and public opinion. Figure 12.1 outlines five major federal laws that have had a significant impact on the rights and operations of labor unions. (Take a few moments to read the basics involved in each of these laws in Figure 12.1 before going on.)

| | |
|---|---|
| Norris-LaGuardia Act, 1932 | Prohibited courts from issuing injunctions against nonviolent union activities; outlawed contracts forbidding union activities; outlawed the use of yellow-dog contracts by employers. (Yellow-dog contracts were contractual agreements forced on workers by employers whereby the employee agreed not to join a union as a condition of employment.) |
| National Labor Relations Act (Wagner Act), 1935 | Gave employees the right to form or join labor organizations (or to refuse to form or join); the right to collectively bargain with employers through elected union representatives; and the right to engage in labor activities such as strikes, picketing, and boycotts. Prohibited certain unfair labor practices by the employer and the union, and established the National Labor Relations Board to oversee union election campaigns and investigate labor practices. This act gave great impetus to the union movement. |
| Fair Labor Standards Act, 1938 | Set a minimum wage and maximum basic hours for workers in interstate commerce industries. The first minimum wage set was 25 cents an hour, except for farm and retail workers. |
| Labor–Management Relations Act (Taft-Hartley Act), 1947 | Amended the Wagner Act; permitted states to pass laws prohibiting compulsory union membership (right-to-work laws); set up methods to deal with strikes that affect national health and safety; prohibited secondary boycotts, closed-shop agreements, and featherbedding (the requiring of wage payments for work not performed) by unions. This act gave more power to management. |
| Labor–Management Reporting and Disclosure Act (Landrum-Griffin Act), 1959 | Amended the Taft-Hartley Act and the Wagner Act; guaranteed individual rights of union members in dealing with their union, such as the right to nominate candidates for union office, vote in union elections, attend and participate in union meetings, vote on union business, and examine union records and accounts; required annual financial reports to be filed with the U.S. Department of Labor. One goal of this act was to clean up union corruption. |

figure 12.1

**MAJOR LEGISLATION AFFECTING LABOR–MANAGEMENT RELATIONS**

The Norris-LaGuardia Act paved the way for union growth in the United States. This legislation prohibited employers from using contracts that forbid union activities such as yellow dog contracts.[13] A **yellow-dog contract** required employees to agree, as a condition of employment, not to join a union. Later, the passage of the National Labor Relations Act (or Wagner Act) provided labor with clear legal justification to pursue other key issues that were strongly supported by Samuel Gompers and the AFL. One of these key issues, **collective bargaining**, is the process whereby union and management representatives negotiate a contract for workers. The Wagner Act expanded labor's right to collectively bargain, and obligated employers to meet at reasonable times and bargain in *good faith* with respect to wages, hours, and other terms and conditions of employment. Gompers believed that collective bargaining was critical to attaining a fairer share of the economic pie for workers and improving work conditions on the job.

**yellow-dog contract**
A type of contract that required employees to agree as a condition of employment not to join a union; prohibited by the Norris-LaGuardia Act in 1932.

**collective bargaining**
The process whereby union and management representatives form a labor–management agreement, or contract, for workers.

The Wagner Act also established an administrative agency, the National Labor Relations Board (NLRB), to oversee labor–management relations.[14] Consisting of five members who are appointed by the president of the United States, the NLRB provides workplace guidelines and offers legal protection to workers who seek to vote on organizing a union to represent them in the workplace. **Certification** is the formal process whereby a labor union is recognized by the NLRB as the authorized bargaining agent for a group of employees. Figure 12.2 on page 326 describes the steps involved in a union-organizing campaign leading to certification. After the election, both the union and management have five days to contest the results to the NLRB.[15] The Wagner Act also provided workers with a clear process to remove a union as its workplace representative.[16] **Decertification**, also described in Figure 12.2, is the process

**certification**
Formal process whereby a union is recognized by the National Labor Relations Board (NLRB) as the bargaining agent for a group of employees.

figure 12.2

**STEPS IN UNION-ORGANIZING AND DECERTIFICATION CAMPAIGNS**

Note that the final vote in each case requires that the union receive over 50 percent of the *votes cast.* Note, too, that the election is secret.

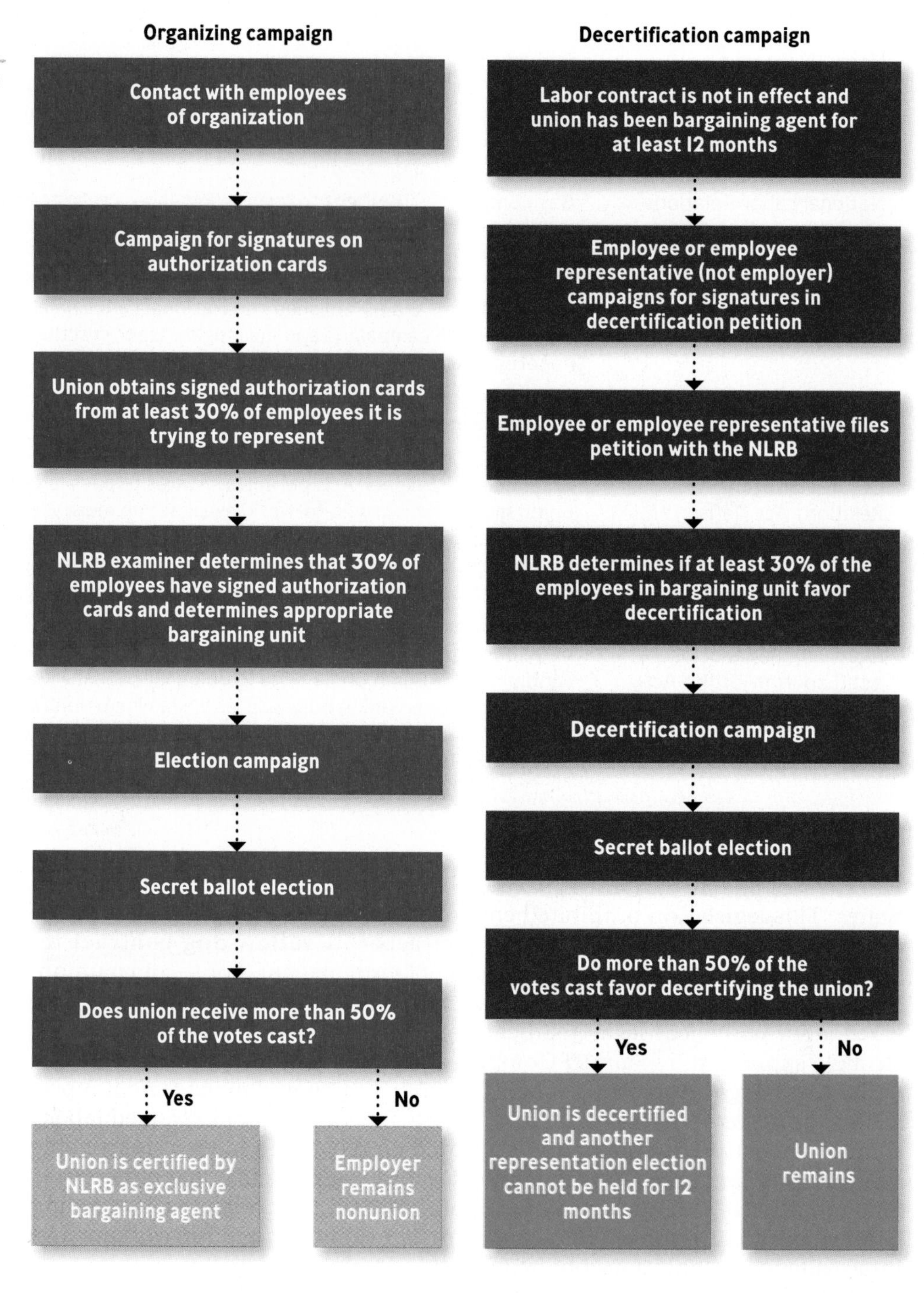


**decertification**
The process by which workers take away a union's right to represent them.

by which workers can take away a union's right to represent them. Read the Dealing with Change box to understand the difficult challenge labor has faced in trying to organize workers at Wal-Mart.

## Objectives of Organized Labor

The objectives of labor unions frequently change due to shifts in social and economic trends. For example, in the 1970s the primary objective of labor unions was additional pay and benefits for their members. Throughout the 1980s, objectives shifted toward issues related to job security and union recognition. In the 1990s and into the 2000s, unions again focused on job

DEALING WITH change

## The Unions versus Wal-Mart

All too often we hear about the potential of war breaking out somewhere in the world. Thankfully, to avoid conflict the opposing sides work hard to deter war and the possible devastation it can cause. No such luck when it comes to organized labor and Wal-Mart. According to Lee Scott, chief executive of Wal-Mart, union leadership has declared war on the company. Joe Hansen, president of the United Food and Commercial Workers Union (UCFW), does not deny it.

Wal-Mart is the nation's largest employer. Not a single one of its 1.3 million workers (or associates, as Wal-Mart calls them) is a union member. The company has always opposed unions in its stores in the United States and has yet to lose an organizing election. After losing a bitter organizing campaign in Las Vegas, the UCFW decided to change its tactics and abandon its strategy of trying to organize Wal-Mart workers store by store. Instead the union, with the help and support of fellow unions and activist groups, has formed the Center for Community and Corporate Ethics (CCCE). The purpose of the CCCE is to organize and build a nationwide grassroots campaign to battle Wal-Mart's efforts at expansion and force the company to offer health care benefits to all its employees. In response, Wal-Mart has increased its spending on national advertising to counter union criticisms. The ads attempt to convince Americans that Wal-Mart is "good for America."

This conflict promises to be long and hard-fought. Scott claims that the unions either want to unionize all Wal-Mart workers or make the company go away; he says neither of these will happen. Unions claim that Wal-Mart employees have to be organized because the economic power of Wal-Mart affects all workers' standard of living. Stewart Acuff, organizing director of the AFL-CIO, states, "Wal-Mart is a third-party negotiator at every bargaining table whether we like it or not." The battle lines are drawn, and it looks like there is little chance for peace.

Sources: Jonathan Birchall, "Battle Between Wal-Mart and the Unions Set to Hot Up," *Financial Times*, April 12, 2005, p. 20; Aaron Bernstein, "Declaring War on Wal-Mart," *BusinessWeek*, February 7, 2005, p. 31; and Amy Joyce and Matthew Mosk, "Unions Hope Wal-Mart Bill Has Momentum," *Washington Post*, January 14, 2006.

www.aflcio.com

security, but the issue of global competition and its effects often took center stage. The AFL-CIO, for example, was a major opponent of the North American Free Trade Agreement (NAFTA) and the Central American Free Trade Agreement (CAFTA), fearing union workers would lose jobs to low-wage workers in other nations.[17] Both agreements were passed by the Congress and signed by the president. Organized labor has also strongly opposed the increase in offshore outsourcing, claiming this practice would cause U.S. workers to lose additional jobs.

The **negotiated labor–management agreement**, more informally referred to as the labor contract, sets the tone and clarifies the terms and conditions under which management and the union will function over a specific period. Negotiations cover a wide range of work topics and can often take a long time before an agreement is reached. Figure 12.3 on page 328 provides a list of topics commonly negotiated by management and labor during contract talks.

Labor unions generally insist that a contract contain a union security clause. A **union security clause** stipulates that employees who reap benefits

**negotiated labor–management agreement (labor contract)**
Agreement that sets the tone and clarifies the terms under which management and labor agree to function over a period of time.

**union security clause**
Provision in a negotiated labor–management agreement that stipulates that employees who benefit from a union must either officially join or at least pay dues to the union.

figure 12.3

**ISSUES IN A NEGOTIATED LABOR–MANAGEMENT AGREEMENT**

Labor and management often meet to discuss and clarify the terms that specify employees' functions within the company. The topics listed in this figure are typically discussed during these meetings.

1. Management rights
2. Union recognition
3. Union security clause
4. Strikes and lockouts
5. Union activities and responsibilities
   a. Dues checkoff
   b. Union bulletin boards
   c. Work slowdowns
6. Wages
   a. Wage structure
   b. Shift differentials
   c. Wage incentives
   d. Bonuses
   e. Piecework conditions
   f. Tiered wage structures
7. Hours of work and time-off policies
   a. Regular hours of work
   b. Holidays
   c. Vacation policies
   d. Overtime regulations
   e. Leaves of absence
   f. Break periods
   g. Flextime
   h. Mealtime allotments
8. Job rights and seniority principles
   a. Seniority regulations
   b. Transfer policies and bumping
   c. Promotions
   d. Layoffs and recall procedures
   e. Job bidding and posting
9. Discharge and discipline
   a. Suspension
   b. Conditions for discharge
10. Grievance procedures
   a. Arbitration agreement
   b. Mediation procedures
11. Employee benefits, health, and welfare

**closed shop agreement**
Clause in a labor–management agreement that specified workers had to be members of a union before being hired (was outlawed by the Taft-Hartley Act in 1947).

**union shop agreement**
Clause in a labor–management agreement that says workers do not have to be members of a union to be hired, but must agree to join the union within a prescribed period.

from a union must either officially join or at least pay dues to the union. After passage of the Wagner Act, labor unions sought strict security in the form of the closed shop agreement. A **closed shop agreement** specified that workers had to be members of a union before being hired for a job. To labor's dismay, the Labor–Management Relations Act (Taft-Hartley Act) outlawed this practice in 1947 (see Figure 12.4). Today, labor unions favor the union shop agreement as the most effective means of ensuring workers' security. Under the **union shop agreement**, workers do not have to be members of a union to be hired for a job but must agree to join the union within a prescribed period (usually 30, 60, or 90 days). However, under a contingency called an **agency shop agreement**, employers may hire nonunion workers who are not required to join the union but must pay a special union fee or pay regular union dues. Labor unions believe that such fees or dues are justified because the union represents all workers in collective bargaining, not just the union's members.

The Taft-Hartley Act recognized the legality of the union shop but granted individual states the power to outlaw such agreements through passage of

figure 12.4

**DIFFERENT FORMS OF UNION AGREEMENTS**

| TYPE OF AGREEMENT | DESCRIPTION |
|---|---|
| Closed shop | The Taft-Hartley Act made this form of agreement illegal. Under this type of labor agreement, employers could hire only current union members for a job. |
| Union shop | The majority of labor agreements are of this type. In a union shop, the employer can hire anyone, but as a condition of employment, employees hired must join the union to keep their jobs. |
| Agency shop | Employers may hire anyone. Employees need not join the union, but are required to pay a union fee. A small percentage of labor agreements are of this type. |
| Open shop | Union membership is voluntary for new and existing employees. Those who don't join the union don't have to pay union dues. Few union contracts are of this type. |

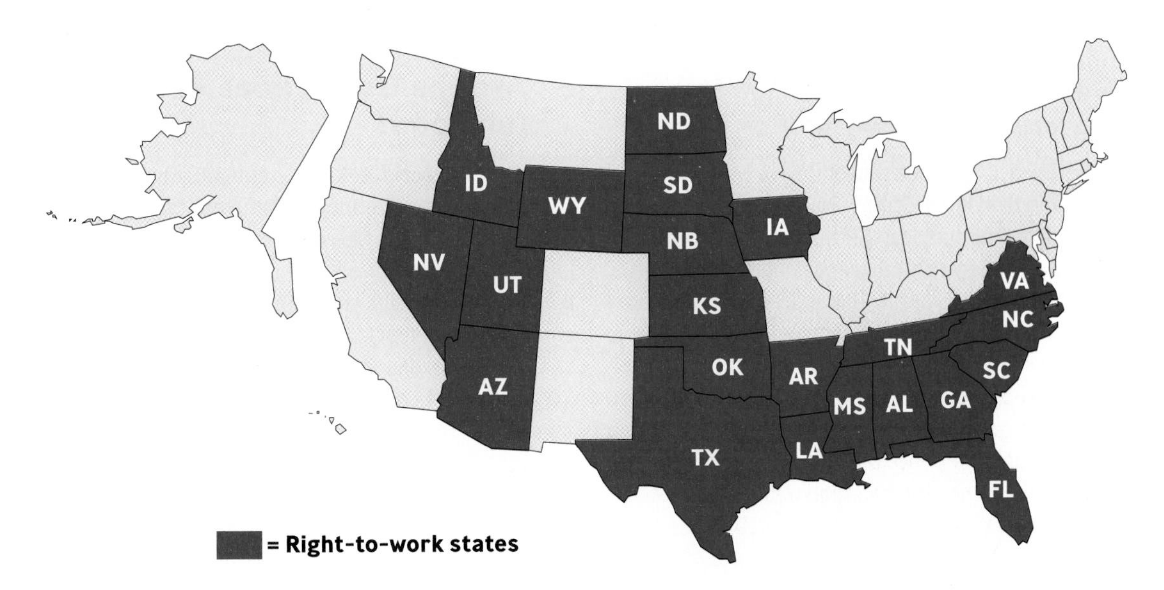


figure 12.5

**STATES WITH RIGHT-TO-WORK LAWS**

**right-to-work laws**. To date, 22 states have passed such legislation (see Figure 12.5). In a right-to-work state, an **open shop agreement** exists that gives workers the option to join or not join a union, if one is present in the workplace. Furthermore, if they choose not to join the certified union in their workplace, they cannot be forced to pay a fee or dues to the union. (The Casing the Web case "Do Right-to-Work Laws Help States?" at www.mhhe.com/ub8e discusses the Taft-Hartley Act in depth.)

In the future, the focus of union negotiations will most likely shift as issues such as child and elder care, worker retraining, two-tiered wage plans, offshore outsourcing, employee empowerment, and even integrity and honesty testing further challenge union members' rights in the workplace. Unions also intend to carefully monitor immigration policies and global agreements such as NAFTA and CAFTA to see that U.S. jobs are not lost.

Labor unions play a key workplace role in countries other than the United States as well. In Europe organized labor is a major force throughout the continent, and unions have historically had a good deal more influence in the workplace than unions have in the United States.[18] The Reaching Beyond Our Borders box on page 330 discusses a formidable challenge European unions face due to changing global markets.

**agency shop agreement**
Clause in a labor–management agreement that says employers may hire nonunion workers; employees are not required to join the union but must pay a union fee.

**right-to-work laws**
Legislation that gives workers the right, under an open shop, to join or not join a union if it is present.

**open shop agreement**
Agreement in right-to-work states that gives workers the option to join or not join a union, if one exists in their workplace.

## Resolving Labor–Management Disagreements

The rights of labor and management are outlined in the negotiated labor–management agreement. Upon acceptance by both sides, the agreement becomes a guide to work relations between union members and managers. However, signing the agreement doesn't necessarily end the employee–management negotiations. There are sometimes differences concerning interpretations of the agreement. For example, managers may interpret a certain clause in the agreement to mean that they are free to select who works overtime. Union members may interpret the same clause to mean that managers must select employees for overtime on the basis of *employee seniority*. If controversies such as this cannot be resolved between the two parties, employees may file a grievance.

A **grievance** is a charge by employees that management is not abiding by or fulfilling the terms of the negotiated labor–management agreement, according to how they perceive it. Overtime rules, promotions, layoffs, transfers, job assignments, and so forth are generally sources of employee grievances. Handling such grievances demands a good deal of contact between union officials

**grievance**
A charge by employees that management is not abiding by the terms of the negotiated labor–management agreement.

REACHING BEYOND our borders

www.europa.eu.int

### Are the Good Times Really Over for Good?

Over the past 30 years, European unions have been the envy of organized labor in the United States. Powerful unions such as IG Metall (the leading labor union in Germany) negotiated some of the most worker-friendly contracts imaginable. For example, in Germany union workers typically had a 35-hour workweek; workers also received paid vacations ranging from five to nine weeks each year. Unions also had considerable control in the company boardrooms. A system known as co-determination gave labor 50 percent of the seats on corporate boards, which laid the foundation for labor peace but limited the power of the management team. In France the situation was similar. According to a law passed in 1998, French workers could be on the job for a maximum of only 35 hours per week, and jobs were complemented by generous vacation benefits. It looks like the life of a union worker in Europe is pretty good. Well, maybe.

As Bob Dylan once sang, "The times, they are a-changin'." European unions, like their American counterparts, are getting used to givebacks (concessions to management). For example, unions at DaimlerChrysler agreed to scrap a pay raise and increase the workweek to 39 hours in exchange for a promise that 6,000 autoworkers jobs would remain in Germany for the next eight years. A similar agreement was reached at the Siemens factories, where workers agreed to a 40-hour workweek if the company agreed not to move jobs to Hungary. Similarly, union workers in Lyon, France, agreed to expand their workweek if the company promised not to relocate to the Czech Republic. Managers feel that the establishment of the euro as the currency of the European Union (EU) laid bare comparative wage costs across Europe. The problem for the unions is that the hourly wage rate varies greatly among the member countries of the EU. Wages in low-labor-cost countries like Poland and the Czech Republic are about 20 percent the cost in France or Germany; workers also spend about 500 more hours on the job each year. These realities have convinced many companies to move their operations to countries in Eastern Europe; some have even talked of moving to China. Talk has also surfaced to end co-determination in Germany. The high unemployment rates in Germany and France are also issues that go against the unions.

Unions in Europe promise to protect the strength they built over the past three decades. Nonetheless, the draw of low-cost operations and declining public opinion may be too strong to fight off. One thing is for certain, though: The notoriously rigid labor markets of a few years back are most likely a thing of the past.

Sources: Jack Ewing and Justin Hibbard, "The Bell Tolls for Germany, Inc.," *BusinessWeek*, August 15, 2005, pp. 40–41; Richard Milne, "German Steel Workers Close to Strike Over Pay," *Financial Times*, May 10, 2005, p. 3; and Matt Moore, "Germany's IG Metall Wants 5 Percent Wage Increase for Its 3.4 Million Members in 2006," AP Worldstream, January 29, 2006.

**shop stewards**
Union officials who work permanently in an organization and represent employee interests on a daily basis.

and managers. Grievances, however, do not imply that a company has broken the law or the labor agreement. In fact, the vast majority of grievances are negotiated and resolved by **shop stewards** (union officials who work permanently in an organization and represent employee interests on a daily basis) and supervisory-level managers. However, if a grievance is not settled at this level, formal grievance procedures will begin.[19] Figure 12.6 illustrates the different steps the formal grievance procedure could follow.

**bargaining zone**
The range of options between the initial and final offer that each party will consider before negotiations dissolve or reach an impasse.

**mediation**
The use of a third party, called a mediator, who encourages both sides in a dispute to continue negotiating and often makes suggestions for resolving the dispute.

## Mediation and Arbitration

During the negotiation process, there is generally what's called a **bargaining zone**, which is the range of options between the initial and final offer that each party will consider before negotiations dissolve or reach an impasse. If labor–management negotiators aren't able to agree on alternatives within this bargaining zone, mediation may be necessary. **Mediation** is the use of a third party, called a mediator, who encourages both sides in a dispute to continue negotiating and often makes suggestions for resolving the dispute. However, it's important to remember that mediators evaluate facts in the dispute and then make suggestions, not decisions.[20] Elected officials (current and past), attorneys, and college professors are often called on to serve as mediators in labor disputes. The National Mediation Board provides federal mediators when requested in a dispute.[21] Continental and Northwest Airlines asked for such assistance in negotiating a new contract with its flight attendants and the mechanics' union.[22]

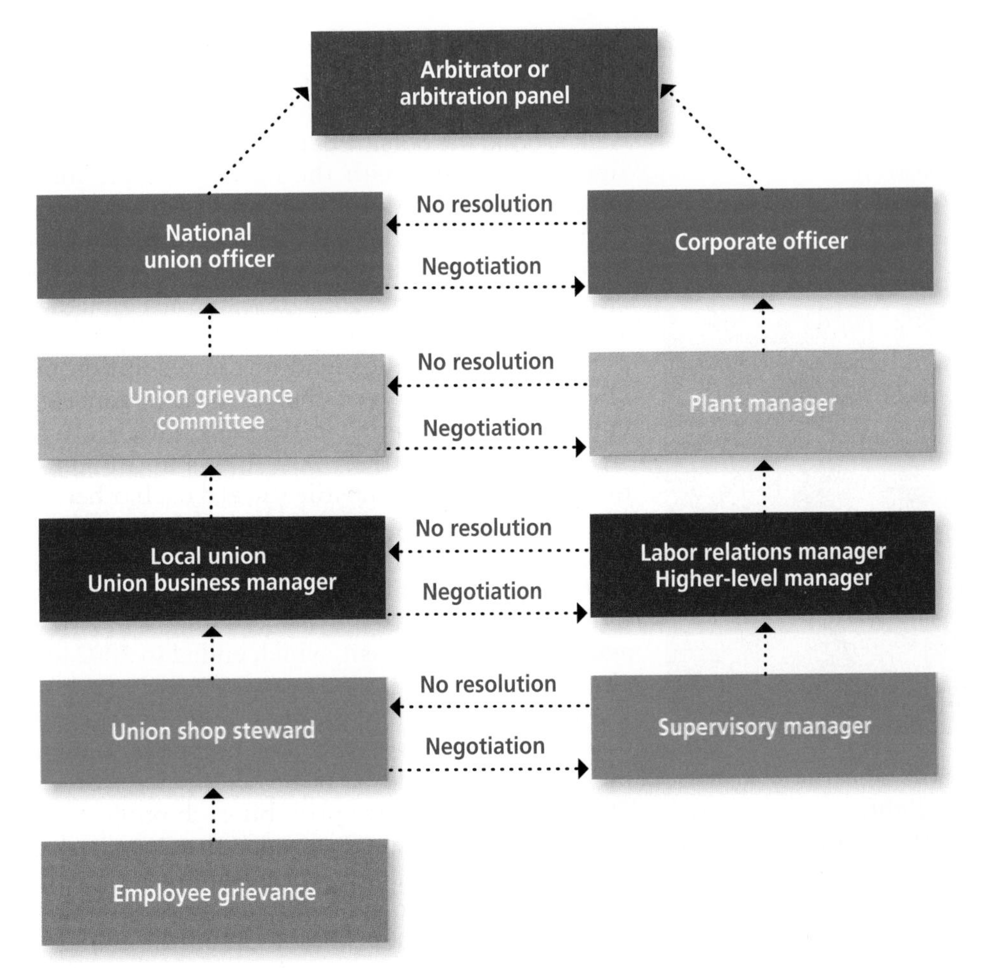


figure 12.6

**THE GRIEVANCE RESOLUTION PROCESS**

The grievance process may move through several steps before the issue is resolved. At each step, the issue is negotiated between union officials and managers. If no resolution comes internally, an outside arbitrator may be mutually agreed on. If so, the decision by the arbitrator is binding (legally enforceable).

A more extreme option used to resolve conflicts is arbitration.[23] **Arbitration** is an agreement to bring in an impartial third party (a single arbitrator or a panel of arbitrators) to render a binding decision in a labor dispute. The arbitrator(s) must be acceptable to both labor and management. You may have heard of baseball players filing for arbitration to resolve a contract dispute with their teams.[24] Many of the negotiated labor–management agreements in the United States call for the use of an arbitrator to end labor disputes. The nonprofit American Arbitration Association is the dominant organization used in dispute resolution.[25]

**arbitration**
The agreement to bring in an impartial third party (a single arbitrator or a panel of arbitrators) to render a binding decision in a labor dispute.

## TACTICS USED IN LABOR–MANAGEMENT CONFLICTS

If labor and management cannot reach an agreement through collective bargaining, and negotiations break down, either side or both sides may use specific tactics to enhance their negotiating position and perhaps sway public opinion. The primary tactics used by organized labor are strikes and boycotts. Unions might also use pickets and work slowdowns to get desired changes. Management, for its part, may implement lockouts, injunctions, and even strikebreakers. The following sections look briefly at each of these tactics.

### Union Tactics

Strikes have historically been the most potent tactic unions have used to achieve their objectives in labor disputes. A **strike** occurs when workers collectively refuse to go to work. Strikes can attract public attention to a labor dispute and at

**strike**
A union strategy in which workers refuse to go to work; the purpose is to further workers' objectives after an impasse in collective bargaining.

As these workers at Boeing illustrate, a strike is still the most potent tactic that unions use in labor disputes with management. Strikes, however, can generate violence and lead to extended bitterness in a company that takes a long time to heal. When do you think workers are justified to strike?

times cause operations in a company to slow down or totally cease. Besides refusing to work, strikers may also picket the company, which means that they walk around the outside of the organization carrying signs and talking with the public and the media about the issues in the labor dispute. Unions also often use picketing as an informational tool before going on strike. The purpose is to alert the public to an issue that is stirring labor unrest, even though no strike has been voted.

Strikes sometimes lead to the resolution of a labor dispute; however, they also have generated violence and extended bitterness. Often after a strike is finally settled, both labor and management remain openly hostile toward each other and mutual complaints of violations of the negotiated labor–management agreement continue. This occurred after the United Auto Workers strike against Caterpillar in the 1990s and the Teamsters strike against Overnite Transit, which ended in 2002 after almost four years.[26]

The public often realizes how important a worker is when he or she goes on strike. Imagine what an economic and social disaster it would be if a town's police force or firefighters went on strike. That's why many states prohibit such public safety workers from striking, even though they can be unionized.[27] Employees of the federal government, such as postal workers, can organize unions but are also denied the right to strike. When strikes are prohibited, workers sometimes exert their frustrations by engaging in sick-outs (often called the blue flu). That is, they arrange in groups to be absent from work and claim illness as the reason.

Under the provisions of the Taft-Hartley Act, the president can ask for a cooling-off period to prevent a strike in what's considered a critical industry. During a **cooling-off period**, workers return to their jobs while the union's bargaining team and management continue negotiations. The cooling-off period can last up to 80 days. Today, both labor and management seek to avoid strikes if at all possible, and very few labor disputes lead to a strike.[28] Changing social perceptions and attitudes also affect the potential for strikes. For example, after President Ronald Reagan fired striking air traffic controllers in 1981 for violating the Public Employees Relations Act and broke their union, other unions hesitated to strike. The Major League Baseball Players strike that canceled the World Series in 1994 generated further hostilities toward strikes, and unions felt the mood of the country was leaning against them. A successful strike against United Parcel Service (UPS) in 1997, however, showed the strike was still a potent tactic for labor to use in conflicts with management. As technological change, offshore outsourcing, and reductions in worker benefits—such as health insurance—continue to alter the workplace, it's unlikely that strikes will disappear. Strikes in health care, air and ground transportation, professional sports, and other major industries have illustrated that the strike is not yet dead as a labor tactic.

**cooling-off period**
When workers in a critical industry return to their jobs while the union and management continue negotiations.

**primary boycott**
When a union encourages both its members and the general public not to buy the products of a firm involved in a labor dispute.

Unions also use boycotts as a means to obtain their objectives in a labor dispute.[29] Boycotts can be classified as primary or secondary. A **primary boycott** occurs when organized labor encourages both its members and the general public not to buy the products or services of a firm involved in a labor dispute. A **secondary boycott** is an attempt by labor to convince others to stop doing business with a firm that is the subject of a primary boycott. For example, a union could not initiate a secondary boycott against a supermarket

**secondary boycott**
An attempt by labor to convince others to stop doing business with a firm that is the subject of a primary boycott; prohibited by the Taft-Hartley Act.

When consumer products giant Nestlé announced it was cutting jobs at its Perrier subsidiary, workers took to the streets to encourage consumers to boycott the popular water. Primary boycotts against a company's products during a labor dispute are legal and often a key tactic of labor unions. Have you ever been asked by a union member to boycott a particular company's products?

chain because that chain carries goods produced by a company that's the target of a primary boycott. Labor unions can legally authorize primary boycotts, but the Taft-Hartley Act prohibits the use of secondary boycotts.

## Management Tactics

Like labor, management also uses specific tactics to achieve its workplace goals. A **lockout** is an attempt by managers to put pressure on union workers by temporarily closing the business. When workers are not working, they are not paid. Today, management rarely uses lockouts to achieve its objectives. However, the lockout of West Coast dockworkers in 2002 and the high-profile lockout of National Hockey League (NHL) players that caused the cancellation of the entire 2004–2005 NHL season remind us this tactic is not dead.[30] Still, management today most often uses injunctions and strikebreakers to counter labor demands it sees as excessive.

**lockout**
An attempt by management to put pressure on unions by temporarily closing the business.

An **injunction** is a court order directing someone to do something or to refrain from doing something. Management has sought injunctions to order striking workers back to work, limit the number of pickets that can be used during a strike, or otherwise deal with actions that could be detrimental to the public welfare. For a court to issue an injunction, management must show a "just cause," such as the possibility of violence or the destruction of property. The use of strikebreakers has been a particular source of hostility and violence in labor relations. **Strikebreakers** (called scabs by unions) are workers who are hired to do the jobs of striking employees until the labor dispute is resolved. Employers have had the right to replace strikers since a 1938 Supreme Court ruling, but it wasn't until the 1980s that this tactic was frequently used. Be sure to read the Making Ethical Decisions box on page 334, which deals with this issue.

**injunction**
A court order directing someone to do something or to refrain from doing something.

**strikebreakers**
Workers hired to do the jobs of striking workers until the labor dispute is resolved.

## The Future of Unions and Labor–Management Relations

As mentioned earlier, many new issues have emerged that have affected labor–management relations. They include increased global competition, advancing technology, offshore outsourcing, and the changing nature of work. To save jobs, many unions have granted concessions, or **givebacks**, to management. In such situations, union members give back previous gains from labor

**givebacks**
Concessions made by union members to management; gains from labor negotiations are given back to management to help employers remain competitive and thereby save jobs.

www.ethics.ubc.ca/resources/business

## MAKING ethical decisions

### Let Your Conscience Be Your Guide

You just checked your wallet and see that only one picture of George Washington is staring back at you. Money is obviously tight, and the cost of your education keeps going up. You read last weekend that More-4-Less, a local grocery chain in your town, is seeking workers to replace members of the United Commercial Food Workers Union who are currently on strike against the company. Several classmates at your college are union members employed at More-4 Less, and many other students are supporting the strike. Several people who live in your neighborhood are also employed by the company. More-4-Less argues that its management has made a fair offer to the union workers, but the demands of the workers are clearly excessive and could ruin the company. More-4-Less is offering an attractive wage rate and flexible schedules to workers willing to cross the picket line and come to work during the strike. There is also the possibility of permanent employment. As a student, you could certainly use the job and the extra money for tuition and expenses. What would you do? What will be the consequences of your decision? Is your choice ethical?

negotiations. For example, unions at airlines such as US Airways, United, American, and Northwest Airlines agreed to give back previous workplace gains just to keep the airlines flying.[31] However, unions seem to be resisting any givebacks affecting retiree benefits.[32]

Organized labor is at a crossroads. Membership in the United Auto Workers has decreased by 60 percent, or 420,000 jobs, since 1979.[33] The unionized share of the workforce has declined from a peak of 35.5 percent in 1945 to just 12.5 percent today.[34] Only 8 percent of workers in the private sector are unionized, and union membership by state varies considerably (see Figure 12.7).[35]

figure 12.7

**UNION MEMBERSHIP BY STATE**

Source: www.aflcio.org, 2006.

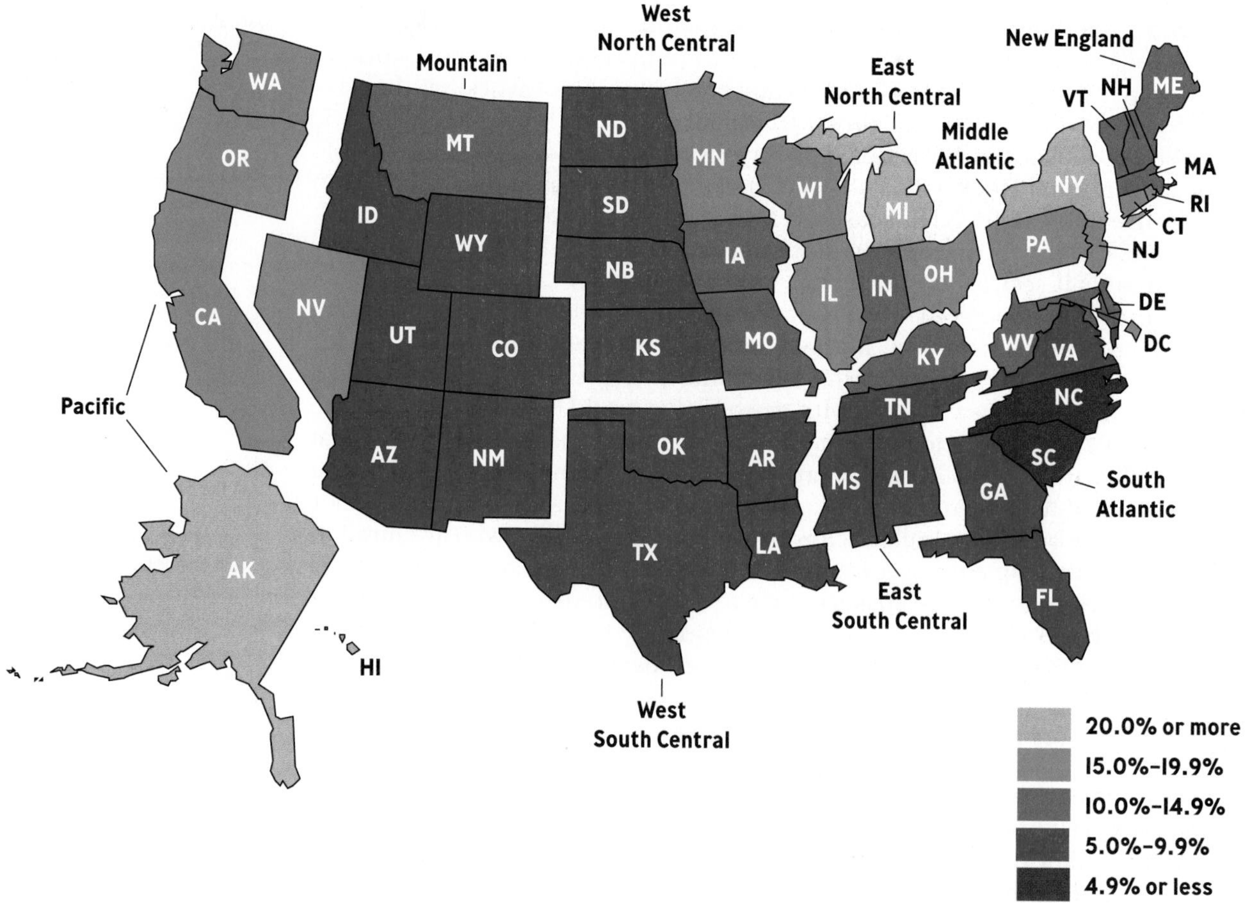

SPOTLIGHT ON small business

## Nursing the Unions Back to Health

The workforce of the United States in the 21st century is expected to be very different from that of the past. Demographic changes are causing alterations in its composition as well as in the characteristics of many jobs. For example, the aging of the baby boomers promises to drive the need for increased health care services and increased numbers of health care professionals. Labor unions have not lost sight of this fact. They see health care as an occupational area prime for growth in union membership. This is particularly true in health care's largest occupation, nursing.

The Service Employees International Union (SEIU) represents approximately 900,000 health care workers, including 80,000 nurses. In 2005, the SEIU split with the AFL-CIO and, along with the Teamsters Union and five other unions, joined the Change to Win coalition. The SEIU is currently planning to expand its organizing efforts with a goal of attracting approximately 1 million nurses into organized labor over the next 10 years. However, it expects a good deal of competition from labor groups such as the United American Nurses, an affiliate of the AFL-CIO; the American Nurses Association, which represents over 100,000 nurses; and the California Nurses Association, which claims over 60,000 members.

For their part, unions promise to deliver the respect and professionalism on the job that nurses deserve and are currently lacking. Labor guarantees it will improve nurses' job life by focusing on issues such as increased pay (including bonus systems), benefits, professional growth and development (including tuition reimbursement), and enhanced patient care through the creation of labor/management councils.

Labor is also not forgetting about physicians. Ever thought about going to the doctor and asking to see a union card before saying "Ahhh"? This is not as absurd as you think. Many private-practice physicians have embraced unionizing as a means to collective bargaining with managed health care organizations such as health maintenance organizations (HMOs). The American Medical Association (AMA) launched a physicians union called Physicians for Responsible Negotiations (PRN) in late 1999, and the PRN has been affiliated with the SEIU since 2004.

The number of union members in the health care industry could grow significantly in the years ahead. Naturally, the care of and well-being of patients must remain the key focus of the industry. However, maybe someday the president of the AFL-CIO may be called away from leading the annual Labor Day parade to perform an emergency appendectomy, deliver a baby, or assist as a surgery nurse.

Sources: Melanie Evans, "State of the Unions: Split in AFL-CIO May Pose Hardships for Bosses," *Modern Healthcare*, August 1, 2005; Jess Jamison, "Unions Role in Behavioral Health Organizations," *Behavioral Health Management*, May 1, 2005; Kris Maher, "The New Union Worker," *The Wall Street Journal*, September 27, 2005, pp. B1 and B11; and William Wan, "SEIU, Civista Discuss New Nurse Contract," *Washington Post*, February 2, 2006.

The largest labor organization in the United States is the National Education Association (NEA), which represents almost 2.7 million members.[36] To grow, unions will have to include more white-collar, female, and foreign-born workers than they have traditionally included. Plans to specifically target membership campaigns to women in relatively low-paying fields, such as health care and garment sewing have taken effect in the Teamsters Union and the Union of Needletrades, Industrial & Textile Employees (UNITE). The Spotlight on Small Business box discusses labor's attempt to organize workers in the health care industry.

It's safe to assume that unions in the 21st century are likely to be quite different from those in the past.[37] Union members understand that U.S. firms must remain competitive with foreign firms, and organized labor must do its best to maintain U.S. competitiveness.[38] Many unions have already taken on a new role in assisting management in training workers, redesigning jobs, and assimilating the changing workforce. They are also helping recruit and train foreign workers, unskilled workers, and any others who need special help in adapting to the job requirements of the new economy. Evidence of such cooperation at unionized companies like Kaiser Permanente and Southwest Airlines highlight how unions taking a leadership role

Membership in labor unions has dropped significantly over the past several decades, making the protection of union jobs paramount to labor's survival. Economic concerns about globalization, free trade, and the relocation of jobs to low-wage countries is a key reason why organized labor has fiercely opposed trade agreements such as NAFTA and CAFTA. Should the U.S. government protect workers from losing their jobs due to free trade agreements?

with management can make things happen.[39] For cooperating with management, unions can expect improved job security, profit sharing, and sometimes increased wages. Management can expect a productive, dedicated workforce to handle the challenges of growing competition.[40] How organized labor and management handle these challenges may well define the future for labor unions. After the Progress Assessment, we will look at other issues facing employees and managers in the 21st century.

**progress assessment**

- What are the major laws that affected union growth, and what does each one cover?
- Why do the objectives of unions change over time?
- What are the major tactics used by unions and by management to assert their power in contract negotiations?
- What types of workers do unions hope to organize in the future?

## CONTROVERSIAL EMPLOYEE–MANAGEMENT ISSUES

This is an interesting time in the history of employee–management relations. Organizations are involved in global expansion, offshore outsourcing, and technology change. The government has eliminated some social benefits to workers and is taking a more active role in mandating what benefits and assurances businesses must provide to workers. In other instances, employees are raising questions of fairness and workplace security. Let's look at several rather controversial issues, starting with that of executive compensation.

### Executive Compensation

Tiger Woods putts his way to over $87 million a year, Will Smith acts his way to $35 million a year, Oprah Winfrey talks her way to over $220 million a year, and George Lucas "has the force with him" for over $290 million a year.[41] Is it out of line, then, for Terry Semel, CEO of Yahoo, to make $120 million a year?[42] In Chapter 2 we explained that the U.S. free-market system is built on incentives that allow top executives to make such large amounts—or more. Today, however, the government, boards of directors, stockholders, unions, and employees are challenging this principle and arguing that executive compensation has gotten out of line.[43] In fact, way out of line. In 2004, the average total compensation (salary, bonuses, and incentives) for a CEO of a major company was $36 million, compared to just $33,176 for the average worker. Even after adjusting for inflation, this represents an enormous increase from the $160,000 average CEO compensation in 1960.

In times past, CEO compensation and bonuses were determined by the firm's profitability or an increase in its stock price.[44] The logic of this assumption was as the fortunes of a company and its stockholders grew, so would the rewards of the CEO. Today, however, executives generally receive stock options (the ability to buy company stock at a set price at a later date) and restricted stock (stock issued directly to the CEO that can't be sold usually for about three or four years)

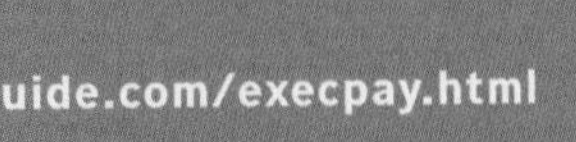

LEGAL briefcase

## Saying Goodbye the Gold-Lined Way

Most workers understand that if they are fired for incompetence, they are lucky to get their last paycheck. Charles Elson, director of the Center for Corporate Governance at the University of Delaware, perhaps said it best: "You shouldn't pay someone to fail." Unfortunately, many companies seem to be missing his point. Some corporate executives, who exited their companies under fire, sometimes wound up better off than if they had stayed—at least in monetary terms. Take CEO Carly Fiorina of Hewlett-Packard (HP), for example. She was behind a hotly debated merger with Compaq Computer Company and presided over a 30 percent drop in the stock price of HP. Her ouster as CEO was welcomed by investors—and quite profitable for her. She left HP with a "golden handshake" that included a $42 million severance package, with about $21 million of that in cash. Similarly, the Michael Ovitz departure at Walt Disney still boggles many people's minds. Ovitz was hired by Disney and fired 14 months later in the mid-1990s; he exited with a severance package worth about $140 million.

In some instances, imprisonment doesn't deter payments to CEOs. Martha Stewart was not paid by Martha Stewart Living Omnimedia while she was in prison, but she did begin to collect a guaranteed salary and bonus of $1.4 million when she started her five months of house arrest. Andrew Wiederhorn, former CEO of Fog Cutter Capital Group, collected about $5.5 million in compensation during his imprisonment for pension-law and income-tax felonies. Steve Madden, CEO of Steve Madden Ltd., received a $700,000 annual salary during his 41-month jail term for stock fraud and money laundering. (By law, a person cannot conduct business while in prison but can collect a paycheck.) Other CEOs have found the golden road to retirement, while their former companies were the ones paving the road. Don Tyson, the son of the founder of Tyson Foods, receives $800,000 a year for 20 hours of work per month. If he dies, the payments go to his survivors.

Such "corporate benevolence" is causing stockholders and lower-level employees to question the disparity of such treatment for top executives. One lawsuit was filed in the Tyson Foods case, and another is pending against Wiederhorn. Stockholders lost court decisions against both Disney and Madden, but Neil Minow, veteran shareholder activist, promises the fight is just beginning. Stay tuned!

Sources: Joann S. Lublin, "Imprisonment Doesn't Bar Pay for Select Group of CEOs," *The Wall Street Journal*, March 2, 2005, p. B1; Pamela Gaynor, "Carly Fiorina's Payoff Share Not Fair, Experts Say," *Pittsburgh Post-Gazette*, February 2, 2005; Louis Lavelle, "Consulting Even Beyond the Grave," *BusinessWeek*, February 28, 2005, p. 14; Geoffrey Colvin, "Hewlett-Packard: Home of the CEO Pay Heist," *Fortune*, May 2, 2005, p. 52; and Patrick McGeehan, "Still Living Large Down on the Farm," *New York Times*, January 8, 2006.

as part of their compensation.[45] In fact, stock options now account for 57 percent of a CEO's compensation, and restricted stock makes up 22 percent.[46] The key problem arises when executives are compensated with stock options and restricted stock even when the company does not meet expectations. John F. Antioco, CEO of Blockbuster Inc., saw his compensation increase by 541 percent even though the company's operating income fell by 51 percent and its stock price dropped by 47 percent.[47] What's even more frustrating to some people, however, is when a CEO whose poor performance forced him or her to resign walks away with lofty compensation.[48] Many CEOs also are awarded fat retainers, consulting contracts, and lavish perks when they retire.[49] Make sure to read the Legal Briefcase box for further discussion of this controversial trend.

The late management consultant Peter Drucker long criticized executive pay levels. He suggested that CEOs should not earn much more than 20 times the salary of the company's lowest-paid employee. Herman Miller, a Michigan producer of office furniture, has followed Drucker's advice. At this company, pay for the chief executive is limited to 20 times the average worker's pay. Not many companies, however, have placed such limits on executive compensation, and today the average CEO of a major corporation makes 160 times the average hourly worker's pay.[50] At times the numbers have been staggering. For example, a hot dog vendor at Disney's Magic Kingdom making minimum wage would need to work 52,327 years to earn what CEO Michael Eisner earned in 1998 ($575 million); a custodian or maintenance worker earning minimum wage at Oracle would have to work 63,468 years to make what CEO Larry Ellison earned in 2001 ($706 million).

Michael Eisner was never one to "duck" the issues during his years as CEO of Walt Disney Company. Even a classic star like Donald Duck has to pat him on the back for his $575 million in compensation that he received in 1998. Eisner increased the value of Disney under his tenure and added such companies as ABC television and ESPN to the Disney media empire. What do you feel is fair compensation for the CEO of a large, multinational company?

As global competition intensifies, it's worth noting that American CEOs typically earn two to three times as much as executives in Europe and Canada.[51] In European countries such as Germany, workers account for 50 percent of the seats on the board of directors of major firms according to a process called *co-determination*.[52] Since boards set executive pay, this could be a reason why the imbalance in pay is less for European executives than for their American counterparts. Graef Crystal, a pay consultant and expert on corporate governance, has long suggested a link between CEO compensation and executive-friendly boards of directors that are often paid well for a modest amount of work.[53] Pressure from the government and from dissatisfied shareholders for full disclosure concerning executive compensation promises to put U.S. boards of directors on notice that they are not there simply to enrich CEOs.[54]

It is important to recognize that most U.S. executives are responsible for multibillion-dollar corporations and that they work 70-plus hours a week. Many can show that their decisions turned potential problems into successes and huge compensation for employees and stockholders as well as themselves.[55] Furthermore, the market is not awash with seasoned, skilled professionals who can manage large companies. This is especially true for troubled companies looking for the right CEO to accomplish a turnaround. Hewlett-Packard, Lucent, and Tyco paid out millions to find CEOs to set them on the right path. Clearly, there is no easy answer to the question of what is fair compensation for executives, but it's a safe bet that the controversy will not go away.

## Pay Equity

Another controversial workplace issue is that of pay equity for women versus men. Put simply, pay equity goes beyond the concept of equal pay for equal work. Federal and state equal-pay laws have been in effect for many years. The Equal Pay Act of 1963 requires companies to give equal pay to men and women who do the same job.[56] For example, it's against the law to pay a female nurse less than a male nurse unless factors such as seniority, merit pay, or performance incentives are involved. Pay equity is the concept that people in jobs that require similar levels of education, training, or skills should receive equal pay. This somewhat thorny issue has become more important as women have become a sizable and permanent part of the labor force. Pay equity centers on comparing the value of jobs such as a bank teller or librarian (traditionally women's jobs) with jobs such as truck driver or plumber (traditionally men's jobs). Such a comparison shows that "women's" jobs tend to pay less—sometimes much less.

In the United States today, women earn approximately 80 percent of what men earn, though the disparity varies considerably by profession, job experience and tenure, and level of education.[57] In the past the primary explanation for this disparity was that women only worked 50 to 60 percent of their available years once they left school (experience and tenure), whereas men, on the whole, worked all of those years. This explanation doesn't hold much substance today because fewer women now leave the workforce for an extended time. Other explanations suggest that many working women devote more time to their families than men do, and thus accept lower-paying jobs with more flexible hours such as retail sales clerks.[58]

In the 1980s, pay critics proposed instituting a concept called comparable worth that required by law that people in jobs that require similar levels of education, training, or skills should receive equal pay. Evidence, however, did not support the idea that comparable worth would lead to better market equilibrium; in fact, many felt it would create more chaos and inequity. In today's knowledge-based economy, women appear to be competing financially with men in growing fields such as health care, biotechnology, and knowledge technology.[59] Studies conducted at the University of Michigan found that earnings of women with baccalaureate degrees were 96 percent of men's. Female engineers and anesthesiology nurses often earn more than what their male counterparts are paid. However, Heather Boushey, an economist at the Economic Policy Institute, believes that the government puts too much faith in the idea that education will automatically close the pay gap. She and other critics claim that because of the rejection of comparable worth, government and other institutions are overlooking the pay gaps, especially gaps that women with children face.[60] As women continue to comprise a large percentage of the labor force, pay equity promises to be a challenging employee–management issue.

**sexual harassment**
Unwelcome sexual advances, requests for sexual favors, and other conduct (verbal or physical) of a sexual nature that creates a hostile work environment.

## Sexual Harassment

**Sexual harassment** refers to unwelcome sexual advances, requests for sexual favors, and other conduct (verbal or physical) of a sexual nature that creates a hostile work environment. In evaluating sexual harassment, a person's conduct on the job can be considered illegal under specific conditions, such as the following:

- The employee's submission to such conduct is made either explicitly or implicitly a term or condition of employment, or an employee's submission to or rejection of such conduct is used as the basis for employment decisions affecting the worker's status. A threat such as "Go out with me or you are fired" or "Go out with me or you will never be promoted here" would constitute *quid pro quo sexual harassment.*
- The conduct unreasonably interferes with a worker's job performance or creates an intimidating, hostile, or offensive work environment. This type of harassment is referred to as *hostile work environment sexual harassment.*

The Civil Rights Act of 1991 governs sexual harassment and, legally, both men and women are covered under this legislation. This fact was reinforced in 1997, when the Supreme Court agreed that same-sex harassment also falls within the purview of sexual harassment law. Women, however, still file the majority of sexual harassment cases. The Supreme Court in 1996 broadened the scope of what can be considered a hostile work environment; the court's keyword seemed to be *unwelcome,* a term that refers to behavior that would offend a reasonable person.[61] The number of sexual

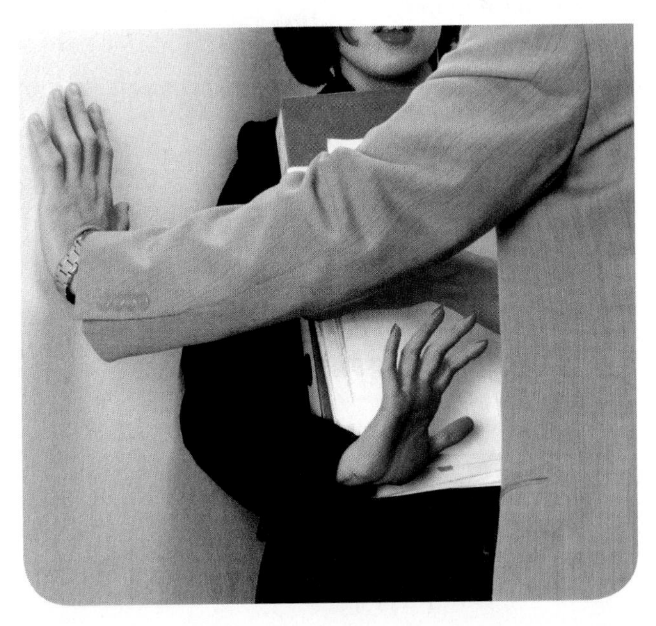

Unwelcomed sexual advances, requests for sexual favors, and other verbal or physical conduct are prohibited under the Civil Rights Act of 1991. While most employees are aware of sexual harassment policies in the workplace, they are often not certain of what sexual harassment actually means. Thus many companies have turned to the Internet to train employees about the dos and don'ts related to acceptable sexual conduct on the job.

harassment complaints filed annually with the Equal Employment Opportunity Commission (EEOC) has leveled off since 2000; additionally, approximately 90 percent of sexual harassment suits are settled out of court. Unfortunately, the number of sexual harassment lawsuits against small companies has increased.[62] For example, Donna Salyers, founder of Donna Salyer's Fabulous Furs, was shocked to find out that the EEOC was suing her firm on behalf of four temporary employees who claimed their supervisor made offensive remarks to them.[63] The lawsuit cost the firm almost $150,000.

There's no question that managers and workers are now much more sensitive to sexual comments and behavior than they were in the past. Still, EEOC statistics report that sexual harassment continues to be a persistent area of employee complaint. A major problem is that workers and managers often know that a policy concerning sexual harassment exists but have no idea what it says. Cari Dominguez, chairwoman of the EEOC, recommends that companies offer management training and require sexual harassment workshops for all employees. A good deal of the training can be done at work through information on the Internet. Many companies have responded by setting up rapid, effective grievance procedures and promptly reacting to an employee's allegation of harassment.[64] Such efforts may save businesses millions of dollars in lawsuits and make the workplace more productive and harmonious.[65] Nonetheless, despite these efforts it's a safe bet that sexual harassment will not disappear soon as a key employee–management issue.

## Child Care

Child care became an increasingly important workplace issue in the late 1990s and remains a workplace concern today. According to the U.S. Census Bureau, a sizable number of today's 50 million working women are likely to bear children during their working years. Such statistics obviously raise concerns among employers for two key reasons: (1) It's estimated that absences related to child care already cost American businesses billions of dollars annually, and (2) Employee child care raises the controversial workplace question of who should pay for child care services.[66] Many workers strongly challenge workplace benefits for parents and single parents, arguing that single workers and single-income families should not subsidize child care for dual-income families. Federal child care assistance rose significantly after the passage of the Welfare Reform Act of 1996. However, in 2005 Congress froze the funding of the Child Care and Development Fund at its current level.[67] Thus, the issue of child care remains an important one to business.

Questions involving responsibilities for child care subsidies, child care programs, and even parental leave have spurred much debate in the private and public sectors of the economy. The number of large companies offering child care as an employee benefit is growing. *Working Mother* magazine highlighted companies such as Bristol-Myers Squibb, IBM, and JP Morgan Chase as being particularly sympathetic and cooperative to working mothers.[68] Other large firms that offer extensive child care programs include Johnson & Johnson, American Express, and Campbell Soup. A few companies even provide emergency child care services for employees whose children are ill or whose regular child care arrangements are disrupted.

Bristol Myers Squibb is not just a leader in the pharmaceutical industry; it's considered one of the 10 most sympathetic and cooperative employers to working mothers according to *Working Mother* magazine. Here at the company's child care facility an employee visits with her child during her lunch break. Who should pay for such employee benefits such as child care, the employee or the company?

However, according to *Inc.* magazine, only 3 percent of businesses with fewer than 100 employees provide child care at work.[69] Some small companies, however, have found that implementing creative child care programs helps them compete with larger organizations in the search to hire qualified employees. For example, Haemonetics Corporation in Braintree, Massachusetts, has a state-of-the-art child care facility called the Kids' Space at Haemonetics. In the summer, the facility includes Camp Haemonetics—the kids come to work with their parents and then get bused off for swimming, hiking, and so forth at a nearby state park. At noon, they come back for lunch with Mom or Dad, and then return for more camp activities until about 5:00 p.m.[70] In 1986, entrepreneurs Roger Brown and Linda Mason recognized the emerging attraction of child care as a benefit in the workplace. The husband-and-wife team started Bright Horizons Family Solutions Inc. to provide child care at worksites for employers. Today, the company runs nearly 600 child care centers for about 400 companies.

What's obvious to businesses of all sizes is that working parents consider safe, affordable child care an issue on which they will not compromise. Companies have responded by providing

- Discount arrangements with national child care chains.
- Vouchers that offer payments toward whatever type of child care the employee selects.
- Referral services that help identify high-quality child care facilities to employees.
- On-site child care centers at which parents can visit children at lunch or during lag times throughout the workday.
- Sick-child centers to care for moderately ill children.

The number of single-parent and two-income households makes it certain that child care will remain a hotly debated employee–management issue. However, a workplace storm is brewing over an issue employees and managers have not faced in times past: elder care.

## Elder Care

The workforce in the United States is aging. The 2000 census showed that since 1990, the number of people ages 65 and over jumped by 12 percent, to 35 million. The number is expected to double by 2040, with 77 million Americans over 65. In 2012, the overall labor force will grow by 12 percent but the percentage of workers ages 55 and older will increase by 49 percent.[71] Most of these workers will not have to concern themselves with finding child care for their children. However, they will confront another problem: how to care for older parents and other relatives. The number of households with at least one adult providing elder care has tripled since 1992. It's estimated that 15 percent of the U.S. workforce now provides care for an older family member or friend, a number that is expected to grow over the next decade. Current estimates suggest that companies are presently losing $11 billion a year in reduced productivity, absenteeism, and turnover from employees who are responsible for aging relatives.[72] Sandra Timmerman, director of MetLife's Mature Market Institute, suggests that elder care is *the* key workplace issue of the next decade.[73]

The U.S. Office of Personnel Management (OPM) found that employees with elder care responsibilities need information on medical, legal, and insurance issues, as well as the full support of their supervisors and company. The OPM also suggested that such caregivers may require moving to flextime, telecommuting, part-time employment, or job sharing. Some firms, in reaction to the effect of elder care on their workforce, have begun to offer employee assistance programs. At JP Morgan Chase, employees are offered elder care management services that include a consultant who conducts a full-fledged needs assessment program for the employee. AAA and UPS offer health-spending accounts in which employees can put aside pretax income for elder care expenses. Unfortunately, few U.S. companies (large, medium, or small) provide any type of elder care programs or benefits; the primary focus has been on the rising cost of employee health insurance. Nor does the government provide much relief with this issue. Both Medicare and Medicaid place heavy financial burdens on family caregivers.

The AARP and the National Alliance of Caregivers expect costs to companies to rise even higher as more and more experienced and high-ranking employees become involved in caring for older parents and other relatives. Their argument makes sense, since the jobs older workers hold are often more critical to a company than those held by younger workers (who are most affected by child care problems). Estimates are that costs to employers could skyrocket to $25 billion annually. Already many firms realize that transfers and promotions are sometimes out of the question for employees whose elderly parents need ongoing care. Unfortunately, as the nation gets older, the elder care situation will grow considerably worse. With an aging workforce, this employee–management issue promises to persist well into the 21st century.

## Drug Testing

Not long ago, acquired immunodeficiency syndrome (AIDS) caused great concern in the workplace. Thankfully, the spread of AIDS has declined in the United States—good news for all Americans and for business. However, alcohol and drug abuse are serious workplace issues that involve far more workers than AIDS does. In fact, the issue of substance abuse reaches far and wide, from the nation's factory floors to its construction sites to the locker rooms of its professional sports teams.

Alcohol is the most widely used drug in the workplace, with an estimated 6.2 percent of full-time employees in the United States believed to be heavy drinkers.[74] Approximately 40 percent of industrial injuries and fatalities can be linked to alcohol consumption. Nearly 8 percent of full-time workers ages 18–49 use illegal drugs, according to the Department of Health and Human Services' Substance Abuse & Mental Health Services Association. Individuals who use illegal drugs are three and a half times more likely to be involved in workplace accidents and are five times more likely to file a workers' compensation claim than employees who do not use drugs. According to the National Institute on Drug Abuse, employed drug users cost their employers about twice as much in medical and workers' compensation claims than drug-free co-workers.[75] The U.S. Department of Labor projects that over a one-year period, drug abuse cost U.S. companies $81 billion in lost productivity.[76] The National Institute of Health estimates that each drug abuser can cost an employer approximately $11,000 annually. Today, over 70 percent of major companies now test workers and job applicants for substance abuse.[77]

## Violence in the Workplace

Employers are also struggling with a growing trend toward violence in the workplace. The Occupational Safety and Health Administration (OSHA) reports that workplace homicides account for 16 percent of all workplace deaths; homicide is the third leading cause of job-related fatalities.[78] The nation first faced the shock of large-scale workplace violence in 1986, when a postal service employee in Oklahoma killed 14 fellow workers before taking his own life. Since then, many employees have perished on the job at the hands of fellow employees.[79] Many executives and managers consider workplace violence a serious issue and have taken action to prevent problems before they occur. To deal with this growing threat, firms have held focus groups to invite employee input, hired managers with strong interpersonal skills, and employed skilled consultants to deal with any growing potential of workplace violence. At software firm Mindbridge, based in Worchester, Pennsylvania, two company officials must be present whenever an employee is disciplined or fired. Nine states presently have passed laws allowing an employer to seek a temporary restraining order on behalf of workers experiencing threats or harassment.

Some companies believe that reports of workplace violence are primarily overblown by the media. According to an American Management Association study, close to half of its member companies do not provide any formal training for dealing with prevention of violence in the workplace. Unfortunately, organizations such as the U.S. Postal Service, Edgewater Technology, and Xerox can attest that workplace violence is all too real and promises to be a major issue for the foreseeable future.

Firms that have healthy employee–management relations have a better chance to prosper than those that don't. As managers, taking a proactive approach is the best way to ensure workable employee–management environments. The proactive manager anticipates potential problems and works toward resolving those issues before they get out of hand—a good lesson to remember for any manager.

### progress assessment

- How does top-executive pay in the United States compare with top-executive pay in other countries?
- What's the difference between pay equity and equal pay for equal work?
- How is the term *sexual harassment* defined, and when does sexual behavior become illegal?
- What are some of the issues related to child care and elder care, and how are companies addressing those issues?

## summary

**1.** Trace the history of organized labor in the United States.

1. Organized labor in the United States dates back almost to the American Revolution.
   - **What was the first union?**

   The cordwainers (shoemakers) organized a craft union of skilled specialists in 1792. The Knights of Labor, which was formed in 1869, was the first national labor organization.
   - **How did the AFL-CIO evolve?**

   The American Federation of Labor (AFL), formed in 1886, was an organization of craft unions. The Congress of Industrial Organizations (CIO), a group of unskilled and semiskilled workers, broke off from the AFL in 1935. Over time, the two organizations saw the benefits of joining together and became the AFL-CIO in 1955. The AFL-CIO is a federation of labor unions, not a national union.

**2.** Discuss the major legislation affecting labor unions.

2. Legislation has had an important effect on the growth of labor unions.
   - **What are the provisions of the major legislation affecting labor unions?**

   See Figure 12.1 on page 325.

**3.** Outline the objectives of labor unions.

3. The objectives of labor unions shift in response to changes in social and economic trends.
   - **What topics typically appear in labor–management agreements?**

   See Figure 12.3 on page 328.

**4.** Describe the tactics used by labor and management during conflicts, and discuss the role of unions in the future.

4. If negotiations between labor and management break down, either or both sides may use certain tactics to enhance their position or sway public opinion.
   - **What are the tactics used by unions and management in conflicts?**

   Unions can use strikes and boycotts. Management can use injunctions and lockouts.
   - **What will unions have to do to cope with declining membership?**

   In order to grow, unions will have to adapt to an increasingly white-collar, female, and culturally diverse workforce. To help keep American businesses competitive in international markets, unions must soften their historic "us-versus-them" attitude and build a new "we" attitude with management. Unions also will have to find a new sense of harmony in its own ranks.

**5.** Explain some of today's controversial employee–management issues, such as executive compensation, pay equity, child care and elder care, drug testing, and violence in the workplace.

5. Some controversial employee–management issues are executive compensation, pay equity, child care and elder care, drug testing, and violence in the workplace.
   - **What is a fair wage for managers?**

   The market and the businesses in it set managers' salaries. What is fair is open to debate. The top executives of the 100 largest public companies were paid, on average, $36 million in 2005.
   - **How is equal pay and pay equity different?**

   The Equal Pay Act of 1963 provides that workers receive equal pay for equal work (with exceptions for seniority, merit, or performance). Pay equity is the demand for equivalent pay for jobs requiring similar levels of education, training, and skills. At one time some suggested implementing a system called comparable worth.
   - **Isn't pay inequity caused by sexism?**

   There is some evidence that supports that statement and counterarguments that refute the charge. It's believed that education and training lead to pay equity, but that is not always the case.
   - **How are some companies addressing the child care issue?**

   Responsive companies are providing child care on the premises, emergency care when scheduled care is interrupted, discounts with child care chains, vouchers to be used at the employee's chosen care center, and referral services.
   - **What is elder care, and what problems do companies face with regard to this growing problem?**

   Workers with older parents or other relatives often need to find some way to care for them. It's becoming a problem that will perhaps outpace the need for child care. Workers who need to care for dependent parents are generally more experienced and vital to the mission of the organization than younger workers are. The cost to business is very large and growing.
   - **Why are more and more companies now testing workers and job applicants for substance abuse?**

   Nearly 8 percent of employed adults between the ages of 18 and 49 in the United States are believed to be current illicit drug users. Individuals who use drugs are three and a half times more likely to be involved in workplace accidents and five times more likely to file a workers' compensation claim than those who do not use drugs.

## key terms

**agency shop agreement** 329
**American Federation of Labor (AFL)** 324
**arbitration** 331
**bargaining zone** 330
**certification** 325
**closed shop agreement** 328
**collective bargaining** 325
**Congress of Industrial Organizations (CIO)** 324
**cooling-off period** 332
**craft union** 323
**decertification** 326
**givebacks** 333
**grievance** 329
**industrial unions** 324
**injunction** 333
**Knights of Labor** 324
**lockout** 333
**mediation** 330
**negotiated labor–management agreement (labor contract)** 327
**open shop agreement** 329
**primary boycott** 332
**right-to-work laws** 329
**secondary boycott** 332
**sexual harassment** 339
**shop stewards** 330
**strike** 331
**strikebreakers** 333
**union** 322
**union security clause** 327
**union shop agreement** 328
**yellow-dog contract** 325

## critical thinking questions

1. Do you believe that union shop agreements are violations of a worker's freedom of choice in the workplace? Do you think that open shop agreements unfairly penalize workers who pay dues to unions they have elected to represent them in the workplace?

2. Should college football coaches be paid the same as college volleyball coaches? Should female basketball players in the Women's National Basketball Association (WNBA) be paid the same as their male counterparts in the National Basketball Association (NBA)? What role should market forces and government play in determining such wages?

3. If a company provides employer-paid child care services to workers with children, should workers who do not have children or the need for child care services be paid extra compensation by the employer?

## developing workplace skills

1. Talk with several health care professionals (doctors, nurses, etc.) about their feelings of possible unionization in health care professions. List the pros and cons they offer concerning unions advancing in the medical profession.

2. Evaluate the following statement: "Labor unions are dinosaurs that have outlived their usefulness in today's knowledge-based economy." After your evaluation, take the position on this statement that differs from your own point of view. Use outside sources such as Web sites for the National Association of Manufacturers (www.nam.org) and the AFL-CIO (www.aflcio.org) to defend your contrary view. Be sure to consider such questions as: Do unions serve a purpose in some industries? Do unions make the United States less competitive in global markets?

3. Find the latest information on federal and state legislation related to child care, parental leave, and elder care benefits for employees. In what direction are the trends moving? Do you favor such movements in workplace legislation? Why or why not?

4. Compile a list of two or three employee–management issues not covered in the chapter. Compare your list with those of several classmates and see what issues you selected in common and ones unique to each individual. Collectively pick which workplace issue you all agree will be important in the future and discuss its likely effects and outcomes.

5. Do businesses and government agencies have a duty to provide additional benefits to employees beyond fair pay and good working conditions? Does providing benefits such as child care and elder care to some employees discriminate against those who do not require such assistance? Propose a benefits system that you consider fair and workable for both employees and employers.

## taking it to the net

### Purpose

To understand why workers choose to join unions and how unions have made differences in certain industries.

### Exercise

Visit the AFL-CIO Web site (www.aflcio.org). Navigate through the site and find information regarding why workers join unions and what the benefits have been.

1. There have been many debates about right-to-work laws. Compare the average wages of workers in right-to-work states with those in other states. Which group of states offers the higher wages? In addition to union pressure, what else could account for the wage differences?
2. What percentage of workers in your state belongs to a union? If the percentage of union workers is higher (or lower) than the national average, explain why unions do (or do not) have strength in your state.
3. Explain how union membership has affected minorities, women, younger and older workers, and part-time workers.
4. The AFL-CIO site presents the union's perspective on labor issues. Choose one of these issues and find other resources that support management's perspective on the issue.

## casing the web

To access the case *"Do Right-to-Work Laws Help States?"* visit **www.mhhe.com/ub8e**

video case

## United We Stand

After reading this chapter, you are familiar with the history of labor unions. You have learned the tactics that labor uses to get new benefits from management, and you have learned the tactics that management uses to respond to labor demands. You are also familiar with the various laws that are involved in labor/management disputes. You may get the impression from the media that labor unions are in decline and don't have much clout any more. In fact, the number of people in labor unions has declined dramatically, but that doesn't mean that labor unions are not very important today or that they have lost their passion for seeking fair treatment by companies.

We are so accustomed to thinking about labor unions in the auto, steel, and other related industries that we tend to overlook some truly key industries where labor unions are very important. No doubt you have heard in passing of the Screen Actors Guild (SAG), the American Federation of TV and Radio Artists, and the Writers Guild of America. But do you have any idea what issues the membership faces in such unions? Are they the same issues that unions have always had: seniority, pay, benefits, and such? Or are they different somehow?

Many young people dream of becoming a "movie star." They see the glamour, the excitement, the adulation of the fans, and the huge paychecks. What they don't see behind the scenes is the constant fight going on to win and keep certain privileges that past actors have won. Back in the 1930s, actors worked unrestricted hours, had no required meal breaks, and had unbreakable seven-year contracts. The producers tried to control who you could marry, what political views to express, and what your morals should be. The Screen Actors Guild won some concessions for the actors in 1937, but the studios pretty much still "owned" their stars. Eventually the stars won the right to better contracts—to the point where independent studios were formed and actors could control their own careers, even demanding a percentage of gross for their pay (Jimmy Stewart in 1950).

Other issues concerned residuals for films shown on TV and in reruns. Other contracts had to do with commercials and how the actors would be paid for them. Today's contracts deal with issues like diversity, salary and work conditions, financial assurances, safety considerations, and so on. Things are constantly changing for actors. For example, independent film producers in the United States and around the world have different rules and requirements. TV commercials now appear on cell phones. The Screen Actors Guild keeps up with such changes to assure fair treatment of its members.

While SAG is for movie actors, The American Federation of Television and Radio Artists is a performer's union for actors, radio and TV announcers and newspersons, singers, and others who perform on radio and TV. It negotiates wages and working conditions much like the SAG, including health care and pensions. You can imagine negotiating an issue like equal pay for equal work when dealing with highly paid actors and actresses with huge egos.

The Writers Guild of America (WGA) represents **writers** in the motion picture, broadcast and new media industries. Like actors, writers have issues dealing with pay, benefits, retirement, and so forth. The more you think about it, the more it will become clear to you that actors and others in the entertainment industry need unions or some other kind of organization to protect them from unfair practices. You can only imagine what treatment actors and others get from independent companies in other countries if they don't have representation.

Unions today are gathering momentum in industries where the pay is traditionally relatively low and the work is hard. That includes nursing, teaching (including college teachers), and other professions (profit, nonprofit, and government).

### Thinking It Over

1. You can imagine what it would be like to try to get a job as an actor on Hollywood. What role might a union play in helping you find a job, negotiate a contract, and otherwise look out for your interests? You might look on the SAG/AFTRA and WGA Web sites for more information.
2. What issues might actors, performers, and writers have that other workers may not have?
3. What is the general attitude in your class toward labor unions? Are there many union workers in your town? Where do you see labor unions gaining strength in the future?

# marketing: BUILDING customer relationships

profile

Getting to Know

X Lance Fried,

Entrepreneur

Lance Fried was not a marketer at first but rather an electrical engineer. He was also a product design whiz who had served as CEO of an apparel company. He is now the CEO of Freestyle Audio. In short, Fried is the kind of person who knows marketing opportunities when he sees them. One day, Fried was watching surfers near his home in Del Mar, California. He thought they might enjoy having a submersible MP3 player to wear while surfing. That thought merely bounced around in his head for a while until a friend dropped an iPod into a cooler full of water and ice, making it useless. Fried began working on a waterproof player. After a while, he completed a lightweight prototype that was capable of holding about 80 songs. Now what?

The fastest way to market such a product would be to go to large retailers and get wide distribution. The problem is that Fried's waterproof MP3 player would not get the personal attention that he felt it needed at such large stores. Furthermore, it would be hard to produce enough products to serve large retail outlets. At smaller surfing shops, however, it would be of major interest. It was sure to be a big hit.

Fried took the MP3 player to a trade show and placed his products at the bottom of a large fish tank with earphones sticking out so that potential customers could try them. As hoped, the players were a big hit and several smaller retailers ordered them. *Surfer* magazine put the waterproof MP3 players at the top of its

## LEARNING goals

After you have read and studied this chapter, you should be able to

1. Define *marketing* and explain how the marketing concept applies in both for-profit and nonprofit organizations.
2. List and describe the four Ps of marketing.
3. Describe the marketing research process, and explain how marketers use environmental scanning to learn about the changing marketing environment.
4. Explain how marketers meet the needs of the consumer market through market segmentation, relationship marketing, and the study of consumer behavior.
5. List ways in which the business-to-business market differs from the consumer market.

CHAPTER 13

www.freestyleaudio.com

Christmas wish list. You can imagine the interest that such exposure caused.

Eventually, Fried will probably sell his waterproof players in major retail stores, but for now he is selling them directly to customers on Freestyle's Web site. The product was so popular the first year that it was sold out before Christmas. Second-year sales were expected to hit $10 million. There are about 5 million surfers, 3 million wakeboarders, and 10 million water rafters and kayakers in the United States, so the market is still wide open.

Every product has its own challenges when it comes to marketing. In this case, most surfers do not go into a surf shop hoping to buy an MP3 player. To attract their attention, there should be good point-of-sale materials explaining how the product works. Endorsements by leading surfers would also help. A video could show surfers using the players, and related TV ads could be developed.

Fried's story illustrates clearly some of the issues that come up with marketing. Marketing begins with watching people to see what their needs are. It then involves developing products that consumers might want. Those products need to be perfected and tested in the marketplace. Then one must decide how to distribute or sell those products. Should we sell them through large retailers, on the Internet, or what? How should we inform the public about the products: advertising, publicity in the media, trade shows, flyers, or what? Making such decisions is difficult, but, if you are successful, you can make a lot of people very happy and make a lot of money as well. That is what marketing is all about.

Sources: Laura Kolodny, "Hands On; Case Study," *Inc.*, April 2005, pp. 44–45; Marc Graser and T. L. Stanley, "Key Function on Xbox 360: Marketing," *Advertising Age*, June 6, 2005, p. 13; Alex Wilson, "Unique Surf Products Stir ASR," www.surfermag.com; and Gary Silverman, "How May I Help You?," *Financial Times Weekend*, February 4/5, 2006, pp. W1 and W2.

## WHAT IS MARKETING?

**marketing**
The process of planning and executing the conception, pricing, promotion, and distribution of goods and services to facilitate exchanges that satisfy individual and organizational objectives.

Many people think of marketing as "selling" or "advertising." Yes, selling and advertising are part of marketing, but, as the Opening Profile shows, marketing involves much more.[1] **Marketing** is the process of planning and executing the conception, pricing, promotion, and distribution of goods and services to facilitate exchanges that satisfy individual and organizational objectives.

What marketers do at any particular time depends on what needs to be done to fill customers' needs. Consumers' wants and needs continually change. Let's take a brief look at how these changes influenced the evolution of marketing.

### The Evolution of the Field of Marketing

The evolution of marketing in the United States involved four eras: (1) production, (2) selling, (3) marketing concept, and (4) customer relationship (see Figure 13.1).

**The Production Era** From the time the first European settlers began their struggle to survive in America until the early 1900s, the general philosophy of business was "Produce as much as you can because there is a limitless market." Given the limited production capability and the vast demand for products in those days, such a philosophy was both logical and profitable. Business owners were mostly farmers, carpenters, and trade workers. There was a need for greater and greater productive capacity, so the goals of business centered on *production*. This was necessary at the time because most goods were bought as soon as they became available. The greatest marketing need was for *distribution and storage*.

**The Selling Era** By the 1920s, businesses had developed mass-production techniques (e.g., automobile assembly lines), and production capacity often exceeded the immediate market demand. Therefore, the business philosophy turned from an emphasis on production to an emphasis on *selling*. Most companies emphasized selling and advertising in an effort to persuade consumers to buy existing products; few offered service after the sale.

**The Marketing Concept Era** After World War II ended, in 1945, there was a tremendous demand for goods and services among the returning soldiers who were starting new careers and beginning families. Those postwar years launched the baby boom (a sudden increase in the birthrate) and a boom in

figure 13.1

**MARKETING ERAS**

The evolution of marketing in the United States involved four eras: (1) production, (2) sales, (3) marketing concept, and (4) customer relationship.

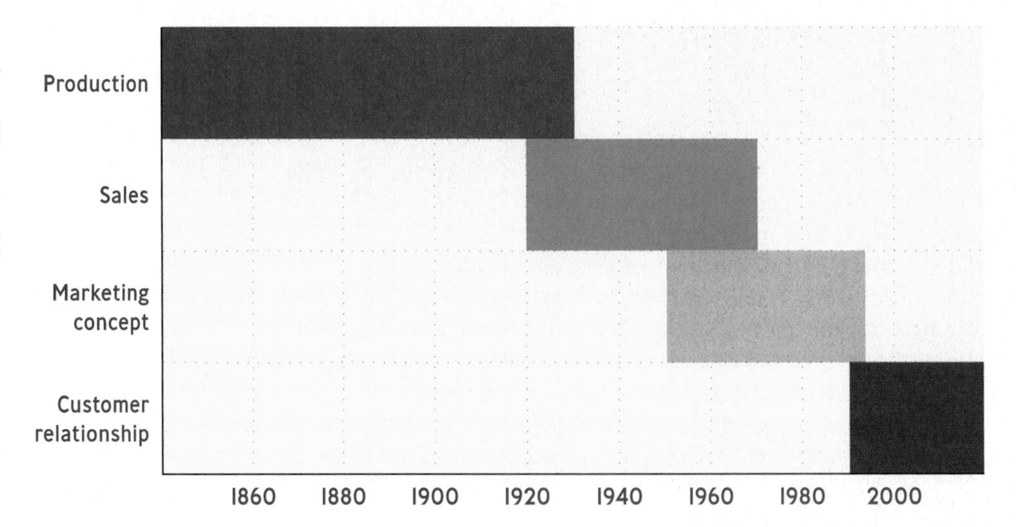

consumer spending. Competition for the consumer's dollar was fierce. Businesses recognized the need to be responsive to consumers if they wanted to get their business, and a philosophy emerged in the 1950s called the marketing concept.

The **marketing concept** had three parts:

1. *A customer orientation.* Find out what consumers want and provide it for them. That's exactly what Lance Fried did with his waterproof MP3 player. (Note the emphasis on meeting consumer needs rather than on promotion or sales.)
2. *A service orientation.* Make sure everyone in the organization has the same objective: customer satisfaction. This should be a total and integrated organizational effort. That is, everyone from the president of the firm to the delivery people should be customer oriented.[2]
3. *A profit orientation.* Focus on those goods and services that will earn the most profit and enable the organization to survive and expand to serve more consumer wants and needs.



Marketers have been using the concept of "Find a need and fill it" for many years. Advertising was used to communicate the fact that the products consumers wanted were now available. What unmet needs do you have that marketers might fill? Why don't you go into that business?

It took a while for businesses to implement the marketing concept. That process went slowly during the 1960s and 70s. During the 1980s, businesses began to apply the marketing concept more aggressively than they had done over the preceding 30 years. That led to the focus on customer relationship management (CRM) that has become so important today.[3] We shall explore that concept next.

**The Customer Relationship Era** In the 1990s and early 2000s managers extended the marketing concept by adopting the concept of customer relationship management. **Customer relationship management (CRM)** is the process of learning as much as possible about customers and doing everything you can to satisfy them—or even exceed their expectations—with goods and services over time.[4] The idea is to enhance customer satisfaction and stimulate long-term customer loyalty. For example, most airlines offer frequent-flier programs that reward loyal customers with free flights.[5]

**marketing concept**
A three-part business philosophy: (1) a customer orientation, (2) a service orientation, and (3) a profit orientation.

**customer relationship management (CRM)**
The process of learning as much as possible about customers and doing everything you can to satisfy them—or even exceed their expectations—with goods and services over time.

## Nonprofit Organizations and Marketing

Even though the marketing concept emphasizes a profit orientation, marketing is a critical part of almost all organizations, whether for-profit or nonprofit. Charities use marketing to raise funds (e.g., to combat world hunger) or to obtain other resources. For example, the Red Cross uses promotion to encourage people to donate blood when local or national supplies run low. Greenpeace uses marketing to promote ecologically safe technologies. Churches use marketing to attract new members and to raise funds. Politicians use marketing to get votes.

States use marketing to attract new businesses and tourists. Many states, for example, have competed to get automobile companies from other countries to locate plants in their area. Schools use marketing to attract new students. Other

How can you help protect
the prairie and the penguin?
Simple. Visit www.earthshare.org and learn how the world's leading environmental groups are working together under one name. And how easy it is for you to help protect the prairies and the penguins and the planet.
www.earthshare.org
Ad Council
One environment. One simple way to care for it.
Earth Share


The Ad Council sponsors many such ads as a public service. The idea is to make the public more aware of various needs that are only being met by nonprofit organizations. The public is then encouraged to get involved somehow, if only by sending money. Have you responded to any Ad Council advertisements that you can remember?

organizations, such as arts groups, unions, and social groups, also use marketing. The Advertising Council, for example, uses marketing to create awareness and change attitudes on such issues as drunk driving and fire prevention. Marketing, in fact, is used to promote everything from environmentalism (Save a Whale) and crime prevention (Take a Bite Out of Crime) to social issues (Choose Life). What nonprofit organizations seemed to have the best fund-raising promotions after Hurricanes Katrina and Rita?

## THE MARKETING MIX

Pleasing customers has become a priority for marketers. Much of what marketing people do has been conveniently divided into four factors, called the four Ps to make them easy to remember and implement. They are

1. Product
2. Price
3. Place
4. Promotion

Managing the controllable parts of the marketing process, then, involves (1) designing a want satisfying *product*, (2) setting a *price* for the product, (3) placing the product in a *place* where people will buy it, and (4) *promoting* the product. These four factors are called the **marketing mix** because they are blended together in a marketing program. A marketing manager designs a marketing program that effectively combines the ingredients of the marketing mix (see Figure 13.2). The Dealing with Change box explores how recent changes in the automobile industry have affected the application of the four Ps to that market.

**marketing mix**
The ingredients that go into a marketing program: product, price, place, and promotion.

### Applying the Marketing Process

The four Ps are a convenient way to remember the basics of marketing, but they don't necessarily include everything that goes into the marketing process for all products. One of the best ways for you to understand the entire marketing process is to take a product or a group of products and follow the process that led to their development and sale (see Figure 13.3 on page 354).

Imagine, for example, that you and your friends want to start a moneymaking business near your college. You have noticed that among your friends there are a lot of vegetarians. You do a quick survey in a couple of dorms, sororities and fraternities, and find that there are many vegetarians—and other students who like to eat vegetarian meals once in a while.[6] Your preliminary research indicates that there may be some demand for a vegetarian restaurant nearby. You check the fast-food stores in the area and find that it is very difficult to find more than one or two vegetarian meals at any one restaurant. In fact, most don't have any except salads and some soups.

Further research indicates that there are a number of different kinds of vegetarians. Some (lacto-ovo) eat dairy products and eggs. Others eat dairy products but no eggs (lacto-vegetarian). Vegans eat neither eggs nor dairy products.

DEALING WITH change

## Four Ps Drive Marketing

You can see the four Ps of marketing in action if you closely follow changes that are occurring in the automobile industry. New products are being designed to meet market niches. There are, for example, sports cars designed to compete with the Porsche Boxster and appeal to successful young executives, and sport-utility vehicles (SUVs) for nearly every taste. Pickup trucks have features like four-wheel drive, grocery-bag hooks, and center armrests that double as laptop workstations.

Never before have there been more choices in cars—from small personal cars to large vans to "green" cars that run on a combination of gas and electric power. And in those cars is every conceivable convenience from phones to CD players, cup holders, satellite radio, and global positioning systems. Automobile companies truly seem to be listening to customers and trying to meet their needs. This is the *product* part of the four Ps.

The latest influence on car buying seems to be gas prices. Big SUVs are losing their popularity, and people are choosing to buy hybrids and smaller cars instead. What would happen if gas prices were to fall back to lower prices? When it comes to *pricing*, there is a whole new revolution going on in this industry. On the Web, sites such as Autobytel.com and Autoweb.com provide product and price information and dealer referrals. Customers can thus determine the best price before going to a dealership. To eliminate one of the most annoying parts of buying a car, some dealers are offering no-haggle pricing. One promotional effort is to offer automobiles at employee prices. Thus, you pay the same for a General Motors (GM) car as a GM employee would, or for a Ford as a Ford employee would, and so on.

Getting cars to a *place* that is convenient for customers is also being done by auto Web sites. Autobytel.com and Autoweb.com help customers find the dealer closest to them that will offer the best price for the automobile they choose. Ford and General Motors (GM) are experimenting with Web sites and factory-owned stores. GM's service, called BuyPower, gives consumers access to every vehicle on participating dealers' lots as well as independent data about competing models. Meanwhile, chains such as AutoNation and Car-Max are selling both new and used cars at convenient locations. Consumers can now order almost any car from anywhere in the world via the Internet. The car will be shipped to a nearby port, and all paperwork is handled with ease.

*Promotion* for new and used cars is also changing. Dealers are trying low-pressure salesmanship because they know that customers are now armed with much more information than in the past. More and more power is being shifted to consumers. They can go on the Internet; learn about various cars and their features, including safety features; pick which features they want; get the best price available; and order the car—all without leaving their homes. In such an atmosphere the marketing task shifts from helping the seller sell to helping the buyer buy. Internet sellers make every effort to help buyers find the car that best meets their needs and minimize the hassle involved in getting that car.

Sources: Jennifer Saranow, "Car Dealers Pile on Extra Discounts," *The Wall Street Journal*, September 15, 2005, pp. D1 and D4; Brooke Capps, "Everyone an Employee as GM Spawns Copycats," *Advertising Age*, September 5, 2005, p. 6; Richard J. Newman, "Running on Fumes," *U.S. News and World Report*, July 25, 2005, p. 40; Alan Reynolds, "Car Wars," *Washington Times*, June 12, 2005, p. B1; and Harry Mauer, "Ford's New Look," *BusinessWeek*, February 6, 2006, p. 32.

www.autobytel.com

Marketing manager

Marketing mix

Product

Price

Place

Promotion

figure 13.2

**MARKETING MANAGERS AND THE MARKETING MIX**

Marketing managers must choose how to implement the four Ps of the marketing mix: product, price, place, and promotion. The goals are to please customers and make a profit.

figure 13.3

THE MARKETING PROCESS WITH THE FOUR Ps

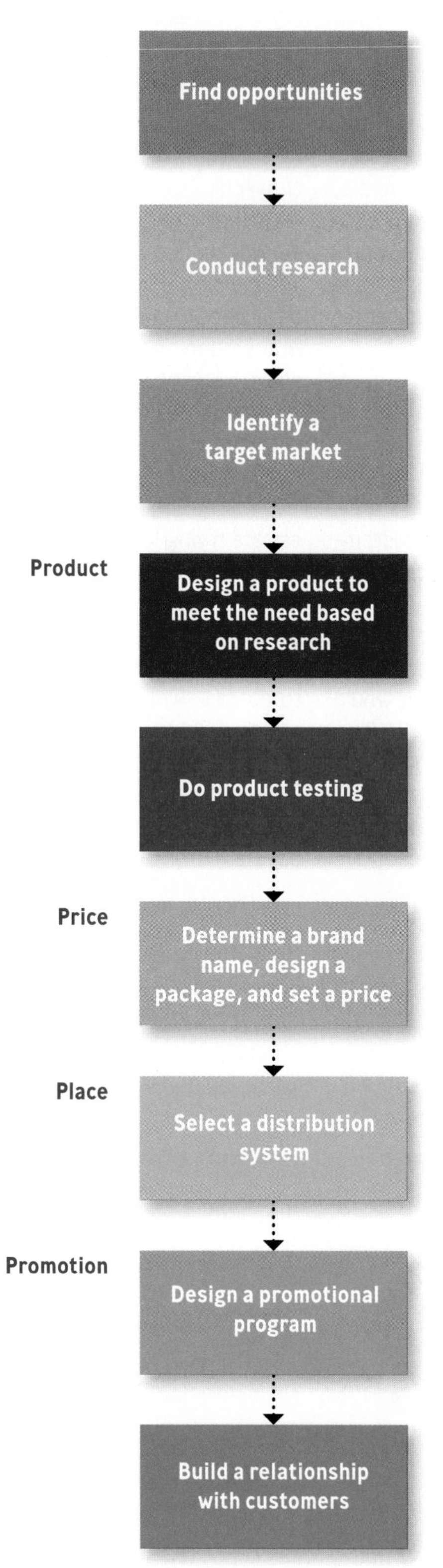


Fruitarians eat mostly raw fruits, grains, and nuts. You conclude that a vegetarian restaurant would have to appeal to all kinds of vegetarians to be a success. Without consciously knowing it, you are performing the first couple of steps in the marketing process. You notice an opportunity (a need for vegetarian food near campus). You also do some preliminary research to see if your idea has any merit at all. And then you identify groups of people who may be very interested in your product. They will be your *target market* (the people you will try to persuade to come to your restaurant).

## Designing a Product to Meet Needs

Once you have researched consumer needs and found a target market (discussed in more detail later) for your product, the four Ps of marketing begin. You start by developing a product or products. A **product** is any physical good, service, or idea that satisfies a want or need plus anything that would enhance the product in the eye of consumers, such as the brand. In this case, your proposed product is a restaurant that would serve different kinds of vegetarian meals.

**product**
Any physical good, service, or idea that satisfies a want or need plus anything that would enhance the product in the eyes of consumers, such as the brand.

It's a good idea at this point to do *concept testing*. That is, you develop an accurate description of your restaurant and ask people, in person or online, whether the concept (the idea of the restaurant and the kind of meals you intend to offer) appeals to them. If it does, you might go to a supplier, like Amy's Kitchen, that makes vegetarian meals to get samples of the products that you take to consumers to test their reactions.[7] The process of testing products among potential users is called **test marketing**.

**test marketing**
The process of testing products among potential users.

If consumers like the product and agree they would buy it, you have the information you need to find investors and to find a convenient location to open a restaurant. You will have to think of a catchy name. (For practice, stop for a minute and try to think of a clever one.) We'll use Very Vegetarian in this text. Meanwhile, let's continue with the discussion of product development.

You may want to offer some well-known brand names to attract people right away. A **brand name** is a word, letter, or group of words or letters that differentiates one seller's goods and services from those of competitors.[8] Brand names of vegetarian products include Tofurky, Mori-Nu, and Yves Veggie Cuisine. We'll

**brand name**
A word, letter, or group of words or letters that differentiates one seller's goods and services from those of competitors.

Kelly Flatley learned in college that her friends "loved" her granola mix. She had found a need. She began making granola in her parent's kitchen and selling it at local markets and sidewalk sales. She named it Bear Naked (bearly processed and utterly naked ingredients). Bear Naked breakfast products can now be found nationwide. The granola is made with real whole grains and has no trans fats, cholesterol, refined sugars, or high fructose corn syrup and is vegetarian friendly. Sound like a good product for Very Vegetarian?

discuss the product development process in detail in Chapter 14. In the following chapters, we will follow the Very Vegetarian case to show you how all marketing and other business decisions tie together. For now, we're simply sketching the whole marketing process to give you an overall picture. So far, we've only covered the first P of the marketing mix: product. Next comes price.

## Setting an Appropriate Price

After you have decided what products and services you want to offer consumers, you have to set appropriate prices.[9] Those prices depend on a number of factors.[10] For example, in the restaurant business, the price could be close to what other restaurants charge to stay competitive. Or you might charge less to attract business, especially at the beginning.[11] Or you may offer high-quality products for which customers are willing to pay a little more (à la Starbucks).[12] You also have to consider the costs involved in producing, distributing, and promoting the product. We shall discuss such pricing issues in more detail in Chapter 14.

## Getting the Product to the Right Place

Once you have opened your restaurant, you have to decide how best to get your products to the consumer. Of course, you can always have people come in, sit down, and eat at the restaurant, but that is not the only alternative, as you have seen with pizza. You could deliver the food to customers' dorms, rooming houses, and other dwelling places. Remember, *place* is the third P in the marketing mix. In addition to having a restaurant, you may want to sell your products to supermarkets or health-food stores, or you may want to sell them through organizations that specialize in distributing food products. Such organizations, called *intermediaries*, are in the middle of a series of organizations that distribute goods from producers to consumers. (The more traditional word for such companies is *middlemen.*) Getting the product to consumers when and where they want it is critical to market success.[13] We'll discuss the importance of marketing intermediaries and distribution in detail in Chapter 15.

## Developing an Effective Promotional Strategy

**promotion**
All the techniques sellers use to motivate people to buy their products or services.

The last of the four Ps of marketing is promotion. **Promotion** consists of all the techniques sellers use to inform people and motivate them to buy their products or services. They include advertising; personal selling; public relations; publicity; word of mouth; and various sales promotion efforts, such as coupons, rebates, samples, and cents-off deals. Promotion is discussed in detail in Chapter 16.

This last step in the marketing process often includes relationship building with customers. That includes responding to suggestions consumers may make to improve the products or their marketing (including price and packaging).[14] Postpurchase, or after-sale, service may include refusing to accept payment for meals that weren't satisfactory and making other adjustments to ensure consumer satisfaction. Marketing is an ongoing process. To remain competitive, companies must continually adapt to changes in the market and to changes in consumer wants and needs. Customers will likely recommend that you stock other vegetarian products that they would like. Listening to customers and responding to their needs is the key to marketing.[15] You don't have to decide every product to carry; your customers will tell you what they want by what they buy and what they request.

**progress assessment**

- What are the three parts of the marketing concept?
- What are the four Ps of the marketing mix?

## Providing Marketers with Information

**marketing research**
The analysis of markets to determine opportunities and challenges, and to find the information needed to make good decisions.

Every step in the marketing process depends on information that is used to make the right decisions. **Marketing research** is the analysis of markets to determine opportunities and challenges, and to find the information needed to make good decisions.

Marketing research helps determine what customers have purchased in the past and what situational changes have occurred to alter not only what consumers want now but also what they're likely to want in the future.[16] In addition, marketers conduct research on business trends, the ecological impact of their decisions, global trends, and more. Businesses need information in order to compete effectively, and marketing research is the activity that gathers that information.[17] Note, too, that in addition to listening to customers, marketing researchers should pay attention to what employees, shareholders, dealers, consumer advocates, media representatives, and other stakeholders have to say.

## The Marketing Research Process

A simplified marketing research process consists of at least four key steps:

1. Defining the question (problem or opportunity) and determining the present situation.
2. Collecting data.
3. Analyzing the research data.
4. Choosing the best solution and implementing it.

The following sections look at each of these steps.

**Defining the Question and Determining the Present Situation** Marketing researchers should be given the freedom to help discover what the present situation is, what the problems or opportunities are, what the alternatives are, what information is needed, and how to go about gathering and analyzing data.

**Collecting Data** Obtaining usable information is vital to the marketing research process. Research can become quite expensive, so some trade-off must often be made between the need for information and the cost of obtaining that information. Normally the least expensive method is to gather information that has already been compiled by others and published in journals and books or made available online. Such existing data are called **secondary data** since you aren't the first one to gather them. Figure 13.4 lists the principal sources of secondary marketing research information. Despite its name, *secondary* data should be gathered *first* to avoid incurring unnecessary expense. To find secondary data about vegetarians, go on the Internet and see what you can find.

**secondary data**
Information that has already been compiled by others and published in journals and books or made available online.

Often, secondary data don't provide all the information managers need for important business decisions. To gather additional, in-depth information, marketers must do their own research. The results of such *new studies* are called **primary data**. One way to gather primary data is to conduct a survey. Telephone surveys, online surveys, mail surveys, and personal interviews are the most common forms. Focus groups (defined below) are another popular method of surveying individuals. What do you think would be the best way to

figure 13.4

**SELECTED SOURCES OF PRIMARY AND SECONDARY INFORMATION**

You should spend a day or two at the library becoming familiar with these sources. You can read about primary research in any marketing research text from the library.

| PRIMARY SOURCES | SECONDARY SOURCES | | |
|---|---|---|---|
| Interviews<br>Surveys<br>Observation<br>Focus groups<br>Online surveys<br>Questionnaires<br>Customer comments<br>Letters from customers | **Government Publications**<br>*Statistical Abstract of the United States*<br>*Survey of Current Business*<br>*Census of Retail Trade* | *Census of Transportation*<br>*Annual Survey of Manufacturers* | |
| | **Commercial Publications**<br>ACNielsen Company studies on retailing and media<br>Marketing Research Corporation of America studies on consumer purchases<br>Selling Areas—Marketing Inc. reports on food sales | | |
| | **Magazines**<br>*Entrepreneur*<br>*BusinessWeek*<br>*Fortune*<br>*Inc.*<br>*Advertising Age*<br>*Forbes*<br>*Harvard Business Review*<br>*Journal of Marketing* | *Journal of Retailing*<br>*Journal of Consumer Research*<br>*Journal of Advertising*<br>*Journal of Marketing Research*<br>*Marketing News* | *Journal of Advertising Research*<br>Trade magazines appropriate to your industry such as *Progressive Grocer*<br>Reports from various chambers of commerce |
| | **Newspapers**<br>*The Wall Street Journal, Barron's* | | |
| | **Internal Sources**<br>Company records<br>Balance sheets | Income statements<br>Prior research reports | |
| | **General Sources**<br>Internet searches<br>Google-type searches | Commercial databases | |

The authors of this text enjoy the benefits of using focus groups. College faculty and students come to these meetings and tell us how to improve this book. We listen carefully and make as many changes as we can in response. Suggestions have included adding these photo essays to the book's pictures and making the text as user-friendly as possible. How are we doing so far?

survey students about your potential new restaurant? Would you do a different kind of survey after you were open for a few months? One question that researchers pay close attention to is this: Would you recommend this product to a friend?[18]

A **focus group** is a small group of people (8 to 14 individuals, for example) who meet under the direction of a discussion leader to communicate their opinions about an organization, its products, or other given issues. This textbook is updated periodically using many focus groups made up of faculty and students. They tell the authors what subjects and examples they like and dislike, and the authors follow their suggestions for changes.

Marketers can now gather both secondary and primary data online. The authors of this text, for example, do much research online, but they also gather data from books, articles, interviews, and other sources.

**Analyzing the Research Data** The data collected in the research process must be turned into useful information. Careful, honest interpretation of the data collected can help a company find useful alternatives to specific marketing challenges.[19] For example, by doing primary research, Fresh Italy, a small Italian pizzeria, found that its pizza's taste was rated superior compared to that of the larger pizza chains. However, the company's sales lagged behind the competition. Secondary research on the industry revealed that free delivery (which Fresh Italy did not offer) was more important to customers than taste. Fresh Italy now delivers—and has increased its market share.

**Choosing the Best Solution and Implementing It** After collecting and analyzing data, market researchers determine alternative strategies and make recommendations as to which strategy may be best and why. This final step in a research effort involves following up on the actions taken to see if the results were as expected. If not, the company can take corrective action and conduct new studies in the ongoing attempt to provide consumer satisfaction at the lowest cost. You can see, then, that marketing research is a continuous process of responding to changes in the marketplace and changes in consumer preferences.[20]

**primary data**
Data that you gather yourself (not from secondary sources such as books and magazines).

**focus group**
A small group of people who meet under the direction of a discussion leader to communicate their opinions about an organization, its products, or other given issues.

In today's customer-driven market, ethics is important in every aspect of marketing. Companies should therefore do what's right as well as what's profitable. This step could add greatly to the social benefits of marketing decisions. (See the Making Ethical Decisions box.)

## The Marketing Environment

**environmental scanning**
The process of identifying the factors that can affect marketing success.

Marketing managers must be aware of the surrounding environment when making marketing mix decisions. **Environmental scanning** is the process of identifying the factors that can affect marketing success. As you can see in Figure 13.5, those factors include global, technological, sociocultural, competitive, and economic influences. We discussed these factors in some detail in Chapter 1, but it is helpful to review them from a strictly marketing perspective as well.

**Global Factors** The most dramatic global change is probably the growth of the Internet.[21] Now businesses can reach many of the consumers in the world relatively easily and carry on a dialogue with them about the goods and

## * * * MAKING ethical decisions

www.kelloggs.com

### No Kidding

Marketers have long recognized that children can be an important influence on their parents' buying decisions. In fact, many direct appeals for products are focused on children. Let's say that you work for a cereal maker that has experienced a great response to a new high-fiber, high-protein cereal among health-conscious adult consumers. The one important group you haven't been able to attract is children. Therefore, the product development team is considering introducing a child-oriented brand to expand the product line.

The new children's cereal may have strong market potential if you follow two recommendations of the research department. First, coat the flakes generously with sugar (significantly changing the cereal's nutritional benefits). Second, promote the product exclusively on children's TV programs. Such a promotional strategy should create a strong demand for the product, especially if you offer a premium (a toy or other surprise) in each box. The consensus among the research department is that kids will love the new taste, plus parents will agree to buy the children's brand because of their positive impression of your best-selling brand. The research director commented, "The chance of a parent actually reading our label and noting the addition of sugar is nil."

Would you introduce the children's cereal following the recommendations of your research department? What are the benefits of doing so? What are the risks involved in following the recommendations? What would you do if you were the marketing manager for this product?

services they want. The Reaching Beyond Our Borders box on page 360 discusses global marketing in more detail. This globalization process puts more pressure on those whose responsibility it is to deliver products. Many marketers outsource that function to companies like FedEx, UPS, and DHL, which have a solid reputation for delivering goods quickly.

**Technological Factors** The most important technological changes also involve the Internet and the growth of consumer databases. Using consumer databases, companies can develop products and services that closely match

figure 13.5

THE MARKETING ENVIRONMENT

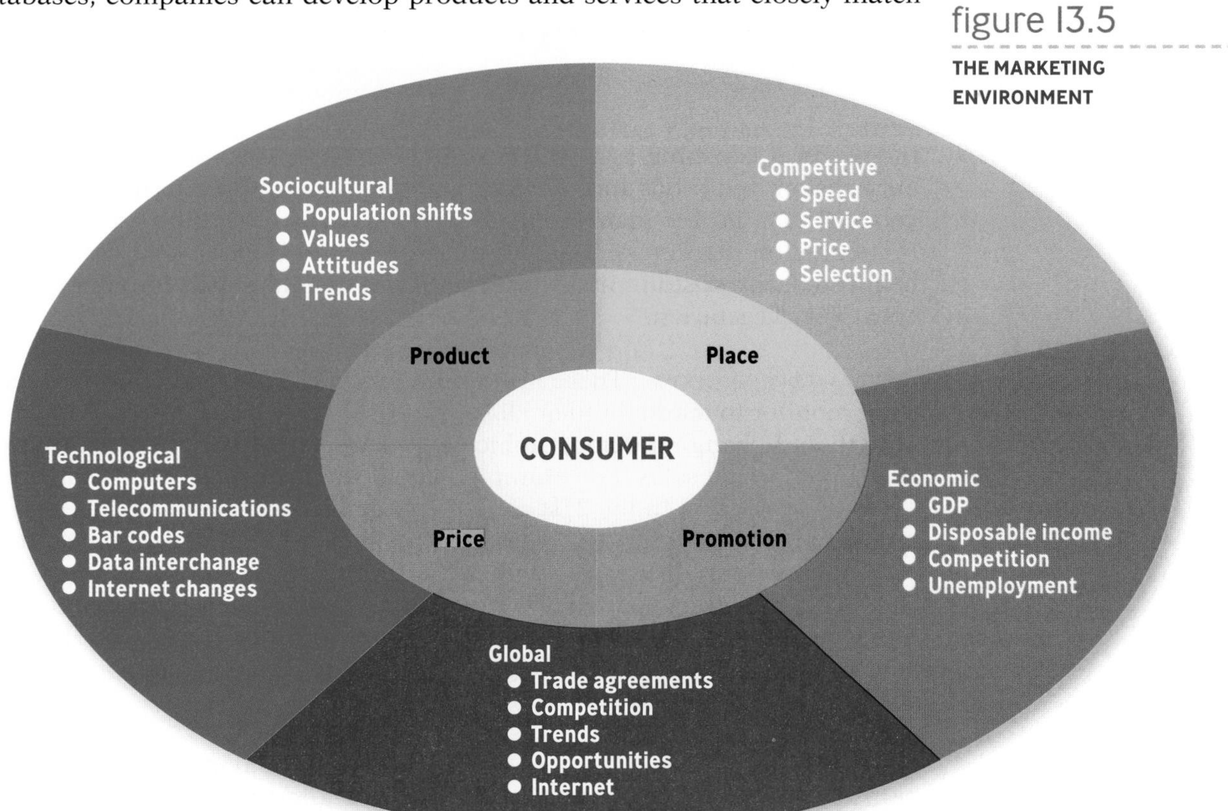

REACHING BEYOND

our borders

## Responding to the Needs of People in Other Countries

Developments in technology, such as the Internet, have led some people to say that the world is "flat." What they mean is that the world is now so integrated economically that companies must think globally as well as locally. It is important to remember that the world is made up of over 6 billion people, and most of them do not live in the United States. Therefore, marketing plans often should include ways to reach global markets. This is especially true in countries like China and India, which have populations of over a billion people.

When the American Chamber of Commerce surveyed companies doing business in China, it learned that some 68 percent of that business was profitable and that 70 percent of the profitable business had margins that exceeded the global average. Motorola says that for many products China will be a larger market than the United States. It is also a huge market for companies like Hewlett-Packard and the auto makers whose markets in the United States are slowing at best.

The secret to success in markets like China and India is to follow *all* the marketing principles outlined in this chapter. That includes listening to customers to determine the unique wants and needs of consumers in other countries. It also means segmenting the market in various ways and developing promotional strategies that are appropriate for each. Haworth Inc., from Holland, Michigan, for example, sells office furniture in China (100,000 chairs and 75,000 work stations each *month*). Showrooms offer free cappuccino and wireless Internet connections. Potential customers can try the ergonomically designed furniture before buying, and the company sends designers and psychologists to companies to create the best workplace environment possible.

Sometimes the need is to develop products to meet the needs of poor people. After all, almost half of the people in the world make less than $2 a day. How do you meet their needs? You may offer creative financing, for one. If the poor can't afford 12 ounces of your product, you might be able to sell them 4 ounces. For those people without electricity, hand-powered products must be developed. As you can see, global marketing is much more than finding markets for already existing products. It is a whole process of learning new cultures, developing products to meet unusual and often unexpected needs, and pricing those products to meet the resources available. Hundreds of Procter & Gamble (P&G) research managers, for example, live with Chinese families in cities and on farms to learn how they use products such as detergents and toothpaste. P&G sells cheaper, more basic versions of Tide and Crest in small villages and cities. Other companies could learn from this example. The potential is awesome. What countries might you enjoy living in while researching the needs of the people?

Sources: Dexter Roberts and Michael Arndt, "It's Getting Hotter in the East," *BusinessWeek*, August 22, 2005, pp. 78–84, C. K. Prahalad, "A New Path to Profit," *Fast Company*, January 2005, pp. 25–26; and John Lancaster, "Building Wealth by the Penny," *Washington Post*, March 14, 2006, p. A13.

the needs of consumers. As you read in Chapter 9, it is now possible to produce customized goods and services for about the same price as mass-produced goods. Thus, flexible manufacturing and mass customization are also major influences on marketers. You can imagine, for example, using databases to help you devise custom-made fruit mixes and various salads for your customers at Very Vegetarian.

**Sociocultural Factors** There are a number of social trends that marketers must monitor to maintain their close relationship with customers. Population growth and changing demographics are examples of social trends that can have an effect on sales. For example, one of the fastest-growing segments of the U.S. population in the 21st century is people over 65. The increase in the number of older Americans creates growing demand for nursing homes, health care, prescription drugs, recreation, continuing education, and more. Other shifts in the American population are creating new challenges for marketers as they adjust their products to meet the tastes and preferences of Hispanic, Asian, and other growing ethnic groups. What might you do to appeal to specific ethnic groups with Very Vegetarian?

**Competitive Factors** Of course, marketers must pay attention to the dynamic competitive environment. Many brick-and-mortar companies must be aware of new competition from the Internet, including those that sell automobiles, insurance, music videos, and clothes. In the book business, Barnes & Noble and Borders Books are still adjusting to the new reality of Amazon.com's huge selection of books at good prices. Now that consumers can literally search the world for the best buys through the Internet, marketers must adjust their pricing policies accordingly. Similarly, they have to adjust to competitors who can deliver products quickly or provide excellent service. Can you see any opportunities for Very Vegetarian to make use of the Internet?

To appeal to diverse ethnic groups, marketers must learn to listen better and be more responsive to unique ethnic needs. What complaints have you heard from your friends from different countries?

**Economic Factors** Marketers must pay close attention to the economic environment. As we began the new millennium, the United States was experiencing unparalleled growth, and customers were eager to buy even the most expensive automobiles, watches, and vacations. But as the economy slowed, marketers had to adapt by offering products that were less expensive and more tailored to consumers with modest incomes. Marketers in countries such as Indonesia had already gone through such an economic fall and are now recovering. You can see, therefore, that environmental scanning is critical to a company's success during rapidly changing economic times. What economic changes are occurring around your school that might affect a new restaurant? Have the war in Iraq and natural disasters affected your area?

## Two Different Markets: Consumer and Business-to-Business (B2B)

Marketers must know as much as possible about the market they wish to serve. As we defined it in Chapter 6, a market consists of people with unsatisfied wants and needs who have both the resources and the willingness to buy. There are two major markets in business: the consumer market and the business-to business market. The **consumer market** consists of all the individuals or households that want goods and services for personal consumption or use and have the resources to buy them. The **business-to-business (B2B) market** consists of all the individuals and organizations that want goods and services to use in producing other goods and services or to sell, rent, or supply goods to others. Oil-drilling bits, cash registers, display cases, office desks, public accounting audits, and business software are examples of B2B goods and services.[22] Traditionally, they have been known as industrial goods and services because they are used in industry.

**consumer market**
All the individuals or households that want goods and services for personal consumption or use.

**business-to-business (B2B) market**
All the individuals and organizations that want goods and services to use in producing other goods and services or to sell, rent, or supply goods to others.

The important thing to remember is that the buyer's reason for buying—that is, the end use of the product—determines whether a product is considered a consumer product or a B2B product. For example, a cup of yogurt bought for a student's breakfast is considered a consumer product. However, if Very Vegetarian purchased the same cup of yogurt to sell to its breakfast customers, the yogurt would then be considered a B2B product. The following sections will outline in more detail consumer and B2B markets.

**progress assessment**

- What are the four steps in the marketing research process?
- What is environmental scanning?
- Can you define the terms *consumer market* and *business-to-business market*?

## THE CONSUMER MARKET

The total potential consumer market consists of the over 6 billion people in global markets. Because consumer groups differ greatly in age, education level, income, and taste, a business usually can't fill the needs of every group. Therefore, it must first decide which groups to serve and then develop products and services specially tailored to their needs.

Take the Campbell Soup Company, for example. You know Campbell for its traditional soups such as chicken noodle and tomato. You may also have noticed that Campbell has expanded its product line to appeal to a number of different tastes. Campbell noticed the population growth in the American South and in the Latino community in cities across the nation, so it introduced a creole soup for the southern market and a red bean soup for the Latino market. In Texas and California, where people like their food with a bit of kick, Campbell makes its nacho cheese soup spicier than in other parts of the country. Campbell is just one company that has had some success studying the consumer market, breaking it down into categories, and then developing products for separate groups of consumers.

**market segmentation**
The process of dividing the total market into groups whose members have similar characteristics.

**target marketing**
Marketing directed toward those groups (market segments) an organization decides it can serve profitably.

The process of dividing the total market into several groups whose members have similar characteristics is called **market segmentation**.[23] Selecting which groups (market segments) an organization can serve profitably is called **target marketing**. For example, a shoe store may choose to sell only women's

What happens when you outgrow the Gap? Gap, Inc. has responded to that question by opening a concept store called Forth & Towne. Its target market is women 35 and older. Such women enjoy the highest income among female shoppers, but had a limited choice of stores where they could buy apparel. Are there groups whose fashion needs are still not being met? How would you describe that target market?

shoes, only children's shoes, or only athletic shoes. The issue is finding the right target market (the segment that would be most profitable to serve) for the new venture. For example, 73 percent of teens use bottled water as opposed to only 43 percent of people over 65.[24] You can see why a company selling water would choose teens as a target market.

## Segmenting the Consumer Market

There are several ways a firm can segment the consumer market (see Figure 13.6). For example, rather than trying to sell a product throughout the United States, you might try to focus on just one or two regions of the country where you might be most successful. One option is to focus on people in southern states such as Florida, Texas, and North Carolina. Dividing the market by geographic area (cities, counties, states, regions, etc.) is called **geographic segmentation**.

Alternatively, you could aim your product's promotions toward people ages 25 to 45 who have some college training and have above-average incomes. Automobiles such as Lexus are often targeted to this audience. Segmentation by

**geographic segmentation** Dividing the market by geographic area.

figure 13.6

**MARKET SEGMENTATION**

This table shows some of the methods marketers use to divide the market. The aim of segmentation is to break the market into smaller units.

| MAIN DIMENSION | SAMPLE VARIABLES | TYPICAL SEGMENTS |
|---|---|---|
| Geographic segmentation | Region | Northeast, Midwest, South, West |
| | City or county size | Under 5,000; 5,000–10,999; 20,000–49,000; 50,000–99,999 |
| | Density | Urban, suburban, rural |
| Demographic segmentation | Gender | Male, female |
| | Age | Under 5; 5–10; 11–18; 19–34; 35–49; 50–64; 65 and over |
| | Education | Some high school or less, high school graduate, some college, college graduate, postgraduate |
| | Race | Caucasian, African American, Indian, Asian, Hispanic |
| | Nationality | American, Asian, Eastern European, Japanese |
| | Life stage | Infant, preschool, child, teenager, collegiate, adult, senior |
| | Income | Under $15,000; $15,000–$24,999; $25,000–$44,999; $45,000–$74,999; $75,000 and over |
| | Household size | 1; 2; 3–4; 5 or more |
| | Occupation | Professional, technical, clerical, sales supervisors, farmers, students, home based business owners, retired, unemployed |
| Psychographic segmentation | Personality | Gregarious, compulsive, extroverted, aggressive, ambitious |
| | Values | Actualizers, fulfillers, achievers, experiencers, believers, strivers, makers, strugglers |
| | Lifestyle | Upscale, moderate |
| Benefit segmentation | Comfort | (Benefit segmentation divides an already established market into smaller, more homogeneous segments. Those people who desire economy in a car would be an example. The benefit desired varies by product.) |
| | Convenience | |
| | Durability | |
| | Economy | |
| | Health | |
| | Luxury | |
| | Safety | |
| | Status | |
| Volume segmentation | Usage | Heavy users, light users, nonusers |
| | Loyalty status | None, medium, strong |

**demographic segmentation**
Dividing the market by age, income, and education level.

**psychographic segmentation**
Dividing the market using the group's values, attitudes, and interests.

**benefit segmentation**
Dividing the market by determining which benefits of the product to talk about.

**volume, or usage, segmentation**
Dividing the market by usage (volume of use).

age, income, and education level are ways of **demographic segmentation**. Also included are religion, race, and profession. This is the most used segmentation variable, but not necessarily the best.

You may want your ads to portray a group's lifestyle. To do that, you could study the group's lifestyle, values, attitudes, and interests. This segmentation strategy is called **psychographic segmentation**.[25] For example, if you decide to target Generation Y, you would do an in-depth study of their values and interests. Such research reveals which TV shows they watch and which actors they like the best. That information could then be used to develop advertisements for those TV shows using those stars. PepsiCo did such a segmentation study for its Mountain Dew brand. The resulting promotion dealt with Generation Y's living life to the limit.

In marketing for Very Vegetarian, what benefits of vegetarianism might you talk about? Should you emphasize freshness, heart-healthiness, taste, or what? Determining which benefits are preferred and using those benefits to promote a product is called **benefit segmentation**.

You can also determine who are the big eaters of vegetarian food. Does your restaurant seem to attract more men or more women? More students or more faculty members? Separating the market by usage (volume of product use) is called **volume, or usage, segmentation**. You may be surprised to find that repeat customers come from the local community or are commuters. Once you know who your customer base is, you can design your promotions to better appeal to that specific group or groups.

The best segmentation strategy is to use all the variables to come up with a consumer profile (a target market) that's sizable, reachable, and profitable. On the one hand, that may mean not segmenting the market at all and instead going after the total market (everyone). On the other hand, it may mean going after smaller and smaller segments. We'll discuss that strategy next.

## Reaching Smaller Market Segments

**niche marketing**
The process of finding small but profitable market segments and designing or finding products for them.

**one-to-one marketing**
Developing a unique mix of goods and services for each individual customer.

**Niche marketing** is the process of finding small but profitable market segments and designing or finding products for them. Just how small such a segment can be is illustrated by Fridgedoor.com. This company sells refrigerator magnets on the Internet. It keeps some 1,500 different magnets in stock and sells as many as 400 a week.

**One-to-one marketing** means developing a unique mix of goods and services for *each individual customer.* Travel agencies often develop such packages, including airline reservations, hotel reservations, rental cars, restaurants, and admission to museums and other attractions for individual customers. This is relatively easy to do in B2B markets where each customer may buy in huge volume. But one-to-one marketing is now becoming possible in consumer markets as well.[26] Dell provides a unique computer system for each customer. Automakers are starting to customize cars as well. Can you envision designing special Very Vegetarian menu items for individual customers?

## Moving toward Relationship Marketing

**mass marketing**
Developing products and promotions to please large groups of people.

In the world of mass production following the Industrial Revolution, marketers responded by practicing mass marketing. **Mass marketing** means developing products and promotions to please large groups of people. That is, there is little segmentation. The mass marketer tries to sell products to as many people as possible. That means using mass media, such as TV, radio, and newspapers. Although mass marketing led many firms to success, marketing

SPOTLIGHT ON small business

www.zanescycles.com

## Marketing Helps Small Firms Compete

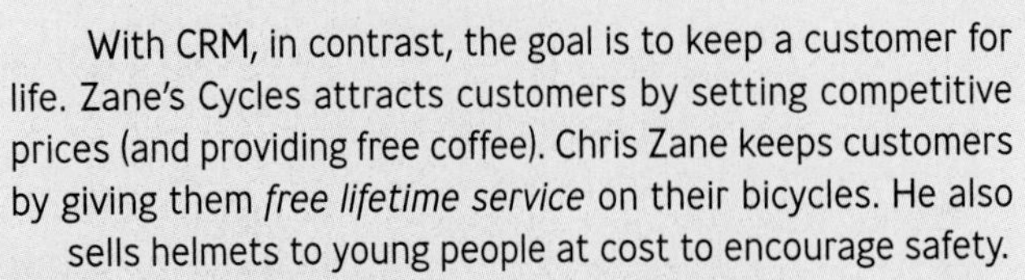

Putting into practice old marketing techniques has enabled small retailers to compete with the giants such as Wal-Mart and Sears. Zane's Cycles in Branford, Connecticut, is a good example. Chris Zane, the owner, began the shop when he was still a teenager. Early on, he learned that to keep customers a store has to offer outstanding service and more. The principle behind such service is a concept now called customer relationship management (CRM). Long before such a concept emerged, however, small stores knew that the secret to long-term success against giant competitors is to give superior service.

Most large stores focus on making the sale; they give follow-up service little thought. The goal is to make the transaction, and that is the end of it; thus, such an approach is called *transactional marketing.*

With CRM, in contrast, the goal is to keep a customer for life. Zane's Cycles attracts customers by setting competitive prices (and providing free coffee). Chris Zane keeps customers by giving them *free lifetime service* on their bicycles. He also sells helmets to young people at cost to encourage safety.

Zane keeps a database on customers so that he knows what they need and when they will need it. For example, if he sells a bicycle with a child's seat, he knows that soon the customer who purchased that bike may be buying a regular bicycle for the child—and he can send out an appropriate brochure at just the right time. Zane encourages people to give him their names, addresses, and other such information by offering to make exchanges without receipts for those people whose transaction information is in the database.

Zane also establishes close community relationships by providing scholarships for local students. Because of Zane's competitive prices, great service, and community involvement, his customers recommend his shop to others. No large store can compete with Zane's in the areas of friendly service and personal attention to each customer. That is what the new style of marketing is all about. Are there stores in your area that offer such great service that they can compete successfully with giant department stores and national chains?

managers often got so caught up with their products and competition that they became less responsive to the market. Airlines, for example, got so caught up in meeting competition that they often annoyed customers.

**Relationship marketing** tends to lead away from mass production and toward custom-made goods and services. The goal is to keep individual customers over time by offering them new products that exactly meet their requirements. The Spotlight on Small Business box shows how a small business can compete with larger firms by using relationship marketing. The latest in technology enables sellers to work with individual buyers to determine their wants and needs and to develop goods and services specifically designed for them (e.g., hand-tailored shirts and unique vacations). One-way messages in mass media give way to a personal dialogue among participants. Relationship marketing, combined with enterprise resource planning (ERP), links firms in

**relationship marketing**
Marketing strategy with the goal of keeping individual customers over time by offering them products that exactly meet their requirements.

a smooth customer-oriented system. The following are just a couple of examples of relationship marketing:

- Airlines, rental car companies, and hotels have frequent-user programs through which loyal customers can earn special services and awards. For example, a traveler can earn bonus miles good for free flights on an airline. He or she can also earn benefits at a car rental agency (that includes no stopping at the rental desk—just pick up a car and go) and special services at a hotel, including faster check-in and check-out procedures, flowers in the room, free breakfasts, and free exercise rooms.
- The Hard Rock Cafe used customer relationship management software to launch a loyalty program, personalize its marketing campaigns, and provide the contact center with more customer information. The result was that response times to customer inquiries were cut from a week to 24 hours. Can you imagine having a loyalty program at Very Vegetarian? What kind of specials might you offer?

## The Consumer Decision-Making Process

A major part of the marketing discipline is called consumer behavior. Figure 13.7 shows the consumer decision-making process and some of the outside factors that influence it. The five steps in the process are often studied in courses on consumer behavior. Problem recognition may occur, say, when your washing machine breaks down. This leads to an information search—you look for ads about washing machines and read brochures about them. You may even consult a secondary data source like *Consumer Reports* or other information sources. And, most likely, you will seek advice from other people who have purchased washing machines. After compiling all this information, you evaluate alternatives and make a purchase decision. But the process does not end here. After the purchase, you may first ask the people you spoke to previously how their machines perform and then do other comparisons. Marketing researchers investigate consumer thought processes and behavior at each stage to determine the best way to facilitate marketing exchanges.

Consumer behavior researchers also study the various influences that impact on consumer behavior. Figure 13.7 shows several such influences that affect consumer buying: marketing mix variables (the four Ps); psychological influences, such as perception and attitudes; situational influences, such as the type of purchase and the physical surroundings; and sociocultural influences, such as reference groups and culture. Other factors important in the consumer decision-making process whose technical definitions may be unfamiliar to you include the following:

- *Learning* involves changes in an individual's behavior resulting from previous experiences and information. For example, if you've tried a particular brand of shampoo and you don't like it, you may never buy it again.
- *Reference group* is the group that an individual uses as a reference point in the formation of his or her beliefs, attitudes, values, or behavior. For example, a college student who carries a briefcase instead of a backpack may see businesspeople as his or her reference group.
- *Culture* is the set of values, attitudes, and ways of doing things that is transmitted from one generation to another in a given society. The American culture, for example, emphasizes education, freedom, and diversity.

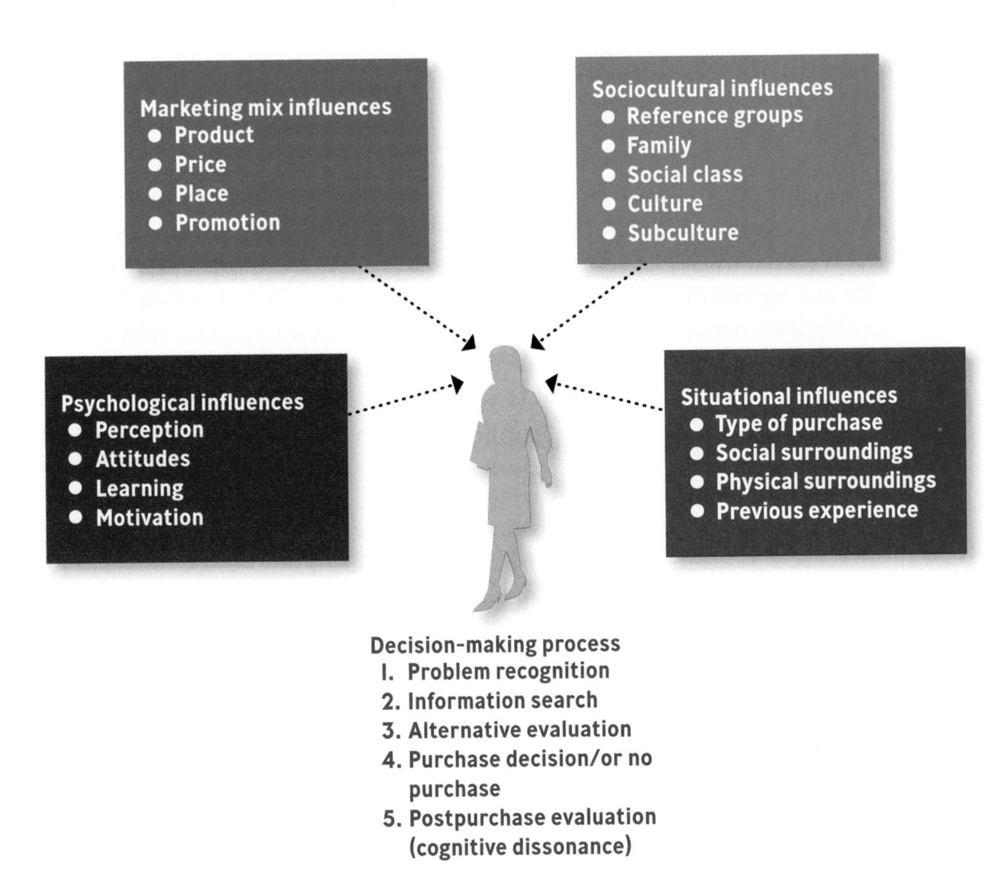


figure 13.7

**THE CONSUMER DECISION-MAKING PROCESS AND OUTSIDE INFLUENCES**

There are many influences on consumers as they decide which goods and services to buy. Marketers have some influence, but it's not usually as strong as sociocultural influences. Helping consumers in their information search and their evaluation of alternatives is a major function of marketing.

- *Subculture* is the set of values, attitudes, and ways of doing things that results from belonging to a certain ethnic group, religious group, racial group, or other group with which one closely identifies (e.g., teenagers). The subculture is one small part of the larger culture. Your subculture may prefer rap and hip-hop music, while your parents' subculture may prefer light jazz.
- *Cognitive dissonance* is a type of psychological conflict that can occur after a purchase. Consumers who make a major purchase like a car may have doubts about whether they got the best product at the best price. Marketers must therefore reassure such consumers after the sale that they made a good decision. An auto dealer, for example, may send positive press articles about the particular car a consumer purchased. The dealer may also offer product guarantees and provide certain free services to the customer.

Consumer behavior courses are a long-standing part of a marketing curriculum. Today, colleges are expanding their offerings in marketing to include courses in business-to-business marketing. The following section will give you some insight into that growing and important area.

## THE BUSINESS-TO-BUSINESS MARKET

Business-to-business (B2B) marketers include manufacturers; intermediaries such as retailers; institutions (e.g., hospitals, schools, and charities); and the government.[27] The B2B market is larger than the consumer market because items are often sold and resold several times in the B2B process before they are sold to the final consumer. The marketing strategies often differ from consumer marketing because business buyers have their own decision-making process. Several factors make B2B marketing different; some of the more important are as follows:

1. The number of customers in the B2B market is relatively few; that is, there are just a few construction firms or mining operations compared to the 70 million or so households in the U.S. consumer market.
2. The size of business customers is relatively large; that is, a few large organizations account for most of the employment and production of various goods and services. Nonetheless, there are many small to medium-sized firms in the United States that together make an attractive market.
3. B2B markets tend to be geographically concentrated. For example, oilfields tend to be concentrated in the Southwest and in Alaska. Consequently, marketing efforts may be concentrated on a particular geographic area and distribution problems can be minimized by locating warehouses near industrial centers.
4. Business buyers are generally thought to be more rational (as opposed to emotional) than ultimate consumers in their selection of goods and services; they use specifications and often more carefully weigh the total product offer, including quality, price, and service.
5. B2B sales tend to be direct, but not always. Manufacturers sell products, such as tires, directly to auto manufacturers but tend to use intermediaries, such as wholesalers and retailers, to sell to ultimate consumers.
6. There is much more emphasis on personal selling in B2B markets than in consumer markets. Whereas consumer promotions are based more on advertising, B2B sales are based on selling. That is because there are fewer customers who demand more personal service.

Figure 13.8 shows some of the differences between buying behavior in the B2B market compared to the consumer market. You will learn all about the business-to-business market if you take advanced marketing courses.

figure 13.8

**COMPARING BUSINESS-TO-BUSINESS AND CONSUMER BUYING BEHAVIOR**

| | BUSINESS-TO-BUSINESS MARKET | CONSUMER MARKET |
|---|---|---|
| **Market Structure** | Relatively few potential customers | Many potential customers |
| | Larger purchases | Smaller purchases |
| | Geographically concentrated | Geographically dispersed |
| **Products** | Require technical, complex products | Require less technical products |
| | Frequently require customization | Sometimes require customization |
| | Frequently require technical advice, delivery, and after-sale service | Sometimes require technical advice, delivery, and after-sale service |
| **Buying Procedures** | Buyers are trained | No special training |
| | Negotiate details of most purchases | Accept standard terms for most purchases |
| | Follow objective standards | Use personal judgment |
| | Formal process involving specific employees | Informal process involving household members |
| | Closer relationships between marketers and buyers | Impersonal relationships between marketers and consumers |
| | Often buy from multiple sources | Rarely buy from multiple sources |

## YOUR PROSPECTS IN MARKETING

There is a wider variety of careers in marketing than in most business disciplines. Therefore, if you were to major in marketing, an array of career options would be available to you. You could become a manager in a retail store like Saks or Target. You could do marketing research or get involved in product management. You could go into selling, advertising, sales promotion, or public relations. You could get involved in transportation, storage, or international distribution. You could design interactive Web sites to implement CRM. These are just a few of the possibilities. As you read through the following marketing chapters, consider whether a marketing career would interest you.

### progress assessment

- Can you name and describe five ways to segment the consumer market?
- What is niche marketing, and how does it differ from one-to-one marketing?
- What are four key factors that make industrial markets different from consumer markets?

## summary

1. Define *marketing* and explain how the marketing concept applies in both for-profit and nonprofit organizations.

1. Marketing is the process of determining customer wants and needs and then providing customers with goods and services that meet or exceed their expectations.
   - **How has marketing changed over time?**
   During the *production era*, marketing was largely a distribution function. Emphasis was on producing as many goods as possible and getting them to markets. By the early 1920s, during the *selling era*, the emphasis turned to selling and advertising to persuade customers to buy the existing goods produced by mass production. After World War II, the tremendous demand for goods and services led to the *marketing concept era*, when businesses recognized the need to be responsive to customers' needs. During the 1990s, marketing entered the *customer relationship era*. The idea became one of trying to enhance customer satisfaction and stimulate long-term customer loyalty.
   - **What are the three parts of the marketing concept?**
   The three parts of the marketing concept are (1) a customer orientation, (2) a service orientation, and (3) a profit orientation (that is, market those goods and services that will earn the firm a profit and enable it to survive and expand to serve more customer wants and needs).
   - **What kinds of organizations are involved in marketing?**
   All kinds of organizations use marketing, including both for-profit and nonprofit organizations (states, charities, churches, politicians, schools, etc.).

2. List and describe the four Ps of marketing.

2. The marketing mix consists of the four Ps of marketing: product, price, place, and promotion.
   - **How do marketers implement the four Ps?**
   The idea is to design a *product* that people want, *price* it competitively, *place* it in a location where consumers can find it easily, and *promote* it so that consumers know it exists.

**3.** Describe the marketing research process, and explain how marketers use environmental scanning to learn about the changing marketing environment.

3. Marketing research is the analysis of markets to determine opportunities and challenges and to find the information needed to make good decisions.
   - **What are the steps to follow when conducting marketing research?**

   (1) Define the problem and determine the present situation, (2) collect data, (3) analyze the research data, and (4) choose the best solution.
   - **What is environmental scanning?**

   Environmental scanning is the process of identifying the factors that can affect marketing success. Marketers pay attention to all the environmental factors that create opportunities and threats.
   - **What are some of the more important environmental trends in marketing?**

   The most important global and technological change is probably the growth of the Internet. An important technological change is the growth of consumer databases. Using consumer databases, companies can develop products and services that closely match the needs of consumers. There are a number of social trends that marketers must monitor to maintain their close relationship with customers—population growth and shifts, for example. Of course, marketers must also monitor the dynamic competitive environment and pay attention to the economic environment.

**4.** Explain how marketers meet the needs of the consumer market through market segmentation, relationship marketing, and the study of consumer behavior.

4. The process of dividing the total market into several groups whose members have similar characteristics is called market segmentation.
   - **What are some of the ways marketers segment the consumer market?**

   *Geographic segmentation* means dividing the market into different regions. Segmentation by age, income, and education level are ways of *demographic segmentation.* We could study a group's values, attitudes, and interests; this segmentation strategy is called *psychographic segmentation.* Determining which benefits customers prefer and using those benefits to promote a product is called *benefit segmentation.* Separating the market by usage (volume of use) is called *volume segmentation.* The best segmentation strategy is to use all the variables to come up with a consumer profile (a target market) that's sizable, reachable, and profitable.
   - **What is the difference between mass marketing and relationship marketing?**

   Mass marketing means developing products and promotions to please large groups of people. Relationship marketing tends to lead away from mass production and toward custom-made goods and services. Its goal is to keep individual customers over time by offering them products or services that meet their needs.
   - **What are some of the factors that influence the consumer decision-making process?**

   See Figure 13.7 on page 367 for some of the major influences on consumer decision making. Some other factors in the process are learning, reference group, culture, subculture, and cognitive dissonance.

**5.** List ways in which the business-to-business market differs from the consumer market.

5. The B2B market consists of manufacturers, intermediaries such as retailers, institutions (e.g., hospitals, schools, and charities), and the government.
   - **What makes the business-to-business market different from the consumer market?**

   The number of customers in the B2B market is relatively small, and the size of business customers is relatively large. B2B markets tend to be geographically concentrated, and industrial buyers generally are more rational than ultimate consumers in their selection of goods and services. B2B sales tend to be direct, and there is much more emphasis on personal selling in B2B markets than in consumer markets.

## key terms

**benefit segmentation** 364
**brand name** 354
**business-to-business (B2B) market** 361
**consumer market** 361
**customer relationship management (CRM)** 351
**demographic segmentation** 364
**environmental scanning** 358
**focus group** 358
**geographic segmentation** 363
**marketing** 350
**marketing concept** 351
**marketing mix** 352
**marketing research** 356
**market segmentation** 362
**mass marketing** 364
**niche marketing** 364
**one-to-one marketing** 364
**primary data** 358
**product** 354
**promotion** 355
**psychographic segmentation** 364
**relationship marketing** 365
**secondary data** 357
**target marketing** 362
**test marketing** 354
**volume, or usage, segmentation** 364

## critical thinking questions

1. Which of your needs are not being met by businesses and/or nonprofit organizations in your area? Are there enough people with similar needs to attract an organization that would meet those needs? How would you find out?

2. When businesses buy goods and services from other businesses, they usually buy in large volume. Salespeople in the business-to-business area usually are paid on a commission basis; that is, they earn a certain percentage of each sale they make. Can you see why B2B sales may be a more financially rewarding career area than consumer sales? Industrial companies sell goods such as steel, lumber, computers, engines, parts, and supplies. Where would you find the names of such companies?

3. What environmental changes are occurring in your community? What environmental changes in marketing are most likely to change your career prospects in the future? How can you learn more about those changes? What might you do to prepare for them?

## developing workplace skills

1. Think of an effective marketing mix for one of the following goods and services: a new electric car, an easy-to-use digital camera, or a car wash for your neighborhood. Be prepared to discuss your ideas in class.

2. Working in teams of five (or on your own if class size is a problem), think of a product or service that your friends want but cannot get on or near campus. You might ask your friends at other schools what's available there. What kind of product would fill that need? Discuss your results in class and how you might go about marketing that new product.

3. Relationship marketing efforts include frequent-flier deals at airlines, special discounts for members at certain supermarkets (e.g., Safeway), and Web sites that keep track of what you've purchased and recommend new

products that you may like (e.g., Amazon.com). Evaluate any one of these programs (if you have no personal experience with them, look up such programs on the Internet). What might they do to increase your satisfaction and loyalty? Be prepared to discuss these programs in class.

4. Working in teams of four or five (or on your own if teams are difficult to form), list as many brand names of pizza as you can, including brands from pizza shops, restaurants, supermarkets, and so on. Merge your list with the lists from other groups. Then try to identify the "target market" for each brand. Do they all seem to be after the same market or are there different brands for different markets? What are the separate appeals?

5. Take a little time to review the concepts in this chapter as they apply to Very Vegetarian, the restaurant used as an example throughout. Have an open discussion in class about (*a*) a different name for the restaurant, (*b*) a location for the restaurant, (*c*) a promotional program, and (*d*) a way to establish a long-term relationship with customers.

## taking it to the net

**Purpose**

To demonstrate how the Internet can be used to enhance relationship marketing.

**Exercise**

Nike wants to help its customers add soul to their soles and express their individuality by customizing their own shoes. See for yourself at www.nike.com. Click on Customize and build a shoe that fits your style.

1. What if you're in the middle of your shoe design and have questions about what to do next? Where can you go for help?
2. How does Nike's Web site help the company strengthen its relationships with its stakeholders? Give examples to support your answer.
3. How do the elements of the Web site reflect Nike's target market?
4. Does Nike invite comments from visitors to its Web site? If so, how does this affect its attempt to build positive relationships with its customers?

## casing the web

To access the case *"Customer-Oriented Marketing Concepts at Thermos,"* visit **www.mhhe.com/ub8e**

## video case

### MTV Goes Everywhere

Marketing begins and ends with the customer. Nowhere is that more true than at MTV. They serve many market segments, but two of the most important to them are the high-school age audience and the college audience. Nothing is more dynamic than these two groups. They adopt new ideas and new products faster than movie stars change spouses. That's why MTV has people on campuses listening and responding to the latest trends, wants, and needs. One result is Urge, an online music subscription service for pre-college students. Another online subscription service, University, does many of the same things as Urge, but for university students. The competition is stiff, so MTV has to offer the right kinds of music and be ready to react to new trends. The four Ps of marketing: product, place, promotion, and price all come into play.

The product is not fixed. Students can develop their own products and work with MTV to make them available to others. The best place to be is everywhere. Today, that means online. But it also includes offering a cable channel, mtvU.com, and various events. The most effective promotions include word-of-mouth marketing, or viral marketing as it's known today. The price has to be competitive, and that's a moving target. Right now, you can buy tracks one at a time for 99 cents, buy an album, or subscribe to a service that provides whatever you want.

Music marketers must understand consumer behavior better than most marketers because the market is so specialized. That means understanding the culture(s) of high-school listeners, the culture of college listeners, and the multiple cultures that exist in different parts of the country and different areas within a city. Sometimes it is easier to let each group make its own videos and music and then help them to spread that new material to different audiences. That's exactly what MTV does. Students like to explore, and MTV provides the means to do that.

This chapter emphasizes relationship building. MTV does everything it can to establish and maintain a close relationship not only with its customers but with its performers as well. There are many stakeholders in the music business, and MTV must listen and respond to all of them. That includes performers, young listeners, college-age customers, parents, and people throughout the world.

Like the authors of this text, the people at MTV conduct periodic focus groups to determine how well they are serving their customer groups. When a new idea like the Digital Incubator comes up, there is a great need to work with various groups to get the service down right. When you give out $25,000 to a group to create something new, you want the product to be one that people will enjoy. That means listening, responding, and listening again.

MTV provides composition courses to teach young people how to create music. By establishing relationships with the music producers of tomorrow, MTV assures itself of being relevant for years to come. When exploring the dynamic world of marketing, no company provides a better example of relationship marketing than MTV. Many students dream of working in the music industry when they graduate. They may find, however, that there are equally interesting marketing jobs in other industries as well. That includes, of course, sports marketing and event marketing of all kinds.

### Thinking It Over

1. There are many ways that MTV tries to reach the college audience. What are some of the ways that members of your class have interacted with the company? Are they familiar with Urge, University, and the various events that MTV sponsors? Who are the most important competitors?
2. Does the move from selling music digitally rather than on physical products represent a change that will be affecting other industries? What trends do you see on campus that affect the music industry and other industries as well?
3. On a scale of 1 to 10, how would you rate the efforts that MTV have made to reach you and your friends? What mistakes are they making, if any? Are there other stakeholders whose needs are not being met?

# developing and pricing products AND services

*

profile

**Getting to Know**

**X Bill and Vieve Gore**

**of W. L. Gore & Associates**

You are probably familiar with Gore-Tex, generally found in sportswear and outdoor apparel, and how effective it is in keeping you free from rain and cold. W. L. Gore & Associates is perhaps most famous for its Gore-Tex fabric and insulation, but when Bill and Vieve (short for Genevieve) Gore started the company in 1958, they were not into fabrics. They made wire and cable insulated with a polymer called polytetrafluoro-ethylene. Bill had worked at DuPont, where the polymer was known as Teflon, a name you have probably seen on pots and pans. The Gores' son, Bob, a sophomore at the University of Delaware at the time, had suggested insulating wire with Teflon, and Bill took the idea back to DuPont. When DuPont passed on the idea, Bill bought the patent. He and Vieve then started their company in the basement of their home.

Bill and Vieve set about establishing a company culture that would be fun and at the same time encourage innovation and individual freedom. At Gore, there are no employees; there are associates. Bill Gore frequently referred to the company simply as "the Associates." The company encourages associates to spend some of their time, about 10 percent typically, on new ideas. A story of guitar strings illustrates the company's innovative climate and its freedom to experiment. In 1993, engineer and Gore associate Dave Meyers found a way to improve bike cables and developed the Ride-On brand. That led him to try to improve the cables that control the movements of large animated puppets. He needed small diameters, so he tried coating guitar strings. That led him to wonder if he could make a better guitar string. Not a musician himself, he sought help from another associate; they worked for two years on the project, but without success. A third colleague heard of their efforts, and the three associates persuaded half a dozen others to join them. Finally, three years after beginning, Meyer and his team were ready to seek the support of the larger company to consider marketing the new product. The result, Elixir, was the first major improvement in the field in three decades and has become the top-selling acoustic guitar string.

Gore now has factories and offices in Europe, Asia, South America, and Australia. Gore's products have been to the moon with NASA, to the tops of mountains, and to the poles of the Earth. Gore-Tex products are used by bikers, hikers, and runners. The company also makes filters, seals, and vents for all sorts of industries. It makes fabrics and stents that are used by surgeons to repair the human body. It also still makes wires,

LEARNING **goals**

After you have read and studied this chapter, you should be able to

1. Explain the concept of a total product offer.
2. Describe the various kinds of consumer and industrial goods.
3. List and describe the functions of packaging.
4. Describe the differences among a brand, a brand name, and a trademark, and explain the concepts of brand equity and brand loyalty.
5. Explain the role of brand managers and the steps of the new-product development process.
6. Draw the product life cycle, describe each of its stages, and describe marketing strategies at each stage.
7. Explain various pricing objectives and strategies.
8. Explain why nonpricing strategies are growing in importance.

CHAPTER 14

www.gore.com

cables, and several hundred other products, including dental floss.

W. L. Gore & Associates was ranked second overall on *Fortune* magazine's 2005 list of the 100 best companies to work for, and first among midsized companies. In the United Kingdom, it was named number one in 2004 and 2005 among the 100 best places to work in the United Kingdom. It was also highly ranked on similar lists in Germany and Italy. In 2004, *Fast Company* magazine named Gore the most innovative company in America.

This chapter is all about developing and pricing new products and services. In the future, the companies that thrive will be the ones that offer new, exciting products like the ones developed by the Gores.

Sources: Chris Markham, "Full Bore at Gore," *Arizona Daily Sun*, January 23, 2005; Alan Deutschman, "What I Know Now," *Fast Company*, September 1, 2005; Alan Deutschman, "The Fabric of Creativity," *Fast Company*, December 2004; "Looking after Their Staff Pays Off for Firm," *Glasgow Daily Record*, March 4, 2005; Ann Harrington, "Hall of Fame," *Fortune*, January 24, 2005; www.gore.com; and Bruce Nussbaum, "Davos Will Be Different," *BusinessWeek*, January 23, 2006, p. 96.

## PRODUCT DEVELOPMENT AND THE TOTAL PRODUCT OFFER

**value**
Good quality at a fair price. When consumers calculate the value of a product, they look at the benefits and then subtract the cost to see if the benefits exceed the costs.

Bill Gore knows that global competition today is so strong that American businesses could lose some part of the market to foreign producers if they are not careful. The only way to prevent such losses is to design and promote better products, meaning products that are perceived to have the best **value**—good quality at a fair price.[1] When consumers calculate the value of a product, they look at the benefits and then subtract the cost to see if the benefits exceed the costs. As we'll see in this chapter, whether consumers perceive a product as the best value depends on many factors, including the benefits they seek and the service they receive. To satisfy consumers, marketers must learn to listen better than they do now and to adapt constantly to changing market demands.[2] For example, traditional phone companies must now learn to adapt to Voice over Internet Protocol (VoIP)—a system that allows people to make phone calls over the Internet.[3] Managers must also constantly adapt to price challenges from competitors.[4] VoIP, for example, is much cheaper than traditional phone services. The Dealing with Change box looks at Panera Bread and how it has changed over time to respond to consumer desires.

McDonald's and other marketers have learned that adapting products to new competition and new markets is an ongoing necessity.[5] An organization can't do a one-time survey of consumer wants and needs, design a group of products to meet those needs, put them in the stores, and then just relax. It must constantly monitor changing consumer wants and needs, and adapt products, policies, and services accordingly.[6] That's why many of the McDonald's stores in France look nothing like those in the United States. Half of the 932 French stores have been upgraded, using at least eight different themes, such as "Mountain." Such stores have a wood-beam ceiling, like a ski chalet. Elsewhere, McDonald's is adding Golden Arches Hotels to its list of products. Two such hotels have been built in western Switzerland. In China, McDonald's

How would you like a beer or glass of wine with your Big Mac? You can get both at this McDonald's in Paris. Also, notice how this McDonald's restaurant in Paris fits into the architectural scheme of the city. The same is true of the menu in McDonald's restaurants in countries other than the United States. In Europe, McDonald's frequently adapts its menus and interior restaurant designs to fit into the taste and cultural demands of each country.

## DEALING WITH change

### Making Bread Making Bread

You may not have a Panera Bread in your town, but just wait. The company now has over 700 stores, about a third of which are company owned and the rest franchised. Panera is one of the hottest quick-service food concepts—a place to sip coffee, eat sandwiches made with fresh-baked bread, and log onto the free Wi-Fi service. Ron Shaich is the CEO and chairman of the company. He was named the 2005 Foodservice Operator of the Year by the International Food Service Manufacturers. How did he earn such an honor? He listens to customers carefully to see how they react to the products being offered in his restaurant. Naturally, he heard about customers following the Atkins diet a couple of years ago. As a result, he had Panera's master bakers develop low-carb breads, bagels, and bread sticks.

The Atkins diet faded, but Shaich was still listening to customers and was able to adapt again. That meant, for one thing, serving hormone-free, humanely raised chicken in salads and sandwiches. It also meant offering breads with whole grains. Adapting is an ongoing struggle. For Panera, it means constantly listening to customers, finding out what they want, and designing the appropriate appetizers, soups, salads, sandwiches, desserts, and more. Consumers seem much more aware of healthy eating these days. They are counting calories and doing everything they can to eat what is best for them. Shaich will be listening and responding.

Sources: Scott Kirsner, "Four Leaders You Need to Know," *Fast Company*, February 2005, p. 70, "Panera Bread to Open in Northern California," *PR Newswire*, January 24, 2005; Bob Krummert, "Panera Founder Nabs IFMA Gold Plate," *Restaurant Hospitality*, July 1, 2005; and Susannah Gardiner, "Our Finest Hour," *Washington Post Magazine*, April 9, 2006, pp. 16–20 and 47–49.

www.panera-ohio.com

is adding rice burgers to the menu.[7] McDonald's and Burger King are now accepting credit cards and offering gift cards to boost sales.[8]

In Kokomo, Indiana, McDonald's is trying waiter service and a more varied menu. In New York, McDonald's is offering McDonuts to compete with Krispy Kreme. In Atlanta and other places, McDonald's computer stations link to the Internet. In Hawaii, McDonald's is trying a Spam breakfast platter, and in Columbus, Ohio, a Mega McDonald's has a karaoke booth. And watch out, Starbucks—McDonald's has a McCafe in Chicago's Loop that sells premium coffee, pastries, and wrapped sandwiches. There are more than 300 such cafés in other countries. McDonald's is also trying premium coffee in its regular outlets,[9] and it has had a great success selling salads. Want a hamburger without a bun? Fine, "I'm lovin' it!"[10] What's really new at McDonald's? Try digital-media kiosks that allow customers to burn custom CDs from a catalog of 70,000 songs, print digital photos, and download ringtones for mobile phones.[11]

Fast-food organizations must constantly monitor all sources of information for new product ideas. McDonald's isn't alone in that. Look at those baguettes and cream cheese croissants at 7-Eleven—they're right next to the cappuccino machine.[12] KFC put in a new line of chicken sandwiches. Arby's introduced a new salad. Burger King tried a new X-treme Double Cheeseburger. Wendy's finally added breakfast to its menu.[13]

Offerings differ in various locations according to the wants of the local community. In Iowa pork tenderloin is big, but in Oklahoma City it's tortilla scramblers. Overseas, companies must adapt to local tastes. At Bob's Big Boy in Thailand, for example, you can get Tropical Shrimp; at Carl's Junior in Mexico, you can order the Machaca Burrito; and at Shakey's Pizza in the Philippines, you can get Cali Shandy, a Filipino beer.

Product development, then, is a key activity in any modern business, anywhere in the world. The Spotlight on Small Business box on page 378 shows how the whole process gets started. There's a lot more to new-product development than merely introducing goods and services, however. What marketers do to create excitement for those products is as important as the products themselves.

SPOTLIGHT ON small business www.dreamdinners.com

### When You Don't Have Time to Cook at Home

Marketing, as you learned in Chapter 13, often begins by looking around to see what people want and need, and seeing whether or not anyone is satisfying those needs. If no one is meeting some need, a marketing opportunity exists. You don't have to look far to see one such opportunity. Men and women today are often very busy with work and don't have much time to be making home-cooked meals. Nonetheless, they would like to offer their families good meals because such meals create more "family time" and because they are often much more nutritious than restaurant fare. So, what could be done to help such people prepare meals? The answer: a company called Dream Dinners. Dream Dinners is like a community kitchen where moms and dads can whip up a couple of weeks' worth of meals in just a couple of hours.

This is how it works: Customers go to a Web site to pick a time and date and the meals they would like to prepare, like herb-crusted flank steak. When they arrive, the ingredients will be ready. Customers then mix the ingredients and take the prepared, but uncooked, meals home to put in the refrigerator until needed. No shopping for food. No looking in cook books for recipes. Just meals ready-to-go. Sound good? The idea has caught on to the extent that Dream Dinners now has over 115 stores in 19 states, with many more to come. Of course, a good idea brings in competitors. Dream Dinners' competitors include companies with names like Designed Dinners and Simply Cook It.

What does such a company offer as its "product"? First of all, it provides a place to meet with others and have a good time preparing meals. Second, it saves time for people too busy to be shopping for food and preparing meals at home every night. Third, it saves a lot of stress and mess. Finally, the company saves people money in that they don't have to buy big supplies of condiments that they will only use sparingly. Perhaps most important, the company offers a quick and easy way to create healthy and satisfying meals for the whole family. What else might such a company add to its product offer? Can you see such a service going into catering? Making desserts? Offering other services for busy families, such as house cleaning? Remember, every unmet need is a potential opportunity for creating a satisfying product offer.

Sources: "Dinner by Design Announces Continued Growth and Expansion; Consumers 'Eating Up' Idea of Do-It-Yourself Meals," PR Newswire, April 21, 2005; Teresa Mendez, "Assembly-Line Cooking," *Washington Times*, September 4, 2005, pp. D1 and D3; and Eileen Gunn, "A New Way to Get a Home-Cooked Meal," *The Wall Street Journal*, February 2, 2006, p. D4.

## Developing a Total Product Offer

From a strategic marketing viewpoint, a total product offer is more than just the physical good or service. A **total product offer** consists of everything that consumers evaluate when deciding whether to buy something. Thus, the basic product or service may be a washing machine, an insurance policy, or a beer, but the total product offer also may consist of the value enhancers that appear in Figure 14.1.

figure 14.1

**POTENTIAL COMPONENTS OF A TOTAL PRODUCT OFFER**

| | | | |
|---|---|---|---|
| Price | Brand name | Convenience | Package |
| Store surroundings | Service | Internet access | Buyer's past experience |
| Guarantee | Speed of delivery | Image created by advertising | Reputation of producer |

When people buy a product, they may evaluate and compare total product offers on all these dimensions. Note that some of the attributes are tangible (the product itself and its package), whereas others are intangible (the reputation of the producer and the image created by advertising). A successful marketer must begin to think like a consumer and evaluate the total product offer as a collection of impressions created by all the factors listed in Figure 14.1. It is wise to talk with consumers to see which features and benefits are most important to them, that is, which value enhancers they want in the final offerings. What questions might you ask consumers when developing the total product offer for Very Vegetarian? (Recall the business idea we

DEALING WITH change

### Using the Web to Differentiate a Product

The real estate market is constantly changing. What can a realtor do to differentiate his or her product from that offered by other realtors? Prices for realtors' services are usually about the same. The houses they sell are often similar. So what value enhancements can a realtor make to the process to attract customers? The answer, according to Elizabeth Gray-Carr of Prudential Real Estate, is to build relationships with potential sellers and buyers by offering interactive tools and unusually detailed information, including personal Web pages.

All realtors are expected to know information about schools, shopping, religious facilities, recreation, mortgage rates, recent prices in various neighborhoods, and so forth. What makes Gray-Carr stand out from the bunch is that she provides all that information on a Web site. As she thinks of new information to add, Gray-Carr puts it on the Web. That includes weather information, nearby golf courses and other recreation sites, and so on. For buyers, the site lists the agency's entire inventory of homes, and provides a virtual tour of each. Buyers can also access extensive information about the neighborhood, including school districts and the prices of homes recently sold.

Sellers can use similar information to determine the right price for their homes. If a seller signs with Gray-Carr, that seller will have 24/7 information about the process of the sale and will have a lot less paperwork to worry about than usual. When there are settled standards for electronic signatures, buyers and sellers will be able to handle all the paperwork from remote locations, making it possible to buy a home from another country and move in as soon as you arrive. Can you imagine what other value-enhancing information Gray-Carr could add to her total product offer? Can you see how her total product offer can be more valuable than those offered by other real estate agents?

www.callelizabeth.com

introduced in Chapter 13.) Remember, the store surroundings are important, as are things like the parking lot and the condition of the bathrooms.

Sometimes an organization can use low prices to create an attractive total product offer. For example, outlet stores often offer brand-name goods for less than regular retail stores do. Shoppers must be careful, however, because outlet stores also carry lower-quality products with similar but not exactly the same features as those carried in regular stores. Consumers like shopping in outlet stores in any case because they believe they are getting quality goods at low prices.

**total product offer**
Everything that consumers evaluate when deciding whether to buy something; also called a *value package*.

Different consumers may want different total product offers, so a company may develop a variety of offerings. For example, auto companies sometimes offer customers a choice between zero-percent financing and a rebate of thousands of dollars. Of course, the autos themselves may have features such as automatic fold-down seats, cup holders, global positioning systems, VCRs, and more—lots more. The consumer is invited to select from a variety of options.[14] The Dealing with Change box looks at the value enhancers that may be provided by a real estate agent.

## Product Lines and the Product Mix

Companies usually don't sell just one product. Rather, they sell several different but complementary products. A **product line** is a group of products that are physically similar or are intended for a similar market. They usually face similar competition. In one product line, there may be several competing brands. Notice, for example, Diet Coke, Diet Coke with Splenda, and Coke Zero. There is also Diet Coke with Lemon, Diet Coke with Lime, Diet Vanilla Coke, and Diet Cherry Coke.[15] Makes it kind of hard to choose, doesn't it? Both Coke and Pepsi have added water and sports drinks to their product lines to meet new consumer tastes.[16]

**product line**
A group of products that are physically similar or are intended for a similar market.

**product mix**
The combination of product lines offered by a manufacturer.

Similarly, Procter & Gamble has many brands in its laundry detergent product line, including Tide, Era, Downy, and Bold.[17] All of P&G's product lines make up its **product mix**, which is the combination of all product lines offered by a manufacturer.

Service providers have product lines and product mixes as well.[18] For example, a bank or credit union may offer a variety of services from savings accounts, automated teller machines, and computer banking to money market funds, safety deposit boxes, loans (home, car, etc.), traveler's checks, online banking, and insurance. AT&T combines services (telephone) with goods (computers, phones) in its product mix.

## PRODUCT DIFFERENTIATION

**product differentiation**
The creation of real or perceived product differences.

**convenience goods and services**
Products that the consumer wants to purchase frequently and with a minimum of effort.

**Product differentiation** is the creation of real or perceived product differences. Actual product differences are sometimes quite small, so marketers must use a creative mix of pricing, advertising, and packaging (value enhancers) to create a unique, attractive image. Various bottled water companies, for example, have successfully attempted product differentiation. The companies made their bottled waters so attractive through pricing and promotion that now restaurant customers often order water by brand name, such as Aquafina, Dasani, or Evian.

There's no reason why you couldn't create a similar attractive image for Very Vegetarian, your vegetarian restaurant. It would be easy to differentiate such a store from the typical burger joint. Small businesses can often win market share with creative product differentiation. For example, yearbook photographer Charlie Clark competes with other yearbook photographers by offering multiple clothing changes, backgrounds, and poses along with special allowances, discounts, and guarantees. He has been so successful that companies use him as a speaker at photography conventions. This is just one more example of how small businesses may have the advantage of being more flexible than big businesses in adapting to customer wants and needs and giving them attractive product differences. How could you be equally creative in responding to the consumer wants of vegetarians? The Reaching Beyond Our Borders box talks about adapting to the needs of the very poor.

How can restaurants differentiate themselves from others? In addition to world-class food, Wolfgang Puck's Postrio restaurant in San Francisco includes a great location, wonderful paintings from leading artists, outstanding service, and more. How have restaurants in your area differentiated their total product offer?

### Marketing Different Classes of Consumer Goods and Services

Several attempts have been made to classify consumer goods and services. One classification, based on consumer purchasing behavior, has four general categories—convenience, shopping, specialty, and unsought.

1. **Convenience goods and services** are products that the consumer wants to purchase frequently and with a minimum of effort (e.g., candy, gum, milk, snacks, gas, banking services). One store that sells mostly convenience goods is 7-Eleven. Location, brand awareness, and image are important for marketers of convenience goods and services. The Internet has taken convenience to a whole new level, especially for banks and other service companies, such as real estate firms. Companies that don't offer such services

www.unilever.com

REACHING BEYOND our borders

## Designing Products for the Poor

When designing products for the world market, it is important to remember that over 2.5 billion people in this world make $2 a day or less. They are not necessarily interested in the latest iPod or DVD player. However, in some countries, people are buying cell phones and renting them out to their neighbors. The owners make a few cents a call, and everyone in the village is able to communicate better with others. To sell in such villages, other companies must learn to make and sell products that are meant to be shared. That often means helping buyers finance the product and teaching them how to begin a business as a renter of goods.

Unilever, the Anglo-Dutch consumer-goods giant, has taken a lead in developing products for people in less developed countries. The idea was to develop small packages with low prices, thus making it possible for people with very little money to have access to products they want. In India, for example, Unilever sells single-use packages of Sunsilk shampoo for as little as two cents. It also has a deodorant stick that sells for 16 cents. The deodorant is a big hit in the Philippines, Bolivia, Peru, and India. There is also a nickel-sized package of Vaseline and a small tube of Close Up toothpaste that sells for eight cents.

Poor people often cannot afford eyeglasses. Scojo Vision out of Brooklyn now sells glasses in El Salvador, India, Haiti, and Guatemala for $2 a pair. Scojo is training entrepreneurs in those countries to use eye charts so they can prescribe the right correction (there are three different ones). London's Freeplay Energy Group is making radios for countries in which electricity doesn't exist and batteries are too expensive—the radios are powered by cranking a handle.

Microlending firms are giving entrepreneurs loans of $100 to $300 or so to start their own businesses. With a little capital, these entrepreneurs are able to generate money to send their children to school and to buy food and other necessities. They can also buy a few "luxury" goods like soap and deodorant, if the price is right. Doing business globally means learning to adapt to the wants and needs of everyone, and that includes the wants and needs of the very poor. As they learn to become entrepreneurs themselves, they will have the resources to buy other products and someday to trade globally themselves.

Sources: Jeffrey E. Garten, "Don't Just Throw Money at the World's Poor," *BusinessWeek*, March 7, 2005, p. 30; William Barlwin, "A Capital Idea," *Forbes*, April 18, 2005, p. 22; Robert J. Samuelson, "The World Is Still Round," *Washington Post*, July 22, 2005, p. A23; and Pete Engardio, "Business Prophet," *BusinessWeek*, January 23, 2006, pp. 68–73.

are likely to lose market share to those that do unless they offer outstanding service to customers who visit in person.

2. **Shopping goods and services** are products that the consumer buys only after comparing value, quality, price, and style from a variety of sellers. Shopping goods and services are sold largely through shopping centers where consumers can make comparisons. Sears is one store that sells mostly shopping goods. Because many consumers carefully compare such products, marketers can emphasize price differences, quality differences, or some combination of the two. Examples include clothes, shoes, appliances, and auto repair services.

3. **Specialty goods and services** are consumer products with unique characteristics and brand identity. Because these products are perceived as having no reasonable substitute, the consumer puts forth a special effort to purchase them. Examples include fine watches, expensive wine, fur coats, jewelry, imported chocolates, and expensive cigars, as well as services provided by medical specialists or business consultants. A Jaguar automobile dealer is an example of a specialty-goods retailer. These products are often marketed through specialty magazines. For example, specialty skis may be sold through sports magazines and specialty foods through gourmet magazines. By establishing interactive Web sites through which customers can place orders, companies that sell specialty goods and services can make buying their goods as easy as or easier than shopping at a local mall.

**shopping goods and services**
Those products that the consumer buys only after comparing value, quality, price, and style from a variety of sellers.

**specialty goods and services**
Consumer products with unique characteristics and brand identity. Because these products are perceived as having no reasonable substitute, the consumer puts forth a special effort to purchase them.

**unsought goods and services**
Products that consumers are unaware of, haven't necessarily thought of buying, or find that they need to solve an unexpected problem.

4. **Unsought goods and services** are products that consumers are unaware of, haven't necessarily thought of buying, or find that they need to solve an unexpected problem. Some examples of unsought products are emergency car-towing services, burial services, and insurance.

The marketing task varies according to the category of product; that is, convenience goods are marketed differently from specialty goods, and so forth. The best way to promote convenience goods is to make them readily available and to create the proper image. Some combination of price, quality, and service is the best appeal for shopping goods. Specialty goods rely on reaching special market segments through advertising. Unsought goods such as life insurance often rely on personal selling; car towing relies heavily on Yellow Pages advertising.

Whether a good or service falls into a particular class depends on the individual consumer. A shopping good for one consumer (e.g., coffee) could be a specialty good for another consumer (e.g., flavored gourmet coffee). Some people shop around to compare different dry cleaners, so dry cleaning is a shopping service for them. Others go to the closest store, making it a convenience service. Therefore, marketers must carefully monitor their customer base to determine how consumers perceive their products.

**industrial goods**
Products used in the production of other products. Sometimes called business goods or B2B goods.

## Marketing Industrial Goods and Services

**Industrial goods** (sometimes called business goods or B2B goods) are products used in the production of other products. They are sold in the business-to-business (B2B) market. Some products can be classified as both consumer goods and industrial goods. For example, personal computers could be sold to consumer markets or B2B markets. As a consumer good, the computer might be sold through electronics stores like Best Buy or through computer magazines. Most of the promotional task would go to advertising. As an industrial good, personal computers are more likely to be sold by salespeople or on the Internet. Advertising would be less of a factor in the promotion strategy. You can see that classifying goods by user category helps determine the proper marketing mix strategy.

Figure 14.2 shows some categories of both consumer and industrial goods and services. *Installations* consist of major capital equipment such as new factories and heavy machinery. *Capital items* are products that last a long time and cost a lot of money. A new factory building would be considered both a capital item and an installation. *Accessory equipment* consists of capital items that are not quite as long-lasting or as expensive as installations. Examples include computers, photocopy machines, and various tools. Other industrial goods and examples are labeled in the chart.

Many goods could be classified as consumer goods or industrial goods, based on their uses. For example, a computer that a person uses at home for personal use would clearly be a consumer good. But that same computer used in a commercial setting, such as an accounting firm or a manufacturing plant, would be classified as an industrial good. What difference does it make how a good is classified?

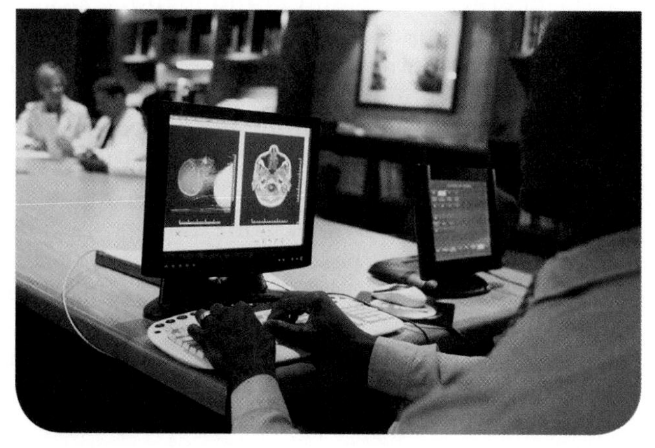

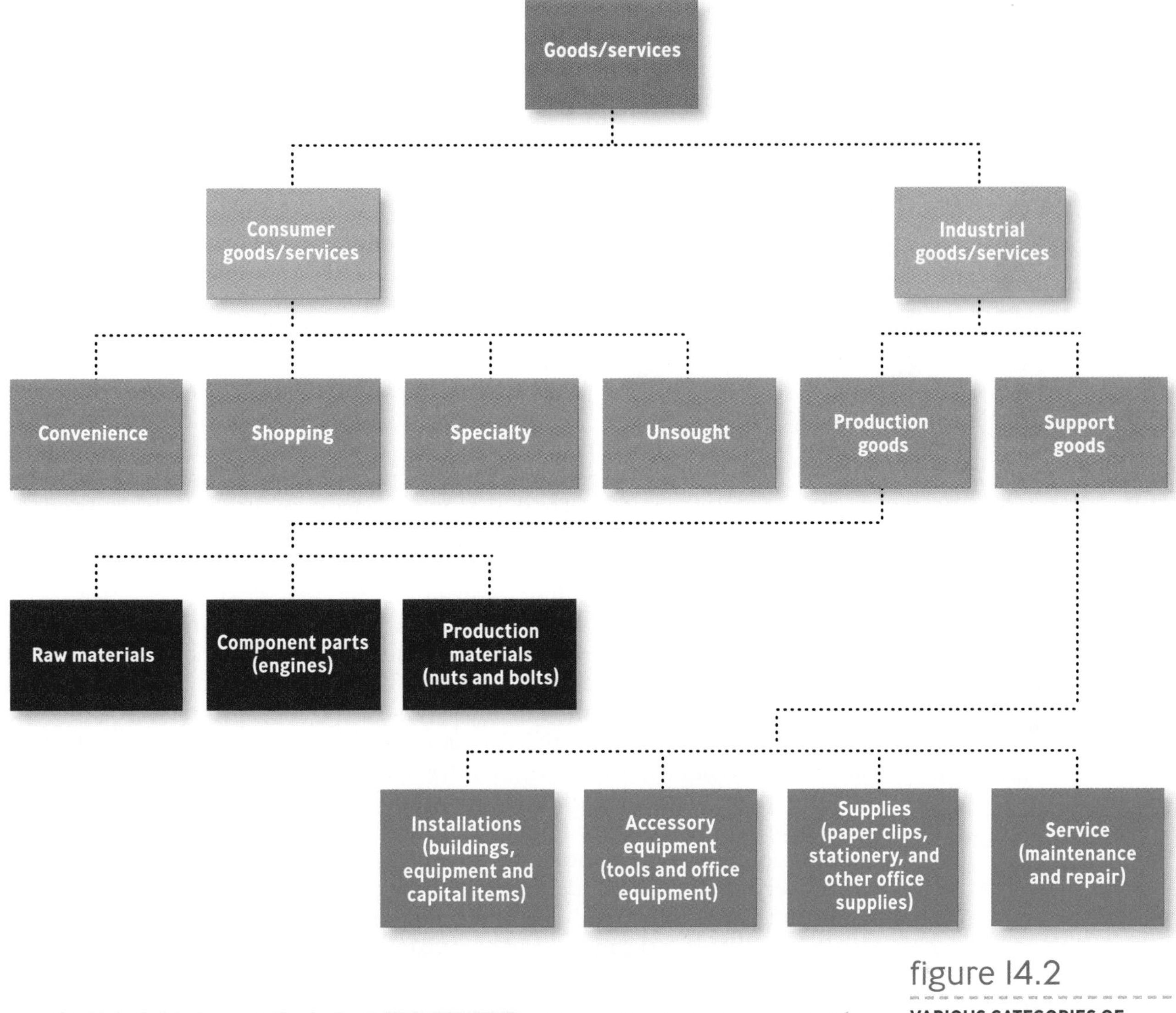


figure 14.2

**VARIOUS CATEGORIES OF CONSUMER AND INDUSTRIAL GOODS AND SERVICES**

**progress assessment**

- What value enhancers may be included in a total product offer?
- What's the difference between a product line and a product mix?
- Name the four classes of consumer goods and services, and give examples of each.
- Describe three different types of industrial goods.

## PACKAGING CHANGES THE PRODUCT

We've said that consumers evaluate many aspects of the total product offer, including the brand. It's surprising how important packaging can be in such evaluations.[19] Many years ago people had problems with table salt because it would stick together and form lumps during humid or damp weather. The Morton Salt Company solved that problem by designing a package that kept salt dry in all kinds of weather; thus the slogan "When it rains, it pours." Packaging made Morton's salt more desirable than competing products, and even though other

Packaging and branding can make a huge difference in the attractiveness of a product. Anybody who has pounded on the bottom of a ketchup bottle trying to get it out may appreciate the squeezable bottles now available. But do cute sayings on the label make ketchup more attractive? You decide.

salt companies developed similar packaging, Morton's is still the best-known salt in the United States.

Other companies have also used packaging to change and improve their basic product. Thus, we've had squeezable ketchup bottles that stand upside down on their caps; square paint cans with screw tops and integrated handles; plastic bottles for motor oil that eliminate the need for funnels; toothpaste pumps; packaged dinners and other foods, like popcorn, that can be cooked in a microwave oven; and so forth. Another interesting innovation is the use of aromatic packaging. For example, Arizona Beverage Company now has aromatic caps on its iced teas.[20] In each case, the package changed the product in the minds of consumers and opened large markets. Do you sometimes have difficulty opening plastic package wraps?[21] We can't wait for a new package for CDs that is more easily opened than the standard plastic jewel case. Can you see some market potential in developing better packaging? Packaging has become a profession. Check out the Michigan State University School of Packaging, for example.[22]

Packaging can help make a product more attractive to retailers. For example, the Universal Product Codes (UPCs) on many packages help stores control inventory; the UPC is the combination of a bar code (those familiar black-and-white lines) and a preset number that gives the retailer information about the product (price, size, color, etc.). In short, packaging changes the product by changing its visibility, usefulness, or attractiveness.

One new technology in tracking products is the radio frequency identification (RFID) chip. Attached to products, these chips send out signals telling a company where the products are at all times. The advantages of RFID chips over bar codes include that the chips can carry more information, that items don't have to be read one at a time (whole pallets can be read in an instant), and that items can be read at a distance. Wal-Mart has been a leader in using RFID technology.[23]

## The Growing Importance of Packaging

Packaging has always been an important aspect of the product offer, but today it's carrying more of the promotional burden than in the past. Many products that were once sold by salespersons are now being sold in self-service outlets, and the package has been given more sales responsibility. The Fair Packaging and Labeling Act was passed so that consumers could get quantity and value comparisons on packaging. As a result, you are now getting much more information on packages than in the past. The package must perform the following functions:

1. Protect the goods inside, stand up under handling and storage, be tamperproof, deter theft, and yet be easy to open and use.
2. Attract the buyer's attention.
3. Describe the contents and give information about the contents.
4. Explain the benefits of the good inside.
5. Provide information on warranties, warnings, and other consumer matters.
6. Give some indication of price, value, and uses.

Packaging of services also has been getting more attention recently. For example, Virgin Airlines includes door-to-door limousine service and in-flight massages in its total package. Financial institutions are offering everything from financial advice to help in purchasing insurance, stocks, bonds, mutual funds, and more. When combining goods or services into one package, it's important not to include so much that the price gets too high. It's best to work with customers to develop value enhancers that meet their individual needs.

Creating a new brand image is very different from managing a brand that is already well known. These three men created and built a highly successful brand called Tommy Bahama. There is no such person as Tommy, but shoppers still have an image of the kind of guy he is: cool, relaxed, and so on. The brand image is carried over by selling the clothes at specialty stores where customers expect higher quality and can get better service. Are you the Tommy Bahama type?

## BRANDING AND BRAND EQUITY

Closely related to packaging is branding. A **brand** is a name, symbol, or design (or combination thereof) that identifies the goods or services of one seller or group of sellers and distinguishes them from the goods and services of competitors. The word *brand* is sufficiently comprehensive to include practically all means of identification of a product. As we noted in Chapter 13, a *brand name* consists of a word, letter, or group of words or letters that differentiates one seller's goods and services from those of competitors. Brand names you may be familiar with include Red Bull, Sony, Del Monte, Campbell, Levi's, Snackwell's, Borden, and Michelob. Such brand names give products a distinction that tends to make them attractive to consumers.[24]

A **trademark** is a brand that has been given exclusive legal protection for both the brand name and the pictorial design. Trademarks such as McDonald's golden arches are widely recognized. Trademarks need to be protected from other companies that may want to trade on the trademark holder's reputation and image. Companies often sue other companies for too-closely matching brand names. McDonald's might sue to prevent a company from selling, say, McDonnel hamburgers.

People are often impressed by certain brand names, even though they say they know there's no difference between brands in a given product category. For example, when people say that all aspirin is alike, put two bottles in front of them—one with the Anacin label and one with the label of an unknown brand. See which they choose. Most people choose the brand name, even when they say there's no difference.

For the buyer, a brand name assures quality, reduces search time, and adds prestige to purchases. For the seller, brand names facilitate new-product introductions, help promotional efforts, add to repeat purchases, and differentiate products so that prices can be set higher.

**brand**
A name, symbol, or design (or combination thereof) that identifies the goods or services of one seller or group of sellers and distinguishes them from the goods and services of competitors.

**trademark**
A brand that has been given exclusive legal protection for both the brand name and the pictorial design.

**manufacturers' brand names**
The brand names of manufacturers that distribute products nationally.

### Brand Categories

Several categories of brands are familiar to you. **Manufacturers' brand names** are the brand names of manufacturers that distribute products nationally—Xerox, Kodak, Sony, and Chevrolet, for example.

**Dealer (private-label) brands** are products that don't carry the manufacturer's name but carry a distributor or retailer's name instead. Kenmore and Diehard are dealer brands sold by Sears. These brands are also known as house brands or distributor brands.

Many manufacturers fear having their brand names become generic names. A *generic name* is the name for a product category. Did you know that aspirin and linoleum, which are now generic names for products, were once brand names? So were nylon, escalator, kerosene, and zipper. All those names became so popular, so identified with the product, that they lost their brand

**dealer (private-label) brands**
Products that don't carry the manufacturer's name but carry a distributor or retailer's name instead.

**generic goods**
Nonbranded products that usually sell at a sizable discount compared to national or private-label brands.

**knockoff brands**
Illegal copies of national brand-name goods.

status and became generic. (Such issues are decided in the courts.) Their producers then had to come up with new names. The original Aspirin, for example, became Bayer aspirin. Companies that are working hard to protect their brand names today include Styrofoam (cups and packaging) and Rollerblade (in-line skates).

**Generic goods** are nonbranded products that usually sell at a sizable discount compared to national or private-label brands. They feature basic packaging and are backed with little or no advertising. Some are of poor quality, but many come close to having the same quality as the national brand-name goods they copy. There are generic tissues, generic cigarettes, generic peaches, and so forth. Consumers today are buying large amounts of generic products because their overall quality has improved so greatly in recent years that it approximates or equals that of more expensive brand names. What has been your experience trying generic products?

**Knockoff brands** are illegal copies of national brand-name goods. If you see an expensive brand-name item such as a Polo shirt or a Rolex watch for sale at a ridiculously low price, you can be pretty sure it's a knockoff.[25] Often the brand name is just a little off, like Palo (Polo) or Bolex (Rolex). Look carefully.[26]

## Generating Brand Equity and Loyalty

**brand equity**
The combination of factors—such as awareness, loyalty, perceived quality, images, and emotions—that people associate with a given brand name.

**brand loyalty**
The degree to which customers are satisfied, like the brand, and are committed to further purchase.

**brand awareness**
How quickly or easily a given brand name comes to mind when a product category is mentioned.

A major goal of marketers in the future will be to reestablish the notion of brand equity. **Brand equity** is the combination of factors—such as awareness, loyalty, perceived quality, images, and emotions—that people associate with a given brand name. Brand names with the highest brand equity ratings include Reynolds Wrap aluminum foil and Ziploc food bags. In the past, companies tried to boost their short-term performance by offering coupons and price discounts to move goods quickly. This eroded consumers' commitment to brand names. Now companies realize the value of brand equity and are trying to measure the earning power of strong brand names.[27]

The core of brand equity is brand loyalty. **Brand loyalty** is the degree to which customers are satisfied, like the brand, and are committed to further purchases. A loyal group of customers represents substantial value to a firm, and that value can be calculated.[28]

**Brand awareness** refers to how quickly or easily a given brand name comes to mind when a product category is mentioned. Advertising helps build strong brand awareness. Established brands, such as Coca-Cola and Pepsi, are usually the highest in brand awareness. Event sponsorship (e.g., football's FedEx Orange Bowl and NASCAR's Nextel Cup Series) helps improve brand awareness.

Perceived quality is an important part of brand equity. A product that's perceived as having better quality than its competitors can be priced accordingly.[29] The key to creating a perception of quality is to identify what consumers look for in a high-quality product and then to use that information in every message the company sends out. Factors influencing the perception of quality include price, appearance, and reputation. Consumers often develop *brand preference*—that is, they prefer one brand over another—because of such cues. When consumers reach the point of *brand insistence*, the product becomes a specialty good. For example, a consumer may insist on Goodyear tires for his or her car.

It's now so easy to copy a product's benefits that off-brand products are being developed to draw consumers away from brand-name goods. Brand-name manufacturers, like Intel Corporation, have to develop new products and new markets faster and promote their names better than ever before to hold off challenges from competitors.

## ethical decisions

www.gotagless.com/retires_mj.html

### Are We Too Star Struck?

Many producers use brand association to sell their products—often to young people. They use famous people, like Paris Hilton, in their ads to attract the attention of the audience. This is true for many products. An ethical question raised by such ads is: "What if the star in the ad doesn't really use the product?" If young people are lured into buying huge soft drinks, too much fast food, and the like because they see their idols on TV or in the movies using them, who is responsible for the harm that may be caused? The producer? The TV show? The network? The person in the ad? Have you been persuaded to buy such products because of celebrity endorsements? Was your experience a positive one? Do you have any feeling of responsibility for your buying behavior? What are the ethical choices?

## Creating Brand Associations

The name, symbol, and slogan a company uses can assist greatly in brand recognition for that company's products. **Brand association** is the linking of a brand to other favorable images. For example, you can link a brand to other product users, to a popular celebrity, to a particular geographic area, or to competitors (see the Making Ethical Decisions box). Note, for example, how ads for Mercedes-Benz and Buick associate those companies' cars with rich people who may spend their leisure time playing or watching golf or polo. Tiger Woods was chosen as a spokesperson for Buick because of his golf popularity. Note, too, the success of associating basketball shoes with stars such as Shaquille O'Neal and LeBron James. The person responsible for building brands is known as a brand manager or product manager. We'll discuss that position next.

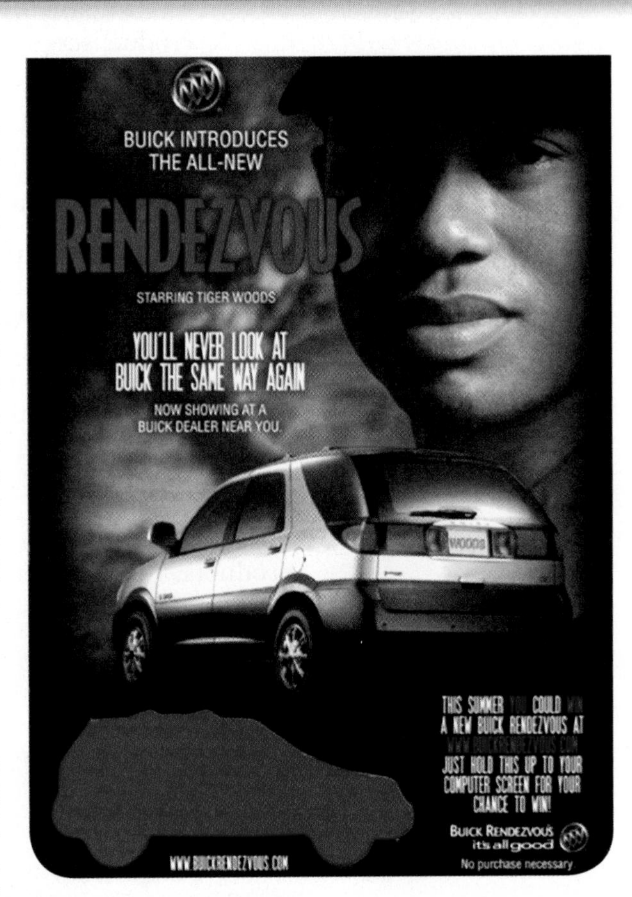


Celebrity endorsements can add (or detract) from a product's attractiveness. Tiger Woods has been a good role model and, therefore, a good spokesperson for the products he endorses. What celebrities have not been chosen to endorse products because they are controversial? Have you been moved to buy anything because of a celebrity endorsement or are the influences too subtle to notice?

## Brand Management

A **brand manager** (known as a product manager in some firms) has direct responsibility for one brand or one product line. This responsibility includes all the elements of the marketing mix: product, price, place, and promotion. Thus, the brand manager might be thought of as a president of a one-product firm. One reason many large consumer-product companies created the position of brand manager was to have greater control over new-product development and product promotion.[30] Some companies have brand-management *teams* to bolster the overall effort.

### progress assessment

- What six functions does packaging now perform?
- What's the difference between a brand name and a trademark?
- Can you explain the difference between a manufacturer's brand, a dealer brand, and a generic brand?
- What are the key components of brand equity?

**brand association** The linking of a brand to other favorable images.

**brand manager** A manager who has direct responsibility for one brand or one product line; called a product manager in some firms.

# THE NEW-PRODUCT DEVELOPMENT PROCESS

Chances that a new product will fail are overwhelmingly high.[31] About 86 percent of products introduced in one year failed to reach their business objectives. Not delivering what is promised is a leading cause of new-product failure. Other reasons for failure include poor positioning, not enough differences from competitors, and poor packaging. Small firms, especially, may experience a low success rate unless they do proper product planning.

As Figure 14.3 shows, new-product development for producers consists of several stages:

1. Idea generation, based on consumer wants and needs.
2. Product screening.
3. Product analysis.
4. Development (including building prototypes).
5. Testing.
6. Commercialization (bringing the product to the market).

**product screening** A process designed to reduce the number of new-product ideas being worked on at any one time.

**product analysis** Making cost estimates and sales forecasts to get a feeling for profitability of new-product ideas.

New products continue to pour into the market every year, and the profit potential looks tremendous. Think, for example, of the potential of home video conferencing, interactive TV, large-screen high-definition TV sets, virtual reality games and products, Internet-connected phones, iPods with video, and other innovations. Where do these ideas come from? How are they tested? What's the life span for an innovation? The following material looks at these issues.

## Generating New-Product Ideas

A strong point can be made for listening to employee suggestions for new products. Most ideas for new industrial products come from company sources (e.g., employees) other than research and development. Employees are also a major source for new consumer goods ideas. Firms should also listen to their suppliers for new-product ideas.

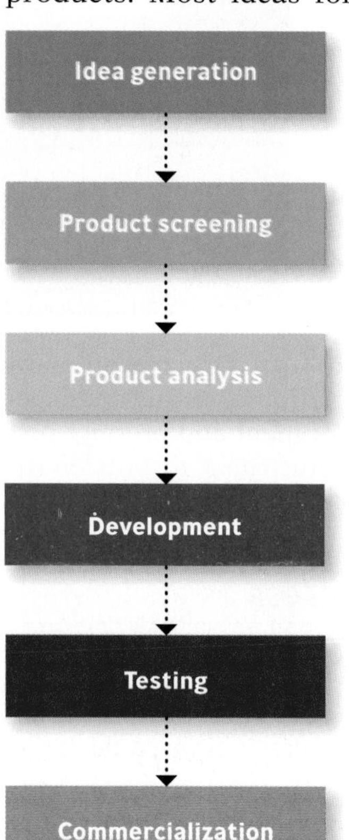


figure 14.3

THE NEW-PRODUCT DEVELOPMENT PROCESS

Product development is a six-stage process. Which stage do you believe to be the most important?

## Product Screening

**Product screening** is designed to reduce the number of new-product ideas being worked on at any one time. Criteria needed for screening include whether the product fits in well with present products, profit potential, marketability, and personnel requirements. Each of these factors may be assigned a weight, and total scores are then computed. It now takes about seven ideas to generate one commercial product.

## Product Analysis

**Product analysis** is done after product screening. It's largely a matter of making cost estimates and sales forecasts to get a feeling for profitability of new-product ideas. Products that don't meet the established criteria are withdrawn from consideration.

## Product Development and Testing

If a product passes the screening and analysis phase, the firm begins to develop it further. A product idea can be developed into many different product concepts, which are alternative product offerings based on the same product idea that have different meanings and values to consumers. For example, a firm that makes packaged meat products may develop the concept of a chicken dog—a hot dog made of chicken that tastes like an all-beef hot dog. A prototype, or sample, may be developed so that consumers can actually try the taste.

**Concept testing** involves taking a product idea to consumers to test their reactions. Do they see the benefits of this new product? How frequently would they buy it? At what price? What features do they like and dislike? What changes would they make? Different samples are tested using different packaging, branding, ingredients, and so forth until a product emerges that's desirable from both production and marketing perspectives. As you plan for Very Vegetarian, can you see the importance of concept testing for new vegetarian dishes?

**concept testing**
Taking a product idea to consumers to test their reactions.

## Commercialization

Even if a product tests well, it may take quite a while before the product achieves success in the market. Take the zipper, for example, the result of one of the longest development efforts on record for a consumer product. After Whitcomb Judson received the first patents for his clothing fastener in the early 1890s, it took more than 15 years to perfect the product—and even then consumers weren't interested. Judson's company suffered numerous financial setbacks, name changes, and relocations before settling in Meadville, Pennsylvania. Finally, the U.S. Navy started using zippers during World War I. Today, Talon Inc. is the leading U.S. maker of zippers, producing some 500 million of them a year.

The example of the zipper shows that the marketing effort must include **commercialization**. This includes (1) promoting the product to distributors and retailers to get wide distribution and (2) developing strong advertising and sales campaigns to generate and maintain interest in the product among distributors and consumers. New products are now getting rapid exposure to global markets by being promoted on the Internet. Interactive Web sites enable consumers to view new products, ask questions, and make purchases easily and quickly.

**commercialization**
Promoting a product to distributors and retailers to get wide distribution, and developing strong advertising and sales campaigns to generate and maintain interest in the product among distributors and consumers.

# THE PRODUCT LIFE CYCLE

Once a product has been developed and tested, it is placed on the market. Products often go through a life cycle consisting of four stages: introduction, growth, maturity, and decline. This is called the product life cycle (see Figure 14.4 on page 390). The **product life cycle** is a *theoretical* model of what happens to sales and profits for a product class (e.g., all dishwasher soaps) over time. However, not all products follow the life cycle, and particular brands may act differently.[32] For example, while frozen foods as a generic class may go through the entire cycle, one brand may never get beyond the introduction stage. Also, some products become classics and never experience much of a decline. Others may be withdrawn from the market altogether. Nonetheless, the product life cycle may provide some basis for anticipating future market developments and for planning marketing strategies. Some products, such as microwave ovens, stayed in the introductory stage for years. Other products, such as fad clothing, may go through the entire cycle in a few months.

**product life cycle**
A theoretical model of what happens to sales and profits for a product class over time.

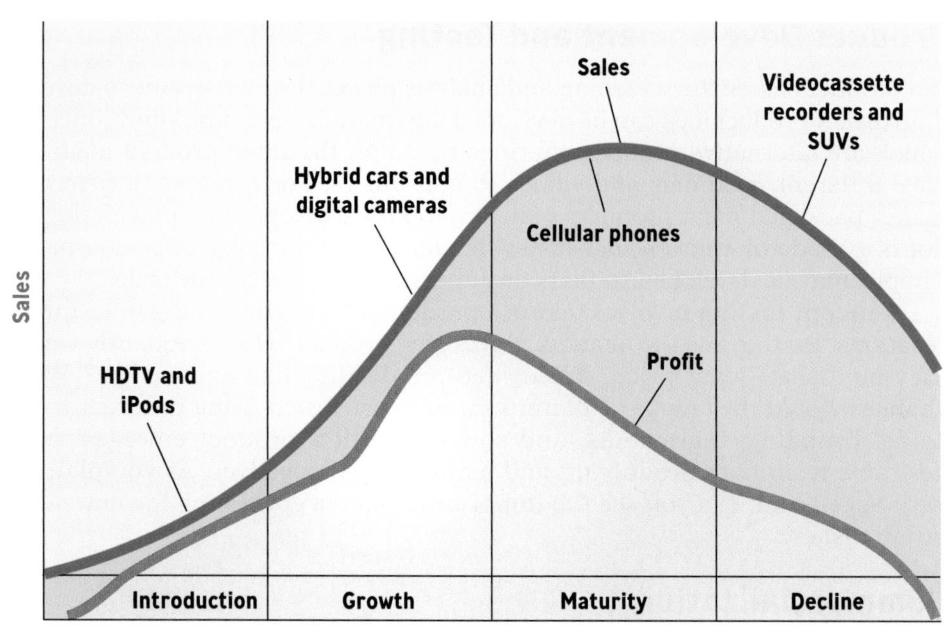


figure 14.4

**SALES AND PROFITS DURING THE PRODUCT LIFE CYCLE**

Note that profit levels start to fall *before* sales reach their peak. This is due to increasing price competition. When profits and sales start to decline, it's time to come out with a new product or to remodel the old one to maintain interest and profits.

## Example of the Product Life Cycle

You can see how the theory works by looking at the product life cycle of instant coffee. When it was introduced, most people didn't like it as well as "regular" coffee, and it took several years for instant coffee to gain general acceptance (introduction stage). At one point, though, instant coffee grew rapidly in popularity, and many brands were introduced (growth stage). After a while, people became attached to one brand and sales leveled off (maturity stage). Sales then went into a slight decline when freeze-dried coffees were introduced (decline stage). Now freeze-dried coffee is, in turn, at the decline stage as consumers are buying fresh specialty beans from companies such as Starbucks and grinding them at home. It's extremely important for marketers to recognize what stage a product is in so that they can make intelligent and efficient marketing decisions.

The product life cycle can give marketers valuable clues as to how to promote a product over time. Some products, like crayons and sidewalk chalk, have very long product life cycles, change very little, and never seem to go into decline. Crayola Crayons has been successful for 100 years!

## The Importance of the Product Life Cycle

The importance of the product life cycle to marketers is this: Different stages in the product life cycle call for different marketing strategies. The table in Figure 14.5 outlines the marketing mix decisions that might be made. As you go through the table, you'll see that each stage calls for multiple marketing mix changes. Remember, these concepts are largely theoretical and should be used only as guidelines. The price strategies mentioned in the table will be discussed later in this chapter.

Figure 14.6 shows in table form the theory of what happens to sales volume, profits, and competition during the product life cycle. You can compare

| | MARKETING MIX ELEMENTS | | | |
|---|---|---|---|---|
| **LIFE CYCLE STAGE** | **PRODUCT** | **PRICE** | **PLACE** | **PROMOTION** |
| Introduction | Offer market-tested product; keep mix small | Go after innovators with high introductory price (skimming strategy) or use penetration pricing | Use wholesalers, selective distribution | Dealer promotion and heavy investment in primary demand advertising and sales promotion to get stores to carry the product and consumers to try it |
| Growth | Improve product; keep product mix limited | Adjust price to meet competition | Increase distribution | Heavy competitive advertising |
| Maturity | Differentiate product to satisfy different market segments | Further reduce price | Take over wholesaling function and intensify distribution | Emphasize brand name as well as product benefits and differences |
| Decline | Cut product mix; develop new-product ideas | Consider price increase | Consolidate distribution; drop some outlets | Reduce advertising to only loyal customers |

figure 14.5

**SAMPLE STRATEGIES FOLLOWED DURING THE PRODUCT LIFE CYCLE**

this table to the graph in Figure 14.4. For instance, both the table and the graph show that a product at the mature stage may reach the top in sales growth while profit is decreasing. At that stage, a marketing manager may decide to create a new image for the product to start a new growth cycle. You may have noticed, for example, how Arm & Hammer baking soda gets a new image every few years to generate new sales. One year it's positioned as a deodorant for refrigerators and the next as a substitute for harsh chemicals in swimming pools. Knowing what stage in the cycle a product has reached helps marketing managers decide when such strategic changes are needed.

### progress assessment

- What are the six steps in the new-product development process?
- Can you draw a product life cycle and label its parts?

| **LIFE CYCLE STAGE** | **SALES** | **PROFITS** | **COMPETITORS** |
|---|---|---|---|
| Introduction | Low sales | Losses may occur | Few |
| Growth | Rapidly rising sales | Very high profits | Growing number |
| Maturity | Peak sales | Declining profits | Stable number, then declining |
| Decline | Falling sales | Profits may fall to become losses | Declining number |

figure 14.6

**HOW SALES, PROFITS, AND COMPETITION VARY OVER THE PRODUCT LIFE CYCLE**

Theoretically, all products go through these stages at various times in their life cycle. What happens to sales as a product matures?

# COMPETITIVE PRICING

Pricing is so important to marketing and the development of total product offers that it has been singled out as one of the four Ps in the marketing mix, along with product, place, and promotion. It is one of the most difficult of the four Ps for a manager to control. That is important because price is a critical ingredient in consumer evaluations of the product. In this section, we'll explore price both as an ingredient of the total product offer and as a strategic marketing tool.

## Pricing Objectives

A firm may have several objectives in mind when setting a pricing strategy. When pricing a new vegetarian offering, we may want to promote the product's image. If we price it high and use the right promotion, maybe we can make it the Evian of vegetarian meals. We also might price it high to achieve a certain profit objective or return on investment. We could also price such a product lower than its competitors because we want poor people and older people to be able to afford this healthy meal. That is, we could have some social or ethical goal in mind. Low pricing may also discourage competition because the profit potential is less in this case. A low price may also help us capture a larger share of the market. The point is that a firm may have several pricing objectives over time, and it must formulate these objectives clearly before developing an overall pricing strategy. Popular objectives include the following:

1. *Achieving a target return on investment or profit.* Ultimately, the goal of marketing is to make a profit by providing goods and services to others. Naturally, one long-run pricing objective of almost all firms is to optimize profit.[33]
2. *Building traffic.* Supermarkets often advertise certain products at or below cost to attract people to the store. These products are called loss leaders. The long-run objective is to make profits by following the short-run objective of building a customer base. The Internet portal Yahoo once provided an auction service for free in competition with eBay. Why give such a service away free? To increase advertising revenue on the Yahoo site and attract more people to Yahoo's other services.
3. *Achieving greater market share.* The U.S. auto industry is in a fierce international battle to capture and hold market share. One way to capture a larger part of the market is to offer low finance rates (e.g., zero-percent financing), low lease rates, or rebates. In 2005–2006, some companies offered autos at employee-discount prices.[34] The result was a large loss in profits.
4. *Creating an image.* Certain watches, perfumes, and other socially visible products are priced high to give them an image of exclusivity and status.
5. *Furthering social objectives.* A firm may want to price a product low so that people with little money can afford the product. The government often gets involved in pricing farm products so that everyone can get basic needs such as milk and bread at a low price.

Note that a firm may have short-run objectives that differ greatly from its long-run objectives. Both should be understood at the beginning and put into the strategic marketing plan. Pricing objectives should be influenced by other marketing decisions regarding product design, packaging, branding, distribution, and promotion. All of these marketing decisions are interrelated.

People believe intuitively that the price charged for a product must bear some relation to the cost of producing the product. In fact, we'd generally agree that prices are usually set somewhere above cost. But as we'll see, prices and cost aren't always related. In fact, there are three major approaches to pricing strategy: cost-based, demand-based (target costing), and competition-based.

It seems like a very good deal to be able to buy a car for the same price as employees from the car company pay. In fact, it was such a good deal that other companies began making the same kind of offer. Are you at all suspicious of such promotions? Why?

## Cost-Based Pricing

Producers often use cost as a primary basis for setting price. They develop elaborate cost accounting systems to measure production costs (including materials, labor, and overhead), add in some margin of profit, and come up with a price. The question is whether the price will be satisfactory to the market as well. In the long run, the market—not the producer—determines what the price will be. Pricing should take into account costs, but it should also include the expected costs of product updates, the objectives for each product, and competitor prices.

## Demand-Based Pricing

An opposing strategy to cost-based pricing is one called target costing. **Target costing** is demand based. It means designing a product so that it satisfies customers and meets the profit margins desired by the firm. Target costing makes the final price an input to the product development process, not an outcome of it. You estimate the selling price people would be willing to pay for a product and subtract the desired profit margin. The result is the target cost of production. Japanese companies such as Isuzu Motors, Komatsu Limited, and Sony all have used target costing.

**target costing**
Designing a product so that it satisfies customers and meets the profit margins desired by the firm.

## Competition-Based Pricing

**Competition-based pricing** is a strategy based on what all the other competitors are doing. The price can be at, above, or below competitors' prices. Pricing depends on customer loyalty, perceived differences, and the competitive climate. **Price leadership** is the procedure by which one or more dominant firms set the pricing practices that all competitors in an industry follow. You may have noticed that practice among oil and cigarette companies.

**competition-based pricing**
A pricing strategy based on what all the other competitors are doing. The price can be set at, above, or below competitors' prices.

**price leadership**
The procedure by which one or more dominant firms set the pricing practices that all competitors in an industry follow.

## Break-Even Analysis

Before you begin selling a new vegetarian sandwich, it may be wise to determine how many sandwiches you'd have to sell before making a profit. You'd then determine whether you could reach such a sales goal. **Break-even analysis** is the process used to determine profitability at various levels of sales. The break-even point is the point where revenues from sales equal all costs. The formula for calculating the break-even point is as follows:

**break-even analysis**
The process used to determine profitability at various levels of sales.

$$\text{Break-even point (BEP)} = \frac{\text{Total fixed cost (FC)}}{\text{Price of one unit (P)} - \text{Variable cost (VC) of one unit}}$$

**total fixed costs**
All the expenses that remain the same no matter how many products are made or sold.

**variable costs**
Costs that change according to the level of production.

**Total fixed costs** are all the expenses that remain the same no matter how many products are made or sold. Among the expenses that make up fixed costs are the amount paid to own or rent a factory or warehouse and the amount paid for business insurance. **Variable costs** change according to the level of production. Included are the expenses for the materials used in making products and the direct costs of labor used in making those goods. For producing a specific product, let's say you have a fixed cost of $200,000 (for mortgage interest, real estate taxes, equipment, and so on). Your variable cost (e.g., labor and materials) per item is $2. If you sold the products for $4 each, the break-even point would be 100,000 items. In other words, you wouldn't make any money selling this product unless you sold more than 100,000 of them:

$$\text{BEP} = \frac{\text{FC}}{\text{P} - \text{VC}} = \frac{\$200{,}000}{\$4.00 - \$2.00} = \frac{\$200{,}000}{\$2.00} = 100{,}000 \text{ boxes}$$

## Other Pricing Strategies

**skimming price strategy**
Strategy in which a new product is priced high to make optimum profit while there's little competition.

**penetration strategy**
Strategy in which a product is priced low to attract many customers and discourage competition.

**everyday low pricing (EDLP)**
Setting prices lower than competitors and then not having any special sales.

**high–low pricing strategy**
Setting prices that are higher than EDLP stores, but having many special sales where the prices are lower than competitors'.

**bundling**
Grouping two or more products together and pricing them as a unit.

Let's say a firm has just developed a new line of products, such as plasma TV sets. The firm has to decide how to price these sets at the introductory stage of the product life cycle. One strategy would be to price them high to recover the costs of developing the sets and to take advantage of the fact that there are few competitors. A **skimming price strategy** is one in which a new product is priced high to make optimum profit while there's little competition. Of course, those large profits will attract competitors.

A second strategy would be to price the new TVs low. This would attract more buyers and discourage other companies from making sets because the profit is so low. This strategy enables the firm to penetrate or capture a large share of the market quickly. A **penetration strategy**, therefore, is one in which a product is priced low to attract more customers and discourage competitors. The Japanese successfully used a penetration strategy with videocassette recorders. No U.S. firm could compete with the low prices the Japanese offered.

There are several pricing strategies used by retailers. One is called **everyday low pricing (EDLP)**. That's the pricing strategy used by Home Depot and Wal-Mart. Such stores set prices lower than competitors and usually do not have many special sales. The idea is to have consumers come to those stores whenever they want a bargain rather than waiting until there is a sale, as they do for most department stores.[35]

Department stores and other retailers most often use a **high–low pricing strategy**. The idea is to have regular prices that are higher than those at stores using EDLP but also to have many special sales in which the prices are lower than those of competitors. The problem with such pricing is that it teaches consumers to wait for sales, thus cutting into profits.[36] As the Internet grows in popularity, you may see fewer stores with a high–low strategy because consumers will be able to find better prices on the Internet and begin buying more and more from online retailers.

Some retailers use price as a major determinant of the goods they carry. For example, there are stores that promote goods that sell for only $1 or only $10. Outlet stores supposedly sell brand-name goods at discount prices, and sometimes they do. Other stores, sometimes called discount stores, sell "seconds," or damaged goods. Consumers must take care to carefully examine such goods to be sure the flaws are not too major.

**Bundling** means grouping two or more products together and pricing them as a unit. For example, a store might price washers and dryers as a unit.

Jiffy Lube offers an oil change and lube, and then checks your car's fluid levels and air pressure and bundles them all into one price. **Psychological pricing** means pricing goods and services at price points that make the product appear less expensive than it is. For example, a house might be priced at $399,000 with the idea that that price sounds like a lot less than $400,000. Gas stations almost always use psychological pricing—$2.99 per gallon sounds less than $3.00.

Psychological pricing sets the price at $19.99 rather than $20.00 because the price seems to be less that way. What is your reaction to such pricing? Does a $300,000 condo seem to be a much better deal because it is priced at "only $299,000"? What about a 99 cent hot dog over one costing $1.00?

## How Market Forces Affect Pricing

Recognizing the fact that different consumers may be willing to pay different prices, marketers sometimes price on the basis of consumer demand rather than cost or some other calculation. That's called *demand-oriented pricing* and is reflected by movie theaters with low rates for children and by drugstores with discounts for senior citizens. The Washington Opera Company in Washington, D.C., for example, raised its prices on prime seating and lowered its pricing on less attractive seating; this strategy raised the company's revenues by 9 percent.

Marketers are facing a new pricing problem: Customers can now compare prices of many goods and services on the Internet. For example, you may want to check out deals on sites such as DealTime.com, MySimon.com, or Buy.com. Priceline.com introduced consumers to a "demand collection system," in which buyers post the prices they are willing to pay and invite sellers to either accept or decline the price. Consumers can get great prices on airlines, hotels, and other products by naming the price they are willing to pay. You can also buy used goods online. Have you or any of your friends bought or sold anything on eBay or Amazon.com? Clearly, price competition is going to heat up as consumers have more access to price information from all around the world. As a result, nonprice competition is likely to increase.

**psychological pricing**
Pricing goods and services at price points that make the product appear less expensive than it is.

## NONPRICE COMPETITION

In spite of the emphasis placed on price in microeconomic theory, marketers often compete on product attributes other than price. You may have noted that price differences are small with products such as gasoline, men's haircuts, candy bars, and even major products such as compact cars and private colleges. Typically, you will not see price used as a major promotional appeal on television. Instead, marketers tend to stress product images and consumer benefits such as comfort, style, convenience, and durability.

Many small organizations promote the services that accompany basic products rather than price in order to compete with bigger firms. The idea is that good service will enhance a relatively homogeneous product. Danny O'Neill, for example, is a small wholesaler who sells gourmet coffee to upscale restaurants. He has to watch competitors' prices and see what services they offer so that he can charge the premium prices he wants. To charge high prices, he has to offer superior service. Larger companies often do the same thing. For example, some airlines stress friendliness, promptness, abundant flights, good meals, and other such services. Many hotels stress "no surprises," business services, health clubs, and other extras.

**progress assessment**

- Can you list two short-term and two long-term pricing objectives? Can the two be compatible?
- What's wrong with using a cost-based pricing strategy?
- What's the purpose of break-even analysis?
- Can you calculate a product's break-even point if producing it costs $10,000 and revenue from the sale of one unit is $20?

## summary

**1. Explain the concept of a total product offer.**

1. A total product offer consists of everything that consumers evaluate when deciding whether to buy something.
   - **What's included in a total product offer?**

   A total product offer includes price, brand name, satisfaction in use, and more.
   - **What's the difference between a product line and a product mix?**

   A product line is a group of physically similar products with similar competitors. A product line of gum may include bubble gum and sugarless gum. A product mix is a company's combination of product lines. A manufacturer may offer lines of gum, candy bars, chewing tobacco, and so on.
   - **How do marketers create product differentiation for their goods and services?**

   Marketers use a mix of pricing, advertising, and packaging to make their products seem unique and attractive.

**2. Describe the various kinds of consumer and industrial goods.**

2. Consumer goods are sold to ultimate consumers like you and me and not to businesses.
   - **What are the four classifications of consumer goods and services, and how are they marketed?**

   There are convenience goods and services (requiring minimum shopping effort); shopping goods and services (for which people go searching and compare price and quality); specialty goods and services (which consumers go out of their way to get, and often demand specific brands); and unsought goods and services (products that consumers are unaware of, haven't necessarily thought of buying, or find that they need to solve an unexpected problem). Convenience goods and services are best promoted by location, shopping goods and services by some price/quality appeal, and specialty goods and services by specialty magazines and interactive Web sites.
   - **What are industrial goods, and how are they marketed differently from consumer goods?**

   Industrial goods are products sold in the business-to-business market (B2B), and are used in the production of other products. They're sold largely through salespeople and rely less on advertising. Installations are major capital equipment such as new factories and heavy machinery. Accessory equipment is capital items that are not quite as long-lasting or as expensive as installations. Examples include computers, photocopy machines, and various tools.

3. Packaging changes the product and is becoming increasingly important, taking over much of the sales function for consumer goods.
   - **What are the six functions of packaging?**

   The six functions are (1) to protect the goods inside, stand up under handling and storage, be tamperproof, deter theft, and yet be easy to open and use; (2) to describe the contents; (3) to explain the benefits of the product inside; (4) to provide information on warranties, warnings, and other consumer matters; (5) to indicate price, value, and uses; and (6) to attract the buyer's attention.

**3.** List and describe the functions of packaging.

4. Branding also changes a product.
   - **Can you give examples of a brand, a brand name, and a trademark?**

   One example of a brand name of crackers is Waverly by Nabisco. The brand consists of the name Waverly as well as the symbol (a red triangle in the corner with *Nabisco* circled in white). The brand name and the symbol are also trademarks, since Nabisco has been given legal protection for this brand. Manufacturers need to protect their brand names from competitors who try to steal their name or image.
   - **What is brand equity, and how do managers create brand associations?**

   Brand equity is the combination of factors such as awareness, loyalty, perceived quality, images, and emotions people associate with a given brand name. Brand association is the linking of a brand to other favorable images. For example, you can link a brand to other product users, to a popular celebrity, to a particular geographic area, or to competitors.

**4.** Describe the differences among a brand, a brand name, and a trademark, and explain the concepts of brand equity and brand loyalty.

5. Brand managers coordinate product, price, place, and promotion decisions for a particular product.
   - **What are the six steps of the product development process?**

   The steps are (1) generation of new-product ideas, (2) product screening, (3) product analysis, (4) development, (5) testing, and (6) commercialization.

**5.** Explain the role of brand managers and the steps of the new-product development process.

6. Once a product is placed on the market, marketing strategy varies as the product class goes through various stages of acceptance called the product life cycle.
   - **What are the theoretical stages of the product life cycle?**

   They are introduction, growth, maturity, and decline.
   - **How do marketing strategies theoretically change at the various stages?**

   See Figures 14.4 and 14.5 on pages 390 and 391.

**6.** Draw the product life cycle, describe each of its stages, and describe marketing strategies at each stage.

7. Pricing is one of the four Ps of marketing.
   - **What are pricing objectives?**

   Objectives include achieving a target profit, building traffic, increasing market share, creating an image, and meeting social goals.
   - **What's the break-even point?**

   At the break-even point, total cost equals total revenue. Sales beyond that point are profitable.

$$\text{The break-even point} = \frac{\text{Total fixed cost}}{(\text{Price of one unit} - \text{Variable cost of one unit})}$$

   - **What strategies can marketers use to determine a product's price?**

   A *skimming price strategy* is one in which the product is priced high to make optimum profit while there's little competition, whereas a *penetration strategy* is one in which a product is priced low to attract more customers and discourage competitors. *Demand-oriented pricing* is based on consumer

**7.** Explain various pricing objectives and strategies.

demand rather than cost. *Competition-oriented pricing* is based on all competitors' prices. *Price leadership* occurs when all competitors follow the pricing practice of one or more dominant companies. *Bundling* means grouping two or more products into a unit and charging one price for them.

**8.** Explain why nonpricing strategies are growing in importance.

8. In spite of the emphasis placed on price in microeconomic theory, marketers often compete on product attributes other than price.
   - **Why do companies use nonprice strategies?**

   Pricing is one of the easiest marketing strategies to copy. Therefore, often it is not a good long-run competitive tool. Instead, marketers may compete using nonprice strategies that are less easy to copy, including offering great service, educating consumers, and establishing long-term relationships with customers.

## key terms

**brand** 385
**brand association** 388
**brand awareness** 386
**brand equity** 386
**brand loyalty** 386
**brand manager** 388
**break-even analysis** 393
**bundling** 394
**commercialization** 389
**competition-based pricing** 393
**concept testing** 389
**convenience goods and services** 381
**dealer (private-label) brands** 386
**everyday low pricing (EDLP)** 394
**generic goods** 386
**high–low pricing strategy** 394
**industrial goods** 382
**knockoff brands** 386
**manufacturers' brand names** 385
**penetration strategy** 394
**price leadership** 393
**product analysis** 388
**product differentiation** 381
**product life cycle** 389
**product line** 380
**product mix** 381
**product screening** 388
**psychological pricing** 395
**shopping goods and services** 381
**skimming price strategy** 394
**specialty goods and services** 382
**target costing** 393
**total fixed costs** 394
**total product offer** 380
**trademark** 385
**unsought goods and services** 382
**value** 376
**variable costs** 394

## critical thinking questions

1. What value enhancers affected your choice of the school you attend? Did you consider size, location, price, reputation, Internet services, library services, sports, placement, and selection of courses offered? What factors were most important? Why? What schools were your alternatives? Why didn't you choose them?

2. In what stage of the product life cycle are laptop computers? What does Figure 14.5 indicate firms should do at that stage? What will the next stage be? What might you do at that stage to optimize profits?

3. Peanut butter is in the maturity or decline stage of the product life cycle. Does that explain why Skippy introduced a reduced-fat version of its

peanut butter? What other variations on older products have been introduced in the last few years?

4. What are some of the things you could do to enhance the product offer of Very Vegetarian other than changing the menu from time to time?

## developing workplace skills

1. Look around your classroom and notice the different types of shoes that students are wearing. What product qualities were they looking for when they chose those shoes? What was the importance of price, style, brand name, and color? Describe the product offerings you would feature in a new shoe store designed to appeal to college students.

2. A total product offer consists of everything that consumers evaluate when choosing among products, including price, package, service, and reputation. Working in teams, compose a list of factors that consumers might consider when evaluating the following products: a vacation resort, a college, a new car.

3. Imagine that you are involved in a money-raising activity for your school. You decide to sell large pizzas for $12 each. You buy a used pizza oven for $12,000. That is the only fixed cost. The variable cost per unit is $6.00. Calculate the break-even point and decide whether or not you should go ahead with the project. That is, do you think you could sell enough pizzas to make a sizable profit?

4. How important is price to you when buying the following products: shoes, milk, computers, hair cuts, and auto rentals? What nonprice factors, if any, are more important in making these choices? How much time does it take to evaluate factors other than price when making such purchases?

5. Determine where in the product life cycle you would place each of the following products and then prepare a marketing strategy for each product based on the recommendations in this chapter:
   a. Alka-Seltzer.
   b. Cellular phones.
   c. Hybrid automobiles.
   d. Campbell's chicken noodle soup.

## taking it to the net * 1

**Purpose**

To assess how the Internet can be used to shop for various goods.

**Exercise**

Shopbots are Internet sites that you can use to find the best prices on goods you need. No shopbot searches the entire Internet, so it's a good idea to use more than one to get the best deals. Furthermore, not all shopbots figure in shipping and handling costs. Here are some to try: MySimon.com, Pricegrabber.com, PriceSCAN.com.

1. Which of the shopbots seem most comprehensive—offering the most goods or the most information?
2. Which shopbot is the easiest to use? The hardest?
3. Write down some of the prices you find on the Internet and then go to a local store, such as Wal-Mart, and compare prices. Does either source—the Net or the store—clearly have the lowest prices, or does it depend on the product?
4. Evaluate shopping on the Internet versus shopping in stores. What are the advantages and disadvantages of each?

## casing the web

To access the case *"Everyday Low Pricing,"* visit **www.mhhe.com/ub8e**

## video case

### SolutionPeople Have the Idea

When most people think about product development, packaging, and branding, they think about goods like cars, furniture, and the like. They don't usually think about services. Yet the bulk of tomorrow's jobs are going to be in the service sector. So it makes sense, when talking about product development, to visit a service company to learn what it's all about. But who has an idea about what company to visit? We need some solutions here. "Hey, I've got an idea," someone says. "How about going to the SolutionPeople?" SolutionPeople is a business to business (B2B) firm that sells services that help other companies create new ideas for products. It is a service organization.

The development and pricing of **services** such as those offered by the SolutionPeople may be more complicated than the development and pricing of **goods**. How do you go about pricing a service? You can't add up the costs involved in producing the service, then add a little for profit, and come up with a price. The cost may be very low and the value quite high. So what do you base your price on? The answer is that you price a service based on the value that service has to the customers you serve. For example, SolutionPeople conducts seminars for companies where many people gather for brainstorming sessions. That is, they sit around and try to come up with new-product ideas that will prove very profitable in the long run. How much is the service (seminars) worth? It depends on how good they are in helping their customers generate profitable ideas. The ideas may be worth millions of dollars or they may be useless. So, as they say, the proof is in the pudding. If the seminars are good and generate many profitable ideas, people will be willing to pay a lot of money. If they are not good, people won't be willing to pay much. It's that simple.

Pricing services is truly an art rather than a science. You have to understand the value of a product to consumers and then you have to be bold in your pricing strategy. In some ways, your service can be viewed as a monopoly in that you are offering a service no one else can duplicate. On the other hand, there may be many competing companies offering services that are similar.

Service companies often come up with products that they use to aid in their work. SolutionPeople has a product called KnowBrainer that helps companies come up with new ideas. The product itself is not very expensive to make—just a few dollars. But it is very valuable to a company that uses it. Over time, the KnowBrainer product can be improved or adapted to be more useful to more companies. For example, it could be adapted for use on an iPod and be called a PodBrainer. In all cases, the pricing depends not on the cost of making the product, but on the value of the product to business buyers.

So, why doesn't someone simply copy the basic concepts and sell them? Good point. It is important for services to have copyright protection. But no one can copy the ability to think creatively. That talent is unique to a few people, and is very valuable.

Services use packaging and branding concepts much like those used for goods. For example, SolutionPeople uses a light bulb logo that distinguishes it from other service providers. The company uses color, fonts, and other means to make its logo memorable. Those images are put onto T-shirts and other products to convey the company's message in as many ways as possible.

Services depend very heavily on word of mouth for promotion—testimonials. But word of mouth only works if you have a product (service) worth telling other people about. The SolutionPeople brainstorming sessions, team-building exercises, and the like must be fun, exciting, and most of all, effective in creating new ideas if they want their customers to tell others about them.

### Thinking It Over

1. What kind of services could you offer others in your area? Think of tutoring, lawn mowing, hair cutting, consulting, etc. How would you go about pricing your service? Can you see how service pricing is more difficult than the pricing of goods?
2. There are lots of professional service organizations trying to sell their services to other companies, including legal, accounting, financial, and consulting services. There are also cleaning services, delivery services, and so on. Which service organizations have been able to create a positive image for themselves that makes their companies stand out from the competition? Try to think of companies in as many areas listed above as you can. How were those positive images created?
3. Has this video given you any new insights into the service sector of the economy? How might you use those new ideas to choose a career different from those that most students are choosing?

# distributing products quickly AND efficiently

*

profile

**Getting to Know**

**X A. Jayson Adair**

**of Copart Inc.**

What happens to cars that are totally destroyed in a wreck or a natural disaster like Hurricane Katrina? Where do stolen cars go when they are recovered after the insurance settlement? How do people learn about the availability of such cars? The answer is a company called Copart Inc., located in Fairfield, California. The president and CEO of the company is A. Jayson Adair. He was born in Australia, but his father is American, so he now lives in the United States. He worked with his father, a chiropractor, and did various construction-type jobs until he helped develop Copart. The idea was to sell damaged cars and parts through auctions.

The buyers of such cars are mostly rebuilders, licensed dismantlers, and used car dealers and exporters. The cars are often sold at traditional auctions. What Copart now offers is an Internet auction that allows buyers to bid on cars they have seen in pictures (they can see 10 online) or have been inspected by people on the site. Copart also sells used parts. It has over 110 facilities in the United States and Canada. Over 20 percent of sales are made overseas to countries as far away as Cambodia or United Arab Emirates.

Clearly one of the major needs of such a company is the ability to ship parts and whole cars anywhere in the world. Copart provides services such as towing and storage to buyers and other salvage companies. But note this: Victor Viaden lives in Minsk, Belarus. He spotted a 1995 Ford Probe on the Internet site and bought it for $150. He paid $3,500 to transport it to Belarus, fixed it up, and sold it for $4,500. Clearly, Viaden could have made a lot more money if he could have cut back on the transportation expenses. That's what this chapter is all about.

Copart's Internet selling process is available (for a price) to other companies selling wrecked cars. The other companies can have an on-site auction on Monday and then have an Internet auction on Thursday to get rid of the cars unsold from Monday. Use of the Internet has enabled Copart and other such companies to go international and greatly expand their businesses.

Copart processes about 40 percent of all cars salvaged in the United States. Because of its size, the company is able to attract major sellers like State Farm. Kemper Auto and Home Group uses Copart exclusively to sell its salvaged vehicles.

This chapter is about distribution. When you buy a new computer from Dell or a book from Amazon.com, you expect

LEARNING **goals**

**After you have read and studied this chapter, you should be able to**

1. Explain the concept of marketing channels and the value of marketing intermediaries.
2. Give examples of how intermediaries perform the six marketing utilities.
3. Describe the various wholesale intermediaries in the distribution system.
4. Explain the distribution strategies retailers use.
5. Explain the various kinds of nonstore retailing.
6. Explain the various ways to build cooperation in channel systems.
7. Describe the emergence of logistics.
8. Outline how intermediaries move goods from producers to consumers through the use of various transportation modes and storage functions.

# CHAPTER 15

**www.copart.com**

to receive your order in a few days. No longer do you hear "Allow six weeks for delivery" from most firms. Jay Adair takes the Internet to a whole new level by selling automobiles and parts. The challenge, however, is much the same. Copart must get those cars to the people who bought them in a timely manner. This chapter will explore all the organizations involved in getting products from manufacturers to consumers. In Copart's case, the organizations involved recycle damaged goods so they can be used again. All such movement of goods is called logistics, as you shall see.

Sources: www.copart.com, 2006; Alex Biesada, "Copart, Inc.," Fact Sheet from Hoovers, 2005; Andrew Tilin, "Top of the Heap," *Business 2.0*, May 2005, p. 54; and Stephen Power, "Take It Back," *The Wall Street Journal*, April 17, 2006, p. R6.

# THE EMERGENCE OF MARKETING INTERMEDIARIES

**marketing intermediaries**
Organizations that assist in moving goods and services from producers to industrial and consumer users.

**channel of distribution**
A whole set of marketing intermediaries, such as wholesalers and retailers that join together to transport and store goods in their path (or channel) from producers to consumers.

**agents/brokers**
Marketing intermediaries who bring buyers and sellers together and assist in negotiating an exchange but don't take title to the goods.

It is easy to overlook the importance of the distribution and storage functions in marketing. That's because so much discussion focuses on advertising, selling, marketing research, and other such functions. But it doesn't take much to realize the importance of distribution. For example, consider shoes made by Timberland. Imagine the challenge of getting the raw materials together, making 12 million pairs of shoes, as Timberland does, and then distributing those shoes to stores throughout the world. That's what thousands of manufacturing firms—making everything from automobiles to toys—have to deal with every day. There are hundreds of thousands of marketing intermediaries whose job it is to help move goods from the raw-material state to producers and then on to consumers. Then, in the case of Copart, from consumers to recyclers and back to manufacturers or assemblers.[1] Managing the flow of goods through those intermediaries has become one of the most important managerial functions for many organizations. Let's look at some of the organizations involved.

**Marketing intermediaries** (they were once called *middlemen*) are organizations that assist in moving goods and services from producers to business and consumer users. They're called intermediaries because they're in the middle of a series of organizations that join together to help distribute goods from producers to consumers. A **channel of distribution** consists of a whole set of marketing intermediaries, such as agents, brokers, wholesalers, and retailers, that join together to transport and store goods in their path (or channel) from producers to consumers. **Agents/brokers** are marketing intermediaries who bring buyers and sellers together and assist in negotiating an exchange, but don't take title to the goods—that is, at no point do they own the goods. A **wholesaler** is a marketing intermediary that sells to other organizations, such as retailers, manufacturers, and hospitals. They are part of the business-to-business (B2B) system. A **retailer** is an organization that sells to ultimate consumers (that is, people like you and me).

Channels of distribution help ensure communication flows *and* the flow of money and title to goods. They also help ensure that the right quantity and assortment of goods will be available when and where needed.[2] Figure 15.1 pictures selected channels of distribution for both consumer and industrial (or B2B) goods.

## Why Marketing Needs Intermediaries

Manufacturers don't always need marketing intermediaries to sell their goods to consumer and business buyers.[3] Figure 15.1 shows that some manufacturers sell directly to buyers. So why have marketing intermediaries at all? The answer is that intermediaries perform certain marketing tasks—such as transporting, storing, selling, advertising, and relationship building—faster and cheaper than most manufacturers could.[4] A simple analogy is this: You could deliver packages in person to people anywhere in the world, but usually you don't. Why not? Because it's usually cheaper and faster for you to have them delivered by the U.S. Postal Service or some private firm such as UPS or FedEx.

The distribution system in the United States is apparent when you are driving on a freeway. You see the thousands of trucks and trains moving goods from here to there. But what are not so visible are the many distribution warehouses that store goods until they are needed. Have you ever thought about the benefits of having food, furniture, and other needed goods close at hand?

Similarly, you could sell your home by yourself or buy stock directly from other people, but you probably wouldn't do so. Why? Again, because there are specialists (agents and brokers) who make the process more efficient and easier than it would be otherwise. Agents and brokers are marketing intermediaries. They facilitate

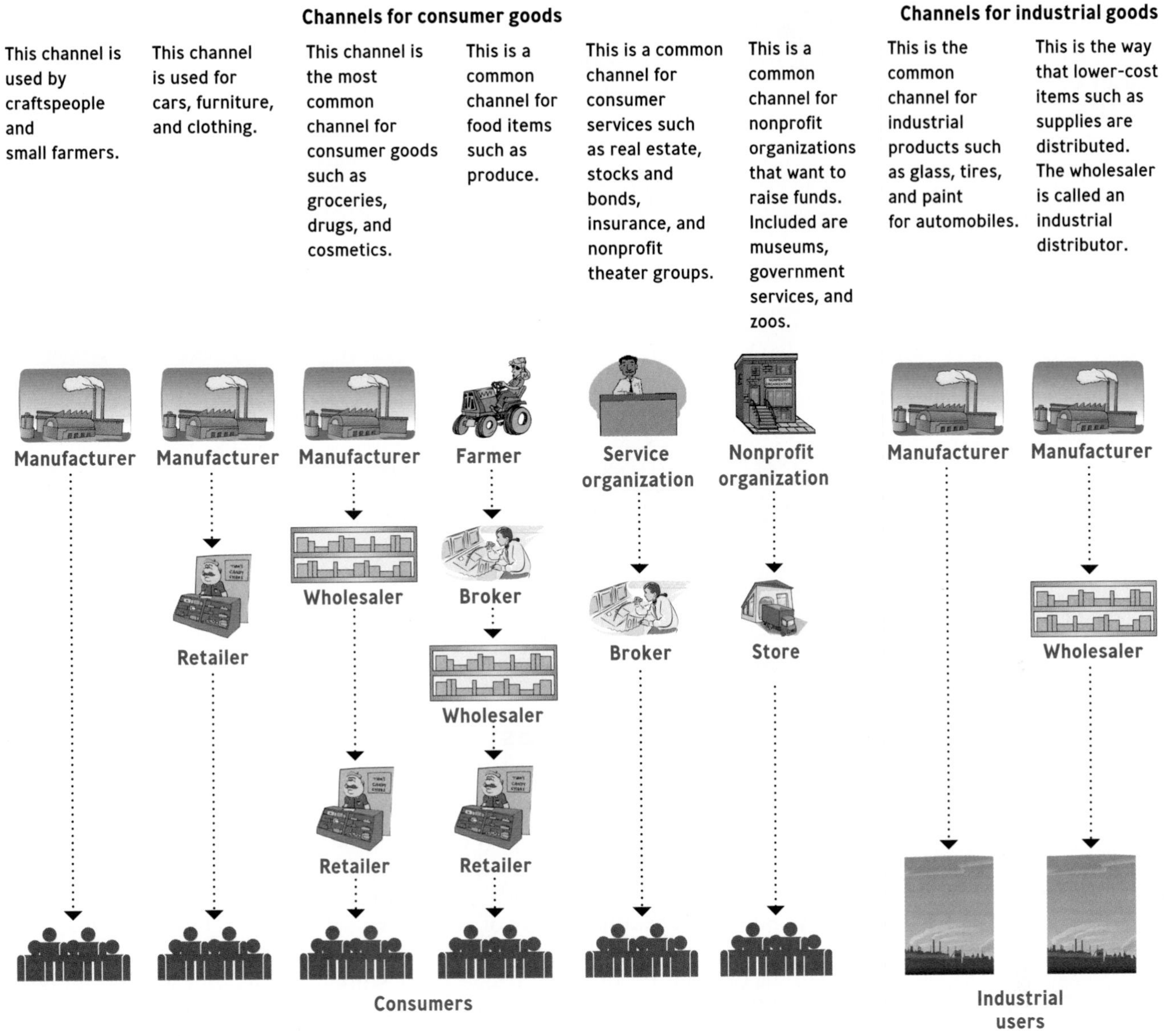

**Channels for consumer goods**

This channel is used by craftspeople and small farmers.
Manufacturer
Consumers

This channel is used for cars, furniture, and clothing.
Manufacturer
Retailer
Consumers

This channel is the most common channel for consumer goods such as groceries, drugs, and cosmetics.
Manufacturer
Wholesaler
Retailer
Consumers

This is a common channel for food items such as produce.
Farmer
Broker
Wholesaler
Retailer
Consumers

This is a common channel for consumer services such as real estate, stocks and bonds, insurance, and nonprofit theater groups.
Service organization
Broker
Consumers

This is a common channel for nonprofit organizations that want to raise funds. Included are museums, government services, and zoos.
Nonprofit organization
Store
Consumers

**Channels for industrial goods**

This is the common channel for industrial products such as glass, tires, and paint for automobiles.
Manufacturer
Industrial users

This is the way that lower-cost items such as supplies are distributed. The wholesaler is called an industrial distributor.
Manufacturer
Wholesaler
Industrial users

**figure 15.1**

**SELECTED CHANNELS OF DISTRIBUTION FOR CONSUMER AND INDUSTRIAL GOODS AND SERVICES**

the exchange process. In the next section, we'll explore how intermediaries improve the efficiency of various exchanges.

## How Intermediaries Create Exchange Efficiency

The benefits of using marketing intermediaries can be illustrated rather easily. Suppose that five manufacturers of various food products each tried to sell directly to five retailers. The number of exchange relationships that would have to be established is 5 times 5, or 25. But picture what happens when a wholesaler enters the system. The five manufacturers would contact one wholesaler to establish five exchange relationships. The wholesaler would have to establish contact with the five retailers. That would also mean five exchange relationships. Note that the number of exchanges is reduced from 25 to only 10 by the addition of a wholesaler. Figure 15.2 on page 406 shows this process.

Some economists have said that intermediaries add *costs* and need to be eliminated. Marketers say that intermediaries add *value* and that the *value greatly exceeds the cost*. In the next section, we shall explore this debate and show you the value that intermediaries provide.

**wholesaler**
A marketing intermediary that sells to other organizations.

**retailer**
An organization that sells to ultimate consumers.

figure 15.2

**HOW INTERMEDIARIES CREATE EXCHANGE EFFICIENCY**

This figure shows that adding a wholesaler to the channel of distribution cuts the number of contacts from 25 to 10. This improves the efficiency of distribution.

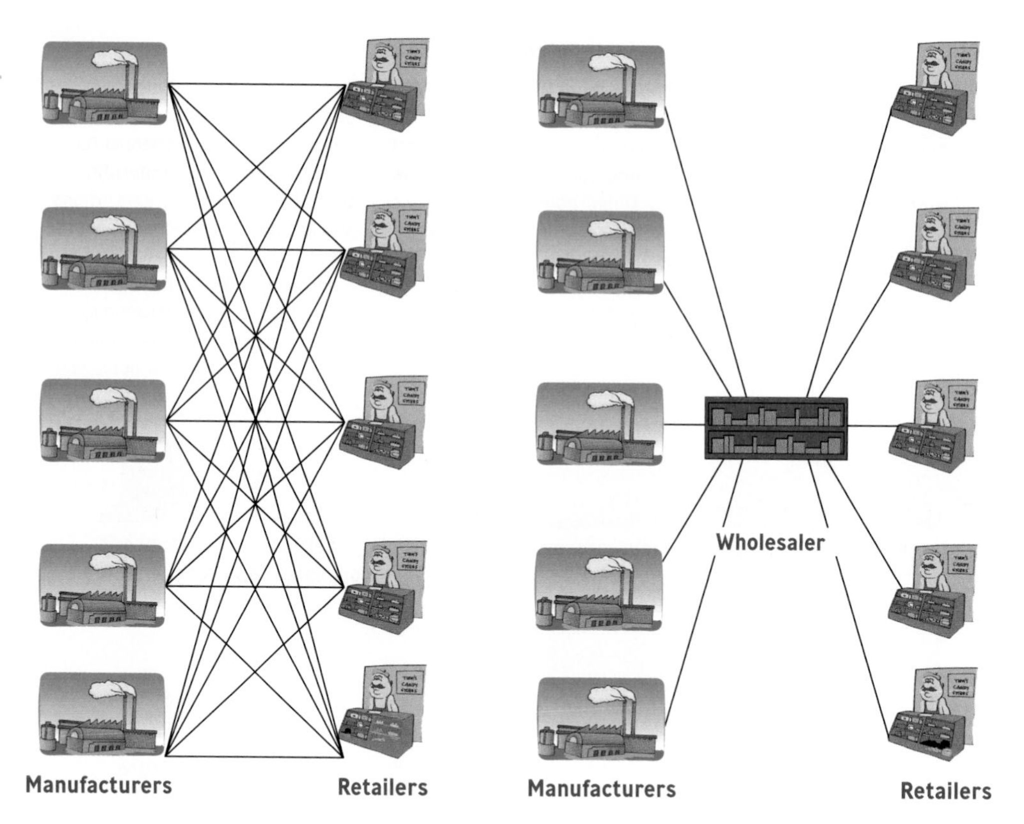


## The Value versus the Cost of Intermediaries

Marketing intermediaries have always been viewed by the public with a degree of suspicion. Some surveys have shown that about half of the cost of the things we buy are marketing costs that go largely to pay for the work of intermediaries. People reason that if we could only get rid of intermediaries, we could greatly reduce the cost of everything we buy. Sounds good, but is the solution really that simple?

Let's take as an example a box of cereal that sells for $4. How could we, as consumers, get the cereal for less? Well, we could all drive to Michigan where some of the cereal is produced and save some shipping costs. But would that be practical? Can you imagine millions of people getting in their cars and driving to Michigan just to buy some cereal? No, it doesn't make sense. It's much cheaper to have intermediaries bring the cereal to major cities. That might involve transportation and warehousing by wholesalers. These steps add cost, don't they? Yes, but they add value as well, the value of not having to drive to Michigan.

The cereal is now in a warehouse somewhere on the outskirts of the city. We could all drive down to the wholesaler and pick it up. But that still isn't the most economical way to buy cereal. If we figure in the cost of gas and time, the cereal would be too expensive. Instead, we prefer to have someone move the cereal from the warehouse to a truck, drive it to the corner supermarket, unload it, unpack it, price it, shelve it, and wait for us to come in to buy it. To make it even more convenient, the supermarket may stay open for 24 hours a day, seven days a week. Think of the costs. But think also of the value! For $4, we can get a box of cereal *when* we want it, and with little effort.

If we were to get rid of the retailer, we could buy a box of cereal for slightly less, but we'd have to drive farther and spend time in the warehouse looking through rows of cereals. If we got rid of the wholesaler, we could save a little more money, not counting our drive to Michigan. But a few cents here and a few cents there add up—to the point where marketing may add up to 75 cents for every 25 cents in manufacturing costs.

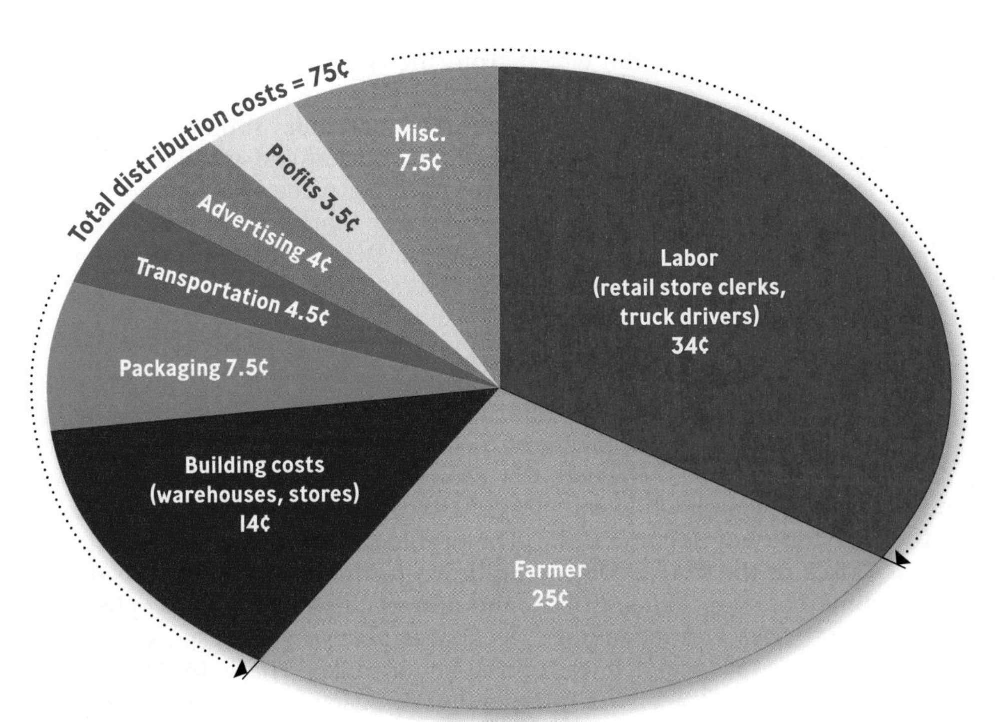


figure 15.3

**DISTRIBUTION'S EFFECT ON YOUR FOOD DOLLAR**

Note that the farmer gets only 25 cents of your food dollar. The bulk of your money goes to intermediaries to pay distribution costs. Their biggest cost is labor (truck drivers, clerks), followed by warehouses and storage.

Figure 15.3 shows where your money goes in the distribution process. Notice that the largest percentage goes to people who drive trucks and work in wholesale and retail organizations. Note also that only 3.5 cents goes to profit. Here are three basic points about intermediaries:

1. Marketing intermediaries can be eliminated, but their activities can't; that is, you can eliminate some wholesalers and retailers, but then consumers or someone else would have to perform the intermediaries' tasks, including transporting and storing goods, finding suppliers, and establishing communication with suppliers.
2. Intermediary organizations have survived in the past because they have performed marketing functions faster and cheaper than others could.[5] To maintain their competitive position in the channel, intermediaries must adopt the latest in technology.[6]
3. Intermediaries add costs to products, but these costs are usually more than offset by the values they create.

## THE UTILITIES CREATED BY INTERMEDIARIES

**Utility,** in economics, is the want-satisfying ability, or value, that organizations add to goods or services when the products are made more useful or accessible to consumers than they were before. Six utilities are added: form, time, place, possession, information, and service. Although some utilities are performed largely by producers, most are performed by marketing intermediaries. We shall explore all the utilities next and describe how intermediaries provide each.

**utility**
In economics, the want-satisfying ability, or value, that organizations add to goods or services when the products are made more useful or accessible to consumers than they were before.

### Form Utility

Traditionally, *form utility* (see Chapter 9) has been provided mostly by producers rather than by intermediaries. It consists of taking raw materials and changing their form so that they become useful products. Thus, a farmer who separates

Think of how many stores provide time utility by having goods and services available to you 24 hours a day, seven days a week. Have you ever needed to renew a drug prescription late at night or buy something from the pharmacy at the last minute? Can you see how time utility offers added value?

the wheat from the chaff and the processor who turns the wheat into flour are creating form utility. Retailers and other marketers sometimes perform form utility as well. For example, retail butchers cut pork chops from a larger piece of meat and trim off the fat. The servers at Starbucks make coffee just the way you want it. Dell assembles computers according to customers' wishes.[7]

## Time Utility

**time utility** Adding value to products by making them available when they're needed.

Intermediaries, such as retailers, add **time utility** to products by making them available when they're needed. For example, Devar Tennent lives in Boston. One winter evening while watching TV with his brother, Tennent suddenly got the urge for a hot dog and Coke. The problem was that there were no hot dogs or Cokes in the house. Devar ran down to the corner delicatessen and bought some hot dogs, buns, Cokes, and potato chips. He also bought some frozen strawberries and ice cream. Devar was able to get these groceries at midnight because the local deli was open 24 hours a day. That's time utility. You can buy goods at any time on the Internet, but you can't beat having them available right around the corner *when you want them*. On the other hand, note the *value* that an Internet company provides by staying accessible 24 hours a day.

## Place Utility

**place utility** Adding value to products by having them where people want them.

Intermediaries add **place utility** to products by having them *where* people want them. For example, while traveling through the badlands of South Dakota, Juanita Ruiz got hungry and thirsty. There are no stores for miles in this part of the country. Juanita saw one of many signs along the road saying that Wall Drug with fountain service was up ahead. Lured by the signs, she stopped at the store for refreshments. She also bought some sunglasses and souvenir items there. The goods and services provided by Wall Drug are in a convenient place for vacationers. Throughout the United States, 7-Eleven stores remain popular because they are usually in easy-to-reach locations. They provide place utility.[8] As more and more sales become global, place utility will grow in importance.

## Possession Utility

**possession utility** Doing whatever is necessary to transfer ownership from one party to another, including providing credit, delivery, installation, guarantees, and follow-up service.

Intermediaries add **possession utility** by doing whatever is necessary to transfer ownership from one party to another, including providing credit. Activities associated with possession utility include delivery, installation, guarantees, and follow-up service. For example, Larry Rosenberg wanted to buy a nice home in the suburbs. He found just what he wanted, but he didn't have the money he needed. So he went with the real estate broker to a local savings and loan and borrowed the money to buy the home. Both the real estate broker and the savings and loan are marketing intermediaries that provide possession utility. For those consumers who don't want to own goods, possession utility makes it possible for them to use goods through renting or leasing.

## Information Utility

**information utility** Adding value to products by opening two-way flows of information between marketing participants.

Intermediaries add **information utility** by opening two-way flows of information between marketing participants. For example, Jerome Washington couldn't decide what kind of TV set to buy. He looked at various ads in the

*** MAKING

## ethical decisions

### Look One Place, Buy Another

After talking with some of your friends, you have discovered a practice that is quite common among them. It goes like this: They go to a local department store or furniture store and shop. They talk to the salespeople and get all kinds of help with the choice of fabrics and other matters. They copy all the information on a piece of paper, including the name of the manufacturer, the model number of the piece they are looking at, and the price. They then call the manufacturer and order the item directly, thus saving the retail markup. Often they simply go online and do the same. For every $1 that consumers spend online, they spend $6 offline (in stores) using the research they did online to find the best deals.

You need a new sofa for your apartment. The retail price at your local furniture store is $2,000. The price directly from the manufacturer is closer to $1,600. You have spent lots of time with the salesperson at the store and she was very helpful. She helped you pick out colors and fabrics. You wonder about the ethical issue of buying the sofa somewhere else. Does the fact that many consumers use the Internet to learn about products and then go to the store to buy them change the ethical situation? You know lots of others are getting information at stores and then buying online, so why not you? Does the excuse "Everyone does it" make it ethical? What would you do? Are there ethical consequences?

Source: Robert Buderi, "E-Commerce Gets Smarter," *Technology Review*, April 2005, pp. 54–59; Richard Waters, "Online Revolution," *Financial Times*, September 21, 2005, p. 1; and Kyle Cattani, Hans Sebastian Heese, Wendell Gilland and Jayashankar Swaminathan, "When Manufacturers Go Retail," *MIT Sloan Management Review*, Winter 2006, p. 9.

newspaper, talked to salespeople at several stores, and read material at the library and on the Internet. He also got some booklets from the government about radiation hazards and consumer buying tips. Newspapers, salespeople, libraries, Web sites, and government publications are all information sources made available by intermediaries.[9] They provide information utility. Check out the Making Ethical Decisions box. It explores an ethical question involved with getting free information utility from one intermediary with the intention of buying from another.

## Service Utility

Intermediaries add **service utility** by providing fast, friendly service during and after the sale and by teaching customers how to best use products over time. For example, Sze Leung bought a personal computer for his office at home. Both the computer manufacturer and the retailer where he bought the computer continue to offer help whenever Leung needs it. He also gets software updates for a small fee to keep his computer up-to-date. What attracted Leung to the retailer in the first place was the helpful, friendly service he received from the salesperson in the store. Service utility is rapidly becoming the most important utility for many retailers because without it they could lose business to direct marketing (e.g., marketing by catalog or on the Internet). Can you see how some of these services could be provided over the Internet?

**service utility**
Adding value by providing fast, friendly service during and after the sale and by teaching customers how to best use products over time.

### progress assessment

- What is a channel of distribution, and what intermediaries are involved?
- Why do we need intermediaries? Can you illustrate how intermediaries create exchange efficiency? How would you defend intermediaries to someone who said that getting rid of them would save millions of dollars?
- Can you give examples of the utilities created by intermediaries and how intermediaries perform them?

# WHOLESALE INTERMEDIARIES

There's often some confusion about the difference between wholesalers and retailers. It's helpful to distinguish wholesaling from retailing, and to clearly define the functions performed in each, so that companies can design effective systems of distribution. Some producers will deal only with wholesalers and won't sell directly to retailers. Some producers give wholesalers a bigger discount than retailers. What confuses the issue is that some organizations sell much of their merchandise to other intermediaries (a wholesale sale) but also sell to ultimate consumers (a retail sale). The office superstore Staples is a good example. It sells office supplies to small businesses and to consumers as well. Warehouse clubs such as Sam's Club and Costco are also examples.

The issue is really rather simple: A *retail sale* is the sale of goods and services to consumers for their own use. A *wholesale sale* is the sale of goods and services to businesses and institutions (e.g., hospitals) for use in the business or to wholesalers or retailers for resale. Wholesalers make business-to-business (B2B) sales. Most people are not as familiar with the various kinds of wholesalers as they are with retailers. Let's explore some of these helpful wholesale intermediaries. Pay attention to this section because such intermediaries provide a lot of marketing jobs that other students don't know about; thus, you have a good opportunity to find a good job in such places.

## Merchant Wholesalers

**merchant wholesalers**
Independently owned firms that take title to (own) the goods they handle.

**Merchant wholesalers** are independently owned firms that take title to the goods they handle. About 80 percent of wholesalers fall in this category. There are two types of merchant wholesalers: full-service wholesalers and limited-function wholesalers. *Full-service wholesalers* perform all of the distribution functions (see Figure 15.4). *Limited-function wholesalers* perform only selected functions, but try to do them especially well. Three common types of limited-function wholesalers are rack jobbers, cash-and-carry wholesalers, and drop shippers.

**rack jobbers**
Wholesalers that furnish racks or shelves full of merchandise to retailers, display products, and sell on consignment.

**Rack jobbers** furnish racks or shelves full of merchandise to retailers, display products, and sell on consignment. This means that they keep title to the goods until they're sold, and then they share the profits with the retailer. Merchandise such as music, toys, hosiery, and health and beauty aids are sold by rack jobbers.

**cash-and-carry wholesalers**
Wholesalers that serve mostly smaller retailers with a limited assortment of products.

**Cash-and-carry wholesalers** serve mostly smaller retailers with a limited assortment of products. Traditionally, retailers went to such wholesalers, paid cash, and carried the goods back to their stores—thus the term *cash-and-carry*. Today, stores such as Office Depot and Staples allow retailers and others to use credit cards for wholesale purchases.

**drop shippers**
Wholesalers that solicit orders from retailers and other wholesalers and have the merchandise shipped directly from a producer to a buyer.

**Drop shippers** solicit orders from retailers and other wholesalers and have the merchandise shipped directly from a producer to a buyer. They own the merchandise but don't handle, stock, or deliver it. That's done by the producer. Drop shippers tend to handle bulky products such as coal, lumber, and chemicals.

## Agents and Brokers

Agents and brokers bring buyers and sellers together and assist in negotiating an exchange. However, unlike merchant wholesalers, agents and brokers never own the products they distribute. Usually they do not carry inventory, provide credit, or assume risks. While merchant wholesalers earn a profit from the sale of goods, agents and brokers earn commissions or fees based on a percentage

figure 15.4

A FULL-SERVICE WHOLESALER

| A FULL-SERVICE WHOLESALER WILL: | THE WHOLESALER MAY PERFORM THE FOLLOWING SERVICES FOR CUSTOMERS: |
|---|---|
| 1. Provide a sales force to sell the goods to retailers and other buyers. | 1. Buy goods the end market will desire and make them available to customers. |
| 2. Communicate manufacturers' advertising deals and plans. | 2. Maintain inventory, thus reducing customers' costs. |
| 3. Maintain inventory, thus reducing the level of the inventory suppliers have to carry. | 3. Transport goods to customers quickly. |
| 4. Arrange or undertake transportation. | 4. Provide market information and business consulting services. |
| 5. Provide capital by paying cash or quick payments for goods. | 5. Provide financing through granting credit, which is especially critical to small retailers. |
| 6. Provide suppliers with market information they can't afford or can't obtain themselves. | 6. Order goods in the types and quantities customers desire. |
| 7. Undertake credit risk by granting credit to customers and absorbing any bad debts, thus relieving the supplier of this burden. | |
| 8. Assume the risk for the product by taking title. | |

Source: Thomas C. Kinnear, *Principles of Marketing*, 4th ed., © 1995, p. 394. Reprinted by permission of Pearson Education, Inc., Upper Saddle River, NJ.

of the sales revenues. Agents and brokers differ in that agents maintain long-term relationships with the people they represent, whereas brokers are usually hired on a temporary basis.

Agents who represent producers are known as *manufacturer's agents* or *sales agents*. As long as they do not represent competing products, manufacturer's agents may represent one or several manufacturers in a specific territory. Manufacturer's agents are often used in the automotive supply, footwear, and fabricated steel industries. Sales agents represent a single producer in a typically larger territory. Sales agents are used by small producers in the textile and home furnishing industries.

Brokers have no continuous relationship with the buyer or seller. Once they negotiate a contract between a buyer and seller, their relationship ends. Brokers are used by the producers of seasonal products (e.g., fruits and vegetables) and in the real estate industry.

## RETAIL INTERMEDIARIES

A supermarket is a retail store. A retailer, remember, is a marketing intermediary that sells to ultimate consumers. The United States boasts approximately 2.3 million retail stores. This does not include the retail Web sites. Retail organizations employ more than 11 million people and are one of the major employers of marketing graduates. Figure 15.5 on page 412 lists, describes, and gives examples of various kinds of retailers. Have you shopped in each kind of store? What seems to be the advantages of each? Would you enjoy working in a retail store of some kind? Some retailers seem to compete mostly on price, but others, such as specialty stores, use variety as a competitive tool.

| TYPE | DESCRIPTION | EXAMPLE |
|---|---|---|
| Department store | Sells a wide variety of products (clothes, furniture, housewares) in separate departments | Sears, JCPenney, Nordstrom |
| Discount store | Sells many different products at prices generally below those of department stores | Wal-Mart, Target |
| Supermarket | Sells mostly food with other nonfood products such as detergent and paper products | Safeway, Kroger, Albertson's |
| Warehouse club | Sells food and general merchandise in facilities that are usually larger than supermarkets and offer discount prices; membership may be required | Costco, Sam's Club |
| Convenience store | Sells food and other often-needed items at convenient locations; may stay open all night | 7-Eleven |
| Category killer | Sells a huge variety of one type of product to dominate that category of goods | Toys "R" Us, Bass Proshops, Office Depot |
| Outlet store | Sells general merchandise directly from the manufacturer at a discount; items may be discontinued or have flaws ("seconds") | Nordstrom Rack, Liz Claiborne, Nike, TJ Maxx |
| Specialty store | Sells a wide selection of goods in one category | Jewelry stores, shoe stores, bicycle shops |

figure 15.5

**TYPES OF RETAIL STORES**

## Retail Distribution Strategy

A major decision marketers must make is selecting the right retailers to sell their products. Different products call for different retail distribution strategies. There are three categories of retail distribution: intensive distribution, selective distribution, and exclusive distribution.

**intensive distribution**
Distribution that puts products into as many retail outlets as possible.

**Intensive distribution** puts products into as many retail outlets as possible, including vending machines. Products that need intensive distribution include convenience goods such as candy, cigarettes, gum, and popular magazines.

**selective distribution**
Distribution that sends products to only a preferred group of retailers in an area.

**Selective distribution** is the use of only a preferred group of the available retailers in an area. Such selection helps to assure producers of quality sales and service. Manufacturers of appliances, furniture, and clothing (shopping goods) usually use selective distribution.

**exclusive distribution**
Distribution that sends products to only one retail outlet in a given geographic area.

**Exclusive distribution** is the use of only one retail outlet in a given geographic area. The retailer has exclusive rights to sell the product and is therefore likely to carry a large inventory, give exceptional service, and pay more attention to this brand than to others. Luxury auto manufacturers often use exclusive distribution, as do producers of specialty goods such as skydiving equipment or fly-fishing products.

**progress assessment**

- Describe the activities of rack jobbers and drop shippers.
- What kinds of products would call for each of the different distribution strategies: intensive, selective, exclusive?

## Nonstore Retailing

Nothing else in retailing has received more attention recently than electronic retailing. Internet retailing, however, is just one form of nonstore retailing. Other categories of nonstore retailing include telemarketing; vending machines, kiosks, and carts; direct selling; multilevel marketing; and direct marketing. Small businesses can use nonstore retailing to open up new channels of distribution for their products.

## Electronic Retailing

**electronic retailing**
Selling goods and services to ultimate customers (e.g., you and me) over the Internet.

**Electronic retailing** consists of selling goods and services to ultimate consumers (e.g., you and me) over the Internet. Because of Web site improvements and discounts, online retail sales were predicted to jump 22 percent in 2005, to $172 billion.[10] But getting customers is only half the battle. The other half is delivering the goods, providing helpful service, and keeping your customers. When electronic retailers fail to have sufficient inventory or fail to deliver goods on time (especially at Christmastime and other busy periods), customers give up and go back to brick-and-mortar stores.

Most Internet retailers now offer e-mail confirmation. But sometimes electronic retailers are not so good at handling complaints, taking back goods that customers don't like, and providing personal help. Some Web sites are trying to improve customer service by adding help buttons that lead customers to almost instant assistance from a real person. RightStart.com, for example, is a seller of children's toys and products. It has added a live chat function to its online retailing. If you have a problem, you click the Live Help link and a customer-service representative answers within minutes.

Old brick-and-mortar stores are rapidly going online also. The result, sometimes called a brick-and-click store, allows customers to choose which shopping technique suits them best.[11] In any case, most companies that want to compete in the future will probably need both a real store presence and an online presence to provide consumers with all the options they want. Part of that strategy is to include the company's phone number in all Internet promotions so that consumers can call in an order as well as place it online.

Traditional retailers like Sears have learned that selling on the Internet calls for a new kind of distribution system. Sears's warehouses were accustomed to delivering truckloads of goods to the company's retail outlets. But they were not prepared to make deliveries, except for large orders like furniture and appliances, to individual consumers. It turns out, therefore, that both traditional retailers and new Internet retailers have to develop new distribution systems to meet the demands of today's Internet-savvy shoppers. The new chairman of Sears Holdings Corporation is Eddie Lampert. The retail world is watching to see how good he is in rebuilding Sears so that it can compete more effectively with Wal-Mart and Target.[12] See the Reaching Beyond Our Borders box on page 414 to see how quickly retailers have learned to respond to customer demand.

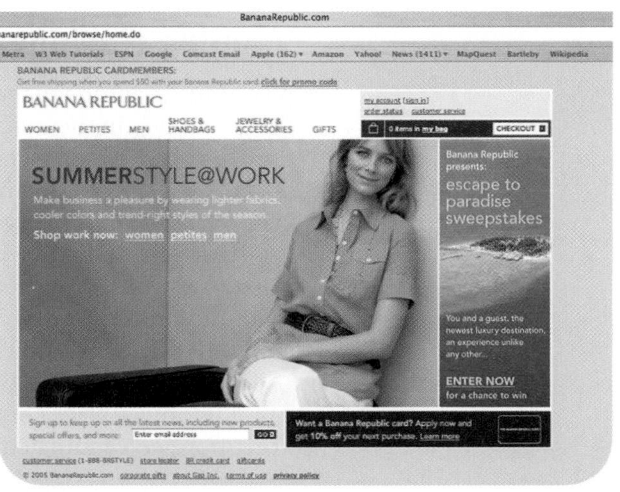


There are many examples of brick-and-mortar stores adding Internet services for their customers for added convenience. Some people shop on the Internet and then go to the store to buy the merchandise. Others both shop and buy on the Internet. What leads you to shop from a store rather than on the Internet? What are the advantages and disadvantages of shopping and buying on the Internet?

REACHING BEYOND our borders

www.inditex.com

## What You Want, When You Want It

You can find what you want at Zara and, if you can't, you only have to wait a couple of days and shop again, because Zara has one of the best supply-chain systems in the world. Zara, owned by parent Inditex, is an apparel store with a flagship store in Madrid, Spain. You can find Zara stores in Germany, Italy, Great Britain, and the United States. There is another one in San Juan, Puerto Rico. In fact, the company added a store a day in 2005 and hopes to have 4,000 stores in 70 countries by the end of the decade.

What is special about these stores is the response they make to consumer wants and needs. Few markets change as rapidly as the consumer fashion industry, and no other store is more responsive than Zara. Store managers use handheld computers to punch in orders as customer demand dictates. Some 200 designers and product managers compile the data from the various stores and decide what to produce next. That information is sent by intranet to a group of nearby factories. Within days, those outfits will be hanging on store shelves. Flexible factories can replace or redesign a pair of jeans faster than a teenager can change her mind.

The clothes are gathered in a huge warehouse that's about nine times bigger than Amazon.com's warehouse (about 90 football fields). The warehouse is connected to 14 factories through a maze of tunnels. Items move into the warehouse and are out the door in a matter of hours. Zara is thus able to have twice-a-week deliveries that bring in fresh designs all the time. Shoppers can come in weekly and find new merchandise that represents the latest in fashion.

Part of what makes Zara's amazing distribution system so fast is that Zara does not go overseas to manufacture its clothes. The merchandise may cost more as a result, but it is much fresher and more up-to-date than clothing sold in other retail stores.

Source: "Zara: A Model Fashion Retailer," CNNInternational.com, July 22, 2004; and Sarah Mower, "The Zara Phenomenon," London (England) *Evening Standard*, January 13, 2006.

## Telemarketing

**telemarketing**
The sale of goods and services by telephone.

**Telemarketing** is the sale of goods and services by telephone. Some 80,000 companies have used telemarketing to supplement or replace in-store selling and to complement online selling. Many send a catalog to consumers and let them order by calling a toll-free number. As we noted, many electronic retailers provide a help feature online that serves the same function. The National Do Not Call Registry, which went into effect in 2003, was expected to eliminate 80 percent of telemarketing calls, so there is likely to be a big dropoff in that kind of telemarketing.

## Vending Machines, Kiosks, and Carts

A vending machine dispenses convenience goods when consumers deposit sufficient money in the machine. Vending machines carry the benefit of location—they're found in airports, office buildings, schools, service stations, and other areas where people want convenience items. Vending machines in Japan sell everything from bandages and face cloths to salads and spiced seafood. Vending by machine will be an interesting area to watch as such innovations are introduced in the United States. You may be surprised to learn that vending machines in the United States are now selling iPods, Bose headphones, sneakers, digital cameras, and DVD movies.[13]

Carts and kiosks have lower overhead costs than stores do; therefore, they can offer lower prices on items such as T-shirts, purses, watches, and umbrellas. You often see vending carts outside stores on the sidewalk or along walkways in malls; mall owners often love them because they're colorful and create a marketplace atmosphere. Kiosk workers often dispense coupons and provide all kinds of helpful information to consumers, who tend to enjoy the interaction. Also, many kiosks serve as gateways to the Internet, so consumers can shop at a store and still have access to all the products available on the Internet in one place.

Direct selling is a great way to reach consumers who are often too busy to go shopping themselves. The salesperson provides immediate attention and help, and the customer saves time. Have you ever bought goods at such a sale? What did you notice about the atmosphere of the sales situation that differed from in-store buying?

## Direct Selling

**Direct selling** involves selling to consumers in their homes or where they work. Major users of this category include cosmetics producers (Avon) and vacuum cleaner manufacturers (Electrolux). Trying to emulate the success of those companies, other businesses are now venturing into direct selling. Lingerie, artwork, and plants are just a few of the goods now sold at "house parties" sponsored by sellers.[14]

Because so many men and women work outside the home and aren't at home during the day, companies that use direct selling are sponsoring parties at workplaces or in the evenings and on weekends. Some companies, such as those in encyclopedia sales, have dropped most of their direct selling efforts in favor of Internet selling.

**direct selling**
Selling to consumers in their homes or where they work.

## Multilevel Marketing

Over 1,000 U.S. companies have had great success using multilevel marketing (MLM). MLM salespeople work as independent contractors. They earn commissions on their own sales, and they also create commissions for the "upliners" who recruited them. In turn, they receive commissions from any "downliners" they recruit to sell. When you have hundreds of downliners—that is, people who have been recruited by the people you recruit—the commissions can be quite sizable. Some people make tens of thousands of dollars a month this way.

The main attraction of multilevel marketing for employees, other than the potential for making money, is the low cost of entry. For a small investment, the average person can start up a business and begin recruiting others. Many people question MLM marketing because some companies using it have been unethical. It is true that *one must be very careful to examine the practices of such firms*. Nonetheless, the success of this form of marketing is revealed by the fact that MLM sales overall have reached $18 billion a year.

## Direct Marketing

**direct marketing**
Any activity that directly links manufacturers or intermediaries with the ultimate consumer.

One of the fastest-growing aspects of retailing is direct marketing. **Direct marketing** includes any activity that directly links manufacturers or intermediaries with the ultimate consumer. Thus, direct retail marketing includes direct mail, catalog sales, and telemarketing as well as online marketing.[15] Popular consumer catalog companies that use direct marketing include Coldwater Creek, L. L. Bean, and Lands' End. Direct marketing has created tremendous competition in some high-tech areas as well.

Direct marketing has become popular because shopping from home or work is more convenient for consumers than going to stores. Instead of driving to a mall, people can "shop" in catalogs and freestanding advertising supplements in the newspaper and then buy by phone, mail, or computer. Interactive

**corporate distribution system**
A distribution system in which all of the organizations in the channel of distribution are owned by one firm.

**contractual distribution system**
A distribution system in which members are bound to cooperate through contractual agreements.

online selling is expected to provide increasing competition for retail stores in the near future.

Direct marketing took on a new dimension when consumers became involved with interactive video. Producers now provide all kinds of information on CD-ROMs or Web sites. The potential of such systems seems almost limitless. Consumers can ask questions, seek the best price, and order goods and services—all by computer. Companies that use interactive video have become major competitors for those who market by regular paper catalogs.

For consumers to receive the maximum benefit from marketing intermediaries, the various organizations must work together to ensure a smooth flow of goods and services to the consumer. Historically, there hasn't always been total harmony in the channel of distribution. As a result, channel members have created certain systems that make the flows more efficient. We'll discuss those systems next.

Harry and David uses a combination of brick-and-mortar stores, catalogs, and a website to sell its gift baskets, fresh fruits, candy, pies, and other goodies. Forget to buy someone a gift? Just go to harryanddavid.com and find something special to send out immediately. What advantages does each option (store, catalog, website) offer consumers?

## BUILDING COOPERATION IN CHANNEL SYSTEMS

One way that traditional retailers can stay competitive with online retailers is to make the whole system so efficient that online retailers can't beat them on cost—given the need for customers to pay for delivery. That means that manufacturers, wholesalers, and retailers (members of the channel of distribution) must work closely together to form a unified system.[16] How can manufacturers get wholesalers and retailers to cooperate in such a system? One way is to somehow link the firms together in a formal relationship. Four systems have emerged to tie firms together: corporate systems, contractual systems, administered systems, and supply chains.

Harry & David
Cool Fruit 2006
Fresh Cherries:
Reserve Yours Now!
Save now at our Summer Sale!
Dark Sweet Cherries (page 3)


### Corporate Distribution Systems

A **corporate distribution system** is one in which all of the organizations in the channel of distribution are owned by one firm. If the manufacturer owns the retail firm, clearly it can maintain a great deal of control over its operations. Sherwin-Williams, for example, owns its own retail stores and thus coordinates everything: display, pricing, promotion, inventory control, and so on. Other companies that have tried corporate systems include General Electric, Firestone, and Xerox.

### Contractual Distribution Systems

If a manufacturer can't buy retail stores, it can try to get retailers to sign a contract to cooperate. A **contractual distribution system** is one in which members are bound to cooperate through contractual agreements. There are three forms of contractual systems:

1. *Franchise systems* such as McDonald's, KFC, Baskin-Robbins, and AAMCO. The franchisee agrees to all of the rules, regulations, and procedures established by the franchisor. This results in the consistent quality and level of service you find in most franchised organizations.

2. *Wholesaler-sponsored chains* such as Ace Hardware and IGA food stores. Each store signs an agreement to use the same name, participate in chain promotions, and cooperate as a unified system of stores, even though each store is independently owned and managed.
3. *Retail cooperatives* such as Associated Grocers. This arrangement is much like a wholesaler-sponsored chain except that it is initiated by the retailers. The same degree of cooperation exists, however, and the stores remain independent. Normally in such a system, retailers agree to focus their purchases on one wholesaler, but cooperative retailers could also purchase a wholesale organization to ensure better service.

## Administered Distribution Systems

If you were a producer, what would you do if you couldn't get retailers to sign an agreement to cooperate? One thing you could do is to manage all the marketing functions yourself, including display, inventory control, pricing, and promotion. A system in which producers manage all of the marketing functions at the retail level is called an **administered distribution system**. Kraft does that for its cheeses; Scott does it for its seed and other lawn care products. Retailers cooperate with producers in such systems because they get a great deal of free help. All the retailer has to do is ring up the sale.

**administered distribution system**
A distribution system in which producers manage all of the marketing functions at the retail level.

## Supply Chains

The latest in systems coordination involves the supply chain.[17] The **supply chain** (sometimes called a **value chain**) consists of the sequence of linked activities that must be performed by various organizations to move goods and services from the source of raw materials to ultimate consumers. The supply chain is longer than a channel of distribution because it includes links from suppliers to manufacturers, whereas the channel of distribution begins with manufacturers. Channels of distribution are part of the overall supply chain (see Figure 15.6). Included in the supply chain are farmers, miners, suppliers of all kinds (e.g., parts, equipment, supplies), manufacturers, wholesalers, and retailers. **Supply-chain management** is the process of managing the movement of raw materials, parts, work in progress, finished goods, and related information through all the organizations involved in the supply chain; managing the return of such goods if necessary; and recycling materials when appropriate.[18]

**supply chain (or value chain)**
The sequence of linked activities that must be performed by various organizations to move goods from the sources of raw materials to ultimate consumers.

**supply-chain management**
The process of managing the movement of raw materials, parts, work in progress, finished goods, and related information through all the organizations involved in the supply chain; managing the return of such goods, if necessary; and recycling materials when appropriate.

One example of a complex supply chain is provided by the automaker Kia's model Sorento. It is assembled in South Korea, named after an Italian resort, and made from components from all over the world. The car has over 30,000 parts. The shock and front-loading system is from AF Sachs AG, the front-wheel drive is from BorgWarner, and the tires are from Michelin. Airbags are sometimes flown in from Swedish company Autoliv Inc., which makes them in Utah. As you can see, supply-chain management is interfirm and international.[19]

figure 15.6

THE SUPPLY CHAIN

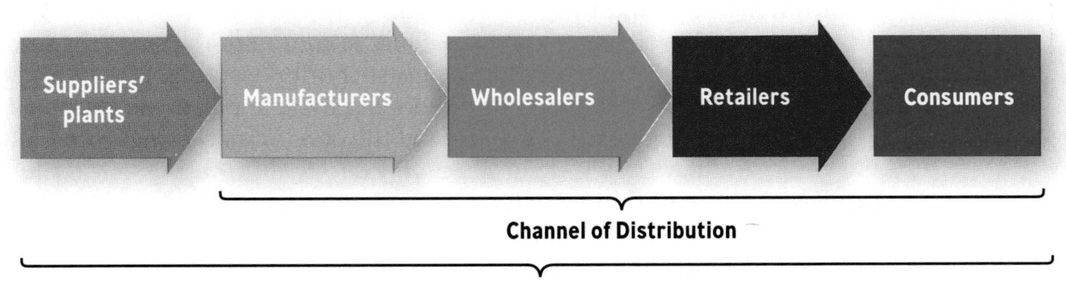

"I'm going to cut the fat ...
as soon as I can find it."


Trimming supply chain costs is tricky business. Cut the wrong thing at the wrong time, and losses can quickly cancel out gains ... and then some. The challenge: fully integrated, real-time supply chain solutions.

People, processes and technology from Menlo Worldwide answer the call: Some of the toughest, most complex logistics challenges in the world are met with the help of customer-specific solutions – engineered, installed and managed by Menlo Worldwide.

When it's time to cut waste and cost from *your* supply chain, think Menlo Worldwide. To learn more, visit us at www.menloworldwide.com.

GLOBAL NETWORK MANAGEMENT 3RD PARTY LOGISTICS SUPPLY CHAIN TECHNOLOGIES INTEGRATED SOLUTIONS CONSULTING LEAN LOGISTICS

Often companies outsource the supply chain process to firms like Menlo Worldwide. Such experts can greatly reduce distribution costs. What distribution firm do you use to send packages to others?

Countries involved in making the Kia Sorento include the United States, Mexico, Thailand, China, and, of course, South Korea.

Companies such as SAP, PeopleSoft, i2, and Manugistics have developed software that makes it possible to coordinate the movement of goods and information so that consumer wants can be translated into products with the least amount of materials, inventory, and time. The flows among firms are often so smooth that it looks like all of the organizations involved are one firm. Computers make such links possible. Naturally, the systems are quite complex and quite expensive, but they can pay for themselves in the long run because of inventory savings, customer service improvement, and responsiveness to market changes. It is because such systems are so effective and efficient that they are sometimes called *value chains* instead of supply chains.

Not all supply chains are as efficient as one would hope.[20] The complexity of supply-chain management often leads firms to outsource the whole process to experts that know how to integrate it. Richardson Electronics of LaFox, Illinois, for example, does business in 125 countries with 37 different currencies. Richardson relies on PeopleSoft's Supply Chain Management and Financial Management solutions. Note that PeopleSoft also provides financial help, making it easier and easier to ship goods anywhere in the world and be sure of payment. Outsourcing of the distribution function is on the rise as more firms realize the complexities involved.

## THE EMERGENCE OF LOGISTICS

Clearly, a major issue in marketing in the future will be: How can I ship goods from city to city or country to country in the fastest way possible and still keep costs low enough to make such exchanges mutually beneficial? This is an especially big challenge when selling bulky merchandise, such as automobiles (see this chapter's Opening Profile). When shipping from country to country, it is often impossible to use trucks or trains because the goods have to travel over water. Shipping by air is often prohibitively expensive. That narrows the choice to moving goods by ship. But how do you get the goods to the ship—and from the ship to the buyer? And how do you handle foreign trade duties and taxes?

To better manage customs problems, many companies are turning to Web-based trade compliance systems. ClearCross and Xporta, for example, determine what paperwork is needed, cross-checking their databases for information about foreign trade duties and taxes, U.S. labor law restrictions, and federal regulations from the Food and Drug Administration or the Bureau of Alcohol, Tobacco, and Firearms. Distributing goods globally is more complicated than you thought, we'd guess. As transportation and distribution issues got more and more complex, marketers responded by developing more sophisticated systems.

Distribution issues have been at the core of marketing from the very beginning. In fact, the first college courses in marketing had titles like "The Distribution of Farm Products." Those courses focused on distribution (mostly transportation), and marketing was defined as "the business activity that directs the flow of goods and services from producer to consumer." We have

How do you move heavy raw materials like timber from one country to another? This photo shows some of the firms involved in the logistics process. A trucking firm brings the logs to a dock where huge cranes lift the logs into the hold of a ship. The ship must be unloaded and the logs put on another truck to move to a processing plant. Why is successfully managing the logistics process a key to surviving in some industries?

come a long way since then, with marketers shifting focus to other issues such as product development, branding, consumer behavior, promotion, and marketing research. But marketing is now coming full circle, and physical distribution is again a major issue. Over time, the term *physical distribution* tended to be replaced by the broader term *logistics*. **Logistics** involves planning, implementing, and controlling the physical flow of materials, final goods, and related information from points of origin to points of consumption to meet customer requirements at a profit.

**Inbound logistics** brings raw materials, packaging, other goods and services, and information from suppliers to producers. **Materials handling** is the movement of goods within a warehouse, from warehouses to the factory floor, and from the factory floor to various workstations. *Factory processes* change raw materials and parts and other inputs into outputs, such as finished goods (e.g., shoes, cars, clothes). **Outbound logistics** manages the flow of finished products and information to business buyers and ultimate consumers (people like you and me). **Reverse logistics** involves bringing goods back to the manufacturer because of defects or for recycling materials.[21]

Logistics is as much about the movement of *information* as it is about the movement of goods. Customer wants and needs must flow through the system all the way to suppliers and must do so in real time. Information must also flow down through the system with no hesitation. That, of course, demands sophisticated hardware and software.

*Third-party logistics* is the term used to describe the use of outside firms to help move goods from here to there. It is part of a larger trend, mentioned earlier, of outsourcing functions that your firm cannot do more efficiently than outside firms. The Dealing with Change box on page 420 discusses how business expertise in logistics might be used in national emergencies.

Moving goods from one place to another is a major part of logistics. Next, we explore alternative means of shipment.

**logistics**
The marketing activity that involves planning, implementing, and controlling the physical flow of materials, final goods, and related information from points of origin to points of consumption to meet customer requirements at a profit.

**inbound logistics**
The area of logistics that involves bringing raw materials, packaging, other goods and services, and information from suppliers to producers.

**materials handling**
The movement of goods within a warehouse, from warehouses to the factory floor, and from the factory floor to various workstations.

**outbound logistics**
The area of logistics that involves managing the flow of finished products and information to business buyers and ultimate consumers (people like you and me).

**reverse logistics**
The area of logistics that involves bringing goods back to the manufacturer because of defects or for recycling materials.

## GETTING GOODS FROM PRODUCER TO CONSUMER EFFICIENTLY

How do you get products to people around the world after the sale? What are your options? You could take the goods to the buyer yourself, but that doesn't seem like the most efficient way of doing things. You could send goods by truck,

DEALING WITH change

### Responding to National Emergencies

In 2005, Hurricanes Katrina and Rita devastated the Gulf Coast region. There were many complaints about the slow response of local, state, and federal governments to the emergency. In contrast, companies like Home Depot, Domino Sugar, and Wal-Mart were up and running in a short time, arriving days before the Federal Emergency Management Agency (FEMA) in many cases. How could the government use the expertise of logistics experts to help in future emergencies? One such expert is Gus Pagonis of Sears. Picture him in charge of government aid.

Recently, the American Society of Transportation & Logistics gave William "Gus" Pagonis the title of Distinguished Logistics Professional. Few people in the world have more expertise in logistics and overall leadership in management than Pagonis. He is widely known for his logistical achievements, particularly during the Gulf War of 1990–91. During the war, Pagonis kept 250,000 GIs fed, clothed, and equipped for battle. During the peak of the military buildup, 5,000 troops arrived on the front each day. Pagonis was responsible for feeding, sheltering, and equipping each one. He used global positioning technology to track the movement of supplies.

After his success in masterminding the logistics for the Gulf War, Pagonis left the army and was appointed executive vice president of logistics for Sears, Roebuck & Company. As head of the Sears Logistics Group, he is the contact person for all of Sears's logistics and is responsible for vendor relations, transportation, home deliveries, outlet stores, international logistics, and the integration of information systems to tie it all together. Sears has millions of dollars' worth of materials on the move daily. The retailer makes 5,000 home deliveries a day and moves 250,000 truckloads of goods each year. It has 30 large distribution centers and 90 smaller outlets. Pagonis must move some 100,000 products to over 2,000 stores through that system. Do you think this kind of expertise would be helpful to the Department of Homeland Security, especially the part dealing with disasters?

Sources: Eric Hellweg, "Supply-Chain Hero," *Business 2.0*, January 2002, pp. 74–75; Howard Schultz, "New Lessons to Learn," *Fortune*, October 3, 2005, pp. 87–88; David Leonard, "The Only Lifeline Was the Wal-Mart," *Fortune*, October 3, 2005, pp. 74–80; and Anne Hull, "A Company Town on the Mississippi," *Washington Post*, January 22, 2006, pp. A1 and A8.

www.sears.com

by train, by ship, or by pipeline. You could use a shipping specialist, such as UPS, FedEx, or the U.S. Postal Service, but often that is too expensive, especially for large items. Nonetheless, some of the most sophisticated marketers outsource the distribution process to such specialists. Seattle-based Groovetech, an online music store catering to DJs, ships 100 time-sensitive orders per day. The company credits UPS OnLine WorldShip with boosting customer satisfaction and cutting order-processing time to one minute. The UPS sorting center in Louisville, Kentucky, processes 304,000 packages an hour, but even this number could be increased to 500,000 if UPS could get planes in and out faster. Choosing the most efficient method of getting goods from producer to consumer requires evaluating both transportation and storage strategies.

## Choosing the Right Transportation Mode

All transportation modes can be evaluated on basic service criteria: cost, speed, dependability, flexibility, frequency, and reach. Figure 15.7 compares the various transportation modes on these criteria.

**Trains Are Great for Large Shipments** The largest percentage of goods in the United States (by volume) is shipped by rail. Railroad shipment is best for bulky items such as coal, wheat, automobiles, and heavy equipment. For the past 20 years or so, railroads have handled about 35 to 40 percent of the total volume of goods in the United States. In piggyback shipping, a truck trailer is detached from the cab; loaded onto a railroad flatcar; and taken to a destination where it will be offloaded, attached to a truck, and driven to the customer's plant. As a result of practices such as piggyback shipments, railroads should continue to hold better than a 38 percent share of the market. Railroad shipment is a relatively energy-efficient way to move goods and could therefore experience significant gains if energy prices continue to climb.

**freight forwarder**
An organization that puts many small shipments together to create a single large shipment that can be transported cost-effectively to the final destination.

| MODE | COST | PERCENTAGE OF DOMESTIC VOLUME | SPEED | ON-TIME DEPENDABILITY | FLEXIBILITY HANDLING PRODUCTS | FREQUENCY OF SHIPMENTS | REACH |
|---|---|---|---|---|---|---|---|
| Railroad | Medium | 38% | Slow | Medium | High | Low | High |
| Trucks | High | 25 | Fast | High | Medium | High | Highest |
| Pipeline | Low | 21 | Medium | Highest | Lowest | Highest | Lowest |
| Ships (water) | Lowest | 15 | Slowest | Lowest | Highest | Lowest | Low |
| Airplane | Highest | 1 | Fastest | Low | Low | Medium | Medium |

figure 15.7

**COMPARING TRANSPORTATION MODES**

Combining trucks with railroads lowers cost and increases the number of locations reached. The same is true when combining trucks with ships. Combining trucks with airlines speeds goods over long distances and gets them to almost any location.

A company may not ship enough goods to even think of using a railroad. However, smaller manufacturers or marketers that don't ship enough products to fill a railcar or truck can get good rates and service by using a freight forwarder. A **freight forwarder** can put many small shipments together to create a single large shipment that can be transported cost-effectively, by truck or train, to the final destination. Some freight forwarders also offer warehousing, customs assistance, and other services along with pickup and delivery. You can see the benefits of such a company to a smaller seller. A freight forwarder is just one of many distribution specialists that have emerged to help marketers move goods from one place to another.

**Trucks Are Good for Small Shipments to Remote Locations** The second largest surface transportation mode is motor vehicles (trucks, vans, and so forth). Such vehicles handle a little over 25 percent of the volume. As Figure 15.7 shows, trucks reach more locations than trains. Trucks can deliver almost any commodity door-to-door. You could buy your own truck to make deliveries, but for widespread delivery you can't beat trucking specialists. Like freight forwarders, they have emerged to supply one important marketing function—transporting goods. Railroads have joined with trucking firms to further the process of piggybacking. The difference lately is that the new 20-foot-high railroad cars, called double stacks, can carry two truck trailers, one on top of the other. The cost of trucking goes up when fuel prices rise. That forces trucking companies to look for ways to cut costs.[22]

**Water Transportation Is Inexpensive but Slow** When sending goods overseas, often the least expensive way is by ship. Obviously, ships are slower than ground or air transportation, so water transportation isn't appropriate for goods that need to be delivered quickly. Ships move a greater volume of goods than you might expect. Over the past 20 years, water transportation has carried 15 to 17 percent of the total. Water transport is local as well as international. If you live near the Mississippi River, for example, you've likely seen towboats hauling as many as 30 barges at a time, with a cargo of up to 35,000 tons. On smaller rivers, about eight barges can be hauled, carrying up to 20,000 tons—that's the equivalent of four 100-car railroad trains. Thus, you can see the importance of river traffic. Add to that Great Lakes shipping, shipping from coast to coast and along the coasts, and international shipments, and water transportation

Containerization makes moving goods much easier. You can put the containers on a railroad car, pull them on a truck, and store them in huge storage lots. They can be used over and over again. Some containers are shaped just like the cargo area in an airplane so that no space is wasted.

takes on a new dimension as a key transportation mode.[23] When truck trailers are placed on ships to travel long distances at lower rates, the process is called *fishyback* (see the explanation of *piggyback*). When they are placed in airplanes, by the way, the process is called *birdyback*.

**Pipelines Are Fast and Efficient** One transportation mode that's not readily visible to the average consumer is movement by pipeline. About 21 percent of the total volume of goods moves this way. Pipelines are used primarily for transporting water, petroleum, and petroleum products—but a lot more products than you may imagine may be sent by pipeline. One company, for example, sent coal by pipeline by first crushing it and mixing it with water.

**Air Transportation Is Fast but Expensive** Today, only a small part of shipping is done by air. Nonetheless, air transportation is a critical factor in many industries. Airlines carry everything from small packages to luxury cars and elephants, and are expanding to be a competitive mode for other goods. The primary benefit of air transportation is speed. No firms know this better than FedEx and UPS. As just two of several competitors vying for the fast-delivery market, FedEx and UPS have used air transport to expand into global markets.

The air freight industry is starting to focus on global distribution. Emery has been an industry pioneer in establishing specialized sales and operations teams aimed at serving the distribution needs of specific industries. KLM Royal Dutch Airlines has cargo/passenger planes that handle high-profit items such as diplomatic pouches and medical supplies. Specializing in such cargo has enabled KLM to compete with FedEx, TNT, and DHL.

**intermodal shipping**
The use of multiple modes of transportation to complete a single long-distance movement of freight.

**Intermodal Shipping** **Intermodal shipping** uses multiple modes of transportation—highway, air, water, rail—to complete a single long-distance movement of freight. Services that specialize in intermodal shipping are known as intermodal marketing companies. Today, railroads are merging with each other and with other transportation companies to offer intermodal distribution.

You can imagine such a system in action. Picture an automobile made in Japan for sale in the United States. It would be shipped by truck to a loading dock, and from there it would be moved by ship to a port in the United States. It may be placed on another truck and then taken to a railroad station for loading on a train that will take it across country to again be loaded on a truck for delivery to a local dealer. No doubt you have seen automobiles being hauled across country by train and by truck. Now imagine that all of that movement was handled by one integrated shipping firm. That's what intermodal shipping is all about.

Now you know about the various ways of shipping goods once you have sold them. But that is only the first step in understanding the system that has been developed to move goods from one point to another. Another important part of a complex logistics system consists of storage.

## The Storage Function

People want goods to be delivered quickly when they finally decide to buy them. That means that marketers must have goods available in various parts of the country ready to be shipped locally when ordered. A good percentage of the total cost of logistics is for storage.[24] This includes the cost of the storage warehouse (distribution facility) and its operation, plus movement of goods within the warehouse. There are two major kinds of warehouses: storage and distribution. A *storage warehouse* holds products for a relatively long time. Seasonal goods such as lawn mowers would be kept in such a warehouse.

*Distribution warehouses* are facilities used to gather and redistribute products. You can picture a distribution warehouse for FedEx or UPS handling

RFID tags are being used in all kinds of situations, from the movement of goods to the tracking of livestock. They contain much more information than the old bar codes. One of the services being offered by delivery firms is tracing your shipment from one place to another. How could RFID tags help you avoid losing your luggage, car keys, and other things?

thousands of packages in a very short time. The packages are picked up at places throughout the country and then processed for reshipment at these centers. General Electric's combination storage and distribution facility in San Gabriel Valley, California, gives you a feel for how large such buildings can be. It is nearly half a mile long and 465 feet wide—that's massive enough to hold almost 27 football fields.

## Tracking Goods

One of the more important aspects of managing the flow of goods from producer to consumer is keeping track of where goods are at any given time. As noted in Chapter 14, companies use Universal Product Codes—the familiar black-and-white bar codes and a preset number—to keep track of inventory. The latest in tracking technology, as we mentioned earlier, involves radio frequency identification (RFID).[25] RFID technology tags merchandise so that it can be tracked from the time it's loaded off the supplier's docks to when the customer takes it out the retailer's door. Wal-Mart, Target, Woolworth, and other organizations have all said that they will require suppliers to use RFID.[26] Few companies are more concerned about the tracking of items than UPS, which now uses a mix of Bluetooth's short-range radio capability and wireless receivers to track merchandise. It claims the system is even better than RFID.[27]

# WHAT ALL THIS MEANS TO YOU

The life or death of a firm often depends on its ability to take orders, process orders, keep customers informed about the progress of their orders, get the goods out to customers quickly, handle returns, and manage any recycling issues.[28] Some of the most exciting firms in the marketplace are those that assist in some aspect of supply-chain management.

What all this means to you is that there are many new jobs becoming available in the exciting area of supply-chain management. These include jobs with the companies providing the various modes of distribution: trains, airplanes, trucks, ships, and pipelines. It also means new jobs handling information flows between and among companies (e.g., Web site development). But there are also jobs that involve processing orders, keeping track of inventory, following the path of products as they move from seller to buyer and back, recycling goods, and more—much more.

### progress assessment

- What are the four systems that have evolved to tie together members of the channel of distribution?
- How does logistics differ from distribution?
- What are inbound logistics, outbound logistics, and reverse logistics?

## summary

**1.** Explain the concept of marketing channels and the value of marketing intermediaries.

1. A channel of distribution consists of a whole set of marketing intermediaries, such as agents, brokers, wholesalers, and retailers, that join together to transport and store goods in their path (or channel) from producers to consumers.
   - **How do marketing intermediaries add value?**

   Intermediaries perform certain marketing tasks—such as transporting, storing, selling, advertising, and relationship building—faster and cheaper than most manufacturers could. Channels of distribution ensure communication flows and the flow of money and title to goods. They also help ensure that the right quantity and assortment of goods will be available when and where needed.
   - **What are the principles behind the use of such intermediaries?**

   Marketing intermediaries can be eliminated, but their activities can't; that is, you can eliminate some wholesalers and retailers, but then consumers or someone else would have to perform the retailer's tasks, including transporting and storing goods, finding suppliers, and establishing communication with suppliers. Intermediary organizations have survived in the past because they have performed marketing functions faster and cheaper than others could. Intermediaries add costs to products, but these costs are usually more than offset by the values they create.

**2.** Give examples of how intermediaries perform the six marketing utilities.

2. Marketing intermediaries perform the following utilities: form, time, place, possession, information, and service.
   - **How do intermediaries perform the six marketing utilities?**

   A retail grocer may cut or trim meat, providing some form utility. But marketers are more often responsible for the five other utilities. Time utility is provided by having goods available *when* people want them. Place utility is provided by having goods *where* people want them. Possession utility is provided by making it possible for people to own things by providing them with credit, delivery, installation, guarantees, and anything else that will help *complete the sale*. Marketers also inform consumers of the availability of goods and services with advertising, publicity, and other means. That provides information utility. Finally, marketers provide fast, friendly, and efficient service during and after the sale (service utility).

**3.** Describe the various wholesale intermediaries in the distribution system.

3. A wholesaler is a marketing intermediary that sells to organizations and individuals, but not to final consumers.
   - **What are some wholesale organizations that assist in the movement of goods from manufacturers to consumers?**

   *Merchant wholesalers* are independently owned firms that take title to (own) goods that they handle. *Rack jobbers* furnish racks or shelves full of merchandise to retailers, display products, and sell on consignment. *Cash-and-carry wholesalers* serve mostly small retailers with a limited assortment of products. *Drop shippers* solicit orders from retailers and other wholesalers and have the merchandise shipped directly from a producer to a buyer.

4. A retailer is an organization that sells to ultimate consumers.
   - **What are three distribution strategies marketers use?**

   Marketers use three basic distribution strategies: intensive (putting products in as many places as possible), selective (choosing only a few stores in a chosen market), and exclusive (using only one store in each market area).

**4.** Explain the distribution strategies retailers use.

5. Nonstore retailing is retailing done outside a store.
   - **What are some of the forms of nonstore retailing?**

   Nonstore retailing includes online marketing; telemarketing (marketing by phone); vending machines, kiosks, and carts (marketing by putting products in convenient locations, such as in the halls of shopping centers); direct selling (marketing by approaching consumers in their homes or places of work); multilevel marketing (marketing by setting up a system of salespeople who recruit other salespeople and help them to sell directly to customers); and direct marketing (direct mail and catalog sales). Telemarketing and online marketing are also forms of direct marketing.

**5.** Explain the various kinds of nonstore retailing.

6. One way of generating more cooperation in channels of distribution is to form unified systems.
   - **What are the four types of distribution systems?**

   The four distribution systems that tie firms together are (1) *corporate systems*, in which all organizations in the channel are owned by one firm; (2) *contractual systems*, in which members are bound to cooperate through contractual agreements; (3) *administered systems*, in which all marketing functions at the retail level are managed by manufacturers; and (4) *supply chains*, in which the various firms in the supply chain are linked electronically to provide the most efficient movement of information and goods possible. Note that the supply-chain system is longer than a channel of distribution because it includes organizations selling to manufacturers while the other systems only merge firms in the channel of distribution *after a product is made*. Supply chains are so efficient that they are sometimes known as value chains.

**6.** Explain the various ways to build cooperation in channel systems.

7. Logistics involves planning, implementing, and controlling the physical flow of materials, final goods, and related information from points of origin to points of consumption to meet customer requirements at a profit.
   - **What is the difference between logistics and distribution?**

   Distribution is a much more basic concept and involves mostly transportation. Logistics is more complex. *Inbound logistics* brings raw materials, packaging, other goods and services, and information from suppliers to producers. *Materials handling* is the moving of goods from warehouses to the factory floor and to various workstations. *Outbound logistics* manages the flow of finished products and information to business buyers and ultimate consumers (people like you and me). *Reverse logistics* involves bringing goods back to the manufacturer because of defects or for recycling materials.

**7.** Describe the emergence of logistics.

8. Various transportation modes are used to move goods from producers to consumers.
   - **What are the differences among the various transportation modes?**

   Rail (for heavy shipments within the country or between bordering countries); trucks (for getting goods directly to consumers); ships (for slow,

**8.** Outline how intermediaries move goods from producers to consumers through the use of various transportation modes and storage functions.

inexpensive movement of goods, often internationally); pipelines (for moving water and oil and other such goods); and airplanes (for shipping goods quickly).

- **What is intermodal shipping?**

Intermodal shipping uses multiple modes of transportation—highway, air, water, rail—to complete a single long-distance movement of freight.

- **What are the different kinds of warehouses?**

A storage warehouse stores products for a relatively long time. Distribution warehouses are facilities used to gather and redistribute products.

## key terms

**administered distribution system** 417
**agents/brokers** 404
**cash-and-carry wholesaler** 410
**channel of distribution** 404
**contractual distribution system** 416
**corporate distribution system** 416
**direct marketing** 415
**direct selling** 415
**drop shippers** 410
**electronic retailing** 413
**exclusive distribution** 412
**freight forwarder** 421
**inbound logistics** 419
**information utility** 408
**intensive distribution** 412
**intermodal shipping** 422
**logistics** 419
**marketing intermediaries** 404
**materials handling** 419
**merchant wholesalers** 410
**outbound logistics** 419
**place utility** 408
**possession utility** 408
**rack jobbers** 410
**retailer** 404
**reverse logistics** 419
**selective distribution** 412
**service utility** 409
**supply chain (or value chain)** 417
**supply-chain management** 417
**telemarketing** 414
**time utility** 408
**utility** 407
**wholesaler** 404

## critical thinking questions

1. Imagine that we have eliminated intermediaries and you have to go shopping for groceries and shoes. How would you find out where the shoes and groceries were? How far would you have to travel to get them? How much money do you think you'd save for your time and effort?

2. Which intermediary do you think is most important today and why? What changes are happening to companies in that area?

3. One of the major scarcities in the future will be water. If you could think of an inexpensive way to get water from places of abundance to places where it is needed for drinking, farming, and other uses, you could become very, very rich. Pipelines are an alternative, but you could also freeze the water and ship it by train or truck. You could put the water into huge rubber or plastic containers and roll the containers on to railroad tracks. You could tie a rope or chain onto icebergs and tow them to warmer climates. Future wealth is awaiting those who develop the most practical and efficient (read inexpensive) way to move water. Do you have any good ideas?

## developing workplace skills

1. The six utilities of marketing are form, time, place, possession, information, and service. Give examples of organizations in your area that perform each of these functions.

2. Form small groups and diagram how Dole might get pineapples from a field in Thailand to a canning plant in California to a store near your college. Include the intermediaries and the forms of transportation each one might use.

3. Discuss the merits of buying and selling goods in stores versus over the Internet. What advantages do stores have? Has anyone in the class tried to sell anything on the Internet? How did he or she ship the product?

4. Many students have worked in retailing, and some want to continue such careers after college, yet few students consider similar jobs in wholesaling. Discuss in class the differences between wholesaling and retailing and why retailing has more appeal. Since there are fewer students seeking jobs in wholesaling, do you think such jobs may be easier to get?

5. One of the fast-growing parts of retailing is using eBay to sell new and used merchandise. This is being done by companies as well as by individuals. Form small groups and discuss group members' experiences using eBay for buying and selling goods. What tricks have they learned? What can be done to minimize the problems associated with shipping?

## taking it to the net

### Purpose

To examine how small businesses can learn to use the Internet to distribute their products directly to customers.

### Exercise

Many small businesses have no idea how to begin selling goods over the Internet. Several free Web sites have been developed to help small businesses get started. Some have links to other sites that provide all kinds of help from setting up the site to doing marketing, handling credit purchases, and more. Many businesses will need help setting up Web sites of their own. You may be able to help if you learn now all that is involved. Begin by going to www.bigstep.com to learn the steps involved. Take the eight-step tour and learn as much as you can.

Then go to www.workz.com, click on "Build Your Web Site," and answer the following questions:

1. What kind of information were you able to gather about starting a Web site?
2. What additional information would you like before getting started? Where might you turn for such help?

3. What other advice would you give a small company about trying to sell on the Internet? What would you say about credit cards, answering consumer questions, distribution, and returns?
4. What issues may come up for foreign visitors to the site?

## casing the web

To access the case *"Multilevel Marketing,"* visit **www.mhhe.com/ub8e**

## video case

### Feeding the Poor of Chicago

Every business, both for-profit and not-for-profit, needs to understand the basic principles of marketing. This video highlights one of the most important marketing functions—distribution. Like all marketing challenges, the Greater Chicago Food Depository began by finding a need and filling it.

Here is the need: Often the many caterers, restaurants, hotels and hospitals in the Chicago area prepare too much food for their customers. It seems like a waste to just throw the food away, but the food is perishable and can't be saved for long. While these businesses have too much food, there are thousands of poor people in the Chicago area who have too little or no food.

Here is the solution: The Greater Chicago Food Depository (GCFD) gathers the food from those with too much and gives it to those with too little. While this may sound simple, consider that the GCFD distributes more than 40 million pounds of food a year to 600 retail outlets (soup kitchens, food pantries and the like). Its warehouse is 268,000 square feet (the size of six football fields).

This video highlights the important role middlemen (intermediaries) play in the GCFD distribution system. It must have people who are willing and able to gather and prepare the food from these various sources and help distribute the food to groups and individuals. It has to have a warehouse where food can be stored, sorted, and then distributed where needed. It has to have retail outlets where people can easily get to the food. And it has to have suppliers who will keep the channel of distribution full of the foods needed.

You can see that the smooth working of this system involves the cooperation of businesses (restaurants, hotels, and so on), nonprofit agencies of all kinds, and the government. It is important to recognize that other stakeholders are involved. Taxpayers, for example, would want to know how you choose what people get the free food and what people do not. The local community would be interested in the location of food distribution centers. Keeping all stakeholders happy is a major concern of the Greater Chicago Food Depository as it is with all organizations.

Once a food distribution center has been established, the next step, as in all such organizations, is to make the system more efficient. Using capital items like the Producemobile, a farmer's market on wheels, to gather produce is just one example. Naturally, such a system calls for a leader who has some experience running a large organization. Such experience does not have to be in logistics, necessarily. It could be in management or IT or similar areas of business. The exciting thing about working for the Greater Chicago Food Depository and the various organizations that work with it is the feeling one has of making a direct major contribution to society.

#### Thinking It Over

1. When you compare the food distribution system being used to feed the poor with the

distribution system used by supermarkets in your area, what other technologies, systems, techniques, or strategies might you recommend for making the logistics of food distribution to the poor more effective and efficient?

2. There are literally billions of poor people throughout the world who need food and other staples. Can you envision a distribution system that would become more global in scope? Would that be a good idea? Why or why not?
3. After reviewing this video, do you see the opportunities such organizations provide for applying business skills you are learning in this class? Do you see yourself volunteering for such an organization? What might you do for them?

# using effective promotional techniques

*

profile

**Getting to Know**

**X Dietrich Mateschitz**

**of Red Bull**

Many a student sits with a can of Red Bull next to him or her when preparing for a big exam. Red Bull, Monster, and Full Throttle are all energy drinks with giant doses of caffeine in them. Dietrich Mateschitz is the man who introduced Red Bull to the U.S. market. Mateschitz graduated from the Vienna University of Economics and Business Administration. His major was world trade. For a while, he worked on the marketing of Procter & Gamble's Blendax toothpaste. He also did some marketing for Unilever and Jacobs Coffee. In 1987, he founded Red Bull with two Thai partners. Now he is a billionaire.

Mateschitz is an example of a billionaire who did not invent a wonderful new product. Instead, he made his money through creative marketing. Mateschitz bought a Thai company that already had an energy drink called Krating Daeng (red water buffalo). He changed the ingredients and the name (a little) and added carbonation. Red Bull is not known for tasting great. Furthermore, the name isn't very appealing and the price is high. So what made it so popular? For one thing, Red Bull has a lot of wake-up power, including 80 milligrams of caffeine. It also has mysterious ingredients such as taurine and glucuronolactone.

CHAPTER 16

LEARNING **goals**

**After you have read and studied this chapter, you should be able to**

1. Define *promotion* and list the four traditional tools that make up the promotion mix.
2. Define *advertising* and describe the advantages and disadvantages of various advertising media, including the Internet.
3. Illustrate the steps of the B2B and B2C selling processes.
4. Describe the role of the public relations department, and tell how publicity fits in that role.
5. Explain the importance of various forms of sales promotion, including sampling.
6. Give examples of word of mouth, viral marketing, blogging, and podcasting.

**www.redbull.com**

But the secret to Red Bull's success is something called guerrilla marketing. Guerrilla (not gorilla) marketing means studying the market for your product very carefully and then going after that market using nontraditional promotional means such as sponsoring sports events and creating word of mouth with sometimes outrageous promotions. Event marketing began with the sponsorship of mountain biking, paragliding, snowboarding, and hang-gliding competitions. Mateschitz also sponsors Red Bull's Flutag (flying day) contest, in which competitors fly homemade contraptions over water. All together, Red Bull supports about 500 world-class extreme sports athletes. It also sponsors parties on various university campuses. You might enjoy talking with your friends about where they first learned about Red Bull.

In addition to sponsoring extreme sports, Mateschitz sponsors the World Stunt Awards. He bought the Formula I team Jaguar Racing from Ford and renamed it Red Bull Racing. In other words, the brand Red Bull has become closely associated with those who live large and are not afraid to take chances, including drinking something that has a lot of kick.

The success of Red Bull led to the introduction of more than 100 competitors, including Monster, whose slogan is "Unleash the Beast." There are lots of energy drinks available today, but Red Bull still stands out in the crowd because of its unusual promotions. This chapter is about effective promotional techniques. You will explore traditional promotional tools such as advertising, selling, and public relations. But you will also delve into some nontraditional promotional tools such as product placement, blogging, podcasting, and viral marketing.

Sources: Kerry A. Dolan, "The Soda with Buzz," *Forbes*, March 28, 2005; Christopher Palmeri, "Hansen Natural," *BusinessWeek*, June 6, 2005; Wikipedia (online encyclopedia); Gwendolyn Bounds, "Move Over, Coke," *The Wall Street Journal*, January 30, 2006, pp. R1 and R3; and Andrew Murr, "Monster vs. Red Bull," *Newsweek*, March 28, 2006, p. E22.

figure 16.1

THE TRADITIONAL PROMOTION MIX

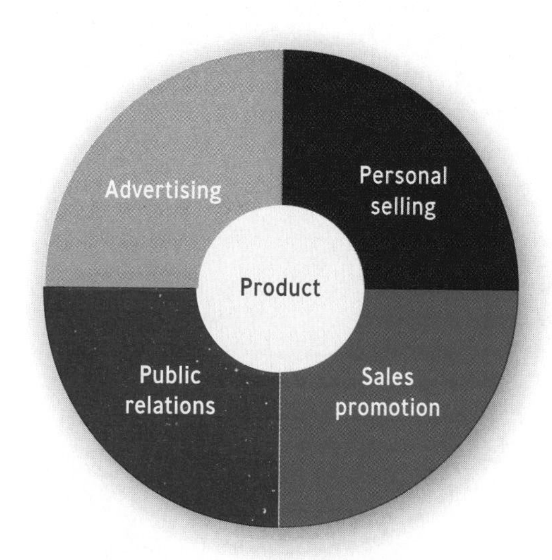


**promotion**
An effort by marketers to inform and remind people in the target market about products and to persuade them to participate in an exchange.

**promotion mix**
The combination of promotional tools an organization uses.

**integrated marketing communication (IMC)**
A technique that combines all the promotional tools into one comprehensive, unified promotional strategy.

## PROMOTION AND THE PROMOTION MIX

**Promotion** is an effort by marketers to inform and remind people in the target market about products, and to persuade them to participate in an exchange. Marketers use many different tools to promote their products and services. Traditionally, as shown in Figure 16.1, those tools included advertising, personal selling, public relations, and sales promotion. The combination of promotional tools an organization uses is called its **promotion mix**. The product is shown in the middle of the figure to illustrate the fact that product design (the product itself) can be a promotional tool (e.g., through giving away free samples).[1] We'll discuss all of these promotional tools in this chapter—and more.

**Integrated marketing communication (IMC)** combines all the promotional tools into one comprehensive, unified promotional strategy. The idea is to use all the promotional tools and company resources to create a positive brand image and to meet the strategic marketing and promotional goals of the firm.[2] Lately, companies have been including a lot of Internet promotions in that mix.[3] Figure 16.2 shows the six steps to follow in establishing a promotional campaign.

As we discuss each of the promotional tools in this chapter, we explore the changes that are occurring in those areas. Then, at the end of the chapter, we

figure 16.2

STEPS IN A PROMOTIONAL CAMPAIGN

1. Identify a target market. (Refer back to Chapter 13 for a discussion of segmentation and target marketing.)
2. Define the objectives for each element of the promotion mix. Goals should be clear and measurable.
3. Determine a promotional budget. The budgeting process will clarify how much can be spent on advertising, personal selling, and other promotional efforts.
4. Develop a unifying message. The goal of an integrated promotional program is to have one clear message communicated by advertising, public relations, sales, and every other promotional effort.
5. Implement the plan. Advertisements must be scheduled to complement efforts being made by public relations and sales promotion. Salespeople should have access to all materials to optimize the total effort.
6. Evaluate effectiveness. Measuring results depends greatly on clear objectives. Each element of the promotional mix should be evaluated separately, and an overall measure should be taken as well. It is important to learn what is working and what is not.

examine the latest promotional strategies and how they can be combined to build better relationships with customers and other stakeholders. We begin the exploration of promotional tools by looking at advertising—the most visible tool.

**advertising**
Paid, nonpersonal communication through various media by organizations and individuals who are in some way identified in the advertising message.

## ADVERTISING: FIGHTING TO KEEP CONSUMER INTEREST

**Advertising** is paid, nonpersonal communication through various media by organizations and individuals who are in some way *identified in the message*. *Propoganda* is nonpersonal communication that *does not have an identified sponsor*. It is often distributed by the government in various countries. Figure 16.3 lists various categories of advertising. Take a minute to look it over, because there is a lot more to advertising than just television commercials.

The importance of advertising in the United States is easy to document; just look at the numbers in Figure 16.4 on page 434. The total ad volume exceeds $245 billion yearly. Television in all its forms (broadcast and cable) is the number one medium. Direct mail is number two, closely followed by newspapers. Internet advertising was up 15.7 percent over the previous year.[4]

The public benefits greatly from advertising expenditures. First, ads are informative. The number three medium, newspaper advertising, is full of information about products, prices, features, and more. So is direct mail advertising, the number two medium. Advertising not only informs us about products but also provides us with free TV and radio programs: The money advertisers spend for commercial time pays for the production costs. Advertising also covers the major costs of producing newspapers and magazines. When

figure 16.3

MAJOR CATEGORIES OF ADVERTISING

**Different Kinds of Advertising Are Used by Various Organizations to Reach Different Market Targets. Major Categories Include the Following:**

- *Retail advertising*—advertising to consumers by various retail stores such as supermarkets and shoe stores.
- *Trade advertising*—advertising to wholesalers and retailers by manufacturers to encourage them to carry their products.
- *Business-to-business advertising*—advertising from manufacturers to other manufacturers. A firm selling motors to auto companies would use business-to-business advertising.
- *Institutional advertising*—advertising designed to create an attractive image for an organization rather than for a product. "We Care about You" at Giant Food is an example. "Virginia Is for Lovers" and "I ❤ New York" are two institutional campaigns by government agencies.
- *Product advertising*—advertising for a good or service to create interest among consumer, commercial, and industrial buyers.
- *Advocacy advertising*—advertising that supports a particular view of an issue (e.g., an ad in support of gun control or against nuclear power plants). Such advertising is also known as cause advertising.
- *Comparison advertising*—advertising that compares competitive products. For example, an ad that compares two different cold care products' speed and benefits is a comparative ad.
- *Interactive advertising*—customer-oriented communication that enables customers to choose the information they receive, such as interactive video catalogs that let customers select which items to view.
- *Online advertising*—advertising messages that appear on computers as people visit different Web sites.

figure 16.4

**ADVERTISING EXPENDITURE BY MEDIA (IN MILLIONS OF DOLLARS)**

| RANK | MEDIUM | U.S. AD SPENDING |
|---|---|---|
| 1 | Direct mail | $48.37 |
| 2 | Newspapers | 44.84 |
| 3 | Broadcast TV | 41.93 |
| 4 | Radio | 19.10 |
| 5 | Cable TV | 18.81 |
| 6 | Yellow Pages | 13.90 |
| 7 | Consumer magazines | 11.44 |
| 8 | Internet | 5.65 |
| 9 | Out of home | 5.44 |
| 10 | Business publications | 4.00 |
| 11 | All other | 31.99 |
| 12 | Total | 245.48 |

Source: *Advertising Age FACTPACK* 2005. Copyright 2005 Crain Communications, Inc. Reprinted with permission.

we buy a magazine, we pay mostly for mailing or promotional costs. Figure 16.5 discusses the advantages and disadvantages of various advertising media to the advertiser. Newspapers, radio, and the Yellow Pages are especially attractive to local advertisers.

Television offers many advantages to national advertisers, but it's expensive. For example, the cost of 30 seconds of advertising during the Super Bowl telecast is about $2.5 million.[5] How many bottles of beer or bags of dog food must a company sell to pay for such commercials? The answer may seem to be "A lot," but few other media besides television have ever allowed advertisers to reach so many people with such impact.

figure 16.5

**ADVANTAGES AND DISADVANTAGES OF VARIOUS ADVERTISING MEDIA**

The most effective media are often very expensive. The inexpensive media may not reach your market. The goal is to use the medium that can reach your desired market most effectively and efficiently.

| MEDIUM | ADVANTAGES | DISADVANTAGES |
|---|---|---|
| Newspapers | Good coverage of local markets; ads can be placed quickly; high consumer acceptance; ads can be clipped and saved. | Ads compete with other features in paper; poor color; ads get thrown away with paper (short life span). |
| Television | Uses sight, sound, and motion; reaches all audiences; high attention with no competition from other material. | High cost; short exposure time; takes time to prepare ads. Digital video recorders skip over ads. |
| Radio | Low cost; can target specific audiences; very flexible; good for local marketing. | People may not listen to ad; depends on one sense (hearing); short exposure time; audience can't keep ad. |
| Magazines | Can target specific audiences; good use of color; long life of ad; ads can be clipped and saved. | Inflexible; ads often must be placed weeks before publication; cost is relatively high. |
| Outdoor | High visibility and repeat exposures; low cost; local market focus. | Limited message; low selectivity of audience. |
| Direct mail | Best for targeting specific markets; very flexible; ad can be saved. | High cost; consumers may reject ad as junk mail; must conform to post office regulations. |
| Yellow Pages–type advertising | Great coverage of local markets; widely used by consumers; available at point of purchase. | Competition with other ads; cost may be too high for very small businesses. |
| Internet | Inexpensive global coverage; available at any time; interactive. | Relatively low readership in the short term (but growing rapidly). |

Product placement is often very subtle. It could be the watch the actors are wearing, or the shoes, or the clothes. It could be the drink they are drinking—or the cars they are driving. In any case, the idea is to influence you to desire having that product yourself. What product placements have you noticed in your favorite TV shows?

TV advertising isn't limited to traditional commercials for products that interrupt TV programming; sometimes the products appear in the programs themselves. **Product placement** means paying to put products into TV shows and movies where they will be seen. Have you noticed products that have been featured in movies and TV shows, like the cars in James Bond movies? Many are more subtle, like the wheeled luggage from Zuca Inc. that appeared on the TV show *CSI*. In just one episode of *King of Queens*, the following products were shown: Cheetos, *People* magazine, Fruit Loops, a Hyatt hotel, and Mrs. Butterworth's syrup.[6] Other TV shows with multiple product placements have included the *Amazing Race: Family Edition* and *The Apprentice*.[7] The Dealing with Change box on page 436 offers other examples of product placement.

**product placement**
Putting products into TV shows and movies where they will be seen.

Marketers must now choose which media can best be used to reach the audience they desire. Radio advertising, for example, is less expensive than TV advertising and often reaches people when they have few other distractions, such as driving in their cars. Radio is especially good, therefore, for selling services that people don't usually read about in print media—services such as banking, mortgages, continuing education, brokerage services, and the like. On the other hand, radio has become so commercial-ridden that some people are switching to Sirius or XM radio or some other commercial-free offer.[8]

While "surfing the channels" one often comes upon an infomercial for some kind of new cookware or cleaning product or tool. Often the demonstration is fascinating and leads you to call the number on the screen. George Foreman has been as successful selling his grills in infomercials as he was in the boxing ring. Have you bought anything after seeing an infomercial? Were you happy with the purchase?

## The Growing Use of Infomercials

A growing form of advertising is the infomercial. An **infomercial** is a full-length TV program devoted exclusively to promoting goods or services. Infomercials have been successful because they show the product in great detail. A great product can often sell itself if there's some means to show the public how it works. Infomercials provide that opportunity. People have said that a half-hour infomercial is the equivalent of sending your very best salespeople to a person's home and allowing them to use everything in their power to make the sale: drama, demonstration, testimonials, graphics, and more. Products that have had over $1 billion in sales through infomercials include Proactiv (acne cream); Soloflex, Total Gym, and Bowflex (exercise machines); and the George Foreman Grill and Ron Popeil's Rotisserie

## DEALING WITH change

### You Can't TiVo Your Way Away from Product Placement

You can avoid watching commercials on TV by using TiVo or a similar digital video recorder (DVR). But advertisers still have ways of reaching viewers. Have you ever been watching a TV show or a movie and noticed that the actors are using brand-name products? They drive a certain kind of car, use a certain kind of camera, and drink a certain kind of drink. Most of the time, such product exposure is no accident. As explained in the text, the term for the promotional tool in which marketers pay to have their products featured on TV shows and in the movies is *product placement.* In the TV series *Lost*, you could see the participants drinking Dasani bottled water (a Coke product) and using survival items from crates prominently displaying the Lowe's logo. Pepsi, however, has earned top honors in product placement for having its brand prominently displayed in seven movies that topped the box office for at least a week.

Nike wasn't identified as the creator of *Road to Paris*, a one-hour documentary about the U.S. cycling team, but you might have guessed had you noticed how often Nike's swoosh showed up. You may also have noticed the Coke cups sitting on the table in front of the judges on *American Idol.* Few viewers missed the Pontiac GTO used in the movie *XXX* with Vin Diesel. The BMW Films series on the Internet called *The Hire* features a BMW and its driver, played by Clive Owen. The fourth season of *The Apprentice* with Donald Trump showed Poggenpohl kitchen cabinets in the Trump Tower apartment where the contestants lived. Cadillac had only to provide free automobiles to get exposure on *The Sopranos*.

The use of product placement is a challenge to traditional advertising agencies and to the networks and studios. They have to adapt to this change in promotional emphasis. Though it is difficult to measure advertising effectiveness, some marketers have found traditional forms of advertising too expensive for the responses they were getting. That is why they turned to product placement. What products have you noticed on TV shows and in the movies? Were you ever tempted to buy a product because you saw actors using it in the course of the program or film?

Sources: Cheryl Lu-Lien Tan, "Best Appliance in a Supporting Role . . . ," *The Wall Street Journal*, September 22, 2005, p. B1; Jeffrey Gangemi, "Product Placement," *BusinessWeek*, August 15, 2005, p. 10; Jessi Hempel, "Mad Ave," *BusinessWeek*, March 7, 2005, p. 14; Jon Fine, "End Run Around TiVo?," *BusinessWeek*, August 8, 2005, p. 22; and Marc Graser, "TV's Savior?," *Advertising Age*, February 6, 2006, p. S1.

**infomercial**
A full-length TV program devoted exclusively to promoting goods or services.

and Grill.[9] Some products, such as personal development seminars or workout tapes, are hard to sell without showing people a sample of their contents and using testimonials.

## Advertisers Are Moving to the Internet

Even though television advertising is still the number one choice for marketers, it is beginning to lose its appeal. Digital video recorders (DVRs) enable consumers to skip the ads on TV.[10] This makes TV less attractive to advertisers unless commercials get so much better that people will want to watch them rather than skip through them.[11] New programming venues, such as video on demand, may make it even more difficult for advertisers to catch consumers' eyes.[12] A popular alternative for some advertisers is to go online with their ads. Visit Oprah.com, for example, and you might see an ad for the Quest minivan. Nissan's online spending was up 40 percent in 2005 (over 2004).[13] Chrysler is expecting to spend 20 percent of its ad budget online. That's money that used to be spent on TV, newspaper, and magazine ads.[14]

When marketers advertise on a big online property, such as Yahoo, they can reach the people they most want to reach—consumers researching vacations, or exploring the car market, or checking stocks.[15] Ultimately, the goal is to get customers and potential customers to a Web site where they can learn more about the company and its products—and vice versa. If users click through an ad to get to the Web site, the company has the opportunity not only to provide information but also to interact with the customer (e.g., gathering names, addresses, opinions, or preferences). Internet advertising thus becomes a means to bring customers and companies together. As a result, McDonald's spent 80 percent of its ad budget on TV four years ago. Today,

McDonald's spends less than half of its budget on prime-time TV. Much of the money is now being spent on the Internet.[16]

**Interactive promotion** allows marketers to go beyond a *monologue*, where sellers try to persuade buyers to buy things, to a *dialogue* in which buyers and sellers work together to create mutually beneficial exchange relationships. For example, Garden.com was an online retailer of garden products and services before its assets were acquired by Burpee. Dionn Schaffner, vice president of marketing, says, "Gardening is an information-intensive activity. Customers obviously want to learn about gardening, but they also seek inspiration by communicating with fellow gardeners and experts." Garden.com's answer was an interactive Web site through which customers could chat with each other and ask gardening questions.

**interactive promotion**
Promotion process that allows marketers to go beyond a monologue, where sellers try to persuade buyers to buy things, to a dialogue in which buyers and sellers work together to create mutually beneficial exchange relationships.

Technology has greatly improved the speed and potential of Internet dialogues. Many companies provide online videos, chat rooms, and other services in a virtual store where they are able to talk to other customers, talk to salespeople, examine goods and services, and buy products.

The Internet is changing the whole approach to working with customers. Note that we said "working with" rather than "promoting to." The current trend is to *build relationships* with customers over time.[17] That means carefully listening to what consumers want, tracking their purchases, providing them with excellent service, and giving them access to a full range of information. Advertisers also like online advertising because the latest technology enables them to see just how many people have clicked on a commercial and how much of it the potential customer has read or watched.[18]

## Global Advertising

Global advertising involves developing a product and promotional strategy that can be implemented worldwide. Certainly global advertising would save companies money in research and design. However, other experts think that promotions targeted at specific countries or regions may be much more successful than global promotions since each country or region has its own culture, language, and buying habits.

The evidence supports the theory that promotional efforts specifically designed for individual countries often work best since problems arise when one campaign is used in all countries. For example, when a Japanese company tried to use English words to name a popular drink, it called the product Pocari Sweat, not a good image for a beverage in the minds of most English-speaking people. In England, the Ford Probe didn't go over too well because the word *probe* made people think of doctors' waiting rooms and medical examinations. People in the United States may have difficulty with Krapp toilet paper from Sweden. But perhaps even that is not as bad as the translation of the Coors slogan "Turn it loose" that became "Suffer from diarrhea." Clairol introduced its curling iron, the Mist Stick, to the German market, not realizing that *Mist* in German can mean "manure." A T-shirt promoting a visit by the Pope in Miami read *la papa,* which means "the potato." The T-shirt

This ad for CoverGirl is designed for the African American female. There are many ads directed toward the Latin market as well. What other groups may prove to be attractive candidates for targeted commercials? Do you find such commercials to be effective?

REACHING BEYOND

our borders

**Let's Stop at Starsbuck for Some Coffee**

Who wouldn't want to reach a market of over 1 billion people? That's why China is such an attractive market for promoters throughout the world. But promoting in China and in other countries calls for caution. For example, Chinese manufacturers often produce counterfeit versions of Prada handbags, Christian Dior sunglasses, and the like. It was reported in the *Washington Times* that more than 90 percent of all CDs, DVDs, and computer programs sold in China are pirated (that is, illegally sold). In Shanghai, you can stop and order your favorite coffee drink at Starsbuck (note the spelling), but you won't be getting what you think. And driving around on a Hongda is not the same as being on a Honda motorcycle. It is important to check out all the rules and regulations regarding promotions in a country like China because the rules are very different from those in the United States, including copyright laws.

Caution in promotions is called for no matter what the country. KFC, for example, has learned that advertisements meant for a European audience may have consequences in the United States, even though the ads are not shown in the states. One ad, for example, has the theme "Servin' up soul." The campaign has been a big success in England and other countries, but has the potential for causing some stir among minorities in America. One has to be careful about stereotypes in advertising, no matter where they are shown. The Internet has united the world to the extent that an ad in one country may reach the rest of the world. It is important, again, to learn the rules and regulations of each country you advertise in, because all countries regulate what you can say and where and how. Furthermore, each culture has its own sense of what is proper and what is not. You can't just promote globally using the same copy and art in every situation.

Sources: Arnold Beichman, "China's Pirates," *Washington Times*, April 11, 2005, p. A16, and Guy Matthews, "KFC 'Soul' Ad Poses Global Issue," *The Wall Street Journal*, January 27, 2005, p. B6.

should have said *el Papa*. As you can see, getting the words right in international advertising is tricky and critical. So is understanding the culture.

People in Brazil rarely eat breakfast, but they treat Kellogg's corn flakes as a dry snack like potato chips. Thus, Kellogg used a promotional strategy that showed people in Brazil how to eat cereal with cold milk in the morning. Many more situations could be cited to show that international advertising calls for researching the wants and needs of people in each specific country and then designing appropriate ads and testing them.

In the United States, selected groups are large enough and different enough to call for specially designed promotions. Masterfoods USA, for example, tried to promote dulce de leche (caramel) M&M's to the Hispanic market in cities like Los Angeles, Miami, and San Antonio. The promotion was not successful, however. Knowing the market had potential, Masterfoods changed course and bought a candy company called the Lucas Group, which has had success selling such candies as Felix Sour Fruit and Lucas Hot and Spicy in Mexico. Masterfoods had much more success selling those candies in the United States. Maybelline, which makes a wide array of cosmetics, is targeting special promotions to African American women. In short, much advertising today is moving from globalism (one ad for everyone in the world) to regionalism (specific ads for each country or for specific groups within a country). In the future, marketers will prepare more custom-designed promotions to reach smaller audiences—audiences as small as one person. The Reaching Beyond Our Borders box discusses issues regarding advertising in other countries.

## PERSONAL SELLING: PROVIDING PERSONAL ATTENTION

**personal selling**
The face-to-face presentation and promotion of goods and services.

**Personal selling** is the face-to-face presentation and promotion of goods and services. It also involves the search for new prospects and follow-up service after the sale. Effective selling isn't simply a matter of persuading others to buy. In fact, it's more accurately described today as helping others satisfy their wants and needs.

Given that perspective, you can see why salespeople are starting to use the Internet, portable computers, paging devices, fax machines, and other technology. They can use this technology to help customers search the Net, design custom-made products, look over prices, and generally do everything it takes to complete the order. The benefit of personal selling is that there is a person there to help you complete a transaction. The salesperson should listen to your needs, help you reach a solution, and do all that is possible to make accomplishing that solution smoother and easier.

You are familiar with all kinds of men and women who do personal selling. They work in the local department store and sell all kinds of goods and services like automobiles, insurance, and real estate. What could they do to be more helpful to you, the customer? Could you be a successful salesperson? What would you like to sell?

It is costly to provide customers with personal attention, especially since some companies are replacing salespeople with Internet services and information. Therefore, those companies that retain salespeople must train them to be especially effective, efficient, and helpful.

To illustrate personal selling's importance in our economy and the career opportunities it provides, let's look at some numbers. First, U.S. census data show that nearly 10 percent of the total labor force is employed in personal selling. When we add those who sell for nonprofit organizations, we find that over 7 million people are employed in sales. With so many companies eager to raise revenues today, the demand for salespeople is increasing dramatically. A recent poll found that 77 percent of the companies polled are hiring more field sales representatives.[19] To lure new salespeople companies are paying them quite well. Top sellers at 90 percent of the companies surveyed made more than their direct supervisor and 19 percent made more than the CEO.[20] The average cost of a single sales call to a potential business-to-business (B2B) buyer is about $400. Surely no firm would pay that much to send out anyone but a highly skilled, professional marketer and consultant.

## Steps in the Selling Process

The best way to understand personal selling is to go through the selling process with a product and see what's involved. Imagine that you are a software salesperson whose job is to show business users the advantages of using various programs. One product that is really hot these days, and one that is becoming critically important to establishing long-term relationships with customers, is customer relationship management (CRM) software.[21] Let's go through the selling process to see what you can do to sell CRM software. Although this is a business-to-business (B2B) example, the process is similar, but less complex, in consumer selling. In both business-to-business and consumer selling, it is critical for the salesperson to know the product well and to know how the product compares to competitors' products. Such product knowledge is needed before the salesperson begins the selling process. The selling process then consists of seven steps, explained in the following paragraphs.

**prospecting**
Researching potential buyers and choosing those most likely to buy.

**qualifying**
In the selling process, making sure that people have a need for the product, the authority to buy, and the willingness to listen to a sales message.

**prospect**
A person with the means to buy a product, the authority to buy, and the willingness to listen to a sales message.

**1. Prospect and Qualify** The first step in the selling process is prospecting. **Prospecting** involves researching potential buyers and choosing those most likely to buy. That selection process is called **qualifying**. To qualify people means to make sure that they have a need for the product, the authority to buy, and the willingness to listen to a sales message. A person who meets these criteria is called a **prospect**. You often meet prospects at trade shows, where they come up to booths sponsored by manufacturers and ask questions.

Other prospects may visit your Web site seeking information. But often the best prospects are people at companies who were recommended to you by others who use your product or know all about it. Salespeople often e-mail potential clients with proposals to see if there is any interest before making a formal visit.

**2. Preapproach** Before making a sales call, you must do further research. In the preapproach phase, you must learn as much as possible about customers and their wants and needs. Before you try to sell the CRM software, you would want to know which people in the company are most likely to buy or use it. What kind of customers do they deal with? What kind of relationship strategies are they now using? All that information should be in a database so that, if one representative leaves the firm, the company can carry information about customers to the new salesperson. Note that the selling process may take a long time and that gathering information before you approach the customer is critical.

**3. Approach** An old saying goes "You don't have a second chance to make a good first impression." That's why the approach is so important. When you call on a customer for the first time, your opening comments are important. The idea is to give an impression of friendly professionalism, to create rapport, to build credibility, and to start a relationship. Often the decision of whether or not to use a software package depends on reliable service from the salesperson. In selling CRM products, you can make it known from the start that you'll be available to help the prospect company train its employees to use the software and to upgrade the package when necessary.

**4. Make Presentation** In the actual presentation of the CRM software, the idea is to match the benefits of your value package to the client's needs. Companies such as Ventaso Inc. and the Sant Group now provide sales proposal software that includes everything from PowerPoint presentations to competitive analysis. Since you've done your homework and know the prospect's wants and needs, you can tailor the presentation accordingly. During the presentation is a great time to use testimonials (letters or statements from users praising the product) to show potential buyers that they are joining leaders in other firms in trying this new software.

**5. Answer Objections** You should anticipate any objections the prospect may raise and determine proper responses. Think of questions as opportunities for creating better relationships, not as challenges to what you're saying. Customers may have legitimate doubts, and you are there to resolve those doubts. Relationships are based on trust, and trust comes from successfully and honestly working with others. Often you can introduce the customer to others in the firm who can answer their questions and provide them with anything they need. Using a laptop computer, you may set up a virtual meeting in which the customer can chat with other members of the firm and begin building a relationship.

**trial close**
A step in the selling process that consists of a question or statement that moves the selling process toward the actual close.

**6. Close Sale** As a salesperson, you have limited time and can't spend forever with one potential customer answering questions and objections. A **trial close** consists of a question or statement that moves the selling process toward the actual close. Questions you might ask in a trial close include "Would you like the blue one or the red one?" and "Do you want to pay for that with your credit card?" The final step is to ask for the order and show the client where to sign. Once a relationship is established, the goal of the sales call may be to get a testimonial from the customer. As you can see, salespeople must learn to close many times before a long-term relationship is established.

**7. Follow Up** The selling process isn't over until the order is approved and the customer is happy. The sales relationship may continue for years as you respond to new requests for information. One salesperson puts it this way: "Salespeople really need to be providers of solutions to their customers and also need to think about what happens after the sale."[22] You can see why selling is often described as a process of establishing relationships, not just a matter of selling goods or services. The follow-up step includes handling customer complaints, making sure that the customer's questions are answered, and quickly supplying what the customer wants. Often, customer service is as important to the sale as the product itself. Most manufacturers have therefore established Web sites where information may be obtained and discussions may take place.

Don't think that making the sale is the end of the relationship with a customer. You should follow up on the sale to make sure the customer is happy and perhaps make a suggestion of something to complement what was purchased. Follow-up is a key part of the selling process. Have salespeople been able to sell you more because of effective follow-up procedures? How did they do it?

The selling process varies somewhat among different goods and services, but the general idea is the same. Your goals as a salesperson are to help the buyer buy and to make sure that the buyer is satisfied after the sale. Sales force automation (SFA), in fact, includes over 400 software programs that help salespeople design products, close deals, tap into company intranets, and more. With SFA, some salespeople can even conduct virtual reality tours of the manufacturing plant for the customer.

## The Business-to-Consumer (B2C) Sales Process

Most sales to consumers take place in retail stores, where the role of the salesperson differs somewhat from that in B2B selling. In both cases, knowing the product comes first. However, in business-to-consumer (B2C) sales the salesperson does not have to do much prospecting or qualifying. Except in sales processes involving expensive products such as automobiles and furniture, during which salespeople may have to ask a few questions to qualify prospective customers before spending too much time with them, it is assumed that most people who come to the store are qualified to buy the merchandise.

Similarly, retail salespeople don't usually have to go through a preapproach step, although it is important to understand as much as possible about the type of people who shop at a given store. One thing for sure, though, is that a salesperson needs to focus on the customer and refrain from talking to fellow salespeople—or, worse, talking on the phone to friends—when customers are around.

The first formal step in the B2C sales process, then, is the approach. Too many salespeople begin with a line like "May I help you?" That is not a good opening because the answer too often is "No." A better approach is "What may I help you with?" or, simply, "How are you today?" The idea is to show the customer that you are there to help and that you are friendly and knowledgeable. Also, you need to discover what the customer wants.

According to what the customer tells you, you then make a presentation. You show customers how the products you have meet their needs. You answer questions that help them choose the products that are right for them. The more you learn about customers' specific wants, the better you are able to help them choose the right product or products to meet those wants.

As in B2B selling, it is important to make a trial close. "Would you like me to put that on hold?" and "Will you be paying for that with your store credit

figure 16.6

**STEPS IN THE BUSINESS-TO-CONSUMER (B2C) SELLING PROCESS**

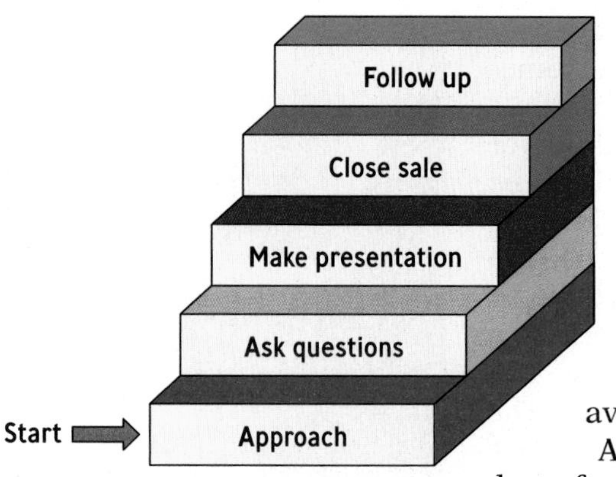


card?" are two such efforts. A store salesperson walks a fine line between being helpful and being pushy. Selling is an art, and a salesperson must learn just how far to go. Often individual buyers need some time alone to think about the purchase. The salesperson must respect that need and give them time and space, but still be clearly available when needed.

After-sale follow-up is an important but often neglected step in B2C sales. If the product is to be delivered, the salesperson should follow up to be sure it is delivered on time. The same is true if the product has to be installed. There is often a chance to sell more merchandise when a salesperson follows up on a sale. Figure 16.6 shows the whole B2C selling process. You can compare that figure to the seven-step process we outlined earlier for B2B selling.

progress assessment

- What are the four traditional elements of the promotion mix?
- What are the three most important advertising media in order of dollars spent?
- What are the seven steps in the B2B selling process?

**public relations (PR)**
The management function that evaluates public attitudes, changes policies and procedures in response to the public's requests, and executes a program of action and information to earn public understanding and acceptance.

## PUBLIC RELATIONS: BUILDING RELATIONSHIPS

**Public relations (PR)** is defined as the management function that evaluates public attitudes, changes policies and procedures in response to the public's requests, and executes a program of action and information to earn public understanding and acceptance. In other words, a good public relations program has three steps:

1. *Listen to the public.* Public relations starts with good marketing research ("evaluates public attitudes").
2. *Change policies and procedures*. Businesses don't earn understanding by bombarding the public with propaganda; they earn understanding by having programs and practices in the public interest. The best way to learn what the public wants is to listen to people often—in different forums, including on the Internet.
3. *Inform people that you're being responsive to their needs.* It's not enough to simply have programs in the public interest. *You have to tell the public* about those programs so that they know you're being responsive. Public relations has more power to influence consumers because the message comes from a source (the media) that is perceived as being more trustworthy.[23]

It is the responsibility of the PR department to maintain close ties with the company stakeholders (customers, media, community leaders, government officials, and other corporate stakeholders).[24]

## Publicity: The Talking Arm of PR

Publicity is the talking arm of public relations. It is one of the major functions of almost all organizations. Here's how it works: Suppose that you want to introduce your store, Very Vegetarian, to consumers but you have very little money to promote it. You need to get some initial sales to generate funds. One effective way to reach the public is through publicity. **Publicity** is any information about an individual, product, or organization that's distributed to the public through the media and that's not paid for, or controlled by, the seller. You might envision preparing a press release describing Very Vegetarian and the research findings that consumers love it, and sending it to the various media. John D. Rockefeller once remarked, "Next to doing the right thing, the most important thing is to let people know that you are doing the right thing."[25] What might Very Vegetarian do to help the community and thus create more publicity?

**publicity**
Any information about an individual, product, or organization that's distributed to the public through the media and that's not paid for or controlled by the seller.

Much skill is involved in writing such releases so that the media will want to publish them.[26] You may need to write different stories for different media. One may talk about the new owners. Another may talk about the unusual product offerings. If the stories are published, release of the news about your store will reach many potential consumers (and investors, distributors, and dealers), and you may be on your way to becoming a wealthy marketer. Publicity works only if the media find the material interesting or newsworthy. The idea, then, is to write publicity that meets those criteria.

Besides being free, publicity has several further advantages over other promotional tools, such as advertising. For example, publicity may reach people who wouldn't read an ad. It may appear on the front page of a newspaper or in some other prominent position, or be given air time on a television news show. Perhaps the greatest advantage of publicity is its believability. When a newspaper or magazine publishes a story as news, the reader treats that story as news—and news is more believable than advertising.

There are several disadvantages to publicity as well. For example, marketers have no control over how, when, or if the media will use the story. The media aren't obligated to use a publicity release, and most are thrown away. Furthermore, the story may be altered so that it's not so positive. There's good publicity (iPod sales are taking off) and bad publicity (GM going bankrupt). Also, once a story has run, it's not likely to be repeated. Advertising, in contrast, can be repeated as often as needed. One way to see that publicity is handled well by the media is to establish a friendly relationship with media representatives, being open with them when they seek information. Then, when you want their support, they're more likely to cooperate.

# SALES PROMOTION: GETTING A GOOD DEAL

**Sales promotion** is the promotional tool that stimulates consumer purchasing and dealer interest by means of short-term activities. These activities include such things as displays, trade shows and exhibitions, event sponsorships, and contests. Figure 16.7 lists some B2B sales promotion techniques. For consumer sales promotion activities, think of those free samples of products that

**sales promotion**
The promotional tool that stimulates consumer purchasing and dealer interest by means of short-term activities.

Trade shows
Portfolios for salespeople
Deals (price reductions)
Catalogs
Conventions

figure 16.7
**BUSINESS-TO-BUSINESS SALES PROMOTION TECHNIQUES**

This International Manufacturing Trade Show in Chicago featured 4,000 booths, giving buyers for other businesses thousands of new products to explore and purchase. Can you see why trade shows in many industries are an efficient and necessary way to stay abreast of the latest developments, your competitors, and consumer reactions and needs?

you get in the mail, the cents-off coupons that you clip from newspapers, the contests that various retail stores sponsor, and the prizes in Cracker Jack boxes (see Figure 16.8). You can stimulate sales in Very Vegetarian by putting half-off coupons in the school paper and in home mailers.

Sales promotion programs are designed to supplement personal selling, advertising, and public relations efforts by creating enthusiasm for the overall promotional program. There was a big increase in such promotions as the 21st century began, especially online. Sales promotion can take place both internally (within the company) and externally (outside the company). Often it's just as important to generate employee enthusiasm about a product as it is to attract potential customers. The most important internal sales promotion efforts are directed at salespeople and other customer-contact people, such as complaint handlers and clerks. Internal sales promotion efforts include (1) sales training; (2) the development of sales aids such as flip charts, portable audiovisual displays, and videotapes; and (3) participation in trade shows where salespeople can get leads. Other employees who deal with the public may also be given special training to improve their awareness of the company's offerings and make them an integral part of the total promotional effort.

After generating enthusiasm internally, it's important to get distributors and dealers involved so that they too are eager to help promote the product. Trade shows are an important sales promotion tool because they allow marketing intermediaries to see products from many different sellers and make comparisons among them. Today, virtual trade shows—trade shows on

figure 16.8

**CONSUMER SALES PROMOTION TECHNIQUES**

| | |
|---|---|
| Coupons | Bonuses (buy one, get one free) |
| Cents-off promotions | Catalogs |
| Sampling | Demonstrations |
| Premiums | Special events |
| Sweepstakes | Lotteries |
| Contests | In-store displays |

the Internet—enable buyers to see many products without leaving the office. Furthermore, the information is available 24 hours a day, seven days a week.

After the company's employees and intermediaries have been motivated with sales promotion efforts, the next step is to promote to final consumers using samples, coupons, cents-off deals, displays, store demonstrations, premiums, contests, rebates, and so on. Sales promotion is an ongoing effort to maintain enthusiasm, so different strategies must be used over time to keep the ideas fresh. You could put food displays in your Very Vegetarian store to show customers how attractive the products look. You could also sponsor in-store cooking demonstrations to attract new vegetarians.

Guerilla marketing street teams go to all kinds of events to hand out samples, engage the customer in a conversation about the products, and create word of mouth. You may have encountered such a team trying to sign you up for a credit card by offering you a free T-shirt or something like that. When are you most receptive to such promotions and when do they annoy you the most?

## Sampling

One popular sales promotion tool is **sampling**—letting consumers have a small sample of the product for no charge. Because many consumers won't buy a new product unless they've had a chance to see it or try it, grocery stores often have people standing in the aisles handing out small portions of food and beverage products. Sampling is a quick, effective way of demonstrating a product's superiority at the time when consumers are making a purchase decision. Standing outside Very Vegetarian and giving out samples would surely attract attention.

Pepsi introduced its FruitWorks product line with a combination of sampling, event marketing, and a new Web site. *Event marketing* means sponsoring events such as rock concerts or being at various events to promote your products. In the case of FruitWorks, Pepsi first sent samples to Panama City, Florida, and South Padre Island, Texas, for spring break. Students got free rides on Pepsi trucks and samples of the drinks. Similar sampling and event marketing efforts had been successful for SoBe (herbal-fortified drinks) and Snapple (fruit drinks and iced teas).

**progress assessment**

- What are the three steps involved in setting up a public relations program?
- What are the sales promotion techniques used to reach consumers?
- What sales promotion techniques are used to reach businesses?

**sampling**
A promotional tool in which a company lets consumers have a small sample of a product for no charge.

## Word of Mouth

Although word of mouth is not normally listed as one of the major promotional efforts (word of mouth is not paid for, so is not considered advertising), it is often one of the most effective tools.[27] This is especially true of Internet word of mouth because it can reach so many people so easily.[28] In **word-of-mouth promotion**, people tell other people about products that they've purchased. Anything that encourages people to talk favorably about an organization may be effective word of mouth. Notice, for example, how stores use clowns, banners, music, fairs, and other attention-getting devices to create word of mouth. Clever commercials can also generate much word of mouth. The whole idea is to get more and more people talking about your products and your brand name so that customers remember them when they go to buy things. You might enjoy brainstorming strategies for creating word of mouth about Very Vegetarian. The Making Ethical Decisions box asks some questions about tobacco companies' strategies.

**word-of-mouth promotion**
A promotional tool that involves people telling other people about products they've purchased.

## MAKING ethical decisions

### A Tobacco Industry Smoke Screen?

Since the number of smokers in the United States is declining rapidly due to the aging population, the tobacco industry must recruit new smokers if it is to survive and prosper. Today, most new smokers are children or teenagers. Obviously, getting young people to start smoking is vitally important to the survival of the tobacco industry.

The tobacco industry claims it doesn't advertise to children. Do you think this is true? Cigarette ads have been illegal on U.S. television and radio since 1970, but the tobacco industry spends millions of dollars each year on other forms of cigarette promotion. Tobacco spokespeople say this promotion is intended to encourage brand loyalty or to encourage adult smokers to try a new brand. Is it ethical to place poster-size cigarette ads where young people often meet, such as near theaters, record stores, and video arcades? What about advertising cigarettes on billboards at sporting and entertainment events? What would you do if a company offered to pay you to put up such ads on your campus?

**Viral Marketing** A number of companies have begun creating word of mouth by paying people to promote their products to others. One such strategy encourages people to go into Internet chat rooms and hype (or talk enthusiastically and favorably about) bands, movies, video games, and sports teams. People who agree to hype products in this way may get what the industry calls *swag*—free tickets, backstage passes, T-shirts, and other such merchandise. What do you think of the ethics of paying ordinary people to promote goods and services?

**viral marketing**
The term now used to describe everything from paying people to say positive things on the Internet to setting up multilevel selling schemes whereby consumers get commissions for directing friends to specific Web sites.

**Viral marketing** is the term now used to describe everything from paying people to say positive things on the Internet to setting up multilevel selling schemes whereby consumers get commissions for directing friends to specific Web sites.

One especially effective strategy for spreading positive word of mouth is to send testimonials (letters or statements from customers praising a product) to current customers. Most companies use testimonials only in promoting to new customers, but testimonials are also effective in confirming customers' belief that they chose the right company. Positive word of mouth from other users further confirms their choice. Therefore, some companies make it a habit to ask customers for referrals.

It is important to note also that negative word of mouth can hurt a firm badly. Taking care of consumer complaints quickly and effectively is one of the best ways to reduce the effects of negative word of mouth. Today, negative word of mouth can spread faster than ever before. Online forums, chat rooms, bulletin boards, and Web sites can all be used as means to spread criticism about a product or company.

**blog**
An online diary (Web log) that looks like a web page but is easier to create and update by posting text, photos, or links to other sites.

**Blogging** A **blog**—short for Web log—is an online diary that looks like a Web page but is easier to create and update by posting text, photos, or links to other sites. There are over 30 million blogs currently on the Internet, and 40,000 new ones are being added each day.[29] You may not be involved in blogging yet, but clearly it is a phenomenon of the future.[30] Here is an example of how it is affecting marketing: A new book came out called *Freakonomics*. The publisher, HarperCollins, sent advanced galleys to 100 bloggers. These bloggers sent reviews to other bloggers (word of mouth) and pretty soon *Freakonomics* was number three on Amazon.com's list of most-ordered books.[31] You can imagine what blogging will do in the future for movies, TV shows, and more—much more. Business information will be revolutionized by bloggers. If you want to know about small-business trends, you would go to SmallBusinesses.blogspot.com. If you want some cool business ideas, you would go to CoolBusinesssideas

.com.[32] Expertise on all areas of business will soon be available from bloggers. We encourage you to try such sites in the Taking It to the Net exercise at the end of this chapter.

**podcasting**
A means of distributing audio and video programs via the Internet that lets users subscribe to a number of files, also known as feeds, and then hear or view the material at the time they choose.

**Podcasting** **Podcasting** is a means of distributing audio and video programs via the Internet that lets users subscribe to a number of files, also known as feeds, and then hear or view the material at the time they choose.[33] The word *podcast* comes from a combination of Apple's iPod digital music player and broadcasting. The term is a bit misleading since you don't need to use an iPod or any other portable player to access the feeds; you can use a computer using "podcatching" software as well. Podcasting allows you to become your own newscaster, since it enables independent producers to create self-published, syndicated "radio shows." Podcasting gives broadcast radio or television programs a new distribution method. It won't be long before people are talking about products, services, and more on podcasts.

Are you getting the idea that traditional promotional methods are slowly but surely being replaced by new technology? If so, you are getting the right idea. Today, high school and college students are way ahead of Madison Avenue when it comes to such technology, but not for long. By keeping up with the latest trends, you may be able to grab a good job in promotion while traditionalists are still wondering what happened.

## How New Technologies Are Affecting Promotion

As people purchase goods and services on the Internet, companies keep track of those purchases and gather other facts and figures about those consumers. Over time, companies learn who buys what, when, and how often. They can then use that information to design catalogs and brochures specifically designed to meet the wants and needs of individual consumers as demonstrated by their actual purchasing behavior. So, for example, a flower company may send you a postcard first reminding you that your spouse's birthday is coming up soon and that you bought a particular flower arrangement last time, and then recommending a new arrangement this time.

Because so much information about consumers is now available, companies are tending to use the traditional promotional tools (e.g., TV advertising) less than before and are putting more money into direct mail and other forms of direct marketing, including catalogs and the Internet. Consumers are reacting favorably to such promotions, so you can expect the trend toward direct sales and Internet sales to accelerate. Promotional programs will change accordingly. See the Spotlight on Small Business box on page 448 for examples of new Internet and creative promotions.

New technology offers consumers a continuous connection to the Internet and enables marketers to send video files and other data to them faster than ever before. Using such connections, marketers can interact with consumers in real time. As you have read in this chapter, that means that you can talk with a salesperson online and chat with other consumers about their experiences with products and services. You can also search the Net for the best price and find any product information you may want in almost any form you want—copy, sound, video, or whatever.

Such technology gives a great deal of power to consumers like you. You no longer have to rely on advertising or other promotions to learn about products. You can search the Net on your own and find as much information as you want, when you want it. If the information is not posted, you can request it and get it immediately. Thus, promotion has become much more interactive than ever before.

More and more it is impossible to get away from commercial messages. You may get a podcast on your iPod. You may see product placement on your video games. Promotional messages are everywhere—on telephone poles, on billboards, on buses and trains, and on the back of park benches. Is there a point where commercials are simply too intrusive on you? What can you do about it?

SPOTLIGHT ON small business

## Help, I'm Getting Married

Getting married can be one of the most stressful times of your life. Wouldn't it be great if you could find a firm that would handle all the details for you? Well, there is one. It is called Knot.com. It will help you find a reception hall, bridesmaids' dresses, a DJ, wedding rings, and more. You can even find gift registries. More than 2.1 million potential customers a *month* visit www.Knot.com, so advertisers are eager to be included on the Web site. Ad revenue for this dot-com company increased by 41 percent in 2004 and was expected to grow even faster in 2005.

If you recently got married, you can go to the related newlywed site at www.thenest.com. Or, if you are merely looking, you can go to www.greatboyfriends.com. Knot.com and its other Web sites illustrate the trend of moving advertising away from the traditional media toward the Internet.

Speaking of weddings, how does a small business that gives bridal shows use creative promotion to win customers at a minimum of cost? Carol Boucher of Valley Forge, Pennsylvania, has a small company called Bridal Event that gives bridal shows. There is a lot of competition for audiences among such shows, and Boucher wanted her company to stand out from the others. An advertising consultant, remembering that satisfied customers provide the best ad copy, recommended using testimonials from attendees at previous shows. Word of mouth is almost always the best way of reaching new customers. Some small companies even pay their previous customers to recommend new customers. For example, they may give previous customers $5 for every new customer who comes to the show because of their recommendation.

Small businesses find that an important part of promotion is getting local papers to print stories about them (publicity). One way a bridal company can get such free publicity is to take a picture of several brides and grooms and write interesting stories about how each couple met and why they went to a bridal show. Other stories could feature new wedding gowns, fun things to do at wedding receptions, or unusual flower arrangements. A small business could set up a blog to let people talk with each other about wedding plans. Would you go to such a blog to learn creative wedding ideas?

Sources: Matthew Boyle, "Take the Plunge: It's Time to Buy the Knot," *Fortune*, April 8, 2005, p. 106; BridalEvent.com, 2005; Lora Kolodny, "The Art of the Press Release," *Inc.*, March 2005, p. 36; Leslie Walker, "The Company That Turns Pages," *Washington Post*, April 7, 2005, pp. E1 and E4; and Allison Fass, "Wedding March," *Forbes*, December 12, 2005, pp. 88–89.

# MANAGING THE PROMOTION MIX: PUTTING IT ALL TOGETHER

Each target group calls for a separate promotion mix. For example, large, homogeneous groups of consumers (i.e., groups whose members share specific similar traits) are usually most efficiently reached through advertising. Large organizations are best reached through personal selling. To motivate people to buy now rather than later, sales promotion efforts such as sampling, coupons, discounts, special displays, and premiums may be used. Publicity adds support to the other efforts and can create a good impression among all consumers. Word of mouth is often the most powerful promotional tool and is generated effectively by listening, being responsive, and creating an impression worth passing on to others. You will be much better at spreading word of mouth if you learn the arts of blogging and podcasting.

**push strategy**
Promotional strategy in which the producer uses advertising, personal selling, sales promotion, and all other promotional tools to convince wholesalers and retailers to stock and sell merchandise.

**pull strategy**
Promotional strategy in which heavy advertising and sales promotion efforts are directed toward consumers so that they'll request the products from retailers.

## Promotional Strategies

There are two key ways to facilitate the movement of products from producers to consumers. The first is called a push strategy. In a **push strategy**, the producer uses advertising, personal selling, sales promotion, and all other promotional tools to convince wholesalers and retailers to stock and sell merchandise. If the push strategy works, consumers will then walk into a store, see the product, and buy it. The idea is to push the product through the distribution system to the stores.

A second strategy is called a pull strategy. In a **pull strategy**, heavy advertising and sales promotion efforts are directed toward consumers so that they'll request the products from retailers. If the pull strategy works, consumers will go to the store and order the products. Seeing the demand for the products, the store owner will then order them from the wholesaler. The wholesaler, in turn, will order them from the producer. Products are thus pulled down through the distribution system. When movie producers keep advertising new films on TV, they use a pull strategy, hoping that viewers will ask for those movies at movie theaters.

Dr Pepper has used TV advertising in a pull strategy to increase distribution. Tripledge, a maker of windshield wipers, also tried to capture the interest of retail stores through a pull strategy. Of course, a company could use both push and pull strategies at the same time in a major promotional effort. The latest in pull and push strategies are being conducted on the Internet, with companies sending messages to both consumers and businesses.

It is important to make promotion part of a total systems approach to marketing. That is, promotion should be part of supply-chain management. In such cases, retailers would work with producers and distributors to make the supply chain as efficient as possible. Then a promotional plan would be developed for the whole system. The idea would be to develop a total product offer that would appeal to everyone: manufacturers, distributors, retailers, and consumers.

### progress assessment

- What is viral marketing?
- What is blogging and podcasting?
- Describe how to implement a push strategy and a pull strategy.

## summary

1. Define *promotion* and list the four traditional tools that make up the promotion mix.

1. Promotion is an effort by marketers to inform and remind people in the target market about products and to persuade them to participate in an exchange.
   - **What are the four traditional promotional tools that make up the promotion mix?**

   The four traditional promotional tools are advertising, personal selling, public relations, and sales promotion. The product itself can be a promotional tool—that's why it is shown in the middle of Figure 16.1.

2. Define *advertising* and describe the advantages and disadvantages of various advertising media, including the Internet.

2. Advertising is limited to paid, nonpersonal (not face-to-face) communication through various media by organizations and individuals who are in some way identified in the advertising message.
   - **What are the advantages of using the various media?**

   You can review the advantages and disadvantages of the various advertising media in Figure 16.5.
   - **Why the growing use of infomercials?**

   Infomercials are growing in importance because they show products in use and present testimonials to help sell goods and services.

3. Illustrate the steps of the B2B and B2C selling process.

3. Personal selling is the face-to-face presentation and promotion of products and services. It also involves the search for new prospects and follow-up service after the sale.

- **What are the seven steps of the B2B selling process?**

The steps of the selling process are (1) prospect and qualify, (2) preapproach, (3) approach, (4) make presentation, (5) answer objections, (6) close sale, and (7) follow-up.

- **What are the steps in the B2C selling process?**

The steps are the approach, which includes asking questions; the presentation, which includes answering questions; the closing; and follow-up.

**4.** Describe the role of the public relations department, and tell how publicity fits in that role.

4. Public relations (PR) is the function that evaluates public attitudes, changes policies and procedures in response to the public's requests, and executes a program of action and information to earn public understanding and acceptance.

- **What are the three major steps in a good public relations program?**

(1) Listen to the public—public relations starts with good marketing research; (2) develop policies and procedures in the public interest—one doesn't earn understanding by bombarding the public with propaganda; rather, one earns understanding by having programs and practices in the public interest; and (3) inform people that you're being responsive to their needs.

- **What is publicity?**

Publicity is the talking part of sales promotion; it is information distributed by the media that's not paid for, or controlled by, the seller. It's an effective way to reach the public. Publicity's greatest advantage is its believability.

**5.** Explain the importance of various forms of sales promotion, including sampling.

5. Sales promotion motivates people to buy now instead of later.

- **How are sales promotion activities used both within and outside the organization?**

Internal sales promotion efforts are directed at salespeople and other customer-contact people to keep them enthusiastic about the company. Internal sales promotion activities include sales training, sales aids, audiovisual displays, and trade shows. External sales promotion (promotion to consumers) involves using samples, coupons, cents-off deals, displays, store demonstrators, premiums, and other such incentives.

**6.** Give examples of word of mouth, viral marketing, blogging, and podcasting.

6. Word of mouth is not considered one of the traditional forms of promotion, but it has always been an effective way of promoting goods and services.

- **How is word of mouth being used in promotion today?**

A number of companies have begun creating word of mouth by paying individuals to promote products. Some pay people to go into Internet chat rooms and hype (talk enthusiastically and favorably about) bands, movies, video games, and sports teams. People who agree to hype products in this way get what the industry calls *swag*—free tickets, backstage passes, T-shirts, and other merchandise. *Viral marketing* is the term now used to describe everything from paying people to say positive things on the Internet to setting up multilevel selling schemes whereby consumers get commissions for directing friends to specific Web sites. Word of mouth is now spread by blogs (Web logs). Podcasting is like blogging, but with more of an audiovisual focus.

- **What are the various promotional strategies?**

In a push strategy, the producer uses advertising, personal selling, sales promotion, and all other promotional tools to convince wholesalers and retailers to stock and sell merchandise. In a pull strategy, heavy advertising and sales promotion efforts are directed toward consumers so that they'll request the products from retailers.

## key terms

**advertising** 433
**blog** 446
**infomercial** 435
**interactive promotion** 437
**integrated marketing communication (IMC)** 432
**personal selling** 438
**podcasting** 447
**product placement** 435
**promotion** 432
**promotion mix** 432
**prospect** 439
**prospecting** 439
**publicity** 443
**public relations (PR)** 442
**pull strategy** 448
**push strategy** 448
**qualifying** 439
**sales promotion** 443
**sampling** 445
**trial close** 440
**viral marketing** 446
**word-of-mouth promotion** 445

## critical thinking questions

1. What kinds of problems can emerge if a firm doesn't communicate with environmentalists, the news media, and the local community? In your area have you seen examples of firms that aren't responsive to the community? What have been the consequences?
2. How much of your buying behavior has moved from stores to the Internet? If you don't actually buy things on the Internet, do you use it to compare goods and prices? Do you or your friends take advantage of the low prices on used goods from eBay? Do you see yourself turning to the Internet over time for an increasing number of purchases? Do you look at ads on the Internet? Do they seem to be effective?
3. Now that there is a greater possibility of interactive communications between companies and potential customers, do you think the importance of traditional advertising will grow or decline? What will be the effect, if any, on the price we consumers must pay for TV programs, newspapers, and magazines?
4. What will be the effect on the media of blogging and podcasting? Are you and your friends involved in such activities? Do you see blogging becoming an important word-of-mouth promotional tool?

## developing workplace skills

1. Using at least two different media—a newspaper, magazine, or any other medium—choose two ads that you consider good and two that you don't consider good. Be prepared to discuss why you feel as you do about each ad.
2. Scan your local newspaper for examples of publicity (stories about new products) and sales promotion (coupons, contests, sweepstakes). Share your examples and discuss the effectiveness of such promotional efforts with the class.
3. Many students shy away from careers in selling, often because they think that salespeople are dishonest or too pushy, or because they think they are not outgoing enough. Prepare a one-page document that discusses your experience with salespeople and what you think of selling as a career.

4. In small groups, discuss whether or not you are purchasing more goods using catalogs and/or the Internet and why. Do you look up information on the Internet before buying goods and services? How helpful are such searches? Present your findings to the class.

5. In small groups or individually, make a list of six products (goods and services) that most students own or use and then discuss which promotional techniques prompt you to buy these goods and services: advertising, personal selling, publicity, sales promotion, or word of mouth. Which tool seems to be most effective for your group? Why do you suppose that is?

## taking it to the net * 1

### Purpose

To learn about business blogs.

### Exercise

Go to Blogger.com to learn how easy it is to start your own blog. Then go to the following business-oriented blogs: Ventureblog.com, Feld.com, and PatentPending.blogs.com.

1. What kind of subjects are covered in each blog?
2. What are the advantages and disadvantages of reading such blogs?
3. Would you like to see a blog for this course? For your school?

## taking it to the net * 2

### Purpose

To learn about online sales promotion efforts.

### Exercise

Many marketers put coupons in magazines and newspapers. Some place coupon dispensers in supermarket and other store displays. The latest in couponing is Internet placement. To find such sites, go to www.couponmountain.com and click on various links to explore what is available. Sometimes the best deal is to pay nothing at all. To check out free offers on the Internet, go to www.yesfree.com and explore what is available there.

1. Are you willing to register at a Web site to get free coupons faxed to you? Why or why not?
2. What could these Web sites do to become more user-friendly for you and your friends?
3. Have you become more price-conscious now that Web sites give so much competitive information about price and coupons for so many products that are readily available? Is that a good thing or not for marketers?
4. Integrated marketing communication efforts are designed to create a good image for a firm, one that is consistent. Do sites like these fit into such a scheme? Why or why not?

## casing the web

To access the case *"Developing a Promotional Strategy for Biltmore Estate,"* visit **www.mhhe.com/ub8e**

## video case

### Promotion Gets a Big Push

Students today are witnessing a major revolution in promotion. They have seen radio change from standard broadcasting to commercial-free satellite radio. They have watched families blank out TV commercials with TIVO and other DVR recording devices. Students spend less time reading newspapers and magazines and more time talking on the phone, playing video games, and listening to their iPods. There are more entertainment options available today and more distractions from traditional promotional tools.

Today's students also have a wonderful opportunity to reinvent promotion, changing it from a one-way stream of sales pitches to an interactive dialogue among promoters and consumers. Traditional promotional tools—selling, advertising, public relations, and sales promotion—have always provided fun and interesting careers. Creating funny and captivating ads for TV has been a real challenge. Selling to businesses and consumers has always been challenging and interesting to those with the needed skills and desire. Public relations has been critical to all kinds of organizations and individuals.

The challenge today is to create promotions for the new realities of the marketplace. That means, for one thing, creating advertising and other promotions on the Internet. One of the cutting edge advertising agencies in this regard is Night Agency. The Night Agency has become an integral part of the marketing process for the firms it serves. It does everything from helping in the design of the product to working with the company to develop a winning brand name, effective packaging, and fast distribution.

A company like Night Agency has to promote itself to other businesses. Like most firms, Night Agency relies heavily on word-of-mouth to spread its name. Publicity in the form of articles written about the company is another powerful promotional tool. Night Agency teaches other firms how to use public relations and publicity to educate the public about the good that the firms do and to give the firm's side of controversies.

Often promotional efforts begin inside of a company. Salespeople, clerks, and other customer-contact people (and that means almost everyone in the firm) often don't understand everything they need to know about the products they make and sell. A worker in a firm making watches, for example, should be able to talk with people on the street about the quality and value the watches provide. That means using internal promotions such as videos, brochures, meetings, and charts to keep employees informed. Full-function advertising agencies get involved in such internal promotions as well as the more traditional external promotions.

One of the more innovative products from Night Agency is interactive Web games and demonstrations. Such promotions get potential customers more deeply involved in promotions than they have been in the past. But such promotions need to be measured like any other promotional tool to make sure they are seen, remembered, and followed.

One of the more memorable of their efforts was called the Darfur Digital Activist Contest that was designed to increase awareness of the desperate need for aid among the people in Darfur, Sudan. It is exciting and rewarding to use promotional tools to make a difference in the world, and doing what you can to end world hunger, poverty, disease, and war is part of that challenge.

Night Agency, as you will see in this video, creates dynamic, exciting promotions.

#### Thinking It Over

1. What kind of promotions have led to you to buy the things that you have purchased lately? That includes the school you attend (what prompted you to go there?), the clothes you have bought, the music you listen to, the restaurants you go to, and so on.
2. What differences did you notice between what Night Agency does and what you are used to seeing in promotions, if anything?
3. What has been your reaction thus far to Internet promotions? Do you pay any attention to them? Are they getting better? If so, in what way?

# understanding financial information AND accounting

*

profile

**Getting to Know**

**X Roxanne Coady**

**of R. J. Julia Booksellers**

When Roxanne Coady first contemplated changing careers and starting her own business, she looked forward to a change of pace. She hoped for a much less demanding job than the one she held as the national tax director at BDO Seidman, a New York–based international accounting firm. Coady, a certified public accountant (CPA), was once called "an accountant's accountant" by *Money* magazine. She spent 20 years in public and private accounting and was familiar with financial analysis, healthy balance sheets, and return on equity and assets. When she made the decision to leave the security of the corporate world to open a bookstore, her colleagues agreed that her new business, R. J. Julia Booksellers, would be in sound financial hands. She almost proved them wrong.

In its first five years, R. J. Julia Booksellers (named after Coady's grandmother who died in a concentration camp in World War II) enjoyed strong growth of 30 to 75 percent a year. The company published a first-class newsletter, had free wine and food at author events, sported stylish extra-strength bags for customers, and had a large, well-compensated staff who received regular bonuses. However, the financial condition of the company was deteriorating. Inventory turnover was unacceptable, and business costs were running too high. The company was failing to turn a profit. The irony was that after Coady's career as a successful accountant, accounting seemed to be the weakest area in the operation of R. J. Julia Booksellers.

Coady realized that as an accountant she had always used her head, but as a bookseller and book lover she was letting her passion take over. R. J. Julia Booksellers was being treated as a personal mission outside the rules of business.

LEARNING goals

**After you have read and studied this chapter, you should be able to**

1. Describe the importance of financial information and accounting.
2. Define and explain the different areas of the accounting profession.
3. List the steps in the accounting cycle, distinguish between accounting and bookkeeping, and explain how computers are used in accounting.
4. Explain how the major financial statements differ.
5. Explain the importance of ratio analysis in reporting financial information.

CHAPTER 17

**www.rjjulia.com**

Coady had ignored budgets and misspent approximately $250,000 of the money she and her husband had saved. Financial standards were lax, cash flow was poor, and return on investment was never thoroughly analyzed. Instead of committing herself to solving the company's problems, she threw more money at them. Finally, she had to face the fact that the firm had no goal-setting procedures and her staff had never been briefed on meeting financial objectives. The company sorely needed a business overhaul, and Coady, the accountant, was ready to implement it.

She gathered her staff and announced major changes at the bookstore, starting with the preparation of monthly profit-and-loss statements and cash flow analyses that monitored all aspects of the business. She knew the company needed to focus intensely on costs, since profit margins in the book business are slim. Coady recognized that as a small-business owner she was not exempt from the financial principles and standards she had expected from larger businesses she worked with as a CPA. She also decided to implement a company training manual and to structure evaluations more carefully. Employees were encouraged to become more efficient. Today, Roxanne Coady is one of the most successful independent bookstore owners in the country. In fact, she recently expanded to a second bookstore by taking ownership of Elm Street Books in New Canaan, Connecticut. She renamed the bookstore R. J. Julia–Elm Street Books. Coady is also the founder of Read to Grow Inc., a nonprofit group devoted to battling illiteracy.

Controlling costs, managing cash flows, understanding profit margins and taxes, and reporting finances accurately are keys to survival for both large and small organizations. This chapter will introduce you to the accounting fundamentals and financial information critical to business success. The chapter also briefly explores the financial ratios that are essential in measuring business performance in a large or small business.

Sources: Cara Baruzzi, "Madison, Conn., Bookseller Gains Ownership of Second Store," *New Haven (Connecticut) Register*, July 7, 2005; Julie Fishman-Lapin, "New Canaan, Conn., Bookstore Gets an Independent Partner," *Stamford (Connecticut) Advocate*, June 23, 2005; and Cara Baruzzi, "Old Saybrook, Conn., Retailer Given Business Award," *New Haven (Connecticut) Register*, August 26, 2005.

# THE IMPORTANCE OF ACCOUNTING INFORMATION

Stories like that of Roxanne Coady and R. J. Julia Booksellers are repeated hundreds of times every day throughout the business community. Small and sometimes large businesses falter or even fail because they do not follow good financial procedures. Financial management is the heartbeat of competitive businesses. Accounting information keeps the heartbeat stable.

You have to know something about accounting if you want to succeed in business. The simple truth is that learning some basic accounting terms is mandatory. You also have to understand how bookkeeping is related to accounting and how accounts are kept. It's almost impossible to run any size business or understand business operations without being able to read, understand, and analyze accounting reports and financial statements. Accounting reports and financial statements reveal as much about a business's health as pulse rate and blood pressure readings tell us about a person's health.

The purpose of this chapter is to introduce you to basic accounting principles and the important financial information obtained from accounting. By the end of the chapter, you should have a good idea of what accounting is, how it works, and why it is important. You should also know some accounting terms and understand the purpose of accounting statements. While it's important to understand how accounting statements are constructed, it's even more important to know what they mean to the business. A few hours invested in learning this material will pay off handsomely as you become more involved in business or simply in understanding what's going on in the world of business and finance.

**accounting**
The recording, classifying, summarizing, and interpreting of financial events and transactions to provide management and other interested parties the information they need to make good decisions.

## What Is Accounting?

Financial information is primarily based on information generated from accounting. **Accounting** is the recording, classifying, summarizing, and interpreting of financial events and transactions to provide management and other interested parties the information they need to make good decisions. Financial transactions can include such specifics as buying and selling goods and services, acquiring insurance, paying employees, and using supplies. Once the business's transactions have been recorded, they are usually classified into groups that have common characteristics. For example, all purchases are grouped together, as are all sales transactions. The method used to record and summarize accounting data into reports is called an *accounting system* (see Figure 17.1).

A major purpose of accounting is to help managers evaluate the financial condition and the operating performance of the firm so that they can make well-informed decisions. Another is to report financial information to interested

figure 17.1

**THE ACCOUNTING SYSTEM**

The inputs to an accounting system include sales documents and other documents. The data are recorded, classified, and summarized. They're then put into summary financial statements such as the income statement and balance sheet and statement of cash flows.

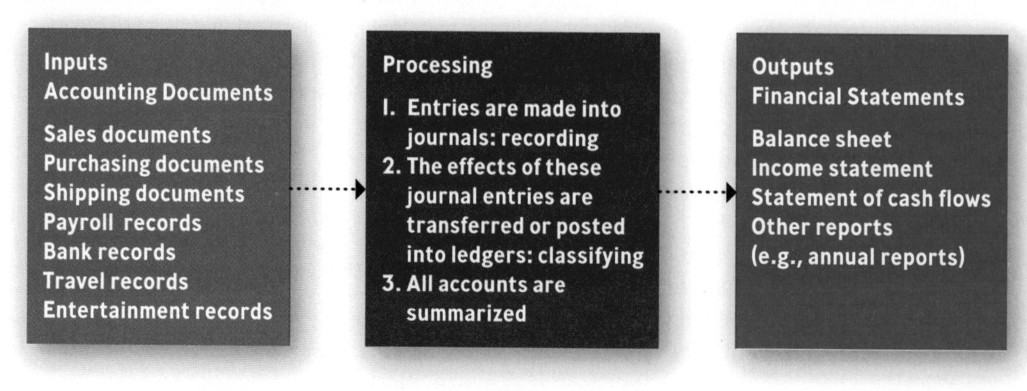

Inputs
Accounting Documents
Sales documents
Purchasing documents
Shipping documents
Payroll records
Bank records
Travel records
Entertainment records
Processing
1. Entries are made into journals: recording
2. The effects of these journal entries are transferred or posted into ledgers: classifying
3. All accounts are summarized
Outputs
Financial Statements
Balance sheet
Income statement
Statement of cash flows
Other reports
(e.g., annual reports)

| USERS | TYPE OF REPORT |
|---|---|
| Government taxing authorities (e.g., the Internal Revenue Service) | Tax returns |
| Government regulatory agencies | Required reports |
| People interested in the organization's income and financial position (e.g., owners, creditors, financial analysts, suppliers) | Financial statements found in annual reports (e.g., income statement, balance sheet, statement of cash flows) |
| Managers of the firm | Financial statements and various internally distributed financial reports |

figure 17.2

**USERS OF ACCOUNTING INFORMATION AND THE REQUIRED REPORTS**

Many types of organizations use accounting information to make business decisions. The reports needed vary according to the information each user requires. An accountant must prepare the appropriate forms.

stakeholders such as employees, owners, creditors, suppliers, unions, community activists, investors, and the government (for tax purposes) regarding the economic activities of the firm (see Figure 17.2). Accounting work is divided into several major areas. Let's look at those areas next.

# AREAS OF ACCOUNTING

Accounting has been called the language of business. It's possible you may think that accounting is only for profit-seeking firms. Nothing could be further from the truth. It is also the language used to report financial information about nonprofit organizations such as churches, schools, hospitals, fraternities, and government agencies. The accounting profession is divided into five key working areas: managerial accounting, financial accounting, auditing, tax accounting, and governmental and not-for-profit accounting. All five areas are important, and all create career opportunities for students willing to put forth the effort to study accounting.[1] Let's briefly explore each area.

## Managerial Accounting

**Managerial accounting** is used to provide information and analyses to managers within the organization to assist them in decision making. Managerial accounting is concerned with measuring and reporting costs of production, marketing, and other functions; preparing budgets (planning); checking whether or not units are staying within their budgets (controlling); and designing strategies to minimize taxes.

**managerial accounting**
Accounting used to provide information and analyses to managers within the organization to assist them in decision making.

If you are a business major, it's almost certain you will be required to take a course in managerial accounting. You may even pursue a career as a certified management accountant. A **certified management accountant (CMA)** is a professional accountant who has met certain educational and experience requirements, passed a qualifying exam in the field, and been certified by the Institute of Certified Management Accountants. With growing emphasis on global competition, outsourcing, and organizational cost-cutting, managerial accounting may be one of the most important areas you study in your college career.

**certified management accountant (CMA)**
A professional accountant who has met certain educational and experience requirements, passed a qualifying exam in the field, and been certified by the Institute of Certified Management Accountants.

## Financial Accounting

**Financial accounting** differs from managerial accounting in that the financial information and analyses it generates are for people primarily *outside* the organization. The information goes not only to company owners, managers, and employees but also to creditors and lenders, employee unions, customers, suppliers,

**financial accounting**
Accounting information and analyses prepared for people outside the organization.

Assembling a marine diesel engine involves many tools, parts, raw materials, and other components. Keeping these costs at a minimum and setting realistic production schedules is critical to industry survival. Management accountants team with managers from production, marketing, and other areas to ensure company competitiveness. Visit www.cma.edu to find out more about managerial accounting.

**annual report**
A yearly statement of the financial condition, progress, and expectations of an organization.

**private accountant**
An accountant who works for a single firm, government agency, or nonprofit organization.

**public accountant**
An accountant who provides accounting services to individuals or businesses on a fee basis.

**certified public accountant (CPA)**
An accountant who passes a series of examinations established by the American Institute of Certified Public Accountants.

government agencies, and the general public. External users are interested in important financial questions such as: Is the organization profitable? Is it able to pay its bills? How much debt does the organization hold? These questions and others are often answered in the company's **annual report**, a yearly statement of the financial condition, progress, and expectations of an organization. As pressure from stakeholders for detailed financial information has grown, companies have poured more information than ever into their annual reports.

It's critical for firms to keep accurate financial information. Therefore, many organizations employ a **private accountant**, who works for a single firm, government agency, or nonprofit organization. However, not all firms or nonprofit organizations want or need a full-time accountant. Fortunately, thousands of accounting firms in the United States provide the accounting services an organization needs through public accountants.

A **public accountant** provides accounting services to individuals or businesses on a fee basis. Public accountants can provide business assistance in many ways. They may design an accounting system for a firm, help select the correct software to run the system, or analyze the financial performance of an organization. An accountant who passes a series of examinations established by the American Institute of Certified Public Accountants (AICPA) and meets the state's requirement for education and experience earns recognition as a **certified public accountant (CPA)**. CPAs find careers as private accountants or public accountants, and are often sought to fill other financial positions within organizations.[2] Today, there are 450,000 CPAs in the United States.[3]

The accounting profession knows that it's vital for users of a firm's financial information to be assured that the information provided is accurate. The independent Financial Accounting Standards Board (FASB) defines the *generally accepted accounting principles (GAAP)* that accountants must follow. If financial reports are prepared in accordance with GAAP, users can expect the information to be reported according to standards agreed on by accounting professionals.[4]

The accounting profession suffered perhaps the darkest period in its history in the early 2000s. Accounting scandals involving companies such as

## DEALING WITH change

### Accountants Reading Between the Lines

In 2004, the U.S. economy lost $660 billion to fraud, according to the Association of Certified Fraud Examiners. Fraud includes things like check kiting (using multiple checking accounts so that checks from one account are written to cover checks from another account), reporting the sale of phantom inventory to nonexistent customers, or inflating company earnings reports to allow the company to qualify for large loans or to look good in front of the stockholders. Finding and, more important, proving fraud is the job of the accounting industry's version of Sherlock Holmes: the forensic accountant.

Forensic accountants have a somewhat sexy job in the normally quiet world of accounting. Forensic accountant Jack Damico describes himself as "an investigative accountant who looks below the surface and reads between the lines." Many companies found out the hard way that even the slightest whiff of accounting irregularities can be detrimental to their health. Unfortunately, the pressure to meet earnings expectations caused some companies to play fast and loose with their financial reporting. Enter the accounting supersleuths.

The forensic accountant sifts for information on computer hard drives, financial papers, bank records, and billing receipts. However, forensic accountants also see part of their job as behavioral, meaning they get out and listen to employees who have concerns about supervisors encouraging them to "cook the books" or "hide some costs." Sue Talkington, a CPA and certified fraud examiner, would prefer to help companies prevent fraud by setting up self-protective internal controls. "Pay me now," she says, "or pay me later, but you're going to pay me more if you pay me later." Also, in the wake of the Sarbanes-Oxley Act, pressures have mounted on companies to provide accurate financial information. Forensic accountants can expect to stay busier than ever.

Sources: Worth Sparkman, "Some CPAs Find a Niche in Forensic Accounting," *Arkansas Business*, July 11, 2005; Kate Berry, "Business Booming for Forensic Accountants," *Los Angeles Business Journal*, June 6, 2005; and Mike Tierney, "Jack Damico: Forensic Accountant Tackles Biggest Cases," *Atlanta Journal and Constitution*, March 13, 2005.

www.forensisgroup.com

WorldCom, Enron, and Tyco raised public suspicions of the profession and corporate integrity in general. The Enron scandal even led to the downfall of one of the nation's major accounting firms, Arthur Andersen, after the firm was convicted of obstruction of justice for its actions in the Enron case (the conviction was later reversed by the U.S. Supreme Court).[5] Scrutiny of the accounting industry intensified and culminated with the U.S. Congress's passage of the Sarbanes-Oxley Act.[6] This legislation created new government reporting standards for publicly traded companies.[7] It also created the Public Company Accounting Oversight Board (PCAOB), which is charged with overseeing the American Institute of Certified Public Accountants.[8] Figure 17.3 on page 460 lists a few of the major provisions of Sarbanes-Oxley.

Today, CPAs on average take 40 hours of continuing education training a year, are subject to recertification, undergo ethics training requirements, and must pass an ethics exam.[9] The accounting profession understands that accountants must be considered as professional as doctors or lawyers. The Dealing with Change box offers an example of just how intense the scrutiny has become in accounting and what some companies are doing about it.

## Auditing

The job of reviewing and evaluating the records used to prepare a company's financial statements is referred to as **auditing**. Private accountants within an organization often perform internal audits to guarantee that proper accounting

**auditing**
The job of reviewing and evaluating the records used to prepare a company's financial statements.

figure 17.3

**KEY PROVISIONS OF THE SARBANES-OXLEY ACT**

- Prohibits accounting firms from providing certain non-auditing work (such as consulting services) to companies they audit.
- Strengthens the protection for whistle-blowers who report wrongful actions of company officers.
- Requires company CEOs and CFOs to certify the accuracy of financial reports and imparts strict penalties for any violation of securities reporting (e.g., earnings misstatements).
- Prohibits corporate loans to directors and executives of the company.
- Establishes the five-member Public Company Accounting Oversight Board under the Securities and Exchange Commission (SEC) to oversee the accounting industry.
- Stipulates that altering or destroying key audit documents will result in felony charges and significant criminal penalties.

procedures and financial reporting are being carried out within the company.[10] Public accountants also conduct independent audits of accounting information and related records. Financial auditors today not only examine the financial health of an organization but also look into operational efficiencies and effectiveness.[11] An accountant who has a bachelor's degree and two years of experience in internal auditing, and who has passed an exam administered by the Institute of Internal Auditors, can earn professional accreditation as a **certified internal auditor (CIA)**. An **independent audit** is an evaluation and unbiased opinion about the accuracy of a company's financial statements. A firm's annual report often includes a written opinion by an auditor.

**certified internal auditor (CIA)**
An accountant who has a bachelor's degree and two years of experience in internal auditing, and who has passed an exam administered by the Institute of Internal Auditors.

**independent audit**
An evaluation and unbiased opinion about the accuracy of a company's financial statements.

After accounting scandals such as the ones previously mentioned, the legitimacy of allowing a company to do both auditing and consulting work for the same firm was questioned.[12] To address this issue, the AICPA put in place new rules concerning auditing and consulting to ensure the integrity of the auditing process.[13]

## Tax Accounting

Taxes are the price we pay for roads, parks, schools, police protection, the military, and other functions provided by government. Federal, state, and local governments require individuals and organizations to file tax returns at specific times and in a precise format. A **tax accountant** is trained in tax law and is responsible for preparing tax returns or developing tax strategies. Since governments often change tax policies according to specific needs or objectives, the job of the tax accountant is constantly challenging. Also, as the burden of taxes grows in the economy, the role of the tax accountant becomes increasingly important to the organization or entrepreneur.[14]

**tax accountant**
An accountant trained in tax law and responsible for preparing tax returns or developing tax strategies.

## Government and Not-for-Profit Accounting

**Government and not-for-profit accounting** involves working for organizations whose purpose is not generating a profit but serving ratepayers, taxpayers, and others according to a duly approved budget. Governments (federal, state, and local) require an accounting system that satisfies the needs of their information users. The primary users of government accounting information are citizens, special interest groups, legislative bodies, and creditors. These users want to ensure that government is fulfilling its obligations and making the proper use of taxpayers' money. Governmental accounting standards are set by

**government and not-for-profit accounting**
Accounting system for organizations whose purpose is not generating a profit but serving ratepayers, taxpayers, and others according to a duly approved budget.

the Governmental Accounting Standards Board (GASB). The Federal Bureau of Investigation, the Internal Revenue Service, the Missouri Department of Natural Resources, and the Cook County Department of Revenue are just a few of the many government agencies that offer career possibilities to accountants seeking to work in government accounting.

Not-for-profit organizations also require accounting professionals. In fact, not-for-profit organizations have a growing need for trained accountants since contributors to nonprofits want to see exactly how and where the funds they contribute are being spent. Charities like the Red Cross, universities and colleges, hospitals, and labor unions all hire accountants to show contributors where their money goes.

As you can see, managerial and financial accounting, auditing, tax accounting, and governmental and not-for-profit accounting each require specific training and skill. After the Progress Assessment we will clarify the difference between accounting and bookkeeping.

**progress assessment**

- What is accounting?
- What is the difference between managerial and financial accounting?
- What is the difference between a private accountant and a public accountant?

## THE ACCOUNTING CYCLE

The **accounting cycle** is a six-step procedure that results in the preparation and analysis of the major financial statements (see Figure 17.4). The accounting cycle involves the work of both the bookkeeper and the accountant. **Bookkeeping** involves the recording of business transactions and is an important part of financial reporting. Accounting, however, goes far beyond the mere recording of financial information. Accountants classify and summarize financial data provided by bookkeepers, and then interpret the data and report the information to management. They also suggest strategies for improving the firm's financial condition and are especially important in financial analysis and income tax preparation.

A bookkeeper's first task is to divide all of the firm's transactions into meaningful categories such as sales documents, purchasing receipts, and shipping documents, being very careful to keep the information organized and manageable. Bookkeepers then record financial data from the original transaction documents (sales slips and so forth) into a record book or computer program called a **journal**. The word *journal* comes from the French word *jour*,

**accounting cycle**
A six-step procedure that results in the preparation and analysis of the major financial statements.

**bookkeeping**
The recording of business transactions.

**journal**
The record book or computer program where accounting data are first entered.

figure 17.4

**STEPS IN THE ACCOUNTING CYCLE**

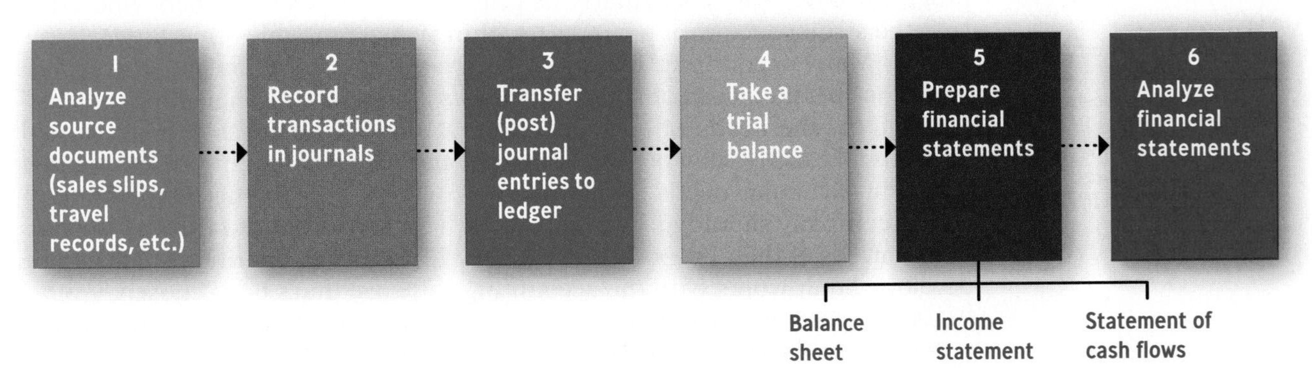

"I'LL TELL YOU HARRIS, THEY DON'T MAKE ACCOUNTANTS LIKE THEY USED TO. THOSE I HAD IN THE 1990'S NEVER BROUGHT ME FIGURES LIKE THESE."

The integrity of a firm's financial statements is vital. Accounting irregularities that occurred in the late 1990s at firms like Enron and WorldCom made the companies look stronger than they actually were. Accountants are now committed to regaining the trust and respect their profession enjoyed in the past. What part should the government play in overseeing the accounting industry?

**double-entry bookkeeping**
The concept of writing every business transaction in two places.

**ledger**
A specialized accounting book or computer program in which information from accounting journals is accumulated into specific categories and posted so that managers can find all the information about one account in the same place.

which means "day." A journal is where the day's transactions are kept.

It's quite possible that a bookkeeper could make a mistake when recording financial transactions. For example, it's possible to enter $10.98 as $10.89. So that they can check one list of transactions against the other to make sure that they add up to the same amount bookkeepers record all transactions in two places. If the amounts are not equal, the bookkeeper knows that he or she made a mistake. The concept of writing every transaction in two places is called **double-entry bookkeeping**. In double-entry bookkeeping, two entries in the journal and the ledgers (discussed next) are required for each company transaction.

To see how this system works, suppose a business wanted to determine how much it paid for office supplies in the first quarter of the year. Without a specific bookkeeping tool, that would be difficult even with accurate accounting journals. Therefore, bookkeepers make use of a specialized accounting book or computer program called a **ledger**, in which information from accounting journals is transferred (or posted) into specific categories so managers can find all the information about a single account (i.e. office supplies, cash, and so on) in one place.

The next step is to prepare a trial balance. A **trial balance** is a summary of all the financial data in the account ledgers to make certain the figures are correct and balanced. If the information in the account ledgers is not accurate, it must be corrected before the firm's financial statements are prepared. The accountant then prepares the firm's financial statements—including a balance sheet, an income statement, and a statement of cash flows—according to generally accepted accounting principles. From the information in the financial statements, the accountant analyzes and evaluates the financial condition of the firm. We will review these last two steps in depth in the following sections.

## Using Computers in Accounting

Computers and accounting software have simplified the accounting process considerably.[15] Today, computerized accounting programs post information from journals instantaneously so that financial information is readily available whenever the organization needs it. Because computers can rapidly handle large amounts of financial information, accountants are freed up to do more important tasks such as financial analysis.[16] Computerized accounting programs have been particularly helpful to small-business owners who often lack the strong accounting support within their companies that larger firms enjoy.[17] Many accounting packages, such as QuickBooks and Peachtree, address the specific needs of small businesses, which are often significantly different from the needs of a major corporation. Yet business owners should understand exactly what computer system and which programs are best suited for their particular needs. That's one reason why entrepreneurs planning to start a company should hire or consult with an accountant to identify the particular needs of their proposed firm. Then, a specific accounting system can be developed that works with the accounting software that's been chosen.[18]

A computer is a wonderful tool for businesspeople and helps ease the monotony of bookkeeping and accounting work, but it's important to remember that no computer has yet been programmed to make good financial decisions by itself. The work of an accountant requires training and very specific competencies.[19] After the Progress Assessment, let's look at the balance sheet, income statement, and statement of cash flows—and the important financial information each provides.

**trial balance**
A summary of all the data in the account ledgers to show whether the figures are correct and balanced.

progress assessment

- What is the difference between accounting and bookkeeping?
- What is the difference between an accounting journal and a ledger?
- Why does a bookkeeper prepare a trial balance?
- What advantages do computers provide businesses in maintaining and compiling accounting information?

## UNDERSTANDING KEY FINANCIAL STATEMENTS

**financial statement**
A summary of all the transactions that have occurred over a particular period.

A **financial statement** is a summary of all the transactions that have occurred over a particular period. Financial statements indicate a firm's financial health and stability, and are key factors in management decision making. That's why stockholders (the owners of the firm), bondholders and banks (people and institutions that lend money to the firm), labor unions, employees, and the Internal Revenue Service are all interested in a firm's financial statements.[20] The following are the key financial statements of a business:

1. The *balance sheet*, which reports the firm's financial condition on a specific date.
2. The *income statement*, which summarizes revenues, cost of goods, and expenses (including taxes), for a specific period and highlights the total profit or loss the firm experienced during that period.
3. The *statement of cash flows*, which provides a summary of money coming into and going out of the firm that tracks a company's cash receipts and cash payments.

The differences among the financial statements can be summarized this way: The balance sheet details what the company owns and owes on a certain day; the income statement shows the revenue a firm earned selling its products compared to its selling costs (profit or loss) over a specific period of time; and the statement of cash flows highlights the difference between cash coming in and cash going out of a business. To fully understand important financial information, you must be able to understand the purpose of an organization's financial statements. To help you with this task, we'll explain each statement in more detail next.

### The Fundamental Accounting Equation

Imagine that you don't owe anybody money. That is, you don't have any liabilities (debts). In this case, your assets (cash and so forth) are equal to what you *own* (equity). However, if you borrow some money from a friend, you have incurred a liability. Your assets are now equal to what you *owe* plus what you own. Translated into business terms, Assets = Liabilities + Owners' equity.

In accounting, this equation must always be balanced. For example, suppose you have $50,000 in cash and decide to use that money to open a small coffee shop. Your business has assets of $50,000 and no debts. The accounting equation would look like this:

| Assets | = Liabilities | + Owners' equity |
|---|---|---|
| $50,000 | = $0 | + $50,000 |

You have $50,000 cash and $50,000 owners' equity (the amount of your investment in the business—sometimes referred to as net worth). However, before opening the business, you borrow $30,000 from a local bank; the equation now changes. You have $30,000 of additional cash, but you also have a debt (liability) of $30,000. Remember, with each business transaction there is a recording of two transactions. (Recall the discussion of double-entry bookkeeping earlier in this chapter.)

Your financial position within the business has changed. The equation is still balanced but is changed to reflect the transaction:

| Assets | = Liabilities | + Owners' equity |
|---|---|---|
| $80,000 | = $30,000 | + $50,000 |

**fundamental accounting equation**
Assets = liabilities + owners' equity; this is the basis for the balance sheet.

This formula, called the **fundamental accounting equation**, is the basis for the balance sheet. As the sample balance sheet in Figure 17.5 (for our hypothetical vegetarian restaurant Very Vegetarian introduced in Chapter 13) highlights, you list assets in a separate column from liabilities and owners' (or stockholders') equity. The assets are equal to or are balanced with the liabilities and owners' (or stockholders') equity. It's that simple. Something that is often complicated is determining what is included in the asset account and what is included in the liabilities and owners' equity accounts. Since it's critical that businesspeople understand the important financial information on the balance sheet, let's take a closer look.

## The Balance Sheet

**balance sheet**
The financial statement that reports a firm's financial condition at a specific time.

A **balance sheet** is the financial statement that reports a firm's financial condition at a specific time. It's composed of three major accounts: assets, liabilities, and owners' equity.[21] The balance sheet is so named because it shows a *balance* between two figures: the company's assets on the one hand, and its liabilities plus owners' equity on the other. The following example will further explain the idea behind the balance sheet.

Let's say that you want to know what your financial condition is at a given time. Maybe you want to buy a new house or car and therefore need to calculate your available resources. One of the best measuring sticks is your balance sheet. First, you would add up everything you own—cash, property, money owed you, and so forth (assets). Subtract from that the money you owe others—credit card debt, IOUs, current car loan, student loan, and so forth (liabilities)—and you have a figure that tells you your net worth (equity). This is fundamentally what companies do in preparing a balance sheet: follow the procedures set in the fundamental accounting equation. In that preparation, however, it's important to follow generally accepted accounting principles (GAAP).

## Classifying Assets

**assets**
Economic resources (things of value) owned by a firm.

**Assets** are economic resources (things of value) owned by a firm. Assets include productive, tangible items (e.g., equipment, buildings, land, furniture, and motor vehicles) that help generate income, as well as intangibles with value (e.g.,

VERY VEGETARIAN
Balance Sheet
December 31, 2007

| | | | |
|---|---|---|---|
| **Assets** | | | |
| ① Current assets | | | |
| Cash | | $ 15,000 | |
| Accounts receivable | | 200,000 | |
| Notes receivable | | 50,000 | |
| Inventory | | 335,000 | |
| Total current assets | | | $600,000 |
| ② Fixed assets | | | |
| Land | | $ 40,000 | |
| Building and improvements | $200,000 | | |
| Less: Accumulated depreciation | −90,000 | | |
| | | 110,000 | |
| Equipment and vehicles | $120,000 | | |
| Less: Accumulated depreciation | −80,000 | | |
| | | 40,000 | |
| Furniture and fixtures | $26,000 | | |
| Less: Accumulated depreciation | −10,000 | | |
| | | 16,000 | |
| Total fixed assets | | | 206,000 |
| ③ Intangible assets | | | |
| Goodwill | | $ 20,0 00 | |
| Total intangible assets | | | 20,000 |
| Total assets | | | $ 826,000 |
| **Liabilities and Owners' Equity** | | | |
| ④ Current liabilities | | | |
| Accounts payable | | $ 40,000 | |
| Notes payable (due June 2008) | | 8,000 | |
| Accrued taxes | | 150,000 | |
| Accrued salaries | | 90,000 | |
| Total current liabilities | | | $ 288,000 |
| ⑤ Long-term liabilities | | | |
| Notes payable (due Mar. 2012) | | $ 35,000 | |
| Bonds payable (due Dec. 2017) | | 290,000 | |
| Total long-term liabilities | | | 325,000 |
| Total liabilities | | | $ 613,000 |
| ⑥ Owners' equity | | | |
| Common stock (1,000,000 shares) | | $ 100,000 | |
| Retained earnings | | 113,000 | |
| Total owners' equity | | | 213,000 |
| Total liabilities & owners' equity | | | $ 826,000 |

**figure 17.5**

**SAMPLE VERY VEGETARIAN BALANCE SHEET**

① Current assets: Items that can be converted to cash within one year.

② Fixed assets: Items such as land, buildings, and equipment that are relatively permanent.

③ Intangible assets: Items of value such as patents and copyrights that don't have a physical form.

④ Current liabilities: Payments that are due in one year or less.

⑤ Long-term liabilities: Payments not due for one year or longer.

⑥ Owners' equity: The value of what stockholders own in a firm (also called stockholders' equity).

patents, trademarks, copyrights, or goodwill). Think, for example, of the value of brand names such as Starbucks, Coca-Cola, McDonald's, and Intel. Intangibles such as brand names can be among the firm's most valuable assets.[22] Goodwill represents the value that can be attributed to factors such as a firm's reputation, location, and superior products.[23] It is included on the balance sheet when a firm acquiring another firm pays more than the value of that firm's tangible assets. Not all companies, however, list intangible assets on their balance sheets.

**liquidity**
How fast an asset can be converted into cash.

**current assets**
Items that can or will be converted into cash within one year.

**fixed assets**
Assets that are relatively permanent, such as land, buildings, and equipment.

**intangible assets**
Long-term assets (e.g., patents, trademarks, copyrights) that have no real physical form but do have value.

**liabilities**
What the business owes to others (debts).

**accounts payable**
Current liabilities involving money owed to others for merchandise or services purchased on credit but not yet paid for.

**notes payable**
Short-term or long-term liabilities that a business promises to repay by a certain date.

**bonds payable**
Long-term liabilities that represent money lent to the firm that must be paid back.

**owners' equity**
The amount of the business that belongs to the owners minus any liabilities owed by the business.

**retained earnings**
The accumulated earnings from a firm's profitable operations that were kept in the business and not paid out to stockholders in dividends.

Assets are listed on the firm's balance sheet according to their liquidity. **Liquidity** refers to how fast an asset can be converted into cash. For example, an account receivable is an amount of money owed to the firm that it expects to be paid within one year. Accounts receivable are considered liquid assets. Land, however, is difficult to turn into cash quickly because it takes time and paperwork to sell land; thus, land is a long-term asset (an asset expected to last more than one year) and not considered liquid. Assets are divided into three categories according to how quickly they can be turned into cash:

1. **Current assets** are items that can or will be converted into cash within one year. Current assets include cash, accounts receivable, and inventory.
2. **Fixed assets** are long-term assets that are relatively permanent such as land, buildings, and equipment. (These assets are also referred to on the balance sheet as property, plant, and equipment.)
3. **Intangible assets** are long-term assets that have no real physical form but do have value. Patents, trademarks, copyrights, and goodwill are examples of intangible assets.

## Liabilities and Owners' Equity Accounts

Another important accounting term is liabilities. **Liabilities** are what the business owes to others (debts). *Current liabilities* are debts due in one year or less; *long-term liabilities* are debts not due for one year or longer. The following are common liability accounts recorded on a balance sheet (see again Figure 17.5):

1. **Accounts payable** are current liabilities involving money owed to others for merchandise or services purchased on credit but not yet paid for. If you have a bill you haven't paid, you have an account payable.
2. **Notes payable** can be short-term or long-term liabilities (e.g., loans from banks) that a business promises to repay by a certain date.
3. **Bonds payable** are long-term liabilities that represent money lent to the firm that must be paid back. (We will discuss bonds in depth in Chapters 18 and 19.)

As the fundamental accounting equation highlighted earlier, the value of things you own (assets) minus the amount of money you owe others (liabilities) is called *equity*. The value of what stockholders own in a firm (minus liabilities) is called *stockholders' equity* (or *shareholders' equity*). Because stockholders are the owners of a firm, stockholders' equity can also be called owners' equity. **Owners' equity** is the amount of the business that belongs to the owners minus any liabilities owed by the business. The formula for owners' equity, then, is assets minus liabilities. Differences can exist in the owners' equity account according to the type of organization. Businesses that are not incorporated identify the investment of the sole proprietor or partner(s) through a *capital account*. For sole proprietors and partners, then, owners' equity means the value of everything owned by the business minus any liabilities of the owner(s), such as bank loans.

For corporations, the owners' equity account records the owners' claims to funds they have invested in the firm (such as capital stock), as well as retained earnings. **Retained earnings** are accumulated earnings from the firm's profitable operations that were kept in the business and not paid out to stockholders in distributions of company profits. (These distributions, called dividends, are discussed in Chapter 19.) Take a few moments to look again at Figure 17.5 and

## SPOTLIGHT ON small business

www.dinkytown.net/java/NetWorth.html

### You Incorporated

How do you think You Inc. stacks up financially? Let's take a little time to find out. You may be pleasantly surprised, or you may realize that you need to think hard about planning your financial future. Remember, your net worth is nothing more than the difference between what you own (assets) and what you owe (liabilities). Be honest, and do your best to give a fair evaluation of your private property's value.

| **Assets** | |
|---|---|
| Cash | $ ________ |
| Savings account | ________ |
| Checking account | ________ |
| Home | ________ |
| Stocks & bonds | ________ |
| Automobile | ________ |
| IRA or Keogh | ________ |
| Personal property | ________ |
| Other assets | ________ |
| Total assets | $ ________ |

| **Liabilities** | |
|---|---|
| Installment loans & interest | $ ________ |
| Other loans & interest | ________ |
| Credit card accounts | ________ |
| Mortgage | ________ |
| Taxes | ________ |
| Cell phone | ________ |
| Total liabilities | $ ________ |

Determine your net worth:

| | |
|---|---|
| Total assets | $ ________ |
| Total liabilities | − ________ |
| Net worth | $ ________ |

see what facts you can determine about the vegetarian restaurant, Very Vegetarian, from its balance sheet. After the Progress Assessment, take a few minutes and try to estimate your own personal net worth, following the directions in the Spotlight on Small Business box.

**progress assessment**

- What is the formula for the balance sheet? What do we call this formula?
- What does it mean to list various assets by liquidity?
- What goes into the account called liabilities?
- What is owners' equity and how is it determined?

## The Income Statement

The financial statement that shows a firm's bottom line—that is, its profit after costs, expenses, and taxes—is the **income statement** (at one time called the profit-and-loss statement). The income statement summarizes all of the resources (called *revenue*) that have come into the firm from operating activities, money resources that were used up, expenses incurred in doing business, and resources left after all costs and expenses, including taxes, were paid. The resources (revenue) left over are referred to as **net income or net loss** (see Figure 17.6 on page 468).

**income statement**
The financial statement that shows a firm's profit after costs, expenses, and taxes; it summarizes all of the resources that have come into the firm (revenue), all the resources that have left the firm, and the resulting net income.

**net income or net loss**
Revenue left over after all costs and expenses, including taxes, are paid.

The income statement reports the firm's financial operations over a particular period of time, usually a year, a quarter of a year, or a month.[24] It's the

figure 17.6

**SAMPLE VERY VEGETARIAN INCOME STATEMENT**

① Revenue: Value of what's received from goods sold, services rendered, and other financial sources.

② Cost of goods sold: Cost of merchandise sold or cost of raw materials or parts used for producing items for resale.

③ Gross profit: How much the firm earned by buying or selling merchandise.

④ Operating expenses: Cost incurred in operating a business.

⑤ Net income after taxes: Profit or loss over a specific period after subtracting all costs and expenses, including taxes.

VERY VEGETARIAN
Income Statement
For the Year Ended December 31, 2007

| | | | |
|---|---|---|---|
| ① Revenues | | | |
| Gross sales | | $720,000 | |
| Less: Sales returns and allowances | $ 12,000 | | |
| Sales discounts | 8,000 | −20,000 | |
| Net sales | | | $700,000 |
| ② Cost of goods sold | | | |
| Beginning inventory, Jan. 1 | | $200,000 | |
| Merchandise purchases | $400,000 | | |
| Freight | 40,000 | | |
| Net purchases | | 440,000 | |
| Cost of goods available for sale | $640,000 | | |
| Less ending inventory, Dec. 31 | | −230,000 | |
| Cost of goods sold | | | −410,000 |
| ③ Gross profit | | | $290,000 |
| ④ Operating expenses | | | |
| Selling expenses | | | |
| Salaries for salespeople | $ 90,000 | | |
| Advertising | 18,000 | | |
| Supplies | 2,000 | | |
| Total selling expenses | | $ 110,000 | |
| General expenses | | | |
| Office salaries | $ 67,000 | | |
| Depreciation | 1,500 | | |
| Insurance | 1,500 | | |
| Rent | 28,000 | | |
| Light, heat, and power | 12,000 | | |
| Miscellaneous | 2,000 | | |
| | | 112,000 | |
| Total operating expenses | | | 222,000 |
| Net income before taxes | | | $ 68,000 |
| Less: Income tax expense | | | 19,000 |
| ⑤ Net income after taxes | | | $ 49,000 |

financial statement that reveals whether the business is actually earning a profit or losing money. The income statement includes valuable financial information for stockholders, lenders, investors (or potential investors), employees, and of course the government. Because of the importance of this financial report, let's take a moment to look at the income statement and learn what each step means. Before we start, however, take a quick look at how the income statement is arranged according to generally accepted accounting principles (GAAP):

Revenue
− Cost of goods sold
= Gross profit (gross margin)
− Operating expenses
= Net income before taxes
− Taxes
= Net income or loss

www.aicpa.org

LEGAL briefcase

### The Last Shall Be First

When valuing a firm's inventory, generally accepted accounting principles (GAAP) sometimes permit an accountant to use different methods of accounting for inventory. Let's look at two possible treatments of inventory that could be used, FIFO and LIFO.

Let's say that a college bookstore buys textbooks for resale to students. It buys 100 copies of a particular textbook in July at a cost of $70 a copy. When classes begin, the bookstore sells 50 copies of the text to students for $90 each. Since the book will be used again next term, the 50 copies not sold are placed in the bookstore's inventory for next term. In late December the bookstore orders 50 additional copies of the text to sell for the coming term. The publisher's price of the book to the bookstore has increased to $80 a copy due to inflation and other costs. The bookstore now has 100 copies of the same textbook from different purchase cycles in its inventory (same book, but different costs to the bookstore). If the bookstore sells 50 copies of the book to students at $100 each at the beginning of the new term, what's the bookstore's cost of the book for accounting purposes? It depends.

The books being sold are identical, but the accounting treatment is different. If the bookstore uses a method called *first in, first out (FIFO)*, the cost of goods sold (cost of 50 textbooks sold) would be $70 each, because the textbook that was bought first cost $70. The bookstore, however, could use another method, called *last in, first out (LIFO)*. Using LIFO, the bookstore's last purchase of the textbooks that cost $80 each would be the cost of each of the 50 textbooks sold. If the book sells for $100, what will be the difference in gross margin using FIFO versus LIFO?

## Revenue

**Revenue** is the value of what a firm received for goods sold, services rendered, and other financial sources. Make note that there is a difference between revenue and sales. Most revenue (money coming into the firm) comes from sales, but there could be other sources of revenue, such as rents received, money paid to the firm for use of its patents, and interest earned, that's included in reporting revenue. Be careful not to confuse the terms *revenue* and *sales*, or to use them as if they were synonymous. Also, a quick glance at the income statement shows you that the term *gross sales* refers to the total of all sales the firm completed. *Net sales* are gross sales minus returns, discounts, and allowances.

**revenue**
The value of what is received for goods sold, services rendered, and other financial sources.

## Cost of Goods Sold (Cost of Goods Manufactured)

The **cost of goods sold (or cost of goods manufactured)** is a measure of the cost of merchandise sold or the cost of raw materials and supplies used for producing items for resale. It makes sense to compare how much a business earned by selling merchandise over the period being evaluated to how much it spent to buy the merchandise. The cost of goods sold includes the purchase price plus any freight charges paid to transport goods plus any costs associated with storing the goods. The valuation of a firm's inventory also presents an interesting accounting application in determining the company's cost of goods sold. In financial reporting, it doesn't matter when a particular item was actually placed in a firm's inventory, but it does matter how an accountant records the cost of the item when it was sold. Sound a bit confusing? Read the Legal Briefcase box about two such inventory valuation methods.

**cost of goods sold (or cost of goods manufactured)**
A measure of the cost of merchandise sold or cost of raw materials and supplies used for producing items for resale.

It's critical that companies accurately report and manage this important income statement item. Recall from this chapter's Opening Profile the problems Roxanne Coady discovered concerning R. J. Julia Booksellers' handling of its costs.

When you subtract the cost of goods sold from net sales, you get what is called gross profit or gross margin. **Gross profit (gross margin)** is how much

**gross profit (gross margin)**
How much a firm earned by buying (or making) and selling merchandise.

a firm earned by buying (or making) and selling merchandise. In a service firm, there may be no cost of goods sold; therefore, net revenue could equal gross profit. In a manufacturing firm, however, it's necessary to estimate the cost of goods manufactured. In either case (selling goods or services), the gross profit doesn't tell you everything you need to know about the financial performance of the firm. The income statement also needs to determine the *net* profit or loss a firm experienced. To get that, you must subtract the business's expenses.

## Operating Expenses

**operating expenses**
Costs involved in operating a business, such as rent, utilities, and salaries.

**depreciation**
The systematic write-off of the cost of a tangible asset over its estimated useful life.

In the process of selling goods or services, a business incurs certain expenses. **Operating expenses** are the costs involved in operating a business. Obvious operating expenses include rent, salaries, supplies, utilities, and insurance. Operating expenses such as depreciation are a bit more complex. **Depreciation** is the systematic write-off of the cost of a tangible asset over its estimated useful life. Have you ever heard the comment that a new car depreciates in market value as soon as you drive it off the dealer's lot? The same principle holds true for assets such as equipment and machinery that are considered depreciable. Subject to accounting rules set by GAAP and the Internal Revenue Service (which are beyond the scope of this chapter), companies are permitted to recapture the cost of these assets over time using depreciation as an operating expense of the business.

Operating expenses can generally be classified into two categories: selling and general expenses. *Selling expenses* are expenses related to the marketing and distribution of the firm's goods or services (such as salaries for salespeople, advertising, and supplies). *General expenses* are administrative expenses of the firm (such as office salaries, depreciation, insurance, and rent). Accountants are trained to help you record all applicable expenses and find other relevant expenses you need to deduct as a part of doing business.

## Net Profit or Loss

After deducting all expenses, we determine the firm's net income before taxes (see again Figure 17.6). Then, after allocating for taxes, we get to what's called the *bottom line*, which is the net income (or perhaps net loss) the firm incurred from revenue minus sales returns, costs, expenses, and taxes. It answers the question "How much did the business earn or lose in the specific reporting period?" Net income can also be referred to as net earnings or net profit.

The terms associated with the balance sheet and income statement may seem a bit confusing to you at this point, but you actually use similar accounting concepts all the time. For example, you know the importance of keeping track of costs and expenses when you prepare your own budget. If your expenses (e.g., rent and utilities) exceed your revenues (how much you earn), you are in trouble. If you need more money (revenue), you may need to sell some of the things you own to meet your expenses. The same is true in business. Companies need to keep track of how much money they earn and spend, how much cash they have on hand, and so on. The only difference is that companies tend to have more complex problems and a good deal more information to record than you as an individual do.

Users of financial statements are also keenly interested in how a firm handles the flow of cash coming into and flowing out of a business. Cash flow problems can plague both businesses and individuals. Keep this in mind as we look at the statement of cash flows in the next section.

## The Statement of Cash Flows

In 1988, the Financial Accounting Standards Board (FASB) required firms to replace the statement of changes in financial position with the statement of cash flows. The **statement of cash flows** reports cash receipts and disbursements related to the three major activities of a firm:

- *Operations* are cash transactions associated with running the business.
- *Investments* are cash used in or provided by the firm's investment activities.
- *Financing* is cash raised from the issuance of new debt or equity capital or cash used to pay business expenses, past debts, or company dividends.

**statement of cash flows**
Financial statement that reports cash receipts and disbursements related to a firm's three major activities: operations, investments, and financing.

Accountants analyze all of the cash changes that have occurred from operating, investing, and financing to determine the firm's net cash position. The statement of cash flows also gives the firm some insight into how to handle cash better so that no cash flow problems (e.g., having no cash on hand) occur.

Figure 17.7 shows a statement of cash flows, again using the example of Very Vegetarian. As you can see, this financial statement answers such questions as: How much cash came into the business from current operations? That is, how much cash came into the firm from buying and selling goods and services? Was cash used to buy stocks, bonds, or other investments? Were some investments sold that brought in cash? How much money came into the firm from issuing stock?

These and other financial transactions are analyzed to see their effect on the cash position of the firm. Understanding cash flow can mean success or failure of any business. We will analyze cash flow a bit more in depth in the next section.

Very Vegetarian

VERY VEGETARIAN
Statement of Cash Flows
For the Year Ended December 31, 2007

| | | |
|---|---|---|
| ① Cash flows from operating activities | | |
| Cash received from customers | $150,000 | |
| Cash paid to suppliers and employees | (90,000) | |
| Interest paid | (5,000) | |
| Income tax paid | (4,500) | |
| Interest and dividends received | 1,500 | |
| Net cash provided by operating activities | | $52,000 |
| ② Cash flows from investing activities | | |
| Proceeds from sale of plant assets | $ 4,000 | |
| Payments for purchase of equipment | (10,000) | |
| Net cash provided by investing activities | | (6,000) |
| ③ Cash flows from financing activities | | |
| Proceeds from issuance of short-term debt | $ 3,000 | |
| Payment of long-term debt | (7,000) | |
| Payment of dividends | (15,000) | |
| Net cash inflow from financing activities | | (19,000) |
| Net change in cash and equivalents | | $27,000 |
| Cash balance (beginning of year) | | (2,000) |
| Cash balance (end of year) | | $25,000 |

figure 17.7

**VERY VEGETARIAN STATEMENT OF CASH FLOWS**

① Cash receipts from sales, commissions, fees, interest, and dividends. Cash payments for salaries, inventories, operating expenses, interest, and taxes.

② Includes cash flows that are generated through a company's purchase or sale of long-term operational assets, investments in other companies, and its lending activities.

③ Cash inflows and outflows associated with the company's own equity transactions or its borrowing activities.

Cash flow is the difference between money coming into and going out of a business. Careful cash flow management is a must for a business of any size, but is particularly important for small businesses and seasonal businesses such as a ski resort. Can you think of any large firms that were forced into bankruptcy because of cash flow problems?

**cash flow**
The difference between cash coming in and cash going out of a business.

## The Importance of Cash Flow Analysis

Cash flow, if not properly managed, can cause a business much concern. Cash flow analysis is really rather simple to understand.[25] Let's say you borrow $100 from a friend to buy a used bike and agree to pay your friend back at the end of the week. In turn, you sell the bike for $150 to someone else, who also agrees to pay you by the end of the week. Unfortunately, at the end of the week the person who bought the bike from you does not have the money as promised; he says that he will have to pay you next month. Meanwhile, your friend wants the $100 you agreed to pay her by the end of the week! What seemed like a great opportunity to make an easy $50 profit is a real cause for concern. Right now, you owe $100 and have no cash. What do you do when your friend shows up at the end of the week and demands to be paid? If you were a business, this might cause you to default on the loan and possibly go bankrupt, even though you had the potential for profits.

It's possible that a business can increase sales and profit yet still suffer greatly from cash flow problems. **Cash flow** is simply the difference between cash coming in and cash going out of a business. Poor cash flow constitutes a major operating problem for many companies and is particularly difficult for small businesses. Careful cash flow analysis is particularly helpful to businesses such as ski resorts, in which the flow of cash into the business is seasonal. Accountants sometimes face tough ethical challenges in reporting the flow of funds into a business. Read the Making Ethical Decisions box to see how such an ethical dilemma can arise.

How do cash flow problems start? What often happens to a business is that, in order to meet the demands of customers, the business buys more and more goods on credit (no cash is involved). Similarly, more and more goods are sold on credit (no cash is involved). This goes on until the firm uses up all the credit it has with its lenders. When the firm requests more money from its lenders to pay a crucial bill, the lender refuses the loan because the credit limit has been reached. All other credit sources refuse funds as well. The company desperately needs funds to pay its bills, or it could be forced into bankruptcy. Unfortunately, all too often, the company does go into bankruptcy because there was no cash available when it was most needed.

Cash flow analysis also points out clearly that a business's relationship with its lender(s) is critical. Maintaining a working relationship with a bank is a path to preventing cash flow problems that often develop. The value that accountants provide to businesses in dealing with cash flow is also critical. Accountants can advise the firm whether it needs cash and, if so, how much. They can also offer advice on how a company is managing its cash position and provide key insights into how, when, and where finance managers can get the money a firm needs. After the Progress Assessment, we will see how accountants analyze financial statements using ratios.

### progress assessment

- What are the three steps in the formula that makes up the income statement?
- What's the difference between revenue and income on the income statement?
- Why is the statement of cash flows important in evaluating a firm's operations?

* * * MAKING

## ethical decisions

www.fasb.gov

### On the Accounting Hot Seat

You are the only accountant employed by a small manufacturing firm. You are in charge of keeping the books for the company, which has been suffering from an economic downturn that shows no signs of reversing course in the near future.

You know that your employer is going to ask the bank for an additional loan so that the company can continue to pay its bills. Unfortunately, the financial statements for the year will not show good results, and your best guess is that the bank will not approve a loan increase on the basis of the financial information you will present.

Your boss approaches you in early January before you have closed the books for the preceding year and suggests that perhaps the statements can be "improved" by treating the sales that were made at the beginning of January as if they were made in December. He also asks you to do a number of other things that will cover up the trail so that the auditors will not discover the padding of the year's sales.

You know that it is against the professional rules of the Financial Accounting Standards Board (FASB), and you argue with your boss. Your boss tells you that, if the company does not get the additional bank loan, there's a good chance the business will close. That means you and everyone else in the firm will be out of a job. You believe your boss is probably right, and you know that with the current economic downturn finding a job will be tough for you and almost impossible for others in the company. What are your alternatives? What are the likely consequences of each alternative? What will you do?

## ANALYZING FINANCIAL STATEMENTS: RATIO ANALYSIS

**ratio analysis**
The assessment of a firm's financial condition and performance through calculations and interpretations of financial ratios developed from the firm's financial statements.

Accurate financial information from the firm's financial statements forms the basis of the financial analysis performed by accountants inside and outside the firm. **Ratio analysis** is the assessment of a firm's financial condition and performance through calculations and interpretation of financial ratios developed from the firm's financial statements. Financial ratios are especially useful in analyzing the actual performance of the company compared to its financial objectives and compared to other firms within its industry.[26] At first glance, ratio analysis may seem complicated; the fact is, though, that most of us already use ratios quite often. For example, in basketball, the number of shots made from the foul line is expressed by a ratio: shots made to shots attempted. A player who shoots 85 percent from the foul line is considered an outstanding free throw shooter, and suggestions are not to foul this player in a close game.

Whether ratios measure an athlete's performance or the financial health of a business, they provide a good deal of valuable information. Financial ratios provide key insights into how a firm compares to other firms in its industry in the important areas of liquidity (speed of changing assets into cash), debt (leverage), profitability, and overall business activity. Understanding and interpreting business ratios is a key to sound financial analysis. Let's look briefly at four key types of ratios businesses use to measure financial performance.

### Liquidity Ratios

As explained earlier, *liquidity* refers to how fast an asset can be converted to cash. Liquidity ratios measure a company's ability to turn assets into cash to pay its short-term debts (liabilities that must be repaid within one year.)[27] These short-term debts are of particular importance to lenders of the firm who expect to be paid on time. Two key liquidity ratios are the current ratio and the acid-test ratio.

The *current ratio* is the ratio of a firm's current assets to its current liabilities. This information can be found on the firm's balance sheet. Look back at Figure 17.5, which details Very Vegetarian's balance sheet. The company lists current assets of $600,000 and current liabilities of $288,000, a current ratio of

2.08, which means Very Vegetarian has $2.08 of current assets for every $1 of current liabilities. See the following calculation:

$$\text{Current ratio} = \frac{\text{Current assets}}{\text{Current liabilities}} = \frac{\$600{,}000}{\$288{,}000} = 2.08$$

An obvious question to ask is: Is Very Vegetarian financially sound for the short term (less than one year)? It depends! Usually a company with a current ratio of 2 or better is considered a safe risk for granting short-term credit since it appears to be performing in line with market expectations. However, it's important to compare Very Vegetarian's current ratio to that of competing firms in its industry. It's also important for the firm to compare its current ratio with its current ratio from the previous year to note any significant changes.

Another key liquidity ratio, called the *acid-test ratio*, or *quick ratio*, measures the cash, marketable securities (such as stocks and bonds), and receivables of a firm, compared to its current liabilities:

$$\text{Acid-test ratio} = \frac{\text{Cash} + \text{Accounts receivable} + \text{Marketable securities}}{\text{Current liabilities}}$$

$$= \frac{\$265{,}000}{\$288{,}000} = 0.92$$

This ratio is particularly important to firms with difficulty converting inventory into quick cash and helps answer such questions as: What if sales drop off and we can't sell our inventory? Can we still pay our short-term debt? Though ratios vary among industries, an acid-test ratio of between 0.50 and 1.0 is usually considered satisfactory but could also be a sign of some cash flow problems. Therefore, Very Vegetarian's acid-test ratio of 0.92 could raise concerns that perhaps the firm may not meet its short-term debt and may therefore have to go to a high-cost lender for financial assistance.

## Leverage (Debt) Ratios

Leverage (debt) ratios measure the degree to which a firm relies on borrowed funds in its operations. A firm that takes on too much debt could experience problems repaying lenders or meeting promises made to stockholders. The *debt to owners' equity ratio* measures the degree to which the company is financed by borrowed funds that must be repaid. Again, we can use Figure 17.5 to measure Very Vegetarian's level of debt:

$$\text{Debt to owners' equity ratio} = \frac{\text{Total liabilities}}{\text{Owners' equity}} = \frac{\$613{,}000}{\$213{,}000} = 287\%$$

Anything above 100 percent shows that a firm has more debt than equity. With a ratio of 287 percent, Very Vegetarian has a rather high degree of debt compared to its equity, which implies that the firm may be perceived as quite risky to lenders and investors. However, again it's always important to compare a firm's debt ratios to those of other firms in its industry because debt financing is more acceptable in some industries than it is in others. Comparisons with past debt ratios can also identify trends that may be occurring within the firm or industry.

## Profitability (Performance) Ratios

Profitability (performance) ratios measure how effectively a firm is using its various resources to achieve profits. Company management's performance is often measured by the firm's profitability ratios. Three of the more important ratios used are earnings per share (EPS), return on sales, and return on equity.

EPS is an important ratio for a company because earnings help stimulate growth in the firm and are available for such things as stockholders' dividends. A 1997 Financial Accounting Standards Board rule requires companies to report their quarterly EPS in two ways: basic and diluted. The *basic earnings per share (basic EPS) ratio* helps determine the amount of profit earned by a company for each share of outstanding common stock. The *diluted earnings per share (diluted EPS) ratio* measures the amount of profit earned by a company for each share of outstanding common stock, but this ratio also takes into consideration stock options, warrants, preferred stock, and convertible debt securities, which can be converted into common stock. For simplicity's sake, we will compute only the basic EPS. Continued earnings growth is well received by both investors and lenders. The basic EPS ratio for Very Vegetarian is calculated as follows:

$$\text{Basic earnings per share} = \frac{\text{Net income after taxes}}{\text{Number of common stock shares outstanding}}$$

$$= \frac{\$49{,}000}{1{,}000{,}000} = \$.049 \text{ per share}$$

Another reliable indicator of performance is obtained by using a ratio that measures the return on sales. Firms use this ratio to see if they are doing as well as the companies they compete against in generating income from the sales they achieve. *Return on sales* is calculated by comparing a company's net income to its total sales. Very Vegetarian's return on sales is 7 percent, a figure that must be measured against competing firms in its industry to judge its performance:

$$\text{Return on sales} = \frac{\text{Net income}}{\text{Net sales}} = \frac{\$49{,}000}{\$700{,}000} = 7\%$$

Risk is a market variable that concerns investors. The higher the risk involved in an industry, the higher the return investors expect on their investment. Therefore, the level of risk involved in an industry and the return on investment of competing firms is important in comparing the firm's performance. *Return on equity* measures how much was earned for each dollar invested by owners. It's calculated by comparing a company's net income to its total owners' equity. Very Vegetarian's return on equity looks reasonably sound:

$$\text{Return on equity} = \frac{\text{Net income after tax}}{\text{Total owners' equity}} = \frac{\$49{,}000}{\$213{,}000} = 23\%$$

It's important to remember that profits help companies like Very Vegetarian grow. Therefore, profitability ratios are considered vital measurements of company growth and management performance.

## Activity Ratios

Converting the firm's resources to profits is a key function of management. Activity ratios measure the effectiveness of a firm's management in using the assets that are available.[28]

Inventory turnover is critical to just about any business. Poor turnover results in old merchandise and implies poor buying decisions. Inventory turnover is particularly important to businesses such as restaurants that serve perishable items like food. It's critical that restaurants turn over tables to keep the flow of food moving and the profits of the restaurant up. Can you think of other businesses that need to watch their inventory turnover ratios closely?

The *inventory turnover ratio* measures the speed of inventory moving through the firm and its conversion into sales. Idle inventory costs a business money. Think of the fixed cost of storing inventory in a warehouse as opposed to the revenue available when companies sell (turn over) inventory. The more efficiently a firm manages its inventory, the higher the return. The inventory turnover ratio for Very Vegetarian is measured as follows:

$$\text{Inventory turnover} = \frac{\text{Cost of goods sold}}{\text{Average inventory}} = \frac{\$410{,}000}{\$215{,}000} = 1.9 \text{ times}$$

A lower-than-average inventory turnover ratio in an industry often indicates obsolete merchandise on hand or poor buying practices. A higher-than-average ratio may signal lost sales because of inadequate stock. An acceptable turnover ratio is generally determined industry by industry.

Managers need to be aware of proper inventory control and expected inventory turnover to ensure proper performance. Have you ever worked as a food server in a restaurant like Very Vegetarian? How many times did your employer expect you to turn over a table (keep changing customers at the table) in an evening? The more times a table turns, the higher the return to the owner.

Accountants and other finance professionals use several other specific ratios, in addition to the ones we have discussed, to learn more about a firm's financial condition. The key purpose here is to acquaint you with what financial ratios are; how they are related to the firm's financial statements; and how investors, creditors, lenders, managers, employees, and others use them. If you can't recall where the accounting information used in ratio analysis comes from, see Figure 17.8 for a quick reference. It's also important for you to keep in mind that financial analysis begins where the accounting financial statements end.

We hope that you can see from this chapter that there is more to accounting than meets the eye. It can be fascinating and is critical to the firm's operations. It's worth saying one more time that, as the language of business, accounting is a worthwhile language to learn.

| Balance Sheet Accounts | | |
|---|---|---|
| **ASSETS** | **LIABILITIES** | **OWNERS' EQUITY** |
| Cash | Accounts payable | Capital stock |
| Accounts receivable | Notes payable | Retained earnings |
| Inventory | Bonds payable | Common stock |
| Investments | Taxes payable | Treasury stock |
| Equipment | | |
| Land | | |
| Buildings | | |
| Motor vehicles | | |
| Goodwill | | |

| Income Statement Accounts | | | |
|---|---|---|---|
| **REVENUES** | **COST OF GOODS SOLD** | **EXPENSES** | |
| Sales revenue | Cost of buying goods | Wages | Interest |
| Rental revenue | Cost of storing goods | Rent | Donations |
| Commissions revenue | | Repairs | Licenses |
| Royalty revenue | | Travel | Fees |
| | | Insurance | Supplies |
| | | Utilities | Advertising |
| | | Entertainment | Taxes |
| | | Storage | |

figure 17.8

**ACCOUNTS IN THE BALANCE SHEET AND INCOME STATEMENT**

### progress assessment

- What's the major benefit of performing ratio analysis on the basis of financial statements?
- What are the four main categories of financial ratios?

## summary

**1.** Describe the importance of financial information and accounting.

1. Financial information is critical to the growth and development of an organization. Accounting provides the information necessary to measure a firm's financial condition.
   - **What is accounting?**

   Accounting is the recording, classifying, summarizing, and interpreting of financial events and transactions that affect an organization. The methods used to record and summarize accounting data into reports are called an accounting system.

**2.** Define and explain the different areas of the accounting profession.

2. The accounting profession covers five major areas: managerial accounting, financial accounting, auditing, tax accounting, and governmental and not-for-profit accounting.
   - **How does managerial accounting differ from financial accounting?**

   Managerial accounting provides information and analyses to managers within the firm to assist them in decision making. Financial accounting provides information and analyses to external users of data such as creditors and lenders.
   - **What is the job of an auditor?**

   Auditors review and evaluate the standards used to prepare a company's financial statements. An independent audit is conducted by a public accountant and is an evaluation and unbiased opinion about the accuracy of company financial statements.
   - **What is the difference between a private accountant and a public accountant?**

   A public accountant provides services for a fee to a variety of companies, whereas a private accountant works for a single company. Private and public accountants do essentially the same things with the exception of independent audits. Private accountants do perform internal audits, but only public accountants supply independent audits.

**3.** List the steps in the accounting cycle, distinguish between accounting and bookkeeping, and explain how computers are used in accounting.

3. The accounting cycle is a six-step procedure that results in the preparation and analysis of the major financial statements.

- **What are the six steps of the accounting cycle?**

The six steps of the accounting cycle are (1) analyzing documents; (2) recording information into journals; (3) posting that information into ledgers; (4) developing a trial balance; (5) preparing financial statements (the balance sheet, income statement, and statement of cash flows); and (6) analyzing financial statements.

- **What is the difference between bookkeeping and accounting?**

Many people confuse bookkeeping and accounting. Bookkeeping is part of accounting and includes the mechanical part of recording data. Accounting also includes classifying, summarizing, interpreting, and reporting data to management.

- **What are journals and ledgers?**

Journals are original-entry accounting documents. This means that they are the first place transactions are recorded. Summaries of journal entries are recorded (posted) into ledgers. Ledgers are specialized accounting books that arrange the transactions by homogeneous groups (accounts).

- **How can computers help accountants?**

Computers can record and analyze data and provide financial reports. Software is available that can continuously analyze and test accounting systems to be sure they are functioning correctly. Computers can help decision making by providing appropriate information, but they cannot make good financial decisions independently. Accounting applications and creativity are still human traits.

**4.** Explain how the major financial statements differ.

4. Financial statements are a critical part of the firm's financial position.

- **What is a balance sheet?**

A balance sheet reports the financial position of a firm on a particular day. The fundamental accounting equation used to prepare the balance sheet is Assets = Liabilities + Owners' equity.

- **What are the major accounts of the balance sheet?**

Assets are economic resources owned by the firm, such as buildings and machinery. Liabilities are amounts owed by the firm to others (e.g., creditors, bondholders). Owners' equity is the value of the things the firm owns (assets) minus any liabilities; thus, owners' equity equals assets minus liabilities.

- **What is an income statement?**

An income statement reports revenues, costs, and expenses for a specific period of time (e.g., for the year ended December 31, 2007). The formula is Revenue − Cost of goods sold = Gross margin; Gross margin − Operating expenses = Net income before taxes; and Net income before taxes − Taxes = Net income (or net loss). Note that the income statement was once called the profit-and-loss statement.

- **What is a statement of cash flows?**

Cash flow is the difference between cash receipts (money coming in) and cash disbursements (money going out). The statement of cash flows reports cash receipts and disbursements related to the firm's major activities: operations, investments, and financing.

**5.** Explain the importance of ratio analysis in reporting financial information.

5. Financial ratios are a key part of analyzing financial information.

- **What are the four key categories of ratios?**

There are four key categories of ratios: liquidity ratios, leverage (debt) ratios, profitability (performance) ratios, and activity ratios.

- **What is the major value of ratio analysis to the firm?**
Ratio analysis provides the firm with information about its financial position in key areas compared to comparable firms in its industry and its past performance.

## key terms

**accounting** 456
**accounting cycle** 461
**accounts payable** 466
**annual report** 458
**assets** 464
**auditing** 459
**balance sheet** 464
**bonds payable** 466
**bookkeeping** 461
**cash flow** 472
**certified internal auditor (CIA)** 460
**certified management accountant (CMA)** 457
**certified public accountant (CPA)** 458
**cost of goods sold (or cost of goods manufactured)** 469
**current assets** 466
**depreciation** 470
**double-entry bookkeeping** 462
**financial accounting** 457
**financial statement** 463
**fixed assets** 466
**fundamental accounting equation** 464
**government and not-for-profit accounting** 460
**gross profit (gross margin)** 469
**income statement** 467
**independent audit** 460
**intangible assets** 466
**journal** 461
**ledger** 462
**liabilities** 466
**liquidity** 466
**managerial accounting** 457
**net income or net loss** 467
**notes payable** 466
**operating expenses** 470
**owners' equity** 466
**private accountant** 458
**public accountant** 458
**ratio analysis** 473
**retained earnings** 466
**revenue** 469
**statement of cash flows** 471
**tax accountant** 460
**trial balance** 463

## critical thinking questions

1. As a potential investor in a firm or perhaps the buyer of a business, would you be interested in evaluating the company's financial statements? Why or why not? What would be the key information you would seek from a firm's financial statements?

2. Why is it important that accounting reports be prepared according to specific procedures (GAAP)? Would it be advisable to allow businesses some flexibility or creativity in preparing financial statements?

3. What value do financial ratios offer in reviewing the financial performance of a firm?

## developing workplace skills

1. Visit, telephone, or e-mail a CPA at a firm in your area, or talk with a CPA in your college's business department. Ask what challenges, changes, and opportunities he or she foresees in the accounting profession in the next five years. List the CPA's forecasts on a sheet of paper and then compare them with the information in this chapter.

2. Go to the Web sites of the American Institute of Certified Public Accountants (www.aicpa.org) and the Institute of Certified Management Accountants (www.imanet.org). Browse through the sites and find information concerning the requirements for becoming a certified public accountant (CPA) and a certified management accountant (CMA). Compare the requirements of the programs and choose which program is most appealing to you.
3. Place yourself in the role of a new board member of an emerging not-for-profit organization that is hoping to attract new donors. Contributors large and small want to know how efficiently not-for-profit organizations use their donations. Unfortunately, your fellow board members see little value in financial reporting and analysis; they feel the organization's good work speaks for itself. Prepare a fact sheet convincing the board of the need for effective financial reporting, and offer arguments why it may help the organization's fund-raising goals.
4. Obtain a recent annual report for a company of your choice. (Hints: *The Wall Street Journal* has a free annual reports service. Also, many companies post their annual reports on their Web sites.) Look over the company's financial statements and see if they match the information in this chapter. Read the auditor's opinion (usually at the end of the report) and record what you think are the most important conclusions of the auditors concerning the company's financial statements.
5. From the annual report you obtained in exercise 4, try your hand at computing financial ratios. Compute the current ratio, debt to owners' equity ratio, and basic earnings per share ratio for the firm. Next, request an annual report of one of the company's competitors and compute the same ratios for that company; then compare the differences.

## taking it to the net

**Purpose**

To calculate and analyze current ratios and quick (acid-test) ratios.

**Exercise**

Thingamajigs and Things, a small gift shop, has total assets of $45,000 (including inventory valued at $30,000) and $9,000 in liabilities. WannaBees, a specialty clothing store, has total assets of $150,000 (including inventory valued at $125,000) and $85,000 in liabilities. Both businesses have applied for loans. Use the calculators at Bankrate.com to answer the following questions:

1. Calculate the current ratio for each company. Comparing the ratios, which company is more likely to get the loan? Why?
2. The quick (acid-test) ratio is considered an even more reliable measure of a business's ability to repay loans than the current ratio. Because inventory is often difficult to liquidate, the value of the inventory is subtracted from the total current assets. Calculate the quick ratio for each business. Do you think either business will get the loan? Why or why not?

## casing the web

To access the case *"Getting Through the Hard Times at Hard Rock,"* visit **www.mhhe.com/ub8e**

video case

## When the Goal Line Meets the Bottom Line

There are a lot of statistics to gather in any sport. Football is no exception. There are the ones that the average fan follows most closely, like win-loss records and the number of passes completed given the number of tries. For the Chicago Rush of the Arena Football League, the regular season statistics were not so wonderful in the 2006 season. They won only seven games and lost nine. Nonetheless, that record was good enough to win them a wildcard spot in the playoffs. Much to their credit, the team went on the win the Foster Trophy.

There are other important statistics for a football team to follow. You can't keep playing the game unless you make enough money to pay the players and keep the games going. Therefore, like all companies, the Chicago Rush has to keep careful accounting records. At the top of the income statement, revenues are a key. Winning a championship should improve that number and, after all costs and expenses are deducted, that bigger number should carry right down to the bottom line—profit after taxes.

A new team in a relatively new sport can't expect the bottom line to be huge. Investing in a team can be a major commitment. So the bottom line score is often as important as the scores on the field. And the person keeping those scores is a major player. That person at the Chicago Rush is Maggie Wirth. She goes through the same six-step accounting process outlined in this chapter.

Accounting can be an interesting and challenging occupation when you consider how important it is to the team and all its owners, players, and fans. When it comes time to be paid, the players are interested in whether or not the cash flow is sufficient. Costs and expenses have to be kept in line—and that includes player salaries. What seem like mere data to the average person turns out to be more important in the long run than wins and losses and championships won. Without the money, the game is over.

With increased revenue comes the opportunity to increase marketing. There are many competing sports in Chicago, and many teams have been around for years. To attract fans, the Rush must consistently provide exciting games and fun entertainment during those games. As in any sports program, the team is looking for revenue from all sorts of sources: parking, various food concessions, team merchandise, and more. Growth often is accompanied by more expenses, including higher-cost players. Going international adds its own expenses, for airline fees, hotels, and related items.

Keeping track of revenues, expenses, and other details may seem a rather remote part of team planning, but, as you can see from this case, such details are at the heart of the enterprise. Just as the offense and the defense need to have their plans and their appraisals over time, the fiscal health (profit and loss) of the team must be measured as well. And, just as there is a football team, there is a financial team. Keeping score is more than keeping track of first downs and touchdowns. In the background are people keeping score of how many fans are coming versus last year, how many hot dogs and sodas were sold, and how much it cost to clean the uniforms and clean the stadium. Boring statistics? Hardly. They determine whether or not the team can stay in business. There are lots of people relying on the results. The same is true in all businesses. The managers, employees, investors, and others are all following the accounting scores as closely as whatever score-keeping the company does (usually sales or profit).

### Thinking It Over

1. Does accounting seem more interesting and important when analyzed in the context of a major sport?
2. Player salaries are a major expense to a sports team. What role might accounting play in helping managers and coaches talk to the players about salaries? Does the fact that arena football is a relatively new sport have anything to do with such negotiations?
3. Do different groups, like managers and stockholders and players and fans, want different figures compiled by the accounting department? What are those differences?

# financial management

profile

**Getting to Know**

**X Jonathan Mariner**

**CFO of Major League Baseball**

Baseball fans are used to studying statistics. The number of hits, home runs, wins, and losses are easy to count. Many fans can calculate a pitcher's earned run average or compute a hitter's total bases or slugging percentage. And near the end of every season, everybody wants to keep track of the first-place team's magic number.

But some numbers aren't magic, and they aren't as easily handled as a batting average or a won-lost percentage. These are the numbers that keep track of baseball's finances. The game on the field may not have changed much in the past hundred years, but baseball financing has become much more complicated. Jonathan Mariner is the man who oversees the financial numbers for Major League Baseball.

Mariner is executive vice president and chief financial officer (CFO) of Major League Baseball (MLB). He is responsible for MLB's central office budgeting, financial reporting, and risk management activities. Mariner graduated from the University of Virginia with a bachelor's degree in accounting and is a certified public accountant. He received his master of business administration degree from Harvard Business School. Mariner began his professional career with MCI Communications Inc., where he served as senior financial analyst and as a senior manager.

Mariner entered the sports industry when he worked for H. Wayne Huizenga as CFO for Pro Player Stadium and as vice president and CEO for the Florida Panthers Hockey Club. Later he became executive vice president and CFO of the Florida Marlins baseball team. He was also president of Marlins Ballpark Development Company, which supported the Marlins' new ballpark in southern Florida.

After serving as chief operating officer and CFO of Charter Schools USA, Mariner returned to the baseball industry to be executive vice president of finance in 2002. Since then he has been responsible for providing updates on the industry's financial health at owners' meetings, overseeing all team-level financial reporting through the teams' CFOs, and providing financial reviews on potential ownership applications. He also serves on league-wide committees, such as finance and compensation, revenue sharing, long-range planning, and debt service.

Another of Mariner's major duties has been to administer MLB's $1.5 billion leaguewide credit facility. This facility is part of MLB's attempt to bring some of the poorer teams into a closer parity, or equality, with richer teams. The New York Yankees, for instance, had a payroll of more than $208 million in 2005, while

LEARNING **goals**

**After you have read and studied this chapter, you should be able to**

1. Describe the importance of finance and financial management to an organization, and explain the responsibilities of financial managers.
2. Outline the financial planning process, and explain the three key budgets in the financial plan.
3. Explain the major reasons why firms need operating funds, and identify various types of financing that can be used to obtain those funds.
4. Identify and describe different sources of short-term financing.
5. Identify and describe different sources of long-term financing

CHAPTER 18

**http://mlb.mlb.com**

the Tampa Bay Devil Rays had only $29 million. The way Mariner has structured the debt facility, each team has access to a $50 million revolving loan and a $25 million term loan. Mariner also administers the league's luxury tax and revenue-sharing systems. The luxury tax is a penalty that teams pay when their payroll exceeds a certain amount. (In 2006, the Yankees were the only team required to pay the tax.) Under revenue sharing, richer teams contribute part of their baseball revenues to a pool that poorer teams can be paid from.

One problem that Mariner faces is that owners are often driven by benefits other than just the bottom line. "There are psychic benefits," says Marvin Goldklang, a limited partner in the Yankees, referring to the benefits of riding up Broadway in a ticker-tape parade. And don't even bother to ask the average fan what he or she thinks of the bottom line. "We tell the owners all the time: fans don't care if you are losing money," says Mariner. "And they shouldn't. It's not their concern. You have to operate in a fiscally responsible way, but at the end of the day, all the fans really care about is winning." Operating in a fiscally responsible way is Mariner's concern.

Risk and uncertainty clearly define the role of financial management, even in unlikely industries like Major League Baseball. In this chapter, you'll explore the role of finance in business and learn about the challenges and tools financial managers like Jonathan Mariner use to seek financial stability and future growth.

Sources: http://mlb.mlb.com, 2006, and Tim Reason, "Squeeze Play: Forget Steroids. It's Spending That Has Baseball in a Bind," *CFO*, April 2004.

# THE ROLE OF FINANCE AND FINANCIAL MANAGERS

**finance**
The function in a business that acquires funds for the firm and manages those funds within the firm.

**financial management**
The job of managing a firm's resources so it can meet its goals and objectives.

**financial managers**
Managers who make recommendations to top executives regarding strategies for improving the financial strength of a firm.

The central goal of this chapter is to answer two major questions: "What is finance?" and "What do financial managers do?" **Finance** is the function in a business that acquires funds for the firm and manages those funds within the firm. Finance activities include preparing budgets; doing cash flow analysis; and planning for the expenditure of funds on such assets as plant, equipment, and machinery. **Financial management** is the job of managing a firm's resources so it can meet its goals and objectives. Without a carefully calculated financial plan, the firm has little chance for survival, regardless of its product or marketing effectiveness. Let's review the role of an accountant and compare it with that of a financial manager.

An accountant could be compared to a skilled laboratory technician who takes blood samples and other measures of a person's health and writes the findings on a health report (in business, the equivalent of a set of financial statements).[1] A financial manager of a business is the doctor who interprets the report and makes recommendations to the patient regarding changes that will improve the patient's health. In short, **financial managers** examine the financial data prepared by accountants and make recommendations to top executives regarding strategies for improving the health (financial performance) of the firm.

It should be clear that financial managers can make sound financial decisions only if they understand accounting information. That's why we examined accounting thoroughly in Chapter 17. Similarly, a good accountant needs to understand finance. It's fair to say that accounting and finance go together like peanut butter and jelly. In large and medium-sized organizations, both the accounting and finance functions are generally under the control of a chief financial officer (CFO) such as Jonathan Mariner, whom you met in the chapter Opening Profile.[2] However, financial management could also be in the hands of a person who serves as the company treasurer or vice president of finance. A comptroller is the chief *accounting* officer.

Figure 18.1 highlights a financial manager's tasks. As you can see, two key responsibilities are to obtain funds and to control the use of those funds effectively. Controlling funds includes managing the firm's cash, credit accounts (accounts receivable), and inventory. Finance is a critical activity in both

figure 18.1
**WHAT FINANCIAL MANAGERS DO**

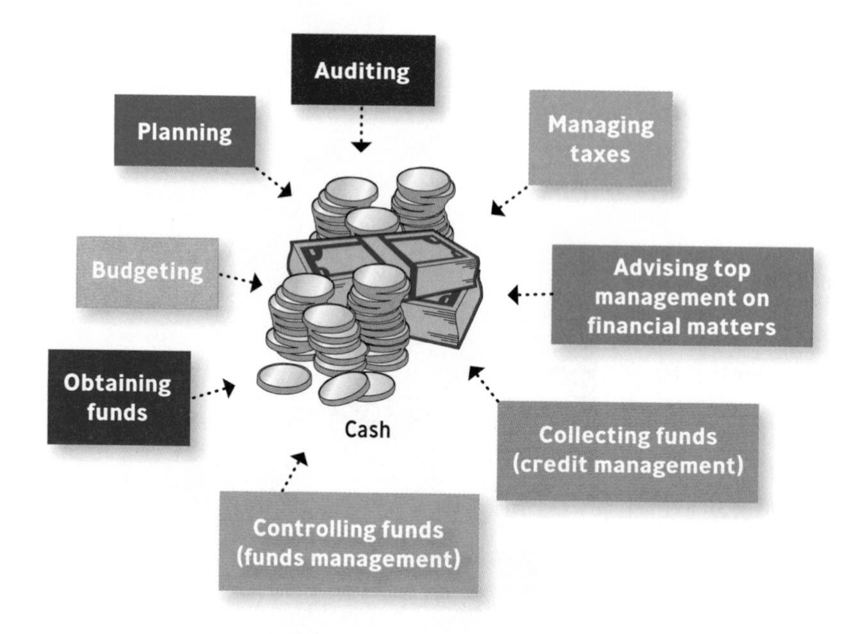

DEALING WITH change

## Bringing Financial Goodwill to Goodwill Industries

www.goodwill.org

When Michael Miller became CEO of an underperforming Goodwill operation in Portland, Oregon, he knew that careful planning and financial management were essential to making his stores successful. He reviewed the organization's financial records and found that a significant part of Goodwill's funding came from government sources to support Goodwill's services to people with disabilities and other special-needs populations. This concerned him because he knew that government funding can swing wildly. He therefore set out to make his Goodwill stores as profitable as possible.

Miller knew that Goodwill's accounting and financial management practices had to change. He analyzed the organization's financial position and initiated strategic planning as if he were running a fast-paced, for-profit business. He found that average donors to Goodwill were women ages 35 to 44 with incomes of approximately $50,000. In contrast, he found the average shoppers at his stores were women ages 25 to 54 who earned $30,000. After a cost analysis of each store, he shut down locations with the lowest sales and opened new stores where the groups of donors and shoppers intersected. Miller also attacked Goodwill's costs with a passion. By collecting goods at off-site trailers located near his stores and bringing them directly to the stores with no detour to Goodwill distribution branches, he cut operating expenses by 30 percent. To increase profitability, Miller set up Starbucks-like coffee stations in Goodwill stores so that shoppers could purchase high-profit products like coffee and books.

Did Miller's efforts pay off? And how! His employees—mostly people who have disabling conditions such as cerebral palsy or Down's syndrome, or who have long depended on welfare—earn wages well above the state's $6.90 minimum wage. The Goodwill stores that had sales of $4 million when Miller took charge today have over $50 million in sales.

Sources: Tom Herman, "Charities May See More Scrutiny," *The Wall Street Journal*, March 2, 2005, p. D3, and www.goodwill.org.

profit-seeking and nonprofit organizations.[3] Read the Dealing with Change box to see how careful financial management helped Goodwill Industries.

Finance is important no matter what the firm's size. As you may remember from Chapter 6, financing a small business is a difficult but essential function if a firm expects to survive its important first five years. But the need for careful financial management goes well beyond the early years and remains a challenge that a business, large or small, must face throughout its existence.[4] Even a market giant cannot afford to ignore finance. Chrysler Corporation, for example, faced extinction in the late 1970s because of severe financial problems. Had it not been for a government-backed loan in 1980 of $1 billion, Chrysler might have joined the ranks of defunct auto companies such as Packard and Hudson instead of becoming part of Daimler-Benz.[5] The following are three of the most common ways for a firm to fail financially:

1. Undercapitalization (lacking enough funds to start the business).
2. Poor control over cash flow.
3. Inadequate expense control.

## The Importance of Understanding Finance

You can see the issues involved with capitalization, control over cash flow, and expense control when you consider the financial problems encountered several years ago by a small organization called Parsley Patch. Two friends, Elizabeth Bertani and Pat Sherwood, started the company on what can best be described as a shoestring budget. It began when Bertani prepared salt-free seasonings for her husband, who was on a no-salt diet. Her friend Sherwood thought the seasonings were good enough to sell. Bertani agreed, and Parsley Patch Inc. was born.

The business began with an investment of $5,000, which was rapidly eaten up for a logo and a label design. Bertani and Sherwood quickly learned the importance of capital in getting a business going. Eventually, the two women personally invested more than $100,000 to keep the business from experiencing severe undercapitalization.

The partners believed that gourmet shops would be an ideal distribution point for their product. Everything started well, and hundreds of gourmet shops adopted the product line. But when sales failed to meet expectations, the women decided that the health-food market offered more potential than gourmet shops because salt-free seasonings were a natural for people with restricted diets. The choice was a good one. Sales soared, approaching $30,000 a month. Still, the company earned no profits.

As children we learned to save our money for a rainy day. Financial managers need to remember this and then some. They are responsible for seeing that a company pays its bills and collects payments from customers on time, takes advantage of buying merchandise on credit, obtains funds when needed, limits bad debts . . . are you exhausted yet? It's no wonder that CFOs are generally the second highest paid executives in a business.

Bertani and Sherwood were not trained in monitoring cash flow or in controlling expenses. In fact, they had been told not to worry about costs, and they hadn't. They eventually hired a certified public accountant (CPA) and an experienced financial manager, who taught them how to compute the costs of the various blends they produced and how to control their expenses. The financial specialists also offered insight into how to control cash coming in and out of the company (cash flow). Soon Parsley Patch earned a comfortable margin on operations that ran close to $1 million a year. Luckily, the owners were able to turn things around before it was too late.

If Bertani and Sherwood had understood finance before starting their business, they may have been able to avoid the problems they encountered. The key word here is *understood.* You do not have to pursue finance as a career to understand finance. Financial understanding is important to anyone who wants to start a small business, invest in stocks and bonds, or plan a retirement fund. In short, finance and accounting are two areas everyone involved in business needs to study. Since accounting was discussed in Chapter 17, let's look more closely at what financial management is all about.

## WHAT IS FINANCIAL MANAGEMENT?

Financial managers are responsible for seeing that the company pays its bills. Finance functions such as buying merchandise on credit (accounts payable) and collecting payment from customers (accounts receivable) are responsibilities of financial managers. Therefore, financial managers are responsible for paying the company's bills at the appropriate time and for collecting overdue payments to make sure that the company does not lose too much money to bad debts (people or firms that don't pay their bills). While these functions are critical to all types of businesses, they are particularly critical to small- and medium-sized businesses, which typically have smaller cash or credit cushions than large corporations.

It's vital that financial managers stay abreast of changes or opportunities in finance and prepare to adjust to them. For example, tax payments represent an outflow of cash from the business. Therefore, financial managers must be involved in tax management and must keep abreast of changes in tax law. Financial managers also carefully analyze the tax implications of various managerial decisions in an attempt to minimize the taxes paid by the business. It's critical that businesses of all sizes concern themselves with managing taxes.

Usually a member of the firm's finance department, the internal auditor, checks on the journals, ledgers, and financial statements prepared by the accounting department to make sure that all transactions have been treated in accordance with generally accepted accounting principles (GAAP).[6] If such audits were not done, accounting statements would be less reliable. Therefore, it is important that internal auditors be objective and critical of any improprieties or deficiencies they might note in their evaluation.[7] Regular, thoroughly conducted internal audits offer the firm assistance in the important role of financial planning, which we'll look at next.

## FINANCIAL PLANNING

Financial planning is a key responsibility of the financial manager in a business. Planning has been a recurring theme of this book. We've stressed planning's importance as a managerial function and offered insights into planning your career. Financial planning involves analyzing short-term and long-term money flows to and from the firm. The overall objective of financial planning is to optimize the firm's profitability and make the best use of its money.[8]

Financial planning involves three steps: (1) forecasting both short-term and long-term financial needs, (2) developing budgets to meet those needs, and (3) establishing financial control to see how well the company is doing what it set out to do (see Figure 18.2). Let's look at each step and the role these steps play in improving the financial health of an organization.

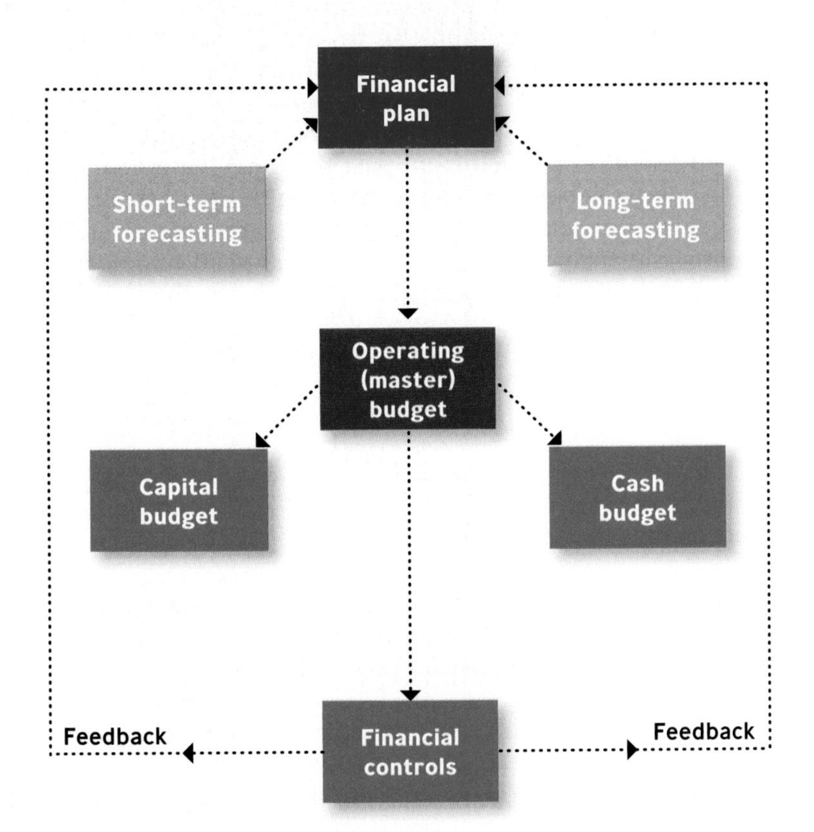


figure 18.2

**FINANCIAL PLANNING**

Note the close link between financial planning and budgeting.

## Forecasting Financial Needs

**short-term forecast**
Forecast that predicts revenues, costs, and expenses for a period of one year or less.

**cash flow forecast**
Forecast that predicts the cash inflows and outflows in future periods, usually months or quarters.

**long-term forecast**
Forecast that predicts revenues, costs, and expenses for a period longer than 1 year, and sometimes as far as 5 or 10 years into the future.

Forecasting is an important part of any firm's financial plan. A **short-term forecast** predicts revenues, costs, and expenses for a period of one year or less. This forecast is the foundation for most other financial plans, so its accuracy is critical. Part of the short-term forecast may be in the form of a **cash flow forecast**, which predicts the cash inflows and outflows in future periods, usually months or quarters. The inflows and outflows of cash recorded in the cash flow forecast are based on expected sales revenues and on various costs and expenses incurred and when they'll come due.[9] The company's sales forecast estimates the firm's projected sales for a particular period. A business often uses its past financial statements as a basis for projecting expected sales and various costs and expenses.[10]

A **long-term forecast** predicts revenues, costs, and expenses for a period longer than 1 year, and sometimes as far as 5 or 10 years into the future. This forecast plays a crucial part in the company's long-term strategic plan which asks questions such as: What business are we in? Should we be in it five years from now? How much money should we invest in technology and new plant and equipment over the next decade? Will there be cash available to meet long-term obligations? Innovations in Web-based software today assist financial managers in dealing with these long-term forecasting questions.

The long-term financial forecast gives top management, as well as operations managers, some sense of the income or profit potential possible with different strategic plans. Additionally, long-term projections assist financial managers with the preparation of company budgets.

## Working with the Budget Process

**budget**
A financial plan that sets forth management's expectations, and, on the basis of those expectations, allocates the use of specific resources throughout the firm.

The budgeting process depends on the accuracy of the firm's financial statements. Put simply, a budget is a financial plan.[11] More specifically, a **budget** sets forth management's expectations for revenues and, on the basis of those expectations, allocates the use of specific resources throughout the firm. The key financial statements—the balance sheet, income statement, and statement of cash flows—form the basis for the budgeting process. Businesses use cost and revenue information derived from past financial statements as the basis for forecasting company budgets. The firm's budgets are compiled from short-term and long-term financial forecasts that need to be as accurate as possible. Since budgeting is clearly tied to forecasting, financial managers must take forecasting responsibilities seriously. A budget becomes the primary guide for the firm's financial operations and financial needs.

There are usually several types of budgets established in a firm's financial plan:

**capital budget**
A budget that highlights a firm's spending plans for major asset purchases that often require large sums of money.

- A capital budget.
- A cash budget.
- An operating (master) budget.

**cash budget**
A budget that estimates a firm's projected cash inflows and outflows that the firm can use to plan for any cash shortages or surpluses during a given period.

A **capital budget** highlights a firm's spending plans for major asset purchases that often require large sums of money. The capital budget primarily concerns itself with the purchase of such assets as property, buildings, and equipment.

A **cash budget** estimates a firm's projected cash inflows and outflows that the firm can use to plan for any cash shortages or surpluses during a given period (e.g., monthly, quarterly). Cash budgets are important guidelines that help managers to anticipate borrowing, debt repayment, operating expenses,

VERY VEGETARIAN
Monthly Cash Budget

| | January | February | March |
|---|---|---|---|
| Sales forecast | $50,000 | $45,000 | $40,000 |
| Collections | | | |
| Cash sales (20%) | | $9,000 | $8,000 |
| Credit sales (80% of past month) | | $40,000 | $36,000 |
| Monthly cash collection | | $49,000 | $44,000 |
| Payments schedule | | | |
| Supplies and material | | $11,000 | $10,000 |
| Salaries | | 12,000 | 12,000 |
| Direct labor | | 9,000 | 9,000 |
| Taxes | | 3,000 | 3,000 |
| Other expenses | | 7,000 | 6,000 |
| Monthly cash payments | | $42,000 | $39,000 |
| Cash budget | | | |
| Cash flow | | $7,000 | $5,000 |
| Beginning cash | | −1,000 | 6,000 |
| Total cash | | $6,000 | $11,000 |
| Less minimum cash balance | | −6,000 | −6,000 |
| Excess cash to market securities | | $0 | $5,000 |
| Loans needed for minimum balance | | 0 | 0 |

figure 18.3

**A SAMPLE CASH BUDGET FOR VERY VEGETARIAN**

and short-term investments.[12] The cash budget is often the last budget that is prepared. A sample cash budget for our ongoing example company, Very Vegetarian, is provided in Figure 18.3.

The **operating budget (master budget)** ties together all the firm's other budgets and summarizes the business's proposed financial activities. It can be defined more formally as the projection of dollar allocations to various costs and expenses needed to run or operate a business, given projected revenues.[13] How much the firm will spend on supplies, travel, rent, advertising, salaries, and so forth is determined in the operating, or master, budget. The operating budget is generally the most detailed and most useful budget that a firm prepares.

**operating budget (master budget)**
The budget that ties together all of a firm's other budgets; it is the projection of dollar allocations to various costs and expenses needed to run or operate the business, given projected revenues.

Clearly, financial planning plays an important role in the operations of the firm. This planning often determines what long-term investments are made, when specific funds will be needed, and how the funds will be generated. Once a company has determined its short-term and long-term financial needs and established budgets to show how funds will be allocated, the final step in financial planning is to establish financial controls. Before you read about such controls, the Spotlight on Small Business box on page 490 challenges you to check your personal financial-planning skill by developing a monthly budget for "You Incorporated."

## Establishing Financial Controls

**Financial control** is a process in which a firm periodically compares its actual revenues, costs, and expenses with its budget. Most companies hold at least monthly financial reviews as a way to ensure financial control. Such

**financial control**
A process in which a firm periodically compares its actual revenues, costs, and expenses with its budget.

SPOTLIGHT ON **small business** www.dinkytown.net/java/HomeBudget.html

## You Incorporated Monthly Budget

In Chapter 17, you compiled a sample balance sheet for You Inc. (see p. 467). Now, let's develop a monthly budget for You Inc. Be honest and think of everything that needs to be included for an accurate monthly budget for You!

| | Expected | Actual | Difference |
|---|---|---|---|
| **Monthly income:** | | | |
| Wages (net pay after taxes) | | | |
| Savings account withdrawal | | | |
| Family support | | | |
| Loans | | | |
| Other sources | | | |
| **Total monthly income** | | | |
| **Monthly expenses:** | | | |
| **Fixed expenses** | | | |
| Rent or mortgage | | | |
| Car payment | | | |
| Health insurance | | | |
| Life insurance | | | |
| Tuition or fees | | | |
| Other fixed expenses | | | |
| **Subtotal of fixed expenses** | | | |
| **Variable expenses** | | | |
| Food | | | |
| Clothing | | | |
| Entertainment | | | |
| Transportation | | | |
| Phone | | | |
| Utilities | | | |
| Publications | | | |
| Internet connection | | | |
| Cable television | | | |
| Other expenses | | | |
| **Subtotal of variable expenses** | | | |
| **Total expenses** | | | |
| **Total income − Total expenses = Cash on hand/(Cash deficit)** | | | |

control procedures help managers identify variances to the financial plan and allow them to take corrective action if necessary. Financial controls also provide feedback to help reveal which accounts, which departments, and which people are varying from the financial plans.[14] Finance managers can judge if such variances may or may not be justified allowing them to make some financial adjustments to the plan when needed. The Making Ethical Decisions box details a situation a manager can face related to financial control. After the Progress Assessment, we shall explore specific reasons why firms need to have funds readily available.

*** MAKING

## ethical decisions

http://ethics.acusd.edu/index.html

### Playing It Safe or Stupid

You have recently assumed a new job as a manager in the auditing department of a major pharmaceutical company. After working there just a few months, you sense that the attitude of most employees at the company is "Who cares?" For example, salespeople don't turn in detailed expense reports for their travel, nor do they provide receipts to receive reimbursement for meals and other expenses. You check and find that the company operations manual states explicitly that such documentation is required. You also notice that employees readily help themselves to office supplies like pens, paper, and staplers with no questions asked. You approach your supervisor and cite the many financial control flaws you have noted and suggest that the company toughen up on lax employee behavior. Your supervisor puts his arm on your shoulder and says, "I've been here for twenty-eight years, and this is the way it's always been. If you want my advice, don't rock the boat." What will you do? What could result from your decision?

### progress assessment

- Name three finance functions important to the firm's overall operations and performance.
- What are the three primary financial problems that cause firms to fail?
- In what ways do short-term and long-term financial forecasts differ?
- What is the organization's purpose in preparing budgets? Can you identify three different types of budgets?

## THE NEED FOR OPERATING FUNDS

In business, the need for operating funds never seems to cease. That's why sound financial management is essential to all businesses. Like our personal financial needs, the capital needs of a business change over time. For example, as a small business grows, its financial requirements shift considerably. (Remember the example of Parsley Patch.) The same is true with large corporations such as Intel, Johnson & Johnson, and PepsiCo. As they venture into new product areas or markets, their capital needs increase, causing a need for funds for different reasons. Virtually all organizations have certain operational needs for which funds must be available. Key areas include:

- Managing day-by-day needs of the business.
- Controlling credit operations.
- Acquiring needed inventory.
- Making capital expenditures.

Let's look carefully at these financial needs, which affect both the smallest and the largest of businesses.

### Managing Day-by-Day Needs of the Business

If workers expect to be paid on Friday, they don't want to have to wait until Monday for their paychecks. If tax payments are due on the 15th of the month, the government expects the money on time. If the interest payment on a business loan is due on the 30th, the lender doesn't mean the 1st of the next month. As you can see, funds have to be available to meet the daily operational costs of the business.

The challenge of sound financial management is to see that funds are available to meet these daily cash needs without compromising the firm's investment potential.[15] Money has what is called a *time value.* In other words, if someone offered to give you $200 today or $200 one year from today, you would benefit by taking the $200 today. Why? It's very simple. You could start collecting interest or invest the $200 you receive today, and over a year's time your money would grow. The same thing is true in business; the interest gained on the firm's investments is important in maximizing the profit the company will gain. That's why financial managers encourage keeping a firm's cash expenditures to a minimum. By doing this, the firm can free up funds for investment in interest-bearing accounts. It's also not unusual for finance managers to suggest that a company pay its bills as late as possible (unless a cash discount is available) but try to collect what's owed to it as fast as possible. This way, they maximize the investment potential of the firm's funds. Efficient cash management is particularly important to small firms in conducting their daily operations because their access to capital is generally much more limited than that of larger businesses.[16]

## Controlling Credit Operations

Financial managers know that making credit available helps keep current customers happy and attracts new customers. In today's highly competitive business environment, many businesses would have trouble surviving without making credit available to customers.

The major problem with selling on credit is that as much as 25 percent or more of the business's assets could be tied up in its credit accounts (accounts receivable). This means the firm needs to use some of its available funds to pay for the goods or services already sold to customers who bought on credit. Financial managers in such firms must develop efficient collection procedures. For example, businesses often provide cash or quantity discounts to buyers who pay their accounts by a certain time. Also, finance managers carefully scrutinize old and new credit customers to see if they have a favorable history of meeting their credit obligations on time.[17] In essence, the firm's credit policy reflects its financial position and its desire to expand into new markets.

It's difficult to think of a business that does not make credit available to customers. However, collecting accounts receivables can often be time-consuming and expensive. Accepting credits cards such as Visa, MasterCard, or American Express can simplify transactions and guarantee payment. What types of products do you regularly use a charge card to purchase?

One way to decrease the time, and therefore expense, involved in collecting accounts receivable is to accept bank credit cards such as MasterCard or Visa.[18] This is convenient for both the customer and the business. The banks that issue such credit cards have already established the customer's creditworthiness, which reduces the business's risk. Businesses must pay a fee to accept credit cards, but the fees are generally not considered excessive compared to the benefits the cards provide.

## Acquiring Needed Inventory

As we noted earlier in the text, effective marketing implies a clear customer orientation. This focus on the customer means that high-quality service and availability of goods are vital if a business expects to prosper in today's markets. Therefore, to satisfy customers, businesses must maintain inventories that often involve a sizable expenditure of funds. Although it's true that firms expect to recapture their investment in inventory through sales to customers, a carefully constructed inventory policy assists in managing the firm's available funds and maximizing profitability. For example, Take-a-Dip, a neighborhood ice cream parlor, ties up more funds in inventory (ice cream) in the summer than in the winter. It's obvious why. Demand for ice cream goes up in the summer.

Innovations such as just-in-time inventory control (discussed in Chapter 9) help reduce the amount of funds a firm must tie up in inventory. Also, by carefully evaluating its inventory turnover ratio (discussed in Chapter 17) a firm can better control its outflow of cash for inventory. It's important for a business of any size to understand that a poorly managed inventory system can seriously impact cash flow and drain its finances dry.

## Making Capital Expenditures

**capital expenditures**
Major investments in either tangible long-term assets such as land, buildings, and equipment or intangible assets such as patents, trademarks, and copyrights.

**Capital expenditures** are major investments in either tangible long-term assets such as land, buildings, and equipment or intangible assets such as patents, trademarks, and copyrights. In many organizations the purchase of major assets—such as land for future expansion, manufacturing plants to increase production capabilities, research to develop new-product ideas, and equipment to maintain or exceed current levels of output—is essential. As you can imagine, these expenditures often require a huge portion of the organization's funds.

Expansion into new markets can also cost large sums of money with no guarantee that the expansion will be commercially successful. Therefore, it's critical that companies weigh all the possible options before committing what may be a large portion of their available resources. For this reason, financial managers evaluate the appropriateness of such purchases or expenditures. Consider the situation in which a firm needs to expand its production capabilities due to increases in customer demand. One option is to buy land and build a new plant. Another option would be to purchase an existing plant or consider renting. Can you think of financial and accounting considerations that would come into play in this decision?

Obviously, the need for operating funds raises several questions in any firm: How does the firm obtain funds to finance operations and other business necessities? Will specific funds be needed by the firm in the long term or short term? How much will it cost to obtain these needed funds? Will these funds come from internal or external sources? We address these questions next.

**debt financing**
Funds raised through various forms of borrowing that must be repaid.

## Alternative Sources of Funds

**equity financing**
Funds raised from operations within the firm or through the sale of ownership in the firm.

**short-term financing**
Borrowed capital that will be repaid within one year.

**long-term financing**
Borrowed capital that will be repaid over a specific period longer than one year.

Earlier in the chapter, finance was described as the function in a business responsible for acquiring and managing funds. Determining the amount of money needed and finding out the most appropriate sources from which to obtain it are fundamental steps in sound financial management. A firm can seek to raise needed capital through borrowing money (debt), selling ownership (equity), or earning profits (retained earnings). **Debt financing** refers to funds raised through various forms of borrowing that must be repaid. **Equity financing** is money raised from within the firm (from operations) or through the sale of ownership in the firm (e.g., the sale of stock). Firms can borrow funds either short-term or long-term. **Short-term financing** refers to funds needed for a period of one year or less. In contrast, **long-term financing** refers to funds needed for a period longer than one year (usually 2 to 10 years). Figure 18.4 on page 494 highlights reasons why firms may need funds short-term and long-term.

figure 18.4

WHY FIRMS NEED FUNDS

| SHORT-TERM FUNDS | LONG-TERM FUNDS |
|---|---|
| Meeting monthly expenses | New product development |
| Unanticipated emergencies | Replacing capital equipment |
| Cash-flow problems | Mergers or acquisitions |
| Expanding current inventory | Expansion into new markets (domestic or global) |
| Temporary promotional programs | Building new facilities |

We'll explore the different sources of short- and long-term financing fully in the next sections. For now it's important to know that businesses can use different methods of raising money. Before we go on, however, pause to check your understanding of what you just read by doing the Progress Assessment.

**progress assessment**

- Money is said to have a time value. What does this mean?
- Why are accounts receivable a financial concern to the firm?
- What's the primary reason an organization spends a good deal of its available funds on inventory and capital expenditures?
- What's the difference between debt and equity financing?

## OBTAINING SHORT-TERM FINANCING

The bulk of a finance manager's job does not involve obtaining *long-term* funds. In fact, in small businesses, long-term financing is often out of the question. Instead, the day-to-day operation of the firm calls for the careful management of *short-term* financial needs. Firms may need to borrow short-term funds for purchasing additional inventory or for meeting bills that come due unexpectedly. Also, as we do in our personal lives, a business sometimes needs to obtain short-term funds when its cash reserves are low. This is particularly true, again, of small businesses.

Most small businesses are primarily concerned with just staying afloat until they are able to build capital and creditworthiness. Firms can obtain short-term financing in several different ways. Also, suppliers of short-term funds can require that the funds provided be secured or unsecured. Let's look at the major forms of short-term financing and what's meant by secured and unsecured financing with regard to different ways of obtaining needed funds.

### Trade Credit

**trade credit**
The practice of buying goods and services now and paying for them later.

The most widely used source of short-term funding, trade credit (an account payable), is the least expensive and most convenient form of short-term financing. **Trade credit** is the practice of buying goods or services now and paying for them later. Small businesses rely heavily on trade credit from firms such as United Parcel Service, as do large firms such as Kmart. When a firm buys merchandise, it receives an invoice (a bill) much like the one you receive when you buy something with a credit card. As you will see, however, the terms businesses receive are often different.

It is common for business invoices to contain terms such as *2/10, net 30.* This means that the buyer can take a 2 percent discount for paying the invoice within 10 days. The total bill is due (net) in 30 days if the purchaser does not take advantage of the discount. Finance managers need to pay close attention to such discounts because they create opportunities to reduce the firm's costs. Think about it for a moment: If the discount offered to the customer is 2/10, net 30, the customer will pay 2 percent more for waiting an extra 20 days to pay the invoice.

Uninformed businesspeople may believe that 2 percent is insignificant, so they pay their bills after the discount period. By doing that, however, such firms lose a tremendous opportunity to save money—and it's much more than 2 percent! In the course of a year, 2 percent for 20 days adds up to a *36 percent* interest rate (because there are eighteen 20-day periods in the year). If the firm is capable of paying within 10 days, it is needlessly (and significantly) increasing its costs by not doing so.

Some suppliers hesitate to give trade credit to organizations with a poor credit rating, no credit history, or a history of slow payment. In such cases, the supplier may insist that the customer sign a promissory note as a condition for obtaining credit. A **promissory note** is a written contract with a promise to pay a supplier a specific sum of money at a definite time. Promissory notes can be sold by the supplier to a bank at a discount (the amount of the note less a fee for the bank's services in collecting the amount due).

**promissory note**
A written contract with a promise to pay a supplier a specific sum of money at a definite time.

## Family and Friends

Many small firms obtain short-term funds by borrowing money from family and friends. Because such funds are needed for periods of less than a year, friends or relatives are sometimes willing to help. Such loans can create problems, however, if the firm does not understand cash flow.[19] As we discussed earlier, the firm may suddenly find itself having several bills coming due at the same time with no sources of funds to pay them. It is better, therefore, not to borrow from friends or relatives; instead, go to a commercial bank that fully understands the business's risk and can help analyze your firm's future financial needs.

Entrepreneurs appear to be listening to this advice. According to the National Federation of Independent Business, entrepreneurs today are relying less on family and friends as a source of borrowed funds than they have in the past. If an entrepreneur does decide to ask family or friends for financial assistance, it's important that both parties (1) agree on specific loan terms, (2) put the agreement in writing, and (3) arrange for repayment in the same way they would for a bank loan. Such actions help keep family relationships and friendships intact.[20]

## Commercial Banks

Banks are highly sensitive to risk and are often reluctant to lend money to small businesses. Nonetheless, a promising and well-organized venture may be able to get a bank loan. In fact, almost half of small business financing today is funded by commercial banks.[21] If a business is able to get such a loan, a small- or medium-sized business should have the person in charge of the finance function keep in close touch with the bank. It's also wise to see a banker periodically (as often as once a month) and send the banker all the firm's financial statements so that the bank is kept up-to-date and continues to supply funds when needed.

It's that time of year, the season to be jolly and the season to shop, shop, shop. Ever wonder how retail stores get the money to buy all the treasures we splurge on during the holiday season? Department stores and other large retailers make extensive use of commercial banks and other lenders to borrow the funds they need to buy merchandise to stock their shelves. Ho! Ho! Ho!

If you try to imagine the different types of businesspeople who go to banks for a loan, you'll get a better idea of the role of financial management. Picture, for example, a farmer going to the bank to borrow funds for seed, fertilizer, equipment, and other needs. The farmer may buy such supplies in the spring and pay for them after the fall harvest. Now picture a local toy store buying merchandise for Christmas sales. The store may borrow the money for such purchases in the summer and pay it back after Christmas. Restaurants may borrow funds at the beginning of the month and pay by the end of the month. It's evident that how much a business borrows and for how long depends often on the kind of business it is and how quickly the merchandise purchased with a bank loan can be resold or used to generate funds.

You can also imagine how important it is for specialists in a company's finance and accounting departments to do a cash flow forecast. Unfortunately, small-business owners generally lack the luxury of such specialists and must monitor cash flow themselves. By anticipating times when many bills will come due, a business can begin early to seek funds or sell other assets to prepare for a possible financial crunch. This is why it's important for businesspeople to keep friendly and close relations with their bankers. An experienced banker may spot cash flow problems early or be more willing to lend money in a crisis if a businessperson has established a strong, friendly relationship built on openness, trust, and sound management practices. It's important to remember that your banker wants you to succeed almost as much as you want to. Bankers can be an invaluable support to any business but especially to small, growing businesses.

## Different Forms of Short-Term Loans

**secured loan**
A loan backed by something valuable, such as property.

Commercial banks offer different types of loans to customers. A **secured loan** is a loan that's backed by something valuable, such as property. The item of value is called *collateral.* If the borrower fails to pay the loan, the lender may take possession of the collateral. For example, an automobile loan is a secured loan. If the borrower fails to pay the loan, the lender will repossess (take back) the car. Collateral thus takes some of the risk out of lending money.

Accounts receivable are assets that are often used by businesses as collateral for a loan; the process is called *pledging*. Some percentage of the value of accounts receivable pledged (usually about 75 percent) is advanced to the borrowing firm.[22] As customers pay off their accounts, the funds received are forwarded to the lender in repayment of the funds that were advanced. Inventory such as raw materials (e.g., coal, steel), is also often used as collateral or security for a business loan. Other assets that can be used as collateral include buildings, machinery, and company-owned stocks and bonds.

The most difficult kind of loan to get from a bank or other financial institution is an unsecured loan. An **unsecured loan** doesn't require the borrower to offer the lending institution any collateral to obtain the loan. In other words, the loan is not backed by any specific assets. Normally, a lender will give unsecured loans only to highly regarded customers (e.g., long-standing customers or customers considered financially stable).

**unsecured loan**
A loan that's not backed by any specific assets.

If a business develops a good relationship with a bank, the bank may open a line of credit for the firm. A **line of credit** is a given amount of unsecured short-term funds a bank will lend to a business, provided the bank has the funds readily available. In other words, a line of credit is not guaranteed to a business; however, a line of credit can speed up the borrowing process so that a firm does not have to go through the hassle of applying for a new loan every time it needs funds. Generally, the funds requested are available as long as the credit limit set by the bank is not exceeded. As businesses mature and become more financially secure, the amount of credit often is increased. Some firms will even apply for a **revolving credit agreement**, which is a line of credit that's guaranteed. However, banks usually charge a fee for guaranteeing such an agreement. Both lines of credit and revolving credit agreements are particularly good sources of funds for unexpected cash needs.

**line of credit**
A given amount of unsecured short-term funds a bank will lend to a business, provided the funds are readily available.

**revolving credit agreement**
A line of credit that is guaranteed by the bank.

If a business is unable to secure a short-term loan from a bank, the financial manager may seek short-term funds from **commercial finance companies**. These non-deposit-type organizations make short-term loans to borrowers who offer tangible assets (e.g., property, plant, and equipment) as collateral. Since commercial finance companies are willing to accept higher degrees of risk than commercial banks, they usually charge higher interest rates than banks. Commercial finance companies often make loans to businesses that cannot get funds elsewhere. General Electric Capital Corporation is the largest commercial finance company in the United States, with $425 billion in assets; GE Capital Corporation has operations in 47 countries around the world.[23]

**commercial finance companies**
Organizations that make short-term loans to borrowers who offer tangible assets as collateral.

## Factoring Accounts Receivable

One relatively expensive source of short-term funds for a firm is **factoring**, which is the process of selling accounts receivable for cash. Factoring dates as far back as 4,000 years, during the days of ancient Babylon. Today, the Internet can help a firm find factors quickly so that they can solicit bids on the firm's accounts receivable promptly.[24] Here's how factoring works: Let's say that a firm sells many of its products on credit to consumers and other businesses, creating a number of accounts receivable. Some of the buyers may be slow in paying their bills, causing the firm to have a large amount of money due to it. A *factor* is a market intermediary (usually a financial institution like a commercial bank) that agrees to buy the firm's accounts receivable, at a discount, for cash. The discount rate charged depends on the age of the accounts receivable, the nature of the business, and the condition of the economy. The factor collects and keeps the money that was owed the firm when it collects the accounts receivable.

**factoring**
The process of selling accounts receivable for cash.

REACHING BEYOND

www.factoring.org

our borders

## Guaranteeing That the Deal Gets Done

With over 6 billion potential customers on planet Earth, the lure of global markets is just too enticing for businesses to ignore. Unfortunately, the path of would-be exporters is often blocked by financing constraints such as the complications of trading in foreign currencies and difficulty in collecting money owed from global accounts. Combine these financing challenges with political instability, high loan defaults, threats of terrorism, and unstable currencies, and the prospects of doing business globally look iffy at best. This shaky global environment requires U.S. companies to use creative financing methods such as international factoring (also called forfeiting) for protection in global markets. International factoring involves negotiating with intermediaries who make sure the payment for products gets from the foreign buyer back to the seller.

There are four parties involved in an international factoring transaction: the exporter (the seller), the U.S. factor (called the export factor), the foreign factor (called the import factor), and the importer (the buyer). It works like this: The exporter and the export factor sign a factoring agreement that transfers the exporter's accounts receivable to the U.S. factor in exchange for coverage against any credit losses that could be incurred globally. In other words, the export factor guarantees the exporter that it will receive the money it is owed (minus fees, of course). The export factor selects an import factor to act on the seller's behalf under the export factor's supervision. The import factor assists in finding local customers in global markets to whom the seller can sell its goods or services.

When an exporter receives an order from a customer, the import factor collects payment from the global buyer. The import factor deducts a fee and gives the remainder to the export factor. The export factor deducts a fee and gives that remainder to the selling company (exporter). Complicated? Yes, but by using these agreements U.S. exporters can do business even in risky global markets without the risk of suffering significant credit losses. Today, international factoring accounts for almost $1 trillion in global trade.

Sources: Michael Rudnick, "Shift Abroad Keeps Fueling Import-Factoring Demand," *Home Furnishing Network*, August 15, 2005, and Lisa Casabona, "Origins of Factoring Come Full Circle," *WWD*, September 19, 2005.

Even though factoring can be an expensive way of raising cash, it is popular among small businesses.[25] Factoring can also be used by large firms. Macy's, the department store chain, for example, used factoring during its reorganization several years ago. Factoring is common in the clothing and furniture businesses, and it is popular in financing growing numbers of global trade ventures.[26] The Reaching Beyond Our Borders box explains how firms use factoring to reduce the risk of selling products in global markets. What's important for you to note is that factoring is not a loan; factoring is the sale of an asset (accounts receivable). And while it's true that discount rates charged by factors are usually higher than loan rates charged by lending institutions, remember that many small businesses cannot qualify for a loan. A company can reduce the cost of factoring if it agrees to reimburse the factor for slow-paying accounts, and it can reduce costs even further if it assumes the risk of those customers who don't pay at all.

## Commercial Paper

**commercial paper**
Unsecured promissory notes of $100,000 and up that mature (come due) in 270 days or less.

Sometimes a large corporation needs funds for just a few months and wants to get lower rates of interest than those charged by banks. One strategy is to sell commercial paper. **Commercial paper** consists of *unsecured* promissory notes, in amounts of $100,000 and up, that mature (come due) in 270 days or less. Commercial paper states a fixed amount of money the business agrees to repay to the lender (investor) on a specific date. The interest rate is stated in the agreement.

Still, because commercial paper is unsecured, only financially stable firms (mainly large corporations with excellent credit reputations) are able

Jennifer Elias and Julie Tucker, Founders, SmartsCo
On a wintry night last year, SmartsCo, a publisher of party games, received a frantic call. A retailer needed stock overnight for a holiday event. So Jen and Julie packed their cars and hand-delivered it. "Likewise," says Jen, "when we sorely needed better cash flow, American Express cared enough to make sure we got it."
OPEN ARMS
OPEN
HOW AMERICAN EXPRESS SERVES SMALL BUSINESS


Ever had a great idea for a new business but unfortunately the financial cupboard was bare? Welcome to the world of the entrepreneur. It's difficult for small businesses to secure financing from commercial banks or other financial institutions. That's why many small business owners are turning to credit cards to finance their formation or first-level expansion. However, credit cards are an expensive way to borrow money and should be used only as a last resort.

to sell it. For these companies it's a way to get short-term funds quickly and for less than the interest charged by commercial banks. Since most commercial paper matures in 30 to 90 days, it's also an investment opportunity for buyers who can afford to put up cash for short periods to earn some interest on their money.

## Credit Cards

Letitia Mulzac seemed to have things going her way as she planned to open an imported gift and furniture shop. She had chosen a great location and lined up reliable business contacts in India, Indonesia, and Morocco. Unfortunately, she didn't have enough money in her savings to start the business.[27] She did, however, have a Small Business Credit Card with a high credit limit from American Express. According to the National Small Business Association, about half of all small businesses like Mulzac's finance their formation or first-level expansion with credit cards. Credit cards provide a readily available line of credit to a business that can save time and the likely embarrassment of being rejected for a bank loan.[28] Of course, in contrast to the convenience credit cards offer, they are extremely risky and costly. For example, interest rates can be exorbitant. There are also considerable penalties users must pay if they fail to make their payments on time. Credit cards are an expensive way to borrow money and are probably best used as a last resort. After checking your progress, we will look into long-term financing options.

### progress assessment

- What does the term *2/10, net 30* mean?
- What's the difference between trade credit and a line of credit at a bank?
- What's the difference between a secured loan and an unsecured loan?
- What is factoring? What are some of the considerations involved in establishing a discount rate in factoring?

# OBTAINING LONG-TERM FINANCING

Forecasting helps the firm to develop a financial plan. This plan specifies the amount of funding the firm will need over various time periods and the most appropriate sources for obtaining those funds. In setting long-term financing objectives, finance managers generally ask three questions:

1. What are the organization's long-term goals and objectives?
2. What are the financial requirements needed to achieve long-term goals and objectives?
3. What sources of long-term capital are available, and which will best fit our needs?

In business, long-term capital is used to buy expensive assets such as plant and equipment, to develop new products, and to finance expansion of the organization. In major corporations, decisions involving long-term financing normally involve the board of directors and top management, as well as finance and accounting managers. Take pharmaceutical giant Pfizer, for example. Pfizer spends over $8 billion a year researching and developing new products.[29] The actual development of a new innovative medicine can sometimes take 10 years and cost close to $1 billion in company funds before the product is ever introduced in the market. It's easy to see why long-term financing decisions involve high-level managers at Pfizer. In small- and medium-sized businesses, it's also obvious that the owners are always actively involved in analyzing long-term financing opportunities that affect their company.

As we noted earlier in the chapter, long-term funding comes from two major types of financing, debt financing or equity financing. Let's look at these two sources of long-term financing next.

## Debt Financing

Debt financing involves borrowing money that the company has a legal obligation to repay. Firms can borrow funds by either getting a loan from a lending institution or possibly issuing bonds.

**Debt Financing by Borrowing Money from Lending Institutions** Firms that establish and develop rapport with a bank, insurance company, pension fund, commercial finance company, or other financial institution often are able to secure a long-term loan. Long-term loans are usually repaid within 3 to 7 years but may extend to 15 or 20 years. For such loans, a business must sign what is called a term-loan agreement. A **term-loan agreement** is a promissory note that requires the borrower to repay the loan in specified installments (e.g., monthly or yearly). A major advantage of using this type of financing is that the interest paid on the long-term debt is tax deductible.

**term-loan agreement**
A promissory note that requires the borrower to repay the loan in specified installments.

Because long-term loans involve larger amounts of funding than short-term loans, they are generally more expensive to the firm than short-term loans are. Also, since the repayment period could be quite long, lenders are not assured that their capital will be repaid in full. Therefore, most long-term loans require collateral, which may be in the form of real estate, machinery, equipment, company stock, or other items of value. Lenders may also require certain restrictions on a firm's operations to force it to act responsibly in its business practices. The interest rate for long-term loans is based on the adequacy of collateral, the firm's credit rating, and the general level of market interest rates. The greater the risk a lender takes in making a

Major League Baseball is big business; building a new stadium is big dollars. When the St. Louis Cardinals needed financing to replace their old stadium with a new state-of-the-art facility, they turned to the community for help. St. Louis County responded by issuing bonds that helped finance the construction of the new home of the Cardinals. Go Cards!

loan, the higher the rate of interest a lender requires. This principle is known as the **risk/return trade-off**.

**risk/return trade-off**
The principle that the greater the risk a lender takes in making a loan, the higher the interest rate required.

**Debt Financing by Issuing Bonds** If an organization is unable to obtain its long-term financing needs by getting a loan from a lending institution, it may try to issue bonds. A bond is a long-term debt obligation of a corporation or government. Figure 18.5 on page 502 lists the organizations that can issue bonds. To put it simply, a bond is like an IOU with a promise to repay the amount borrowed on a certain date. To be more specific, a bond is a binding contract through which the organization issuing the bond agrees to specific terms with investors in return for the money those investors lend to the company. The terms of the agreement in a bond issue are referred to as the **indenture terms**.

**indenture terms**
The terms of agreement in a bond issue.

You are probably somewhat familiar with bonds. For example, you may own investments like U.S. government savings bonds, or perhaps you have volunteered your time to help a local school district pass a bond issue. Maybe your community is building a new stadium or cultural center that requires selling bonds. It's fair to say that businesses compete with the government when issuing bonds. Potential investors (individuals and institutions) in bonds measure the risk involved in purchasing a bond against the return (interest) the bond promises to pay and the company's ability to repay the bond when promised.

Like other forms of long-term debt, bonds can be secured or unsecured. A **secured bond** is issued with some form of collateral, such as real estate, equipment, or other pledged assets. If the bond's indenture terms are violated, the bondholder can issue a claim on the collateral. An **unsecured bond** (called a debenture bond) is a bond backed only by the reputation of the issuer. Investors in such bonds simply trust that the organization issuing the bond will make good on its financial commitments. Bonds are a key means of long-term financing for many organizations. They can also be valuable investments for private individuals or institutions. Given this importance, we will discuss bonds more in depth in Chapter 19.

**secured bond**
A bond issued with some form of collateral.

**unsecured bond**
A bond backed only by the reputation of the issuer; also called a debenture bond.

figure 18.5

**WHO CAN ISSUE BONDS?**

Source: *The Wall Street Journal Guide to Money and Markets.*

1. Federal, state, and local governments

2. Federal government agencies

3. Corporations

4. Foreign governments and corporations

## Equity Financing

If a firm cannot obtain a long-term loan from a lending institution, or if it is unable to sell bonds to investors, it may look for long-term funding from equity financing. Equity financing comes from the owners of the firm. Therefore, equity financing involves selling ownership in the firm in the form of stock, or using earnings that have been retained by the company to reinvest in the business (retained earnings). A business can also seek equity financing by selling ownership in the firm to venture capitalists. Figure 18.6 compares debt and equity financing options.

**Equity Financing by Selling Stock** Regardless of whether or not a firm can obtain debt financing, there usually comes a time when it needs additional funds. One way to obtain such funds is to sell ownership shares (called *stock*) in the firm to private investors. The key word to remember here is *ownership*.

figure 18.6

**DIFFERENCES BETWEEN DEBT AND EQUITY FINANCING**

| | Type of Financing | |
|---|---|---|
| **CONDITIONS** | **DEBT** | **EQUITY** |
| Management influence | There's usually none unless special conditions have been agreed on. | Common stockholders have voting rights. |
| Repayment | Debt has a maturity date. | Stock has no maturity date. |
| | Principal must be repaid. | The company is never required to repay equity |
| Yearly obligations | Payment of interest is a contractual obligation. | The firm isn't legally liable to pay dividends. |
| Tax benefits | Interest is tax deductible. | Dividends are paid from after-tax income and aren't deductible. |

The purchasers of stock become owners in the organization. The number of shares of stock that will be available for purchase is generally decided by the corporation's board of directors. The first time a company offers to sell its stock to the general public is called an *initial public offering (IPO).* (IPOs are discussed further in Chapter 19.)

Selling stock to the public to obtain funds is by no means easy or automatic. U.S. companies can issue stock for public purchase only if they meet requirements set by the Securities and Exchange Commission (SEC) as well as by various state agencies.[30] Companies can issue different types of stock, such as common and preferred stock. Both types of stock ownership (common and preferred) are discussed further in Chapter 19.

**Equity Financing from Retained Earnings** Have you ever heard a businessperson say that he or she reinvests the firm's profits right back into the business? You probably remember from Chapter 17 that the profits the company keeps and reinvests in the firm are called *retained earnings*. Retained earnings often are a major source of long-term funds, especially for small businesses, which have fewer financing alternatives, such as selling bonds or stock, than large businesses do. However, large corporations also depend on retained earnings for needed long-term funding. In fact, retained earnings are usually the most favored source of meeting long-term capital needs since a company that uses them saves interest payments, dividends (payments for investing in stock), and any possible underwriting fees for issuing bonds or stock. Also, if a firm uses retained earnings, there is no new ownership created in the firm, as occurs with selling stock.

Unfortunately, many organizations do not have sufficient retained earnings on hand to finance extensive capital improvements or business expansion. If you think about it for a moment, it makes sense. What if you wanted to buy an expensive personal asset such as a new car? The ideal way to purchase the car would be to go to your personal savings account and take out the necessary cash. No hassle! No interest! Unfortunately, few people have such large amounts of cash available. Most businesses are no different. Even though they would like to finance long-term needs from operations, few have the resources on hand to accomplish this.

**Equity Financing from Venture Capital** The hardest time for a business to raise money is when it is just starting or moving into early stages of expansion. A start-up business typically has few assets and no market track record, so the chances of borrowing significant amounts of money from a bank are slim. **Venture capital** is money that is invested in new or emerging companies that are perceived as having great profit potential. Venture capital has helped dozens of firms—such as Intel, Apple Computer, and Cisco Systems—get started. Venture capital firms are a potential source of start-up capital for new companies or companies moving into expanding stages of business.

**venture capital**
Money that is invested in new or emerging companies that are perceived as having great profit potential.

The venture capital industry originally began as an alternative investment vehicle for wealthy families. The Rockefeller family, for example (whose vast fortune came from John D. Rockefeller's Standard Oil Company, started in the 19th century), financed Sanford McDonnell when he was operating his company from an airplane hangar. That small venture grew into McDonnell Douglas, a large aerospace and defense contractor that merged with Boeing Corporation in 1997. The venture capital industry grew significantly in the 1980s, when many high-tech companies such as Intel and Apple were being started. In the 1990s the industry grew immensely, especially in high-tech centers such as California's Silicon Valley, where venture capitalists concentrated primarily on Internet-related companies. In the early 2000s, however, problems in the technology industry and the slowdown in the overall economy reduced venture capital expenditures considerably. Today, venture capitalists are treading cautiously and holding companies to strict standards before investing their capital.[31]

An entrepreneur or finance manager must remember that venture capitalists invest in a business in return for part ownership of the business. Venture capitalists admit that they expect higher-than-average returns and competent management performance for their investment. Therefore, a start-up company has to be careful when choosing a venture capital firm. The dangers of financing with venture capitalists can be illustrated by the experience of Jon Birck, who started Northwest Instrument Systems with venture capital money. Birck worked until 11:00 or 12:00 each night to build the company. After having dedicated three years to the company, he was asked to leave by the venture capital firm, which wanted a more experienced chief executive officer to protect its investment. Birck had left a secure job, put his marriage on the line, taken out a second mortgage on his house, and given himself a below-average salary to get Northwest on its feet; then, just when the firm was ready for rapid growth, he was asked to resign.

As this story shows, financing a firm's long-term needs through venture capital can involve a high degree of risk. Still, it's obvious there are risks whenever firms borrow funds. Knowing this, you might be inclined to ask: Why do firms borrow funds at all? Why not just use the other forms of equity funding, especially selling stock? The reason involves the use of leverage (debt). Next, let's look briefly at why companies use leverage.

**leverage**
Raising needed funds through borrowing to increase a firm's rate of return.

## Making Decisions on Using Financial Leverage

Raising needed funds through borrowing to increase the firm's rate of return is referred to as **leverage**. While it's true that debt increases the risk of the firm, it also enhances the firm's ability to increase profits. Remember, two key jobs of the finance manager or chief financial officer (CFO) are to forecast the need for borrowed funds and to plan how to manage these funds once they are obtained.

**cost of capital**
The rate of return a company must earn in order to meet the demands of its lenders and expectations of its equity holders.

Firms are concerned with the cost of capital. **Cost of capital** is the rate of return a company must earn in order to meet the demands of its lenders and expectations of its equity holders (stockholders or venture capitalists). If the firm's earnings are larger than the interest payments on the funds borrowed, business owners can realize a higher rate of return than if they used equity financing. Figure 18.7 describes an example involving our vegetarian restaurant, Very Vegetarian (introduced in Chapter 13). If Very Vegetarian needed $500,000 in financing, it could consider selling bonds (debt) or stock (equity) to raise funds. Comparing the two options in this situation, you can see that

figure 18.7

**USING LEVERAGE VERSUS EQUITY FINANCING**

Very Vegetarian needs to raise $500,000; compare its two options for doing so.

| OPTION A | | OPTION B | |
|---|---|---|---|
| Raise 10% by selling stock (equity); raise 90% by issuing bonds (debt). | | Raise 100% by selling stock (equity). | |
| Common stock | $ 50,000 | Common stock | $500,000 |
| Bonds (@ 10% interest) | 450,000 | | |
| | $500,000 | | $500,000 |
| Earnings | $ 125,000 | Earnings | $ 125,000 |
| Less bond interest | 45,000 | | |
| Net earnings/income | $ 80,000 | Net earnings/income | $ 125,000 |
| Return to stockholders | $\frac{\$80,000}{\$50,000} = 160\%$ | Return to stockholders | $\frac{\$125,000}{\$500,000} = 25\%$ |

Very Vegetarian would benefit by selling bonds since the company's earnings are greater than the interest paid on borrowed funds (bonds). However, if the firm's earnings were less than the interest paid on borrowed funds (bonds), the owners could lose money on their investment. It's also important to remember that bonds, like all debt, have to be repaid at a specific time.

Normally, it's up to each individual firm to determine exactly how to balance debt and equity financing. For example, Trump Hotels and Casino deals with billions of dollars of debt in financing its operations. In contrast, chewing-gum maker Wm. Wrigley Jr. Company carried no long-term debt until it issued bonds to help finance the company's purchase of Kraft Food's candy business in 2005.[32] Leverage ratios (which we discussed in Chapter 17) give companies a standard of the comparative leverage of firms in their industries. According to Standard & Poor's and Moody's Investor Services (firms that provide corporate and financial research), the debt of a large industrial corporation typically ranges between 33 and 40 percent of its total assets. Small-business debt varies considerably.

As the requirements of financial institutions become more stringent and investors more demanding, it's certain that the job of the finance manager will become more challenging. Chapter 19 takes a closer look at bonds (debt) and stocks (equity) both as financing tools for businesses and as investment options for private investors. You will learn about bond and stock issues, the securities exchanges, how to buy and sell stock, how to choose the right investment strategy, how to read stock and bond quotations, and more. Finance takes on a whole new dimension when you see how you can participate in financial markets yourself.

### progress assessment

- What are the two major forms of debt financing available to a firm?
- How does debt financing differ from equity financing?
- What are the major forms of equity financing available to a firm?
- What is leverage, and why would firms choose to use it?

## summary

1. Finance is that function in a business responsible for acquiring funds for the firm, managing funds within the firm (e.g., preparing budgets and doing cash flow analysis), and planning for the expenditure of funds on various assets.
   - **What are the most common ways firms fail financially?**

   The most common financial problems are (1) undercapitalization, (2) poor control over cash flow, and (3) inadequate expense control.
   - **What do financial managers do?**

   Financial managers plan, budget, control funds, obtain funds, collect funds, audit, manage taxes, and advise top management on financial matters.

**1.** Describe the importance of finance and financial management to an organization, and explain the responsibilities of financial managers.

2. Financial planning involves forecasting short- and long-term needs, budgeting, and establishing financial controls.
   - **What are the three budgets of finance?**

   The capital budget is the spending plan for expensive assets such as property, plant, and equipment. The cash budget is the projected cash balance

**2.** Outline the financial planning process, and explain the three key budgets in the financial plan.

at the end of a given period. The operating (master) budget summarizes the information in the other two budgets; it projects dollar allocations to various costs and expenses given various revenues.

**3.** Explain the major reasons why firms need operating funds, and identify various types of financing that can be used to obtain those funds.

3. During the course of a business's life, its financial needs shift considerably.
   - **What are the major financial needs for firms?**

   Businesses have financial needs in four major areas: (1) managing day-by-day needs of the business, (2) controlling credit operations, (3) acquiring needed inventory, and (4) making capital expenditures.
   - **What's the difference between debt financing and equity financing?**

   Debt financing refers to funds raised by borrowing (going into debt), whereas equity financing is raised from within the firm (through retained earnings) or by selling ownership in the company by issuing stock or selling ownership to venture capitalists.
   - **What's the difference between short-term and long-term financing?**

   Short-term financing refers to funds that will be repaid in less than one year, whereas long-term financing refers to funds that will be repaid over a specific time period of more than one year.

**4.** Identify and describe different sources of short-term financing.

4. Sources of short-term financing include trade credit, promissory notes, family and friends, commercial banks and other financial institutions, factoring, commercial paper, and credit cards.
   - **Why should businesses use trade credit?**

   Trade credit is the least expensive and most convenient form of short-term financing. Businesses can buy goods today and pay for them sometime in the future.
   - **What's a line of credit?**

   It is an agreement by a bank to lend a specified amount of money to the business at any time, if the money is available. A revolving credit agreement is a line of credit that guarantees a loan will be available—for a fee.
   - **What's the difference between a secured loan and an unsecured loan?**

   An unsecured loan has no collateral backing it. Secured loans have collateral backed by assets such as accounts receivable, inventory, or other property of value.
   - **Is factoring a form of secured loan?**

   No, factoring means selling accounts receivable at a discounted rate to a factor (an intermediary that pays cash for those accounts).
   - **What's commercial paper?**

   Commercial paper is a corporation's unsecured promissory note maturing in 270 days or less.

**5.** Identify and describe different sources of long-term financing.

5. One of the important functions of a finance manager is to obtain long-term financing.
   - **What are the major sources of long-term financing?**

   Debt financing involves the sale of bonds and long-term loans from banks and other financial institutions. Equity financing is obtained through the sale of company stock, from the firm's retained earnings, or from venture capital firms.
   - **What are the two major forms of debt financing?**

   Debt financing comes from two sources: selling bonds and borrowing from individuals, banks, and other financial institutions. Bonds can be secured by some form of collateral or can be unsecured. The same is true of loans.
   - **What's leverage, and how do firms use it?**

   Leverage is raising funds from borrowing. It involves the use of borrowed funds to invest in such undertakings as expansion, major asset purchases, and research and development. Firms measure the risk of borrowing (leverage) against the potential for higher profits.

## key terms

budget 488
capital budget 488
capital expenditures 493
cash budget 488
cash flow forecast 488
commercial finance companies 497
commercial paper 498
cost of capital 504
debt financing 493
equity financing 493
factoring 497
finance 484
financial control 489
financial management 484
financial managers 484
indenture terms 501
leverage 504
line of credit 497
long-term financing 493
long-term forecast 488
operating budget (master budget) 489
promissory note 495
revolving credit agreement 497
risk/return trade-off 501
secured bond 501
secured loan 496
short-term financing 493
short-term forecast 488
term-loan agreement 500
trade credit 494
unsecured bond 501
unsecured loan 497
venture capital 503

## critical thinking questions

1. What sources of short-term funds would a new business owner be most likely to count on in trying to grow his or her business? What sources of long-term funds?

2. Why is it necessary for a finance manager to understand accounting information if the firm has a trained accountant on its staff?

3. Why do firms generally prefer to borrow funds rather than issue shares of stock to obtain long-term financing?

## developing workplace skills

1. Visit the Web site Bankrate.com. Check the current interest rate; then see what rate small businesses would pay for short-term and long-term loans. See what forms borrowers use to apply for loans that are available from Bankrate.com. Share these forms with your class and explain what type of information the bank is seeking.
2. Go to your college's Web site and see if the college's operating budget is online. If not, go to the campus library and see if the reference librarian has a copy of your college's operating budget for the current year. Try to identify major capital expenditures planned at your college for the future.
3. One of the most difficult concepts to get across to small-business owners is the need to take all the trade credit they can get. For example, we know that credit terms 2/10, net 30 can save businesses more than 36 percent a year if they pay their bills in the first 10 days. Work with a group of classmates to build a convincing argument of the benefits of using this concept.

4. Go online and check the financial requirements needed to open a franchise of your choice (e.g., Subway, McDonald's.) You can also go to the library and use a copy of the *Franchise Opportunities Handbook* as a resource. Check out the capitalization requirements for the franchise and see if the franchisor offers financial assistance to prospective franchisees. Evaluate the cost of the franchise versus its business potential using the risk/return trade-off.
5. Contact a lending officer at a local bank in your community or visit the bank's Web site and check the bank's policies on providing a business a line of credit and a revolving line of credit? Evaluate the potential of a small business receiving either form of short-term loan.

## taking it to the net

### Purpose

To learn how small-business owners can obtain equity financing by finding investors willing to buy a stake in their companies.

### Exercise

When it comes to finding equity capital, many small-business owners have a difficult time finding investors. The Access to Capital Electronic Network (ACE-Net) is an Internet-based listing service developed by the Small Business Administration that allows entrepreneurs to present information about their small, growing company to venture capitalists and institutional and accredited individual investors across the country. ACE-Net encourages entrepreneurs who meet certain criteria to list their businesses and then makes their listing available to qualified investors. Go to http://activecapital.org/entrepreneurs_enroll and see if the following businesses qualify for participation on ACE-Net:

1. Growing Like a Weed is a lawn care service business organized as a limited liability company. It needs $25,000 to buy additional equipment in order to expand. Does it meet ACE-Net's listing criteria? Why or why not?
2. Allied Technology is a corporation that produces computer chips. It needs $6 million to build a new manufacturing plant. Does it meet ACE-Net's listing criteria? Why or why not?
3. Bells'n Whistles is a pinball refurbishing company. Partners Merv and Marv need $300,000 to buy inventory. Do they meet ACE-Net's listing criteria? Why or why not?
4. Lettuce Entertain You is a corporation that needs $500,000 to remodel an old warehouse to house its latest restaurant. Does it meet ACE-Net's listing criteria? Why or why not?

## casing the web

To access the case *"Survival Financially in the Nonprofit World,"* visit **www.mhhe.com/ub8e**

video case

## It's My Money

Entrepreneurs tend to be an independent bunch of people, but few are as independently minded as Todd McFarlane. He started out working for others as a cartoonist and eventually started his own firm. Now he focuses more on making toys; that is, collectibles of sports personalities, musicians, movie heroes, and the like. You can see in the video that McFarlane takes a rather casual approach to business. That doesn't mean, however, that he is not constantly aware of his need for financing. Nor does it mean that he doesn't know everything he needs to know about financing options.

Of course, the number one financing option is to put up your own money. The advantage of doing that is that no one can tell you what to do. And that means a lot to McFarlane. But usually your own money won't pay for everything that you need. In that case, you have to go out to the banks and other sources to get funding. It helps to have a financial expert on board to help determine what funds are needed, to budget those funds, and to keep track of spending. Steve Peterson is that guy at McFarlane. Nonetheless, McFarlane has trained himself to be able to read the reports and keep track of everything that's going on in the finance area. All entrepreneurs could learn from that.

McFarlane knows that it is easy to spend too much money on something—and to lose lots of money in the bargain. That means being wise in both long-term and short-term financing. Usually McFarlane stays away from investors, but that isn't possible when funding a major project like a movie. Furthermore, when you get into ownership financing, you also lose some control over the project. Normally, McFarlane doesn't like to lose such control, but in some cases, like making a cartoon movie, that is necessary.

One way to keep loan costs down is to be a good customer of the bank. If you pay your loans back in time, you can get lower interest rates. But McFarlane also knows the benefit of having a budget and sticking to it. That's as true in your personal finances as it is in business. If you make $25,000, you need to spend less than $25,000. And if you make a million dollars, you have to spend less than a million dollars. It's the same principle.

Sometimes people spend money for a passion. In McFarlane's case, that means baseball. He once paid several million dollars for a home-run ball hit by one of the home-run leaders. The problem was that he didn't remain the leader very long, and the ball was not worth nearly as much money. So? The publicity that McFarlane got for buying the ball—and losing millions—made up for the loss. It earned him licensing agreements with many ball clubs, and the right to make the images he sells. He expects to make millions from the investment in the long run.

So, what do you do with your money when you have millions more than you need? For McFarlane, it means giving money to the ALS Association, the one that fights Lou Gehrig's disease. Again, the publicity that McFarlane gets from investing in home-run balls attracts more donors to the cause.

So, what can we learn from this video? You learn that every entrepreneur needs to understand finance to be successful in the long run. You can be as casual as you want about business, but, when it comes to finance, you better know what you're doing. And the money you make is yours to spend. You can have a good time buying what you want, but you can also make a difference in the world by helping some cause to raise money.

### Thinking It Over

1. Why do you suppose a free thinker like McFarlane tries to avoid getting other investors involved in his business? What is the advantage, in this instance, of debt financing?
2. What is the advantage of having a "line of credit" at the bank? What can a business do to keep loan charges at a minimum?
3. Do businesspeople have a special obligation to give some of their money to charity? What famous businesspeople have been in the news because of their giving? Should others follow their example?

# securities markets

## Financing and Investing Opportunities

profile

Getting to Know

X Jim Cramer

The Mad Man of Wall Street

When the stock market was skyrocketing in the late 1990s, television sets across the country were tuned in to financial channels such as CNBC. It seemed that everywhere you looked there was a TV screen with stock quotes scrolling across the bottom as the latest stock gurus touted the hottest stocks. These stock "experts" included players from all edges of the market: CEOs, CFOs, stock analysts, and financial advisors of every kind. Many of these commentators had a style you might expect from professional businesspeople (i.e., formal, deliberate, dry) as they droned on about their view of their businesses or the market in general.

In March 2005, a new image came on the scene as Jim Cramer began hosting the investment show *Mad Money*. Cramer doesn't drone; rather, he declaims, he rants, he yells, and he screams. He recommends some stocks and he trashes others. He throws chairs, computer keyboards, water bottles. He uses a sound effects board to produce applause, raspberries, babies crying, truck noises, or "The Stars and Stripes Forever" to underline some point. His antics are circus-like, but attention-getting. His frenetic pace pulls in callers to his "Lightning Round," during which he shouts out opinions on stocks suggested by the callers who usually greet him with "Booyah, Jim!"

In some ways Cramer's life leading up to *Mad Money* was as wild as his act on the show. He graduated from Harvard in 1977 and worked as a reporter for several newspapers. He hit bottom after his home was burglarized and his checking account was wiped out. He ended up homeless and lived in his beat-up Ford Fairmont for seven months.

Friends and family helped him get back on his feet. In 1981, he entered Harvard Law School and graduated in 1984. It was during law school that Cramer's love of stock trading reignited. As a kid he had memorized ticker symbols and had built a fantasy stock portfolio. While at Harvard, Cramer began trading for real, using money he earned working as a researcher for a law professor. The more he traded, the more excited he became about the market. He even left stock tips on his answering machine: "I'm not here right now. Take a look at . . ., which has a good business model." After following a few of those stock tips, a friend asked him to manage a $500,000 portfolio. In two years, the portfolio had gained $150,000.

Cramer's prowess led to a position as a broker for the prestigious Goldman Sachs. In 1987, Cramer and partner Jeff Berkowitz formed the hedge fund Cramer Berkowitz, which was so successful that Cramer routinely made $10 million or more a year. But success like that frequently comes at a cost.

LEARNING goals

**After you have read and studied this chapter, you should be able to**

1. Identify and explain the functions of securities markets, and discuss the role of investment bankers.
2. Compare the advantages and disadvantages of debt financing by issuing bonds, and identify the classes and features of bonds.
3. Compare the advantages and disadvantages of equity financing by issuing stock, and explain the differences between common and preferred stock.
4. Describe the various stock exchanges where securities are traded.
5. Explain how to invest in securities markets and various investment objectives such as long-term growth, income, cash, and protection from inflation.
6. Analyze the opportunities bonds offer as investments.
7. Explain the opportunities stocks offer as investments.
8. Explain the opportunities in mutual funds and exchange-traded funds (ETFs) as investments, and the benefits of diversifying investments.
9. Discuss specific high-risk investments, including junk bonds, buying stock on margin, and commodity trading.
10. Explain securities quotations listed in the financial section of a newspaper, and describe how stock market indicators like the Dow Jones Industrial Average affect the market.

CHAPTER 19

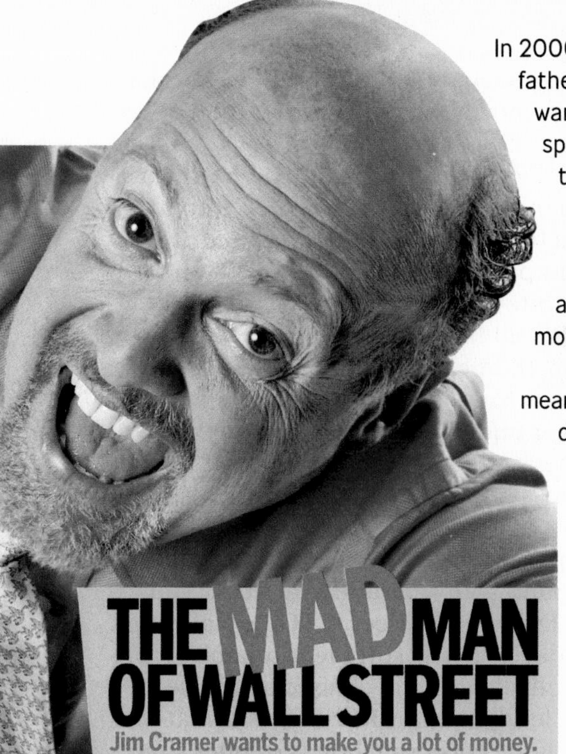

THE MAD MAN OF WALL STREET
Jim Cramer wants to make you a lot of money. He's got plenty himself, so why does he bother?
BY ROBEN FARZAD


In 2000, Cramer's wife, father, and daughter warned him he was spending too much time on the fund. He sold out to his partner and began to plan around his family more.

But that doesn't mean Cramer slowed down much. He wrote three books. He co-founded the online investment site TheStreet.com and wrote a column for it. He wrote columns for SmartMoney.com and for *New York* magazine. He had a daily syndicated radio show. He was a commentator on a CNBC program called *Squawk Box* and was Cramer on *Kudlow and Cramer*, a news interview show. He was the subject of a *BusinessWeek* cover story and a *Sixty Minutes* profile on CBS.

Despite the chaotic look of *Mad Money*, Cramer's intentions are serious. "I want people to understand the stocks they own, understand things like dividends. . . . I approach this with as much rigor as I can," he says. "But you have to make this stuff come alive, or no one will watch." Some of his critics don't agree with his approach, but others are willing to listen. Says Scot Rothbort of Seton Hall University's Stillman School of Business, "You have to filter out some of the histrionics, but if you listen carefully, his message is to do your homework."

Sources: Charles Gasparino, "The 'Mad' Money Man," *Newsweek*, March 21, 2005; Matthew Futterman, "Who Is This Jim Cramer, and Why Is He Yelling at You?," *Syracuse Post-Standard*, October 16, 2005; Alan T. Saracevic, "Taking Stock of Jim Cramer's 'Mad Money' Picks," *San Francisco Chronicle*, July 31, 2005; David Kadlec, "Stock-Raving Mad," *Time*, August 15, 2005; Roben Farzad, "The Mad Man of Wall Street," *BusinessWeek*, October 31, 2005; and Miriam Hill, "'Mad Money' Host Turns Financial Show Conventions on Their Head," *Philadelphia Inquirer*, January 19, 2006.

## THE FUNCTION OF SECURITIES MARKETS

Securities markets, such as the New York Stock Exchange (NYSE) and the NASDAQ (pronounced *nazz-dak*), are financial marketplaces for stocks and bonds. These institutions serve two major functions: First, they assist businesses in finding long-term funding to finance capital needs, such as beginning operations, expanding their businesses, or buying major goods and services. Second, they provide private investors a place to buy and sell securities (investments)—such as stocks, bonds, and mutual funds—that can help them build their financial future. In this chapter, we will look at securities markets such as the NYSE and the NASDAQ from the perspectives of both businesses and private investors.

**initial public offering (IPO)** The first public offering of a corporation's stock.

Securities markets are divided into primary and secondary markets. *Primary markets* handle the sale of *new* securities. This is an important point to understand. Corporations make money on the sale of their securities only once—when they are first sold on the primary market. The first public offering of a corporation's stock is called an **initial public offering (IPO)**. After that, the *secondary market* handles the trading of securities between investors, with the proceeds of a sale going to the investor selling the stock, not to the corporation whose stock is sold. For example, imagine that your vegetarian business has grown into a chain of restaurants and that your products are now available in many retail stores throughout the country. You would like to raise money to expand further. If you, the owner of Very Vegetarian, offer 1 million shares of stock in your company at $10 a share, you would raise $10 million at this initial offering. However, if Shareholder Jones sells 100 shares of her Very Vegetarian stock to Investor Smith, Very Vegetarian collects nothing from this transaction. Smith bought the stock from Jones, not from Very Vegetarian. However, it's possible for companies like Very Vegetarian to offer additional shares of stock to raise additional capital.

David and Tom Gardner, the Motley Fools, are passionate to spread the message that securities markets can provide opportunities for all. The brothers have built their careers on providing quality financial information to investors—regardless of education or income. Visit their Web site at www.fool.com for more information.

As Chapter 18 implied, the importance of long-term funding to businesses can't be overemphasized. Unfortunately, many new companies start without sufficient capital, and many established firms fail to do adequate long-term financial planning. If given a choice, businesses normally prefer to meet long-term financial needs by using retained earnings or by borrowing from a lending institution (bank, pension fund, insurance company). However, if such types of long-term funding are not available, a company may be able to raise funds by issuing corporate bonds (debt) or selling stock (ownership). Recall that issuing corporate bonds is a form of debt financing and selling stock in the corporation is a form of equity financing. These forms of debt or equity financing are not available to all companies, especially small businesses. However, many firms use such financing options to meet long-term financial needs.

For example, what if you needed long-term financing to expand your operations at Very Vegetarian? Your chief financial officer (CFO) explains that the company doesn't have sufficient retained earnings, and it's unlikely the firm can secure the needed funds from a lender. The CFO suggests that you might want to issue corporate bonds or offer shares of stock to private investors to secure the financing needed. She warns, however, that being able to issue corporate bonds or shares of stock in the company is not an automatic right. Getting approval for bond or stock issues requires extensive financial disclosures and detailed scrutiny by the U.S. Securities and Exchange Commission (SEC). Because of such requirements, she recommends that the company turn to an investment banker for assistance. Let's see why.

## The Role of Investment Bankers

**Investment bankers** are specialists who assist in the issue and sale of new securities. Investment banking firms, such as Goldman Sachs, or large financial institutions, like Citigroup and Bank of America, help companies prepare the extensive financial analyses necessary to gain SEC approval for stock or bond issues.

**investment bankers**
Specialists who assist in the issue and sale of new securities.

Investment bankers also underwrite new issues of bonds or stocks.[1] That is, an investment banking firm buys the entire bond or stock issue a company wants to sell at an agreed-on discount, which can be quite sizable, and then sells the issue to private or institutional investors at full price. **Institutional investors** are large organizations—such as pension funds, mutual funds, insurance companies, and banks—that invest their own funds or the funds of others. Because of their vast buying power (these institutions control over 53 percent of U.S. stocks), institutional investors are a powerful force in securities markets.[2]

**institutional investors**
Large organizations—such as pension funds, mutual funds, insurance companies, and banks—that invest their own funds or the funds of others.

Raising needed long-term funding using debt financing (bonds) is an option many companies pursue. Let's look in more depth at bonds as a long-term financing alternative.

# DEBT FINANCING BY SELLING BONDS

A **bond** is a corporate certificate indicating that a person has lent money to a firm. A company that issues bonds has a legal obligation to make regular interest payments to investors and to repay the entire bond principal amount at a prescribed time. Let's explore the language of bonds more carefully so that you understand exactly what's involved.

**bond**
A corporate certificate indicating that a person has lent money to a firm.

## Learning the Language of Bonds

A more comprehensive definition of a bond than the one just given is that a bond is a contract of indebtedness issued by a corporation or government unit that promises payment of a principal amount at a specified future time, plus interest. Interest is paid to the holder of the bond until the principal amount is due. Thus, in this context, **interest** is the payment the issuer of a bond makes to the bondholders for use of the borrowed money. The interest rate paid on a bond may also be called the bond's *coupon rate.* This term dates back to when bonds were issued as bearer bonds and the holder, or bearer, was considered the owner. The company issuing the bond kept no accounts of transfers in ownership, and the interest on the bond was obtained by clipping coupons attached to the bond and sending them to the issuing company for payment. Today, bonds are registered to particular owners and changes in ownership are recorded electronically.

**interest**
The payment the issuer of the bond makes to the bondholders for use of the borrowed money.

The interest rate paid on a bond varies according to factors such as the state of the economy, the reputation of the company issuing the bond, and the going interest rate for government bonds or bonds of similar companies. Once an interest rate is set for a corporate bond issue (except in the case of what's called a floating-rate bond), it cannot be changed. The interest rate being paid by U.S. government bonds clearly affects the interest rate a firm must agree to pay, since government bonds are considered safe investments. (Remember the risk/return trade-off defined in Chapter 18.) Figure 19.1 on page 514 lists and describes several types of government bonds that compete in securities markets with U.S. corporate bonds.

figure 19.1

**TYPES OF GOVERNMENT SECURITIES THAT COMPETE WITH CORPORATE BONDS**

| BOND | DESCRIPTION |
|---|---|
| U.S. government bond | Issued by the federal government; considered the safest type of bond investment |
| Treasury bill (T-bill) | Matures in less than a year; issued with a minimum denomination of $1,000 |
| Treasury note | Matures in 10 years or less; sold in denominations of $1,000 and $5,000 |
| Treasury bond | Matures in 25 years or more; sold in denominations of $1,000 and $5,000 |
| Municipal bond | Issued by states, cities, counties, and other state and local government agencies; usually exempt from federal taxes |
| Yankee bond | Issued by a foreign government; payable in U.S. dollars |

Bonds of all types are evaluated (rated) in terms of their risk to investors by independent rating firms such as Standard & Poor's and Moody's Investors Service.[3] Bond ratings can range from high-quality, gilt-edged bonds to bonds considered junk (which we discuss later in this chapter). Figure 19.2 describes the range of ratings these two firms attach to bond issues. Bonds are issued with a *denomination*, which is the amount of debt represented by one bond. (Bonds are almost always issued in multiples of $1,000.) The *principal* is the face value of a bond. The issuing company is legally bound to repay the bond principal to the bondholder in full on the **maturity date**. For example, if Very Vegetarian issues a $1,000 bond with an interest rate of 5 percent and a maturity date of 2025, the company is agreeing to pay a bondholder a total of $50 in interest each year until a specified date in 2025, when the full $1,000 must be repaid. Though bond interest is quoted for an entire year, it is usually paid in two installments (semiannually). Maturity dates for bonds can vary. For example, firms such as Disney and Coca-Cola have issued bonds with 50-year maturity dates.[4]

**maturity date**
The exact date the issuer of a bond must pay the principal to the bondholder.

## Advantages and Disadvantages of Issuing Bonds

Bonds offer several long-term financing advantages to an organization. Advantages of issuing bonds include the following:

- Bondholders are creditors, not owners, of the firm and seldom have a vote on corporate matters; thus, management maintains control over the firm's operations.

figure 19.2

**BOND RATINGS: MOODY'S INVESTORS SERVICE AND STANDARD & POOR'S INVESTOR SERVICE**

| Rating | | |
|---|---|---|
| MOODY'S | STANDARD & POOR'S | DESCRIPTIONS |
| Aaa | AAA | Highest quality (lowest default risk) |
| Aa | AA | High quality |
| A | A | Upper medium grade |
| Baa | BBB | Medium grade |
| Ba | BB | Lower medium grade |
| B | B | Speculative |
| Caa | CCC, CC | Poor (high default risk) |
| Ca | C | Highly speculative |
| C | D | Lowest grade |

- Interest paid on bonds is tax deductible to the firm issuing the bond. Chapter 17 explained how certain interest expenses help a firm limit its tax responsibilities to the government.
- Bonds are a temporary source of funding for a firm. They're eventually repaid and the debt obligation eliminated.
- Bonds can be repaid before the maturity date if they contain a call provision, and can also be convertible to common stock. (Both features are discussed below.)

But bonds also have their drawbacks:

- Bonds increase debt (long-term liabilities) and may adversely affect the market's perception of the firm.
- Paying interest on bonds is a legal obligation. If interest is not paid, bondholders can take legal action to force payment.
- The face value (denomination) of bonds must be repaid on the maturity date. Without careful planning, this repayment can cause cash flow problems when the bonds come due.

## Different Classes of Bonds

As mentioned in Chapter 18, corporations can issue two different classes of corporate bonds. The first class is *unsecured bonds*, which are not backed by any collateral (such as equipment). These bonds are usually referred to as **debenture bonds**. Generally, only well-respected firms with excellent credit ratings can issue debenture bonds, since the only security the bondholder has is the reputation and credit history of the company.

**debenture bonds**
Bonds that are unsecured (i.e., not backed by any collateral such as equipment).

The second class of bonds is *secured bonds*, which are backed by some tangible asset (collateral) that is pledged to the bondholder if bond interest isn't paid or the principal isn't paid back when promised. For example, a mortgage bond is a bond secured by company assets such as land and buildings. In issuing bonds, a company can choose to include different features in the various bond issues. Let's look at some possible special bond features.

## Special Bond Features

By now you should understand that bonds are issued with an interest rate, are unsecured or secured by some type of collateral, and must be repaid at their maturity date. This repayment requirement often leads companies to establish a reserve account called a **sinking fund**, whose primary purpose is to ensure that enough money will be available to repay bondholders on the bond's maturity date. Firms issuing sinking-fund bonds periodically retire (set aside) some part of the bond principal prior to maturity so that enough capital will be accumulated by the maturity date to pay off the bond. Sinking funds can be attractive to issuing firms and potential investors for several reasons:

**sinking fund**
A reserve account in which the issuer of a bond periodically retires some part of the bond principal prior to maturity so that enough capital will be accumulated by the maturity date to pay off the bond.

- They provide for an orderly retirement (repayment) of a bond issue.
- They reduce the risk the bond will not be repaid.
- The market price of the bond is supported because the risk of the firm's not repaying the principal on the maturity date is reduced.

Another special feature that can be included in a bond issue is a call provision. A *callable bond* permits the bond issuer to pay off the bond's principal (i.e., call the bond) prior to its maturity date. Call provisions must be indicated when a bond is issued, and bondholders should be aware of whether or not a bond is callable. Callable bonds give companies some discretion in their long-term forecasting. For example, suppose Very Vegetarian issued $10 million in 20-year bonds with an interest rate of 10 percent. The yearly interest expense would be $1 million ($10 million times 10 percent). If in a couple of years market conditions change, and bonds issued of the same quality are only paying 7 percent, Very Vegetarian would be paying 3 percent, or $300,000 ($10 million times 3 percent), in excess interest yearly. Obviously, the company could benefit if it could call in (pay off) the old bonds and issue new bonds at the lower interest rate. If a company calls a bond before maturity, investors in the bond are often paid a price above the bond's face value.

Another feature sometimes included in bonds is convertibility. A *convertible bond* is a bond that can be converted into shares of common stock in the issuing company.[5] This feature is often an incentive for an investor to buy a bond. Why, you may ask, would bond investors want to convert their investment to stock? That's easy. If the value of the firm's common stock grows sizably over time, bondholders can compare the value of continued bond interest with the possible sizable profit they could gain by converting to a specified number of shares of common stock. When we discuss common stock in the next section, this advantage will become more evident to you.

**progress assessment**

- Why are bonds considered to be a form of debt financing?
- What does it mean when a firm states that it is issuing a 9 percent debenture bond due in 2025?
- Explain the difference between an unsecured and a secured bond.
- Why might convertible bonds be attractive to investors?

## EQUITY FINANCING BY SELLING STOCK

Equity financing is the other form of long-term funding first introduced in Chapter 18. One form of equity financing is obtaining funds through the sale of ownership (stock) in the corporation. As we did previously with bonds, let's look first at the language of stock.

**stocks**
Shares of ownership in a company.

**stock certificate**
Evidence of stock ownership that specifies the name of the company, the number of shares it represents, and the type of stock being issued.

**dividends**
Part of a firm's profits that may be distributed to stockholders as either cash payments or additional shares of stock.

### Learning the Language of Stock

**Stocks** are shares of ownership in a company. A **stock certificate** is evidence of stock ownership that specifies the name of the company, the number of shares it represents, and the type of stock being issued (see Figure 19.3). Today, stock is generally held electronically for the owners of the stock; that is, the owners don't get any paper certificate. Certificates sometimes indicate a stock's *par value*, which is a dollar amount assigned to each share of stock by the corporation's charter. Some states use par value as a basis for calculating the state's incorporation charges and fees; but today, since par values do not reflect the market value of the stock, most companies issue "no-par" stock. **Dividends** are part of a firm's profits that may be distributed to stockholders as either cash payments or additional shares of stock. Dividends are declared by a corporation's board of directors and are generally paid quarterly.[6] Although it's a legal obligation for companies that issue *bonds* to pay interest, companies that issue *stock* are not required to pay dividends.[7]

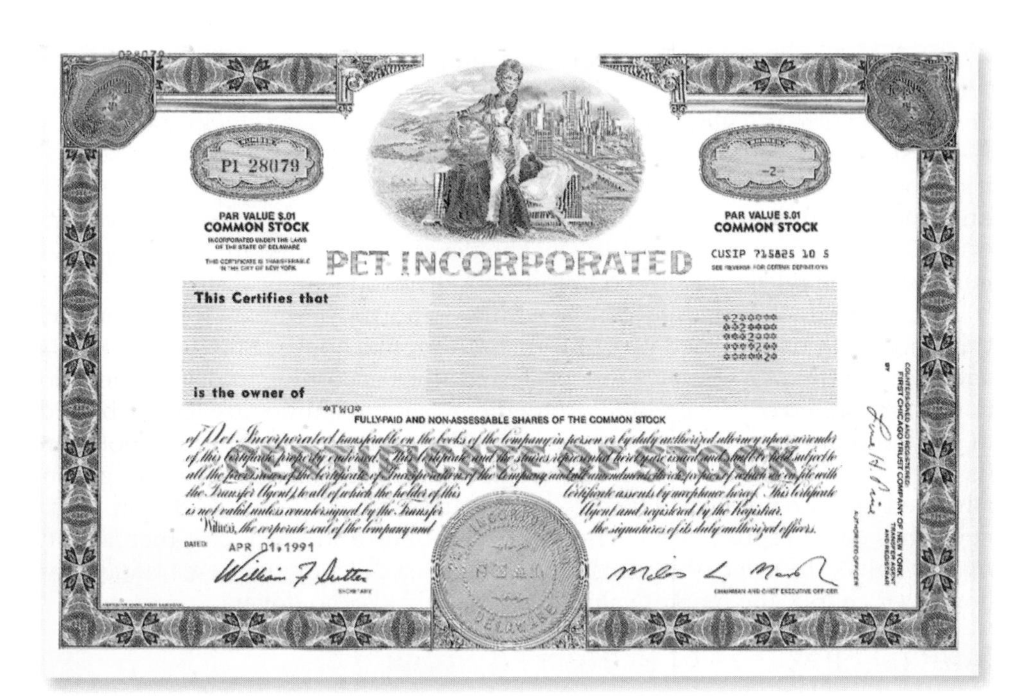


figure 19.3

**STOCK CERTIFICATE FOR PET INC.**

Examine this certificate for key information about this stock.

## Advantages and Disadvantages of Issuing Stock

The following are some advantages to the firm of issuing stock:

- As owners of the business, stockholders never have to be repaid.
- There's no legal obligation to pay dividends to stockholders; therefore, income (retained earnings) can be reinvested in the firm for future financing needs.
- Selling stock can improve the condition of a firm's balance sheet since issuing stock creates no debt. (A corporation may also buy back its stock to improve its balance sheet and make the company appear stronger financially.)

Disadvantages of issuing stock include the following:

- As owners, stockholders (usually only common stockholders) have the right to vote for the company's board of directors. Typically, one vote is granted for each share of stock. Hence, the direction and control of the firm can be altered by the sale of additional shares of stock.
- Dividends are paid out of profit after taxes and are not tax deductible.
- Management's decisions can be affected by the need to keep stockholders happy.

Companies can issue two classes of stock: preferred and common. Let's see how these two forms of equity financing differ.

## Issuing Shares of Preferred Stock

Owners of **preferred stock** enjoy a preference (hence the term *preferred*) in the payment of dividends; they also have a prior claim on company assets if the firm is forced out of business and its assets sold. Normally, however, preferred stock does not include voting rights in the firm. Preferred stock is frequently referred to as a hybrid investment because it has characteristics of both bonds and stocks. To illustrate this, consider the treatment of preferred stock dividends.

**preferred stock**
Stock that gives its owners preference in the payment of dividends and an earlier claim on assets than common stockholders if the company is forced out of business and its assets sold.

Preferred stock dividends differ from common stock dividends in several ways. Preferred stock is generally issued with a par value that becomes the base for the dividend the firm is willing to pay. For example, if a preferred stock's par value is $100 a share and its dividend rate is 4 percent, the firm is committing to a $4 dividend for each share of preferred stock the investor owns (4 percent of $100 = $4). An owner of 100 shares of this preferred stock is promised a fixed yearly dividend of $400. In addition, the preferred stockholder is also assured that this dividend must be paid in full before any common stock dividends can be distributed.

Preferred stock is therefore quite similar to bonds: both have a face (or par) value and both have a fixed rate of return.[8] Also, like bonds, Standard & Poor's and Moody's Investors Service rate preferred stock according to risk. So how do bonds and preferred stock differ? Remember that companies are legally bound to pay bond interest and to repay the face value (denomination) of the bond on its maturity date. In contrast, even though preferred stock dividends are generally fixed, they do not legally have to be paid; also, stock (preferred or common) never has to be repurchased. Though both bonds and stock can increase in market value, the price of stock generally increases at a higher percentage than bonds. Of course, the market value of both could also go down.

## Special Features of Preferred Stock

Preferred stock can have other special features that do not apply to common stock. For example, like bonds, preferred stock can be callable. This means that preferred stockholders could be required to sell back their shares to the corporation. Preferred stock can also be convertible to shares of common stock. Another important feature of preferred stock is that it can be cumulative. That is, if one or more dividends are not paid when promised, the missed dividends will be accumulated and paid later to cumulative preferred stockholders. This means that all dividends, including any back dividends, must be paid in full before any common stock dividends can be distributed.

**common stock**
The most basic form of ownership in a firm; it confers voting rights and the right to share in the firm's profits through dividends, if approved by the firm's board of directors.

## Issuing Shares of Common Stock

**Common stock** is the most basic form of ownership in a firm. In fact, if a company issues only one type of stock, it must be common. Holders of common stock have the right (1) to vote for company board directors and important issues affecting the company and (2) to share in the firm's profits through dividends, if approved by the firm's board of directors. Having voting rights in a corporation allows common stockholders to influence corporate policy since the elected board chooses the firm's top management and makes many major policy decisions. Common stockholders also have what is called a *preemptive right*, which is the first right to purchase any new shares of common stock the firm decides to issue. This right allows common stockholders to maintain a proportional share of ownership in the company.

Now that we have looked at stocks and bonds from a company's perspective as a source of long-term financing, let's look at them from an investor's perspective. Before we do that, though, it's important to explore and understand stock exchanges—the places where stocks and bonds are traded.

**progress assessment**

- Name at least two advantages and two disadvantages of issuing stock as a form of equity financing.
- What are the major differences between preferred stock and common stock?
- In what ways is preferred stock similar to bonds? How are they different?

DEALING WITH change

## A Change at the Exchange

On December 6, 2005, John Thain, CEO of the New York Stock Exchange (NYSE), began a historic meeting of the exchange's members by reading a letter from a member who had inherited her seat on the exchange from her father. While many NYSE seats were held by corporations, many others were still held by individuals who took a certain pride in saying, "I've been a member since . . ." After all, there were only 1,336 seats, and membership meant ownership and the right to trade on the floor of the exchange.

The results of this meeting changed that. The members overwhelmingly approved a merger with Archipelago Holdings Inc. of Chicago. Archipelago is a securities trading company that specializes in electronic trading. Its customers can access all marketplaces, rather than be limited to a single market.

www.nyse.com

The merger made the New York Stock Exchange a publicly traded company, now called the NYSE Group. The NYSE and Archipelago are divisions of the NYSE Group. The new company has the capability to trade not only stocks listed at the NYSE but also those on NASDAQ and over-the-counter stocks through Archipelago's electronic trading system.

NYSE seat holders had a wild ride during 2005. Seats sold for as low as $975,000 in January and for a record $4 million at the end of November. In the merger, seat holders were paid $5 million in stock and $300,000 in cash. Licenses to trade on the NYSE are still called "seats," but the revenues from sale of those licenses now go to the exchange rather than to the individual seat holders. And there are no more members; they are now simply stockholders.

Sources: Susan Diesenhouse, "Venerable NYSE Trades In on New Technology from Chicago's Archipelago," *Chicago Tribune*, December 6, 2005; Pradnya Joshi, "New York Stock Exchange Members Approve Merger to Take Institution Public," *Newsday*, December 7, 2005; "NYSE Seat Owners Vote to Buy Archipelago," AP Online, December 7, 2005; and Marcy Gordon, "SEC Approves NYSE-Archipelago Merger," AP Online, February 28, 2006.

## STOCK EXCHANGES

As its name implies, a **stock exchange** is an organization whose members can buy and sell (exchange) securities for companies and individual investors. U.S. stock exchanges are regulated by the Securities and Exchange Commission (SEC). U.S. investors can also purchase shares on foreign stock exchanges.

**stock exchange**
An organization whose members can buy and sell (exchange) securities for companies and individual investors.

### U.S. Exchanges

The largest stock exchange in the United States, the New York Stock Exchange (NYSE), was founded in 1792. The NYSE is a floor-based exchange (trades take place on the floor of the stock exchange) that lists about 2,800 companies, mostly very large, with a total market value of about $20 trillion.[9] Because of such a large market value, the NYSE is often referred to as the Big Board. Until recently, brokerage firms such as A. G. Edwards and Merrill Lynch purchased memberships, or seats, on the NYSE. However, this changed in 2005 when the NYSE merged with Archipelago. Archipelago is a securities trading company that specializes in electronic trading (see the Dealing with Change box).[10]

The second largest floor-based U.S. exchange is the American Stock Exchange (AMEX).[11] The AMEX and NYSE are considered national exchanges because they handle stocks of companies from all over the United States.

In addition to the national exchanges, there are several regional exchanges in cities such as Chicago, San Francisco, Philadelphia, Cincinnati, Spokane, and Salt Lake City. The regional exchanges deal mostly with firms in their own

If you stroll along Times Square in New York City, you never have to wonder how stocks on the NASDAQ exchange are performing. The NASDAQ price wall continuously updates prices and the number of shares being traded. Originally the NASDAQ dealt primarily with small companies; today it competes with the NYSE for new stock listings.

areas and handle the stock of many large corporations listed on the Big Board. Regional exchanges are often used by big institutional investors to trade stock since the transaction costs are less than those of large exchanges like the NYSE.

Not all securities are traded on registered stock exchanges. The **over-the-counter (OTC) market** provides companies and investors with a means to trade stocks not listed on the national securities exchanges. The OTC market is a network of several thousand brokers that maintain contact with one another and buy and sell securities through a nationwide electronic system.

The **NASDAQ** (originally known as the National Association of Securities Dealers Automated Quotations) evolved from the OTC market but is no longer part of it. As of this writing, the SEC is considering NASDAQ's application for exchange registration.[12] Unlike a floor-based exchange like the NYSE, the NASDAQ is a telecommunications network. It links dealers across the nation so that they can buy and sell securities electronically rather than in person. Originally the NASDAQ dealt mostly with small firms. Today, however, well-known companies such as Microsoft, Intel, Starbucks, Cisco, and Dell trade their stock on the NASDAQ. The NASDAQ also handles federal, state, and city government bonds. Today, the NASDAQ lists approximately 3,300 companies and its average is reported every business day.[13]

Figure 19.4 lists the requirements for registering (listing) stocks on the various exchanges. It's important to note that stocks can be delisted from an exchange if a company fails to meet the exchange's minimum requirements.[14] Adding a company to an exchange is a highly competitive undertaking, and the battle between the stock exchanges is often fierce.[15]

**over-the-counter (OTC) market**
Exchange that provides a means to trade stocks not listed on the national exchanges.

## Securities Regulations and the Securities and Exchange Commission

The Securities Act of 1933 helps protect investors by requiring full disclosure of financial information by firms selling bonds or stock.[16] The U.S. Congress passed this legislation to deal with the free-for-all atmosphere that existed in the securities markets during the Roaring Twenties and the early 1930s. The Securities and Exchange Act of 1934 created the **Securities and Exchange Commission (SEC)**, which has responsibility at the federal level for regulating activities in the various exchanges. Companies trading on the national exchanges must register with the SEC and provide it annual updates. The 1934 act also established specific guidelines that companies must follow when issuing financial securities such as bonds or stock. For example, before issuing either bonds or stock for sale to the public, a company must file a detailed registration statement with the SEC that includes extensive economic and financial information relevant to the firm. The condensed version of that registration document—called a **prospectus**—must be sent to prospective investors.

| EXCHANGE | REQUIREMENTS | TYPE OF COMPANY |
|---|---|---|
| New York Stock Exchange (NYSE) | Pretax income of $2.5 million; 2,000 shareholders holding at least 100 shares; market value of $50 million | Oldest, largest, and best-known companies |
| American Stock Exchange (AMEX) | Pretax income of $750,000; 500,000 shares publicly held at a minimum market value of $3 million; minimum of 400 public shareholders | Midsized growth companies |
| NASDAQ | Total market value of all shares of $8 million; 400 shareholders holding at least 100 shares | Large, midsized, and small growth companies |

figure 19.4

**REQUIREMENTS FOR LISTING STOCK ON THE NEW YORK, AMERICAN, AND NASDAQ EXCHANGES**

The 1934 act also established guidelines to prevent company insiders from taking advantage of privileged information they may have. *Insider trading* involves the use of knowledge or information that individuals gain through their position that allows them to benefit unfairly from fluctuations in security prices.[17] The key words here are *benefit unfairly.* Insiders within a firm are permitted to buy and sell stock in the company they work for so long as they do not take unfair advantage of information.

Originally, the Securities & Exchange Commission (SEC) defined the term *insider* rather narrowly as consisting of a company's directors, employees, and relatives. Today the term has been broadened to include just about anyone with securities information that is not generally available to the general public.[18] For example, say that the chief financial officer of Very Vegetarian tells her next-door neighbor that she is finalizing paperwork to sell the company. The neighbor buys the stock on this information. A court may well consider the purchase an insider trade. Penalties for insider trading can include fines or imprisonment. The Legal Briefcase box on page 522 describes situations that could involve insider trading. See how well you interpret this important legal issue. After that, judge the manager's dilemma in the Making Ethical Decisions box on page 523, which could also involve the question of insider actions.

**NASDAQ**
A nationwide electronic system that links dealers across the nation so that they can buy and sell securities electronically.

**Securities and Exchange Commission (SEC)**
Federal agency that has responsibility for regulating the various exchanges.

**prospectus**
A condensed version of economic and financial information that a company must file with the SEC before issuing stock; the prospectus must be sent to prospective investors.

## Global Stock Exchanges

It's important to remember that we live in a global economy and that the United States is not the only country offering investment opportunities. Stock exchanges operate globally, even in former communist-bloc countries like Poland and Hungary. Expanded communications and the relaxation of many legal barriers now enable investors to buy securities from companies almost anywhere in the world. For example, if you hear of a foreign company that you feel has great potential for growth, you can obtain shares of its stock with little difficulty from U.S. brokers who have access to foreign stock exchanges. In fact, 470 foreign firms from 51 different countries are listed on the NYSE with a market value of $5 trillion.[19] The Reaching Beyond Our Borders box on page 524 offers advice on how U.S. investors can become active in the global market.

Foreign investors can also easily invest in U.S. securities. Large exchanges like the London and Tokyo stock exchanges trade large amounts of U.S. securities daily. The number of U.S. companies that are listed on foreign stock exchanges is also growing. In addition to the London and Tokyo exchanges, other major stock exchanges are located in Paris, Sydney, Buenos Aires, Frankfurt, Zurich, Hong Kong, and Taiwan.[20]

LEGAL briefcase

www.sec.gov

### Ins and Outs of Insider Trading

Insider trading involves buying or selling a stock on the basis of company information not available to the investing public. It's sometimes difficult to identify insider trading. The following hypothetical examples will give you an idea of what's legal and what's illegal. See how many of the questions you can answer. The answers are at the end of this box.

1. You work in research and development at a large company and have been involved in a major effort that should lead to a blockbuster new product coming to the market. News about the product is not public, and very few other workers even know about it. Can you purchase stock in the company?
2. Pertaining to the above situation, you are in a local coffee bar and mention to a friend about what's going on at the company. Another customer seated at an adjoining table overhears your discussion. Can this person legally buy stock in the company before the public announcement?
3. You work as an executive secretary at a major investment banking firm. You are asked to copy documents that detail a major merger about to happen that will keenly benefit the company being taken over. Can you buy stock in the company before the announcement is made public?
4. Your stockbroker recommends that you buy shares in a little-known company. The broker seems to have some inside information, but you don't ask any questions about his source. Can you buy stock in this company?
5. You work as a cleaning person at a major securities firm. At your job you come across information from the trash cans and computer printers of employees of the firm that provide detailed information about several upcoming deals the firm will be handling. Can you buy stock in the companies involved?

Answers: 1. No; 2. Yes; 3. No; 4. Yes; 5. No.

Sources: Mike Dano, "Inside Insider Trading," *RCR Wireless News*, September 12, 2005, and Jenny Anderson, "Insider-Trading Microscope Now Shifts to Laboratories," *International Herald Tribune*, August 10, 2005.

## HOW TO INVEST IN SECURITIES

**stockbroker**
A registered representative who works as a market intermediary to buy and sell securities for clients.

Investing in bonds, stocks, or other securities is not difficult. First, you decide what bond or stock you want to buy. After that, it's necessary to find a registered representative authorized to trade stocks and bonds who can call a member of the stock exchange to execute your order. A **stockbroker** is a registered representative who works as a market intermediary to buy and sell securities for clients. Stockbrokers place an order with a stock exchange member who goes to the place at the exchange where the bond or stock is traded and negotiates a price. After the transaction is completed, the trade is reported to your broker, who notifies you to confirm your purchase. Large brokerage firms like Merrill Lynch or A. G. Edwards maintain automated order systems that allow their brokers to enter your order the instant you make it. Seconds later, the order can be confirmed. Online brokers (discussed next), such as Ameritrade or E*Trade, can also confirm investor trades in a matter of seconds.[21]

The same procedure is followed if you wish to sell stocks or bonds. Brokers historically held on to stock or bond certificates for investors to ensure safekeeping and to allow investors to sell their securities easily and quickly. As mentioned earlier, brokers now keep most records of bond or stock ownership electronically, and transactions are almost instantaneous. A broker can be a valuable source of information about what stocks or bonds would best meet your financial objectives. It's important, however, that you learn about and follow stocks and bonds on your own, because investment analysts' advice may not always meet your specific expectations and needs.[22] In fact, several years back, a Stockholm newspaper gave five Swedish stock analysts and a chimpanzee each the equivalent of $1,250 to make as much money as they could in the stock market. The chimp made his selections by throwing darts—and won the competition. *The Wall Street Journal* also periodically compares the

* * * MAKING

## ethical decisions

www.nasdaq.com

### What Will It Be: Your Bark or Your Bite?

After 35 years of hard work you finally made it to the post of chief executive officer of Laddie Come Home, a large producer of pet foods. As part of your new compensation package, you are entitled to bonuses based on the company's stock performance. If the stock price of Laddie Come Home exceeds $50 a share during the current fiscal year, you could realize a windfall of close to $3 million in bonuses. The company's stock is currently selling for $42 per share. It's been brought to your attention by an investment-banking firm that a major competitor, Barking up the Wrong Tree, has an interest in acquiring your company. The investment banker hinted that Barking up the Wrong Tree would pay upward of $50 a share for Laddie Come Home. Your attorney says the merger is perfectly legal and would have no antitrust problems. You realize the company board of directors would probably follow your recommendation if you suggested selling the company, but you also know that at least half of the current employees (many who have been at the company for over 20 years) would lose their jobs in the takeover.

You plan to retire within the next two years, and $3 million could make life easier. What are the ethical considerations in this situation? What are your alternatives? What are the consequences of each alternative? What will you do?

predictions of a panel of experts to those of "dart throwers." Make sure to look for these contests in the *Journal.* You might want to compete against the experts to test your knowledge.

## Investing Online

As we have stressed throughout this book, technology has affected virtually every aspect of business, and trading in investment securities is no exception. Investors can use online trading services to buy and sell stocks and bonds in place of using traditional brokerage services. Ameritrade, E*Trade, and Charles Schwab are a few of the leading providers of Web-based stock trading services. The commissions charged by these trading services are far less than those of regular stockbrokers. Trades that may have cost hundreds of dollars with traditional brokerage firms may cost as low as $5 each on the Web.[23] Traditional brokerage companies, such as Merrill Lynch, have introduced their own online capabilities to serve customers who want to trade electronically.[24]

Today, customers interested in online trading services are primarily investors willing to do their own research and make their own investment decisions without the assistance of a broker.[25] The leading online services, however, do provide important market information such as company financial data, price histories of a stock, and consensus analysts' reports. Often the level of information services provided by online brokers depends on the size of your account and level of trading. Online brokers are also exploring other financial services alternatives. For example, online broker E*Trade has recast itself as a financial services supermarket. The company offers banking services, checking accounts, mortgages, car loans, credit cards, and insurance.[26]

Whether you decide to trade stocks and bonds using an online broker or decide to invest through a traditional stockbroker, it is important to remember that investing means committing (and risking) your money with the expectation of making a profit. As the market downturn in the early 2000s highlighted, investing is certainly a risky business.

Have a feeling about a stock you believe is going to become the next Microsoft, but don't have a stockbroker? Well, relief is just a click away. Investors can use online trading services such as E*Trade for their investment needs for a fraction of the cost charged by traditional brokers. Investors, however, must do their own research and make their own decisions. Check out www.etrade.com for more information.

REACHING BEYOND our borders

www.ml.com

### It Really Is a Small World

Given the volatility (ups and downs) of the U.S. stock market, investors might wonder if investing in global markets is even worth considering. After all, investing in global markets appears riskier than investing in the U.S. market. Still, financial analysts argue that putting some money overseas might be a good idea. Many believe that global markets in the 21st century will perform better than the U.S. market. In fact, signs of this have already started. In 2004, global markets outperformed the U.S. market by a wide margin.

As an investor, or perhaps a future investor, you may want to consider the advice of such experts (this advice is not foolproof, of course). Check out the following tips, and you may find that global nugget that helps you meet your long-term financial goals:

- Consider mutual funds. In 1990, 116 mutual stock funds held part of their money in multinational stocks. Today, there are over 1,700 mutual funds that invest in international stocks. Mutual funds can offer global portfolios that include U.S. stocks, funds totally international in scope, or funds that invest in individual countries or regions such as Asia or Latin America.
- Look into American depository receipts (ADRs), which can be purchased from American brokers. ADRs represent a set number of shares in a foreign company held on deposit at a foreign branch of an American bank.
- Invest in global companies listed on U.S. stock exchanges. Companies listed on U.S. securities markets must comply with U.S. accounting procedures, and rules of the Securities and Exchange Commission.
- Trade with a domestic broker (such as Merrill Lynch and Morgan Stanley) that has an office abroad. Many U.S. brokers also produce detailed research on foreign companies.
- Invest in global companies that have a solid track record like Shell Oil, Nestlé, Sony, and Siemens.
- Be wary of investing in countries that have a history of currency problems or political instability.

As Americans become more global in their perspectives, it's likely that global investments will grow. However, it's important to remember that markets have varying degrees of risk. Keep the risk/return trade-off in mind in considering any investments, especially global ones.

Sources: Andrei Postelnicu, "NYSE and NASDAQ Apply to Open Outposts in China," *Financial Times*, March 10, 2005; Ruchir Sharma, "The Grand Illusion," *Newsweek International*, May 2, 2005; and Theresa Molloy, "International Investing," *Research*, September 1, 2005.

Therefore, the first step in any investment program is to analyze such factors as desired income, cash requirements, growth prospects, level of risk, and the need to hedge against inflation. You are never too young or too old to get involved in investments, so let's look at some alternatives and questions you should consider before investing.

## Choosing the Right Investment Strategy

As you might suspect, investment objectives change over the course of a person's life. Key investment decisions often center on personal objectives such as growth and income. For example, a young person can afford more high-risk investment options (such as stocks) than a person nearing retirement. Often younger investors are looking for significant growth in the value of their investments over time. Therefore, if stocks go into a tailspin and decrease in value, the younger person has time to wait for stocks to rise again. An older person, perhaps on a fixed income, doesn't have the luxury of waiting, and may be inclined to invest in bonds that offer a steady return as a protection against inflation. To an elderly investor, additional income is probably more important than potential growth.

What's inherent in any investment strategy is the risk/return trade-off. Investors must evaluate investment strategies related to growth, income, inflation protection, or liquidity. For example, should you consider stocks or bonds? Do you want common or preferred stock? Do you want corporate-issued or government-issued bonds? These are tough questions whose answers vary investor by investor. That's why it's important for investors to consider five key criteria when selecting investment options:

1. **Investment risk**. The chance that an investment will be worth less at some future time than it's worth now.
2. **Yield**. The expected rate of return on an investment, such as interest or dividends, usually over a period of one year.
3. **Duration**. The length of time your money is committed to an investment.
4. **Liquidity**. How quickly you can get back your invested funds if you want them or need them.
5. **Tax consequences**. How the investment will affect your tax situation.

Since new investors are not generally well versed in the world of investing or in choosing proper investment strategies, an investment planner such as a chartered financial analyst (CFA) or a certified financial planner (CFP) can be helpful. A short course in investments can also be useful. Setting investment objectives such as growth or income should clearly set the tone for your investment strategy.



Bonds, stocks, and mutual funds all offer opportunities for investors to enhance their financial future. We will look first at the potential of bonds as an investment, then move on to stocks and mutual funds. Before we do that, though, check your understanding by doing the Progress Assessment.

Securities markets are like financial supermarkets; lots of investment choices to choose from. That's why it's important before committing your money to determine what investment strategy is right for you. The risk/return tradeoff is a good starting point. Assistance from a certified financial planner (CFP) or a chartered financial analyst (CFA) can also help. How do investment objectives change over a person's lifetime?

**progress assessment**

- What is the primary purpose of a stock exchange? Can you name the largest stock exchange in the United States?
- What does NASDAQ stand for? How does this exchange work?
- What is the key advantage to online investing?

## INVESTING IN BONDS

For investors who desire low risk and guaranteed income, U.S. government bonds are a secure investment because these bonds have the financial backing and full faith and credit of the federal government. Municipal bonds, also secure, are offered by local governments and often have advantages such as tax-free interest. Some may even be insured. Corporate bonds are a bit more risky and challenging.

Two questions often arise with first-time corporate bond investors. The first is "If I purchase a corporate bond, do I have to hold it until the maturity date?" The answer is no, you do not have to hold a bond until maturity. Bonds are bought and sold daily on major securities exchanges (remember the secondary market discussed earlier). However, if you decide to sell your bond to another investor before its maturity date, you are not guaranteed to get the

"YOU CAN COME BACK IN. IT'S JUST A CORRECTION."


The tough reality of investing is "what goes up can also go down." Investing in stock is always a risky venture as many investors found out in the bear market in 2000–2002. It's important to set an overall investment strategy and continuously monitor your investments. Doing homework before committing your money also helps. What type of investment most interests you?

face value of the bond (usually $1,000). For example, if your bond does not have features (high interest rate, early maturity, etc.) that make it attractive to other investors, you may be forced to sell your bond at a *discount*, that is, a price less than the bond's face value. But if your bond is highly valued by other investors, you may be able to sell it at a *premium*, that is, a price above its face value. Bond prices generally fluctuate inversely with current market interest rates. *As interest rates go up, bond prices fall, and vice versa.* Thus, like all investments, bonds have a degree of risk.

The second question is "How can I assess the investment risk of a particular bond issue?" Standard & Poor's and Moody's Investors Service rate the level of risk of many corporate and government bonds (refer back to Figure 19.2). Naturally, the higher the market risk of a bond compared to other bonds, the higher the interest rate the issuer of the bond might offer to investors. This again refers to the risk/return trade-off discussed in Chapter 18. Investors will invest in a bond considered risky only if the potential return to them is high enough. It's important to remember that investors have many investment options besides bonds. One such option is to buy stock.

## INVESTING IN STOCKS

Buying stock makes the investor a partial owner of the firm. Stocks provide investors an opportunity to participate in the success of emerging or expanding companies. In fact, since 1925, the average annual return on stocks has been about 12 percent, the highest return of any popular investment. As owners, however, stockholders can also lose money if a company does not do well or the overall stock market is declining. The early 2000s were proof of that. Again, it's up to investors to choose the investment that best fits their overall investment objectives.

According to investment analysts, the market price (and growth potential) of a common stock depends heavily on the overall performance of the corporation in meeting its business objectives. If a company reaches its stated objectives, there are great opportunities for capital gains. **Capital gains** are the positive difference between the price at which you bought a stock and what you sell it for. For example, a $1,000 investment made in Microsoft when its stock was first offered to the public would be worth over $1 million today. Stocks can be subject to a high degree of risk, however. Drops in the stock market such as the ones in 1987, 1997, and 2000–2002 (discussed later in this chapter) certainly caught investors' attention.

**capital gains**
The positive difference between the purchase price of a stock and its sale price.

Stock investors are often called bulls or bears according to their perceptions of the market. *Bulls* are investors who believe that stock prices are going to rise; they buy stock in anticipation of the increase. When overall stock prices are rising, the market is called a bull market. *Bears* are investors who expect stock prices to decline. Bears sell their stocks in anticipation of falling prices. When the prices of stocks decline steadily, the market is called a bear market.[27]

As we discussed previously, setting investment objectives such as growth, income, inflation protection, or cash can set the tone for your investment strategy. Investors may select several different investment opportunities in stock depending on their strategy. *Growth stocks*, for example, are stocks of corporations (often technology, biotechnology, or Internet-related firms) whose earnings are expected to grow at a rate faster than other stocks in the market. While often considered risky, such stocks offer investors the potential for high returns. Another option is *income stocks*. These are stocks that offer investors a rather high dividend yield on their investment. Public utilities are often considered good income stocks that will generally keep pace with inflation.

The stock of high-quality companies such as Coca-Cola, General Electric, and Procter & Gamble are referred to as *blue-chip stocks.* These stocks pay regular dividends and generally experience consistent growth in the company's stock price. However, as the market decline in 2000–2002 proved, even blue-chip stocks are not immune from falling prices. Investors can even invest in a type of stock called a penny stock. *Penny stocks* are stocks that sell for less than $2 (some analysts say less than $5).[28] Such stocks frequently represent ownership in firms, such as mining or oil exploration companies, that compete in high-risk industries. Penny stocks are usually considered risky investments.

Investors who buy stock have more options for placing an order than investors buying and selling bonds. Stock investors, for example, can place a *market order*, which tells a broker to buy or to sell a stock immediately at the best price available. This type of order can be processed quickly, and the trade price can be given to the investor almost instantaneously. A *limit order* tells the broker to buy or to sell a particular stock at a specific price, if that price becomes available. Let's say, for example, that a stock is selling for $40 a share; you believe that the price will go up eventually but that it might drop a little before it goes higher. You could place a limit order at $36. The broker will buy the stock for you at $36 if the stock drops to that price. If the stock never falls to $36, the broker will not purchase it.

## Stock Splits

Companies and brokers prefer to have stock purchases conducted in *round lots*, that is, purchases of 100 shares at a time. However, investors often buy stock in *odd lots*, or purchases of less than 100 shares at a time. Many investors cannot afford to buy 100 shares of a stock in companies that may be selling for perhaps as high as $100 per share. Such high prices often induce companies to declare **stock splits**; that is, they issue two or more shares for every share of stock that's currently outstanding. For example, if Very Vegetarian stock were selling for $100 a share, Very Vegetarian could declare a two-for-one stock split. Investors who owned one share of Very Vegetarian would now own two shares; each share, however, would now be worth only $50 (one half as much as before the split). As you can see, there is no change in the firm's ownership structure and no change in the investment's value after the stock split.[29] Investors, however, generally approve of stock splits because often the demand for the stock at $50 per share may be greater than the demand at $100 per share. Thus, the $50 stock price may go up in the near future. It's important to note that a company can never be forced to split its stock. For example, Berkshire Hathaway has never had a stock split and its shares have sold for as much as over $90,000 for one share.

**stock splits**
An action by a company that gives stockholders two or more shares of stock for each one they own.

One of the most popular and simplest ways of investing in bonds and stocks is through mutual funds. Let's see why.

# INVESTING IN MUTUAL FUNDS AND EXCHANGE-TRADED FUNDS

A **mutual fund** buys stocks and bonds and then sells shares in those securities to the public. A mutual fund is like an investment company that pools investors' money and then buys stocks or bonds in many companies in

**mutual fund**
An organization that buys stocks and bonds and then sells shares in those securities to the public.

It's fun to stop and enjoy a Dairy Queen sundae especially if you own the company. Warren Buffett, America's most successful investor, built his fortune through prudent investing and is now the second wealthiest person (after Bill Gates) in the United States. In 2006, Buffett announced that he was giving the bulk of his fortune to the Gates Foundation. The $30 billion gift will be distributed in annual amounts of $1.5 billion.

accordance with the specific purpose of the fund. Mutual fund managers are experts who pick what they consider to be the best stocks and bonds available. Investors can buy shares of the mutual funds and thus take part in the ownership of many different companies that they could not afford to invest in individually. Thus, for a normally small fee, mutual funds provide professional investment management and help investors diversify.

Funds available range in purpose from very conservative funds that invest only in government securities or secure corporate bonds to others that specialize in emerging high-tech firms, Internet companies, foreign companies, precious metals, and other investments with greater risk. Some mutual funds even invest exclusively in socially responsible companies.[30]

For young people, the best choice is usually to buy a few index funds and to diversify those investments among different kinds of stock. An *index fund* is a fund that invests in a certain kind of stock. The most-recommended is an index fund that covers the whole stock market. *To diversify* means to invest in a variety of index funds. For example, you can put your money into an index fund that focuses on large companies, one that focuses on small companies, one that invests in emerging countries, and one that invests mainly in real estate (real estate investment trusts, or REITs). We cannot go into great detail here about the benefits and drawbacks of all the choices. A stockbroker, certified financial planner (CFP), or banker can help you find the mutual fund that best fits your investment objectives. In addition, the newsletter *Morningstar Investor* is an excellent resource for evaluating mutual funds, as are business publications such as *BusinessWeek*, *The Wall Street Journal*, *Money*, and *Investor's Business Daily*. Figure 19.5 gives you a list of just some of the options you have in terms of mutual fund investments.

One key advantage of mutual funds is that you can buy most funds directly and save any fees or commissions. The Internet has made access in and out of mutual funds easier than ever. A true *no-load fund* is one that charges no commission to investors to either buy or sell its shares. A *load fund* would charge a commission to investors to buy shares in the fund or would charge a commission when investors sell shares in the fund. It's important to check the costs involved in a mutual fund, such as fees and charges imposed in the managing of a fund, because these can differ significantly. It's also important to check the long-term performance record of the fund's management.[31] Some funds, called open-end funds, will accept the investments of any interested investors. Closed-end funds offer a specific number of shares for investment; once a closed-end fund reaches its target number, no new investors can buy into the fund.

**exchange-traded funds (ETFs)**
Collections of stocks that are traded on exchanges but are traded more like individual stocks than like mutual funds.

A newer way that investors can diversify is through buying **exchange-traded funds (ETFs)**. ETFs are collections of stocks that are traded on exchanges but are traded more like individual stocks than like mutual funds.[32] The Dealing with Change box discusses the differences between mutual funds and ETFs, and identifies a few of the most frequently traded ETFs. The key points to remember about both mutual funds and ETFs is that they offer small

## DEALING WITH change

### Diamonds and Spiders and Vipers, Oh My!

Just like Dorothy in *The Wizard of Oz*, some new investors may feel like visitors in a strange new world when they first enter the land of stock markets. The big boards dazzle investors with streaming stock quotes, and analysts point in all different directions as they try to guide investors toward their financial goals. The yellow brick road that leads the way to financial success may not really be paved in gold, but adventurers can run into all sorts of things along their way—things like Diamonds and Spiders and Vipers. These intriguing entities are not as exotic as they sound. They belong to a type of investment group known as exchange-traded funds (ETFs).

ETFs are similar to mutual funds in that they are collections of stocks that are traded on exchanges. However, unlike mutual funds that are traded only at the end of the trading day, ETFs can be traded throughout the entire trading day just like individual stocks. This offers investors significant trading flexibility. Another advantage of ETFs is that while they do charge fees, these fees are usually much lower than those charged by mutual funds. ETFs, then, are a flexible, low-cost way for investors to diversify their portfolios.

There are ETFs for most types of asset classes and market sectors such as technology, biotechnology, emerging markets, and energy. For example, Dow Industrial Average Model New Depositary Shares (Diamonds) is an ETF that tracks the Dow stocks; Standard & Poor's Depositary Receipts (SPDRs, or Spiders) track nine sectors of the S&P 500 Index; and Vanguard's Index Participation Equity Receipts (Vipers) track the 10 sectors of the MSCI US Investable Market 2500 Index, as well as the Morgan Stanley REIT Index.

The number of ETFs is growing as more and more investors are moving away from high-cost mutual funds that are actively managed (and in recent years subjects of high-profile management scandals). With sector focus, diversification, short-term trading, and low cost all in one package, ETFs can be a useful means of reaching your financial goals.

Sources: Ronald L. Delegge, "Into the ETF Arena: Vanguard VIPERs," *Research*, April 1, 2005; Lars Hamich, "Gearing Up for an ETF Boom," *Investment Adviser*, May 23, 2005; and Aaron Pressman, "Funds to Cover Every Angle," *BusinessWeek*, March 27, 2006, pp. 102–4.

www.etrade.com

investors a way to spread the risk of stock and bond ownership and a way to have their investments managed by a trained specialist for a nominal fee. Most financial advisers put mutual funds and ETFs high on the list of recommended investments for small or beginning investors.

| | | | |
|---|---|---|---|
| AB | Investment-grade corporate bonds | MP | Stock and bond fund |
| AU | Gold oriented | MT | Mortgage securities |
| BL | Balanced | MV | Mid-cap value |
| EI | Equity income | NM | Insured municipal bonds |
| EM | Emerging markets | NR | Natural resources |
| EU | European region | PR | Pacific region |
| GL | Global | SB | Short-term corporate bonds |
| GM | General municipal bond | SC | Small-cap core |
| GT | General taxable bonds | SE | Sector funds |
| HB | Health/Biotech | SG | Small-cap growth |
| HC | High-yield bonds | SM | Short-term municipal bonds |
| HM | High-yield municipal bonds | SP | S&P 500 |
| IB | Intermediate-term corporate bonds | SQ | Specialty |
| IG | Intermediate-term government bonds | SS | Single-state municipal bonds |
| IL | International | SU | Short-term government bonds |
| IM | Intermediate-term municipal bonds | SV | Small-cap value |
| LC | Large-cap core | TK | Science & technology |
| LG | Large-cap growth | UN | Unassigned |
| LT | Latin America | UT | Utility |
| LU | Long-term U.S. bonds | WB | World bonds |
| LV | Large-cap value | XC | Multi-cap core |
| MC | Mid-cap core | XG | Multi-cap growth |
| MG | Mid-cap growth | XV | Multi-cap value |

Sources: *The Wall Street Journal*, and *Investor's Business Daily*.

figure 19.5

**MUTUAL FUND OBJECTIVES**

Mutual funds have a wide array of investment categories. They range from low-risk, conservative funds to others that invest in high-risk industries. Listed here are abbreviations of funds and what these abbreviations stand for.

## Diversifying Investments

**diversification**
Buying several different investment alternatives to spread the risk of investing.

**Diversification** involves buying several different investment alternatives to spread the risk of investing. For example, an investor may put 20 percent of his or her money into growth stocks that have relatively high risk. Another 30 percent may be invested in conservative government bonds, 15 percent in income stocks, 20 percent in a mutual fund, and the rest placed in the bank for emergencies and possible other investment opportunities. By diversifying investments, investors decrease the chance of losing everything they have invested. This type of investment strategy is often referred to as a *portfolio strategy* or *allocation model.*

Both stockbrokers and certified financial planners are trained to give advice about the portfolio that would best fit each client's financial objectives. However, the more investors read and study the market on their own, the higher their potential for gain. It's also important for investors not to forget the risk/return trade-off and be aware that some investments carry rather heavy risks. Let's take a look at several such high-risk investments.

# INVESTING IN HIGH-RISK INVESTMENTS

At a racetrack some bettors always pick the favorites; others like the long shots. The same thing is true in the investment market. Some investors think that high-rated corporate bonds are clearly the investment of choice; others want to take more market risk. Let's look at three relatively risky investment options: junk bonds, buying stock on margin, and commodities.

## Investing in High-Risk (Junk) Bonds

**junk bonds**
High-risk, high-interest bonds.

Although bonds are generally considered relatively safe investments, some investors look for higher returns through riskier bonds called **junk bonds**. Standard & Poor's Investment Advisory Service and Moody's Investors Service consider non-investment-grade bonds (bonds rated BB or lower) to be junk bonds because of their high risk and high bond-default rates. Junk bonds rely on the firm's ability to pay investors interest as long as the value of the company's assets remains high and its cash flow stays strong.[33] Although the interest rates are attractive and often tempting, if the company can't pay off the bond, the investor is left with a bond that isn't worth more than the paper it's written on—in other words, junk.[34]

## Buying Stock on Margin

**buying stock on margin**
Purchasing stocks by borrowing some of the purchase cost from the brokerage firm.

**Buying stock on margin** involves purchasing stocks by borrowing some of the purchase cost from the brokerage firm. The margin is the amount of money an investor must invest in the stock. The board of governors of the Federal Reserve System sets margin rates in the U.S. market. (You will read about this in more detail in Chapter 20.) Briefly, if the margin rate is 50 percent, an investor who qualifies for a margin account may borrow 50 percent of the stock's purchase price from a broker. Although buying on margin sounds like an easy way to buy more stocks, the downside is that investors must repay the credit extended by the broker, plus interest. Additionally, if the investor's account goes down in market value, the broker will issue a margin call, requiring the investor to come up with more money to cover the losses the investor's portfolio has suffered. If the investor is unable to make the margin call, the broker can legally sell off shares of the investor's stock to reduce the broker's chance of loss. Margin calls can force the investor to repay a significant portion of his or her account's loss within days or even hours.

## Investing in Commodities

Commodities can be high-risk investments for most investors. Investors willing to speculate in commodities hope to profit handsomely from the rise and fall of prices of items such as coffee, wheat, pork bellies (slabs of bacon), petroleum, and other articles of commerce (commodities) that are scheduled for delivery at a given (future) date. Trading in commodities is not for the novice investor; it demands much expertise. Small shifts in the prices of certain items can result in significant gains and losses. It's estimated, in fact, that 75 to 80 percent of the investors who speculate in commodities lose money in the long term.[35]

Trading in commodities, however, can also be used as a means of protecting businesspeople, farmers, and others from wide fluctuations in commodity prices and thus for them can be a very conservative investment strategy. A **commodity exchange** specializes in the buying and selling of precious metals and minerals (e.g., silver, foreign currencies, gasoline) and agricultural goods (e.g., wheat, cattle, sugar). The Chicago Board of Trade (CBOT), with its 60,000-square-foot trading floor, is the largest commodity exchange in terms of floor size. The CBOT is involved with a wide range of commodities, including corn, plywood, silver, gold, and U.S. Treasury bonds.[36]

**commodity exchange**
A securities exchange that specializes in the buying and selling of precious metals and minerals (e.g., silver, foreign currencies, gasoline) and agricultural goods (e.g., wheat, cattle, sugar).

Commodity exchanges operate much like stock exchanges: Members of the exchange meet on the exchange's floor to transact deals. Yet a commodities exchange looks quite different from a stock exchange, and is interesting to observe. Transactions for a specific commodity take place in a specific trading area, or "pit," that can only be described as an exciting spectacle. Trades result from the meeting of a bid and offer in an open competition among exchange members. The bids and offers are made in a seemingly impossible-to-understand blend of voices, with all participants shouting at once. Today, however, the old color and excitement of the pits are becoming somewhat obsolete. More and more traders and brokers are working electronically at computer screens where millions of contracts are zipping around on global computer networks.[37] In fact, the CBOT has relinquished its long-standing title as the largest trading futures exchange in the world to the Eurex exchange, based in Frankfurt, Germany.[38]

Many companies use commodities markets to their advantage by dealing in the futures market. **Futures markets** involve the purchase and sale of goods for delivery sometime in the future. Take, for example, a farmer who has corn growing in the field. The farmer is not sure what price the corn will sell for at harvest time. To be sure of a price, the farmer could sell the corn on the commodity floor for delivery in the future at a fixed price. Since the price is now fixed, the farmer can plan the farm's budget and expenses accordingly. In contrast, as the owner of Very Vegetarian, you may be worried about the possibility that corn prices will rise. If you buy the corn in the futures market, you know what you will have to pay and, like the farmer, can also plan accordingly. All of this is possible because of commodity exchanges. Figure 19.6 on page 532 evaluates bonds, stocks, mutual funds, and commodities according to risk, income, and possible investment growth (capital gain).

**futures markets**
Commodities markets that involve the purchase and sale of goods for delivery sometime in the future.

**progress assessment**

- What is a stock split? Why do companies sometimes split their stock?
- What is a mutual fund? How do such funds benefit small investors?
- What is meant by buying stock on margin?

figure 19.6
COMPARING INVESTMENTS

| Investment | Degree of risk | Expected income | Possible growth (capital gain) |
|---|---|---|---|
| Bonds | Low | Secure | Little |
| Preferred stock | Medium | Steady | Little |
| Common stock | High | Variable | Good |
| Mutual funds | Medium | Variable | Good |
| Commodities | Very high | Very volatile | Very volatile |

## UNDERSTANDING INFORMATION FROM SECURITIES MARKETS

You can find a wealth of investment information in newspapers, in magazines, on television, and on Web sites. Such information is useless, however, until you understand what it means. Look through *The Wall Street Journal*, *Barron's*, *Investor's Business Daily*, *USA Today*, and your local newspaper's business section; listen carefully to business reports on radio and TV for investment analysis and different viewpoints; and visit different sites on the Internet that provide information about companies and markets. But keep in mind that investing is an inexact science and few people are consistently right in predicting future market movements. Every time someone sells a stock believing it will fall, someone else is buying it, believing it will go higher. By reading the following sections carefully, you will begin to better understand investment information.

It's never too early to start thinking about investments. All you have to do is commit yourself to doing some extra homework. A wealth of information is available in the library or on the Internet. Financial publications like *The Wall Street Journal*, *Barron's*, and *Investor's Business Daily* can start you on the path to becoming one of America's great investors. Do you have the commitment it takes?

### Understanding Bond Quotations

Bonds, remember, are debt issued by corporations and governments. Government issues are covered in *The Wall Street Journal* in a table called Treasury Issues. These issues are traded on the over-the-counter (OTC) market. The price of a bond is quoted as a percentage of $1,000. The interest rate is often followed by an *s* for easier pronunciation. For example, 9 percent bonds due in 2015 are called 9s of 15.

Figure 19.7 gives a sample of bond quotes for corporate bonds. Look at the quotes and note the variation in interest rates and maturity dates. The more you know about the bond market, the better prepared you will be to talk intelligently with investment counselors and brokers. You want to be sure that their advice is consistent with your best interests and investment objectives.

### Understanding Stock Quotations

If you look in the Money & Investing section of *The Wall Street Journal*, you will see stock quotations from the NYSE, the AMEX, and the NASDAQ. Look at the top of the columns and notice the headings. To understand the headings better, look carefully at Figure 19.8. This example highlights the information on the NYSE and the AMEX. Stocks are quoted in decimal amounts. The NYSE officially shifted in late 2000 from trading stocks in fractions to trading in decimals. The NASDAQ converted to the decimal program in the spring of 2001. Preferred stocks are listed separately

figure 19.7

**UNDERSTANDING BOND QUOTATIONS**

| Bonds | Yld | Vol | Bond Close | Chg |
|---|---|---|---|---|
| GMA zr 5 | ... | 27 | 368.88 | ... |
| Hilton 5.06 | cv | 30 | 96.13 | –0.13 |
| Honywhl zr09 | ... | 5 | 68.13 | ... |
| HousF 6.750,11 | 6.8 | 10 | 99.00 | +2.00 |
| IBM 7.500,13 | 6.5 | 4 | 115.00 | ... |
| IBM 8.375,19 | 6.8 | 94 | 123.00 | ... |
| IBM 6.500,28 | 6.2 | 10 | 104.38 | ... |
| JCPL 7.125,04 | 7.1 | 10 | 101.00 | ... |

This is a zero-coupon bond.*

CV means this is a convertible bond

These IBM bonds pay 8.375% interest and mature in 2019

This bond is currently yielding 6.2%

Number of bonds traded this day

The price of this bond increased $20 from the previous day

This bond is currently selling at a premium (1010.00)

*Zero-coupon bonds pay no interest prior to maturity. The return to the investor comes from the difference between the purchase price and the bond's face value.

Source: *Investor's Business Daily.*

in *The Wall Street Journal*. If a publication does not list preferred stock issues separately, preferred stock is identified by the letters *pf* following the abbreviated company name. Corporations can have several different preferred stock issues.

Let's look at the columns and headings more closely. Moving from left to right, the stock quote tells us the following:

- The percent of change in the stock's price for the year to date (YTD).
- The highest and lowest price the stock has sold for over the past 52 weeks.
- The company name and the company's stock symbol.
- The last dividend paid per share.
- The stock's dividend yield (annual dividend as a percentage of the price per share).

figure 19.8

**UNDERSTANDING STOCK QUOTATIONS**

Source: *The Wall Street Journal.*

| YTD % CHG | 52-WEEK HI | 52-WEEK LO | STOCK (SYM) | DIV | YLD % | PE | VOL 100s | CLOSE | NET CHG |
|---|---|---|---|---|---|---|---|---|---|
| 16.7 | 22.36 | 15.05 | Mattel MAT | .05 | .2 | 21 | 9838 | 20.08 | 0.13 |
| 4.4 | 19.15 | 8.21↓ | MayrckTube MVK | | ... | cc | 2300 | 13.52 | 0.60 |
| –6.2 | 7.90 | 1.77 | Maxtor MXO | | ... | dd | 28648 | 5.95 | 0.05 |
| –36.5 | 38.86 | 20.10 | MayDeptStrs' MAY | .95 | 4.0 | 13 | 10482 | 23.47 | 0.17 |
| –10.9 | 47.94 | 18.84 | Maytag MYG | .72 | 2.6 | 13 | 5707 | 27.66 | 0.56 |
| 19.9 | 65.55 | 45.10 | McClatchy A MNI x | .40 | .7 | 23 | 1561 | 56.35 | 0.52 |
| 13.7 | 27.25 | 20.67 | McCrmkCo MKC s | .44f | 1.8 | 21 | 3053 | 23.85 | 0.05 |
| –70.3 | 17.29 | 2.34 | McDermint MDR | | ... | dd | 15706 | 3.65 | 0.64 |
| –34.3 | 30.72 | 15.75 | McDonalds MCD | .24f | 1.4 | 14 | 57791 | 17.40 | 0.20 |
| –2.5 | 69.70 | 50.71 | McGrawH MHP | 1.02 | 1.7 | 26 | 6296 | 59.48 | –0.69 |
| –27.8 | 42.09 | 24.99 | McKesson MCK | .24 | .9 | 17 | 15741 | 27.01 | 0.16 |
| –15.2 | 6.35 | 2.54 | McMoRanExpl MMR | .35p | ... | dd | 196 | 4.91 | 0.16 |
| 21.6 | 4.14 | 1.55↓ | MdwbrkinsGp MIG | | ... | 20 | 416 | 2.42 | –0.02 |
| –25.1 | 36.50 | 15.57 | MeadWVaco MWV | .92 | 4.0 | dd | 4169 | 23.15 | –0.43 |
| 30.8 | 4.50 | 1.57 | MediaArts MDA | | ... | dd | 45 | 3.44 | 0.14 |
| 16.0 | 69.49 | 46.55 | MediaGen A MEG | .72 | 1.2 | dd | 644 | 57.80 | –0.03 |
| –34.7 | 29.75 | 9.25 | MedStaffNtwk MRN n | | ... | ... | 454 | 14.04 | –0.05 |
| –25.0 | 64.60 | 33.85 | MediclsPhrm MRX | | ... | 31 | 5997 | 48.45 | –0.42 |

Price of Mattel stock is 21 times its earnings

Closing price of May Department Stores stock

Stock yields a 1.8% dividend

McKesson went up 16¢ since the previous close

Stock pays a dividend of 72¢

High and low price for last 52 weeks

Change in stock price for year to date

Symbol for company

599,700 shares of this stock traded today

- The price/earnings ratio (P/E), which is the price of the stock divided by the firm's per share earnings. (For example, if the price of Very Vegetarian stock were $50, and the company earnings were $5 per share, Very Vegetarian's price/earnings ratio would be 10. Take a look again at the discussion of financial ratios at the end of Chapter 17.)
- The number of shares of stock in the company traded that day, in 100s.
- The stock's closing price for the day.
- The net change in the stock's price from the previous day.

Look down the columns and find the stock that's had the biggest price change over the past 52 weeks, the stock that pays the highest dividend, and the stock that has the highest and lowest price/earnings ratio. The more you look through the figures, the more sense they begin to make. You might want to build a hypothetical portfolio of stocks and track how they perform over the next six months. (See the Developing Workplace Skills and Taking It to the Net exercises at the end of this chapter for suggested exercises.)

## Understanding Mutual Fund Quotations

As we explained earlier, buying mutual funds is a way to get investment advice and diversify your investments at a minimum cost. Look up the listing of mutual funds in *The Wall Street Journal* (see Figure 19.9). You will see that many companies offer mutual funds. The various funds offer alternatives to meet investors' objectives. For example, the American Century mutual funds listed in Figure 19.9 highlight many different kinds of funds available from that company. You can learn about the specifics of the various funds by contacting a broker or contacting the fund directly by phone or through its Web page. Business publications can also guide you to free information from various mutual funds.

As you look across the columns in the mutual fund quotations, the information is rather simple to understand. The fund's name is in the first column, followed by the fund's net asset value (NAV), which is the market value of the mutual fund's portfolio divided by the number of shares it has outstanding. The NAV is the price per share of the mutual fund. The next column lists the net change in the NAV from the previous day's trading. The fund's year-to-date (YTD) return is in the next column. Finally, in this example, the fund's three-year return is listed. Publications like *The Wall Street Journal* list a fund's

figure 19.9

**UNDERSTANDING MUTUAL FUND QUOTATIONS**

Source: *The Wall Street Journal.*

| FUND | NAV | NET CHG | YTD %RET | 3-YR %RET |
|---|---|---|---|---|
| American Century Ist | | | | |
| DivBnd | 10.33 | –0.01 | 7.1 | 8.3 |
| EqIndex | 3.62 | –0.01 | –20.3 | –12.9 |
| EqGro | 15.58 | –0.01 | –18.4 | –12.0 |
| EqInc | 6.58 | –0.03 | –4.7 | 9.3 |
| IncGro | 22.29 | –0.03 | –17.6 | –10.8 |
| IntlDisc r | 9.01 | 0.04 | –12.4 | –13.7 |
| IntlGr | 6.51 | 0.02 | –18.4 | –16.8 |
| Select | 29.49 | –0.05 | –20.7 | –15.1 |
| StrMod | 5.32 | ... | –8.6 | NS |
| Ultra | 22.05 | –0.03 | –20.7 | –15.8 |
| Value | 6.03 | –0.02 | –11.8 | 6.6 |

Name of the fund family

The price at which a fund's shares can be purchased or sold; called net asset value

Name of the specific fund

The rate of percentage return of the fund year to date

Change from the previous day's net asset value (NAV)

Rate of percentage return of the fund for the past 3 years

13-week return, one-year return, and five-year return on different days of the week to provide investors with detailed information about funds that are listed.

It's simple to change your investment objectives with mutual funds. Switching your money, for example, from a bond fund to a stock fund and back is generally no more difficult than calling an 800 number or clicking a mouse. Mutual funds are a great way to begin investing to meet your financial objectives.

## Stock Market Indicators

When you listen to news reports on television or on radio, you often hear announcers say things like "The Dow Industrials are up 90 points today in active trading." Wonder what's going on? The **Dow Jones Industrial Average (the Dow)** is the average cost of 30 selected industrial stocks and is used to give an indication of the direction (up or down) of the stock market over time. A man named Charles Dow began the practice of measuring stock averages in 1884, using the prices of 12 important stocks. The 12 original stocks and the 30 current stocks in the Dow are illustrated in Figure 19.10. Do you recognize any of the 12 original companies?

**Dow Jones industrial Average (the Dow)**
The average cost of 30 selected industrial stocks, used to give an indication of the direction (up or down) of the stock market over time.

New stocks are substituted on the Dow when it's deemed appropriate. For example, the Dow was broadened in 1982 to include 30 stocks. In 1991, Disney was added to the Dow to reflect the increased importance of the service sector (again, see Figure 19.10). In 1997, the list was again altered, with Hewlett-Packard, Johnson & Johnson, Wal-Mart, and Citigroup replacing Texaco, Woolworth, Bethlehem Steel, and Westinghouse. In 1999, the Dow added Home Depot and SBC Communications along with its first NASDAQ stocks, Intel and Microsoft. Chevron, Sears Roebuck, Union Carbide, and Goodyear were eliminated. In 2004, American International Group, Pfizer, and Verizon replaced AT&T, International Paper, and Eastman Kodak. In 2005, AT&T rejoined the Dow when it merged with SBC.[39] The 30 current stocks in the Dow Jones Industrial Average also include such long-standing notables as General Electric, IBM, and Coca-Cola.

Critics argue that if the purpose of the Dow is to give an indication of the direction of the broader market over time, the 30-company sample is too small to get a good statistical representation. Many investors and market analysts

figure 19.10

**THE ORIGINAL DOW AND CURRENT DOW**

| THE ORIGINAL DOW 12 | THE 30 CURRENT DOW COMPANIES | |
|---|---|---|
| American Cotton Oil | Alcoa | Honeywell International |
| American Sugar Refining Co. | Altria | Intel |
| American Tobacco | American Express | International Business Machines (IBM) |
| Chicago Gas | American International Group | Johnson & Johnson |
| Distilling & Cattle Feeding Co. | AT&T | J. P. Morgan |
| General Electric Co. | Boeing | McDonald's |
| Laclede Gas Light Co. | Caterpillar | Merck |
| National Lead | Citigroup | Microsoft |
| North American Co. | Coca-Cola | Minnesota Mining & Manufacturing (3M) |
| Tennessee Coal, Iron & Railroad Co. | Du Pont | Pfizer |
| U.S. Leather | Exxon Mobil | Procter & Gamble |
| U.S. Rubber Co. | General Electric | United Technologies |
| | General Motors | Verizon |
| | Hewlett-Packard | Wal-Mart Stores |
| | Home Depot | Walt Disney |

therefore prefer to follow stock indexes like the Standard & Poor's 500 (S&P 500), which tracks the performance of 400 industrial, 40 financial, 40 public utility, and 20 transportation stocks. Investors also closely follow the NASDAQ average, which is quoted each trading day to show the trends that are occurring in this important exchange.

Staying abreast of what's happening in the market will help you decide what investments seem most appropriate to your needs and objectives. However, it's important to remember two key investment realities: The first is that your personal financial objectives and needs change over time. The second is that markets can be volatile. Let's look at the volatility that's inherent in the market and the challenges in the 21st century that promise to present investors with new risks and opportunities.

**program trading** Giving instructions to computers to automatically sell if the price of a stock dips to a certain point to avoid potential losses.

## The Market's Roller-Coaster Ride

Throughout the 1900s, the stock market had its ups and downs, spiced with several major tremors. The first "crash" occurred on Tuesday, October 29, 1929, when the stock market lost almost 13 percent of its value in a single day. That "Black Tuesday" brought home to investors the reality of market volatility, especially to those who were heavily margined. Many investors lost everything they had invested. On October 19, 1987, the stock market suffered the largest one-day drop in its history: The Dow Jones Industrial Average fell 508 points and lost over 22 percent of the market's value. The loss caused $500 billion to vanish before bewildered investors' eyes.

On October 27, 1997, investors felt the fury of the market once again. The Dow fell 554 points, primarily because of investors' fears of an impending economic crisis in Asian markets. Luckily, the market regained its strength after a short downturn. The market was not so fortunate in the early 2000s. The Dow, S&P 500, and NASDAQ all declined significantly in value from 2000 to 2002. Not since 1939–41 had the S&P declined three years in a row, and the NASDAQ had never fallen three consecutive years. All told, investors lost $7 trillion in market value from 2000 through 2002.

You can't say the stock market isn't exciting. Consider these freefalls: On October 29, 1929, the stock market crashed causing many investors to lose everything they owned. On October 19, 1987 (pictured here), stocks experienced the largest one-day drop in history. From 2000–2002, investors saw $7 trillion in market value disappear. What did we learn and what does the future hold?

What caused the market turmoil of 1929, 1987, 1997, and 2000–2002? Ask a dozen financial analysts and you will probably get a dozen different answers.[40] In 1987, however, many analysts agreed that program trading was a big cause of the disastrous fall. In **program trading**, investors give their computers instructions to sell automatically if the price of their stock dips to a certain point to avoid potential losses. On October 19, 1987, the computers became trigger-happy; sell orders caused many stocks to fall to unbelievable depths on that day.

The crash of 1987 prompted the U.S. exchanges to create mechanisms to restrict program trading whenever the market moves up or down by a large number of points in a trading day. The two major restrictions are called *curbs* and *circuit breakers*. Program trading curbs are put in effect when the Dow moves up or down more than a certain number of points (2 percent of the previous quarter's average value). Basically this means a key computer is turned off, so program trading must be done "by hand" rather than automatically by computer. When these restrictions are triggered, you'll see the phrase *curbs in* if you watch programming like CNBC or MSNBC.

Circuit breakers are more drastic restrictions that are triggered when the Dow falls 10, 20, or 30 percent in a day. Depending on the rate of decline and the time of day, the circuit breakers will halt trading for anywhere from half an hour to two hours so that traders have time to assess the situation. If the Dow drops 30 percent, however, trading closes for the entire day. Circuit breakers were triggered for the first and only time on October 27, 1997, when the Dow fell 350 points at 2:35 p.m. and 550 points at 3:30 p.m. That reflected an approximate 7 percent overall decline and shut the market for the remainder of the day. Many market watchers believe that the 1997 market drop could have been much worse had it not been for the new rules. Still, it's inevitable that market gyrations will persist, causing investors many headaches and sleepless nights.

## Investing Challenges in the 21st-Century Market

It's obvious from the market slides discussed above that in dealing with the stock market, what goes up can also go down. Furthermore, it's safe to presume that 21st-century markets will undergo changes and experience events that will only heighten their risk. The September 11, 2001, terrorist attacks on the World Trade Center and the Pentagon certainly proved that even a superpower like the United States is not immune to outside forces. They also reinforced the fact that today we live in a global market where all the economies of the world are closely linked. As we saw with the Asian financial crisis in 1997, negative events that affect one region economically affect other nation's economies as well.

Investor confidence and trust in corporations and the stock market also eroded in the early 2000s. Investor trust that the real value of companies was fairly reflected in company financial statements was shattered by disclosures of financial fraud at companies such as WorldCom, Enron, and Tyco. Investment analysts also came under fire as information revealed that they often provided wildly optimistic evaluations about companies they knew were not worth their current prices. Dramatic change has impacted the securities exchanges as well. The NYSE and the NASDAQ are intensely competitive in the search for investors' dollars.

Traditional brokers such as Merrill Lynch and A. G. Edwards have changed the way they do business due to challenges from online brokers like E*Trade, which attracted more and more investors. These challenges and changes, along with the growing influence and activity of institutional investors, promise to make securities markets exciting but not always stable places to be in the 21st century.

The basic lessons to keep in mind are the importance of diversifying your investments and understanding the risks of investing. Taking a long-term perspective is also a wise idea. The 1990s saw the market reach unparalleled heights only to collapse into a deep bear market in 2000–2002 and then slowly recover through the mid-2000s. Advertisements by brokerage firms in print and on television could make you think that investing in the market is guaranteed money in the bank. Don't be fooled, and don't be driven by greed. It's critical for you to know that there's no such thing as easy money or a sure thing. Investing is a challenging and interesting field that's always changing. If you carefully research companies and industries, keep up with the news, and make use of investment resources—such as newspapers, magazines, newsletters, the Internet, and TV programs—the payoff can be highly rewarding. You may want to refer to this chapter again when you read about personal finance in the bonus chapter at the end of book.

**progress assessment**

- What does the Dow Jones Industrial Average measure? Why is it important?
- Why do the 30 companies comprising the Dow change periodically?
- Explain program trading and the problems it can create.

# summary

**1.** Identify and explain the functions of securities markets, and discuss the role of investment bankers.

1. Securities markets provide opportunities for businesses and investors.
   - **What opportunities are provided to businesses and individual investors by securities markets?**

   Businesses are able to raise much-needed funding to help finance major expenses of the firm. Individual investors can share in the success and growth of emerging firms by having the opportunity of investing in the firm.
   - **What role do investment bankers play in securities markets?**

   Investment bankers are specialists who assist in the issue and sale of new securities.

**2.** Compare the advantages and disadvantages of debt financing by issuing bonds, and identify the classes and features of bonds.

2. Companies can raise capital by debt financing, which involves issuing bonds.
   - **What are the advantages and disadvantages of issuing bonds?**

   The advantages of issuing bonds include the following: (1) Management retains control since bondholders cannot vote; (2) interest paid on bonds is tax deductible; (3) bonds are only a temporary source of financing, and after they are paid off the debt is eliminated; and (4) bonds can be paid back early if they are issued with a call provision and often bonds can be convertible to common stock. The disadvantages of bonds include the following: (1) Because bonds are an increase in debt, they may affect the market's perception of the company adversely; (2) interest on bonds must be paid; and (3) the bond's face value must be repaid on the maturity date.
   - **Are there different types of bonds?**

   Yes. There are unsecured (debenture) and secured bonds. Unsecured bonds are not supported by collateral, whereas secured bonds are backed by tangible assets such as mortgages, buildings, and equipment.

**3.** Compare the advantages and disadvantages of equity financing by issuing stock, and explain the differences between common and preferred stock.

3. Companies can also raise capital by equity financing, which involves selling stock.
   - **What are the advantages and disadvantages of selling stock?**

   The advantages of selling stock include the following: (1) The stock price never has to be repaid since stockholders are owners in the company; (2) there is no legal obligation to pay dividends; and (3) no debt is incurred, so the company is financially stronger. Disadvantages of selling stock include the following: (1) Stockholders become owners of the firm and can affect its management by voting for the board of directors; (2) it is more costly to pay dividends, since they are paid after taxes; and (3) managers may be tempted to make stockholders happy in the short term rather than plan for long-term needs.
   - **What are the differences between common and preferred stock?**

   Holders of common stock have voting rights in the company. Holders of preferred stock generally have no voting rights. In exchange for having no voting rights, preferred stocks offer a fixed dividend that must be paid in full before common stockholders receive a dividend. Preferred stockholders are also paid back their investment before common stockholders if the company is forced out of business.

**4.** Describe the various stock exchanges where securities are traded.

4. Stock exchanges afford investors the opportunity of investing in securities markets through the different investment options that are offered.
   - **What is a stock exchange?**

   Stock exchanges are securities markets whose members are involved in buying and selling securities such as bonds and stocks.

- **What are the different exchanges?**

There are stock exchanges all over the world. The largest U.S. exchange is the New York Stock Exchange (NYSE). It and the American Stock Exchange (AMEX) together are known as national exchanges because they handle stock of companies all over the country. In addition, there are several regional exchanges that deal primarily with companies in their own areas.

- **What is the over-the-counter (OTC) market?**

The OTC market is a system for exchanging stocks not listed on the national exchanges.

5. Securities markets provide opportunities to buy and sell investments.

**5.** Explain how to invest in securities markets and various investment objectives such as long-term growth, income, cash, and protection from inflation.

- **How do investors normally make purchases in securities markets?**

Investors generally purchase investments through market intermediaries called stockbrokers, who provide many different services. Online investing is also very popular.

- **What are the criteria for selecting investments?**

Investors should determine their overall financial objectives. Are they interested in growth, income, cash, or a hedge against inflation? Investments should be evaluated with regard to (1) risk, (2) yield, (3) duration, (4) liquidity, and (5) tax consequences.

- **How are securities exchanges regulated?**

The Securities and Exchange Commission (SEC) is responsible for regulating securities exchanges. Also, according to SEC rules, companies that intend to sell bonds or stock to the public must provide a prospectus to potential investors.

- **What is insider trading?**

Insider trading involves the use of information or knowledge that individuals gain through their position that allows them to benefit unfairly from fluctuations in security prices.

6. Bonds present opportunities for investors.

**6.** Analyze the opportunities bonds offer as investments.

- **What is the difference between a bond selling at a discount and a bond selling at a premium?**

A bond selling at a premium is a bond that can be sold in securities markets (secondary market) at a price above its face value. A bond selling at a discount is a bond that can be sold in securities markets (secondary market) but at a price below its face value.

7. Stocks present opportunities for investors to enhance their financial position.

**7.** Explain the opportunities stocks offer as investments.

- **What is a market order?**

A market order tells a broker to buy or to sell a security immediately at the best price available. A limit order tells the broker to buy or sell at a specific price if the stock reaches that price.

- **What does it mean when a stock splits?**

When a stock splits, stockholders receive two or more shares of stock for each share they own. Each share is then worth half or less of the original share. Therefore, while the number of the shares in the company increases, the total value of the stockholders' holdings stays the same. The lower price per share may increase demand for the stock.

8. Mutual funds are attractive investments for small or beginning investors.

**8.** Explain the opportunities in mutual funds and exchange-traded funds (ETFs) as investments, and the benefits of diversifying investments.

- **How can mutual funds help individuals diversify their investments?**

A mutual fund is an organization that buys stocks and bonds and then sells shares in those securities to the public. Individuals who buy shares in a mutual fund are able to invest in many different companies they could not afford to invest in otherwise.

- **What is diversification?**

Diversification means buying several different types of investments (government bonds, corporate bonds, preferred stock, common stock, etc.) with different degrees of risk. The purpose is to reduce the overall risk an investor would assume by just investing in one type of security.

- **What are ETFs?**

ETFs are similar to mutual funds in that they are collections of stocks that are traded on exchanges, but are traded more like individual stocks.

**9.** Discuss specific high-risk investments, including junk bonds, buying stock on margin, and commodity trading.

9. Other types of speculative investments are available for investors seeking large returns on their investments.

- **What is a junk bond?**

Junk bonds are high-risk (rated BB or below), high-interest debenture bonds that speculative investors often find attractive.

- **What does buying on margin mean?**

It means that the investor borrows up to 50 percent of the cost of a stock from the broker so he or she can get shares of stock without paying the full price of the stock.

- **What are commodity exchanges?**

Commodity exchanges specialize in the buying and selling of precious metals and minerals (e.g., silver, oil) and agricultural goods (e.g., wheat, cattle, sugar).

**10.** Explain securities quotations listed in the financial section of a newspaper, and describe how stock market indicators like the Dow Jones Industrial Average affect the market.

10. Security quotations and Dow Jones Industrial Averages are listed daily in newspapers.

- **What information do stock quotations give you?**

The stock quotations give you all kinds of information: the highest price in the last 52 weeks; the lowest price; the dividend yield; the price/earnings ratio; the total shares traded that day; and the close and net change in price from the previous day. Bond quotations give you information regarding trading bonds in securities markets, as do quotations concerning mutual funds.

- **What is the Dow Jones Industrial Average?**

The Dow Jones Industrial Average is the average price of 30 specific stocks used to indicate a direction (up or down) of the stock market.

## key terms

**bond** 513
**buying stock on margin** 530
**capital gains** 526
**commodity exchange** 531
**common stock** 518
**debenture bonds** 515
**diversification** 530
**dividends** 516
**Dow Jones Industrial Average (the Dow)** 535
**exchange-traded funds (ETFs)** 528
**futures markets** 531
**initial public offering (IPO)** 512
**institutional investors** 513
**interest** 513
**investment bankers** 513
**junk bonds** 530
**maturity date** 514
**mutual fund** 527
**NASDAQ** 521
**over-the-counter (OTC) market** 520
**preferred stock** 517
**program trading** 536
**prospectus** 521
**Securities and Exchange Commission (SEC)** 521
**sinking fund** 515
**stockbroker** 522
**stock certificate** 516
**stock exchange** 519
**stocks** 516
**stock splits** 527

## critical thinking questions

1. Why do companies like callable bonds? Why do investors dislike them?
2. Imagine that you inherited $50,000 and that you want to invest it to meet two of your financial goals: (1) to save for a wedding you plan to have in two years and (2) to save for your retirement a few decades from now. How would you invest the money? Explain your answer.
3. If you are considering investing in the bond market, how could information provided by Standard & Poor's and Moody's Investors Service help you?
4. If you are considering investing in the stock market, would you prefer individual stocks, mutual funds, or ETFs? What are the advantages and disadvantages of each?
5. Why would manufacturers of products such as candy, coffee, and bread be interested in the futures market?

## developing workplace skills

1. Go to the Web sites of Charles Schwab (www.schwab.com), E*Trade (www.etrade.com), and Ameritrade (www.ameritrade.com). Investigate each of the brokerage companies and compare what they offer to investors in terms of research and advice and how their fee structures work. Evaluate each of the brokers according to services they offer, and decide which service you consider most appropriate to your investment objectives. Be prepared to defend your choice to the class.
2. Read *The Wall Street Journal*, *Investor's Business Daily*, or the business section of your local newspaper each day for two weeks and then select three stocks for your portfolio from the New York Stock Exchange and three from the NASDAQ. Track the stocks in your portfolio and use a computer to graphically display the trends of each one on a weekly basis. See how market trends and information affect your stocks and write out a brief explanation of why your stocks were affected.
3. U.S. government bonds compete with corporations for investors' dollars. Check out the different types of savings bonds that are offered by the federal government and make a list of the types most appealing to you.
4. See if anyone is interested in setting up an investment game in your class. Each student should choose one stock and one mutual fund. Record each student's selections and the corresponding prices on a chart. In six weeks, look up and chart the prices again. Discuss the results in terms of percentage gain or loss.
5. Many businesses try to raise funds by offering new stock offerings called initial public offerings (IPOs). Go to the library, obtain recent financial publications like *The Wall Street Journal* or *Investor's Business Daily*—or go to www.schwab.com, www.etrade.com, or www.ameritrade.com—to find two IPOs that have been offered during the past six months. Track the performance of each IPO from its introduction to its present price.

## taking it to the net

**Purpose**

To evaluate the advantages and disadvantage of ETFs.

**Exercise**

Exchange-traded funds (ETFs) have become a popular investment option for those who are looking for a low-cost, flexible way to diversify their portfolios. To learn more about ETFs, go to www.etrade.com and click on the "Mutual Funds, ETFs, and Bonds" tab.

1. What are the pros and cons of investing in ETFs?
2. What are the five most actively traded ETFs?
3. Which funds had the most growth in the last three years?
4. In which industry sectors and/or countries do these high-growth funds specialize?

## casing the web

To access the case *"Making Dreams Come True,"* visit **www.mhhe.com/ub8e**

## video case

### A Fool and His Money: Motley Fool

Matthew-Emmert is no fool, but he loves working for Motley Fool, the company that provides people with financial advice. He enjoys talking about stocks and bonds, and Motley Fool gives him the chance to do that—and make money as well. What a deal! Being a typical broker was not Matt's idea of a good time. The Motley Fool atmosphere is much more relaxed and customer oriented.

David and Tom Gardner started Motley Fool to help people with their investments. They got started by sending out a newsletter and expanded into books, a Web site, and more. Now they have their own radio show and give seminars. Basically, they do whatever they think might help their clients become better investors.

One investment people can make is to buy stock (ownership of the firm). Stocks are sold on the various exchanges: NYSE, AMEX, and NASDAQ. When you buy a stock, you don't care as much where it is sold; you just want to buy a company that will prosper and grow and earn you money. Most people buy common stock. Others buy preferred stock. That is a kind of stock that pays dividends (a share of the profits) and has a certain preference when it comes to dividing a firm's assets if it fails. You can buy income stocks that pay a large dividend; growth stocks that don't pay a dividend, but are expected to grow faster than most companies; or penny stocks that cost a few dollars, but could rise dramatically if conditions are right.

So how does a person know what stocks to buy and when? That's where the Motley Fool organization comes in. For college students, they would recommend starting with an index fund. An index fund is made up of a bundle of stocks (such as 500 stocks chosen by Standard & Poor's). The idea is to own a whole bunch of companies so that your risk is spread among different companies in different industries. The broader the index, the better. That is, an index of the whole stock exchange is better than one that buys just high-tech stocks or just growth stocks.

Another investment people can make is to buy bonds (lending money to firms). Bonds pay interest, much like the interest you would make by putting your money in a bank. Since a bond is a loan, it states when the loan is due (maturity date) and how much interest it will pay. Some bonds, called junk bonds, are quite risky, but pay high interest. Other bonds are convertible into shares of stock if the price goes up high enough. You are likely to get a better return from investing in stocks rather than bonds. But stocks are said to be more risky, so there is a risk/reward trade-off you have to explore.

To the average investor, there are simply too many choices—too many decisions to make. So Motley Fool tries to help by making the process as simple and as understandable as possible. They wouldn't encourage you, for example, to buy stock on margin (that is, borrow money to buy stock). They wouldn't encourage you to become a day trader either (buying and selling stock often, sometimes within hours). Rather, they would encourage you to buy into an index fund or two and then buy a few shares of stock in companies they recommend. Investing can be fun, especially when you fool around with the "fools" at Motley Fool. But you can lose a lot of money if you are not careful. That's why Matt Emmert and the other employees are there—to help you be a little less foolish with your money.

### Thinking It Over

1. What have you learned in this video that might help you to become a better investor in the future?
2. Would you like to receive advice from a company like Motley Fool? Just go to www.fool.com and you can sign up easily.
3. What have you learned about stocks and bonds that would lead you to invest in index funds of stock rather than bonds? Would that be as true for someone just about to retire? Why?
4. Why do you suppose it is important to learn about stocks and bonds now rather than later in your life when you have more money to invest?

# understanding money, financial institutions, AND THE federal reserve

profile

**Getting to Know**

X *Ben S. Bernanke*

**of the Federal Reserve**

In 2006, President George W. Bush appointed Ben Bernanke (pronounced ber-*nan*-kee) as chairman of the Federal Reserve Board. Bernanke was born in Augusta, Georgia. He taught himself calculus and got 1590 out of 1600 on his college board exams. He graduated from Harvard summa cum laude with a bachelor's degree in economics and then earned a PhD from MIT. For seven years, he was an economics professor and department chair at Princeton. He was a member of the Board of Governors at the Fed from 2002 to 2005, serving alongside Alan Greenspan, who was the head of the U.S. Federal Reserve System from 1987 to 2006. Bernanke was previously appointed chairman of the President's Council of Economic Advisers in 2005.

As head of the Federal Reserve, Bernanke is now one of the most powerful men in the United States. You can understand how important this position is by reviewing what Alan Greenspan did as chairman. Under Greenspan's leadership, the United States enjoyed the longest economic expansion in its history. Greenspan had control over the nation's money supply. One tool he used was interest rates. He raised interest rates several times in 1999/2000 to slow the growth of the economy. He felt it was overheated; that is, he feared

LEARNING goals

After you have read and studied this chapter, you should be able to

1. Explain what money is and how its value is determined.
2. Describe how the Federal Reserve controls the money supply.
3. Trace the history of banking and the Federal Reserve System.
4. Classify the various institutions in the U.S. banking system.
5. Explain the importance of the Federal Deposit Insurance Corporation and other organizations that guarantee funds.
6. Discuss the future of the U.S. banking system.
7. Evaluate the role and importance of international banking, and the role of the World Bank and the International Monetary Fund.

CHAPTER 20

www.bog.frb.fed.us

inflation. As it turned out, the economy slowed too fast (due to many circumstances, including the higher interest rates), and Greenspan began cutting interest rates to get the economy moving again. He ended up cutting them 13 times. Those cuts were not as effective as hoped; the stock market stalled, and the United States entered a recession. Some people believed that cutting taxes and lowering interest rates together would get the economy moving again. The economy *did* begin growing, and Greenspan raised interest rates time after time to slow the rate of growth. People are now watching Bernanke to see how he will respond to the ups and downs of the economy. One thing Bernanke did early in his tenure as Fed Chairman was to continue raising interest rates.

Bernanke said, "My first priority will be to maintain continuity with the policies and policy strategies established during the Greenspan years." His challenges include managing the nation's trade deficit, a possible cooling of the housing market, and the possible continuation of high energy prices. The country will be watching Bernanke to see how effective he will be in keeping the economy growing.

The major difference between Bernanke and Greenspan is said to be Bernanke's view of inflation. Greenspan tended to use his own judgment when changing interest rates. He didn't follow any set prescription. Bernanke, however, will likely follow something called inflation targeting. The idea is to choose some level of inflation, say 2 percent, and then use monetary policy to reach that rate. If inflation is above that rate, the Fed will raise interest rates and vice versa. Having such targets gives the public a better idea of what the Fed is likely to do in the future. Furthermore, Bernanke has the ability to explain his policies in a clear and concise manner, something that didn't always occur with Greenspan. You will learn more about the Federal Reserve and the banking system in general in this chapter. Using that information, you can better understand the decisions being made by the new head of the Federal Reserve.

Sources: Justin Fox, "The Fed's Glory Days Are Over," *Fortune*, April 4, 2005, pp. 26–28; Greg Ip, "Bernanke Is Named to Lead the Fed," *The Wall Street Journal*, October 25, 2005, pp. A1 and A17; Robert J. Barro, "Goodbye Mr. Big Chips," *The Wall Street Journal*, January 30, 2006, p. A18: James C. Cooper, "Bernanke May Have His Work Cut Out for Him," *BusinessWeek*, February 6, 2006, p. 29; and Nell Henderson, "From Fed, More of the Same," *Washington Post*, March 29, 2006, pp. D1 and D2.

# WHY MONEY IS IMPORTANT

The U.S. economy depends heavily on money: its availability and its value relative to other currencies. Economic growth and the creation of jobs depend on money. Money is so important to the economy that many institutions have evolved to manage money and to make it available to you when you need it. Today you can easily get cash from an automated teller machine (ATM) almost anywhere in the world, but in many places cash isn't the only means of payment you can use. Most organizations will accept a check, credit card, debit card, or smart card for purchases. The Bank of Japan reported the first drop ever in the number of coins in circulation. One reason is the electronic cash stored in smart cards and even mobile phones.[1] Behind the scenes of this free flow of money is a complex system of banking that makes it possible for you to do all these things.

The complexity of the banking system has increased as the electronic flow of money from country to country has become as free as that from state to state. Each day, more than $1.5 *trillion* is exchanged in the world's currency markets. Therefore, what happens to any major country's economy has an effect on the U.S. economy and vice versa. Clearly, there's more to money and its role in the economies of the world than meets the eye. There's no way to understand the U.S. economy without understanding global money exchanges and the various institutions involved in the creation and management of money.

We'll explore such institutions in this chapter. Let's start at the beginning by discussing exactly what people mean when they say "money" and how the supply of money affects the prices you pay for goods and services.

**money**
Anything that people generally accept as payment for goods and services.

**barter**
The trading of goods and services for other goods and services directly.

## What Is Money?

**Money** is anything that people generally accept as payment for goods and services. In the past, objects as diverse as salt, feathers, stones, rare shells, tea, and horses have been used as money. In fact, until the 1880s, cowrie shells were one of the world's most abundant currencies. **Barter** is the trading of goods and services for other goods and services directly. Though barter may sound like something from the past, many people have discovered the benefits of bartering online. Others still barter goods and services the old-fashioned way—face-to-face. For example, in Siberia two eggs have been used to buy one admission to a movie, and customers of Ukraine's Chernobyl nuclear plant have paid in sausages and milk. Some of the trade in Russia over recent years has been done in barter.

The problem is that eggs and milk are difficult to carry around. People need some object that's portable, divisible, durable, and stable so that they can trade goods and services without carrying the actual goods around with them. One answer to that problem over the years was to create coins made of silver or gold. Coins met five standards for a useful form of money:

- **Portability**. Coins are a lot easier to take to market than are pigs or other heavy products.
- **Divisibility**. Different-sized coins could be made to represent different values. For example, prior to 1963, a U.S. quarter had half as much silver content as a half dollar, and a dollar had four times the silver of a quarter. Because silver is now too expensive, today's coins are made of other metals, but the accepted values remain.
- **Stability**. When everybody agrees on the value of coins, the value of money is relatively stable. In fact, U.S. money has become so stable that

much of the world has used the U.S. dollar as the measure of value.

- **Durability**. Coins last for thousands of years, even when they've sunk to the bottom of the ocean, as you've seen when divers find old Roman coins in sunken ships.
- **Uniqueness**. It's hard to counterfeit, or copy, elaborately designed and minted coins. But with the latest color copiers, people are able to duplicate the look of paper money relatively easily. Thus, the government has had to go to extra lengths to make sure real dollars are readily identifiable. That's why you have new paper money with the picture slightly off center and with new invisible lines that quickly show up when reviewed by banks and stores. Note the blue, peach, and green colors in the new $20 bill. Other denominations of bills also have new colors.[2]

Newly engraved bills make it much harder to counterfeit money. The bills look a little different and are different colors from previous engravings. If you owned a store, would you teach your employees how to recognize a legitimate bill?

When coins and paper money became units of value, they simplified exchanges. Most countries now have their own coins and paper money, and they're all about equally portable, divisible, and durable. However, they're not always equally stable.

Electronic cash (e-cash) is the latest form of money. In addition to being able to make online bill payments using software programs such as Quicken or Microsoft Money, you can e-mail e-cash to anyone using Web sites such as Pay Pal (owned by eBay). Recipients get an e-mail message telling them they have several choices for how they can receive the money: automatic deposit (the money will be sent to their bank), e-dollars for spending online, or a traditional check in the mail. Foreign nationals who work in America can cash checks, pay bills, and send money home by using kiosks at over a thousand 7-Eleven stores throughout the United States. Companies are also developing ways to send money across national boundaries using mobile phones.[3]

## What Is the Money Supply?

This chapter's opening profile features Ben Bernanke. As Fed Chairman, he is in control of the money supply. Two questions emerge from that simple statement: (1) What is the money supply? and (2) Why does it need to be controlled?

The **money supply** is the amount of money the Federal Reserve Bank makes available for people to buy goods and services. There are several ways of referring to the money supply. They're called M-1, M-2, and so on. The *M* stands for money, and the *1* and *2* stand for different definitions of the money supply. **M-1**, for example, includes coins and paper bills, money that's available by writing checks (demand deposits and share drafts), and money that's held in traveler's checks—that is, money that can be accessed quickly and easily. **M-2** includes everything in M-1 plus money in savings accounts, and money in money market accounts, mutual funds, certificates of deposit, and the like—that is, money that may take a little more time to obtain than coins and paper bills. M-2 is the most commonly used definition of money. M-3 is M-2 plus big deposits (e.g., institutional money-market funds and agreements among banks).

**money supply**
The amount of money the Federal Reserve Bank makes available for people to buy goods and services.

**M-l**
Money that can be accessed quickly and easily (coins and paper money, checks, traveler's checks, etc.).

**M-2**
Money included in M-l plus money that may take a little more time to obtain (savings accounts, money market accounts, mutual funds, certificates of deposit, etc.).

## Why Does the Money Supply Need to Be Controlled?

Imagine what would happen if governments (or in the case of the United States, the Federal Reserve, a nongovernmental organization) were to generate twice as much money as exists now. There would be twice as much money available, but there would be the same amount of goods and services. What would happen to prices in that case? Think about the answer for a minute. (Hint: Remember the laws of supply and demand from Chapter 2.) The answer is that prices would go up because more people would try to buy goods and services with their money and would bid up the price to get what they wanted. This is called inflation. That is why some people define inflation as "too much money chasing too few goods."

Now think about the opposite: What would happen if the Fed took some of the money out of the economy? What would happen to prices? Prices would go down because there would be an oversupply of goods and services compared to the money available to buy them; this is called deflation. If too much money is taken out of the economy, a recession might occur. That is, people would lose jobs and the economy would stop growing.

Now we come to a second question about the money supply: Why does the money supply need to be controlled? The money supply needs to be controlled because doing so allows us to manage the prices of goods and services somewhat. And controlling the money supply affects employment and economic growth or decline. That's why Ben Bernanke is so important. He is the person in charge of the money supply.

## The Global Exchange of Money

A *falling dollar value* means that the amount of goods and services you can buy with a dollar decreases. A *rising dollar value* means that the amount of goods and services you can buy with a dollar goes up. Thus, in real terms, the price you pay for a German car would be lower if the American dollar rose relative to the euro (Europe's current unit of money).[4] However, if the euro gained strength and rose in value relative to the U.S. dollar, the cost of cars from Germany would go up.[5]

What makes the dollar weak (falling dollar value) or strong (rising dollar value) is the position of the U.S. economy relative to other economies. When the economy is strong, the demand for dollars is high and the value of the dollar rises.[6] When the economy is perceived as weakening, however, the demand for dollars declines and the value of the dollar falls.[7] The value of the dollar thus depends on a strong economy. Clearly, control over the money supply is important. In the following section, we'll discuss in more detail the money supply and how it's managed. Then we'll explore the U.S. banking system and how it lends money to businesses and individuals, such as you and me.

# CONTROL OF THE MONEY SUPPLY

You already know that money plays a huge role in the American economy and in the economies of the rest of the world. Therefore, it's important to have an organization that controls the money supply to try to keep the U.S. economy from growing too fast or too slow. Theoretically, with the proper monetary policy, you can keep the economy growing without causing inflation. (See Chapter 2 to review monetary policy.) The organization in charge of monetary policy is the Federal Reserve System (the Fed).

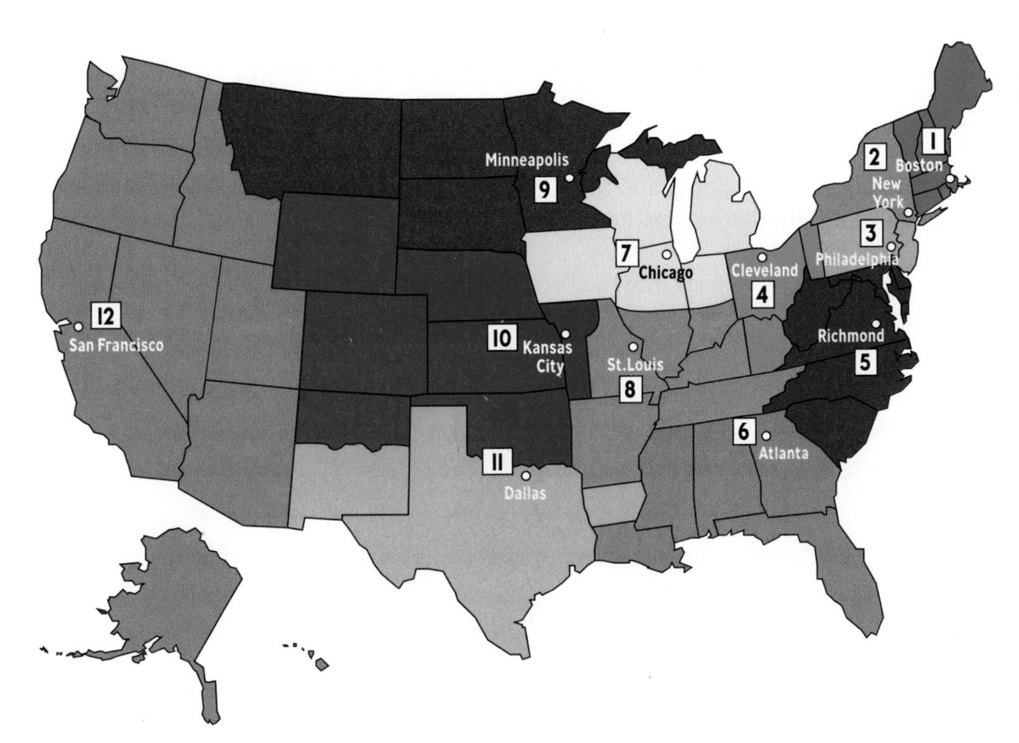


figure 20.1

**THE 12 FEDERAL RESERVE DISTRICT BANKS**

## Basics about the Federal Reserve

The Federal Reserve System consists of five major parts: (1) the board of governors; (2) the Federal Open Market Committee (FOMC); (3) 12 Federal Reserve banks; (4) three advisory councils; and (5) the member banks of the system. Figure 20.1 shows where the 12 Federal Reserve banks are. Member banks may be chartered by the federal government or by the state in which they're located.

The board of governors administers and supervises the 12 Federal Reserve banks. The seven members of the board are appointed by the president and confirmed by the Senate. The board's primary function is to set monetary policy. The Federal Open Market Committee (FOMC) has 12 voting members and is the policymaking body. The committee is made up of the seven-member board of governors plus the president of the New York reserve bank. Four others rotate in from the other reserve banks. The advisory councils offer suggestions to the board and to the FOMC. The councils represent the various banking districts, consumers, and member institutions, including banks, savings and loan institutions, and credit unions.

The Fed buys and sells foreign currencies, regulates various types of credit, supervises banks, and collects data on the money supply and other economic activity. As part of monetary policy, the Fed determines the reserve requirement, that is, the level of reserves that must be kept at the 12 Federal Reserve banks by all financial institutions. It also lends money to member banks and sets the rate for such loans (called the *discount rate*). Finally, it buys and sells government securities in what are known as open-market operations. It is important to understand how the Fed controls the money supply, so we'll explore that in some depth next. As noted, the three basic tools the Fed uses to manage the money supply are reserve requirements, open-market operations, and the discount rate (see Figure 20.2 on page 550). Let's explore how each of these is administered.

| CONTROL METHOD | IMMEDIATE RESULT | LONG-TERM EFFECT |
|---|---|---|
| **Reserve Requirements** | | |
| A. Increase. | Banks put more money into the Fed, *reducing* money supply; thus, there is less money available to lend to customers. | Economy slows. |
| B. Decrease. | Banks put less money into the Fed, *increasing* the money supply; thus, there is more money available to lend to customers. | Economy speeds up. |
| **Open-Market Operations** | | |
| A. Fed sells bonds. | Money flows from economy to the Fed. | Economy slows. |
| B. Fed buys bonds. | Money flows into the economy from the Fed. | Economy speeds up. |
| **Managing the Discount Rate** | | |
| A. Rate increases. | Banks borrow less from the Fed; thus, there is less money to lend. | Economy slows. |
| B. Rate decreases. | Banks borrow more from the Fed; thus, there is more money to lend. | Economy speeds up. |

figure 20.2

**HOW THE FEDERAL RESERVE CONTROLS THE MONEY SUPPLY**

**reserve requirement**
A percentage of commercial banks' checking and savings accounts that must be physically kept in the bank.

## The Reserve Requirement

The **reserve requirement** is a percentage of commercial banks' checking and savings accounts that must be physically kept in the bank (e.g., as cash in the vault) or in a non-interest-bearing deposit at the local Federal Reserve district bank. The reserve requirement is one of the Fed's most powerful tools. When the Fed increases the reserve requirement, banks have less money for loans and thus make fewer loans. Money becomes scarcer, which in the long run tends to reduce inflation. For instance, if Omaha Security Bank holds deposits of $100 million and the reserve requirement is, say, 10 percent, then the bank must keep $10 million on reserve. If the Fed were to increase the reserve requirement to 11 percent, then the bank would have to put an additional $1 million on reserve, thus reducing the amount it could lend out. Since this increase in the reserve requirement would affect all banks, the money supply would be reduced and prices would likely fall.

A decrease of the reserve requirement, in contrast, increases the funds available to banks for loans, so banks make more loans and money becomes more readily available. An increase in the money supply stimulates the economy to achieve higher growth rates, but it can also create inflationary pressures. That is, the prices of goods and services may go up.

**open-market operations**
The buying and selling of U.S. government bonds by the Fed with the goal of regulating the money supply.

## Open-Market Operations

**Open-market operations** are a commonly used tool by the Fed; they consist of buying and selling government bonds. To decrease the money supply, the federal government sells U.S. government bonds to the public. The money it gets as payment is no longer in circulation, decreasing the money supply. If the Fed wants to increase the money supply, it buys government bonds from individuals, corporations, or organizations that are willing to sell. The money paid by the Fed in return for these securities enters circulation, resulting in an increase in the money supply.

## The Discount Rate

The Fed has often been called the bankers' bank. One reason for this is that member banks can borrow money from the Fed and then pass it on to their customers in the form of loans. The **discount rate** is the interest rate that the Fed charges for loans to member banks. An increase in the discount rate by the Fed discourages banks from borrowing and consequently reduces the number of available loans, resulting in a decrease in the money supply. In contrast, lowering the discount rate encourages member banks to borrow money and increases the funds available for loans, which increases the money supply. The discount rate is one of two interest rates the Fed controls. The Fed also sets the rate that banks charge each other (the *federal funds rate*).

**discount rate**
The interest rate that the Fed charges for loans to member banks.

## The Federal Reserve's Check-Clearing Role

One of the functions of the Federal Reserve System is to help process your checks. If you write a check to a local retailer, that retailer will take the check to its bank. If your account is also at that bank, it is a simple matter to reduce your account by the amount of the check and increase the amount in the retailer's account. But what happens if you write a check to a retailer in another state? That retailer will take the check to its bank. That bank will deposit the check for credit in the closest Federal Reserve bank. That bank will send the check to your local Federal Reserve bank for collection. The check will then be sent to your bank and the amount of the check will be withdrawn. Your bank will authorize the Federal Reserve bank in your area to deduct the amount of the check. That bank will pay the Federal Reserve bank that began the process in the first place. It will then credit the deposit account in the bank where the retailer has its account. That bank will then credit the account of the retailer. (See Figure 20.3 on page 552 for a diagram of such an interstate transaction.) This long and involved process is a costly one; therefore, banks take many measures to lessen the use of checks. Such efforts include the use of credit cards, debit cards, and other electronic transfers of money.

As you can see, the whole economy is affected by the Federal Reserve System's actions. In the following sections, we'll briefly discuss the history of banking to give you some background information on why the Fed came into existence. Then we'll explore what's happening in banking today.

### progress assessment

- What is money?
- What are the five characteristics of useful money?
- What is the money supply, and why is it important?
- What are the various ways the Federal Reserve controls the money supply, and how do they work?
- What are the major functions of the Federal Reserve? What other functions does it perform?

# THE HISTORY OF BANKING AND THE NEED FOR THE FED

It will be easier for you to understand why we have a Federal Reserve System and why it is so important to the economy if we trace the history of banking in the United States. At first, there were no banks. Strict laws in Europe limited

figure 20.3

**CHECK-CLEARING PROCESS THROUGH THE FEDERAL RESERVE BANK SYSTEM**

Suppose Mr. Brown, a farmer from Quince Orchard, Maryland, purchases a tractor from a dealer in Austin, Texas.

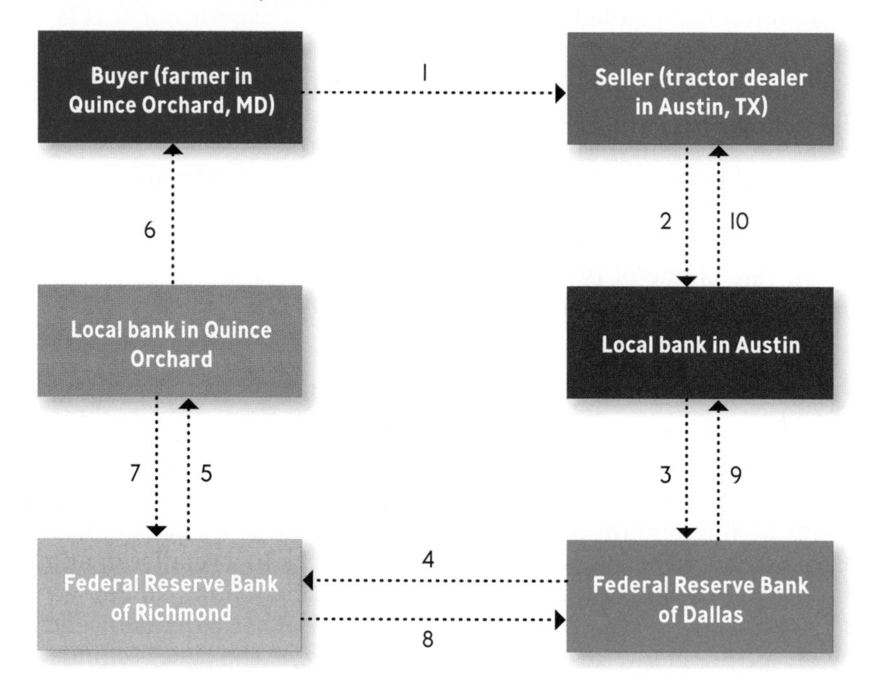


1. Mr. Brown sends his check to the tractor dealer.
2. The dealer deposits the check in his account at a local bank in Austin.
3. The Austin bank deposits the check for credit in its account at the Federal Reserve Bank of Dallas.
4. The Federal Reserve Bank of Dallas sends the check to the Federal Reserve Bank of Richmond for collection.
5. The Federal Reserve Bank of Richmond forwards the check to the local bank in Quince Orchard, where Mr. Brown opens his account.
6. The local bank in Quince Orchard deducts the check amount from Mr. Brown's account.
7. The Quince Orchard bank authorizes the Federal Reserve Bank of Richmond to deduct the check amount from its deposit account with the Federal Reserve Bank.
8. The Federal Reserve Bank of Richmond pays the Federal Reserve Bank of Dallas.
9. The Federal Reserve Bank of Dallas credits the Austin bank's deposit account.
10. The Austin bank credits the tractor dealer's account.

the number of coins that could be brought to the colonies in the New World. Thus, colonists were forced to barter for goods; for example, cotton and tobacco may have been traded for shoes and lumber.

The demand for money was so great that Massachusetts issued its own paper money in 1690, and other colonies soon followed suit. But continental money, the first paper money printed in the United States, became worthless after a few years because people didn't trust its value.

*Land banks* were established to lend money to farmers. But Great Britain, still in charge of the colonies at that point, ended land banks by 1741. The colonies rebelled against these and other restrictions on their freedom, and a new bank was formed in Pennsylvania during the American Revolution to finance the war against England.

In 1791, after the United States gained independence, Alexander Hamilton persuaded Congress to form a *central bank* (a bank at which other banks could keep their funds and borrow funds if needed), over the objections of Thomas Jefferson and others.[8] This first version of a federal bank closed in 1811, only to be replaced in 1816 because state-chartered banks couldn't support the War of 1812. The battle between the Second (Central) Bank of the United States and state banks got hot in the 1830s. Several banks in Tennessee were hurt by pressure from the Central Bank. The fight ended when the bank was closed in 1836. You can see that there was great resistance to a central bank through much of U.S. history.

By the time of the Civil War, the banking system was a mess. Different banks issued different kinds of currencies. During the Civil War, coins were hoarded because they were worth more as gold and silver than as coins. The chaos continued long after the war ended, reaching something of a climax in 1907, when many banks failed. People got nervous about the safety of banks and attempted to withdraw their funds. This is now known as "a run on the banks." Soon the cash was depleted and some banks had to refuse money to depositors. This caused people to distrust the banking system in general.

Despite the long history of opposition to a central bank, the cash shortage problems of 1907 led to the formation of an organization that could lend money to banks—the Federal Reserve System. It was to be a "lender of last resort" in such emergencies. Under the Federal Reserve Act of 1913, all federally chartered banks had to join the Federal Reserve. State banks could also join. The Federal Reserve became the bankers' bank. If banks had excess funds, they could deposit them in the Fed; if they needed extra money, they could borrow it from the Fed. The Federal Reserve System has been intimately related to banking ever since.

## Banking and the Great Depression

The Federal Reserve System was designed to prevent a repeat of the 1907 panic. Nevertheless, the stock market crash of 1929 led to bank failures in the early 1930s. When the stock market began tumbling, people hurried to banks to make withdrawals. In spite of the Federal Reserve System, the banks ran out of money and states were forced to close banks. President Franklin D. Roosevelt extended the period of the bank closings in 1933 to gain time to come up with some solution to the problem.

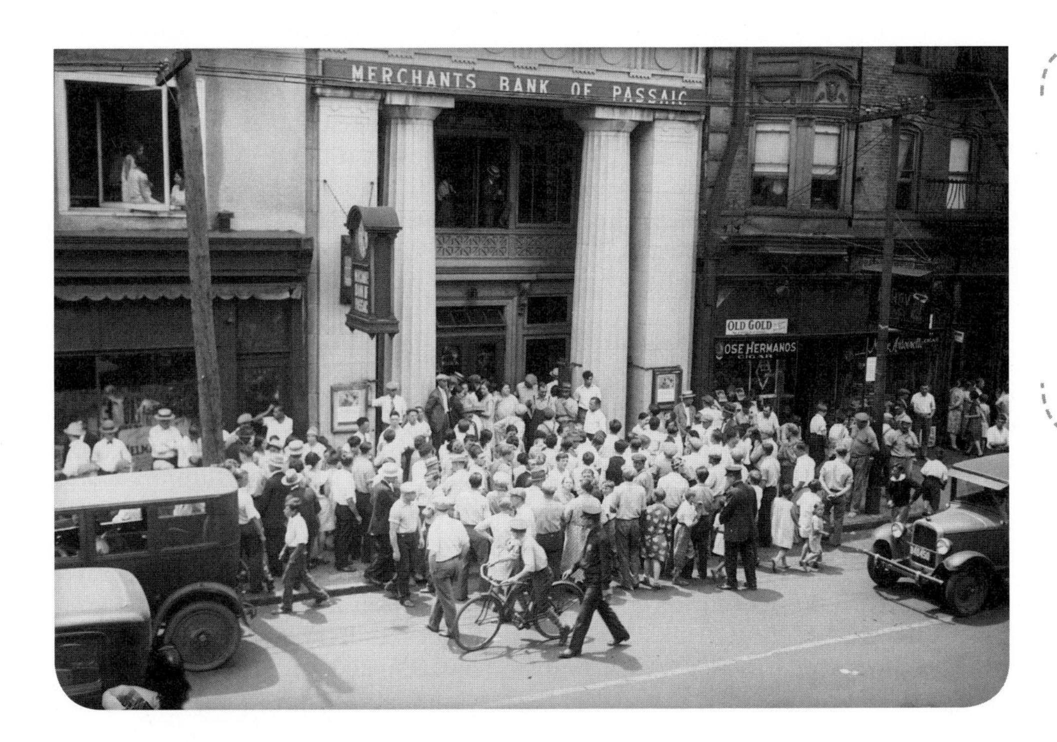


The Federal Reserve System was designed to prevent the run on the banks that occurred in 1907. The stock market crash of 1929, however, caused depositors to make another run on their banks and make withdrawals. Federal deposit insurance was established in 1933 to protect depositor's money.

In 1933 and 1935, Congress passed legislation to strengthen the banking system. The most important move was to establish federal deposit insurance, which you'll learn more about later in this chapter. At this point, it's important for you to know that in the 1930s, during the Great Depression, the government started an insurance program to further protect the public from bank failures.

**nonbanks**
Financial organizations that accept no deposits but offer many of the services provided by regular banks (pension funds, insurance companies, commercial finance companies, consumer finance companies, and brokerage houses).

## THE AMERICAN BANKING SYSTEM

The American banking system consists of commercial banks, savings and loan associations, credit unions, and mutual savings banks. In addition, there are various financial organizations, often called **nonbanks**, that accept no deposits but offer many of the services provided by regular banks. Nonbanks include pension funds, insurance companies, commercial finance companies, consumer finance companies, and brokerage houses. In the following sections we'll discuss the activities and services provided by each of these institutions, starting with commercial banks.

**commercial bank**
A profit-seeking organization that receives deposits from individuals and corporations in the form of checking and savings accounts and then uses some of these funds to make loans.

### Commercial Banks

A **commercial bank** is a profit-seeking organization that receives deposits from individuals and corporations in the form of checking and savings accounts and then uses some of these funds to make loans. Commercial banks have two types of customers: depositors and borrowers (those who take out loans). A commercial bank is equally responsible to both types of customers. Commercial banks try to make a profit by efficiently using the funds depositors give them. In essence, a commercial bank uses customer deposits as inputs (on which it pays interest) and invests that money in interest-bearing loans to other customers (mostly businesses). Commercial banks make a profit if the revenue generated by loans exceeds the interest paid to depositors plus all other operating expenses.

**demand deposit**
The technical name for a checking account; the money in a demand deposit can be withdrawn anytime on demand from the depositor.

**Services Provided by Commercial Banks** Individuals and corporations that deposit money in a checking account have the privilege of writing personal checks to pay for almost any purchase or transaction. The technical name for a checking account is a **demand deposit** because the money is available on demand from the depositor. Typically, banks impose a service charge for check-writing privileges or demand a minimum deposit. Banks might also charge a small handling fee for each check written. For corporate depositors, the amount of the service charge depends on the average daily balance in the checking account, the number of checks written, and the firm's credit rating and credit history.

In the past, checking accounts paid no interest to depositors, but interest-bearing checking accounts have experienced phenomenal growth in recent years. Most commercial banks offer negotiable order of withdrawal (NOW) and Super NOW accounts to their depositors. A NOW account typically pays an annual interest rate but requires depositors always to maintain a certain minimum balance in the account (e.g., $500) and may restrict the number of checks that depositors can write each month.

A Super NOW account pays higher interest to attract larger deposits. However, Super NOW accounts require a larger minimum balance. They sometimes offer free, unlimited check-writing privileges. Individual banks determine the specific terms for their NOW and Super NOW accounts. The longer you keep your funds in such accounts, the more interest they pay.

* * * MAKING

# ethical decisions

## To Tell the Teller or Not

You have been banking at the same bank for some time, but the tellers at the bank keep changing, so it is difficult to establish a relationship with any one teller. You do not like using the automated teller machine. Therefore, you are working with a teller and withdrawing $300 for some expenses you expect to incur. The teller counts out your money and says: "OK, here's your $300." Before you leave the bank, you count the money once more. You notice that the teller has given you $350 by mistake. You return to the teller and say, "I think you have made a mistake in giving me this money." She replies indignantly, "I don't think so. I counted the money in front of you."

You are upset by her quick denial of a mistake and her attitude. You have to decide whether or not to give her back the overpayment of $50. What are your alternatives? What would you do? Is that the ethical thing to do?

In addition to these types of checking accounts, commercial banks offer a variety of savings account options. A savings account is technically called a **time deposit** because the bank can require a prior notice before withdrawal. Recently, you could make much more money in an online bank than in a regular neighborhood bank.[9] You should check around to find where your money can earn the most interest.

**time deposit**
The technical name for a savings account; the bank can require prior notice before the owner withdraws money from a time deposit.

A **certificate of deposit (CD)** is a time-deposit (savings) account that earns interest to be delivered at the end of the certificate's maturity date. The depositor agrees not to withdraw any of the funds in the account until the end of the specified period. CDs are now available for periods of three months up to many years; the longer the CD is to be held, the higher the interest. The interest rates also depend on economic conditions and the prime rate at the time of the deposit. In addition to the checking and savings accounts discussed above, commercial banks offer a variety of other services to their depositors, including automated teller machines and credit cards. The Making Ethical Decisions box discusses the kind of situation that led to more automated banking.

**certificate of deposit (CD)**
A time-deposit (savings) account that earns interest to be delivered at the end of the certificate's maturity date.

Commercial banks also offer credit cards to creditworthy customers, life insurance, inexpensive brokerage services, financial counseling, automatic payment of telephone bills, safe deposit boxes, tax-deferred individual retirement accounts (IRAs) for qualified individuals and couples, traveler's checks, trust departments, and overdraft checking account privileges. The latter means that preferred customers can automatically get loans at reasonable rates when they've written checks exceeding their account balance. Because of competition, banks will be offering even more services, such as staying open longer hours and offering more online services.[10] Wal-Mart has applied for a banking permit. This makes traditional banks nervous because of Wal-Mart's reputation for offering services at low prices.[11]

Automated teller machines (ATMs) give customers the convenience of 24-hour banking at a variety of outlets such as supermarkets, department stores, and drugstores in addition to the bank's regular branches.[12] Depositors can—almost anywhere in the world—transfer funds, make deposits, and get cash at their own discretion with the use of a computer-coded personalized plastic

It's amazing what you can do at local ATMs in some locations. You can get maps, phone cards, postage stamps, and more. What is the most unique service you have seen at an ATM machine? What other products or services would you like to have?

SPOTLIGHT ON small business

## You Won't Loan Me Money? Isn't That What Banks Are For?

The founders of many new companies go to the bank or other local financial institution to get a loan, but most often they are turned down. Why? Because so many new businesses fail. Banks and other financial institutions simply cannot take on such risk. If you do go to a local bank to get a loan, it is often better to go to a smaller, local bank (if you can find one after all the mergers). You are more likely to get better service and advice. Despite its name, the Small Business Administration is not likely to give small businesses money either, for the same reason. Of course, some do get money, so check it out.

Commercial banks often charge outrageous amounts to borrow money. What about nonbanks? Small businesses are too small to borrow from pension funds, insurance companies, or brokerage firms. Often small businesses use a whole batch of credit cards to get started, but the fees can be extremely high if the bills are not paid monthly. Many small businesses turn to friends and family for loans, but that too can be dicey if the business does not do well.

Angel investors are wealthy individuals who use their own money to fund start-up companies at the early stages of their development. That would seem to be a good place to look for money, but angel investors usually seek out high-growth companies in fields like technology and biotech that might issue stock or get bought out in a few years. Local companies like restaurants, roofers, and deck cleaners usually cannot get a hearing, much less a loan. The same is true of venture capital firms. They pool the money of people and invest in companies; but usually not small, local companies.

One way to get money is to apply for a government grant. The process is tedious and demands a lot of work, but the funds are often available, especially for start-up businesses in hard-pressed areas. These may be called enterprise or empowerment zones. Such grants are likely to be available in Louisiana, Mississippi, Florida, and other areas hit by natural disasters, especially if the grants are for educational or construction purposes. Go to the Business Owners' Idea Café online (www.businessownersideacafe.com) for help. You can also apply for grants from foundations and corporations. You might seek professional help from an organization like AllWrite Communications (www.allwritecommunications.com). AllWrite will write your grant application for you and help you in other ways. In short, banks and nonbanks are often reluctant to loan money to small businesses. That opens the door for angel investors and others to fill the gaps.

Sources: Sheryl Nance-Nash, "Seeking Seed Money," *Black Enterprise*, May 2005, pp. 89–97; Lee Gomez, "The Angels Are Back, and This Time They Have a Trade Group," *The Wall Street Journal*, April 11, 2005, p. B1; and Crystal Detamore-Rodman, "Work with Me," *Entrepreneur*, April 2006, p. 65.

access card. Beyond all that, today's ATMs are doing even more. New ATMs can dispense maps and directions, phone cards, and postage stamps. They can sell tickets to movies, concerts, sporting events, and so on. They can even show movie trailers, news tickers, and video ads. Some can take orders for flowers and DVDs, and download music and games. The convenience chain 7-Eleven is testing machines that cash checks and send wire transfers. What next? A bank in Japan enables customers to play a slot machine while it processes their transactions. Customers push a button to stop three spinning wheels on the screen. Hit triple 7s, and the bank waives its transaction fee. Get three golds in a row, you win a certificate worth 1,000 yen.[13]

**Services to Borrowers** Commercial banks offer a variety of services to individuals and corporations in need of a loan. Generally, loans are given on the basis of the recipient's creditworthiness. Banks want to manage their funds effectively and are supposed to screen loan applicants carefully to ensure that the loan plus interest will be paid back on time. Small businesses and minority businesses often search out banks that cater to their needs. The Spotlight on Small Business box discusses the problems small businesses often have in finding people to lend them money.

## Savings and Loan Associations (S&Ls)

**savings and loan association (S&L)**
A financial institution that accepts both savings and checking deposits and provides home mortgage loans.

A **savings and loan association (S&L)** is a financial institution that accepts both savings and checking deposits and provides home mortgage loans. S&Ls are often known as thrift institutions because their original purpose (starting in 1831) was to promote consumer thrift and home ownership. To help them encourage home ownership, thrifts were permitted for many years to offer slightly higher interest rates on savings deposits than banks. Those rates attracted a large pool of funds, which were then used to offer long-term fixed-rate mortgages at whatever the rate was at the time. S&Ls no longer offer better rates than banks.

Between 1979 and 1983, about 20 percent of the nation's S&Ls failed. There were many reasons for these failures, but the largest may be the fact that capital gains taxes were raised, making investments in real estate less attractive. Investors walked away from their real estate loans, leaving S&Ls with lots of property that was worth less than the money they had lent to investors. When those properties were sold, the S&Ls lost money. In the mid-2000s, many people were concerned about a possible "housing bubble." If that bubble burst, housing prices would again fall.[14] Such a fall could have severe consequences for S&Ls, banks, and the economy in general.

In the past, the government stepped in to strengthen S&Ls. To improve the financial power of S&Ls, the federal government permitted them to offer NOW and Super NOW accounts, to allocate up to 10 percent of their funds to commercial loans, and to offer mortgage loans with adjustable interest rates based on market conditions. In addition, S&Ls were permitted to offer a variety of other banking services, such as financial counseling to small businesses and credit cards. As a result, S&Ls became much more similar to commercial banks than before the fall.

## Credit Unions

**credit unions**
Nonprofit, member-owned financial cooperatives that offer the full variety of banking services to their members.

**Credit unions** are nonprofit, member-owned financial cooperatives that offer the full variety of banking services to their members. Typically, credit unions offer their members interest-bearing checking accounts at relatively high rates, short-term loans at relatively low rates, financial counseling, life insurance policies, and a limited number of home mortgage loans. Credit unions may be thought of as financial cooperatives organized by government agencies, corporations, unions, or professional associations.

As nonprofit institutions, credit unions enjoy an exemption from federal income taxes. You might want to visit a local credit union and see if you are eligible to belong and then compare the rates you get to local banks. Credit unions often have fewer branches than banks and less access to ATMs, and many don't have online banking. It's best to determine what services you need and then compare *those* services to the same services offered by banks.[15]

## Other Financial Institutions (Nonbanks)

As we explained earlier, *nonbanks* are financial organizations that accept no deposits but offer many of the services provided by regular banks. Nonbanks include life insurance companies, pension funds, brokerage firms, commercial finance companies, and corporate financial services (such as

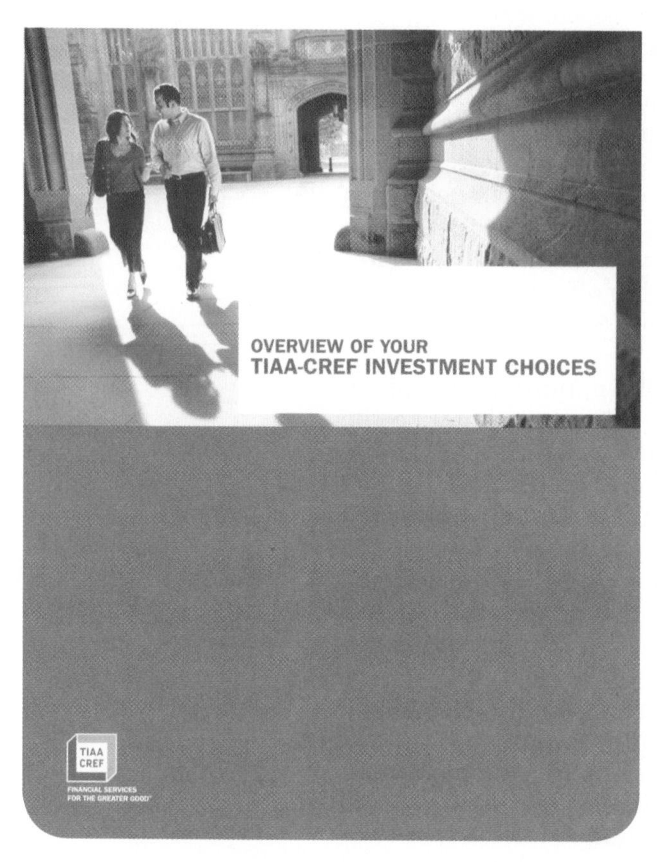


Financial services organizations like TIAA-CREF are becoming a major force in U.S. financial markets. Such organizations lend money to corporations.

Ford Motor Credit). As competition between these organizations and banks has increased, the dividing line between banks and nonbanks has become less and less apparent. This is equally true in Europe, where U.S. companies such as Fidelity Investment and GE Capital Corporation compete with European banks. The diversity of financial services and investment alternatives offered by nonbanks has led banks to expand the services they offer.[16] In fact, many banks have merged with brokerage firms to offer full-service financial assistance.

Life insurance companies provide financial protection for policyholders, who periodically pay premiums. In addition, insurers invest the funds they receive from policyholders in corporate and government bonds. In recent years, more insurance companies have begun to provide long-term financing for real estate development projects.

**Pension funds** are amounts of money put aside by corporations, nonprofit organizations, or unions to cover part of the financial needs of members when they retire. Contributions to pension funds are made either by employees, by employers, or by both employers and employees. A member may begin to collect a monthly draw on this fund upon reaching a certain retirement age. To generate additional income, pension funds typically invest in low-return but safe corporate stocks or in other conservative investments such as government securities and corporate bonds.

**pension funds**
Amounts of money put aside by corporations, nonprofit organizations, or unions to cover part of the financial needs of members when they retire.

Many financial services organizations that provide retirement and health benefits such as TIAA-CREF are becoming a major force in U.S. financial markets. Such organizations lend money directly to corporations.

Brokerage firms have traditionally offered services related to investments in the various stock exchanges in this country and abroad. However, brokerage houses have made serious inroads into regular banks' domain by offering high-yield combination savings and checking accounts. In addition, brokerage firms offer checking privileges on accounts (money market accounts). Also, investors can get loans from their broker, using their securities as collateral.

Commercial and consumer finance companies offer short-term loans to businesses or individuals who either cannot meet the credit requirements of regular banks or have exceeded their credit limit and need more funds. These finance companies' interest rates are higher than those of regular banks. The primary customers of these companies are new businesses and individuals with no credit history. In fact, college students often turn to consumer finance companies for loans to pay for their education. One should be careful when borrowing from such institutions because the interest rates can be quite high.

Corporate financial systems established at major corporations such as General Electric, Sears, General Motors, and American Express offer considerable financial services to customers. To compete with such nonbank organizations, banks have had to offer something extra—guaranteed savings.

progress assessment

- Why did the United States need a Federal Reserve Bank?
- What's the difference between a bank, a savings and loan association, and a credit union?
- What is a consumer finance company?

## HOW THE GOVERNMENT PROTECTS YOUR FUNDS

The American economic system learned a valuable lesson from the depression of the 1930s. To prevent investors from being completely wiped out during an economic downturn, several organizations evolved to protect your money. The three major sources of financial protection are the Federal Deposit Insurance Corporation (FDIC); the Savings Association Insurance Fund (SAIF), originally called the Federal Savings and Loan Insurance Corporation (FSLIC); and the National Credit Union Administration (NCUA). All three insure deposits in individual accounts up to $100,000.

### The Federal Deposit Insurance Corporation (FDIC)

**Federal Deposit Insurance Corporation (FDIC)**
An independent agency of the U.S. government that insures bank deposits.

The **Federal Deposit Insurance Corporation (FDIC)** is an independent agency of the U.S. government that insures bank deposits. If a bank were to fail, the FDIC would arrange to have that bank's accounts transferred to another bank or pay off depositors up to a certain amount ($100,000 per account). The FDIC covers about 13,000 institutions, mostly commercial banks. What would happen if one of the top 10 banks in the United States were to fail? The FDIC has a contingency plan to nationalize the bank so that it wouldn't fail. The idea is to maintain confidence in banks so that if one happens to falter, others do not fail.

### The Savings Association Insurance Fund (SAIF)

**Savings Association Insurance Fund (SAIF)**
The part of the FDIC that insures holders of accounts in savings and loan associations.

The **Savings Association Insurance Fund (SAIF)** insures holders of accounts in savings and loan associations. It's now part of the FDIC. It was originally called the Federal Savings and Loan Insurance Corporation (FSLIC) and was an independent agency. A brief history will show why the association was created.

Both the FDIC and the FSLIC were started during the Great Depression. The FDIC was begun in 1933, and the FSLIC in 1934. Some 1,700 bank and thrift institutions had failed during the previous few years, and people were losing confidence in them. The FDIC and FSLIC were designed to create more confidence in banking institutions. In the 1980s, to get more control over the banking system in general, the government placed the FSLIC under the Federal Deposit Insurance Corporation (FDIC) and gave it a new name: the Savings Association Insurance Fund. Like the FDIC, it insures accounts for up to $100,000.

### The National Credit Union Administration (NCUA)

The National Credit Union Administration (NCUA) provides up to $100,000 coverage per individual depositor per institution. This coverage includes all accounts, including checking, savings or money market accounts, and

LEGAL briefcase

### What Are Your Rights?

If your checkbook is stolen, the practice in the past has been that you were not liable if a thief used your checks to buy things. Similarly, if a thief steals your credit card, most banks will forgive any loss above $50; many will even waive that $50. That's not the case for *business* cards, however. Most banks make corporate customers assume far more liability for cards issued to their employees.

What about fraud involving debit cards and electronic funds transfers? Federal law says that you are responsible for the first $50 if you report the loss within *two* days and $500 if you report the loss within 60 days. If you wait more than two months, the bank may not cover any of the loss. Of course, there are exceptions to every rule; that's why we have lawyers and courts.

It has been reported that one out of six people in the United States is vulnerable to identity theft. Be careful when giving out your Social Security number. When a business asks for a Social Security number, ask to give it your driver's license number instead. Be sure to destroy anything that has your bank numbers, Social Security number, or other ID. You must protect yourself from identity theft because the losses can be serious.

Sources: Carla Freid, "ID Theft: It's Only a Matter of Time," *Money*, August 2005, p. 27; Dean Foust, "Forget Those Comfy Old Rules about Fraud," *BusinessWeek*, March 28, 2005, p. 35; Sid Kirchheimer, "Stamp Out Identity Theft," *AARP Bulletin*, February 2005, p. 27; and Eric Schoeniger, "How to Plug the $13 Billion Leak," *BusinessWeek*, March 20, 2006, pp. 2–5.

certificates of deposit. Additional protection can be obtained by holding accounts jointly or in trust. Individual retirement accounts (IRAs) are also separately insured. The Legal Briefcase box looks at identity theft and other issues regarding self-protection of your money.

## THE FUTURE OF BANKING

Banking in the future is likely to change dramatically. One cause of change is the repeal of the Glass-Steagall Act of 1933, which prohibited banks from owning brokerages. The newer law—the Gramm-Leach-Bliley Act of 1999—allows banks, insurers, and securities firms (brokers) to combine and sell each other's services. This allows you and other consumers one-stop shopping for all your financial needs. One company can provide you with banking services, including credit and debit cards; mortgages; insurance of all kinds, including life and car; and brokerage services, including the ability to buy stocks, bonds, and mutual funds. Furthermore, since all of your financial records can be kept in the same company, it may be easier for you to compute your taxes. In fact, the financial firm may do much of that work for you.

You can expect banks to be doing many new things to win customers from competitors. Umpqua Bank of Roseburg, Oregon, for example, gives out Umpqua chocolate and has a digital kiosk for burning tunes onto CDs. The Wainright Bank & Trust in Boston has a lounge—with a plasma TV and free coffee and doughnuts. And the First National Bank of Hermitage, Pennsylvania has a Lifestyle 50 club that organizes trips for fiftysomethings.[17] Who knows what might be next?

### Electronic Banking on the Internet

Not only have banking, insurance, and brokerage services been combined in one company, but they are also available online. All of the nation's top 25 retail banks now allow customers access to their accounts online, and most have bill-paying capacity. Thus, you are now able to do all of your financial transactions from home, using your telephone or your computer. That includes banking transactions such as transferring funds from one account to another (e.g., savings to checking), paying your bills, and finding out how much is in your various accounts. You can apply for a car loan or mortgage online and get a response almost immediately. The company can check your financial records and give you a reply while you wait. Buying and selling stocks and bonds is equally easy.

New Internet banks (e.g., NetBank) have been created that offer online banking only; they do not have physical branches. Such banks can offer customers high interest rates and low fees because they do not have the costs of physical overhead that traditional banks have. While many consumers are pleased with the savings and convenience, not all are entirely happy with the service they receive with Internet banks.[18] Why are they dissatisfied? First, they are nervous about security. People fear putting their financial information into cyberspace, where others may see it. Despite all the assurances of privacy, people are still concerned. Furthermore, some people want to be able to talk to a knowledgeable person when they have banking problems. They miss the service, the one-on-one help, and the security of local banks.

Because of these issues, the future seems to be with organizations like Wells Fargo, Citigroup, and Bank One, which are traditional banks that offer both online services and brick-and-mortar facilities. Combined online and brick-and-mortar banks not only offer online services of all kinds but also have automated teller machines (ATMs), places to go to deposit and get funds, and real people to talk to in person. Even small, local banks offer online services now.

## Using Technology to Make Banking More Efficient

The way things have traditionally been done in banking—depositing money, writing checks, protecting against bad checks, and so on—is expensive. Imagine the cost to the bank of approving a check, processing it through the banking system, and mailing it back to you. Bankers have long looked for ways to make the system more efficient.

One step in the past was to issue credit cards.[19] Credit cards reduce the flow of checks, but they too have their costs: There's still paper to process. Using Visa and MasterCard costs retailers about $2 per $100 purchase; using Amex costs them about $2.50.[20] The future will see much more electronic exchange of money because it is the most efficient way to transfer funds. In an **electronic funds transfer (EFT) system**, messages about a transaction are sent from one computer to another. Thus, funds can be transferred more quickly and more economically than with paper checks. EFT tools include electronic check conversion, debit cards, smart cards, direct deposits, and direct payments.

**electronic funds transfer (EFT) system**
A computerized system that electronically performs financial transactions such as making purchases, paying bills, and receiving paychecks.

**Electronic check conversion (ECC)** converts a traditional paper check into an electronic transaction at the cash register (called a point-of-sale terminal) and processes it through the Federal Reserve's Automated Clearing House (ACH). ECC saves time and money while reducing the risks of bounced checks. When a customer makes payment with a check, it is run through a check reader, where magnetic ink character recognition (MICR) information is captured. The check is verified against a database for acceptance. The transaction is electronically transferred through the ACH, where funds are debited directly from the customer's account and deposited automatically into the merchant's

**electronic check conversion (ECC)**
An electronic funds transfer tool that converts a traditional paper check into an electronic transaction at the cash register and processes it through the Federal Reserve's Automated Clearing House.

account. Since checks are electronically deposited, there are no trips to the bank, deposit slips, or risks of lost or stolen checks.

**debit card**
An electronic funds transfer tool that serves the same function as checks: it withdraws funds from a checking account.

Whereas ECC *reduces* the paper-handling processes of using checks, debit cards *eliminate* them. A **debit card** serves the same function as checks: It withdraws funds from a checking account. Debit cards look like credit cards but work very differently. The difference between a debit card and a credit card is that you can spend no more money than is already in your account. That makes them good for people who may need some discipline when it comes to spending.[21]

You put the card into a slot in a point-of-sale terminal at a retailer. When the sale is recorded, an electronic signal is sent to the bank, transferring funds from your account to the store's account automatically. A record of transactions appears immediately online. Debit cards are a real challenge to credit cards. Today, one of three retail transactions involves the use of a debit card. There are some 294 million cards in use.[22]

Some companies are now using payroll debit cards. Employees who sign up for the program each receive a debit card. They can access the funds in their accounts immediately after they are posted. They can withdraw their funds from an ATM, pay bills online, or transfer funds to another cardholder. The system is much cheaper for companies than issuing checks and more convenient for employees.[23]

**smart card**
An electronic funds transfer tool that is a combination credit card, debit card, phone card, driver's license card, and more.

A **smart card** is an electronic funds transfer tool that is a combination of credit card, debit card, phone card, driver's license card, and more. Smart cards replace the typical magnetic strip on a credit or debit card with a microprocessor. The card can then store a variety of information, including the holder's bank balance. Merchants can use this information to check the card's validity and spending limits, and transactions can debit the amount on the card. Visa USA introduced its smart Visa card in 2000. It is embedded with a chip that transmits information online via a card reader plugged into the user's computer. American Express had one of its most successful launches ever with its Blue Card, a smart card with an embedded chip that holds a "certificate of authenticity." That certificate, along with a personal identification number (PIN), secures information that makes Internet shopping safe and convenient.

Some smart cards have embedded radio-frequency antennae that make it possible to access buildings and secure areas within buildings, and to buy gas and other items with a swipe of the card. A biometric function lets you use your fingerprint to boot up your computer. Students are using smart cards to open locked doors to dorms and identify themselves to retailers near campus and on the Internet. The cards also serve as ATM cards.

Need to stop by the office, get gas in your car, then get some cash at the ATM? No problem. Smart cards with embedded radio-frequency antennae can take care of these tasks and then some. Has cash become a thing of the past?

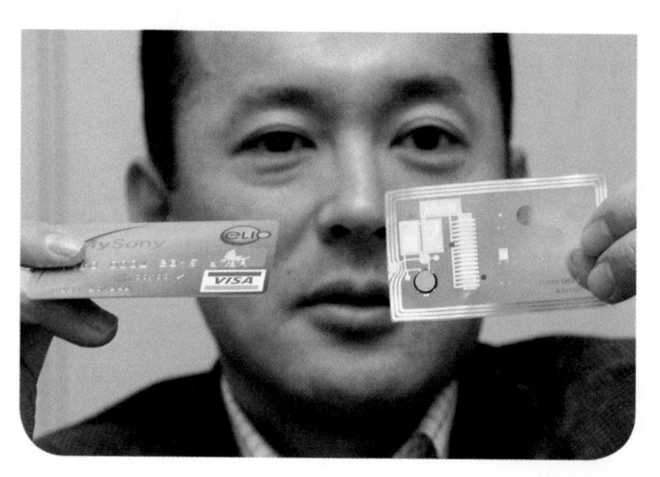


Visa Buxx and Cobalt-card have new debit cards for teenagers. They work like this: Parents can deposit or withdraw funds from their child's account over the phone or the Internet. That amount is then added to or subtracted from the value on the card. The company then reports where the money is being spent over time. Thus, parents can monitor their children's transactions. Such cards are also made available to employees, nannies, and others. The idea is to have an easy-to-use source of money that can be controlled. It is easier to use such a card than to drive to an ATM every time you need a few dollars.

For many, the ultimate convenience in banking involves automatic transactions such as direct deposit and direct payments. A *direct deposit* is a credit made directly to a checking or savings account. Because of direct deposit, some workers today receive no paycheck. Rather, their employer contacts the bank and orders it to transfer funds from the employer's account to the worker's account. Individuals can use direct deposits to transfer funds to other accounts, such as from a checking account to a savings account.

Not only can you deposit funds directly into bank accounts automatically, but you can also withdraw them automatically. A *direct payment* is a preauthorized electronic payment. Customers sign a separate authorization form for each company they would like the bank to pay automatically. This form authorizes the designated company to collect funds for the amount of the bill from the customer's checking or savings account on the specified date. The customer's financial institution provides information regarding the transaction on the monthly statement.

## INTERNATIONAL BANKING AND BANKING SERVICES

Banks help companies conduct business in other countries by providing three services: letters of credit, banker's acceptances, and money exchange. If a U.S. company wants to buy a product from Germany, the company could pay a bank to issue a letter of credit. A **letter of credit** is a promise by the bank to pay the seller a given amount if certain conditions are met. For example, the German company may not be paid until the goods have arrived at the U.S. company's warehouse. A **banker's acceptance** promises that the bank will pay some specified amount at a particular time. No conditions are imposed. Finally, a company can go to a bank and exchange American dollars for euros to use in Germany; that's called *currency* or *money exchange*.

**letter of credit**
A promise by the bank to pay the seller a given amount if certain conditions are met.

**banker's acceptance**
A promise that the bank will pay some specified amount at a particular time.

Banks are making it easier than ever before for travelers and businesspeople to buy goods and services overseas as well. Automated teller machines now provide yen, euros, and other foreign currencies through your personal Visa, MasterCard, Cirrus, Plus, or American Express card.

### Leaders in International Banking

This chapter has focused on banking within the United States. In the future, though, it's likely that many crucial financial issues will be international. In today's financial environment, it's foolish to discuss the American economy apart from the world economy. If the Federal Reserve decides to lower interest rates, foreign investors can withdraw their money from the United States in minutes and put it in countries with higher rates. Of course, the Fed's increasing interest rates can draw money to the United States equally quickly.

Today's money markets form a global market system. The United States is just a part of that system. There are banks larger than U.S. banks all over the world. International bankers tend not to be nationalistic in their dealings. That is, they make investments in any country where they can get a maximum return for their money at a reasonable risk.[24] That's how more than $1.5 trillion is traded daily! The net result of international banking and finance has been to link the economies of the world into one interrelated system with no regulatory control. American firms must compete for funds with firms all over the world. An efficient firm in London or Tokyo is more likely to get international financing than a less efficient firm in Detroit or Chicago.

What all this means to you is that banking is no longer a domestic issue; it's an international issue. To understand the U.S. financial system, you must learn about the global financial system. To understand America's economic condition, you'll have to learn about the economic condition of countries throughout the world. What has evolved, basically, is a world economy financed by international banks. The United States is just one player in the game. To be a winning player, America must stay financially secure and its businesses must stay competitive in world markets.

**World Bank**
The bank primarily responsible for financing economic development; also known as the International Bank for Reconstruction and Development.

## The World Bank and the International Monetary Fund (IMF)

To understand what is happening in the global banking world, you have to understand what the World Bank and the International Monetary Fund (IMF) are. The World Bank and the IMF are twin intergovernmental pillars that support the structure of the world's banking community.

The **World Bank** (also known as the International Bank for Reconstruction and Development) is primarily responsible for financing economic development. For example, it lent money to countries in Western Europe after World War II so they could rebuild.[25] Today, the World Bank lends most of its money to less developed nations to improve productivity and help raise the standard of living and quality of life. That includes trying to eliminate diseases that kill millions of people each year.[26]

Recently, the World Bank has come under considerable criticism, with major protests taking place in Seattle, Washington; Washington, D.C.; and other places. There have been a variety of protesters at such events. Environmentalists charge that the World Bank finances projects that damage the ecosystem.[27] Human rights activists and unionists argue that the bank supports countries that restrict religious freedoms and tolerate sweatshops. AIDS activists complain that the bank does not do enough to get low-cost AIDS drugs to developing nations. As a result of such protests, the World Bank is trying to develop strategies that focus more on the poor and do less to damage the environment.[28] Despite its efforts to improve, the World Bank still has many critics.[29] Some want the bank to forgive the debts of less developed countries and others want the bank to stop making such loans until the countries institute free markets and private property.[30] Recently, the World Bank has withheld money from some countries because of perceived corruption.[31] You can read more about the World Bank in the Reaching Beyond Our Borders box.

U2's Bono is one star who has taken on the issue of the unpayable debt poor countries owe to the United States. There are many such countries. What would happen if the United States were to forgive all such debts?

Protesters have been upset with the IMF as well. In contrast to the World Bank, the **International Monetary Fund (IMF)** was established to foster cooperative monetary policies that stabilize the exchange of one national currency

REACHING BEYOND

our borders

## What Can Be Done to Help the World's Poor?

Many, if not most, people are confused about the role of the World Bank. You can't cash a check there. The mother of one woman who works at the bank thinks her daughter is a teller, but, of course, she is not. There are no bank branches. So what is the World Bank?

Basically, the World Bank's role is to help poor nations become less poor. In the past, it has done that by financing large projects, like the building of dams, which have not proved to be that beneficial. The new head of the bank, Paul Wolfowitz, hopes to change the priorities. For one thing, not much has been done about agriculture in the past. Wolfowitz will focus much more on agricultural development, especially in Africa. He will also give much more for small-business support rather than the big projects of the past. Also, he will spend more on infrastructure (projects such as roads and utilities, water, electricity, schools, and irrigation). Recently, for example, a $3 billion loan was given to India to build roads, provide drinking water, and install irrigation devices.

The World Bank is owned by 184 *countries* (both developed countries and developing countries) that are its members. The United States is the largest shareholder (about 16 percent), so the U.S. president gets to select the president of the bank. Other countries, such as France (4.3 percent ownership), also have a big say in what the bank does. China, Russia, and Saudi Arabia own about 3 percent each.

It is not easy to get agreement on the best way to go about helping poorer nations develop. Some people complain that the World Bank gives too much money to poor countries with no results. Others complain that the World Bank does not give enough money. Each year the bank lends about $20 billion to developing countries. The goals include ending poverty and hunger, insuring primary education for all children (the focus is especially on education for young women), establishing equal rights for women, fighting corruption, and lessening disease. These, we could probably all agree, are noble causes. What people cannot agree on is the best way to achieve these ends.

Sources: Ann Gerhart, "World Bank's Loan Rangers," *Washington Post*, June 9, 2005, pp. C1 and C4; Andrew Balls and Chris Giles, "Leadership Key in Poor Nations, Says Wolfowitz," *Financial Times*, September 26, 2005, p. 2; David Frum, "The World's Banker," *National Review*, April 11, 2005, p. 22; Fareed Zakaria, "The Education of Paul Wolfowitz," *Newsweek*, March 28, 2005, p. 37; Sebastian Mallaby, "Wolfowitz's Corruption Agenda," *Washington Post*, February 20, 2006, p. A21; and Edward T. Pound and Danielle Knight, "Cleaning Up the World Bank," *U.S. News & World Report*, April 3, 2006, pp. 40–51.

for another. About 184 countries are members of the IMF. It requires those members (who are voluntary) to allow their own money to be exchanged for foreign money freely, to keep the IMF informed about changes in monetary policy, and to modify those policies on the advice of the IMF to accommodate the needs of the entire membership. The IMF is not supposed to be a lending institution primarily, as is the World Bank. Rather, it is designed to be an overseer of member countries' monetary and exchange rate policies. The IMF's goal is to maintain a global monetary system that works best for all nations so that world trade can be enhanced.[32] Members of the IMF contribute funds (rich countries pay more, poor countries pay less). Those funds are available to countries when they get into financial difficulty.

**International Monetary Fund (IMF)**
Organization that assists the smooth flow of money among nations.

The IMF was in the news almost daily in the late 1990s and early part of this century because it was lending money (billions of dollars) to nations whose currencies had fallen dramatically and whose banks were failing (e.g., Asian and Latin American countries and Russia). Recent IMF failures have taken place in Turkey, Argentina, Uruguay, and Brazil. When Argentina got into financial difficulty, some people believed that it would be better off if the IMF didn't intervene. Many of the protesters in Seattle and Washington were there to protest actions taken by the World Bank and the IMF. Debt relief advocates want the World Bank and IMF to forgive the debts of poor countries because many of them cannot afford to feed their people, much less pay back huge loans. But the failure of such loans shows that the World Bank and IMF's actions have not been very successful. Therefore, they are both under attack from all directions and are planning to change their policies.[33] Only time will tell what will finally emerge.

**progress assessment**

- What's the difference between the FDIC and the SAIF?
- Describe an electronic funds transfer (EFT) system. What are its benefits?
- What are the limitations of online banking?
- What are the roles of the World Bank and the International Monetary Fund?

## summary

**1.** Explain what money is and how its value is determined.

1. Money is anything that people generally accept as payment for goods and services.
   - **How is the value of money determined?**

   The value of money depends on the money supply; that is, how much money is available to buy goods and services. Too much money in circulation causes inflation. Too little money causes deflation, recession, and unemployment.

**2.** Describe how the Federal Reserve Controls the money supply.

2. Because the value of money is so important to the domestic economy and international trade, an organization was formed to control the money supply.
   - **What's that organization and how does it work?**

   The Federal Reserve makes financial institutions keep funds in the Federal Reserve System (reserve requirement), buys and sells government securities (open-market operations), and lends money to banks (the discount rate). To increase the money supply, the Fed can cut the reserve requirement, buy government bonds, and lower the discount rate.

**3.** Trace the history of banking and the Federal Reserve System.

3. In the American colonies, there were no banks at first and coins were limited. The colonists traded goods for goods instead of using money.
   - **How did banking evolve in the United States?**

   Massachusetts issued its own paper money in 1690; other colonies followed suit. British land banks lent money to farmers but ended such loans by 1741. After the American Revolution, there was much debate about the role of banking, and there were heated battles between the Central Bank of the United States and state banks. Eventually, a federally chartered and state-chartered system was established, but chaos continued until many banks failed in 1907. The system was revived by the Federal Reserve only to fail again during the Great Depression. The Fed, banks, and S&Ls were in the news during the 1990s because many banks and S&Ls failed and the Federal Reserve kept raising interest rates. The Fed then cut interest rates 13 times.

4. Savings and loans, commercial banks, and credit unions are all part of the banking system.
   - **How do they differ from one another?**

   Before deregulation in 1980, commercial banks were unique in that they handled both deposits and checking accounts. At that time, savings and loans couldn't offer checking services; their main function was to encourage thrift and home ownership by offering high interest rates on savings accounts and providing home mortgages. Deregulation closed the gaps between banks and S&Ls so that they now offer similar services.
   - **What kinds of services do they offer?**

   Banks and thrifts offer such services as savings accounts, NOW accounts, CDs, loans, individual retirement accounts (IRAs), safe-deposit boxes, online banking, insurance, stock, and traveler's checks.
   - **What is a credit union?**

   A credit union is a member-owned cooperative that offers everything that a bank does. That is, it takes deposits, allows you to write checks, and makes loans. It also may sell life insurance and make home loans. Because credit unions are member-owned cooperatives rather than profit seeking businesses like banks, credit union interest rates are sometimes higher than those from banks, and loan rates are often lower.
   - **What are some of the other financial institutions that make loans and do other bank-like operations?**

   Nonbanks include life insurance companies that lend out their funds, pension funds that invest in stocks and bonds and make loans, brokerage firms that offer investment services, and commercial finance companies.

**4.** Classify the various institutions in the U.S. banking system.

5. The government has created organizations to protect depositors from losses such as those experienced during the Great Depression.
   - **What agencies ensure that the money you put into a bank, S&L, or credit union is safe?**

   Money deposited in banks is insured by an independent government agency, the Federal Deposit Insurance Corporation (FDIC). Money in S&Ls is insured by another agency connected to the FDIC, the Savings Association Insurance Fund (SAIF). Money in credit unions is insured by the National Credit Union Administration (NCUA). These organizations protect your savings up to $100,000 per account.

**5.** Explain the importance of the Federal Deposit Insurance Corporation and other organizations that guarantee funds.

6. There will be many changes in the banking system in coming years.
   - **What are some major changes?**

   One important change will be more services offered by banks, including insurance, securities (stocks, bonds, and mutual funds), and real estate sales. Electronic funds transfer (EFT) systems will make it possible to buy goods and services with no money. Automated teller machines enable you to get foreign money whenever and wherever you want it. Online banking may change the banking process dramatically as people become more used to paying bills and conducting other transactions online. ATMs will offer more services, including the ability to pick up tickets to events and download music.

**6.** Discuss the future of the U.S. banking system.

7. Today's money markets aren't national; they are global.
   - **What do we mean by global markets?**

   Global markets mean that banks do not necessarily keep their money in their own countries. They make investments where they get the maximum return.

**7.** Evaluate the role and importance of international banking, and the role of the World Bank and the International Monetary Fund.

- **What are the roles of the World Bank and the IMF?**

The World Bank (also known as the International Bank for Reconstruction and Development) is primarily responsible for financing economic development. The International Monetary Fund (IMF), in contrast, was established to assist the smooth flow of money among nations. It requires members (who join voluntarily) to allow their own money to be exchanged for foreign money freely, to keep the IMF informed about changes in monetary policy, and to modify those policies on the advice of the IMF to accommodate the needs of the entire membership.

## key terms

**banker's acceptance** 563
**barter** 546
**certificate of deposit (CD)** 555
**commercial bank** 554
**credit unions** 557
**debit card** 562
**demand deposit** 554
**discount rate** 551
**electronic check conversion (ECC)** 561
**electronic funds transfer (EFT) system** 561
**Federal Deposit Insurance Corporation (FDIC)** 559
**International Monetary Fund (IMF)** 565
**letter of credit** 563
**M-1** 547
**M-2** 547
**money** 546
**money supply** 547
**nonbanks** 554
**open-market operations** 550
**pension funds** 558
**reserve requirement** 550
**savings and loan association (S&L)** 557
**Savings Association Insurance Fund (SAIF)** 559
**smart card** 562
**time deposit** 555
**World Bank** 564

## critical thinking questions

1. If you were Ben Bernanke, chairman of the Federal Reserve, what economic figures might you use to determine how well you were doing?
2. How much cash do you usually carry with you? What other means do you use to pay for items you buy at the store or on the Internet? What trends do you see in such payments? How might those trends make your experience more satisfactory?
3. If the value of the dollar declines relative to the euro, what will happen to the price of French wine sold in U.S. stores? Would people in France be more or less likely to buy an American car? Why or why not?
4. Do you keep your savings in a bank, an S&L, a credit union, or some combination? Have you compared the benefits you could receive from each? Where would you expect to find the best loan values?

## developing workplace skills

1. In a small group, discuss the following: What services do you use from banks and S&Ls? Does anyone use Internet banking? What seem to be the pluses and minuses of online banking? Use this opportunity to compare the rates and services of various local banks and S&Ls.
2. Poll the class to see who uses banks and who uses a credit union. Have class members compare the services at each (interest rates given on accounts, the services available, and the loan rates). If anyone uses an online service, see how those rates compare. If no one uses a credit union or online bank, discuss the reasons.
3. One role of the Federal Reserve is to help process your checks. Break up into small groups and discuss when and where you use checks versus credit cards and cash. Do you often write checks for small amounts? Would you stop doing that if you calculated how much it costs to process such checks? Discuss your findings with others in the class.
4. While in your small groups, take out some bills ($1 and $5) and look at them closely. Note that it says "Federal Reserve Note" on the top. Look at your $1 notes. You will find a jagged circle in the middle of the left side. What states are they from? Note also the words "This note is legal tender for all debts, public and private." What role does the Fed play in making such money?
5. Write a one-page paper on the role of the World Bank and the International Monetary Fund in providing loans to countries. Is it important for U.S. citizens to lend money to people in other countries through such organizations? Why or why not? Be prepared to debate the value of these organizations in class.

## taking it to the net

### Purpose

To learn a few fun facts about U.S. currency.

### Exercise

Your parents always told you money doesn't grow on trees. Other than that, what else do you know about money? Go to the Web site of the Bureau of Engraving and Printing (BEP) at www.moneyfactory.com and answer the following questions:

1. What is currency paper made of?
2. How much ink does the BEP use to print money each day?
3. How much does it cost to produce a paper currency note?
4. Approximately how many times could you fold a piece of currency before it would tear?
5. How long is the life span of a $1 bill?

6. What is the origin of the dollar sign ($)?
7. Why did the BEP print paper notes in 3-, 5-, 10-, 25-, and 50-cent denominations during the Civil War?
8. If you had 10 billion $1 bills and spent one every second of every day, how long would it take you to go broke?
9. Who was the only woman whose portrait appeared on a paper U.S. currency note?
10. When did "In God We Trust" become part of the U.S. currency design?
11. Whose picture is on a $100 bill? (If you're still a kid at heart, you might enjoy playing the money trivia games at the Treasury Dome at www.bep.treas.gov/kids_site/tdome.html.)

## casing the web

To access the case *"Learning about the Federal Reserve System,"* visit **www.mhhe.com/ub8e**

## video case

### Would You Like Banking with that Insurance?

It's not unusual to hear employees at a fast-food restaurant ask, "Would you like fries with that?" But you don't expect your insurance agent to ask, "Would you like banking services with your insurance coverage?" Nonetheless that's exactly what is happening at State Farm. This chapter is all about money and banking, and the latest trends in banking. One of those trends is to combine banking with insurance, as you'll see in this video.

You won't see a State Farm bank in your neighborhood shopping center or downtown. And you won't see any State Farm ATMs in your local grocery store or on the corner. That's because State Farm is a virtual bank; that is, an online bank. As you read in this chapter, recent legislation made it possible for financial institutions to provide services they couldn't provide before. For example, stock brokers can offer insurance, and insurance companies can offer banking. At State Farm Bank, you can get regular banking services such as checking accounts, loans, CDs, credit cards, IRAs, and more.

So, how do you get such services? State Farm Insurance agents will handle any of your banking needs. But, like most online banks, you can do most of your banking online via the Internet. Customer service is available 24 hours a day. Any remaining questions can be directed at your State Farm agent.

This chapter talked about banks and savings and loans (thrift agencies). State Farm falls into the thrift category. Its deposits are insured by the Federal Deposit Insurance Corporation, like banks and other thrifts. State Farm, however, does not have strategic partnerships with car dealerships or other firms like General Motors Acceptance Corporation does.

Because it is in the health and banking business, State Farm offers products like health insurance plans that are low cost and high deductible. Although State Farm's insurance and banking operations have been integrated, that integration was not as easy as might be imagined. Two different corporate cultures had to be merged, but that merger has gone relatively smoothly. Now, when a customer suffers a major loss because of a flood or hurricane or something similar, the bank can easily respond and adjust insurance payments and house payments accordingly.

Like all corporations, State Farm has ethical issues to confront. For example, agents make sure that customers understand that they can buy insurance and not get involved in banking and vice versa. The whole idea is to listen to customers to determine their wants and needs. If they want to buy a new car, financing can be made available—and insurance. Because of their good products and good service, State Farm mostly relies on word of mouth to promote their products. Of course, they have highly trained salespeople to help customers as well.

### Thinking It Over

1. What advantages and disadvantages do you see with doing both insurance and banking with the same company?
2. Are you as comfortable doing banking online as with a clerk in a brick and mortar bank? Would it help to be able to work with your insurance agent instead of a banking clerk?
3. What kind of services do you get from a brick and mortar bank (such as ATMs) that you might not get as easily from an online bank?

# WORKING WITHIN THE legal environment OF business

profile

**Getting to Know**

**X** David Boies

**Corporate Attorney**

In sports, the go-to guy is the person a team relies on when they need someone whose exceptional skills can change the momentum of a game. Attorney David Boies is such a go-to guy. However, Boies's skill doesn't lie in getting his team the winning base hit, touchdown, or three-point shot. His expertise is representing the special needs and challenges of clients that range the entire spectrum of business and society.

According to *Time* magazine, Boies has an "extraordinary ability to take complex issues and present them simply." He has been called "the best trial lawyer in America." One look at his diverse, wide-ranging client list makes you think there is a great deal of truth to that statement. Boies has represented corporate giants such as IBM, CBS, Calvin Klein, Napster, and the New York Yankees. He was legal counsel to the Federal Deposit Insurance Corporation (FDIC) in its litigation to recover losses suffered from the failed savings-and-loan associations in the early 1990s, and was special trial counsel for the U.S. Department of Justice in its antitrust suit against Microsoft in the early 2000s. New clients include insurance giant AIG and the New York Mets Baseball Club. In perhaps his most famous case, Boies served as chief legal counsel to Al Gore during the disputed presidential election in 2000.

Boies's success did not come easily. Due to a learning disability called dyslexia, Boies did not learn to read until he was in the third grade. Dyslexia slows his reading ability to this day.

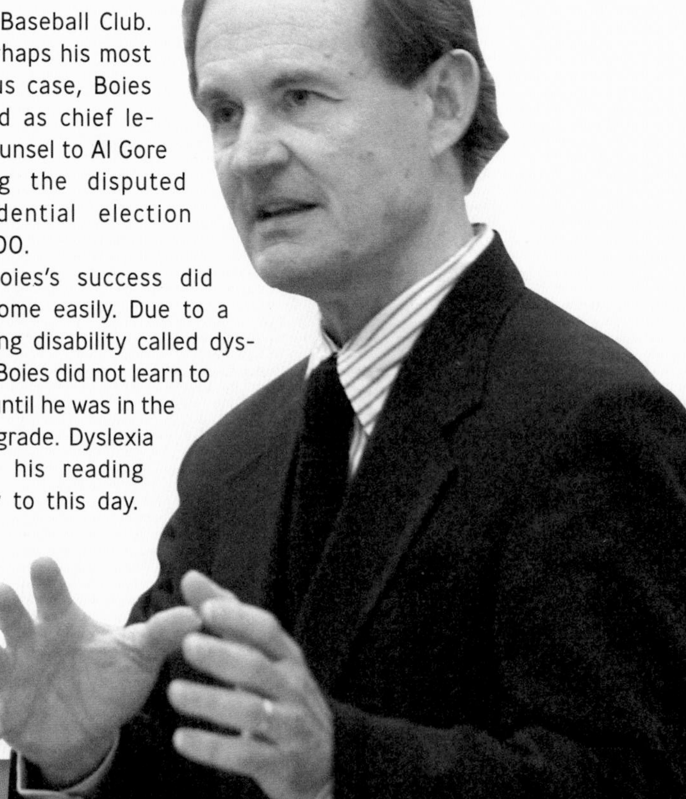

# BONUS CHAPTER A

## LEARNING goals

**After you have read and studied this chapter, you should be able to**

1. Define *business law*, distinguish between statutory and common law, and explain the role of administrative agencies.
2. Define tort law and explain the role of product liability in tort law.
3. Identify the purposes and conditions of patents, copyrights, and trademarks.
4. Describe warranties and negotiable instruments as covered in the Uniform Commercial Code.
5. List and describe the conditions necessary to make a legally enforceable contract, and describe the possible consequences if such a contract is violated.
6. Summarize several laws that regulate competition and protect consumers in the United States.
7. Explain the role of tax laws in generating income for the government and as a method of discouraging or encouraging certain behaviors among taxpayers.
8. Distinguish among the various types of bankruptcy as outlined by the Bankruptcy Code.
9. Explain the role of deregulation as a tool to encourage competition.

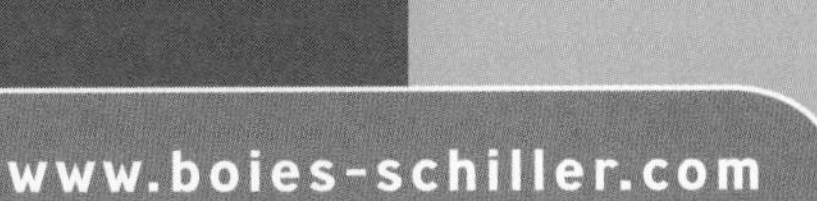


Still, Boies did not let this challenge overwhelm his inner drive and desire to make a difference. He studied hard and completed his undergraduate degree at Redlands University in three years. He then graduated from Northwestern University's law school. Boies credits the intense concentration his dyslexia requires as the root of his ability to recall key facts and legal citations in the course of his work. Dyslexia has also made him sensitive to others with disabilities. His law firm has six employees with developmental disabilities who sort and deliver interoffice mail.

Boies has taught courses at New York University Law School and is the author of many publications, including *Courting Justice* (2004). In this book he details butting heads with Bill Gates during the Microsoft case and representing George Steinbrenner, owner of the New York Yankees, in a legal battle with Major League Baseball. Today, he heads Boies, Schiller & Flexner, a 190-member law firm in New York. What new cases will come across his desk in the future? It's hard to say, but according to Stephen Gillars, a law professor at New York University, "David Boies is on the cusp of becoming one of those lawyers who has achieved legendary status." There doesn't seem to be anyone objecting to that statement.

Legal issues affect almost every area of our lives; they also impact every aspect of business. Don't expect that situation to change anytime soon. The United States has more lawyers than any other developed nation in the world and is clearly the world's most litigious society. In this chapter, we will look briefly at the history and structure of the U.S. legal system. Then we will discuss key areas of business law such as torts, patents, copyrights, and trademarks, sales law, contract law, laws to protect competition and consumers, tax law, and bankruptcy law. You probably won't be able to go head-to-head with David Boies after reading this chapter, but if you use it as a foundation to the study of law, who knows what your future may be?

Sources: Michael Saul, "Stadium May Miss Deadline, Boies Sez," *New York Daily News,* March 17, 2005; "March 31st WCA Event to Feature Renowned Trial Lawyer David Boies," *Westchester County Business Journal*, March 21, 2005; and James Bernstein, "Big-Time Lawyer Boies to Defend AIG's Former Chairman," *Newsday*, May 4, 2005.

**judiciary**
The branch of government chosen to oversee the legal system through the court system.

**business law**
Rules, statutes, codes, and regulations that are established to provide a legal framework within which business may be conducted and that are enforceable by court action.

**statutory law**
State and federal constitutions, legislative enactments, treaties of the federal government, and ordinances—in short, written law.

**common law**
The body of law that comes from decisions handed down by judges; also referred to as unwritten law.

# THE NEED FOR LAWS

Imagine a society without laws. Just think, no speed limits, no age restrictions on the consumption of alcoholic beverages, no limitations on who can practice law or medicine—a society where people are free to do whatever they choose, with no interference. Obviously, the more we consider this possibility, the more unrealistic we realize it is. Laws are an essential part of a civilized nation. Over time, though, the depth and scope of the body of laws must change to reflect the needs and changes in society. The **judiciary** is the branch of government chosen to oversee the legal system through the court system.

The U.S. court system is organized at the federal, state, and local levels. At both the federal and state levels, trial courts hear cases involving criminal and civil law. *Criminal law* defines crimes, establishes punishments, and regulates the investigation and prosecution of people accused of committing crimes. *Civil law* involves legal proceedings that do not involve criminal acts; it includes laws regulating marriage, payment for personal injury, and so on. Both federal and state systems have appellate courts. Such courts hear appeals of decisions made at the trial-court level brought by the losing party in the case. Appellate courts can review and overturn decisions made at the trial-court level.

The judiciary also governs the activities and operations of business. Thus, you see laws and regulations regarding sexual harassment on the job, hiring and firing practices, unpaid leave for family emergencies, environmental protection, worker safety, and more. As you may suspect, businesspeople prefer to set their own standards of behavior and often complain that the government is overstepping its bounds in governing business. Unfortunately, the U.S. business community generally has not implemented acceptable standards fast enough, causing government to expand its control and enforcement procedures. In this chapter we shall look at some of the laws and regulations in place and how they affect business.

**Business law** refers to rules, statutes, codes, and regulations that are established to provide a legal framework within which business may be conducted and that are enforceable by court action. A businessperson should be familiar with laws regarding product liability, sales, contracts, fair competition, consumer protection, taxes, and bankruptcy. Let's start by discussing the foundations of law and find out what law is all about.

## Statutory and Common Law

There are two major kinds of law: statutory law and common law. Both are important for businesspeople.

In the U.S. judicial system, judges are guided in their decisions by common law. Common law is often referred to as unwritten law because it is based on previous decisions handed down by judges. Such decisions become precedent and guide other judges in making legal rulings.

**Statutory law** includes state and federal constitutions, legislative enactments, treaties of the federal government, and ordinances—in short, written law. You can read the statutes that make up this body of law, but they are often written in language whose meaning must be determined in court. That's one reason why there are more than 900,000 lawyers in the United States.

**Common law** is the body of law that comes from decisions handed down by judges. Common law is often referred to as *unwritten law* because it does not appear in any legislative enactment, treaty, or other such document. Under common law principles, what judges have decided in previous cases is very important in deciding today's cases. Such decisions are called **precedent**, and they guide judges in the handling of new cases. Common law evolves through decisions made in trial courts, appellate courts, and special courts. Lower courts (trial courts) must abide by the precedents set by higher courts (appellate courts) such as the U.S. Supreme Court. In law classes, students study case after case to learn about common law as well as statutory law.

**precedent**
Decisions judges have made in earlier cases that guide the handling of new cases.

## Administrative Agencies

Different organizations within the government issue many rules, regulations, and orders. **Administrative agencies** are federal or state institutions and other government organizations created by Congress or state legislatures with delegated power to create rules and regulations within their given area of authority. Legislative bodies can create administrative agencies and also terminate them. Some administrative agencies hold quasi-legislative, quasi-executive, and quasi-judicial powers. This means an agency is allowed to pass rules and regulations within its area of authority, conduct investigations in cases of suspected rules violations, and hold hearings when it feels the rules and regulations have been violated. Administrative agencies issue more rulings affecting business and settle more business disputes than courts do.[1] Such agencies include the Securities and Exchange Commission (SEC) and the Equal Employment Opportunity Commission (EEOC). Figure A.1 lists and describes the powers and functions of several administrative agencies at the federal, state, and local levels of government. How many of these agencies have you heard about?

**administrative agencies**
Federal or state institutions and other government organizations created by Congress or state legislatures with delegated power to pass rules and regulations within their mandated area of authority.

### progress assessment

- What is business law?
- What is the difference between statutory and common law?

figure A.I

**EXAMPLES OF FEDERAL, STATE, AND LOCAL ADMINISTRATIVE AGENCIES**

| EXAMPLES | POWERS AND FUNCTIONS |
|---|---|
| **Federal Agencies** | |
| Federal Trade Commission | Enforces laws and guidelines regarding unfair business practices and acts to stop false and deceptive advertising and labeling. |
| Food and Drug Administration | Enforces laws and regulations to prevent distribution of adulterated or misbranded foods, drugs, medical devices, cosmetics, and veterinary products, as well as any hazardous consumer products. |
| **State Agencies** | |
| Public utility commissions | Set rates that can be charged by various public utilities to prevent unfair pricing by regulated monopolies (e.g., natural gas, electric power companies). |
| State licensing boards | License various trades and professions within a state (e.g., state cosmetology board, state real estate commission). |
| **Local Agencies** | |
| Maricopa County Planning Commission | Oversees land-use proposals, long-term development objectives, and other long-range issues in Maricopa County, Arizona. |
| City of Chesterfield Zoning Board | Sets policy regarding zoning of commercial and residential property in the city of Chesterfield, Missouri. |

# TORT LAW

**tort**
A wrongful act that causes injury to another person's body, property, or reputation.

**negligence**
In tort law, behavior that causes unintentional harm or injury.

Tort law is an example of common law at work. A **tort** is a wrongful act that causes injury to another person's body, property, or reputation. Although torts often are noncriminal acts, victims can be awarded compensation if the conduct that caused the harm is considered intentional. An *intentional* tort then is a willful act that results in injury. The question of intent was a major factor in the lawsuits against the U.S. tobacco industry.[2] Courts had to decide whether cigarette makers intentionally withheld information from the public about the harmful effects of their products. **Negligence**, in tort law, deals with behavior that causes *unintentional* harm or injury. Decisions involving negligence can often lead to huge judgments against businesses. In a highly publicized case several years ago, McDonald's lost a lawsuit to a person severely burned by hot coffee she bought at a drive-through window. The jury felt McDonald's failed to provide an adequate warning on the cup. Product liability is another example of tort law that's often controversial, especially regarding torts related to business actions.[3] Let's take a closer look at this issue.

## Product Liability

**product liability**
Part of tort law that holds businesses liable for harm that results from the production, design, sale, or use of products they market.

**strict product liability**
Legal responsibility for harm or injury caused by a product regardless of fault.

Few issues in business law raise as much debate as product liability. Critics believe product liability laws have gone too far and deter product development; others feel these laws should be expanded.[4] **Product liability** holds businesses liable for harm that results from the production, design, sale, or use of products they market. At one time the legal standard for measuring product liability was whether a producer knowingly placed a hazardous product on the market. Many states have extended product liability to the level of **strict product liability**—legally meaning liability without regard to fault. Thus, a company could be held liable for damages caused by placing a defective product on the market even if the company did not know of the defect at the time of sale. In such cases, the company is required to compensate the injured party financially.

The rule of strict liability has caused serious problems for businesses. It's estimated that more than 70 companies have been forced into bankruptcy due to asbestos litigation.[5] Companies that produced lead-based paint could also be subjected to expensive legal cases even though lead paint has been banned in the United States for nearly three decades.[6] Manufacturers of chemicals and drugs are also susceptible to lawsuits under strict product liability. A producer may place a drug or chemical on the market that everyone feels is safe. However, if a side effect or other health problem emerges, the manufacturer can, under the doctrine of strict liability, be held liable. Pharmaceutical giant Merck faces such liability due to problems with its painkiller Vioxx.[7]

There are many interesting liability cases. Gun manufacturers have been sued by cities such as Newark, Philadelphia, Chicago, New Orleans, and Miami. The cities sought financial payments to cover the costs of police work and medical care necessitated by gun violence. Lawsuits have also been filed on behalf of private individuals affected by gun violence. (Thus far, most of the lawsuits have been dropped or dismissed by courts.) Fast food has also been on the strict liability front burner.[8] McDonald's was the subject of a liability suit charging that its food caused obesity, diabetes, and other health problems in children.[9] The initial lawsuit against the company was dismissed by a trial judge, but part of the lawsuit was reinstated at the appellate court level.[10] Few expect the issue to go away anytime soon.[11]

Meaningful tort reform would set limits on the amount of damages for which companies are liable should their products harm consumers. Such reform has been a key objective of business for many years.[12] Congress took a first step with passage of the Class Action Fairness Act.[13] Businesses and insurance companies, however, argue that much more needs to be done. Figure A.2 highlights several major product liability awards that cost companies dearly.

## LAWS PROTECTING IDEAS: PATENTS, COPYRIGHTS, AND TRADEMARKS

Many people, including you perhaps, have invented products that are assumed to have commercial value. The question is what to do next. One step may be to apply for a patent.[14] A **patent** is a document that gives inventors exclusive rights to their inventions for 20 years from the date they file the patent applications.[15] Approximately 350,000 patent requests are filed with the U.S. Patent and Trademark Office (USPTO) a year; about 180,000 of these requests are granted.[16] In addition to filing forms with the USPTO, the inventor must make sure the product is truly unique.[17] Approval for a patent may take up to 24 months.[18] Approval time is expected to increase to 45 months by 2008 if the USPTO does not hire additional patent examiners.[19] Patent applicants are recommended to seek the advice of a lawyer; in fact, less than 2 percent of product inventors file on their own. How good are your chances of receiving a patent if you file for one? Close to 70 percent of patent applications are approved, each at a minimum cost to the inventor of $6,600 in fees over the life of the patent.[20]

**patent**
A document that gives inventors exclusive rights to their inventions for 20 years.

Patent owners have the right to sell or license the use of the patent to others. Foreign companies, also eligible to file for U.S. patents, account for nearly half the U.S. patents issued. The penalties for violating a patent can be severe. Dr. Gary Michelson received a settlement of $1.35 billion from Medtronic Inc.

figure A.2

**MAJOR PRODUCT LIABILITY CASES**

| COMPANY | YEAR | SETTLEMENT |
|---|---|---|
| Ford Motor Company | 1978 | $125 million in punitive damages awarded in the case of a 13-year-old boy severely burned in a rear-end collision involving a Ford Pinto |
| A. H. Robins | 1987 | Dalkon Shield intrauterine birth-control devices recalled after eight separate punitive-damage awards |
| Playtex Company | 1988 | Considered liable and suffered a $10 million damage award in the case of a toxic shock syndrome fatality in Kansas; removed certain types of tampons from the market |
| Jack in the Box | 1993 | Assessed large damages after a two-year-old child who ate at Jack in the Box died of *E. coli* poisoning and others became ill |
| Sara Lee Corporation | 1998 | Costly company recall necessitated when tainted hot dogs caused food-poisoning death of 15 people |
| General Motors | 1999 | Suffered $4.8 billion punitive award in faulty fuel-tank case |
| Major Tobacco Firms | 2004 | $130 billion sought by the federal government for smoking cessation programs (settled for $10 billion) |

Source: U.S. Department of Justice; American Trial Lawyers Association.

Recording artist LL Cool J testified during a U.S. Senate hearing on illegal file sharing on peer-to-peer networks and the impact of technology on the entertainment industry. Musicians are protected by copyright laws and can charge a fee to anyone wanting to use their work. The music industry challenged the free exchange of their work by the online entertainment industry. Does the music industry have a reasonable case?

to end litigation and license patents covering a range of back-surgery products.[21] Sony, the manufacturer of PlayStation, was ordered to pay Immersion Corporation $90.7 million for violating Immersion's patents on technology used to make games more realistic.[22] The USPTO, however, cannot take action on behalf of patent holders if infringement of a patent occurs. The defense of patent rights is solely the job of the patent holder and can be quite expensive.[23]

The U.S. Congress made a change in patent law with passage of the American Inventor's Protection Act, which requires patent applications to be made public after 18 months regardless of whether a patent has been granted. This law was passed in part to address critics who argued that some inventors intentionally delayed or dragged out a patent application because they expected others to develop similar products or technology. When someone filed for a similar patent, the inventor surfaced to claim the patent—referred to as a *submarine patent*—and demanded large fees for its use.[24] The late engineer Jerome Lemelson, for example, reportedly collected more than $1 billion in patent royalties for a series of long-delayed patents, including forerunners of the fax machine, the Walkman, and the bar-code scanner.[25] A new problem faces the USPTO with the growth of business-method patents, which involve different business applications using the Internet. The issue of such patents first surfaced when Amazon.com sued competitor Barnes & Noble for violating its One-Click online purchasing system.[26] Today, companies that were issued business-method patents in the 1980s and 1990s are claiming wide control over almost any online-type transaction. Some suggest that a lack of reform will slow the pace of technological innovation, increase legal costs, and exclude small businesses from the patent process.[27] The USPTO has agreed to take steps to tighten the issuing of such patents.

**copyright**
A document that protects a creator's rights to materials such as books, articles, photos, and cartoons.

Just as a patent protects an inventor's right to a product or process, a **copyright** protects a creator's rights to materials such as books, articles, photos, paintings, and cartoons. Copyrights are filed with the Library of Congress and involve a minimum of paperwork. They last for the lifetime of the author or artist, plus 70 years, and can be passed on to the creator's heirs. The Copyright Act of 1978, however, gives a special term of 75 years from publication to works published before January 1, 1978, whose copyrights had not expired by that date. The holder of an exclusive copyright may charge a fee to anyone who wishes to use the copyrighted material. If a work is created by an employee in the normal course of a job, the copyright belongs to the employer and lasts 95 years from publication or 120 years from creation, whichever comes first.

A *trademark* is a legally protected name, symbol, or design (or combination of these) that identifies the goods or services of one seller and distinguishes them from those of competitors. Trademarks generally belong to the owner forever, as long as they are properly registered and renewed every 10 years.[28] Some well-known trademarks include the Pillsbury Doughboy, the Disney Company's Mickey Mouse, the Nike swoosh, and the golden arches of McDonald's. Like a patent, a trademark is protected from infringement.[29] Companies fight hard to protect trademarks, especially in global markets where pirating can be extensive.[30] We discuss trademarks in more detail in Chapter 14.

**progress assessment**

- What is tort law?
- What is product liability?
- How long is a patent enforceable?
- What is a trademark? Can you give an example of a trademark?

## SALES LAW: THE UNIFORM COMMERCIAL CODE

At one time, laws involving businesses varied from state to state, making interstate trade extremely complicated. Today, all states have adopted the same commercial law. The **Uniform Commercial Code (UCC)** is a comprehensive commercial law that covers sales laws and other commercial laws. Since all 50 states have adopted the law (although it does not apply in certain sections of Louisiana), the UCC simplifies trading across state lines.

**Uniform Commercial Code (UCC)**
A comprehensive commercial law, adopted by every state in the United States, that covers sales laws and other commercial laws.

The UCC has 11 articles, which contain laws covering sales; commercial paper such as promissory notes and checks; bank deposits and collections; letters of credit; bulk transfers; warehouse receipts, bills of lading, and other documents of title; investment securities; and secured transactions. We do not have space to discuss all 11 articles, but we would like to discuss at least two of them: Article 2, which contains laws regarding warranties, and Article 3, which covers negotiable instruments.

### Warranties

A *warranty* guarantees that the product sold will be acceptable for the purpose for which the buyer intends to use it. There are two types of warranties. **Express warranties** are specific representations by the seller that buyers rely on regarding the goods they purchase. The warranty you receive in the box with an iPod, a DVD player, or a toaster, is the express warranty. It spells out the seller's warranty agreement. **Implied warranties** are legally imposed on the seller. It is implied, for example, that the product will conform to the customary standards of the trade or industry in which it competes. For example, it's

**express warranties**
Specific representations by the seller that buyers rely on regarding the goods they purchase.

**implied warranties**
Guarantees legally imposed on the seller.

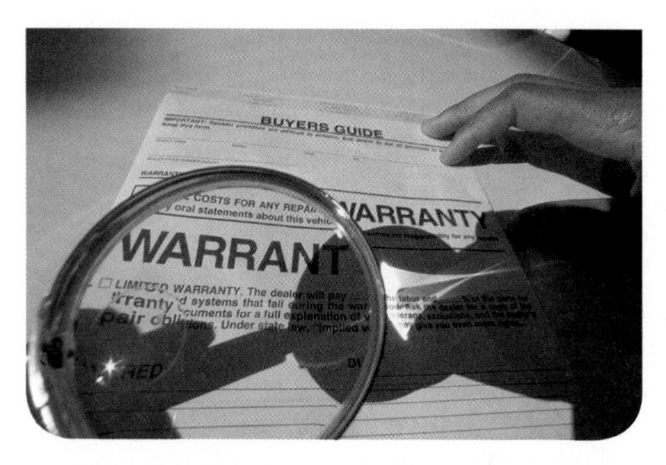


Would you buy a new car if the dealer offered no warranty on your purchase? How about an iPod or liquid crystal television with no guarantee of performance? Warranties are an important part of a product and generally of major concern to purchasers. It's important that you check if a product's warranty is a full or limited warranty. Should colleges offer students warranties with their degree programs?

expected that a toaster will toast your bread to your desired degree (light, medium, dark) or that food bought for consumption off an establishment's premises is fit to eat.

Warranties offered by sellers can be either full or limited. A full warranty requires a seller to replace or repair a product at no charge if the product is defective, whereas a limited warranty typically limits the defects or mechanical problems that are covered. Many of the rights of buyers, including the acceptance and rejection of goods, are spelled out in Article 2 of the UCC. Both buyers and sellers should become familiar with the UCC. You can read more about it on the Internet or in business law books in the library.

## Negotiable Instruments

**Negotiable instruments** are forms of commercial paper (such as checks) that are transferable among businesses and individuals and represent a promise to pay a specified amount. Article 3 of the Uniform Commercial Code requires negotiable instruments to follow four conditions. They must (1) be written and signed by the maker or drawer, (2) be made payable on demand or at a certain time, (3) be made payable to the bearer (the person holding the instrument) or to specific order, and (4) contain an unconditional promise to pay a specified amount of money. Checks or other forms of negotiable instruments are transferred (negotiated for payment) when the payee signs the back. The payee's signature is referred to as an *endorsement*.

**negotiable instruments**
Forms of commercial paper (such as checks) that are transferable among businesses and individuals and represent a promise to pay a specified amount.

# CONTRACT LAW

If I offer to sell you my bike for $50 and later change my mind, can you force me to sell the bike, saying we had a contract? If I lose $120 to you in a poker game, can you sue in court to get your money? If I agree to sing at your wedding for free and back out at the last minute, can you claim I violated a contract? These are the kinds of questions that contract law answers.

A **contract** is a legally enforceable agreement between two or more parties. **Contract law** specifies what constitutes a legally enforceable agreement. Basically, a contract is legally binding if the following conditions are met:

**contract**
A legally enforceable agreement between two or more parties.

**contract law**
Set of laws that specify what constitutes a legally enforceable agreement.

1. **An offer is made**. An offer to do something or sell something can be oral or written. If I agree to sell you my bike for $50, I have made an offer. That offer is not legally binding, however, until other conditions are met.
2. **There is a voluntary acceptance of the offer**. The principle of mutual acceptance means that both parties to a contract must agree on the terms. If I use duress in getting you to agree to buy my bike, the contract would not be legal. Duress occurs if there is coercion through force or threat of force. You couldn't use duress to get me to sell my bike, either. Even if we both agree, though, the contract is still not legally binding without the next four conditions.
3. **Both parties give consideration**. **Consideration** means something of value. If I agree to sell you my bike for $50, the bike and the $50 are consideration, and we have a legally binding contract. If I agree to sing

**consideration**
Something of value; consideration is one of the requirements of a legal contract.

at your wedding and you do not give me anything in return (consideration), we have no contract.

4. **Both parties are competent**. A person under the influence of alcohol or drugs, or a person of unsound mind (one who has been legally declared incompetent), cannot be held to a contract. In many cases, a minor may not be held to a contract either. For example, if a 15-year-old agrees to pay $10,000 for a car, the seller will not be able to enforce the contract due to the buyer's lack of competence.
5. **The contract must involve a legal act**. A contract covering the sale of illegal drugs or stolen merchandise is unenforceable since both of the sales are violations of criminal law. (If gambling is prohibited by state law, you cannot collect the poker debt.)
6. **The contract is in proper form**. An agreement for the sale of goods worth $500 or more must be in writing. Contracts that cannot be fulfilled within one year also must be put in writing. Contracts regarding real property (land and everything attached to it) must be in writing.

## Breach of Contract

**breach of contract**
When one party fails to follow the terms of a contract.

**Breach of contract** occurs when one party fails to follow the terms of a contract. Both parties may voluntarily agree to end a contract; but if one person violates the contract, the following may occur:

1. **Specific performance**. The person who violated the contract may be required to live up to the agreement if money damages would not be adequate.[31] For example, if I legally offered to sell you a rare painting, I would have to sell you that painting.
2. **Payment of damages**. The term **damages** refers to the monetary settlement awarded to a person who is injured by a breach of contract. If I fail to live up to a contract, you can sue me for damages, usually the amount you would lose from my nonperformance.[32] If we had a legally binding contract for me to sing at your wedding, for example, and I failed to come, you could sue me for the cost of hiring a new singer.
3. **Discharge of obligation**. If I fail to live up to my end of a contract, you could agree to drop the matter. Generally you would not have to live up to your end of the agreement either.

**damages**
The monetary settlement awarded to a person who is injured by a breach of contract.

Lawyers would not be paid so handsomely if the law were as simple as implied in these rules of contracts. That's why it's always best to have a contract in writing even though oral contracts can be enforceable under contract law. The offer and consideration in a contract should be clearly specified, and the contract should be signed and dated. A contract does not have to be complicated as long as it has these elements: (1) It is in writing, (2) mutual consideration is specified, and (3) there is a clear offer and agreement.

### progress assessment

- What is covered in the Universal Commercial Code? What are express warranties as opposed to implied warranties?
- What are the four elements of a negotiable instrument, according to the UCC?
- What are the six conditions for making a contract legally binding? What could happen if a contract is broken?

# LAWS TO PROMOTE FAIR AND COMPETITIVE PRACTICES

One objective of legislators is to pass laws that the judiciary will enforce to ensure a competitive atmosphere among businesses and promote fair business practices. Chapter 2 explained how competition is a cornerstone of the free-market system. In the United States, the Justice Department's antitrust division and other government agencies serve as watchdogs to ensure that competition among sellers flows freely and that new competitors have open access to the market.[33] The scope of the government is broad and extensive. The Justice Department's antitrust division has tackled the competitive practices of market giants such as Microsoft, Visa, and MasterCard.[34] Figure A.3 highlights key high-profile antitrust cases.

There was, however, a time when big businesses were able to drive smaller competitors out of business with little resistance. The following brief history shows how government responded to these troubling situations in the past and how business must deal with new challenges facing them today.[35]

## The History of Antitrust Legislation

In the late 19th century, big oil companies, railroads, steel companies, and other industrial firms dominated the U.S. economy. The fear was that such large and powerful companies would be able to crush any competitors and then charge high prices. It was in that atmosphere that Congress passed the Sherman Antitrust Act in 1890. The Sherman Act was designed to prevent large organizations from stifling the competition of smaller or newer firms. The Sherman Act forbids the following: (1) contracts, combinations, or conspiracies in restraint of trade, and (2) actual monopolies or attempts to monopolize any part of trade or commerce.

figure A.3

**HISTORY OF HIGH-PROFILE ANTITRUST CASES**

| CASE | OUTCOME |
|---|---|
| *United States* v. *Standard Oil*<br>1911 | Standard Oil broken up into 34 companies; Amoco, Chevron, and Exxon Mobil are results of the breakup |
| *United States* v. *American Tobacco*<br>1911 | American Tobacco split into 16 companies; British Tobacco and R. J. Reynolds are results of the breakup |
| *United States* v. *E. I. du Pont de Nemours*<br>1961 | DuPont ordered to divest its 23 percent ownership stake in General Motors |
| *United States* v. *AT&T*<br>1982 | Settled after Ma Bell agreed to spin off its local telephone operations into seven regional operating companies |
| *United States* v. *Microsoft*<br>2000 | Microsoft ordered to halt prior anticompetitive practices. |

Source: U.S. Department of Justice.

Because of the act's vague language, there was some doubt about just what practices it prohibited. The following laws were passed later to clarify some of the legal concepts in the Sherman Act:

- **The Clayton Act of 1914**. The Clayton Act prohibits exclusive dealing, tying contracts, interlocking directorates, and buying large amounts of stock in competing corporations. *Exclusive dealing* is selling goods with the condition that the buyer will not buy goods from a competitor (when the effect lessens competition). A *tying contract* requires a buyer to purchase unwanted items in order to purchase desired items. For example, let's say I wanted to purchase 20 cases of Pepsi-Cola per week to sell in my restaurant. Pepsi, however, says it will sell me the 20 cases only if I also agree to buy 10 cases each of its Mountain Dew and Diet Pepsi products. My purchase of Pepsi-Cola would be *tied* to the purchase of the other two products. An *interlocking directorate* occurs when a board of directors includes members of the board of competing corporations.
- **The Federal Trade Commission Act of 1914**. The Federal Trade Commission Act prohibits unfair methods of competition in commerce. This legislation set up the five-member Federal Trade Commission (FTC) to enforce compliance with this act. The FTC deals with wide-ranging competitive issues—everything from preventing companies from making misleading "Made in the USA" claims and regulating telemarketers' practices, to insisting that funeral providers give consumers accurate, itemized price information about funeral goods and services. The involvement and activity of the FTC typically depends on the members serving on the board at the time.[36] The FTC is now responsible for overseeing mergers and acquisitions in the health care, energy, computer hardware, automotive, and biotechnology industries. (Mergers and acquisitions were discussed in depth in Chapter 5.) The Wheeler-Lea Amendment of 1938 gave the FTC additional jurisdiction over false or misleading advertising. It also gave the FTC power to increase fines if its requirements are not met within 60 days.
- **The Robinson-Patman Act of 1936**. The Robinson-Patman Act prohibits price discrimination. An interesting aspect of the legislation is that it applies to both sellers and buyers who "knowingly" induce or receive an unlawful discrimination in price.[37] It also stipulates that certain types of price cutting are criminal offenses punishable by fine and imprisonment. Specifically, the legislation outlaws price differences that "substantially" weaken competition unless these differences can be justified by lower selling costs associated with larger purchases. It also prohibits advertising and promotional allowances unless they are offered to all retailers, large and small. This act applies to business-to-business transactions and does not apply to consumers in business transactions.

The changing nature of business from manufacturing to knowledge technology has led the call for new levels of regulation from federal agencies.[38] For example, Microsoft's competitive practices were the focus of an intense investigation. The major accusation was that the company hindered competition by refusing to sell its Windows operating system to computer manufacturers who did not agree to sell Windows-based computers exclusively. Computer manufacturers had a choice of buying only Windows or buying no Windows at all. Given that consumers wanted Windows, the buying companies had little choice but to agree. Read the description of the Clayton Act again. Do you think Microsoft violated the law? The U.S. Justice Department settled the case with Microsoft, but the company still faces antitrust charges from the European Union (EU).[39]

**consumerism**
A social movement that seeks to increase and strengthen the rights and powers of buyers in relation to sellers.

## LAWS TO PROTECT CONSUMERS

**Consumerism** is a social movement that seeks to increase and strengthen the rights and powers of buyers in relation to sellers. Consumerism is also the people's way of getting a fair share in marketing exchanges. Although consumerism is not a new movement, the corporate scandals of the early 2000s involving companies such as Enron, Global Crossing, and WorldCom led the movement to take on new vigor and direction. Consumers were particularly critical of federal agencies such as the Securities and Exchange Commission (SEC) for their lack of oversight and action in the securities markets.[40] (The SEC was discussed in depth in Chapters 17 and 19.) To help allay consumer fears concerning falsified financial statements (such as WorldCom's $11 billion accounting "mistake"), the Public Company Accounting Reform and Investor Protection Act (Sarbanes/Oxley Act) requires CEOs to verify the accuracy of their firms' financial statements to the SEC.

It's vital that businesses recognize consumer needs and interests in making important decisions. In the 1960s, President John F. Kennedy proposed four basic rights of consumers: (1) the right to safety, (2) the right to be informed, (3) the right to choose, and (4) the right to be heard. These rights will only be achieved if businesses and consumers recognize them and take action in the marketplace. Figure A.4 lists major consumer protection laws.

**taxes**
How the government (federal, state, and local) raises money.

## TAX LAWS

Mention the word *taxes* and most people frown. That's because taxes affect almost every individual and business in the United States. **Taxes** are how the government (federal, state, or local) raises money. Traditionally, taxes have been used primarily as a source of funding for government operations and programs. They can also be used as a method of discouraging or encouraging certain behaviors among taxpayers. For example, if the government wishes to reduce consumer use of certain classes of products (cigarettes, liquor, etc.), it passes what are referred to as *sin taxes*.[41] The additional cost of the product from increased taxes perhaps discourages additional consumption of these products. In other situations, the government may encourage businesses to hire new employees or purchase new equipment by offering a tax credit. A tax credit is an amount that can be deducted from a tax bill.[42]

Taxes are levied from a variety of sources. Income (personal and business), sales, and property are the major bases of tax revenue. The federal government receives its largest share of taxes from income. States and local communities often make extensive use of sales taxes. School districts generally depend on property taxes. The tax policies of states and cities are important considerations when businesses seek to locate operations. Tax policies also affect personal decisions such as retirement. A tax issue sure to be debated further involves Internet taxation, especially taxing Internet transactions (e-commerce). States claim they are losing over $15 billion in sales taxes from such sales transactions.[43] The European Union already levies certain Internet taxes, so expect the debate in the United States to continue. Figure A.5 on page 586 highlights the primary types of taxes levied on individuals and businesses.

| LEGISLATION | PURPOSE |
|---|---|
| Pure Food and Drug Act (1906) | Protects against the adulteration and misbranding of foods and drugs sold in interstate commerce. |
| Food, Drug, and Cosmetic Act (1938) | Protects against the adulteration and sale of foods, drugs, cosmetics, or therapeutic devices and allows the Food and Drug Administration to set minimum standards and guidelines for food products. |
| Wool Products Labeling Act (1940) | Protects manufacturers, distributors, and consumers from undisclosed substitutes and mixtures in manufactured wool products. |
| Fur Products Labeling Act (1951) | Protects consumers from misbranding, false advertising, and false invoicing of furs and fur products. |
| Flammable Fabrics Act (1953) | Prohibits the interstate transportation of dangerously flammable wearing apparel and fabrics. |
| Automobile Information Disclosure Act (1958) | Requires auto manufacturers to put suggested retail prices on all new passenger vehicles. |
| Textile Fiber Products Identification Act (1958) | Protects producers and consumers against misbranding and false advertising of fiber content of textile fiber products. |
| Cigarette Labeling Act (1965) | Requires cigarette manufacturers to label cigarettes as hazardous to health. |
| Fair Packaging and Labeling Act (1966) | Makes unfair or deceptive packaging or labeling of certain consumer commodities illegal. |
| Child Protection Act (1966) | Removes from sale potentially harmful toys and allows the FDA to pull dangerous products from the market. |
| Truth-in-Lending Act (1968) | Requires full disclosure of all finance charges on consumer credit agreements and in advertisements of credit plans. |
| Child Protection and Toy Safety Act (1969) | Protects children from toys and other products that contain thermal, electrical, or mechanical hazards. |
| Fair Credit Reporting Act (1970) | Requires that consumer credit reports contain only accurate, relevant, and recent information and are confidential unless a proper party requests them for an appropriate reason. |
| Consumer Product Safety Act (1972) | Created an independent agency to protect consumers from unreasonable risk of injury arising from consumer products and to set safety standards. |
| Magnuson–Moss Warranty–Federal Trade Commission Improvement Act (1975) | Provides for minimum disclosure standards for written consumer products warranties and allows the FTC to prescribe interpretive rules and policy statements regarding unfair or deceptive practices. |
| Alcohol Labeling Legislation (1988) | Provides for warning labels on liquor saying that women shouldn't drink when pregnant and that alcohol impairs a person's abilities. |
| Nutrition Labeling and Education Act (1990) | Requires truthful and uniform nutritional labeling on every food the FDA regulates. |

figure A.4

**CONSUMER PROTECTION LAWS**

## BANKRUPTCY LAWS

**Bankruptcy** is the legal process by which a person, business, or government entity unable to meet financial obligations is relieved of those debts by a court. The court divides any assets among creditors, allowing creditors to get at least part of their money and freeing the debtor to begin anew. The U.S.

figure A.5

**TYPES OF TAXES**

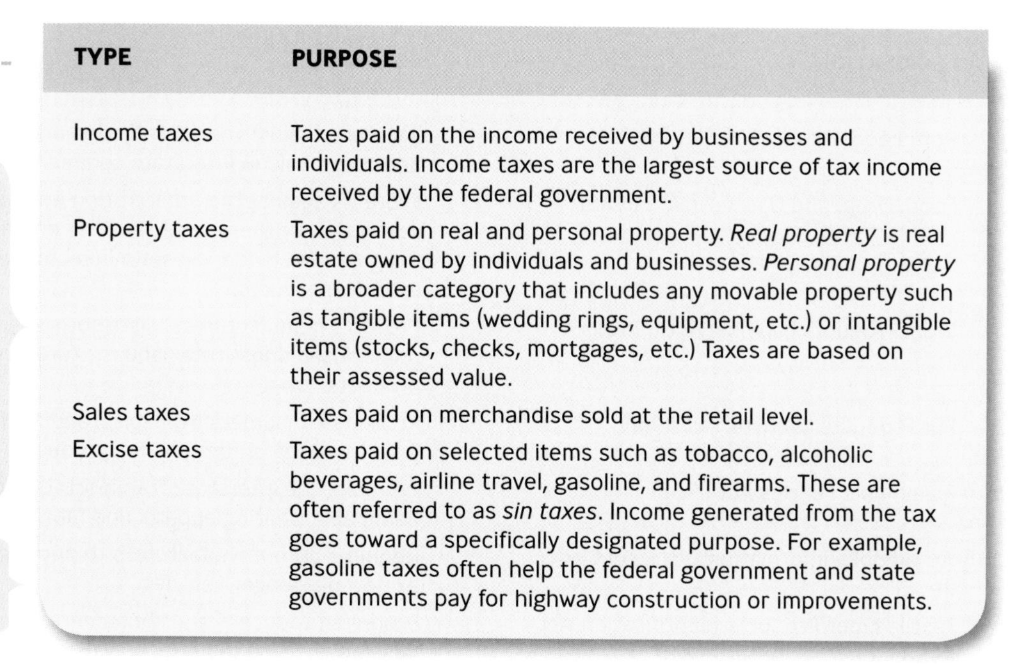

| TYPE | PURPOSE |
| --- | --- |
| Income taxes | Taxes paid on the income received by businesses and individuals. Income taxes are the largest source of tax income received by the federal government. |
| Property taxes | Taxes paid on real and personal property. *Real property* is real estate owned by individuals and businesses. *Personal property* is a broader category that includes any movable property such as tangible items (wedding rings, equipment, etc.) or intangible items (stocks, checks, mortgages, etc.) Taxes are based on their assessed value. |
| Sales taxes | Taxes paid on merchandise sold at the retail level. |
| Excise taxes | Taxes paid on selected items such as tobacco, alcoholic beverages, airline travel, gasoline, and firearms. These are often referred to as *sin taxes*. Income generated from the tax goes toward a specifically designated purpose. For example, gasoline taxes often help the federal government and state governments pay for highway construction or improvements. |

**bankruptcy**
The legal process by which a person, business, or government entity unable to meet financial obligations is relieved of those obligations by a court that divides any assets among creditors, allowing creditors to get at least part of their money and freeing the debtor to begin anew.

**voluntary bankruptcy**
Legal procedures initiated by a debtor.

**involuntary bankruptcy**
Bankruptcy procedures filed by a debtor's creditors.

Constitution gives Congress the power to establish bankruptcy laws, and there has been bankruptcy legislation since the 1890s. Major amendments to the bankruptcy code include the Bankruptcy Amendments and Federal Judgeships Act of 1984, the Bankruptcy Reform Acts of 1994, and the Bankruptcy Abuse Prevention and Consumer Protection Act of 2005.[44] The 1984 legislation allows a person who is bankrupt to keep part of the equity (ownership) in a house, $1,200 in a car, and some other personal property. The Bankruptcy Reform Act of 1994 amended more than 45 sections of the bankruptcy code and created reforms to speed up and simplify the process. The Bankruptcy Reform Act of 2005 made it harder for individuals to eliminate most debts from a bankruptcy.[45]

In 2004, a record 1.59 million Americans filed for bankruptcy; by contrast, only 780,000 did so in 1990.[46] The number of bankruptcies began to increase in the late 1980s and grew tremendously in the 1990s. Bankruptcy attorneys attributed the increase in filings to a lessening of the stigma of bankruptcy, the changing economy, an increase in understanding of bankruptcy law and its protections, increased advertising by bankruptcy attorneys, and the ease with which some consumers can get credit. While high-profile bankruptcies of businesses—such as Kmart, United Airlines, and Trump Hotels and Casinos—sometimes dominate the news, over 90 percent of bankruptcy filings each year are by individuals.[47] The bankruptcy legislation passed in 2005 makes it more difficult for people to escape overwhelming debt from credit cards, medical bills, student loans, or other loans that are not secured through a home or other asset. The new legislation also requires debtors to receive credit counseling and raises the cost of filing for bankruptcy.

Under Chapter II bankruptcy law, the mighty can fall and then rise again. Retail giant Kmart was forced to declare bankruptcy when it could not repay its suppliers. Under the leadership of Edward S. Lampert (on left), the company emerged from bankruptcy as a better-managed business and merged with Sears to create Sears Holding Company.

Bankruptcy can be either voluntary or involuntary. In **voluntary bankruptcy** cases the debtor applies for bankruptcy, whereas in **involuntary bankruptcy** cases the creditors start legal action against the debtor. Most bankruptcies are voluntary because creditors usually want to wait in hopes that they will be paid all of the money due them rather than settle for only part of it.

Bankruptcy procedures begin when a petition is filed with the court under one of the following sections of the Bankruptcy Code:

Chapter 7—"straight bankruptcy" or liquidation (used by businesses and individuals).

Chapter 11—reorganization (used almost exclusively by businesses).

Chapter 13—repayment (used by individuals).

Chapter 7 calls for straight bankruptcy, which requires the sale of nonexempt assets of debtors. Under federal exemption statutes, a debtor may be able to retain up to $7,500 of equity in a home ($15,000 in a joint case); up to $1,200 of equity in an automobile; up to $4,000 in household furnishings, apparel, and musical instruments; and up to $500 in jewelry. States may have different exemption statutes. When the sale of assets is over, the remaining cash is divided among creditors, including the government. Chapter 7 has been the most popular form of bankruptcy among individuals, with about 70 percent of bankruptcies following Chapter 7 procedures. Chapter 7 stipulates the order in which the assets are distributed among creditors. First, creditors with secured claims receive the collateral for their claims or repossess the claimed asset (such as an automobile or home). Then unsecured claims (backed by no asset) are paid in this order:

1. Costs involved in the bankruptcy case.
2. Any business costs incurred after bankruptcy was filed.
3. Wages, salaries, or commissions (limited to $2,000 per person).
4. Contributions to employee benefit plans.
5. Refunds to consumers who paid for products that weren't delivered (limited to $900 per claimant).
6. Federal and state taxes.

See Figure A.6 for the steps used in liquidating assets under Chapter 7.

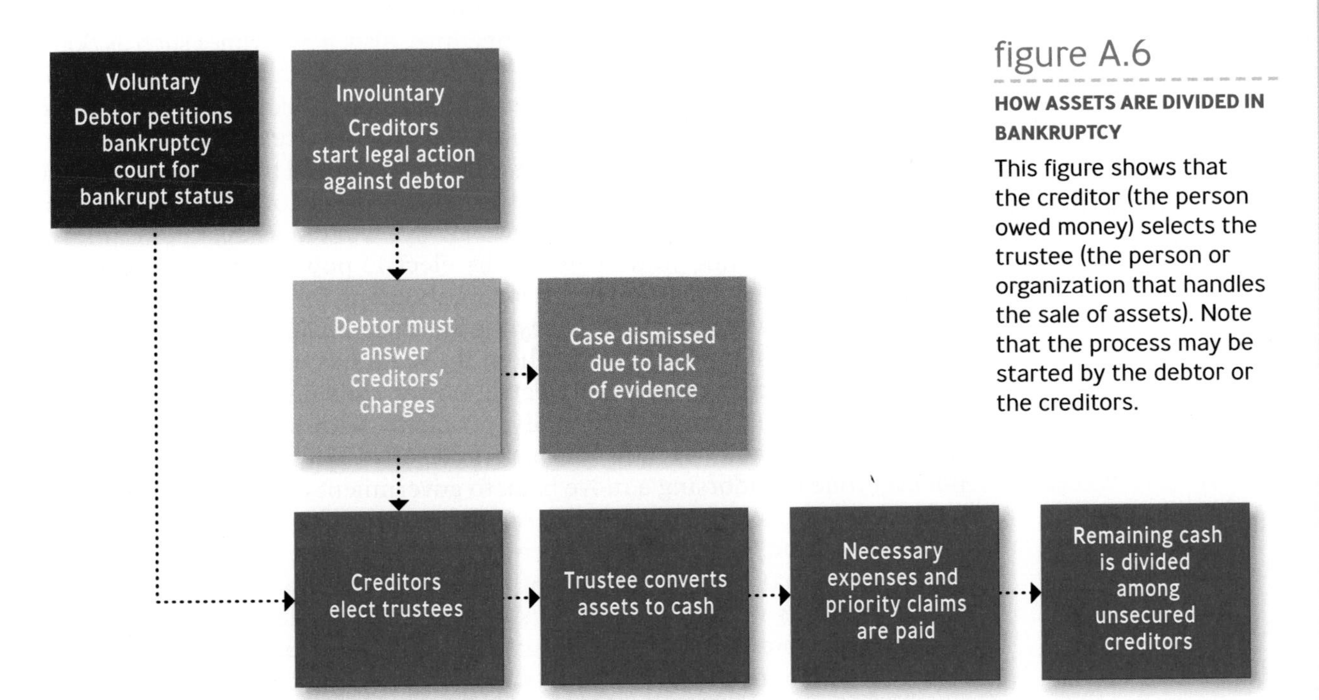


figure A.6

**HOW ASSETS ARE DIVIDED IN BANKRUPTCY**

This figure shows that the creditor (the person owed money) selects the trustee (the person or organization that handles the sale of assets). Note that the process may be started by the debtor or the creditors.

Chapter 11 bankruptcy allows a company to reorganize and continue operations while paying only a limited proportion of its debts. Under Chapter 11, a company continues to operate but has court protection against creditors' lawsuits while it tries to work out a plan for paying off its debts. A company does not have to be insolvent in order to file for relief under Chapter 11. In theory, it is a way for sick companies to recover and is designed to help both debtors and creditors find the best solution. A trustee appointed by the court to protect the interests of creditors usually supervises all such matters. Under certain conditions, the company can sell assets, borrow money, and change company officers to strengthen its market position. In reality, less than one-third of Chapter 11 companies survive—usually the firms with lots of cash available. The Bankruptcy Reform Act of 1994 provides a fast-track procedure for small businesses filing under Chapter 11. Though it's not commonly used, individuals can also file under Chapter 11.

Chapter 13 bankruptcy permits individuals, including small-business owners, to pay back creditors over a period of three to five years. Chapter 13 proceedings are less complicated and less expensive than Chapter 7 proceedings. The debtor files a proposed plan for paying off debts to the court. If the plan is approved, the debtor pays a court-appointed trustee in monthly installments as agreed on in the repayment plan. The trustee then pays each creditor. The bankruptcy legislation passed by the U.S. Congress in 2005, means more debtors will have to file bankruptcy under Chapter 13.[48]

## DEREGULATION

**deregulation**
Government withdrawal of certain laws and regulations that seem to hinder competition.

By 1980, the United States had developed laws and regulations covering almost every aspect of business. Concerns arose that there were too many laws and regulations, and that these laws and regulations were costing the public money (see Figure A.7). Thus began the movement toward deregulation. **Deregulation** means that the government withdraws certain laws and regulations that seem to hinder competition. Perhaps the most publicized examples of deregulation have been those in the airline and telecommunications industries. At one time, the government restricted airlines with regard to where they could land and fly. When the restrictions were lifted, airlines began competing for different routes and charging lower prices. Consumers clearly benefited from the deregulation, but established airlines were challenged to be more competitive. Also, new airlines such as Southwest were born to take advantage of the opportunities. Passage of the Telecommunications Act in 1996 brought similar deregulation to telecommunications and gave consumers a flood of options in local telephone service markets.[49] New regulations in the banking and investments industries changed the nature of financial markets and made them more competitive with stronger consumer protections.[50]

Unfortunately, deregulation has not always worked as desired. California became the first state to deregulate the electric power industry in the late 1990s. State leaders envisioned customers shopping for electricity in a market packed with power suppliers jockeying for their business—with consumers choosing the best option.[51] Since then, the state has experienced significant problems, with deregulation of electric power causing several states to halt deregulation programs. Additionally, problems with phony energy transactions from companies such as Enron soured some states on deregulation. Still, not everyone is endorsing a move back to government-controlled regulation in utilities. In Texas and New York, deregulation programs have been somewhat successful. Time will tell if utility deregulation will survive.

It seems that some regulation of business is necessary to ensure fair and honest dealings with the public. Businesses may dispute this by arguing that they have adapted to laws and regulations, and have done much toward producing safer, more effective products. Unfortunately, corporate scandals in the

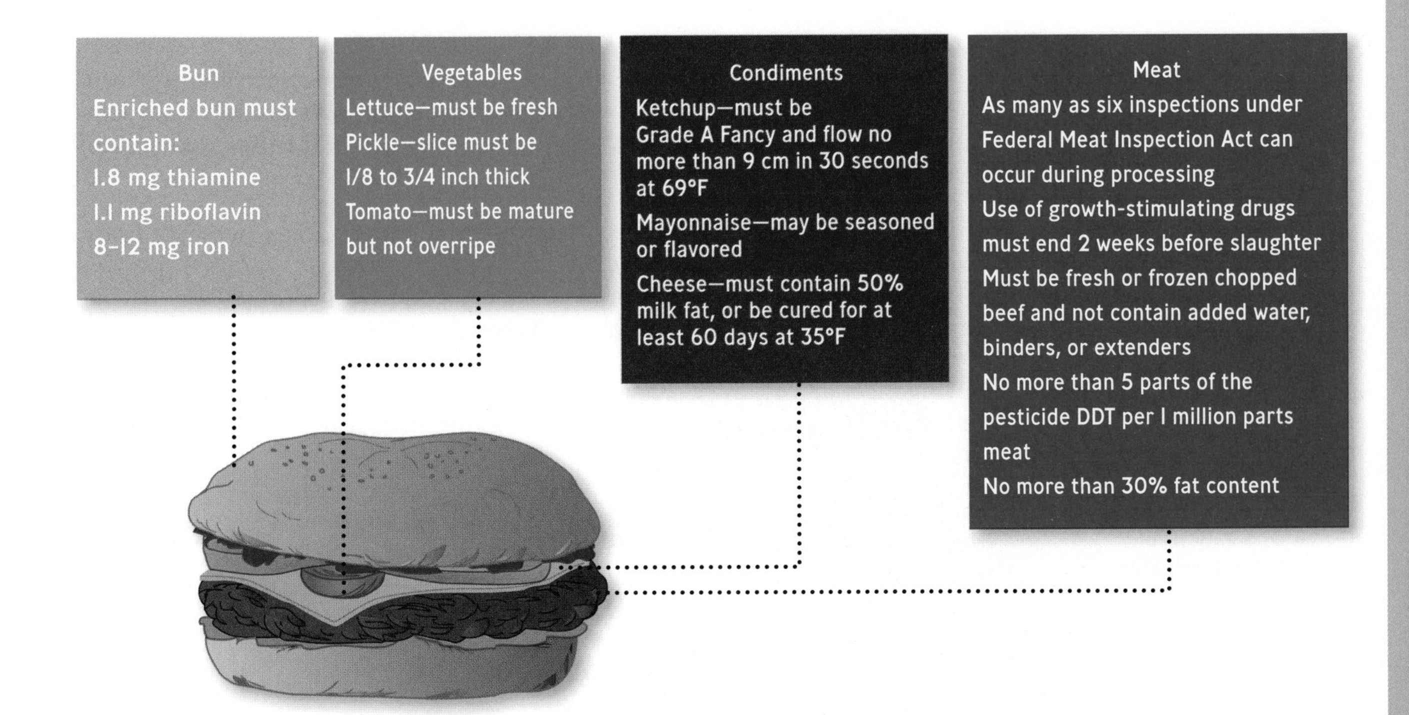
Bun
Enriched bun must contain:
1.8 mg thiamine
1.1 mg riboflavin
8–12 mg iron
Vegetables
Lettuce—must be fresh
Pickle—slice must be 1/8 to 3/4 inch thick
Tomato—must be mature but not overripe
Condiments
Ketchup—must be Grade A Fancy and flow no more than 9 cm in 30 seconds at 69°F
Mayonnaise—may be seasoned or flavored
Cheese—must contain 50% milk fat, or be cured for at least 60 days at 35°F
Meat
As many as six inspections under Federal Meat Inspection Act can occur during processing
Use of growth-stimulating drugs must end 2 weeks before slaughter
Must be fresh or frozen chopped beef and not contain added water, binders, or extenders
No more than 5 parts of the pesticide DDT per 1 million parts meat
No more than 30% fat content

figure A.7

**HAMBURGER REGULATIONS**

Does this amount of regulation seem just right, too little, or too much for you?

early 2000s remain on the minds of many. These events soured what was assumed to be better dialogue and cooperation between business and government. The scandals led to a cry for even more government regulation and control of business operations to protect investors and workers. With global competition increasing and small- and medium-sized businesses striving to capture selected markets, business and government need to continue to work together to create a competitive environment that is fair and open. If businesses do not want additional regulation they must follow current regulation and accept their responsibilities to all stakeholders.

### progress assessment

- What is covered in the Clayton Act, the Federal Trade Commission Act, and the Robinson-Patman Act?
- Describe bankruptcy under Chapters 7, 11, and 13.
- What is deregulation? Give examples of when deregulation has been successful and unsuccessful.

## summary

1. Business law refers to rules, statutes, codes, and regulations that are established to provide a legal framework within which business may be conducted and that are enforceable by court action.

   • **What is the difference between statutory law and common law?**

   Statutory law includes state and federal constitutions, legislative enactments, treaties of the federal government, and ordinances—in short, written law. Common law is the body of unwritten law that comes from decisions handed down by judges.

1. Define *business law*, distinguish between statutory and common law, and explain the role of administrative agencies.

- **What are administrative agencies?**

Administrative agencies are federal or state institutions and other government organizations created by Congress or state legislatures with delegated power to create rules and regulations within their mandated area of authority.

**2.** Define tort law and explain the role of product liability in tort law.

2. A tort is wrongful conduct that causes injury to another person's body, property, or reputation.
- **What is an intentional tort?**

An intentional tort is a willful act that results in injury.
- **What is negligence?**

Negligence, in tort law, deals with behavior that causes *unintentional* harm or injury. Decisions involving negligence can often lead to huge judgments against businesses.

**3.** Identify the purposes and conditions of patents, copyrights, and trademarks.

3. Patents and copyrights protect the rights of inventors, writers, and other developers of original products.
- **What are patents and copyrights?**

A patent is a document that gives inventors exclusive rights to their inventions for 20 years from the date they file the patent applications. A copyright protects a creator's rights to materials such as books, articles, photos, paintings, and cartoons.
- **What is a trademark?**

A trademark is a legally protected name, symbol, or design (or combination of these) that identifies the goods or services of one seller and distinguishes them from those of competitors.

**4.** Describe warranties and negotiable instruments as covered in the Uniform Commercial Code.

4. The Uniform Commercial Code (UCC) is the law that covers sales laws and other commercial law in all states.
- **What does Article 2 of the UCC cover?**

Article 2 contains laws regarding warranties. Express warranties are guarantees made by the seller, whereas implied warranties are guarantees imposed on the seller by law.
- **What does Article 3 of the UCC cover?**

It covers negotiable instruments (such as checks). It states that a negotiable instrument must (1) be written and signed by the maker or drawer, (2) be made payable on demand or at a certain time, (3) be made payable to the bearer (the person holding the instrument) or to specific order, and (4) contain an unconditional promise to pay a specified amount of money.

**5.** List and describe the conditions necessary to make a legally enforceable contract, and describe the possible consequences if such a contract is violated.

5. Contract law specifies what a legally enforceable agreement is.
- **What makes a contract enforceable under the law?**

An enforceable contract must meet six conditions: (1) An offer must be made, (2) the offer must be voluntarily accepted, (3) both parties must give consideration, (4) both parties must be competent, (5) the contract must be legal, and (6) the contract must be in proper form.
- **What are the possible consequences if a contract is violated?**

If a contract is violated, one of the following may be required: (1) specific performance, (2) payment of damages, or (3) discharge of obligation.

**6.** Summarize several laws that regulate competition and protect consumers in the United States.

6. Several laws were passed that regulate competition and protect consumers.
- **What does the Sherman Act cover?**

The Sherman Act forbids contracts, combinations, or conspiracies in restraint of trade and actual monopolies or attempts to monopolize any part of trade or commerce.

- **What does the Clayton Act add?**

The Clayton Act prohibits exclusive dealing, tying contracts, interlocking directorates, and buying large amounts of stock in competing corporations.

- **Which act regulates false and deceptive advertising?**

The Federal Trade Commission Act prohibits unfair methods of competition in commerce, including deceptive advertising.

- **Which act prohibits price discrimination and demands proportional promotional allowances?**

The Robinson-Patman Act applies to both sellers and buyers who "knowingly" induce or receive an unlawful discrimination in price.

7. Taxes are how the government (federal, state, and local) raises money.
   - **How does the government use taxes to encourage or discourage certain behavior among taxpayers?**

   If the government wishes to do something such as improve its citizens' health, it can reduce consumer use of certain classes of products (cigarettes, liquor, etc.) by passing what are referred to as *sin taxes*. In other situations, the government may offer tax credits to encourage businesses to hire new employees or purchase new equipment.

**7.** Explain the role of tax laws in generating income for the government and as a method of discouraging or encouraging certain behaviors among taxpayers.

8. When businesses or individuals become buried in debt they can file for bankruptcy.
   - **What are the bankruptcy laws?**

   Chapter 7 calls for straight bankruptcy, in which all of the assets are divided among creditors after exemptions. Chapter 11 allows a firm to reorganize and continue operation after paying only a limited portion of its debts. Chapter 13 allows individuals to pay their creditors over an extended period of time. The Bankruptcy Reform Act of 2005 requires most individuals to file under Chapter 13 making it harder for them to eliminate most debts from a bankruptcy.

**8.** Distinguish among the various types of bankruptcy as outlined by the Bankruptcy Code.

9. Deregulation means that the government withdraws certain laws and regulations that seem to hinder competition.
   - **What are a few of the most published examples of deregulation?**

   Perhaps the most publicized examples of deregulation have been those in the airline and telecommunications industries.

**9.** Explain the role of deregulation as a tool to encourage competition.

## key terms

**administrative agencies** 575
**bankruptcy** 586
**breach of contract** 581
**business law** 574
**common law** 574
**consideration** 580
**consumerism** 584
**contract** 580
**contract law** 580
**copyright** 578
**damages** 581
**deregulation** 588
**express warranties** 579
**implied warranties** 579
**involuntary bankruptcy** 586
**judiciary** 574
**negligence** 576
**negotiable instruments** 580
**patent** 577
**precedent** 575
**product liability** 576
**statutory law** 574
**strict product liability** 576
**taxes** 584
**tort** 576
**Uniform Commercial Code (UCC)** 579
**voluntary bankruptcy** 586

## critical thinking questions

1. Do you think the laws that promote fair and competitive practices are effective in the United States? What evidence do you have of that?
2. More and more individuals continue to file bankruptcy each year. Do you think the U.S. Congress was correct in toughening the bankruptcy laws?
3. Pick a side: Should there be increased government action to deal with deceptive business practices or should business be counted on to regulate itself to prevent deceptive business practices? Which do you think is better for society and business in the long run?

## developing workplace skills

1. Go to the Web site of the U.S. Patent and Trademark Office (www.uspto.gov) and view the information provided about obtaining a patent. See if you can estimate how long the process will take to complete and what your cost will be.
2. Call your local real estate board or visit a realtor and obtain a copy of a real estate contract. Read the contract carefully to see how it meets the six requirements stated in the chapter for a contract to be legal and binding.
3. See how your state and your local community stack up in the tax game. Does your state have an income tax? What percentage do you have to pay the state on your income? What about property taxes and sales taxes? How do these taxes in your area compare to other states and communities? Compare your tax rates with three other states and communities of your choice.
4. In 2005, the U.S. Congress passed bankruptcy reform legislation that the president signed into law. The new law makes it more difficult for individuals to file for bankruptcy under Chapter 7 and limits certain debts that could not be eliminated by bankruptcy. Research the changes in the new law and offer reasons why you support or oppose the new law.
5. Supporters of tort reform argue that it's unfair that plaintiffs (the parties bringing lawsuits) don't have to pay damages to the defendants (the parties subject to the lawsuits) if they lose the case. Should plaintiffs be subject to paying damages if they lose a case? Why or why not?

## taking it to the net

Imagine that you and several of your musician friends decide to start a band that you want to call Indented Fish. You want to protect the band name and the new songs you've written so that other groups can't use them. Go to the U.S. Patent and Trademark Office's Web site (www.uspto.gov) to find out how to get the protection you seek.

1. Do you need to apply for patents, copyrights, or trademarks, or some combination of these to protect your band name and songs?
2. When can you use the trademark symbols ™ and ®?
3. How can you secure a copyright of your songs?
4. What are the advantages of registering copyrights?
5. What do you have to do to register a copyright on your songs?

## casing the web

To access the case *"A Whopper of a Decision,"* visit **www.mhhe.com/ub8e**

# using technology to manage information

profile

**Getting to Know**

**X** *Eva Chen*

**Cofounder and CEO of Trend Micro**

When the NIMDA worm crashed thousands of computers around the world in 2001, Eva Chen was more annoyed than usual that her company could respond to viruses only after they had infected computers and networks. All the company could do was to tell the customers to shut down their systems and then give them the tools to repair the damage. As chief technology officer at Trend Micro, a company that develops security software, she took the shortcoming personally, especially since her company's own network was shut down by the virus.

Over the next year she kept coming back to the problem. At meetings with many of Trend Micro's 300 engineers and 2,000 employees throughout Asia, Europe, and the United States, she would ask for ideas on how to stop such viruses before they could spread their damage. One night at dinner with her two bickering children, the answer occurred to her. Just as parents sometimes have to separate the kids to calm them down, perhaps there was some way to separate parts of a network so that viruses could be detected and disarmed before they harmed the whole system.

Chen's idea was to design a box that would scan packets of data and hold on to those that might contain worms. There the questionable data would be compared with Trend Micro's current virus-tracking information, and any detected worms would be destroyed. The only problem with Chen's idea was that it involved hardware, and Trend Micro makes software. At first, executives at Trend Micro were reluctant to expand into hardware. But Chen won them over with a convincing demonstration. Chen called her new product Network VirusWall and made it bright red so that it would stand out in the racks of gray and black servers that dominate information technology departments. Network VirusWall sales were so strong that the company's stock price soared while prices of other tech companies plummeted.

Chen is a native of Taiwan. She earned a bachelor's degree in philosophy at Chen Chi University before moving to the United States and completing a master of science in management information systems and international management from the University of Texas, Dallas. She then returned to Taiwan, where she found a job with Acer Computers. "I found I was good at bridging the marketing need and the engineering capability. I have a technical degree and know how to talk computer language, but at the same time I have empathy with what the users need."

LEARNING goals

After you have read and studied this chapter, you should be able to

1. Outline the changing role of business technology.
2. List the types of business information, identify the characteristics of useful information, and discuss how data are stored and mined.
3. Compare the scope of the Internet, intranets, extranets, and virtual private networks as tools in managing information.
4. Review the hardware most frequently used in business, and outline the benefits of the move toward computer networks.
5. Classify the computer software most frequently used in business.
6. Evaluate the human resource, security, privacy, and stability issues in management that are affected by information technology.

BONUS CHAPTER B

www.trendmicro.com

In 1988, she cofounded Trend Micro with Steve and Jenny Chang in California. She was executive vice president from 1988 to 1996 and chief technology officer (CTO) from 1996 to 2004. The company now is headquartered in Tokyo and has more than 2,500 employees, representing 30 countries worldwide. In the beginning, many potential customers were reluctant to work with a woman CTO. When Trend Micro first began to enter the Japanese market, Chen had special cards that identified her as an "engineering secretary." When she attended meetings with one of the company's male engineers, she pretended to take notes while actually she was writing him instructions. By the end of 2003, there was no need for such tricks; Chen was recognized by *Information Security* magazine as one of the five most influential "Women of Vision." In 2004, Eva Chen was named CEO of Trend Micro.

Chen says her management style is to be a good listener: "I listen and respect others' opinions and try to match their innovations with what the customer needs. A software company's main asset is its people's intelligence, so the most important thing is to let them grow and reveal their talents."

Sources: Jessie Ho, "Trend Micro Founder Shares Tricks of the Trade," *Taipei Times*, October 10, 2005; Kim Girard, "Sometimes Worms Just Need a Time-Out," *Business2.0*, May, 2004; "Eva Chen Is CTO of Trend Micro," *Diversity Careers*, January 2005; and www.trendmicro.com.

# THE ROLE OF INFORMATION TECHNOLOGY

Throughout this text, we have emphasized the need for managing information flows among businesses and their employees, businesses and their suppliers, businesses and their customers, and so on. Since businesses are in a constant state of change, those managers who try to rely on old ways of doing things will simply not be able to compete with those who have the latest in technology and know how to use it.

**data processing (DP)** Name for business technology in the 1970s; included technology that supported an existing business and was primarily used to improve the flow of financial information.

Business technology has often changed names and roles. In the 1970s, business technology was known as **data processing (DP)**. (Although many people use the words *data* and *information* interchangeably, they are different. Data are raw, unanalyzed, and unorganized facts and figures. Information is the processed and organized data that can be used for managerial decision making.) DP was used to support an existing business; its primary purpose was to improve the flow of financial information. DP employees tended to be hidden in a back room and rarely came in contact with customers.

**information systems (IS)** Technology that helps companies do business; includes such tools as automated teller machines (ATMs) and voice mail.

In the 1980s, business technology became known as **information systems (IS)**. IS moved out of the back room and into the center of the business. Its role changed from supporting the business to doing business. Customers began to interact with a wide array of technological tools, from automated teller machines (ATMs) to voice mail. As business increased its use of information systems, it became more dependent on them.

**information technology (IT)** Technology that helps companies change business by allowing them to use new methods.

Until the late 1980s, business technology was just an addition to the existing way of doing business. Keeping up-to-date was a matter of using new technology on old methods. But things started to change as the 1990s approached. Businesses shifted to using new technology on new methods. Business technology then became known as **information technology (IT)**, and its role became to change business.

Obviously, the role of the IT staff has changed as the technology itself has evolved. The chief information officer (CIO) has moved out of the back room and into the boardroom. Eva Chen (from the Opening Profile) is just one example. Because improved hardware and software keep computers running more smoothly than in the past, the average CIO can spend less time worrying about keeping the systems running and more time finding ways to use technology to boost business by participating in purchasing decisions, operational strategy, and marketing and sales.[1] Today the role of the CIO is to help the business use technology to communicate better with others while offering better service and lower costs.[2]

## How Information Technology Changes Business

Time and place have always been at the center of business. Customers long had to go to the business during certain hours to satisfy their needs. We went to the store to buy clothes. We went to the bank to arrange for a loan. Businesses decided when and where we did business with them. Today, IT allows businesses to deliver goods and services whenever and wherever it is convenient for the customer. Thus, you can order clothes from the Home Shopping Network, arrange a home mortgage loan by phone or computer, or buy a car on the Internet at any time you choose.

Consider how IT has changed the entertainment industry. If you wanted to see a movie 35 years ago, you had to go to a movie theater. Thirty years ago, you could wait for it to be on television. Twenty years ago, you could wait for it to be on cable television. Fifteen years ago, you could go to a video store and rent it. Now you can order video on demand by satellite or cable, or download the movie over the Internet to watch on your TV, computer, or even cell phone or iPod whenever and wherever you wish.[3]

As IT breaks time and location barriers, it creates organizations and services that are independent of location. For example, the NASDAQ and the SOFFEX are electronic stock exchanges without trading floors. Buyers and sellers make trades by computer.

Being independent of location brings work to people instead of people to work. With IT, data and information can flow more than 8,000 miles in a second, allowing businesses to conduct work around the globe continuously. We are moving toward what is called **virtualization**, which is accessibility through technology that allows business to be conducted independently of location.[4] For example, you can carry a virtual office in your pocket or purse. Such tools as cellular phones, pagers, laptop computers, and personal digital assistants allow you to access people and information as if you were in an actual office. Likewise, people who otherwise would not have met are forming virtual communities through computer networks.

The way people do business drastically changes when companies increase their technological capabilities. Electronic communications can provide substantial time savings whether you work in an office, at home, or on the road. E-mail has put an end to tedious games of telephone tag and is far faster than paper-based correspondence. Instant messaging (IM), best known as the preferred way for millions of teenagers to find out who likes whom, is now a favorite real-time communication tool for businesses. For example, you may turn on your computer first thing in the morning to see who else is logged on. You may participate in half a dozen IM conversations at once through a cascade of pop-up windows. You might try to respond to a client in one window and agree to meet a colleague for lunch in another. (However, not everyone can tolerate the many interruptions that IM brings, so many people choose to keep IM turned off.)

Internet and intranet communication using shared documents and other methods allow contributors to work on a common document without time-consuming meetings. See Figure B.1 on page 598 for other examples of how information technology is changing business.

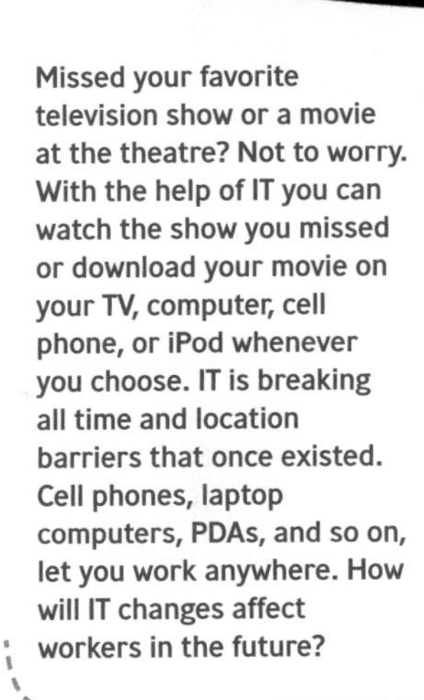

Missed your favorite television show or a movie at the theatre? Not to worry. With the help of IT you can watch the show you missed or download your movie on your TV, computer, cell phone, or iPod whenever you choose. IT is breaking all time and location barriers that once existed. Cell phones, laptop computers, PDAs, and so on, let you work anywhere. How will IT changes affect workers in the future?

**virtualization**
Accessibility through technology that allows business to be conducted independent of location.

## Moving from Information toward Knowledge and Business Intelligence

In the mid-1990s, yet another change occurred in the terminology of business technology: We started moving away from IT and toward knowledge technology (KT). *Knowledge* is information charged with enough intelligence to make it relevant and useful. KT adds a layer of intelligence to filter appropriate information and deliver it when it is needed. For example, consider the number 70. Alone, it doesn't mean much. Change it to 70 percent and it means a little more but still doesn't tell us a lot. Make it a 70 percent chance of rain and we have more meaning.

Now let's imagine that you are the first one on your block with a wristwatch featuring KT. As you walk out the door, the watch signals you that it has a message: "70 percent chance of rain in your city today." KT just gave you relevant and useful information at the moment you needed it. Now you can head for class with an umbrella under your arm, knowing that you made an informed decision.

figure B.1

**HOW INFORMATION TECHNOLOGY IS CHANGING BUSINESS**

This table shows a few ways that information technology is changing businesses, their employees, suppliers, and customers.

| | |
|---|---|
| **Organization** | Technology is breaking down corporate barriers, allowing functional departments or product groups (even factory workers) to share critical information instantly. |
| **Operations** | Technology shrinks cycle times, reduces defects, and cuts waste. Service companies use technology to streamline ordering and communication with suppliers and customers. |
| **Staffing** | Technology eliminates layers of management and cuts the number of employees. Companies use computers and telecommunication equipment to create "virtual offices" with employees in various locations. |
| **New products** | Information technology cuts development cycles by feeding customer and marketing comments to product development teams quickly so that they can revive products and target specific customers. |
| **Customer relations** | Customer service representatives can solve customers' problems instantly by using companywide databases to complete tasks from changing addresses to adjusting bills. Information gathered from customer service interactions can further strengthen customer relationships. |
| **New markets** | Since it is no longer necessary for customers to walk down the street to get to stores, online businesses can attract customers to whom they wouldn't otherwise have access. |

KT changes the traditional flow of information; instead of an individual going to the database, the database comes to the individual. For example, using KT business training software, AT&T can put a new employee at a workstation and then let the system take over everything from laying out a checklist of the tasks required on a shift to answering questions and offering insights that once would have taken up a supervisor's time. Knowledge databases may one day replace the traditional mentors who helped workers up the corporate ladder.

**business intelligence (BI)** Any of a variety of software applications that analyze an organization's raw data and take out useful insights from it.

KT "thinks" about the facts according to an individual's needs, reducing the time that a person must spend finding and getting information. As KT became more sophisticated in the mid-2000s it became better known as **business intelligence (BI)**. BI refers to a variety of software applications that analyze an organization's raw data and take out useful insights from it. BI activities include data mining (which we will discuss later in this chapter), online analytical process, querying, and reporting.[5]

Businesspeople who use BI can focus on what's important: deciding about how to react to problems and opportunities. For example, imagine you are a sales rep who just closed a big deal. While you celebrate your success, someone else in the finance department is upset because your customer never pays on time, which costs the company a lot of money. By using BI that provides the right information to the right person at the right time, you could have negotiated different payment terms with the customer, thus connecting the sales activity to the financial requirements in a seamless process.[6]

The businesses that build flexible information infrastructures will have a significant competitive advantage. Constant changes in technology interact with each other to create more change. Maintaining the flexibility to successfully integrate these changes is crucial to business survival.[7] History is filled with stories of once-mighty companies that couldn't keep up with the challenge of change: Packard Bell and RCA once dominated their industries but failed to compete effectively and have lost market share. They had size and money, but not flexibility. Knowledge sharing is at the heart of keeping pace with change.

progress assessment

- How has the role of information technology changed since the days when it was known as data processing?
- How has information technology changed the way we do business?

## TYPES OF INFORMATION

Today, information flows into and through an organization from many different directions. The types of information that are available to businesses today include:[8]

- **Business process information**. This includes all transaction data gathered at the point of sale as well as information gained through operations such as enterprise resource planning, supply chain management, and customer relationship management systems. It is estimated that the amount of corporate data available doubles every six months.
- **Physical-world observations**. These observations result from the use of radio frequency identification (RFID) devices, miniature cameras, wireless access, global positioning systems, and sensor technology—all of which have to do with where people or items are located and what they are doing. Computer chips cost pennies apiece and can be found in a wide range of products including credit cards, printer ink cartridges, baseballs, tire valves, running shoes, vacuum cleaners, and even beer mugs. That's right—Mitsubishi has produced a "smart" beer mug that senses when it is time for a refill and sends a signal to the bartender.[9]
- **Biological data**. Forms of identification include fingerprinting, which while not new can now be taken and shared more easily than ever before. Biometric devices can scan retinas, recognize faces and voices, and analyze DNA. Although such information is usually used for security purposes, it may be used to customize products and services in the future.
- **Public data**. Free and accessible, public data include electronic traces that people leave when posting to the Internet, sending e-mail, and using instant messaging. More and more, public data are being stored, shared, or sold.
- **Data that indicate personal preferences or intentions**. Internet shoppers leave a trail of information that can reveal personal likes and dislikes. Considering that in just one month, approximately 84 million people (half of all U.S. Internet users) used either the eBay or Amazon Web sites, you can imagine the volume of information that is available. And this information is valuable. In fact, eBay now sells blinded transaction data to third parties.

Your finger can be used as a form of identification using a simple biometric device such as the one shown below. Currently, such technology is used primarily for security purposes, but in the future it could be used to customize products and provide key services. Can you think of ways businesses could make use of this technology?

The volume and complexity of all of this information is staggering. While data appear in all forms and formats—including text, numbers, audio, and video—computing systems have been developed that can search through the data and identify, categorize, and refine relevant opinions on any topic imaginable.[10]

## Managing Information

Even before the use of computers, managers had to sift through mountains of information to find what they needed to help them make decisions. Today, businesspeople are faced with *infoglut*, an overabundance of data. Have you seen the classic episode of TV's *I Love Lucy* with Lucy and Ethel on the candy line? Everything was going OK until the candy started coming too fast for them. Then mayhem broke loose. That's what's happening to many managers today. Instead of candy, it is information that is passing by too quickly. Too much information can confuse issues rather than clarify them. How can managers keep from getting buried in the infoglut? Stepping back to gain perspective is the key to managing the flood of information.

The most important step toward gaining perspective is to identify the four or five key goals you wish to reach. Eliminating the information that is not related to those top priorities can reduce the amount of information flowing into your office by half. For example, as we were gathering information to include in this chapter, we collected several hundred journal articles. Feeling the pressure of information overload, we identified the goals we wanted the chapter to accomplish and eliminated all the articles that didn't address those goals. As we further refined our goals, the huge stack of paper gradually dropped to a manageable size.

Obviously, not all of the information that ends up on your desk will be useful. The usefulness of management information depends on four characteristics:

1. **Quality**. Quality means that the information is accurate and reliable. When the clerk at a fast-food restaurant enters your order into the cash register, it may be automatically fed to a computer, and the day's sales and profits can be calculated as soon as the store closes. The sales and expense data must be accurate, or the rest of the calculations will be wrong. This can be a real problem when, for example, a large number of calculations are based on questionable sales forecasts rather than actual sales.
2. **Completeness**. There must be enough information to allow you to make a decision but not so much as to confuse the issue. Today, as we have noted, the problem is often too much information rather than too little.
3. **Timeliness**. Information must reach managers quickly. If a customer has a complaint, that complaint should be handled instantly if possible and certainly within no more than one day. In the past, a salesperson would make a report to his or her manager; that report would go to a higher-level manager, and the problem would not be resolved for days, weeks, or months. E-mail, instant messaging, and other developments make it possible for marketing, engineering, and production to hear about a problem with a product the same day the salesperson hears about it. Product changes can be made on the spot using computer-integrated manufacturing, as discussed in Chapter 9.
4. **Relevance**. Different managers have different information needs. Again, the problem today is that information systems often make too much data available. Managers must learn which questions to ask to get the answers they need.

The important thing to remember when facing information overload is to relax. You can never read everything that is available. Set goals for yourself, and do the best you can.

## Storing and Mining Data

It doesn't matter how interesting your information is if nobody's paying attention or people can't get to the information they need when they need it. Storing, sorting, and getting useful information to the right people at the right time are the goals in managing information. How do businesses organize a data glut so that it becomes useful information? The answer for many companies is a data warehouse. A *data warehouse* stores data on a single subject over a specific period of time.

The whole purpose of a data warehouse is to get data out. *Data mining* is looking for hidden patterns in a data warehouse. Data-mining software discovers previously unknown relationships among the data. The legendary example of data mining is a study by a retail chain that revealed a spike in beer sales coincided with a spike in diaper sales on weekdays between 5:00 and 7:00 p.m. The conclusion that thirsty dads pick up diapers on the way home from work prompted store managers to consider moving the diapers next to the beer to boost sales. The retail chain never did pair the Heineken with the Huggies, but the story led to a new science of tracking what's selling where and who's buying it.

Wal-Mart is the poster child for data mining. The retail giant has massive data warehouses that track sales on a minute-by-minute basis in order to reveal regional and local sales trends. Using this information, Wal-Mart customizes each store's offerings on the basis of local demand, keeping it and its suppliers informed about how each of the 70,000 products in the stores is selling and what it anticipates will sell next. For example, Wal-Mart used its sophisticated data-mining capabilities to predict the demand for umbrellas in rain-drenched parts of California during a recent winter. It analyzed historical sales data from stores in the region, National Weather Service predictions, and satellite weather patterns. It was able to predict not only the needed umbrella inventory but also the styles and colors most desired by its customers. The system was even able to identify the locations in specific stores that were best for increasing umbrella sales.[11]

The success of data mining depends on a number of factors, but perhaps the most important is access to data to mine in the first place. Frequently, organizations have a multitude of data storage systems that run on incompatible platforms. The divergent systems must be integrated in some way before the data can be connected. Such integration is possible today, but getting departments and divisions to hand over the keys to their data can be difficult.

**progress assessment**

- What types of information are available to businesses today?
- What are the four characteristics of information that make it useful?
- What is data mining and how do businesses use it?

# THE ROAD TO KNOWLEDGE: THE INTERNET, INTRANETS, EXTRANETS, AND VIRTUAL PRIVATE NETWORKS

The importance of business knowledge is nothing new—what is new is the recognition of the need to manage it like any other asset. To manage knowledge, a company needs to learn how to share information throughout the organization and to implement systems for creating new knowledge. This need is leading to

Social networking sites such as MySpace.com link old friends and new friends in an ever-expanding community. Such sites provide a virtual meeting place that is available 24/7. How do technology tools like social networking and blogging change the way people communicate and build relationships with each other?

new technologies that support the exchange of information among staff, suppliers, and customers. Who wins and who loses will be decided by who harnesses the technology that provides the pipeline of interaction and information flows between individuals and organizations. At the heart of knowledge management are the Internet, intranets, extranets, and virtual private networks.

You already know that the Internet is a network of computer networks. The Internet has evolved from a tool that allowed only one-to-one communications (usually through e-mail) to a one-to-many broadcast communication tool. Today the Internet allows many-to-many communication through such things as file sharing, Web logs (blogs), and social networking services that connect masses of people to each other at once.[12]

Internet users can point and click their way from site to site with complete freedom. But what if you don't want just anybody to have access to your Web site? You might create an intranet. An **intranet** is a companywide network, closed to public access, that uses Internet-type technology. To prevent unauthorized outsiders (particularly the competition) from accessing their sites, companies can construct a firewall between themselves and the outside world. A firewall can consist of hardware, software, or both. Firewalls allow only authorized users to access the intranet. Some companies use intranets only to publish information for employees, such as phone lists and employee policy manuals. These companies do not enjoy as high a return on their investment as other companies that create interactive intranet applications. Such applications include allowing employees to update their addresses or submit company forms such as supply requisitions, time sheets, or payroll forms online. These applications save money or generate revenue increases because they eliminate paper handling and enable decision making. AmeriKing, the largest independent Burger King franchisee in the United States, estimates that it saves about a half a million dollars a year on printing and distribution costs for things such as physician directories, employee profiles, and employee contact information.

**intranet**
A companywide network, closed to public access, that uses Internet-type technology.

**extranet**
A semiprivate network that uses Internet technology and allows more than one company to access the same information or allows people on different servers to collaborate.

Many businesses choose to open their intranets to other, selected companies through the use of extranets. An **extranet** is a semiprivate network that uses Internet technology and allows more than one company to access the same information or allows people on different servers to collaborate. One of the most common uses of extranets is to extend an intranet to outside customers. Extranets change the way we do business. No longer are the advantages of electronic data interchange (EDI) available only to the large companies that can afford such a system. Now almost all companies can use extranets to share data and process orders, specifications, invoices, and payments.

Notice that we described an extranet as a semiprivate network. This means that outsiders cannot access the network easily; but since an extranet does use public lines, knowledgeable hackers (people who break into computer systems for illegal purposes such as transferring funds from someone's bank account to their own without authorization) can gain unauthorized access. Most companies want a network that is as private and secure as possible. One way to increase the probability of total privacy is to use dedicated lines (lines reserved solely for the network). There are two problems with this method: (1) It's expensive, and (2) it limits use to computers directly linked to those lines. What if your company needs to link securely with another firm or an individual for just a short time? Installing dedicated lines between companies in this case would be too expensive and time-consuming. Virtual private networks are a solution.

A **virtual private network (VPN)** is a private data network that creates secure connections, or "tunnels," over regular Internet lines.[13] The idea of the VPN is to give the company the same capabilities as an extranet at much lower cost by using shared public resources rather than private ones. This means that companies no longer need their own leased lines for wide-area communication but can instead use public lines securely. Just as phone companies provide secure shared resources for voice messages, VPNs provide the same secure sharing of public resources for data. This allows for on-demand networking: An authorized user can join the network for any desired function at any time, for any length of time, while keeping the corporate network secure.

**virtual private network (VPN)**
A private data network that creates secure connections, or "tunnels," over regular Internet lines.

## The Front Door: Enterprise Portals

How do users log on to an organization's network? Frequently, they do so through an enterprise portal that centralizes information and transactions. Portals serve as entry points to a variety of resources, such as e-mail, financial records, schedules, and employment and benefits files. They can even include streaming video of the company's day care center. Portals are more than simply Web pages with links. They identify users and allow them access to areas of the intranet according to their roles: customers, suppliers, employees, and so on. They make information available in one place so that users don't have to deal with a dozen different Web interfaces. The challenge to the CIO is to integrate resources, information, reports, and so on—all of which may be in a variety of places—so that they appear seamless to the user.

The ease of searching and navigating different information systems that is gained by having the information easily accessible in one place saves money as well as time. Compuware, a software developer, estimates that enterprise portals save each employee 30 minutes a day. That adds up to 125 hours an employee a year. Multiply that by the number of employees and the average hourly salary, and you can see how much money a company can save.[14]

## Broadband Technology

**broadband technology**
Technology that offers users a continuous connection to the Internet and allows them to send and receive mammoth files that include voice, video, and data much faster than ever before.

As traffic on the Internet increases, the slower the connection becomes. New technologies unlock many of the traffic jams on the Internet. For example, **broadband technology** offers users a continuous connection to the Internet and allows them to send and receive mammoth files that include voice, video, and data much faster than ever before. The more bandwidth, the bigger the pipe for data to flow through—and the bigger the pipe, the faster the flow. Whether the broadband connection is by cable modem, digital subscriber line (DSL), satellite, or fixed wireless, the impact is much the same. With broadband, data can reach you more than 50 times faster than with a dial-up connection using a 56k modem (the kind that came with most computers in the late 1990s and early 2000s).[15]

Even with broadband technology, the traffic on the Internet has become so intense that early Net settlers—scientists and other scholars—have found themselves being squeezed off the crowded Internet and thus unable to access, transmit, and manipulate complex mathematical models, data sets, and other digital elements of their craft. Their answer? Create another Internet, reserved for research purposes only.

**Internet2**
The private Internet system that links government supercomputer centers and a select group of universities; it runs more than 22,000 times faster than today's public infrastructure and supports heavy-duty applications.

The private system, **Internet2**, runs more than 22,000 times faster than today's public infrastructure and supports heavy-duty applications such as videoconferencing, collaborative research, distance education, digital libraries, and full-body simulations known as teleimmersion. A key element of Internet2 is a network called very-high-speed backbone network service (vBNS), which was set up in 1995 as a way to link government supercomputer centers and a select group of universities. The power of Internet2 makes it possible for a remote medical specialist to assist in a medical operation over the Internet without having to contend with deterioration of the connection as, say, home users check sports scores.

Although Internet2 became available to only a few select organizations in late 1997, there are now more than 200 member universities.[16] Whereas the public Internet divides bandwidth equally among users (if there are 100 users, they each get to use 1 percent of the available bandwidth), Internet2 is more capitalistic. Users who are willing to pay more can use more bandwidth.

Cynics say that soon Internet2 itself will be overrun by networked undergrads engaged in song swapping and other resource-hogging pursuits. But the designers of Internet2 are thinking ahead. Not only do they expect Internet history to repeat itself, but they are counting on it. They are planning to filter the Internet2 technology out to the wider Internet community in such a way that there is plenty of room on the road for all of us—at a price, of course.

**progress assessment**

- What is an extranet and how does it differ from an intranet?
- What is an enterprise portal?

## THE ENABLING TECHNOLOGY: HARDWARE

We hesitate to discuss the advances that have been made in computer hardware because what is powerful as we write this may be obsolete by the time you read it. In the mid-1970s the chairman of Intel Corporation, Gordon E. Moore, predicted that the capacity of computer chips would double every year or so. This has since been called Moore's law.[17] The million-dollar vacuum-tube computers that awed people in the 1950s couldn't keep up with a pocket calculator today. In fact, a greeting card that plays "Happy Birthday" contains more computing power than existed before 1950.

The speed of evolution in the computer industry has slowed little since Moore's remark, although in 1997 Moore did say that his prediction cannot hold good for much longer because chip makers will sooner or later run into a fundamental law of nature, which is that the finite size of atomic particles will prevent infinite miniaturization. That, however, won't stop computer companies from improving chips in other ways than shrinking them.[18] Rapid advances make one product after another obsolete, helping create demand for newer chips. For example, a three-year-old personal computer (PC) is considered out-of-date. So rather than add potentially outdated facts to your information overload, we offer you a simple overview of the current computer technology.

Hardware includes computers, pagers, cellular phones, printers, scanners, fax machines, personal digital assistants (PDAs), and so on. The mobile worker can find travel-size versions of computers, printers, and fax machines that are almost as powerful and feature-laden as their big brothers. All-in-one devices that address the entire range of your communications needs are also available. For example, there are handheld units that include a wireless phone, camera, fax, and e-mail capabilities, Web browsers, and a personal information manager (PIM).

## Cutting the Cord: Wireless Information Appliances

Some experts think we have entered the post-PC era—that is, they believe we are moving away from a PC-dominant environment and toward an array of Internet appliance options. Internet appliances are designed to connect people to the Internet and to e-mail. They include equipment like PDAs (e.g., PalmPilot and Blackberry), smart phones, two-way paging devices, and in-dash computers for cars.

The standardization of wireless networking has set the common PC free as well. No longer chained to their desks, laptop computer users find it liberating to have the mobility and flexibility to work on the Internet or company network anywhere they can tap into a wireless network. Wireless networks use a technology called Wi-Fi, from the term *wireless fidelity.* (Techies call Wi-Fi by its official name, 802.11, but Wi-Fi will do just fine for us.) Wireless local-area networks in hotel rooms, coffee shops, and airport lounges allow users with laptops outfitted with wireless modems to connect to the Web and download at 50 times the speed of typical dial-up connections. People are taking the Internet with them, tapping in anytime and anywhere to gather information and transact business.

It's getting late and you have got a term paper that's due. Unfortunately, you also have a craving for a steaming cup of Starbuck's coffee. Oh my, the challenges of getting an education. Simple answer, why not do both? With wireless networks available at locations such as Starbucks you can work on that term paper and enjoy that latte without feeling guilty.

## Computer Networks

Perhaps the most dynamic change in business technology has been the move away from mainframe computers that serve as the center of information processing and toward network systems that allow many users to access information at the same time. In an older system, the mainframe performed all the tasks and sent the results to a "dumb" terminal that could not perform those tasks itself. In a **network computing system** (also called **client/server computing**), personal computers (clients) can obtain needed information from huge databases in a central computer (the server). Networks connect people to people and people to data; they allow companies the following benefits:

**network computing system (client/server computing)**
Computer systems that allow personal computers (clients) to obtain needed information from huge databases in a central computer (the server).

- Saving time and money.
- Providing easy links across functional boundaries.
- Allowing employees to see complete information.

Here's how networks helped software giant Lotus Development. Instead of waiting for the information gained from 4 million annual phone calls to be summarized by technical support people, Lotus Development sends the information straight into a database, where it's available on demand. Rather than accepting someone else's idea of what information is needed, any Lotus development employee can access the data and search according to his or her needs. The result is that many more employees than before have direct access to market information and can act accordingly.

Networks have their drawbacks as well. Maintaining a fleet of finicky desktop PCs can be expensive. The cost of the computer itself is just the down payment. Computing costs go up with productivity losses as you upgrade and troubleshoot equipment and train employees to use it. By the time you've recouped your costs, it's time for another upgrade. A large part of PC support costs comes from adding software that causes conflicts or disables other software on the system. Making upgrades to two or three PCs in a small home office is annoying; making them to dozens or hundreds of PCs in a corporation is daunting. Using networks requires so many organizational changes and incurs such high support and upgrade costs that some companies that tried networking PCs are now looking at other options.

One option is a hybrid of mainframe and network computing. In this model, applications and data reside on a server, which handles all of the processing needs for all the client machines on the networks. The client machines look like the PCs that most people use, but they lack the processing power to handle applications on their own. Called *thin-client networks*, these networks may resemble the ill-tempered dumb terminals of the 1980s, but the execution is much better. Users can still use the Windows applications that they had been using. In a thin-client network, software changes and upgrades need to be made only on the server, so the cost of ownership can be reduced by 20 percent.

Another option is to rent software and hardware access by way of the Internet as needed instead of trying to maintain a proprietary network. Back in the Web boom, companies called application service providers (ASPs) ran software at data centers and rented access to these functions to customers who didn't want to buy expensive servers and software. Most ASPs went out of business because CIOs were slow to hand over their critical data to companies with no track record or little experience in their specific industries. But the fall of little ASPs didn't stop the flow of outsourcing IT functions to big service providers like IBM. IBM offers pay-as-you-go computing, even hourly rentals, involving all types of IT, from server access to supply-chain-management software.

## SOFTWARE

Computer software provides the instructions that enable you to tell the computer what to do. Although many people looking to buy a computer think first of the equipment, it is important to find the right software before finding the right hardware. The type of software you want dictates the kind of equipment you need.

Some programs are easier to use than others. Some are more sophisticated and can perform more functions than others. A businessperson must decide what functions he or she wants the computer system to perform and then choose the appropriate software. That choice will help determine what brand of computer to buy, how much power it should have, and what other peripherals it needs.

**shareware**
Software that is copyrighted but distributed to potential customers free of charge.

**public domain software (freeware)**
Software that is free for the taking.

Although most software is distributed commercially through suppliers like retail stores or electronic retailers, there is some software, called **shareware**, that is copyrighted but distributed to potential customers free of charge. The users are asked to send a specified fee to the developer if the program meets their needs and they decide to use it. The shareware concept has become popular and has dramatically reduced the price of software. **Public domain software (freeware)** is software that is free for the taking. The quality of shareware and freeware varies greatly. To help you have an idea of the quality of such programs, find a Web site that rates shareware and freeware programs. For example, Sharewarejunkies.com lists the programs downloaded most often, editors' picks, and links to downloadable programs.

Businesspeople most frequently use software for (1) writing (word processors), (2) manipulating numbers (spreadsheets), (3) filing and retrieving data (databases), (4) presenting information visually (graphics), (5) communicating (e-mail and instant messaging), and (6) accounting. Integrated software or a software suite can perform many functions. Another class of software program, called groupware, is used on networks. Figure B.2 describes these types of software.

| | |
|---|---|
| **Word Processing Programs** | With word processors, standardized letters can be personalized quickly, documents can be updated by changing only the outdated text and leaving the rest intact, and contract forms can be revised to meet the stipulations of specific customers. The most popular word-processing programs include Corel WordPerfect, Microsoft Word, and Lotus WordPro. |
| **Desktop Publishing (DTP) Software** | DTP combines word processing with graphics capabilities that can produce designs that once could be done only by powerful page-layout design programs. Popular DTP programs include Microsoft Publisher, Adobe PageMaker Plus, and Corel Print Office. |
| **Spreadsheet Programs** | A spreadsheet program is simply the electronic equivalent of an accountant's worksheet plus such features as mathematical function libraries, statistical data analysis, and charts. Using the computer's speedy calculations, managers have their questions answered almost as fast as they can ask them. Some of the most popular spreadsheet programs are Lotus 1-2-3, Quattro Pro, and Excel. |
| **Database Programs** | A database program allows users to work with information that is normally kept in lists: names and addresses, schedules, inventories, and so forth. Using database programs, you can create reports that contain exactly the information you want in the form you want it to appear in. Leading database programs include Q&A, Access, Approach, Paradox, PFS: Professional File, PC-File, R base, and FileMaker Pro for Apple computers. |
| **Personal Information Managers (PIMs)** | PIMs or contact managers are specialized database programs that allow users to track communication with their business contacts. Such programs keep track of everything—every person, every phone call, every e-mail message, every appointment. Popular PIMs include Goldmine, Lotus Organizer, ACT, and ECCO Pro. |
| **Graphics and Presentation Programs** | Computer graphics programs can use data from spreadsheets to visually summarize information by drawing bar graphs, pie charts, line charts, and more. Inserting sound clips, video clips, clip art, and animation can turn a dull presentation into an enlightening one. Some popular graphics programs are Illustrator and Freehand for Macintosh computers, Microsoft PowerPoint, Harvard Graphics, Lotus Freelance Graphics, Active Presenter, and Corel Draw. |
| **Communications Programs** | Communications software enables a computer to exchange files with other computers, retrieve information from databases, and send and receive electronic mail. Such programs include Microsoft Outlook, ProComm Plus, Eudora, and Telik. |
| **Message Center Software** | Message center software is more powerful than traditional communications packages. This new generation of programs has teamed up with fax/voice modems to provide an efficient way of making certain that phone calls, e-mail, and faxes are received, sorted, and delivered on time, no matter where you are. Such programs include Communicate, Message Center, and WinFax Pro. |
| **Accounting and Finance Programs** | Accounting software helps users record financial transactions and generate financial reports. Some programs include online banking features that allow users to pay bills through the computer. Others include "financial advisers" that offer users advice on a variety of financial issues. Popular accounting and finance programs include Peachtree Complete Accounting, Simply Accounting, Quicken, and QuickBooks Pro. |
| **Integrated Programs** | Integrated software packages (also called suites) offer two or more applications in one package. This allows you to share information across applications easily. Such packages include word processing, database management, spreadsheet, graphics, and communications. Suites include Microsoft Office, Lotus SmartSuite, and Corel WordPerfect Suite. |
| **Groupware** | Groupware is software that allows people to work collaboratively and share ideas. It runs on a network and allows people in different areas to work on the same project at the same time. Groupware programs include Lotus Notes, Frontier's Intranet Genie, MetaInfo Sendmail, and Radnet Web Share. |

figure B.2

**TYPES OF POPULAR COMPUTER SOFTWARE**

progress assessment

- How do computer networks change the way employees gather information?
- What are the major types of computer software used in business?

# EFFECTS OF INFORMATION TECHNOLOGY ON MANAGEMENT

The increase of information technology has affected management greatly and will continue to do so. Four major issues arising out of the growing reliance on information technology are human resource changes, security threats, privacy concerns, and stability.

## Human Resource Issues

By now, you may have little doubt that computers are increasingly capable of providing us with the information and knowledge we need to do our daily tasks. The less creative the tasks, the more likely they will be managed by computers. For example, many telemarketing workers today have their work structured by computer-driven scripts. That process can apply to the work lives of customer service representatives, stockbrokers, and even managers. Technology makes the work process more efficient as it replaces many bureaucratic functions. We talked in Chapter 8 about tall versus flat organization structures. Computers often eliminate middle-management functions and thus flatten organization structures.

One of the major challenges technology creates for human resource managers is the need to recruit employees who know how to use the new technology or train those who already work in the company. Often companies hire consultants instead of internal staff to address these concerns. Outsourcing technical training allows companies to concentrate on their core businesses. Even techno-savvy companies outsource technology training. Computer companies such as 3Com, Cisco, and Microsoft often hire a technology training company called Information Management Systems to train employees to use their own systems.

Perhaps the most revolutionary effect of computers and the increased use of the Internet and intranets is that of telecommuting. Mobile employees, using computers linked to the company's network, can transmit their work to the office, and back, from anywhere as easily as (and sometimes more easily than) they can walk into the boss's office.[19]

Naturally, such work decreases travel time and overall costs, and often increases productivity. Telecommuting helps companies save money by allowing them to retain valuable employees during long pregnancy leaves or to tempt experienced employees out of retirement. Companies can also enjoy savings in commercial property costs, since having fewer employees in the office means that a company can get by with smaller, and therefore less expensive, offices than before.[20] At AT&T, 90 percent of the managers telecommute at least some of the time and 10 percent of all other employees telecommute full-time, saving the company $34 million a year just in real estate costs.[21]

Telecommuting enables men and women to stay home with small children. It has also been a tremendous boon for workers with disabilities. Employees who can work after hours on their home computers rather than at the office report lowered stress and improved morale. Studies show that telecommuting is most successful among people who are self-starters, who don't have home distractions, and whose work doesn't require face-to-face interaction with coworkers.

Even as telecommuting has grown in popularity, however, some telecommuters report that a consistent diet of long-distance work gives them a dislocated feeling of being left out of the office loop. Some feel a loss of the increased energy people can get through social interaction. In addition to the isolation issue is the intrusion that work brings into what is normally a personal setting. Often people working from home don't know when to turn the work off. Some companies are pulling away from viewing telecommuting as an either–or proposition: either at home or at the office. Such companies are using telecommuting as a part-time alternative. In fact, industry now defines telecommuting as working at home a minimum of two days a week.

Electronic communication can never replace human communication for creating enthusiasm and esprit de corps. Efficiency and productivity can become so important to a firm that people are treated like robots. In the long run, such treatment decreases efficiency and productivity. Computers are a tool, not a total replacement for managers or workers, and creativity is still a human trait. Computers should aid creativity by giving people more freedom and more time. Often they do, but unfortunately many Americans take the results of their productivity gains not in leisure (as do the Europeans), but in increased consumption, making them have to work even harder to pay for it all. Information technology allows people to work at home, on vacation, and in the car at any time of the day. Now U.S. citizens work longer hours than people in any other nation on earth.

Figure B.3 illustrates how information technology changes the way managers and workers interact. For additional information about telecommuting and home-based workers, review Chapters 6 and 11.

## Security Issues

According to the FBI about 40 percent of all U.S. companies between 2000 and 2003 (the latest data available) combated an attempt to steal information from their computer networks. Recent headlines reported major breaches,

figure B.3

**WHEN INFORMATION TECHNOLOGY ALTERS THE WORKPLACE**

| MANAGERS MUST | WORKERS MUST |
|---|---|
| • Instill commitment in subordinates rather than rule by command and control.<br>• Become coaches, training workers in necessary job skills, making sure they have resources to accomplish goals, and explaining links between a job and what happens elsewhere in the company.<br>• Give greater authority to workers over scheduling, priority setting, and even compensation.<br>• Use new information technologies to measure workers' performance, possibly based on customer satisfaction or the accomplishment of specific goals. | • Become initiators, able to act without management direction.<br>• Become financially literate so they can understand the business implications of what they do and changes they suggest.<br>• Learn group interaction skills, including how to resolve disputes within their work group and how to work with other functions across the company.<br>• Develop new math, technical, and analytical skills to use newly available information on their jobs. |

MyDoom is a mass-mailing worm flooding e-mail servers worldwide. The worm steals e-mail addresses from the infected machine and generates e-mails with a fake From: field, so incoming messages may appear to be from people you know. The worm also attempts to open a port on an infected PC, allowing a remote hacker to gain control of the system. How can you protect your computer against such an infectious virus?

**virus**
A piece of programming code inserted into other programming to cause some unexpected and, for the victim, usually undesirable event.

such as the loss of backup tapes containing the account information of 1.2 million Bank of America credit card holders, stolen information on 145,000 people from data aggregator ChoicePoint; and unauthorized access to shoe retailer DSW's credit card data for 1.4 million accounts.[22] "Secure" information is typically stolen by hackers who break into companies' networks; employees who steal it; or companies who lose it through incompetence, poor gatekeeping, or bad procedures.[23]

Data security issues are not limited to businesses, of course. Officials were unable to find the hackers who broke into Pentagon computers through the Internet and stole, altered, and erased numerous records. Ironically, one of the Pentagon systems to which the hackers gained access was that of computer security research.

Computer security is more complicated today than ever before. When information was processed on mainframes, the single data center was easier to control because there was limited access to it. Today, however, computers are accessible not only in all areas within the company but also in all areas of other companies with which the firm does business.

An ongoing security issue involves the spread of computer viruses over the Internet. A **virus** is a piece of programming code inserted into other programming to cause some unexpected and, for the victim, usually undesirable event. Viruses are spread by downloading infected programming over the Internet or by sharing an infected disk. Often the source of the file you downloaded is unaware of the virus. The virus lies dormant until circumstances cause its code to be executed by the computer. Some viruses are playful ("Kilroy was here!"), but some can be quite harmful, erasing data or causing your hard drive to crash. Programs such as Norton's AntiVirus "inoculate" your computer so that it doesn't catch a known virus. But because new viruses are being developed constantly, antivirus programs may have only limited success. Therefore, you should keep your antivirus protection program up-to-date and, more important, practice "safe computing" by not downloading files from unknown sources and by using your antivirus program to scan disks before transferring files from them.[24]

*Phishing* is another type of online security threat. A scammer will embellish an e-mail with a stolen logo for a well-recognized brand such as eBay, PayPal, or Citibank that make the message look authentic. Phishing messages often state something like "account activation required" or "Your account will be canceled if you do not verify." When the victims click the link contained in the message, they are sent to a phony Web site that takes their personal data and uses it to commit fraud. The best way to avoid a phishing scam is to never access a Web site through a link in an e-mail message. Instead, open a new window and go to the Web site directly.[25]

Existing laws do not address the problems of today's direct, real-time communication. As more and more people log on to the Internet, the number of legal issues will likely increase. Today, copyright and pornography laws are crashing into the virtual world. Other legal questions—such as those involving intellectual property and contract disputes, online sexual and racial harassment, and the use of electronic communication to promote crooked sales schemes—are being raised as millions of people log on to the Internet. Cybercrimes cost the United States billions of dollars a year.

Until September 11, 2001, corporate and government security officials worried mostly about online theft, credit card fraud, and hackers. Today, however, they are most concerned about cyberterrorism.[26] Terrorist hackers could shut down the entire communications, money supply, electricity, and transportation systems. For instance, an attempt to shut down Web browsing in 2002 occurred when a powerful electronic attack crippled 9 of the 13 computers that manage Internet traffic globally. If one more of the critical computers had been hit, it would have disrupted e-mails and Web browsing across many parts of the Internet. It was considered by officials to be the most sophisticated large-scale assault against crucial computers in the history of the Internet. Although most Internet users didn't notice the attack (it lasted only one hour, and most Internet providers routinely store, or cache, popular Web directory information), the attack demonstrated the Internet's vulnerability.

The Critical Infrastructure Protection Board, a part of the U.S. Office of Homeland Defense, was created after September 11, 2001, to devise a plan for improving the security of America's critical infrastructure. In order to do this, the agency needs the cooperation of businesses across the country because 85 percent of the system it needs to protect is in the private sector. If the government doesn't know what's going on there (e.g., hacker attacks, viruses), how can it help defend it? You might think that companies would eagerly give this information to the government in exchange for increased protection, but CIOs are reluctant to file such reports for fear that the public will find out about the security breaches and lose faith in their companies' ability to protect their assets. To encourage the sharing of information about critical infrastructure, Congress passed the Critical Infrastructure Information Act of 2002. The act provides that critical infrastructure information voluntarily submitted to a covered federal agency is exempt from disclosure under the Freedom of Information Act.[27] This gives businesses the assurance that any information they provide the Department of Homeland Security will remain secret. This is only a start on what is likely to be a long effort to improve security technologies that keep the bad guys out of cyberspace.[28]

## Privacy Issues

The increasing use of technology creates major concerns about privacy. For example, e-mail is no more private than a postcard. You don't need to be the target of a criminal investigation to have your e-mail snooped. More than one-fourth of U.S. companies scan employee e-mail regularly and legally. Just as employers can log and listen to employees' telephone conversations, they can track e-mail in a search for trade secrets, non-work-related traffic, harassing messages, and conflicts of interest. Also, most e-mail travels over the Internet in unencrypted plain text. Any hacker with a desire to read your thoughts can trap and read your messages. Some e-mail systems, such as Lotus Notes, can encrypt e-mail so that you can keep corporate messages private. If you use browser-based e-mail, you can obtain a certificate that has an encryption key from a company such as VeriSign; the cost is about $10 a year. Of course, legitimate users who want to decrypt your mail need to get an unlocking key.

The Internet presents increasing threats to your privacy, as more and more personal information is stored in computers and people are able to access that data, legally or illegally. The Internet allows Web surfers to access all sorts of information about you. For example, some Web sites allow people to search for vehicle ownership from a license number or to find individuals' real estate property records. One key question in the debate over protecting our privacy is "Isn't this personal information already public anyway?" Civil libertarians have long fought to keep certain kinds of information available to the public. If access to such data is restricted on the Internet, wouldn't we have to reevaluate our policies on public records entirely? The privacy advocates don't think so. After all, the difference is that the Net makes obtaining personal information too easy. Would your neighbors or friends even consider going to the appropriate local agency and sorting through public documents for hours to find your driving records or to see your divorce settlement? Probably not. But they might dig into your background if all it takes is a few clicks of a button.

**cookies**
Pieces of information, such as registration data or user preferences, sent by a Web site over the Internet to a Web browser that the browser software is expected to save and send back to the server whenever the user returns to that Web site.

Average PC users are concerned that Web sites have gotten downright nosy. In fact, many Web servers track users' movements online. Web surfers seem willing to swap personal details for free access to online information. This personal information can be shared with others without your permission. Web sites often send **cookies** to your computer that stay on your hard drive. These are pieces of information, such as registration data or user preferences, sent by a Web site over the Internet to a web browser that the browser is expected to save and send back to the server whenever the user returns to that Web site. These little tidbits often simply contain your name and a password that the Web site recognizes the next time you visit it so that you don't have to reenter the same information again. Other cookies track your movements around the Web and then blend that information with a database so that a company can tailor the ads you receive accordingly. Some software, known as *spyware*, can be installed on your computer without your knowledge. The spyware can then infect your system with viruses and track your online behavior.[29]

Do you mind someone watching over your shoulder while you're on the Web? Tim Berners-Lee, the researcher who invented the World Wide Web, led the development of a way to prevent you from receiving cookies without your permission. His Platform for Privacy Preferences, or P3, allows a Web site to automatically send information on its privacy policies. With P3 you can set up your Web browser to communicate only with those Web sites that meet certain criteria.[30] You need to decide how much information about yourself you are willing to give away. Remember, we are living in an information economy, and information is a commodity—that is, an economic good with a measurable value.

## Stability Issues

Although technology can provide significant increases in productivity and efficiency, instability in technology also has a significant impact on business. For example, candy maker Hershey discovered the Halloween trick was on it one year when the company couldn't get its treats to the stores on time. Failure of its new $115 million computer system disrupted shipments, and retailers were forced to order Halloween treats from other companies. Consequently, Hershey suffered a 12 percent decrease in sales that quarter.

Every once in a while a computer glitch could work in your favor, though. At least it did for a Swedish woman who checked her bank account to see if her monthly child allowance from the Swedish government had arrived and discovered her balance was more than $10 billion, twice the size of Sweden's defense budget. Apparently, someone had punched in a few too many zeros. When the woman notified her bank, the transaction was canceled, and the $1.6 million of interest that accrued over the three days it took to correct the error was taken out of her account. (But she did get a little something—the bank sent her flowers as a thank you for reporting the error quickly.) The list of computer glitches that have caused delays, outages, garbled data, and general snafus could go on and on.

What's to blame? Experts say it is a combination of computer error; human error; malfunctioning software; and an overly complex marriage of software, hardware, and networking equipment. Some systems are launched too quickly to be bug-proof, and some executives are too naive to challenge computer specialists. As critical as technology is to business, some of it is not built for rigorous engineering, and people aren't properly trained to use it. As things get more complex, we will probably be prone to more errors.

## TECHNOLOGY AND YOU

If you are beginning to think that being computer illiterate may be occupational suicide, you are getting the point. Workers in every industry come in contact with computers to some degree. Even fast-food workers read orders on computer screens. As information technology eliminates old jobs while creating new ones, it is up to you to learn and maintain the skills you need to be certain you aren't left behind.

### progress assessment

- How has information technology changed the way people work?
- What management issues have been affected by the growth of information technology?

## summary

1. Business technology is continuously changing names and changing roles.
   - **What have been the various names and roles of business technology since 1970?**

   In the 1970s, business technology was called data processing (DP) and its role was to support existing business. In the 1980s, its name became information systems (IS) and its role changed to doing business. In the 1990s, business technology became information technology (IT) and its role is now to change business.
   - **How does information technology change business?**

   Information technology has minimized the importance of time and place to businesses. Business that is independent of time and location can deliver products and services whenever and wherever it is convenient for the customer. See Figure B.1 for examples of how information technology changes business.
   - **What is knowledge technology?**

   Knowledge technology adds a layer of intelligence to filter appropriate information and deliver it when it is needed.
   - **What is business intelligence?**

   Business intelligence refers to a variety of software applications that analyze an organization's raw data and take out useful insights from it.

**1.** Outline the changing role of business technology.

**2.** List the types of business information, identify the characteristics of useful information, and discuss how data are stored and mined.

2. Information technology multiplies the mountains of information available to businesspeople.
   - **What types of information are available to businesses today?**

   The types of information available to businesses today include: (1) business process information, (2) physical-world observations, (3) biological data, (4) public data, and (5) data that indicate personal preferences or intentions.
   - **How can you deal with information overload?**

   The most important step in dealing with information overload is to identify your four or five key goals. Eliminate information that will not help you meet your key goals.
   - **What makes information useful?**

   The usefulness of management information depends on four characteristics: quality, completeness, timeliness, and relevance.
   - **What are data storage and data mining?**

   Data storage is a way businesses organize data into useful information. A *data warehouse* stores data on a single subject over a specific period of time. *Data mining* is looking for hidden patterns in a data warehouse. Data-mining software discovers previously unknown relationships among data.

**3.** Compare the scope of the Internet, intranets, extranets, and virtual private networks as tools in managing information.

3. To become knowledge-based, businesses must know how to share information and design systems for creating new knowledge.
   - **What information technology is available to help business manage information?**

   The heart of information technology involves the Internet, intranets, and extranets. The Internet is a massive network of thousands of smaller networks open to everyone with a computer and a modem. An intranet is a companywide network protected from unauthorized entry by outsiders. An extranet is a semiprivate network that allows more than one company to access the same information.

**4.** Review the hardware most frequently used in business, and outline the benefits of the move toward computer networks.

4. Computer hardware changes rapidly.
   - **What was one of the most dynamic changes in computer hardware in the past decade?**

   One of the most dynamic changes was the move away from mainframe computers that serve as the center of information processing toward network systems that allow many users to access information at the same time.
   - **What are the major benefits of networks?**

   Networks' major benefits are (1) saving time and money, (2) providing easy links across functional boundaries, and (3) allowing employees to see complete information.

**5.** Classify the computer software most frequently used in business.

5. Computer software provides the instructions that enable you to tell the computer what to do.
   - **What types of software are used by managers most frequently?**

   Managers most often use word processing, electronic spreadsheet, database, graphics, e-mail and instant messaging, and accounting programs. Another class of software, called groupware, allows people to work collaboratively and share ideas.

**6.** Evaluate the human resource, security, privacy, and stability issues in management that are affected by information technology.

6. Information technology has a tremendous effect on the way we do business.
   - **What effect has information technology had on business management?**

   Computers eliminate some middle management functions and thus flatten organization structures. Computers also allow employees to work from their own homes. On the negative side, computers sometimes allow information to fall into the wrong hands. Managers must find ways to prevent stealing by hackers. Concern for privacy is another issue affected by the vast store of information available on the Internet. Finding the balance between freedom to access private information and individuals' right to privacy will require continued debate.

## key terms

**broadband technology** 603
**business intelligence** 598
**cookies** 612
**data processing (DP)** 596
**extranet** 602
**information systems (IS)** 596
**information technology (IT)** 596
**Internet2** 604
**intranet** 602
**network computing system (client/server computing)** 605
**public domain software (freeware)** 606
**shareware** 606
**virtual private network (VPN)** 603
**virtualization** 597
**virus** 610

## critical thinking questions

1. What information, either for your personal life or for your job, would you like to receive exactly when and where you need it?
2. If you could design a system to provide the information you identified in question 1, what might it look like and what would it do?
3. What are the implications for world trade given the ability firms and government organizations now have to communicate across borders?
4. Could the cooperation needed among telecommunications firms worldwide lead to increased cooperation among other organizations on issues such as world health care and worldwide exchanges of technical information? How?

## developing workplace skills

1. Imagine that you have $3,000 to buy a computer system or to upgrade a computer you already have. Research the latest in hardware and software in computer magazines and on Web sites such as www.zdnet.com. Then go to a computer store or to online computer sites such as Dell, Gateway, and Micron to find the best value. Make a list of what you would buy, and then write a summary explaining the reasons for your choices.
2. Interview someone who bought a computer system to use in his or her business. Ask why that person bought that specific computer and how it is used. Ask about any problems that occurred during the purchase process

or in installing and using the system. What would the buyer do differently next time? What software does he or she find especially useful?

3. If you have worked with computers, you've probably experienced times when the hard drive crashed or the software wouldn't perform as it should have. Describe one computer glitch you've experienced and what you did to resolve it. Analyze and discuss the consequences of the interruption (e.g., decreased productivity, increased stress). If you haven't had a problem with a personal computer, talk with a friend or classmate who has.

4. Choose a topic that interests you and then, on the Internet, use two search engines to find information about the topic. If the initial result of your search is a list of thousands of sites, narrow your search using the tips offered by the search engine. Did both search engines find the same Web sites? If not, how were the sites different? Which engine found the most appropriate information?

5. Discuss how technology has changed your relationship with specific businesses or organizations such as your bank, your school, and your favorite places to shop. Has it strengthened or weakened your relationship? On a personal level, how has technology affected your relationship with your family, friends, and community? Take a sheet of paper and write down how technology has helped build your business and personal relationships on one side. On the other side of the paper, list how technology has weakened the relationships. What can you and others do to use technology more effectively to reduce any negative impact?

## taking it to the net

### Purpose

To experience the functions and benefits of an enterprise portal.

### Exercise

Log on to www.dynamicintranet.com and try the demo to see what an enterprise portal can do and how it can help businesses and their employees. (Click through the demo to get a general idea of the benefits of enterprise portals; don't try to understand the technical descriptions—you can save that for another course.) Business-to-employee (B2E) portals are not accessible to outsiders, but you can see what one looks like and experiment using some of its tools by logging on to the demo portal of Toasters Inc. at http://demo.dynamicintra.net/toaster_en.asp.

1. Using the calendar feature in the demo portal, schedule a meeting with three other employees. (Hint: Click "Calendar" and then "Search Public Calendar" to get started.) What are the benefits of using this tool rather than calling a meeting personally?

2. Suppose you want to work from home one day a week, but you aren't sure what Toasters' policy is on telecommuting. Find the policy in the human resources directory.

3. You're a team leader for Project 996. What's your reward if your team meets its goal?
4. Some of the folks in marketing have a sick sense of humor. See if you can find why office humor isn't reserved for the water cooler anymore. Obviously, Toasters Inc. allows individual employees to post information to the portal without supervisory approval. What are the advantages and disadvantages of unmoderated postings?

## casing the web

To access the case *"The Super Bowl of Networks,"* visit **www.mhhe.com/ub8e**

# managing risk

profile

**Getting to Know**

**X A. G. Gaston**

**Insurance Entrepreneur and Risk Taker**

Arthur George (A. G.) Gaston was born in Demopolis, Alabama, on July 4, 1892. The grandson of slaves, he was born into poverty. He went into the military and served in an all-black regiment in World War I. When he came back from the war, he went to work in the mines. Not a promising start.

Gaston was one of very few men in the mines who brought a box lunch with him. Being a nice guy, Gaston was willing to share his sandwiches with others. But soon the entrepreneur in him took hold, and he began selling quality sandwiches to his fellow miners. Gaston took the earnings from his sandwich business and began lending money to the miners at interest. He also sold them peanuts and popcorn. The secret to successful entrepreneurship, as you have learned, is to find a need and fill it. So far, Gaston was quite successful at doing this.

One more need that he noticed among the people he worked with was the need for proper funeral services. The miners had difficulty saving the money for such events. In 1923, Gaston started the Booker T. Washington Burial Society. He went door-to-door selling insurance to cover funerals. In 1932, the company became the Booker T. Washington Insurance Company. It became the largest black-owned insurance company in Alabama. Eventually his business interests included two radio

After you have read and studied this chapter you should be able to

1. Discuss the environmental changes that have made risk management more important.
2. Explain the four ways of managing risk.
3. Distinguish between insurable and uninsurable risk.
4. Explain the rule of indemnity.
5. Discuss the various types of insurance that businesses may buy.
6. Explain why businesses must carry workers' compensation insurance.
7. Tell others why businesses cannot manage environmental damage on their own.

BONUS CHAPTER C

stations, two cemeteries, motels, the Citizens' Federal Savings Bank in downtown Birmingham, and more. He was on the board of trustees of the Tuskegee Institute. *Black Enterprise* magazine chose Gaston as the "Entrepreneur of the Century" in honor of his contributions.

Gaston became wealthy as an entrepreneur—his worth was estimated at about $130 million. By the way, he worked until he was over 100 years old. He is a true inspiration to those who begin with little but strive for a lot.

Becoming a successful entrepreneur means assuming a lot of risk. Once a company gets started, more risks emerge, such as the risk of fires and accidents. Recent hurricanes damaged or destroyed many, many businesses in New Orleans and throughout the Gulf Coast region. Similar natural catastrophes occur every day somewhere in the nation and throughout the world. Clearly, the management of such risks has become more and more important over time. Entrepreneurs can lose their money as fast as they earned it if they don't handle risk properly. This bonus chapter is about risk management. You will learn how people like A. G. Gaston manage risk in their companies. One of the ways is to buy insurance, but there are others as well.

Sources: Carol Jenkins and Elizabeth Gardner Hines, *Black Titan: A. G. Gaston and the Making of a Black Millionaire* (One World/Ballantine), 2004; http://en.wikipedia.org/wiki/a.g._gaston; James C. Johnson, "A. G. Gaston: Rough Road to Riches," *Black Enterprise*, August 2005; and Nitin Nohria, "Risk, Uncertainty, and Doubt," *Harvard Business Review*, February 2006, pp. 39–40.

## UNDERSTANDING BUSINESS RISKS

The management of risk is a major issue for businesses throughout the country.[1] Almost every day you hear about a hurricane, earthquake, flood, fire, airplane crash, riot, or car accident that destroyed property or injured someone. An accident that involves a major personality may be front-page news for weeks. Such reports are so much a part of the news that we tend to accept these events as part of everyday life. But events involving loss mean a great deal to the businesspeople involved. They must pay to restore the property and compensate those who are injured. A survey presented in *Quality Digest* found that more than 90 percent of 271 executives are building or want to build enterprise risk management (ERM) into their organizations.[2] An ERM program usually has a few well-defined goals, such as (1) defining which risks the program will manage; (2) what risk management processes, technologies, and investments will be required; and (3) how these efforts will be coordinated across the firm.[3]

Given the 9/11 attack, two wars (Afghanistan and Iraq), corporate and government scandals, several major hurricanes and tornadoes, and the threat of terrorists and bird flu, it is no surprise that risk management is getting more attention.[4] The risks of serious information security failures are manifold. Computer hackers and computer viruses have become a real threat, and identity theft has become commonplace.[5]

In addition to the newsmaking stories, thousands of other incidents involve businesspeople in lawsuits. Lawsuits in recent years have covered everything from job-related accidents to product liability. In some states, insurance is not available or is too expensive for high-risk businesses. New legislation has been passed in some areas to lessen some of these risks so that companies can obtain insurance coverage again at a reasonable price.[6]

You may have read about the incident at Wendy's in which a woman fraudulently claimed to have found part of a person's finger in her chili. Business at that facility went down by half until the company could prove the fraud.[7] It is hard to anticipate such losses, but that is what risk management is all about—minimizing the losses from unexpected events.

The Secretary of the Interior, Gale Norton, presented a discussion of U.S. efforts to prepare for a possible outbreak of bird flu. Although the flu may be spread to the United States by migratory birds, the possibility of person-to-person spreading of the flu seems to be relatively remote. Have you done anything to prepare for such an outbreak?

## How Rapid Change Affects Risk Management

Changes are occurring so fast in the business world that it is difficult to keep up with the new risks involved. For example, who in the organization can evaluate the risks of buying or selling products over the Internet? As companies reach global markets over the Internet, who in the company watches for fluctuations in the world's currencies and how they may affect profits? Will global warming affect weather conditions? How will climate change affect farms and cattle raising? What would happen to the economy if there were a series of terrorist attacks on the country? What would happen if a flu (e.g., bird flu) epidemic would occur?[8] As you can see, risk management is getting more complex and more critical for all businesses. Those who do business in other countries face increasing risk from social unrest—think of the damage businesses suffered in France as a result of riots in 2005 and 2006.[9] Let's explore how companies go about managing risk. We'll begin by going over a few key terms.

# MANAGING RISK

The term **risk** refers to the chance of loss, the degree of probability of loss, and the amount of possible loss. There are two different kinds of risk:

**risk**
The chance of loss, the degree of probability of loss, and the amount of possible loss.

- **Speculative risk** involves a chance of either profit or loss. It includes the chance a firm takes to make extra money by buying new machinery, acquiring more inventory, and making other decisions in which the probability of loss may be relatively low and the amount of loss is known.[10] An entrepreneur takes speculative risk on the chance of making a profit.[11] In business, building a new plant is a speculative risk because it may result in a loss or a profit.[12]
- **Pure risk** is the threat of loss with no chance for profit. Pure risk involves the threat of fire, accident, or loss. If such events occur, a company loses money; but if the events do not occur, the company gains nothing.[13]

**speculative risk**
A chance of either profit or loss.

**pure risk**
The threat of loss with no chance for profit.

The risk that is of most concern to businesspeople is pure risk. Pure risk threatens the very existence of some firms. Once such risks are identified, firms have several options:

1. Reduce the risk.
2. Avoid the risk.
3. Self-insure against the risk.
4. Buy insurance against the risk.

We'll discuss the option of buying insurance in detail later in this bonus chapter. In the next sections, we will discuss each of the other alternatives for managing risk. These steps should be taken to lower the need for outside insurance.

## Reducing Risk

A firm can reduce risk by establishing loss-prevention programs such as fire drills, health education, safety inspections, equipment maintenance, accident prevention programs, and so on. Many retail stores, for example, use mirrors, video cameras, and other devices to prevent shoplifting. Water sprinklers and smoke detectors are used to minimize fire loss. In industry, most machines have safety devices to protect workers' fingers, eyes, and so on.

Product recalls can also reduce risk. A classic example is the highly publicized decision by Johnson & Johnson Company to pull its Tylenol pills off the shelves across the country when sabotaged capsules killed several people. More recently, when an estimated 400 deaths in traffic accidents were blamed on faulty tires, Firestone and Ford recalled thousands of tires before more people were killed or hurt.

Employees, as well as managers, can reduce risk. For example, truck drivers can wear seat belts to minimize injuries from accidents, operators of loud machinery can wear earplugs to reduce the chance of hearing loss, and those who lift heavy objects can wear back braces. The beginning of an effective risk management strategy is a good loss-prevention program. However, high insurance rates have forced some people to go beyond merely preventing risks to the point of avoiding risks, and in extreme cases by going out of business.

## Avoiding Risk

Many risks cannot be avoided. There is always the chance of fire, theft, accident, or injury. But some companies are avoiding risk by not accepting hazardous jobs and by outsourcing shipping and other functions.[14] The threat of lawsuits has driven away some drug companies from manufacturing vaccines, and some consulting engineers refuse to work on hazardous sites. Some companies are losing outside members of their boards of directors for lack of liability coverage protecting them from legal action against the firms they represent. Many companies cut back on their investments in the early 2000s to avoid losses.[15]

## Self-Insuring

**self-insurance**
The practice of setting aside money to cover routine claims and buying only "catastrophe" policies to cover big losses.

Many companies and municipalities have turned to self-insurance because they either can't find or can't afford conventional property/casualty policies. Such firms set aside money to cover routine claims and buy only "catastrophe" insurance policies to cover big losses. **Self-insurance**, then, lowers the cost of insurance by allowing companies to take out insurance only for larger losses.

Hurricane damage such as this cannot be accurately estimated by a business before the event happens. That is the whole idea of having insurance. What happens, though, when the insurance company says that the damage was from water, not wind, and the loss is not covered in your policy? Can you see why it is important to understand fully the coverage you or your company has?

Self-insurance is most appropriate when a firm has several widely distributed facilities. The risk from fire, theft, or other catastrophe is then more manageable. Firms with huge facilities, in which a major fire or earthquake could destroy the entire operation, usually turn to insurance companies to cover the risk.

One of the more risky strategies for self-insurance is for a company to "go bare," paying claims straight out of its budget. The risk here is that the whole firm could go bankrupt over one claim, if the damages are high enough. A less risky alternative is to form risk retention group-insurance pools that share similar risks. It is estimated that about one-third of the insurance market is using such alternatives.

## Buying Insurance to Cover Risk

Although well-designed, consistently enforced risk-prevention programs reduce the probability of claims, accidents do happen. Insurance is the armor individuals, businesses, and nonprofit organizations use to protect themselves from various financial risks. For this protection, such organizations spend about 10 percent of gross domestic product (GDP) on insurance premiums. Some insurance protection is provided by the federal government (see Figure C.1), but most risks must be covered by individuals and businesses on their own.[16] To reduce the cost of insurance, some companies buy a business ownership policy (BOP)—a package that includes property and liability insurance.[17] We will continue our discussion of insurance by identifying the types of risks that are uninsurable, followed by those that are insurable.

**What Risks Are Uninsurable?** Not all risks are insurable, even risks that once were covered by insurance. An **uninsurable risk** is one that no insurance company will cover. Examples of things that you cannot insure include market risks (e.g., losses that occur because of price changes, style changes, or new products that make your product obsolete); political risks (e.g., losses from war or government restrictions on trade); some personal risks (such as loss of a job); and some risks of operation (e.g., strikes or inefficient machinery).

**uninsurable risk**
A risk that no insurance company will cover.

figure C.1
**PUBLIC INSURANCE**
State or federal government agencies that provide insurance protection.

| TYPE OF INSURANCE | WHAT IT DOES |
|---|---|
| Unemployment Compensation | Provides financial benefits, job counseling, and placement services for unemployed workers. |
| Social Security | Provides retirement benefits, life insurance, health insurance, and disability income insurance. |
| Federal Housing Administration (FHA) | Provides mortgage insurance to lenders to protect against default by home buyers. |
| National Flood Insurance Association | Provides compensation for damage caused by flooding and mud slides to properties located in flood-prone areas. |
| Federal Crime Insurance | Provides insurance to property owners in high-crime areas. |
| Federal Crop Insurance | Provides compensation for damaged crops. |
| Pension Benefit Guaranty Corporation | Insures pension plans to prevent loss to employees if the company declares bankruptcy or goes out of business. |

**insurable risk**
A risk that the typical insurance company will cover.

**insurable interest**
The possibility of the policyholder to suffer a loss.

**What Risks Are Insurable?** An **insurable risk** is one that the typical insurance company will cover. Generally, insurance companies use the following guidelines when evaluating whether or not a risk is insurable:

1. The policyholder must have an **insurable interest**, which means that the policyholder is the one at risk to suffer a loss. You cannot, for example, buy fire insurance on your neighbor's house and collect if it burns down.
2. The loss should be measurable.
3. The chance of loss should be measurable.
4. The loss should be accidental.
5. The risk should be dispersed; that is, spread among different geographical areas so that a flood or other natural disaster in one area would not bankrupt the company.
6. The insurance company can set standards for accepting the risk.

**progress assessment**

- What events have created more awareness of the need for risk management in companies?
- What is the difference between pure risk and speculative risk?
- What are the four major options for handling risk?
- What are some examples of uninsurable risk?

**insurance policy**
A written contract between the insured and an insurance company that promises to pay for all or part of a loss.

**premium**
The fee charged by an insurance company for an insurance policy.

**law of large numbers**
Principle that if a large number of people are exposed to the same risk, a predictable number of losses will occur during a given period of time.

## UNDERSTANDING INSURANCE POLICIES

An **insurance policy** is a written contract between the insured (an individual or organization) and an insurance company that promises to pay for all or part of a loss. A **premium** is the fee charged by the insurance company or, in other words, the cost of the insurance policy to the insured.

Like all other private businesses, an insurance company is designed to make a profit. Insurance companies therefore gather data to determine the extent of various risks. What makes the acceptance of risk possible for insurance companies is the law of large numbers.

The **law of large numbers** states that if a large number of people or organizations are exposed to the same risk, a predictable number of losses will occur during a given period of time. Once the insurance company predicts the number of losses likely to occur, it can determine the appropriate premiums for each policy it issues. The premium is supposed to be high enough to cover expected losses and yet earn a profit for the firm and its stockholders. Today, many insurance companies are charging high premiums not for past risks but for the anticipated costs associated with the increasing number of court cases and high damage awards.

**rule of indemnity**
Rule saying that an insured person or organization cannot collect more than the actual loss from an insurable risk.

### Rule of Indemnity

The **rule of indemnity** says that an insured person or organization cannot collect more than the actual loss from an insurable risk. One cannot gain from risk management; one can only minimize losses. One cannot, for example, buy two insurance policies and collect from both for the same loss. If a company or person carried two policies, the two insurance companies would calculate any loss and divide the reimbursement.

## Types of Insurance Companies

There are two major types of insurance companies. A **stock insurance company** is owned by stockholders, just like any other investor-owned company. A **mutual insurance company** is owned by its policyholders. A mutual insurance company, unlike a stock company, does not earn profits for its owners. It is a nonprofit organization, and any excess funds (over losses, expenses, and growth costs) go to the policyholders/investors in the form of dividends or premium reductions.

**stock insurance company**
A type of insurance company owned by stockholders.

**mutual insurance company**
A type of insurance company owned by its policyholders.

**progress assessment**

- What is the law of large numbers?
- What is the rule of indemnity?

# INSURANCE COVERAGE FOR VARIOUS KINDS OF RISK

As we have discussed, risk management consists of reducing risk, avoiding risk, self-insuring, and buying insurance. There are many types of insurance that cover various losses: property and liability insurance, health insurance, and life insurance. Property losses result from fires, accidents, theft, or other perils. Liability losses result from property damage or injuries suffered by others for which the policyholder is held responsible. Let's begin our exploration of insurance by looking at health insurance.

## Health Insurance

Businesses and nonprofit organizations may offer their employees an array of health care benefits to choose from. Everything from hospitalization to physician fees, eye exams, dental exams, and prescriptions can be covered. Often, employees may choose between options from health care providers (e.g., Blue Cross/Blue Shield); health maintenance organizations (HMOs, e.g., Kaiser Permanente); preferred provider organizations (PPOs); or Medical Savings Accounts (MSAs).

**health maintenance organizations (HMOs)**
Health care organizations that require members to choose from a restricted list of doctors.

**Health Maintenance Organizations (HMOs)** **Health maintenance organizations (HMOs)** offer a full range of health care benefits. Emphasis is on helping members stay healthy instead of on treating illnesses. Two nice features typical of HMOs are that members do not receive bills and do not have to fill out claim forms for routine service. HMOs employ or contract with doctors, hospitals, and other systems of health care, and members must use those providers. In other words, they cannot choose any doctor they wish but can select one doctor from the approved list to be their primary care physician. That doctor will then recommend specialists, if necessary. The HMO system is called managed care.

HMOs are less expensive than comprehensive health insurance providers, but members sometimes complain about not being able to choose doctors or to get the care they want or need. Some physicians also complain that they lose some freedom to do what is needed to make people well and often receive less compensation than they feel is appropriate for the services they provide. To save money, HMOs usually must

Aflac insurance policies may help you with those expenses not covered by your major medical plan. Has your curiosity been raised by Aflac commercials on TV?

**preferred provider organizations (PPOs)**
Health care organizations similar to HMOs except that they allow members to choose their own physicians (for a fee).

**medical savings accounts (MSAs)**
Tax-deferred accounts that allow people to save money for medical expenses.

approve treatment before it is given. People who prefer to have their doctor make such decisions often choose a PPO, as we shall see next.

**Preferred Provider Organizations (PPOs)** **Preferred provider organizations (PPOs)** also contract with hospitals and physicians, but unlike an HMO, a PPO does not require its members to choose only from those physicians. However, members do have to pay more if they don't use a physician on the preferred list. Also, members usually have to pay a deductible (e.g., $250) before the PPO will pay any bills. When the plan does pay, members usually have to pay part of the bill. This payment is called co-insurance. Some people feel that the added expense of PPOs over HMOs is worth the freedom to select their own physicians.

Since both HMOs and PPOs can cost as much as 80 percent less than comprehensive individual health insurance policies, most businesses and individuals choose to join one.

**Medical savings accounts (MSAs)** are tax-deferred accounts that allow people to save money for medical expenses. Employers (or you) would put part of the money currently spent on health insurance into an MSA. The part would be used to buy a catastrophic insurance policy that covers major medical expenses (less a deductible). The idea is to allow you to go to almost any doctor, get the services you need, and pay for them with the funds in your MSA. It is expected that you would go to the doctor less often than under an HMO or PPO and would bargain for a good price. The use of MSAs is expected to lower overall health costs in the United States. If you don't spend the money in your account in any one year, you can save the money (tax-free) for future medical expenses (any interest is also tax-free). Or you can withdraw the money at the end of the year, as long as you maintain a minimum balance. MSAs are a relatively new form of insurance that you may want to investigate further.

## Disability Insurance

Disability insurance replaces part of your income (50 to 70 percent) if you become disabled and thus unable to work. There usually is a period during which you must be disabled (e.g., 60 days) before you can begin collecting. Many employers provide this type of insurance, but some do not. In either case, insurance experts recommend that you get disability insurance because the chances of becoming disabled by a disease or accident when young are much higher than the chance of dying. The premiums for such insurance vary according to age, occupation, and income.

## Workers' Compensation

Workers' compensation insurance guarantees payment of wages, medical care, and rehabilitation services (e.g., retraining) for employees who are injured on the job. Employers in all 50 states are required to provide this insurance. This insurance also provides benefits to the survivors of workers who die as a result of work-related injuries. The cost of insurance varies by the company's safety record, its payroll, and the types of hazards faced by workers. For example, it costs more to insure a steelworker than an accountant.

## Liability Insurance

*Professional* liability insurance covers people who are found liable for professional negligence. For example, if a lawyer gives advice carelessly and the client loses money, the client may then sue the lawyer for an amount equal to that lost; the insurance would cover the lawyer's loss. Professional liability insurance is also known as malpractice insurance. While you may think of doctors and dentists when you hear that term, the fact is that many professionals, including mortgage brokers and real estate appraisers, are buying professional liability insurance because of large lawsuits their colleagues have faced.

*Product* liability insurance covers liability arising out of products sold. If a person is injured by, say, a ladder or some other household good, he or she may sue the manufacturer for damages. Insurance usually covers such losses.

## OTHER BUSINESS INSURANCE

It is impossible in an introductory course like this to discuss in detail all the insurance coverage that businesses may buy. Naturally, businesses must protect themselves against property damage, and they must buy car and truck insurance and more. Figure C.2 on page 628 will give you some idea of the types of insurance available. Many businesses were happy that they had business interruption insurance after Hurricane Katrina caused so much damage on the Gulf Coast.[18] The same was true when tornadoes ripped through the Midwest in April 2006.

The point to be made in this bonus chapter is that risk management is critical in all firms. That includes the risk of investing funds and the risk of opening your own business (speculative risk). Remember from Chapter 1, though, that risk is often matched by opportunity and profits. Taking on risk is one way for an entrepreneur to prosper. Regardless of how careful we are, however, we all face the prospect of death, even entrepreneurs. To ensure that those left behind will be able to continue the business, entrepreneurs often buy life insurance that will pay partners and others what they will need to keep the business going. We'll explore that next.

### Life Insurance for Businesses

We discuss life insurance in Bonus Chapter D. There, the focus is on life insurance for you and your family. Everything said there applies to life insurance for business executives as well. The best kind of insurance to cover executives in the firm is term insurance, but dozens of new policies with interesting features have been emerging recently.

### Insurance Coverage for Home-Based Businesses

Homeowner's policies usually don't have adequate protection for a home-based business. For example, they may have a limit of $2,500 for business equipment. For more coverage, you may need to add an endorsement (sometimes called a *rider*) to your homeowner's insurance. For about $25 a year, you can increase the coverage to $10,000. Check with your insurance agent for details. If clients visit your office or if you receive deliveries regularly, you may need home-office insurance. It costs around $150 a year, but it protects you from slip-and-fall lawsuits and other risks associated with visitors. For more elaborate businesses, such as custom cabinetry shops and other types of manufacturing or inventory-keeping businesses, a business-owner policy may be needed. That costs $300 a year or more. Unless you are an expert on insurance, you will need to consult an insurance agent about the best insurance for your home-business needs.

### The Risk of Damaging the Environment

The risk of environmental harm reaches international proportions in issues such as global warming. The 1986 explosion at the Chernobyl nuclear power plant in what was then the Soviet Union caused much concern throughout the world. Due to violations of various safety standards, several U.S. nuclear power plants have been shut down. Yet since coal-fired power plants are said to cause acid rain (and global warming), and other inexpensive fuel sources haven't been fully developed, figure C.2

PRIVATE INSURANCE

| TYPES OF INSURANCE | WHAT IT DOES |
|---|---|
| **Property and Liability** | |
| Fire | Covers losses to buildings and their contents from fire. |
| Automobile | Covers property damage, bodily injury, collision, fire, theft, vandalism, and other related vehicle losses. |
| Homeowner's | Covers the home, other structures on the premises, home contents, expenses if forced from the home because of an insured peril, third-party liability, and medical payments to others. |
| Computer coverage | Covers loss of equipment from fire, theft, and sometimes spills, power surges, and accidents. |
| Professional liability | Protects from suits stemming from mistakes made or bad advice given in a professional context. |
| Business interruption | Provides compensation for loss due to fire, theft, or similar disasters that close a business. Covers lost income, continuing expenses, and utility expenses. |
| Nonperformance loss protection | Protects from failure of a contractor, supplier, or other person to fulfill an obligation. |
| Criminal loss protection | Protects from loss due to theft, burglary, or robbery. |
| Commercial credit insurance | Protects manufacturers and wholesalers from credit losses due to insolvency or default. |
| Public liability insurance | Provides protection for businesses and individuals against losses resulting from personal injuries or damage to the property of others for which the insured is responsible. |
| Extended product liability insurance | Covers potentially toxic substances in products; environmental liability; and, for corporations, director and officer liability. |
| Fidelity bond | Protects employers from employee dishonesty. |
| Surety bond | Covers losses resulting from a second party's failure to fulfill a contract. |
| Title insurance | Protects buyers from losses resulting from a defect in title to property. |
| **Health Insurance** | |
| Basic health insurance | Covers losses due to sickness or accidents. |
| Major medical insurance | Protects against catastrophic losses by covering expenses beyond the limits of basic policies. |
| Hospitalization insurance | Pays for most hospital expenses. |
| Surgical and medical insurance | Pays costs of surgery and doctor's care while recuperating in a hospital. |
| Dental insurance | Pays a percentage of dental expenses. |
| Disability income insurance | Pays income while the insured is disabled as a result of accident or illness. |
| **Life Insurance** | |
| Group life insurance | Covers all the employees of a firm or members of a group. |
| Owner or key executive insurance | Enables businesses of sole proprietors or partnerships to pay bills and continue operating, saving jobs for the employees. Enables corporations to hire and train or relocate another manager with no loss to the firm. |
| Retirement and pension plans | Provides employees with supplemental retirement and pension plans. |
| Credit life insurance | Pays the amount due on a loan if the debtor dies. |

nuclear power plants are still considered by some to be a necessity. How to make nuclear power plants safer will be an issue well into the next century.

Many U.S. businesses, such as Home Depot and FedEx, are doing what they can to reduce greenhouse gases. Around the world, companies such as BP (Britain), Bayer (Germany), and BT (Britain) are doing their part.[19]

Many people feel there is a need for a more careful evaluation of environmental risks than currently is done. How much risk is there in global warming? We don't know all the details yet, but the risks may be substantial.[20] Therefore, many companies are going out of their way to protect the environment.[21]

Clearly, risk management now goes far beyond the protection of individuals, businesses, and nonprofit organizations from known risks. It means the evaluation of worldwide risks such as global warming.[22] It also means prioritizing these risks so that international funds can be spent where they can do the most good. No insurance company can protect humanity from such risks. These risks are the concern of businesses and governments throughout the world, with the assistance of the international scientific community.[23] They should also be your concern as you study risk management in all its dimensions.

### progress assessment

- What's the difference between an HMO and a PPO?
- How are medical savings accounts (MSAs) expected to save the government money?
- Why should someone buy disability insurance?
- How many different kinds of private insurance can you name?

## summary

1. Risk management is becoming a critical part of management in most firms.
   - **What changes have made risk management more important?**

   Global warming, terrorist threats, natural disasters, war, and an unstable economy have all contributed to additional risk and the need for more risk management.

**1.** Discuss the environmental changes that have made risk management more important.

2. There are several ways of handling risk.
   - **What are the four major ways of managing risk?**

   The major ways of avoiding risk are: (1) reduce risk, (2) avoid risk, (3) self-insure, and (4) buy insurance.

**2.** Explain the four ways of managing risk.

3. Some risks are insurable and others are not.
   - **What's the difference between insurable and uninsurable risk?**

   Uninsurable risk is risk that no insurance company will cover. Examples of things that you cannot insure include market risks, political risks, some personal risks (such as loss of a job); and some risks of operation (e.g., strikes or inefficient machinery). An insurable risk is one that the typical insurance company will cover. Generally, insurance companies use the following guidelines when evaluating whether or not a risk is insurable: (1) the policyholder must have an insurable interest, (2) the loss should be measurable, (3) the chance of loss should be measurable, (4) the loss should be accidental, (5) the risk should be dispersed, and (6) the insurance company can set standards for accepting risks.

**3.** Distinguish between insurable and uninsurable risk.

**4.** Explain the rule of indemnity.

4. There are some things one should know about insurance company rules.
   - **What is the rule of indemnity?**

   The rule of indemnity says that an insured person or organization cannot collect more than the actual loss from an insurable risk.
   - **What are the two kinds of insurance companies?**

   A stock insurance company is owned by stockholders, just like any other investor-owned company. A mutual insurance company is owned by its policyholders.

**5.** Discuss the various types of insurance that businesses may buy.

5. There are insurance policies to cover all different kinds of risk.
   - **What kind of policy covers health risks?**

   Health maintenance organizations (HMOs) offer a full range of health care benefits. Emphasis is on helping members stay healthy instead of on treating illnesses. Preferred provider organizations (PPOs) also contract with hospitals and physicians, but unlike an HMO, a PPO does not require its members to choose from only those physicians. Medical savings accounts (MSAs) enable you to pay for your doctors out of a savings account and buy insurance for catastrophes. This is supposed to lower overall insurance costs for the country.

**6.** Explain why businesses must carry workers' compensation insurance.

6. Businesses must explore many kinds of insurance.
   - **What kinds of insurance do most businesses have?**

   Workers' compensation insurance guarantees payment of wages, medical care, and rehabilitation services (e.g., retraining) for employees who are injured on the job. Employers in all 50 states are required to provide this insurance. Professional liability insurance covers people who are found liable for professional negligence. Product liability insurance provides coverage against liability arising out of products sold. If a person is injured by a ladder or some other household good, he or she may sue the manufacturer for damages. Most businesses also have some kind of life insurance for the executives. If you conduct business from home, you should also have some form of home-office insurance to cover liabilities.

**7.** Tell others why businesses cannot manage environmental damage on their own.

7. There is much discussion in the news about whether or not businesses are ruining the environment.
   - **What are businesses doing to cover the risks of harming the environment?**

   Many businesses are doing what they can to minimize damage to the environment. Such risks, however, are often beyond what businesses can manage. They are the concern of governments around the world.

## key terms

**health maintenance organizations (HMOs)** 625
**insurable interest** 624
**insurable risk** 624
**insurance policy** 624
**law of large numbers** 624
**medical savings accounts (MSAs)** 626
**mutual insurance company** 625
**preferred provider organizations (PPOs)** 626
**premium** 624
**pure risk** 621
**risk** 621
**rule of indemnity** 624
**self-insurance** 622
**speculative risk** 621
**stock insurance company** 625
**uninsurable risk** 623

## critical thinking questions

1. Are you self-insuring your apartment (or where you live) and your assets? What have you done to reduce the risk? Have you done anything to avoid risk? How much would it cost to buy insurance for your dwelling and the contents?

2. What risks do you take that cannot be covered by insurance?
3. What actions have you taken to avoid risk?
4. What can you do to lower the risk of natural disasters such as floods, hurricanes, and tornadoes?

## developing workplace skills

1. Write a one-page paper about ways you could reduce risk in your life (e.g., drive slower). Form into small groups and share what you have written. Then discuss everything that you and your classmates might do to reduce the risk of loss or harm.
2. You cannot insure yourself against speculative risk. However, you can minimize the risks you take when investing. Compare and contrast the risks of investing in stocks versus bonds for the long term. Be prepared to discuss your results in class.
3. Much of risk management is observing the behavior of others and then acting to reduce risky behavior. What kind of risky behavior have you observed among college students? What is being done, if anything, to inform them of such risks and to minimize them? What has been the response? What can you learn from such observation? Discuss the merits of having a risk manager for education facilities.
4. Form into small groups and discuss liability insurance, automobile insurance, renter's insurance, life insurance, and disability insurance. Develop a list of questions to discuss openly in class so that everyone is more informed about these issues.
5. Write a short (two-page) essay on the perceived risks of a terrorist attack, a natural disaster, or a major health disaster such as bird flu. Which risk do you perceive as most likely? Most dangerous? Discuss what you could do to warn others of such risks and motivate them to do something about them.

## taking it to the net

### Purpose

To learn about insurance for your dwelling and property, and to examine the issue of liability.

### Exercise

Go to the Information Insurance Institute at www.iii.org. Explore the site and then answer the following questions:

1. What is homeowner's insurance?
2. What is in a standard policy?
3. What different types of homeowner's policies are there?
4. What is renter's insurance?
5. Is an umbrella policy a wise purchase? Why or why not?

MANAGING

# personal finances

profile

## Getting to Know × Millionaires You Can Follow to Financial Success

There are about 8.9 million households in the United States with more than $1 million in financial assets. These are the people we call millionaires. They don't have to make a million dollars a year; they only have to have that much money in assets. A marketing research firm projects that the number of millionaire households will jump by about 52 percent by 2009. One of the best ways to learn how to become a millionaire is to do what companies do: benchmark those who are successful. That is, you should find out what all those millionaires did to make their money. For over 20 years, Thomas Stanley has been doing just that—studying wealthy people. His research is available in a book called *The Millionaire Next Door: The Surprising Secrets of America's Wealthy*, which he coauthored with William Danko.

Stanley and Danko found that the majority of millionaires are entrepreneurs who own one or more small businesses. Self-employed people are about *five times* as likely to be millionaires as people who earn a paycheck working for others. The average income of American millionaires is about $131,000 a year. So how did they get to be millionaires? They saved their money! To become a millionaire by the time you are 50 or so, you have to save about 15 percent of your income every year—starting when you are in your 20s. If you start later, you have to save an even larger

LEARNING goals

After you have read and studied this chapter, you should be able to

1. Describe the six steps of learning to control your assets.
2. Explain ways to build a financial base, including investing in real estate, saving money, and managing credit.
3. Explain how buying the appropriate insurance can protect your financial base.
4. Outline a strategy for retiring with enough money to last a lifetime.

# BONUS CHAPTER D

www.armchairmillionaire.com

percentage. The secret is to put your money in a place where it will grow without your having to pay taxes on it. You'll learn how to do that in this chapter.

To save that 15 percent a year, you have to spend less than you earn. Discipline in spending must begin with your first job and stay with you all your life. To save money, the millionaires Stanley studied tended to own modest homes and to buy used cars. In short, becoming a millionaire has as much or more to do with thrift than with how much you earn.

Stanley's newest book is called *Millionaire Women Next Door*. Female millionaires, according to Stanley, are on average 52 years old. They work about 50 hours a week and have an average net worth of $4.75 million. Some 70 percent took on leadership roles before they were teenagers. Over 60 percent have college degrees, and over half of those with degrees paid for their own tuition and fees! Almost 100 percent are homeowners. They are goal oriented and they persevere. Like the men who are millionaires, they are frugal: They buy used cars and homes, and save. They are often, however, generous, donating about 7 percent of their annual incomes to charities and other such groups.

Do you want to be a millionaire? If so, then you need to do what other rich people have done. You need to get an education, work hard, save your money, and make purchases carefully. This chapter will give you more insight into how to manage your finances. Are you ready to do the hard work it takes to become a millionaire? You are not likely to win a million dollars on a TV show, but you are quite likely to become a millionaire if you become an entrepreneur and save your money carefully.

Sources: Thomas J. Stanley, *Millionaire Women Next Door* (Kansas City: Andrews McMeel, 2004); Robert Frank, "Millionaire Ranks Hit New High," *The Wall Street Journal*, May 25, 2005, pp. D1 and D5; David Futrelle, Jon Birger, and Pat Regnier, "Getting Rich in America," *Money*, May 2005, pp. 99–104; "Picture of Wealth Is a Study in Contrasts," *Barron's*, March 20, 2006, p. 14; and Luisa Kroll and Allison Fass, "Billionaire Bacchanalia," *Forbes*, March 27, 2006, p. 111.

# THE NEED FOR PERSONAL FINANCIAL PLANNING

America is largely a capitalist country. It follows, then, that the secret to success in such a country is to have capital. With capital, you can take nice vacations, raise a family, invest in stocks and bonds, buy the goods and services you want, give generously to others, and retire with enough money to see you through. Money management, however, is not easy. You have to earn the money in the first place. Then you have to learn how to save money; spend money wisely; and insure yourself against the risks of serious accidents, illness, or death. We shall discuss each of these issues in this bonus chapter so that you can begin making financial plans for the rest of your life. With a little bit of luck, you may be one of the millionaires Stanley and Danko interview for their next book.

You will likely need some help. Recently high school students averaged a grade of 52 percent (failing) on a test of personal finance and economics.[1] Another report found that college students are also poorly educated about financial matters such as IRAs, 401(k) plans, and the like.[2] This bonus chapter will give you the basics so that you will be far ahead of the game. This subject is so important to your fiscal health that you may enjoy taking an entire class on it.

## Financial Planning Begins with Making Money

A major reason for studying business is that it prepares you for finding and keeping a good job. Today, that usually means learning how to communicate well, how to use a computer, and how to apply some of the skills you have learned in your college classes and in life. It also means staying out of financial trouble, if you want to keep the money you earn.

You already know that one of the secrets to finding a well-paying job is to have a good education. Throughout history, an investment in education has paid off regardless of the state of the economy or political ups and downs. Benjamin Franklin said, "If a man empties his purse into his head, no one can take it away from him. An investment in knowledge always pays the best interest." Education has become even more important since we entered the information age. A typical full-time worker in the United States with a four-year college degree earns about $50,000—62 percent more than one with only a high school diploma.[3] The lifetime income of families headed by individuals with a bachelor's degree will be about $1.6 million more than the incomes of families headed by those with a high school diploma. One way to begin to be a millionaire, therefore, is to finish college.

The government is eager for you to go to college and is willing to help you by giving you various tax breaks to do so. For example, with education savings accounts, funds grow free of taxes. Many people use their education to find successful careers and to improve their earning potential, but at retirement they have little to show for their efforts.[4] Making money is one thing; saving, investing, and spending it wisely is something else. Less than 10 percent of the U.S. population has accumulated enough money by retirement age to live comfortably. Following the six steps listed in the next section will help you become one of those with enough to live in comfort after retirement.

## Six Steps in Learning to Control Your Assets

The only way to save enough money to do all of the things you want to do in life is to make more than you spend. Although you may find it hard to save today, saving money is not only possible but imperative if you want to accumulate enough to be financially secure. In spite of that necessity, 36.8 percent of U.S. households don't have a retirement account.[5] You should not become one of them. The following are six steps you can take today to get control of your finances.

**Step 1: Take an Inventory of Your Financial Assets** To take inventory, you need to develop a balance sheet for yourself. Remember, a balance sheet starts with the fundamental accounting equation: Assets = Liabilities + Owners' equity. You can develop your own balance sheet similar to the one presented in Chapter 17 by listing your assets (e.g., TV, DVR player, iPod, computer, bicycle, car, jewelry, and clothes) on one side and liabilities (e.g., mortgage, credit card debt, and auto loans) on the other. Assets include anything you own. For our purpose, evaluate your assets on the basis of their current value, not purchase price as required in formal accounting statements. If you have no debts (liabilities), then your assets equal your net worth (in a corporation it's called owners' equity). If you do have debts, you have to subtract them from your assets to get your net worth.

If the value of your liabilities exceeds the value of your assets, you aren't on the path to financial security. You may need more financial discipline in your life.

Since we're talking about accounting, let's talk again about an income statement. At the top of the statement is revenue (everything you take in from your job, investments, etc.). You subtract all your costs and expenses to get net income or profit. Software programs such as Quicken and Web sites such as Dinkytown.net have a variety of tools that can easily help you with these calculations.

This may also be an excellent time to think about how much money you will need to accomplish all your goals. The more you visualize your goals, the easier it is to begin saving for them.

**Step 2: Keep Track of All Your Expenses** Often you may find yourself running out of cash (a cash flow problem). In such circumstances, the only way to trace where the money is going is to keep track of every cent you spend. Keeping records of your expenses can be a rather tedious but necessary chore if you want to learn discipline. Actually, it could turn out to be an enjoyable task because it gives you such a feeling of control. Here's what to do: Carry a notepad with you wherever you go and record *everything* you spend as you go through the day. That notepad is your journal. At the end of the week, record your journal entries into a record book or computerized accounting program.

Develop certain categories (accounts) to make the task easier and more informative. For example, you can have a category called "Food" for all food you bought from the grocery or the convenience store during the week. You might want to have a separate account for meals eaten away from home because you can dramatically cut such costs if you make your meals at home. Other accounts could include automobile, clothing, utilities, entertainment, donations to charity, and gifts. Most people like to have a category called "Miscellaneous" where they put expenditures for things like caffe latte. You won't believe how much you fritter away on miscellaneous items unless you keep a *detailed* record for at least a couple of months.

You can develop your accounts on the basis of what's most important to you or where you spend the most money. Once you have recorded all of

People need to take some time to balance income with expenses to be sure that there is money left to invest. Most people do not do such calculations and cannot retire as a result. What kind of savings plan have you started?

your expenses, it is relatively easy to see where you are spending too much money and what you have to do to save more money. A venti mocha frappuccino in a local Starbucks costs about $4.25. If you cut back from five to one a week, you would save $17 a week, or over $850 a year. Over 10 years, that could mean an extra $12,000 for retirement if the money is invested wisely.

**Step 3: Prepare a Budget** Once you know your financial situation and your sources of revenue and expenses, you're prepared to make a personal budget.[6] Remember, budgets are financial plans. Items that are important in a household budget include mortgage or rent, utilities, food, clothing, vehicles, furniture, life insurance, car insurance, and medical care. You'll need to make choices regarding how much to allow for such expenses as eating out, entertainment, and so on. Keep in mind that what you spend now reduces what you can save later. For example, spending $3.50 a day for cigarettes adds up to about $25 a week, $100 a month, $1,200 a year. If you can save $4 or $5 a day, you'll have almost $1,800 saved by the end of the year. Keep this up during four years of college and you'll have saved more than $7,000 by graduation. And that's before adding any interest earned. Cost-saving choices you might consider to reach this goal are listed in Figure D.1.

You'll learn that running a household is similar to running a small business. It takes the same careful record keeping, the same budget processes and forecasting, the same control procedures, and often (sadly) the same need to periodically borrow funds. Suddenly, concepts such as credit and interest rates become only too real. This is where some knowledge of finance, investments, and budgeting pays off. Thus, the time you spend learning budgeting techniques will benefit you throughout your life.

**Step 4: Pay Off Your Debts** The first thing to do with the money remaining after you pay your monthly bills is to pay off your debts. Start with the debts that carry the highest interest rates. Credit card debt, for example, may be costing you 16 percent or more a year. Merely paying off such debts will set you on a path toward financial freedom. It's better to pay off a debt that costs 16 percent than to put the money in a bank account that earns, say, only 3 percent or less.

figure D.1

**POSSIBLE COST-SAVING CHOICES**

The effect of the choices you make today can have a dramatic impact on your financial future. Compare the differences these few choices you can make now would mean to your future net worth. If you would make the lower-cost choices every month during your four years of college, and invest the savings in a mutual fund earning 6 percent compounded annually, you would double your money every 12 years.

| FIRST CHOICE COST PER MONTH | ALTERNATE CHOICE COST PER MONTH | SAVINGS PER MONTH |
|---|---|---|
| Starbucks caffe latte $3.00 for 20 day = $60.00 | Quick Trip's Cappuccino $.60 for 20 days = $12.00 | $48.00 |
| Fast-food lunch of burger, fries, and soft drink $4.00 for 20 days = $80.00 | Lunch brought from home $2 for 20 days = $40.00 | 40.00 |
| Evian bottled water $1.50 for 20 days = $30.00 | Generic bottled water $.50 for 20 days = $10.00 | 20.00 |
| CD = $15.00 | Listen to your old CDs = $0.00 | 15.00 |
| Banana Republic T-shirt = $34.00 | Old Navy T-shirt = $10.00 | 24.00 |
| | Total savings per month | $147.00 |
| | | × 48 months |
| | Total savings through 4 years of college | $7,056.00 |

| | Annual Rate of Return | | | |
|---|---|---|---|---|
| TIME | 2% | 5% | 8% | 11% |
| 5 years | $5,520 | $ 6,381 | $ 7,347 | $ 8,425 |
| 10 years | 6,095 | 8,144 | 10,795 | 14,197 |
| 15 years | 6,729 | 10,395 | 15,861 | 23,923 |
| 20 years | 7,430 | 13,266 | 23,305 | 40,312 |
| 25 years | 8,203 | 16,932 | 34,242 | 67,927 |

figure D.2

**HOW MONEY GROWS**

This chart illustrates how $5,000 would grow at various rates of return. Recent savings account interest rates were very low (less than 2 percent), but in earlier years they've been over 5 percent. Annual rates of return of the S&P 500 have varied widely, but the average annual return between 1970 and 2003 was 11 percent.

**Step 5: Start a Savings Plan** It's important to save some money each month in a separate account for large purchases you're likely to make (such as a car or house). Then, when it comes time to make that purchase, you'll have more cash. You should save at least enough for a significant down payment on a loan so that you can reduce the finance charges.

The best way to save money is to *pay yourself first.* That is, take your paycheck, take out money for savings, and then plan what to do with the rest.[7] You can arrange with your bank or mutual fund to deduct a certain amount every month. You will be pleasantly surprised when the money starts accumulating and earning interest over time. With some discipline, you can eventually reach your goal of becoming a millionaire. It's not as difficult as you may think. Figure D.2 shows how $5,000 grows over various time periods at different rates of return. If you start at age 40, you'll have 25 years in by the time you reach 65.

**Step 6: Borrow Money Only to Buy Assets That Have the Potential to Increase in Value or Generate Income** Don't borrow money for ordinary expenses; you'll only get into more debt that way. If you have budgeted for emergencies, such as car repairs and health care costs, you should be able to stay financially secure. Most financial experts will tell you to save about six months of earnings for contingency purposes. That means keeping the money in highly liquid accounts, such as the bank or money market fund.

Only the most unexpected of expenses should cause you to borrow. It is hard to wait until you have enough money to buy what you want, but learning to wait is a critical part of self-discipline. Of course, you can always try to produce more income by working overtime or by working on the side for extra revenue.

If you follow all six of these steps, you'll not only have money for investment but you'll have developed most of the financial techniques needed to become financially secure. At first you may find it hard to live within a budget. Nonetheless, the payoff is well worth the pain.

## BUILDING YOUR FINANCIAL BASE

The path to success in a capitalist system is to have capital (money) to invest, yet the trend today for graduates is to be not only capital-poor but also in debt. As you've read, accumulating capital takes discipline and careful planning. With the money you save, however, you can become an entrepreneur, one of the fastest ways to wealth. As you read in the Opening Profile, that often means living frugally.

Living frugally is extremely difficult for the average person.[8] Most people are eager to spend their money on a new car, furniture, iPods, clothes, HDTV, and the like.[9] They tend to look for a fancy apartment with all the amenities. A capital-generating strategy may require forgoing most (though not all) of these purchases to accumulate investment money. The living style required is similar to the one adopted by most college students: a relatively inexpensive apartment furnished in hand-me-downs from parents, friends, and resale shops.

For five or six years, you can manage with the old sound system, a used car, and a few nice clothes. The necessary living style is one of sacrifice, not luxury. It's important not to feel burdened by this plan; instead, feel happy knowing that your financial future will be more secure. That's the way the majority of millionaires got their money. If living frugally seems too restrictive for you, you can still save a little. It's better to save a smaller amount than none at all.

People are wise to plan their financial future with the same excitement and dedication they bring to other aspects of their lives. When you get married, for example, it is important to discuss financial issues with your spouse. Conflicts over money are a major cause of divorce, so agreeing on a financial strategy before marriage is very important. A great strategy is to try to live on one income and to save the other. The longer you wait before marriage, the more likely it will be that one or the other of you can be earning enough to do that—as college graduates. If the second spouse makes $18,000 a year after taxes, saving that income for five years quickly adds up to $90,000 (plus interest).

What do you do with the money you accumulate? The first investment might be a low-priced home.[10] You should make this investment as early as possible. The purpose of this investment is to lock in payments for your shelter at a fixed amount. This is possible by owning a home, but not by renting. Through the years, homeownership has been a wise investment. However, many young people take huge risks by buying too much home for their income, something the millionaires in the Opening Profile simply don't do. Furthermore, young people may take out interest-only loans or other such loans that are very, very risky. The old maxim "Don't buy a home that costs more than two and a half times your income" still stands.[11] Some people believe that we have lately been in a housing bubble that is starting to deflate; in fact, real estate prices are falling in some areas. That won't affect you if you are buying for the long term. Just stay within your means.[12]

## Real Estate: Historically, a Relatively Secure Investment

Homes do provide several investment benefits. First, a home is the one investment that you can live in. Second, once you buy a home, the payments are relatively fixed (though taxes and utilities go up). As your income rises, the house payments get easier and easier to make, but renters often find that rents tend to go up at least as fast as income. Paying for a home is a good way of forcing yourself to save. You must make the payments every month. Those payments are an investment that prove very rewarding over time for most people.

Some couples have used the seed money accumulated from saving one income (in the strategy outlined above) to buy a duplex home (two attached homes). They live in one part of the duplex and rent out the other. The rent covers a good part of the payments for both homes, so the couple can be housed cheaply while their investment in a home appreciates. They learn that it's quite possible to live comfortably, yet inexpensively, for several years. In this way they accumulate capital. As they grow older, they see that such a strategy has put them years ahead of their peers in terms of financial security. As capital accumulates and values

Buying a home has usually been a very good and very safe investment. But that is not always the case. Sometimes housing prices may rise too fast and can fall just as fast. What has happened to housing prices in your area over the last couple of years?

| | | Interest Rates | | | |
|---|---|---|---|---|---|
| INCOME | MONTHLY PAYMENT | 5% | 6% | 7% | 15% |
| $ 30,000 | $ 700 | $106,263 | $ 98,303 | $ 91,252 | $56,870 |
| 50,000 | 1,167 | 180,291 | 167,081 | 155,376 | 98,606 |
| 80,000 | 1,867 | 287,213 | 266,056 | 247,308 | 155,916 |
| 100,000 | 2,333 | 361,240 | 334,832 | 311,433 | 198,013 |

Source: Federal Housing Finance Board.

figure D.3

**HOW MUCH HOUSE CAN YOU AFFORD?**

Monthly mortgage payments—including interest, principal, real estate taxes, and insurance—generally shouldn't amount to more than 28 percent of monthly income. Here's how much people in various income categories can afford to pay for a home if they use a 30-year mortgage and make a 10 percent down payment. How do you think the changes in mortgage interest rates affect the average price of homes?

rise, they can sell and buy an even larger apartment building or a single-family home. Many fortunes have been made in real estate in just such a manner. Furthermore, a home is a good asset to use when applying for a loan.

Once you understand the benefits of homeownership versus renting, you can decide whether those same principles apply to owning the building if you set up your own business—or owning versus renting equipment, vehicles, and the like. Furthermore, you may start thinking of real estate as a way to earn a living. You could, for example, buy older homes, fix them up, and sell them—a path many millionaires have taken to attain financial security. Figure D.3 will give you some idea of how expensive a house you can afford, given your income. You can find current mortgage interest rates and mortgage calculators at www.interest.com.

**Tax Deduction and Homeownership** Buying a home is likely to be the largest and perhaps the most important investment you'll make. It's nice to know that the federal government is willing to help you with that investment. Here's how: Interest on your home mortgage payments is tax deductible. So are your real estate taxes. Since during the first few years, virtually all the mortgage payments go for interest on the loan, almost all the early payments are tax-deductible—a tremendous benefit for homeowners and investors. If, for example, your payments are $1,000 a month and your income is in the 25 percent tax bracket, then during the early years of your mortgage Uncle Sam will, in effect, give you credit for about $250 of your payment, lowering your real cost to $750. This makes homeownership much more competitive with renting than it may appear on the surface.

Experienced real estate investors will tell you that there are three keys to getting the optimum return on a home: location, location, and location. A home in the best part of town, near schools, shopping, and work, is usually a sound financial investment. Often young people tend to go farther away from town, where homes are often less expensive, but such homes may appreciate in value much more slowly than homes in the city or town center. It's important to learn where the best place to buy is. It's usually better, from a financial viewpoint, to buy a smaller home in a great location than a large home in a not-so-great setting.

## Where to Put Your Savings

What are some other good places to save your money? For a young person, one of the worst places to keep long-term investments is in a bank or savings and loan. It is important to have about six months' savings in the bank for emergencies, but the bank is not the best place to invest. Internet banks pay higher interest than your local bank, but even their rates are relatively low.[13]

One of the best places to invest over time has been the stock market. The stock market does tend to go up and down, but over a longer period of time it has proved to be one of the best investments. That's important because about half of U.S. households own stock and roughly the same percentage own mutual funds. Most financial experts believe that the stock market will grow more slowly in the future than it has over the last 50 years, but that may not be true. The U.S. economy has always managed to rise up after a crisis like the stock market fall of recent years.

The future always looks gloomy during a financial crisis, but that doesn't mean you shouldn't take risks. Remember, the greater the risk, the greater the return (usually). When stocks are low, that is the time to *buy*. Actually, when stocks collapse, that is an opportunity to get into the stock market, not avoid it. The average investor buys when the market is high and sells when it is low. Clearly, that is not a good idea. It takes courage to buy when everyone else is selling. That is called a **contrarian approach** to investing. In the long run, however, that's the way the rich get richer.

**contrarian approach**
Buying stock when everyone else is selling or vice versa.

Chapter 19 gave you a foundation for starting an investment program. That chapter also talked about bonds, but bonds have traditionally lagged behind stocks as a long-term investment.

## Learning to Manage Credit

Known as *plastic* to young buyers, credit cards are no doubt familiar to you. Names like Visa, MasterCard, American Express, Discover, and Diners Club are well known to most people. Finance charges on credit card purchases usually amount to anywhere from 12 to 20 percent annually. This means that if you finance a TV, home appliances, and other purchases with a credit card, you may end up spending much more than if you pay with cash. A good manager of personal finances, like a good businessperson, pays on time and takes advantage of savings made possible by paying early. People who've established a capital fund can tap that fund to make large purchases and pay the fund back (with interest if so desired) rather than pay a bank finance charges. Some 23 percent of college students owe more than $3,000 on their credit cards.[14] That is not a good start. There are much cheaper ways to finance your college fees and books than using a credit card—like borrowing from a bank.[15]

Credit card companies like First USA are quite willing to give you a credit card, and are usually willing to give you a free gift for signing with them. Why do you suppose they are so willing to give you a card?

Credit cards are, however, an important element in a personal financial system, even if they're rarely used. First, you may have to own a credit card to buy certain goods or even rent a car because some businesses require one for identification and assured payment.[16] Second, you can use a credit card to keep track of purchases. A gasoline credit card, for example, gives you records of purchases over time for income tax and financial planning purposes. It's sometimes easier to write one check at the end of the month for several purchases than to carry cash around. Besides, when cash is stolen or lost, it is simply gone; a stolen credit card can be canceled to protect your account.

Finally, a credit card is simply more convenient than cash or checks. If you come upon a special sale and need more money than you usually carry, paying by credit is quick and easy. You can carry less cash and don't have to worry about keeping your checkbook balanced as often.

If you do use a credit card, you should pay the balance in full during the period when no interest is charged. Not having to pay 16 percent interest is as good as earning 16 percent tax free. Also, you may want to choose a card that pays you back in cash, like the Discover card, or others that offer paybacks like credits toward the purchase of a car, free long-distance minutes, or frequent-flier miles. The value of these givebacks can be from 1 to 5 percent.[17] Rather than pay 16 percent, you earn a certain percentage—quite a difference. Some cards have no annual fees; others have lower interest rates.[18] To compare credit cards, check out www.cardratings.com.

The danger of a credit card is the flip side of its convenience. Too often, consumers buy goods and services that they wouldn't normally buy if they had to pay cash or write a check on funds in the bank. Using credit cards, consumers often pile up debts to the point where they're unable to pay. If you aren't the type who can stick to a financial plan or household budget, *it may be better not to have a credit card at all.*

This illustration should help you see the problem. Imagine a customer who has a $10,000 balance on his or her credit card with a 16 percent interest rate, and who pays the minimum 4 percent monthly payment. How long do you think it would take to pay off the debt, and what would the cost for interest be? The answers: 14 years and nearly $5,000—and that's without using the card again to purchase so much as a candy bar.[19] (Prior to 2006, the minimum payment was 2 percent. The lower minimum payment may have been enticing for the short term, but over time that same $10,000 balance would have taken over 30 years to repay and cost over $18,000 interest if only the 2 percent minimum were paid.)

Some people would be better off with a *debit* card. Debit cards are like credit cards, but they won't let you spend more than you have in the bank, a great benefit for those who are not as careful with their spending as they should be.

In sum, credit cards are a helpful tool to the financially careful buyer. They're a financial disaster to people with little financial restraint and tastes beyond their income.[20] College students take note: Of the debtors seeking help at the National Consumer Counseling Service, more than half were between 18 and 32.

**progress assessment**

- What are the six steps you can take to control your finances?
- What steps should a person follow to build capital?
- Why is real estate a good investment?

## PROTECTING YOUR FINANCIAL BASE: BUYING INSURANCE

One of the last things young people think about is the idea that they may get sick or have an accident and die. It is not a pleasant thought. Even more unpleasant, though, is the reality of young people dying every day in accidents and other unexpected ways. You have to know only one of these families to see the emotional and financial havoc such a loss causes.

Today, with so many husbands and wives both working, the loss of a spouse means a sudden drop in income. To provide protection from such risks, a couple or business should buy life insurance.

figure D.4

WHY BUY TERM INSURANCE?

| INSURANCE NEEDS IN EARLY YEARS ARE HIGH. | INSURANCE NEEDS DECLINE AS YOU GROW OLDER. |
|---|---|
| 1. Children are young and need money for education. | 1. Children are grown. |
| 2. Mortgage is high relative to income. | 2. Mortgage is low or completely paid off. |
| 3. Often there are auto payments and other bills to pay. | 3. Debts are paid off. |
| 4. Loss of income would be disastrous. | 4. Insurance needs are few. |
| | 5. Retirement income is needed. |

**term insurance**
Pure insurance protection for a given number of years.

Today, the least expensive and simplest form of life insurance is **term insurance.**[21] It is pure insurance protection for a given number of years that typically costs less the younger you buy it (see Figure D.4). Every few years, however, you might have to renew the policy, and the premium could go higher. It's helpful to check out prices for term insurance through a Web-based service. For example, try Quickeninsurance.com or Insweb.com. Be sure to enter as much information as possible to get the most accurate and best rates.

How much insurance do you need? *Newsweek* magazine posed this question: We just had our first baby; how much life insurance should we have? Answer: Seven times your family income plus $100,000 for college. To be fair, apportion it so that a spouse earning 60 percent of the income carries 60 percent of the insurance.

It is a good idea before buying life insurance to check out the insurance company through a rating service such as A. M. Best (www.ambest.com) or Moody's Investors Service (www.moodys.com). One of the newer forms of term insurance is something called multiyear level-premium insurance. It guarantees that you'll pay the same premium for the life of the policy. Recently, 40 percent of new term policies guaranteed a set rate for 20 years or more. Some companies allow you to switch your term policy for a more expensive whole or universal life policy.

**whole life insurance**
Life insurance that places part of the premium in savings and the other part toward pure insurance.

**Whole life insurance** is another type of life insurance. Some part of the money you pay for whole life insurance goes toward pure insurance and another part goes toward savings, so you are buying both insurance and a savings plan. This may be a good idea for those people who have trouble saving money. A universal life policy lets you choose how much of your payment should go to insurance and how much to investments. The investments traditionally were very conservative but paid a steady interest rate.

**variable life insurance**
Whole life insurance that invests the cash value of the policy in stocks or other high-yielding securities.

**Variable life insurance** is a form of whole life insurance that invests the cash value of the policy in stocks or other high-yielding securities. Death benefits may thus vary, reflecting the performance of the investments. Some people, seeing the stock market go up for so many years, switched out of whole life policies to get the higher potential returns of variable life insurance. When the stock market plunged, they were not so certain of the wisdom of their choice. In the long run, however, stocks should rise again.

**annuity**
A contract to make regular payments to a person for life or for a fixed period.

Life insurance companies recognized the desire that people had for higher returns on their insurance (and for protecting themselves against running out of money before they die) and began selling annuities. An **annuity** is a contract to make regular payments to a person for life or for a fixed period. With an annuity, you are guaranteed to have an income until you die. There are two kinds of annuities: fixed and variable. *Fixed annuities* are investments that pay the policyholder a specified interest rate. They are not as popular as *variable* *annuities*, which provide investment choices identical to mutual funds. Such annuities are gaining in popularity relative to term or whole life insurance. Clearly, people have been choosing more risk to get greater returns when they retire. This means, however, that people must be more careful in selecting an insurance company and what investments are made with their money.

Because life insurance is getting much more complex, before buying any insurance, it may be wise to consult a financial adviser who is not an insurance agent. He or she can help you make the wisest decision about insurance.

## Health Insurance

Individuals need to consider protecting themselves from losses due to health problems.[22] You may have health insurance coverage through your employer. If not, you can buy insurance from a health insurance provider (e.g., Blue Cross/Blue Shield), a health maintenance organization (HMO), or a preferred provider organization (PPO)—see Bonus Chapter C for an explanation of how these differ. For quick online help in picking a health insurance provider, try EHealthInsurance.com or Healthaxis.com (not available in all areas). You may be able to buy health insurance for less by buying it through a professional organization. Be sure to do a careful search to find the best program for you and your family. One of the more popular alternatives to traditional health insurance these days is a health savings account (HSA).[23] Check this plan out if you have to choose a health insurance plan for yourself.

It's dangerous financially not to have any health insurance. Hospital costs are simply too high to risk financial ruin by going uninsured. In fact, it's often a good idea to supplement health insurance policies with **disability insurance** that pays part of the cost of a long-term sickness or an accident. Your chances of becoming disabled at an early age are much higher than your chances of dying from an accident. Therefore, it's important to have the proper amount of disability insurance.[24] Call an insurance agent or check the Internet for possible costs of such insurance. The cost is relatively low to protect yourself from losing your income for an extended period.

**disability insurance**
Insurance that pays part of the cost of a long-term sickness or an accident.

## Homeowner's or Renter's Insurance

As you begin to accumulate possessions, you may want to seriously consider getting insurance to cover their loss. You may be surprised to see how much it would cost to replace all the clothes, furniture, pots and pans, appliances, sporting goods, electronic equipment (e.g., computers, VCRs, and the like), and the other things you own. Apartment insurance or homeowner's insurance covers such losses. But you must be careful to specify that you want *guaranteed replacement cost*. That means that the insurance company will give you whatever it costs to buy all of those things *new*. Such insurance costs a little bit more than a policy without guaranteed replacement, but you will get a lot more if you have a loss.

The other option is to buy insurance that covers the depreciated cost of the items. For example, a sofa you bought five years ago for $600 may only be worth $150 now. The current value is what you would get from insurance, not the $700 or more you may need to buy a brand-new sofa. The same is true for a computer you paid $950 for a few years ago. If it were to be stolen, you would get only a few hundred dollars for it rather than the replacement cost.

Most policies don't cover expensive items like engagement and wedding rings and silver pieces of all kinds. You can buy a *rider* to your insurance policy that will cover such items at a reasonable cost. Ask your agent about such coverage.

**umbrella policy**
A broadly based insurance policy that saves you money because you buy all your insurance from one company.

**Social Security**
The term used to describe the Old-Age, Survivors, and Disability Insurance Program established by the Social Security Act of 1935.

**individual retirement account (IRA)**
A tax-deferred investment plan that enables you (and your spouse, if you are married) to save part of your income for retirement; a traditional IRA allows people who qualify to deduct from their reported income the money they put into an account.

### Other Insurance

You should buy insurance for your car. In fact, most states require that drivers have automobile insurance. Get a large deductible of $500 or so to keep the premiums lower, and cover small damages on your own. Be sure to include insurance against losses from uninsured motorists.

You'll also need liability insurance to protect yourself against being sued by someone accidentally injured by you. Often you can get a discount by buying all your insurance (life, health, homeowner's, automobile, etc.) with one company. This is called an **umbrella policy**. Also, look for other discounts. GEICO, for example, gives discounts for safe driving, good grades, and more.

## PLANNING YOUR RETIREMENT

It may seem a bit early to be planning your retirement; however, not doing so would be a big mistake. Successful financial planning means long-range planning, and retirement is a critical phase of life. What you do now could make a world of difference in your quality of life after age 65, or whenever you retire.

### Social Security

**Social Security** is the term used to describe the Old-Age, Survivors, and Disability Insurance Program established by the Social Security Act of 1935. There's little question that by the time you retire, there will have been significant changes in the Social Security system. There is talk today of making part of the system private.[25] Although the media talk about it all the time, there really is no Social Security trust fund. The money you receive when you retire comes directly from the Social Security taxes being paid by others. The problem is that the number of people retiring and living longer is increasing dramatically, though the number of workers paying into Social Security per retiree is declining. The results are likely to include serious cuts in benefits, a much later average retirement age, reduced cost-of-living adjustments (COLAs), and/or much higher Social Security taxes.

One purpose of doing personal financial planning is to have enough money for retirement, maybe even early retirement. If you plan to relax and travel when you retire, you need to begin saving now. Is it too soon for you to be thinking about retirement? It may not be since you need to do the proper financial planning early in your career.

The moral of the story is: Don't count on Social Security to provide you with ample funds for retirement. Rather, plan now to save funds for your nonworking years. Recognizing Social Security's potential downfall, the government has established incentives for you to save money now for retirement. The following section gives the specifics.

### Individual Retirement Accounts (IRAs)

Traditionally, an **individual retirement account (IRA)** has been a tax-deferred investment plan that enables you (and your spouse, if you are married) to save part of your income for retirement. A traditional IRA allows people who qualify to deduct from their reported income the money they put into an account. **Tax-deferred contributions** are those for which you pay no current taxes, but the earnings gained in the IRA are taxed as income when they are withdrawn from your IRA after retirement.

Let's see why a traditional IRA is a good deal for an investor. The tremendous benefit is the fact that the invested money is not taxed. That means fast, and good, returns for you. For example, say you put $4,000 into an IRA each year. (The maximum IRA contribution was $4,000 in 2006 and will gradually increase to $5,000 in 2008.[26] If you're 50 or older, you can make an additional $500–$1,000 "catch-up" contribution.) Normally, you'd pay taxes on that $4,000 when you receive it as income. But because you put the money into an IRA, you won't have to pay those taxes. If you're in the 25 percent tax bracket, that means you save $1,000 in taxes! Put another way, the $4,000 you save only costs you $3,000—a huge bargain.

**tax-deferred contributions**
Retirement account deposits for which you pay no current taxes, but the earnings gained are taxed as regular income when they are withdrawn at retirement.

The earlier you start saving, the better—because your money has a chance to double and double again. If you save $4,000 a year for 35 years in an IRA and earn 11 percent a year, you'll accumulate savings of more than $1.5 million. If you start when you are just out of school, you'll be a millionaire by the time you're 55. All you have to do is save $4,000 a year and earn 11 percent. If you increase your contribution to the maximum allowable each time it is raised, you can reach your million-dollar goal even earlier. The actual rate of return depends on the type of investments you choose. It is important to remember that future rates of return can't be predicted with certainty and that investments that pay higher rates of return also have higher risk and volatility. For example, the stock market was booming in the mid to late 1990s and then plummeted for several years starting in 1999. The actual rate of return on investments can vary widely over time, but the average for the S&P 500 between 1970 and 2004 was 11.5 percent a year. Some analysts expect it to be lower in the coming years, so you may need to save more to reach the same goals.[27]

The earlier you start, the better. Consider this: If you were to start contributing $4,000 to an IRA earning 11 percent when you're 22 years old and do so for only five years, you'd have over $27,000 by the time you're 27. Even if you *never added another penny* to the IRA, by the time you're 65 you'd have almost $1.5 million. If you waited until you were 30 to start saving, you would need to save $4,000 every year for 35 years to have the same nest egg. And what would you have if you started saving at 22 *and* continued nonstop every year until 65? More than $3.5 million! Can you see why investment advisers often say that an IRA is the best way to invest in your retirement?

A more recent kind of IRA is called a **Roth IRA**.[28] People who invest in a Roth IRA don't get up-front deductions on their taxes as they would with a traditional IRA, but the earnings grow tax-free and are also tax-free when they are withdrawn. *This is usually the best deal for college-age students*. Traditional IRAs offer tax savings when they are deposited and Roth IRAs offer tax savings when they are withdrawn. For those who invested in a regular IRA, it is possible to transfer the money into a Roth IRA (if you make less than $100,000 a year). You will have to pay taxes first, but the long-term benefits often make this exchange worthwhile if you believe your tax rate is likely to be higher when you retire than it is now.

**Roth IRA**
An IRA where you don't get up-front deductions on your taxes as you would with a traditional IRA, but the earnings grow tax-free and are also tax-free when they are withdrawn.

Financial planners highly recommend IRAs, but they differ as to which kind is best. It depends on the circumstances of each individual. Both have advantages and disadvantages, so you should check with a financial adviser to determine which would be best for you. You may decide to have both kinds of accounts. For more details about IRAs, check out the MoneyChimp Web site (www.moneychimp.com), run by a group of self-proclaimed amateur investors.

One key point to remember is that you can't take the money out of either type of IRA until you are 59½ years old without paying a 10 percent penalty and paying taxes on the income. On the one hand, that's a benefit for you, because it can keep you from tapping into your IRA when an emergency comes up or you're tempted to make a large impulse purchase. On the other hand, the money is there if a real need or emergency arises. For example, the government now allows you to take out some funds to invest in an education or a first home. But check the rules; they change over time.

A wide range of investment choices is available when you open an IRA. Your local bank, savings and loan, and credit union all have different types of IRAs. Insurance companies offer such plans as well. You may prefer to be a bit aggressive with this money to earn a higher return. In that case, you can put your IRA funds into stocks, bonds, mutual funds, or precious metals. Some mutual funds have multiple options (gold stocks, government securities, high-tech stocks, and more). You can switch from fund to fund or from investment to investment with your IRA funds. You can even open several different IRAs as long as the total amount invested doesn't exceed the government's limit. You might consider contributing to an IRA through payroll deductions to ensure that the money is invested before you're tempted to spend it. Opening an IRA may be one of the wisest investments you make.

**Simple IRAs** Companies with 100 or fewer employees can provide their workers with a simple IRA. Basically, that means that employees can contribute a larger part (up to $10,000) of their income annually than they can with the regular IRAs ($4,000–$5,000). The company matches the contribution. This new plan enables people to save much more money over time and makes for a good employee benefit for smaller companies. Simple IRAs can help companies with 100 or fewer employees compete for available workers.

**401(k) plan**
A savings plan that allows you to deposit pretax dollars and whose earnings compound tax free until withdrawl, when the money is taxed at ordinary income tax rates.

## 401(k) Plans

A **401(k) plan** is a savings plan that allows you to deposit pretax dollars and whose earnings compound tax-free until withdrawal, when the money is taxed at ordinary income tax rates. 401(k) plans now account for 49 percent of America's private pension savings. More than 220,000 companies now offer 401(k) retirement plans covering some 55 million workers. For 28 percent of these employees, a 401(k) or similar defined-contribution plan is their only pension. One problem is that only about 80 percent of eligible employees make any contributions.[29] That is a huge mistake, as you will see.

These plans have three benefits: (1) The money you put in reduces your present taxable income, (2) tax is deferred on the earnings, and (3) employers often

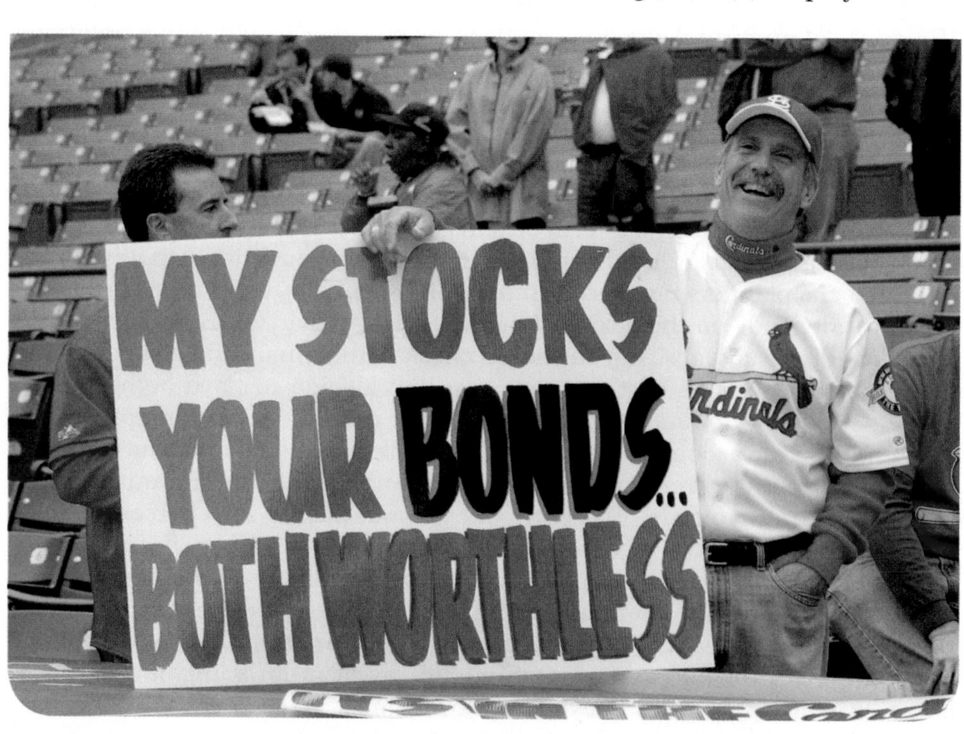


Falling investments is no laughing matter. If the value of your retirement account plunges as it did for many in the late 1990s and early 2000s, your dream of an early retirement may be knocked out of the park. If you have already started to save for your retirement, is your portfolio well diversified?

match part of your deposit. More than 80 percent of 401(k) plans offer a match, sometimes 50 cents on a dollar. No investment will give you a better deal than an instant 50 percent return on your money. You should deposit at least as much as your employer matches, often up to 15 percent of your salary. You can usually select how the money in a 401(k) plan is invested: stocks, bonds, and in some cases real estate. Be careful not to invest all your money in the company where you work. Although the company may be doing quite well, it could collapse and leave you with almost nothing. It is always best to diversify your funds among different companies and among stocks, bonds, and real estate investment trusts.

Like the simple IRA, there is a simple 401(k) plan for those firms that employ 100 or fewer employees. Employees again are allowed to invest an amount (maximum of $10,000 in 2005) that is matched by the employer. This is a rather new program, but it should also prove popular among small businesses in attracting new workers.

## Keogh Plans

Millions of small-business owners don't have the benefit of a corporate retirement system.[30] Such people can contribute to an IRA, but the amount they can invest is limited. The alternative for all those doctors, lawyers, real estate agents, artists, writers, and other self-employed people is to establish their own Keogh plan. It's like an IRA for entrepreneurs. You can also check into simplified employee pension (SEP) plans, which are the best types of IRAs for sole proprietors.

The advantage of Keogh plans is that participants can invest up to $40,000 per year. The original amount was much lower, but the government wanted to encourage self-employed people to build retirement funds.

Like traditional IRAs, Keogh funds aren't taxed until they are withdrawn, nor are the returns the funds earn. Thus, a person in the 25 percent tax bracket who invests $10,000 yearly in a Keogh saves $2,500 in taxes. That means, in essence, that the government is financing 25 percent of his or her retirement fund. As with an IRA, this is an excellent deal.

As with an IRA, there's a 10 percent penalty for early withdrawal. Also like an IRA, funds may be withdrawn in a lump sum or spread out over the years. However, the key decision is the one you make now—to begin early to put funds into an IRA, a Keogh plan, or both so that the "magic" of compounding can turn that money into a sizable retirement fund.

## Financial Planners

If the idea of developing a comprehensive financial plan for yourself or your business seems overwhelming, relax; help is available. The people who assist in developing a comprehensive program that covers investments, taxes, insurance, and other financial matters are called financial planners. Be careful, though—anybody can claim to be a financial planner today. It's often best to find a person who has earned the distinction of being a certified financial planner (CFP). To earn the distinction of CFP, a person must complete a curriculum on 106 financial topics and a 10-hour examination. In the United States today there are about 36,000 planners with the CFP distinction. Unfortunately, many so-called financial planners are simply life insurance salespeople or mutual fund salespeople. Businesspeople often turn to their accountants or finance department for legitimate financial planning help.

In the past few years, there has been an explosion in the number of companies offering financial services. Such companies are sometimes called one-stop financial centers or financial supermarkets because they provide a variety of financial services, ranging from banking service to mutual funds, insurance, tax assistance, stocks, bonds, and real estate. It pays to shop around for financial advice. Ask around among your friends and family. Find someone who understands your situation and is willing to spend some time with you.

Most financial planners begin with life insurance. They feel that most people should have basic term insurance coverage. They also explore your health insurance plans. They look for both medical expense and disability coverage. They may also recommend major medical protection to cover catastrophic illnesses.

Financial planning covers all aspects of investing, all the way to retirement and death. Financial planners can advise you on the proper mix of IRAs, stocks, bonds, real estate, and so on.

## Estate Planning

It is never too early to begin thinking about estate planning, although you may be far from the time when you may retire. You may even help your parents or others to do such planning. If so, you need to know some basics. An important first step is to select a guardian for your minor children. That person should have a genuine concern for your children as well as a parental style and moral beliefs that you endorse. As part of the process you should ensure that you leave sufficient resources to rear your children, not only for living expenses but also for medical expenses, college, and other major expenses. Often life insurance is a good way to assure such a fund. Be sure to discuss all these issues with the guardian and choose a contingent guardian in case the first choice is unable to perform the functions.

**will**
A document that names the guardian for your children, states how you want your assets distributed, and names the executor for your estate.

**executor**
A person who assembles and values your estate, files income and other taxes, and distributes assets.

A second step is to prepare a will. A **will** is a document that names the guardian for your children, states how you want your assets distributed, and names the executor for your estate. An **executor** assembles and values your estate, files income and other taxes, and distributes assets.

A third step is to prepare a durable power of attorney. This document gives an individual you name the power to take over your finances if you become incapacitated. A durable power of attorney for health care delegates power to a person named to make health decisions for you if you are unable to make such decisions yourself.

There are other steps to follow that are beyond the scope of this text. You may need to contact a financial planner/attorney to help you prepare the paper work and do the planning necessary to preserve and protect your investments for your children and spouse (and others). There are whole books on estate planning, so we can only give you a hint as to what is involved. But it all begins with a strong financial base.

As you have read thus far, accumulating enough funds to be financially secure is a complex and difficult matter. Investing that money and protecting it from loss makes the process even more involved. It is never too early to start a saving and investment program. As you have learned, there are many, many millionaires in the United States and around the world. They have taken various paths to their wealth, but the most common ones are entrepreneurship and wise money management.[31] We hope this chapter helps you join their ranks.

**progress assessment**

- What are three advantages of using a credit card?
- What kind of life insurance is recommended for most people?
- What are the advantages of investing through an IRA? A Keogh account? A 401(k) account?
- What are the main steps to take in estate planning?

## summary

1. There are six steps you can take today to get control of your finances.
   - **What are the six steps to managing personal assets?**

   (1) Take an inventory of your financial assets. That means that you need to develop a balance sheet for yourself: Assets − Liabilities = Net worth. (2) Keep track of all your expenses. (3) Prepare a budget. (4) Pay off your debts. (5) Start a savings plan (the best way to save money is to pay yourself first; that is, take your paycheck, take out money for savings, and then plan what to do with the rest). (6) If you have to borrow money, borrow only when it's to buy assets that have the potential to increase in value or generate income, such as a house or business.

1. Describe the six steps of learning to control your assets.

2. You can build a financial base so that you feel financially secure.
   - **How can I accumulate funds?**

   First, find a job. Try to live as frugally as possible. The savings can then be invested to generate even more capital. One such investment is a duplex home where the renter helps pay the mortgage.
   - **Why is real estate such a good investment?**

   First, a home is the one investment that you can live in. Second, once you buy a home, the payments are relatively fixed (though taxes and utilities go up). As your income rises, the house payments get easier and easier to make, but renters often find that rents tend to go up at least as fast as income.
   - **How does the government help you buy real estate?**

   The government allows you to deduct interest payments on the mortgage, which allows you to buy more home for the money than you could otherwise.
   - **Where is the best place to keep savings?**

   It is not wise to keep long-term savings in a bank or savings and loan. It is best, in the long run, to invest in stock. It is a good idea to diversify among mutual funds and other investments. Bonds have not traditionally been as good an investment. Although stocks go up and down, in the long run they earn more than most other investments.
   - **What is a good way to handle credit cards?**

   You should pay the balance in full during the period when no interest is charged. Not having to pay 16 percent interest is as good as earning 16 percent tax free. Often a debit card is better than a credit card because it limits you to the amount you have in the bank.

2. Explain ways to build a financial base, including investing in real estate, saving money, and managing credit.

3. It is as important to preserve capital as it is to accumulate it.
   - **What is the role of insurance in protecting capital?**

   Insurance protects you from loss. For example, if you were to die, you would lose the income that you would have earned. You can buy life insurance that will make up for some or all of that loss. Term insurance is pure insurance protection for a given number of years.
   - **Why is term insurance preferred?**

   You can buy much more term insurance than whole life insurance for the same amount of money.
   - **Do I need other insurance?**

   It is important to have health insurance to protect against large losses. You also need car insurance (get a large deductible—$500 or so) and liability insurance in case you injure someone. You should also have homeowner's or rental insurance. Often an umbrella policy will provide all your insurance protection for a lower cost.

3. Explain how buying the appropriate insurance can protect your financial base.

**4.** Outline a strategy for retiring with enough money to last a lifetime.

4. It may seem too early to begin planning your retirement, but not to do so would be a big mistake. Successful financial planning means long-range planning, and retirement is a critical phase of life.
   - **Can I rely on Social Security to cover my retirement expenses?**
   You cannot rely on Social Security to cover your retirement expenses. Social Security depends on payments from young people to cover the needs of retired people. The problem is that there are fewer and fewer young people paying into the system.
   - **What are the basics of saving for retirement?**
   Supplement Social Security with savings plans of your own. Everyone should have an IRA or some other retirement program. A Roth IRA is especially good for young people because your money grows tax-free and it is tax-free when you withdraw it. For entrepreneurs, a Keogh plan or a simplified employee pension (SEP) plan is wise. If you work for someone else, check out the 401(k) plan. Find a financial adviser who can recommend the best savings plan and help you make other investments.
   - **What are the basics of estate planning?**
   You need to choose a guardian for your children. You need to prepare a will. You need an executor for your estate. You need to sign a durable power of attorney to enable someone else to handle your finances if you are not capable. The same is true of a health durable power of attorney. Estate planning is complex and often calls for the aid of a financial planner/attorney, but the money is well spent to protect your assets.

## key terms

**401(k) plan** 646
**annuity** 642
**contrarian approach** 640
**disability insurance** 643
**executor** 648
**individual retirement account (IRA)** 644
**Roth IRA** 645
**Social Security** 644
**tax-deferred contributions** 645
**term insurance** 642
**umbrella policy** 644
**variable life insurance** 642
**whole life insurance** 642
**will** 648

## critical thinking questions

1. Have you given any thought to becoming an entrepreneur? Do the statistics in this bonus chapter about millionaires give you some courage to pursue such a venture?

2. There has been much talk about a housing bubble, meaning that houses in the United States may be overpriced—but that is only true in certain areas. What is the situation in your area? Would you recommend that a college graduate buy a home or rent?

3. What kinds of questions must a person ask before considering the purchase of a home?

4. What insurance coverage do you now have? According to this bonus chapter, what insurance do you need to buy next?

## developing workplace skills

1. Check your local paper or use an online realtor to gather information regarding the cost to rent a two-bedroom apartment and to buy a two-bedroom condominium in your area. Go to www.dinkytown.net and use the site's "rent-versus-buy calculator" to compare the costs. How do the costs compare? Discuss your findings in small groups.
2. Talk with your parents or others you know who have invested in a family home. What appreciation have they gained on the purchase price? (Or, conversely, how has the price depreciated?) What other benefits has the home brought? Compose a list of the benefits and the drawbacks of owning a home and real estate in general as an investment. Be prepared to give a one-minute presentation on what you learned.
3. Check with your family or others in your area to determine the cost of major medical/hospital treatments. Ask them about medical insurance and the dangers of not having any. What insurance program would they recommend? Discuss your results with the class.
4. The best time to start saving for the future is *now.* To prove this point to yourself, calculate how much you will have at age 65 if you begin saving $100 a month now versus $100 a month 10 years from now. You can go onto the Internet to find such calculations. Just type in "compound interest" in Google and find an appropriate site.
5. Check out the benefits and drawbacks of both traditional and Roth IRAs. Be prepared to make a two-minute presentation on the benefits of each and to discuss your findings in class.

## taking it to the net

### Purpose

To use online resources to make smart personal finance decisions.

### Exercise

Use the calculators at Dinkytown.net to answer the following questions:

1. You need $5,000 for a trip to Europe in two years. How much would you have to deposit monthly in a savings account paying 3 percent in order to meet your goal?
2. Investing $1,000 at 6 percent for five years, what is the difference in purchasing power of your savings if inflation increases by 2 percent annually during that time? By 4 percent?
3. Starting today, how much would you need to save each month in order to become a millionaire before you retire?

4. You need a new car. What car can you afford if you have $1,500 for a down payment, can make monthly payments of $300, and get $1,000 for trading in your old clunker?
5. How much house can you afford if you earn $36,000 a year and have $10,000 savings for a down payment, a $6,000 car loan balance, and no credit card debts?

## casing the web

To access the case *"Becoming Financially Secure,"* visit **www.mhhecom/ub8e**

# chapter notes

## PROLOGUE

1. "College Degree Nearly Doubles Annual Earnings, Census Bureau Reports," *U.S. Census Bureau News*, March 28, 2005, and "How Much Is That Degree Worth?" *Salt Lake City Deseret News*, April 23, 2006.
2. Kemba Dunham, "Job Growth for African-Americans Varies Based on Education Level," *The Wall Street Journal Online*, March 10, 2005; Paul Kaihla, "Climbing the Pay Scale," *Business 2.0*, March 2005, pp. 99–104; Gary Emerling, "Women Zip by Men in Attending College," *Washington Times*, March 31, 2005, p. B2; and Fred A. Mohr "College Grads Making More," *Syracuse (New York) Post-Standard*, February 2, 2006.
3. Tim Aylsworth, "Purpose of College Is Not Boosting Salaries," University Wire, February 8, 2006.
4. Laura G. Knapp et al., "Enrollment in Postsecondary Institutes," *Education Statistics Quarterly* 5, no. 4 (August 2004), and Jennifer Torres, "More Options for Adult Students," *Bergen County (New Jersey) Record*, April 17, 2006.
5. Bill Coplin, "10 Things Employers Want You to Learn in College," *Community College Journal*, April/May 2005, p. 10.
6. Blanca Torres, "Offer Could Hinge on Good Table Manners," *St. Louis Post-Dispatch*, March 27, 2005, p. F3; Roger Kimball, "On Academic Celebrity," *The Wall Street Journal*, April 8, 2005, p. W13; and "ODU Students Brush Up on Etiquette, *Richmond Times Dispatch*, April 21, 2006.
7. Marilyn Much, "Stopping Workplace Incivility," *Investors Business Daily*, February 24, 2005, p. A7, and "Etiquette Sometimes Lacking, Still Needed in Corporate World," *Augusta Chronicle*, April 30, 2006.
8. "Networking, Not the Internet, Remains the Number One Way to Land a New Position Say Experts at Lee Hecht Harrison," PR Newswire, September 15, 2005, and Megan Riley, "Networking Essential to Graduates," University Wire, April 12, 2006.
9. Laura Egodigwe, "How Networking Really Works," *Black Enterprise*, February 1, 2005, and Marshall Lager, "Social Networking: Getting in Touch the CRM Way," *CRM*, March 1, 2006.
10. Jessica Mintz, "Social Networking Sites Catch Employers' Eyes," The Wall Street Journal Online, March 31, 2005; Julie Forster "No Secrets: It's Not Uncommon for Job Recruiters to Peruse Online Networking Sites," *Saint Paul (Minnesota) Pioneer Press*, March 10, 2006; and Nikki Caiafa, "Potential Employers May Discover Information on Personal Web Sites," University Wire, April 17, 2006.
11. Megan Ballinger, "Niche Job Sites," The Wall Street Journal Online, March 17, 2005, and "JobCentral Expands," Business Wire, January 17, 2006.
12. Sarah E. Needleman, "Jobs Blog Where to Find Diversity Minded Employers," The Wall Street Journal Online, April 18, 2005, and "This Year's Nominee List is in for Business-Related Web Sites," *Colorado Springs Gazette*, April 17, 2006.
13. Deb Koen, "The Job-Seeker's Experience Dilemma," The Wall Street Journal Online, March 24, 2005.
14. Paula Szuchman, "The Job You Want with an A-List Internship," The Wall Street Journal Online, February 25, 2005, and Courtney O. Walker, "Internships Can Help Prepare Students," University Wire, March 29, 2006.
15. Marshall Loeb, "Pattern Your Resume on Leaders in Your Field," The Wall Street Journal Online, April 12, 2005, and Maryann Haggerty, "Make It Short and Sweet for the Right Impression," *Washington Post*, January 1, 2006.
16. Marshall Loeb, "Polish Your Speech to Excel in Interviews," The Wall Street Journal Online, April 18, 2005, and Rich Heintz, "Ten Things You Don't Want to Hear in a Job Interview," *Job Journal*, January 8, 2006.
17. Arlene S. Hirsch, "How to Answer Questions About Your Weaknesses," The Wall Street Journal Online, March 3, 2005; Perri Capell, "Don't Be Blindsided by Recruiters' Questions," The Wall Street Journal Online, March 23, 2005; Sarah E. Needleman, "Recruiters Reveal Their Top Interview Questions," The Wall Street Journal Online, February 25, 2005; and "What Questions Should I Ask in a Job Interview?" *Buffalo News*, May 1, 2006.

## CHAPTER 1

1. "Billionaire Bacchanalia," *Forbes,* March 27, 2006, p. 111.
2. Leigh Buchanan, "The Inner City 100," *Inc. Magazine,* June 2006, pp. 109–120.
3. Aaron Bernstein, "A Social Strategist for Wal-Mart," *BusinessWeek,* February 6, 2006, p. 11.
4. Pete Engardio, "The Future of Outsourcing," *BusinessWeek,* January 30, 2006, pp. 50–58.
5. Erin White, "Smaller Companies Join the Outsourcing Trend," *The Wall Street Journal,* May 8, 2006, p. B3.
6. Pete Engardio and Bruce Einhorn, "Outsourcing Innovation," *BusinessWeek,* March 21, 2005, pp. 84–94.
7. Joann Muller and Robyn Meredith, "Last Laugh," *Forbes,* April 18, 2005, pp. 98–104.
8. Anne Fisher, "Bringing the Jobs Home," *Fortune,* March 20, 2006, p. 23.
9. William Foster and Jeffrey Bradach, "Should Nonprofits Seek Profits?," *Harvard Business Review,* February 2005, pp. 92–100.
10. Steve Case, "Purpose and Profit Go Together," *The Wall Street Journal,* May 10, 2005, p. B2.
11. Amanda Bower, "Meet the Hard-Nosed Do-Gooders," *Time Inside Business,* January 2006, p. A24.
12. Foster and Bradach, "Should Nonprofits Seek Profits?"
13. Krissah Williams and Cecilia Kang, "The Latino Small-Business Boom," *Washington Post,* March 22, 2006, pp. A1 and A10.
14. "The Nation's Largest Black-Owned Business," *Black Enterprise,* June 2006, pp. 93–194.
15. Alison Overholt, "25 Top Women Business Builders," *Fast Company,* May 2005, pp. 67–79.
16. "CEO Justice," *The Wall Street Journal,* March 16, 2005, p. A24.

17. Brad Stone, "High Techs New Day," *Newsweek,* April II, 2005, pp. 60–64.
18. Paul Sloan, "Retail Without the Risk," *Business 2.0,* March 2006, p. II8.
19. Michael V. Copeland, "Everyone's Investing in B to B," *Business 2.0,* April 2006, p. 30.
20. Fred Reichheld, "The Microeconomics of Customer Relationships," *MIT Sloan Management Review,* Winter 2006, pp. 73–78.
21. Tom Lester, "The Cost of Not Caring for Your Customers," *Financial Times,* January 30, 2006, p. 10.
22. Robin Sidel, "Security Breach Hits Credit Cards," *The Wall Street Journal,* April 14, 2005, pp. DI and D2.
23. Eric Schoeniger, "How to Plug the $13 Billion Leak," an ad in *BusinessWeek,* March 20, 2006, pp. 2–5.
24. Mike Richman, "The Quest for Zero Defects," *Quality Digest,* April 2005, pp. 40–43.
25. James P. Womack and Daniel T. Jones, "Lean Consumption," *Harvard Business Review,* March 2005, pp. 58–68.
26. Chad Terhune, "Pepsi, Vowing Diversity Isn't Just Image Polish, Seeks Inclusive Culture," *The Wall Street Journal,* April 19, 2005, p. BI.
27. David Wessel, "The Basics of Social Security," *The Wall Street Journal,* February I, 2005, p. BI.
28. Sean Tuffnell, "Preparing for a Tough Fight," *Washington Times*, March 4, 2005, p. AI7.
29. "Social Security Deficits in the Outyears," *The Wall Street Journal,* February 25, 2005, p. AI8.
30. Fred Frailey, "Fix It Now, or Fix It Later," *Kiplinger's Personal Finance,* March 2005, p. 16.
31. "The Private-Account Option," *The Wall Street Journal,* February I, 2005, p. B4.
32. "Will Globalization Survive?," *Washington Times*, April 10, 2005, p. B2.
33. "A Lemon for Lenovo?," *BusinessWeek*, February 21, 2005, p. 13.
34. Mary Anastasia O'Grady, "Wish They All Could Be Like Estonia," *The Wall Street Journal*, January 4, 2006, p. AI0.

## CHAPTER 2

1. Donald Lambro, "Pessimism Fact Check," *Washington Times,* January 30, 2006, p. AI7.
2. Moon Ihlwan, "Hands Across the DMZ," *BusinessWeek,* March 20, 2006, p. 48.
3. Mark Henricks, "The New China?," *Entrepreneur,* February 2006, pp. 17–18.
4. Anne Underwood, "Designing the Future," *Newsweek,* May 16, 2005, pp. 40–45.
5. Kristin Ohlson, "Burst of Energy," *Entrepreneur,* February 2006, pp. 46–47.
6. "Net Is Cast for Fish Farms," *Washington Times,* April 4, 2005, p. A8.
7. Michael Novak, "Troubled Continent," *National Review,* February 13, 2006, pp. 36–38.
8. Thomas Homer-Dixon, "Of Human Fallout," *Worth,* January 2004, p. 38.
9. "Comrade Capitalists," *The Wall Street Journal,* January 31, 2006, p. AI4.
10. "Quirky Causes," *Forbes,* March 28, 2005, p. 172.
11. Amanda Ripley and Amanda Bower, "From Riches to Rags," *Time,* December–January 2006, pp. 72–88.
12. Ibid.
13. Marilyn Chase, "Gates to Donate Extra $250 Million for Health Grants," *The Wall Street Journal,* May 17, 2005, p. D7.
14. Sean O'Neill, "My Teen Dream: Owning an Ice Cream Shop," *Kiplinger's Personal Finance,* April 2005, p. 120.
15. Rich Karlgaard, "World's Worst Disease," *Forbes,* January 9, 2006, p. 31.
16. Jon Surmacz, "In a League of Its Own," www.cio.com, April 15, 2005, pp. 66–71.
17. Bruce Bartlett, "Flogging the Income Icon," *Washington Times,* May 18, 2005, p. AI9.
18. Alan Reynolds, "For the Record," *The Wall Street Journal,* May 18, 2005, p. AI4.
19. "Sox and Stocks," *The Wall Street Journal,* April 19, 2005, p. A20.
20. Richard Rahn, "Weapons of Mass Disinformation," *Washington Times,* March 21, 2005, p. AI5.
21. Brian M. Carney, "Europe Hasn't Outgrown 'That '70s Show,'" *The Wall Street Journal,* May 9, 2005, p. A23.
22. Mary Anastasia O'Grady, "Overcoming Castro's 'Culture of Fear,'" *The Wall Street Journal,* May 6, 2005, p. AI5.
23. Mary Anastasia O'Grady, "The New Tehran-Caracas Axis," *The Wall Street Journal,* January 13, 2006, p. AI3.
24. Mark Henricks, "The New China?," *Entrepreneur,* February 2006, pp. 17–18.
25. Dexter Roberts, "How Rising Wages Are Changing the Game in China," *BusinessWeek,* March 27, 2006, pp. 32–35.
26. Laura D'Andrea Tyson, "How Europe Is Revving Its Engine," *BusinessWeek,* February 21, 2005, p. 24.
27. Eric J. Savitz, "Look Who's Storming the Net," *Smart Money,* June 2005, pp. 40–48.
28. Willard R. Sparks, "World Growth in 2005," *Business Perspectives,* Forecast 2005, pp. 32–35.
29. James C. Cooper and Kathleen Madigan, "The GDP Report: No Reason to Sweat," *BusinessWeek,* May 16, 2005, p. 21.
30. Julie L. Hotchkiss, "Employment Growth and Labor Force Participation: How Many Jobs Are Enough?," *Economic Review,* First Quarter 2005, pp. I–3, and James C. Cooper, "One Big Reason to Expect a Decent Year for Jobs," *BusinessWeek,* January 23, 2006, p. 27.
31. Nell Henderson, "Inflation Hit Five-Year High of 3.4% Last Year," *Washington Post,* January 19, 2006, p. DI.
32. James C. Cooper, Kathleeen Madigan, Michael Arndt, and Rich Miller, "Is That a Whiff of Inflation?," *BusinessWeek,* March 7, 2005, pp. 34–37.
33. David Pilling, "Japan Still in Grip of Deflation as Prices Fall," *Financial Times,* April 27, 2005, p. 7.
34. E. S. Browning, "Stagflation Fear Puts a Chill into Blue Chips," *The Wall Street Journal,* April 29, 2005, pp. CI and C4.
35. Alfred Tella, "Foot-Dragging on Price-Index Repair," *Washington Times,* February 3, 2005, p. AI9.
36. Richard S. Dunham, "The Struggle to Sell the Economy's Sizzle," *BusinessWeek,* January 23, 2006, p. 43.
37. Steven Gray, "Coffee on the Double," *The Wall Street Journal,* April 12, 2005, p. BI.
38. Victor Zarnowitz and Dara Lee, "Can U.S. Business Cycles Still Be Dated by Monthly Coincident Indicators Alone?," *Business Cycle Indicator,* March 2005, pp. 3–4.
39. Peter Navarro, "Principles of the Master Cyclist," *MIT Sloan Management Review,* Winter 2004, pp. 20–24.
40. Lakshman Achuthan, "How Anyone Can Forecast Booms and Busts," *Bottom Line Personal,* June I, 2005, pp. 3–4.
41. "Ledger," *Washington Post,* February 13, 2005, p. B5.
42. "States of Plenty," *The Wall Street Journal,* January II, 2006, p. A4.
43. Dunham, "The Struggle to Sell the Economy's Sizzle."

## CHAPTER 3


1. Erin White, "Executives with Global Experience Are Among the Most In-Demand," *The Wall Street Journal*, January 25, 2005, p. B6.
2. Christopher Swann, "Concerns Grow over New Record Deficit in U.S. Trade," *Financial Times*, April 13, 2005, p. 7; Victoria Ruan, "China Expects 15% Jump in Trade," *The Wall Street Journal*, January 13, 2006; and Murray Hiebert, "China's Trade Surplus Tripled, Topping $100 Billion Last Year," *The Wall Street Journal*, January 12, 2006.
3. Paul McDougall, "Tech Powerhouse," *Information Week*, April 19, 2005, pp. 20–22.
4. Tom Lowry, "Wow Yao!," *BusinessWeek*, October 25, 2004, pp. 87–90.
5. Tim Burt, "Close-Up on Hollywood's Leading Lady," *Financial Times*, April 24, 2005, p. W3.
6. Thuy-Doan Le, "U.S. Wine Exports Jump 28 Percent," *Sacramento Bee*, February 19, 2005.
7. Peter Coy, Adrienne Carter, and Michael Arndt, "The Export Engine Needs a Turbocharge," *BusinessWeek*, February 14, 2005, p. 32, and Martin Ladner, "Trade Offs: Understand Legal Basics of Importing and Exporting," *Houston Business Journal,* January 13, 2006.
8. Erin White, "Future CEOs May Need to Have Broad Liberal-Arts Foundation," *The Wall Street Journal*, April 12, 2005, p. B4.
9. Guy DeJonquieres, "Going Global Is Always a Risky Business," *Financial Times*, March 8, 2005, p. 15, and Christine Hall, "Understanding Culture Is Key to Global Mindset," *Houston Business Journal*, January 13, 2006.
10. Frank Vargo, "U.S. Trade Policy: Free Trade Agreements Level the Playing Field for Everyone," *Rubber & Plastics News*, May 2, 2005, and "Free Trade Winds in the Mideast," *The Wall Street Journal*, January 11, 2006.
11. Greg Hitt, "Congress Set to Debate Free Trade," *The Wall Street Journal*, April 13, 2005, p. A17.
12. Chris Smith, "Globalization Provides Mixed Blessings," University Wire, April 19, 2005, and Robert Batterson, "Resolutions for 2006 Start with Embracing Free Trade," *St. Louis Post-Dispatch*, January 1, 2006.
13. Paul Magnusson, "Globalization Is Great—Sort Of," *BusinessWeek*, April 25, 2005, p. 25.
14. Elizabeth Wasserman, "Happy Birthday WTO," *Inc.*, January 2005, pp. 21–23.
15. Alan Hughes, "Time to Venture Abroad: Exporting Is a Multibillion-Dollar Industry That Can be Extremely Lucrative—If You're Properly Prepared," *Black Enterprise*, June 1, 2004, and Martin Ladner, "Trade Offs: Understand Legal Basics of Importing and Exporting," *Houston Business Journal*, January 13, 2006.
16. Brad Stone, "Grande Plans: Yes It Seems Like There's a Starbucks on Every Corner, but Howard Schultz Says His Company Is Just Warming Up," *Newsweek*, November 4, 2004.
17. Jonathan Birchall, "The Business Blend That Brought Starbucks to the World," *Financial Times*, March 29, 2005, p. 8, and Steven Gray and Kate Kelly, "Starbucks Plans to Debut in the Movie Business," *The Wall Street Journal*, January 12, 2006.
18. "Anheuser-Busch Raises Tsingtao Stake," *Financial Times*, April 12, 2005, p. 25.
19. "Anheuser-Busch Triples Tsingtao Stake," *St. Louis Post-Dispatch*, April 12, 2005, p. B1.
20. "Herbalife Selects GlobalSight Software to Automate Globalization Efforts for Both Print and Web," *PR Newswire,* August 23, 2005.
21. www.doc.gov.
22. Greg Hitt, "Trade Gap Widens, Fuels Calls for Tougher Stance on China," *The Wall Street Journal*, April 13, 2005, p. A2.
23. John Zarocostas, "EU Prepared to Impose Sanctions on the U.S.," *WWD*, April 1, 2005, and "Mandelson Warns China It Must Crack Down on Illegal Dumping," AP Worldstream, January 10, 2006.
24. Rick Barrett, "Tariffs on Foreign Steel Spark Debate," *Milwaukee Journal Sentinel*, April 19, 2005, and "Prime Minister Must Take Action in the Softwood Lumber Dispute," PR Newswire, February 9, 2005.
25. "Tokyo Disney Parks Operator Sees Sales, Profit Fall," *Kyodo World News Service*, May 9, 2005.
26. Nicholas Zamiska and Vanessa O'Connell, "Altria Is in Talks to Make Marlboros in China," *The Wall Street Journal*, April 21, 2005, pp. B1–B2.
27. www.export.gov/comm_svc/eac.html
28. Hughes, "Time to Venture Abroad."
29. www.rockymountainchocolatefactory.com.
30. Gil Bassak, "Homegrown Outsourcing," *Product Design & Development*, March 1, 2005, and S. Srinivasan, "U.S. Senator Supports Outsourcing to India," AP Online, January 13, 2006.
31. Stephanie Kang, "Just Do It: Nike Gets Revelatory," *The Wall Street Journal*, April 13, 2005, p. A12.
32. Lee Hawkins Jr. and Joann S. Lublin, "Emergency Repairman: GM's Wagoner Aims to Make Auto Company More Global," *The Wall Street Journal*, April 6, 2005, p. B1; "Shanghai Automotive Industry Corporation Guide to China's Auto Market," *Automotive News,* March 9, 2005; and Martin Strathnairn, "SAIC Car Sales to Get Boost From GM," *Birmingham Post,* January 9, 2006.
33. Kenneth Fox, "Seeing the Invisible," *Business & Economics Review*, April–June 2005, p. 17.
34. Haig Simonian, "A Case of Two Heads Being Better Than One," *Financial Times*, March 4, 2005, p. 9.
35. "Chevron Establishes Multimillion-Dollar Strategic Research Alliance in Australia; Global Scope to Benefit Chevron's Worldwide Operations," PR Newswire, April 7, 2005.
36. Tom Wright, "Nestlé Focuses on Health to Fatten Its Profit-Bucking Global Trend," *International Herald Tribune*, April 9, 2005.
37. Mark Srite, "Levels of Culture and Individual Behavior: An Integrative Perspective," *Journal of Global Information Management*, April 1, 2005.
38. Keith Naughton, "Red, White, & Bold," *Newsweek*, April 25, 2005, pp. 34–35.
39. Jim Mateja, "Reputation Only Style Top-Selling Camry Needs," *Chicago Tribune*, February 25, 2005.
40. Eric Bellman and Kris Hudson, "Wal-Mart Trains Sights on India's Retail Market," *The Wall Street Journal,* January 18, 2006, p. A9.
41. Timothy Aeppel, "Weak Dollar, Strong Sales," *The Wall Street Journal*, January 20, 2005, pp. B1–B2, and Rick Carew, "China Takes Further Step Toward Freeing Up Yuan," *The Wall Street Journal*, January 4, 2006.
42. Christopher Swan, "U.S. Exporters Fail to Reap the Full Benefits of a Weaker Greenback," *Financial Times*, March 22, 2005, p. 3.
43. Ed Zwirn, "Dollar Doldrums," *CFO*, May 2005, pp. 35–38.

44. www.hbfuller.com.
45. Angie C. Marek and Nisha Ramachandran, "Wanna Swap?" *U.S. News & World Report*, September 6, 2004; Rob Kaiser, "Bartering Makes a Comeback Through Evolving Business Networks," *Chicago Tribune*, October 4, 2004; and Steve Gutterman, "Russia, Ukraine Gas Companies Reach Deal," AP Online, January 4, 2006.
46. "The Jails Where Time Is Money," *Financial Times*, February 17, 2005, p. 8.
47. Glenn R. Simpson, "Multinational Companies Unite to Fight Bribery," *The Wall Street Journal*, January 27, 2005, p. A2.
48. Peter Fritsch and Timothy Mapes, "In Indonesia, a Tangle of Bribes Creates Trouble for Monsanto," *The Wall Street Journal*, April 5, 2005, pp. A1–A6.
49. "Mercantilism," *Columbia Encyclopedia,* February 24, 2005.
50. Greg Hitt, "Trade and Aid Clash Over Shrimp Tariffs," *The Wall Street Journal*, April 25, 2005, p. A4.
51. Stephan Vitvitsky, "Failure of the Cuban Embargo," University Wire, November 2, 2004, and Rob Reuteman, "The Cuba Question: To Trade or Not to Trade," *Denver Rocky Mountain News*, January 14, 2006.
52. Robert Block, "U.S Cracks Down on Technology Exports to Iran," *The Wall Street Journal*, February 25, 2005, p. A1.
53. John Zarocostas, "WTO to Focus on Barriers," *Footwear News*, January 10, 2005, and Evan Ramstad, "Tech Companies Push for Tariff Overhauls as Products Converge," *The Wall Street Journal*, December 15, 2005.
54. Chester Dawson, "A China Price for Toyota," *BusinessWeek*, February, 21, 2005, pp. 50–51, and Clay Chandler, "Full Speed Ahead," *Fortune,* February 7, 2005, pp. 79–84.
55. Bill Emmott, "Japan, Inc. RIP," *The Wall Street Journal*, March 10, 2005, p. A16.
56. Elizabeth Wasserman, "Happy Birthday WTO," *Inc.*, January 2005, pp. 21–23, and Julian Morris, "The Future of World Trade," *The Wall Street Journal*, December 20, 2005.
57. Claude Barfield, "The Cause of World Trade Demands a Powerful Patron," *Financial Times*, February 15, 2005, p. 15, and "U.S. Official Optimistic About Talks on Vietnam's WTO Accession," AP Worldstream, January 13, 2006.
58. Marton Dunai, "The New EU: Work in Progress," *The Wall Street Journal*, April 5, 2005, p. A15.
59. Graham Bowley, "Enlarged EU Portrayed as a 'Job Machine,'" *International Herald Tribune*, May 21, 2005, and Paul Ames, "EU Mulls Plan to Create Rival to MIT in Bid to Counter Trans-Atlantic Brain Drain," AP Worldstream, January 13, 2006.
60. www.doc.gov/nafta.
61. Randy L. Gahn, "Trade Agreement Would Harm Workers," *Fresno Bee*, May 12, 2005.
62. Diego Cervallas, "Immigration—U.S. New Curbs Draw Angry Response from Mexico," *IPS*, May 13, 2005.
63. Stuart E. Eizenstat and David Marchick, "Trade Wins," *The Wall Street Journal*, March 8, 2005, p. A20; Juan Carlos Llorca, "CAFTA to Miss Jan. 1 Deadline, but Countries Still Scrambling to Join Soon," AP Worldstream, December 31, 2005; and Jenalia Moreno, "High Hopes Greet CAFTA's Entrance," *Houston Chronicle*, January 1, 2006.
64. Juan Carlos Llorca, "Latin Free-Trade Accord Hits Delay," *Bergen County (New Jersey) Record,* January 1, 2006.
65. Susan Segal and Eric Farnsworth, "Hemispheric Threads; Mutual Sustenance Is the Key," *Washington Times,* January 16, 2006.
66. *The 2005 CIA World Fact Book* (www.cia.gov/cia/publications/factbook), and "Exporting An Uber-Brand," *BusinessWeek*, April 4, 2005, p. 74.
67. Frances Williams, "China Overtakes Japan as Third Largest Exporter," *Financial Times*, April 15, 2005, p. 4.
68. Elliot Blair Smith, "Companies Belly Up to Juicy Buffet in China," *USA Today*, January 26, 2005, p. B1.
69. Andrei Posteinicu, Richard McGregor, and Norma Cohen, "NYSE and Nasdaq Apply to Open Outposts in China," *Financial Times*, March 10, 2005, p. 1.
70. Chester Dawson, "A 'China Price' for Toyota," *BusinessWeek*, February 21, 2005, pp. 50–51.
71. Joe Studwell, "China's Boom Has Led to Only Partial Change," *Financial Times*, April 4, 2005, p. 15.
72. Frederik Balfour, "Fake's," *BusinessWeek*, February 7, 2005, pp. 54–64.
73. Peter Mandelson, "India's New Leadership Role: An Economic Giant," *International Herald Tribune*, January 15, 2005, and Foster Klug, "Lawmaker Says Tour of China and India a 'Reality Check on Asia's Growing Economies,'" AP Worldstream, January 6, 2006.
74. Mary Dejevsky, "Forget the China Story, Russia Offers a Greater Prize for Western Investors," *Independent*, April 22, 2005.
75. Richard Ernsberger, "The Big Squeeze: A 'Second Wave' of Offshoring Could Threaten Middle-Income, White-Collar and Skilled Blue-Collar Jobs," *Newsweek International*, May 30, 2005.
76. Ibid.
77. Pete Engardio, "The Future of Outsourcing," *BusinessWeek,* January 30, 2006, pp. 50–58.
78. Anne Fisher, "Offshoring Could Boost Your Career," *Fortune*, January 24, 2005, p. 36.


## CHAPTER 4


1. Lewis Krauskopf, "2004 Saw No Letup in Corporate Scandals, Amid Expanded Probes of Wrongdoing," *Hackensack (New Jersey) Record,* January 2, 2005; "They Fought the Law," *BusinessWeek*, January 10, 2005; Bethany McLean, "The Fall of Fannie Mae," *Fortune*, January 24, 2005; Betsy Streisand, "Giving the Boot," *U.S. News & World Report*, March 28, 2005; James T. Madore, "Former ImClone CEO to Pay Fine, Forgo Civil Trial for Insider Trading," *South Florida Sun-Sentinel,* January 20, 2005; "The Cleanup Crew," *BusinessWeek*, January 10, 2005; Charles Pope, "Ex-Boeing Executive Jailed for 4 Months, Meanwhile Contract Woes Mount with New GAO Ruling," *Seattle Post-Intelligencer*, February 19, 2005; Gloria Borger, "Who's Minding Congress?" *U.S. News & World Report*, March 28, 2005, p. 46.
2. Jennifer Alsever, "The Ethics Monitor," *Fast Company,* May 2005, p. 33.
3. Andrea Jones, "File-Sharing Legalities Downloaded at Forum" *Atlanta Journal-Constitution,* April 6, 2005.
4. Scott Eyman, "Ethical Behavior, Convictions Sadly Lacking, Author Says," *Palm Beach Post,* January 21, 2005.
5. Alicia Shepherd, "Psst . . . What's the Answer?" *People Weekly*, January 24, 2005; Camille Breland, "U. Mississippi Business School Warns Prospective Cheaters," University Wire, January 21, 2005; and Jennifer Smith Richards, "OSU Sniffing Out Cheaters: Penalties Being Stiffened, More Cases Being Pursued in University Crackdown," *Columbus Dispatch*, January 17, 2006.
6. David F. Martin, "Plagiarism and Technology: A Tool for Coping with Plagiarism," *Journal of Business Education*, January 1, 2005.

7. Kenneth Blanchard and Norman Vincent Peale, *The Power of Ethical Management* (New York: William Morrow, 1996), and Shoshana Zuboff, "A Starter Kit for Business Ethics," *Fast Company*, January 1, 2005.
8. Rebecca M. Chory-Assad, "Motivating Factors: Perceptions of Justice and Their Relationship with Managerial and Organizational Trust," *Communication Studies*, March 1, 2005; Dan Roberts and Alison Maitland, "New Puritanism Blurs Professional Ethics," *Financial Times*, March 8, 2005, p. 23; Brenda Helps, "Managers' Actions Create Environments of Integrity, Trust," *Hotel & Motel Management*, January 10, 2005; and Kevin Kemper, "Scandals Taint Execs' Perceptions, Survey Finds," *Columbus Business First*, January 13, 2006.
9. "Pressure to Meet Unrealistic Business Objectives and Deadlines Is Leading Factor for Unethical Corporate Behavior, New Survey Suggests," Business Wire, January 17, 2006.
10. Booz Allen Hamilton, "New Study Finds Link between Financial Success and Focus on Corporate Values," Business Wire, February 3, 2005.
11. Kathryn Tyler, "Do the Right Thing: Ethics Training Programs Help Employees Deal with Ethical Dilemmas," *HRMagazine*, February 1, 2005.
12. Alison Maitland, "How Ethics Codes Can Be Made to Work," *Financial Times,* March 7, 2005, p. 9.
13. Barbara Jorgensen, "Oaths of Office: Complex Regulations Prompt More Companies to Hire Compliance Chiefs," *Electronic Business*, February 1, 2005; and "New Year, New Name: EOA Becomes the Ethics and Compliance Officer Association," Business Wire, January 13, 2006.
14. John S. McClenahen, "Defining Social Responsibility," *Industry Week*, March 1, 2005.
15. Thomas Donaldson, "Defining the Value of Doing Good Business," *FT Mastering Corporate Governance*, June 3, 2005, pp. 2–3.
16. William Damon, "Saints and Sinners in Business," *Security Management,* January 1, 2005.
17. Andy Serwer, "Still a Great Job: Making Sure Bill Gates Stays Rich," *Fortune,* May 3, 2005, p. 73, and Wendy Zellner, "The Gates Effect," *Fast Company*, January 1, 2006.
18. Adam Geller, "Corporate Giving to Tsunami Victims Rivaled Only by Post-9/11 Assistance," AP Worldstream, January 10, 2005; "Good Works: Tsunami," *Atlanta Journal Constitution*, January 15, 2005; Edward Iwata, "Tsunami Donors Creative in Giving," *USA Today*, January 18, 2005; Kimberly Blanton, "Charities Are Swamped by Offers of Aid from Corporations," *Boston Globe*, January 19, 2005; and Clay Chandler, "A Wave of Corporate Charity," *Fortune,* January 24, 2005.
19. "Trading Places," *M2 Presswire*, January 31, 2005.
20. Jessi Hempel, "A Corporate Peace Corps Catches On," *BusinessWeek,* January 31, 2005.
21. "Fast Channel Partners with Ad Council and USA Freedom Corps to Distribute Tsunami Relief Campaign," PR Newswire, January 10 2005, and "Mobilizing Americans Toward Community Service," University Wire, February 28, 2005.
22. Anita Lienhart, "She Drove, He Drove Mercedes C320," Gannett News Service, January 9, 2001; Menke-Gluckert, "Baby Benz Faces the Moose," *Europe,* February 2, 1998, pp. 40–44; and Earle Eldridge, "Luxury Sales Up: 'Move Up' Market Strong," *Edmonton Sun,* June 21, 2002, p. DR16.
23. Rober Kuttner, "Dishonest Capitalism Won't Go Unpunished," *BusinessWeek*, May 23, 2005, p. 32.
24. Rice Turner, "Aiming to Do Well by Doing Good," *Investors Business Daily,* June 1, 2005, p. A8.
25. Floyd Norris, "Preserving the Right to Insider Tips," *International Herald Tribune*, February 4, 2005; Andrew Caffrey, "Wife of Former Lexington, Massachusetts, Drug Firm CEO Charged with Insider Trading," *Boston Globe,* January 14, 2005; and Mark Jewell, "Ex-Biogen Exec. Settles Insider Trade Case," AP Online, January 12, 2006.
26. Leslie Rose McDonald, "To Increase Profitability, Treat Employees Well," *Syracuse (New York) Post-Standard,* March 23, 2005, and "Dedicated Employees Get Nurturing They Need," *Chain Drug Review*, January 2, 2006.
27. "Hiring Is Stymied by the Search for the Perfect Candidate," Business Wire, January 6, 2005; Lynda V. Mapes, "Good Business: Two Local Companies Are Proving It Pays to Do Well by Workers," *Seattle Times*, January 31, 2005; and Andrea K. Walker, "Workers Cheer Bill Requiring Wal-Mart to Pay More for Employee Health Care," *Baltimore Sun*, January 14, 2006.
28. B. Kreisler, "Onsite Theft: Bilked, Betrayed and Bewildered," *Units*, June 1, 2005, and Rosemary Barnes, "Employee Theft Can Ruin Firm," *San Antonio Express-News*, January 14, 2006.
29. Jared Gilbert, "Alcoa Does Its Bit for the World—and Its Own Image—with Earthwatch Projects," *Workforce Management*, March 1, 2005, and Katherine Mangu-Ward, "The Age of Corporate Environmentalism: Surprise—Big Business Has Learned That It's Pretty Easy Being Green," *Reason*, February 1, 2006.
30. Elizabeth Laurienzo, "Calvert Social Index Quarterly Adjustments," PR Newswire, March 17, 2005, and "Corporate Social Concerns: Are They Good Citizenship, or a Rip-Off for Investors?" *The Wall Street Journal*, December 6, 2005.
31. Peter Debreceny, "CSR—Does It Have a Place in Corporate PR?" PR Newswire, February 2, 2005; "In 2005, How to Align Your Money with Your Values," *Christian Science Monitor*, January 24, 2005; "Barclays Global Investors Announces the First U.S. Exchange-Traded Fund for Socially Responsible Investors," Business Wire, January 31, 2005; "New ETFs Focus on Social Responsibility," AP Online, February 3, 2005; Joe Feuerherd, "Socially Responsible Investing Movement Grows Up," *National Catholic Reporter,* March 11, 2005; and "Go Green by Trading, Says Goldman," *Economic Times*, December 31, 2005.
32. Jim Carlton, "J. P. Morgan Adopts 'Green' Lending Policies," *The Wall Street Journal*, April 25, 2005, pp. B1 and B6.
33. Jay Greene and Mike France, "Culture Wars Hit Corporate America," *BusinessWeek*, May 23, 2005, pp. 90–93.
34. Aaron Bernstein, "A Major Swipe at Sweatshops," *BusinessWeek*, May 23, 2005, pp. 98–100; "Stamping Out Sweatshops," *BusinessWeek*, May 23, 2005, p. 136; and Mari Herreras, "Recent Court Cases Might Help Rewrite Company Policies: Employment Law Update," *Wenatchee Business Journal*, January 1, 2006.
35. Karl Schoenberger, "U.S. Companies Must Follow U.S. Anti-Corruption Law Abroad," *San Jose Mercury News*, March 13, 2005.
36. Eric Green, "Inter-American Group Wants Anti-corruption Treaty Strengthened," *Washington File*, March 8, 2005.
37. Rice University, "World of Business Without Rules," *Ascribe Business & Economic News Service*, January 28, 2005.

38. "ISO Takes on Social Responsibility," *Quality Digest*, May 2005.

## CHAPTER 5

1. Rick Mayes, "Even Small Businesses Need to See the Big Picture," *Research*, April 1, 2005, and "Business Opportunity Series and Expo Helps Americans Realize Their No. 1 Goal: Owning a Small Business," Business Wire, January 18, 2006.
2. U.S. Internal Revenue Service.
3. Jill Elswick, "Loaded Statements: Web-based Total Compensation Statements Keep Employees in the Know," *Employee Benefit News*, May 1, 2005.
4. Linda Tischler, "Power Couple," *Fast Company*, March 2005, pp. 44–51.
5. Jeff Opdyke, "When Business and Friendship Don't Mix," *The Wall Street Journal*, March 17, 2005, and Paulette Thomas, "One Sweet Solution to a Sour Partnership," *The Wall Street Journal,* March 23, 2005.
6. Rocky Scott, "Bill Fights 'Delaware Flight,' " *Tallahassee Democrat*, June 21, 2005.
7. www.parcorpsvcs.com/statefees.htm.
8. U.S. Internal Revenue Service.
9. Joyce M. Rosenberg, "Small Businesses Face Tax Law Changes for 2004," Associated Press, February 8, 2005.
10. Greg W. Smith, "C Corps vs. S Corps: How Tax Law Changes May Prompt Switching," *Financial Executive,* May 1, 2005, and Crystal Detamore-Rodman, "Focus on Finances: S Corps Are Coming Under Closer Scrutiny," *Entrepreneur*, January 1, 2006.
11. Tim Smith, "Macroeconomics and Entrepreneurship in 2005," *Wiglaf Journal*, May 2005.
12. Megan E. Mowrey, "Choice of Business Entity after JGTRRA and AJCA," *Strategic Finance,* March 1, 2005.
13. Thomas D. Scholtes, "Board Guidance for Going Private," *Directors & Boards*, March 22, 2005.
14. Matthew Benjamin, "Deal Mania," *U.S. News & World Report,* April 18, 2005.
15. Elaine Kurtenbach, "Failure to Acquire U.S. Oil Company Unlikely to Deter Chinese Expansion," *Bergen County (New Jersey) Record,* August 7, 2005, and Peter S. Goodman, "CNOOC Buys Oil Interest in Nigeria; Overseas Deal First Since Unocal Bid," *Washington Post*, January 10, 2006.
16. 26th Annual Franchise 500," *Entrepreneur*, January 1, 2005, and "*Entrepreneur*'s 27th Annual Franchise 500," *Entrepreneur*, January 1, 2006.
17. Peter Shea, "Sunny Franchise Days Ahead," *Franchising World*, January 1, 2005; Christopher Swan, "Franchising: Broadening Appeal Lifts Sector," *Financial Times*, June 8, 2005; and Michelle Kearns, "Franchises Give a National Twist to Local Businesses," *Buffalo News*, January 16, 2006.
18. April Y. Pennington, "An American Icon," *Entrepreneur*, January 1, 2005, and Geoff Williams, "Behind the Arches," *Entrepreneur*, January 1, 2006.
19. Tiesha Higgins, "Franchising Not Just for Fast Food Anymore," *Gazette Business,* January 5, 2005, p. A31, and Ed Duggan, "Playing the Franchising Game Can Be a Risky Business," *South Florida Business Journal,* May 13, 2005.
20. Mark N. Howard, "Be Your Own Boss: Affordable Franchises," *Black Enterprise,* April 2005, and Dolly Penland, "Picking a Business," *Jacksonville Business Journal*, November 25, 2005.
21. Nina Wu, "Couple Takes Fitness Road to Fiscal Fitness," *Pacific Business Journal*, December 2, 2006, and Rebecca Reisner, "Finding a Whole New Grind," BusinessWeek Online, January 20, 2006.
22. Julie Bennett, "A Franchiser's Path to International Success Is Often Paved with Pitfalls," *The Wall Street Journal*, April 7, 2005, p. D7, and Anne Fisher, "Hidden Risk," *Fortune*, December 26, 2005.
23. Stacy Perman, "Extending the Front Lines of Franchising," *BusinessWeek,* April 12, 2005, and Karen E. Klein, "The Capital Gender Gap," *BusinessWeek*, May 23, 2005.
24. "Women Business Owners' Access to Capital," Center for Women's Business Research Press Release, March 23, 2005, and Stacy Perman, "Act II: A Biz of One's Own," BusinessWeek Online, January 17, 2006.
25. "Minority-Owned Businesses Boost Local Economies," *La Prensa de San Antonio*, February 20, 2005.
26. "Marriott Seeks to Double Its 270 Minority Proprietors," PR Newswire, April 14, 2005.
27. www.mcdonalds.com.
28. "NRECA Programs Benefit 825 Co-ops, 37 Million Consumers Nationwide," *Rural Cooperative Magazine,* May/June 2005.

## CHAPTER 6

1. Shera Dalin, "Future Entrepreneurs Get Tips," *St. Louis Post-Dispatch,* June 26, 2005.
2. Tiana Velez, "New Generation of High-Tech Entrepreneurs Gathers Steam," *Arizona Daily Star*, January 31, 2005.
3. Philipp Harper, "History's 10 Greatest Entrepreneurs," MSNBC Interactive, 2005.
4. John A. Challenger, "As Entrepreneurs, Seniors Lead U.S. Start-ups," *Franchising World*, August 1, 2005; Dawn R. DeTienne, "Prior Knowledge, Potential Financial Reward, Opportunity Identification," *Entrepreneurship: Theory and Practice,* January 1, 2005; "List of Richest People Was Topped by Microsoft Corp. Founder Bill Gates for 11th Year in a Row," *Capper's*, March 29, 2005; and John Fried, "How I Did It," *Inc.*, March 2005, pp. 88–90.
5. Sarah Kwak, "Students Succeed as Entrepreneurs," University Wire, June 3, 2005; Karen E. Klein, "Rekindling an Entrepreneur's Passion," BusinessWeek Online, December 15, 2005; and Pallavi Gogoi, "Startup Secrets of the Successful," BusinessWeek Online, January 18, 2006.
6. Amy Joyce, "After the Pink Slip, a Rosier Outlook; Laid-Off Workers Take Chances as Entrepreneurs," *Washington Post,* July 4, 2002, p. T5.
7. Thomas M. Cooney, "What Is an Entrepreneurial Team?" *International Small Business Journal*, June 1, 2005, and "Management Advisory Group to Advise Paxson," *South Florida Business Journal*, January 16, 2006.
8. Helle Neergaard, "Networking Activities in Technology-Based Entrepreneurial Teams," *International Small Business Journal*, June 1, 2005.
9. Leyland M. Lucas, "Not Just Domestic Engineers: An Exploratory Study of Homemaker Entrepreneurs," *Entrepreneurship: Theory and Practice*; January 1, 2005, and Shirley Henderson, "Mothers of Invention: As Home-Based Businesses Grow, Moms Find Their Creative Niche," *Ebony*, May 1, 2005.
10. Sammi King, "Internet a Boon to Home-Based Businesses," *Arlington Heights (Illinois) Daily Herald,* February 22, 2005; Steve Jones, "Home Businesses Can Be Path to Freedom," *Myrtle Beach (South Carolina) Sun News,* May 15, 2005; and Kristen Millares Bolt, "Moms Setting Up Online Businesses," *Seattle Post-Intelligencer*, February 5, 2005.

11. Deb Gruver, "Small-Business Owners Face Pros, Cons of Home-Based Enterprises," *Wichita Eagle,* June 3, 2005; Deb Gruver, "Home-Based Businesses Need to Use Caution with Deductions," *Wichita Eagle*, March 18, 2005; "Parenting, Work-at-Home Experts Join to Author Book Series for Busy Moms," PR Newswire, January 31, 2005; and Janel Stephens, "Disciplined Commute from Bed to Home Office," *Sarasota Herald Tribune*, March 17, 2005.
12. Sucharita Mulpuru, "2005 U.S. eCommerce: The Year in Review," *Forrester Research*, January 20, 2006, and Doris Hajewski, "New Year's Retail Forecast Not as Rosy as 2005," *Milwaukee Journal Sentinel*, January 17, 2006.
13. Richard Waters, "Trial and Error Shows the Path to Success," *Financial Times,* March 9, 2005, p. 9; Kim Thomas, "Icing on Slice of Web Sales," *Financial Times,* March 9, 2005, p. 7; and Susan Kuchinskas, "Online Sales Up, Service Down," *InternetNews*, January 11, 2006.
14. Mark Henricks, "The Fast Lane: There Are Tried-and-True Rules for Growing a Company," *Entrepreneur*, April 1, 2005, and Gregory J. Gilligan, "PoshTots Bought by BabyUniverse," *Richmond Times-Dispatch*, January 19, 2006.
15. Simon Avery, "Pioneers of E-Commerce," *Cincinnati Post*, August 6, 2005.
16. Larry Olmsted, "Nonstop Innovation: How One Company Transforms Its Employees into Entrepreneurs," *Inc.,* July 2005, p. 34; Alan Deutschman, "Building a Better Skunk Works," *Fast Company*, March 2005, pp. 68–73; and Nicole Marie Richardson, "What It Takes to Be a Successful Intrapreneur," *Black Enterprise*, December 1, 2005.
17. Phil Bishop, "Strengthening the Innovation Chain," *Electronic Business*, December 1, 2004, and Robert D. Ramsey, "Gaining the Edge over the Competition," *Supervision*, May 1, 2005.
18. U.S. Citizenship and Immigration Services.
19. Dan Strempel, "UConn Mulls Stamford Tech Incubator," *Fairfield County (Connecticut) Business Journal*, April 11, 2005; Emily Le Coz, "Incubators Provide Tools for Entrepreneurs," *Northeast Mississippi Daily Journal*, January 6, 2006; and Nancy Cambria, "'Incubator' Loan Program Will Foster Small Businesses," *St. Louis Post-Dispatch*, January 19, 2006.
20. Emily Le Coz, "Incubators Flip Startup Numbers," *Northeast Mississippi Daily Journal*, January 7, 2006.
21. Gwendolyn Bounds, "SBA Reconsiders What Small Means," *The Wall Street Journal,* March 25, 2005, and "Small Business Owners Expose SBA Efforts to Hurt Small Businesses," Business Wire, June 2, 2005.
22. Martin Wolk, "Small Business Having a Big Impact on Jobs," MSNBC Interactive, August 2005; U.S. Census Bureau; and SBA Office of Advocacy.
23. Jon Bonne, "Big Store or Small? Why Consumers Care," MSNBC Interactive, 2005; Paulette Thomas, Small Competitors Can Conquer Tough Markets," *The Wall Street Journal*, April 2005; and Emily Bryson York, "To Fight the Gorilla, Be Nimble, Unique," *Crain's Chicago Business*, August 8, 2005.
24. Eileen Blass, "The New Entrepreneurs," *USA Today*, January 18, 2005.
25. Mark Henricks, "Honor Roll: By Teaching Everything from Planning to Perseverance, the Schools in Our 3rd Annual Top 100 Colleges and Universities Give Their Students a Competitive Advantage in the Real World," *Entrepreneur*, April 1, 2005; Dennis Seid, "Can Entrepreneurship Be Taught? Experts Believe So," *Northeast Mississippi Daily Journal*, January 6, 2006; and Hillary Wool, "Dartmouth Business School Offering Class in Entrepreneurship," University Wire, January 6, 2006.
26. "BBB Tips Give Entrepreneurs the Inside Track on Small Business Start-Up," Business Wire, August 24, 2005, and Perri Capell, "Typical Funding Mistakes That You Should Avoid," *The Wall Street Journal,* April 12, 2005.
27. Brian Hindo, "Money from Home," *BusinessWeek SmallBiz*, Spring 2005, p. 30.
28. Jim Melloan, "Angels with Angles," *Inc.*, July 2005, pp. 93–104; Lee Gomes, "Angel Investors Return and They Are Serious," *The Wall Street Journal,* April 12, 2005; Kevin Allison, "Angel Investing Takes Flight Again," *Financial Times*, May 3, 2005, p. 12; and Arlene Weintraub, "Where VCs Fear to Tread," *BusinessWeek*, March 7, 2005, pp. 86–87.
29. "Venture Capitalists Invested $4.63 Billion During the First Three Months of 2005," *Purchasing*, May 19, 2005; Amanda Fung, "Startups Find Few VC Funds," *Crain's New York Business*, August 1, 2005; and Tricia Bishop, "Fewer Venture Capital-Funded Companies Go Public in 2005," *Baltimore Sun*, January 4, 2006.
30. Gwendolyn Bounds, "Unusual Collateral Rescues a Small Business," *The Wall Street Journal,"* February 25, 2005, and Chris Penttila, "Easy Target? Budget-Cutters in Congress Have Set Their Sights on the SBA," *Entrepreneur*, January 1, 2006.
31. Carrie Mason-Draffen, "SBA's Micro Loan Program Helps Tiny Businesses Get Off the Ground," *Newsday*, February 15, 2005; Kathy Mayer, "Small Business Bucks," *Indiana Business Magazine*, January 1, 2005; Tinana Velez, "Senate Amendment Would Bolster SBA Funding," *Arizona Daily Star*, March 28, 2005; Jim Wyss, "Microloans Provide Massive Assistance," *Miami Herald,* April 18, 2005; and Rachel Stone, "Small Business Administration Approves More Than $2.5 Billion in Disaster Loans," *Beaumont (Texas) Enterprise,* January 16, 2006.
32. www.sba.gov.
33. "Growing with SBA Loans," *Florida Trend,* June 1, 2005; Shera Dalin, "SBA Budget Would Trim Funds for Low-Income Entrepreneurs," *St. Louis Post-Dispatch*, February 8, 2005; and Dave Gallagher, "Small Businesses Are Confident These Days: Borrowing, Start-Ups in Smaller Cities Are on Rise," *Bellingham Herald*, January 8, 2006.
34. Robert Rodriguez, "Family Matters," *Fresno Bee,* March 27, 2005, and Kathryn A. Morris, "Keeping It All in the Family," *Journal of Leadership & Organizational Studies,* January 1, 2005.
35. John Canter, "How and Why I Hired My Tax Accountant," *The Wall Street Journal*, February 25, 2005.
36. Shabnam Mogharabi, "Justice for All: Small Businesses Sometimes Can't Afford Full-Time Lawyers," *Pool & Spa News,* August 8, 2005, and Mike Sunnucks, "Law Firms Offer Flat Fees, Technology to Help Small, Midsize Clients," *Business Journal*, December 23, 2005.
37. Marilyn Carpenter, "Charlotte Businesses Benefit with SCORE," *Sarasota Herald Tribune,* January 19, 2005; Rick Moriarty, "Group Knows the Score," *Syracuse Post Standard,* January 16, 2005; and Greg Stiles, "SCORE Gets Renewed Presence in Southern Oregon," *Mail Tribune*, January 5, 2006.
38. www.sbea.org.


## CHAPTER 7


1. Roderick M. Kramer, "The Great Intimidators," *Harvard Business Review*, February 2006, pp. 88–96.

2. Jack Welch and Suzy Welch, "How to Be a Good Leader," *Newsweek*, April 4, 2005, pp. 45–48.
3. Gary Hamel, "The Why, What, and How of Management Innovation, " *Harvard Business Review*, February 2006, pp. 72–84.
4. Peter Cappelli and Monika Hamori, "The New Road to the Top," *Harvard Business Review*, January 2005, pp. 25–32.
5. Marcus Buckingham, "What Great Managers Do," *Harvard Business Review*, March 2005, pp. 70–79.
6. Elizabeth Fenner, "Happiness," *Fortune*, February 21, 2005, p. 36.
7. Kenneth R. Brousseau, Michael J. Driver, Gary Hourihon, and Rikard Larsson. "The Seasoned Executive's Decision-Making Style," *Harvard Business Review*, February 2006, pp. 111–121.
8. John E. West, "Listening to the Customer," *Quality Digest*, February 2006, p. 16.
9. Jack Welch, "It's All in the Sauce," *Fortune*, April 18, 2005, pp. 138–144.
10. Sholnn Freeman, "What Drives Them," *Washington Post*, January 11, 2006, pp. D1 and D3.
11. Jonathan Fahey, "Hydrogen Gas," *Forbes*, April 25, 2005, pp. 78–83.
12. Bill Breen, "The Clear Leader," *Fast Company*, March 2005, pp. 65–67.
13. Janel M. Radtke, "How to Write a Mission Statement," TCCI Magazine Online, 2005.
14. Giovanni Gavetti and Jan W. Rivkin, "How Strategists Really Think," *Harvard Business Review*, April 2005, pp. 54–63.
15. Neal E. Boudette, "Powerful Nostalgia," *The Wall Street Journal*, January 10, 2006, p. B1.
16. Michael C. Mankins and Richard Steele, "Stop Making Plans: Start Making Decisions," *Harvard Business Review*, January 2006, pp. 76–84.
17. Robert J. Samuelson, "No Joke: CEOs Do Some Good," *Newsweek*, April 18, 2005, p. 49.
18. Gary Silverman, "How May I Help You?," *Financial Times*, February 4/5, 2006, pp. W1 and W2.
19. Leigh Buchanan and Andrew O'Connell, "A Brief History of Decision Making," *Harvard Business Review*, January 2006, pp. 32–51.
20. Paul Rogers and Marcia Blenko, "Who Has the D?," *Harvard Business Review*, January 2006, pp. 53–61.
21. Chris Penttila, "Musical Chairs," *Entrepreneur*, April 2006, p. 24.
22. Andreas Priestland and Robert Hanig, "Developing First-Level Leaders," *Harvard Business Review*, June 2005, pp. 113–120.
23. P. Fraser Johnson and Robert D. Klassen, "E-Procurement," *MIT Sloan Management Review*, Winter 2005, pp. 7–10.
24. Mahender Singh, "Supply Chain Reality Check," *MIT Sloan Management Review*, Spring 2005, p. 96.
25. Lee Ann Jackson, "Relax Your Grip," *Black Enterprise*, February 2006, p. 71.
26. Joe Raelin, "Finding Meaning in the Organization, "*Sloan Management Review*, Spring 2006, pp. 64–68.
27. Peter F. Drucker, "What Makes an Effective Executive," *Harvard Business Review*, June 2004, pp. 58–63.
28. Lucy Kellaway, "Beware the Senseless Dumbing Up of Management Thinking," *Financial Times*, May 23, 2005, p. 8.
29. David Rooke and William R. Torbert, "Transformations of Leadership," *Harvard Business Review*, April 2005, pp. 67–76.
30. Thaddeus Herrick, "Leadership as Layup? Lessons from Basketball," The Wall Street Journal Online, March 21, 2005.
31. Amy Joyce, "Big Bad Boss Tales," *Washington Post*, May 29, 2005, pp. F1 and F4.
32. Simon London, "Why Managers Have Little Time for Management Theory," *Financial Times*, January 18, 2006, p. 10.
33. Andrew Baxter, "Keeping the Know-How of a Retiring Generation," *Financial Times*, January 25, 2006, p. 1 of a Special Report.
34. "Corporate Social Responsibility: Good Citizenship or Investor Rip-Off?," *The Wall Street Journal*, January 9, 2006, pp. R6 and R7; and Ryan Underwood, "In Tune with the Environment," *Fast Company*, February 2005, p. 26.


## CHAPTER 8


1. Bernard Simon and James Mackintosh, "Ford to Axe 25,000 Jobs and Close Seven Plants," *Financial Times*, Janurary 24, 2006, p. 1.
2. Lee Hawkins Jr., "GM Posts a $4.78 Billion Loss, Vows Turnaround; Shares Fall 3.4%," *The Wall Street Journal*, January 27, 2006, p. A3.
3. Jerry Flint, "Bankruptcy, Shmankruptcy," *Forbes*, February 13, 2006, p. 105.
4. Jeremy Grant, "Kraft to Shut 20 Plants and Axe 8,000 Jobs as Costs Soar," *Financial Times*, January 31, 2006, p. 17.
5. Mike Esterl, "Siemens Chief Is Setting a Higher Bar," *The Wall Street Journal*, January 24, 2006, p. C3.
6. Rob Hof, "How Good Are Google's Extras?," *BusinessWeek*, January 16, 2006, pp. 88–89.
7. Thomas A. Stewart, "Architects of Change," *Harvard Business Review*, April 2006, p. 10.
8. Robert J. Samuelson, "The World Is Still Round," *Washington Post*, July 22, 2005, p. A23.
9. Fred Reichheld, "The Microeconomics of Customer Relations," *MIT Sloan Management Review*, Winter 2006, pp. 73–78.
10. Charles Forelle, "IBM Restructuring, Job Cuts," *The Wall Street Journal*, May 5, 2005, p. A3.
11. Brian Grow, "Renovating Home Depot," *BusinessWeek*, March 6, 2006, pp. 50–58.
12. Cait Murphy, "Sara Lee Cleans Out Its Cupboards," *Fortune*, March 7, 2005, p. 38.
13. Mark Tatge, "Brenda the Liquidator," *Forbes*, March 14, 2005, p. 48.
14. Pui-Wing Tam, "H-P Net Rises on Gains Across Units," *The Wall Street Journal*, February 16, 2006, p. A3.
15. Rob Cross, Jeanne Liedtka and Leigh Weiss, "A Practical Guide to Social Networks," *Harvard Business Review*, March 2005, pp. 124–132.
16. Steven Gray, "Beyond Burgers," *The Wall Street Journal*, February 18–19, 2006, pp. A1 and A7.
17. Robert Simons, "Designing High Performance Jobs," *Harvard Business Review*, July–August 2005, pp. 54–62.
18. Dick Baynton, "The China Connection," *Update* (Woodworking Machinery Industry Association newsletter), April 2005.
19. Harry Maurer, "News You Need to Know," *BusinessWeek*, February 6, 2006, p. 32.
20. Ranjay Gulati and James B. Oldroyd, "The Quest for Customer Focus," *Harvard Business Review*, April 2005, pp. 92–101.
21. Robert Buderi, "E-Commerce Gets Smarter," *Technology Review*, April 2005, pp. 54–59.
22. Ron Adner, "Innovation Ecosystem," *Harvard Business Review*, April 2006, pp. 98–107.
23. Jon R. Katzenbach and Douglas K. Smith, "The Discipline of Teams," *Harvard Business Review*, July–August 2005, pp. 162–71.

24. Jeff Weiss and Jonathan Hughes, "Want Collaboration?," *Harvard Business Review*, March 2005, pp. 93–101.
25. Bill Fischer and Andy Boynton, "Virtuoso Teams," *Harvard Business Review*, July–August 2005, pp. 117–21.
26. John E. (Jack) Wert, "Listening to the Customer," *Quality Digest*, February 2006, p. 16.
27. Philip Evans and Bob Wolf, "Collaboration Rules," *Harvard Business Review*, July–August 2005, pp. 96–104.
28. Jerker Denrell, "Selection Bias and the Perils of Benchmarking," *Harvard Business Review*, April 2005, pp. 114–19.
29. Amy Barrett, "Cracking the Whip at Wyeth," *BusinessWeek*, February 6, 2006, pp. 70–71.
30. Chris Noon, "Lampert's New Sears Post Loss as Brands Combine," Forbes.com, June 7, 2005.
31. Amy Barrett, "Man with Scalpel," *BusinessWeek*, April 18, 2005, p. 42.
32. David Ernst and James Bamford, "Your Alliances Are Too Stable," *Harvard Business Review*, June 2005, pp. 133–141.
33. Jean Halliday, "Ford Puts Consumers at Center of 'Rebirthing,'" *Advertising Age*, January 30, 2006, p. 31.
34. Keith Naughton, "Detroit Hoping for a Small Victory," *Newsweek*, February 6, 2006, p. 10.
35. Erin White, "Savvy Job Hunters Research Office Culture," The Wall Street Journal Online, April 12, 2005.
36. Tom Lester, "The Cost of Not Caring for Your Customers," *Financial Times*, January 30, 2006, p. 10.
37. Steven Watters, "The Organization Woman," *Business 2.0*, April 2006, pp. 106–110.

## CHAPTER 9

1. A. Gary Shilling, "What's Bad for GM . . .," *Forbes*, April 25, 2005, p. 112.
2. Alex Taylor III, "GM Hits the Skids," *Fortune*, April 4, 2005, pp. 71–74.
3. David Welch and Dan Beuke, "Why GM's Plan Won't Work . . . And the Ugly Road Ahead," *BusinessWeek*, May 9, 2005, pp. 85–93.
4. Moon Ihlwan and Jason Bush, "Hyundai: Crowding into the Fast Lane," *BusinessWeek*, June 20, 2005, p. 54, and Andrew Tilin, "The Smartest Company of the Year," *Business 2.0*, February 2005, pp. 65–72.
5. David Welch and Adam Aston, "Fill" Er Up—But With What?" *BusinessWeek*, May 22, 2006, pp. 60–63.
6. Walter Williams, "Vanishing Manufacturing Jobs?," *Washington Times*, May 8, 2006, p. A17.
7. George F. Will, "Labor Since the Overpass," *Newsweek*, August 15, 2005; Jeffrey Mccracken and Jamie Butters, "'04 Bodes Well for U.S. Market Share," *Detroit Free Press*, January 3, 2004; and Alex Taylor III, "Can One Man Save GM?" *Fortune*, September 19, 2005.
8. Alan Reynolds, "Car Wars," *Washington Times*, June 12, 2005, p. B1.
9. Pete Engardio, "The Future of Outsourcing," *BusinessWeek*, January 30, 2006, pp. 50–58.
10. David Welch and Dean Foust, "The Good News about America's Auto Industry," *BusinessWeek*, February 13, 2006, pp. 32–35.
11. Alan Reynolds, "Manufacturing and Trade," *Washington Times*, May 29, 2005, p. B4, and Brian S. Wesbury, "Resilient Economy," *The Wall Street Journal*, September 8, 2005, p. A18.
12. James Mehring, "Full Throttle on the Factory Floor," *BusinessWeek*, February 13, 2006, p. 28.
13. Ibid.
14. H. James Harrington and Thomas McNellis, "Mobilizing the Right Lean Metrics for Success," *Quality Digest*, May 2006, pp. 32–38.
15. Fred Reichheld, "The Microeconomics of Customer Relationships," *MIT Sloan Management Review*, Winter 2006, pp. 73–78.
16. David H. Freedman, "Freeing Your Inner Think Tank," *Inc.*, May 2005, pp. 65–66.
17. Norman R. Augustine and Burton Richter, "Our Ph.D. Deficit," *The Wall Street Journal*, May 4, 2005, p. A18.
18. Burt Helm, "The Next Tiny Thing," *BusinessWeek*, September 5, 2005, p. 22, and Renée Comet, "iPod to the Max," *Kiplinger's*, January 2006, pp. 100–101.
19. Jennifer Merritt and Louis Lavelle, "Tomorrow's B-School? It Might Be a D-School," *BusinessWeek*, August 1, 2005, pp. 80–81.
20. Robyn Waters, "The Secret of Feel-Good Shopping," *Kiplinger's*, January 2006, pp. 20–22.
21. Christina S.N. Lewis and Jessica E. Vascellaro, "Finding the Perfect Pair of Jeans—on the Internet," *The Wall Street Journal*, January 19, 2006, p. D4.
22. Derrell S. James, "Using Lean and Six Sigma in Project Management," *Quality Digest*, August 2005, pp. 49–55, and Bill Ritsch, "Breaking the Bottleneck," *Quality Digest*, March 2006, p. 41.
23. Shoshana Zuboff, "The Personalized Economy," *CIO*, April 2005, pp. 32–37, and Christina S.N. Lewis and Jessica E. Vascellaro, "Finding the Perfect Pair of Jeans—on the Internet," *Wall Street Journal*, January 19, 2006, p. D4.
24. Julia Boorstin, "Adidas Expands Its Footprint," *Fortune*, May 30, 2005, p. 33.
25. Robyn Waters, "The Secret of Feel-Good Shopping," *Kiplinger's*," January 2006, pp. 20–22.
26. Gail Edmondson, William Boston and Andrea Zammert, "Detroit East," *BusinessWeek*, July 25, 2005, pp. 48–51.
27. Richard Wilding, "The Ghost in the Machine," *Financial Times*, April 7, 2006, p. 5 of a section called Mastering Uncertainty.
28. Douglas M. Lambert and A. Michael Knemeyer, "We're in This Together," *Harvard Business Review*, December 2004, pp. 114–22.
29. Richard Waters, "Manufacturing Glitches Dent Xbox Sales," *Financial Times*, January 27, 2006, p. 17.
30. Michelle Conlin, "Call Centers in the Rec Room," *BusinessWeek*, January 23, 2006, pp. 76–77.
31. Michael V. Copeland, "The Mighty Micro-multinational," *Business 2.0*, July 2006, pp. 106–14.
32. Joseph Weber and Ann Therese Palmer, "How the Net Is Remaking the Mall," *BusinessWeek*, May 9, 2005, pp. 60–61, and Avery Johnson, "Hotels Take 'Know Your Customer' to a New Level," *Wall Street Journal*, February 7, 2006, pp. D1 and D3.
33. Janet Bealer Rodie, "Brückner, M-Tec Partner to Provide Carpet Solutions," *Textile World*, May 1, 2005.
34. Brian Nadel, "Enterprise Resource Working" (ad), *Fortune*, July 25, 2005, pp. S1–S5, and V. Kumar, Rajkumar Venkatesan and Werner Reinartz, "Knowing What to Sell, When, and to Whom," *Harvard Business Review*, March 2006, pp. 131–137.
35. Horst-Henning Wolf, "Making the Transition to Strategic Purchasing," *MIT Sloan Management Review*, Summer 2005, pp. 17–24.
36. P. Fraser Johnson and Robert D. Klassen, "E-Procurement," *MIT Sloan Management Review*, Winter 2005, pp. 7–10.
37. Connie Robbins Gentry, "Million-Dollar Savings," *Chain Store Age*, February 2005, pp. 54–55.

38. H. James Harrington, "Six Sigma: Quality's Viagra?," *Quality Digest*, August 2005, p. 14.
39. Davis Balestracci, "When Processes Moonlight as Trends," *Quality Digest*, June 2005, p. 18.
40. Laura Smith, "And the Winners Are . . .," *Quality Digest*, January 2006, p. 6.
41. Laura Smith, "Profiles in Quality," *Quality Digest*, July 2005, pp. 53–54.
42. Smith, "And the Winners Are . . ."
43. John E. (Jack) West, "Continuous Improvement and Your QMS," *Quality Digest*, April 2006, p. 16.
44. Scott M. Paton, "The Cost of Quality," *Quality Digest*, January 2006, p. 128.
45. Leonard Berry, Venkatesh Shankar, Janet Turner Parish, Susan Cadwallader, and Thomas Dotzel, "Creating New Markets Through Service Innovation," *MIT Sloan Management Review*, Winter 2006, pp. 56–63.


## CHAPTER 10


1. "How Employee Satisfaction and Motivation Are Tied to Customer Satisfaction," *Managing Training & Development*, January 1, 2005; Michael Skapinker, "Measures of Success Must Go Beyond Financial Results," *Financial Times*, March 2, 2005; and "Employee Retention and Succession Programs Lead to Higher Retention, Increased ROI, Says AberdeenGroup," Business Wire, January 9, 2006.
2. "Employee Turnover Picking Up Speed—Ensure Employee Loyalty," PR Newswire, June 30, 2005, and Barbara Rose, "Better Job Market Puts Retention at Premium," *Chicago Tribune*, January 10, 2006.
3. Michael Wilson, "The Psychology of Motivation and Employee Retention," *Maintenance Supplies*, July 1, 2005; Jeff Kirby, "Light Their Fires: Find Out How to Improve Employee Motivation and Increase Overall Company Productivity," *Security Management*, June 1, 2005; and Michael Arndt, "Nice Work If You Can Get It," *BusinessWeek*, January 9, 2006.
4. Jane Gaboury, "Tension Invention," *Industrial Engineer*, July 1, 2005.
5. Richard DiPaolo, "Ergonomically Inclined," *Maintenance Supplies*, June 1, 2005.
6. Jay Velury, "Empowerment to the People," *Industrial Engineer*, May 1, 2005.
7. Horst Brand, "Working in the Digital Age," *Monthly Labor Review*, January 1, 2005.
8. Steven Bratman, "The Double-Blind Gaze," *Altadena (California) Skeptic*, January 1, 2005.
9. John A. Byrne, "The 21st Century Corporation: Back to the Future: Visionary vs. Visionary," *BusinessWeek*, August 28, 2000, p. 210, and Richard S. Tedlow, "The Education of Andy Grove," *Fortune*, December 12, 2005.
10. Pamela Babcock, "Find What Workers Want," *HRMagazine*, April 1, 2005.
11. Cliff Edwards, "Inside Intel," *BusinessWeek*, January 9, 2006.
12. Nadira A. Hira and Christopher Tkaczyk, "Hall of Fame," *Fortune*, January 24, 2005, pp. 94–95, and Geoff Colvin, "The 100 Best Companies to Work For 2006," *Fortune*, January 23, 2006.
13. Michael Wilson, "The Psychology of Motivation and Employee Retention," *Maintenance Supplies*, July 1, 2005; Jeff D. Opdyke, "Money Can't Buy Job Happiness," *The Wall Street Journal*, April 19, 2005; and "Incentives on the Rise," *Financial & Insurance Meetings*, January 1, 2006.
14. "Organizing for Empowerment: An Interview with AES's Roger Sant and Dennis Bakke," *Harvard Business Review*, January 1, 1999, p. 110; Dave Hemsath, "301 More Ways to Have Fun at Work," *HRMagazine*, July 1, 2005; Sandy McCrarey, "Motivating the Workforce with a Positive Culture," *Franchising World*; March 1, 2005; Linda F. Jarrett, "Helping Drive Enterprise," *St. Louis Commerce*, March 2005, pp. 14–21; Alan Schwarz, "How I Did It," *Inc.*, April 2005, pp. 116–18; and Mark Dominiak, "Use Creative Tactics to Retain Staff; Management Rewards Such as Outings, Time Off, Group Activities Can Revitalize Hard-Working Employees," *TelevisionWeek*, January 16, 2006.
15. Margaret Heffernan, "The Morale of the Story," *Fast Company*, March 2005, pp. 79–81.
16. "A New Era for Japanese Banks," *Pensions Management*, January 1, 2005, and "Japanese Icon Sony Brings in American Boss to Battle Slump," Agence France Presse, English, March 7, 2005.
17. "Japan's Economy Best in Decade But Still Faces Many Problems," Kyodo World News Service, January 20, 2005; "Japan 21st in World Competitiveness," *Kyodo News International*, May 12, 2005; and Joanna Sullivan, "Reaching Out: Japanese Banker Launches Business to Match Employers with Hispanics Eager to Work," *Baltimore Business Journal*, January 16, 2006.
18. Richard A. Roberts, "Success Means Change," *Supervision*, April 1, 2005, and Dawn Sagario, "With a Plan, Delusional Office Slackers Can Be Put Back on Track," Gannett News Service, June 30, 2005.
19. Patricia M. Buhler, "Managing in the New Millennium: Human Resources," *Supervision*, January 1, 2005, and Jena McGregor, "The Struggle to Measure Performance," *BusinessWeek*, January 9, 2006.
20. Karen van Dam, "Employee Attitudes Toward Job Changes," *Journal of Occupational and Organizational Psychology*, June 1, 2005, and Goutam Challagalla, "Adapting Motivation, Control, and Compensation Research to a New Environment," *Journal of Personal Selling & Sales Management*, March 22, 2005.
21. David Nadler and Edward Lawler, "Motivation—a Diagnostic Approach," in *Perspectives on Behavior in Organizations* (New York: McGraw-Hill, 1977).
22. Rebecca M. Chory-Assad, "Motivating Factors: Perceptions of Justice and Their Relationship with Managerial and Organizational Trust," *Communication Studies*, March 1, 2005, and Christine A. Henle, "Predicting Workplace Deviance from the Interaction Between Organizational Justice and Personality," *Journal of Managerial Issues*, June 22, 2005.
23. Dean B. McFarlin, "Wage Comparisons with Similar and Dissimilar Others," *Journal of Occupational and Organizational Psychology*, March 1, 2005, and Katherine Reynolds Lewis, "If You Think You're Underpaid, Think Again," *Post-Standard*, January 18, 2006.
24. Holly J. Payne, "Reconceptualizing Social Skills in Organizations: Exploring the Relationship between Communication Competence, Job Performance, and Supervisory Roles," *Journal of Leadership & Organizational Studies*, January 1, 2005.
25. John E. Guiniven, "Making Employee Communication Work," *Journal of Employee Assistance*, March 1, 2005; Dean A. Hill, "Communication Strategy: Conquer the Hurdles That Are Inhibiting Dialogue with Your Employees," *Detroiter*, January 1, 2005; Mark Faircloth, "Eight Strategies for Building a Sales Culture," *Community*

*Banker*, August I, 2005; "Communications Q&A," *Pensions Management*, August I, 2005; and Mark Henricks, "The Truth? Your Employees Can Handle it, so Just Communicate with Them, Already," *Entrepreneur*, July I, 2005.
26. Dee-Ann Durbin, "Ford Sales Fall, but Mustang Coupe a Hit," AP Online, June I, 2005, and Amy Wilson, "Lasso a Mustang? Maybe; Dealers Scramble to Meet Demand," *Automotive News*, April 4, 2005.
27. "Ford to Increase Mustang Production to Meet Runaway Consumer Demand," PR Newswire, March I7, 2005 and "Ford Achieves First Car Sales Increase Since I999," PR Newswire, January 4, 2006.
28. Don Mecoy, "Baby Boomers Staying on Job Longer, Experts Say," *Daily Oklahoman*, January 8, 2006.
29. "Managing Older Workers Sometimes Awkward for Generation X, Y Bosses," *San Luis Obispo (California) Tribune*, July 25, 2005; John Foltz, "Managing Multiple Generations at Work," *Feed & Grain*, August I, 2005; Gregory B. Turner, "Understanding Generation X . . . Boom or Bust Introduction," *Business Forum*, December 22, 2005; and Leah Thayer, "Deconstructing Generation X: Log On, Open Up, and Take the Time to Explain Things," *Remodeling*, January I, 2006.
30. Shirleen Holt, "Four Generations Deep, a New Work Force Fights to Find What It Values," *Seattle Times*, March 22, 2005, and Kyra Kyles, "The Age of Y," *Chicago Tribune*, December 27, 2005.
3I. Chuck Roberts, "Are We Ready for Generation Y?" *Fleet Equipment*; April I, 2005; Shelly Garcia, "Generation Y Proves Challenge for Boomer Managers," *San Fernando Valley Business Journal*, January I7, 2005; Peter Brandow, "Bring On Generation Y," *Ward's Dealer Business*, March I, 2005; and "The Generation Game," *New Zealand Management*, December I, 2005.
32. Leslie Rose Mcdonald, "Employee Recognition Reduces Turnover," *Syracuse (New York) Post-Standard*, July 27, 2005, and Leslie McIntyre-Tavella, "Just Say 'Thank You,'" *Westchester County Business Journal*, February I4, 2005.

## CHAPTER II

I. Sally Coleman Selden, "Human Resource Management in American Counties," *Public Personnel Management*, April I, 2005, and Robert Rodriguez, "HR's New Breed," *HRMagazine*, January I, 2006.
2. Michael Keating, "Infrastructure Crucial When Establishing Nanotech Operations, but the U.S. Faces a Shortage of Skilled Workers to Staff Such Facilities," *Expansion Management*, February I, 2005.
3. Jason Stein, "The Search for Skilled Labor," *Wisconsin State Journal,* April I, 2005; "ATS Survey Shows Looming Skilled Labor Shortage Will Cost Manufacturers an Average $50 Million," Business Wire, June 7, 2005; Jennifer Curry and Dan Reynolds, "Some Industries Face Skilled Worker Shortage," *Pittsburgh Business Times*, December 3I, 2005; and Rob Varnon, "Firms Help Laid-Off Bic Employees," *Connecticut Post*, January I9, 2006.
4. Robert J. Grossman, "The Truth about the Coming Labor Shortage," *HRMagazine*, March I, 2005; James Detar, "Education Key to Firms Finding Skilled Workers," *Investors' Business Daily*, April 4, 2005; and "Employers Tackle a Tricky Math Problem," *Inc.,* March 2005.
5. J. Albert Diaz, "2030 Forecast: Mostly Gray," *USA Today*, April 2I, 2005; Richard Lee, "High Incomes, Retiring Baby Boomers Put Dent in Economic Development," *Stamford (Connecticut) Advocate,* April 29, 2005; Ellen M. Heffes, "Dramatic Workforce Trends Require Planning Now," *Financial Executive*, July I, 2005; Neal Conan, "Analysis: Post-Boomer Work Force," *Talk of the Nation* (National Public Radio), September 2I, 2005; and Don Mecoy, "Baby Boomers Staying on Job Longer, Experts Say," *Daily Oklahoman*, January 8, 2006.
6. John J. Fitzpatrick Jr., "State Labor Legislation Enacted in 2004," *Monthly Labor Review,* January I, 2005, and "Labor Law: What You Should Know," *Florida Trend*, June I, 2005.
7. Ronald G. Breshears, "Family Issues in the Workplace," *Journal of Education for Business*; January I, 2005, and H. J. Cummins, "Keeping Baby Close to Work," *Minneapolis (Minnesota) Star Tribune*, January 2I, 2006.
8. Adam Geller, "Steep Decline in Worker Satisfaction May Have Leveled Off," *St. Louis Post-Dispatch*, March I, 2005.
9. Gilbert Chan, "HP Workers Prepare for Uncertainty; Layoffs Take Toll on Employee Morale," *Sacramento Bee,* July 20, 2005, and Michael Crom, "Communicate Well to Restore Motivation to Workers Facing Downsizing," Gannett News Service, July 28, 2005.
I0. Jeffrey Sparshott, "Lucent to Shut Maryland Facility; II0 Jobs Being Shifted to India," *Washington Times*, March I0, 2005; John P. McDermott, "North Charleston Firm Sending Jobs Overseas," *Charleston (South Carolina) Post and Courier*, January 26, 2005; and Richard, Ernsberger Jr., "The Big Squeeze: A 'Second Wave' of Offshoring Could Threaten Middle-Income, White-Collar and Skilled Blue-Collar Jobs," *Newsweek International*, May 30, 2005.
II. Carl Grassi, "New Grace Period Beefs Up Cafeteria Benefit Plans," *Crain's Cleveland Business*, July II, 2005, and Len Boselovic and Christopher Snowbeck, "Future of Health, Pension Benefits Cloudy," *Seattle Post-Intelligencer*, January I6, 2006.
I2. Lisa Kovach, "High Health-Care Costs Weigh Heavily on Firms," *San Diego Business Journal*, February 28, 2005; Della Pacheco, "Aging Employees, Parents Face Care-Giving Challenges," *Indianapolis Business Journal*, April II, 2005; Linda Wasmer Andrews, "Hiring People with Intellectual Disabilities," *HRMagazine*, July I, 2005; and Anne E. Winkler, "Does Affirmative Action Work?" *Regional Review*, January I, 2005.
I3. "Employee Turnover Picking Up Speed—Ensure Employee Loyalty," PR Newswire, June 30, 2005; "Surveys Reveal Turnover Rates Are on the Rise," *Report on Salary Surveys*, May I, 2005; and "70 Percent of HR Managers Concerned about Workforce Retention, According to Monster Study," Business Wire, January 9, 2006.
I4. Elena Malykhina, "Supplying Labor to Meet Demand," *Informationweek*, March 2I, 2005, pp. 69–72.
I5. Anthony R. Wheeler, "Post-Hire Human Resource Management Practices and Person-Organization Fit: A Study of Blue-Collar Employees," *Journal of Managerial Issues*, March 22, 2005.
I6. "What to Do Now That Training Is Becoming a Major HR Force," *HR Focus*, February I, 2005.
I7. Tom Shehan, "How to Retain Employees: A High Turnover Rate Is Costly in Both Direct and Indirect Costs," *Detroiter*, January I, 2005, and "Hiring Is Stymied by the Search for the Perfect Candidate," Business Wire, January 6, 2005.
I8. Michelle V. Rafter, "Unicru Breaks Through in the Science of 'Smart Hiring,'" *Workforce Management*, May I, 2005, and "PetSmart Selects Unicru to Find People Passionate About Pets," Business Wire, January I7, 2006.

19. Liz Kislik, "A Hire Authority," *Catalog Age*, April 1, 2005, and "HR by Numbers: How to Hire the Right People and Then Lead Them to Success," *Prosales*, January 1, 2006.
20. Marcela Creps, "What Not to Ask Applicants at a Job Interview," *Bloomington (Indiana) Herald-Times*, May 31, 2005.
21. Tara Pepper, "Inside the Head of an Applicant," *Newsweek*, February 21, 2005, and "Personality Assessment Tests," PR Newswire, April 12, 2005.
22. "Experts Available to Discuss Court Ruling That Personality Tests for Job Applicants Are Prohibited Under the ADA," Business Wire, July 5, 2005.
23. David Hench, "Maine Overwhelmed as Background Checks Balloon," *Portland (Maine) Press Herald*, April 18, 2005; Carol Hymowitz, "Add Candidate's Character to Boards' Lists of Concerns," *The Wall Street Journal*, March 17, 2005; James Swann, "Guarding the Gates with Employee Background Checks," *Community Banker*, August 1, 2005; Carol Patton, "To Tell the Truth: It's an Institution's Duty to Ensure that New Hires Are Who They Say They Are," *University Business*, January 1, 2006; and Mary Jane Maytum, "Look a Little Closer: Investigators Say Employers Can Thwart Value of Background Checks; Some Should Dig Deeper," *Business First*, January 27, 2006.
24. "Employers Continue to Order More Sophisticated Drug Testing," *Drug Detection Report*, September 1, 2005.
25. Deborah J. Myers, "You're Fired! Letting an Employee Go Isn't Easy for Any Manager," *Alaska Business Monthly*, May 1, 2005.
26. "Why HR Must Act as a Strategic Gatekeeper for Contingent Staffing," *Human Resource Department Management Report*, January 1, 2005; Shelly Garcia, "Use of Temporary Workers May Be Permanent Solution for Businesses," *San Fernando Valley Business Journal*, November 22, 2004; H. Lee Murphy, "Temps Are Back, and Cheaper," *Crain's Chicago Business*, February 14, 2005; and "Temp Jobs' Climb Hints at Broader Growth to Come," *Washington Post*, January 16, 2006.
27. Maria Mallory White, "Student Gives Temp Work 'A' Experience, Pay Found Rewarding," *Atlanta Journal and Constitution,* July 14, 2002, p. R1.
28. Alison Maitland, "Employers Nurse the Stress Bug," *Financial Times,* April 19 2005, p. 12.
29. Laurie Bassi and Daniel McMurrer, "How's Your Return on People?" *Harvard Business Review,* March 2004, p. 18, and Beth Earnest, "Coaching Employees to Be Their Best," *Business Journal of Milwaukee*, January 13, 2006.
30. Robert Green, "Effective Training Programs: How to Design In-House Training on a Limited Budget," *CADalyst*, March 1, 2005, and Lynne M. Connelly, "Welcoming New Employees," *Journal of Nursing Scholarship*, June 22, 2005.
31. "Big Boy Restaurants Launches National Online Training Program for Employees," Business Wire, March 28, 2005.
32. Sunwoo Kang, "Perceived Usefulness and Outcomes of Intranet-Based Learning," *Journal of Instructional Psychology*, March 1, 2005.
33. Patrick J. Sauer, "The Problem: Magnetech Wants to Triple Its Workforce," *Inc.*, January 2005, pp. 38–39.
34. Leah Carlson, "Spending on Employee Training Remains Stable," *Employee Benefit News*, February 1, 2005, and Kirstin Dorsch, "Small BizU Offers Training Whenever It's Convenient," *Jacksonville Business Journal*, January 6, 2006.
35. Jeffrey Pfeffer, "A Blueprint for Success," *Business 2.0,* April 2005, p. 66.
36. Anne Fisher, "How to Network—and Enjoy It," *Fortune*, April 4, 2005, p. 38; Daisy Wademan, "The Best Advice I Ever Got," *Harvard Business Review*, January 2005, pp. 35–38; and E. R. 'Bud' Giesinger, "A Formal Mentoring Program Puts Informal Goodwill to Work," *Houston Business Journal*, January 6, 2006.
37. Meredith Levinson, "Shmooze or Lose," *CIO,* March 15, 2005, p. 26, and Bob Nelson, "The Mentor Experience Has a Power to Transform a Career," *Portland (Maine) Business Journal*, January 20, 2006.
38. "The Puzzle of the Lost Women," *Financial Times*, March 1, 2005, p. 10.
39. Laura Egodigwe, "How Networking Really Works," *Black Enterprise,* February 2005, pp. 98–102.
40. "Networking Should Cross Ethnic Lines," *Orange County Register*, August 18, 2005; Dean Takahashi, "Ethnic Network Helps Immigrants Succeed," *The Wall Street Journal Interactive Edition,* July 28, 1999; and Benita Newton, "National Networking Event Makes Its Way to Virginia for First Time," *Norfolk, (Virginia) Virginian-Pilot,* July 21, 2005.
41. Perry Pascarella, "Compensating Teams," *Across the Board,* February 1997, pp. 16–23, and Goutam Challagalla, "Adapting Motivation, Control, and Compensation Research to a New Environment," *Journal of Personal Selling & Sales Management,* March 22, 2005.
42. Glen Fest, "Incentive Pay: Compensating for Good Relationships," *Bank Technology News*, June 1, 2005.
43. Jill Elswick, "Loaded Statements: Web-Based Total Compensation Statements Keep Employees in the Know," *Employee Benefit News*, May 1, 2005.
44. Christine Larson, "Time Out," *U.S. News & World Report,* February 28, 2005; Lynda V. Mapes, "Two Local Companies Are Proving It Pays to Do Well by Workers," *Seattle Times*, January 31, 2005; Danielle Sacks, "Not the Retiring Sort," *Fast Company*, May 2005; and "Baby Boomer and Generation X Workers Agree When It Comes to Voluntary Benefits, Says Aon Consulting," PR Newswire, January 31, 2006.
45. Jennifer Gill, "Here Are Nine Remedies to Soothe Your Health Care Woes Now," *Inc.*, April 2005, pp. 105–12; Vanessa Fuhrmans, "One Cure for High Health Costs," *The Wall Street Journal,* February 11, 2005, pp. A1 and A8; and "The Top 10 Funding Issues for HSA Account Owners and Employers," *Employee Benefit News*, January 1, 2006.
46. Michael Hayes, "Outrageous Employee Benefits," *Journal of Accountancy*, May 1, 2005.
47. Leah Carlson, "Businesses Decry Proposed Tax on Flex Benefits," *Employee Benefit News*, May 1, 2005.
48. "What Role Will HRIS Be Playing This Year?" *Human Resource Department Management Report*, January 1, 2005, and "Outsourcing Benefits Administration?" *Payroll Manager's Report*, February 1, 2005.
49. Samuel Greengard, "Sun's Shining Example," *Workforce Management*, March 1, 2005, and Ellen Gragg, "Are Telecommuting and Flextime Dead?" *OfficeSolutions*, January 1, 2006.
50. Linda Stern, "Just Don't Ask If They're in PJs," *Newsweek*, February 21, 2005, and Michelle Conlin, "Call Centers in the Rec Room," *BusinessWeek*, January 23, 2006.
51. "How New Style Exit Interviews Can Help You Reduce Turnover," *Human Resource Department Management Report*, April 1, 2005; Lee Conrad, "Hated Working Here? Log On and Vent," *Bank Technology News,* April 1, 2005; and Robert Half, "Enlightening Departures," *NZ Business*, August 1, 2005.

52. Betsy Morris, "How Corporate America Is Betraying Women," *Fortune*, January 10, 2005, pp. 64–74, and Mitchell Pacelle, "Citigroup Faces Gender-Bias Suit Over Broker-Account Assignments," *The Wall Street Journal*, April 1, 2005, p. C4.
53. Justin Miller, "Group Responds in Affirmative Action Case at U. Michigan," University Wire, February 2, 2005.
54. "Deliberate Bias Not Needed to Win Age Suits," *USA Today*, March 30, 2005.

## CHAPTER 12

1. Jennifer C. Kerr, "Dissident Unions Press AFL-CIO," *Capital Times*, June 16, 2005, and John B. Schnapp, "Auto Workers of the World Unite . . ." *The Wall Street Journal*, January 25, 2006.
2. John Hoerr, "Lucky Strike," *Harper's*, June 1, 2005, and Kris Maher, "Share of the U.S. Work Force in Unions Held Steady in 2005," *The Wall Street Journal*, January 21, 2006.
3. Paolo Quattrone, "Is Time Spent, Passed, or Counted? The Missing Link Between Time and Accounting History," *Accounting Historian's Journal*, June 1, 2005, and Paula Dobbyn, "Alaska High in Union Tally," *Anchorage Daily News*, January 21, 2006.
4. Danielle Welty, "U. Nebraska Student Plans Mock Sweatshop to Raise Student Awareness," University Wire, March 21, 2005, and Schnapp, "Auto Workers of the World Unite . . ."
5. Robert Ross, "Sweated Work, Weak Bodies: Anti-Sweatshop Campaign and Languages of Labor," *Journal of Social History*, June 22, 2005.
6. Shelia Burt, "Festival Gears to Honor Legendary Labor Leader Mother Jones," *St. Louis Post-Dispatch*, June 13, 2005.
7. Stephan Franklin, "Sunday Not Just Another Working Day," *Chicago Tribune*, May 2, 2005.
8. www.aflcio.org, and William Glanz, "Sweeney Smooths Over Split in Labor; AFL-CIO Still a Player with Clout," *Washington Times*, January 17, 2006.
9. "A Crack in Big Labor's Armor," *Washington Times*, June 23, 2005.
10. William Glanz, "Unions to Quit AFL-CIO; Four Dissatisfied Groups Walk Out on Convention," *Washington Times*, July 25, 2005.
11. Terence Chea, "Service Workers Board OKs AFL-CIO Split," AP Online, June 11, 2005; Stephen Franklin, "Child-Care Coup Only a Baby Step for Labor," *Chicago Tribune*, January 7, 2006; and Will Lester, "United Farm Workers Leave AFL-CIO," AP Online, January 13, 2006.
12. www.aflcio.org, and William Glanz, "Farm Union Leaves AFL-CIO," *Washington Times*, January 13, 2006.
13. James Pope, "How Americans Lost the Right to Strike, and Other Tales," *Michigan Law Review*, December 1, 2004.
14. Ritu Kalra, "Labor Paints a Target on Union-Election Law," *Hartford Courant*, June 14, 2005.
15. Brad Dawson, "Goodyear Asheboro Workers Again Opt for Union," *Rubber & Plastics News*, June 27, 2005, and Damian J. Troise, "NLRB Judge Cites Commercial Bakery Chef Solutions for Labor Law Violations," *New Haven Register*, January 27, 2006.
16. "Big Labor's Secrets," *The Wall Street Journal*, April 25, 2005, p. A14.
17. Rick S. Bender, "Like Its Big Brother, CAFTA Hurts Labor," *Seattle Post-Intelligencer*, May 10, 2005.
18. Jack Ewing, "The Decline of Germany," *BusinessWeek International,* February 17, 2003, p. 46, and Karen Lowry Miller, "A Danish Conspiracy," *Newsweek International*, January 19, 2006.
19. "AFGE Wins $20 Million Initial Payment for DHS Employees in National Grievance Over Unpaid Overtime," PR Newswire, June 9, 2005, and "Steelworkers Announce Members Ratified First Union Contract for Oroville Hospital Employees," PR Newswire, January 3, 2006.
20. "National Mediation Board Puts UPS Talks with IPA in Recess," Business Wire, June 23, 2005, and Paul Monies, "Settlements Offered in DHL-Teamsters Dispute," *Daily Oklahoman*, January 6, 2006.
21. Jennifer Koons, "National Mediation Board," *National Journal*, June 18, 2005, and "World Airways, Pilots Resume Negotiations," AP Online, January 25, 2006.
22. "Continental Airlines Seeks Federal Mediation with Its Flight Attendant Union," PR Newswire, June 21, 2005, and "Strike Potential Grows as Northwest Mechanics Request End to Mediation," Business Wire, July 5, 2005.
23. Samuel Estreicher, Michael Heise, and David Sherwyn, "Assessing the Case for Employment Arbitration: A New Path for Empirical Research," *Stanford Law Review*, April 1, 2005.
24. Dennis Maffezzoli, "Life Isn't Fair . . . and Neither Is Baseball's Draft," *Sarasota Herald Tribune*, June 7, 2005, and Mike Fitzpatrick, "Willis, Soriano File for Arbitration," AP Online, January 14, 2006.
25. Joshua S. Lipshutz, "The Courts Inplicit Roadmap: Charting the Prudent Course at the Juncture of Mandatory Arbitration Agreements and Class Action Lawsuits," *Stanford Law Review*, April 1, 2005; "New York City Firefighters Union Introduces Online Voting for Members in the Military Serving in Iraq and Afghanistan," PR Newswire, June 14, 2005; and David Nakamura and Thomas Heath, "Baseball to Seek Arbitration Over D.C. Stadium," *Washington Post*, January 4, 2006.
26. Terrence Nguyen, "UPS Deal Sparks Overnite-Teamsters Uncertainty," *Fleet Owner*, May 19, 2005.
27. Terry Ganey, "Governor Rescinds Collective Bargaining," *St. Louis Post-Dispatch*, May 10, 2005, p. B1, and Mike Wells, "Deputies' Vote Accepts Pay Deal with Sheriff," *Tampa Tribune*, January 1, 2006.
28. Diane E. Lewis, "A New Breed of Union Chief in Midst of Risky Strike Move," *Boston Globe*, May 24, 2005.
29. Rachel Osterman, "UFW Ready to Boycott Gallo—Again," *Sacramento Bee*, June 14, 2005.
30. Tim Panaccio, "Charities Also a Casualty of NHL Lockout," *Philadelphia Inquirer*, January 8, 2005, and "NHL Lockout Chronology," AP Online, July 13, 2005.
31. Martin J. Moylan, "Northwest Airlines Mechanics, Cleaners Union to Accept Concessions," *St. Paul Pioneer Press*, June 25, 2005; Dave Carpenter, "Deal Removes Strike Threat to United Employee Wage and Benefit Concession Should Help Company Emerge from Bankruptcy," *St. Louis Post-Dispatch*, June 1, 2005; and Susan Carey, "Northwest Machinists Pact Could Save Jobs," *The Wall Street Journal*, January 23, 2006.
32. Rick Popely, "Union: GM Retirees' Benefits Are Off Limits," *Chicago Tribune*, June 15, 2005.
33. Joseph B. White, Lee Hawkins Jr., and Karen Lundegaard, "UAW Is Facing Biggest Battles in Two Decades," *The Wall Street Journal*, June 10, 2005, p. B1.
34. "Labor of Politics," *The Wall Street Journal*, March 4, 2005, p. A14.

35. Lou Dobbs, "Disorganized Labor," *U.S. News & World Report*, March 7, 2005, p. 48, and Michael L. Diamond, "Unions Enjoying Growth in State," *Asbury Park Press*, January 21, 2006.
36. George Archibald, "NEA Bolsters Gays on Policy, Practices; Conservative Discussion Stifled," *Washington Times*, July 8, 2005.
37. Norm Brodsky, "Why the Union Can't Win," *Inc.,* March 2005, pp. 55–56.
38. Hoyt N. Wheeler, "The Third Way," *Business & Economic Review*, January–March 2005, pp. 6–8.
39. Jeffrey Pfeffer, "In Praise of Organized Labor," *Business 2.0*, June 2005, p. 80.
40. Caroline Daniel, "A Top-Flight Employee Strategy," *Financial Times*, April 4, 2005, p. 8.
41. Kurt Badenhausen, Kiri Blakeley, Allison Fass, Sasha Haines-Stiles, Tomas Kellner, Peter Newcomb, Dorothy Pomerantz, Brett Pulley, and Amanda Schupak, "The Celebrity 100," *Forbes*, July 4, 2005, p. 102.
42. Louis Lavelle, "A Payday for Performance," *BusinessWeek*, April 18, 2005, pp. 78–80.
43. Betty Sosnin, "A Fresh Look at Executive Pay," *HRMagazine*, May 1, 2005, and Becky Yerak, "SEC Wants Executive Pay, Perks Spelled Out," *Chicago Tribune*, January 18, 2006.
44. Jeffrey Pfeffer, "The Pay-for-Performance Fallacy," *Business 2.0*, July 2005, p. 64.
45. Michael Sisk, "Taking Stock," *Inc*., April 2005, p. 34.
46. David Nicklaus, "CEO Pay and Performance," *St. Louis Post-Dispatch*, April 18, 2005, p. B1.
47. Geoffrey Colvin, "Hewlett-Packard: Home of the CEO Pay Heist," *Fortune*, May 2, 2005, p. 52, and Louis Lavelle, "A Payday for Performance," *BusinessWeek*, April 18, 2005, pp. 78–80.
48. William F. Buckley, "Capitalism's Boil," *National Review*, May 23, 2005, p. 58, and David Barkholz, "Delphi Compensation Plan Troubles Lenders; Banks Want to Base Pay on Performance," *Automotive News*, January 9, 2006.
49. Louis Lavelle, "Consulting Even Beyond the Grave," *BusinessWeek*, February 28, 2005, p. 14.
50. Joann S. Lublin, "CEO Bonuses Rose 46.4% at 100 Big Firms in 2004," *The Wall Street Journal*, February 25, 2005, p. A1; "Tax 'Gross-Ups' in the Stratosphere," *St. Louis Post-Dispatch*, January 31, 2006; and Lauren Etter, "Are CEOs Worth Their Weight in Gold?" *The Wall Street Journal*, January 21, 2006.
51. Blanca Torres, "Pace of Chief Executive Compensation Continues Rapid Rise," *Baltimore Sun*, May 15, 2005.
52. Jack Ewing and Justin Hibbard, "The Bell Tolls for Germany Inc.," *BusinessWeek*, August 15, 2005, pp. 40–41.
53. Geoffrey Colvin, "CEO Knockdown," *Fortune*, April 5, 2005, pp. 19–20.
54. Kate O'Sullivan, "Targeting Executive Pay," *CFO*, March 2005, p. 15, and Becky Yerak, "SEC Wants Executive Pay, Perks Spelled Out," *Chicago Tribune*, January 18, 2006.
55. Robert J. Samuelson, "No Joke: CEOs Do Some Good," *Newsweek*, April 18, 2005, p. 49.
56. Janet Stiles, "Equal Pay for the Sexes," *HRMagazine*, May 1, 2005, p. 64.
57. John Leo, "Of Men, Women, and Money," *U.S. News & World Report*, March 21, 2005, p. 64.
58. Donald L. Schunk, "The Gender Wage and Participation Gap," *Business & Economic Review*, July–September 2005, pp. 8–12.
59. Linda Tischler, "Bridging the (Gender Wage) Gap," *Fast Company*, January 2005, pp. 85–87.
60. Carol Kleiman, "Worklife Column," *Chicago Tribune*, August 23, 2005.
61. Michael Zwieg and Danielle Kiwak, "Legal Perspectives (Sexual Harrassment/Discrimination)," *Delaney Report*, March 21, 2005.
62. Jennifer Gill, "Gender Issues," *Inc.,* April 2005, pp. 38–39.
63. Ibid.
64. William Warful, "Sex Ed: Insulating Yourself from Sexual Harassment Litigation," *Risk Management*, February 1, 2005, and Elizabeth Feigin Befus, "New Sexual Harassment Prevention Measures," *National Real Estate Investor*, January 1, 2006.
65. Mary-Kathryn Zachary, "Labor Law for Supervisors: Insurance Issues in Sexual Harassment Cases," *Supervision*, August 1, 2005.
66. Melissa Hennessy, "Adventures in Babysitting," *Human Capital 2005 CFO*, 2005, pp. 53–55.
67. "Senate Proposes FY06 Freeze for Key Child Care Services," *Report on Preschool Programs*, July 27, 2005, and "Final Spending Bills Cut 1 Percent from Child Care, Other Programs," *Report on Preschool Programs*, January 11, 2006.
68. www.workingmother.com.
69. Nadine Heintz, "Can I Bring the Kids?" *Inc*., June 2004, and H. J. Cummins, "Keeping Baby Close to Work," *Star Tribune*, January 21, 2006.
70. www.haemonetics.com.
71. "HR Sees Lack of Core Competencies in New Workers," PR Newswire, June 19, 2005, and Charley Hannagan, "Elder Care Becomes Issue in Workplace," Syracuse (New York) *Post-Standard*, January 1, 2006.
72. Della Pacheco, "Aging Employees, Parents Face Care-Giving Challenges," *Indianapolis Business Journal*, April 11, 2005, p. 20.
73. Marlon Manuel, "Bridging the Distance; Adult Kids Spend More Time on Road to Help Aging Parents," *Atlanta Journal and Constitution*, May 5, 2005.
74. Marilyn Blake, "Creating a Drug-Free Workplace: Sobering Facts That May Impact Your Safety Efforts," *Rural Telecommunications*, July 1, 2005.
75. Ngina Jackson, "There Is a Bottom Line to Workplace Drug Testing," *Washington Informer*, January 12, 2005.
76. Ericka C. Wheeler, "Workplace Drug Abuse on the Rise," *Indianapolis Recorder*, February 18, 2005.
77. "Employers Continue to Order More Sophisticated Drug Testing," *Drug Detection Report*, September 1, 2005, and Chad Umble, "Testing Times," *Lancaster New Era*, January 10, 2006.
78. "OSHA Prepares to Turn the Spotlight on Workplace Homicides," *OSHA Security Director's Report*, January 1, 2005.
79. John Strahinich, "Workplace Violence, Death Threats Surging," *Boston Herald*, May 6, 2005, and Tim Molloy, "Deaths in Calif. Shootings Rise to Seven," AP Online, February 1, 2006.


## CHAPTER 13


1. George Potts, "Deconstructing the M Word," *Inc.*, January 2006, pp. 16–17.
2. Jena McGregor, "Would You Recommend Us?," *BusinessWeek*, January 30, 2006, pp. 94–95.
3. V. Kumar, Rajkumar Venkatesan and Werner Reinartz, "Knowing What to Sell, When, and to Whom," *Harvard Business Review*, March 2006, pp. 131–137.
4. Michael Lowenstein, "What Do Customers Want?" *Deliver*, March 2006, p. 17.

5. Joseph C. Nunes and Xavier Dréze, "Your Loyalty Program Is Betraying You," *Harvard Business Review*, April 2006, pp. 124–131.
6. Daniel Yee, "Students Demand Veggies," *Washington Times*, January 12, 2006, p. A2.
7. Lora Kolodny, "Things I Can't Live Without: Andy Berliner," *Inc.*, July 2005, p. 64.
8. John Wilman, "Valued Measure of Success," *Financial Times*, April 3, 2006, pp. 1 and 4 of a Special Report called Global Branch.
9. "Priced to Sell," *Entrepreneur*, February 2006, p. 100.
10. Geoff Williams, "Name Your Price," *Entrepreneur*, September 2005, pp. 108–15.
11. Peter Lattman, "Cheapskates," *Forbes*, July 4, 2005, pp. 76–77.
12. Rafi Mohammed, "Pick the Right Price Point to Pull in Profits," *Entrepreneur*, January 2006, p. 27.
13. Geoffrey Colvin, "The FedEx Edge," *Fortune*, April 3, 2006, pp. 77–84.
14. Stephanie Clifford, "Running Through the Legs of Goliath," *Inc.*, February 2006, pp. 103–9.
15. John E. (Jack) West, "Listening to the Customer," *Quality Digest*, February 2006, p. 16.
16. Louise Lee, "Too Many Surveys, Too Little Passion?," *BusinessWeek*, August 1, 2005, p. 38.
17. Thomas H. Davenport, "Competing on Analytics," *Harvard Business Review*, January 2006, pp. 99–107.
18. Jena McGregor, "Would You Recommend Us?," *BusinessWeek*, January 30, 2006, pp. 94–95.
19. Thomas H. Davenport, "Competing on Analytics," pp. 99–107.
20. Kim Thomas, "Anthropologists Get to the Bottom of Customers' Needs," *Financial Times*, May 24, 2005, p. 7.
21. Steven Levy and Brad Stone, "The New Wisdom of the Web," *Newsweek*, April 3, 2006, pp. 47–53.
22. Steve Hamm, "An eBay for Business Software," *BusinessWeek*, September 19, 2005, pp. 78–79.
23. Daniel Yankelovich and David Meer, "Rediscovering Market Segmentation," *Harvard Business Review*, February 2006, pp. 122–31.
24. Magali Rheault, "The Kiplinger Monitor," *Kiplinger's*, July 2005, p. 22.
25. Americus Reed II and Lisa E. Bolton, "The Complexity of Identity," *MIT Sloan Mangement Review*, Spring 2005, pp. 18–22.
26. Robyn Waters, "The Secrets of Feel-Good Shopping," *Kiplinger's*, January 2006, pp. 20–22.
27. Michael V. Copeland, "Everyone Is Investing in B-to-¢ B," *Business 2.0,* April 2006, p. 30.


## CHAPTER 14


1. Michael D. Lemonick, "Are We Losing Our Edge?," *Time*, February 13, 2006, pp. 22–31.
2. Avery Johnson, "Hotels Take 'Know Your Customer' to New Level," *The Wall Street Journal*, February 7, 2006, pp. D1 and D3.
3. Paul Taylor, "Can There Be Any Future for Traditional Telephony?" *Financial Times*, February 22, 2006, p. 1.
4. Mike Hogan, "Go the Distance," *Entrepreneur*, April 2006, p. 57.
5. Steven Gray, "Beyond Burgers," *The Wall Street Journal*, February 18–19, 2006, pp. A1 and A7.
6. Kathleen Kingsbury, "McMakeover Deluxe," *Time Inside Business*, March 2006, p. A17.
7. Jeremy Grant, "Golden Arches Bridge Local Tastes," *Financial Times*, February 9, 2006, p. 10.
8. Jeremy Grant, "Appetite for Plastic Makes Fast Food a Short Order," *Financial Times*, January 3, 2006, p. 17.
9. Kate MacArthur, "BK, McD's Wake Up to Premium Coffee," *Advertising Age*, April 11, 2005, p. 14.
10. Kate MacArthur, "McD's '05 Strategy Hinges on Balance,'" *Advertising Age*, January 10, 2005, p. 6.
11. Kate MacArthur, "Beyond Burgers: McD's Tests CDs, Photos, Rings," *Advertising Age*, May 23, 2005, pp. 3 and 147.
12. Elizabeth Esfahani, "7-Eleven Gets Sophisticated," *Business 2.0*, January–February 2005, pp. 92–110.
13. Jeremy Grant, "Wendy's Hopes Breakfast Will Restore Sales and Profits," *Financial Times*, February 7, 2006, p. 18.
14. David Welch and David Kiley, "Chrysler Slips Out of Cruise Control," *BusinessWeek*, February 6, 2006, p. 39.
15. Kate MacArthur, "Sweet Nothings?," *Advertising Age*, March 28, 2005, p. 3.
16. Katrina Booker, "The Pepsi Machine," *Fortune*, February 6, 2006, pp. 68–72.
17. Jack Neff, "Small Ball: Marketers Rely on Line Extensions," *Advertising Age*, April 11, 2005, pp. 10–11.
18. Leonard L. Berry, Venkatesh Shankar, Janet Turner Parish, Susan Cadwallader, and Thomas Dotzel, "Creating New Markets Through Service Innovation," *MIT Sloan Management Review*, Winter 2006, pp. 56–63.
19. Pascal Zachary, "Evolution of an Envelope," *Business 2.0,* April 2006, p. 70.
20. Margaret Webb Pressler, "Appealing to the Senses," *Washington Post,* February 19, 2006, pp. F1 and F5.
21. Joyce Gemperlein, "But the Dang Thing Won't Open," *Washington Post*, June 12, 2005, p. F5.
22. Kathy Lally, "Leaders of the Packed," *Washington Post*, March 27, 2005, pp. F1 and F4.
23. "RFID on the Rise," *Quality Digest*, February 2006, p. 9.
24. Paul Kaihla, "Sexing Up a Piece of Meat," *Business 2.0*, Arpril 2006, pp. 72–76.
25. Mure Dickie and Raphael Minder, "China Makes Progress Against Sellers of Fakes," *Financial Times*, January 17, 2006, p. 6.
26. Julia Boorstin, "Louis Vuitton Tests a New Way to Fight the Faux," *Fortune*, May 16, 2005, p. 34.
27. Michele Kayal, "Brand Quest: This Summer, Aston Hotels Will Rebrand as ResortQuest Hawaii," *TravelAge West*, May 30, 2005.
28. Jonathan Drew, "Limited Brands Shifts Focus to Beauty Products," *St. Louis Post-Dispatch*, June 12, 2005.
29. Nanette Byrnes, Rober Berner, Wendy Zellner and William C. Symonds, "Branding: Five New Lessons," *BusinessWeek*, February 14, 2005, pp. 26–28.
30. Niraj Dawar, "What Are Brands Good For?," *Sloan Management Review*, Fall 2004, pp. 31–37.
31. Susumu Ogawa and Frank T. Piller, "Reducing the Risks of New Product Development," *MIT Sloan Management Review*, Winter 2006, pp. 65–71.
32. Youngme Moon, "Break Free from the Product Life Cycle," *Harvard Business Review*, May 2005, pp. 86–94.
33. Alison Stein Wellner, "Boost Your Bottom Line by Taking the Guesswork Out of Pricing," *Inc.*, June 2005, pp. 72–82.
34. Bradley Johnson, " 'Discount' Ploy Could Bite Detroit," *Advertising Age*, July 11, 2005, pp. 1 and 33.
35. Julian Hunt, "Losing Their Religion? Julian Hunt Finds Worshipers at the Altar of EDLP Are Having Their Faith Challenged," *Grocer*, March 12, 2005.
36. John Springer, "Better Pricing, Promotions Required, Speakers Say," *Supermarket News*, May 9, 2005.

## CHAPTER 15


1. Lorraine Woellert, "HP Wants Your Old PCs Back, " *BusinessWeek*, April 10, 2006, pp. 82–83.
2. Rob Carter, "The FedEx Edge," *Fortune*, April 3, 2006, pp. 77–84.
3. Kyle Cattani, Hans Sebastian Heese, Wendell Gilland, and Jayashankar Swaminathan, "When Manufacturers Go Retail," *MIT Sloan Management Review*, Winter 2006, p. 9.
4. Daniel Nissanoff, "Futureshop," *Fast Company*, January–February 2006, p. 103.
5. Judith Turnock, "Victories in Capitalism," an ad in *Forbes*, June 5, 2006, pp. 83ff.
6. Chad Terhune, "Supply-Chain Fix for Pepsi," *The Wall Street Journal*, June 6, 2006, p. B3.
7. Jeffrey Ressner, "Long Tail's Tribe," *Time Inside Business*, July 2006, pp. A11–A12.
8. Thomas M. Anderson, "Checkups on the Run," *Kiplinger's*, May 2006, p. 96.
9. Chris Taylor, "Imagining the Google Future," *Business 2.0*, January–February 2006, pp. 79–86.
10. Daniel Nisanoff, "Join the Online Bazaar," *Kiplinger's*, May 2006, pp. 22–24.
11. Greg Holden, "Fast Forward," *Entrepreneur*, May 2006, pp. 63–69.
12. Mya Frazier, "Lampert Can Make Money, but Can He Remake Retail?," *Advertising Age*, September 26, 2005, pp. 16–17.
13. Nick Wingfield, "Buying an iPod from a Vending Machine," *The Wall Street Journal*, September 1, 2005, pp. D1 and D2.
14. Alan Farnham, "The Party That Crashed Retailing," *Forbes*, November 1, 2005, pp. 80–81.
15. Lawrence M. Kimmel, "Direct Marketing Can't Get Lost in the Mail," *Advertising Age*, January 16, 2006, p. 15.
16. Brian Nadel, "Business Process Management for Dummies," *Fortune*, March 21, 2005, pp. 163ff.
17. Richard Wilding, "The Ghost in the Supply Chain," *Financial Times*, a special part called Mastering Uncertainty, April 7, 2006, p. 5.
18. Hau L. Lee, "The Triple-A Supply Chain," *Harvard Business Review*, October 2004, pp. 102–12.
19. Mahender Singh, "Supply Chain Reality Check," *Sloan Management Review*, Spring 2005, p. 96.
20. Ibid.
21. Lorraine Woellert, "HP Wants Your Old PCs Back, " OP at
22. Michael Aneiro, "Shipping Woes Boost Freight Co-ops," *Inc.*, March 2005, p. 25.
23. Robert Wright, "Growing Ships," *Financial Times*, May 23, 2005, p. 6.
24. Gianpaolo Callioni, Xavier de Mongros, Regine Slagmulder, Luk N. Van Wassenhove, and Linda Wright, "Inventory-Driven Costs," *Harvard Business Review*, March 2005, pp. 135–40.
25. Myra Frazier, "The Store of the Future," *Advertising Age*, January 16, 2006, pp. 1 and 23.
26. Glenn Townes, "Looking at RFID?," *Black Enterprise*, May 2005, p. 58, and Roger Morton, "RFID compliance: Year Two," *Logisticstoday*, January 1, 2006.
27. Tom Mashberg, "Brown Goes Bluetooth," *Technology Review*, June 2005, p. 42.
28. Tom Lester, "The Cost of Not Caring for Your Customer," *Financial Times*, January 30, 2006, p. 10.


## CHAPTER 16


1. Bruce Nussbaum, "Davos Will Be Different," *BusinessWeek*, January 23, 2006, p. 96.
2. Randall Rothenberg, "Despite All the Talk, Ad and Media Shops Aren't Truly Integrated," *Advertising Age*, March 27, 2006, p. 24.
3. Stephen Baker, "Wiser About the Web," *BusinessWeek*, March 27, 2006, pp. 54–58.
4. "Fact Pack," a supplement to *Advertising Age*, 2005.
5. Abbey Klaassen, "Fourth and Goal: Eight Spots Left in Super Bowl," *Advertising Age*, January 9, 2006, p. 3.
6. Suzanne Vrancia, "Advertising Spotlight," *The Wall Street Journal*, February 1, 2006, p. B3A.
7. Dan Beucke, "Pitching In," *BusinessWeek*, January 30, 2006, p. 13.
8. Westin Renehart, "What Your Targets Are Saying," *Advertising Age*, March 28, 2005, p. 94.
9. Thomas Mucha, "Stronger Sales in Just 28 Minutes," *Business 2.0*, June 2005, pp. 56–60.
10. David Kiley, "Counting the Eyeballs," *BusinessWeek*, January 16, 2006, pp. 84–85.
11. Anne Marie Fink, "Press Fast-Forward for TV Salvation," *Advertising Age*, June 20, 2005, p. 18.
12. Aline van Duyn, "Demand for 'On Demand,'" *Financial Times*, January 3, 2006, p. 9.
13. Megan Barnett, "All the News," *U.S. News & World Report*, August 1, 2005, pp. 36–38.
14. Fred Vogelstein, "Yahoo's Brilliant Solution," *Fortune*, August 8, 2005, pp. 42–55.
15. Stephanie N. Mehta, "How the Web Will Save the Commercial," *Fortune*, August 8, 2005, pp. 58–60.
16. Ronald Grover, "Mad Ave Is Starry-Eyed Over Net Video," *BusinessWeek*, May 23, 2005, pp. 36–39.
17. Rieva Lesonsky, "The Doctor Is In," *Entrepreneur*, March 2006, p. 10.
18. Matthew Maier, "Online Video Ads Get Ready to Grab You," *Business 2.0*, May 2005, pp. 25–26.
19. Anne Fisher, "Salespeople in the Catbird Seat," *Fortune*, June 13, 2005, p. 130.
20. Ibid.
21. V. Kumar, Rajkumar Venkatesan and Werner Reinartz, "Knowing What to Sell, When, and to Whom," *Harvard Business Review*, March 2006, pp. 131–137.
22. Chip Jones, "This Salesman's Alive and Focused," *Richmond Times-Dispatch*, May 22, 2005, pp. A1 and A8.
23. Paul Holmes, "Programs That Demonstrate the Value of Public Relations," *Advertising Age*, January 24, 2005, pp. C12–C16.
24. Paul Holmes, "Senior Marketers Are Sharply Divided About the Role of PR in the Overall Mix," *Advertising Age*, January 24, 2005, pp. C1 and C2.
25. "The Birth of PR," *Forbes*, January 9, 2006, p. 34.
26. Lora Kolodny, "The Art of the Press Release," *Inc.*, March 2005, p. 36.
27. Julie Bennett, "The New World of Marketing: Word-of-Mouth Campaigns Replace Traditional Tools," *The Wall Street Journal*, February 7, 2006, p. B7.
28. Matthew Creamer, "Word of Mouth Gaining Respect of Marketers," *Advertising Age*, January 23, 2006, pp. 3 and 28.
29. Frank ahrens, "30 million Blogs and Counting," *The Washington Post*, February 26, 2006, p. F7.
30. Simon Dumenco, "Oh Please, a Blogger Is Just a Writer with a Cooler Name," *Advertising Age*, January 16, 2006, p. 18.
31. David Kirkpatrick, "Book Buzz—Via Blogs," *Fortune*, May 16, 2005, p. 198.
32. Hillary Johnson, "Why I Read Business Blogs Every Day," *Inc.*, August 2005, pp. 105–6.
33. www.wikipedia.org.

## CHAPTER 17


1. Ellen Heffes, "Accounting: Trends Affecting the Next Generation of Accountants," *Financial Executive*, September 1, 2005.
2. Scott Leibs, "Who's Counting?" *CFO*, May 2005, p. 15, and Maureen Nevin Duffy, "Oh, The Places You'll Go! CPA's Today Have Career Options Even They Never Envisioned 100 Years Ago," *Journal of Accountancy*, October 1, 2005.
3. Paramjit Mahli, "The CPAs Are Coming," *Financial Planning*, September 30, 2005.
4. Robert Tie, "The Case for Private Company GAAP," *Journal of Accountancy*, May 1, 2005; Ian P. N. Hague, "Convergence: In Search of the Best: CPAs Should Understand How U.S. and Foreign Accounting Standards Influence Each Other," *Journal of Accountancy*, January 1, 2006; and C. J. Prince, "Closing the GAAP," *Entrepreneur*, January 1, 2006.
5. Mary Flood, "Andersen Document Shredding Conviction Overturned," *Houston Chronicle*, June 1, 2005, and Elwin Green, "Scandal also Brought Arthur Andersen Down," *Pittsburgh Post-Gazette*, January 31, 2006.
6. J. Bonasia, "Deloitte Going Against the Grain in 'Mixing' Accounting, Consulting," *Investors Business Daily*, February 24, 2005, p. A4.
7. Steve Hamm, "Death, Taxes, & Sarbanes-Oxley," *BusinessWeek*, January 17, 2005, pp. 28–32, and Terence O'Hara, "Excavations in Accounting; To Monitor Internal Controls, Firms Dig Ever Deeper into Their Books," *Washington Post*, January 30, 2006.
8. Paul Barr, "Hard to Handle: New Guidance Helps Boards Navigate Sarbanes-Oxley," *Modern Healthcare*, August 8, 2005, and "Exercising Leadership: Tougher Internal Controls Are on the Way as the PCAOB Flexes Its Oversight Muscles," *Controller's Report*, December 1, 2005.
9. Kate O'Sullivan, "School Days," *CFO*, September 2004, pp. 106–7, and Kathe McKimmie, "Choosing an Accountant: Tips to Find the Right Firm for Your Business," *Indiana Business Magazine*, March 1, 2005.
10. Christopher J. Zinski, "Whistling to the Audit Committee: How an Internal Investigation Begins," *Community Banker*, August 1, 2005, and Joseph T. Wells, "When the Boss Trumps Internal Controls: What a Difference a Hotline, a Routine Audit and the Right Reporting Chain Could Have Made," *Journal of Accountancy*, February 1, 2006.
11. Richard Brody, "A Proactive Approach to Combating Fraud: Seven Preemptive Measures Can Help Internal Auditors Deliver a Knockout to Fraudulent Activity," *Internal Auditor*, April 1, 2005, and Joanne Sammer, "New Kids on the Block: More Companies Are Hiring Chief Accounting Officers," *Journal of Accountancy*, February 1, 2006.
12. Robert D. Novak, "Threat of the Auditors," *Washington Post*, April 7, 2005, p. A31, and Michael P. Rose, "Internal Audit Can Deliver More Value," *Financial Executive*, January 1, 2006.
13. Alan Reinstein, "Issues in Accounting," *RMA Journal*, February 1, 2005.
14. Floyd Norris, "How KPMG Was Given a Lesson in Humility," *International Herald Tribune*, August 30, 2005, and Celia Whitaker, "Bridging the Book-Tax Accounting Gap," *Yale Law Journal*, December 1, 2005.
15. Mark Henricks, "Over-the-Counter Accounting Help," *Crain's Chicago Business*, May 9, 2005.
16. Randy Johnston, "Management & Compliance: Accounting Software Is Morphing to Business Management Software," *CPA Technology Advisor*, August 1, 2005.
17. Nicole Torres, "Count Me In: Scared of Numbers? With These Accounting Tips You Won't Be," *Entrepreneur*, April 1, 2005.
18. Randy Johnston, "Your Accounting Software Should Have Business Management & Analytics," *CPA Technology Advisor*, September 1, 2005, and Gregory L. LaFollette, "The Dream Team: Meet America's Tax and Accounting Technology Dream Team," *CPA Technology Advisor*, January 1, 2006.
19. Barbara Hagenbaugh, "Rules Spur Demand for Accountants," *USA Today*, January 18, 2005, p. B1, and "Back to Basics Necessitated by Law," *USA Today*, December 1, 2005.
20. Richard W. Rahn, "Where Is the Balance Sheet?" *Washington Times*, April 21, 2005, and Lisa Kianoff, "Financial Statements: An Often Unused Tool for the Masses," *CPA Technology Advisor*, January 1, 2006.
21. Mike Vorster, "Balance Sheet Basics," *Construction Equipment*, February 1, 2005, and Joseph S. Eastern, "How to Read a Balance Sheet," *Family Practice News*, January 1, 2006.
22. David Whelan, "Beyond the Balance Sheet: Hot Brand Values," *Forbes*, June 20, 2005, pp. 113–15.
23. Kenneth Dogra, "Accounting for Goodwill: Why Are Firms Willing to Pay So Much for Takeovers When the Goodwill Burden Is Onerous?" *Financial Management*, May 1, 2005, and Greg Paeth, "Scripps Weighs Sale of Channel," *Cincinnati Post*, February 3, 2006.
24. Jennifer Heebner, "Snapshot of an Income Statement," *Jewelers Circular Keystone*, May 1, 2005, and "Here's a Sweet Lesson on Income Statements," *The Bergen County (New Jersey) Record*, April 14, 2005.
25. Virginia Munger Kahn, "Beating the Cash Crunch," *BusinessWeek Small Biz*, Spring 2005; Kenneth L. Parkinson, "Cash Flow Forecasting: Do It Better and Save," *Financial Executive*, January 1, 2006; and John S. McClenahen and Traci Purdum, "Cash Flow Is King," *Industry Week*, February 1, 2006.
26. Sativa Ross, "All in the Numbers: Does Your Income Statement and Balance Sheet Provide a Winning Combination?," *Aftermarket Business*, May 1, 2005.
27. Tom Judge, "Liquidity Ratio Can Help Spot Cash Gap," *Powersports Business*, March 14, 2005.
28. Martin Labbe, "Devil's in the Details," *Fleet Owner*, May 1, 2005.


## CHAPTER 18


1. Jane von Bergen, "Calling All Accountants," *Philadelphia Enquirer*, October 12, 2005; David Simanoff, "Accountants Can Count on More Job Offers," *Tampa Tribune*, June 26, 2005; and Mike Allen, "Supply and Demand Works in Accountants' Favor: Firms Are Desperately Seeking Skilled CPAs," *San Diego Business Journal*, January 16, 2006.
2. Tom Lowry, "The CFO Behind Adelphia's Rescue," *BusinessWeek*, April 11, 2005; and Gregory J. Millman, "Two Generations of CFOs: How Different Are They?," *Financial Executive*, November 1, 2005; "Paradigm Shifts," *CFO*, March 2005, pp. 37–54; and Terry Maxon, "EDS Loses CFO to eBay: Swan, Who Helped Lead Turnaround, to Take Similar Job at eBay," *Dallas Morning News*, February 22, 2006.
3. Tom Herman, "Charities May See More Scrutiny," *The Wall Street Journal*, March 2, 2005, p. D3.
4. Don Durfee, "The Top Spot," *CFO*, October 2005, pp. 52–60.
5. Fara Warner, "Keeping the Crisis in Chrysler," *Fast Company*, September 1, 2005, pp. 68–73.

6. Chris Cather, "The World According to GAAP," *Motley Fool*, April 25, 2005; Robert Tie, "The Case for Private Company GAAP," *Journal of Accountancy*, May 1, 2005; and William A. Grimm, "Raising Capital? Then Make Sure to Mind the GAAP," *Orlando Business Journal*, February 17, 2006.
7. Joseph V. Hermanson and Dana R. Raghunandan, "Factors Associated with U.S. Companies' Investment in Internal Auditing," *Accounting Horizons*, June 1, 2005.
8. Gary McWilliams, "Dell Puts Cash Flow to Work," *The Wall Street Journal*, April 25, 2005, p. C3.
9. Michael Hunstad, "Better Forecasting: Know Your Cash Flows," *Financial Executive*, May 1, 2005, and Kenneth L. Parkinson, "Cash Flow Forecasting: Do It Better and Save," *Financial Executive*, January 1, 2006.
10. Patrick Kilts, "Effective Cash Flow Management Improves Investment Outlook," *Crain's Cleveland Business*, September 19, 2005; Bruce Perryman, "Grow with the Flow," *Stitches Magazine*, January 1, 2005; and Andi Gray, "The Optimum Growth Model," *Fairfield County Business Journal*, January 30, 2006.
11. Tim Reason, "Budgeting in the Real World," *CFO*, July 2005, pp. 43–48.
12. Charles Mulford, "A Best Practices Approach to Cash Flow Reporting: Implications for Analysis," *Business Credit*, January 1, 2005.
13. Jordan I. Shifrin, "All Boards Must Grapple with Budget Issues," *Daily Herald*, June 4, 2005.
14. Jennifer M. Mueller, "Evaluating Internal Financial Reporting Controls," *Health Care Financial Management*, August 1, 2005; Andrea Morrow, "Financial Solutions for Nonprofit Organizations: Out of Control," *Michigan Chronicle*, July 12, 2005; and "Financial Executives Research Foundation Issues Study of Internal Controls Reporting," PR Newswire, May 27, 2005.
15. Andrew Ashby, "Do's and Don'ts for Good Cash Management," *Financial Executive*, October 1, 2005.
16. Nathan Parmelee, "Why Free Cash Flow Matters," *Motley Fool*, August 28, 2005, and Chris Cather, "Operating Cash Flow Tricks," *Motley Fool*, March 28, 2005.
17. Phyllis Micahnik, "Credit Collection and Cash Flow," *Contracting Business*, August 1, 2005, and Tom Diana, "Changing Ways of Managing Collection and Deduction," *Business Credit*, September 1, 2005.
18. "Visa Says Its Check Card Is Transforming the Way People Pay for Goods," *Wireless News*, September 27, 2005; Jeff DeMoss, "Credit Card Companies Increase Minimum Monthly Payment Requirements," *Standard-Examiner*, January 1, 2006; and Yasmin Assemi, "Credit, Debit Cards Helped Revolutionize Shopping," *Stockton (California) Record*, February 12, 2006.
19. Susan C. Thompson, "Mixing Personal, Business Funds Is a Formula for Bankruptcy," *St. Louis Post-Dispatch*, August 5, 2005, and Carolyn M. Brown, "Borrowing from Dad: Financing from Relatives and Friends Has Risks and Rewards," *Black Enterprise*, January 1, 2005.
20. Kate Ashford, "Lend to a Friend (Without Regret): Four Things to Do When a Pal Asks for a Loan," *Money*, November 1, 2005.
21. Deanna Galbraith, "Borrowing Money Effectively," *San Fernando Valley Business Journal*, August 29, 2005, and Kerry Hall, "Stable Financing Is a Constant Concern for Small Businesses," *Charlotte Observer*, January 11, 2006.
22. David Barkholz, "Delphi Crisis May Hurt Vendors: CEO Miller Says Company Can Pay Its Bills—Even If It Is Bankrupt," *Automotive News*, September 26, 2005, and Marc Heller, "Despite Co-Op's Bankruptcy, Executive Says Farmers Served Best by DFA, Others," *Watertown Daily Times*, January 1, 2006.
23. www.gecapital.com.
24. Liza Casabona, "Origins of Factoring Come Full Circle," *WWD*, September 19, 2005, and "Texas Oil Drill Bit Manufacturer Taps into a $1 Million Factoring Credit Line," PR Newswire, February 1, 2006.
25. Jan Norman, "Accounts Receivable Financing Helps Some Small Businesses Grow," *Orange County Register*, August 9, 2005, and Joseph Ingrassia, "Venture Merchant Banking: Financing 'Sales' vs. 'Assets,'" *Financial Executive*, January 1, 2006.
26. Paulette Thomas, "For Sale: Unpaid Invoices," *Crain's Chicago Business*, May 9, 2005, and Liza Casabona, "CIT: Consolidation Remains a 'Huge Issue,'" *WWD*, February 13, 2006.
27. Jean Ende, "Card Issuers Charge After Owners," *Crain's New York Business*, July 18, 2005.
28. James C. Johnson, "Plastic Debt," *Black Enterprise*, September 1, 2005; Rick Archer, "Credit Card Issuers Targeting Small Businesses," *Westchester County Business Journal*, May 23, 2005; and Mark Calvey, "Small Biz Charge Is On," *San Francisco Business Times*, January 20, 2006.
29. Amy Barrett, "Pfizer's Funk," *BusinessWeek*, February 28, 2005, and Jennifer Bayot, "Pfizer's Pain Inflamed by Weak Sales," *International Herald Tribune*, April 6, 2005.
30. Amy Borrus, "The SEC: Cracking Down on Spin," *BusinessWeek*, September 26, 2005.
31. Randy Myers, "Stuck on Yellow," *CFO*, October 2005, pp. 81–86; and "Venture Capital: Not-So-Easy Money," *CFO*, October 2005, p. 20; and Michael Liedtke, "Venture Capital Investment Remained Level in 2005," AP Worldstream, January 24, 2006.
32. Suzette Parmley, "Trump Banking on Bankruptcy Reorganization Approval Tuesday," *Philadelphia Inquirer*, April 4, 2005, and James P. Miller, "Wrigley Bond Issue Would Come with a Pleasant Flavor," *Chicago Tribune*, April 7, 2005.


## CHAPTER 19


1. John J. Oslund, "JARGON; Investment Bankers," *Minneapolis Star Tribune*, March 24, 2006.
2. "U.S. Institutional Investors Boost Control of U.S. Equity Market Assets," *Conference Board*, October 10, 2005, and Paula L. Rechner, "A Meta-Analysis of the Effects of Executive and Institutional Ownership on Firm Performance," *Journal of Managerial Issues*, December 22, 2005.
3. David Henry, "Debt Valley Days," *BusinessWeek*, March 20, 2006, pp. 50–51.
4. Joanna Chung, Jennifer Hughes, and Gillian Tett, "Into the Unknown: Long Bonds Are Back, but Can We Be Sure of the World of 2055?" *Financial Times*, May 16, 2005, p. 15; Rich Miller, "Betting Big on Low Yields," *BusinessWeek*, May 16, 2005, p. 38; and Ben White and Nell Henderson, "Strong Demand Greets Return of the Long Bond," *Washington Post*, February 10, 2006.
5. Richard Lehmann, "The Year of the Convertible," *Forbes*, February 14, 2005, p. 134, and Stan Luxenberg, "Convertible Opportunities," *Registered Rep*, September 1, 2005.
6. David Landis, "Dividends with Room to Grow," *Kiplinger's Personal Finance*, February 1, 2006.
7. Jim Mueller, "Dividend Myths Foolishly Debunked, Part 2," *Motley Fool*, March 9, 2006.

8. "Preferred Stock, Explained," *Motley Fool*, January 26, 2006.
9. www.nyse.com.
10. Joseph Weber, Mara Der Hovanesian, Amy Burrus, and Mike McNamee, "The Tremors form Two Trading Titans," *BusinessWeek*, May 9, 2005, pp. 82–93; Joseph Weber, "The Merc's Bad Example," *BusinessWeek*, May 16, 2005, p. 85; and Susan Diesenhouse, "NYSE, Archipelago Complete Merger: Marriage Called Likely to Transform Industry," *Chicago Tribune*, March 8, 2006.
11. www.amex.com.
12. Peter Chapman, "In the Footsteps of NASDAQ at Chicago Stock Exchange, *Traders*, March 1, 2005, and Gregory Bresiger, "Traders, Lawmakers Back NASDAQ Exchange Plan," *Traders*, January 1, 2006.
13. www.nasdaq.com.
14. Andrew McIntosh, "Taser Stock Faces Delisting," *Sacramento Bee*, November 26, 2005, and Tom Murphy, "Standard Stock Sinks Close to Crucial Mark," *Indianapolis Business Journal*, February 20, 2006.
15. Matt Krantz, "NASDAQ, NYSE Wage 'Interesting Battle' Over ECNs," *USA Today*, April 25, 2005, and John Gapper, "Stock Exchanges Go Peer-to-Peer," *Financial Times*, April 28, 2005, p. 15.
16. Robert Kuttner, "Cox's SEC: Investors Beware," *BusinessWeek*, June 27, 2005, p. 134, and Amy Borrus, "The Unlikely Hardnose at the SEC," *BusinessWeek*, January 23, 2006.
17. Greg Griffin, "Feds Investigate Insider Trading, False Reporting by Former Qwest Officials," *Denver Post*, August 28, 2005, and Tom Webb and Tim Huber, "SEC Targets Nash Finch: Food Company, Under Insider Trading Cloud, Replaces CEO, General Counsel" *Saint Paul Pioneer Press*, February 17, 2006.
18. Mike Pramik, "Former Marketing Professor Faces Civil Trial After Insider-Trading Conviction," *Columbus Dispatch*, June 22, 2005, and "Former Broker Admits Insider Trading," AP Online, March 7, 2006.
19. www.nyse.com.
20. Jeremy Grant, "Taifex Raises Its International Profile," *Financial Times*, March 29, 2005; Jeremy Grant, "Getting a Jump on the Competition," *Financial Times*, May 4, 2005; and Jennifer Hughes, "Eurex Issues a Challenge to CME," *Financial Times*, June 17, 2005.
21. www.etrade.com.
22. Toddi Gutner, "Broker or Advisor?" *BusinessWeek*, April 11, 2005, p. 104; Gregory Crawford, "Wall Street's Scramble; Brokerage Firms Offer New Services, but Money Managers Seek Elimination of Conflicts of Interest," *Pensions & Investments*, August 22, 2005; and Brooke Southall, "Smith Barney's Use of 'Advisor' Irks NAPFA; Organization Contends the Term Is Misleading," *Investment News*, January 9, 2006.
23. Virgil Larson, "Online Stock Brokerage Ameritrade Tests $5 Trading Model," *Omaha World-Herald*, January 14, 2005.
24. "At the Bell; Schwab Reduces Online Trading Fee," Investment News, February 7, 2005, and Don Mecoy, "Oklahomans Trade Stocks from Home," *Daily Oklahoman*, March 8, 2006.
25. Toni Hansen, "Placing Electronic Orders," *SFO*, April 2006, pp. 88–93.
26. Joseph Weber, "E*Trade Rises from the Ashes," *BusinessWeek*, January 17, 2005.
27. Allan Sloan, "Beware the Quiet Bear," *Newsweek*, March 21, 2005, and Mark Davis, "Bulls and Bears See the Same Signs but Interpret Them Differently," *The Kansas City Star*, December 31, 2005.
28. Will Deener, "Penny Stocks Almost Always Promise More Than They Deliver," *Dallas Morning News*, October 27, 2005, and Dan O'Connell, "Spamming Penny Stocks," *Kiplinger's Personal Finance*, January 1, 2006.
29. "Apple's Board Approves 2-For-1 Stock Split," AP Worldstream, February 11, 2005, and David Nicklaus, "When It Comes to Stocks, Is It Better to Split Hairs or Shares?" *St. Louis Post-Dispatch*, February 10, 2006.
30. Meg Richards, "Socially Responsible Funds a Challenge," AP Online, October 12, 2005, and Julie Tripp, "Social(k) Funds Aim for Greener Portfolios," *Oregonian*, February 26, 2006.
31. Walter Updegrave, "Crystal Ball on the Fritz? Try These Funds," *Money*, August 1, 2005, and R. C. Balaban, "Mutual Funds Must Fit the Investor, Each Other," *Waterloo Courier*, March 12, 2006.
32. Matt Blackman, "The Secret to Winning the ETF Game," *Stocks, Futures & Options Magazine*, May 2005, pp. 69–71, and Joseph B. James III, "Exchange Traded Funds Offer New Means to Buy into Stock Market," *San Antonio Business Journal*, March 3, 2006.
33. James Mackintosh, Bernard Simon, and Richard Beales, "GM and Ford Are Cut to Junk," *Financial Times*, May 6, 2005; Tom Walker, "As Rates Rise, Junk Bonds Lose Luster," *Atlanta Journal & Constitution*, October 29, 2005; and David Henry, "Why Junk Bonds Are Getting Junked," *BusinessWeek*, February 13, 2006.
34. Meg Richards, "Beware of Putting Too Much into Junk Bonds," Bergen County (New Jersy) *Record*, June 24, 2005; and Ilana Polyak, "Time to Trash Your Junk," *Kiplinger's Personal Finance*, March 1, 2006.
35. Peter Garnham, "A Wild Ride for Coffee as Speculators Jump on Price Swings," *Financial Times*, May 11, 2005, p. 24; David Silverman, "It's All About Supply and Demand," *Stocks, Futures & Options Magazine*, November 2005, pp. 69–73; and Gail Marks Jarvis, "Commodities Best Digested in Small Bites," *Chicago Tribune*, February 12, 2006.
36. Oliver Ryan, "Chicago's Making a Contracts Killing," *Fortune*, November 11, 2005.
37. Kate Ryan, "Future Still on Hold at Board of Trade," *Crain's Chicago Business*, November 11, 2005, and "Chicago Board of Trade to Become More Accessible," *Kiplinger Agriculture Letter*, February 3, 2006.
38. Kate Ryan, "Eurex Aims at Merc's Currency Futures Biz," *Crain's Chicago Business*, September 19, 2005.
39. www.djindexes.com.
40. Brad Delong and Konstantin Magin, "The Last Bubble Was Brief, but It Was Still Irrational," *Financial Times*, April 19, 2005, p. 19.


## CHAPTER 20


1. David Rocks and Hiroko Tashiro, "Coins Lose Cachet in Japan," *BusinessWeek*, October 31, 2005, p. 12, and Ben King, "The Mobile Phone That Puts Cash Out of Business," *Financial Times*, December 16, 2005, p. 9.
2. "Anybody Got a Ten-spot?," *Money*, November 2005, pp. 166–70, and "Government Debuts Colorful $10 Currency," *Washington Times*, March 3, 2006, p. C11.
3. Michael Freedman, "The Invisible Bankers," *Forbes*, October 17, 2005, pp. 94–104.
4. Reshma Kapadia, "Will the Greenback Rise?" *SmartMoney*, August 2005, p. 34, and Ralph Atkins, "Heading Up or Tailing Off?," *Financial Times*, February 16, 2006, p. 11.

5. Andrea Lehman, "Dark Dollar Signs," *Hispanic Business*, June 2005, pp. 22–24.
6. Mortimer B. Zuckerman, "Don't Look Now, But . . .," *U.S. News & World Report*, August 29, 2005, p. 90.
7. Reshma Kapadia, "After Three Years of Doldrums, Will the Greenback Rise?," *Smart Money*, August 2005, p. 34.
8. Editorial called "Hamilton and Jefferson," *St. Croix Review*, January 2005, pp. 2–6.
9. Jeffrey R. Kosnett, "Finally, Banks Take Savers Seriously," *Kiplinger's*, June 2005, pp. 23–24.
10. Terence O'Hara, "Area Gets an All-Day Bank Fight," *Washington Post*, June 2, 2005, pp. A1 and A8, and Crystal Detamore-Rodman, "Work with Me," *Entrepreneur*, April 2006, p. 65.
11. Kathleen Terence O'Hara, "Piggy Banker," *Washington Post*, February 12, 2006, pp. F1 and F6.
12. Jonathan Birchall, "Wal-Mart Ignites Bank Regulatory Debate," *Financial Times*, February 21, 2006, p. 20.
13. Addison Wiggin, "Play the Slots at Your Bank!," *AGORA Financial Forum*, September 2005, p. 3.
14. James B. Stewart, "Inflation Is Back," *Smart Money*, June 2005, pp. 43–44.
15. Anne Kadet, "How to Dump Your Bank," *Smart Money*, January 2005, pp. 84–88.
16. Terence O'Hara, "Area Gets All-Day Bank Fight," *Washington Post*, June 2, 2005, pp. A1 and A8.
17. Mara Der Hovanesian, "Coffee, Tea, or Mortgage?," *BusinessWeek*, April 3, 2006, pp. 48–49.
18. Megan Johnston, "Five Questions to Ask Before You Bank Online," *Money*, April 2005, p. 57.
19. Frank Norton, "Buried Alive," *Washington Times*, January 31, 2006, pp. C1 and C8.
20. Bernard Condon, "Pyrrhic Victory," *Forbes*, May 23, 2005, p. 52.
21. Jane Bryant Quinn, "Capital Ideas," *Newsweek*, March 21, 2005, p. E26.
22. "The Rise of Debit Cards," *Kiplinger's*, April 2005, p. 24.
23. Nicole Gull, "Taking the Pain Out of Payday," *Inc.*, January 2005, p. 36.
24. Kate Linebaugh, "How Foreign Banks Scaled the Chinese Wall," *The Wall Street Journal*, February 23, 2006, pp. C1 and C5.
25. Bruce Bartlett, "Wolfowitz in Bank Clothing?," *Washington Times*, March 23, 2005, p. A14.
26. Fareed Zakaria, "The Education of Paul Wolfowitz," *Newsweek*, March 28, 2005, p. 37.
27. Ann Gerhart, "World Bank's Loan Rangers," *Washinton Post*, June 9, 2005, pp. C1 and C4.
28. Edward T. Pound and Danielle Knight, "On Top of the World," *U.S. News & World Report*, April 3, 2006, p. 28.
29. David Frum, "The World's Banker," *National Review*, April 11, 2005, p. 22.
30. Richard Rahn, "A Run on the World Bank," *Washington Times*, June 3, 2005, p. A18, and Edward T. Pound and Danielle Knight, "Cleaning Up the World Bank," *U.S. News & World Report*, April 3, 2006, pp. 40–51.
31. Sebastian Mallaby, "Wolfowitz's Corruption Agenda," *Washington Post*, February 20, 2006, p. A21.
32. Chris Giles and Andrew Balls, "Call for IMF Reform Draws Muted Echo," *Financial Times*, February 24, 2006, p. 3.
33. Martin Wolf, "The World Needs a Tough and Independent Monetary Fund," *Financial Times*, February 22, 2006, p. 13.


## BONUS CHAPTER A


1. Aaron Bernstein, "Wal-Mart vs. Class Actions," *BusinessWeek*, March 21, 2005, pp. 73–74, and Caroline E. Mayer, "Rules Would Limit Lawsuits; U.S. Agencies Seek to Preempt States," *Washington Post*, February 16, 2006.
2. John Schmeltzer, "Altria Prepares for Breakup," *Chicago Tribune*, November 5, 2004, and "Altria Preparing to Break Up Company," *National Petroleum News*, January 1, 2005.
3. Lori Becker, "Persistence of New Piper," *Palm Beach Post*, May 22, 2005.
4. Lanny R. Berke, "Design for Safety—The Next Hot Button: How to Stay Out of Court," *Machine Design*, February 17, 2005, and Edward Martin, "Athwart Torts: Why the Case Politicians and Special-Interest Groups Make That Lawsuits Are Crippling the Economy Doesn't Stand Up," *Business North Carolina*, January 1, 2006.
5. Deb Riechmann, "Bush Takes Aim at Asbestos Lawsuits," AP Online, January 7, 2005, and Tom Ramstack, "Senate OKs Asbestos Bill, 98-1; Debate Set on Trust Fund, Plan to End Lawsuits," *Washington Times*, February 8, 2006.
6. Nena Groskind, "Landlords: Lead Pain Can Lead to Lawsuits," *Boston Herald*, May 20, 2005, and Eric Tucker, "Jury Finds Former Lead Paint Makers Liable," AP Online, February 23, 2006.
7. Alex Berensen, "Bitter Pill: New Chief Seeks Remedy for Ailing Merck," *International Herald Tribune*, May 21, 2005; Janet McConnaughey, "Jury Gives Merck Victory in Federal Vioxx Lawsuit," *St. Louis Post-Dispatch*, February 18, 2006; and John Curran, "Vioxx Lawyers Burn the Midnight Oil," *St. Louis Post-Dispatch*, March 28, 2006.
8. Matthew Boyle, "Can You Really Make Fast Food Healthy?" *Fortune*, August 9, 2004, pp. 135–39 and Andrew Johnson, "Food Industry Faces Challenges, Culver Says: Obesity Lawsuits, Customer Demands Are Top Concerns," *Milwaukee Journal Sentinel*, March 14, 2006.
9. Rupal Parekh, "Court Reinstates Portion of McDonald's Obesity Suit," *Business Insurance*, January 31, 2005, and "McDonald's Facing Lawsuits over French Fry Wheat, Dairy Ingredients," AP Worldstream, February 19, 2006.
10. Bill Condie, "Lawsuit Setback for McDonald's," *Evening Standard*, January 26, 2005.
11. "Restaurants Are Urged to Give Customers Nutrition Information," *The Wall Street Journal*, February 15, 2005, and Matthew Kish, "Banning 'McLawsuits,'" *Indianapolis Business Journal*, February 27, 2006.
12. Jack Stack, "How to Save American Business," *Inc.*, February 1, 2005, and Gail Appleson, "Companies Like Missouri's Tort Reforms," *St. Louis Post-Dispatch*, March 27, 2006.
13. Mark A. Hoffmann, "Tort Reform Backers Hope to Stay on Winning Streak," *Business Insurance*, January 9, 2006.
14. Gwendolyn Bounds, "You Have a Great Idea. Now What?," *The Wall Street Journal*, May 9, 2005, pp. R1–R3.
15. Raymund Flandez, "Get a Patent," *The Wall Street Journal*, May 9, 2005, p. R9.
16. Larry Greenemeier, "The Impossibility of Patents," *Information Week*, March 21, 2005, pp. 14–16, and Michael Orey, "The Patent Epidemic," *BusinessWeek*, January 9, 2006.
17. Bounds, "You Have a Great Idea. Now What?," p. R1.
18. Peter Busbaum, "Safeguarding Intellectual Property," *Fortune*, March 12, 2005, pp. S2–S4.
19. Peter Davidson, "Patents Out of Control," *USA Today*, January 13, 2004, p. B1.
20. www.uspto.org.

21. Thomas M. Burton, "Medtronic Settles Patent Fight," *The Wall Street Journal*, April 25, 2005, p. B4.
22. Nick Wingfield, "Ruling Threatens Sony's U.S. Sales of PlayStations," *The Wall Street Journal*, March 29, 2005, p. A3.
23. Anne Field, "How to Knockout Knockoffs," *BusinessWeek Small Biz*, Spring 2005, pp. 71–76.
24. Susan Kuchinskas, "Mr. Smith Went to Washington for Patent Reform," www.Internet.com, March 10, 2005.
25. Sean Michael Kerner, "A Primer on Software Patents," www.*Internet.com*, May 20, 2005 and Greg Griffin, "Trolling for Patents," *Denver Post*, March 12, 2006.
26. Steven R. Hansen, "Patent Rules Makes Process Protection a Challenge," *Los Angeles Business Journal*, May 2, 2005.
27. Greenemeier, "The Impossibility of Patents," and Andrew Bridges, "Justices Take on Question of Patents," AP Online, March 21, 2006.
28. Lee Wilson, *A Friendly Handbook to Protecting and Profiting from Trademarks* (New York, New Yorker, Allworth Press, 2005).
29. "Federal Court Orders Otamedia to Pay Philip Morris USA $173 Million in Damages for Trademark Infringement," Business Wire, March 14, 2005, and Greg Griffin, "Indian Motorcycle Trademark Lives On Despite Bumps," *Denver Post*, February 6, 2006.
30. Frederik Balfour, "Fakes!," *BusinessWeek*, February 7, 2005, pp. 55–64, and "Czech Brewery Wins Trademark Dispute over Anheuser-Busch in Finland," AP Worldstream, January 5, 2006.
31. "Independent Film and Television Producer Leigh Ann Burton Files Civil Complaint Alleging Defendant Lions Gate and Dellaverson Breached Their Contract and Misrepresented Facts Related to Usher Film 'Dying for Dolly,'" Business Wire, April 4, 2005, and Beth Musgrave, "Judge Rules Lawyers in Diet Drug Case Breached Contract," *Lexington Herald-Leader*, March 10, 2006.
32. Ken Bensinger, "Spanish Soap Opera: Televisa-Univision Suit May Mask Deeper Struggle," *Variety*, May 16, 2005, and "Former Manager Sues the Killers, Alleging Breach of Contract," AP Worldstream, February 23, 2006.
33. Thomas A. Hemphill, "Modernizing U.S. Antitrust Law: the Role of Technology and Innovation," *Business Economics*, April 1, 2005, and Dan Wallach, "Four U.S. Chemical Companies Served Subpoenas for Possible Antitrust Violations," *Beaumont Enterprise*, March 19, 2006.
34. Raf Casert, "Microsoft Meets Deadline to Submit Papers for Landmark Antitrust Case," AP Worldstream, June 1, 2005, and Becky Yerak, "Discover Takes on Rivals with Signature Debit Card," *Chicago Tribune*, February 14, 2006.
35. Jeffery Silva, "Antitrust Law's Future in Doubt," *RCR Wireless News*, May 23, 2005.
36. Tim Reason, "The Limits of Mercy," *CFO*, April 2005, pp. 61–66.
37. Lisa Aichlmayr, "Is It Unfair Pricing? Dealer Sues Goodyear, Florida Competitors: Claims Violations of Robinson-Patman Act," *Tire Business*, October 11, 2004, and "Supreme Court Rejects Ruling Against Volvo," AP Worldstream, January 11, 2006.
38. Lawrence B. Lindsey, "Assuring U.S. Competitiveness: Fair Antitrust Enforcement is Critical," *Washington Times*, June 3, 2005, and James P. Miller, "Lawsuits over 'Tying' Are Knottier after New Ruling," *Chicago Tribune*, March 2, 2006.
39. Jack Ewing, "Speak Softly and Carry a Thick Brief," *BusinessWeek*, March 20, 2006, pp. 46–48.
40. "SEC Tightening Oversight of Mutual Funds," *United Press International*, January 14, 2004, and Eileen Alt Powell, "AIG to Pay $1.64 Billion to Settle Charges," AP Online, February 10, 2006.
41. M. R. Kropko, "Ohio Lawmakers May Double Tax on Beer, Wine," *Cincinnati Post*, May 24, 2005; "Sensible Sin Tax?" *Chicago Tribune Business News*, May 28, 2005; and Gregory Hahn, "When We Indulge, the State Profits," *Idaho Statesman*, March 7, 2006.
42. Nancy Nall Derringer, "State Fund Gets $60 Million to Use for New Tax Credits," *Crain's Detroit Business*, May 23, 2005.
43. "States Line Up for Voluntary Internet Sales Tax Program," *Internet Week*, May 19, 2005.
44. "Fitch: 2005 Bankruptcy Reform Legislation a S-T Negative, L-T Positive for U.S. Credit Card ABS," Business Wire, March 15, 2005.
45. Sandra Block, "Filing Chapter 7 Bankruptcy Will Get Tougher Soon," *USA Today*, April 21, 2005, and Jennifer Brooks, "Harsher Bankruptcy Law Benefits Banks, Could Crush Some Consumers," Gannett News Service, February 10, 2006.
46. Michael Schroeder and Suein Hwang, "Sweeping New Bankruptcy Law to Make Life Harder for Debtors," *The Wall Street Journal*, April 6, 2005, pp. A1–A4, and "Personal Bankruptcy Filings Up 30 Pct," AP Online, March 25, 2006.
47. "Fitch: 2005 Bankruptcy Reform Legislation," and Michael J. Martinez, "Survey: New Bankruptcy Law Isn't Working," AP Online, February 22, 2006.
48. Ed Roberts, "Late-2005 Rush to File Bankruptcy Pushes Earnings to a 20-Year Low," *Credit Union Journal*, February 27, 2006.
49. David G. Loomis, "Competition in Local Telecommunications: There's More Competition Than You Think," *Business Economics*, April 1, 2005.
50. Ken Herman, "Chairman of SEC to Depart; Critics Say Donaldson Too Fond of Regulation," *Atlanta Journal and Constitution*, June 2, 2005.
51. Elaine Misonzhnik, "Grid Changes Taking the Strain," *Real Estate Weekly*, February 23, 2005, and Amit R. Paley and Terence O'Hara, "Electricity Deregulation: High Cost, Unmet Promises," *Washington Post*, March 12, 2006.


## BONUS CHAPTER B


1. Beth Stackpole, "Virtually Flawless?" *CIO*, May 15, 2005, pp. 58–64, and Allan Holmes, "The Changing CIO Role: The Dual Demands of Strategy and Execution," *CIO*, January 1, 2006.
2. Christopher Koch, "Who's Mining the Store?" *CIO*, May 15, 2005, pp. 52–56; Marianne Kolbasuk McGee and Chris Murphy, "Facing the Challenge," *InformationWeek*, March 28, 2005, pp. 22–24; and Jaime Capella, "The CIO's First 100 Days," *Optimize*, March 2006.
3. Daniel McGinn, "Movies on the Move," *Newsweek*, October 17, 2005, p. E4; Michael Hastings, "A Click Away: Internet TV," *Newsweek*, January 31, 2005, p. E10; Rana Foroohar, "Hi! The Net Is Calling," *Newsweek*, January 31, 2005, p. E4; Steven Levy, "Life Isn't Just as You Want It? Remix It!," *Newsweek*, March 28, 2005, p. 17; Karen Breslau and Daniel McGinn, "A Movie Classic for a New Age," *Newsweek*, October 17, 2005, pp. E6–E10; and "Google Enters Video-on-Demand Domain," *Screen Digest*, January 1, 2006.
4. Steve Hamm, "A Virtual Revolution," *BusinessWeek*, June 20, 2005, pp. 98–102, and Robert L. Mitchell, "Virtualization's Real Impact," *Computerworld*, March 13, 2006.
5. Meridith Levinson, "The Brain Behind the Big, Bad Burger," *CIO*, March 15, 2005, pp. 49–58, and Meridith Levinson, "Business Intelligence: Not Just for Bosses Anymore," *CIO*, January 15, 2006.

6. "Operational BI Comes of Age," *BusinessWeek*, May 23, 2005, pp. S2–S10, and Jennifer McAdams and Heather Havenstein, "What's Next: Business Intelligence," *Computerworld*, January 2, 2006.
7. Rick Whiting and Charles Babcock, "Integrate or Disintegrate," *InformationWeek*, March 21, 2005, pp. 20–22, and Alan Cane, "Super-Fast Blue Gene Looks for Answers," *Financial Times*, May 6, 2005, pp. 10.
8. Glover Ferguson, Sanjay Mathur, and Baiju Shah, "Evolving from Information to Insight," *MIT Sloan Management Review*, Winter 2005, pp. 51–58.
9. David H. Freedman, "What's Next," *Inc.*, April 2005, pp. 61–62; Laurie Sullivan, "Wal-Mart Assesses New Uses for RFID," *InformationWeek*, March 28, 2005, p. 30; Laurie Sullivan, "RFID Help from the Outside," *InformationWeek*, March 28, 2005, pp. 54–58; and Marc L. Songini, "Some Manufacturers Get Early RFID Payoff," *Computerworld*, March 13, 2006.
10. Accenture Technology Labs, "Sentiment Monitoring Services," case study, www.accenture.com.
11. Kevin M. Fickenscher, "The New Frontier of Data Mining," *Health Management Technology*, October 1, 2005.
12. Robert D. Hof, "The Future of Tech," *BusinessWeek*, June 20, 2005, pp. 73–82; Steven Levy, "Ma Bell's Kids Will Live on the Net," *Newsweek*, February 28, 2005, pp. 14; and Richard Waters, "It's the Internet, but Not as We Know It," *Financial Times*, April 20, 2005, p. 1.
13. Tom Nolle, "IP VPNs," *Telecommunications Americas*, June 1, 2005, and "Network-Based IP VPN Equipment Enabling Key Services for Service Providers Reports In-Stat," *Business Wire*, January 4, 2006.
14. "Enterprise Portals: Measurable Productivity and ROI Tools," Africa News Service, May 6, 2002, and Drew Robb, "Unifying Your Enterprise with a Global HR Portal," *HR Magazine*, March 1, 2006.
15. Michael V. Copeland, "How to Ride the Fifth Wave," *Business 2.0*, July 2005, pp. 78–85.
16. www.internet2.edu, and Scott Canon, "To Build a Better Net: Many Say Cyberspace Is in Need of Rethinking and Repair, Becoming as Perilous as It Is Valuable," *Kansas City Star*, January 22, 2006.
17. Michael Singer. "Moore's Law Relevant but Not Forever," *Internet News*, April 15, 2005, and John Markoff, "Moore's Law Enforcement," *International Herald Tribune*, February 21, 2006.
18. Mark David, "Will Moore's Law Run into a Power Roadblock?" *Electronic Design*, March 2, 2006, and Clint Boulton, "IBM Chip Path to Cheat Moore's Law?" *Internet News*, February 21, 2006.
19. Jay Greene, "Combat over Collaboration," *BusinessWeek*, April 18, 2005, pp. 64–66, and Brad Foss, "Telecommuters Tout Perks of Lifestyle," AP Online, March 14, 2006.
20. Cliff Edwards, "Wherever You Go, You're on the Job," *BusinessWeek*, June 20, 2005, pp. 87–96, and Roger Fillion, "Doing Homework: Telecommuting Jobs Benefit Workers, Help Companies Cut Costs," *Rocky Mountain News*, February 6, 2006.
21. Carol Kleiman, "Big Firms Like Working from Home," *Chicago Tribune*, August 9, 2005, and Brendan Sullivan, "New Options for CIOs in a Wire, Wired World," *CIO*, March 15, 2005, p. 24.
22. Daniel Roth, "The Great Data Heist," *Fortune*, May 16, 2005, pp. 66–75, and Dean Foust, "Keeping a Grip on Identity," *BusinessWeek*, March 28, 2005, pp. 32–33.
23. Michael Sivy, Pat Regnier, and Carolyn Bigda, "What No One Is Telling You about Identity Theft," *Money*, July 2005, pp. 95–99, and Julie Tripp, "Stolen PINs Expose Debit Cards to Fraud; Hundreds of Thousands Were Taken, Unlocking Access to Victims' Bank Accounts," *Post-Standard*, March 23, 2006.
24. Philip E. Ross, "Our Frankenputer," *Forbes*, March 14, 2005, pp. 64–68; Stephen Manes, "Ounces of Protection," *Forbes*, March 14, 2005, pp. 70; and Quentin Hardy, "Saving Software from Itself," *Forbes*, March 14, 2005, pp. 60–62.
25. Brian Grow, "New Sharks in the Web Surf," *BusinessWeek*, March 28, 2005, p. 14; Joan Caplin, "That Smell? Something Truly Phishy," *Money*, January 2005, p. 28; Steven Marlin, "Phishers Try to Reel in Small Businesses," *InformationWeek*, March 21, 2005, pp. 78–79; Scott Berinato, "How to Save the Internet," *CIO*, March 15, 2005, pp. 70–80; and Phyllis Furman, "Don't Get Hooked by Phishing Scam," *New York Daily News*, March 30, 2006.
26. Douglas Schweitzer, "Be Prepared for Cyberterrorism," *Computerworld*, March 28, 2005; John Mallery, "Cyberterrorism: Real Threat or Media Hype?" *Security Technology & Design*, May 1, 2005; "Are We Prepared for the Latest Type of Terrorism—Cyberterrorism?" Business Wire, September 20, 2005; and Ted Bridis, "U.S. Concludes 'Cyber Storm' Mock Attacks," AP Online, February 10, 2006.
27. Heather Zachary, "Navigating Communications Regulation in the Wake of 9/11," *Federal Communications Law Journal*, May 1, 2005.
28. Brian Grow, "Hacker Hunters," *BusinessWeek*, May 30, 2005, pp. 72–82.
29. Michael Myser, "Invasion of the Corporate Spyware," *Business 2.0*, March 2005, p. 30; Stephen H. Wildstrom, "Fighting Spyware: Microsoft to the Rescue?" *BusinessWeek*, February 7, 2005, p. 22; Martin J. Garvey, "Uncovering Spyware," *InformationWeek*, March 21, 2005, pp. 45–48; and "Spyware Companies Beware: New Consumer Protection Initiative to Combat Spyware and Other 'Badware,'" US Newswire, January 25, 2006.
30. www.w3.org/P3P.


## BONUS CHAPTER C


1. Nitin Nohria, "Risk, Uncertainty, and Doubt," *Harvard Business Review*, February 2006, pp. 39–40.
2. "Risk Management Gains Popularity," *Quality Digest*, September 2005, p. 11.
3. Kevin Hopkins, "The New Risk Environment," a special advertising section in *BusinessWeek*, October 24, 2005, pp. 131ff.
4. Andrew Jack, "The Bird Flu Issue Has Landed," *Financial Times*, January 10, 2006, p. 8.
5. Eric Schoeniger, "How to Plug the $13 Billion Leak," *BusinessWeek*, March 20, 2006, pp. 2–5, and M. Eric Johnson, "A Broader Context for Information Security," a special section in *Financial Times* called "Mastering Risk," September 16, 2005, pp. 1–12.
6. Charlie Ross, "Jackson Action," *The Wall Street Journal*, September 15, 2005, p. A21.
7. Jack Schuessler, "Food for Thought," *The Wall Street Journal,* May 17, 2005, p. A12.
8. James Altucher, "Living with Bird Flu, Sharks and Hurricanes," *Financial Times*, April 4, 2006, p. 10.
9. Andrea Felsted, "Doing Business in a Dangerous World," *Financial Times*, April 25, 2006, p. 1.
10. Deborah Wince-Smith, "Innovate at Your Own Risk," *Harvard Business Review*, May 2005, p. 25.
11. Keith Goffin and Rick Mitchell, "The Risks of Innovation," a special section in *Financial Times* called "Managing Risk," September 30, 2005, pp. 1–12.

12. Norm Brodsky, "How Much Risk Can You Take?," *Inc.*, December 2005, pp. 73–74.
13. Maggie Urry, "Business Stands By and Sees Profits Go to Blazes," *Financial Times*, April 25, 2006, p. 4.
14. Erin White, "Smaller Companies Join the Outsourcing Trend," *The Wall Street Journal*, May 8, 2006, p. B3.
15. Jack Kemp, "How Congress Stalks the Economic Upturn," *Washington Times*, August 4, 2005, p. A17.
16. Amy Borrus, Mike McNamee, and Howard Gleckman, "Up to His Neck in the Risk Pool," *BusinessWeek*, June 6, 2005, pp. 109–11.
17. Andrea Siedsma, "Insurance Well Spent," *Hispanic Business,* March 2006, pp. 48–50.
18. Jennifer Reingold, "Mastering Disaster," *Fast Company,* July/August 2006, pp. 38–39.
19. Katherine Mangu-Ward, "The Age of Corporate Environmentalism," *Reason*, February 2006, pp. 36–41.
20. Jeffrey Kluger, "Global Warming," *Time*, April 3, 2006, pp. 28–42, and Thomas G. Donlan, "Take the Hot Air Out of Global Warming," *Barron's*, December 5, 2005, p. 47.
21. David Ignatius, "Corporate Green," *Washington Post*, May 11, 2005, p. A17.
22. Holman W. Jenkins, "A Global Warming Worksheet," *The Wall Street Journal*, February 1, 2006, p. A15.
23. Chip Giller and David Roberts, "Green Gets Going," *Fast Company*, March 2006, pp. 73–78.


## BONUS CHAPTER D


1. Associated Press, "Teens Short of Knowledge When Asked About Money," *Washington Times*, April 6, 2006, pp. C10 and C11, and Cal Thomas, "Take Care of Yourself," *Washington Times*, February 13, 2005, p. B1.
2. Gill Plimmer, "A Race Between Education and Disaster," *Financial Times,* June 19, 2006, pp. 1 & 2.
3. Lauren Etter, "College Admissions: Is Gate Open or Closed?," *The Wall Street Journal*, March 25–26, 2006, p. A7.
4. Cox News Service, "Americans Unprepared for Retirement," *Washington Times*, April 5, 2006, p. C7.
5. Pamela Ginsberg, "Saving for the Future," *Washington Post*, March 28, 2005, pp. E1 and E9.
6. Jane Bennett Clark, "Budgets That Work (Honest)," *Kiplinger's*, January 2005, pp. 72–78.
7. Sakina P. Spruell, "Here's to 5 Years of DOFE," *Black Enterprise*, January 2005, pp. 61–64.
8. Kelly Greene, "Workers Lag on Retirement Savings," *The Wall Street Journal*, April 5, 2005, p. D2.
9. Robert J. Samuelson, "Our Vanishing Savings Rate," *Newsweek*, August 22, 2005, p. 38.
10. Matthew S. Scott, "5 Trends That Will Make You Rich," *Black Enterprise*, August 2005, p. 46.
11. Jane Bryant Quinn, "Escaping the Trap," *Newsweek*, September 15, 2005, p. 63.
12. James K. Glassman, "Where's the Bubble?" *Kiplinger's*, May 2005, pp. 30–32.
13. Rekha, "Banks Are Exploring Online Channels for a Share of the Pie," *Financial Times*, March 29, 2006, p. 4.
14. George Mannes, "I Owe U," *Money*, September 2005, pp. 106–10.
15. Michelle Singletary, "Hitting the Books on Personal Finance," *Washington Post*, August 25, 2005, p. D2.
16. Janet Bodnar, "Give Kids Credit? Not So Fast," *Kiplinger's*, March 2005, p. 91.
17. Maggie Dunphy, "The Best Credit Card for You," *SmartMoney*, August 2005, pp. 94–99, and Brooke Kosofsky Glassberg, "Go Ahead, Pick a Card, but Not Just Any Card," *Budget Travel*, April 2006, pp. 55–56.
18. Amanda Gengler, "Nab a Lower Credit-Card Rate," *Money*, May 2006, p. 45.
19. Mara Der Hovanesian, "Tough Love for Debtors," *BusinessWeek*, April 25, 2005, pp. 98–99.
20. Frank Norton, "Buried Alive," *Washington Times*, January 31, 2006, pp. C7 and C8.
21. Jane Bryant Quinn, "Planning for Trouble," *Newsweek*, January 9, 2006, pp. 57–59.
22. Elizabeth Warren, "Sick and Broke," *Washington Post*, February 9, 2005, p. A23.
23. Sarah Rubenstein, "A Hitch on Health Insurance," *Wall Street Journal,* June 10–11, 2006, p. B4.
24. David Futrelle, "Fear Factor," *Money*, October 2005, p. 86.
25. Barbara Basler, "Risky Business," *AARP Bulletin*, February 2005, pp. 10 and 13.
26. "Save More Tax Free," *Money*, March 2005, p. 78.
27. Jeanne Sahadi, "Will the Market Really Pay You Double Digits?" *Money*, May 2005, p. 54.
28. Mary Beth Franklin, "Family-Friendly Relief," *Kiplinger's,* July 2006, p. 88.
29. Mary Beth Franklin, "Retire Hassle Free," *Kiplinger's*, September 2005, pp. 94–95, and Lee Eisenberg, "The New Rest of Your Life," *Kiplinger's*, February 2006, pp. 65–66.
30. Laura D'Andrea Tyson, "Retirement Savings: A Boost for the Needy," *BusinessWeek*, June 6, 2005, p. 30.
31. Justin Steele, "How to Make a Million," *Kiplinger's*, May 2006, pp. 77–85.

# glossary

**401(k) plan (p. 646)** A savings plan that allows you to deposit pretax dollars and whose earnings compound tax free until withdrawal, when the money is taxed at ordinary income tax rates.

**absolute advantage (p. 62)** The advantage that exists when a country has a monopoly on producing a specific product or is able to produce it more efficiently than all other countries.

**accounting (p. 456)** The recording, classifying, summarizing, and interpreting of financial events and transactions to provide management and other interested parties the information they need to make good decisions.

**accounting cycle (p. 461)** A six-step procedure that results in the preparation and analysis of the major financial statements.

**accounts payable (p. 466)** Current liabilities involving money owed to others for merchandise or services purchased on credit but not yet paid for.

**acquisition (p. 132)** One company's purchase of the property and obligations of another company.

**administered distribution system (p. 417)** A distribution system in which producers manage all of the marketing functions at the retail level.

**administrative agencies (p. 575)** Federal or state institutions and other government organizations created by Congress or state legislatures with delegated power to pass rules and regulations within their mandated area of authority.

**advertising (p. 433)** Paid, nonpersonal communication through various media by organizations and individuals who are in some way identified in the advertising message.

**affirmative action (p. 311)** Employment activities designed to "right past wrongs" by increasing opportunities for minorities and women.

**agency shop agreement (p. 329)** Clause in a labor–management agreement that says employers may hire nonunion workers; employees are not required to join the union but must pay a union fee.

**agents/brokers (p. 404)** Marketing intermediaries who bring buyers and sellers together and assist in negotiating an exchange but don't take title to the goods.

**American Federation of Labor (AFL) (p. 324)** An organization of craft unions that championed fundamental labor issues; founded in 1886.

**annual report (p. 458)** A yearly statement of the financial condition, progress, and expectations of an organization.

**annuity (p. 642)** A contract to make regular payments to a person for life or for a fixed period.

**apprentice programs (p. 298)** Training programs involving a period during which a learner works alongside an experienced employee to master the skills and procedures of a craft.

**arbitration (p. 331)** The agreement to bring in an impartial third party (a single arbitrator or a panel of arbitrators) to render a binding decision in a labor dispute.

**assembly process (p. 239)** That part of the production process that puts together components.

**assets (p. 464)** Economic resources (things of value) owned by a firm.

**auditing (p. 459)** The job of reviewing and evaluating the records used to prepare a company's financial statements.

**autocratic leadership (p. 195)** Leadership style that involves making managerial decisions without consulting others.

**balance of payments (p. 64)** The difference between money coming into a country (from exports) and money leaving the country (for imports) plus money flows from other factors such as tourism, foreign aid, military expenditures, and foreign investment.

**balance of trade (p. 64)** The total value of a nation's exports compared to its imports over a particular period.

Note: Terms and definitions printed in italics are considered business slang, or jargon.

**balance sheet (p. 464)** The financial statement that reports a firm's financial condition at a specific time.

***ballyhooed*** *Talked about in an exaggerated way.*

**banker's acceptance (p. 563)** A promise that the bank will pay some specified amount at a particular time.

**bankruptcy (p. 586)** The legal process by which a person, business, or government entity unable to meet financial obligations is relieved of those obligations by a court that divides any assets among creditors, allowing creditors to get at least part of their money and freeing the debtor to begin anew.

**bargaining zone (p. 330)** The range of options between the initial and final offer that each party will consider before negotiations dissolve or reach an impasse.

**barter (p. 546)** The trading of goods and services for other goods and services directly.

***bear market*** *Situation where the stock market is declining in value and investors feel it will continue to decline.*

***been there, done that*** *Prior experience.*

**benchmarking (p. 221)** Comparing an organization's practices, processes, and products against the world's best.

**benefit segmentation (p. 364)** Dividing the market by determining which benefits of the product to talk about.

**blog (p. 446)** An online diary (Web log) that looks like a Web page but is easier to create and update by posting text, photos, or links to other sites.

**bond (p. 513)** A corporate certificate indicating that a person has lent money to a firm.

**bonds payable (p. 466)** Long-term liabilities that represent money lent to the firm that must be paid back.

**bookkeeping (p. 461)** The recording of business transactions.

***bottom line*** *The last line in a profit and loss statement; it refers to net profit or loss.*

**brain drain (p. 41)** The loss of the best and brightest people to other countries.

**brainstorming (p. 189)** Coming up with as many solutions to a problem as possible in a short period of time with no censoring of ideas.

**brand (p. 385)** A name, symbol, or design (or combination thereof) that identifies the goods or services of one seller or group of sellers and distinguishes them from the goods and services of competitors.

**brand association (p. 388)** The linking of a brand to other favorable images.

**brand awareness (p. 386)** How quickly or easily a given brand name comes to mind when a product category is mentioned.

**brand equity (p. 386)** The combination of factors—such as awareness, loyalty, perceived quality, images, and emotions—that people associate with a given brand name.

**brand loyalty (p. 386)** The degree to which customers are satisfied, like the brand, and are committed to further purchase.

**brand manager (p. 388)** A manager who has direct responsibility for one brand or one product line; called a product manager in some firms.

**brand name (p. 354)** A word, letter, or group of words or letters that differentiates one seller's goods and services from those of competitors.

**breach of contract (p. 581)** When one party fails to follow the terms of a contract.

**break-even analysis (p. 393)** The process used to determine profitability at various levels of sales.

***brightest days*** *The best of times for a person or organization.*

**broadband technology (p. 603)** Technology that offers users a continuous connection to the Internet and allows them to send and receive mammoth files that include voice, video, and data much faster than ever before.

**budget (p. 488)** A financial plan that sets forth management's expectations, and, on the basis of those expectations, allocates the use of specific resources throughout the firm.

***bull market*** *Situation where the stock market is increasing in value and investors feel it will continue to grow.*

**bundling (p. 394)** Grouping two or more products together and pricing them as a unit.

**bureaucracy (p. 210)** An organization with many layers of managers who set rules and regulations and oversee all decisions.

**business (p. 4)** Any activity that seeks to provide goods and services to others while operating at a profit.

**business cycles (p. 49)** The periodic rises and falls that occur in all economies over time.

**business environment (p. 10)** The surrounding factors that either help or hinder the development of businesses.

**business intelligence (p. 598)** Any of a variety of software applications that analyze an organization's raw data and take out useful insights from it.

**business law (p. 574)** Rules, statutes, codes, and regulations that are established to provide a legal framework within which business may be conducted and that are enforceable by court action.

**business plan (p. 165)** A detailed written statement that describes the nature of the business, the target market, the advantages the business will have in relation to competition, and the resources and qualifications of the owner(s).

**business-to-business (B2B) market (p. 361)** All the individuals and organizations that want goods and services to use in producing other goods and services or to sell, rent, or supply goods to others.

**buying stock on margin (p. 530)** Purchasing stocks by borrowing some of the purchase cost from the brokerage firm.

**cafeteria-style fringe benefits (p. 304)** Fringe benefits plan that allows employees to choose the benefits they want up to a certain dollar amount.

***cannibalize a business*** *One franchise pulls business away from another franchise.*

**capital budget (p. 488)** A budget that highlights a firm's spending plans for major asset purchases that often require large sums of money.

**capital expenditures (p. 493)** Major investments in either tangible long-term assets such as land, buildings, and equipment or intangible assets such as patents, trademarks, and copyrights.

**capital gains (p. 526)** The positive difference between the purchase price of a stock and its sale price.

**capitalism (p. 34)** An economic system in which all or most of the factors of production and distribution are privately owned and operated for profit.

**cash-and-carry wholesalers (p. 410)** Wholesalers that serve mostly smaller retailers with a limited assortment of products.

**cash budget (p. 488)** A budget that estimates a firm's projected cash inflows and outflows that the firm can use to plan for any cash shortages or surpluses during a given period.

**cash flow (p. 472)** The difference between cash coming in and cash going out of a business.

**cash flow forecast (p. 488)** Forecast that predicts the cash inflows and outflows in future periods, usually months or quarters.

***center stage*** *A very important position.*

**centralized authority (p. 211)** An organization structure in which decision-making authority is maintained at the top level of management at the company's headquarters.

**certificate of deposit (CD) (p. 555)** A time-deposit (savings) account that earns interest to be delivered at the end of the certificate's maturity date.

**certification (p. 325)** Formal process whereby a union is recognized by the National Labor Relations Board (NLRB) as the bargaining agent for a group of employees.

**certified internal auditor (CIA) (p. 460)** An accountant who has a bachelor's degree and two years of experience in internal auditing, and who has passed an exam administered by the Institute of Internal Auditors.

**certified management accountant (CMA) (p. 457)** A professional accountant who has met certain educational and experience requirements, passed a qualifying exam in the field, and been certified by the Institute of Certified Management Accountants.

**certified public accountant (CPA) (p. 458)** An accountant who passes a series of examinations established by the American Institute of Certified Public Accountants.

**chain of command (p. 210)** The line of authority that moves from the top of a hierarchy to the lowest level.

**channel of distribution (p. 404)** A whole set of marketing intermediaries, such as wholesalers and retailers that join together to transport and store goods in their path (or channel) from producers to consumers.

***climbed the ladder*** *Promoted to higher-level jobs.*

**closed shop agreement (p. 328)** Clause in a labor–management agreement that specified workers had to be members of a union before being hired (was outlawed by the Taft-Hartley Act in 1947).

**collective bargaining (p. 325)** The process whereby union and management representatives form a labor–management agreement, or contract, for workers.

**command economies (p. 43)** Economic systems in which the government largely decides what goods and services will be produced, who will get them, and how the economy will grow.

**commercial bank (p. 554)** A profit-seeking organization that receives deposits from individuals and corporations in the form of checking and savings accounts and then uses some of these funds to make loans.

**commercial finance companies (p. 497)** Organizations that make short-term loans to borrowers who offer tangible assets as collateral.

**commercialization (p. 389)** Promoting a product to distributors and retailers to get wide distribution, and developing strong advertising and sales campaigns to generate and maintain interest in the product among distributors and consumers.

**commercial paper (p. 498)** Unsecured promissory notes of $100,000 and up that mature (come due) in 270 days or less.

**commodity exchange (p. 531)** A securities exchange that specializes in the buying and selling of precious metals and minerals (e.g., silver, foreign currencies, gasoline) and agricultural goods (e.g., wheat, cattle, sugar).

**common law (p. 574)** The body of law that comes from decisions handed down by judges; also referred to as unwritten law.

**common market (p. 77)** A regional group of countries that have a common external tariff, no internal tariffs, and a coordination of laws to facilitate exchange; also called a *trading bloc*. An example is the European Union.

**common stock (p. 518)** The most basic form of ownership in a firm; it confers voting rights and the right to share in the firm's profits through dividends, if offered by the firm's board of directors.

**communism (p. 42)** An economic and political system in which the state (the government) makes almost all economic decisions and owns almost all the major factors of production.

**comparative advantage theory (p. 62)** Theory that states that a country should sell to other countries those products that it produces most effectively and efficiently, and buy from other countries those products that it cannot produce as effectively or efficiently.

**competition-based pricing (p. 393)** A pricing strategy based on what all the other competitors are doing. The price can be set at, above, or below competitors' prices.

**compliance-based ethics codes (p. 96)** Ethical standards that emphasize preventing unlawful behavior by increasing control and by penalizing wrongdoers.

**compressed workweek (p. 307)** Work schedule that allows an employee to work a full number of hours per week but in fewer days.

**computer-aided design (CAD) (p. 240)** The use of computers in the design of products.

**computer-aided manufacturing (CAM) (p. 240)** The use of computers in the manufacturing of products.

**computer-integrated manufacturing (CIM) (p. 240)** The uniting of computer-aided design with computer-aided manufacturing.

**concept testing (p. 389)** Taking a product idea to consumers to test their reactions.

**conceptual skills (p. 192)** Skills that involve the ability to picture the organization as a whole and the relationship among its various parts.

**conglomerate merger (p. 132)** The joining of firms in completely unrelated industries.

**Congress of Industrial Organizations (CIO) (p. 324)** Union organization of unskilled workers; broke away from the American Federation of Labor (AFL) in 1935 and rejoined it in 1955.

**consideration (p. 580)** Something of value; consideration is one of the requirements of a legal contract.

**consumerism (p. 584)** A social movement that seeks to increase and strengthen the rights and powers of buyers in relation to sellers.

**consumer market (p. 361)** All the individuals or households that want goods and services for personal consumption or use.

**consumer price index (CPI) (p. 48)** Monthly statistics that measure the pace of inflation or deflation.

**contingency planning (p. 188)** The process of preparing alternative courses of action that may be used if the primary plans don't achieve the organization's objectives.

**contingent workers (p. 295)** Workers who do not have the expectation of regular, full-time employment.

**continuous process (p. 239)** A production process in which long production runs turn out finished goods over time.

**contract (p. 580)** A legally enforceable agreement between two or more parties.

**contract law (p. 580)** Set of laws that specify what constitutes a legally enforceable agreement.

**contract manufacturing (p. 69)** A foreign country's production of private-label goods to which a domestic company then attaches its brand name or trademark; also called *outsourcing*.

**contractual distribution system (p. 416)** A distribution system in which members are bound to cooperate through contractual agreements.

**contrarian approach (p. 640)** Buying stock when everyone else is selling or vice versa.

**controlling (p. 185)** A management function that involves establishing clear standards to determine whether or not an organization is progressing toward its goals and objectives, rewarding people for doing a good job, and taking corrective action if they are not.

**convenience goods and services (p. 381)** Products that the consumer wants to purchase frequently and with a minimum of effort.

**conventional (C) corporation (p. 124)** A state-chartered legal entity with authority to act and have liability separate from its owners.

**cookies (p. 612)** Pieces of information, such as registration data or user preferences, sent by a Web site over the Internet to a Web browser that the browser software is expected to save and send back to the server whenever the user returns to that Web site.

***cooking the books*** *Making accounting information look better than it actually is to outside observers and users of financial information of a company.*

**cooling-off period (p. 332)** When workers in a critical industry return to their jobs while the union and management continue negotiations.

**cooperative (p. 141)** A business owned and controlled by the people who use it—producers, consumers, or workers with similar needs who pool their resources for mutual gain.

**copyright (p. 578)** A document that protects a creator's rights to materials such as books, articles, photos, and cartoons.

**core competencies (p. 223)** Those functions that the organization can do as well as or better than any other organization in the world.

**core time (p. 306)** In a flextime plan, the period when all employees are expected to be at their job stations.

**corporate distribution system (p. 416)** A distribution system in which all of the organizations in the channel of distribution are owned by one firm.

**corporate philanthropy (p. 99)** Dimension of social responsibility that includes charitable donations.

**corporate policy (p. 100)** Dimension of social responsibility that refers to the position a firm takes on social and political issues.

**corporate responsibility (p. 100)** Dimension of social responsibility that includes everything from hiring minority workers to making safe products.

**corporate social initiatives (p. 100)** Dimension of social responsibility that includes enhanced forms of corporate philanthropy directly related to the company's competencies.

**corporate social responsibility (p. 99)** A business's concern for the welfare of society.

**corporation (p. 118)** A legal entity with authority to act and have liability separate from its owners.

**cost of capital (p. 504)** The rate of return a company must earn in order to meet the demands of its lenders and expectations of its equity holders.

**cost of goods sold (or cost of goods manufactured) (p. 469)** A measure of the cost of merchandise sold or cost of raw materials and supplies used for producing items for resale.

***couch potatoes*** *People who sit and watch TV for hours at a time.*

**countertrading (p. 74)** A complex form of bartering in which several countries may be involved, each trading goods for goods or services for services.

***counting on it*** *Expecting it.*

**craft union (p. 323)** An organization of skilled specialists in a particular craft or trade.

**credit unions (p. 557)** Nonprofit, member-owned financial cooperatives that offer the full variety of banking services to their members.

**critical path (p. 251)** In a PERT network, the sequence of tasks that takes the longest time to complete.

**cross-functional self-managed teams (p. 219)** Groups of employees from different departments who work together on a long-term basis.

**current assets (p. 466)** Items that can or will be converted into cash within one year.

**customer relationship management (CRM) (p. 351)** The process of learning as much as possible about customers and doing everything you can to satisfy them—or even exceed their expectations—with goods and services over time.

**damages (p. 581)** The monetary settlement awarded to a person who is injured by a breach of contract.

**database (p. 15)** An electronic storage file where information is kept; one use of databases is to store vast amounts of information about consumers.

**data processing (DP) (p. 596)** Name for business technology in the 1970s; included technology that supported an existing business and was primarily used to improve the flow of financial information.

**dealer (private-label) brands (p. 386)** Products that don't carry the manufacturer's name but carry a distributor or retailer's name instead.

**debenture bonds (p. 515)** Bonds that are unsecured (i.e., not backed by any collateral such as equipment).

**debit card (p. 562)** An electronic funds transfer tool that serves the same function as checks: it withdraws funds from a checking account.

**debt financing (p. 493)** Funds raised through various forms of borrowing that must be repaid.

**decentralized authority (p. 211)** An organization structure in which decision-making authority is delegated to lower-level managers more familiar with local conditions than headquarters management could be.

**decertification (p. 326)** The process by which workers take away a union's right to represent them.

**decision making (p. 189)** Choosing among two or more alternatives.

**deflation (p. 47)** A situation in which prices are declining.

**demand (p. 37)** The quantity of products that people are willing to buy at different prices at a specific time.

**demand deposit (p. 554)** The technical name for a checking account; the money in a demand deposit can be withdrawn anytime on demand from the depositor.

**demographic segmentation (p. 364)** Dividing the market by age, income, and education level.

**demography (p. 16)** The statistical study of the human population with regard to its size, density, and other characteristics such as age, race, gender, and income.

**departmentalization (p. 214)** The dividing of organizational functions into separate units.

**depreciation (p. 470)** The systematic write-off of the cost of a tangible asset over its estimated useful life.

**depression (p. 49)** A severe recession.

**deregulation (p. 588)** Government withdrawal of certain laws and regulations that seem to hinder competition.

**devaluation (p. 73)** Lowering the value of a nation's currency relative to other currencies.

**direct marketing (p. 415)** Any activity that directly links manufacturers or intermediaries with the ultimate consumer.

**direct selling (p. 415)** Selling to consumers in their homes or where they work.

**disability insurance (p. 643)** Insurance that pays part of the cost of a long-term sickness or an accident.

**discount rate (p. 551)** The interest rate that the Fed charges for loans to member banks.

**disinflation (p. 47)** A situation in which price increases are slowing (the inflation rate is declining).

**diversification (p. 530)** Buying several different investment alternatives to spread the risk of investing.

**dividends (p. 516)** Part of a firm's profits that may be distributed to stockholders as either cash payments or additional shares of stock.

**double-entry bookkeeping (p. 462)** The concept of writing every business transaction in two places.

**Dow Jones Industrial Average (the Dow) (p. 555)** The average cost of 30 selected industrial stocks, used to give an indication of the direction (up or down) of the stock market over time.

**drop shippers (p. 410)** Wholesalers that solicit orders from retailers and other wholesalers and have the merchandise shipped directly from a producer to a buyer.

**dumping (p. 65)** Selling products in a foreign country at lower prices than those charged in the producing country.

**e-commerce (p. 15)** The buying and selling of goods and services over the Internet.

***economic pie*** *The money available in the economy.*

**economics (p. 31)** The study of how society chooses to employ resources to produce goods and services and distribute them for consumption among various competing groups and individuals.

**economies of scale (p. 208)** The situation in which companies can reduce their production costs if they can purchase raw materials in bulk; the average cost of goods goes down as production levels increase.

**electronic check conversion (ECC) (p. 561)** An electronic funds transfer tool that converts a traditional paper check into an electronic transaction at the cash register and processes it through the Federal Reserve's Automated Clearing House.

**electronic funds transfer (EFT) system (p. 561)** A computerized system that electronically performs financial transactions such as making purchases, paying bills, and receiving paychecks.

**electronic retailing (p. 413)** Selling goods and services to ultimate customers (e.g., you and me) over the Internet.

***e-mail snooped*** *When someone other than the addressee reads e-mail messages.*

**embargo (p. 76)** A complete ban on the import or export of a certain product or stopping all trade with a particular country.

**employee orientation (p. 297)** The activity that introduces new employees to the organization; to fellow employees; to their immediate supervisors; and to the policies, practices, and objectives of the firm.

**empowerment (p. 16)** Giving frontline workers the responsibility, authority, and freedom to respond quickly to customer requests.

**enabling (p. 196)** Giving workers the education and tools they need to make decisions.

**enterprise resource planning (ERP) (p. 247)** A computer application that enables multiple firms to manage all of their operations (finance, requirements planning, human resources, and order fulfillment) on the basis of a single, integrated set of corporate data.

**enterprise zones (p. 158)** Specific geographic areas to which governments try to attract private business investment by offering lower taxes and other government support.

**entrepreneur (p. 4)** A person who risks time and money to start and manage a business.

**entrepreneurial team (p. 154)** A group of experienced people from different areas of business who join together to form a managerial team with the skills needed to develop, make, and market a new product.

**entrepreneurship (p. 150)** Accepting the risk of starting and running a business.

**environmental scanning (p. 358)** The process of identifying the factors that can affect marketing success.

**equity financing (p. 493)** Funds raised from operations within the firm or through the sale of ownership in the firm.

**equity theory (p. 275)** The idea that employees try to maintain equity between inputs and outputs compared to others in similar positions.

**ethics (p. 90)** Standards of moral behavior, that is, behavior that is accepted by society as right versus wrong.

**everyday low pricing (EDLP) (p. 394)** Setting prices lower than competitors and then not having any special sales.

**exchange rate (p. 73)** The value of one nation's currency relative to the currencies of other countries.

**exchange-traded funds (ETFs) (p. 528)** Collections of stocks that are traded on exchanges but are traded more like individual stocks than like mutual funds.

**exclusive distribution (p. 412)** Distribution that sends products to only one retail outlet in a given geographic area.

**executor (p. 648)** A person who assembles and values your estate, files income and other taxes, and distributes assets.

**expectancy theory (p. 274)** Victor Vroom's theory that the amount of effort employees exert on a specific task depends on their expectations of the outcome.

**exporting (p. 60)** Selling products to another country.

**express warranties (p. 579)** Specific representations by the seller that buyers rely on regarding the goods they purchase.

**external customers (p. 198)** Dealers, who buy products to sell to others, and ultimate customers (or end users), who buy products for their own personal use.

**extranet (p. 602)** A semiprivate network that uses Internet technology and allows more than one company to access the same information or allows people on different servers to collaborate.

**extrinsic reward (p. 260)** Something given to you by someone else as recognition for good work; extrinsic rewards include pay increases, praise, and promotions.

**facility layout (p. 245)** The physical arrangement of resources (including people) in the production process.

**facility location (p. 242)** The process of selecting a geographic location for a company's operations.

**factoring (p. 497)** The process of selling accounts receivable for cash.

**factors of production (p. 9)** The resources used to create wealth: land, labor, capital, entrepreneurship, and knowledge.

**Federal Deposit Insurance Corporation (FDIC) (p. 559)** An independent agency of the U.S. government that insures bank deposits.

**finance (p. 484)** The function in a business that acquires funds for the firm and manages those funds within the firm.

**financial accounting (p. 457)** Accounting information and analyses prepared for people outside the organization.

**financial control (p. 489)** A process in which a firm periodically compares its actual revenues, costs, and expenses with its projected ones.

**financial management (p. 484)** The job of managing a firm's resources so it can meet its goals and objectives.

**financial managers (p. 484)** Managers who make recommendations to top executives regarding strategies for improving the financial strength of a firm.

**financial statement (p. 463)** A summary of all the transactions that have occurred over a particular period.

**fiscal policy (p. 50)** The federal government's efforts to keep the economy stable by increasing or decreasing taxes or government spending.

**fixed assets (p. 466)** Assets that are relatively permanent, such as land, buildings, and equipment.

**flat organization structure (p. 213)** An organization structure that has few layers of management and a broad span of control.

**flexible manufacturing (p. 240)** Designing machines to do multiple tasks so that they can produce a variety of products.

**flextime plan (p. 306)** Work schedule that gives employees some freedom to choose when to work, as long as they work the required number of hours.

**focus group (p. 358)** A small group of people who meet under the direction of a discussion leader to communicate their opinions about an organization, its products, or other given issues.

**foreign direct investment (p. 70)** The buying of permanent property and businesses in foreign nations.

**foreign subsidiary (p. 70)** A company owned in a foreign country by another company (called the *parent company*).

**form utility (p. 238)** The value added by the creation of finished goods and services, such as the value added by taking silicon and making computer chips or putting services together to create a vacation package.

**formal organization (p. 227)** The structure that details lines of responsibility, authority, and position; that is, the structure shown on organization charts.

**franchise (p. 135)** The right to use a specific business's name and sell its products or services in a given territory.

**franchise agreement (p. 134)** An arrangement whereby someone with a good idea for a business sells the rights to use the business name and sell a product or service to others in a given territory.

**franchisee (p. 135)** A person who buys a franchise.

**franchisor (p. 134)** A company that develops a product concept and sells others the rights to make and sell the products.

***free-for-all atmosphere*** *A situation where all order seems to be lost in conducting business.*

**free-market economies (p. 43)** Economic systems in which the market largely determines what goods and services get produced, who gets them, and how the economy grows.

**free-rein leadership (p. 195)** Leadership style that involves managers setting objectives and employees being relatively free to do whatever it takes to accomplish those objectives.

**free trade (p. 61)** The movement of goods and services among nations without political or economic barriers.

**freight forwarder (p. 421)** An organization that puts many small shipments together to create a single large shipment that can be transported cost-effectively to the final destination.

**fringe benefits (p. 304)** Benefits such as sick-leave pay, vacation pay, pension plans, and health plans that represent additional compensation to employees beyond base wages.

***from scratch*** *From the beginning.*

**fundamental accounting equation (p. 464)** Assets = liabilities + owners' equity; this is the basis for the balance sheet.

**futures markets (p. 531)** Commodities markets that involve the purchase and sale of goods for delivery sometime in the future.

**Gantt chart (p. 251)** Bar graph showing production managers what projects are being worked on and what stage they are in at any given time.

**General Agreement on Tariffs and Trade (GATT) (p. 76)** A 1948 agreement that established an international forum for negotiating mutual reductions in trade restrictions.

**general partner (p. 122)** An owner (partner) who has unlimited liability and is active in managing the firm.

**general partnership (p. 121)** A partnership in which all owners share in operating the business and in assuming liability for the business's debts.

**generic goods (p. 386)** Nonbranded products that usually sell at a sizable discount compared to national or private-label brands.

**geographic segmentation (p. 363)** Dividing the market by geographic area.

***get in on the dough*** *Take the opportunity to make some money.*

**givebacks (p. 333)** Concessions made by union members to management; gains from labor negotiations are given back to management to help employers remain competitive and thereby save jobs.

***go for the gold*** *To work to be the very best (figuratively winning a gold medal).*

***go out with me*** *Go with me to dinner or to a movie or some other entertainment.*

**goals (p. 185)** The broad, long-term accomplishments an organization wishes to attain.

**goal-setting theory (p. 273)** The idea that setting ambitious but attainable goals can motivate workers and improve performance if the goals are accepted, accompanied by feedback, and facilitated by organizational conditions.

***gone off the deep end*** *Doing something risky, almost crazy—like jumping into the deep end of a swimming pool when you can't swim.*

**goods (p. 20)** Tangible products such as computers, food, clothing, cars, and appliances.

***goofing off*** *Doing things at work not associated with the job, such as talking with others at the drinking fountain.*

**government and not-for-profit accounting (p. 460)** Accounting system for organizations whose purpose is not generating a profit but serving ratepayers, taxpayers, and others according to a duly approved budget.

**grievance (p. 329)** A charge by employees that management is not abiding by the terms of the negotiated labor–management agreement.

**gross domestic product (GDP) (p. 46)** The total value of final goods and services produced in a country in a given year.

**gross profit (gross margin) (p. 469)** How much a firm earned by buying (or making) and selling merchandise.

***hard copy*** *Copy printed on paper.*

**Hawthorne effect (p. 263)** The tendency for people to behave differently when they know they are being studied.

**health maintenance organizations (HMOs) (p. 625)** Health care organizations that require members to choose from a restricted list of doctors.

***heart*** *The most important part of something; the central force or idea.*

**hierarchy (p. 210)** A system in which one person is at the top of the organization and there is a ranked or sequential ordering from the top down of managers who are responsible to that person.

**high–low pricing strategy (p. 394)** Setting prices that are higher than EDLP stores, but having many special sales where the prices are lower than competitors'.

**horizontal merger (p. 132)** The joining of two firms in the same industry.

***hot second*** *Immediately.*

**human relations skills (p. 192)** Skills that involve communication and motivation; they enable managers to work through and with people.

**human resource management (p. 288)** The process of determining human resource needs and then recruiting, selecting, developing, motivating, evaluating, compensating, and scheduling employees to achieve organizational goals.

**hygiene factors (p. 265)** In Herzberg's theory of motivating factors, job factors that can cause dissatisfaction if missing but that do not necessarily motivate employees if increased.

***If it isn't broken, don't fix it*** *Don't risk making things worse by changing things that don't need to be changed.*

**implied warranties (p. 579)** Guarantees legally imposed on the seller.

**importing (p. 60)** Buying products from another country.

**import quota (p. 76)** A limit on the number of products in certain categories that a nation can import.

**inbound logistics (p. 419)** The area of logistics that involves bringing raw materials, packaging, other goods and services, and information from suppliers to producers.

**income statement (p. 467)** The financial statement that shows a firm's profit after costs, expenses, and taxes; it summarizes all of the resources that have come into the firm (revenue), all the resources that have left the firm, and the resulting net income.

**incubators (p. 159)** Centers that offer new businesses low-cost offices with basic business services.

**identity theft (p. 15)** The obtaining of private information about a person, such as Social Security number and/or credit card number, and using that information for illegal purposes, such as buying things with it.

**indenture terms (p. 501)** The terms of agreement in a bond issue.

**independent audit (p. 460)** An evaluation and unbiased opinion about the accuracy of a company's financial statements.

**individual retirement account (IRA) (p. 644)** A tax-deferred investment plan that enables you (and your spouse, if you are married) to save part of your income for retirement; a traditional IRA allows people who qualify to deduct from their reported income the money they put into an account.

**industrial goods (p. 382)** Products used in the production of other products. Sometimes called business goods or B2B goods.

**industrial unions (p. 324)** Labor organizations of unskilled and semiskilled workers in mass-production industries such as automobiles and mining.

**inflation (p. 47)** A general rise in the prices of goods and services over time.

**infomercial (p. 435)** A full-length TV program devoted exclusively to promoting goods or services.

**informal organization (p. 227)** The system of relationships and lines of authority that develops spontaneously as employees meet and form power centers; that is, the human side of the organization that does not appear on any organization chart.

**information systems (IS) (p. 596)** Technology that helps companies do business; includes such tools as automated teller machines (ATMs) and voice mail.

**information technology (IT) (p. 596)** Technology that helps companies change business by allowing them to use new methods.

**information utility (p. 408)** Adding value to products by opening two-way flows of information between marketing participants.

**initial public offering (IPO) (p. 512)** The first public offering of a corporation's stock.

**injunction (p. 333)** A court order directing someone to do something or to refrain from doing something.

**insider trading (p. 102)** An unethical activity in which insiders use private company information to further their own fortunes or those of their family and friends.

**institutional investors (p. 513)** Large organizations—such as pension funds, mutual funds, insurance companies, and banks—that invest their own funds or the funds of others.

**insurable interest (p. 624)** The possibility of the policyholder to suffer a loss.

**insurable risk (p. 624)** A risk that the typical insurance company will cover.

**insurance policy (p. 624)** A written contract between the insured and an insurance company that promises to pay for all or part of a loss.

**intangible assets (p. 466)** Long-term assets (e.g., patents, trademarks, copyrights) that have no real physical form but do have value.

**integrated marketing communication (IMC) (p. 432)** A technique that combines all the promotional tools into one comprehensive and unified promotional strategy.

**integrity-based ethics codes (p. 96)** Ethical standards that define the organization's guiding values, create an environment that supports ethically sound behavior, and stress a shared accountability among employees.

**intensive distribution (p. 412)** Distribution that puts products into as many retail outlets as possible.

**interactive promotion (p. 437)** Promotion process that allows marketers to go beyond a monologue, where sellers try to persuade buyers to buy things, to a dialogue in which buyers and sellers work together to create mutually beneficial exchange relationships.

**interest (p. 513)** The payment the issuer of the bond makes to the bondholders for use of the borrowed money.

**intermittent process (p. 239)** A production process in which the production run is short and the machines are changed frequently to make different products.

**intermodal shipping (p. 422)** The use of multiple modes of transportation to complete a single long-distance movement of freight.

**internal customers (p. 198)** Individuals and units within the firm that receive services from other individuals or units.

**International Monetary Fund (IMF) (p. 565)** Organization that assists the smooth flow of money among nations.

**Internet2 (p. 604)** The private Internet system that links government supercomputer centers and a select group of universities; it runs more than 22,000 times faster than today's public infrastructure and supports heavy-duty applications.

**intranet (p. 602)** A companywide network, closed to public access, that uses Internet-type technology.

**intrapreneurs (p. 158)** Creative people who work as entrepreneurs within corporations.

**intrinsic reward (p. 260)** The personal satisfaction you feel when you perform well and complete goals.

**inverted organization (p. 224)** An organization that has contact people at the top and the chief executive officer at the bottom of the organization chart.

**investment bankers (p. 513)** Specialists who assist in the issue and sale of new securities.

**invisible hand (p. 32)** A phrase coined by Adam Smith to describe the process that turns self-directed gain into social and economic benefits for all.

**involuntary bankruptcy (p. 586)** Bankruptcy procedures filed by a debtor's creditors.

***IOUs*** *Debt; abbreviation for "I owe you."*

**ISO 14000 (p. 250)** A collection of the best practices for managing an organization's impact on the environment.

**ISO 9000 (p. 250)** The common name given to quality management and assurance standards.

**job analysis (p. 291)** A study of what is done by employees who hold various job titles.

**job description (p. 291)** A summary of the objectives of a job, the type of work to be done, the responsibilities and duties, the working conditions, and the relationship of the job to other functions.

**job enlargement (p. 269)** A job enrichment strategy that involves combining a series of tasks into one challenging and interesting assignment.

**job enrichment (p. 267)** A motivational strategy that emphasizes motivating the worker through the job itself.

**job rotation (p. 269)** A job enrichment strategy that involves moving employees from one job to another.

**job sharing (p. 308)** An arrangement whereby two part-time employees share one full-time job.

**job simulation (p. 299)** The use of equipment that duplicates job conditions and tasks so that trainees can learn skills before attempting them on the job.

**job specifications (p. 291)** A written summary of the minimum qualifications required of workers to do a particular job.

**joint venture (p. 69)** A partnership in which two or more companies (often from different countries) join to undertake a major project.

**journal (p. 461)** The record book or computer program where accounting data are first entered.

**judiciary (p. 574)** The branch of government chosen to oversee the legal system through the court system.

***jumped headfirst*** *Began quickly and eagerly without hesitation.*

**junk bonds (p. 530)** High-risk, high-interest bonds.

**just-in-time (JIT) inventory control (p. 247)** A production process in which a minimum of inventory is kept on the premises and parts, supplies, and other needs are delivered just in time to go on the assembly line.

***key player*** *Important participant.*

***kick back and relax*** *To take a rest.*

**Knights of Labor (p. 324)** The first national labor union; formed in 1869.

**knockoff brands (p. 386)** Illegal copies of national brand-name goods.

***know-how*** *A level of specific expertise.*

**knowledge management (p. 197)** Finding the right information, keeping the information in a readily accessible place, and making the information known to everyone in the firm.

***latchkey kids*** *School-age children who come home to empty houses since all of the adults are at work.*

**law of large numbers (p. 624)** Principle that if a large number of people are exposed to the same risk, a predictable number of losses will occur during a given period of time.

**leading (p. 185)** Creating a vision for the organization and guiding, training, coaching, and motivating others to work effectively to achieve the organization's goals and objectives.

**lean manufacturing (p. 241)** The production of goods using less of everything compared to mass production.

**ledger (p. 462)** A specialized accounting book or computer program in which information from accounting journals is accumulated into specific categories and posted so that managers can find all the information about one account in the same place.

**letter of credit (p. 563)** A promise by the bank to pay the seller a given amount if certain conditions are met.

***level playing field*** *Treating everyone equally.*

**leverage (p. 504)** Raising needed funds through borrowing to increase a firm's rate of return.

**leveraged buyout (LBO) (p. 132)** An attempt by employees, management, or a group of investors to purchase an organization primarily through borrowing.

**liabilities (p. 466)** What the business owes to others (debts).

**licensing (p. 66)** A global strategy in which a firm (the licensor) allows a foreign company (the licensee) to produce its product in exchange for a fee (a royalty).

**limited liability (p. 122)** The responsibility of a business's owners for losses only up to the amount they invest; limited partners and shareholders have limited liability.

**limited liability company (LLC) (p. 122)** A company similar to an S corporation but without the special eligibility requirements.

**limited liability partnership (LLP) (p. 122)** A partnership that limits partners' risk of losing their personal assets to only their own acts and omissions and to the acts and omissions of people under their supervision.

**limited partner (p. 122)** An owner who invests money in the business but does not have any management responsibility or liability for losses beyond the investment.

**limited partnership (p. 121)** A partnership with one or more general partners and one or more limited partners.

**line of credit (p. 497)** A given amount of unsecured short-term funds a bank will lend to a business, provided the funds are readily available.

**line organization (p. 217)** An organization that has direct two-way lines of responsibility, authority, and communication running from the top to the bottom of the organization, with all people reporting to only one supervisor.

**line personnel (p. 217)** Employees who are part of the chain of command that is responsible for achieving organizational goals.

**liquidity (p. 466)** How fast an asset can be converted into cash.

**lockout (p. 333)** An attempt by management to put pressure on unions by temporarily closing the business.

**logistics (p. 419)** The marketing activity that involves planning, implementing, and controlling the physical flow of materials, final goods, and related information from points of origin to points of consumption to meet customer requirements at a profit.

**long-term financing (p. 493)** Borrowed capital that will be repaid over a specific period longer than one year.

**long-term forecast (p. 488)** Forecast that predicts revenues, costs, and expenses for a period longer than 1 year, and sometimes as far as 5 or 10 years into the future.

**loss (p. 4)** When a business's expenses are more than its revenues.

**M-1 (p. 547)** Money that can be accessed quickly and easily (coins and paper money, checks, traveler's checks, etc.).

**M-2 (p. 547)** Money included in M-1 plus money that may take a little more time to obtain (savings accounts, money market accounts, mutual funds, certificates of deposit, etc.).

**macroeconomics (p. 31)** The part of economics study that looks at the operation of a nation's economy as a whole.

**management (p. 182)** The process used to accomplish organizational goals through planning, organizing, leading, and controlling people and other organizational resources.

**management by objectives (MBO) (p. 273)** A system of goal setting and implementation that involves a cycle of discussion, review, and evaluation of objectives among top and middle-level managers, supervisors, and employees.

**management development (p. 299)** The process of training and educating employees to become good managers and then monitoring the progress of their managerial skills over time.

**managerial accounting (p. 457)** Accounting used to provide information and analyses to managers within the organization to assist them in decision making.

**manufacturers' brand names (p. 385)** The brand names of manufacturers that distribute products nationally.

**market (p. 170)** People with unsatisfied wants and needs who have both the resources and the willingness to buy.

**marketing (p. 350)** The process of planning and executing the conception, pricing, promotion, and distribution of goods and services to facilitate exchanges that satisfy individual and organizational objectives.

**marketing concept (p. 351)** A three-part business philosophy: (1) a customer orientation, (2) a service orientation, and (3) a profit orientation.

**marketing intermediaries (p. 404)** Organizations that assist in moving goods and services from producers to industrial and consumer users.

**marketing mix (p. 352)** The ingredients that go into a marketing program: product, price, place, and promotion.

**marketing research (p. 356)** The analysis of markets to determine opportunities and challenges, and to find the information needed to make good decisions.

**market price (p. 38)** The price determined by supply and demand.

**market segmentation (p. 362)** The process of dividing the total market into groups whose members have similar characteristics.

***marriage of software, hardware, etc.*** *Combination of various technologies.*

**Maslow's hierarchy of needs (p. 263)** Theory of motivation based on unmet human needs from basic physiological needs to safety, social, and esteem needs to self-actualization needs.

**mass customization (p. 241)** Tailoring products to meet the needs of individual customers.

**mass marketing (p. 364)** Developing products and promotions to please large groups of people.

**master limited partnership (MLP) (p. 122)** A partnership that looks much like a corporation (in that it acts like a corporation and is traded on a stock exchange) but is taxed like a partnership and thus avoids the corporate income tax.

**materials handling (p. 419)** The movement of goods within a warehouse, from warehouses to the factory floor, and from the factory floor to various workstations.

**materials requirement planning (MRP) (p. 246)** A computer-based production management system that uses sales forecasts to make sure that needed parts and materials are available at the right time and place.

**matrix organization (p. 218)** An organization in which specialists from different parts of the organization are brought together to work on specific projects but still remain part of a line-and-staff structure.

**maturity date (p. 514)** The exact date the issuer of a bond must pay the principal to the bondholder.

***measuring stick*** *Tool used to evaluate or compare something.*

**mediation (p. 330)** The use of a third party, called a mediator, who encourages both sides in a dispute to continue negotiating and often makes suggestions for resolving the dispute.

**medical savings accounts (MSAs) (p. 626)** Tax-deferred accounts that allow people to save money for medical expenses.

**mentor (p. 299)** An experienced employee who supervises, coaches, and guides lower-level employees by introducing them to the right people and generally being their organizational sponsor.

**merchant wholesalers (p. 410)** Independently owned firms that take title to (own) the goods they handle.

**merger (p. 132)** The result of two firms forming one company.

***Mickey D's*** *Nickname for McDonald's.*

**microeconomics (p. 31)** The part of economics study that looks at the behavior of people and organizations in particular markets.

**micropreneurs (p. 154)** Entrepreneurs willing to accept the risk of starting and managing the type of business that remains small, lets them do the kind of work they want to do, and offers them a balanced lifestyle.

**middle management (p. 191)** The level of management that includes general managers, division managers, and branch and plant managers who are responsible for tactical planning and controlling.

***mine the knowledge*** *Make maximum use of the knowledge employees have.*

**mission statement (p. 185)** An outline of the fundamental purposes of an organization.

**mixed economies (p. 44)** Economic systems in which some allocation of resources is made by the market and some by the government.

**monetary policy (p. 51)** The management of the money supply and interest rates.

**money (p. 546)** Anything that people generally accept as payment for goods and services.

**money supply (p. 547)** The amount of money the Federal Reserve Bank makes available for people to buy goods and services.

**monopolistic competition (p. 39)** The market situation in which a large number of sellers produce products that are very similar but that are perceived by buyers as different.

**monopoly (p. 40)** A market in which there is only one seller for a product or service.

***more than meets the eye*** *More than one can see with his or her own eyes; much is happening that is not visible.*

**motivators (p. 265)** In Herzberg's theory of motivating factors, job factors that cause employees to be productive and that give them satisfaction.

***mouse-click away*** *Ease of doing something by using the computer or Internet.*

***muddy the water*** *Making things even more difficult than they currently are.*

**multinational corporation (p. 70)** An organization that manufactures and markets products in many different countries and has multinational stock ownership and multinational management.

**mutual fund (p. 527)** An organization that buys stocks and bonds and then sells shares in those securities to the public.

**mutual insurance company (p. 625)** A type of insurance company owned by its policyholders.

**NASDAQ (p. 521)** A nationwide electronic system that communicates over-the-counter trades to brokers.

**national debt (p. 50)** The sum of government deficits over time.

**negligence (p. 576)** In tort law, behavior that causes unintentional harm or injury.

**negotiable instruments (p. 580)** Forms of commercial paper (such as checks) that are transferable among businesses and individuals and represent a promise to pay a specified amount.

**negotiated labor-management agreement (labor contract) (p. 327)** Agreement that sets the tone and clarifies the terms under which management and labor agree to function over a period of time.

**net income or net loss (p. 467)** Revenue left over after all costs and expenses, including taxes, are paid.

**network computing system (client/server computing) (p. 605)** Computer systems that allow personal computers (clients) to obtain needed information from huge databases in a central computer (the server).

**networking (p. 220)** Using communications technology and other means to link organizations and allow them to work together on common objectives.

**networking (p. 299)** The process of establishing and maintaining contacts with key managers in one's own organization and other organizations and using those contacts to weave strong relationships that serve as informal development systems.

**niche marketing (p. 364)** The process of finding small but profitable market segments and designing or finding products for them.

**nonbanks (p. 554)** Financial organizations that accept no deposits but offer many of the services provided by regular banks (pension funds, insurance companies, commercial finance companies, consumer finance companies, and brokerage houses).

**nonprofit organization (p. 7)** An organization whose goals do not include making a personal profit for its owners or organizers.

**North American Free Trade Agreement (NAFTA) (p. 78)** Agreement that created a free-trade area among the United States, Canada, and Mexico.

**notes payable (p. 466)** Short-term or long-term liabilities that a business promises to repay by a certain date.

**objectives (p. 185)** Specific, short-term statements detailing how to achieve the organization's goals.

**off-the-job training (p. 298)** Training that occurs away from the workplace and consists of internal or external programs to develop any of a variety of skills or to foster personal development.

**oligopoly (p. 39)** A form of competition in which just a few sellers dominate the market.

**one-to-one marketing (p. 364)** Developing a unique mix of goods and services for each individual customer.

**online training (p. 298)** Training programs in which employees "attend" classes via the Internet.

**on-the-job training (p. 297)** Training in which the employee immediately begins his or her tasks and learns by doing, or watches others for a while and then imitates them, all right at the workplace.

**open shop agreement (p. 329)** Agreement in right-to-work states that gives workers the option to join or not join a union, if one exists in their workplace.

**open-market operations (p. 550)** The buying and selling of U.S. government bonds by the Fed with the goal of regulating the money supply.

**operating budget (master budget) (p. 489)** The budget that ties together all of a firm's other budgets; it is the projection of dollar allocations to various costs and expenses needed to run or operate the business, given projected revenues.

**operating expenses (p. 470)** Costs involved in operating a business, such as rent, utilities, and salaries.

**operational planning (p. 188)** The process of setting work standards and schedules necessary to implement the company's tactical objectives.

**operations management (p. 236)** A specialized area in management that converts or transforms resources (including human resources) into goods and services.

**organization chart (p. 190)** A visual device that shows relationships among people and divides the organization's work; it shows who is accountable for the completion of specific work and who reports to whom.

**organizational (or corporate) culture (p. 225)** Widely shared values within an organization that provide unity and cooperation to achieve common goals.

**organizing (p. 184)** A management function that includes designing the structure of the organization and creating conditions and systems in which everyone and everything work together to achieve the organization's goals and objectives.

***out of the office loop*** *Out of the line of communication that occurs in the workplace.*

**outbound logistics (p. 419)** The area of logistics that involves managing the flow of finished products and information to business buyers and ultimate consumers (people like you and me).

**outsourcing (p. 6)** Assigning various functions, such as accounting, production, security, maintenance, and legal work, to outside organizations.

**over-the-counter (OTC) market (p. 520)** Exchange that provides a means to trade stocks not listed on the national exchanges.

**owners' equity (p. 466)** The amount of the business that belongs to the owners minus any liabilities owed by the business.

**participative (democratic) leadership (p. 195)** Leadership style that consists of managers and employees working together to make decisions.

**partnership (p. 118)** A legal form of business with two or more owners.

**patent (p. 577)** A document that gives inventors exclusive rights to their inventions for 20 years.

***pave the way*** *Process of making a task easier.*

***peanut butter and jelly*** *Popular combination for sandwich; the two are seen as perfect complementary products.*

**penetration strategy (p. 394)** Strategy in which a product is priced low to attract many customers and discourage competition.

**pension funds (p. 558)** Amounts of money put aside by corporations, nonprofit organizations, or unions to cover part of the financial needs of members when they retire.

***perks*** *Short for* perquisites; *compensation in addition to salary, such as day care or a company car.*

**perfect competition (p. 39)** The market situation in which there are many sellers in a market and no seller is large enough to dictate the price of a product.

**performance appraisal (p. 300)** An evaluation in which the performance level of employees is measured against established standards to make decisions about promotions, compensation, additional training, or firing.

**personal selling (p. 438)** The face-to-face presentation and promotion of goods and services.

**place utility (p. 408)** Adding value to products by having them where people want them.

**planning (p. 184)** A management function that includes anticipating trends and determining the best strategies and tactics to achieve organizational goals and objectives.

***piece of the action*** *A share in the opportunity.*

***pink slip*** *A notice that you've lost your job.*

***pitch in*** *To help as needed.*

**PMI (p. 189)** Listing all the pluses for a solution in one column, all the minuses in another, and the implications in a third column.

**podcasting (p. 447)** A means of distributing audio and video programs via the Internet that lets users subscribe to a number of files, also known as feeds, and then hear or view the material at the time they choose.

**possession utility (p. 408)** Doing whatever is necessary to transfer ownership from one party to another, including providing credit, delivery, installation, guarantees, and follow-up service.

***poster child*** *Best example.*

**precedent (p. 575)** Decisions judges have made in earlier cases that guide the handling of new cases.

**preferred provider organizations (PPOs) (p. 626)** Health care organizations similar to HMOs except that they allow members to choose their own physicians (for a fee).

**preferred stock (p. 517)** Stock that gives its owners preference in the payment of dividends and an earlier claim on assets than common stockholders if the company is forced out of business and its assets sold.

**premium (p. 624)** The fee charged by an insurance company for an insurance policy.

**price leadership (p. 393)** The procedure by which one or more dominant firms set the pricing practices that all competitors in an industry follow.

**primary boycott (p. 332)** When a union encourages both its members and the general public not to buy the products of a firm involved in a labor dispute.

**primary data (p. 358)** Data that you gather yourself (not from secondary sources such as books and magazines).

**principle of motion economy (p. 262)** Theory developed by Frank and Lillian Gilbreth that every job can be broken down into a series of elementary motions.

**private accountant (p. 458)** An accountant who works for a single firm, government agency, or nonprofit organization.

**problem solving (p. 189)** The process of solving the everyday problems that occur. Problem solving is less formal than decision making and usually calls for quicker action.

**process manufacturing (p. 239)** That part of the production process that physically or chemically changes materials.

**producer price index (PPI) (p. 49)** An index that measures prices at the wholesale level.

**product (p. 354)** Any physical good, service, or idea that satisfies a want or need plus anything that would enhance the product in the eyes of consumers, such as the brand.

**product analysis (p. 388)** Making cost estimates and sales forecasts to get a feeling for profitability of new-product ideas.

**product differentiation (p. 381)** The creation of real or perceived product differences.

**product liability (p. 576)** Part of tort law that holds businesses liable for harm that results from the production, design, sale, or use of products they market.

**product life cycle (p. 389)** A theoretical model of what happens to sales and profits for a product class over time.

**product line (p. 380)** A group of products that are physically similar or are intended for a similar market.

**product mix (p. 381)** The combination of product lines offered by a manufacturer.

**product placement (p. 435)** Putting products into TV shows and movies where they will be seen.

**product screening (p. 388)** A process designed to reduce the number of new-product ideas being worked on at any one time.

**production (p. 236)** The creation of finished goods and services using the factors of production: land, labor, capital, entrepreneurship, and knowledge.

**production management (p. 236)** The term used to describe all the activities managers do to help their firms create goods.

**productivity (p. 13)** The amount of output you generate given the amount of input.

**profit (p. 4)** The amount of money a business earns above and beyond what it spends for salaries and other expenses.

**program evaluation and review technique (PERT) (p. 250)** A method for analyzing the tasks involved in completing a given project, estimating the time needed to complete each task, and identifying the minimum time needed to complete the total project.

**program trading (p. 536)** Giving instructions to computers to automatically sell if the price of a stock dips to a certain point to avoid potential losses.

**promissory note (p. 495)** A written contract with a promise to pay a supplier a specific sum of money at a definite time.

**promotion (p. 355)** All the techniques sellers use to motivate people to buy their products or services.

**promotion (p. 432)** An effort by marketers to inform and remind people in the target market about products and to persuade them to participate in an exchange.

**promotion mix (p. 432)** The combination of promotional tools an organization uses.

***pros and cons*** *Arguments for and against something.*

**prospect (p. 439)** A person with the means to buy a product, the authority to buy, and the willingness to listen to a sales message.

**prospecting (p. 439)** Researching potential buyers and choosing those most likely to buy.

**prospectus (p. 521)** A condensed version of economic and financial information that a company must file with the SEC before issuing stock; the prospectus must be sent to prospective investors.

**psychographic segmentation (p. 364)** Dividing the market using the group's values, attitudes, and interests.

**psychological pricing (p. 395)** Pricing goods and services at price points that make the product appear less expensive than it is.

**public accountant (p. 458)** An accountant who provides his or her accounting services to individuals or businesses on a fee basis.

**public domain software (freeware) (p. 606)** Software that is free for the taking.

**public relations (PR) (p. 442)** The management function that evaluates public attitudes, changes policies and procedures in response to the public's requests, and executes a program of action and information to earn public understanding and acceptance.

**publicity (p. 443)** Any information about an individual, product, or organization that's distributed to the public through the media and that's not paid for or controlled by the seller.

**pull strategy (p. 448)** Promotional strategy in which heavy advertising and sales promotion efforts are directed toward consumers so that they'll request the products from retailers.

***pump up the profits*** *Making profits in a company appear larger than they actually are under recognized accounting rules.*

**purchasing (p. 247)** The function in a firm that searches for quality material resources, finds the best suppliers, and negotiates the best price for goods and services.

**pure risk (p. 621)** The threat of loss with no chance for profit.

**push strategy (p. 448)** Promotional strategy in which the producer uses advertising, personal selling, sales promotion, and all other promotional tools to convince wholesalers and retailers to stock and sell merchandise.

**qualifying (p. 439)** In the selling process, making sure that people have a need for the product, the authority to buy, and the willingness to listen to a sales message.

**quality (p. 248)** Consistently producing what the customer wants while reducing errors before and after delivery to the customer.

**quality of life (p. 5)** The general well-being of a society in terms of political freedom, a clean natural environment, education, health care, safety, free time, and everything else that leads to satisfaction and joy.

***quid pro quo*** *Latin phrase meaning "something given in return for something else."*

***quite a stir*** *Something that causes a feeling of concern.*

**rack jobbers (p. 410)** Wholesalers that furnish racks or shelves full of merchandise to retailers, display products, and sell on consignment.

**ratio analysis (p. 473)** The assessment of a firm's financial condition and performance through calculations and interpretations of financial ratios developed from the firm's financial statements.

**real time (p. 221)** The present moment or the actual time in which something takes place.

**recession (p. 49)** Two or more consecutive quarters of decline in the GDP.

**recruitment (p. 292)** The set of activities used to obtain a sufficient number of the right people at the right time.

**reinforcement theory (p. 274)** Theory that positive and negative reinforcers motivate a person to behave in certain ways.

**relationship marketing (p. 365)** Marketing strategy with the goal of keeping individual customers over time by offering them products that exactly meet their requirements.

**reserve requirement (p. 550)** A percentage of commercial banks' checking and savings accounts that must be physically kept in the bank.

**resource development (p. 31)** The study of how to increase resources and to create the conditions that will make better use of those resources.

**restructuring (p. 223)** Redesigning an organization so that it can more effectively and efficiently serve its customers.

**retailer (p. 404)** An organization that sells to ultimate consumers.

**retained earnings (p. 466)** The accumulated earnings from a firm's profitable operations that were kept in the business and not paid out to stockholders in dividends.

**revenue (p. 4)** The total amount of money a business takes in during a given period by selling goods and services.

**revenue (p. 469)** The value of what is received for goods sold, services rendered, and other financial sources.

**reverse discrimination (p. 312)** Discrimination against whites or males in hiring or promoting.

**reverse logistics (p. 419)** The area of logistics that involves bringing goods back to the manufacturer because of defects or for recycling materials.

**revolving credit agreement (p. 497)** A line of credit that is guaranteed by the bank.

**right-to-work laws (p. 329)** Legislation that gives workers the right, under an open shop, to join or not join a union if it is present.

**risk (p. 5)** The chance an entrepreneur takes of losing time and money on a business that may not prove profitable.

**risk (p. 621)** The chance of loss, the degree of probability of loss, and the amount of possible loss.

**risk/return trade-off (p. 501)** The principle that the greater the risk a lender takes in making a loan, the higher the interest rate required.

**Roth IRA (p. 645)** An IRA where you don't get upfront deductions on your taxes as you would with a traditional IRA, but the earnings grow tax-free and are also tax-free when they are withdrawn.

**rule of indemnity (p. 624)** Rule saying that an insured person or organization cannot collect more than the actual loss from an insurable risk.

***rules-of-the-road orientation*** *Introduction to the proper procedures within an organization.*

**sales promotion (p. 443)** The promotional tool that stimulates consumer purchasing and dealer interest by means of short-term activities.

**sampling (p. 445)** A promotional tool in which a company lets consumers have a small sample of a product for no charge.

**savings and loan association (S&L) (p. 557)** A financial institution that accepts both savings and checking deposits and provides home mortgage loans.

**Savings Association Insurance Fund (SAIF) (p. 559)** The part of the FDIC that insures holders of accounts in savings and loan associations.

**scientific management (p. 261)** Studying workers to find the most efficient ways of doing things and then teaching people those techniques.

**S corporation (p. 129)** A unique government creation that looks like a corporation but is taxed like sole proprietorships and partnerships.

***sea of information*** *Lots of information, often too much to process.*

**secondary boycott (p. 332)** An attempt by labor to convince others to stop doing business with a firm that is the subject of a primary boycott; prohibited by the Taft-Hartley Act.

**secondary data (p. 357)** Information that has already been compiled by others and published in journals and books or made available online.

**secured bond (p. 501)** A bond issued with some form of collateral.

**secured loan (p. 496)** A loan backed by something valuable, such as property.

**Securities and Exchange Commission (SEC) (p. 521)** Federal agency that has responsibility for regulating the various exchanges.

**selection (p. 294)** The process of gathering information and deciding who should be hired, under legal guidelines, for the best interests of the individual and the organization.

**selective distribution (p. 412)** Distribution that sends products to only a preferred group of retailers in an area.

**self-insurance (p. 622)** The practice of setting aside money to cover routine claims and buying only "catastrophe" policies to cover big losses.

**Service Corps of Retired Executives (SCORE) (p. 172)** An SBA office with volunteers from industry, trade associations, and education who counsel small businesses at no cost (except for expenses).

**service utility (p. 409)** Adding value by providing fast, friendly service during and after the sale and by teaching customers how to best use products over time.

**services (p. 21)** Intangible products (i.e., products that can't be held in your hand) such as education, health care, insurance, recreation, and travel and tourism.

**sexual harassment (p. 339)** Unwelcome sexual advances, requests for sexual favors, and other conduct (verbal or physical) of a sexual nature that creates a hostile work environment.

***shaky ground*** *Idea that possible problems lie ahead.*

**shareware (p. 606)** Software that is copyrighted but distributed to potential customers free of charge.

***Sherlock Holmes*** *A famous fictional detective who was particularly adept at uncovering information to solve very difficult mysteries.*

***shoestring budget*** *A budget that implies the company is short on funds and only includes a minimal amount of financial expenditures (i.e., it's as thin as a shoestring).*

**shop stewards (p. 330)** Union officials who work permanently in an organization and represent employee interests on a daily basis.

**shopping goods and services (p. 381)** Those products that the consumer buys only after comparing value, quality, price, and style from a variety of sellers.

**short-term financing (p. 493)** Borrowed capital that will be repaid within one year.

**short-term forecast (p. 488)** Forecast that predicts revenues, costs, and expenses for a period of one year or less.

***sift through mountains of information*** *Sort through large volumes of information.*

**sinking fund (p. 515)** A reserve account in which the issuer of a bond periodically retires some part of the bond principal prior to maturity so that enough capital will be accumulated by the maturity date to pay off the bond.

**six sigma quality (p. 248)** A quality measure that allows only 3.4 defects per million opportunities.

**skimming price strategy (p. 394)** Strategy in which a new product is priced high to make optimum profit while there's little competition.

**small business (p. 160)** A business that is independently owned and operated, is not dominant in its field of operation, and meets certain standards of size (set by the Small Business Administration) in terms of employees or annual receipts.

**Small Business Administration (SBA) (p. 168)** A U.S. government agency that advises and assists small businesses by providing management training and financial advice and loans.

**Small Business Investment Company (SBIC) Program (p. 169)** A program through which private investment companies licensed by the Small Business Administration lend money to small businesses.

**smart card (p. 562)** An electronic funds transfer tool that is a combination credit card, debit card, phone card, driver's license card, and more.

***smoking gun*** *An issue or other disclosure that proves a person or organization has done something wrong.*

**social audit (p. 106)** A systematic evaluation of an organization's progress toward implementing programs that are socially responsible and responsive.

**Social Security (p. 644)** The term used to describe the Old-Age, Survivors, and Disability Insurance Program established by the Social Security Act of 1935.

**socialism (p. 41)** An economic system based on the premise that some, if not most, basic businesses should be owned by the government so that profits can be evenly distributed among the people.

**sole proprietorship (p. 118)** A business that is owned, and usually managed, by one person.

**span of control (p. 212)** The optimum number of subordinates a manager supervises or should supervise.

**specialty goods and services (p. 382)** Consumer products with unique characteristics and brand identity. Because these products are perceived as having no reasonable substitute, the consumer puts forth a special effort to purchase them.

**speculative risk (p. 621)** A chance of either profit or loss.

***squeezing franchisees' profits*** *Tightening or reducing profits.*

**staff personnel (p. 217)** Employees who advise and assist line personnel in meeting their goals.

**staffing (p. 193)** A management function that includes hiring, motivating, and retaining the best people available to accomplish the company's objectives.

**stakeholders (p. 5)** All the people who stand to gain or lose by the policies and activities of a business.

**standard of living (p. 5)** The amount of goods and services people can buy with the money they have.

***state-of-the-art*** *The most modern type available.*

**statement of cash flows (p. 471)** Financial statement that reports cash receipts and disbursements related to a firm's three major activities: operations, investments, and financing.

**statistical process control (SPC) (p. 248)** The process of taking statistical samples of product components at each stage of the production process and plotting those results on a graph. Any variances from quality standards are recognized and can be corrected if beyond the set standards.

**statistical quality control (SQC) (p. 248)** The process some managers use to continually monitor all phases of the production process to assure that quality is being built into the product from the beginning.

**statutory law (p. 574)** State and federal constitutions, legislative enactments, treaties of the federal government, and ordinances—in short, written law.

***staying afloat*** *Staying in business during tough times.*

**stockbroker (p. 522)** A registered representative who works as a market intermediary to buy and sell securities for clients.

**stock certificate (p. 516)** Evidence of stock ownership that specifies the name of the company, the number of shares it represents, and the type of stock being issued.

**stock exchange (p. 519)** An organization whose members can buy and sell (exchange) securities for companies and investors.

**stock insurance company (p. 625)** A type of insurance company owned by stockholders.

**stocks (p. 516)** Shares of ownership in a company.

**stock splits (p. 527)** An action by a company that gives stockholders two or more shares of stock for each one they own.

**strategic alliance (p. 69)** A long-term partnership between two or more companies established to help each company build competitive market advantages.

**strategic planning (p. 186)** The process of determining the major goals of the organization and the policies and strategies for obtaining and using resources to achieve those goals.

**strict product liability (p. 576)** Legal responsibility for harm or injury caused by a product regardless of fault.

**strike (p. 331)** A union strategy in which workers refuse to go to work; the purpose is to further workers' objectives after an impasse in collective bargaining.

**strikebreakers (p. 333)** Workers hired to do the jobs of striking workers until the labor dispute is resolved.

**supervisory management (p. 191)** Managers who are directly responsible for supervising workers and evaluating their daily performance.

**supply (p. 37)** The quantity of products that manufacturers or owners are willing to sell at different prices at a specific time.

**supply chain (or value chain) (p. 417)** The sequence of linked activities that must be performed by various organizations to move goods from the sources of raw materials to ultimate consumers.

**supply-chain management (p. 417)** The process of managing the movement of raw materials, parts, work in progress, finished goods, and related information through all the organizations involved in the supply chain; managing the return of such goods, if necessary; and recycling materials when appropriate.

**SWOT analysis (p. 186)** A planning tool used to analyze an organization's strengths, weaknesses, opportunities, and threats.

**tactical planning (p. 187)** The process of developing detailed, short-term statements about what is to be done, who is to do it, and how it is to be done.

**tall organization structure (p. 213)** An organizational structure in which the pyramidal organization chart would be quite tall because of the various levels of management.

**target costing (p. 393)** Designing a product so that it satisfies customers and meets the profit margins desired by the firm.

**target marketing (p. 362)** Marketing directed toward those groups (market segments) an organization decides it can serve profitably.

**tariff (p. 75)** A tax imposed on imports.

**tax accountant (p. 460)** An accountant trained in tax law and responsible for preparing tax returns or developing tax strategies.

**tax-deferred contributions (p. 645)** Retirement account deposits for which you pay no current taxes, but the earnings gained are taxed as regular income when they are withdrawn at retirement.

**taxes (p. 584)** How the government (federal, state, and local) raises money.

**technical skills (p. 192)** Skills that involve the ability to perform tasks in a specific discipline or department.

**technology (p. 13)** Everything from phones and copiers to computers, medical imaging devices, personal digital assistants, and the various software programs that make business processes more efficient and productive.

***telecom*** *Short for telecommunications.*

**telemarketing (p. 414)** The sale of goods and services by telephone.

***telephone tag*** *To leave a telephone message when you attempt to return a message left for you.*

**term insurance (p. 642)** Pure insurance protection for a given number of years.

**term-loan agreement (p. 500)** A promissory note that requires the borrower to repay the loan in specified installments.

**test marketing (p. 354)** The process of testing products among potential users.

***thorny issue*** *An issue that can cause pain or difficulty (as a thorn on a rose bush may).*

***through the grapevine*** *Information communication; stories told by one person to the next.*

**time deposit (p. 555)** The technical name for a savings account; the bank can require prior notice before the owner withdraws money from a time deposit.

***time in the trenches*** *Working with the other employees and experiencing what they contend with as opposed to managing from an office and relying solely on reports about what is happening in the workplace.*

**time utility (p. 408)** Adding value to products by making them available when they're needed.

**time-motion studies (p. 261)** Studies, begun by Frederick Taylor, of which tasks must be performed to complete a job and the time needed to do each task.

***to take a break*** *To slow down and do something besides work.*

**top management (p. 190)** Highest level of management, consisting of the president and other key company executives who develop strategic plans.

**tort (p. 576)** A wrongful act that causes injury to another person's body, property, or reputation.

**total fixed costs (p. 394)** All the expenses that remain the same no matter how many products are made or sold.

**total product offer (p. 380)** Everything that consumers evaluate when deciding whether to buy something; also called a *value package*.

**trade credit (p. 494)** The practice of buying goods and services now and paying for them later.

**trade deficit (p. 64)** An unfavorable balance of trade; occurs when the value of a country's imports exceeds that of its exports.

**trade protectionism (p. 75)** The use of government regulations to limit the import of goods and services. Advocates of trade protectionism believe that it allows domestic producers to survive and grow, producing more jobs.

**trademark (p. 385)** A brand that has been given exclusive legal protection for both the brand name and the pictorial design.

**training and development (p. 297)** All attempts to improve productivity by increasing an employee's ability to perform. Training focuses on short-term skills, whereas development focuses on long-term abilities.

**transparency (p. 221)** A concept that describes a company being so open to other companies working with it that the once-solid barriers between them become see-through and electronic information is shared as if the companies were one.

**trial balance (p. 463)** A summary of all the data in the account ledgers to show whether the figures are correct and balanced.

**trial close (p. 440)** A step in the selling process that consists of a question or statement that moves the selling process toward the actual close.

***trigger-happy*** *Term that refers to people reacting too fast to the circumstances facing them in a difficult situation.*

***turn a blind eye*** *Ignore something of importance.*

***turn the work off*** *Stop working.*

**umbrella policy (p. 644)** A broadly based insurance policy that saves you money because you buy all your insurance from one company.

**unemployment rate (p. 46)** The number of civilians at least 16 years old who are unemployed and tried to find a job within the prior four weeks.

**Uniform Commercial Code (UCC) (p. 579)** A comprehensive commercial law, adopted by every state in the United States, that covers sales laws and other commercial laws.

**uninsurable risk (p. 623)** A risk that no insurance company will cover.

**union (p. 322)** An employee organization that has the main goal of representing members in employee-management bargaining over job-related issues.

**union security clause (p. 327)** Provision in a negotiated labor–management agreement that stipulates that employees who benefit from a union must either officially join or at least pay dues to the union.

**union shop agreement (p. 328)** Clause in a labor–management agreement that says workers do not have to be members of a union to be hired, but must agree to join the union within a prescribed period.

**unlimited liability (p. 119)** The responsibility of business owners for all of the debts of the business

**unsecured bond (p. 501)** A bond backed only by the reputation of the issuer; also called a debenture bond.

**unsecured loan (p. 497)** A loan that's not backed by any specific assets.

**unsought goods and services (p. 382)** Products that consumers are unaware of, haven't necessarily thought of buying, or find that they need to solve an unexpected problem.

**utility (p. 407)** In economics, the want-satisfying ability, or value, that organizations add to goods or services when the products are made more useful or accessible to consumers than they were before.

**value (p. 376)** Good quality at a fair price. When consumers calculate the value of a product, they look at the benefits and then subtract the cost to see if the benefits exceed the costs.

**variable costs (p. 394)** Costs that change according to the level of production.

**variable life insurance (p. 642)** Whole life insurance that invests the cash value of the policy in stocks or other high-yielding securities.

**venture capital (p. 503)** Money that is invested in new or emerging companies that are perceived as having great profit potential.

**venture capitalists (p. 168)** Individuals or companies that invest in new businesses in exchange for partial ownership of those businesses.

**vertical merger (p. 132)** The joining of two companies involved in different stages of related businesses.

**vestibule training (p. 298)** Training done in schools where employees are taught on equipment similar to that used on the job.

**viral marketing (p. 446)** The term now used to describe everything from paying people to say positive things on the Internet to setting up multilevel selling schemes whereby consumers get commissions for directing friends to specific Web sites.

**virtual corporation (p. 221)** A temporary networked organization made up of replaceable firms that join and leave as needed.

**virtual private network (VPN) (p. 603)** A private data network that creates secure connections, or "tunnels," over regular Internet lines.

**virtualization (p. 597)** Accessibility through technology that allows business to be conducted independent of location.

**virus (p. 610)** A piece of programming code inserted into other programming to cause some unexpected and, for the victim, usually undesirable event.

**vision (p. 185)** An encompassing explanation of why the organization exists and where it's trying to head.

**volume, or usage, segmentation (p. 364)** Dividing the market by usage (volume of use).

**voluntary bankruptcy (p. 586)** Legal procedures initiated by a debtor.

***walk out the door*** *Leave the company; quit your job.*

***watching over your shoulder*** *Looking at everything you do.*

**whistleblowers (p. 97)** People who report illegal or unethical behavior.

**whole life insurance (p. 642)** Life insurance that stays in effect until age 100.

**wholesaler (p. 404)** A marketing intermediary that sells to other organizations.

**will (p. 648)** A document that names the guardian for your children, states how you want your assets distributed, and names the executor for your estate.

**word-of-mouth promotion (p. 445)** A promotional tool that involves people telling other people about products they've purchased.

**World Bank (p. 564)** The bank primarily responsible for financing economic development; also known as the International Bank for Reconstruction and Development.

**World Trade Organization (WTO) (p. 76)** The international organization that replaced the General Agreement on Tariffs and Trade, and was assigned the duty to mediate trade disputes among nations.

**yellow-dog contract (p. 325)** A type of contract that required employees to agree as a condition of employment not to join a union; prohibited by the Norris-LaGuardia Act in 1932.

# photo credits

## PROLOGUE

Page 4: © Digital Vision
Page 6: © PhotoDisc/Getty Images
Page 8: © Digital Vision
Page 10: The McGraw-Hill Companies, Inc./Christopher Kerrigan, photographer
Page 12: The Studio Dog/Getty Images
Page 13: © Blend Images/SuperStock
Page 16: Robert Nickelsberg/Getty Images
Page 22: PRNewsFoto/CareerBuilder.com/AP/Wide World Photos.

## CHAPTER 1

Page 3: Photo courtesy of Michele Foods
Page 4: © John Madere/Corbis
Page 5: Samantha Sin/AFP/Getty Images
Page 8: AP/Wide World Photos
Page 12: AP/Wide World Photos
Page 13: © Mark Richards/PhotoEdit
Page 14 (top): AP/Wide World Photos
Page 14 (bottom): AP/Wide World Photos
Page 15: PRNewsFoto/NEWSWEEK/AP/Wide World Photos
Page 17: Ad courtesy of Cargill, Incorporated ©2006
Page 19: © CLARO CORTES IV/Reuters/Corbis
Page 20: Photo by Bob Nichols, USDA Natural Resources Conservation Service.

## CHAPTER 2

Page 28: Photo by Ojo Newspaper/Getty Images
Page 30 (left): © Royalty Free/Corbis
Page 30 (right): AP/Wide World Photos
Page 32: Saeed Khan/AFP/Getty Images
Page 33: © Naashon Zalk/Corbis
Page 34: AP/Wide World Photos
Page 35 (top): © Tom Thaves
Page 35: (bottom): AP/Wide World Photos
Page 36: AP/Wide World Photos
Page 41: © Francis Dean/The Image Works
Page 42: © Claudia Daut/Reuters/Corbis
Page 46: © Monika Graff/The Image Works
Page 48: © Hulton-Deutsch Collection/Corbis
Page 50: © James Marshal/The Image Works.

## CHAPTER 3

Page 58 (left): Steve Finn/Getty Images
Page 58 (right): MTV Networks Asia
Page 63: AP/Wide World Photos
Page 64: PRNewsFoto/Build-A-Bear Workshop/AP/Wide World Photos
Page 65: Danziger/Cartoon Arts International/NY Times Syndicate
Page 66: Yoshikazu Tsuno/AFP/Getty Images
Page 67: Courtesy of Domino's Pizza
Page 68: Alexander Nemenov/AFP/Getty Images
Page 71: Photo courtesy of The Tuscaloosa News, Tuscaloosa, Ala.
Page 73: Credit © European Community, 2006
Page 75: AP/Wide World Photos
Page 77: AP/Wide World Photos
Page 80: Kevin Lee/Bloomberg News/Landov
Page 81: AP/Wide World Photos.

## CHAPTER 4

Page 89: AP/Wide World Photos
Page 90: John Gress/Getty Images
Page 94: Darryl Lester, Hindsight Consulting
Page 98: Gregory Heisler/Time Inc./Time Life Pictures/Getty Images
Page 99: John Gillooly, Professional Event Images, Inc.
Page 102: AP/Wide World Photos
Page 103: Mike Segar/Reuters
Page 105: © Todd Selby
Page 106: PRNewsFoto/P&G/AP/Wide World Photos
Page 108: © Deanne Fitzmaurice/San Francisco Chronicle/Corbis.

## CHAPTER 5

Page 117: Courtesy of Cold Stone Creamery
Page 119: © Max Hirshfeld
Page 121: © Gillian Laub
Page 123: John Costello/Philadelphia Inquirer
Page 128: © Craig Sands
Page 133: © 2005 Ted Rice, All rights are reserved
Page 136: InterContinental Hotels Group
Page 139: © Stacy Kranitz
Page 141: Reuters/Claro Cortes IV/Landov.

## CHAPTER 6

Page 148: Photo courtesy of Pinnacle
Page 150: ©2005 Matthew Gilson/All Rights Reserved
Page 155: AP/Wide World Photos
Page 157: AP/Wide World Photos
Page 158: © Bill Varie/Corbis
Page 159: John Roca/New York Daily News
Page 160: © Pier Nicola D'Amico
Page 164: © Chris Fanning
Page 165: Copyright 2005, USA TODAY. Reprinted with permission
Page 166: Ron Tarver/Philadelphia Inquirer
Page 170: AP/Wide World Photos
Page 172: Laura Mueller/Charlotte Observer.

## CHAPTER 7

Page 181: © Scott McDermott/Corbis
Page 182: AP/Wide World Photos
Page 183: © Fred Prouser/Reuters/Corbis
Page 184: Courtesy of Monster
Page 186: Alex Wong/Getty Images
Page 189: AP/Wide World Photos
Page 191: David W. Harbaugh
Page 193: © Catherine Karnow/Corbis
Page 194: AP/Wide World Photos.

## CHAPTER 8

Page 204: Courtesy of Xerox Corporation
Page 209: Courtesy of German Information Center, NY
Page 212: © John Gress/Reuters/Corbis
Page 213: © The New Yorker Collection 2005 Drew Dernavich from cartoonbank.com. All Rights Reserved
Page 220 PRNewsFoto/Rubbermaid Home Products/AP Wide World Photos
Page 221: Comstock/PictureQuest
Page 222: Photo courtesy of K2 Sports
Page 223: Laura Skelding/The Austin American-Statesman
Page 226: AP/Wide World Photos.

## CHAPTER 9

Page 232: REUTERS/Rebecca Cook
Page 234: Brian Schoenhals/Getty Images
Page 236: Chicago Tribune photo by Charles Osgood. All rights reserved. Used with permission
Page 237: Courtesy of The Ritz Carlton
Page 238: Reprinted from the July 4, 2005 issue of Business Week by permission. Copyright 2005 by The McGraw-Hill Companies
Page 240: © Brownie Harris/CORBIS
Page 241: © Rainer Holz/Corbis
Page 242: © Ann States
Page 249: © Jeff Sciortino Photography.

## CHAPTER 10

Page 259 (left): Justin Sullivan/Getty Images
Page 259 (right): Photo Courtesy of Hot Topic
Page 261: Justin Sullivan/Getty Images
Page 262: Property of AT&T Archives. Reprinted with permission of AT&T.
Page 264: © Intel
Page 268: Courtesy of Southwest Airlines
Page 270: Courtesy of Ruckus Wireless
Page 271: Courtesy of Mini Maids
Page 277: Courtesy of Ford Motor Co.
Page 278: © Mark Richards/PhotoEdit.

## CHAPTER 11

Page 286: Courtesy of Wegmans
Page 295: © Juliana Sohn
Page 297 © Jay LaPrete/ Bloomberg News /Landov
Page 298: Photo courtesy of NASA
Page 300: © Jon Silla
Page 305: AAA World, Sept/Oct '01, Vol. 3, No. 5, page 13
Page 306: Courtesy of Caterpillar
Page 307: Photo courtesy of Jet Blue
Page 309: Steve Maisey/TopFoto.co.uk/The Image Works
Page 313: Keith Brofsky/Getty Images.

## CHAPTER 12

Page 321: © John Gress/Reuters/Corbis
Page 322: © Viviane Moos/Corbis
Page 327: Mike Simons/Getty Images
Page 332: AP/Wide World Photos
Page 333: Clavieres Virginie/SIPA
Page 336: Cavannaugh/EPA/Landov
Page 338: © Steven Georges/Press-Telegram/Corbis
Page 339: © Royalty-Free/Corbis
Page 340: AP/Wide World Photos.

## CHAPTER 13

Page 348: Daniel Hennessy Photography
Page 351: The Procter and Gamble Company
Page 352: Courtesy of Earth Share and The Advertising Council
Page 355: Courtesy of Bear Naked
Page 358: © Spencer Grant/PhotoEdit
Page 361: AZN Television/International Networks
Page 362: AP/Wide World Photos
Page 365: Photo Courtesy of Zane's Cycles.

## CHAPTER 14

Page 375: W. L. Gore & Associates, Inc.
Page 376: © Ray Reiss Photography
Page 380: © Stewart Cohen/Getty Images
Page 382 (left): © age fotostock/SuperStock
Page 382 (right): © Comstock/SuperStock
Page 384: David Young-Wolff/PhotoEdit
Page 385: © Dennis Kleiman Photography
Page 387: American Paper Optics, HO/AP/Wide World Photos
Page 390: Scott S. Hamrick/Philadelphia Inquirer
Page 393: AP/Wide World Photos
Page 395: © Dennis MacDonald/PhotoEdit.

## CHAPTER 15

Page 403: © Robin Twomey
Page 404: AP/Wide World Photos
Page 408: © Al Anderer
Page 413 (left): The McGraw-Hill Companies, Inc./Andrew Resek, photographer
Page 413 (right): Used with permission from Gap Inc.
Page 414: Santi Burgos/Bloomberg News/Landov
Page 415: Mel Nathanson/The News and Observer
Page 416: © 2006 Harry and David
Page 418: © Menlo Worldwide, LLC
Page 419: © Gary Braasch/Woodfin Camp
Page 421: © Royalty Free/Corbis
Page 423 (left and right): AP/Wide World Photos.

## CHAPTER 16

Page 430: REUTERS/Calle Toernstroem
Page 435 (top): AP/Wide World Photos
Page 435 (bottom): HORST OSSINGER/DPA/Landov
Page 437: Photo provided by Grey Worldwide, © Grey Worldwide; www.covergirl.com
Page 439: Thinkstock/Jupiter Images
Page 441: Digital Vision/Getty Images
Page 444: International Manufacturing Technology Show
Page 445: © Susan Van Etten/PhotoEdit
Page 447: The McGraw-Hill Companies, Inc./John Flournoy, photographer.

## CHAPTER 17

Page 454: Courtesy of Roxanne Coady; photo by Tricia Bohan Photography
Page 458: Michael Rosenfeld/Getty Images
Page 459: Stockbyte/Getty Images
Page 462: © Dave Carpenter
Page 472: AP/Wide World Photos
Page 476: © age fotostock/SuperStock.

## CHAPTER 18

Page 483: Gino Domenico/Bloomberg News/Landov
Page 485: AP/Wide World Photos
Page 486: Don Farrall/Getty Images
Page 492: © Comstock Images
Page 496: AP/Wide World Photos
Page 499: Provided by American Express
Page 501: © Peter Newcomb/Reuters/Corbis.

## CHAPTER 19

Page 511: Reprinted from the October 31, 2005 issue of Business Week by permission. Copyright 2005 by The McGraw-Hill Companies
Page 512: Courtesy of The Motley Fool
Page 519: AP/Wide World Photos
Page 520: © Robert Brenner/Photo Edit
Page 523: © Brand X/SuperStock
Page 525: © 2006 Charles Schwab & Co., all rights reserved.
Page 526: Mick Stevens
Page 528: AP/Wide World Photos
Page 532: © Digital Vision
Page 536: © Bettmann/CORBIS.

## CHAPTER 20

Page 544: © Ken Cedeno/Corbis
Page 547: Robin Weiner/U.S. Newswire; The U.S. Department of the Treasury Bureau of Engraving and Printing
Page 553: © Bettmann/CORBIS
Page 555: AP/Wide World Photos
Page 558: © TIAA-CREF
Page 562: AP/Wide World Photos
Page 564: AP/Wide World Photos.

## BONUS CHAPTER A

Page 572: © Reuters
Page 574: © Royalty Free/Corbis
Page 578: Mark Wilson/Getty Images
Page 580: © Mark Richards/PhotoEdit
Page 586: © PETER MORGAN/Reuters/Corbis.

## BONUS CHAPTER B

Page 595: Courtesy of Trend Micro
Page 597: AP/Wide World Photos
Page 599: AP/Wide World Photos
Page 602: PRNewsFoto/Newsweek/AP/Wide World Photos
Page 605: Justin Sullivan/Getty Images
Page 610: Lucas Schifres/Landov.

## BONUS CHAPTER C

Page 618: The Birmingham News
Page 620: AP/Wide World Photos
Page 622: AP/Wide World Photos
Page 625: PRNewsFoto/Aflac Incorporated/AP/Wide World Photos.

## BONUS CHAPTER D

Page 632: © Don Farrall/Photodisc/Getty Images
Page 635: Ryan McVay/Getty Images
Page 638: Ryan McVay/Getty Images
Page 640: © Keith Meyers/The New York Times
Page 644: © Royalty Free/Corbis
Page 646: AP/Wide World Photos.

# name index


## A

Abrams, Joel, 88
Abrams, Rhonda, 269
Achuthan, Lakshman, N-2
Ackerly, Leona, 271
Acuff, Stewart, 327
Adair, A. Jayson, 402–403
Adner, Ron, N-8
Aeppel, Timothy, N-3
Ahrens, Frank, N-16
Aichlmayr, Lisa, N-21
Alexander, Whit, 226
Allen, Margaret, 149
Allen, Mike, N-17
Allison, Kevin, N-7
Alsever, Jennifer, N-4
Altucher, James, N-22
Ames, Paul, N-4
Anderson, Jenny, 522
Anderson, Thomas M., N-16
Andrews, Linda Wasmer, N-11
Aneiro, Michael, N-16
Antioco, John F., 337
Arches, Rick, N-18
Archibald, George, N-14
Ariniello, Ed, 294
Aristotle, 91
Arndt, Michael, 360, N-2, N-3, N-10
Ashby, Andrew, N-18
Ashby, Marty, 161
Ashford, Kate, N-18
Assemi, Yasmin, N-18
Aston, Adam, N-9
Atkins, Ralph, N-19
Audretsch, David, 235–236
Augustine, Norman R., N-9
Avery, Simon, N-7
Aylsworth, Tim, N-1

## B

Babcock, Charles, N-22
Babcock, Pamela, N-10
Badenhausen, Kurt, N-14
Baker, Stephen, N-16
Balaban, R. C., N-19
Balestracci, Davis, N-10
Balfour, Frederik, N-4, N-21
Ballinger, Megan, N-1
Balls, Andrew, 565, N-20
Bamford, James, N-9
Barbaro, Michael, 186
Barfield, Claude, N-4
Barker, Robert, 134
Barkholz, David, N-14, N-18
Barnes, Brenda, 211
Barnes, Rosemary, N-5
Barnett, Megan, N-16
Barr, Paul, N-17
Barrett, Amy, N-9, N-18
Barrett, Rick, N-3
Barro, Robert J., 545
Bartlett, Bruce, N-2, N-20
Bartwin, William, 381
Baruzzi, Cara, 455
Basler, Barbara, N-23
Bassak, Gil, N-3
Bassi, Laurie, N-12
Batterson, Robert, N-3
Baxter, Andrew, N-8
Baynton, Dick, N-8
Bayot, Jennifer, N-18
Beales, Richard, N-19
Becker, Lori, N-20
Beckloff, Mark, 128
Befus, Elizabeth Feigin, N-14
Beichman, Arnold, 438
Bellman, Eric, N-3
Bender, Rick S., N-13
Benjamin, Matthew, N-6
Bennett, Julie, N-6, N-16
Bensinger, Ken, N-21
Berensen, Alex, N-20
Berinato, Scott, N-22
Berke, Lanny R., N-20
Berkowitz, Harry, 134
Berkowitz, Jeff, 510
Bernanke, Ben, 544, 545, 568
Berner, Robert, N-15
Berners-Lee, Tim, 612
Bernstein, Aaron, 321, 327, N-1, N-5, N-20
Bernstein, James, 573
Berry, Kate, 459
Berry, Leonard, N-10, N-15
Bertani, Elizabeth, 486
Beucke, Dan, N-9, N-16
Bezos, Jeff, 14, 150
Biesada, Alex, 403
Bigda, Carolyn, N-22
Birchall, Jonathan, 327, N-3, N-20
Birck, Jon, 504
Birger, Jon, 188, 633
Birnbaum, Jeffrey H., 244
Bishop, Phil, N-7
Bishop, Tricia, N-7
Blackman, Matt, N-19
Blake, Marilyn, N-14
Blakeley, Kiri, N-14
Blanchard, Kenneth, N-5
Blanton, Kimberly, N-5
Blass, Eileen, N-7
Blenko, Marcia, N-8
Block, Robert, N-4
Block, Sandra, N-21
Bodnar, Janet, N-23
Bohnengel, Andrew, 173
Boies, David, 572–573
Bolles, Richard Nelson, P-19
Bolt, Kristen Millares, N-6
Bolton, Lisa E., N-15
Bonaminio, Jim, 150
Bonasia, J., N-17
Bonne, Jon, N-7
Bono, 564
Booker, Katrina, N-15
Boorstein, Julia, 68
Boorstin, Julia, N-9, N-15
Borger, Gloria, N-4
Borrus, Amy, N-18, N-23
Boselovic, Len, N-11
Boston, William, N-9
Boucher, Carol, 448
Boudette, Neal E., N-8
Boulton, Clint, N-22
Bounds, Gwendolyn, 431, N-7, N-20
Boushey, Heather, 339
Bower, Amanda, N-1, N-2
Bowley, Graham, N-4
Boyle, Matthew, 287, 448, N-20
Boynton, Andy, N-9
Bradach, Jeffrey, N-1
Brand, Horst, N-10
Brandow, Peter, N-11
Bratman, Steven, N-10
Breen, Bill, N-8
Breland, Camille, N-4
Breshears, Ronald G., N-11
Bresiger, Gregory, N-19
Breslau, Karen, N-21
Bridis, Ted, N-22
Brodsky, Norm, N-14, N-23
Brody, Richard, N-17
Brooks, Jennifer, N-21
Brousseau, Kenneth R., N-8
Brown, Carolyn M., N-18
Brown, Karla, 169
Brown, Roger, 341
Brown, Warren, 119
Browning, E. S., N-2
Buchanan, Leigh, N-1, N-8
Buchholz, Todd G., 321
Buckingham, Marcus, N-8
Buckley, William F., N-14
Buderi, Robert, 13, 409, N-8
Buffett, Warren, 528
Buhler, Patricia M., N-10
Burghart, Tara, 181
Burk, Ken, 116
Burrows, Peter, 224
Burrus, Amy, N-19
Burt, Shelia, N-13
Burt, Tim, N-3
Burton, Thomas M., N-21
Busbaum, Peter, N-20
Bush, George W., 97, 100, 544
Bush, Jason, N-9
Butrym, Daniel, 296
Butters, Jamie, N-9
Bylinsky, Gene, 233
Byrne, John A., N-10
Byrnes, Nanette, N-15

## C

Cadwallader, Susan, N-10, N-15
Caffrey, Andrew, N-5
Caiafa, Nikki, N-1
Callioni, Gianpaolo, N-16
Calvey, Mark, N-18
Cambria, Nancy, N-7
Cane, Alan, N-22
Canion, Rod, 128
Canli, Turhan, 295
Canon, Scott, N-22
Canter, John, N-7

Capell, Perri, N-1, N-7
Capella, Jaime, N-21
Caplin, Joan, N-22
Capobianco, Faust, 160
Cappelli, Peter, N-8
Capps, Brooke, 353
Carew, Rick, N-3
Carey, Ron, 320
Carey, Susan, N-13
Carlson, Leah, N-12
Carlton, Jim, N-5
Carlyle, Thomas, 31
Carney, Brian M., N-2
Carpenter, Dave, N-13
Carpenter, Marilyn, N-7
Carrington, Jerrold, 166
Carter, Adrienne, N-3
Carter, Rob, N-16
Casabona, Liza, 498, N-18
Case, Steve, N-1
Casert, Raf, N-21
Cather, Chris, N-18
Catlette, Bill, 104
Cattani, Kyle, 409, N-16
Causey, Richard, 91
Celello, Michael, 166
Cervallas, Diego, N-4
Challagalla, Goutam, N-10, N-12
Challenger, John A., N-6
Chan, Gilbert, N-11
Chandler, Clay, 183, N-4, N-5
Chang, Jenny, 595
Chang, Steve, 595
Chapman, Peter, N-19
Chase, Marilyn, N-2
Chea, Terence, N-13
Chen, Eva, 594–595, 596
Chenault, Kenneth I., 8
Chmielewski, Dawn C., 93
Chory-Assad, Rebecca M., N-5, N-10
Chung, Joanna, N-18
Clark, Charlie, 380
Clark, Jane Bennett, N-23
Clark, Maxine, 64
Clifford, Stephanie, N-15
Coady, Roxanne, 454–455, 456
Cohen, Norma, N-4
Collins, Jim, 186
Colvin, Geoff, 259, N-10
Colvin, Geoffrey, N-14, N-15
Comet, Renée, N-9
Conan, Neal, N-11
Condie, Bill, N-20
Condon, Bernard, 44, N-20
Confucius, 91
Conley, Lucas, 188, 269
Conlin, Michelle, N-9, N-12
Connelly, Lynne M., N-12
Conrad, Lee, N-12
Contreras, Guillermo, 98
Cook, Scott, 150
Cooney, Thomas M., N-6
Cooper, James C., 545, N-2
Copeland, Michael V., N-2, N-9, N-15, N-22
Coplin, Bill, N-1
Coy, Peter, 233, N-3
Cramer, Jim, P-6, 510–511
Crawford, Gregory, N-19
Crawford, Samuel, 138–139
Creamer, Matthew, N-16
Creps, Marcela, N-12
Crock, Stan, 207
Crom, Michael, N-11
Cross, Rob, N-8
Crystal, Graef, 338
Cummins, H. J., N-11, N-14
Curran, John, N-20
Curry, Jennifer, N-11


# D


Dalin, Shera, N-6, N-7
Damico, Jack, 459
Damon, William, N-5
Daniel, Caroline, N-14
Danko, William, 632, 634
Dano, Mike, 522
Darman, Jonathan, 181
Dauch, Richard, 232–233
Dauten, Dale, 152
Davenport, Thomas H., N-15
David, Mark, N-22
Davidson, Peter, N-20
Davis, Erroll B., Jr., 8
Davis, Mark, N-19
Dawar, Niraj, N-15
Dawson, Brad, N-13
Dawson, Chester, N-4
De George, Richard T., 110
De Soto, Hernando, 28–29
Dean, Jason, 43
Debreceny, Peter, N-5
Deener, Will, N-19
Dejevsky, Mary, N-4
DeJonquieres, Guy, N-3
Delegge, Ronald L., 529
Dell, Michael, 150
Delong, Brad, N-19
DeMello, Tim, 120
Deming, W. Edwards, 248
DeMoss, Jeff, N-18
Denrell, Jerker, N-9
Depp, Johnny, 60
Derringer, Nancy Nall, N-21
Detamore-Rodman, Crystal, 556, N-6, N-20
Detar, James, N-11
Deutschman, Alan, 375, N-7
DeVage, James, 98
Diamond, John, 61
Diamond, Michael L., N-14
Diana, Tom, N-18
Diaz, J. Albert, N-11
Dickie, Mure, N-15
Diesel, Vin, 436
Diesenhouse, Susan, 519, N-19
Dikel, Margaret Riley, P-23
DiPaolo, Richard, N-10
Disney, Walt, 151
Dobbin, Ben, 174
Dobbs, Lou, N-14
Dobbyn, Paula, N-13
Dogra, Kenneth, N-17
Dolan, Kerry A., 431
Dolloff, J. Holly, 293
Domb, Ellen, 249
Dominguez, Cari, 340
Dominiak, Mark, N-10
Donaldson, Thomas, N-5
Donlan, Thomas G., N-23
Dorsch, Kirstin, N-12
Dotzel, Thomas, N-10, N-15
Dow, Charles, 535
Drayton, Bill, 7
Drew, Jonathan, N-15
Dréze, Xavier, N-15
Driver, Michael J., N-8
Drucker, Peter, 9, 273, 337, N-8
Du Pont de Nemours, Éleuthère Irénée, 150
Ducey, Doug, 116–117
Duffy, Maureen Nevin, N-17
Duggan, Ed, N-6
Duke, Lynne, 321
Dumenco, Simon, N-16
Dunai, Marton, N-4
Dunham, Kemba, N-1
Dunham, Richard S., N-2
Dunphy, Maggie, N-23
Durbin, Dee-Ann, N-11
Durfee, Don, N-17
Dye, Dan, 128
Dylan, Bob, 330


# E


Earnest, Beth, N-12
Easter, Bill, III, 8
Eastern, Joseph S., N-17
Eastman, George, 150
Ebbers, Bernard, 91, 102
Edison, Thomas, 142
Edmondson, Gail, N-9
Edwards, Cliff, N-10, N-22
Egodigwe, Laura, N-1, N-12
Eig, Jonathan, 244
Einhorn, Bruce, N-1
Eisenberg, Lee, N-23
Eisner, Michael, 337, 338
Eizenstat, Stuart E., N-4
Eldridge, Earle, N-5
Elgin, Ben, 224
Ellison, Larry, 337
Ellos, William J., 110
Elson, Charles, 337
Elswick, Jill, N-6, N-12
Emerling, Gary, N-1
Emmert, Matthew, 542
Emmott, Bill, N-4
Ende, Jean, N-18
Engardio, Pete, 381, N-1, N-4, N-9
Ernsberger, Richard, N-4, N-11
Ernst, David, N-9
Esfahani, Elizabeth, N-15
Esterl, Mike, N-8
Estreicher, Samuel, N-13
Etter, Lauren, N-14, N-23
Evans, Melanie, 335
Evans, Philip, N-9
Ewing, Jack, 330, N-13, N-14, N-21
Eyman, Scott, N-4


# F


Fahey, Jonathan, N-8
Faircloth, Mark, N-10
Fang, Bay, 183
Fanning, Shawn, 93
Farnham, Alan, N-16
Farnsworth, Eric, N-4
Farr, Michael, P-19
Farzad, Roben, 511
Fass, Allison, 633, N-14
Fayol, Henri, 208–209, 227
Feldman, Henry, 139–140
Feldman, Paula, 139–140
Feldstein, Mary Jo, 64
Felsted, Andrea, N-22
Fenner, Elizabeth, N-8
Ferguson, Glover, N-22
Fest, Glen, N-12
Feuerherd, Joe, N-5
Fickenscher, Kevin M., N-22
Field, Anne, 293, N-21
Field, Carla, 560
Fillion, Roger, N-22
Fine, Jon, 436
Fink, Anne Marie, N-16

Fiorina, Carleton (Carly), 211, 224, 337
Fischer, Bill, N-9
Fisher, Anne, 290, N-1, N-4, N-6, N-12, N-16
Fishman-Lapin, Julie, 455
Fitzpatrick, John J., Jr., N-11
Fitzpatrick, Mike, N-13
Flandez, Raymund, N-20
Flatley, Kelly, 355
Flexman, Nancy, 151
Flint, Jerry, N-8
Flood, Mary, N-17
Foltz, John, N-11
Foos, Richard, 113
Forbes, Malcolm, 142
Ford, Bill, 225
Ford, Henry, 142, 150
Forelle, Charles, N-8
Foreman, George, 435
Foroohar, Rana, N-21
Forster, Julie, N-1
Foss, Brad, N-22
Fosse, Lynn, 259
Foster, Lauren, 68
Foster, William, N-1
Fournier, Ron, 321
Foust, Dean, 560, N-9, N-22
Fox, Justin, 545
Fox, Kenneth, N-3
Frailey, Fred, N-2
France, Mike, N-5
Frank, Robert, 633
Franklin, Mary Beth, N-23
Franklin, Stephan, N-13
Franklin, Stephen, N-13
Frazier, Mya, N-16
Freedman, David H., N-9, N-22
Freedman, Michael, 44, N-19
Freeman, Sholnn, N-8
Frey, James, 181
Fried, John, N-6
Fried, Lance, 348–349, 351
Friedman, Milton, 99
Fritsch, Peter, N-4
Frum, David, 565, N-20
Fry, Art, 158
Fudge, Ann M., 8
Fuhrmans, Vanessa, N-12
Fung, Amanda, N-7
Fuquay, Jim, 149
Furman, Phyllis, N-22
Futrelle, David, 633, N-23
Futterman, Matthew, 511

## G

Gaboury, Jane, N-10
Gahn, Randy L., N-4
Galbraith, Deanna, N-18
Gallagher, Dave, N-7
Galvin, Robert W., 110
Gamble, James, 150
Ganey, Terry, N-13
Gangemi, Jeffrey, 43, 436
Gantt, Henry L., 251, 262, 280
Gapper, John, N-19
Garcia, Shelly, N-11, N-12
Gardiner, Susannah, 377
Gardner, David, 512, 542
Gardner, Tom, 512, 542
Garnham, Peter, N-19
Garry, Michael, 287
Garten, Jeffrey E., 381
Garvey, Martin J., N-22
Gasparino, Charles, 511
Gaston, A. G., 618–619
Gates, Bill, 4, 5, 33, 150, 151, 260, 573
Gates, Melinda, 33
Gavetti, Giovanni, N-8
Gaynor, Pamela, 337
Geller, Adam, N-5, N-11
Gemperlein, Joyce, N-15
Gengler, Amanda, N-23
Gentry, Connie Robbins, N-9
Gerhart, Ann, 565, N-20
Gerstner, Louis, 205
Giesinger, E. R. 'Bud', N-12
Gilbert, Jared, N-5
Gilbreth, Frank, 262, 280
Gilbreth, Lillian, 262, 280
Giles, Chris, 565, N-20
Gill, Jennifer, N-12, N-14
Gilland, Wendell, 409, N-16
Gillars, Stephen, 573
Giller, Chip, 207, N-23
Gilligan, Gregory J., N-7
Ginsberg, Pamela, N-23
Girard, Kim, 595
Glanz, William, N-13
Glassberg, Brooke Kosofsky, N-23
Glassman, James K., N-23
Gleckman, Howard, N-23
Glenn, Don, 13–14
Goffin, Keith, N-22
Gogoi, Pallavi, N-6
Goldklang, Marvin, 483
Gomes, Lee, 556, N-7
Gompers, Samuel, 324, 325
Gooch, Heather, 293
Goodman, Peter S., N-6
Gordon, Marcy, 519
Gore, Al, 572
Gore, Bill, 374–375, 376
Gore, Bob, 374
Gore, Vieve, 374–375
Gragg, Ellen, N-12
Grant, Jeremy, N-8, N-15, N-19
Graser, Marc, 349, 436
Grassi, Carl, N-11
Graves, Earl, 139
Gray, Andi, N-18
Gray, Steven, N-2, N-3, N-8, N-15
Gray-Carr, Elizabeth, 379
Green, Elwin, N-17
Green, Eric, N-5
Green, Robert, N-12
Greene, Jay, N-5, N-22
Greene, Kelly, N-23
Greenemeier, Larry, N-20, N-21
Greengard, Samuel, N-12
Greenspan, Alan, 544–545
Griffin, Greg, N-19, N-21
Grimm, William A., N-18
Groskind, Nena, N-20
Grossman, Robert J., N-11
Grove, Andrew S., 238–239, 264–265
Grover, Ronald, N-16
Grow, Brian, N-8, N-22
Gruver, Deb, N-7
Guest, Greta, 174
Guiniven, John E., N-10
Gulati, Ranjay, N-8
Gull, Nicole, N-20
Gunn, Eileen, 378
Gutner, Toddi, N-19
Gutterman, Steve, N-4

## H

Hadden, Richard, 104
Hagenbaugh, Barbara, N-17
Haggerty, Maryann, N-1
Hague, Ian P. N., N-17
Hahn, Gregory, N-21
Haines-Stiles, Sasha, N-14
Hajewski, Doris, N-7
Half, Robert, N-12
Hall, Christine, N-3
Hall, Kerry, N-18
Halliday, Jean, N-9
Hamel, Gary, N-8
Hamich, Lars, 529
Hamilton, Alexander, 552
Hamm, Steve, N-15, N-17, N-21
Hammond, Dave, 174
Hammonds, Keith H., 7, 205
Hamori, Monika, N-8
Han Dexun, 43
Hancock, Dain, 245
Hanig, Robert, N-8
Hannagan, Charley, N-14
Hansen, Joe, 327
Hansen, Steven R., N-21
Hansen, Toni, N-19
Hardy, Quentin, N-22
Harper, Philipp, N-6
Harrington, Ann, 375
Harrington, H. James, N-9, N-10
Hastings, Michael, N-21
Hastings, Reed, 157
Havenstein, Heather, N-22
Hawkins, Lee, Jr., N-3, N-8, N-13
Hay, Edward, 302
Hayes, John, 174
Hayes, Michael, N-12
Heath, Thomas, N-13
Heebner, Jennifer, N-17
Heese, Hans Sebastian, 409, N-16
Heffernan, Margaret, N-10
Heffes, Ellen, N-11, N-17
Heffron, Pat, 101
Heintz, Nadine, N-14
Heintz, Rich, N-1
Heise, Michael, N-13
Heller, Marc, N-18
Hellweg, Eric, 420
Helm, Burt, N-9
Helps, Brenda, N-5
Hempel, Jessi, 436, N-5
Hemphill, Thomas A., N-21
Hemsath, Dave, N-10
Hench, David, N-12
Henderson, Nell, 545, N-2, N-18
Henderson, Shirley, N-6
Henle, Christine A., N-10
Hennessy, Melissa, N-14
Henricks, Mark, N-2, N-7, N-11, N-17
Henry, David, N-18, N-19
Herman, Ken, N-21
Herman, Tom, 485, N-17
Hermanson, Joseph V., N-18
Herreras, Mari, N-5
Herrick, Thaddeus, N-8
Herzberg, Frederick, 265–267, 268, 281
Hibbard, Justin, 330, N-14
Hiebert, Murray, N-3
Higgins, Tiesha, N-6
Hill, Dean A., N-10
Hill, Miriam, 511
Hilton, Paris, 387
Hindo, Brian, N-7
Hines, Elizabeth Gardner, 619
Hira, Nadira A., N-10
Hirsch, Arlene S., N-1
Hirschfeld, Bob, 117
Hitt, Greg, N-3, N-4
Ho, David, 137
Ho, Jessie, 595
Hoerr, John, N-13

Hof, Rob, N-8
Hof, Robert D., N-22
Hoffa, James P., 320–321
Hoffa, Jimmy, 320
Hoffmann, Mark A., N-20
Hogan, Mike, N-15
Holden, Greg, N-16
Holmes, Allan, N-21
Holmes, Paul, N-16
Holmes, Stanley, 207
Holt, Shirleen, N-11
Homer-Dixon, Thomas, N-2
Hopkins, Kevin, N-22
Hoskins, Michele, 2–3, 4, 8
Hotchkiss, Julie L., N-2
Hourihon, Gary, N-8
Hovanesian, Mara Der, N-19, N-20, N-23
Howard, Mark N., N-6
Huber, Tim, N-19
Hudson, Kris, N-3
Hughes, Alan, N-3
Hughes, Jennifer, N-18, N-19
Hughes, Jonathan, N-9
Huizenga, H. Wayne, 482
Hull, Anne, 244, 420
Hunstad, Michael, N-18
Hunt, Julian, N-15
Hurd, Mark, 211, 224
Hymowitz, Carol, N-12

## I

Iacocca, Lee, 233
Iger, Robert, 183
Ignatius, David, N-23
Ihlwan, Moon, N-2, N-9
Ingrassia, Joseph, N-18
Ip, Greg, 545
Iwata, Edward, N-5

## J

Jack, Andrew, N-22
Jackson, Lee Ann, N-8
Jackson, Ngina, N-14
Jackson, Phil, 194, 195
Jackson, Victoria, 170
Jacobs, Jeff, 180–181
James, Derrell S., N-9
James, Joseph B., III, N-19
Jamison, Jess, 335
Jarrett, Linda F., N-10
Jarvis, Gail Marks, N-19
Jefferson, Thomas, 90, 552
Jenkins, Carol, 619
Jenkins, Holman W., N-23
Jewell, Mark, N-5
Jobs, Steve, 128, 150, 154
Johnson, Andrew, N-20
Johnson, Avery, N-9, N-15
Johnson, Bradley, N-15
Johnson, Carrie, 91
Johnson, Hillary, N-16
Johnson, James C., 619, N-18
Johnson, Jo, 61
Johnson, M. Eric, N-22
Johnson, P. Fraser, N-8, N-9
Johnson, Robert Wood, 96
Johnston, Megan, N-20
Johnston, Randy, N-17
Jones, Andrea, N-4
Jones, Chip, N-16
Jones, Daniel T., N-2
Jones, Steve, N-6
Jorgensen, Barbara, N-5
Joshi, Pradnya, 519
Jotkowitz, Joe, 296
Joyce, Amy, 327, N-6, N-8
Judge, Tom, N-17
Judson, Whitcomb, 389

## K

Kadet, Anne, N-20
Kadlec, David, 511
Kahn, Virginia Munger, N-17
Kaihla, Paul, N-1, N-15
Kalru, Ritu, N-13
Kang, Cecilia, N-1
Kang, Stephanie, N-3
Kang, Sunwoo, N-12
Kapadla, Reshma, 205, N-19, N-20
Kaplan, Dan, 271
Karan, Donna, 9
Karlgaard, Rich, N-2
Karmali, Naazneen, 44
Katzenbach, Jon R., N-8
Kayal, Michele, N-15
Kearns, Michelle, N-6
Keating, Michael, N-11
Keith, Bob, 137
Kellaway, Lucy, N-8
Kelleher, Herb, 268
Kellner, Tomas, N-14
Kelly, Gary, 268
Kelly, Kate, N-3
Kemp, Jack, N-23
Kemper, Kevin, N-5
Kempfer, Lisa M., 259
Kennedy, John F., 584
Kerner, Sean Michael, N-21
Kerr, Jennifer C., N-13
Kianoff, Lisa, N-17
Kiley, David, N-15, N-16
Kilts, Patrick, N-18
Kimball, Roger, N-1
Kimmel, Lawrence M., N-16
King, Sammi, N-6
Kingsbury, Kathleen, N-15
Kinnear, Thomas C., 411
Kinsella, N. Stephan, 29
Kirby, Jeff, N-10
Kirchheimer, Sid, 560
Kirchhoff, Bruce, 162
Kirkpatrick, David, N-16
Kirsner, Scott, 377
Kish, Matthew, N-20
Kislik, Liz, N-12
Kiwak, Danielle, N-14
Klaassen, Abbey, N-16
Klassen, Robert D., N-8, N-9
Kleiman, Carol, N-14, N-22
Klein, Karen E., N-6
Klug, Foster, N-4
Kluger, Jeffrey, N-23
Knapp, Laura G., N-1
Knemeyer, A. Michael, N-9
Knight, Danielle, 565, N-20
Koch, Christopher, N-21
Koen, Deb, N-1
Kohrs, Kenneth, 277
Kolodny, Laura, 349
Kolodny, Lora, 448, N-15, N-16
Koons, Jennifer, N-13
Kosnett, Jeffrey R., N-20
Kovach, Lisa, N-11
Kozlowski, Dennis, 91
Kramer, Roderick M., N-7
Krannich, Caryl, P-19
Krannich, Ron, P-19
Krantz, Matt, N-19
Krauskopf, Lewis, N-4
Kreisler, B., N-5
Kroll, Luisa, 633
Kropko, M. R., N-21
Krummert, Bob, 377
Kshanika, Anthony, 306
Kuchinskas, Susan, N-7, N-21
Kumar, V., N-9, N-14, N-16
Kurtenbach, Elaine, N-6
Kuttner, Robert, N-5, N-19
Kwak, Sarah, N-6
Kyles, Kyra, N-11

## L

Labbe, Martin, N-17
Ladner, Martin, N-3
LaFollette, Gregory L., N-17
Lally, Kathy, N-15
Lambert, Douglas M., N-9
Lambro, Donald, 10, N-2
Lampert, Edward S., 223, 586
Lancaster, John, 360
Landis, David, N-18
Lapin, Aaron, 152
Larkin, John, 61
Larson, Christine, N-12
Larson, Jane, 117
Larson, Virgil, N-19
Larsson, Rikard, N-8
Lattman, Peter, 174, N-15
Laurienzio, Elizabeth, N-5
Lavelle, Louis, 337, N-9, N-14
Lawler, Edward, 274, N-10
Lay, Kenneth, 91
Le, Thuy-Doan, N-3
Le Coz, Emily, N-7
Lee, Dara, N-2
Lee, Daryl, 172
Lee, Hau L., N-16
Lee, Louise, N-15
Lee, Maria, 140
Lee, Richard, N-11
Lee, Sharon, 172
Lee, Tony, 133
Lehman, Andrea, N-20
Lehmann, Richard, N-18
Leibs, Scott, N-17
Lemelson, Jerome, 578
Lemonick, Michael D., N-15
Leo, John, N-14
Leonard, David, 420
Lesonsky, Rieva, N-16
Lester, Tom, N-2, N-9, N-16
Lester, Will, N-13
Leung, Sze, 409
Levinson, Meridith, N-12, N-21
Levy, Steven, N-15, N-21, N-22
Lewis, Christina S. N., N-9
Lewis, Diane E., N-13
Lewis, John L., 324
Lewis, Katherine Reynolds, N-10
Li Yifei, 58–59
Liedtke, Jeanne, N-8
Liedtke, Michael, N-18
Lienhart, Anita, N-5
Lindsey, Lawrence B., N-21
Linebaugh, Kate, 44, N-20
Lipshutz, Joshua S., N-13
LL Cool J, 578
Llorca, Juan Carlos, N-4
Lo, Selina, 270
Loeb, Marshall, N-1
London, Simon, N-8
Loomis, David G., N-21
Lowenstein, Michael, N-14
Lowry, Tom, N-3, N-17
Lublin, Joann S., 337, N-3, N-14
Lucas, George, 336

Lucas, Leyland M., N-6
Lukaszuk, Wanda, 35
Lundegaard, Karen, N-13
Lutz, Jason, 161
Luxenberg, Stan, N-18
Lynn, Kathleen, 154

## M

McAdams, Jennifer, N-22
MacArthur, Kate, N-15
McClam, Erin, 91
McClenahen, John S., N-5, N-17
McConnaughey, Janet, N-20
McConnell, David, 150
McCormick, Cyrus, 20
McCracken, Jeffrey, N-9
McCrarey, Sandy, N-10
McDermott, John P., N-11
McDonald, Ian, 134
McDonald, Leslie Rose, N-5, N-11
McDonnell, Sanford, 503
McDougall, Paul, 61, N-3
McFarlin, Dean B., N-10
McGee, Marianne Kolbasuk, N-21
McGeehan, Patrick, 337
McGinn, Daniel, N-21
McGregor, Douglas, 269–271, 281, N-4
McGregor, Jena, N-10, N-14, N-15
McIntosh, Andrew, N-19
McIntyre-Tavella, Leslie, N-11
McKimmie, Kathe, N-17
Mackintosh, James, N-8, N-19
McLaughlin, Elizabeth, 258–259, 260
McLean, Bethany, N-4
Mcmasters, Paul K., 98
McMurrer, Daniel, N-12
McNamee, Mike, N-19, N-23
McNellis, Thomas, N-9
McPherson, Sue, 259
McWilliams, Gary, N-18
Madden, Normandy, 59
Madden, Steve, 337
Madigan, Kathleen, N-2
Madore, James T., N-4
Maffezzoli, Dennis, N-13
Mageto, Tabitha, 151–152
Magin, Konstantin, N-19
Magnusson, Paul, N-3
Maher, Kris, 335, N-13
Mahli, Paramjit, N-17
Maier, Matthew, N-16
Main, Jeremy, 29
Maitland, Alison, N-5, N-12
Malanson, James R., 290
Mallaby, Sebastian, 565, N-20
Mallery, John, N-22
Malone, Michael S., 224
Malthus, Thomas, 31, 32, 52
Malykhina, Elena, N-11
Mandelson, Peter, 61, N-4
Manes, Stephen, N-22
Mangu-Ward, Katherine, 89, N-5, N-23
Mankins, Michael C., N-8
Mannes, George, N-23
Manuel, Marlon, N-14
Mapes, Lynda V., N-5, N-12
Mapes, Timothy, N-4
Marchick, David, N-4
Marek, Angie C., N-4
Mariner, Jonathan, 482–483, 484
Markham, Chris, 375
Markkula, Mike, 154
Markoff, John, N-22
Markoff, Katrina, 164
Marlin, Steven, N-22
Martin, David F., N-4
Martin, Edward, N-20
Martin, Franny, 165
Martinez, Michael J., N-21
Marx, Groucho, 260
Mashberg, Tom, N-16
Maslow, Abraham, 263–265, 281
Mason, Linda, 341
Mason-Draffen, Carrie, N-7
Mateja, Jim, N-3
Mateschitz, Dieter, 430–431
Mathur, Sanjay, N-22
Matthews, Guy, 438
Mauer, Harry, 353
Maurer, Harry, N-8
Maxon, Terry, N-17
Mayer, Caroline E., N-20
Mayer, Kathy, N-7
Mayes, Rick, N-6
Mayo, Elton, 262–263, 281
Maytum, Mary Jane, N-12
Meany, George, 324
Mecoy, Don, N-11, N-19
Meer, David, N-15
Mehring, James, N-9
Mehta, Stephanie N., N-16
Melloan, Jim, N-7
Melton, Mark, 139
Mendez, Teresa, 378
Meredith, Robyn, N-1
Merritt, Jennifer, N-9
Mervis, Scott, 93
Meyers, Dave, 374
Micahnik, Phyllis, N-18
Michelson, Gary, 577–578
Miller, Aaron, 258, 259
Miller, James P., N-18, N-21
Miller, Jeanne Marie, 155
Miller, Justin, N-13
Miller, Karen Lowry, N-13
Miller, Michael, 485
Miller, Rich, N-2, N-18
Miller, Robert, 149
Millman, Gregory J., N-17
Milne, Richard, 330
Minder, Raphael, N-15
Minow, Nell, 337
Mintz, Jessica, N-1
Misonzhnik, Elaine, N-21
Mitchell, Rick, N-22
Mitchell, Robert L., N-21
Mogharabi, Shabnam, N-7
Mohammed, Rafi, N-15
Mohr, Fred A., N-1
Molloy, Theresa, 524
Molloy, Tim, N-14
Mongros, Xavier de, N-16
Monies, Paul, N-13
Moon, Youngme, N-15
Moore, Gordon E., 604
Moore, Matt, 330
Moorthy, R. S., 110
Moreno, Jenalia, N-4
Moriarty, Rick, N-7
Morrill, Debra, 293
Morris, Angela, 300
Morris, Betsy, 205, N-13
Morris, Julian, N-4
Morris, Kathryn A., N-7
Morrow, Andrea, N-18
Morse, Susan, 244
Mosk, Matthew, 327
Mower, Sarah, 414
Mowrey, Megan E., N-6
Moylan, Martin J., N-13
Much, Marilyn, N-1
Mucha, Thomas, N-16
Mueller, Jennifer M., N-18
Mueller, Jim, N-18
Mulcahey, Anne, 204–205
Mulcahey, Michael, 91
Mulford, Charles, N-18
Mulherin, Pat, 156–157
Muller, Joann, N-1
Mulpuru, Sucharita, N-7
Mulrine, Anna, 34
Mulzac, Letitia, 499
Murphy, Cait, N-8
Murphy, Chris, N-21
Murphy, H. Lee, N-12
Murphy, Tom, N-19
Murr, Andrew, 431
Musgrave, Beth, N-21
Myers, Deborah J., N-12
Myers, Randy, N-18
Myser, Michael, N-22

## N

Nacchio, Joseph P., 134
Nadel, Brian, N-9, N-16
Nadler, David, 274, N-10
Nakamura, David, N-13
Nance-Nash, Sheryl, 556
Naughton, Keith, 103, N-3, N-9
Navarro, Peter, N-2
Needleman, Sarah E., N-1
Neergaard, Helle, N-6
Neff, Jack, N-15
Nelson, Bob, N-12
Newcomb, Peter, N-14
Newman, Richard J., 353
Newton, Benita, N-12
Nguyen, Terrence, N-13
Nicklaus, David, N-14, N-19
Nisanoff, Daniel, N-16
Nissanoff, Daniel, N-16
Noble, Eric, 235
Nohria, Nitin, 619, N-22
Nolle, Tom, N-22
Noon, Chris, N-9
Norman, Jan, N-18
Norris, Floyd, N-5, N-17
Norton, Frank, N-20, N-23
Norton, Gale, 620
Novak, Michael, N-2
Novak, Robert D., N-17
Nunes, Joseph C., N-15
Nussbaum, Bruce, 375, N-16

## O

O'Brien, Chris, 89
O'Connell, Andrew, N-8
O'Connell, Dan, N-19
O'Connell, Vanessa, N-3
Ogawa, Susumu, N-15
O'Grady, Mary Anastasia, 10, N-2
Oh, Helena, 13
O'Hara, Kathleen Terence, N-20
O'Hara, Terence, N-17, N-20, N-21
Ohlson, Kristin, N-2
Oldroyd, James B., N-8
Olmsted, Larry, N-7
O'Neill, Danny, 395
O'Neill, Sean, N-2
Opdyke, Jeff, N-6, N-10
Oreck, Thomas, 244
Orey, Michael, N-20
Oslund, John J., N-18
Osterman, Rachel, N-13
O'Sullivan, Kate, N-14, N-17
Ouchi, William, 271–272, 281

Overholt, Allison, 149, N-1
Ovitz, Michael, 337
Owen, Clive, 436

## P

Pacelle, Mitchell, N-13
Pacheco, Della, N-11, N-14
Paeth, Greg, N-17
Pageon, Remi, 152
Pagonis, William "Gus," 420
Paley, Amit R., N-21
Palmer, Ann Therese, N-9
Palmeri, Christopher, 431
Panaccio, Tim, N-13
Paoletta, Michael, 59
Parekh, Rupal, N-20
Parish, Janet Turner, N-10, N-15
Parkinson, Kenneth L., N-17, N-18
Parmalee, Nathan, N-18
Parmley, Suzette, N-18
Pascarella, Perry, N-12
Paton, Scott M., N-10
Patton, Carol, N-12
Patton, Susannah, 290
Paulson, Steven K., 110
Payne, Holly J., N-10
Peale, Norman Vincent, N-5
Pelton, Ben, 172
Penland, Dolly, N-6
Penney, J. C., 142
Pennington, April Y., 117, N-6
Penttila, Chris, N-7, N-8
Pepper, Tara, N-12
Perman, Stacy, N-6
Perot, H. Ross, 150
Perryman, Bruce, N-18
Peterson, William, 10
Pfeffer, Jeffrey, N-12, N-14
Phillips, Bruce, 150
Pierce, Elizabeth, 258
Piller, Frank T., N-15
Pilling, David, N-2
Plimmer, Gill, N-23
Polyak, Ilana, N-19
Pomerantz, Dorothy, N-14
Pope, Charles, N-4
Pope, James, N-13
Popeil, Ron, 435–436
Popely, Rick, N-13
Postelnicu, Andrei, 524, N-4
Potts, George, N-14
Pound, Edward T., 565, N-20
Powell, Eileen Alt, N-21
Power, Stephen, 403
Prahalad, C. K., 360
Pramik, Mike, N-19
Pressler, Margaret Webb, N-15
Pressman, Aaron, 529
Prevor, Barry, 174
Priestland, Andreas, N-8
Prince, C. J., N-17
Procter, William, 150
Puck, Wolfgang, 380
Pulley, Brett, N-14
Purdum, Traci, N-17

## Q

Quattrone, Paolo, N-13
Quinlan, Anna, 59
Quinn, Jane Bryant, N-20, N-23

## R

Radtke, Janet M., N-8
Raelin, Joe, N-8
Rafter, Michelle V., N-11
Raghunandan, Dana R., N-18
Rahn, Richard, N-2, N-17, N-20
Ramachandran, Nisha, N-4
Ramsey, Robert D., N-7
Ramstack, Tom, N-20
Ramstad, Evan, N-4
Rattray, Celine, 269
Reagan, Ronald, 332
Reason, Tim, 483, N-18, N-21
Rechner, Paula L., N-18
Reed, Americus, II, N-15
Regnier, Pat, 633, N-22
Reichheld, Fred, N-2, N-8, N-9
Reinartz, Werner, N-9, N-14, N-16
Reingold, Jennifer, N-23
Reisner, Rebecca, N-6
Rekha, N-23
Renehart, Westin, N-16
Ressner, Jeffrey, N-16
Reuteman, Rob, N-4
Reynolds, Alan, 353, N-2, N-9
Reynolds, Dan, N-11
Rheault, Magali, N-15
Ricardo, David, 62
Richards, Jennifer Smith, N-4
Richards, Meg, N-19
Richardson, Karen, 137
Richardson, Nicole Marie, N-7
Richman, Mike, N-2
Richter, Allan, 117
Richter, Burton, N-9
Riechmann, Deb, N-20
Rigas, John, 91
Rigas, Michael, 91
Rigas, Timothy, 91
Riley, Megan, N–1
Ripley, Amanda, N-2
Ritsch, Bill, N-9
Rivkin, Jan W., N-8
Robb, Drew, N-22
Roberts, Chuck, N-11
Roberts, Dan, N-5
Roberts, David, 207, N-23
Roberts, Dexter, 43, 360, N-2
Roberts, Ed, N-21
Roberts, Julia, 60
Roberts, Richard A., N-10
Rockefeller, John D., 443, 503
Rocks, David, N-19
Rodie, Janet Bealer, N-9
Rodriguez, Julie, 188
Rodriguez, Robert, N-7, N-11
Roebuck, Alvah C., 142
Roehm, Frances E., P-23
Rogers, Paul, N-8
Rooke, David, N-8
Roosevelt, Franklin D., 36, 553
Rose, Barbara, N-10
Rose, Michael P., N-17
Rosenberg, Joyce M., N-6
Rosenberg, Larry, 408
Ross, Charlie, N-22
Ross, Philip E., N-22
Ross, Robert, N-13
Ross, Sativa, N-17
Roth, Daniel, N-22
Rothbort, Scott, 511
Rothenberg, Randall, N-16
Ruan, Victoria, N-3
Rubenstein, Sarah, N-23
Rudnick, Michael, 498
Ruiz, Juanita, 408
Ryan, Kate, N-19
Ryan, Oliver, N-19

## S

Sacks, Danielle, 269, N-12
Sagario, Dawn, N-10
Sahadi, Jeanne, N-23
Salter, Chuck, 188
Salyers, Donna, 340
Sammer, Joanne, N-17
Samuelson, Robert J., 381, N-8, N-14, N-23
Sant, Roger, 268
Saracevic, Alan T., 511
Saranow, Jennifer, 353
Sauer, Patrick J., N-12
Saul, Michael, 573
Savitz, Eric J., N-2
Scanlan, Thomas, 151
Schaffner, Dionn, 437
Schmeltzer, John, N-20
Schmid, John, 161
Schnapp, John B., N-13
Schoenberger, Karl, N-5
Schoeniger, Eric, 560, N-2, N-22
Scholtes, Thomas D., N-6
Schroeder, Michael, N-21
Schuessler, Jack, N-22
Schultz, Howard, 63, 88–89, 150, 420
Schulze, Horst, 237
Schumpeter, Joseph, 49
Schunk, Donald L., N-14
Schupak, Amanda, N-14
Schuster, Jay, 303–304
Schwarz, Alan, N-10
Schweitzer, Douglas, N-22
Scott, Lee, 327
Scott, Matthew S., N-23
Scott, Rocky, N-6
Sears, Richard Warren, 142
Segal, Susan, N-4
Seid, Dennis, N-7
Selden, Sally Coleman, N-11
Sellers, Patricia, 181, 279
Semel, Terry, 336
Serwer, Andy, N-5
Shah, Baiju, N-22
Shaich, Ron, 377
Shakespeare, William, 91
Shankar, Venkatesh, N-10, N-15
Sharma, Ruchir, 524
Shea, Peter, N-6
Sheets, Mary Ellen, 139
Shehan, Tom, N-11
Shellenbarger, Sue, 13
Shepherd, Alicia, N-4
Sherwell, Philip, 103
Sherwood, Pat, 486
Sherwyn, David, N-13
Shifrin, Jordan I., N-18
Shilling, A. Gary, N-9
Shir, Mark, 300
Shlachter, Barry, 149
Shore, Steve, 174
Shutts, Carole, 140
Sidel, Robin, N-2
Siedsma, Andrea, N-23
Silva, Jeffery, N-21
Silverman, David, N-19
Silverman, Gary, 349, N-8
Sima, Katherine, 279
Simanoff, David, N-17
Simmons, Gene, 268
Simon, Bernard, N-8, N-19
Simonian, Haig, N-3
Simons, Robert, N-8
Simpson, Glenn R., N-4
Singer, Michael, N-22
Singh, Mahender, N-8, N-16

Singletary, Michelle, N-23
Sisk, Michael, N-14
Sivy, Michael, N-22
Slagmulder, Regine, N-16
Sloan, Alan, N-19
Sloan, Paul, N-2
Slusser, Sarah, 276
Smith, Adam, 32, 34, 52, 99
Smith, Chris, N-3
Smith, Douglas K., N-8
Smith, Elliott Blair, N-4
Smith, Ethan, 93
Smith, Greg W., N-6
Smith, Laura, N-10
Smith, Marguerite, 290
Smith, Tim, N-6
Smith, Will, 60, 336
Snowbeck, Christopher, N-11
Solomon, Robert C., 110
Songini, Marc L., N-22
Sonnenfeld, Jeffrey, 103
Sosnin, Betty, N-14
Southall, Brooke, N-19
Spade, Andy, 121
Spade, Kate, 121
Sparkman, Worth, 459
Sparks, Willard R., N-2
Sparshott, Jeffrey, N-11
Spedalle, Natasha, 159
Springer, John, N-15
Spruell, Sakina P., N-23
Srinivasan, S., N-3
Srite, Mark, N-3
Stack, Jack, N-20
Stackpole, Beth, N-21
Stanley, T. L., 349
Stanley, Thomas, 632, 633, 634
Stavro, Steve, 133
Stead, Jerry, 276–277
Steele, Justin, N-23
Steele, Richard, N-8
Stein, Jason, N-11
Steinbrenner, George, 573
Stephens, Janet, N-7
Stephens, Uriah Smith, 324
Stern, Linda, N-12
Stewart, James B., N-20
Stewart, Martha, 12, 102, 103, 337
Stewart, Thomas A., N-8
Stiles, Greg, N-7
Stiles, Janet, N-14
Stollenwerk, John, 173
Stone, Brad, N-2, N-3, N-15
Stone, Rachel, N-7
Strahinich, John, N-14
Strathnairn, Martin, N-3
Strauss, Levi, 142
Streisand, Betsy, N-4
Strempel, Dan, N-7
Studwell, Joe, N-4
Sullivan, Brendan, N-22
Sullivan, Joanna, N-10
Sullivan, Laurie, N-22
Sunnucks, Mike, N-7
Surmacz, Jon, N-2
Sutherland, Donald, 116–117, 118
Sutherland, Susan, 116–117, 118
Swaminathan, Jayashankar, 409, N-16
Swan, Christopher, N-3, N-6
Swann, Christopher, N-3
Swann, James, N-12
Swartz, Mark, 91
Symonds, William C., N-15
Szuchman, Paula, N-1

## T

Tait, Richard, 226
Takahashi, Dean, N-12
Talkington, Sue, 459
Tam, Pul-Wing, 224, N-8
Tan, Cheryl Lu-Lien, 436
Tashiro, Hiroko, N-19
Tatge, Mark, N-8
Taylor, Alex, III, N-9
Taylor, Chris, N-16
Taylor, Frederick, 260–262, 280
Taylor, Paul, N-15
Tedlow, Richard S., N-10
Tella, Alfred, N-2
Tennent, Devar, 408
Terhune, Chad, N-2, N-16
Terrell, Dorothy, 161
Tett, Gillian, N-18
Thain, John, 519
Thayer, Leah, N-11
Thomas, Cal, N-23
Thomas, Kim, N-7, N-15
Thomas, Paulette, 161, N-6, N-7, N-18
Thompson, John W., 8
Thompson, Susan C., N-18
Thurlow, Heida, 171
Tie, Robert, N-17, N-18
Tierney, Mike, 459
Tilin, Andrew, 403, N-9
Timmerman, Sandra, 341
Tischler, Linda, N-6, N-14
Tkaczyk, Christopher, N-10
Torbert, William R., N-8
Torres, Blanca, N-1, N-14
Torres, Jennifer, N-1
Torres, Nicole, N-17
Townes, Glenn, N-16
Tripp, Julie, N-19, N-22
Troise, Damian J., N-13
Trudeau, Garry, 108
Trujillo, Solomon, 134
Trump, Donald, 436
Tsuruoka, Doug, 149, 161
Tucker, Eric, N-20
Tuffnell, Sean, N-2
Turner, Gregory B., N-11
Turner, Rice, N-5
Turner, Ted, 150
Turnock, Judith, N-16
Tyler, Kathryn, 290, N-5
Tyson, Don, 337
Tyson, Laura D'Andrea, N-2, N-23

## U

Umble, Chad, N-14
Underwood, Anne, N-2
Underwood, Ryan, N-8
Updegrave, Walter, N-19
Urry, Maggie, N-23

## V

Vaca, Nina, 148–149
van Dam, Karen, N-10
van Duyn, Aline, N-16
Van Voorhis, Kenneth R., 153
Van Wassenhove, Luk N., N-16
Vanderbilt, Cornelius, 164
Vargo, Frank, N-3
Varnon, Rob, N-11
Vascellaro, Jessica E., N-9
Velez, Tiana, N-6, N-7
Velury, Jay, N-10
Venkatesan, Rajkumar, N-9, N-14, N-16
Vernon, Lillian, 9
Verschoor, Curtis, 98
Vitvitsky, Stephan, N-4
Vladen, Victor, 402
Vogelstein, Fred, N-16
Von Bergen, Jane, N-17
Vorster, Mike, N-17
Vrancia, Suzanne, N-16
Vroom, Victor, 273–274, 282

## W

Wademan, Daisy, N-12
Walker, Andrea K., N-5
Walker, Bob, 13
Walker, Courtney O., N-1
Walker, Tom, N-19
Wallace, Richard, P-19
Wallach, Dan, N-21
Walton, Sam, 4, 5, 30, 151, 152, 222
Wan, William, 335
Warful, William, N-14
Warner, Fara, N-17
Warren, Elizabeth, N-23
Washington, America, 2
Washington, Jerome, 408–409
Wasserman, Elizabeth, N-3, N-4
Waters, Richard, 409, N-7, N-9, N-22
Waters, Robyn, N-9, N-15
Watkins, Sherron, 98
Watters, Steven, N-9
Webb, Tom, N-19
Weber, Harry R., 261
Weber, Joseph, N-9, N-19
Weber, Max, 209, 227
Wegman, Danny, 287
Wegman, John, 286
Wegman, Robert, 287
Wegman, Walter, 286
Weintraub, Arlene, 64, N-7
Weiss, Jeff, N-9
Weiss, Leigh, N-8
Weixel, Marilyn, 290
Welch, David, N-9, N-15
Welch, Jack, N-8
Welch, Suzy, N-8
Wellner, Alison Stein, N-15
Wells, Joseph T., N-17
Wells, Mike, N-13
Welty, Danielle, N-13
Wen Jiabao, 61
Wert, John E., N-9
Wessel, David, N-2
West, John E. (Jack), N-8, N-10, N-15
Wheeler, Anthony R., N-11
Wheeler, Ericka C., N-14
Wheeler, Hoyt N., N-14
Whelan, David, N-17
Whitaker, Celia, N-17
White, Ben, N-18
White, Erin, N-1, N-3, N-9, N-23
White, Joseph B., N-13
White, Maria Mallory, N-12
Whiting, Rick, N-22
Whitney, John, 302–303
Wiederhorn, Andrew, 337
Wiggin, Addison, N-20
Wilding, Richard, N-9, N-16
Wildstrom, Stephen H., N-22
Will, George F., N-9
Williams, Andy, 296
Williams, Frances, N-4
Williams, Geoff, N-6, N-15
Williams, Joe, 161
Williams, Krissah, N-1
Williams, Walter, N-9
Wilman, John, N-15

Wilson, Alex, 349
Wilson, Amy, N-11
Wilson, Lee, N-21
Wilson, Michael, N-10
Wince-Smith, Deborah, N-22
Winfrey, Oprah, 9, 180–181, 194, 336
Wingfield, Nick, N-16, N-21
Winkler, Anne E., N-11
Woellert, Lorraine, N-16
Woldt, Jeffrey, 287
Wolf, Bob, N-9
Wolf, Horst-Henning, N-9
Wolf, Martin, N-20
Wolfowitz, Paul, 565
Wolk, Martin, N-7
Womack, James P., N-2
Woods, Tiger, 336, 386
Wool, Hillary, N-7
Wozniack, Steve, 154
Wright, Linda, N-16
Wright, Robert, N-16
Wright, Tom, N-3
Wu, Nina, N-6
Wyss, Jim, N-7

**Y**

Yankelovich, Daniel, N-15
Yao Ming, 60, 183
Yate, Martin, P-19
Yee, Daniel, N-15
Yerak, Becky, N-14, N-21
York, Emily Bryson, N-7
Yu Chengyu, 43

**Z**

Zachary, G. Pascal, 183
Zachary, Heather, N-22
Zachary, Mary-Kathryn, N-14
Zachary, Pascal, N-15
Zakaria, Fareed, 565, N-20
Zamiska, Nicholas, N-3
Zammert, Andrea, N-9
Zane, Chris, 365
Zarnowitz, Victor, N-2
Zarocostas, John, N-3, N-4
Zellner, Wendy, N-5, N-15
Zhou, Flora, 276
Zinski, Christopher J., N-17
Zirkelbach, Linda, 93
Zuboff, Shoshana, N-5, N-9
Zuckerman, Gregory, 134
Zuckerman, Mortimer B., N-20
Zweig, Michael, N-14
Zwirn, Ed, N-3

# organization index

**A**

A. G. Edwards, 519, 522, 537
A. H. Robins, 577
A. M. Best, 642
AAA, 342
AAM; *see* American Axle & Manufacturing
AAMCO, 416
AARP, 342
ABB, 173
Acadian Ambulance, 57
Ace Hardware, 142, 417
Acer Computers, 594
Adelphia Communications, 91
Adidas, 160, 241
Advertising Council, 351
AES Corporation, 268, 276
AF Sachs AG, 417
AFL-CIO, 321, 324, 345, 346
AICPA; *see* American Institute of Certified Public Accountants
AIG; *see* American International Group
Albertson's, 2, 412
Alcoa, 535
Allen-Bradley, 240–241
Alliant Energy, 8
AllWrite Communications, 556
Alteon Websystems, 270
Altria, 66, 535
Amazon.com, 14, 150, 186, 361, 372, 395, 402, 414, 446, 578, 599
America Online (AOL), 134
American Airlines, 334
American Arbitration Association, 331
American Axle & Manufacturing (AAM), 232–233
American Century, 534
American Cotton Oil, 535
American Express, 8, 101, 340, 492, 499, 535, 558, 561, 562, 563, 640
American Federation of Television and Radio Artists, 347
American Institute of Certified Public Accountants (AICPA), 458, 459, 460, 480
American International Group (AIG), 535, 572
American Management Association, 343
American Medical Association, 335
American Motors, 232
American Nurses Association, 335
American Society of Transportation & Logistics, 420
American Sugar Refining Co., 535
American Tobacco, 535, 582
AmeriKing, 602
Ameritrade, 522, 523, 541
Amgen, 244
Amy's Ice Creams parlors, 226
Amy's Kitchen, 354
Anheuser-Busch, 63, 244
AOL; *see* America Online
AOL Time Warner, 134
Apple Computer, 128, 150, 154, 447, 503
Archipelago Holdings Inc., 519
Arena Football League, 481
Arizona Beverage Company, 384
Arm & Hammer, 391
Arthur Andersen, 90, 91, 123, 459
Artisan Bakery, 152
Ashoka, 7
Associated Grocers, 417
Associated Press, 142
Association of Certified Fraud Examiners, 104, 459
AT&T, 17, 195, 380, 535, 582, 598, 608
Au Bon Pain, 203
Auntie Anne's Pretzels, 139, 140
Autobytel.com, 353
Autoliv Inc., 417
AutoNation, 353
Autoweb.com, 353
Avon, 150, 415

**B**

Bagel Works, 102
Bama Company, 249–250
Bank of America, 151, 513, 610
Bank One, 561
Barnes & Noble, 361, 578
Baskin-Robbins, 135, 416
Bass Pro Shops, 412
Bayer, 386, 629
Baylor University, 58
BCF; *see* Birmingham Change Fund
BDO Seidman, 454
Bear Naked, 355
Behlen Manufacturing, 304

BellSouth, 294–295
Berkshire Hathaway, 527
Bertelsmann, 93
Best Buy, 382
Bethlehem Steel, 535
Better Business Bureau, 172
Big Boy Restaurants, 297
Bill and Melinda Gates Foundation; *see* Gates Foundation
Birmingham Change Fund (BCF), 94
Blockbuster Inc., 294, 337
BLS; *see* Bureau of Labor Statistics
Blue Cross/Blue Shield, 625, 643
Blue Diamond, 142
BMW, 134, 436
Bob's Big Boy, 377
Boeing, 62, 218, 332, 503, 535
Boies, Schiller & Flexner, 573
Booker T. Washington Insurance Company, 618
Borders Books, 361
BorgWarner, 417
BP, 629
Brandt's Cafe, 172
Bridal Event, 448
Briggs & Stratton, 242
Bright Horizons Family Solutions, Inc., 341
Bristol-Myers Squibb, 81, 244, 340
British Airways, 297
British Motors, Ltd., 125
Broadway, 258
BT, 629
Build-A-Bear Workshop Inc., 64
Bureau of Alcohol, Tobacco, and Firearms, 418
Bureau of Economic Analysis, 56
Bureau of Engraving and Printing, 569
Bureau of Labor Statistics (BLS), 56
Burger King, 377, 602
Burpee, 437
Burson-Marsteller, 58
Business Owners' Idea Cafe, 556
Buy.com, 395

## C

Cable News Network, 150
Cakelove, 119
California Nurses Association, 335
Calvin Klein, 572
Campbell Soup Company, 69, 340, 362, 385
Capital Protective Insurance (CPI), 241
Car Lab, 235
Careerbuilder.com, 293, 294
Carl's Junior, 377
Car-Max, 353
Caterpillar, 332, 535
CBS, 572
CCTV, 59
CDnow, 14
Census Bureau, P-3, 26, 340
Center for Community and Corporate Ethics, 327
Center for Corporate Governance, 337
Change to Win, 321, 324, 335
Chantal Cookware, 171
Charles Schwab & Company, 523, 541
Charter Schools USA, 482
Chem-Dry, 101
Chevrolet, 232, 385
Chevron, 69, 80–81, 535
Chicago Gas, 535
Chicago Rush, 481
Chicago White Sox, 36
Children of God for Life, 107
ChoicePoint, 15, 610
Chrysler, 133, 134, 225, 232–233, 436, 485
Church's Chicken, 2
Ciba Specialty Chemicals, 106
Cirque du Soleil, 27
Cisco Systems, 166, 195, 503, 520, 608
Citibank, 610
CITIC Pacific, 80
Citigroup, 44, 149, 513, 535, 561
Citizen's Federal Savings Bank, 619
City of Chesterfield Zoning Board, 575
Clairol, 437
CNBC, 510, 511
CNOOC, 133–134
Coca-Cola, 66, 72, 379, 386, 436, 465, 514, 527, 535
Coca-Cola Retailing Research Council, 287
Coco's Chocolate Dreams, 155
Cold Stone Creamery, 116–117
Coldwater Creek, 415
Communication Development Associates, 296
Communist Youth League, 183
Community Foundation of Greater Birmingham, 94
Compaq Computer, 128, 224, 337
Compuware, 603
Concurrent Pharmaceuticals, 166
Container Store, 284
Continental Airlines, 330
Cook County Department of Revenue, 461
Cookies on Call, 165
Coors Brewing Company, 73, 437
Copart Inc., 402–403, 404
Costco, 104, 412
Council of Economic Advisers, 544
Count Basie Orchestra, 161
Cover Girl, 437
Coverall Cleaning Franchises, 139
CPI; *see* Capital Protective Insurance
CPI Process Systems, 173–174
Cramer Berkowitz, 510–511
Cranium, 226
Crayola, 390
Critical Infrastructure Protection Board, 611
Curves, 68
Custom Foot, 241

## D

Daimler-Benz, 101–102, 133, 485
DaimlerChrysler, 133, 134, 214, 330
Dairy Queen, 528
Decorating Den, 139
Del Monte, 385
Dell Computer, 61, 69, 72, 148, 150, 205, 223, 364, 402, 408, 520
Denny's, 2
Designed Dinners, 378
DHL, 359, 422
Digital Domain, 256–257
Digital Equipment Corporation, 279
Dine Across America, 101
Diners Club, 640
Dip 'N' Strip, 141
Discover, 640
Disney Company, 16, 66, 87, 183, 337, 338, 514, 535, 579
Distilling & Cattle Feeding Co., 535
DistributorMatch.com, 158
Dolan Industries, 249
Dole, 427
Domino Sugar, 420
Domino's, 67, 68
Donna Salyer's Fabulous Furs, 340
Dow Chemical, 108, 111
Dr Pepper, 449
Dream Dinners, 378
Drkoop.com, 14
DSW, 610
Duke Energy, 8
Dun & Bradstreet, 162
Dunkin' Donuts, 67
Dupont, 150, 374, 535, 582

## E

E*Trade, 522, 523, 537, 541
Eastman Chemical Company, 304
Eastman Kodak, 535; *see also* Kodak
eBay, 14, 137, 393, 395, 427, 547, 599, 610
Ecofashion, 105
Economic Development Authority, 166
Economic Policy Institute, 339
Ecoprint, 293
Edgewater Technology, 343
Electrolux, 73, 415
Electronic Data Systems, 150
Eli Lilly, 244
Emery, 422
Enron, 12, 90, 91, 97, 98, 114, 459, 537, 584, 588
Epic Divers & Marine, 188
Ernst & Young, 108, 149
Ethics and Compliance Officers Association, 97
Ethos Water, 88–89
EToys, 14
Excite.com, 278
Exxon, 124
Exxon Mobil, 80–81, 535

## F

Families and Work Institute, 266
Farmers Home Administration, 166
Federal Emergency Management Agency (FEMA), 209, 420
Federal Reserve Bank of Minneapolis, 55
Federated Department Stores, 17
FedEx, 100, 195, 261, 297, 359, 386, 404, 420, 422–423, 629
FEMA; *see* Federal Emergency Management Agency
Fidelity Investments, 558
FINCA; *see* Foundation for International Community Assistance
Firestone, 416, 622
First National Bank of Hermitage, PA, 560
Flextronics, 69, 244
Florida Marlins, 482
Florida Panthers Hockey Club, 482
Florida Power and Light, 40
Florida Public Service Commission, 40
Fog Cutter Capital Group, 337
Food and Drug Administration, 418
Ford Motor Company, 46, 62, 72, 74, 124, 150, 206, 208, 223, 225, 229, 230, 273, 277, 299, 353, 437, 577, 622
Ford Motor Credit, 558
Forrester Research, 81
Foundation for International Community Assistance (FINCA), 43
Freeplay Energy Group, 381
Freestyle Audio, 348–349
Fresh Italy, 358
Fridgedoor.com, 364

## G

Gap, 21, 107, 362
Garden.com, 437
Gates Foundation, 33, 100, 528
GCFD; *see* Greater Chicago Food Depository
GE; *see* General Electric
GEICO, 644

General Electric Capital Corporation, 497, 558
General Electric (GE), 8, 107, 124, 249, 289, 299, 416, 423, 527, 535, 558
General Foods, 302
General Motors Acceptance Corporation, 570
General Motors (GM), 69, 80, 124, 125, 134, 184, 206, 208, 223, 225, 233, 234, 353, 535, 558, 577
General Nutrition Center (GNC), 241
G.I. Joe's, 294
Gifts in Kind International, 101
Gillette, 134, 527
Global Crossing, 584
GlobalSight Corporation, 63
GM; *see* General Motors
GNC; *see* General Nutrition Center
Goldman Sachs, 510, 513
Goodwill Industries, 485
Goodyear, 535
Google, 193, 206, 289
Gore; *see* W. L. Gore & Associates
Grameen, 43
Greater Chicago Food Depository (GCFD), 428
Greater Dallas Hispanic Chamber of Commerce, 149
Greenpeace, 351
Grupo Moraira (Grupo M), 243

## H

H. B. Fuller Company, 73
Haemonetics Corporation, 341
Hallmark, 135
Harbour Consulting, 234
Hard Rock Cafe, 366
HarperCollins, 446
Harpo, Inc., 180–181
Harry and David, 416
Harvard University, 262
Haworth Inc., 360
HealthSouth, 98
Herman Miller, 337
Hershey Foods Corporation, 72, 256, 612
Hertz Rental Corporation, 271
Hewlett-Packard (HP), 61, 69, 211, 223, 224, 279, 289, 290, 337, 338, 360, 535
Hitachi, 69
Holiday Inn, 67, 136
Home Depot, 211, 394, 420, 535, 629
Honda, 6, 46, 71, 243
Honeywell, 249, 535
Hoover's, P-26
Hot Topic, 258–259, 284–285
Houston Rockets, 60
HP; *see* Hewlett-Packard
Hypermart.com, 158
Hyundai, 6, 234

## I

I2 Technologies, 418
IBM, 8, 14, 18, 19, 61, 62, 72, 100, 102, 124, 125, 195, 205, 206, 210, 223, 292, 305, 308, 340, 535, 572, 606
ICIC; *see* Initiative for Competitive Inner City
IG Metall, 330
IGA, 417
Igus, 241
ImClone, 103
Immersion Corporation, 578
Inditex, 414
Information Management Systems, 608
Ingram Micro, 276–277
Initiative for Competitive Inner City (ICIC), 159, 161
Inroads Capital Partners, 166
Institute for Development Strategies, 235
Institute for Liberty and Democracy, 29
Institute of Certified Management Accountants, 457, 480
Institute of Internal Auditors, 460
Insurance Information Institute, 631
Intel, 72, 166, 238, 264, 300, 386, 465, 491, 503, 520, 535, 604
InterActive Custom Clothes, 241
International Brotherhood of Teamsters, 320–321
International Council of Shopping Centers, 174
International Food Service Manufacturers, 377
International Franchise Association, 138
International Paper, 535
International Truck and Engine, 231
Internet Capital Group, 14
Intuit, 150
Isuzu Motors, 393

## J

J. P. Morgan, 535
J. P. Morgan Chase, 107, 340, 342
Jack in the Box, 577
Jacobs Coffee, 430
Jaguar, 381
Jaguar Racing, 431
Jazzercise, 68, 136, 139
JCPenney, 211–212, 412
JetBlue Airways, 307, 308
Jiffy Lube, 394
JohnsByrne, 240
Johnson & Johnson, 96, 100, 340, 491, 535, 622
Jungle Jim's International Market, 150

## K

K2, 222
Kaiser Permanente, 335, 625
KEH Camera Brokers, 156–157
Kellogg, 244, 438
Kemper Auto and Home Group, 402
KFC, 68, 73, 377, 416, 438
Kia, 417–418
KLM Royal Dutch Airlines, 422
Kmart, 103, 186, 223, 494, 586
Knot.com, 448
Kodak, 17, 150, 204, 206, 223, 385
Komatsu Limited, 393
Kraft, 206, 417, 505
Krispy Kreme, 136, 377
Kroger, 412

## L

L. L. Bean, 415
Laclede Gas Light Co., 535
Lacrad International, 90
Land O Lakes, 142
Lands' End, 415
Lenovo Group Ltd., 18, 19, 61
Levi-Strauss, 81, 385
Library of Congress, 578
LILL, 178–179
Liz Claiborne, 412
Lockheed Martin Corporation, 158, 218, 245
L'Oréal, 69
Los Angeles Lakers, 195
Lotus Development, 102, 605
Lowe's, 436
Lucas Group, 438
Lucent Technologies, 338
LVMH, 134

## M

McDonald's, 67, 68, 72, 100, 108, 135, 137, 140, 212, 225, 242, 261, 299, 376–377, 416, 436–437, 465, 535, 576, 579
McDonnell Douglas, 503
McFarlane, 509
McKinsey, 7
Macy's, 498
Majestic Athletic, 160
Major League Baseball (MLB), 160, 482–483, 573
Manchester Craftsman Guild, 161
Manugistics, 418
Maple Leaf Gardens Ltd., 133
Maria's Bakery, 140
Maricopa County Planning Commission, 575
Marlins Ballpark Development Company, 482
Marriott, 139
Martha Stewart Omnimedia, 103, 337
Maryland Technology Development Center, 159
MasterCard, 492, 561, 563, 582, 640
Masterfoods USA, 438
Maybelline, 438
MCI Communications, 482
Medtronic Inc., 577–578
Meineke Discount Muffler Shops, Inc., 136–137
Menlo Worldwide, 418
Mercedes, 71, 243
Merck, 535, 576
Merrill Lynch, 519, 522, 523, 524, 537
Merry Maids, 140
Mervyn's, 186
MetLife Mature Market Institute, 341
Michele Foods, 2–3
Michelin, 417
Michigan State University School of Packaging, 384
Microsoft, 4, 5, 124, 150, 151, 289, 520, 523, 527, 535, 572, 573, 582, 583–584, 608
Millers Outpost, 258
Mindbridge, 343
Mini Maid, Inc., 271
Missouri Department of Natural Resources, 461
Mitsubishi, 599
MLB; *see* Major League Baseball
Money Mailer, Inc., 139–140
Monster, 431
Monster.com, 293, 294
Monte Jade, 300
Moody's Investor Services, P-26, 505, 514, 518, 526, 530, 642
Morgan Stanley, 524
Morton Salt Company, 383–384
Motley Fool, 512, 542–543
Motorola, 110, 231, 236, 249, 299, 360
MTV, 372–373
MTV Networks China, 58–59
mtvU.com, 373
Muhairy Group, 67–68
MySimon.com, 395

## N

Nakano Vinegar Company, 69
Nantucket Nectars, 69
Napster, 93, 572
NASA, 374
NASCAR, 386
Nathan's Famous, 140
National Alliance of Caregivers, 342
National Association of Manufacturers, 345
National Basketball Association (NBA), 60, 183, 195, 345

National Bicycle Industrial Company, 241
National Business Incubator Association (NBIA), 159
National Conference of Commissioners on Uniform State Laws, 130
National Consultant Referrals Inc., 172
National Cooperative Business Association, 141
National Education Association (NEA), 335
National Federation of Independent Business, 495
National Federation of Independent Business Research Foundation, 150
National Football League, 60
National Geographic Society, 305
National Hockey League (NHL), 333
National Institute of Health, 342
National Institute on Drug Abuse, 342
National Lead, 535
National Mediation Board, 330
National Small Business Association, 499
National Venture Capital Association, 168
NBA; *see* National Basketball Association
NBC, 103
NBIA; *see* National Business Incubator Association
NCR, 224
NEA; *see* National Education Association
Nestlé, 69, 70, 333, 524
NetBank, 561
Netflix, 157
NetworkforGood.org, 100
New England Pottery Company, 79
New York Mets, 572
New York Yankees, 482, 483, 572, 573
Nextel, 386
NHL; *see* National Hockey League
Night Agency, 453
Nike, 69, 72, 81, 108–109, 160, 223, 372, 412, 436, 579
Nissan, 436
Nordstrom, 16, 211, 266, 412
Nordstrom Rack, 412
North American Co., 535
Northwest Airlines, 133, 330, 334
Northwest Instrument Systems, 504
Norton, 610
NYSE Group, 519

## O

Occupational Safety and Health Administration (OSHA), 261, 342
Ocean Spray, 142
OECD; *see* Organization for Economic Cooperation and Development
Office Depot, 308, 410, 412
Office of Personnel Management, 341
1154 LILL, 178–179
One Smooth Stone, 231
Oracle Corporation, 337
Oreck, 244
Organization for Economic Cooperation and Development (OECD), 74, 109
Organization of American States, 109
Oriental Land Company, 66
OSHA; *see* Occupational Safety and Health Administration
Overnite Transit Company, 332

## P

Packard Bell, 598
Palo Alto Software, 166
Panera Bread, 203, 377
Parsley Patch, 486, 491
Patagonia, 109, 318–319
PayPal, 547, 610
Peapod, 14
Pencom Systems, 148
People's Commercial Bank, 166
PeopleSoft, 418
PeopleWise, 295
PepsiCo, 73, 364, 379, 386, 436, 445, 491, 583
Perdue Chicken, 73
Pets.com, 14
Pfizer, 244, 535
Philip Morris, 66
Phillips-Van Heusen, 108, 111
Physicians for Responsible Negotiations, 335
Pillsbury, 579
Pinnacle Technical Resources Inc., 148–149
Pizza Hut, 68
Playtex Company, 577
Plum Pictures, 269
Polaroid, 223
Polo Ralph Lauren, 15
Pontiac, 180
Porsche, 134
Postrio restaurant, 380
Priceline.com, 395
Pro Player Stadium, 482
Procter & Gamble, 18, 81, 106, 117, 134, 150, 360, 380, 430, 535
Prudential Real Estate, 379

## Q

Quanta Computer, 69
Qwest Communications, 134

## R

R. J. Julia Booksellers, 454–455, 456
Rainforest Action Network (RAN), 107
Randstad North America, 296
Raven Biotechnologies, 113–114
Raytheon Vision Systems, 290
RCA, 598
Read To Grow Inc., 455
Recording Industry Association of America (RIAA), 93
Red Bull, 385, 430–431
Red Bull Racing, 431
Red Cross, 34, 351, 461
Reebok, 160
Rhino Entertainment, 113
RIAA; *see* Recording Industry Association of America
Riceland Foods, 142
Richardson Electronics, 418
Richland College, 250
Rightstart.com, 413
Ritz-Carlton Hotel Company, 237
RJR Nabisco, 133
Robert Half International, 266–267
Rockwell Automation, 240
Rocky Mountain Chocolate Factory, 67–68, 140
Rowe Furniture, 213
Roxio, 93
Rug Doctor Pro, 140

## S

S&P; *see* Standard & Poor's
Safeway, 371, 412
St. Louis Bread Company, 203
St. Louis Cardinals, 501
Saks Fifth Avenue, 369
Sam's Club, 412
Samsung, 69, 105–106
Samuel Adams, 63
San Fernando Valley Economic Research Center, 296
Sant Group, 440
SAP, 418
Sara Lee Corporation, 211, 577
SBC Communications Inc., 17, 535
SCI Systems, 244
Scojo Vision, 381
Scott, 417
Screen Actors Guild, 347
Sears, Roebuck & Company, 95–96, 103, 108, 109, 111, 186, 223, 365, 381, 385, 412, 413, 420, 535, 558
Sears Holding Company, 586
Second Bank of the United States, 553
Service Employees International Union (SEIU), 324, 335
7-Eleven, 377, 380, 408, 412, 556
Shakey's Pizza, 377
Shanghai Automotive Industrial Corporation, 69
Shell Oil, 524
Sherwin-Williams, 416
Siemens, 206, 330, 524
Simply Cook It, 378
Sirius, 435
Sitecritique.net, 158
Small Business Exporters Association, 64
SmartMoney.com, 511
Sneaker Villa, 161
Solectron, 244
SolutionPeople, 400–401
Sonic, 146–147
Sony, 72, 93, 385, 393, 478, 524
Southwest Airlines, 268, 335, 588
SpeeDee Oil Change & Tune-Up, 140
Springs Industries, 244
SRA International Inc., 135
Standard & Poor's, P-26, 505, 514, 518, 526, 530
Standard Oil, 503, 582
Staples, 170, 410
Starbucks, 48, 63, 88–89, 117, 140, 150, 185, 355, 377, 390, 408, 438, 520, 605
StarKist, 106
State Farm, 402, 570–571
Steve & Barry's University Sportswear, 174
Steve Madden Ltd., 337
Stop & Shop, 2
Students for Responsible Business, 100
Substance Abuse & Mental Health Services Association, 342
Sun Microsystems, 231, 307
Sunkist, 142
Sunny Fresh Foods, 249
Sunoco, Inc., 121
Sunoco Logistics (SXL), 121
Superior Products, 73
Suzuki, 101
Symantec, 8
Synovus, 266

## T

T. J. Maxx, 412
Talon, Inc., 389
Tampa Bay Devil Rays, 483
Target, 186, 222, 223, 294, 369, 412, 423
T.B.S. Inc., 138
TCBY, 137
Teamsters Union, 261, 320–321, 332, 335
Tennessee Coal, Iron & Railroad Co., 535
Texaco, 535
TheStreet.com, 511
3Com, 608
3M, 158, 535
TIAA-CREF, 558
Timberland, 266, 404
Time Warner, 134

TNT, 422
Tompkins Associates, 258
Torrid, 285
Toyota Motor, 6, 71–72, 134, 206, 234
Toys "R" Us, 133, 412
Trend Micro, 594–595
Tropical Blossom Honey Company, 63
True Value Hardware, 142
Trump Hotels and Casinos, 505, 586
Tsingtao Brewing, 63
Tuskegee Institute, 619
Two Men and a Truck, 139
Tyco International, 91, 338, 459, 537
Tyson Foods, 337

## U

Ugly Dolls, 63
Umpqua Bank, 560
Unicru, 294
Unilever, 381, 430
Union Carbide, 535
Union of Needletrades, Industrial & Textile Employees, 335
United Airlines, 334, 586
United American Nurses, 335
United Auto Workers, 332, 334
United Food and Commercial Workers Union, 327
United Parcel Service (UPS), 60, 100, 209, 244, 261, 262, 332, 342, 359, 404, 420, 422–423, 494
U.S. Air Force, 245
U.S. Department of Commerce, 26, 62, 64, 67, 139, 173
U.S. Department of Health and Human Services, 342
U.S. Department of Homeland Security, 209, 420
U.S. Department of Justice, 572, 582
U.S. Department of Labor, P-18, 79, 104, 342
U.S. Government Printing Office, 63–64
U.S. Hispanic Chamber of Commerce, 149
U.S. Marines, 245
U.S. Navy, 245, 389
U.S. Office of Homeland Defense, 611
U.S. Patent and Trademark Office (USPTO), 577, 578, 592
U.S. Postal Service, 342, 343, 404, 420
U.S. Supreme Court, 91, 300, 312, 333, 339, 459, 575
United Technologies, 535
Universal Engineering Corporation, 28
University, 373
University of California at Berkeley, 265, 270
University of California–Los Angeles, 271
University of Maryland, 92, 158, 172
University of Michigan, 312, 339
University of Pittsburgh, 69
Unocal, 133–134
UPS; *see* United Parcel Service
UPS Store, 135
Urge, 373
US Airways, 334
U.S. Leather, 535
U.S. Rubber Co., 535
U.S. Web Corporation, 140
US West, 134

## V

Vanguard, 529
Ventaso, Inc., 440
VeriSign, 611
Verizon, 149, 535
Viacom, 58, 59
Victoria Jackson Cosmetics Company, 170
Virgin Airlines, 385
Virginia Tech, 172
Visa, 492, 561, 563, 582, 640
Visual Networks, 159
Vivendi Universal, 93
Volkswagen, 69, 232, 243
Volunteerconnections.org, 100
VolunteerMatch.org, 100
Vosges Haut-Chocolat, 164

## W

W. L. Gore & Associates, 266, 374–375
Wainright Bank & Trust, 560
Walgreen's, 408
Wall Drug, 408
Wall Street Games, Inc., 120
Wal-Mart, 2, 4, 5, 18, 30, 57, 80, 104, 124, 150, 151, 152, 186, 195, 222, 223, 242, 244, 327, 365, 384, 394, 412, 420, 423, 535, 555, 601
Walt Disney Company; *see* Disney Company
Walt Disney Imagineering, 87
Washington Opera Company, 395
Wedbush Morgan Securities, 258
Wegmans Food Markets, 286–287
Welch's, 142
Wells Fargo Bank, 100, 561
Wendy's, 237, 377
West Paces Hotel Group, 237
Western Australia Energy Research Alliance, 69
Western Electric, 262
Westinghouse, 535
WIF; *see* Women in Franchising
Wizard Vending, 174
Women in Franchising (WIF), 138–139
Women's Foodservice Forum, 2
Women's National Basketball Association, 345
Woolworth, 423, 535
Workforce Solutions, 305
Workz.com, 172
World Environment Center, 88
WorldCom, 91, 102, 104, 134, 459, 537, 584
Wrigley Company, 505
Writers Guild of America, 347
Wyeth, 222

## X

Xerox Corporation, 100, 125, 204–205, 223, 343, 385, 416
XM radio, 435
XSAg.com, 14

## Y

Yahoo, 182, 336, 393, 436
Young & Rubicam Brands, 8

## Z

Zane's Cycles, 365
Zara's, 414
Zuca Inc., 435

# subject index


## A

Absolute advantage, 62
Accessory equipment, 382
Accountants
  certified management, 457
  certified public, 458, 459
  forensic, 459
  private, 458
  public, 458
Accounting
  areas
    auditing, 459–460, 486
    financial, 457–459
    forensic, 459
    government and not-for-profit, 460–461
    managerial, 457
    tax, 460
  defined, 456
  distinction from bookkeeping, 461
  ethical issues, 473
  fundamental equation, 463–464
  generally accepted principles, 458, 469, 470
  journals, 461–462
  ledgers, 462
  oversight of profession, 459, 460
  purposes, 456–457
  relationship to finance, 484
  reports, 457
  scandals, 12, 458–459
  in small businesses, 171, 462
  technology used in, 462–463
  users of information, 457
Accounting cycle, 461–462
Accounting firms
  consulting work, 460
  scandals, 458–459
Accounting system, 456
Accounts payable, 466
Accounts receivable, 497–498
ACH; *see* Automated Clearing House
Acid-test (quick) ratio, 474
Acquisitions, 132–133; *see also* Mergers and acquisitions
Activity ratios, 475–476
ADA; *see* Americans with Disabilities Act
Administered distribution systems, 417
Administrative agencies, 575
ADRs; *see* American depository receipts
Advantage
  absolute, 62
  comparative, 61–62
Advertising
  categories, 433
  celebrity endorsements, 387
  to children, 446
  defined, 433
  direct mail, 415, 433, 434
  expenditures, 433, 434
  false or misleading, 583
  in foreign countries, 72, 73, 360, 438
  global, 437–438
  infomercials, 435–436
  Internet, 433, 434, 436–437, 448
  magazine, 434
  media, 433, 434
  newspaper, 433, 434
  outdoor, 434
  product placement, 435, 436
  public benefits of, 433–434
  radio, 435
  television, 433, 434, 436
  testimonials, 436, 446, 448
  Yellow Pages, 434
Affirmative action, 311–312
AFL; *see* American Federation of Labor
AFL-CIO, 324, 327, 335, 343, 345, 346
African Americans; *see also* Minorities
  affirmative action, 311–312
  business leaders, 8
  entrepreneurs, 161, 618–619
  franchising opportunities, 139
  managers, 300
  small business owners, 160
Age; *see* Aging of population; Demography
Age Discrimination in Employment Act of 1967, 312, 313
Agency shop agreements, 328
Agents/brokers, 404–405, 410–411
Aging of population
  baby boomers, 17–18, 289, 290
  of consumers, 17, 360
  discrimination issues, 313
  elder care, 341–342
  in United States, 17–18, 360
  of workforce, 289, 290, 313
Agriculture; *see also* Food industry
  cooperatives, 141–142
  history, 20–21
  number of farmers, 20
  technology used in, 13–14, 20–21
AIDS, 342
Air transportation, 422
Airlines
  costs of increased security, 19
  deregulation, 588
  problems, 206
Alcohol abuse, 342
Alcohol Labeling Legislation (1988), 585
Alliances
  of Japanese firms, 76
  strategic, 69
American depository receipts (ADRs), 524
American Federation of Labor (AFL), 324, 325, 343
American Indians; *see* Minorities
American Inventor's Protection Act, 578
American Stock Exchange (AMEX), 519, 532
Americans with Disabilities Act (ADA) of 1990, 312, 313
AMEX; *see* American Stock Exchange
Andean Pact, 78
Angel investors, 168, 556
Annual reports, P-25, 458, 460
Annuities, 642–643
Antiglobalization protesters, 77, 564, 565
Antitrust laws, 40, 582–584
Application forms, 294
Application service providers (ASPs), 606
Application software; *see* Software
Apprentice programs, 298
Arbitration, 331
Argentina
  economic problems, 565
  Mercosur, 78
Articles of incorporation, 129
Asia; *see also individual countries*
  franchises, 140, 141
  manufacturing in, 18–19
  markets, 81
  sweatshop labor, 108–109
Asian Americans; *see also* Minorities
  entrepreneurs, 8, 161
  managers, 300
  small business owners, 160
Asian tsunami, 100
ASPs; *see* Application service providers
Assembly line layouts, 245–246
Assembly process, 239
Assets
  accounts receivable, 497
  on balance sheet, 464–466
  capital expenditures, 493
  as collateral for loans, 497
  current, 466
  defined, 464–465
  depreciation, 470
  division of in bankruptcies, 587
  fixed, 466
  goodwill, 465
  intangible, 464–465, 466
  liquidity, 466
  personal, 634–637
ATMs; *see* Automated teller machines
Auctions, online, 402
Auditing, 459–460, 486, 491
Audits, social, 106–108
Authority
  centralized, 208, 211–212
  decentralized, 211–212
  line versus staff, 217
  managerial, 208
Autocratic leadership, 195
Automated Clearing House (ACH), 561–562
Automated teller machines (ATMs), 555–556, 563
Automation; *see* Technology
Automobile industry
  change in, 225
  Chinese, 69, 80
  demand, 39
  fuel-efficient cars, 225
  market shares of U.S. companies, 392
  marketing, 353
  mass production, 208
  mergers, 133–134
  non-U.S. manufacturers, 6, 71–72, 206, 234
  operations management, 236–237
  reorganizations, 206
Automobile Information Disclosure Act (1958), 585
Automobile insurance, 644

## B


B2B; *see* Business-to-business (B2B) market
B2C; *see* Business-to-consumer (B2C) transactions
Baby boomers
- aging of, 17–18, 289, 290
- births of, 350–351
- differences from Generation X members, 17–18, 278–279, 280

Balance of payments, 64–65
Balance of trade, 64
Balance sheets; *see also* Ratio analysis
- accounts, 477
- assets, 464–466
- defined, 463, 464
- liabilities and owners' equity, 466–467
- personal, 463, 467, 635
- sample, 465

Baldrige Awards, 248–250, 256, 304
Bank of Japan, 546
Banker's acceptances, 563
Bankruptcies; *see also* Business failures
- corporate, 134
- defined, 585–586
- division of assets, 587
- involuntary, 586
- laws, 586–588
- number of, 586
- procedures, 587–588
- voluntary, 586–587

Bankruptcy Abuse Prevention and Consumer Protection Act of 2005, 586
Bankruptcy Amendments and Federal Judgeships Act of 1984, 586
Bankruptcy Reform Act of 1994, 586, 588
Bankruptcy Reform Act of 2005, 586
Banks; *see also* Central banks; Investment bankers
- automated teller machines (ATMs), 555–556, 563
- banker's acceptances, 563
- certificates of deposit (CDs), 555
- check-clearing, 551, 552, 561–562
- commercial, 554–556
- credit cards; *see* Credit cards
- debit cards, 562, 641
- demand deposits, 554
- failures, 553
- federal deposit insurance, 554, 559
- fees, 561, 562
- future of, 560–563
- global markets, 44
- history in United States, 551–554
- international, 563–564
- IRAs, 646
- letters of credit, 563
- loans; *see* Loans
- online banking, 242–243, 560–561
- relationships with, 472, 495–496
- reserve requirements, 550
- short-term financing, 495–496
- small businesses and, 166, 172, 556
- technology used in, 561–563
- time deposits, 555
- trade financing, 563

Bar codes, 15, 384, 423
Bargaining zone, 330
Barriers to trade; *see* Trade barriers
Barter, 73–74, 546
Baseball
- financing, 482–483
- major league, 60, 160, 332, 482–483
- stadiums, 501
- strikes, 332

Basic earnings per share, 475
"Basic Guide to Exporting," 63–64
Bearer bonds, 513
Benchmarking, 221–222
Benefit segmentation, 364
Benefits; *see* Fringe benefits
BI; *see* Business intelligence
Bible, 91
Bicycles, 365
Billboards, 434
Biometric devices, 599
*Black Enterprise* magazine, 300, 619
Blogs, 446–447
Blue-chip stocks, 527
Boards of directors, 127, 622
Bolivia, 7
Bonds
- advantages and disadvantages, 514–515
- debenture, 515
- defined, 501, 513
- features
  - call provisions, 515–516
  - convertible, 516
  - sinking funds, 515
- government, 513, 514, 525
- indenture terms, 501
- interest, 513, 514, 525–526
- investing in, 525–526
- issuing, 501, 512–513
- junk, 530
- maturity dates, 514
- quotations, 532, 533
- ratings, 514, 526
- secured, 501, 515
- terminology, 513–514
- underwriting, 513
- unsecured, 501, 515

Bonds payable, 466
Bonus plans, 303
Bookkeeping, 461
Booms, 49
Bootstrapping, 149
Borrowing; *see* Credit; Debt; Loans
Boycotts, 332–333
Brain drain, 41
Brainstorming, 189
Brand associations, 387
Brand awareness, 386
Brand equity, 386
Brand loyalty, 386
Brand managers, 387
Brand names, 354, 385, 465
Brands; *see also* Trademarks
- categories, 385–386
- defined, 385
- knockoff, 386

Brazil
- bribery, 108
- cereal eating, 438
- dumping disputes, 65
- Mercosur, 78

Breach of contract, 581
Break-even analysis, 393–394
Breweries, 63
Bribery, 74, 108, 109; *see also* Corruption
Bridal shows, 448
Britain
- corporations, 125
- currency, 77
- Defense Ministry, 245

Broadband technology, 603–604
Brokerage firms
- exchange memberships, 519
- online, 522, 523
- owned by banks, 560
- services, 558
- stockbrokers, 522, 530

Brokers; *see* Agents/brokers
Budget deficits, 50
Budgets
- capital, 488
- cash, 488–489
- defined, 488
- developing, 488–489
- operating (master), 489
- personal, 490, 636

Bundling, 394–395
Bureaucracy, 28, 209, 210
Burundi, 10
Business
- benefits to community, 32–33
- defined, 4
- evolution in United States, 20–21
- future careers in, 21
- government ownership, 12

Business cycle, 49–50
Business environment; *see also* Legal environment
- competitive environment, 15–16
- defined, 10
- economic and legal environment, 11–12, 72–74, 361
- elements of, 10–11
- global environment, 18–20
- social environment, 16–18, 71–72, 360
- technological environment, 12–15

Business ethics; *see* Ethics
Business failures; *see also* Bankruptcies
- banks, 553
- causes, 162, 485
- Internet companies, 14–15, 158
- number of, 4, 162
- savings and loan associations, 557, 572
- small businesses, 162

Business information systems; *see* Information technology
Business intelligence (BI), 598
Business law, 574; *see also* Legal environment
Business leaders; *see also* Entrepreneurs
- African-American, 8
- global, 58–59
- successful, 142

Business ownership forms
- comparison, 131
- cooperatives, 141–142
- corporations, 118; *see also* Corporations
- franchises, 134–135; *see also* Franchises
- numbers of and total receipts, 118
- partnerships, 118, 122–123
- public ownership, 12
- selecting, 142
- sole proprietorships, 118, 119–120

Business Plan Pro, 166
Business plans, 165–166, 167–168
Business process information, 599
*BusinessWeek*, 528
Businesses, starting
- business plans, 165–166, 167–168
- ethical issues, 164
- number of new businesses, 118
- organizing, 206
- small businesses, 159–160

Business-method patents, 578
Business-to-business (B2B) companies, 14, 247; *see also* Marketing intermediaries
Business-to-business (B2B) market
- comparison to consumer market, 367–368
- defined, 361

industrial goods and services, 382, 383
personal selling, 364, 439–441
sales promotion techniques, 443
Business-to-business (B2B) transactions, 14
Business-to-consumer (B2C) transactions, 14, 441–442; *see also* Consumer market
Buying behavior; *see* Consumer behavior
Buying stock on margin, 530


## C


C corporations, 124–125
CAD; *see* Computer-aided design
Cafeteria-style fringe benefits, 304–305
CAFTA; *see* Central American Free Trade Agreement
California
Silicon Valley, 503
utility deregulation, 588
Callable bonds, 515–516
CAM; *see* Computer-aided manufacturing
Canada; *see also* North American Free Trade Agreement
corporations, 125
executive compensation, 338
exports, 65
franchises, 140
Capital; *see also* Equity financing
cost of, 504
as factor of production, 9, 10
Capital budgets, 488
Capital expenditures, 493
Capital gains, 526
Capital items, 382
Capitalism; *see also* Markets
defined, 34, 43
foundations of, 35–36
history, 34–35
rights in, 36
in United States, 35
Careers
changing, P-29
in future, 21
in global business, 60–61, 70, 82
information sources, P-18 to P-19
in marketing, 369
in operations management, 252
in sales, 439
self-assessments, P-4 to P-5, P-16, P-17
in supply chain management, 423
working for large businesses, 8
Cars; *see* Automobile industry
Carts and kiosks, 414–415
Cash budgets, 488–489
Cash flow
defined, 472
personal, 635
Cash flow analysis, 472
Cash flow forecasts, 488
Cash flow statement; *see* Statement of cash flows
Cash-and-carry wholesalers, 410
Catalog sales, 415–416
Category killer stores, 412
CBOT; *see* Chicago Board of Trade
CDs; *see* Certificates of deposit
Celebrity endorsements, 387
Cell phones, P-8
Cellular layouts; *see* Modular layouts
Central American Free Trade Agreement (CAFTA), 79, 327
Central banks; *see also* Federal Reserve System
history, 552–553
influence on interest rates, 51, 544–545, 551
Centralized authority, 208, 211–212
CEOs (chief executive officers); *see* Managers
Certificates of deposit (CDs), 555
Certification, 325, 326
Certified financial planners (CFPs), 525, 530, 647–648
Certified internal auditors (CIAs), 460
Certified management accountants (CMAs), 457
Certified public accountants (CPAs), 458, 459
CFAs; *see* Chartered financial analysts
CFOs; *see* Chief financial officers
CFPs; *see* Certified financial planners
Chain of command, 210
Change
adapting to, 206, 223–227
management of, 207
risk management and, 621
Channels of distribution, 404, 405; *see also* Distribution
Chapter 7 bankruptcies, 587
Chapter 11 bankruptcies, 587, 588
Chapter 13 bankruptcies, 587, 588
Charitable giving; *see also* Nonprofit organizations
corporate philanthropy, 99–100
by entrepreneurs, 33, 181
giving circles, 94
myths about, 101
by small businesses, 101
Web sites, 100, 101
Chartered financial analysts (CFAs), 525
Check-clearing, 551, 552, 561–562
Chernobyl, 627
Chicago Board of Trade (CBOT), 531
Chief executive officers (CEOs); *see* Managers
Chief financial officers (CFOs), 484
Chief information officers (CIOs), 596
Child Care and Development Fund, 340
Child care benefits, 18, 340–341
Child Protection Act (1966), 585
Child Protection and Toy Safety Act (1969), 585
Children
advertising tobacco products to, 446
guardians, 648
marketing to, 359
China; *see also* Hong Kong
automobile industry, 69, 80
breweries, 63
bribery in, 108
competition with United States, 18
economic growth, 61
economic reforms, 42
entrepreneurs, 43
exports, 43, 60, 65, 80, 108
factors of production, 9
foreign investment, 66, 80
incomes, 30
intellectual property issues, 80, 438
joint ventures in, 69
McDonald's franchises, 376–377
manufacturing in, 18–19, 81
as market, 80, 183, 360
MTV Networks China, 58–59
oil companies, 133–134
population, 61
prison labor, 108
women's roles, 59
WTO membership, 77, 80
CIAs; *see* Certified internal auditors
Cigarette Labeling Act (1965), 585
CIM; *see* Computer-integrated manufacturing
CIO; *see* Congress of Industrial Organizations
CIOs; *see* Chief information officers
Circuit breakers, 536–537
Citizens Corps, 100
Civil law, 574
Civil Rights Act of 1964, 311, 312
Civil Rights Act of 1991, 312, 339
Clayton Act of 1914, 583
Client/server computing; *see* Network computing systems
Closed shop agreements, 328
Closed-end mutual funds, 528
Clothing
import tariffs, 174
T-shirt prices, 36
CMAs; *see* Certified management accountants
Coattail effect, 137
Codes of ethics, 13, 96–97
Coffee production, 88
Cognitive dissonance, 367
Collection procedures, 492
Collective bargaining, 325
Colleges and universities; *see also* Education; Students
Baldrige Award winners, 250
value of education, P-3, 634
Colombia, 78
Command economies, 43; *see also* Communism; Socialism
Commercial banks, 554–556; *see also* Banks
Commercial finance companies, 497
Commercial law, 579–580; *see also* Legal environment
Commercial paper, 498–499
Commercialization, 389
Commissions, 303
Commodities, 531
Commodity exchanges, 531
Common law, 574–575
Common markets, 77–78; *see also* European Union
Common stock, 518; *see also* Stocks
Communication, open, 276–277
Communications technology; *see* Cell phones; Internet; Networks; Technology
Communism, 42, 43, 44
Community service, 100
Comparable worth, 339
Comparative advantage theory, 61–62
Compensation
comparable worth, 339
employee retention and, 104
executive, 336–338
exit packages, 337
in foreign countries, 306
objectives, 302
pay equity, 338–339
pay systems, 302–303
of teams, 303–304
wages, 303
Competition
antitrust laws, 40, 582–584
in capitalism, 36
effects on marketing, 360–361
empowerment and, 16
in free markets, 39–40
global, 18–19, 20
monopolistic, 39

Competition—*Cont.*
nonprice, 395
perfect, 39
world-class businesses produced by, 15–16
Competition-based pricing, 393
Competitive environment, 15–16
Compliance-based ethics codes, 96
Comprehensive Employment and Training Act of 1973, 312
Compressed workweek, 307, 308
Comptrollers, 484
Computer chips, 604
Computer viruses, 610
Computer-aided design (CAD), 240
Computer-aided manufacturing (CAM), 240
Computer-integrated manufacturing (CIM), 240
Computers; *see* Information technology
Concept testing, 354, 389
Conceptual skills, 192
Conglomerate mergers, 133
Congress of Industrial Organizations (CIO), 324, 343
Consideration, 580–581
Constitution, U.S., 585–586
Consultants, 460
Consumer behavior, 366–367
Consumer credit; *see* Credit cards; Personal financial planning
Consumer market
comparison to business-to-business market, 367–368
defined, 361
goods and services classification, 380–382, 383
mass marketing, 364–365
niche marketing, 364
one-to-one marketing, 364
relationship marketing, 365–366
sales promotion techniques, 443–444
segmentation, 362–364
Consumer price index (CPI), 48
Consumer Product Safety Act (1972), 585
Consumer protection, 584, 585
Consumerism, 584
Consumers; *see* Consumer market; Customers
Contingency planning, 188
Contingent workers, 295–296; *see also* Temporary employees
Continuous process, 239
Contract law, 580–581
Contract manufacturing, 69
Contracts
breach of, 581
conditions for legal enforcement, 580–581
defined, 580
Contractual distribution systems, 416–417
Contrarian approach, 640
Control procedures
Gantt charts, 251, 252
PERT charts, 250–251
Controlling
defined, 184, 185
performance standards, 197–198
steps, 197
Convenience goods and services, 380–381
Convenience stores, 412
Conventional (C) corporations, 124–125
Convertible bonds, 516
Convertible preferred stock, 518
Cookies, 612
Cooling-off periods, 332
Cooperatives
agricultural, 141–142
defined, 141
food, 141
retail, 417
Copyright Act of 1978, 579
Copyrights, 93, 578–579, 610; *see also* Intellectual property protection
Core competencies, 222–223
Core time, 306–307
Corporate and Criminal Fraud Accountability (Sarbanes-Oxley) Act, 97, 98, 459, 460, 584
Corporate bonds; *see* Bonds
Corporate culture; *see* Organizational culture
Corporate distribution systems, 416
Corporate income taxes, 127–128, 584, 586
Corporate philanthropy, 99–100; *see also* Charitable giving
Corporate policy, 100
Corporate responsibility, 100; *see also* Corporate social responsibility
Corporate scandals
accounting-related, 12, 458–459
compensation for imprisoned executives, 338
criticism of regulatory agencies, 584
effects, 12
efforts to prevent, 588–589
recent, 90, 91, 102, 103, 537
Corporate social initiatives, 100
Corporate social responsibility
activities, 107
community service by employees, 100
competitive benefits, 101–102
debates on, 99
defined, 99
elements of, 99–100
environmental issues, 88, 102, 105, 106, 107
international standards, 109
investors and, 107
responsibilities to stakeholders
customers, 101–102, 107, 225
employees, 104
investors, 102–104
society and environment, 105–106
social audits, 106–108
watchdogs, 107–108
Corporations
advantages, 125–127
articles of incorporation, 129
boards of directors, 127, 622
bylaws, 129
conventional (C), 124–125
defined, 118
disadvantages, 127–128
financing sources, 125–126
incorporation process, 129
individuals as, 128
limited liability companies, 130–131
S, 129
separation of ownership and management, 127
sizes, 124, 126
taking private, 133
taxes, 127–128, 584, 586
types, 126
virtual, 221, 222
Corruption; *see also* Corporate scandals
bribery in foreign countries, 74, 108
in business, 40
in developing countries, 12, 74
international agreements on, 109
laws against, 12, 74
Cost accounting, 393
Cost of capital, 504
Cost of goods sold (or cost of goods manufactured), 469–470
Cost-based pricing, 393
Costs; *see also* Expenses
cutting, 239–240
forecasting, 488
operating, 470
total fixed, 394
variable, 394
Counterfeiting, 547
Countertrading, 74
Coupons, bond, 513
Court system, 574; *see also* Legal environment
Cover letters, P-18, P-24 to P-25
CPAs; *see* Certified public accountants
CPI; *see* Consumer price index
Craft unions, 323, 324
Credit; *see also* Debt; Loans; Short-term financing
managing, 640–641
microlending firms, 43, 381
trade, 494–495
Credit cards
financing small businesses, 499
interest rates, 636
managing, 640–641
processing costs, 561
stolen, 560
Credit lines, 497
Credit operations, 492
Credit unions, 557, 559–560, 646
Crime; *see also* Corruption
cyber-, 602, 609–610
employee theft, 104
identity theft, P-22 to P-23, 15, 16, 560
imprisonment, 337
insider trading, 102–103, 521, 522
intellectual property piracy, 80, 438
music piracy, 93
victims' rights, 560
Criminal law, 574
Crisis planning, 188
Crisis response, 244
Critical path, 251
CRM; *see* Customer relationship management
Cross-functional teams; *see* Self-managed cross-functional teams
Cuba
economy, 42
embargo on, 76
Cultural diversity; *see also* Diversity
ethical issues, 110
in global markets, 71–72
within teams, 278, 279
in United States, 71
Culture; *see also* Organizational culture
high- or low-context, 279
influences on buying decisions, 366–367
Cumulative preferred stock, 518
Currencies
convertible, 12
devaluations, 73–74
euro, 73, 77, 330
exchange rates, 73, 548
trading, 73, 546
U.S. dollar, 73, 548
Current assets, 466
Current liabilities, 466

Current ratio, 473–474
Customer databases
  determining preferences from, 359–360, 599
  information included in, 447, 599
  in small businesses, 365
  uses of, 15, 447, 599
Customer group departmentalization, 215, 216
Customer relationship era, 351
Customer relationship management (CRM)
  activities, 356
  defined, 351
  in small businesses, 365
  software, 439
Customer service
  in corporate cultures, 225
  improving, 211
Customers
  aging of population, 17, 360
  buying decisions, 366–367
  complaints, 446
  consumer protection, 584, 585
  corporate responsibility to, 101–102, 107, 225
  databases; *see* Customer databases
  diverse population, 17
  external, 198
  focus on, 225
  internal, 198
  involvement in product development, 220
  knowing, 170
  listening to, 192
  online dialogues with, 437, 447
  prospects, 439–440
  qualifying, 439
  responsiveness to, 15
  satisfaction, 198
  of small businesses, 170
Customization, 241
Cybercrime, 609–610
Cyberspace; *see* Internet
Cyberterrorism, 610–611
Cyclical unemployment, 47


## D


Damages, 581
Data
  for marketing research, 357–358
  primary, 357–358
  secondary, 357, 358
Data mining, 601
Data processing (DP), 596; *see also* Information technology
Data security, 602–603
Data warehouses, 601
Databases, 15; *see also* Customer databases
Day care; *see* Child care benefits
Dealer (private-label) brands, 385
Debenture bonds, 515
Debit cards, 560, 562, 641
Debt; *see also* Bonds; Credit cards; Loans
  leverage ratios, 474, 504, 505
  personal, 636, 637
Debt financing
  balancing with equity, 505
  bonds, 501, 513–516
  compared to equity financing, 502
  defined, 493
  loans, 500–501
Debt to owner's equity ratio, 474
Decentralized authority, 211–212
Decertification, 325–326
Decision making
  centralized or decentralized, 208, 211–212
  defined, 189
  empowering employees, 196, 211; *see also* Empowerment
  rational model, 189
Defense Department, U.S., 273, 610
Defense industry, 19, 245
Deficits
  budget, 50
  trade, 64, 65
Defined-contribution plans, 646–647
Deflation, 47–48
Demand, 37
Demand curve, 37, 38
Demand deposits, 554
Demand-based pricing, 393
Deming cycle, 248
Democratic leadership, 195
Demographic segmentation, 363–364
Demography; *see also* Aging of population; Diversity
  defined, 16
  multicultural population, 360
  population growth, 31–32
  single parents, 18
  two-income families, 18
  world population by continent, 60
Denmark
  currency, 77
  nontariff barriers, 76
  public transportation, 41
Department of Motor Vehicles (DMV), 209
Department stores, 412
Departmentalization, 206, 214–215, 216
Depreciation, 470
Depressions, 49; *see also* Great Depression
Deregulation, 40, 588–589
Devaluations, 73–74
Developing countries
  corruption, 12, 74
  countertrading, 74
  currencies, 12
  development programs, 565
  legal environments, 12
  marketing in, 360
  obstacles to entrepreneurship, 28–29
  obstacles to trade with, 74–75
  per capita incomes, 10
  population growth, 31–32
  poverty, 10, 31–32, 565
  products for markets in, 72, 360, 381
  promotion of entrepreneurship, 11–12
  standard of living, 72, 360
  tariffs, 76
  transportation and storage systems, 74
  wealth and freedom in, 10
Diamonds (Dow Industrial Average Model New Depositary Shares), 529
Digital video recorders, 436
Diluted earnings per share, 475
Direct deposit, 563
Direct mail, 415, 433, 434
Direct marketing, 415–416
Direct payments, 563
Direct selling, 415
Directing, 196
Directors, corporate, 127, 622
Disability insurance, 626, 643
Disabled individuals; *see also* Diversity
  accommodations, 313
  laws protecting, 310, 312, 313
  telecommuters, 608
Disaster aid, 34, 100
Disaster response, 244, 420
Discount rate, 551
Discount stores, 412
Discrimination
  age-related, 313
  in employment tests, 294–295
  gender-based, 338–339
  laws prohibiting, 310, 311, 312, 313
  price, 583
  reverse, 312
Disinflation, 47
Distance learning, 298
Distribution; *see also* Marketing intermediaries; Supply chain management
  administered systems, 417
  channels of, 404, 405
  contractual systems, 416–417
  cooperation in, 416
  corporate systems, 416
  of new products, 355
  outsourcing, 419
  physical, 419–422
  retail strategies, 412
Distributor brands, 385
Distributors, 220; *see also* Marketing intermediaries
Diversification, 528, 530
Diversity
  of customers, 17
  in franchising, 138–139
  generational differences, 17–18, 278–280
  groups, 17
  of U.S. population, 16–17
  of workforce, 17
Dividends
  common stock, 516
  preferred stock, 517–518
Division of labor, 206, 208
DMV; *see* Department of Motor Vehicles
Dollar, U.S., 548
Dot-coms; *see* Internet companies
Double-entry bookkeeping, 462
Dow Industrial Average Model New Depositary Shares (Diamonds), 529
Dow Jones Industrial Average, 535–536
DP; *see* Data processing
Drop shippers, 410
Drug companies; *see* Pharmaceutical companies
Drug testing, 342
Dumping, 65


## E


EACs; *see* Export Assistance Centers
Earnings; *see also* Compensation
  of college graduates, P-3, 634
  retained, 466, 503
Earnings per share (EPS)
  basic, 475
  diluted, 475
  price/earnings ratios, 534
Earnings statement; *see* Income statement
ECC; *see* Electronic check conversion
E-commerce; *see also* Internet
  automobile shopping, 353
  combined with traditional retail stores (click-and-brick)
    competition from Internet-only retailers, 360–361
    competitiveness, 413

E-commerce—*Cont.*
combined with traditional retail stores—*Cont.*
distribution systems, 413
successes, 186
Web kiosks in stores, 245
competition with brick-and-mortar retailers, 409
customer relationships, 437
defined, 15
distribution systems, 413
in franchising, 140
global opportunities, 79, 402
growth, 14–15
implementing, 413
information captured, 599
risks, 621
setting up Web-based businesses, 156–158
taxation of, 584
Economic and legal environment, 11–12, 72–74, 361
Economic systems; *see also* Capitalism; Markets
command economies, 43
communism, 42, 43, 44
comparison, 45
free-market, 43
mixed economies, 44
socialism, 41–42, 43, 44
Economics
allocation of resources, 31
defined, 31
as "dismal science," 31–32
growth, 32
macro-, 31–32
micro-, 31
Economies of scale, 208
Ecuador, Andean Pact, 78
EDI; *see* Electronic data interchange
EDLP; *see* Everyday low pricing
Education; *see also* Students; Training and development
economic development and, 32
investing in, P-3, 634
tax incentives, 634
value of, 634
EEOA; *see* Equal Employment Opportunity Act
EEOC; *see* Equal Employment Opportunity Commission
Efficiency, 13
EFT; *see* Electronic funds transfer (EFT) systems
Elder care, 341–342
Elderly; *see* Senior citizens
Electric utilities, 40; *see also* Utilities
Electronic cash, 547
Electronic check conversion (ECC), 561–562
Electronic data interchange (EDI), 602
Electronic funds transfer (EFT) systems, 561
Electronic retailing, 413; *see also* E-commerce
E-mail; *see also* Internet
netiquette, P-7 to P-8
privacy issues, 611
Embargoes, 76
Emerging markets; *see* Developing countries; Global markets
Employee benefits; *see* Fringe benefits
Employee Retirement Income Security Act (ERISA) of 1974, 312
Employee–management relations; *see also* Unions
arbitration, 331
bargaining zone, 330
ethical values in, 94
fairness in, 104
future of, 333–336
grievances, 329–330
impact of technology, 609
in informal organizations, 227
issues, 322–323
AIDS testing, 342
child care, 340–341
comparable worth, 339
drug testing, 342
elder care, 341–342
executive compensation, 336–338
pay equity, 338–339
sexual harassment, 339–340
violence in workplace, 342–343
lockouts, 333
mediation, 330
resolving disagreements, 329–331
in small businesses, 170–171
tactics used in conflicts, 331–333
trust in, 182
Employees; *see also* Compensation; Diversity; Empowerment; Human resource management; Labor; Recruitment; Staffing; Teams; Training and development
aging of, 289, 290, 313
community service, 100
corporate responsibility to, 104
enabling, 196
job-sharing, 308–309
line personnel, 217
losing, 310–311
orientation, 297
part-time, 295–296
pensions, 558
performance appraisals, 300–301
promotions, 309
retention, 104, 310
retirements, 310, 313
safety issues, 207
scheduling, 306–307
staff personnel, 217
terminating, 309–310, 313
theft by, 104
transfers, 309
Employment; *see* Careers; Jobs; Recruitment
Empowerment; *see also* Self-managed cross-functional teams
as competitive advantage, 16
decision making, 196, 211
defined, 16
effects on managerial authority, 208
increased span of control, 212–213
knowledge needed for, 196–197
as motivator, 271
open communication and, 276
restructuring for, 223–225
role of managers in, 184, 196
of self-managed teams, 220
Theory Y management and, 271
Empowerment zones, 556
EMS; *see* Environmental management system
Enabling, 196
Endorsements, celebrity, 387
Energy drinks, 430–431
England; *see* Britain
Enterprise portals, 603
Enterprise resource planning (ERP), 246–247
Enterprise risk management (ERM), 620
Enterprise zones, 158, 159, 556
Entertainment industry; *see* Movies; Television
*Entrepreneur* magazine, 116
Entrepreneurial teams, 154
Entrepreneurs; *see also* Women business owners
advice for, 154
charitable giving, 33, 181
defined, 4
innovation sources, 152
micropreneurs, 154
millionaires, 632–633
minority group members, 8, 161, 618–619
opportunities for, 8–9
personality traits, 151–152
readiness questionnaire, 152–153
retirement planning, 647
social, 7
successful, 4, 150, 151–152
wealth creation by, 9–10
Entrepreneurship; *see also* Businesses, starting; Home-based businesses; Small businesses
advantages, 8
compared to working in large businesses, 8
defined, 150
in developing countries, 28–29
as factor of production, 9, 10
within firms, 158
government support of, 159
history, 150
jobs created by, 150
laws encouraging, 11–12
motivations, 151
Environment; *see* Business environment
Environmental issues
antiglobalization protesters, 77, 564, 565
clean water, 88–89
corporate responsibility and, 88, 102, 105, 106, 107
global warming, 627, 629
of individual companies, 207
ISO 14000 standards, 250
risks, 627–629
tuna fishing, 106
Environmental management system (EMS), 250
Environmental scanning, 358
EPS; *see* Earnings per share
Equal Employment Opportunity Act (EEOA), 311, 312
Equal Employment Opportunity Commission (EEOC)
ADA guidelines, 313
influence on business, 575
powers, 311, 312
sexual harassment complaints to, 339–340
Equal Pay Act of 1963, 312, 338
Equilibrium prices, 37–38
Equipment, 382
Equity, owners'; *see* Owners' equity
Equity financing; *see also* Stocks
balancing with debt, 505
compared to debt financing, 502
defined, 493
retained earnings, 503
selling stock, 502–503
venture capital, 168, 503–504, 556
Equity theory, 274–275
ERISA; *see* Employee Retirement Income Security Act
ERM; *see* Enterprise risk management
ERP; *see* Enterprise resource planning
Estate planning, 648

ETFs; *see* Exchange-traded funds
Ethics; *see also* Corporate scandals; Corporate social responsibility; Corruption
- in accounting, 473
- in auditing, 491
- in banks, 555
- cheating by students, 92
- cigarette advertising, 446
- cultural differences and, 110
- defined, 90
- dilemmas, 92–94
- disaster aid, 34
- enforcement, 97
- formal policies, 13, 96–97
- in global markets, 74, 108–110
- improving, 96–97
- individual responsibility, P-9, 13, 91–94
- insider trading, 521, 522
- legality and, 90
- in marketing, 359
- organizational, 94–96, 194
- orientation questionnaire, 95
- outsourcing, 82, 123, 235
- personal dilemmas, 13
- promoting, 194
- safety issues, 207
- shopping, 409
- standards, 90–91
- starting businesses, 164
- strikebreakers, 334
- subcontracting, 123
- takeover decisions, 523
- values in organizational cultures, 225

Ethics codes, 13, 96–97
Ethics offices, 97
Ethnic groups, marketing to, 360; *see also* Cultural diversity; Minorities
Ethnocentricity, 71
Etiquette, P-6 to P-9
Eurex exchange, 531
Euro
- currencies replaced by, 73
- effects on wages and unions, 330
- introduction, 77

Europe; *see also individual countries*
- codetermination, 330, 338
- executive compensation, 338
- financial institutions, 558
- unions in, 329, 330

European Economic Community, 77
European Union (EU); *see also* Euro
- bribery condemned by, 109
- history, 77
- Internet taxation, 584
- members, 78
- quality standards, 250
- wage differences, 330

Event marketing, 431, 445
Everyday low pricing (EDLP), 394
Exchange rates
- defined, 73
- effects on global business, 73
- floating, 73
- movements, 548

Exchanges; *see* Commodity exchanges; Stock exchanges
Exchange-traded funds (ETFs), 528–529
Exclusive dealing, 583
Exclusive distribution, 412
Executive compensation, 336–338
Executives; *see* Managers
Executors, 648
Exit interviews, 310–311
Expectancy theory, 273–274
Expenses; *see also* Costs
- forecasting, 488
- operating, 470
- personal, 635–636, 637–638

Export Administration Act of 1979, 76
Export Assistance Centers (EACs), 67
Exporting; *see also* Global markets; Trade
- challenges, 173
- competition in, 60
- defined, 60
- export-trading companies, 67
- financing, 175, 498
- government assistance, 63–64, 67
- information on, 63–64, 174
- jobs created by, 19–20, 63
- letters of credit and, 563
- obstacles, 74–75
- opportunities, 63–64
- by small businesses, 67, 79, 82, 173–174

Export-trading companies, 67
Express warranties, 579
Expropriation, 70
External customers, 198
Extranets, 602
Extrinsic rewards, 260

## F

Facility layout, 245–246
Facility location
- defined, 242
- in foreign countries, 243
- in future, 245
- government incentives, 245
- for manufacturers, 243–244

Factoring, 497–498
Factors of production, 9–10, 236
Failures; *see* Business failures
Fair Credit Reporting Act (1970), 585
Fair Labor Standards Act of 1938, 312, 325
Fair Packaging and Labeling Act (1966), 384, 585
False Claims Act, 98
Families; *see also* Children
- elder care, 341–342
- financing from, 495
- single parents, 18

Family and Medical Leave Act of 1993, 312
Family-friendly fringe benefits, 18
Farming; *see* Agriculture
FASB; *see* Financial Accounting Standards Board
*Fast Company*, 149, 375
FBI; *see* Federal Bureau of Investigation
FDA; *see* Food and Drug Administration
FDIC; *see* Federal Deposit Insurance Corporation
Federal budget deficit, 50
Federal Bureau of Investigation (FBI), 461, 609
Federal Deposit Insurance Corporation (FDIC), 559, 572
Federal government; *see* U.S. government
Federal Open Market Committee (FOMC), 549
Federal Reserve Act of 1913, 553
Federal Reserve System
- banks, 55, 549
- Bernanke as chairman, 544, 545
- check-clearing role, 551, 552, 561–562
- control of money supply, 548, 549–551
- discount rate, 551
- formation, 553
- functions, 549
- Greenspan as chairman, 544–545
- interest rates, 544–545, 551
- margin rates, 530
- monetary policy, 50–51, 549
- need for, 553–554
- open-market operations, 549, 550
- organization of, 549
- reserve requirements, 550

Federal Savings and Loan Insurance Corporation (FSLIC), 559
Federal Trade Commission Act of 1914, 583
Federal Trade Commission (FTC), 15, 137, 575, 583, 585
FIFO (first in, first out), 469
Films; *see* Movies
Finance; *see also* Financial management
- defined, 484
- importance, 486
- relationship to accounting, 484

Financial accounting, 457–459; *see also* Accounting
Financial Accounting Standards Board (FASB), 458, 471, 473, 475
Financial control, 489–490
Financial institutions; *see* Banks; Credit unions; Nonbanks; Savings and loan associations
Financial leverage, 504, 505
Financial management; *see also* Financial planning; Short-term financing
- debt financing, 493, 500–501
- defined, 484
- equity financing, 493, 502–504
- leverage, 504–505
- long-term financing, 493–494, 500
- operating funds, 491–494
- reasons for business failures, 485
- in small businesses, 166–168, 485
- sources of funds, 493–494
- tax management, 486–487

Financial managers
- defined, 484
- tasks, 484–485, 486–487
- titles, 484

Financial markets; *see* Securities markets
Financial planning
- budgets, 488–489
- controls, 489–490
- forecasts, 488
- importance, 489
- personal; *see* Personal financial planning
- steps, 487

Financial ratios; *see* Ratio analysis
Financial services; *see* Banks
Financial statements
- annual reports, P-25, 458, 460
- auditing, 459–460, 486
- balance sheet
  - accounts, 477
  - assets, 464–466
  - defined, 463, 464
  - liabilities and owners' equity, 466–467
  - personal, 463, 467
- defined, 463
- income statement, 477
  - accounts, 477
  - cost of goods sold, 469–470

Financial statements—*Cont.*
income statement—*Cont.*
defined, 463, 467–468
gross profit, 469–470
net income, 468, 470
operating expenses, 470
personal, 635
revenue, 469
statement of cash flows, 463, 471
Firewalls, 602
Firing employees, 309–310, 313
Firms; *see* Corporations
First in, first out (FIFO), 469
First-line managers, 191, 194
Fiscal policy, 50
Fixed assets, 466
Fixed-position layouts, 246
Flammable Fabrics Act (1953), 585
Flat organization structures, 213–214
Flexible manufacturing, 240–241
Flextime plans, 306–307
Floating exchange rates, 73
Focus groups, 358
FOMC; *see* Federal Open Market Committee
Food, Drug, and Cosmetic Act (1938), 585
Food and Drug Administration (FDA), 575
Food industry; *see also* Agriculture; Supermarkets
cooperatives, 141
marketing intermediaries, 406–407
meal preparation businesses, 378
regulation of, 585, 589
Forecasts, 488
Foreign Corrupt Practices Act of 1978, 74
Foreign currencies; *see* Currencies
Foreign direct investment
in China, 80
defined, 70
Foreign exchange; *see* Currencies
Foreign markets; see Global markets; Trade
Foreign stock exchanges, 521, 524
Foreign subsidiaries, 70
Forensic accountants, 459
Forfeiting, 498
Form utility, 238, 407–408
Formal organization, 226, 227
Forms of business ownership; *see* Business ownership forms
*Fortune*
Best Companies to Work For, 89, 258, 266, 286, 304, 375
Most Admired Companies, 89
Rising Stars, 59
Four Ps of marketing, 352–356
401(k) plans, 646–647
France
McDonald's stores, 376
unions, 330
Franchise agreements, 134–135
Franchisees, 134
Franchises
advantages, 135–136
defined, 135
disadvantages, 136–137
as distribution system, 416
diversity in, 138–139
e-commerce use, 140
evaluation checklist, 138
fast-growing, 116
home-based, 139–140
international, 67–68, 140–141
scams, 137
start-up costs, 136
success rates, 135, 136
technology used in, 140
Web sites, 140
Franchisors, 134
Fraud; *see also* Corporate scandals
by franchisors, 137
investigations, 459
phishing scams, 610
victims' rights, 560
*Freakonomics*, 446
Free markets; *see* Markets
Free trade; *see also* Trade
defined, 61
laws to ensure fairness, 65
pros and cons, 62
Free trade agreements; *see* Central American Free Trade Agreement; Common markets; North American Free Trade Agreement
Free Trade Area of the Americas (FTAA), 79
Freedom, 10, 36
Freedom of Information Act, 611
Free-market economies, 43; *see also* Capitalism; Markets
Free-rein leadership, 195–196
Freight forwarders, 420, 421
Frequent-user programs, 366
Frictional unemployment, 47
Fringe benefits
cafeteria-style, 304–305
child care, 18, 340–341
defined, 304
employee retention and, 104
examples, 18
family-friendly, 18
in foreign countries, 306
401(k) plans, 646–647
health insurance, 304, 625–626
objectives, 302
outsourcing, 293, 305
vacation time, 304, 305
FSLIC; *see* Federal Savings and Loan Insurance Corporation
FTAA; *see* Free Trade Area of the Americas
FTC; *see* Federal Trade Commission
Full-service wholesalers, 410, 411
Functional departmentalization, 214–215, 216
Fundamental accounting equation, 463–464
Funds; *see* Financial management; Mutual funds
Fur Products Labeling Act (1951), 585
Futures markets, 531

## G

GAAP; *see* Generally accepted accounting principles
Gantt charts, 251, 252
GASB; *see* Governmental Accounting Standards Board
GATT; *see* General Agreement on Tariffs and Trade
GDP (gross domestic product), 46
Gender; *see also* Women
discrimination based on, 338–339
earnings differences, 338–339
General Agreement on Tariffs and Trade (GATT), 76
General partners, 121
General partnerships, 121
Generally accepted accounting principles (GAAP), 458, 469, 470
Generation X, 278–280
Generation Y, 278, 280, 364
Generational differences, 17–18, 278–280
Generic goods, 386
Generic names, 385–386
Geographic departmentalization, 215, 216
Geographical segmentation, 363
Germany
automakers, 71–72
codetermination, 330, 338
imported beer, 63
inflation, 48
standard of living, 5
unions, 330
Givebacks, 333–334
Glass-Steagall Act of 1933, 560
Global business; *see also* Multinational corporations
careers in, 60–61, 70, 82
challenges, 183
opportunities, 62–64
Global environment, 18–20
Global markets; *see also* Exporting; Importing; Trade
adapting products for, 376–377
adapting to other cultures, 68, 71–72, 437–438
advertising, 437–438
banking, 563–564
business etiquette, P-8
contract manufacturing, 69
countertrading, 74
currency markets, 73, 546
developing countries, 72, 360, 381
distribution, 418
effects on marketing process, 358–359
ethical concerns in, 74, 108–110
forces affecting
economic, 72–74
legal and regulatory, 74
physical and environmental, 74–75
sociocultural, 71–72
foreign direct investment, 80
future of, 78–82
joint ventures, 69
large businesses, 62
licensing, 66–67
local contacts, 74
logistics companies, 418
marketing strategies, 72, 73, 360, 438
measuring, 64–65
reaching via Internet, 402
risk management, 629
securities markets, 521, 524
service sector, 44
size of, 60
small businesses, 62–64, 82, 173–174
stock exchanges, 521, 524
strategic alliances, 69
strategies for reaching, 66, 70
Global warming, 627, 629
Globalization, protests against, 77, 564, 565
Goals, 185
Goal-setting theory, 273
Going public; *see* Initial public offerings; Stocks
Golden handshakes, 310
Golden Rule, 91
Goods; *see also* Products
defined, 20
industrial, 382, 383
Goodwill, 465
Government and not-for-profit accounting, 460–461
Government bonds, 513, 514, 525
Governmental Accounting Standards Board (GASB), 461

Governments; *see also* Local governments; State governments; U.S. government
- accounting, 460–461
- bribery of officials, 74, 108
- businesses owned by, 12
- competition to attract businesses, 245
- economic policies, 50–51
- entrepreneurship encouraged by, 159
- fiscal policy, 50
- monetary policy, 50–51, 549
- promotion of entrepreneurship, 11–12
- regulations; *see* Regulations
- relations with businesses, 11–12, 44
- spending policies, 50
- taxes; *see* Taxes
- using business principles in, 21

Gramm-Leach-Bliley Act of 1999, 560
Grapevine, 226–227
Great Britain; *see* Britain
Great Depression, 49, 553–554, 559
Grievances, 329–330
Grocery stores; *see* Supermarkets
Gross domestic product (GDP), 46
Gross margin, 469–470
Gross profit, 469–470
Growth economics, 32
Growth stocks, 526–527
Guerrilla marketing, 431
Gulf War, 420

## H

Hackers, 602, 610
Haiti, 10, 72
Hamburger University (McDonald's), 135, 299
Hardware, 604
Hawthorne effect, 263
Hawthorne studies, 262–263
Health
- AIDS, 342
- threats, 620

Health care; *see also* Pharmaceutical companies
- unions, 335

Health insurance
- buying, 643
- for employees, 304, 625–626
- types, 628

Health maintenance organizations (HMOs), 625–626, 643
Health savings accounts (HSAs), 643
Herzbergs motivating factors, 265–267, 268
Hierarchy, 190–191, 208, 209, 210
Hierarchy of needs, 263–265, 267
High-context cultures, 279
Higher education; *see* Colleges and universities; Education
High–low pricing strategy, 394
High-tech companies; *see* Internet companies; Technology
Hiring; *see* Recruitment
Hispanic Americans, 160, 161
HMOs; see Health maintenance organizations
Home countries, 70
Home-based businesses; *see also* Small businesses
- advantages, 139
- challenges, 155–156
- disadvantages, 139
- franchises, 139–140
- insurance coverage, 627
- number of, 154
- potential areas, 156
- reasons for growth of, 154–155
- scams, 157
- technology used in, 155
- types, 156

Home-based work; *see* Telecommuting
Homeland security, 100
Homeowners insurance, 627, 643
Homes, buying, 638–639
Homosexuals; *see* Diversity
Hong Kong; *see also* China
- Disney theme park, 183
- factors of production, 9
- franchises, 68, 141
- wealth and freedom in, 10

Horizontal mergers, 133
Host countries, 70
Hotels, 237–238
House brands, 385
HSAs; *see* Health savings accounts
Human relations skills, 192
Human resource management; *see also* Recruitment; Training and development
- activities, 288
- challenges, 289–290
- cultural differences, 72, 306
- defined, 288
- global workforce and, 306
- laws affecting, 311–314
- performance appraisals, 300–301
- planning, 290–292
- promotions and transfers, 309
- technology-related issues, 608–609
- terminations, 309–310, 313
- trends, 288–290

Hurricane Katrina, 34, 188, 207, 244, 420
Hurricane Rita, 420
Hygiene factors, 265–266

## I

Identity theft, P-22 to P-23, 15, 16, 560
IMC; *see* Integrated marketing communication
IMF; *see* International Monetary Fund
Immigrants; *see also* Cultural diversity; Minorities
- employees, 290
- entrepreneurs, 8, 159

Immigration Act of 1990, 159
Immigration Reform and Control Act of 1986, 312
Implied warranties, 579–580
Import quotas, 76
Importing; *see also* Global markets; Tariffs; Trade
- defined, 60
- letters of credit and, 563
- logistics companies and, 418
- opportunities, 62–63

Inbound logistics, 419
Income; *see also* Compensation; Earnings
- net, 467, 470
- retained earnings, 466, 503

Income statement
- accounts, 477
- cost of goods sold, 469–470
- defined, 463, 467–468
- gross profit, 469–470
- net income, 468, 470
- operating expenses, 470
- personal, 635
- revenue, 469

Income stocks, 527
Income taxes; *see* Taxes
Incorporation; *see also* Corporations
- articles of, 129
- of individuals, 128
- process, 129

Incubators, 159
Indenture terms, 501
Independent audits, 460
Index funds, 528
India
- competition with United States, 18
- economic growth, 60, 61
- incomes, 72
- legal environment, 12
- McDonald's franchises, 68
- manufacturing in, 81–82
- as market, 80, 360, 381
- outsourcing to, 81–82
- population, 61

Individual retirement accounts (IRAs)
- Roth, 645
- SEP plans, 647
- Simple, 646
- traditional, 644–645

Indonesia
- as market, 81, 361
- Samsung in, 105–106

Industrial goods, 382, 383
Industrial Revolution, 323
Industrial unions, 324
Infant industries, 76
Inflation, 47–48
Infomercials, 435–436
Informal organization, 226–227
Information
- distinction from knowledge, 597
- managing, 600
- public, 599, 611–612
- sharing, 601–603
- types, 599

Information overload, 600
*Information Security*, 595
Information systems (IS), 596
Information technology (IT); *see also* Internet; Networks; Software; Technology
- computer-aided design and manufacturing, 240
- defined, 596
- effects on management, 608–609
- for employee training and development, 297–298
- hardware, 604
- impact on businesses, 12–15, 609
- outsourcing, 606
- privacy issues, 611–612
- role in business, 596–597, 598
- security issues, 602–603, 609–611
- skills needed, 608, 613
- stability issues, 612–613
- training, 608
- use in manufacturing, 240, 246–247

Information utility, 408–409
Initial public offerings (IPOs), 503, 512
Injunctions, 333
Inner-city businesses, 161
Innovation; *see also* Product development
- by entrepreneurs, 152
- in United States, 236

Insider trading, 102, 521, 522
Insourcing, 6, 234–235
Installations, 382
Institutional investors, 513
Insurable interest, 624
Insurable risk, 624

Insurance; *see also* Health insurance
annuities, 642–643
automobile, 644
for boards of directors, 622
business, 627
business ownership policies, 623
disability, 626, 643
government programs, 623
for home-based businesses, 627
homeowners, 627, 643
liability, 626–627, 628, 644
life, 627, 628, 642–643
premiums, 624
property, 628
renters, 643
rule of indemnity, 624
self-, 622–623
for small businesses, 172
types, 628
umbrella policies, 644
uninsurable risks, 623
workers compensation, 626
Insurance companies
IRAs with, 646
life, 558
mutual, 625
ratings, 642
services, 560
stock, 625
Insurance policies, 624
Intangible assets, 464–465, 466
Integrated marketing communication (IMC), 432
Integrity-based ethics codes, 96, 97
Intellectual property protection
copyrights, 93, 578–579, 610
lack of in China, 80, 438
online file sharing and, 93, 578
patents, 577–578
plagiarism from Internet, 92
trademarks, 385, 579
Intensive distribution, 412
Interactive promotion, 437
Inter-American Convention Against Corruption, 109
Interest rates
on bonds, 513, 514, 525–526
central bank influence on, 51, 544–545, 551
discount rate, 551
Intermediaries; *see* Marketing intermediaries
Intermittent process, 239
Intermodal shipping, 422
Internal customers, 198
Internal Revenue Service (IRS), 130, 461, 470
International Bank for Reconstruction and Development; *see* World Bank
International banking, 563–564; *see also* Banks
International business; *see* Global business; Multinational corporations
International Manufacturing Trade Show, 444
International markets; *see* Global markets
International Monetary Fund (IMF), 564–566
International Organization for Standardization (ISO), 109, 250
International trade; *see* Global markets; Trade
Internet; *see also* E-commerce
advertising on, 433, 434, 436–437, 448
agriculture-related Web sites, 13–14
application service providers, 606
auctions, 402
banking, 242–243, 560–561
blogs, 446–447
connections to, 447, 603
cybercrime, 609–610
dialogues with customers, 437, 447
e-mail, P-7 to P-8, 611
file sharing services, 93, 578
impact on businesses, 12–15
intellectual property violations, 92, 93, 610
interactions among firms, 220–221, 245
investment information, 532
job search resources, P-18, P-19 to P-20
learning portals, 290
marketing on, 359–360
netiquette, P-7 to P-8
online brokers, 522, 523
operations management using, 244
phishing scams, 610
podcasting, 447
privacy issues, P-22 to P-23, 15, 611–612
reaching global customers, 402
real estate information, 379
recruiting employees, 293, 294
résumés posted on, P-21 to P-23
security issues, 602, 610
small business Web sites, 171–172, 174
social networking sites, 602
training programs, 290, 298
viral marketing, 446
viruses, 594, 610
Internet appliances, 605
Internet companies; *see also* E-commerce
failures, 14–15, 158
setting up, 156–158
venture capital investments, 503
Internet2, 603–604
Interviews, P-18, P-25 to P-27, 294
Intranets, 602
Intrapreneurs, 158
Intrinsic rewards, 260
Inventory
acquiring, 492–493
as collateral for loans, 496–497
just-in-time, 247–248, 493
valuation, 469
Inventory turnover ratio, 476
Inverted organizations, 224–225
Investing; *see also* Mutual funds; Securities markets
in bonds, 525–526
buying securities, 522
capital gains, 526
commodities, 531
comparing investments, 532
contrarian approach, 640
diversification, 528, 530
401(k) plans, 646–647
futures, 531
in global markets, 524
high-risk investments, 530–531
information sources, 532
IRAs, 644–646
in real estate, 638–639
selling securities, 522
in stocks, 526–527, 640
strategies, 524–525, 530
in 21st century, 537
Investment, foreign direct, 70, 80
Investment advisers, 525, 530
Investment bankers, 513
Investors; *see also* Owners' equity; Venture capitalists
angels, 168, 556
corporate responsibility to, 102–104
institutional, 513
socially conscious, 107
*Investor's Business Daily*, 528
Invisible hand, 32–33
Involuntary bankruptcy, 586
IPOs; *see* Initial public offerings
Iraq war, 19
IRAs; *see* Individual retirement accounts
IRS; *see* Internal Revenue Service
IS; *see* Information systems
ISO 9000 standards, 250
ISO 14000 standards, 250
Israel, McDonald's franchises, 68
IT; *see* Information technology
Italy
bribery in, 108
joint ventures in, 69

## J

Jamaica, 74
Japan
automakers, 71–72, 206, 234
bribery scandal, 108
dumping disputes, 65
executive compensation, 338
exports, 65
factors of production, 9
joint ventures in, 69
keiretsu (corporate alliances), 76
management approach, 271–272
mass customization, 241
nontariff barriers, 76
standard of living, 5
Tokyo Disneyland, 66
vending machines, 414
JIT; *see* Just-in-time (JIT) inventory control
Job analysis, 291
Job descriptions, 291
Job enlargement, 269
Job enrichment, 267–268
Job interviews, 294
Job rotation, 269, 299
Job searches; *see also* Recruitment; Résumés
Internet resources, P-18, P-19 to P-20
interviews, P-18, P-25 to P-27
self-assessments, P-4 to P-5, P-16, P-17
sources of jobs, P-18
strategies, P-16 to P-18
traits sought by recruiters, P-27
Job simplification, 268
Job simulation, 299
Job specialization, 206
Job specifications, 291
Jobs; *see also* Careers; Outsourcing; Recruitment
created by small businesses, 160, 161
displaced by technology, 21
lost due to free-trade agreements, 79
Job-sharing plans, 308–309
Joint Initiative on Corporate Accountability and Workers' Rights, 109
Joint ventures, international, 69
Journals, 461–462
Journeymen, 298
Judiciary, 574; *see also* Legal environment
Junk bonds, 530
Just-in-time (JIT) inventory control, 247–248, 493

## K


Keiretsu, 76
Keogh plans, 647
Key economic indicators, 46–48
Knights of Labor, 324, 343
Knockoff brands, 386
Knowledge
 distinction from information, 597
 as factor of production, 9, 10
 retention, P-5
Knowledge management, 196–197
Knowledge technology (KT), 597–598
Knowledge workers, 9
Koran, 63, 72, 91
Korea; *see* North Korea; South Korea
Koreans, immigrant entrepreneurs, 8
KT; *see* Knowledge technology


## L


Labor; *see also* Employee–management relations; Employees; Unions
 as factor of production, 9, 10
 legislation related to, 324–326, 332
 productivity, 13
Labor–Management Relations Act (Taft-Hartley Act)
 cooling-off periods, 332
 passage, 324
 provisions, 325, 328–329
 secondary boycotts prohibited, 332
Labor–Management Reporting and Disclosure Act (Landrum-Griffin Act), 324
Land, as factor of production, 9
Land banks, 552
Landrum-Griffin Act, 324
Last in, first out (LIFO), 469
Latin America
 common markets, 78
 relations between managers and workers, 72
Law of large numbers, 624
Laws; *see* Legal environment
Lawsuits
 product liability, 576, 577, 627
 threat of, 620, 622
 wrongful discharge, 309, 310
Lawyers, 171, 572–573
Layoffs; *see* Terminating employees
Layout, facility, 245–246
LBOs; *see* Leveraged buyouts
Leadership
 autocratic, 195
 free-rein, 195–196
 need for, 193–194
 participative (democratic), 188, 195
 styles, 194–196
Leading
 defined, 184, 185
 empowering workers, 196
 knowledge management, 196–197
 need for, 193–194
 styles, 194–196
Lean manufacturing, 241
Learning, from peers, 276; *see also* Training and development
Ledgers, 462
Legal environment; *see also* Lawsuits; Regulations; Taxes
 administrative agencies, 575
 antitrust laws, 40, 582–584
 bankruptcy laws, 586–588
 consumer protection, 584, 585
 contract law, 580–581
 deregulation, 40, 588–589
 effects on global markets, 74
 human resource management, 311–314
 intellectual property protection, 93, 385, 577–579
 labor laws, 324–326, 332
 need for laws, 574
 negotiable instruments, 580
 partnership laws, 122, 124
 product liability, 576–577
 punishment for corporate wrongdoing, 90
 restrictions on business, 11–12
 sales law, 579–580
 tort law, 576–577
 trade-related laws, 65
 types of laws, 574–575
 Uniform Limited Liability Company Act, 130
 warranties, 579–580
Legislation; *see* Legal environment
Less-developed countries; *see* Developing countries
Letters of credit, 563
Leverage, 504–505
Leverage ratios, 474, 504, 505
Leveraged buyouts (LBOs), 132, 133
Liabilities; *see also* Debt
 current, 466
 defined, 466
 long-term, 466
Liability
 limited, 121, 125
 unlimited, 119–120, 122–123
Liability insurance, 626–627, 628, 644
Libya, 10
Licensing, 66–67
Life cycle, product, 389–391
Life insurance, 627, 628, 642–643
Life insurance companies, 558
LIFO (last in, first out), 469
Limit orders, 527
Limited liability, 121, 125
Limited liability companies (LLCs), 130–131
Limited liability partnerships (LLPs), 121–122
Limited partners, 121
Limited partnerships, 121
Limited-function wholesalers, 410
Line organizations, 217
Line personnel, 217
Line-and-staff organizations, 217, 218
Lines of credit, 497
Liquidity, 466
Liquidity ratios, 473–474
LLCs; *see* Limited liability companies
LLPs; *see* Limited liability partnerships
Loans; *see also* Credit; Debt
 bank, 556
 from commercial finance companies, 497
 long-term, 500–501
 microlending firms, 43, 381
 secured, 496–497
 short-term, 496–497
 unsecured, 497
Local governments
 administrative agencies, 575
 municipal bonds, 514, 525
 taxes, 584
Location, facility; *see* Facility location
Lockouts, 333
Logistics
 defined, 419
 disaster response, 420
 inbound, 419
 international, 418
 need for, 418–419
 outbound, 419
 reverse, 419
 storage, 422–423
 third-party, 419
Logistics companies, 419
Long-term financing
 balancing debt and equity, 505
 debt, 493, 500–501
 defined, 493
 equity, 493, 502–504
 objectives, 500
Long-term forecasts, 488
Long-term liabilities, 466
Loss leaders, 392
Losses
 defined, 4
 net, 467, 470
Low-context cultures, 279


## M


M-1, 547
M-2, 547
M&A; *see* Mergers and acquisitions
Macroeconomics, 31–32
*Mad Money*, 510, 511
Magazine advertising, 434
Magnuson–Moss Warranty–Federal Trade Commission Improvement Act (1975), 585
Mail; *see* Direct mail; E-mail
Mail-order firms; *see* Catalog sales
Malaysia, 81
Malcolm Baldrige National Quality Awards, 248–250, 256, 304
Management; *see also* Employee–management relations; Empowerment; Motivation; Small business management
 boards of directors, 127, 622
 challenges, 182
 of change, 207
 contrast between American and Japanese styles, 271–272
 controlling, 184, 185, 197–198
 decision making, 189–190
 defined, 182–183
 directing, 196
 effects of information technology, 608–609
 ethics in, 94–96, 194
 functions, 182–184
 leading
  defined, 184, 185
  empowering workers, 196
  knowledge management, 196–197
  need for, 193–194
  styles, 194–196
 levels
  bureaucracies, 210
  middle, 191, 210
  number of, 213–214
  supervisory, 191, 194
  tasks and skills, 191–192
  top, 190–191
 organizing; *see* Organizing
 planning
  contingency, 188
  defined, 183–184
  forms, 187
  goals and objectives, 185
  importance, 184–185, 188
  mission statements, 185
  operational, 188

Management—*Cont.*
planning—*Cont.*
performance standards, 197–198
questions answered by, 185–186
strategic, 186–187, 488
SWOT analysis, 186, 187
tactical, 187–188
vision creation, 184–185
problem solving, 189–190
separation from ownership, 127
tactics used in conflicts with labor, 333
Management by objectives (MBO), 273
Management development, 299–300
Managerial accounting, 457
Managers
authority, 208
changing roles, 182
compensation, 336–338
differences from leaders, 193–194
exit packages, 337
in Latin America, 72
mentors, 299–300
progressive, 180, 182, 196
roles, 16
span of control, 212–213
supervisory, 191, 194
Managing diversity; *see* Diversity
Manpower Development and Training Act of 1962, 312
Manufacturer's agents, 411
Manufacturers' brand names, 385
Manufacturing; *see also* Automobile industry; Operations management
competition in, 235–236
contract, 69
costs, 239–240
decline of, 288
facility layout, 245–246
facility location, 243–244
foreign companies in United States, 234–235, 243
jobs replaced by technology, 21
mass production, 208
production techniques
computer-aided design and manufacturing, 240
flexible manufacturing, 240–241
improving, 239–240
Internet purchasing, 247
just-in-time inventory control, 247–248
lean manufacturing, 241
mass customization, 241
productivity improvements, 20, 21, 49
technology used in, 21, 246–247
in United States, 234–236
Margin
buying stock on, 530
gross, 469–470
Market indices, 535–536
Market orders, 527
Market prices, 37–38, 39, 394
Market segmentation, 362–364
Marketable securities; *see* Securities markets
Marketing; *see also* Personal selling; Promotion
careers in, 369
to children, 359
consumer decision-making process, 366–367
defined, 350
in developing countries, 360
eras, 350–351
ethical issues, 359
evolution of, 350–351
four Ps, 352–356
guerrilla, 431
on Internet, 359–360
mass, 364–365
by nonprofit organizations, 351–352
one-to-one, 364
test, 354
transactional, 365
Marketing concept, 351
Marketing concept era, 350–351
Marketing environment, 358–361
Marketing intermediaries; *see also* Business-to-business (B2B) companies; Retail industry; Wholesalers
cooperation among, 416–418
defined, 404
exchange efficiency created by, 405, 406
in food industry, 406–407
need for, 404–405, 406–407
roles, 355
sales promotion to, 444–445
types, 404
utilities created by, 407–409
value versus cost of, 405–407
Marketing managers, 352, 353
Marketing mix, 352, 353, 390–391
Marketing research
in China, 360
data analysis, 358
data collection, 357–358
data sources, 357
defined, 356
focus groups, 358
process, 356–358
strategy implementation, 358
surveys, 357–358
Markets; *see also* Business-to-business (B2B) market; Consumer market; Global markets; Securities markets
competition in, 39–40
defined, 170
demand, 37
free, 40
functioning of, 36–38
inequality in, 40
price determination, 36–38
supply, 37
Maslow's hierarchy of needs, 263–265, 267
Mass customization, 241
Mass marketing, 364–365
Mass production, 208
Master limited partnerships (MLPs), 121
Materials handling, 419
Materials requirement planning (MRP), 246
Matrix organizations, 217–219
Maturity dates, 514
MBO; *see* Management by objectives
Media, 443; *see also* Advertising; Television
Mediation, 330
Medical savings accounts (MSAs), 626
Medicine; *see* Health care
Mentors, 290, 299–300
Mercantilism, 75
Merchant wholesalers, 410
Mercosur, 78
Mergers and acquisitions
conglomerate mergers, 133
defined, 132–133
ethical issues, 523
foreign companies involved in, 133–134
horizontal mergers, 133
in late 1990s, 131, 134
leveraged buyouts, 132, 133
regulation of, 583
types, 132, 133
vertical mergers, 133
Mexico, 79; *see also* North American Free Trade Agreement
Microeconomics, 31; *see also* Prices
Microlending firms, 43, 381
Micropreneurs, 154
Middle management, 191, 210
Middlemen; *see* Marketing intermediaries
Millionaires, 632–633
MiniPlan, 166
Minorities; *see also* African Americans; Asian Americans; Discrimination; Diversity
businesses owned by, 160
entrepreneurs, 8, 161
franchisees, 139
Hispanic Americans, 160, 161
Mission statements, 185
Mississippi River, 421
Mixed economies, 44
MLM; *see* Multilevel marketing
MLPs; *see* Master limited partnerships
MNCs; *see* Multinational corporations
Model Business Corporation Act, 124
Modular layouts, 245–246
Monetary policy, 50–51, 549
Money
coins, 546–547
counterfeiting, 547
defined, 546
electronic cash, 547
history, 546–547, 551–552
importance, 546
time value of, 492
*Money* magazine, 454, 528
Money management; *see* Personal financial planning
Money supply, 51, 547–548, 549–551
Monopolies
absolute advantage, 62
antitrust laws, 40, 582–584
defined, 40
Monopolistic competition, 39
Moore's law, 604
Moral values, 91; *see also* Ethics
*Morningstar Investor*, 528
Mortgage bonds, 515
Mortgages, 639
Motion pictures; *see* Movies
Motivation
equity theory, 274–275
ethical issues, 278
expectancy theory, 273–274
extrinsic rewards, 260
in future, 278–280
goal-setting theory, 273
Herzberg's factors, 265–267, 268
importance, 260
intrinsic rewards, 260
job enrichment and, 267–268
management by objectives, 273
Maslow's hierarchy of needs, 263–265, 267
by money, 263, 265, 266
reinforcement theory, 274–275
in small businesses, 269
Theory X and Theory Y, 269–271, 273
Theory Z, 271–272, 273
Motivators, 265–267
Motor vehicles; *see* Automobile industry
Movies
global market, 60, 183
product placement, 435, 436
production companies, 269
MRP; *see* Materials requirement planning

MSAs; *see* Medical savings accounts
Multicultural population, 360
Multilevel marketing (MLM), 415
Multinational corporations (MNCs)
in China, 80
defined, 70
economic power, 70
ethical issues, 109, 110
foreign direct investment, 80
foreign subsidiaries, 70
largest, 70
protests against, 77
Municipal bonds, 514, 525
Music industry, 93, 161, 578
Muslims, 63, 72
Mutual funds
closed-end, 528
defined, 527–528
fees, 528
index funds, 528
international stocks, 524
investing in, 527–529
no-load, 528
objectives, 529
quotations, 534–535
Mutual insurance companies, 625
Myspace.com, 602

## N

NAFTA; *see* North American Free Trade Agreement
NASDAQ
competition with NYSE, 519, 537
defined, 521
as electronic stock exchange, 520, 597
functions, 512
performance, 536
stock quotations, 532
stocks and bonds traded on, 520
Times Square price wall, 520
National Association of Securities Dealers Automated Quotations; *see* NASDAQ
National banks, 552–553
National Credit Union Administration (NCUA), 559–560
National debt, 50, 51
National Do Not Call Registry, 414
National Labor Relations Act of 1935 (Wagner Act), 312, 324, 325–326, 328
National Labor Relations Board (NLRB), 325
NCUA; *see* National Credit Union Administration
Needs, hierarchy of, 263–265, 267
Negligence, 576
Negotiable instruments, 580
Negotiated labor–management agreements (labor contracts), 327–329
Neo-Malthusians, 31
Nepal, 7
Net; *see* Internet
Net income or net loss, 467, 470
Netiquette, P-7 to P-8
Network computing systems (client/server computing), 605–606
Networking
among firms, 220–221
by entrepreneurs, 7
in job searches, P-16 to P-18
by managers, 299–300
online, 602
by students, P-6
Networks; *see also* Internet
broadband, 603–604
extranets, 602
firewalls, 602
intranets, 602
portals, 603
virtual private, 603
wireless, 605
New businesses; *see* Businesses, starting
New product development; *see* Product development
New York City, September 11 terrorist attacks, 537
New York Stock Exchange (NYSE)
companies listed on, 121
competition with NASDAQ, 519, 537
electronic trading, 519
foreign companies listed on, 521
functions, 512
international offices, 80
market value, 519
members, 519
as public company, 519
stock quotations, 532–534
*New York Times*, 293
News releases, 443
Newspapers
advertising, 433, 434
bond quotations, 532
mutual fund quotations, 534–535
stock quotations, 532–534
Niche marketing, 364
NLRB; *see* National Labor Relations Board
No-load mutual funds, 528
Nonbanks, 497, 554, 557–558
Nonprice competition, 395
Nonprofit organizations; *see also* Charitable giving
accounting, 460–461
defined, 7
marketing, 351–352
objectives, 7
using business principles in, 7, 21
volunteering for, 100
Nonstore retailing, 412–416
Nontariff barriers, 76
Norris-LaGuardia Act, 325
North American Free Trade Agreement (NAFTA), 78–79, 327
North Korea
famine, 42
incomes, 30
Notes payable, 466
Not-for-profit organizations; *see* Nonprofit organizations
Nuclear power plants, 627–629
Nutrition Labeling and Education Act (1990), 585
NYSE; *see* New York Stock Exchange

## O

Objectives, 185
Occupational Safety and Health Act of 1970, 312
Occupations; *see* Careers
Odd lots, 527
Off-the-job training, 298
Old-Age, Survivors, and Disability Insurance Program; *see* Social Security
Older customers, 17, 360
Older employees, 313
Older Workers Benefit Protection Act, 312
Oligopolies, 39–40
One-to-one marketing, 364
Online banking, 242–243, 560–561
Online brokers, 522, 523
Online business; *see* E-commerce; Internet
Online retailing; *see* E-commerce
Online training, 298
On-the-job training, 297–298
Open communication, 276–277
Open shop agreements, 329
Open-end mutual funds, 528
Open-market operations, 549, 550
Operating (master) budgets, 489
Operating expenses, 470
Operating funds
for capital expenditures, 493
credit operations, 492
day-to-day needs, 491–492
for inventory, 492–493
need for, 491
sources, 493–494
Operational planning, 188
Operations management
careers in, 252
control procedures, 250–251
defined, 236
in manufacturing, 236–237, 238–239
in service industries, 237–238
use of Internet, 244
Operations management planning
facility location, 242–245
materials requirement planning, 246
quality control; *see* Quality control
Opportunities; *see* SWOT analysis
*Oprah Winfrey Show*, 119, 180
Options, stock, 303, 336–337
Organization charts, 189, 210
Organizational (or corporate) culture
defined, 225
informal organization, 226–227
open communication in, 276–277
Organizational design; *see also* Self-managed cross-functional teams
bureaucracy, 209, 210
centralization, 208, 211–212
chain of command, 210
decentralization, 211–212
departmentalization, 206, 214–215
division of labor, 206, 208
Fayol's principles, 208–209
functional structures, 214–215
hierarchy, 190–191, 208, 209, 210
historical development, 208–211
hybrid forms, 215
informal organization, 226–227
inverted structures, 224–225
line organizations, 217
line-and-staff organizations, 217, 218
matrix organizations, 217–219
principles, 206–207
pyramid structures, 209, 210, 213, 224
resistance to change, 225
restructuring, 223–225
span of control, 212–213
tall versus flat structures, 213–214
traditional principles, 208–210
Weber's principles, 209
Organized labor; *see* Unions
Organizing
challenges, 192–193
change in, 207, 223–227
defined, 184
interactions among firms, 220–223

Organizing—*Cont.*
levels of management, 190–192, 210
new businesses, 206
stakeholder-oriented organizations, 192–193, 198
OTC; *see* Over-the-counter (OTC) markets
Outbound logistics, 419
Outdoor advertising, 434
Outlet stores, 412
Outsourcing
contract manufacturing, 69
defined, 6, 222
distribution, 419
employee benefits, 293, 305
ethical issues, 82, 123, 235
examples, 223
to home-based businesses, 155
information technology services, 606
offshore, 81–82
problems with, 81, 222
production, 81, 234, 243
supply chain management, 418
sweatshop labor issue, 108–109
training, 608
Over-the-counter (OTC) markets, 520
Owners' equity; *see also* Stocks
defined, 466
ratio of debt to, 474
return on, 475
Ownership, separation from management, 127; *see also* Business ownership forms

## P

Packaging, 383–385
Pakistan
bribery in, 108
foreign companies in, 72
relations with India and China, 61
Par value, of stock, 516
Paraguay, 78
Parent companies, 70
Parents, single, 18; *see also* Children; Families
Participative (democratic) leadership, 188, 195
Partnerships
advantages, 122
agreements, 124
choosing partners, 125
defined, 118
disadvantages, 122–123
general, 121
limited, 121
limited liability, 121–122
master limited, 121
Part-time employees, 295–296
Patents, 577–578; *see also* Intellectual property protection
Pay equity, 338–339
Pay systems, 302–303; *see also* Compensation
P/E; *see* Price/earnings ratio
Penetration pricing strategy, 394
Penny stocks, 527
Pension funds, 558
Pentagon; *see* Defense Department, U.S.
People's Republic of China; *see* China
PEOs; *see* Professional employer organizations
Perfect competition, 39
Performance appraisals, 300–301
Performance ratios, 474–475
Personal financial planning
advisers, 647–648
balance sheets, 464, 467, 635
budgets, 490, 636
building financial base, 637–638
debts, 636, 637
estate planning, 648
expenditures, 635–636, 637–638
income statements, 635
insurance, 641–644
investments; *see* Investing
need for, 634
real estate, 638–639
retirement planning
401(k) plans, 646–647
IRAs, 644–646
Keogh plans, 647
Social Security, 17–18, 644
savings, 637, 639–640
steps, 634–637
Personal selling; *see also* Sales representatives
in business-to-business market, 364, 439–441
defined, 438–439
relationships with customers, 441
software, 440, 441
steps, 439–441
Personnel; *see* Human resource management
PERT (program evaluation and review technique) charts, 250–251
Peru
Andean Pact, 78
foreign companies in, 72
Pharmaceutical companies, 244, 576
Philanthropy; *see* Charitable giving
Philippines
franchises, 140
as market, 81
Phishing, 610
Physical distribution; *see* Distribution
Physically challenged; *see* Disabled individuals
Piecework pay systems, 303
Pipelines, 422
Place utility, 408
Planning; *see also* Business plans; Financial planning; Operations management planning
contingency, 188
defined, 183–184
forms, 187
goals and objectives, 185
human resources, 290–292
importance, 184–185, 188
mission statements, 185
operational, 188
performance standards, 197–198
questions answered by, 185–186
in small businesses, 165–166
strategic, 186–187, 488
SWOT analysis, 186, 187
tactical, 187–188
vision creation, 184–185
Plastic money; *see* Credit cards
PMI (pluses, minuses, implications), 189–190
Podcasting, 447
Poland, capitalism in, 35
Political economy, 75
Pollution; *see* Environmental issues
Population growth, 31–32; *see also* Demography
Portals, 603
Possession utility, 408
Post-it Notes, 158
Poverty
in developing countries, 10, 31–32, 381
programs to combat, 565
relationship to freedom, 10
relationship to population growth, 31–32
PPI; *see* Producer price index
PPOs; *see* Preferred provider organizations
PR; *see* Public relations
Precedents, 574–575
Preferred provider organizations (PPOs), 626, 643
Preferred stock, 517–518, 532–533
Premiums, 624
Press releases, 443
Price discrimination, 583
Price indexes, 47–48
Price leadership, 393
Price/earnings ratio (P/E), 534
Prices
comparing on Internet, 394
determination of, 36–38
equilibrium, 37–38
inflation and deflation, 47–48
market, 37–38, 39, 394
market forces and, 36, 39, 394
of new products, 355, 392–393
Pricing strategies
break-even analysis, 393–394
bundling, 394–395
competition-based pricing, 393
cost-based pricing, 393
demand-based pricing, 393
everyday low pricing, 394
high–low pricing, 394
penetration, 394
psychological pricing, 395
in retail, 394
skimming, 394
Primary boycotts, 332
Primary data, 357–358
Principle of motion economy, 262
Privacy, on Internet, P-22 to P-23, 15, 611–612
Private accountants, 458
Private enterprise system; *see* Capitalism
Private property, 35–36
Private-label brands, 385
Problem solving, 189–190, 249
Process departmentalization, 215, 216
Process layouts, 246
Process manufacturing, 239
Producer price index (PPI), 48
Product analysis, 388
Product departmentalization, 215, 216
Product development
commercialization, 389
concept testing, 354, 389
design, 354
for developing countries, 72, 360, 381
importance, 377
process, 354–355, 388–389
prototypes, 389
test marketing, 354
total product offer, 378–379
value enhancers, 378, 379, 380
Product differentiation, 39–40, 380
Product liability
defined, 576
insurance, 627

major awards, 577
strict, 576
Product life cycle, 389–391
Product lines, 379–380
Product managers, 387
Product mix, 380
Product placement, 435, 436
Product screening, 388
Production; *see also* Manufacturing; Quality
computer-aided design and manufacturing, 240
control procedures, 250–251
costs, 393
defined, 236
factors of, 9–10, 236
flexible manufacturing, 240–241
just-in-time inventory control, 247–248, 493
lean manufacturing, 241
mass, 208
mass customization, 241
outsourcing of, 81, 234, 243
processes, 238–239
Production era, 350
Production management, 236, 239–240
Productivity
benefits of flextime plans, 307
defined, 13
impact of training, 297
increases in
in manufacturing, 20, 21, 49
in United States, 48, 49
use of technology, 13–14, 49, 240
labor, 13
scientific management and, 260–262
in service sector, 48–49, 236
in United States, 48–49
Products
adapting to other cultures, 376–377
brands, 385–387; *see also* Brand names
complaints about, 446
consumer goods and services, 380–382, 383
customized, 241
defined, 354
development; *see* Product development
distribution; *see* Distribution
failures, 388
generic goods, 386
industrial goods and services, 382, 383
packaging, 383–385
pricing, 355
recalls, 622
tracking technology, 384, 423, 599
Professional behavior, P-6 to P-9
Professional business strategies, P-5 to P-6
Professional employer organizations (PEOs), 293
Profit and loss statement; *see* Income statement
Profitability ratios, 474–475
Profits
defined, 4
gross, 469–470
matching risk and, 4–5
net, 470
Profit-sharing plans, 303
Program evaluation and review technique (PERT) charts, 250–251
Program trading, 536
Project management
Gantt charts, 251, 252
PERT charts, 250–251
Project managers, 218, 219
Promissory notes, 495
Promotion; *see also* Advertising; Personal selling
campaign steps, 432
defined, 355–356, 432
integrated marketing communication, 432
interactive, 437
on Internet, 436–437
sales, 443–445
by small businesses, 448
strategies, 448–449
techniques, 355–356
use of technology, 447
Promotion mix, 432, 448
Promotions, of employees, 309
Property, private ownership, 35–36
Property insurance, 627, 643
Property taxes, 584, 586, 639
Prospecting, 439
Prospects, 439–440
Prospectuses, 520
Protectionism, 75–76
Protective tariffs, 75–76
Prototypes, 389
Psychographic segmentation, 364
Psychological pricing, 395
Public, business responsibility to; *see* Corporate social responsibility
Public accountants, 458
Public Company Oversight Board, 459
Public domain software (freeware), 606
Public Employees Relations Act, 332
Public information, 599, 611–612
Public insurance, 623
Public ownership, 12
Public relations (PR), 442, 443
Public sector; *see* Governments
Public utilities; *see* Utilities
Publicity, 443
Publicity releases, 443
Pull strategy, 448–449
Purchasing, 247; *see also* Suppliers; Supply chain management
Pure Food and Drug Act (1906), 585
Pure risk, 621
Push strategy, 448, 449

Q

Qualifying, 439
Quality
Baldrige Awards, 248–250, 256, 304
as competitive advantage, 15–16
defined, 248
ISO 9000 standards, 250
perceived, 386
six sigma, 248, 249
Quality control
continuous improvement process, 248
at end of production, 248
*Quality Digest*, 249, 620
Quality of life, 5, 244
Quick ratio, 474

R

Race; *see* Diversity; Minorities
Rack jobbers, 410
Radio advertising, 435
Radio frequency identification (RFID), 384, 423, 599
Railroads, 420–421
Ratio analysis
activity ratios, 475–476
defined, 473
leverage ratios, 474, 504, 505
liquidity ratios
acid-test (quick) ratio, 474
current ratio, 473–474
purpose, 473
profitability ratios
basic earnings per share, 475
diluted earnings per share, 475
return on equity, 475
return on sales, 475
use of, 476
Real estate; *see also* Property taxes
investing in, 638–639
ownership in developing countries, 28, 29
Real time, 221
Realtors, 379, 408
Recessions, 49
Recruitment, employee; *see also* Job searches
affirmative action and, 311–312
application forms, 294
background investigations, 295
challenges, 292–293
of contingent workers, 295–296
defined, 292
employment tests, 294–295
interviews, P-18, P-25 to P-27, 294
as management function, 193
online services, 293, 294
physical exams, 295
selecting employees, 294–295
sources, 292, 293
traits sought, P-27
trial periods, 295
Reference groups, 366
Regional stock exchanges, 519–520
Registered bonds, 513
Regulations; *see also* Legal environment
advertising, 583
banking, 560
consumer protection, 584, 585
deregulation, 40, 588–589
direct marketing, 415–416
effects on global markets, 74
on hamburgers, 589
packaging, 384
securities markets, 519, 520–521
support for, 589
Reinforcement theory, 274–275
Relationship marketing, 365–366
Religious differences, 72
Renter's insurance, 643
Research; *see* Marketing research; Product development
Reserve requirements, 550
Resignations, 310–312
Resource development, 31, 32
Resource files, P-5
Resources; *see* Factors of production
Restrictions on trade; *see* Trade barriers
Restructuring, 223–225
Résumés
cover letters, P-18, P-24 to P-25
key words, P-20

Résumés—*Cont.*
posting on Internet, P-21 to P-23
sample, P-21
writing, P-18, P-20
Retail industry; *see also* E-commerce; Supermarkets
catalog companies, 415–416
competition among large companies, 186
decentralized authority, 211
distribution strategies, 412
fashion, 258–259
jobs in, 21
nonstore retailing, 412–416
number of stores in United States, 411
pricing strategies, 394
relations with suppliers, 193
salespersons, 441–442
shopping malls, 414–415
supply chain management, 414
types of stores, 411, 412
Retailers, 404, 405, 410
Retained earnings, 466, 503
Retirement planning
defined-contribution plans, 646–647
401(k) plans, 646–647
IRAs, 644–646
Keogh plans, 647
Social Security, 17–18, 644
Retirements, 290, 310, 313
Return on equity (ROE), 475
Return on investment (ROI), 392, 475
Return on sales, 475
Revenue tariffs, 76
Revenues
defined, 4, 469
forecasting, 488
Reverse discrimination, 312
Reverse logistics, 419
Revolving credit agreements, 497
RFID; *see* Radio frequency identification
Right-to-work laws, 328–329
Risk
avoidance, 622
defined, 4–5, 621
insurable, 624
investment, 524–525
matching profits and, 4–5
pure, 621
reduction, 621–622
return on equity, 475
speculative, 621
uninsurable, 623
Risk management; *see also* Insurance
global, 629
importance, 620, 627
options, 621–624
rapid change and, 621
Risk/return trade-off, 500–501
Robinson-Patman Act of 1936, 583
Rockefeller family, 503
ROE; *see* Return on equity
ROI; *see* Return on investment
Ronald McDonald Houses, 100
Roth IRAs, 645
Royalties, 66
Rule of indemnity, 624
Russia
barter trade, 546
dumping disputes, 65
exports, 65
factors of production, 9
income tax rates, 42
as market, 80–81
WTO membership, 77

## S

S corporations, 129
S&Ls; *see* Savings and loan associations
Safety, 207, 261
SAIF; *see* Savings Association Insurance Fund
Salaries, 303; *see also* Compensation
Sales; *see also* Personal selling
difference from revenues, 469
gross, 469
net, 469
return on, 475
Sales agents, 411
Sales force automation (SFA), 441
Sales law, 579–580
Sales promotion
defined, 443
internal, 444
to marketing intermediaries, 444–445
sampling, 445
techniques, 443–444
word of mouth, 445–447, 448
Sales representatives; *see also* Personal selling
careers, 439
compensation, 439
in retail stores, 441–442
sales promotion to, 444
Sales taxes, 584, 586
Sampling, 445
Sarbanes-Oxley Act, 97, 98, 459, 460, 584
Saudi Arabia
franchises in, 68, 72
imports, 63
Savings; *see also* Retirement planning
personal, 637, 639–640
rates of return, 637
Savings accounts, 555
Savings and loan associations (S&Ls)
defined, 557
failures, 557, 572
federal deposit insurance, 559
IRAs, 646
as marketing intermediaries, 408
services, 557
Savings Association Insurance Fund (SAIF), 559
SBA; *see* Small Business Administration
SBDCs; *see* Small Business Development Centers
SBIC; *see* Small Business Investment Company
Scandals; *see* Corporate scandals; Corruption
Scientific management
Hawthorne studies, 262–263
Taylor's work, 260–262
at UPS, 252, 261
SCM; *see* Supply chain management
SCORE; *see* Service Corps of Retired Executives
Seasonal unemployment, 47
Seasonal workers; *see* Temporary employees
SEC; *see* Securities and Exchange Commission
Secondary boycotts, 332–333
Secondary data, 357, 358
Secured bonds, 501, 515
Secured loans, 496–497
Securities; *see* Bonds; Securities markets; Stocks
Securities Act of 1933, 520
Securities and Exchange Act of 1934, 520
Securities and Exchange Commission (SEC)
accounting investigations, 204
Arthur Andersen investigation, 91
criticism of, 584
defined, 521
establishment, 520
fair disclosure regulation, 103
influence on business, 575
insider trading regulations, 102, 103, 521, 522
regulation of markets, 519, 520–521, 524
regulation of stock and bond issuance, 503, 513, 520
Securities markets; *see also* Investing; Stock exchanges
functions, 512–513
indicators, 535–536
information on, 532
insider trading, 102–103, 521, 522
over-the-counter (OTC), 520
primary, 512
quotations, 532–535
regulation of, 519, 520–521
secondary, 512
volatility, 536–537
Security, information technology, 602–603, 609–611
Selection of employees, 294–295
Selective distribution, 412
Self-insurance, 622–623
Self-managed cross-functional teams, 219–220, 277
Selling; *see* Personal selling; Retail industry; Sales promotion
Selling era, 350
Senior citizens; *see also* Aging of population
as consumers, 17, 360
elder care, 341–342
employees, 313
September 11 terrorist attacks, 537
Service Corps of Retired Executives (SCORE), 172
Service industries
facility layout, 245
global markets, 44
growth, 236, 288
home-based businesses, 154, 156
inverted organizations, 224–225
jobs in, 21
operations management, 237–238
outsourcing jobs, 81–82
packaging, 385
product lines and product mixes, 380
productivity, 48–49, 236
types of organizations, 22
in United States, 236
Service utility, 409
Services, defined, 21
Sexual harassment, 339–340
Sexual orientation; *see* Diversity
SFA; *see* Sales force automation
Shareholders; *see* Stockholders
Shareware, 606

Sherman Antitrust Act, 582–583
Shipping; *see* Transportation
Ships, 421–422
Shop stewards, 330
Shopping goods and services, 381
Shopping malls, 414–415
Short-term financing
  banks, 495–496
  commercial paper, 498–499
  defined, 493
  factoring, 497–498
  family and friends, 495
  lines of credit, 497
  loans, 496–497
  promissory notes, 495
  revolving credit agreements, 497
  for small businesses, 495
  trade credit, 494–495
Short-term forecasts, 488
Simple IRAs, 646
Sin taxes, 584
Singapore, 10
Single parents, 18
Sinking funds, 515
Site selection; *see* Facility location
Six sigma quality, 248, 249
Skill-based pay, 304
Skills
  conceptual, 192
  human relations, 192
  management, 191–192
  technical, 192, 608, 613
Skimming price strategy, 394
Small Business Administration (SBA)
  Access to Capital Electronic Network, 508
  business financing from, 166, 168–169
  BusinessLaw.com, 171
  defined, 168
  definition of small business, 160
  directory of venture capitalists, 168
  failure rate of small businesses, 162
  information on exporting, 64
  international business resources, 174
  LLC information, 131
  programs, 168–169
  Web sites, 169, 174
Small Business Development Centers (SBDCs), 169
Small Business Investment Company (SBIC) Program, 169
Small business management
  accounting systems, 171, 462
  employee management, 170–171
  financial management, 166–168, 485
  financing
    credit cards, 499
    government grants, 556
    retained earnings, 503
    short-term, 495
    sources, 166–168, 556
    venture capital, 168, 556
  functions, 165
  insurance, 172
  learning about, 163–165
  marketing, 170, 172
  MBA students as interns, 172
  planning, 165–166
  recruiting employees, 293
  retirement plans, 646, 647
  Web sites, 171
Small businesses; *see also* Businesses, starting; Entrepreneurship; Home-based businesses
  banks and, 166, 172, 556
  customer relationship management, 365
  defined, 160
  in developing countries, 43
  exporting, 67, 79, 82, 173–174
  failures, 162
  family-run, 170–171
  global markets, 62–64, 82, 173–174
  importance, 161
  jobs created by, 160, 161
  legal environment, 11–12
  markets, 170
  minority-owned, 160
  motivating employees, 269
  nonprice competition, 395
  number of, 160
  philanthropy, 101
  product differentiation, 380
  promotion, 448
  success factors, 162–163, 170–171
  taking over existing firms, 164–165
  Web sites, 171–172, 174
  women-owned, 160
Smart cards, 562
Social audits, 106–108
Social entrepreneurship, 7
Social environment, 16–18, 71–72, 360
Social justice, 105
Social responsibility, 32–33; *see also* Corporate social responsibility
Social Security, 17–18, 644
Social Security Act of 1935, 644
Socialism
  benefits, 41
  command economies, 43
  defined, 41
  government functions, 41
  income tax rates, 41
  negative consequences, 41–42, 44
Socially responsible investing (SRI), 107
Society, responsibility to; *see* Corporate social responsibility
SOFFEX, 597
Soft benefits, 304
Software; *see also* Information technology
  accounting, 462–463
  antivirus, 610
  business intelligence, 598
  business plan, 166
  customer relationship management, 439
  employee application screening, 294
  functions, 606
  Microsoft's competitive practices, 572, 583–584
  public domain, 606
  security, 594
  shareware, 606
  supply chain management, 418
  types, 606, 607
Sole proprietorships
  advantages, 119
  defined, 118
  disadvantages, 119–120
  owner's equity, 466
South Africa
  diamond production, 62
  franchises, 140
South Korea
  bribery in, 108
  incomes, 30
  as market, 81
Soviet Union (former); *see* Russia
Span of control, 212–213
SPC; *see* Statistical process control
Specialty goods and services, 381
Specialty stores, 412
Speculative risk, 621
Spending; *see* Expenses
Spiders (Standard & Poor's Depositary Receipts), 529
SQC; *see* Statistical quality control
SRI; *see* Socially responsible investing
Staff personnel, 217
Staffing; *see also* Employees; Recruitment
  defined, 193
  retention, 104, 310
Stakeholder-oriented organizations, 192–193, 198
Stakeholders
  balancing needs of, 5–6
  defined, 5
  examples, 6
  relationships with, 442
  responding to, 5–6, 198
  responsibilities to, 100
Standard & Poor's 500, 529, 536, 645
Standard & Poor's Depositary Receipts (Spiders), 529
Standard of living
  contribution of business, 5
  defined, 5
  in developing countries, 72, 360
  measuring, 5
Standards; *see also* Regulations
  accounting, 458, 469, 470
  ISO, 250
Start-up companies; *see* Businesses, starting
State governments
  administrative agencies, 575
  competition to attract businesses, 245, 351
  right-to-work laws, 328–329
  taxes, 584
Statement of cash flows, 463, 471
Statement of financial position; *see* Balance sheets
Statement of income and expenses; *see* Income statement
Statistical process control (SPC), 248
Statistical quality control (SQC), 248
Statutory law, 574; *see also* Legal environment
Steel industry, 75
Stock exchanges; *see also* NASDAQ; New York Stock Exchange; Securities markets
  crash of 1929, 553
  defined, 519
  electronic, 519, 520, 597
  global, 521, 524
  indicators, 535–536
  listing requirements, 520, 521
  members, 519
  program trading, 536
  regional, 519–520
  U.S., 519–520
  volatility, 536–537
Stock insurance companies, 625
Stock options, 303, 336–337
Stock splits, 527

Stockbrokers, 522, 530; *see also* Brokerage firms
Stockholders, 127, 466; *see also* Owners' equity
Stocks
advantages and disadvantages, 517
American depository receipts (ADRs), 524
buying on margin, 530
defined, 516
dividends, 516
in 401(k) plans, 647
initial public offerings, 503, 512
investing in, 526–527, 640
issuing, 125, 502–503, 512–513, 518
preferred, 517–518, 532–533
price/earnings ratios, 534
quotations, 532–534
terminology, 516
underwriting, 513
Storage, 422–423
Stores; *see* Retail industry; Supermarkets
Strategic alliances, 69
Strategic planning, 186–187, 488
Strengths; *see* SWOT analysis
Strict product liability, 576
Strikebreakers, 333, 334
Strikes
defined, 331–332
laws prohibiting, 332
potential for, 332
at UPS, 261, 332
Structural unemployment, 47
Students
cheating, 92
internships, 172
knowledge retention, P-5
professional behavior, P-6 to P-9
resource files, P-5
study hints, P-9 to P-11
test-taking hints, P-11 to P-12
time management, P-12
Study hints, P-9 to P-11
Subcontracting, 123; *see also* Outsourcing
Submarine patents, 578
Subsidiaries, foreign, 70
Substance abuse, 342
Supermarkets
defined, 412
employees, 286–287
sampling, 445
Supervisory management, 191, 194
Suppliers
including in cross-functional teams, 220
just-in-time inventory control, 247–248
locations, 243
quality improvements, 249
relationships with, 193, 247
sweatshop labor issue, 108–109
use of Internet, 247
Supply, 37
Supply chain, 417; *see also* Marketing intermediaries
Supply chain management (SCM)
careers in, 423
defined, 417
outsourcing, 418
in retail industry, 414
software, 418
Supply curve, 37, 38
Surcharges; *see* Tariffs
Surface transportation, 420–421
Surveys, marketing research, 357–358
Sweatshop labor, 108–109, 323–324
Sweden, 77
SWOT analysis, 186, 187

## T

Tactical planning, 187–188
Taft-Hartley Act; *see* Labor–Management Relations Act
Taiwan
computer manufacturing, 69
incomes, 30
Tall organization structures, 213
Target costing, 393
Target marketing, 362–363
Tariffs
on clothing imports, 174
in common markets, 77
defined, 75
on imported steel, 75
lowered by international agreements, 76
protective, 75–76
revenue, 76
Tax accountants, 460
Tax-deferred contributions, 644
Taxes
defined, 584
effects on business, 12
excise, 586
government policies, 50
income
corporate, 127–128, 584, 586
deductions for homeowners, 639
education incentives, 634
federal, 584, 586
personal, 41, 584, 586
rates, 41
on Internet transactions, 584
laws, 584
management of, 486–487
property, 584, 586, 639
sales, 584, 586
sin, 584
Social Security, 644
types, 584, 586
value-added, 41
Teams
compensation, 303–304
cultural differences of members, 278, 279
entrepreneurial, 154
global, 278, 279
open communication and, 276–277
organizing, 207
self-managed cross-functional, 219–220, 277
Technical skills, 192
Technological environment, impact on businesses, 12–15
Technology; *see also* Information technology; Internet; Networks; Telecommuting
in banking, 561–563
benefits, 13–14
customer-responsiveness and, 15
defined, 13
digital video recorders, 436
effects on marketing, 359–360
jobs displaced by, 21
in manufacturing, 21, 246–247
product tracking, 384, 423, 599
productivity improvements, 13–14, 49, 240
speed of evolution, 604
Telecommunications Act of 1996, 588
Telecommunications deregulation, 588
Telecommuting
benefits to employee, 307–308, 608–609
benefits to employer, 308, 608
challenges, 308
disadvantages, 609
effects on facility location decisions, 245
Telemarketing, 414
Television
advertising, 433, 434, 436
digital video recorders, 436
financial programs, 510, 511
infomercials, 435–436
*Oprah Winfrey Show*, 119, 180
product placement, 435, 436
Temporary employees
hiring, 293, 295–296
motivating, 278
number of, 296
Ten Commandments, 90
Term insurance, 642
Terminating employees, 309–310, 313
Term-loan agreements, 500
Terrorism
companies linked to, 108
costs of increased security, 19
cyber-, 610–611
September 11 attacks, 537
threat of, 19, 620
Test marketing, 354
Testimonials, 436, 446, 448
Testing
drug, 342
of potential employees, 294–295
Test-taking hints, P-11 to P-12
Textile Fiber Products Identification Act (1958), 585
Thailand, 81
Theory X management, 269–270, 273
Theory Y management, 269–271, 273
Theory Z management, 271–272, 273
Therbligs, 262
Third-party logistics, 419
Threats; *see* SWOT analysis
360-degree reviews, 301
Thrift institutions; *see* Savings and loan associations
*Time*, 572
Time deposits, 555
Time management, P-12
Time utility, 408
Time value of money, 492
Time-motion studies, 261–262
Title VII, Civil Rights Act of 1964, 311, 312
TiVo, 436
Tobacco industry
advertising, 446
lawsuits, 576, 577
regulation of, 585
Top management, 190–191
Tort law, 576–577

Total fixed costs, 394
Total product offer, 378–379
Tourism; *see* Travel industry
Trade; *see also* Exporting; Global markets; Importing
  balance of, 64
  common markets, 77–78
  comparative advantage theory, 61–62
  dumping disputes, 65
  financing, 563
  free, 61, 62
  future issues, 79–81
  importance, 60
  international agreements, 76–77, 78–79
  jobs created by, 19–20
  largest trading countries, 65
  laws to ensure fairness, 65
  measuring, 64–65
  motives for, 61–62
  opportunities, 62–64
  organized labor and, 327
  surpluses, 64
Trade barriers; *see also* Tariffs
  embargoes, 76
  import quotas, 76
  lowered by international agreements, 76–77
  nontariff, 76
Trade credit, 494–495
Trade deficits, 64, 65
Trade protectionism, 75–76
Trade shows, 444
Trade unions; *see* Unions
Trademarks, 385, 579; *see also* Brand names; Intellectual property protection
Trading blocs, 77–78
Trading securities; *see* Brokerage firms; Securities markets
Training and development
  activities, 297–299
  apprentice programs, 298
  computer systems, 297–298
  defined, 297
  by franchisors, 135
  impact on productivity, 297
  job simulation, 299
  management development, 299–300
  mentoring, 290
  off-the-job, 298
  online programs, 290, 298
  on-the-job, 297–298
  outsourcing, 608
  technical, 608
  vestibule training, 298, 299
Trains, 420–421
Transactional marketing, 365
Transfers, employee, 309
Transparency, 221
Transportation; *see also* Distribution; Logistics
  air, 422
  intermodal, 422
  mode comparison, 421
  pipelines, 422
  railroads, 420–421
  surface, 420–421
  water, 421–422
Travel industry, 19
Treasurers, 484
Treasury bills, 514, 525
Treasury bonds, 514, 525
Treasury notes, 514, 525
Trial balances, 462
Trial close, 440, 441–442
TRIZ (theory of inventive problem solving), 249
Trucking, 420, 421
Truth-in-Lending Act (1968), 585


## U


UCC; *see* Uniform Commercial Code
Ukraine, 546
Umbrella policies, 644
Underwriting, 513
Unemployment, 46–47
Unemployment rate, 46–47
Unethical behavior; *see* Ethics
Uniform Commercial Code (UCC), 579
Uniform Limited Liability Company Act, 130
Uniform Partnership Act (UPA), 122
Uninsurable risk, 623
Union security clause, 327–328
Union shop agreements, 328–329
Unions; *see also* Employee–management relations
  accounting staff of, 461
  apprentice programs, 298
  boycotts, 332–333
  certification, 325, 326
  collective bargaining, 325
  contracts, 327–329
  corporate responsibility and, 107
  craft, 323, 324
  decertification, 325–326
  decline of, 321, 322, 334
  defined, 322
  in Europe, 329, 330
  future of, 322–323, 329, 333–336
  givebacks, 333–334
  history, 322, 323–324
  industrial, 324
  leaders, 320–321
  membership by state, 334
  objectives, 326–329
  organizing campaigns, 325, 326
  picketing, 332
  protectionist views, 75
  relations with Wal-Mart, 327
  resistance to management, 227
  shop stewards, 330
  strikes, 261, 331–333
  tactics used in conflicts, 331–333
  views of immigration, 290
United Arab Emirates, 67–68
United Kingdom; *see* Britain
United Mine Workers, 324
United Nations, 58, 107
United States
  comparative advantage, 62
  Constitution, 585–586
  economic development, 20–21, 361
  economic system
    business cycle, 49–50
    key economic indicators, 46–48
    mixed economy, 44
    productivity, 48–49
  incomes, 79
  NAFTA and, 78–79, 327
  standard of living, 5
  trade deficits, 65
  trade laws, 65
  unemployment, 46–47
  wealth and freedom in, 10
U.S. dollar, 548
U.S. government
  administrative agencies, 575
  assistance for exporters, 63–64, 67
  budget deficits, 50
  debt, 50, 51
  Defense Department, 273, 610
  employees, 44
  insurance programs, 623
  revenues and expenditures, 50
  role in economy, 44
U.S. government bonds, 513, 514, 525
*United States v. American Tobacco*, 582
*United States v. AT&T*, 582
*United States v. E.I. du Pont de Nemours*, 582
*United States v. Microsoft*, 572, 573, 582
*United States v. Standard Oil*, 582
United Steelworkers Union, 75
Universal Commercial Code, 12
Universal Product Codes (UPCs), 15, 384, 423
Universities; *see* Colleges and universities
Unlimited liability, 119–120, 122–123
Unsecured bonds, 501, 515
Unsecured loans, 497
Unsought goods and services, 382
UPA; *see* Uniform Partnership Act
UPCs; *see* Universal Product Codes
Uruguay, Mercosur, 78
Uruguay Round, 76
USA Freedom Corps, 100
Usage segmentation, 364
Utilities
  deregulation of, 40, 588
  electric, 40
  monopolies, 40
  regulators, 575
Utility
  defined, 407
  form, 238, 407–408
  information, 408–409
  place, 408
  possession, 408
  service, 409
  time, 408


## V


Value, 376
Value chain; *see* Supply chain
Value enhancers, 378, 379, 380
Value package; *see* Total product offer
Value-added taxes, 41
Values, corporate, 194; *see also* Ethics
Vanguard's Index Participation Equity Receipts (Vipers), 529
Variable costs, 394
Variable life insurance, 642
Vending machines, 414
Vendors; *see* Suppliers
Venezuela, 78
Venture capital, 503–504, 556
Venture capitalists, 168, 503, 556
Vertical mergers, 133
Vestibule training, 298, 299
Vietnam, 42

Violence in workplace, 342–343
Vipers (Vanguard's Index Participation Equity Receipts), 529
Viral marketing, 446
Virtual corporations, 221, 222
Virtual private networks (VPNs), 603
Virtualization, 597
Viruses, 594, 610
Visions, 184–185, 194
Vocational Rehabilitation Act of 1973, 313
Volume, or usage, segmentation, 364
Voluntary bankruptcy, 586–587
Volunteerism; *see* Community service; Nonprofit organizations
VPNs; *see* Virtual private networks

## W

Wages, 303; *see also* Compensation
Wagner Act; *see* National Labor Relations Act of 1935
*Wall Street Journal*, 522–523, 528, 532–534
Warehouse clubs, 412
Warehouses, 422–423
Warranties, 579–580
Water, clean, 88–89
Water transportation, 421–422
Weaknesses; *see* SWOT analysis
Wealth creation
  by entrepreneurs, 9–10
  millionaires, 632–633
  relationship to freedom, 10
Web; *see* Internet
Wedding planning, 448
Welfare Reform Act of 1996, 340
Western Europe; *see* Europe
Wheeler-Lea Amendment of 1938, 583
Whistleblowers, 97, 98
Whole life insurance, 642
Wholesale prices, 48
Wholesalers; *see also* Marketing intermediaries
  cash-and-carry, 410
  defined, 404, 405
  difference from retailers, 410
  full-service, 410, 411
  limited-function, 410
  merchant, 410
  stores sponsored by, 417
Wi-Fi, 605
Wills, 648
Wireless technology, 605
Women
  comparable worth, 339
  in labor force, 18, 339–340
  managers, 300
  millionaires, 633
  pay equity, 338–339
Women business owners
  franchisees, 138–139
  growing number of, 8–9
  small businesses, 160
Wool Products Labeling Act (1940), 585
Word-of-mouth promotion, 445–447, 448
Work teams; *see* Teams
Workers; *see* Employees; Labor
Workers' compensation insurance, 626
Workforce diversity; *see* Diversity
*Working Mother* magazine, 340
World Bank, 564, 565–566
World market; *see* Global markets
World trade; *see* Global markets; Trade
World Trade Organization (WTO), 76, 77, 80
World Wide Web (WWW); *see* Internet
Wrongful discharge lawsuits, 309, 310
WTO; *see* World Trade Organization
WWW (World Wide Web); *see* Internet

## Y

Yankee bonds, 514
Yellow Pages, 434
Yellow-dog contracts, 325
YoungEntrepreneur.com, 172

## Z

Zaire, bribery in, 108
Zippers, 389